Politics:
Canada
FIFTH
EDITION

McGraw-Hill Ryerson Series in Canadian Politics

General Editor – Paul W. Fox

POLITICS: CANADA, 5th Ed., Paul W. Fox
CANADIAN FOREIGN POLICY, D.C. Thomson & R.F. Swanson
THE CONSTITUTIONAL PROCESS IN CANADA, 2nd Ed.,
  R.I. Cheffins & R.N. Tucker
NATIONALISM IN CANADA, P. Russell
POLITICAL PARTIES AND IDEOLOGIES IN CANADA,
  W. Christian & C. Campbell
PRESSURE GROUP BEHAVIOUR IN CANADIAN POLITICS,
  A. Paul Pross
POLITICAL PARTIES IN CANADA, C. Winn & J.C. McMenemy
GOVERNMENT IN CANADA, T.A. Hockin
CANADIAN POLITICS: AN INTRODUCTION TO SYSTEMATIC
  ANALYSIS, J. Jenson & B.W. Tomlin
LOCAL GOVERNMENT IN CANADA, C.R. Tindal & S. Nobes Tindal
PUBLIC POLICY AND PROVINCIAL POLITICS, M. Chandler & W.
  Chandler
POLITICAL CHOICE IN CANADA (Abridged Edition), Harold D.
  Clarke, Jane Jenson, Lawrence LeDuc, Jon H. Pammett
CANADIAN FOREIGN POLICY: CONTEMPORARY ISSUES AND
  THEMES, Michael Tucker
CANADA IN QUESTION: FEDERALISM IN THE EIGHTIES, 3rd
  Ed., D.V. Smiley
THE L-SHAPED PARTY: THE LIBERAL PARTY OF CANADA
  1958-1980, Joseph Wearing

FORTHCOMING

POLITICS AND THE MEDIA IN CANADA, Arthur Siegel

Politics: Canada

FIFTH EDITION

Paul W. Fox
Erindale College
University of Toronto

McGraw-Hill Ryerson Limited

Toronto Montreal New York St. Louis San Francisco
Auckland Bogotá Guatemala Hamburg Johannesburg
Lisbon London Madrid Mexico New Delhi Panama
Paris San Juan São Paulo Singapore Sydney Tokyo

POLITICS: CANADA, Fifth Edition

1 2 3 4 5 6 7 8 9 10 HR 10 9 8 7 6 5 4 3 2

Printed and bound in Canada

Care has been taken to trace ownership of copyright material contained in this text. The publishers will gladly take any information that will enable them to rectify any reference or credit in subsequent editions.

Canadian Cataloguing in Publication Data

Main entry under title:
Politics: Canada

(McGraw-Hill Ryerson series in Canadian politics)
Includes bibliographies
ISBN 0-07-548024-7

1. Canada - Politics and government - 1963-   - Addresses, essays, lectures.   I. Fox, Paul W., date   II. Series.

JL11.P65 1982   320.971   C82-094988-4

PREFACE TO THE FIFTH EDITION

This is the fifth edition of *Politics: Canada*. This book began twenty years ago as a modest collection of readings to supplement existing text books in Canadian politics but at some point along the way it seems to have evolved into a text itself. With each edition the contents have become more extensive and intensive and the book has grown so much in size that the present edition is about twice the length of the first.

Politics: Canada now contains a good deal of original material. While some of it is my own, most of it has been contributed by colleagues who have either prepared it especially for *Politics: Canada* or allowed me to publish it for the first time. I am greatly indebted to them for their labours and also for revising their material when it has appeared in a previous edition. In some cases the authors have completely rewritten their articles for this fifth edition.

Such generosity deserves recognition and my thanks which I would like to express here. Following the order in which their work appears in *Politics: Canada,* I want to thank Brian Land for his very helpful "Guide to Canadian Government Publications," Professor David Bell for his stimulating analysis of "Regionalism in the Canadian Community," Professor Hugh Whalen for his definitive article on public opinion polling, Professor John McMenemy for his trenchant critique of the Senate, Professor Peter Russell for his synoptic review of "The Supreme Court's Interpretation of the Constitution," and Loren Simerl for his meticulous and thorough compilation of the results of provincial elections. I am grateful to each of these authors for contributions which make *Politics: Canada* unique.

I would like to express my gratitude and thanks also to the authors and publishers who have given me permission to reproduce material which appeared originally elsewhere. In each case I have indicated the source in a footnote to the title. I should add that on occasion the titles are my own invention, having been designed to link material together in a particular way for this book. I have taken the liberty also of editing the text of much of the reprinted work. Although at times I have had to reduce it to a shadow of its former self to make it fit the space available, I have tried very hard to maintain the author's meaning and his or her points of view.

Readers will note that the opinions expressed are often controversial or contradictory. I have chosen such articles deliberately as a pedagogic device to stimulate debate among students using this book. Not all of the pieces are argumentative, of course. Many of them are straightforward factual accounts conveying the sort of basic information one would expect to find in a text book. I hope that the mixture of fact and opinion has been judicious. If not, I would be glad to hear from critics.

I have received some comments from readers in the past objecting to items from the popular press being included with scholarly material. My reply is that I have found from experience that students can learn a good deal from different kinds of literature and that variety adds spice to learning as well as to life.

For the same reasons I have included more graphic material in recent editions. The test in selecting items is whether they add to the knowledge of readers.

Unfortunately, because of lack of space, it is not possible to use all of the good material available. The hardest task of an editor is to decide what to include and what to omit. Inevitably, his choice is determined by his conception of what is important at the moment. Though no editor is infallible, one can hope that he comes close to catching the public mood.

With this in mind, it is interesting to glance at the successive editions of *Politics: Canada* and note how the structure and contents of the book have changed. Since the editions have appeared at intervals of four to seven years, the alterations may give some indication of the way the study of Canadian politics and the system of government itself have developed during the past twenty years.

The first edition, which was published in 1962, was a rather scanty collection of "recent readings" reflecting the institutional approach to government that was then common. There was a good deal about the organs of the federal government (the cabinet, Commons, Senate, judiciary, and crown) and on federalism, constitutional amendment, political parties and representation, and even public opinion, but precious little else. The bibliographies were astonishingly brief, revealing quite accurately, I believe, how little scholarly material there was on Canadian politics only two decades ago.

The second edition in 1966 changed the sub-title to "Problems in Canadian Government" — a sure sign of progress — and true to its label, devoted a chapter to French Canada and more attention to federalism, the civil service, and political parties, all of which were generating problems at the time. There was a new chapter on political science as a discipline and the bibliographies grew considerably longer.

In the third edition in 1970 the sub-title was altered to "Culture and Process" and the contents — and the bibliographies — were expanded to add material on subjects under those headings: nationalism, bilingualism, regionalism, voting behaviour, and civil rights. The chapter on the cabinet now became an examination of "the executive process" which dwelt on Prime Minister Trudeau's reforms and innovations while the chapter on the civil service was converted into a study of "the administrative process" which was emerging in the burgeoning bureaucracy.

The fourth edition in 1977 followed the format of its predecessor but reflected the concerns of the period by giving a lot of space to recent attempts at conferences in Victoria and elsewhere to revise the constitution. More attention was paid also to policy-making and management in the public service. The focus of the book was broadened by adding an extensive set of data on provincial election results since 1905 while the bibliographies continued to lengthen.

The present edition marks the successful culmination of the long struggle to amend and patriate the constitution and add a charter of rights. The background to the settlement is reviewed and the new Constitution Act (Canada Act) 1981 is reprinted in its entirety. There is also an excerpt from the Supreme Court's history-making decision on the constitution in September 1981. Fiscal problems are also prominent, as one might expect in a period of economic adversity and when the federal and provincial governments are locked in bitter financial disputes. There is renewed interest in regional economic disparities and in regional assertions, particularly in the West where separatism attracts the sort of attention it used to get in Quebec.

Clearly, the provinces bulk larger and Ottawa smaller. There seems to be less interest in federal parliamentary institutions — the House of Commons, Senate, and cabinet — and even in Mr. Trudeau's "presidential" prime ministership and its trappings in the Prime Minister's Office and the Privy Council Office. Although the making of public policy at both levels of government continues to fascinate observers and accountability for it excites their indignation, increasing interest is displayed in provincial government policies and legislatures. The present edition, for instance, contains three articles on provincial legislatures, two of them by Mr. Robert J. Fleming who is one of the new breed of provincial legislative administrators responsible for advancing the study of assemblies. Since actual growth and the potential for future growth have been greatest recently at the provincial and municipal levels of government, it is likely that these two sectors will receive even more attention in the future.

The bibliographies in this edition reflect these trends. The great increase in their overall size testifies to the extent of the scholarship that is now being conducted in many different aspects of Canadian government and politics. In twenty years there has been a quantum leap in the magnitude of the work done, in the amount of material published, and in the range of subjects studied. In this edition, for instance, the total bibliography runs to more than a hundred pages, which is about ten times the size of the bibliography in the first edition. The lengthiest individual bibliographies, moreover, deal with subjects as diverse as the administrative process, the constitution, political parties, and social issues.

In spite of their length, the current bibliographies are far from exhaustive. Most historical works have been omitted and references to material published prior to the mid-sixties have been deleted, except for some classics which no one would want to ignore. If a reader wishes to check earlier publications, he can consult the bibliographies in previous editions of *Politics: Canada.*

It should be noted that most entries are listed only once, having been put in the bibliography in the chapter which seemed to be most appropriate. To assist those who might look elsewhere, the bibliographies have frequently been cross-referenced.

In some cases sections of a bibliography from a chapter in the fourth edition have been transferred to another chapter in this edition. Probably the biggest change is the consolidation of material in Chapter 1. Since this chapter now brings together Robert Dahl's introduction to political science,

John Meisel's commentary on the state of government today, and Brian Land's guide to Canadian government publications, the bibliography lists references to those topics. But it also adds entries on a number of other subjects: Canadian politics in general, Canadian political science, Canadian foreign policy, political leadership, and a host of sub-categories under social issues. I hope that all of the bibliographies in the book will be useful to instructors and students searching for further material.

To save space, I have abbreviated in the bibliographies the titles of a number of periodicals and publishers whose names would otherwise have appeared over and over again. The abbreviations are listed below.

Finally, a word about the introductions to each chapter. I have designed them to give readers a quick summary of recent major developments in the particular field and to lead into the selections in the chapter. When I have omitted from this edition material which appeared in the previous edition, I have noted its location in case a reader still wishes to consult it. Occasionally, I have also directed readers to additional sources of information on the subjects in a chapter, such as the books in the McGraw-Hill Ryerson Series in Canadian Politics.

There is now a wealth of literature on Canadian government and politics, which is a tribute to the scholars and authors who have been working diligently during the past two decades. They have accomplished a great deal.

Erindale College,   Paul Fox,
University of Toronto   March 31, 1982

BIBLIOGRAPHICAL ABBREVIATIONS

Publications

C.B.R.	*The Canadian Bar Review*
C.J.E.	*Canadian Journal of Economics*
C.J.E.P.S.	*Canadian Journal of Economics and Political Science*
C.J.I.S.	*Canadian Journal of Information Science*
C.J.P.S.	*Canadian Journal of Political Science*
C.P.A.	*Canadian Public Administration*
C.P.P.	*Canadian Public Policy*
C.R.S.A.	*The Canadian Review of Sociology and Anthropology*
C.T.J.	*Canadian Tax Journal*
D.L.R.	*Dalhousie Law Review*
J.C.S.	*Journal of Canadian Studies*
McG.L.J.	*McGill Law Journal*
M.J.P.S.	*Midwest Journal of Political Science*
O.L.R.	*Ottawa Law Review*
Q.Q.	*Queen's Quarterly*
U. of T. Faculty of Law Review	*University of Toronto Faculty of Law Review*

Publishing Companies, Associations, Councils, Institutes, Foundations, etc.

B. and M.	Burns and MacEachern
C.B.C.	Canadian Broadcasting Corporation
C.E.L.A.	Canadian Environmental Law Association
C.I.I.A.	Canadian Institute of International Affairs
C.I.P.A.	Canadian Institute on Public Affairs
C.L.I.C.	Canadian Law Information Council
C.P.S.A.	Canadian Political Science Association
C.T.F.	Canadian Tax Foundation
C.M.H.C.	Central Mortgage and Housing Corporation
C.U.C.S.	Centre for Urban and Community Studies
C.-M	Collier-Macmillan
C.P.A.	Community Planning Association
C.C.	Copp Clark
D. and G.	Deneau and Greenberg
E.C.C.	Economic Council of Canada
F. and W.	Fitzhenry and Whiteside
H.R.W.	Holt Rinehart and Winston
H.M.	Houghton Mifflin
I.C.	Information Canada
I.R.P.P.	Institute for Research on Public Policy
I.I.R.	Institute of Intergovernmental Relations
I.P.A.C.	Institute of Public Administration of Canada

I.U.S.	Institute of Urban Studies
J.L.S.	James, Lewis and Samuel
K.P.	King's Printer
L. & O.	Lester and Orpen
M. & S.	McClelland and Stewart
McG.- Q.U.P.	McGill-Queen's University Press
McG.-H.	McGraw-Hill
McG.-H.R.	McGraw-Hill Ryerson
O.E.C.	Ontario Economic Council
O.I.S.E.	Ontario Institute for Studies in Education
O.U.P.	Oxford University Press
P.-H.	Prentice-Hall
Q.P.	Queen's Printer
R.M.	Rand McNally
R.K.P.	Routledge, Kegan, Paul
S. and S.	Supply and Services
U.A.P.	University of Alberta Press
U.B.C.P.	University of British Columbia Press
U.O.P.	University of Ottawa Press
U.T.P.	University of Toronto Press
W.L.U.P.	Wilfrid Laurier University Press

TABLE OF CONTENTS

I CULTURE

1

POLITICAL SCIENCE —
SCOPE AND SOURCES

This chapter serves as an introduction to the study of political science in general and Canadian politics in particular.

Professor Dahl's article touches on most of the basic issues in political science and outlines the major aspects of the discipline. John Meisel confronts the fundamental question that many people are asking: can any government really govern under current conditions in which competing interests are demanding so much? Brian Land's article, which has been updated again for this edition and moved to this chapter, explains the nature of Canadian government publications and how to find material in the voluminous and confusing maze of official publications.

The lengthy bibliography at the end of the chapter contains items relevant to the three articles and a new and extensive list of references to textbooks in Canadian politics, articles about Canadian political science, and works about Canadian foreign policy, political leadership, and social issues in Canada. The latter is broken down into a dozen sub-categories to assist those who wish to pursue further an individual subject.

WHAT IS POLITICAL SCIENCE?*

Robert A. Dahl

What is political science?

To begin, political science is, of course, the study of politics. One might better say, it is the *systematic* study of politics, that is, an attempt by

* From *American Politics and Government*, the Forum Lectures broadcast and published by the Voice of America, Washington, D.C., 1965, pp. 1-19. By permission.

systematic analysis to discover in the confusing tangle of specific detail whatever principles may exist of wider and more general significance.

At the very outset, then, we must distinguish political science as the systematic *study* of politics from the *practice* of politics.

The same person may of course both study and practise politics. The student of politics may serve as an adviser to the political practitioner. Plato, the great Greek philosopher and political theorist, is said to have gone to Syracuse, in Sicily, in 367 B.C. to advise the ruler of that city—who, I am sorry to say, was a tyrant. . . .

Sometimes, though less often, a political scientist may be not only an adviser but also an active practitioner of the political arts. That astounding man of the Italian Renaissance, Niccolo Machiavelli, served as a secretary of the Republic of Florence for fourteen years. . . . [He also wrote] such masterpieces of political science as *The Prince* and *The Discourses* and even a great comic and rather scabrous play, *La Mandragola*. Machiavelli's descriptions and prescriptions are so lacking in ordinary standards of morality that his name has come to be associated with notions of ruthless egoism in politics. To many people, I imagine, he represents the essence of political evil. Yet the man himself loathed despotism and believed devoutly in the virtues of republican institutions. . . .

Machiavelli began his career as a politician and became a political scientist when his political career ended; with Woodrow Wilson the sequence was just the reverse. Wilson was a historian and political scientist long before he began the political career that propelled him into the White House. . . . It has sometimes been said that Wilson himself unfortunately ignored his own advice when he became President. But the practising politician often does ignore the political scientist—even, as in Wilson's case, when the political scientist happens to be himself.

I mention these examples less to show that political scientists are typically involved in politics than the contrary. I want to emphasize that actually engaging in politics is not at all the same thing as studying politics in order to develop principles of general relevance. Political science means the study, not the practice, of politics.

An Ancient Study

As you may have noticed from these examples, the study of politics is an ancient field of learning. It is also a study that has received unusual emphasis in those Western cultures that derive from the worlds of Greek and Roman civilization. For the Greeks and Romans were immensely concerned with political things.

The modern study of politics, in fact, can be traced to that magnificent and unbelievably creative people, the Greeks of the fifth and the fourth centuries before Christ and, most of all, to the Athenians. It was in Athens that Socrates, Plato, and Aristotle raised to the highest level of intellectual endeavour the kinds of questions about politics that concern thoughtful men down to the present day. I have in mind such questions as:

How do we acquire knowledge about politics and about political life? How do we distinguish politics from other aspects of human life? In what ways are political systems similar to one another? In what ways do political systems differ from one another? What is the role of authority and power in political systems? How do men behave in politics? What are the special characteristics, if any, of *homo politicus,* political man? What kinds of conditions make for stability, for change, or for revolution in a political system? What is required if social peace is to be maintained and violence to be avoided? What sort of political system is the best? How should we and how do we decide questions about what is "the best" in politics?

Every age has produced one or two men who provide great answers to these great questions . . . [such as] the three Greeks: Socrates, Plato, and Aristotle. Let us consider several others. Cicero, who was both witness to and participant in the death agony of the Roman Republic; St. Augustine, born in North Africa in the fourth century; St. Thomas Aquinas, born near Naples in the thirteenth century; Machiavelli, born in Florence in the fifteenth century; Thomas Hobbes, the Englishman, born in the next century; John Locke, also an Englishman, born in the seventeenth century; at the end of seventeenth century, a Frenchman, Montesquieu, who greatly influenced the men who drafted the United States Constitution; in the eighteenth century another Frenchman, Rousseau; in the nineteenth century the Germans, Hegel, Marx, and Engels, the Englishmen Jeremy Bentham and John Stuart Mill, the Frenchman Alexis de Tocqueville. . . .

What Is Politics?

What is politics? This innocent question is rather like asking a biologist, "What is life?" Biology, it is said, is the science of life or living matter in all its manifestations. Very well. But what is living matter? It turns out that this question is extremely difficult to answer and that biologists do not exactly agree on the answer. Yet they are quite confident that some kinds of matter—one-celled animals, for example—are clearly at the centre of biology, while others—a piece of granite, for example—are clearly outside the field. So, too, in political science. We pretty well agree on the kinds of things that are definitely political. Thus the governments of the United States, the Soviet Union, and any other nation, province, state, city, town, or colony are unquestionably political and therefore in the domain of political science. The government of an ant colony is not; at any rate I have not noticed any of my colleagues writing about party politics or imperialism in ant colonies. Yet if we can say with confidence what lies at the centre of politics, we are, like the biologist, confronted with the question of life, not so sure of the exact boundaries.

Let me therefore describe what is at the centre. To begin, wherever we find politics, most authorities agree, we necessarily encounter human beings living together in some kind of an association. . . . Wherever we find politics we encounter some special relationship among the human beings living together, a relationship variously called "rule," "authority," or "power". To refer once again to Aristotle, the very first page of the *Politics* contains references to different kinds of authority, what distinguishes the authority of the statesman from the authority of the head of the household or of the master over his slave, and the like. Wherever we find politics we discover conflict and ways in which the human beings cope with conflict. Indeed, when human beings live together in associations and create the rules, authorities, or governments to deal with these conflicts, the very attempts to rule also help to generate conflicts. Which comes first, power or conflict, need not detain us; we find both conflict and power wherever human beings live together. Politics arises, then, whenever there are people living together in associations, whenever they are involved in conflicts, and wherever they are subject to some kind of power, rulership, or authority.

These phenomena exist everywhere, therefore politics is everywhere. But not all associations have equal power. You can very easily test this—though I strongly urge you not to try—by having your family, which is one association, attempt to take over your neighbour's property, which, I am sure, happens to be protected by a more powerful association, the national state in which you reside. The state is the association that has the greatest power within some particular territory. Thus the *government* of the state is obviously at the very centre of politics, and therefore of political science. And the various organized institutions that make up the government of a state —the executive, the legislature, the judiciary, regional organizations, provinces, and local governments—all involve politics.

There are associations, organizations, and institutions that help to determine what the organs of government actually do; what rules the government adopts and enforces. In the modern world the most important are obviously political parties, such as the Republican and Democratic parties in the United States, Conservatives, Labourites, and Liberals in Britain, the Communist party in the Soviet Union, and so on. In many countries the political parties are so influential that one can consider them as a kind of informal government that rules the rulers. Thus political parties are pretty clearly at or near the centre of politics and therefore of political science.

In addition to the parties, other organizations help to determine what the state does, even though they may not run candidates in elections and are not directly and openly represented in parliament. These associations are sometimes called interest groups; any association that tries to secure from the state policies favourable to its members or followers is an interest group. In the United States interest groups include such organizations as the American Medical Association, which represents physicians and has been involved in the struggle over a national program of medical care; labour unions, including the great national organization, the AFL-CIO, which frequently descends on Congress in an attempt to secure legislation favourable to trade unions in particular and the working people in general; farm organizations, which seek to gain favourable treatment for farms. One could go on endlessly simply listing examples of interest-group organizations in the United States. Not long ago the United States House of Representatives debated and passed a bill increasing the legal authority of the federal government to protect the rights of Negroes. A recently published list of the groups who were actively working in Washington to persuade congressmen to support the bill shows: six civil rights organizations, fifteen labour unions, nineteen religious organizations, and ten other groups.

Neither can we ignore ordinary citizens. Election, voting, and other forms of participation by citizens in civic life are also elements of politics.

Have we now reached the boundaries of politics? Hardly. In fact some political scientists would extend the meaning of politics to include *any* activity involving human beings associated together in relationships of power and authority where conflicts occur. In this sense, politics truly does exist everywhere: within trade unions, within the interest-group organizations of doctors or farmers, in business organizations, even in private clubs, indeed anywhere that human beings assemble together. Viewed in this way, the domain of politics and therefore of political science does not stop simply with the institutions of the state, or even with such familiar political institutions as political parties and organized interest groups, but extends to an enormous range of human activity. The question of how far the boundaries of political science extend is a lively one among political scientists at the present time, but we need not linger over it any more. For it is perfectly obvious that no matter how they draw their boundaries, political scientists have more than enough to do.

Is Politics a Science?

. . . In what sense is the study of politics a science? In what sense *can* it be? Even if it can be, should it be a science? These questions, as you might imagine, are also the subjects of a great deal of discussion; it is not too much to say that the discussion has gone on for a very long time, if not, in fact, from the time of the Greeks.

The term "science" has, of course, many meanings. And the word does not mean quite the same thing in one language as it does in another. In some countries, scholars do not consider that political science is a single subject, like biology, but many subjects. Some scholars speak not of political science but of the political *sciences.* In France, until recently, one heard of *les sciences politiques* and in Italy *le scienze politiche*—that is, the political sciences. What do we mean, then, by the *science* of politics? To some people the word "science" simply means any systematic approach to human knowledge; so that one could speak of the science of physics, the science of mathematics, or perhaps even a science of theology. To others, and this is a good deal more common in English-speaking countries nowadays, the word "science" tends to be restricted to the natural sciences, studies that involve the observation of nature and the development of laws and theories explaining the phenomena of nature such as chemistry, physics, and the biological sciences. In recent years, particularly in the United States, we have come to speak of the social and behavioural sciences, that is, those that seek by observation to develop explanations of human behaviour.

To confuse the matter even more, science is thought of sometimes as an achievement in being, sometimes as a method, and sometimes as a goal.

Physics is a science in the first sense. When one speaks of physics as a "real" science, he probably does not mean that physicists are simply hoping to develop theories that someday will explain the nature of physical reality; he means that they already have such theories, and they are of impressive power to explain the physical world.

But science also refers to the *methods* by which scholars investigate their subject. One might say that a century ago medicine was not very "scientific" because its methods were extremely crude; it was difficult to distinguish the charlatan from the honest inquirer after medical knowledge. Today, on the contrary, medical research in the most advanced laboratories uses highly sophisticated methods of inquiry very much like those used in physics, chemistry, and biology. Yet almost everyone would agree that in its laws, theories, and explanations medicine is not so far advanced as, say, physics.

One might also think of science as a goal, as something to be arrived at by rigorous methods of inquiry, even if present knowledge is somewhat sparse.

In which of these three senses is the study of politics a science? Despite the fact that the best minds of every age have tended to turn their attention to the study of politics, as I pointed out above, certainly the study of politics is not an already achieved science like physics. We simply do not have a body of theories about political systems that enables us to predict the outcome of complex events with anything like the reliability that a physicist, a chemist, or even a biologist generally can predict the outcome of complex events in his field. If you believe that there is such a theory in politics, I am bound to say that you are, in my opinion, deluding yourself. It is true that from time to time a writer, sometimes even a great writer, has claimed that he possesses a full-fledged predictive science of politics. So far, however, no comprehensive theory of politics that undertakes to predict the outcome of complex events has stood the test of experience. The most notable modern example of failure is, I think, Marx. If you examine his predictions carefully and test them against actual developments, he proves to be wrong in so many cases that only those who regard Marxism as a kind of religion to take on faith, and against all evidence, can remain persuaded that it is a truly predictive scientific theory. Nonetheless, political scientists do have an enormous amount of knowledge about politics, much of it extremely reliable knowledge.

•   •   •

We can say, then, that political science is the study of politics by methods and procedures designed to give us the greatest reliability in a highly complex world. As a body of knowledge, modern political science is definitely not a highly perfected science like physics or chemistry. Our knowledge of politics is continually and rapidly growing; however, this knowledge is of varying degrees of reliability, for some of it is highly speculative and about as reliable as anything one is ever likely to learn about human beings.

Matters Studied

What objects or phenomena do we actually study in political science? I have already mentioned most of these when I discussed the boundaries of politics, but let me now enumerate the main phenomena, the "objects" of political science. First, we study individual citizens, voters, leaders. Strange as it may seem, study of the ways in which individuals actually behave in politics is one of the newest developments in the field. It is true, of course, that the behaviour of individuals in politics has never been ignored. Machiavelli's *The Prince* describes how many Renaissance political leaders did act and prescribes how they had to act if they were to succeed in the ruthless and tempestuous political jungle that was Renaissance Italy. Even though few writers had as much to say about the seamy side of political life as did Machiavelli, insights about man's political behaviour are scattered in works over the centuries.

Our understanding of man has made a quantum jump since Sigmund Freud and the advent of modern psychology, psychoanalysis, and psychiatry made us all acutely aware of man's capacity for irrational, nonrational, impulsive, neurotic, and psychotic action—in politics, unfortunately, as much as elsewhere. Partly as a result of this change, in the last several decades political scientists have begun to observe individuals and politics with a concern for detail and accuracy that, if not entirely new, is at least highly uncommon. What is new, perhaps, is a search for reliable generalizations. We are no longer content to observe a few individuals engaged in politics and to describe their behavours, to investigate a few great, unusual leaders or a few simple yet possibly rare citizens. Rather, we want to know how widely our generalizations apply.

. . . [For instance] the independent voter is often thought to be, at least by comparison, a model citizen, rational, thoughtful, responsible, open-minded, in contrast to the partisan who, it is often thought, is less reflective, less thoughtful, and perhaps even less interested in a campaign because he made up his mind long ago and nothing will budge him. The view is, surely, plausible. Beginning with the presidential election of 1940, however, studies by American social scientists began to destroy this happy picture of the independent voter. In one study after another it was discovered that, far from being a thoughtful, attentive, responsible citizen, a person who lacks any spirit of partisanship more than likely has no great interest in politics, is quite ignorant about politics, does not pay much attention to political campaigns, and makes up his mind at the last possible moment, frequently on the basis of rather trivial or accidental influences. . . .

This finding has forced us to do some rethinking of our notions about the roles of the partisan and independent in American politics and perhaps in democratic systems in general. We cannot yet be sure how widespread this phenomenon is. Some studies indicate that it holds in certain European countries, in nations as different, for example, as Britain and Italy. But it may not hold in others. A recent analysis suggests that perhaps our model citizen, the thoughtful, reflective, interested man who does not make up his mind until he has tried to hear both sides of the argument, does actually exist in the United States and may play no negligible role in elections, even though his numbers are pretty tiny.

A second phenomenon studied by political scientists is the private or semipublic associations to which many individuals belong. The most visible of these, as I suggested earlier, are political parties. There are a vast number of studies of political parties throughout the world: how they are organized, how nominations are made, what the parties do in campaigns and elections, the characteristics of party leaders, members, and followers, and differences and similarities in the party systems of various countries.

Perhaps the most significant development during the last several decades has been the discovery of the tremendous importance of interest groups, particularly in the United States. Because class lines are rather weak, vague, and uncertain in this country, despite considerable differences in social standing, prestige, and income, and because our political parties, unlike many European parties, are neither tightly organized nor highly centralized, it was natural, I suppose, that American political scientists were the first to turn their attention to interest groups. It is fair to say, in fact, that they pioneered investigation in this area. In the last decade, however, concern with the role of interest groups in politics has spread to European political scientists, who have also begun to demonstrate that social classes and political parties are by no means the only significant political forces in European politics and that a variety of interest groups are active in the political parties and influence cabinet ministers, the civil servants, and other governmental officials. It would be impossible to understand the operation of any democratic system if one ignored the decisive role often played by representatives of the party of interests that exists in a modern industrialized and urbanized society.

A third focus for study is, of course, the political institutions themselves —the parliaments, the cabinets, the courts, the civil service, and the like. These are such obvious and familiar subjects for political science, therefore, that I will not comment on them further.

A fourth focus is a political system as a whole. A lively question of enduring interest to American political scientists is how to distinguish democracies from other systems and, perhaps more important, what conditions are required for the stability of democratic institutions. As political scientists learn more about the actual operation of democratic political systems, it becomes obvious that . . . the ideals formulated by classical spokesmen for democracy, such as Locke, Rousseau, and Jefferson, are not only a long way from achievement (a fact that in itself would hardly be a new discovery) but may even have to be reformulated for fear that, as unattainable and utopian goals, they serve merely to discredit democracy as an ideal.

The existence of many new nations only recently liberated from colonial rule and still struggling with problems of independence, internal peace, and self-government presents as great an intellectual challenge to political scientists as they have ever faced: to discover the conditions under which these countries can develop stable constitutional governments based on the consent and support of the bulk of the population and capable of an orderly solution to staggering problems of economic growth and social development. It is fair to state that the study of politics in its 2,000-year development in the West has been rather parochial.

Now that we are confronted by the need for moderately reliable knowledge about the political systems developing in Africa, Asia, and even in Latin America, we find that facts and theories drawn from the experience of European and English-speaking countries are inadequate. As a consequence, during the last decade or so, tremendous efforts have been made in the United States to develop scholars with an understanding of the problems and politics of the non-Western world. . . .

I must discuss one other focus of political science that is so painfully important to all of us that it might even be placed at the very centre of the stage. I have in mind, of course, the relation among political systems, that is, international relations. Here, too, the challenge strains our capacities to the very limit if not, indeed, beyond. In their attempt to grapple with the portentous and enormously complicated problems of international politics, political scientists in recent years have resorted to an amazing variety of techniques of inquiry and analysis, not excluding even the use of electronic computers to simulate negotiation and conflict among several countries in international politics. Although some of these efforts might seem absurd and unrealistic, my view is that we are so desperately in need of solutions that we can ill afford to mock any serious intellectual effort to discover them; and help may come from quite unexpected quarters.

Methods of Study

These, then, are some of the phenomena studied by modern political scientists. You might want to know *how* we study these things? To answer this question properly would require many chapters. Politics, as everyone knows, is not something one can directly observe in either a laboratory or a library. Indeed, direct observation of politics is often extremely difficult or downright impossible. Consequently, we often have to study politics by indirect observation, through historical materials, records, papers, statistical data, and the like. This process, I have no doubt, conveys the customary image of nearsighted scholars consulting the works of one another without ever emerging from the library into the heat and turmoil of political life. Yet one of the oldest though often neglected traditions of political science is the tradition of direct observation.

It is worth recalling that the great Greek students of politics, Socrates, Aristotle, and Plato, were able to and did observe politics in the compact laboratory of the city-state. They did not make the sharp division that modern scholars often make between the world of books and study and the world of affairs. Eighteen centuries later, Machiavelli was able to observe the political life of Renaissance Italy from his post in the Republic of Florence. I rather think there are many scholars today who believe that their fragile dignity would be damaged should they leave their libraries to mingle with the ordinary folk in the noisy byways of politics. Nonetheless, a most interesting development over the last several decades has been the growing insistence that wherever possible the scholar should observe as directly as he can the objects of his study. As a result, never before in history have there been so many scholars seeking to interview politicians, civil servants, and ordinary citizens.

. . . This development is, in my view, an enormously healthy one, for just as the biologist is no less a biologist, but a good deal more, because he observes in his laboratory the organisms with which he works, and just as the physician gains knowledge from studying patients and not merely from reading what others have written about disease, so too the study of political

science has gained from the growing conviction that one cannot know politics merely by traversing the path between the classroom and the library.
Yet to observe politics directly is much more difficult for us than it was for
Aristotle or for Machiavelli; for the world we study is larger and more complicated, the population is greater, and the slice of the world we see—we
now know—is not likely to be truly representative of the world.

The political scientist's laboratory, then, is the world—the world of politics. And he must work in that laboratory with the same caution and the
same rigorous concern for the accuracy and reliability of his observation
that is true of the natural scientist in his laboratory; with a good deal less
chance, nonetheless, of succeeding. Because direct observation is no simple
matter of casual and accidental interview, the political scientist finds that
for every hour he spends observing politics he may have to spend a dozen
analyzing his observations. Raw observations are all but useless, so the
scholar still must work at his desk, in the silence of his study, reading and
reflecting, trying to pierce the veil that seems always to keep truth half- hidden. Now that we have brought our political scientist back to his desk, far
from the hurly-burly of politics, let us leave him there. But if he is to study
politics he cannot stay there long. You may run into him at the next political
meeting you attend.

CAN GOVERNMENTS GOVERN? —
CITIZEN DEMANDS AND GOVERNMENT RESPONSE*

John Meisel

> There is no absolute governability or ungovernability. Governability is
> always a function of tasks, both imposed from the outside and generated
> from the inside, and of capabilities, of both the elite and the masses.
> Joji Watanuki

Social science—like motorcars, hemlines and slang—is subject to the vicis-
situdes of fashion. The "in" thing, at one time, was to relate everything to
Riesman's s curve and the other-directed personality: other periods were in-
trigued by Rostow's stages of economic growth, Hartzian fragment theory,
Lijphart's consociationalism, or Bell's end of ideology. At the present time,
one of the mind-catching concerns stresses the so-called ungovernability of
democracies and the related demand overload.

Most of these new perspectives have contributed to our understanding of
social reality but none has provided completely satisfying insights—the recent agonizing over stresses in democratic politics being no exception. The
"demand overload" thesis must therefore be examined and evaluated although, as I shall argue, it is not a completely persuasive perspective on our
current discontents. . . .

* From *Canadian Public Policy*, II, 4, Autumn, 1976. By permission of the publisher and
author who was a member of the Department of Political Studies, Queen's University, and is
now Chairman of the Canadian Radio-Television and Telecommunications Commission.

A thesaurus of the Cassandra-like chorus would have to include at least the following ideas: post-industrial society in the liberal democracies of the '70s is marked by a lack of purpose, an absence of community spirit, and a declining legitimacy of private and public authority. Technology has become a self-generating, uncontrollable force which has triggered a mindless, massive consumption of resources which, if it continues unchecked, will drag mankind towards certain disaster. Citizens, partly because of the expansion of educational opportunities and growing affluence, incessantly generate ever more numerous and vehemently articulated demands, the satisfaction of which is either impossible because of the unavailability of resources or because it requires a level of social control that people are no longer willing to accept. The decline in economic growth precludes the amelioration of conditions of the worst-off groups without adversely affecting the better-off. Political parties are less and less able to perform their traditional functions; governments are becoming impotent observers, and even abettors of disastrous social and economic developments, most notably at present, with respect to stagflation. The industrialized West's shocking profligacy and growing incapacity to reconcile dwindling resources with a stubbornly uncontrollable demographic explosion is beginning to endanger civilization as we have come to know it. Even the heat generated by industrial man ultimately threatens his survival. . . .

From the viewpoint of a student of Canadian politics, satisfied to contemplate the world from a time perspective short of apocalyptic upheaval, these observations can be reduced to three groups of propositions:

(1) The lack of a sense of community, citizen duty and discipline, and the accompanying acquisitive particularism have resulted in people making unreasonable and impossibly high demands on governments.

(2) The demands are impossible to meet or dangerous for at least three reasons. (a) Resources are simply not adequate for their satisfaction and even their partial gratification may have crippling consequences for the effectiveness of the whole system. (b) Governments lack the decision-making capacity to deal with the plethora of demands and the ability to reconcile them into viable programs. (c) The excessive competition for favours among organized particular groups prevents the system from meeting critically important general interests of the community. This is exacerbated by the decline of political parties and by the new rules assumed by interest groups and the media.

(3) Among the drastic consequences of this system overload is the ungovernability of democracies: growing political and economic chaos, a further decline in civility, and the coming to an end of a system which, whatever its shortcomings, has done much to improve the quality of life of virtually all citizens.

How justified are these *cris de coeur*? One cannot but be impressed by the accuracy of many of the perceptions of those who worry about the future of democracy. We *are* unmistakably in the middle of a major upheaval and of fundamental change and we *do* face unprecedented challenges. But while one would not wish to quarrel over the symptoms identified by the writers whose ideas I have just summarized, considerable controversy surrounds their overall diagnosis. It would be nice to be able to test the matter by pitting the overload-ungovernability case against a rigorous theory of liberal democracy in a no-growth economic phase, but no such completely satisfactory theory is available, nor does it seem to spring, ready-made, from my brow. I shall thus content myself with identifying a number of points which will enable us to evaluate the implications of the interaction between current citizen demands and the governmental response.

First, distinction must be made between socio-political forces common to all post-industrial democracies and those unique to Canada. There is great danger that among the former—the general factors—developments unique to the United States or Britain are taken to have universal applicability. Much of the "ungovernability" literature originates in the States and as often happens with the intellectual wares of a super-power, tends to assume that American experience is prototypal. . . .

Second, we must also clearly differentiate between the two sides of our equation. It is the *relationship* between demands and capabilities which is crucial; one cannot evaluate one without bearing in mind the other.

Third, and we are at last getting into the substance of the case, the major change in western societies has been in their value systems. We have witnessed, and are witnessing, an epoch-making decline or transformation of traditional middle class values and their replacement by a new, still evolving, pattern of beliefs and priorities. Such critically important aspects of life as sex, family relations, as well as attitudes to work, authority, the state, and fellow man are all changing, often into paths diametrically opposed to previous directions. This volcanic upheaval affects political demands and behaviour, and since the direction of the change is *away* from the time-honoured middle class virtues, one must expect that the political consequences of the moral and ethical metamorphosis will offend those who evaluate public life from the viewpoint of an established middle class perspective.

In Canada, government is subject to changes additional to those just mentioned. Political values appear to be shifting, particularly with respect to the manner in which the federal and provincial spheres are viewed by the politically active population. Quebec independentism, western regionalism, and the assertion of local and regional rights throughout the country—not to mention the rights of the native peoples—are altering the atmosphere and context in which the respective levels of government can perform the tasks assigned them by the constitution and the services expected by their citizens. The governability of Canada is, in other words, being affected by a changing value system with respect to the very definition of the country and the relationship which should prevail among its people and its constituent parts. The resulting need for adjustments does not mean that Canada is becoming ungovernable but it points to the desirability of our fashioning political and administrative mechanisms suitable for coping with the current and impending situations.

Fourth, whatever the emerging shape of the class structure is likely to be —and it is too soon to be able to say—there is little doubt that the immediate future, at least, will increasingly be dominated by a new class.

The term "class" in the foregoing discussion, like much else in my argument, is perforce ill-defined. Without being able to pinpoint its exact meaning here I should elaborate by mentioning that I see a massive change occurring in post-industrial societies, involving a radical re-allocation of the powers and privileges of various social groups. This realignment is related to both the economic and occupational background of groups and to the values dominating life. The heretofore critical role of property in assuring power and privilege is not likely to disappear altogether but it is being increasingly overshadowed by technical knowledge, particularly skills related to the manipulation of people, and by closeness to the dominant decision-making sites in the private and public sectors. The latter, it must be noted, is growing considerably in importance. The emerging dominant groups or classes derive their strength from the power of their institutional "homes" and the interests they tend to press are those of their institutional bases and of their own role in society.

. . . There is considerable evidence to support the contention that we are living through an era witnessing the waning of the middle classes, as we have known them, and the emergence of a new class alignment. If our analysis is correct, if middle class values are giving way to new values, if the middle class is in the process of being replaced as a dominant force by a new class, then it would not surprise us to find that the equation between demands and the government response was also assuming new, as yet unanticipated, forms. In that event the countries heretofore supporting so-called democratic regimes may be evolving new ways of being governed, which is not to say that they are becoming ungovernable. Whether the new forms are democratic, in the conventional sense, remains to be seen and certainly depends on one's definition of democracy.

Canada offers a dramatic example of the trends we have noted and has probably given more visible signs of the privileged position of its mandarinate than have most liberal democracies. Although the administrative class includes others than public servants, the latter are a typical and all-important component. Many straws in the wind attest to their rising power. Here are a few; not only have the numbers, and the senior positions, within the federal public service risen remarkably in recent years (and the provinces have not been far behind) but its salary scales and rate of pay increase have greatly surpassed those of the rest of the population . . . , even if no account is taken of its exceptionally favourable fringe benefits, including a truly phenomenal (and for the country probably ruinous) factor—pensions indexed to the cost of living. . . . The federal government in trying to implement its incomes policy exhorted the country to cut back expenditures or at least to hold the line, without being able to prevent the rise in numbers of its own bureaucrats, and without succeeding in keeping its own expenditures within the indicated guidelines. This suggests that politicians—no matter how keen their motivation—may be unable to control the work of their officials. . . . There has, in short, emerged a vast number of officials in both the private and public sectors, bolstered by powerful institutional bases, who exercise enormous influence on governmental decisions and on private life. They can be found not only in governments but in unions, educational institutions, health and social service agencies, research and consulting firms, in voluntary associations, even in professional and learned societies. Not infrequently they move from one such organization to another. And wherever they are, they play a critical role in the stimulation of demands.

And this brings us to my fifth point. Demands rarely arise in a spontaneous fashion in society. For needs to become wants, and wants demands, opinion leaders, animators, vanguards of the proletariat, or just plain elites have to mobilize their clientele. In Canada, many of the policies and programs which have undoubtedly contributed to strains in the system are traceable to what could be described as non-spontaneous, engineered, or created demands. It has always been thus, of course; what is changing is the extent or proportion of mobilization which is imposed from above and/or outside the groups directly affected. In our case, it is well known that the introduction of family allowances resulted from the Keynesian spell cast over our political and bureaucratic elites towards the end of the Second World War, reinforced by Gallup polls showing impressive CCF gains. Similarly, medicare, the LIP and OFY schemes, the indexing of pensions, the lavish terms of Canada's Unemployment Insurance Act or regional government were not introduced in response to the claims of existing beneficiaries. In some instances, in fact, the programs brought into being groups whose demands they allegedly met.

Another indication of the key role played in the articulation of demands by the newly emerging managerial class can be found in occupations like teaching or nursing, where the militancy or even unionization met resistance and became acceptable only after the organizational bureaucrats and activist leaders succeeded in persuading the majority of the desirability of pursuing confrontation tactics. . . .

I must stress that by citing the various foregoing examples in illustrating the extent to which demands are now created by public and private officials, I do not necessarily question the desirability of the programs or practices to which they have led. Some, I believe, are eminently worthy and others not. . . .

. . . Have our new elites inside and outside the government released the kindly genie in Aladdin's lamp or have they unleashed the sorcerer's apprentice? I would reply affirmatively to both questions. Many of the new governmental outputs are clearly defensible and contribute to the improvement of the conditions of life of previously ill-favoured Canadians. On the other hand, some programs are wasteful and in many respects counter- productive; the overall performance of the government has been both inflationary and ineffective in reducing unemployment levels, particularly among certain sections of the population.

Sixth, without denying that we are beset by many of the foibles and even calamities identified by the pessimists we can also admit to the presence of encouraging signs.

On the mass or public side, Canada seems much better off than its southern neighbour. Whereas in the U.S.A. students have observed a decline in electoral turnout, party identification, and a sense of efficacy, Canadian participation in elections remains essentially unchanged, a larger number of people identify with political parties and they do so more intensively than previously, although there is some inconclusive evidence suggesting that there appears to be a decline in the sense of citizen trust and in political effectiveness. At another level, we have taken imaginative steps to strengthen the citizens' capacity to participate in decision-making and so, presumably, to maintain or increase their sense of involvement: public funds are being made available to native peoples and environmental groups so that they can make more effective presentations to the Berger Commission . . . ; the federal government experimentally subsidizes the Consumers Association of Canada, enabling it to challenge on more equal terms the corporate giants when they appear before regulatory agencies and changes in the laws affecting election costs have introduced some openness into party finance and have encouraged the financial participation of small donors. . . . More generally, some scholars have produced evidence indicating that the "post-bourgeois" values of young west Europeans are less self-seeking and more community responsive than older ones and that in the United States, contrary to the gloomsayers' argument, there is a growth of ideological politics and that "the dependent voter has been replaced by the responsive voter". . . .

These and similar glimmers of light may perhaps reflect no more than superficial and misleading palliatives: democratic politics in the eyes of many of its doubters on both the Left and the Right requires considerably more radical attention. But it is at least plausible to argue that the political process through which the mass public articulates and aggregates its demands is showing some signs of adjusting to emerging conditions, that participatory processes may emerge in which varieties of formerly excluded citizens can become involved in policy-making and that this experience may ultimately lead to a capacity for screening communal demands so as to assure that the most deserving problems are met without causing hardship to those who can ill afford them.

What about the other side: the elites and particularly those responsible for the governmental process? Do they offer any reassurance? At the risk of resembling witless Pollyanna I derive some cheer from speculating about the future of governments as well. As I have indicated above, I am convinced that governability as such is not, and never has been, an issue: *some* form of allocation of resources will continue to be made by the public sector and government will go on, probably responding differently to public needs than was the case in the heyday of middle class dominance. The question we thus confront is not whether governments can govern but in whose interests they do so. Even if massive inflation continues it is likely that *in the long run* the present middle and upper middle income groups will be most severely hit. As the economy stabilizes new policies will lead towards a new slicing of the pie. The administrative, technological elite will, as elites always do, itself benefit from the new order but other groups will also, of course, do comparatively well. The best organized, most effectively skilled, and the most strategically placed groups are likely to rise to new prominence and to new rewards.

This prospect does not fill me with alarm. The powerful managerial class, particularly in the public sector, embodies—and is likely to continue embodying—many of the best traditions of what is becoming the old order, including a strong sense of public duty and concern for excellence. While some of its technocratic elements may be disposed to taking a mechanistic, soulless approach to human problems, the administrative class in Canada has, as a whole, an impressive record of dedicated public service. Despite numerous recent gaffes, it can withstand comparison with its predecessors, particularly with what we might term the plutocratic, commercial and industrial-dominated elite. If compelled to choose between depending on the recommendations of the mandarins of the oil industry, for instance, or on those of the federal government, there would be no doubt about my choice. The constantly expanding responsibility of public, as distinct from private decision-making, irrespective of ownership, thus strikes me as an encouraging sign, despite its obvious dangers: it promises that publicly responsible allocative processes, rather than the selfishly manipulated market mechanisms will increasingly affect outputs and ever more extensive areas of life. . . .

To link the changing character of the relationship between citizen demands and government response to underlying secular changes in the social structure and to react sanguinely to them is not, of course, to deny that problems of adjustment exist. . . . We cannot enter into a discussion of the available solutions here but should note that they can, and indeed should, be applied on several fronts. Richard Rose has correctly stressed that the "concept of overloaded government emphasizes that the contemporary crisis cannot be understood solely in terms of absolute properties of polity and society, but rather, by considering ratio relationships between different parts. Because overloading reflects a ratio there is more than one way in which to resolve stress". . . . Rose further suggests that "politicians may find some hope in considering that the Chinese ideograph for 'crisis' can also be translated as 'opportunity'," and identifies four fronts on which action can occur: increasing resources, improving government institutions, improving the impact of government programs, and reducing expectations. . . . Which options receive the greatest attention will depend on the values, attitudes, and skills of the new mandarin class. The first thing we need to do—and this is by far the most important point of my argument —is to learn more than we know about ongoing changes within the middle class and about its relations to other sectors of society. Another thing is clear: the most promising strategy is not to expend energy on making the present and future differ as little as possible from the past but to make the future avoid past errors. The need everywhere is to keep breaking down the constantly present and re-emerging elite-mass barriers. In Canada we must also make additional efforts to reduce obstacles impeding free and equal centre-periphery interaction, whether this dimension is conceived spatially or in terms of social and economic power.

A DESCRIPTION AND GUIDE TO THE USE OF CANADIAN GOVERNMENT PUBLICATIONS*

Brian Land

A government publication has been defined as "any printed or processed paper, book, periodical, pamphlet or map, originating in, or printed with the imprint of, or at the expense and by the authority of, any office of le-

* Revised June 1981, for this book by the author who is Director, Ontario Legislative Library, Research and Information Services and Professor of Library Science, University of Toronto. By permission.

gally organized government." ** Government publications range in scope from the formal papers, debates and journals of our legislatures, and from the annual reports of the various departments and agencies to the more popular periodicals and pamphlets for tourists, and to "how to do it" booklets for the handyman or housewife.

The following paragraphs describe some of the more important serial publications of the federal government such as the debates, journals, statutes, and gazettes, and review some of the guides, catalogues, indexes and checklists of government publications.

A. The Major Serial Publications

1. DAILY AGENDA

Order Paper and Notices
The *Order Paper and Notices* is issued daily in bilingual form by the House of Commons when it is in session. On Monday, or on the first sitting day of the week, it is comprehensive and includes the present and past status of all business of the House plus unresolved notices of motions for the production of papers or unanswered questions. For the other sitting days of the week, it is abbreviated, giving only routine proceedings, government orders, private members' business for that day, and notices. The *Order Paper and Notices* is not cumulated or republished.

Order of Business
In the case of the Senate, a section dealing with the "Order of Business" appears each day in the *Minutes of the Proceedings*. This section constitutes the agenda for each day's business of the Senate and is not subsequently republished in its *Journals*.

2. PROCEEDINGS AND JOURNALS

Votes and Proceedings and Journals of the House of Commons
The *Votes and Proceedings* include the daily transactions of the House, the Speech from the Throne, the Address in Reply to the Speech from the Throne, proclamations regarding the summoning and dissolution of Parliament, titles of bills read and assent to bills, recorded votes in the House, Speaker's rulings, lists of returns and reports deposited with the Clerk, a summary of Orders-in-Council passed each month, rosters of committees and committee reports. Everything printed above the Speaker's signature in the daily *Votes and Proceedings* appears at the end of each session in the bound *Journals* of the House of Commons, which then become the official records of the House. Everything printed below the Speaker's signature in the *Votes and Proceedings*, such as notices of committee meetings, is omitted from the *Journals*. The *Journals* are so named because they provide

* * American Library Association, Committee on Library Terminology, *A.L.A. Glossary of Library Terms, with a Selection of Terms in Related Fields*, Chicago, American Library Association, 1943, p. 65.

a complete and concise record of the proceedings of the House in chronological order, day by day.

The bound *Journals* contain a list of sessional papers and a list of appendices consisting mainly of reports of standing committees. Occasionally, the report of a special joint committee of the House of Commons and the Senate is published in the bound *Journals*. An index to the *Journals* is included in the final volume for each session. To locate a Commons committee report in its *Journals*, it is necessary to look in the index under the name of the committee concerned.

Minutes of the Proceedings and Journals of the Senate

The *Minutes of the Proceedings* of the Senate, the official record of proceedings, are issued daily when the Senate is in session and correspond to the *Votes and Proceedings* of the House of Commons. At the end of each session, the *Minutes of the Proceedings* and such appendices as it is decided to include are published with an index in the *Journals* of the Senate. Reports of standing and special committees of the Senate are included in the *Journals*. To locate a Senate committee report in its *Journals*, it is necessary to look in the index under "Committees" where the references to various committees are gathered together.

3. DEBATES

Debates of the House of Commons (Hansard)

The most familiar of the legislative publications are the debates which give a verbatim account of what is said in Parliament. The several volumes each session record the daily debates of the House, messages of the Governor-General and varying information such as lists of members of the House and of the Ministry. Like those of the British Parliament, the Canadian debates are referred to as Hansard in honour of the Hansard family which reported and published the British debates in the nineteenth century.

The only example of printed debates as we know them today which were published before Confederation are the *Parliamentary Debates on the Subject of the Confederation of the British North American Provinces*, published in 1865 and republished in 1951. This volume was indexed by the Public Archives of Canada under the title *Index to Parliamentary Debates on the Subject of the Confederation of the British North American Provinces*, compiled by M.A. Lapin and edited and revised by J.S. Patrick.

The debates of the early Canadian Parliaments, as in most countries, were not officially reported and the only records are, with a few exceptions, the so-called *Scrapbook Debates* which are in the Library of Parliament. These debates consist of clippings from contemporary newspapers, which have been mounted in scrapbooks and for which handwritten indexes have been made. The *Scrapbook Debates* cover the period from Confederation to 1874, and are available on microfilm, published by the Canadian Library Association, Ottawa, 1954. From 1870 to 1872, three volumes of debates of both Houses were published but were unofficial in origin. These are referred to as the *Cotton Debates* after the name of the Ottawa *Times* reporter, John Cotton, who covered the sessions. Not until 1875 did the House of Commons itself begin reporting its debates. From 1875 to 1879, the contract for reporting these debates was awarded to private reporters, but from 1880 on, an official staff of reporters was appointed to secure continuity and uniformity.

As a Centennial project of the Parliament of Canada under the auspices of the Library of Parliament, the Debates of the House of Commons for the years from 1867 to 1875 are being edited by Professor Peter B. Waite of Dalhousie University and published by the Queen's Printer. This reconstructed edition is principally a collation of the debates published during these years in the Ottawa *Times* and Toronto *Globe*. To date, debates for the years from 1867 to May 1870 have been published. The House debates for the years 1870 to 1874 are also to be reconstituted from the same sources for publication.

The daily edition of the *Debates: Official Report (Hansard)* is issued in pamphlet form during each session of Parliament on the morning following each day's sitting and contains the speeches in English as delivered and the English translation of speeches delivered in French. Similarly, a daily edition of the *Debates* containing the speeches in French as delivered and the French translation of speeches delivered in English is also issued on the day following delivery. Following publication of the daily edition, proofs of their speeches or remarks are sent to members for suggested changes which must be confined to the correction of errors and essential minor alterations. At the end of each session, revised bound volumes are published. At the present time, each Wednesday's edition of the daily *Debates* includes an alphabetical list of members with their constituencies, party affiliations and addresses; a complete list of standing, special and joint committees with the membership of each; members of the Ministry according to precedence; and a list of parliamentary secretaries.

In recent years, an index to the daily House of Commons *Debates* has been issued in pamphlet form at intervals during the session. The complete index is either included in the final bound volume of the *Debates* for the session or published separately.

Debates of the Senate (Hansard)

This series is also referred to as Hansard from its prototype, the Parliamentary debates of Great Britain. For the years 1870-1872 inclusive, unofficial non-verbatim versions of the Senate debates appear in the *Cotton Debates* referred to above. The *Debates* of the Senate covering the first three sessions of the first Parliament, November 6, 1867 to May 12, 1870, have been edited by Professor Waite and published as part of the Centennial project of the Parliament of Canada referred to above. In 1871, the Senate began publishing its own *Debates*. From 1871 to 1899, they were published in English only, and from 1871 to 1916, the contract for reporting was awarded to various persons, but in 1917, an official reporter was appointed.

The *Debates: Official Report (Hansard)* of the Senate are, like those of the House of Commons, recorded and printed day by day. The same opportunity is afforded its members to amend or correct errors and omissions in the daily *Debates*, so that the bound volume at the end of the session may be complete and correct. The amount and extent of corrections in Hansard are subject to discussion and agreement in each House respectively. The issue of the *Debates* for the first Tuesday of each month appends a list of

Senators arranged according to seniority, alphabetically and by province. Officers and committees of the Senate are also listed.

In recent years, an index to the daily *Debates* of the Senate has sometimes been issued in pamphlet form at intervals during the session. The complete index is included in the final bound volume of the *Debates* for each session.

4. SESSIONAL PAPERS AND ANNUAL DEPARTMENTAL REPORTS

Sessional Papers
During the course of each session of Parliament, certain reports and papers are received which, when deposited with the Clerk and tabled in the House or Senate, are designated as sessional papers. In the case of the House, each paper, whether printed or unprinted, is assigned a distinctive number and listed in the daily *Votes and Proceedings* along with the name of the Minister who deposited the paper with the Clerk. Published papers are listed in the various checklists and catalogues issued by the Canadian Government Publishing Centre; photocopies of unpublished papers are available for a fee from the Journals Branch of the House of Commons.

In the case of sessional papers deposited with the Clerk of the Senate, photocopies are available for a fee from the Minutes and Journals Branch of the Senate.

From 1867/68 to 1925, sessional papers were published in a collected series. This series included most of the reports that came before Parliament and were ordered printed, with the exception of the reports of committees which were printed as appendices to the *Journals* of each House. There were several volumes of sessional papers for each session, and each volume includes both an alphabetical and numerical list of the papers for that session. They are not paged continuously and indexes refer to the number of each document rather than to pages. Much of the material published in the *Sessional Papers* was also published elsewhere, e.g., a branch report might appear in the *Sessional Papers*, be published separately, and published as part of a departmental report as well as being issued in both English and French. The government ceased publication of the *Sessional Papers* series in 1925 after having published some 923 volumes since Confederation, but the departmental reports formerly included were continued in the series of *Annual Departmental Reports.*.

General Indexes to the Journals of the House and to Sessional Papers
In order to facilitate their use, a consolidated *General Index to the Journals of the House of Commons of Canada, and of the Sessional Papers of Parliament* was published on five occasions covering the following periods: 1867-1876; 1877-1890; 1891-1903; 1904-1915; and 1916-1930. General indexes to the *Journals* of the House of Commons are planned to cover the period since 1930.

Annual Departmental Reports
From 1924/25 to 1929/30, *Annual Departmental Reports* were issued in a series. This series included reports of some commissions as well as continuing the departmental reports issued in *Sessional Papers* up to 1924. Since

this series also duplicated material issued in other forms, it was dropped in 1930 as an economy measure. Annual departmental reports are now published separately by the respective departments, agencies, boards and commissions.

5. PARLIAMENTARY COMMITTEES AND THEIR PUBLICATIONS

Unlike the royal commission or commission of inquiry, which are creatures of the executive, the parliamentary committee is a vital part of the legislative arm of the government—the House of Commons and Senate. Parliamentary committees are of three kinds: the Committee of the Whole House, standing committees, and special committees.

The main function of the Committee of the Whole House is deliberation, rather than inquiry, and clause-by-clause discussion of the bills under consideration, which is facilitated by relaxation of the formal rules of debate and party discipline. The proceedings of the Committee of the Whole House are reported without a break in the *Debates* and in the *Journals* and there is no special problem in locating them.

House of Commons Committees
Under the Standing Orders of the House of Commons adopted June 1978, all public bills except those based on a supply or ways and means motion are referred at the end of second reading to a standing committee of the House or to a special or joint committee for clause-by-clause deliberation. In addition, all governmental estimates for expenditures are also referred to a standing committee.

The effect of recent changes in House procedure has been to extend significantly the functions of its standing committees and, as a consequence, their influence and importance. The standing committees are permanently provided for in the Standing Orders, and are set up at the commencement of each session of Parliament to consider all subjects of a particular type arising or likely to arise in the course of the session, e.g., agriculture; communications and culture; external affairs and national defence; finance, trade and economic affairs; fisheries and forestry; health, welfare and social affairs; Indian affairs and northern development; justice and legal affairs; labour, manpower and immigration; management and members' services; miscellaneous estimates; miscellaneous private bills and standing orders; national resources and public works; privileges and elections; procedure and organization; public accounts; regional development; transport; and veterans' affairs. The deliberations of standing committees are published as *Minutes of Proceedings and Evidence* as their meetings occur. An index is issued for each committee at the end of the session.

Special committees are frequently set up to consider and report on particular bills or upon special subjects. The chief function of the special committee is to investigate, and it is the legislative prototype of the executive's commission of inquiry except that its members must be members of Parliament. Deliberations of special committees are also published as they occur as *Minutes of Proceedings and Evidence*.

Reports of standing committees of the House are published in the daily *Votes and Proceedings*; reports of most special committees, however, are published separately. A list of committee reports appears in the "List of Appendices" in the *Journals* of the House of Commons for each session. These are indexed under the name of the Committee.

Senate Committees

Standing committees set up under the Rules of the Senate are: agriculture; banking, trade and commerce; internal economy, budgets and administration; foreign affairs; health, welfare and science; legal and constitutional affairs; national finance; standing rules and orders; and transport and communication. Reports of standing committees of the Senate are usually published in its *Minutes of the Proceedings*, frequently as an appendix, and are republished in the *Journals* of the Senate. Reports of special committees of the Senate may be published separately as monographs. A list of Senate committee reports appears in the index of the *Journals* under "Committees."

Joint Committees of the House of Commons and Senate

A "joint committee" is one appointed from the membership of both the House of Commons and Senate, e.g., the Joint Committee on Regulations and Other Statutory Instruments, and may be either a standing or special committee.

Committee reports of the House of Commons and of the Senate that are published separately are listed in the checklists and catalogues described below.

6. BILLS, ACTS AND STATUTES

Bills

All Bills originating in the House of Commons or Senate are printed in pamphlet form after first reading. Bills originating in the House of Commons are distinguished by the letter "C" and numbered chronologically as introduced. The numbers from C-2 to C-200 have been reserved for government bills; numbers from C-201 to C-1000 have been allocated to Private Members' bills; and C-1001 upwards to Private Members' private bills. All bills are printed in a bilingual format with English and French text in parallel columns. The progress of bills through the three readings and committee stage is recorded in the *Order Paper and Notices* previously cited. At the end of each session, a list of bills is included in the index to the *Journals* of the House.

Bills originating in the Senate are distinguished by the letter "S" and numbered chronologically as introduced. They also are printed in pamphlet form in a bilingual format. The progress of bills through the three readings and committee stage is recorded in the *Minutes of the Proceedings* of the Senate previously cited. At the end of each session, a list of bills is included in the index to the *Journals* of the Senate.

Parliament issues no bound volume of bills which have failed to pass, and few libraries other than legislative libraries keep such bills beyond the session during which they were proposed.

Acts

When a bill has successfully passed through three readings of both the House of Commons and Senate and received Royal Assent from the Governor-General, it becomes an Act. Each Act is then assigned a chapter number coupled with the name of the reigning sovereign and the regnal year, e.g., 29 Eliz. II 1979, c. 4. Individual Acts are published in pamphlet form by the Queen's Printer. New Acts are also published in Part III of *The Canada Gazette* in order to expedite their distribution to the public. Acts may also be made available from time to time in unofficial pamphlet form as office consolidations, with or without the related regulations.

Statutes of Canada

The Acts passed during each session are gathered together in one or more volumes entitled *Acts of the Parliament of Canada*. In bound form the Acts are more commonly known as the *Statutes of Canada*. Part I of the *Statutes* consists of Public General Acts; Part II of Local and Private Acts. Currently, each sessional volume of *Statutes* has a table of contents listing Acts by their short title, a separate English and French index to Public General Acts, a list of Proclamations of Canada, and a Table of Public Statutes from 1907 to date.

Revised Statutes of Canada

The *Revised Statutes of Canada*, which bring legislation amended since its original passage up to date, have been issued five times since Confederation: 1886, 1906, 1927, 1952 and 1970. When the 1970 *Revised Statutes* were proclaimed in force, the proclamation had the effect of repealing those public general statutes included in the revision and replacing them by the statutes in the revision. For the first time in the history of the Canadian Parliament, the 1970 *Revised Statutes* were tabled in the House of Commons both in the form of magnetic tape containing the machine-readable data base used in their production, as well as in the traditional form of bound volumes. The 1970 revision is in two-language, English-French page format for the first time and each volume contains a table of contents and index. There is also a separate index volume which forms part of the eleven-volume set of the 1970 *Revised Statutes*.

Special Compilations of Statutes

After third reading and Royal Assent, an Act may be published in pamphlet form as a "separate chapter" for public distribution. From time to time, the government also issues unofficial "office consolidations" of certain statutes and regulations for the convenience of court officials, lawyers, and the public generally. For special compilations and indexes to legislation of the federal government prior to 1932, one should consult Marion V. Higgins, *Canadian Government Publications*, described below.

7. THE CANADA GAZETTE, ORDERS-IN-COUNCIL AND REGULATIONS

The Canada Gazette

The Canada Gazette, published in three parts in a bilingual format, is the official gazette of Canada. All matters under the control of Parliament and requiring publication are published in *The Canada Gazette* unless some other mode of publication is required by law.

The Canada Gazette, Part I, is published every Saturday and contains notices of a general character, proclamations, Orders-in-Council required to be published by the enabling Act but not by the Statutory Instruments Act, and various other classes of statutory notices. Orders-in-Council are designated by the letters PC (for Privy Council), followed by the year and a chronological number. Extras and supplements of Part I are published as required. Each issue is indexed and there are also non-cumulative quarterly indexes but no annual index.

The *Canada Gazette, Part II,* is published under the authority of the Statutory Instruments Act on the second and fourth Wednesday of each month with special editions as required. It contains all regulations as defined by the Statutory Instruments Act, and certain other classes of statutory instruments and documents required to be published therein. Each item in Part II is listed by its registration number assigned in the Privy Council Office as either SOR (regulations) or SI (other than regulations) and the numbers are consecutive within each series and year. All regulations and other statutory instruments (other than regulations), and other documents that have been made under statutory or other authority and that were in force at any time since January 1 of the current calendar year, are indexed in the *Consolidated Index of Statutory Instruments,* a quarterly publication. For instruments in force in other than the current calendar year, reference should be made to the *Consolidated Index* of December 31st of the year in question.

The *Canada Gazette, Part III,* is published under the authority of the Statutory Instruments Act. Its purpose is to publish Public Acts as soon as is reasonably practicable after they have received Royal Assent in order to expedite their distribution. Part III contains certain other ancillary information, including a list of proclamations of Canada showing when Acts have been proclaimed in force. From time to time, a Table of Public Statutes from 1907 to date and a Table of Acts and the Ministers responsible for their administration are published.

Orders-in-Council and Regulations
Orders-in-Council were first published in the *Statutes of Canada* for 1872. From 1874 to 1939, certain statutory orders and regulations having the force of law were published in the preliminary section of the *Statutes of Canada.* On two occasions during this period, consolidations were published by the federal government: *Orders-in-Council, Proclamations, Departmental Regulations, etc., Having the Force of Law in the Dominion of Canada* (1875), and *Consolidated Orders-in-Council of Canada* (1889).

Since 1939, there has been a steady increase in the number of statutes which confer power to make orders and regulations on the Minister. The systematic publication of statutory orders "of general or widespread interest or concern" is a fairly recent development. It began in 1940 with the publication of *Proclamations and Orders-in-Council [relating to the War].* Eight volumes of this series were published covering the period from August 26, 1939 to September 30, 1942. During the period from 1940 to 1942, the federal government also published three volumes of the consolidated *Defence of Canada Regulations.* In October 1942, a new publication, *Cana-*

dian War Orders and Regulations, began. Its title changed to *Statutory Orders and Regulations* in October 1945 and it ceased publication in January 1947.

Since January 1, 1947, provision has been made for publication of statutory orders and regulations in Part II of *The Canada Gazette.* In 1950, a *Statutory Orders and Regulations Consolidation* was published, bringing together all statutes which conferred the power to make orders or regulations, and all orders and regulations having a general effect. A later consolidation was published in 1955.

For the period 1867-1975, the Privy Council Office has prepared an annual index of Orders-in-Council which is available on microfilm from the Public Archives of Canada.

A monthly "Summary of Orders-in-Council Passed During the Month" is tabled in the House of Commons and is listed in the *Votes and Proceedings.*

Consolidated Regulations of Canada

In 1978, the *Consolidated Regulations of Canada* were published in 19 volumes. Briefly stated, the consolidation includes: (a) statutory orders and regulations published in the 1955 consolidation of *Statutory Orders and Regulations*; (b) regulations, statutory instruments and other documents published in *The Canada Gazette, Part II,* since the 1955 consolidation; and (c) regulations that, prior to the date of the coming into force of the Statutory Instruments Act, were not published in *The Canada Gazette* but were registered after that date with the Clerk of the Privy Council and were in force on December 31, 1977 and are of general application. It includes as well certain regulations not included in the 1955 consolidation and certain unpublished statutory orders that are still in force and of general application.

To assist users in updating the *Consolidated Regulations of Canada, 1978,* a special two-volume issue of *The Canada Gazette, Part II* was published. The material contained in the special issue is essentially a republication of regulations and other instruments published in 1978 that amend or revoke regulations found in the 1978 consolidation. It does not include regulations published as new regulations during that period.

Each amending regulation and other instrument appearing in the first 16 issues of Part II of *The Canada Gazette* in 1979 was footnoted by title and section number or subdivision thereof to indicate its relation to the 1978 *Consolidated Regulations* where applicable. Commencing with the 17th issue, any material published in Part II of *The Canada Gazette* and affecting the 1978 consolidation refers in the body of the text to a chapter number and, if re-numbering has taken place, to new section numbers. In addition, each amendment or revocation of a regulation or other instrument is footnoted to cite previous relevant amendments of each section or subdivision thereof that is being amended or revoked.

For information about regulations and other instruments in force since January 1, 1978, reference should be made to the *Consolidated Index of Statutory Instruments* for the most recent year. This is a quarterly index that cumulates annually from the date of the consolidation.

8. COMMISSIONS OF INQUIRY AND TASK FORCES

Reports of Royal Commissions and Commissions of Inquiry
Royal commissions, or commissions of inquiry as they are now generally called, are appointed under the terms of the Inquiries Act by the executive arm of government, i.e., the Cabinet, to carry out full and impartial investigations of specific problems and to report their findings so that decisions may be reached and appropriate action taken. When the Cabinet has approved of the setting up of a royal commission or commission of inquiry, it issues an Order-in-Council which is published in *The Canada Gazette, Part I,* giving the terms of reference, powers and names of the commissioners. The commission is usually empowered to call witnesses and to hold public hearings. When the commission has completed its investigation and made its report to the Prime Minister, the report is subsequently published. There has been a recent trend towards the commissioning of special studies which are prepared as supplements to the main report; for example, 26 special studies were published as supplements to the Report of the Royal Commission on Health Services. Usually commissions are popularly referred to by the names of their chairmen; hence the so-called "Lambert report" is the *Final Report* of the Royal Commission on Financial Management and Accountability, chaired by Allen T. Lambert.

A useful reference work for locating royal commission reports is *Federal Royal Commissions in Canada, 1867-1966; A Checklist,* by George F. Henderson, published by the University of Toronto Press in 1967. From 1940 to 1970-71, each edition of the *Canada Year Book* contained a list of newly appointed royal commissions, both federal and provincial, indicating their terms of reference and their date of appointment. This feature was resumed with the 1974 edition.

Reports of Task Forces
The term "task force" became a common expression during World War II when it was used to describe a military force, frequently involving different services, assembled to undertake a specific task. In the jargon of government, the term is used to describe a group of experts gathered together to tackle a particular problem of public concern. In Canada, the use of task forces to help formulate government policy on such topics as labour relations, the government's role in sport, and housing, became fashionable in the late 1960s. In its composition and operation, the task force stands somewhere between a royal commission and a Parliamentary committee. Usually, the task force is made up of academics and other experts from outside government who work closely with senior civil servants. The task force may commission special studies, invite briefs and hold public hearings.

An example of a task force report is: *A Future Together: Observations and Recommendations,* a report of the Task Force on Canadian Unity, published in 1979.

9. PUBLICATIONS OF THE FEDERAL COURTS

The principal publications of the judicial arm of the federal government consist of the reports of cases tried before the two federal courts, the

Federal Court of Canada (formerly known as the Exchequer Court of Canada), and the Supreme Court of Canada. From 1876 to 1922, there was a series of *Reports of the Exchequer Court of Canada*; from 1923 to 1969, the series was known as *Canada Law Reports: Exchequer Court of Canada*; in 1970, the title was changed to *Canada Exchequer Court Reports*, and when the Federal Court replaced the Exchequer Court in 1971, its judgements were contained in a new series called *Canada Federal Court Reports*. From 1876 to 1922, there was also a series known as the *Reports of the Supreme Court of Canada*; from 1923 to 1969, the series was called *Canada Law Reports: Supreme Court of Canada*; and, since 1970, the series has been known as *Canada Supreme Court Reports*.

B. Bibliographies and Catalogues of Government Publications

1. FEDERAL GOVERNMENT PUBLICATIONS

Bibliographies
A useful guide is *Canadian Federal Government Publications; A Bibliography of Bibliographies*, by Mohan Bhatia, which was published in 1971 by the University of Saskatchewan and is divided into three parts: general bibliographies, bibliographies of parliamentary publications, and bibliographies of departmental publications.

Although out-of-date, the manual on *Canadian Government Publications*, compiled by Marion V. Higgins and published in 1935 by the American Library Association, remains the outstanding descriptive bibliography in its field. It includes federal publications beginning with the united province of Canada, 1841-1867. Publications are arranged according to the issuing office, and brief histories of the various governmental agencies are supplied along with a list of their publications. These publications are divided into two large groups: serial publications and special publications. For serials, inclusive dates of publication are shown with a note as to whether or not the reports appeared in the *Sessional Papers* and *Annual Departmental Reports*. The section on special publications includes all of those publications issued by each governmental agency which were not published in the *Journals* or *Sessional Papers*. There is a general subject index.

Government Catalogues Issued Before 1953
For federal government publications issued prior to 1953, the indexes and catalogues available were incomplete, spasmodic, and originated from many different sources. From 1892 to 1938, the *Annual Report* of the Department of Public Printing and Stationery contained a list of government pamphlets and miscellaneous monographs issued during the fiscal year and arranged according to the issuing agency. No bibliographical details were given except paging. From 1894 to 1927, this department also issued a *Price List of Government Publications* which was superseded in 1928 by the *Catalogue of Official Publications of the Parliament and Government of Canada*. This latter publication was issued from 1928 to 1948 in different forms, later being known as the *Government Publications*

Annual Catalogue. It was simply a list of titles and prices of all official publications procurable from the King's Printer and no bibliographical details were supplied. It had supplements at intervals up to 1952, when it was replaced by a new series of daily, monthly and annual catalogues.

Government Catalogues Issued Since 1953

In 1953, the Queen's Printer published the *Canadian Government Publications Consolidated Annual Catalogue*, a basic work which superseded the old *Annual Catalogue* of 1948 and its supplements to 1952. The *Consolidated Annual Catalogue* attempted to include all federal government publications in print as of September, 1953. The *Canadian Government Publications Annual Catalogue*, 1954, supplemented the *Consolidated Annual Catalogue*, 1953, and listed federal government publications issued between October 1953 and December 1954. Both the 1953 and 1954 editions were also published separately in French.

From 1955 to 1977, a bilingual annual *Catalogue* was published. This annual *Catalogue* superseded issues of the bilingual *Canadian Government Publications Monthly Catalogue* which, in turn, cumulated issues of the bilingual *Daily Checklist of Canadian Government Publications.* The purpose of these catalogues was to provide a comprehensive listing of all official publications, public documents and papers, not of a confidential nature, printed or processed at government expense by authority of Parliament or of a government agency, or bought at public expense for distribution to members of Parliament, public servants, or the public. These publications made it possible to check the bibliographic details, price and distribution policy of any current federal government publication. The *Monthly Catalogue* and the annual *Catalogue* were indexed by personal author, title and subject. From 1963 to 1978, the *Monthly Catalogue* also indexed articles in about two dozen Canadian government periodicals by personal author, title and subject. From 1963 to 1977, this index was cumulated in the annual *Catalogue.*

Since 1978, the federal government has introduced a number of changes for economic reasons in the content and frequency of its major checklists and catalogues. In November 1978, a *Weekly Checklist of Canadian Government Publications* superseded the *Daily Checklist.* In 1979, the *Government of Canada Publications Quarterly Catalogue* replaced the *Monthly Catalogue* and the indexing of government periodicals was dropped. The final cumulated edition of the annual *Catalogue* covered the year 1977. Since 1978, a *Government of Canada Publications Index* has been issued annually but, because this publication does not cumulate the contents of the *Quarterly Checklist*, it is necessary to refer from the annual *Index* to the *Quarterly Catalogue* for full information about publications.

The Canadian Government Publishing Centre of the Department of Supply and Services periodically issues a *Special List of Canadian Government Publications*, a bilingual pamphlet highlighting selected publications available free from the issuing department, as well as a selection of publications for sale by the Publishing Centre. In 1976, the Publishing Centre began to issue a new series of bilingual *Subject Lists* of priced Canadian government publications. Each *Subject List* is devoted to a topic of current interest such as Energy, Environment, and Business. *Publishing News*, also issued by the

Publishing Centre, contains information about new titles and editions, out-of-print items etc., and is distributed to booksellers and libraries.

Sectional and Departmental Catalogues
From 1963 to 1970, the federal government published seven sectional catalogues which were especially useful for providing a detailed subject approach to the many hundreds of publications issued by selected departments and agencies. The sectional catalogues were: 10, Labour (1963); 11, Northern Affairs and National Resources (1963); 12, Mines Branch (1967); 13, Forestry (1963); 14, Dominion Bureau of Statistics (1964); 15, Canada Treaty Series (1967); and 16, National Museums of Canada (1970). There are no plans to continue this series.

Certain federal government departments and agencies, such as the Department of Agriculture, the Geological Survey, Statistics Canada, and the National Research Council of Canada, periodically issue excellent guides or indexes to their respective publications giving greater detail than is possible in the general catalogues issued by the Publications Centre.

Canadiana
In 1951, the National Library of Canada (then known as the Canadian Bibliographic Centre) began issuing *Canadiana*, a national monthly bibliography listing books about Canada, published in Canada, or written by Canadians. Since 1952, one part of *Canadiana* has been devoted to federal government publications and all listings are in full bibliographic form giving author, title, edition, publisher, date and place of publication, paging, series notes, and other pertinent information. Coverage of federal government publications in *Canadiana* is not quite as comprehensive as is the case with the *Quarterly Catalogue*. Nevertheless, the bibliographical description for each item listed is considerably more complete, often supplying details about previous publications in the same series. Since 1953, another part of *Canadiana* has listed current publications of the ten provincial governments. *Canadiana* is cumulated annually.

Commercial Indexes
In January 1977, Micromedia Limited of Toronto began publication of *Publicat Index*, a bibliographic reference tool covering Canadian federal government publications of general reference value. Designed to supplement the *Daily Checklist* and *Special List* issued by the Publishing Centre, the *Publicat Index* provided comprehensive coverage of current publications and serials not appearing in the government's own checklists and catalogues. In addition, the *Publicat Index* included selected monographs of reference value which might also have appeared on the government checklists. The *Publicat Index*, which was published monthly and cumulated annually, was superseded in 1979 by the *Microlog Index*, which includes not only Canadian federal publications but also selected provincial and municipal government publications. The *Microlog Index*, issued monthly and cumulated annually by Micromedia Limited, is divided into three parts: main entry section, subject section, and title section; it also has a bilingual index.

2. PROVINCIAL AND TERRITORIAL GOVERNMENT PUBLICATIONS

In general, publications of the provincial governments parallel the types issued by the federal government. Most provinces publish debates, votes and proceedings, journals, sessional papers, annual departmental reports, and gazettes. Because of a dearth of published indexes or catalogues, provincial government publications have in the past been much more difficult to locate than those of the federal government. The situation has improved considerably in recent years but some provinces still do not publish catalogues of their publications on a regular basis. A useful reference work is *Canadian Provincial Government Publications; Bibliography of Bibliographies*, compiled by Mohan Bhatia and published by the Library of the University of Saskatchewan, 1971.

Another valuable reference work for provincial government publications was *Profile Index* which was issued monthly from 1973 to 1978 and cumulated annually. Published by Micromedia Limited of Toronto, *Profile Index* was superseded in 1979 by *Microlog Index*, described above, which includes selected provincial government publications.

A Guide to the Identification and Acquisition of Canadian Provincial Government Publications, prepared by Catherine and Paul Pross, and published in 1977 by the Dalhousie University Libraries and the School of Library Service, is an extremely useful manual for those seeking information about publications issued by provincial governments.

3. RETROSPECTIVE BIBLIOGRAPHIES AND CURRENT CHECKLISTS

Retrospective bibliographies and current checklists and catalogues of provincial and territorial government publications are listed below:

Alberta

Retrospective
MacDonald, Christine. *Publications of the Government of the North-West Territories, 1876-1905, and of the Province of Saskatchewan, 1905-1952.* Regina: Legislative Library, 1952. Includes early material relating to the area which is now Alberta.

Forsyth, Joseph. *Government Publications Relating to Alberta: A Bibliography of Publications of the Government of Alberta from 1905 to 1968, and of Publications of the Government of Canada Relating to the Province of Alberta from 1867 to 1968.* 8 vol. Ann Arbor, Mich: University Microfilms International, 1979. (F.L.A. thesis).

Current
In 1974, the Alberta Government Services Public Affairs Bureau issued a *Publications Catalogue* covering the year 1973. Since 1974, the *Publications Catalogue* has been issued quarterly and cumulated annually.

British Columbia

Retrospective
British Columbia. Provincial Archives. *Dictionary Catalogue of the Provincial Archives of British Columbia.* 8 vol. Boston: G.K. Hall, 1971. Includes government publications.

Lowther, Barbara. *A Bibliography of British Columbia: Laying the Foundations, 1849-1899.* Victoria: University of Victoria, 1968. Includes government publications.

Holmes, Marjorie C. *Publications of the Government of British Columbia, 1871-1947.* Victoria: Provincial Library, 1950.

Current
British Columbia Government Publications Monthly Checklist, compiled and issued by the Legislative Library of British Columbia, Victoria, dates from January 1970.

Manitoba

Retrospective
Morley, Marjorie. *A Bibliography of Manitoba from Holdings in the Legislative Library of Manitoba.* Winnipeg: Legislative Library, 1970.

Current
Manitoba Government Publications Received in the Legislative Library of Manitoba dates from 1970 and was issued three times a year. It was superseded by *Manitoba Government Publications* which has been issued monthly since 1975 and is published by the Department of Cultural Affairs and Historical Resources. An annual cumulation of the monthly checklists is published by the Queen's Printer.

New Brunswick

Retrospective
Bishop, Olga B. *Publications of the Governments of Nova Scotia, Prince Edward Island, New Brunswick, 1758-1952.* Ottawa: National Library, 1957.

Guilbeault, Claude. *Guide to Official Publications of New Brunswick 1952-1970.* Ottawa: University of Ottawa Library School, 1974. (M.L.S. thesis).

Current
New Brunswick Government Documents is an annual checklist of provincial publications received at the Legislative Library in Fredericton and dates from 1955.

Newfoundland

Retrospective
O'Dea, Agnes C. *A Newfoundland Bibliography.* (Preliminary). St. John's: Memorial University of Newfoundland, 1960. Includes government publications.

Current
List of Publications Offered by Government of Newfoundland and Labrador was issued by the Newfoundland Information Service on an irregular basis from 1974 to 1978 when it suspended publication.

Nova Scotia

Retrospective
Bishop, Olga B. *Publications of the Governments of Nova Scotia, Prince Edward Island, New Brunswick, 1758-1952.* Ottawa: National Library, 1957.

Current
Publications of the Province of Nova Scotia is an annual checklist of provincial publications compiled by the Legislative Library. The first issue covered the year 1967. In June 1980, *Publications of the Province of Nova Scotia: Quarterly Checklist*, a list of publications received at the Legislative Library during the quarter, began publication.

Ontario

Retrospective
Bishop, Olga B. *Publications of the Government of the Province of Canada, 1841-1867.* Ottawa: National Library of Canada, 1963. The Province of Canada consisted of Canada West (Ontario) and Canada East (Quebec.)

Bishop, Olga B. *Publications of the Government of Ontario, 1867-1900.* Toronto: Ministry of Government Services, 1976.

MacTaggart, Hazel I. *Publications of the Government of Ontario, 1901-1955: A Checklist Compiled for the Ontario Library Association.* Toronto: University of Toronto Press for the Queen's Printer, 1964.

MacTaggart, Hazel I., and Sundquist, Kenneth E. *Publications of the Government of Ontario, 1956-1971: A Checklist.* Toronto: Ministry of Government Services, 1975.

Current
Ontario Government Publications Monthly Checklist, compiled and edited by the Legislative Library, has been published by the Ministry of Government Services since May 1971. It is cumulated into the *Ontario Government Publications Annual Catalogue*, the first one of which was issued for the year 1972.

Catalogue des publications en français du gouvernement de l'Ontario is a quarterly publication compiled and edited by the Legislative Library and published by the Ministry of Government Services. The first issue was published in 1979.

Prince Edward Island

Retrospective
Bishop, Olga B. *Publications of the Governments of Nova Scotia, Prince Edward Island, New Brunswick, 1758-1952.* Ottawa: National Library, 1957.

Current
P.E.I. Provincial Government Publications Checklist, published since 1976 by the Island Information Service, is issued eleven times a year.

Quebec

Retrospective
Hare, John E. and Wallot, Jean-Pierre. *Les imprimés dans le Bas-Canada, 1801-1941.* Montréal: Presses de l'Université de Montréal, 1967. First of a series; includes government publications.

Bishop, Olga B. *Publications of the Government of the Province of Canada 1841-1867.* Ottawa: National Library of Canada, 1963. The Province of Canada consisted of Canada West (Ontario) and Canada East (Quebec).

Beaulieu, André; Bonenfant, Jean-Charles; and Hamelin, Jean. *Répertoire des publications gouvernementales du Québec,1867-1964.* Québec: Imprimeur de la Reine, 1968.

Beaulieu, André; Hamelin, Jean; and Bernier, Gaston. *Répertoire des publications gouvernementales du Québec: Supplément 1965-1968.* Québec: Editeur officiel du Québec, 1970.

Current
Bibliographie du Québec; Liste mensuelle des publications québécoises ou relatives au Québec établie par la Bibliothèque nationale du Québec, published in Montreal since 1968, contains a section on current government publications of the province.

Catalogue de l'Editeur Officiel has been issued from time to time since 1966 and lists legislative and departmental publications for sale by the Bureau de l'Editeur Officiel. The same agency also publishes *Choix des publications gouvernementales,* an irregular selected annotated list arranged by subject with author and title indexes.

Liste mensuelle des publications du gouvernement du Québec, issued by Service de Diffusion, Ministère des Communications, began monthly publication in April 1981.

Répertoire des publications gouvernementales gratuites, a directory of free publications, is issued from time to time by the Ministère des communications.

Saskatchewan

Retrospective
MacDonald, Christine. *Publications of the Governments of the North-West Territories, 1876-1905, and of the Province of Saskatchewan, 1905-1952.* Regina: Legislative Library, 1952.

Current
Checklist of Saskatchewan Government Publications has been issued every two or three months since 1976 by the Legislative Library of Saskatchewan, Regina.

Northwest Territories

Retrospective
MacDonald, Christine. *Publications of the Governments of the North-West Territories, 1876-1905, and of the Province of Saskatchewan, 1905-1952.* Regina: Legislative Library, 1952.

Current
Government Publications Catalogue is published annually by the Department of Information. The first annual covered the year 1977.

Yukon Territory

Retrospective
Yukon Bibliography. [1897-1963] Ottawa: Department of Northern Affairs and National Resources, 1964. *Update* 1963-1970; 1971-1973; 1974-1975; 1976-1977. Edmonton: Boreal Institute of Northern Studies. Biennial. Includes some government publications.

BIBLIOGRAPHY

Guide to Government Publications

Banks, M.A., *Using a Law Library: A Guide for Students and Lawyers in the Common Law Provinces of Canada*, Toronto, Carswell, 3rd ed., 1980.

Bishop, O.B., *Canadian Official Publications*, Oxford, Pergamon Press, 1981. (Guides to Official Publications, Vol. 9.)

Canada, Treasury Board, Administrative Policy Branch, *Administrative Policy Manual, Chapter 335, Publishing, December 1978*, Ottawa, 1979.

Cherns, J.J., *Official Publishing*, London, Pergamon, 1979.

Dodson, S.C., "Government Publishing in Microform in Canada," *Government Publications Review*, 7A (no. 3, 1980): 253-56.

Dykstra, G.S., *How to Update a Statute for All Canadian Jurisdictions (as of April 1980)*, Ottawa, C.L.I.C., 1980.

Hardisty, A.P., and Graham, M., "Problems Relating to the Acquisition of Federal and Provincial Publications and Some Possible Solutions," *CALL Newsletter*, 4, Nov./Dec. 1978, 55-62.

Janisch, A., "Towards a Subject Index for Legislation in Canada," C.J.I.S., 3, May, 1978, 44-61.

Ward, J., *The Hansard Chronicles*, Ottawa, D. and G., 1980.

Political Science — Introductory

Alker, H.R., Jr., *Mathematics and Politics*, Toronto, C.M., 1965.

Backstrom, C.H., and Hursh, G.D., *Survey Research*, Chicago, Northwestern University Press, 1963.

Benson, O., *Political Science Laboratory*, Columbus, Charles E. Merrill, 1969.

Bergeron, G., Painchaud, P., Sabourin, L., Tournon, J., *L'état actuel de la théorie politique*, Ottawa, 1964, Vol. 1, Cahiers de la Société canadienne de science politique.

Bluhm, W.T., *Theories of the Political System: Classics of Political Thought and Modern Political Analysis*, Englewood Cliffs, N.J., P.-H., 1965.

Charlesworth, J.D., (ed.), *A Design for Political Science: Scope, Objectives, and Methods*, [A Symposium], Monograph 6 in a Series sponsored by The American Academy of Political and Social Science, Philadelphia, 1966.

Connery, R.H. (ed.), *Teaching Political Science: A Challenge to Higher Education*, Don Mills, B. and M., 1965.

Dahl, R.A., *Modern Political Analysis*, Englewood Cliffs, N.J., P.-H., 3rd ed., 1976.

Dion, L., *Le statut théorique de la science politique*, Montréal, le centre de documentation et de recherches politiques, Collège Jean-de-Brébeuf, 1964.

Duverger, M., *The Idea of Politics, the Uses of Power in Society*, Toronto, Methuen, 1966.

Easton, D., *A Framework for Political Analysis*, Englewood Cliffs, N.J., P.-H., 1965.

Easton, D., *A Systems Analysis of Political Life*, New York, Wiley and Sons, 1965.

Easton, D., *The Political System, An Inquiry Into the State of Political Science*, New York, Knopf, 2nd ed., 1971.

Golembiewski, R.T., Welsh, N.A., Crotty, W.J., *A Methodological Primer for Political Scientists*, Chicago, R.M., 1969.

Gould, J., and Kolb, W.D., (eds.), *A Dictionary of the Social Sciences*, New York, The Free Press, 1965.

Gravel, R.J., *Guide méthodologique de la recherche*, Montréal, Les Presses de l'Université du Québec, 1978.

Isaak, A.C., *Scope and Methods of Political Science*, Homewood, Illinois, Dorsey, rev. ed., 1975.

Kalvelage, C., Segal, M., and Anderson, P.J., *Research Guide for Undergraduates in Political Science*, Morristown, N.J., General Learning Press, 1972.

Khan, R.A., MacKown, S.A., and McNiven, J.D., *An Introduction to Political Science*, Georgetown, Ontario, Irwin-Dorsey, 1972.

Landry, R. (dir.), *Introduction à l'analyse des politiques*, Québec, Les Presses de l'Université Laval, 1981.

Mackenzie, W.J.M., *The Study of Political Science Today*, London, Macmillan, 1970.

Merritt, R.L., and Puszka, G.J., *The Student Political Scientist's Handbook*, Cambridge, Mass., Schenkman, 1969.

Monière, D., *Critique épistémologique de l'analyse systématique*, Ottawa, Les Editions de l'Université d'Ottawa, 1976.

Polsby, N., Dentler, R., Smith, P., *Politics and Social Life: An Introduction to Political Behaviour*, Boston, H.M., 1963.

Ranney, A., *The Governing of Men: An Introduction to Political Science*, New York, H.R.W., rev. ed., 1966.

Simeon, R., "The 'Overload Thesis'

and Canadian Government,''
C.P.P., 2, 4, Autumn, 1976.
Sorauf, F.J., *Political Science, An
Informal Overview*, Columbus,
Charles E. Merrill, 1965.
Strum, P., and Shmidman, M.D., *On
Studying Political Science*, Califor-
nia, Goodyear, 1969.
Wallis, W.A.; and Roberts, H.V., *The
Nature of Statistics*, New York, The
Free Press, 1965.
Wiseman, H.V., *Political Systems,
Some Sociological Approaches*, Lon-
don, R.K.P., 1966.

Canadian Politics — General

Albinski, H.S., *Canadian and
Australian Politics in Comparative
Perspective*, Toronto, O.U.P., 1973.
Bell, D., and Tepperman, L., *First
Principles: A Study of Canadian Po-
litical Culture*, Toronto, M. & S.,
1979.
Bernard, A., *La politique au Canada
et au Québec*, Montréal, Les Presses
de l'Université du Québec, 1976.
Byers, R.B., and Saywell, J., *Canadian
Annual Review of Politics and
Public Affairs 1978*, Toronto,
U.T.P., 1980.
Campbell, C., *Canadian Political
Facts: 1945-1976*, Toronto,
Methuen, 1977.
Canada, [Treasury Board], *Organiza-
tion of the Government of Canada,
1980*, Ottawa, S. and S., 13th ed.,
1980.
Dawson, R.M., and Ward, N., *The
Government of Canada*, Toronto,
U.T.P., 5th ed., 1970.
Forcese, D., *The Canadian Class
Structure*, Toronto, McG.-H.R.,
1975.
Godfrey, W.G., *Canadian Political
Cultures*, Toronto, Butterworths,
1981.
Hockin, T.A., *Government in Canada*,
Toronto, McG.-H.R., 1976.
Irvine, W.P., *Public Policy Statistics
in Canada: An Introductory Course*,
Kingston, Queen's University, 1977.
Jenson, J., and Tomlin, B.W., *Cana-

dian Politics: An Introduction to
Systematic Analysis*, Toronto,
McG.-H.R., 1977.
Kahn, C., *Government and You*,
Toronto, M. & S., 1979.
Mallory, J.R., *The Structure of Cana-
dian Government*, Toronto, Mac-
millan, 1974.
Manzer, R., *Canada: A Socio-Political
Report*, Toronto, McG.-H.R., 1974.
Marchak, M.P., *Ideological Perspec-
tives on Canada*, Toronto, McG.-
H.R., 1975.
McMenemy, J., *The Language of
Canadian Politics: A Guide to Im-
portant Terms and Concepts*, Toron-
to, Wiley, 1980.
Rea, K.J., and McLeod, J.T., (eds.),
*Business and Government in
Canada: Selected Readings*, Toron-
to, Methuen, 2nd ed., 1976.
Redekop, J.H., (ed.), *Approaches to
Canadian Politics*, Toronto, P.-H.,
1978.
Schultz, R., *et al.*, *The Canadian
Political Process*, Toronto, H.R.W.,
3rd ed., 1979.
Smiley, D.V., *Canada in Question:
Federalism in the Eighties*, Toronto,
McG.-H.R., 3rd ed., 1980.
Van Loon, R.J., and Whittington,
M.S., *The Canadian Political
System: Environment and Structure
and Process*, Toronto, McG.-H.R.,
3rd ed., 1981.
White, W.L., Wagenberg, R.H., and
Nelson, R.C., *Introduction to Cana-
dian Politics and Government*,
Toronto, H.R.W., 2nd ed., 1977.
Whittington, M., and Williams, G.,
(eds.), *Canadian Politics in the
1980's: Introductory Readings*,
Toronto, Methuen, 1981.

Canadian Political Science

Briggs, E.D., ''Introductory Interna-
tional Relations Course in Canadian
Universities,'' Paper presented at the
Annual Meeting of the C.P.S.A.,
1977.
Cairns, A.C., ''Alternative Styles in
the Study of Canadian Politics,''
C.J.P.S., VII, 1, March, 1974.

Cairns, A.C., "Political Science in Canada and the Americanization Issue," *C.J.P.S.*, VIII, 2, June, 1975. (Comment by D.P. Shugurman, *ibid.*, IX, 1, March, 1976.)

Cairns, A.C., "National Influences on the Study of Politics," *Q.Q.*, 81, 3, Autumn, 1974.

Fox, P.W., *et al.*, *Report of the Committee on Canadian Content*, Toronto, C.P.S.A., mimeo, 1973.

Higgins, D.J.H., "Municipal Politics and Government: Development of the Field in Canadian Political Science," *C.P.A.*, 22, 3, Fall, 1979.

Hodgetts, J.E., "Canadian Political Science: A Hybrid with a Future?," in Hubbard, R.H., (ed.), *Scholarship in Canada*, Toronto, U.T.P,, 1968.

Hull, W.H.N., "The 1971 Survey of the Profession," *C.J.P.S.*, VI, 1, March, 1973.

Kornberg, A., and Thorp, A., "The American Impact on Canadian Political Science and Sociology," in Preston, R., (ed.), *The Influence of the United States on Canadian Development*, Durham, N.C., 1974.

Macpherson, C.B., "After Strange Gods: Canadian Political Science, 1973," in Guinsburg, T.N., and Reuber, G.L., (eds.), *Perspectives on the Social Sciences in Canada*, Toronto, U.T.P., 1974.

Mandlowitz, J., and Assaad, F., "The Nature of Comparative Politics in Canada," Paper presented at the Annual Meeting of the C.P.S.A., 1976.

March, R.R., and Jackson, R.J., "Aspects of the State of Political Science in Canada," *M.J.P.S.*, 11, November, 1967.

Pross, A.P., and Wilson, V.S., "Graduate Education in Canadian Public Administration: Antecedents, Present Trends and Portents," *C.P.A.*, 19, 4, Winter, 1976.

Redekop, J.H., "Authors and Publishers: An Analysis of Textbook Selection in Canadian Departments of Political Science and Sociology," *C.J.P.S.*, IX, 1, March, 1976.

Smiley, D.V., "Contributions to Canadian Political Science Since the Second World War," *C.J.E.P.S.*, XXXIII, 4, November, 1967.

Smiley, D.V., "Must Canadian Political Science be a Miniature Replica?," *J.C.S.*, 9, 1, February, 1974.

Thorburn, H.G., *Political Science in Canada: Graduate Studies and Research*, Kingston, Ontario, mimeo, 1975.

Foreign Policy

(See also Bibliography in Chapter 5)

Clarkson, S., (ed.), *An Independent Foreign Policy for Canada*, Toronto, M. & S., 1968.

Dobell, P.C., *Canada's Search for New Roles: Foreign Policy in the Trudeau Era*, Toronto, O.U.P., 1972.

Donneur, A.P., *Politique Etrangère Canadienne, Bibliographie, 1972-75*, Notes de recherche, Numéro 1, Département de Science politique, Université du Québec à Montréal, 1976.

Eayrs, J., *In Defence of Canada:* Vol. I, *From the Great War to the Great Depression;* Vol. II, *Appeasement and Rearmament;* Vol. III, *Peacemaking and Deterrence;* Vol. IV, *Growing Up Allied*, Toronto, U.T.P., 1961, 1965, 1972, 1980 respectively.

Farrell, B., *The Making of Canadian Foreign Policy*, Toronto, P.-H., 1969.

Hillmer, N., and Stevenson, G., (eds.), *A Foremost Nation: Canadian Foreign Policy and a Changing World*, Toronto, M. & S., 1977.

Holmes, J.W., *The Shaping of Peace: Canada and the Search for World Order, 1943-57*, Toronto, U.T.P., Vol. I, 1979.

Johnson, B., and Zaeher, M.W., (eds.), *Canadian Foreign Policy and the Law of the Sea*, Vancouver, U.B.C.P., 1977.

Lyon, P.V., and Tomlin, B.W.,
Canada as an International Actor,
Toronto, Macmillan, 1979.
Painchaud, P., (dir.), *Le Canada et le Québec sur la scène internationale*.
Montréal, Les Presses de l'Université du Québec à Montréal, 1977.
Thomson, D.C., and Swanson, R.F.,
Canadian Foreign Policy, Options and Perspectives, Toronto,
McG.-H.R., 1972.
Thordarson, B., *Trudeau and Foreign Policy: A Study in Decision-Making*,
Toronto, Oxford, 1972.
Tomlin, B., (ed.), *Canada's Foreign Policy: Analysis and Trends*, Toronto, Methuen, 1977.
Tucker, M.J., *Canadian Foreign Policy: Contemporary Issues and Themes*, Toronto, McG.-H.R., 1980.

Political Leadership

Courtney, J.C., "Prime Ministerial Character: An Examination of Mackenzie King's Political Leadership," *C.J.P.S.*, IX, 1, March, 1976, (with Comment by J.E. Esberey, *ibid.*, and Rejoinder by J.C. Courtney, *ibid.*, IX, 2, June, 1976).
Dion, L., "The Concept of Political Leadership," *C.J.P.S.*, I, 1, March, 1968.
Esberey, J.E., *Knight of the Holy Spirit: A Study of William Lyon MacKenzie King*, Toronto, U.T.P., 1980.
Esberey, J.E., "Personality and Politics: A New Look at the King-Byng Dispute," *C.J.P.S.*, VI, 1, March, 1973.
Fox, P.W., "Psychology, Politics, and Hegetology," *C.J.P.S.*, XIII, 4, December, 1980.
Hockin, T., *Apex of Power: The Prime Minister and Political Leadership in Canada*, Scarborough, P.-H., 2nd ed., 1977.
Schiffer, I., *Charisma: A Psychoanalytic Look at Mass Society*, Toronto, U.T.P., 1973.

Social Issues

Business and Society

Banner, D.K., *Business and Society: Canadian Issues*, Toronto, McG.-H.R., 1979.
Finkel, A., *Business and Social Reform in the Thirties*, Toronto, Lorimer, 1979.
Niosi, J., *The Renaissance of Canadian Business*, Toronto, Lorimer, 1981.
Stanbury, W.T., *Business Interests and the Reform of Canadian Competition Policy, 1971-1975*, Toronto, Methuen, 1977.
Traves, T., *The State and Enterprise: Canadian Manufacturers and the Federal Government, 1917-31*, Toronto, U.T.P., 1979.

Elites and Power

Black, E.R., "The Fractured Mosaic: John Porter Revisited," *C.P.A.*, 17, 4, Winter, 1974.
Bourassa, G., "Les élites politiques de Montréal: de l'aristocratie à la démocratie," *C.J.E.P.S.*, XXXI, 1, February, 1965.
Clement, W., *The Canadian Corporate Elite: An Analysis of Economic Power*, Foreword by J. Porter, Carleton Library, No. 89, M. & S., 1975.
Clement, W., *Continental Corporate Power: Economic Linkages Between Canada and the United States*, Toronto, M. & S., 1977.
Heap, J.L., (ed.), *Everybody's Canada: The Vertical Mosaic Reviewed and Reexamined*, Toronto, B. and M., 1974.
Hunter, A.A., *Class Tells: On Social Inequality in Canada*, Toronto, Butterworths, 1981.
Love, R., *Income Distribution and Inequality in Canada*, Ottawa, E.C.C., 1980.
Newman, P.C., *The Canadian Establishment*, Toronto, M. & S., Vol. 1, 1979; *The Acquisitors*, Vol. 2, 1981.
Olsen, D., *The State Elite*, Toronto, M. & S., 1980.

Osberg, L., *Economic Inequality in Canada*, Toronto, Butterworths, 1981.

Ossenberg, R., (ed.), *Power and Change in Canada*, Toronto, M. & S., 1979.

Park, L., and Park, F., *Anatomy of Big Business*, Toronto, J.L.S., 1973.

Porter, J., *The Vertical Mosaic: An Analysis of Social Class and Power in Canada*, Toronto, U.T.P., 1965.

Presthus, R., *Elite Accommodation in Canadian Politics*, Toronto, Macmillan, 1973.

Presthus, R., *Elites in the Policy Process*, Toronto, Macmillan, 1974.

Smith, D., and Tepperman, L., "Changes in the Canadian Business and Legal Elites, 1870-1970," *C.R.S.A.*, II, 2, May, 1974.

Energy and Resources

Beale, B., *Energy and Industry: The Potential of Energy Development Projects for Canada in the Eighties*, Toronto, Lorimer, 1980.

Berndt, E., *et al.*, *Oil in the Seventies: Essays on Energy Policy*, Vancouver, Fraser Institute, 1977.

Bocking, R.C., *Canada's Water: For Sale?*, Toronto, J.L.S., 1972.

Bourassa, R., *James Bay*, Montreal, Harvest House, 1973.

Bregha, F., *Bob Blair's Pipeline: The Business and Politics of Northern Energy Development Projects*, Toronto, Lorimer, 1979.

Cook, C.E., *Nuclear Power and Legal Advocacy: The Environmentalists and the Courts*, Toronto, D.C. Heath, 1980.

Crabbe, P., and Spry, I.M., (eds.), *Natural Resource Development in Canada*, A Multi-Disciplinary Seminar, Ottawa, U.O.P., 1973.

Cross, M.S., *et al.*, "Energy Sell-out: A Counter-Report," *The Canadian Forum*, LIII, 629-30, June-July, 1973.

Editorial Board, *et al.*, "Energy Policy," *C.P.P.*, 1, 1, Winter, 1975.

Foster, H.D., and Sewell, W.R.D., *Water: The Emerging Crisis in Canada*, Toronto, Lorimer, 1981.

Foster, P., *The Blue-Eyed Sheiks: The Canadian Oil Establishment*, Don Mills, Collins, 1979.

Hooker, C.A., MacDonald, R., Van Hulst, R., and Victor, P., *Energy and the Quality of Life: Understanding Energy Policy in Canada*, Toronto, U.T.P., 1980.

Kilbourn, W., *Pipeline*, Toronto, Clarke, Irwin, 1970.

Knelman, F., *Nuclear Energy: The Unforgiving Technology*, Edmonton, Hurtig, 1977.

Laxer, J., *Canada's Energy Crisis*, Toronto, J.L.S., 1974.

McDougall, J.N., *Fuels and the National Policy*, Toronto, Butterworths, 1981.

Mitchell, B., and Sewell, W.R.D., *Canadian Resource Policies: Problems and Prospects*, Toronto, Methuen, 1981.

Pearse, P., (ed.), *The Mackenzie Pipeline: Arctic Gas and Canadian Energy Policy*, Toronto, M. & S., 1974.

Powrie, T.L., and Gainer, W.D., *La politique canadienne du pétrole et du gaz naturel*, Ottawa, Conseil Economique, 1976.

Pratt, L., *The Tar Sands, Syncrude and the Politics of Oil*, Edmonton, Hurtig, 1977.

Rohmer, R., *The Arctic Imperative: An Overview of the Energy Crisis*, Toronto, M. & S., 1973.

Rowland, W., *Fuelling Canada's Future*, Toronto, Macmillan, 1974.

Salisbury, R.F., *et al.*, *Development and James Bay: Socio-Economic Implications of the Hydro-Electric Project*, Montreal, McGill University, 1972.

Scheffer, W.F., (ed.), *Energy Impacts on Public Policy and Administration*, Toronto, B. and M., 1976.

Scott, A., *Natural Resources: The Economics of Conservation*, Carleton Library No. 67, Toronto, 1973.

Sykes, P., *Sellout: The Giveaway of Canada's Energy Resources*, Edmonton, Hurtig, 1973.

Thur, O.M., (ed.), *Energy Policy and Federalism*, Toronto, Seminar Publication, I.P.A.C., 1980.

Watkins, G.C., and Walker, M.A., (eds.), *Reaction: The National Energy Program*, Vancouver, Fraser Institute, 1981.

Wilson, B., *Canada's Energy Policy*, Toronto, Lorimer, 1980.

Wilson, B.F., *The Energy Squeeze, Canadian Policies for Survival*, Toronto, Lorimer, 1980.

Ethnic Groups and Immigration

Anderson, A.B., and Frideres, J., *Ethnicity in Canada*, Toronto, Butterworths, 1980.

Avery, D., *"Dangerous Foreigners": European Immigrant Workers and Labour Radicalism in Canada, 1896-1932*, Toronto, M. & S., 1979.

Bolaria, B.S., *Oppressed Minorities in Canada*, Toronto, Butterworths, 1980.

Clairmont, D.H., and Magill, D.W., *Africville: The Life and Death of a Canadian Black Community*, Toronto, M. & S., 1974.

Dahlie, J., and Fernando, T., (eds.), *Ethnicity, Power and Politics in Canada*, Toronto, Methuen, 1980.

Davis, M., and Krauter, J.F., *The Other Canadians*, Toronto, Methuen, 1971.

Dirks, G.E., *Canada's Refugee Policy: Indifference or Opportunism*, Montreal, McG.-Q.U.P., 1978.

Driedger, L., (ed.), *The Canadian Ethnic Mosaic: A Quest for Identity*, Toronto, M. & S., 1978.

Finnigan, B., and Gonick, C., (ed.), *Making It: The Canadian Dream*, Toronto, M. & S., 1972.

Forcese, D., and Richer, S., (eds.), *Issues in Canadian Society*, Scarborough, P.-H., 1975.

Goldstein, J.E., and Bienvenue, R.M., (eds.), *Ethnicity and Ethnic Relations in Canada*, Toronto, Butterworths, 1980.

Gutkin, M., *Journey Into Our Heritage: The Story of the Jewish People in the Canadian West*, Toronto, L. and O., 1980.

Hayes, S., "Canadian Jewish Culture: Some Observations," *Q.Q.*, 84, 1, Spring, 1977.

"Immigration," Symposium, *C.P.P.*, I, 3, Summer, 1975.

Isajiw, W., (ed.), *Impact of Ethnicity on Canadian Society*, Toronto, Peter Martin, 1977.

Lupul, M.R., (ed.), *Ukrainian Canadians, Multiculturalism, and Separatism: An Assessment*, Edmonton, U.A.P., 1978.

Mannion, J.J., *Irish Settlements in Eastern Canada: A Study of Cultural Transfer and Adaptation*, Toronto, U.T.P., 1981.

Maxwell, T.R., *The Invisible French: The French in Metropolitan Toronto*, Waterloo, W.L.U.P., 1977.

Menezes, J., (ed.), *Decade of Adjustment: Legal Perspectives on Contemporary Social Issues*, Toronto, Butterworths, 1980.

Potrekenko, H., *No Streets of Gold: A Social History of Ukrainians in Alberta*, Vancouver, New Star, 1977.

Ramcharan, S., *Non-White Immigrants in Canada*, Toronto, Butterworths, 1980.

Sawchuk, J., *The Métis of Manitoba: Reformulation of an Ethnic Identity*, Toronto, Peter Martin, 1978.

Sealey, D.B., and Lussier, A.S., *The Métis: Canada's Forgotten People*, Winnipeg, Manitoba, Métis Federation Press, 1975.

Ujimoto, K.V., and Hirabayashi, G., (eds.), *Visible Minorities and Multiculturalism: Asians in Canada*, Toronto, Butterworths, 1980.

Ward, W.P., *White Canada Forever: Popular Attitudes and Public Policy Toward Orientals in British Columbia*, Montreal, McG.-Q.U.P., 1978.

Winks, R.W., *The Blacks in Canada: A History*, New Haven, Yale University Press, McG.-Q.U.P., 1971.

Environment

Chant, D.A., (ed.), *Pollution Probe*, Toronto, New Press, 1972.

Dwivedi, O.P., (ed.), *Protecting the Environment: Issues and Choices — Canadian Perspectives*, Toronto, C.C., 1974.

Elder, P.S., (ed.), *Environmental Management and Public Participation*, Toronto, C.E.L.A., 1975.

Emond, P., (ed.), *Stop It! A Guide for Citizen Action to Protect the Environment of Nova Scotia*, Ottawa, C.P.A., 1976.

Freeman, M.M.R., *People Pollution*, Montreal, McG.-Q.U.P., 1974.

Howard, R., *Poisons in Public: Case Studies of Environmental Pollution in Canada*, Toronto, Lorimer, 1980.

Krueger, R., and Mitchell, B., (eds.), *Managing Canada's Renewable Resources*, Toronto, Methuen, 1977.

Larkin, P.A., *Freshwater Pollution, Canadian Style*, Montreal, McG.-Q.U.P., 1974.

Leiss, W., (ed.), *Ecology versus Politics in Canada*, Toronto, U.T.P., 1978.

Lundquist, L.J., "Do Political Structures Matter in Environmental Politics? The Case of Air Pollution Control in Canada, Sweden, and the United States," *C.P.A.*, 17, 1, Spring, 1974.

McNairn, C.H., "Airport Noise Pollution: The Problem and the Regulatory Response," *C.B.R.*, L, 2, May, 1972.

Marsden, L.R., *Population Probe: Canada*, Toronto, C.C., 1972.

Raynauld, A., "Protection of the Environment: Economic Perspectives," *C.P.A.*, 15, 4, Winter, 1972.

Richardson, A.H., *Conservation by the People*, Toronto, U.T.P., 1974.

Solomon, L., *The Conserver Solution: A Blueprint for the Conserver Society*, Toronto, Pollution Probe Foundation and Doubleday, 1978.

Stein, S.B., "Environmental Control and Different Levels of Government," *C.P.A.*, 14, 1, Spring, 1971.

Swainson, N.A., (ed.), *Managing the Water Environment*, Vancouver, U.B.C.P., 1976.

Health

Blomqvist, A., *The Health Care Business*, Vancouver, The Fraser Institute, 1979.

Brown, M.C., *The Financing of Personal Health Services in New Zealand, Canada, and Australia*, Canberra, Australian National University, 1977.

Canada, [Hall, E.M.], *Canada's National Provincial Health Program for the 1980's — A Commitment for Renewal*, Ottawa, S. and S., 1980.

Culyer, A.J., *Measuring Health: Lessons for Ontario*, Toronto, O.E.C., 1978.

Evans, R.G., and Williamson, M.F., *Extending Canadian Health Insurance: Options for Pharmacare and Denticare*, Toronto, U.T.P., 1978.

Guest, D., *The Emergence of Social Security in Canada*, Vancouver, U.B.C.P., 1980.

"Health," Symposium, *C.P.P.*, II, 2, Spring, 1976.

Lee, S.S., *Quebec's Health System: A Decade of Change, 1967-1977*, Toronto, I.P.A.C., 1978.

Migué, J.-L., and Belanger, G., *The Price of Health*, Toronto, Macmillan, 1974.

Mishler, W., and Campbell, D.B., "The Healthy State: Legislative Responsiveness to Public Health Care Needs in Canada, 1920-1970," *Comparative Politics*, 10, July, 1978.

Shillington, C.H., *The Road to Medicare in Canada*, Toronto, Del Graphics, 1972.

Soderstrom, L., *The Canadian Health System*, Toronto, Macmillan, 1978.

Taylor, M.G., *Health Insurance and Canadian Public Policy: The Seven Decisions That Created the Canadian Health Insurance System*, Toronto, I.P.A.C., 1978.

Wilkins, R., *L'État de santé au Canada, 1926-1976*, Toronto, I.R.P.P., 1980.

Wolfson, A.D., and Tuohy, C.J., *Opting Out of Medicare: Private Medical Markets in Ontario*, Toronto, U.T.P., 1980.

Labour, Poverty, Housing

Adams, I., *The Poverty Wall*, Toronto, M. & S., 1970.

Adams, I., *et al.*, *The Real Poverty Report*, Edmonton, Hurtig, 1972.

Barber, C., and McCallum, J., *Unemployment and Inflation: The Canadian Experience*, Toronto, Lorimer, 1980.

Canada, Senate, Special Committee on Poverty, *Poverty in Canada*, Ottawa, Q.P., 1972.

Caragata, W., *Alberta Labour: A Heritage Untold*, Toronto, Lorimer, 1979.

Cullingworth, J.B., *Canadian Housing Policy Research: Some Initial Impressions*, Toronto, C.U.C.S., University of Toronto, 1980.

Dennis, M., and Fish, S., *Programs in Search of a Policy: Low Income Housing in Canada*, Toronto, Hakkert, 1972.

Harp, J., and Hofley, J.R., (eds.), *Poverty in Canada*, Scarborough, Ontario, P.-H., 1971.

Johnson, L.A., *Incomes, Disparity and Improvement in Canada Since World War II*, Toronto, New Hogtown Press, 1973.

Lithwick, N.H., "Poverty in Canada: Recent Empirical Findings," *J.C.S.*, VI, 1, May, 1971.

Lithwick, N.H., *Urban Poverty*, Research Monograph No. 1 in the *Urban Canada, Problems and Prospects Series*, Ottawa, C.M.H.C., 1971.

Mann, W.E., (ed.), *Poverty and Social Policy in Canada*, Toronto, C.C., 1970.

Markson, E.W., and Botra, G.R., *Public Policies for An Aging Population*, Toronto, D.C. Heath, 1980.

Montgomery, R., and Marshall, D.R., (eds.), *Housing Policy for the 1980s*, Toronto, Lexington Books, 1980.

New Brunswick, *Participation and Development: The New Brunswick Task Force Report on Social Development and Social Welfare*, Fredericton, Q.P., 1971.

Pentland, H.C., *Labour and Capital in Canada*, Toronto, Lorimer, 1981.

Rose, A., *Canadian Housing Policies, 1935-1980*, Toronto, Butterworths, 1980.

Ross, D.P., *The Working Poor: Wage Earners and the Failure of Income Security Policies*, Toronto, Lorimer, 1981.

Ryan, T.J., *Poverty and the Child—A Canadian Study*, Toronto, McG.-H.R., 1972.

Smith, A., *et al.*, *Poverty and Government Income Support in Canada, 1971-1975: Characteristics of the Low Income Population*, Ottawa, E.C.C., 1979.

Steele, M., *The Demand for Housing in Canada*, Ottawa, Statistics Canada, 1979.

Stone, L.O., and Fletcher, S., *A Profile of Canada's Older Population*, Montreal, I.R.P.P., 1980.

Swidinsky, R., and Wales, T.J., "Poverty and the Welfare State I & II," *BC Studies*, 13, Spring, 1973.

Native People

Adams, H., *Prisons of Grass: Canada from the Native Point of View*, Toronto, New Press, 1975.

Canada, *A Survey of the Contemporary Indians of Canada*, [Hawthorn-Tremblay Report], Ottawa, Q.P., 1966.

Canada, Mackenzie Valley Pipeline Inquiry, *Northern Frontier, Northern Homeland: The Report of the Mackenzie Valley Pipeline Inquiry*, [Berger Report], Ottawa, S. and S., 1977, 2 volumes.

Cardinal, H., *The Unjust Society: The Tragedy of Canada's Indians*, Edmonton, Hurtig, 1969.

Cardinal, H., *The Rebirth of Canada's Indians*, Edmonton, Hurtig, 1977.

Chrétien, J., *Statement of the Government of Canada on Indian Policy, 1969*, Ottawa, Q.P., 1969.

Cox, B., (ed.), *Cultural Ecology: Readings on the Canadian Indians and Eskimos*, Toronto, M. & S., 1973.

Cumming, P.A., and Mickenberg, N.H., (eds.), *Native Rights in Canada*, Toronto, Indian-Eskimo Association, 2nd ed., 1972.

Davis, R., and Zannis, M., *The Genocide Machine in Canada—The*

Pacification of the North, Montreal, Black Rose, 1973.

Denton, T., "Migration from a Canadian Indian Reserve," *J.C.S.*, VII, 2, May, 1972.

Dosman, E.J., *Indians, The Urban Dilemma*, Toronto, M. & S., 1972.

Eisenberg, J., and Troper, H., *Native Survival*, Toronto, O.I.S.E., 1973.

Frideres, J.S., *Canada's Indians: Contemporary Conflicts*, Scarborough, Ontario, P.-H., 1974.

Fuller, W.A., "Northern Frontier, Northern Homeland," *Q.Q.*, 85, 2, Summer, 1978.

Getty, I.A.L., and Smith, D.B., *One Century Later: Western Canadian Reserve Indians Since Treaty 7*, Vancouver, U.B.C.P., 1979.

Green, L.C., "Canada's Indians: Federal Policy, International and Constitutional Law," *O.L.R.*, 4, 1, Summer, 1970.

Krotz, L., *Urban Indians: The Strangers in Canada's Cities*, Edmonton, Hurtig, 1980.

La Violette, P., *The Struggle for Survival, Indian Cultures and the Protestant Ethic in B.C.*, Toronto, U.T.P., 1973.

Manuel, G., *The Fourth World: An Indian Reality*, Toronto, C.-M., 1974.

Nagler, M., *Natives Without a Home: The Canadian Indian*, Montreal, Academic Press, 1975.

Ponting, J.R., and Gibbins, R., *Out of Irrelevance: A Socio-Political Introduction to Indian Affairs in Canada*, Toronto, Butterworths, 1980.

Price, R., (ed.), *The Spirit of the Alberta Indian Treaties*, Toronto, Butterworths, 1979.

Robertson, H., *Reservations are for Indians*, Toronto, J.L.S., 1970.

Ryan, J., *Wall of Words: The Betrayal of the Urban Indian*, Toronto, Peter Martin, 1978.

Smith, D.G., (ed.), *Canadian Indians and the Law: Selected Documents, 1663-1972*, Carleton Library No. 87, Toronto, M. & S., 1975.

Watkins, M., (ed.), *Dene Nation —*

The Colony Within, Toronto, U.T.P., 1977.

Weaver, S.M,, *Making Canadian Indian Policy: The Hidden Agenda, 1968-1970*, Toronto, U.T.P., 1980.

Political Economy Tradition
(See also Bibliography, Chapter 4)

Christian, W., *Harold Innis as Economist and Moralist*, Occasional Paper No. 2, Department of Political Studies, University of Guelph, Guelph, Ontario, Winter, 1981.

Christian, W., "Harold Innis as Political Theorist," *C.J.P.S.*, X, 1, March, 1977.

Christian, W., (ed.), *The Idea File of Harold Adams Innis*, Toronto, U.T.P., 1980.

Clement, W., and Drache, D., *A User's Guide to Canadian Political Economy*, Toronto, Lorimer, 1978.

Drache, D., "Rediscovering Canadian Political Economy," *J.C.S.*, 11, 3, August, 1976.

Knox, P., and Resnick, P., (eds.), *Essays in B.C. Political Economy*, Vancouver, New Star, 1974.

Panitch, L., (ed.), *The Canadian State: Political Economy and Political Power*, Toronto, U.T.P., 1977.

Parker, I., "Harold Innis, Karl Marx, and Canadian Political Economy," *Q.Q.*, 84, 4, Winter, 1977.

Roussopoulos, D., (ed.), *The Political Economy of the State — Canada/ Quebec/U.S.A.*, Montreal, Black Rose, 1973.

Science Policy

Aucoin, P., and French, R., *Knowledge, Power and Public Policy*, Science Council of Canada Background Study No. 31, Ottawa, I.C., 1974.

Canada, Senate, Special Committee on Science Policy, *A Science Policy for Canada: Report*, Ottawa, Q.P., 1970-77, 4 volumes.

Doern, G.B., *Science and Politics in Canada*, Montreal, McG.-Q.U.P., 1972.

Globerman, S., "Canadian Science

Policy and Technological Sovereignty," *C.P.P.*, IV, 1, Winter, 1978.

Hayes, F.R., *The Chaining of Prometheus: Evolution of a Power Structure for Canadian Science*, Toronto, U.T.P., 1973.

Lithwick, N.H., *Canada's Science Policy and the Economy*, London, Methuen, 1969.

Rabkin, Y.M., "Transnational Invariables in Science Policies: Canadian and Soviet Experiences," *C.P.A.*, 24, 1, Spring, 1981.

Women's Rights

Andrews, M.W., "Attitudes in Canadian Women's History, 1945-1975," *J.C.S.*, 12, 4, 1977.

Armstrong, P., and Armstrong, H., *The Double Ghetto: Women and Their Work in Canada*, Toronto, M. & S., 1978.

Bohnen, L.S., "Women Workers in Ontario: A Socio-Legal History," *U. of T. Faculty of Law Review*, Vol. 31, August, 1973.

Canada, "Cultural Tradition and Political History of Women in Canada," *Studies of the Royal Commission on the Status of Women in Canada*, No. 8, Ottawa, I.C., 1971.

Canada, *Report of the Royal Commission on the Status of Women*, Ottawa, I.C., 1970.

Canada (Lalonde, Marc), *Status of Women in Canada*, Ottawa, I.C., 1975.

Cleverdon, C.L., *The Women's Suffrage Movement in Canada*, Toronto, U.T.P., 1974. (First Published in 1950.)

Cochrane, J., *Women in Canadian Life: Politics*, Don Mills, Ontario, F. and W., 1977.

Connelly, M.P., *Last Hired, First Fired: Woman and the Canadian Work Force*, Toronto, Women's Press, 1979.

Matheson, G., (ed.), *Women in the Canadian Mosaic*, Toronto, Peter Martin, 1976.

Stephenson, M., (ed.), *Women in Canada*, Toronto, New Press, 1973.

Miscellaneous

Keating, D.R., *The Power to Make It Happen: Mass Based Community Organizing, What It is and How It Works*, Toronto, Green Tree, 1975.

Keith, W.J., and Shek, B.Z., *The Arts in Canada: The Last Fifty Years*, Toronto, U.T.P., 1980.

Kroeker, H.V., *Sovereign People or Sovereign Governments*, Montreal, I.R.P.P., 1981.

Martell, G., (ed.), *The Politics of the Canadian Public School*, Toronto, Lorimer, 1975.

Massey, H.J., (ed.), *The Canadian Military*, Toronto, C.C., 1972.

Rotstein, A., (ed.), *The Prospect of Change*, Toronto, McG-H., 1965.

Roussopoulos, D., (ed.), *Canada and Radical Social Change*, Montreal, Black Rose, 1973.

Stewart, W., *Hard to Swallow: Why Food Prices Keep Rising and What Can Be Done About It?*, Toronto, Macmillan, 1974.

Warnock, J.W., *Profit Hunger: The Food Industry in Canada*, Vancouver, New Star, 1978.

Ziegel, J.S., "The Future of Canadian Consumerism," *C.B.R.*, Vol. LI, No. 2, 1973.

2

THE CONSTITUTION

Constitutional developments have been so significant since the fourth edition of this book appeared in 1977 that the contents of this chapter have been transformed.

After more than fifty years of repeated effort, Canadian federal and provincial governments except Quebec finally reached agreement on a new constitution which the Canadian Parliament approved in December, 1981, under the title the *Constitution Act, 1981 (Canada Act)*.

Earlier attempts to achieve the same goal in the 1960s and 1970s have been described in the introduction to Chapter 2 in the fourth edition, pp. 14-15. Readers who wish to review the process and study the major documents that emerged at various points in the past twenty years should consult that chapter and previous editions of *Politics: Canada* which contained verbatim accounts or excerpts from the documents.

See, for instance, the first edition, pp. 81-90, for the steps prior to 1960, pp. 91-94 for the "Fulton Formula" in 1960, and pp. 94-98 for an abridgement of Saskatchewan's objections to it. See also the second edition, pp. 135-151, for developments from 1960 to 1964, the verbatim text of the "Fulton-Favreau Formula," and an exchange of letters between Prime Minister L.B. Pearson and Premier Jean Lesage which terminated that phase of the negotiations. The third edition, pp. 462-471, summarized events to 1970 and repeated the "Fulton-Favreau Formula." It also contained on pp. 65-69 extracts from the Official Languages Act (1969) and objections to it.

The fourth edition included the following: the introductory review mentioned above (pp.14-15), an excerpt from the *Final Report* of the Special Joint Committee of the Senate and the House of Commons on the Constitution making certain recommendations for a new constitution (pp. 16-20), a list of the constitutional conferences held between 1967 and 1971 (pp. 20-21), a statement of the conclusions reached at the constitutional conference held in Victoria, B.C., from June 14–16, 1971 (pp. 21-22), the entire text of the Canadian Constitutional Charter, 1971, (more popularly known as the Victoria Charter) which, except for Quebec's repudiation, would have become a new Canadian constitution (pp. 22-32), and a letter from Prime Minister Trudeau to the premiers in 1976 summarizing the negotiations which had been resumed in 1975 on a new constitution, and offering in a draft proclamation a variant of the Victoria Charter (pp. 33-40). The fourth edition contained also a list of five recent Canadian Parliamentary amendments to the British North America Act (pp. 40-41) and an excerpt from the Report of the [Second] Bilingual Districts Advisory Board proposing the creation of federal bilingual districts (pp. 41-44).

Most of this material has been omitted from this edition since it has been eclipsed by a somewhat different settlement that emerged from a final round of negotiations. A hectic and dramatic series of federal-provincial conferences and meetings that commenced in September, 1980 culminated in November, 1981, in an agreement by the federal government and all provinces except Quebec on yet another draft of a revised constitution which was approved by the Canadian Parliament in December, 1981, under the title the *Constitution Act, 1981* (the *Canada Act*).

Professor Alexander Brady's article in this edition reviews the background to the constitutional controversy and the immediate events that led to the determination of the new constitution, including its reference to the provincial courts and the Supreme Court of Canada. (For the Supreme Court's judgement, see *infra*, Chapter 16.)

The next item gives the verbatim text of the Joint Resolution containing the *Constitution Act, 1981 (Canada Act)* passed by the House of Commons on December 2, 1981, and sent to the Queen-in-Parliament at Westminster with a request that it be enacted to replace the B.N.A. Act. When it was proclaimed on April 17, 1982, the new act completed the half-century of struggle to provide Canada with its own constitution. The *Constitution Act, 1982,* as it now became, incorporated the B.N.A. Act and its amendments and included the *Canadian Charter of Rights and Freedoms.* It also located the constitution in Canada rather than in Britain and provided a method for its amendment in Canada.

A final item in this chapter summarizes amendments made to the B.N.A. Act by the Canadian Parliament and the United Kingdom Parliament between 1949 and the adoption of the new constitution in 1981.

The items mentioned above are only some highlights in the very extensive literature which had been produced by the protracted debate on the patriation and revision of the constitution. The bibliography at the end of this chapter lists some of the books and articles that have been published on the subject in recent years. Separate sections contain references to recent major constitutional documents, articles and books on bilingualism and biculturalism, and published works dealing with the amendment of the constitution. The section entitled "Federal Problems," which appeared in Chapter 2 in the fourth edition, has been transferred to Chapter 3 in this edition since that is a more appropriate location. However, many of the items listed in the bibliography in Chapter 3 are relevant to this chapter also.

For comprehensive, succinct accounts of the Canadian constitution, see two books in the McGraw-Hill Ryerson Series in Canadian Politics: D.V. Smiley, *Canada in Question: Federalism in the Eighties,* Toronto, McGraw- Hill Ryerson, 3rd ed., 1980, and R.I. Cheffins and R.N. Tucker, *The Constitutional Process in Canada,* Toronto, McGraw-Hill Ryerson, 2nd ed., 1976. R.M. Dawson and N. Ward, *The Government of Canada,* Toronto, University of Toronto Press, 1970, is a standard text.

BACKGROUND TO THE CONSTITUTIONAL CONTROVERSY AND SETTLEMENT*

Alexander Brady

B.N.A. Act, 1867

In 1867 Canadians expressed much of their constitution in the British North America Act, wherein section 91 listed the wide-ranging powers of the national Parliament, section 92 the exclusive powers of provincial legislatures, and sections 102 to 126 the basic financial relations of the entire system. Thus, in a few slim paragraphs, the main features of the federal structure were outlined, and subsequent law reports depicted the court judgements and opinions that interpret the statute. However significant, this British act has not been the sole written part of the constitution. It is supplemented by other British and Canadian statutes, especially its own amendments, the Statute of Westminster of 1931, and such Canadian enactments as the Succession to the Throne Act, the Senate and House of Commons Acts, and the Elections Act. Aside from statutes, the constitution embraces the unwritten conventions, principles and practices of British parliamentary and responsible government, adapted and amplified to suit the Canadian circumstances.

The major and perhaps most serious omission in the original British North America Act was a procedure for achieving within Canada formal changes when needed in the federal structure. The act provided in section 92(1) that each province could amend its own constitution except the office of lieutenant-governor. The failure to include an overall amending procedure for the entire system did not result merely from absent-mindedness or a naive view of the future. It appears to have been deliberate, grounded in conviction and explicable in the light of colonial circumstances in the critical era of the American civil war. The achievement of union, even to its final drafting in London, required in colonial leaders endless bargaining and dexterous diplomacy. Sir John A. Macdonald, chief architect of the federal scheme, clung tenaciously to a British Conservative bias against contrivances more specific and rigid than what appeared necessary for the immediate occasion. His cautious mind sought the minimum in written elements, fearing that anything more might create deadlock or restrict the flexibility of *ad hoc* solutions that commanded his devotion. At the Quebec Conference he remarked that "we should keep before us the principles of the British constitution. It (our constitution) should be a mere skeleton and framework that would not bind us down. We have now all the elasticity which has kept England together."

* From *Canadian Banker & ICB Review*, 88, 3, June, 1981, with the permission of the publisher and author who is Professor Emeritus, Department of Political Economy, University of Toronto.

Strongly Centralized Federation

Macdonald and colleagues were determined upon a strongly centralized federation, wherein an elaborate amending procedure, involving direct participation of the provinces, was thought to be needless. . . . To Macdonald the provinces were no more than a "decentralized system of minor legislatures for local purposes." He evidently assumed that in future amendments the initiative must dwell with the national Parliament. All that would be needed was a joint address from the Senate and Commons to Westminster. With little difficulty the national Parliament thus secured successive amendments like that of 1871, which eliminated doubts on its capacity to carve new provinces out of the western territories, or that of 1875 which settled the nature of its own privileges.

The influence wielded by the national authority over amendments merely reflected that general employment of centralized power manifest elsewhere in the British North America Act, such as the national executive's nomination of senators for life; its appointment of lieutenant-governors; its selection of judges holding office during good behaviour; the location of residual legislative power in the national Parliament; and provision for the exercise of federal reservation and disallowance over provincial enactments.

Soon after Confederation, however, the centralized bias in the constitution came under vigorous attack. In Ontario Oliver Mowat, a tireless Grit, a Father of Confederation, and a premier of his province for 24 years (1872-96), launched repeated assaults on the centralist pretensions of politicians in Ottawa. He rarely missed an opportunity to employ the courts in defining the powers of provincial legislatures. In successive decisions, beginning with *Hodge v. The Queen* (1883), the Judicial Committee of the Privy Council clearly attempted to illustrate that the constitution of Canada was unambiguously federal, and in no sense had evolved into a unitary system wherein major legislative power is firmly restricted to the Parliament in Ottawa. The Judicial Committee upheld the autonomy of the provinces within areas of their strict jurisdiction. Their decisions remained a solid and enduring fact in the constitution.

Yet despite this fact, some features in the British North America Act continued to seem inconsistent with genuine federalism, such as the reservation and disallowance powers of the federal executive over provincial enactments. These are not now applicable in the ordinary conduct of government as they had been in the early years of Confederation, although they still remain in the letter if not the spirit of the constitution.

Common Partnership

In the twentieth century events demonstrated the wide and ever expanding role of the provinces. They also demonstrated the close interdependence and interrelationships between federal and provincial governments. All administrations had to accept their common partnership. In the early years of the century the constitution in general had to adjust to major changes in the country's life: an accelerated inflow of people, extended railways, rapid western settlement, creation of new provinces out of territories, and participation of Canada in two world wars. The second war in particular profoundly altered the conditions under which at both levels federalism operated. It promoted the pace of industrialization, enlarged urban communities, created a greater need for local services, quickened the exploitation of natural resources, and stimulated a fresh and potent sense of French-Canadian nationality.

The war magnified the ambitions and multiplied the tasks of the national government in seeking economic stability and social progress. Wartime leaders effectively mobilized efforts to secure national survival. Thereby they acquired an accepted authority similar almost to that of rulers in a unitary state, for under wartime powers the normal financial controls of federalism were restricted. Encouraged by the current climate of opinion they launched new public programs in the post-war era. Everywhere in the western world national economic planning was in the air. Keynesian faith in contracyclical budgets appealed to practical policy-makers. Wide visions of public social welfare were prevalent. The bureaucracy, trained and disciplined in wartime Ottawa, saw a rising productivity elevate standards of living and enhance the capacity of the public to pay for welfare.

The national Liberal party, firmly established in office, promptly perceived the electoral advantages of using national funds to satisfy popular appetites for welfare services. In 1944 it initiated family allowances, the boldest and most costly welfare service hitherto attempted. Soon it was sponsoring a proliferation of conditional grants from the federal treasury to further national standards and circumvent limits on federal legislative powers. These new shared-cost programs permitted an unparalleled expansion of federal activity in areas of exclusive provincial jurisdiction, such as natural resources, social welfare, local government, highway construction, and education.

This phase of what was then called co-operative federalism resulted from the strength, initiative, and pressures of the central government, and served substantially the material interests of many Canadians. But by the 1960s it exhibited serious contradictions and faults. The provinces, faced by a national administration endowed with an impressive spending power, frequently complained of being hurried into programs without adequate prior consultation. Each province was naturally anxious to determine its own order of priorities to suit its circumstances. Each wanted sufficient room in which to operate and manoeuvre within its competence, and resented undue pressure from Ottawa.

No Enduring Equilibrium

Since the federal government made grants to the provinces solely in fulfilment of detailed agreements, it actually controlled the provinces by dictating their spending priorities. Its attempt after 1945 to maintain the wartime rental system for basic taxes on personal income, corporations, and inheritance failed to create an enduring fiscal equilibrium. Quebec rejected the rental device. Ontario tried it as a stop-gap, but finally rejected it as too inflexible for an era of peace and dynamic change. All provinces, whenever the agreements emerged for renewal, forcibly contended for higher payments from the federal treasury. They had little choice, since provincial developments and population growth made larger revenues imperative.

Thus by the 1960s federal-provincial fiscal relations became more contentious and complex. The provinces under the hard compulsions of an industrial society were driven to ever higher expenditures on services for which the constitution held them responsible. They constantly faced the soaring costs of education at all levels, mounting expenses of health and welfare, and relentless demand for highways and more highways. In the light of these facts agreements between federal and provincial authorities seemed seldom more than temporary expedients, unsatisfactory not long after negotiation, if not when negotiated. The system worked only when pervaded by a spirit of equitable compromise among divergent interests. Compromise was the indispensable glue holding Confederation together, and when absent the system was unlikely to operate smoothly or effectively.

Quebec Nationalism

With this cumbersome and complicated structure Canada entered its centennial year in 1967. Since then, not surprisingly, federal complexities and contradictions have increased rather than diminished. One factor that soon after the Second World War augmented federal strains was a quickened sense of French-Canadian nationalism which fomented a mood of dissatisfaction and unsettlement in Quebec, and threatened a peaceful and viable Canada. From the outset Quebec differed from other provinces as the homeland of a distinct people, language, and culture. Its special social character was illustrated in civil law, party politics, Roman Catholicism in education, health and welfare institutions, and those customs that for generations demonstrated the tight social integration of the French parish. Yet this old traditional Quebec did not seriously menace or diminish federalism. On the contrary it justified the federal principle as a means to preserve Quebec's own peculiar pattern of life.

In 1960, however, the electoral victory of Jean Lesage and his Liberals brought about the Quiet Revolution (1960-66). More than any previous group of politicians they tried to transform many of Quebec's institutions and make its people masters in their own house. With a passion for modernization, they rapidly enlarged the role of government in the society, especially at the expense of the church in managing schools, colleges, hospitals and welfare. They were determined to carve out an extensive public sector in the economy, accelerate the use of water and other resources, and encourage new industries under Francophone control. They sought in Ottawa more funds to achieve for their province much needed innovations. Their activities contributed to a narrow form of Quebec nationalism that seemed to rival Canadian nationalism. Jean Lesage and most of his colleagues, however, had no ambition to lead Quebec out of Confederation, but their reforms severely wrenched old traditions, and made it easier for new and separatist forms of thinking to emerge.

In replacing the Liberals in 1966, Daniel Johnson and the Union Nationale pressed for a new constitution, ensuring more scope for all provinces and especially Quebec, with its distinct cultural aspirations. At the same time small separatist groups were aggressive and sometimes violent, notably in the centennial year when General de Gaulle made his historic descent on Montreal. The explosion of bombs in post boxes added a violent footnote to the upsurge of local nationalism. These incidents created in the country profound concern.

Constitutional Reform

They inspired Premier John Robarts of Ontario to convene in Toronto the provincial premiers for a Confederation of Tomorrow Conference, which took stock of federalism and discussed ways to ensure its vitality and survival. Conspicuous in these debates was Daniel Johnson's plea for a sweeping constitutional change. At the time most English-speaking provincial leaders, although they admitted flaws in the constitution, advocated no dramatic or drastic changes. Some however found themselves responding to Johnsonian argument and rhetoric on how to stem the rising tide of Quebec separatism.

The Confederation of Tomorrow Conference influenced not merely the provincial leaders, but even in some degree the national government. It partly inspired the prime minister, Lester Pearson, to convene in February 1968 an official conference on constitutional reform, thus initiating discussions which were continued under Prime Minister Trudeau. In only one meeting, in Victoria in June 1971, did these efforts come near success. There a complete constitutional charter for the country was drafted, including provisions for patriation and an amending formula. Yet the conference failed because in the eyes of Quebec's ministers it did not secure an adequate re-allocation of powers relative to social security. At intervals in the next nine years fresh initiatives were attempted, but all fell short of achieving agreement, and were deficient in satisfying Quebec, which in November 1976 elected the Parti Québécois government with its ambition to achieve a stronger and more independent status for the province.

Western Concerns

In the meantime profound economic forces, especially the higher cost of energy, promptly added fresh complexities and frictions to Canada's federation. Some western provinces became anxious about both economic prospects and constitutional rights. At the beginning of 1973 the price of OPEC oil stood at three dollars a barrel. In little more than a year it quadrupled. OPEC policies transformed the world's energy picture and shook the global balance of economic power. With the rise in world prices, the national government in Ottawa strove to check Canadian internal prices from moving to or above the world level. These efforts were viewed by the oil-producing provinces as a serious threat to their asserted right for a maximum benefit from their own resources. Regional self-interest, an in-

digenous and inescapable feature in the country, now assumed bitter proportions as authorities in Ottawa undertook to fix the price for domestic oil.

With OPEC's increased strength, the international price for oil advanced,
and Alberta naturally hoped that its own sales would continue to augment
its wealth and security. Premier Davis of Ontario however was prompt in
complaint to the prime minister: "There is no question that one and a half
million Albertans must have their fair share. But you have the tough task of
speaking for 22 million Canadians who also have their rights and expectations." Mr. Trudeau needed little advice. The national government long felt
obligated to establish an energy policy that would secure an adequate supply
and an appropriate price. But the bounty of nature is distributed differently
in different provinces. Some have oil and some not. The balancing of
regional fortunes is a critical part of the federal task, invariably difficult to
effect, and always generating tensions. A policy that satisfies Ontario may
alienate Alberta.

The Fathers of Confederation believed that they were wise to concede the
provinces a power to control and tax natural resources for the benefit of
residents. From the outset this right was deemed an essential element in the
federal bargain and a cherished part of the British North America Act (sections 92 and 109). Yet it was denied to the three Prairie provinces in
their early years, because the national government then managed their lands
in the presumed general interest of Canada. They were treated as a semi-
colonial community. But in 1930 the Prairie provinces won control over
their lands and resources, and thereby might seem to acquire an equality
with the central provinces. Yet no such equality actually resulted or could
result. Without industrial power and a large demographic base from which
to exert a voting strength in the national Parliament and cabinet, they
remained inferior in influence to the provinces of the St. Lawrence valley.

Hence the sense of a harsh regional struggle has continued within the present federation. The Prairie West is no monolith, and remains unable to
speak with a single and potent political voice. It still feels isolated by
geography, remote from the great centres of continental population, ill-
served by the transportation system, and precariously dependent on the processing of staples. It has impressive natural wealth, but subordinate political
power. Consequently each province has continued to have constant anxieties and fears in dealing with the government in Ottawa.

Alberta is not the least anxious although it is now the wealthiest of the
Prairie provinces, with more than $8 billion in its heritage savings funds,
a mound of money growing at a rapid rate from resource revenue and intended as a protection against the day when the oil runs out. The magnitude
and character of this wealth feeds provincial anxiety because it is exposed to
the potential taxes and other assertions of the national authority. Before the
Leduc oil discovery of 1947, less than 5 per cent of its public revenue was
derived from oil and gas royalties and land-lease payments. Now in the
1980s 60 per cent is obtained from oil and gas. The oil producing provinces
and the federal government have become unremitting competitors in a common drive for tax revenues from natural products. Not surprisingly western
political passions, even separatist sentiments, grow as fiscal frictions between the two levels of government intensify.

Regional Criticism

The Supreme Court in some judgements has incurred regional criticism for appearing to restrict the western provinces in utilizing their resources to the best advantage, especially when these are traded abroad. In a notable decision (the *Canadian Industrial Gas and Oil — CIGOL — vs the Government of Saskatchewan*) the court rejected the validity of provincial legislation designed to cope with the consequences of the sharp rise in oil prices in 1973. When North American prices rose with the action of OPEC, the Saskatchewan government had decided that windfall profits should accrue, not to the oil and gas companies, but to the people of Saskatchewan. The court however ruled that the Saskatchewan tax was not a direct tax, the sole kind open to the province. Thus the provincial attempt to manage its resource in a special way met frustration.

Another controversial decision concerned the action of the Central Canada Potash Company against the Saskatchewan Government, which had established a potash pro-rationing system with an established minimum price. The Supreme Court pronounced the system unconstitutional because most potash went to consumers outside. The provincial administration was really trying to regulate exports and fix prices, a procedure that infringed upon Ottawa's exclusive jurisdiction over interprovincial trade and commerce. Not least significant in provoking a hostile western response is the fact that in court the federal authority is seen to take positive sides with the large and mainly foreign-owned resource companies against the provinces. In such judicial collisions and unpopular alliances between private corporations and federal authorities, the anguished spirit of western alienation found sustenance.

Natural resources have also emerged as a major issue in many other federal-provincial disputations. The national government has always tenaciously asserted a claim to control off-shore mineral resources, and re-emphasized its position in the Federal-Provincial Constitutional Conference of September 1980, especially in rejecting the vehement arguments of Premier Brian Peckford.

For other reasons, however, this conference established for itself a large and distinctive place in the federal-provincial calendar. It witnessed the prime minister's urgent plea for certain major constitutional changes on which he set a priority. His proposals were submitted as non-negotiable, especially the patriation of the constitution, an amending formula, and an entrenched charter of rights and liberties, including language rights binding on both levels of government. If the conference failed to accept his plan, he was firmly determined to pursue it unilaterally and directly through an appeal from Ottawa to Westminster. He was as good as his word. After some days of heated debate he wound the September conference down to an abrupt conclusion without an agreement, and by October 2 he and his ministers were busily engaged in preparing measures designed to secure the passage of a joint parliamentary resolution for submission to London.

Court Cases

To achieve its end the national government utilized a joint parliamentary committee, representing the two chambers and the three major parties. This body within its terms of reference on the whole operated effectively, and with aid from opposition parties did much to collect and marshal evidence that gave concrete substance to the case for an entrenched declaration of rights. Nevertheless the six provinces hostile to Ottawa's unilateralism continued to campaign against it. They sought, by appeals to the senior courts of Manitoba, Newfoundland, and Quebec, to have Mr. Trudeau's procedure condemned as a violation of the constitution. Seldom has the character of the constitution come under such critical scrutiny.

Early in February 1981 the Manitoba Court of Appeal in a split decision (3-2) ruled that the national government had ample right on its side. Such positive encouragement, however, was severely shaken on March 31 when the Newfoundland Court of Appeal unanimously declared that any constitutional change in federal and provincial relations necessitated the consent of the provinces. Although in external relations and foreign policy the national government may speak for the entire country, in the area of constitutional amendments the plenitude of its authority is restricted; it must respect the division of powers and the rights of the provinces, for otherwise the constitution would lack a federal quality. The Newfoundland judges were emphatic that the proposed Charter of Rights and Freedoms threatened to infringe on the powers of the provinces to legislate on property and civil rights.

An immediate result of the Newfoundland opinion was to reverse Mr. Trudeau's former unwillingness to submit the constitutional resolution to the Supreme Court for examination before its transmission to Westminster. . . .

The prolonged hearings before the Supreme Court between April 28 and May 4 brought to a sharp and dramatic focus the conflicting opinions involved in the debates of preceding months. The national government primarily aimed to demonstrate that its action on the constitution rested on reliable law. It had the legal power to do what it did and thereby advanced the interests of the country. It was equally convinced that it was not obligated to consult and accept advice from the provinces. The government's confident sense of power was emphatically conveyed by its chief legal advisers, Messrs. John Robinette and Richard Robert, and notably also by Roy McMurtry, the attorney-general of Ontario, one of the two provinces committed to support Mr. Trudeau's unilateral policy.

The attorney-general, in the course of defending this policy, declared that the national Parliament commanded such complete power that, if it were necessary, it could even advise Westminster to abolish the provinces and promptly transform Canada into a unitary state, although he admitted that political realities rendered this unlikely.

The national government also expressed the conviction that under an unbending convention, the British Parliament must act on constitutional requests from the Canadian Parliament for appropriate amendments. These views are generally consonant with the spirit of those founding fathers who at the outset failed to provide a democratic amending formula. But in 1981, time and circumstances differ greatly from those in 1867. In the interval the federal system has grown profoundly. Although its basic law may have altered little, in a century its political realities, scale of performance, practices, conventions, and workable assumptions have vastly changed. No longer are the provinces the minor political agencies which John A. Macdonald and his associates sought to manipulate and manage according to their designs. They are keenly self-conscious communities, striving to administer substantial local affairs in response to regional necessities and the wide ambit of their jurisdictions under section 92.

A Federal Constitution

Any realistic assessment of Canada's constitution must consider these features in interpreting the basic law. As federal lawyers in the Supreme Court thrashed over some narrow legal points in their brief, Mr. Justice Brian Dickson cut in with a crucial question: "Is the federal status of Canada irrelevant in all this?" The short answer may be that it cannot be irrelevant, because the federal system has hitherto compelled many national administrations to consult the provinces on countless matters, including amendment of the constitution. Consultation has arisen spontaneously because of its urgent necessity. In *Federalism for the Future* (1968) Prime Minister Lester Pearson emphasized that "the relationships between the federal and provincial governments have multiplied as their policies and programmes have multiplied: an elaborate structure of federal-provincial conferences and committees, never contemplated in the constitution, has developed to meet this need." He extolled as imperative this joint and consultative mode of procedure. For him it appeared to be a basic part of Canadian federalism, and must be utilized in coping with the urgencies of constitutional amendment. . . .

Mr. Trudeau at the outset took from Mr. Pearson a similar view. In the Victoria Conference of June, 1971 he carried the technique of collaboration close to success. In September, 1980, however, he impatiently rejected it because in his opinion it had hitherto failed, and he was unwilling to face another failure. Doubtless also he was irritated by what seemed the uncompromising and uncooperative spirit exhibited by some provincial leaders, especially Levesque, Lougheed and Peckford. His federal militancy was partly a response to provincial militancy. But his proposal for unilateral action was a mistake. He thus appeared to reject flatly the federality of Canada, provoked in all provinces, except Ontario and New Brunswick, a fierce hostility, and helped to generate harsh political tensions and confusions that ultimately compelled an appeal to the Supreme Court. Resort to the court was an act of wisdom, since through its able members it could best perform as a dispassionate and final arbiter. . . .

[Editor's note: Following the date at which Professor Brady's article concludes, the Supreme Court of Canada rendered its judgements on the Constitution Act on September 28, 1981. By a 7-2 decision, the Court found that the federal government had the legal right to request the United Kingdom Parliament to amend the B.N.A. Act to implement the new constitution, including a charter of rights, without obtaining the consent of the provinces. Nevertheless, by a 6-3 decision, the Court also concluded that there was a constitutional convention requiring provincial consent for such action. However, the judges were careful to state that such conventions were not enforceable by the courts and they rejected the argument made by seven provinces that unanimous provincial consent was necessary for an amendment. They wisely avoided specifying "what measure of provincial agreement is necessary," remarking that it would be up to "the political actors" to decide. (See *infra*, Chapter 16, for a verbatim extract from the Supreme Court's decision.)

Under pressure from public opinion and taking their cue from the Supreme Court's judgement, the federal and provincial premiers came together in Ottawa on November 2, 1981 for one final attempt to reach consensus on a new constitution. After four days of intense and rather dramatic bargaining, the federal government and all the provinces except Quebec reached agreement on a considerably diluted resolution. It provoked bitter reaction not only from Quebec's Premier Lévesque, who felt that his province had been betrayed and isolated, but from women and native peoples, who believed that their rights to equality had not been adequately safeguarded. Following a massive public protest and further discussion among the premiers, the women secured the emphasis on Section 28 that they desired while the native peoples received less than what they wanted in Section 35.

The amended resolution was then put before both Houses of Parliament and, after limited discussion, it was passed in the House of Commons by a vote of 246-24 on December 2, 1981, and in the Senate by a vote of 59-23 on December 8.

Following a brief ceremony of transmittal to the Governor-General at Rideau Hall, the joint resolution was despatched immediately to the Queen for the attention of the U.K. Parliament at Westminster.

After four days of debate the House of Commons at Westminster gave the Canada Bill final reading and passed it without amendment by a vote of 177-33 on March 8, 1982. The House of Lords passed the bill on third reading without a recorded vote on March 25. The Queen signified her royal assent in Britain on March 26 and the *Constitution Act, 1982* was proclaimed in the presence of the Queen in Ottawa on April 17, 1982.

(See *infra*, the next item for the text of the resolution passed by the Canadian House of Commons, December 2, 1981.)]

CONSTITUTION ACT (CANADA ACT), 1981-82, AND THE CANADIAN CHARTER OF RIGHTS AND FREEDOMS*

THE CONSTITUTION

RESOLUTION RESPECTING CONSTITUTION ACT, 1981

The House resumed, from Tuesday, December 1, consideration of the amended motion of Mr. Chrétien:

THAT, WHEREAS in the past certain amendments to the Constitution of Canada have been made by the Parliament of the United Kingdom at the request and with the consent of Canada;

AND WHEREAS it is in accord with the status of Canada as an independent state that Canadians be able to amend their Constitution in Canada in all respects;

AND WHEREAS it is also desirable to provide in the Constitution of Canada for the recognition of certain

---

* From *House of Commons Debates*, December 2, 1981, pp. 13632-13658. By permission of the Minister of Supply and Services Canada. The *Constitution Act, 1981* became the *Constitution Act, 1982* since it was passed in Britain and proclaimed in Canada in 1982. The *Canada Act, 1982* was the United Kingdom statute which gave Westminster's assent to the *Constitution Act*. Since the U.K. Parliament did not amend the *Constitution Act, 1981* in any respect, the *Constitution Act, 1982* is identical to the *Constitution Act, 1981*.

fundamental rights and freedoms and to make other amendments to that Constitution;

A respectful address be presented to Her Majesty the Queen in the following words:

To the Queen's Most Excellent Majesty:
Most Gracious Sovereign:

We, Your Majesty's loyal subjects, the House of Commons of Canada in Parliament assembled, respectfully approach Your Majesty, requesting that you may graciously be pleased to cause to be laid before the Parliament of the United Kingdom a measure containing the recitals and clauses hereinafter set forth:

An Act to give effect to a request by the Senate and House of Commons of Canada

Whereas Canada has requested and consented to the enactment of an Act of the Parliament of the United Kingdom to give effect to the provisions hereinafter set forth and the Senate and the House of Commons of Canada in Parliament assembled have submitted an address to Her Majesty requesting that Her Majesty may graciously be pleased to cause a Bill to be laid before the Parliament of the United Kingdom for that purpose.

Be it therefore enacted by the Queen's Most Excellent Majesty, by and with the advice and consent of the Lords Spiritual and Temporal, and Commons, in this present Parliament assembled, and by the authority of the same, as follows:

Constitution Act, 1981 enacted

1. The *Constitution Act, 1981* set out in Schedule B to this Act is hereby enacted for and shall have the force of law in Canada and shall come into force as provided in that Act.

Termination of power to legislate for Canada

2. No Act of the Parliament of the United Kingdom passed after the *Constitution Act, 1981* comes into force shall extend to Canada as part of its law.

French version

3. So far as it is not contained in Schedule B, the French version of this Act is set out in Schedule A to this Act and has the same authority in Canada as the English version thereof.

Short title   4. This Act may be cited as the *Canada Act.*

SCHEDULE B

CONSTITUTION ACT, 1981

PART I

CANADIAN CHARTER OF RIGHTS AND FREEDOMS

Whereas Canada is founded upon principles that recognize the supremacy of God and the rule of law:

Guarantee of Rights and Freedoms

Rights and freedoms in Canada   1. The *Canadian Charter of Rights and Freedoms* guarantees the rights and freedoms set out in it subject only to such reasonable limits prescribed by law as can be demonstrably justified in a free and democratic society.

Fundamental Freedoms

Fundamental freedoms   2. Everyone has the following fundamental freedoms:
(*a*) freedom of conscience and religion;
(*b*) freedom of thought, belief, opinion and expression, including freedom of the press and other media of communication;
(*c*) freedom of peaceful assembly; and
(*d*) freedom of association.

Democratic Rights

Democratic rights of citizens   3. Every citizen of Canada has the right to vote in an election of members of the House of Commons or of a legislative assembly and to be qualified for membership therein.

Maximum duration of legislative bodies   4. (1) No House of Commons and no legislative assembly shall continue for longer than five years from the date fixed for the return of the writs at a general election of its members.

Continuation in special circumstances   (2) In time of real or apprehended war, invasion or insurrection, a House of Commons may be continued by Parliament and a legislative assembly may be continued by the legislature beyond five years if such continuation is not opposed by the votes of more than one-third of the members of the House of Commons or the legislative assembly, as the case may be.

Annual sitting of legislative bodies

5. There shall be a sitting of Parliament and of each legislature at least once every twelve months.

Mobility Rights

Mobility of citizens

6. (1) Every citizen of Canada has the right to enter, remain in and leave Canada.

Rights to move and gain livelihood

(2) Every citizen of Canada and every person who has the status of a permanent resident of Canada has the right
(*a*) to move to and take up residence in any province; and
(*b*) to pursue the gaining of a livelihood in any province.

Limitation

(3) The rights specified in subsection (2) are subject to
(*a*) any laws or practices of general application in force in a province other than those that discriminate among persons primarily on the basis of province of present or previous residence; and
(*b*) any laws providing for reasonable residency requirements as a qualification for the receipt of publicly provided social services.

Affirmative action programs

(4) Subsections (2) and (3) do not preclude any law, program or activity that has as its object the amelioration in a province of conditions of individuals in that province who are socially or economically disadvantaged if the rate of employment in that province is below the rate of employment in Canada.

Legal Rights

Life, liberty and security of person

7. Everyone has the right to life, liberty and security of the person and the right not to be deprived thereof except in accordance with the principles of fundamental justice.

Search or seizure

8. Everyone has the right to be secure against unreasonable search or seizure.

Detention or
imprisonment

9. Everyone has the right not to be arbitrarily detained or imprisoned.

Arrest or
detention

10. Everyone has the right on arrest or detention
(a) to be informed promptly of the reasons therefor;
(b) to retain and instruct counsel without delay and to be informed of that right; and
(c) to have the validity of the detention determined by way of *habeas corpus* and to be released if the detention is not lawful.

Proceedings in
criminal and
penal matters

11. Any person charged with an offence has the right
(a) to be informed without unreasonable delay of the specific offence;
(b) to be tried within a reasonable time;
(c) not to be compelled to be a witness in proceedings against that person in respect of the offence;
(d) to be presumed innocent until proven guilty according to law in a fair and public hearing by an independent and impartial tribunal;
(e) not to be denied reasonable bail without just cause;
(f) except in the case of an offence under military law tried before a military tribunal, to the benefit of trial by jury where the maximum punishment for the offence is imprisonment for five years or a more severe punishment;
(g) not to be found guilty on account of any act or omission unless, at the time of the act or omission, it constituted an offence under Canadian or international law or was criminal according to the general principles of law recognized by the community of nations;
(h) if finally acquitted of the offence, not to be tried for it again and, if finally found guilty and punished for the offence, not to be tried or punished for it again; and
(i) if found guilty of the offence and if the punishment for the offence has been varied between the time of commission and the time of sentencing, to the benefit of the lesser punishment.

Treatment or
punishment

12. Everyone has the right not to be subjected to any cruel and unusual treatment or punishment.

Self-crimination

13. A witness who testifies in any proceedings has the right not to have any incriminating evidence so given used to incriminate that witness in any other proceedings, except in a prosecution for perjury or for the giving of contradictory evidence.

Interpreter

14. A party or witness in any proceedings who does not understand or speak the language in which the proceedings are conducted or who is deaf has the right to the assistance of an interpreter.

Equality Rights

Equality before and under law and equal protection and benefit of law

15. (1) Every individual is equal before and under the law and has the right to the equal protection and equal benefit of the law without discrimination and, in particular, without discrimination based on race, national or ethnic origin, colour, religion, sex, age or mental or physical disability.

Affirmative action programs

(2) Subsection (1) does not preclude any law, program or activity that has as its object the amelioration of conditions of disadvantaged individuals or groups including those that are disadvantaged because of race, national or ethnic origin, colour, religion, sex, age or mental or physical disability.

Official Languages of Canada

Official languages of Canada

16. (1) English and French are the official languages of Canada and have equality of status and equal rights and privileges as to their use in all institutions of the Parliament and government of Canada.

Official languages of New Brunswick

(2) English and French are the official languages of New Brunswick and have equality of status and equal rights and privileges as to their use in all institutions of the legislature and government of New Brunswick.

Advancement of status and use

(3) Nothing in this Charter limits the authority of Parliament or a legislature to advance the equality of status or use of English and French.

Proceedings of Parliament

17. (1) Everyone has the right to use English or French in any debates and other proceedings of Parliament.

Proceedings of New Brunswick legislature

(2) Everyone has the right to use English or French in any debates and other proceedings of the legislature of New Brunswick.

Parliamentary statutes and records

18. (1) The statutes, records and journals of Parliament shall be printed and published in English and French and both language versions are equally authoritative.

New Brunswick statutes and records

(2) The statutes, records and journals of the legislature of New Brunswick shall be printed and published in English and French and both language versions are equally authoritative.

Proceedings in courts established by Parliament

19. (1) Either English or French may be used by any person in, or in any pleading in or process issuing from, any court established by Parliament.

Proceedings in New Brunswick courts

(2) Either English or French may be used by any person in, or in any pleading in or process issuing from, any court of New Brunswick.

Communications by public with federal institutions

20. (1) Any member of the public in Canada has the right to communicate with, and to receive available services from, any head or central office of an institution of the Parliament or government of Canada in English or French, and has the same right with respect to any other office of any such institution where

(a) there is a significant demand for communications with and services from that office in such language; or

(b) due to the nature of the office, it is reasonable that communications with and services from that office be available in both English and French.

Communications by public with New Brunswick institutions

(2) Any member of the public in New Brunswick has the right to communicate with, and to receive available services from, any office of an institution of the legislature or government of New Brunswick in English or French.

Continuation of existing constitutional provisions

21. Nothing in sections 16 to 20 abrogates or derogates from any right, privilege or obligation with respect to the English and French languages, or either of them, that exists or is continued by virtue of any other provision of the Constitution of Canada.

Rights and privileges preserved

22. Nothing in sections 16 to 20 abrogates or derogates from any legal or customary right or privilege acquired or enjoyed either before or after the coming into force of this Charter with respect to any language that is not English or French.

Minority Language Educational Rights

Language of instruction

23. (1) Citizens of Canada

(a) whose first language learned and still understood is that of the English or French linguistic minority population of the province in which they reside, or

(b) who have received their primary school instruction in Canada in English or French and reside in a province where the language in which they received that instruction is the language of the English or French linguistic minority population of the province, have the right to have their children receive primary and secondary school instruction in that language in that province.

Continuity of language instruction

(2) Citizens of Canada of whom any child has received or is receiving primary or secondary school instruction in English or French in Canada, have the right to have all their children receive primary and secondary school instruction in the same language.

Application where numbers warrant

(3) The right of citizens of Canada under subsections (1) and (2) to have their children receive primary and secondary school instruction in the language of the English or French linguistic minority population of a province

(a) applies wherever in the province the number of children of citizens who have such a right is sufficient to warrant the provision to them out of public funds of minority language instruction; and

(b) includes, where the number of those children so warrants, the right to have them receive that instruction in minority language educational facilities provided out of public funds.

Enforcement

Enforcement of guaranteed rights and freedoms

24. (1) Anyone whose rights or freedoms, as guaranteed by this Charter, have been infringed or denied may apply to a court of competent jurisdiction to obtain such remedy as the court considers appropriate and just in the circumstances.

Exclusion of evidence bringing administration of justice into disrepute

(2) Where, in proceedings under subsection (1), a court concludes that evidence was obtained in a manner that infringed or denied any rights or freedoms guaranteed by this Charter, the evidence shall be excluded if it is established that, having regard to all the circumstances, the admission of it in the proceedings would bring the administration of justice into disrepute.

General

Aboriginal rights and freedoms not affected by Charter

25. The guarantee in this Charter of certain rights and freedoms shall not be construed so as to abrogate or derogate from any aboriginal, treaty or other rights or freedoms that pertain to the aboriginal peoples of Canada including

(a) any rights or freedoms that have been recognized by the Royal Proclamation of October 7, 1763; and

(b) any rights or freedoms that may be acquired by the aboriginal peoples of Canada by way of land claims settlement.

Other rights and freedoms not affected by Charter

26. The guarantee in this Charter of certain rights and freedoms shall not be construed as denying the existence of any other rights or freedoms that exist in Canada.

Multicultural heritage

27. This Charter shall be interpreted in a manner consistent with the preservation and enhancement of the multicultural heritage of Canadians.

Rights guaranteed equally to both sexes

28. Notwithstanding anything in this Charter, the rights and freedoms referred to in it are guaranteed equally to male and female persons.

Rights respecting certain schools preserved

29. Nothing in this Charter abrogates or derogates from any rights or privileges guaranteed by or under the Constitution of Canada in respect of denominational, separate or dissentient schools.

Application to territories and territorial authorities

30. A reference in this Charter to a province or to the legislative assembly or legislature of a province shall be deemed to include a reference to the Yukon Territory and the Northwest Territories, or to the appropriate legislative authority thereof, as the case may be.

Legislative powers not extended

31. Nothing in this Charter extends the legislative powers of any body or authority.

Application of Charter

Application of Charter

32. (1) This Charter applies

(a) to the Parliament and government of Canada in respect of all matters within the authority of Parliament including all matters relating to the Yukon Territory and Northwest Territories; and

(b) to the legislature and government of each province in respect of all matters within the authority of the legislature of each province.

Exception

(2) Notwithstanding subsection (1), section 15 shall not have effect until three years after this section comes into force.

Exception where
express declaration

33. (1) Parliament or the legislature of a province may expressly declare in an Act of Parliament or of the legislature, as the case may be, that the Act or a provision thereof shall operate notwithstanding a provision included in section 2 or sections 7 to 15 of this Charter.

Operation of
exception

(2) An Act or provision of an Act in respect of which a declaration made under this section is in effect shall have such operation as it would have but for the provision of this Charter referred to in the declaration.

Five year
limitation

(3) A declaration made under subsection (1) shall cease to have effect five years after it comes into force or on such earlier date as may be specified in the declaration.

Re-enactment

(4) Parliament or a legislature of a province may re-enact a declaration made under subsection (1).

Five year
limitation

(5) Subsection (3) applies in respect of a re-enactment made under subsection (4).

Citation

Citation

34. This Part may be cited as the *Canadian Charter of Rights and Freedoms.*

PART II

RIGHTS OF THE ABORIGINAL PEOPLES OF CANADA

Recognition of
existing aboriginal
and treaty
rights

35. (1) The existing aboriginal and treaty rights of the aboriginal peoples of Canada are hereby recognized and affirmed.

Definition of
"aboriginal peoples
of Canada"

(2) In this Act, "aboriginal peoples of Canada" includes the Indian, Inuit and Métis peoples of Canada.

PART III

EQUALIZATION AND REGIONAL DISPARITIES

Commitment to
promote equal
opportunities

36. (1) Without altering the legislative authority of Parliament or of the provincial legislatures, or the rights of any of them with respect to the exercise of their legislative authority, Parliament and the legislatures, together with the government of Canada and the provincial governments, are committed to *(a)* promoting equal opportunities for the well-being of Canadians;

(b) furthering economic development to reduce disparity in opportunities; and

(c) providing essential public services of reasonable quality to all Canadians.

Commitment respecting public services

(2) Parliament and the government of Canada are committed to the principle of making equalization payments to ensure that provincial governments have sufficient revenues to provide reasonably comparable levels of public services at reasonably comparable levels of taxation.

PART IV

CONSTITUTIONAL CONFERENCE

Constitutional conference

37. (1) A constitutional conference composed of the Prime Minister of Canada and the first ministers of the provinces shall be convened by the Prime Minister of Canada within one year after this Part comes into force.

Participation of aboriginal peoples

(2) The conference convened under subsection (1) shall have included in its agenda an item respecting constitutional matters that directly affect the aboriginal peoples of Canada, including the identification and definition of the rights of those peoples to be included in the Constitution of Canada, and the Prime Minister of Canada shall invite representatives of those peoples to participate in the discussions on that item.

Participation of territories

(3) The Prime Minister of Canada shall invite elected representatives of the governments of the Yukon Territory and the Northwest Territories to participate in the discussions on any item on the agenda of the conference convened under subsection (1) that, in the opinion of the Prime Minister, directly affects the Yukon Territory and the Northwest Territories.

PART V

PROCEDURE FOR AMENDING
CONSTITUTION OF CANADA

General procedure for amending Constitution of Canada

38. (1) An amendment to the Constitution of Canada may be made by proclamation issued by the Governor General under the Great Seal of Canada where so authorized by

(a) resolutions of the Senate and House of Commons; and

(b) resolutions of the legislative assemblies of at least two-thirds of the provinces that have, in the aggregate, according to the then latest general census, at least fifty per cent of the population of all the provinces.

Majority of members

(2) An amendment made under subsection (1) that derogates from the legislative powers, the proprietary rights or any other rights or privileges of the legislature or government of a province shall require a resolution supported by a majority of the members of each of the Senate, the House of Commons and the legislative assemblies required under subsection (1).

Expression of dissent

(3) An amendment referred to in subsection (2) shall not have effect in a province the legislative assembly of which has expressed its dissent thereto by resolution supported by a majority of its members prior to the issue of the proclamation to which the amendment relates unless that legislative assembly, subsequently, by resolution supported by a majority of its members, revokes its dissent and authorizes the amendment.

Revocation of dissent

(4) A resolution of dissent made for the purposes of subsection (3) may be revoked at any time before or after the issue of the proclamation to which it relates.

Restriction on proclamation

39. (1) A proclamation shall not be issued under subsection 38(1) before the expiration of one year from the adoption of the resolution initiating the amendment procedure thereunder, unless the legislative assembly of each province has previously adopted a resolution of assent or dissent.

Idem

(2) A proclamation shall not be issued under subsection 38(1) after the expiration of three years from the adoption of the resolution initiating the amendment procedure thereunder.

Compensation

40. Where an amendment is made under subsection 38(1) that transfers provincial legislative powers relating to education or other cultural matters from provincial legislatures to Parliament, Canada shall provide reasonable compensation to any province to which the amendment does not apply.

Amendment by unanimous consent

41. An amendment to the Constitution of Canada in relation to the following matters may be made by pro-

clamation issued by the Governor General under the Great Seal of Canada only where authorized by resolutions of the Senate and House of Commons and of the legislative assembly of each province:

(a) the office of the Queen, the Governor General and the Lieutenant Governor of a province;

(b) the right of a province to a number of members in the House of Commons not less than the number of Senators by which the province is entitled to be represented at the time this Part comes into force;

(c) subject to section 43, the use of the English or the French language;

(d) the composition of the Supreme Court of Canada; and

(e) an amendment to this Part.

Amendment by general procedure

42. (1) An amendment to the Constitution of Canada in relation to the following matters may be made only in accordance with subsection 38(1):

(a) the principle of proportionate representation of the provinces in the House of Commons prescribed by the Constitution of Canada;

(b) the powers of the Senate and the method of selecting Senators;

(c) the number of members by which a province is entitled to be represented in the Senate and the residence qualifications of Senators;

(d) subject to paragraph 41(*d*), the Supreme Court of Canada;

(e) the extension of existing provinces into the territories; and

(f) notwithstanding any other law or practice, the establishment of new provinces.

Exception

(2) Subsections 38(2) to (4) do not apply in respect of amendments in relation to matters referred to in subsection (1).

Amendment of provisions relating to some but not all provinces

43. An amendment to the Constitution of Canada in relation to any provision that applies to one or more, but not all, provinces, including

(a) any alteration to boundaries between provinces, and

(b) any amendment to any provision that relates to the use of the English or the French language within a province,

may be made by proclamation issued by the Governor General under the Great Seal of Canada only where so authorized by resolutions of the Senate and House of Commons and of the legislative assembly of each province to which the amendment applies.

Amendments by
Parliament

44. Subject to sections 41 and 42, Parliament may exclusively make laws amending the Constitution of Canada in relation to the executive government of Canada or the Senate and House of Commons.

Amendments by
provincial
legislatures

45. Subject to section 41, the legislature of each province may exclusively make laws amending the constitution of the province.

Initiation of
amendment
procedures

46. (1) The procedures for amendment under sections 38, 41, 42 and 43 may be initiated either by the Senate or the House of Commons or by the legislative assembly of a province.

Revocation of
authorization

(2) A resolution of assent made for the purposes of this Part may be revoked at any time before the issue of a proclamation authorized by it.

Amendments
without Senate
resolution

47. (1) An amendment to the Constitution of Canada made by proclamation under section 38, 41, 42 or 43 may be made without a resolution of the Senate authorizing the issue of the proclamation if, within one hundred and eighty days after the adoption by the House of Commons of a resolution authorizing its issue, the Senate has not adopted such a resolution and if, at any time after the expiration of that period, the House of Commons again adopts the resolution.

Computation
of period

(2) Any period when Parliament is prorogued or dissolved shall not be counted in computing the one hundred and eighty day period referred to in subsection (1).

Advice to issue
proclamation

48. The Queen's Privy Council for Canada shall advise the Governor General to issue a proclamation under this Part forthwith on the adoption of the resolutions required for an amendment made by proclamation under this Part.

Constitutional
conference

49. A constitutional conference composed of the Prime Minister of Canada and the first ministers of the provinces shall be convened by the Prime Minister of Canada within fifteen years after this Part comes into force to review the provisions of this Part.

PART VI

AMENDMENT TO THE CONSTITUTION ACT, 1867

Amendment to
*Constitution Act,
1867*

50. The *Constitution Act, 1867* (formerly named the *British North America Act, 1867)* is amended by adding thereto, immediately after section 92 thereof, the following heading and section:

*"Non-Renewable Natural Resources, Forestry
Resources and Electrical Energy*

Laws respecting
non-renewable
natural resources,
forestry resources
and electrical energy

92A. (1) In each province, the legislature may exclusively make laws in relation to

(a) exploration for non-renewable natural resources in the province;

(b) development, conservation and management of non-renewable natural resources and forestry resources in the province, including laws in relation to the rate of primary production therefrom; and

(c) development, conservation and management of sites and facilities in the province for the generation and production of electrical energy.

Export from
provinces of
resources

(2) In each province, the legislature may make laws in relation to the export from the province to another part of Canada of the primary production from non-renewable natural resources and forestry resources in the province and the production from facilities in the province for the generation of electrical energy, but such laws may not authorize or provide for discrimination in prices or in supplies exported to another part of Canada.

Authority of
Parliament

(3) Nothing in subsection (2) derogates from the authority of Parliament to enact laws in relation to the matters referred to in that subsection and, where such a law of Parliament and a law of a province conflict, the law of Parliament prevails to the extent of the conflict.

Taxation of
resources

(4) In each province, the legislature may make laws in relation to the raising of money by any mode or system of taxation in respect of

(a) non-renewable natural resources and forestry resources in the province and the primary production therefrom, and

(b) sites and facilities in the province for the generation of electrical energy and the production therefrom,

whether or not such production is exported in whole or in part from the province, but such laws may not authorize or provide for taxation that differentiates between production exported to another part of Canada and production not exported from the province.

"Primary
production"

(5) The expression "primary production" has the meaning assigned by the Sixth Schedule.

Existing powers
or rights

(6) Nothing in subsections (1) to (5) derogates from any powers or rights that a legislature or government of a province had immediately before the coming into force of this section."

Idem

51. The said Act is further amended by adding thereto the following Schedule:

"THE SIXTH SCHEDULE

Primary Production from Non-Renewable Natural Resources and Forestry Resources

1. For the purposes of section 92A of this Act,
(a) production from a non-renewable natural resource is primary production therefrom if
(i) it is in the form in which it exists upon its recovery or severence from its natural state, or
(ii) it is a product resulting from processing or refining the resource, and is not a manufactured product or a product resulting from refining crude oil, refining upgraded heavy crude oil, refining gases or liquids derived from coal or refining a synthetic equivalent of crude oil; and
(b) production from a forestry resource is primary production therefrom if it consists of sawlogs, poles, lumber, wood chips, sawdust or any other primary wood product, or wood pulp, and is not a product manufactured from wood."

PART VII

GENERAL

Primacy of Constitution of Canada

52. (1) The Constitution of Canada is the supreme law of Canada, and any law that is inconsistent with the provisions of the Constitution is, to the extent of the inconsistency, of no force or effect.

Constitution of Canada

(2) The Constitution of Canada includes
(a) the *Canada Act,* including this Act;
(b) the Acts and orders referred to in Schedule I; and
(c) any amendment to any Act or order referred to in paragraph (*a*) or (*b*).

Amendments to Constitution of Canada

(3) Amendments to the Constitution of Canada shall be made only in accordance with the authority contained in the Constitution of Canada.

Repeals and new names

53. (1) The enactments referred to in Column I of Schedule I are hereby repealed or amended to the extent indicated in Column II thereof and, unless repealed, shall continue as law in Canada under the names set out in Column III thereof.

Consequential amendments

(2) Every enactment, except the *Canada Act*, that refers to an enactment referred to in Schedule I by the name in Column I thereof is hereby amended by substituting for that name the corresponding name in Column III thereof, and any British North America Act not referred to in Schedule I may be cited as the *Constitution Act* followed by the year and number, if any, of its enactment.

Repeal and consequential amendments

54. Part IV is repealed on the day that is one year after this Part comes into force and this section may be repealed and this Act renumbered, consequential upon the repeal of Part IV and this section, by proclamation issued by the Governor General under the Great Seal of Canada.

French version of Constitution of Canada

55. A French version of the portions of the Constitution of Canada referred to in Schedule I shall be prepared by the Minister of Justice of Canada as expeditiously as possible and, when any portion thereof sufficient to warrant action being taken has been so prepared, it shall be put forward for enactment by proclamation issued by the Governor General under the Great Seal of Canada pursuant to the procedure then applicable to an amendment of the same provisions of the Constitution of Canada.

English and French versions of certain constitutional texts

56. Where any portion of the Constitution of Canada has been or is enacted in English and French or where a French version of any portion of the Constitution is enacted pursuant to section 55, the English and French versions of that portion of the Constitution are equally authoritative.

English and French versions of this Act

57. The English and French versions of this Act are equally authoritative.

Commencement

58. Subject to section 59, this Act shall come into force on a day to be fixed by proclamation issued by the Queen or the Governor General under the Great Seal of Canada.

Commencement of paragraph 23(1)(a) in respect of Quebec

59. (1) Paragraph 23(1)(a) shall come into force in respect of Quebec on a day to be fixed by proclamation issued by the Queen or the Governor General under the Great Seal of Canada.

Authorization of Quebec

(2) A proclamation under subsection (1) shall be issued only where authorized by the legislative assembly or government of Quebec.

Repeal of this
section

(3) This section may be repealed on the day paragraph 23(1)(*a*) comes into force in respect of Quebec and this Act amended and renumbered, consequential upon the repeal of this section, by proclamation issued by the Queen or the Governor General under the Great Seal of Canada.

Short title and
citations

60. This Act may be cited as the *Constitution Act, 1981,* and the Constitution Acts 1867 to 1975 (No. 2) and this Act may be cited together as the *Constitution Acts, 1867 to 1981.*

SCHEDULE 1

to the

CONSTITUTION ACT, 1981

MODERNIZATION OF THE CONSTITUTION

Item	Column I Act Affected	Column II Amendment	Column III New Name
1.	British North America Act, 1867, 30-31 Vict., c. 3 (U.K.)	(1) Section 1 is repealed and the following substituted therefore: "1. This Act may be cited as the *Constitution Act, 1867.*" (2) Section 20 is repealed. (3) Class 1 of section 91 is repealed. (4) Class 1 of section 92 is repealed.	Constitution Act, 1867
2.	An Act to amend and continue the Act 32-33 Victoria chapter 3; and to establish and provide for the Government of the Province of Manitoba, 1870, 33 Vict., c. 3 (Can.)	(1) The long title is repealed and the following substituted therefor: *"Manitoba Act, 1870."* (2) Section 20 is repealed.	Manitoba Act, 1870
3.	Order of Her Majesty in Council admitting Rupert's Land and the North-Western Terri- into the Union, dated the 23rd day of June, 1870		Rupert's Land and North-Western Territory Order
4.	Order of Her Majesty in Council admitting British Columbia into the Union, dated the 16th day of May, 1871		British Columbia Terms of Union
5.	British North America Act, 1871, 34-35 Vict., c. 28 (U.K.)	Section 1 is repealed and the following substituted therefor: "1. This Act may be cited as the *Constitution Act, 1871.*"	Constitution Act, 1871

6. Order of Her Majesty in Council admitting Prince Edward Island into the Union, dated the 26th day of June, 1873		Prince Edward Island Terms of Union
7. Parliament of Canada Act, 1875, 38-39 Vict., c. 38 (U.K.)		Parliament of Canada Act, 1875
8. Order of Her Majesty in Council admitting all British possessions and Territories in North America and islands adjacent thereto into the Union, dated the 31st day of July, 1880		Adjacent Territories Order
9. British North America Act, 1886, 49-50 Vict., c. 35 (U.K.)	Section 3 is repealed and the following substituted therefor: "3. This Act may be cited as the *Constitution Act, 1886.*"	Constitution Act, 1886
10. Canada (Ontario Boundary) Act, 1889, 52-53 Vict., c. 28 (U.K.)		Canada (Ontario Boundary) Act, 1889
11. Canadian Speaker (Appointment of Deputy) Act, 1895, 2nd Sess., 59 Vict., c. 3 (U.K.)	The Act is repealed.	
12. The Alberta Act, 1905, 4-5 Edw. VII, c. 3 (Can.)		Alberta Act
13. The Saskatchewan Act, 1905, 4-5 Edw. VII, c. 42 (Can.)		Saskatchewan Act
14. British North America Act, 1907, 7 Edw. VII, c. 11 (U.K.)	Section 2 is repealed and the following substituted therefor: "2. This Act may be cited as the *Constitution Act, 1907.*"	Constitution Act, 1907
15. British North America Act, 1915, 5-6 Geo. V, c. 45 (U.K.)	Section 3 is repealed and the following substituted therefor: "3. This Act may be cited as the *Constitution Act, 1915.*"	Constitution Act, 1915
16. British North America Act, 1930, 20-21 Geo. V, c. 26 (U.K.)	Section 3 is repealed and the following substituted therefor: "3. This Act may be cited as the *Constitution Act, 1930.*"	Constitution Act, 1930
17. Statute of Westminster, 1931, 22 Geo. V, c. 4 (U.K.)	In so far as they apply to Canada, (*a*) section 4 is repealed; and (*b*) subsection 7(1) is repealed.	Statute of Westminster, 1931

18.	British North America Act, 1940, 3-4 Geo. VI, c. 36 (U.K.)	Section 2 is repealed and the following substituted therefor: "2. This Act may be cited as the *Constitution Act, 1940.*"	Constitution Act, 1940
19.	British North America Act, 1943, 6-7 Geo. VI, c. 30 (U.K.)	The Act is repealed.	
20.	British North America Act, 1946, 9-10 Geo. VI, c. 63 (U.K.)	The Act is repealed.	
21.	British North America Act, 1949, 12-13 Geo. VI, c. 22 (U.K.)	Section 3 is repealed and the following substituted therefor: "3. This Act may be cited as the *Newfoundland Act.*"	Newfoundland Act
22.	British North America (No. 2) Act, 1949, 13 Geo. VI, c. 81 (U.K.)	The Act is repealed.	
23.	British North America Act, 1951, 14-15 Geo. VI, c. 32 (U.K.)	The Act is repealed.	
24.	British North America Act, 1952, 1 Eliz. II, c. 15 (Can.)	The Act is repealed.	
25.	British North America Act, 1960, 9 Eliz. II, c. 2 (U.K.)	Section 2 is repealed and the following substituted therefor: "2. This Act may be cited as the *Constitution Act, 1960.*"	Constitution Act, 1960
26.	British North America Act, 1964, 12-13 Eliz. II, c. 73 (U.K.)	Section 2 is repealed and the following substituted therefor: "2. This Act may be cited as the *Constitution Act, 1964.*"	Constitution Act, 1964
27.	British North America Act, 1965, 14 Eliz. II, c. 4, Part I (Can.)	Section 2 is repealed and the following substituted therefor: "2. This Part may be cited as the *Constitution Act, 1965.*"	Constitution Act, 1965
28.	British North America Act, 1974, 23 Eliz. II, c. 13, Part I (Can.)	Section 3, as amended by 25-26 Eliz. II, c. 28, s. 38(1) (Can.), is repealed and the following substituted therefor: "3. This Part may be cited as the *Constitution Act, 1974.*"	Constitution Act, 1974
29.	British North America Act, 1975, 23-24 Eliz. II, c. 28, Part I (Can.)	Section 3, as amended by 25-26 Eliz. II, c. 28, s. 31 (Can.), is repealed and the following substituted therefor: "3. This Part may be cited as the *Constitution Act (No. 1), 1975.*"	Constitution Act (No. 1), 1975

| 30. | British North America Act, (No. 2), 1975, 23-24 Eliz. II, c. 53 (Can.) | Section 3 is repealed and the following substituted therefor: "3. This Act may be cited as the *Constitution Act (No. 2), 1975.*" | Constitution Act (No. 2), 1975 |

RECENT CANADIAN AND UNITED KINGDOM PARLIAMENTARY AMENDMENTS OF THE B.N.A. ACT*

Paul Fox

Amendment (No. 2) 1949 of the British North America Act conferred on the Canadian Parliament the power to amend "the Constitution of Canada" in certain respects. Under this power, which became Section 91(1) of the B.N.A. Act, the Canadian Parliament has enacted five amendments which may be summarized as follows:

1952—c.15, cited as the *B.N.A. Act, 1952,* which provided for the readjustment of representation in the House of Commons.

1965—c.4, cited as the *B.N.A. Act, 1965,* which provided for the retirement of certain senators at 75 years of age (incumbents opting for retirement and subsequent newly appointed senators).

1974-75-76—c.13, cited as the *B.N.A. Act (No. 2, 1974),* which again provided for an adjustment of representation in the House of Commons.

1974-75-76—c.28, cited as the *B.N.A. Act, 1975,* which confirmed the representation in the House of Commons of one member of Parliament from the Yukon Territory and increased the representation in the Commons of the Northwest Territories to two members.

1974-75-76—c.53, cited as the *B.N.A. Act (No. 2), 1975,* which increased the number of senators by adding two, one each for the Yukon and Northwest Territories.

(There was no *B.N.A. Act (No. 1), 1974,* since the Bill originally submitted under this designation ultimately became *B.N.A. Act (No. 2), 1975.)*

From 1949 to March 9, 1976, there were three additional amendments passed by the United Kingdom Parliament. The *British North America Act, 1960, 9 Eliz. II, c.2 (U.K.)* repealed the existing Section 99 of the B.N.A. Act and substituted a new Section 99 which altered the tenure of judges of provincial superior courts from life to 75 years of age. The *British North America Act, 1951, 14-15 Geo. VI, c.32 (U.K.)* added Section 94A to the B.N.A. Act, enabling the Parliament of Canada to make laws in relation to old age pensions in Canada. The *British North America Act, 1964, 12-13 Eliz. II, c.73 (U.K.)* altered the foregoing amendment to permit the Parliament of Canada to make laws in relation to old age pensions and sup-

---

* From information verified by the courtesy of Mrs. Madeline Basta, Constitutional and International Law Section, Department of Justice, Ottawa, January 26, 1982.

plementary benefits, including survivors' and disability benefits irrespective of age. Both amendments specified that no such law shall affect the operation of any law present or future of a provincial legislature in relation to such matters.

BIBLIOGRAPHY
(See also Bibliographies in Chapters 3 and 16)

Constitution

Abel, A.S., *Towards a Constitutional Charter for Canada*, Toronto, U.T.P., 1980.

Asplund, C.T., "Mr. Trudeau's Constitution: Going in Style," *Q.Q.*, 87, 4, Winter, 1980.

Bergeron, G., "Lecture du Livre blanc et du Livre Beige selon une perspective 'super-féderaliste'," *C.P.P.*, VI, 3, Summer, 1980.

Bissonnette, B., *Essai sur la constitution du Canada*, Montréal, Editions du jour, 1963.

Black, E.R., "How to Watch the Constitution Game," *Q.Q.*, 86, 4, Winter, 1979.

Black, E.R., "Trudeau's Constitutional Coup d'Etat,"*Q.Q.*, 87, 4, Winter, 1980.

Boadway, R.W., and Norrie, K.H., "Constitutional Reform Canadian-Style: An Economic Perspective," *C.P.P.*, VI, 3, Summer, 1980.

Bohemier, A., *Faillite en droit constitutionnel Canadien*, Montréal, Les Presses de l'Université de Montréal, 1972.

Brossard, J., *L'immigration: Les droits et pouvoirs du Canada et du Québec*, Montréal, Les Presses de l'Université de Montréal, 1967.

Cairns, A.C., "The Living Canadian Constitution," *Q.Q.*, LXXVII, 4, 1970.

Cairns, A.C., "Recent Federalist Constitutional Proposals: A Review Essay," *C.P.P.*, V, 3, Summer, 1979.

"Canada and Quebec: A Proposal for a New Constitution," *Canadian Forum*, LVII, 672, June-July, 1977.

Canada Committee, *Declaration by English- and French-Speaking Canadians*, Montreal, 1966.

Canadian Bar Association, Committee on the Constitution, *Towards a New Canada*, Montreal, 1978.

Canadian Study of Parliament Group, *Seminar on the Constitutional Resolution and Legislative Authority in Canada*, held in Ottawa, January 9, 1981, Ottawa, Q.P., 1981.

Cheffins, R.I., Tucker, R.N., *The Constitutional Process in Canada*, Toronto, McG.H.-R., 2nd ed., 1976.

Clyne, J.V., "The Case for a Constitutional Assembly," *Policy Options*, 2, 1, March-April, 1981.

Council for Canadian Unity, *Final Report of Confederation '78*, A Colloquium on the First Report of the Ontario Advisory Committee on Confederation, Glendon College, York University, June 28-30, 1978.

Dawson, R.M., and Ward, N., *The Government of Canada*, Toronto, U.T.P., 1970.

Driedger, E.A., *A Consolidation of the British North America Acts 1867 to 1975*, Ottawa, Minister of S. and S., 1975.

Faribault, M., and Fowler, R., *Ten to One, the Confederation Wager*, Toronto, M. & S., 1965.

Federation of Canadian Municipalities, *Municipal Government in a New Canadian Federal System*, 1980.

Forsey, E.A., *Freedom and Order: Collected Essays*, Carleton Library No. 73, Toronto, M. & S., 1974.

Forsey, E.A., "The Constitution Bill," *Q.Q.*, 87, 4, Winter, 1980.

Gibson, D., "Constitutional Jurisdiction over Environmental Management in Canada," *U. of T. Law Journal*, 23, 1973.

Hogg, P.W., *Constitutional Law of Canada*, Toronto, Carswell, 1978.

Institute of Intergovernmental Relations, *The Response to Quebec: The Other Provinces and the Constitutional Debate — Documents of Debate No. 2*, Kingston, Ontario, Queen's University, 1980.

Kear, A.R., "The Unique Character of the Constitution," *Policy Options*, 1, 3, September-October, 1980.

Kwavnick, D., *The Tremblay Report*, Carleton Library No. 64, Toronto, M. & S., 1973.

La Forest, G.V., "Delegation of Legislative Power in Canada," *McG.L.J.*, 21, 1, Spring, 1975.

La Forest, G.V., *Disallowance and Reservation of Provincial Legislation*, Ottawa, Department of Justice, 1955.

La Forest, G.V., *Natural Resources and Public Property Under the Canadian Constitution*, Toronto, U.T.P., 1969.

Lajoie, A., *Le pouvoir déclaratoire du Parlement*, Montréal, Les Presses de l'Université de Montréal, 1969.

Landry, R., "Les projets de reformes constitutionnelles des grands partis politiques fédéraux et de la Commission Pepin-Robarts: Essai d'évaluation," *C.P.P.*, V, 2, Spring, 1979.

Laskin, B., *Canadian Constitutional Law: Cases, Text, and Notes on Distribution of Legislative Power*, Toronto, Carswell, 4th ed., 1973.

Lederman, W.R., (ed.), *The Courts and the Canadian Constitution*, Carleton Library, No. 16, Toronto, M. & S., 1964.

Lederman, W.R., *Continuing Canadian Constitutional Dilemmas: Essays on the Constitutional History, Public Law, and Federal Systems of Canada*, Toronto, Butterworths, 1981.

Lyon, J.N., and Atkey, R.G., *Canadian Constitutional Law in a Modern Perspective*, Toronto, U.T.P., 1970.

McConnell, W.H., "A Western View of Constitution-Building," *Q.Q.*, 87, 4, Winter, 1980.

McConnell, W.H., *Commentary on the British North America Act*, Toronto, Macmillan, 1977.

McWhinney, E., *Constitution-making: Principles, Process, Practice*, Toronto, U.T.P., 1981.

McWhinney, E., *Quebec and the Constitution, 1960-78*, Toronto, U.T.P., 1979.

O'Hearn, P.J.T., *Peace, Order and Good Government: A New Constitution for Canada*, Toronto, Macmillan, 1964.

Olling, R.D., and Westmacott, M.W., *The Confederation Debate: The Constitution in Crisis*, Dubuque, Kendall/Hunt, 1980.

Pepin, G., *Les Tribunaux Administratifs et La Constitution: Etude des articles 96 à 101 de l'A.A.N.B.*, Montréal, Les Presses de l'Université de Montréal, 1969.

Russell, P.H., (ed.), *Leading Constitutional Decisions*, Ottawa, Carleton Library Series, rev. and enlarged ed., 1982.

Simeon, R., *A Citizen's Guide to the Constitutional Question*, Business Council on National Issues, Toronto, Gage, 1980.

Smiley, D.V., *Canada in Question: Federalism in the Eighties*, Toronto, McG.H.-R., 3rd ed., 1980.

Stanley, G.F.G., *A Short History of the Canadian Constitution*, Toronto, Ryerson, 1969.

Tremblay, A., *Les compétences législatives au Canada et les pouvoirs provinciaux en matière de propriété et de droits civils*, Ottawa, Edition de l'Université, 1967.

Usher, D., "How Should the Redistributive Power of the State be Divided between Federal and Provincial Governments?," *C.P.P.*, VI, 1, Winter, 1980.

Ward, N., "The Realities of Constitutional Change," *Q.Q.*, 86, 2, Summer, 1979.

West, E.G., and Winer, S.L., "The Individual, Political Tension, and Canada's Quest for a New Constitution," *C.P.P.*, VI, 1, Winter, 1980.

Wiktor, C.L., and Tanguay, G.,
(eds.), *Constitutions of Canada*,
Dobbs Ferry, N.Y., Oceana Publica-
tions, 1978.
York University and Ontario Advisory
Committee on Confederation,
Destiny Canada: Final Report, 1977.

Selected Constitutional Documentation

1946-1974

Canada, *Dominion-Provincial and In-
terprovincial Conferences from 1887
to 1926*, Ottawa, Q.P., 1951.
Canada, *Dominion-Provincial Con-
ferences, 1927, 1935, 1941*, Ottawa,
Q.P., 1951.
Canada, *Dominion-Provincial Con-
ference, (1945)*, Ottawa, Q.P., 1946.
Canada, Proceedings of the Federal-
Provincial Conference, 1955,
Ottawa, Q.P., 1955.
Canada, *Dominion-Provincial Con-
ference, 1957*, Ottawa, Q.P., 1958.
Canada, *Proceedings of the Federal-
Provincial Conference, 1963*,
Ottawa, Q.P., 1964.
Canada, *Constitutional Conference,
Proceedings of First Meeting,
February 5-7, 1968*, Ottawa, Q.P.,
1968.
Canada, *Constitutional Conference,
Proceedings of Second Meeting,
February 10-12, 1969*, Ottawa, Q.P.,
1969.
Canada, *Constitutional Conference,
Proceedings of Third Meeting,
December 8-10, 1969*, Ottawa, Q.P.,
1970.
Canada, *Constitutional Conference
Proceedings, Victoria, B.C., June
14, 1971*, Ottawa, i.C., 1971.
Canada, [Benson, E.J.], *The Taxing
Powers and the Constitution of
Canada*, Ottawa, Q.P., 1969.
Canada, [Lalonde, M.], *Working
Paper on Social Security in Canada*,
Ottawa, I.C., 1973.
Canada, [Martin, P.], *Federalism and
International Relations*, Ottawa,
Q.P., 1968.

Canada, [Pearson, L.B.], *Federalism
for the Future*, Ottawa, Q.P., 1968.
Canada, [Sharp, M.], *Federalism and
International Conferences on Educa-
tion*, Ottawa, Q.P., 1968.
Canada, Special Joint Committee of
the Senate and the House of Com-
mons on the Constitution of
Canada, *Final Report*, Ottawa, I.C.,
1972.
Canada, [Trudeau, P.E.], *A Canadian
Charter of Human Rights*, Ottawa,
Q.P., 1968.
Canada, [Trudeau, P.E.], *Federal-
Provincial Grants and the Spending
Power of Parliament*, Ottawa, Q.P.,
1969.
Canada, [Trudeau, P.E.], *Income
Security and Social Services*, Ottawa,
Q.P., 1969.
Canada, [Trudeau, P.E.], *The Con-
stitution and the People of Canada*,
Ottawa, Q.P., 1969.
Canadian Intergovernmental Con-
ference Secretariat, *The Constitu-
tional Review, 1968-71, Secretary's
Report*, Ottawa, I.C., 1974.

1975-1981

Alberta, *Harmony in Diversity: A New
Federalism for Canada*, Alberta
Government Position Paper on Con-
stitutional Change, Edmonton, 1978.
British Columbia, *British Columbia's
Constitutional Proposals: Towards a
Revised Constitution for Canada*,
Victoria, 1978.
British Columbia, *Distribution of
Legislative Powers*, Discussion Paper
No. 8, Victoria, 1978.
Canada, [Chrétien, J.], *Securing the
Canadian Economic Union in the
Constitution*, Ottawa, 1980.
Canada, *The Constitutional Amend-
ment Bill, Text and Explanatory
Notes*, Ottawa, 1978.
Canada, Federal-Provincial Relations
Office, *Trade Realities in Canada
and the Issue of Sovereignty
Association*, Ottawa, 1978.
Canada, [Lalonde, M., and Basford,
R.], *The Canadian Constitution and*

Constitutional Amendment, Ottawa, 1978.

Canada, *Proposed Resolution for a Joint Address to Her Majesty the Queen Respecting the Constitution of Canada*, Ottawa, S. and S., 1980.

Canada, Senate, House of Commons, *Minutes of Proceedings and Evidence of the Special Joint Committee on the Constitution of Canada, Report to Parliament*, Ottawa, S. and S., February 13, 1981.

Canada, Standing Senate Committee on Legal and Constitutional Affairs, *Report on Certain Aspects of the Canadian Constitution*, Ottawa, S. and S., 1980.

Canada, Task Force on Canadian Unity, [Pepin-Robarts Report], Vol. I, *A Future Together: Observations and Recommendations*; Vol. II, *Coming to Terms: The Words of the Debate*; Vol. III, *A Time to Speak: The Views of the Public*, Ottawa, S. and S., 1979.

Canada, [Trudeau, P.E.], *A Time for Action: Toward the Renewal of the Canadian Federation*, Ottawa, 1978.

Canadian Unity Information Office, *Government of Canada Constitutional Review, 1968-1971*, Ottawa, 1977.

Newfoundland, *Discussion Paper on Major Bilateral Issues: Canada-Newfoundland*, St. John's, Q.P., 1980.

Newfoundland, *Towards the Twenty-First Century Together — The Position of the Government of Newfoundland Regarding Constitutional Change*, St. John's, Q.P., 1980.

Ontario, *Report of the Select Committee on Constitutional Reform*, Toronto, Ontario Government Bookstore, 1980.

Québec, Conseil executif, *La nouvelle entente Québec-Canada; Propositions du gouvernement du Québec pour une entente d'égal à égal: la souveraineté-association*, Québec, Editeur officiel, 1979. (English version: *Québec-Canada, A New Deal*, 1979.)

Quebec, *Constitutional Reform and the Traditional Claims of Quebec — Main Points*, Quebec, 1979.

Quebec, Constitutional Committee of the Quebec Liberal Party, *A New Canadian Federation*, [The Beige Paper], Montreal, 1980.

Saskatchewan, *The Constitution of Canada*, A Background Paper, Regina, Office of Intergovernmental Affairs, Executive Council, 1978.

Saskatchewan, *The Future of Canada — A Saskatchewan Perspective*, Regina, 1980.

Bilingualism and Biculturalism

(See also Bibliography in Chapter 15, "Bilingualism and Biculturalism")

Albinski, H.S., "Politics and Biculturalism in Canada: The Flag Debate," *Australian Journal of Politics and History*, XIII, 2, August, 1967.

Arès, R., *Les positions ethniques, linguistiques et religieuses des Canadiens francais à la suite du recensement de 1971*, Montréal, Bellarmin, 1975.

Beaujot, R.P., "A Demographic View on Canadian Language Policy," *C.P.P.*, V, 1, Winter, 1979.

Benjamin, J., "La minorité et État bicommunautaire: quatre études de cas," *C.J.P.S.*, IV, 4, December, 1971.

Bonenfant, J.-C., "Les études de la Commission royale d'enquête sur le bilinguisme et le biculturalisme," *C.J.P.S.*, IV, 3, September, 1971; V, 2, June, 1972 and 3, September, 1972; and VI, 1, March, 1973.

Breton, A., and Breton, R., *Why Disunity? An Analysis of Linguistic and Regional Cleavages in Canada*, Montreal, I.R.P.P., 1980.

Canada, *A Preliminary Report of the Royal Commission on Bilingualism and Biculturalism*, Ottawa, Q.P., 1965.

Canada, Commissioner of Official Languages, *Annual Report*, Ottawa, I.C., annually, 1971-1981.

Canada, [First] Bilingual Districts Advisory Board, *Report*, [Duhamel Report], Ottawa, I.C., 1971.

Canada, [Second] Bilingual Districts Advisory Board, *Report*, [Fox Report], Ottawa, I.C., 1975.

Canada, *Report of the Royal Commission on Bilingualism and Biculturalism*, Ottawa, Q.P., Book I, *General Introduction and the Official Languages*, 1967; Book II, *Education*, 1968; Book III, *The Work World*, 2 vols., 1969; Book IV, *The Cultural Contributions of the Other Ethnic Groups*, 1970; Books V, VI, *Federal Capital, and Voluntary Associations*, 1970.

Carson, J.J., "Bilingualism Revisited: or the Confessions of a Middle-aged and Belated Francophile," *C.P.A.*, 21, 4, Winter, 1978.

Cartwright, D.C., *Official Language Populations in Canada: Patterns and Contacts*, Montreal, I.R.P.P., 1980.

Castonguay, C., "Why Hide the Facts? The Federalist Approach to the Language Crisis in Canada," *C.P.P.*, V, 1, Winter, 1979.

Comeau, P.-A., "Acculturation ou assimilation: technique d'analyse et tentative de mesure chez les Franco-ontariens," *C.J.P.S.*, II, 2, June, 1969.

Gibson, F.W., (ed.), *Cabinet Formation and Bicultural Relations: Seven Case Studies*, Studies of the Royal Commission on Bilingualism and Biculturalism, No. 6, Ottawa, Q.P., 1970.

Innis, H.R., *Bilingualism and Biculturalism*, (An abridged version of the Royal Commission Report), Toronto, M. & S., 1973.

Joy, R., *Languages in Conflict: The Canadian Experience*, Carleton Library No. 61, Toronto, M. & S., 1972.

Lachapelle, R., et Henripin, J., *La situation démolinguistique au Canada*, Toronto, I.R.P.P., 1980.

La Féderation des Francophones hors Québec, *The Heirs of Lord Durham: Manifesto of a Vanishing People*, Toronto, B. and M., 1978.

Lalande, G., *The Department of External Affairs and Biculturalism*, Studies of the Royal Commission of Bilingualism and Biculturalism, No. 3, Ottawa, Q.P., 1969.

McRae, K.D., "Bilingual Language Districts in Finland and Canada: Adventures in Transplanting of an Institution," *C.P.P.*, IV, 3, Summer, 1978.

Paradis, J.B., "Language Rights in Multicultural States: A Comparative Study," *C.B.R.*, XLVIII, 4, December, 1970.

Phillips, D., *Interest Groups and Intergovernmental Relations: Language Policy-Making in Canada*, Discussion Paper 3, Kingston, I.I.R., Queen's University, 1978.

Russell, P., *The Supreme Court of Canada as a Bilingual and Bicultural Institution*, Documents of the Royal Commission on Bilingualism and Biculturalism, No. 1, Ottawa, Q.P., 1969.

Amending the Constitution

(See also *supra*, other sections in this Bibliography)

Alexander, E.R., "A Constitutional Strait Jacket for Canada," *C.B.R.*, XLIII, 3, March, 1965.

Angers, F.A., "Le problème du rapatriement de la constitution," *L'Action nationale*, LIV, novembre, 1964.

Brady, A., "Constitutional Amendment and the Federation," *C.J.E.P.S.*, XXIX, 4, November, 1963.

Cook, R., *Provincial Autonomy, Minority Rights and the Compact Theory, 1867-1921*, Studies of the Royal Commission on Bilingualism and Biculturalism, No. 4, Ottawa, Q.P., 1969.

Favreau, G., *The Amendment of the Constitution of Canada*, Ottawa, Q.P., 1965.

Gérin-Lajoie, P., *Constitutional Amendment in Canada*, Toronto, U.T.P., 1950.

Laskin, B., "Amendment of the Constitution: Applying the Fulton-Favreau Formula," *McG.L.J.*, XI, 1, January, 1965.

Marion, S., "Le pacte fédératif et les

minorités françaises au Canada,"
Cahiers des dix, 29, 1964.

Miller, D.R., "The Canadian Constitutional Amendment Scheme,"
C.J.P.S., VI, 1, March, 1973.

Morin, J.Y., "Le rapatriement de la constitution," *Cité libre*, XVI, 2, décembre, 1964.

Stanley, G.F.G., "Act or Pact? Another Look at Confederation," *Canadian Historical Association Annual Report*, Ottawa, 1956.

3

FEDERALISM AND FINANCES

This chapter deals with federal problems and in particular with financial relations between Ottawa and the provinces.

Disputes about fiscal matters have been the most characteristic, enduring, and vexatious feature of Confederation. Since 1867 federal and provincial governments have argued continually about the control and allocation of public monies. While the underlying issue has remained unresolved, the individual problems have become more numerous and the settlement of them much more complex. Controversial items now include tax sharing and tax rights, subsidies, grants, equalization and stabilization payments, natural resource revenues, expenditures for health care, higher education and welfare, opting out, compensation, economic development costs, and the discussion of monetary and fiscal policies.

Under the exigencies of war, Ottawa and the provinces entered into a tax-sharing agreement in 1942 which has been renewed quinqennially ever since. Each five-year agreement became more complicated as additional items were included and the formulae for their settlement became more elaborate. For instance, equalization payments were only one of a number of matters provided for by the Federal- Provincial Fiscal Arrangements and Established Programs Financing Act, 1977, that governed the period 1977-82, but the formula for calculating the payments was based on no fewer than 29 different provincial revenue sources. The details of these involved federal-provincial fiscal agreements can be found in various publications produced by the Canadian Tax Foundation, in particular in its annual serial, *The National Finances.*

This chapter has been constructed to acquaint the reader with current federal problems, especially fiscal and economic issues, to provide some of the basic data, and to note some of the suggestions that have been made for improving the machinery for negotiating settlements.

Professor Donald Smiley's perceptive article is an excellent brief review of the major problems in contemporary Canadian federalism. Since he devotes considerable attention to the financial and economic aspects of federalism, his article is a very useful introduction to this chapter. The extract from Professor Richard Simeon's article contains some suggestions for improving collaboration between the federal and provincial governments. Mr. Veilleux's article reviews the main financial and economic issues which have been discussed at federal-provincial conferences during the past two decades. Noting the recent shift in the balance of revenues from the federal to the provincial-municipal sector, the author expresses some concern about the trend in the future and offers alternatives to cope with it.

The next item explains the essential ingredients of the federal government's fiscal procedures. To help students grasp some of the fundamentals quickly, the editor has assembled pie-shaped diagrams showing the components of federal budgetary revenues and expenditures in 1980-81. The provincial comparison is illustrated by taking Ontario as an example and using similar diagrams.

The final item summarizes current federal fiscal transfers to the provinces and payments to all governments. The tables included are particularly useful because they give a very clear picture of how significant federal payments and transfers have become and how great is their impact on the federal system of government. Not only does the federal role now cost Ottawa an enormous sum in cold cash and foregone revenues — something in excess of $20 billion per year — but a large portion of the amount is spent on supporting functions which formerly were deemed to be entirely provincial responsibilities, such as health and welfare and education.

Two items which appeared in this chapter in the fourth edition have been omitted here: the British Columbia budget, 1976-77 (p. 68) and *The Toronto Star's* diagram illustrating government spending as a percentage of every dollar spent in Canada (p. 69). Data comparable to the latter are contained in Mr. Veilleux's article, especially in his Table. Unfortunately, this chapter lacks a description of current federal-provincial fiscal arrangements. The explanation of the 1977-82 agreement which appeared on pp. 71-73 of the fourth edition has been omitted because the agreement expired on March 31, 1982. It has not been replaced since, at the time of writing, although the federal and provincial governments were negotiating a new agreement, they had failed to reach an accord.

There is a considerable growing literature on the subject of Canadian federalism, though rather less on federal-provincial and provincial-municipal financial problems. While the various governments generate most of the data and produce many position papers and some commentaries, the Canadian Tax Foundation continues to be a very valuable source of much useful information. The Institute of Public Administration of Canada also publishes a good deal of relevant literature in its various monographs and in its quarterly journal, *Canadian Public Administration.* A new quarterly, *Canadian Public Policy,* is also an important source of commentary. The Institute of Intergovernmental Relations at Queen's University has started publishing recently a significant amount of useful material on federal issues, as have various organizations such as the Fraser Institute, the C.D. Howe Research Institute, and the Institute for Research on Public Policy. The last began to publish in 1980 a bimonthly journal, *Policy Options,* which contains many articles on federal problems.

A reader should consult also Professor Donald Smiley's book, *Canada in Question: Federalism in the Eighties,* Toronto, McGraw-Hill Ryerson, third edition, 1980, especially Chapter 6, which is a masterly analysis of the economic dimensions of Canadian federalism.

Reflecting the literature available, the bibliography at the end of the chapter contains a long section on "Federalism and Federal Problems," a few references to "Consociationalism and Pluralism," and a medium-length list of publications dealing with "Finances."

THE STRUCTURAL PROBLEM OF CANADIAN FEDERALISM*

Donald V. Smiley

• • •

In general terms, a federal system of government sustains and is sustained by geographically based diversities. People in the states, regions or provinces have from the first to develop attitudes, traditions and interests both specific to these areas and significant for politics and government. The master-solution of federalism to the problem of territorial diversity is to confer jurisdiction over those matters where diversity is most profound and most divisive to state or provincial governments. However, in the interdependent circumstances of the contemporary world there can be no complete hiving off of such matters. What economists call "spill-overs" of state or provincial policies are so ubiquitous that a matter of jurisdiction which concerns only the residents of particular regions will not be of crucial importance even to them. Enough integration on national lines to secure the continuing survival of the federation will eventually bring about demands that the national government take steps towards country-wide standards of services, taxation burdens and economic opportunities even where such actions involve federal involvement in matters within the constitutional jurisdiction of the states or provinces. There is another kind of conflict involving territorial particularisms which the federal division of powers is not able to resolve: those situations where the various states and regions impose contradictory demands upon the national government. In summary then, a constitutional division of powers between national and regional governments by itself cannot under modern circumstances resolve problems caused by geographical diversities. The stability of political systems is overwhelmingly a matter of the relation between the internal conflicts of these systems and their institutional capacity to give authoritative resolution to such conflicts. If conflicts are not numerous or profound, the institutions and procedures for handling such differences need be neither elaborate nor effective. The opposite is of course true. Obviously too, the institutional structures condition the kinds of conflicts that arise for resolution and in turn are conditioned by these conflicts.

It is the argument of this paper that in the Canadian federal system, territorial particularisms have come to find outlets almost exclusively through the provinces. This situation has come about largely as a result of the working of the institutions of the central government which from time to time operate so as to deny provincial and regional interests an effective share in central decision-making. Thus these interests turn to the provinces and continue to do so even after future circumstances provide them with more power in the central government. Canada is now experiencing a number of profound domestic conflicts where the contending forces follow territorial lines along with a relative institutional incapacity for giving authoritative resolution to these conflicts.

* From *Canadian Public Administration*, 14, 3, Fall, 1971, published by the Institute of Public Administration of Canada. By permission.

The Substance of the Present Conflicts

The major conflicts in Canadian politics along territorial lines are the following.
1. *Those related to interprovincial and interregional equalization by the federal government.* In recent years equalization has been extended much beyond the Rowell-Sirois recommendation that each province should have at its disposal adequate revenues to provide services at national average levels without imposing on its citizens taxation at rates above the national average. Equalization now involves a complex of federal and federal- provincial programs to encourage economic growth and enhance economic opportunities in the less favoured parts of Canada, particularly in Quebec and the Atlantic provinces.
2. *Those related to national economic policies.* The traditional economic cleavages between central Canada and the peripheral provinces to the east and west of the heartland remain, even though the peripheral economies — and in particular those of western Canada — have become more diversified. These continuing conflicts involve national trade, transportation and monetary policies as well as newer differences with respect to the development and sale of natural resources.
3. *Those relating to cultural duality in Canada.* The response of the provinces with English-speaking majorities to the French fact in Canada is most positive in those with large French-speaking minorities and least so where this minority is small. These differences are evident whether the claims of duality are expressed through recognition of the two official languages, some sort of special arrangement for Quebec or support for constitutional revision.

If we classify the interests and policies of the provinces toward each of these areas of conflict the result is something like that shown in Table 1. In these terms, Quebec and the western provinces are ranged against each other on each of the axes of conflict. This conflict is more marked in the case of Alberta and British Columbia than in Saskatchewan or Manitoba. These two latter provinces are on the borderline between "have" and "have not" provinces and if favourable economic circumstances should push them toward the former category the country would be clearly divided on the issue of interprovincial equalization by the Ottawa River.

There appears to be an emergent conflict involving provincial and regional particularisms in respect to economic nationalism. Influences toward nationalism can be expected to be more insistent at the federal level than at the provincial. From about the mid-1950s onward, the provincial governments have assumed major responsibilities for attracting foreign capital for development and have shown little concern whence such capital comes. It can be expected that economic nationalism will come to have influences on the politics and policies of some if not all of the provinces but it seems likely that these influences will be weaker at the provincial than at the federal level. More generally, it seems almost certain that the incidence of nationalistic sentiments and interests will vary significantly among the various provinces and regions.

TABLE I

	Contending Provinces		Provinces Whose Attitudes are Ambiguous
Interprovincial equalization	Quebec and the Atlantic provinces	Ontario Alberta BC	Saskatchewan Manitoba
National economic policies	Quebec Ontario	Atlantic and western provinces	
Cultural duality	Quebec Ontario New Brunswick	BC Alberta Saskatchewan Newfoundland	NS Manitoba PEI

Possible Procedures for Resolving Territorially Based Conflicts

There are several possible ways of resolving conflicts where the contending interests are limited to the various provinces or regions.

It seems unlikely that in the immediate future judicial review of the constitution will have more than a subsidiary role in giving authoritative resolution to the conflicting claims of territorial particularism. Significantly, the very great changes in English-French relations from 1960 onward have not been accompanied by any judicial decision which affected these relations in a crucial way, and successive Quebec governments have challenged the legitimacy of the Supreme Court of Canada in its present form as the final appellate court in constitutional matters. The various conflicts between Ottawa and the provinces over fiscal matters are inappropriate for judicial resolution. More generally, the delineation of federal and provincial legislative powers through judicial review relates for the most part to the regulatory activities of government and although these are of continuing importance they do not involve the most decisive of conflicts between the two levels.

A second device for resolving conflicts with a geographical base is through the party system, particularly in the relations between the federal and provincial wings of the two major parties. I can present here only in summary form the conclusions I have reached on this matter without giving the evidence for these conclusions. In general, there has been a long-term trend toward the mutual insulation of federal and provincial party systems. Although this matter is extraordinarily complex and has never been adequately analyzed on a country-wide scale, federal and provincial parties appear less electorally interdependent than in earlier periods of Canadian history. At the provincial level there are several parties which are exclusively or almost exclusively oriented toward provincial affairs (Parti Quebecois, Union Nationale, Social Credit in Alberta and British Columbia). At both levels there has been the development of extra-legislative party organizations involved both in leadership choice and increasingly in policy matters; such federal and provincial wings of the same party tend to be independent of one another. Career patterns of elected politicians have come to involve service at only one level more frequently than in earlier times. Increasingly, federal and provincial wings of the same party have financial resources at their disposal independent of the other level. In the two major parties, distinctive ideologies are not important integrative forces on federal-provincial lines. Thus intra-party interactions are not very effective in giving authoritative resolution to federal-provincial conflict.

The usual solution proposed for the problems of conflict between Ottawa and the provinces is more institutionalized collaboration between the executives of the two levels. There are two quite different possibilities here: they will be labelled "functional federalism" and "political federalism."

Under functional federalism the major responsibilities for federal-provincial collaboration are given to officials of the two levels concerned with relatively specialized public activities. These activities are carried on with a relatively high degree of independence from control by officials and public agencies with more comprehensive concerns and tend to be regulated in accord with the perceptions, procedures and standards prevailing among specialists in these fields. The most characteristic device of functional federalism is the conditional grant arrangement.

Political federalism is characterized by a situation in which the most crucial of intergovernmental relations are those between political and bureaucratic officials with jurisdiction-wide concerns. In Canadian terms these may be departments of finance or specialized treasury agencies, first ministers and their staffs, agencies concerned specifically with constitutional reform or departments or sub-departmental agencies whose main or exclusive responsibilities are federal-provincial relations as such. Under contemporary circumstances there will be a great deal of inter-level collaboration between individuals and agencies with specialized concerns but under the political federalism alternative these are controlled in terms of more comprehensive policies and goals. As the most characteristic device of functional federalism is the conditional grant, so political federalism is manifested by the Federal-Provincial Conference of Prime Ministers and Premiers and by the departments, committees and agencies whose major or exclusive concerns are the government-wide management of relations between the two levels.

During the past decade Canada has passed from functional to political federalism, although great variations persist among the various jurisdictions as to the degree to which specific concerns are controlled in terms of broader goals. In, say, the mid-1950s the most important kinds of federal-provincial interactions were of two kinds. There was first an increasing number of collaborative schemes between agencies and officials with specialized concerns, often, though by no means always, within the framework of shared-cost arrangements. Then there was the periodic renegotiation of the tax agreements for the forthcoming five-year periods, a process involving in the first instance the treasury and finance departments but also inevitably the heads of government. Although agencies with government-wide concerns were never entirely without involvement in specific federal-provincial programs, there was relatively little integration between the two sorts of activities. Arrangements between Ottawa and the provinces related to specialized programs and services were for the most part devised and executed within the context of particularized problems. The tax agreements on the other hand were concluded in terms of considerations which in the main did not include individual services or facilities.

The coming to power of the Lesage government after the Quebec general election of June, 1960 was crucial in the transition from functional to political federalism. For understandable reasons, successive Quebec administrations have been more suspicious of particularized federal-provincial interactions than have been other provinces, and in his speech to the November, 1963 Conference of Prime Ministers and Premiers Mr. Lesage said, "The present policy of making decisions behind hermetically closed doors is no longer acceptable." The new Quebec government established a Department of Federal-Provincial Relations in 1961 . . . and the Department has played a central role in Quebec's relations with Ottawa, the other provinces and foreign countries. Thus particularized aspects of Quebec's relations within the federal system have been subordinated to the more comprehensive goal of defending and enlarging the province's range of autonomy. In Ontario there was the establishment during the 1960s of an impressive aggregation of bureaucratic talent and influence in federal-provincial relations within the Department of Treasury and Economics. So far as the other provinces are concerned, there is with varying degrees a less complete integration of specific and comprehensive objectives than is the case with Ontario and Quebec. However, the trend toward political federalism continues. The increasing involvement of heads of government and their senior cabinet colleagues and advisors in federal-provincial relations, and the increasingly frequent meetings of prime ministers and premiers and of political and appointed members of treasury and finance departments all indicate the development of permanent institutional apparatus involving ministers and deputies where formerly such collaboration was at the middle levels of the federal and provincial bureaucracies. This general development toward subsuming even very particularized goals and activities under more comprehensive ones has been strengthened by the process of constitutional revision and review begun in February, 1968. To take a crucial example of what has happened, conditional grants in the 1945-60 period were for the most part dealt with within the frame of reference of particular services. Now the exercise of the federal spending power on matters within provincial legislative jurisdiction is a subject of constitutional debate at the most fundamental level.

There are several consequences of the relative failure of federal-provincial interactions to give authoritative resolution to conflicts based on geographical particularisms. First, in some cases there is a stand-off where necessary public action is being frustrated. Effective policies in respect to many aspects of urban problems await federal-provincial agreement. . . .

Second, governments avoid collaboration by taking unilateral action with respect to matters where the interests of the other level are involved. Provinces take it for granted that it is appropriate without consulting Ottawa to devise and implement policies concerning, say, higher education or most aspects of natural resource development or the circumstances under which local governments may borrow on the capital market. In these circumstances as in others, important federal interests are directly or indirectly involved. However, it is equally easy to give examples of federal unilateralism — the decision about medical insurance in 1965, the 1966 policies providing for a new formula for federal assistance to post-secondary education, and more recently by federal legislation to deal with environmental pollution. In the constitutional field, parliament has recently enacted important changes in the jurisdiction of the Supreme Court of Canada in a period where the role and function of the Court was a matter of discussion in the process of constitutional review.

Third, the provinces have successfully asserted their influence over matters which in the 1945-60 period were believed to be mainly or exclusively federal. Ottawa can be effective in regulating the general levels of income, prices and employment only with provincial collaboration, if at all. The federal tax system is now a matter for federal-provincial negotiation. Ottawa is on the defensive about the exercise of its spending power on matters within provincial jurisdiction. Broadcasting and some aspects of foreign affairs are the objective of provincial claims. At the Federal-Provincial Conference of 1963 Premier Lesage advanced his formulation of cooperative federalism. The first element was a fastidious respect by Ottawa for provincial jurisdiction. But because major federal policies in the economic field has a direct impact on provincial responsibilities, these matters should be regulated by joint federal-provincial institutions designed for that purpose. The institutionalization of collaborative procedures for designing national economic policies has not proceeded as the then Quebec premier wished, but the basic elements of his solution have in considerable part been achieved.

To an alarming extent, Canadian interests and attitudes which are territorially delimited have come to find an outlet exclusively through the provincial governments. This, I shall argue, has occurred largely because federal institutions have inadequately represented these particularisms. It has been too little stressed that during the first three years of the Quiet Revolution in Quebec there was in power in Ottawa a government less attuned to French-Canadian sensibilities than any other in Canadian history, with the exception of the administration emerging out of the conscription election of 1917. Similarly, the current regionalism in the prairie provinces can be explained partly by the relative lack of representation of the prairies in successive federal Liberal governments from 1963 onward.

The Confederation Settlement and its Passing

To repeat, in broad terms a federal system can deal with territorial particularisms by two kinds of procedures: (i) by conferring jurisdiction over several of the most crucial of these particularisms on the states or provinces, (ii) by securing for each of the major territorial interests a permanent influence on the decision-making processes of the central government. It is my argument that the Canadian system has come to rely too much on the first device and too little on the second.

The confederation settlement of 1864-67 contemplated a centralized federal system. But although this settlement provided for the dominance of the central government, it seems to have been taken for granted that the incidence of Dominion power would be localized. This condition has been attenuated. To trace the development away from localism in federal affairs would be to write the history of these institutions. However, it is perhaps useful to look at some important aspects of the federal government as it emerged at confederation in relation to where we are today.

The Senate. (*a*) At confederation. The composition of the upper legislature chamber was the most contentious issue resolved by the Fathers of Confederation. Further, it seems that these men believed in the crucial importance of this body in the working of the new institutions. Peter Waite has said,

> . . . most members of the Canadian Coalition government thought of federation largely in terms of the composition of the central legislature. In the lower house there would be "rep by pop"; in the upper house there would be representation by territory. . . . Of course local powers would be given to local bodies, but that was taken as a matter presenting little difficulty. The basis of the federal principle lay in the central legislature and in the balance between the House of Commons on the one hand and the Senate on the other.

(*b*) Today. Whatever the usefulness of the contemporary Senate, it does not provide an effective outlet for interests which are localized.

The Parties in the House of Commons. (*a*) At confederation. It was not until the end of the nineteenth century that two cohesive national parties came into existence in Canada. As in the pre-confederation period, political parties in the House of Commons during the early days of the dominion were coalitions, often a relatively loose nature, around political leaders, and many of these leaders themselves had a base of support which was exclusively regional.

(*b*) Today. It is unnecessary to emphasize the cohesiveness of political parties in the Canadian House of Commons, particularly in the case of the government party. Although there are countervailing influences at work to enhance the independence of private MPs, the more decisive developments have been in the other direction. So far as the government party is concerned, the dominance of the prime minister is strengthened by the circumstances that many MPs owe their election to his popularity, his powers of bringing about a dissolution and his control of preferments which members desire.

The Cabinet. (*a*) At confederation. An historian [Jean Hamelin] has said of the first government of the dominion:

> It would have been wrong to suppose that Macdonald was leading a centralized party. He was rather the chief of a coalition of groups in which each obeyed a regional leader, rather than Macdonald himself. To keep the confidence of the majority, Macdonald knew that he must negotiate with these leaders. In this spirit the cabinet was to be, in a certain sense, a chamber of political compensation, where the provincial spokesmen traded their support in return for concessions to their regions.

(*b*) Today. Canadian prime ministers have come increasingly to dominate their cabinets. There have been many reasons for this which need only to be mentioned here — access to the media, the development of staff assistance in the prime minister's and Privy Council offices, the size of the cabinets and the complexity of issues which decrease the possibilities of genuinely collegial decisions and enhance the power of the head of government to impose his own solutions, the influence of the procedure by which leaders are chosen by party conventions. However, a crucial aspect of prime ministerial dominance is the relative decline in the position of cabinet ministers as representatives of provinces or regions, although the cabinet is usually constituted in terms of such representation. Since the departure of the late James G. Gardiner and of Jack Pickersgill it is difficult to think of any minister who has had an important base of provincial or regional political support independent of the head of government. Further, as Donald Gow has pointed out, ministers have virtually no staff involved with regions the ministers allegedly represent, and the departments are "oriented to stress values associated with industrial and social structures and aggregates" rather than particular cultures and regions.

The Federal Bureaucracy. (a) At confederation. At the time of confederation, and for some decades after, the departments of government had a very high degree of autonomy in the recruitment of federal civil servants and positions were characteristically filled by political patronage. Thus to the extent that the cabinet included members of the various provinces and regions, the federal bureaucracy was in a broad sense representative of these localized sentiments and interests.

(b) Today. The establishment of the merit system in the Canadian public service, particularly with the reform measures of 1918, has had the effect of making the federal bureaucracy less representative in its composition. Current efforts of the federal government are to enhance the proportion of francophones at all levels. It is too early to assess the implications of this policy — and the related policy of increasing the number of anglophone civil servants who are bilingual — on the composition of the federal bureaucracy from various parts of English-speaking Canada. Up until the present, cultural and linguistic duality in the federal service has been explicitly concerned with two sorts of considerations: (i) the ability of citizens to deal with federal institutions in whichever of the official languages the citizen chooses, (ii) the ability of federal employees to advance their careers largely or exclusively in the official language milieu of choice. There has been little discussion of the federal bureaucracy as a locus of influence in which cultural and other territorially based particularisms should be represented.

Broadly speaking, the party which forms the government has come increasingly to dominate parliament, and the prime minister, the government party. These developments have the effect of denying strong regional interests a permanent influence in national decision-making. Two other institutions work in the same direction.

1. The national party conventions. Since 1919 and 1927 respectively the Liberals and Conservatives have selected their leaders by national party conventions. In the 1960s the constitutions of these parties have provided for regular conventions even when the leadership was not at stake, although the role of these gatherings in forming or influencing party policy is still in process of evolution. The voting rules of leadership conventions, by which the leader is chosen by an absolute majority compiled through successive secret ballots, enormously enhance the power of individual delegates and

decrease that of provincial leaders. Unlike an American convention, the winning of a national leadership is something other than building a coalition of support from regional chieftains.

2. The electoral system. Alan C. Cairns has demonstrated how the electoral system has both exacerbated sectionalism in Canadian politics and made sectional conflicts more difficult to resolve. . . . From the point of view of my analysis, the crucial factor is that from time to time important regions are denied representation in the governing party, even while giving a significant proportion of the popular vote to this party. In general terms:

> The electoral system has made a major contribution to the identification of particular sections/provinces with particular parties. It has undervalued the partisan diversity within each section/province. By doing so it has rendered the parliamentary composition of each party less representative of the sectional interests in the political system than is the party electorate from which that representation is derived. The electoral system favours minor parties with concentrated sectional support, and discourages those with diffuse national support. The electoral system has consistently exaggerated the significance of cleavages demarcated by sectional/provincial boundaries and has thus tended to transform contests between parties into contests between sections/provinces.

But as the electoral system exacerbates sectionalism it makes such interests more difficult to reconcile through intra-party accommodation in the House of Commons. [To quote Cairns again:]

> The significance of the electoral system for party policy is due to its consistent failure to reflect with even rough accuracy the distribution of partisan support in the various sections/provinces of the country. By making the Conservatives far more of a British and Ontario-based party, the Liberals far more a French and Quebec party, the CCF [NDP] far more a prairie and BC party, and even Social Credit far more of an Alberta party up until 1953, than the electoral support of these parties "required," they were deprived of intra-party spokesmen proportionate to their electoral support from the sections where they were relatively weak. The relative, or on occasion total, absence of such spokesmen for particular sectional communities seriously affects the image of the parties as national bodies, deprives the party concerned of articulate proponents of particular sectional interests in caucus and in the House, and, it can be deductively suggested, renders the members of the parliamentary party personally less sensitive to the interests of the unrepresented sections than they otherwise would be. As a result the general perspectives and policy orientations of a party are likely to be skewed in favour of those interests which, by virtue of strong parliamentary representation, can vigorously assert their claims.

A Brief Digression: The American Experience

If we compare the American and Canadian federal system it is immediately evident that the national government of the United States has a crucial range of powers and responsibilities which is withheld from its Canadian counterpart. Judicial interpretation of congressional power over interstate commerce has given the national authorities a kind of control over economic matters which the courts have denied parliament by restricting the meaning of trade and commerce. The Americans up to now have had no tradition of unconditional subsidies to the states, and conditional grants have tended to be more specific and to impose more restraints on the receiving governments than has been the case in Canada. Treaties concluded by the president and ratified by the U.S. Senate are the "supreme law of the land" and thus Congress has the power to override state jurisdiction in implementing such international arrangements; the Parliament of Canada acquires no powers it would not otherwise have by virtue of the executive concluding an international agreement. There has developed in the United States a pattern of direct federal-local relations which in Canada the sensibilities of the provinces have prevented. Control over the defence establishment is of course relatively more important in the United States than is the same function in Canada.

The American federal system is thus more highly centralized than the Canadian in the scope of powers wielded by the national government. However, the fragmented power system prevailing in Washington allows geographical particularisms to play a more important role than is the case in Ottawa. . . .

• • •

Conclusion and Recommendations

It may be that Canada is governable, if at all, only by adherence to John C. Calhoun's principle of the concurrent majority which "gives to each division or interest through its appropriate organ either a concurrent voice in making and executing the laws or a veto on their execution." The concurrent majority principle might of course be embodied in the operation of federal-provincial relations and to some degree this has come to be so. However, as I have argued, Canada cannot be governed effectively by these means. To be realistic, the predisposition of British parliamentary institutions is against institutional restraints on the powers of government. Thus, although these institutions in Canada as elsewhere have proved very flexible, their thrust, in Calhoun's terms, is toward the rule of the numerical rather than the concurrent majority.

The following implications of my general argument are made in a very tentative way. 1. Any restructuring of federal institutions to give territorial particularisms a more effective outlet should recognize other diversities than those of Anglophone and Francophone. In the past decade the dominant currents of thought and policy in central Canada have emphasized cultural and linguistic duality to the neglect of other attitudes and interests which divide Canadians. The price of this neglect is the resurgence of regionalism in the western provinces. While such a formulation is inevitably somewhat arbitrary, it appears to me that a five-region division of Canada corresponds fairly closely with continuing territorial diversities which merit recognition as such in the institutions of the federal government.

2. Unless and until the government of Canada ceases to operate within British parliamentary traditions, the Senate can play only a restricted role in

representing geographically delimited interests whatever changes are made in the way members of this body are appointed or in its functions. So long as the prime minister and his important ministers sit in the House of Commons and must retain the continuing support of a majority in that House to retain office, the Senate will remain in a secondary position.

3. A strong case can be made for the explicit recognition of representative bureaucracy in the federal government. Such an alternative does not imply that civil servants are primarily ambassadors of such territorial interests. W.R. Lederman has made an argument for regional quotas on the Supreme Court of Canada in terms which have direct relevance to the federal bureaucracy. Professor Lederman rejects in the name of the tradition of judicial independence that members of a final court of appeal are — or should be — the delegates of the government which appointed them. However, he asserts:

> The [regional] quotas are necessary and proper because Canada is a vast country differing in some critical ways region by region. There are common factors but there are unique ones too. If we ensure that judges are drawn from the various regions . . . we ensure that there is available within the Court collective experience and background knowledge of all parts of Canada. In judicial conferences and other contacts within the Court membership, the judges are able to inform and educate one another on essential facts and background from their respective parts of Canada.

4. In terms of Professor Gow's bold proposals, a strong case can be made for a radical restructuring of the federal cabinet and departments of government to make these institutions more effectively representative of regional and cultural interests. One of his suggestions is that the cabinet should "consist of ten to twelve ministers: five regional ministers and others drawn from External Affairs, Finance and a few other departments." The regional minister's deputy "would be a regional minister stationed in a central location within the area served by the minister. He would be the eyes and ears of the minister in the region reporting to him on any matter having to do with the coordination of the activities of the federal departments with one another, or with provincial or municipal departments." Several of the departments with field staffs should have an assistant deputy minister stationed in each of the five regions of Canada. "They would have coordinate standing with the most senior of existing assistant deputies. With such a status, it would be necessary that conflicts between a regional and functional or occupational point of view would be resolved at the level of the deputy minister and minister."

5. Consideration should be given to the reform of the electoral system. In such a reform it seems to me that the first consideration should be to ensure that the regional composition of parties in the House of Commons conforms more closely to their respective regional strengths in popular votes than is the case under the existing electoral law.

6. In broader terms, the kinds of reforms I am suggesting are advanced by measures which attenuate the dominance of the prime minister over his own cabinet and caucus and of the governing party over the House of Commons. Thus an increase in the independence and effectiveness of parliamentary committees is to be welcomed. A case can be made for increasing the

number of free votes in the House of Commons and for a rule by which a government would be required to resign only after defeat on an explicit vote of confidence. There should be a reversal of the current trend toward giving the majority in the House the power to determine the time allowed to debate particular measures. Some attenuation of the power of the prime minister to obtain a dissolution would be desirable. The effective and continuing representation of all important regional interests is clearly incompatible with the degree of dominance of the federal political system by the office of the prime minister that we are now experiencing.

The kinds of reforms I am suggesting would move our political institutions to be more like those of the United States. For this reason alone these recommendations might well be thought unworthy of consideration by Canadians. However, I have nowhere suggested an American-type separation of executive and legislative powers at the federal level. Responsible parliamentary government is a flexible instrument and, if I understand the circumstances of a century ago, the Fathers of Confederation believed it compatible with the highly localized incidence of federal power. It is perhaps more reasonable to argue that the present unsatisfactory results of federal-provincial interaction are at least as palatable as a constitutional system where many crucial political decisions are regulated by regional concurrent majorities at the federal level. On the other hand, the existing regime appears to me to be reducing the sphere in which the national government can act without provincial constraints to a dangerously restricted scope. If my argument is even broadly accurate, the solution — if there is one — is to make federal institutions more effectively representative of territorially based attitudes and interests.

SOME SUGGESTIONS FOR IMPROVING INTERGOVERNMENTAL RELATIONS*

Richard Simeon

• • •

The problems of intergovernmental relations lie at the heart of the crisis of the Canadian federal system. Indeed that crisis can be defined largely as one not so much of our social or economic systems, but of our political institutions — of the relations between them, and of the ways in which they deal with each other. For while the underlying roots of the crisis of federalism lie in differing concepts of community, in regional economic tensions, in linguistic differences, all those tensions are mobilized, channelled and expressed through Canada's federal and provincial governments and their leaders. Any resolution requires if not a redefinition of the powers of these governments, then at least a new consensus on the structure of political

* From an article entitled "Intergovernmental Relations and the Challenges to Canadian Federalism" in *Canadian Public Administration*, 23, 1, Spring, 1980, published by the Institute of Public Administration of Canada. By permission.

authority. Thus, intergovernmental relations, expressed mainly through the federal-provincial conference, are simultaneously the arena within which the multiple tensions of Canadian life are expressed and fought out, and the forum which is expected to work out and resolve those tensions. Partly as a result of the failure of other mechanisms of accommodation, notably the national party system, the executive and administrative process of federal-provincial conferences bears an immense political burden. It has become the main device for national integration. . . .

Before outlining some of the tensions in Canadian federalism and launching into criticisms of the intergovernmental process as it now exists, two qualifications must be stated. First, Canadian governments are not alone in finding it harder to manage the conflicts and contradictions of the contemporary world; nor are they alone in finding it difficult to generate coherent policies. Indeed, the fragmentation of authority between federal and provincial governments is merely our Canadian version of a more general phenomenon — one which is expressed in the United States, for example, in the immobilism resulting from fragmentation of authority within Congress and between it and the President. . . .

Secondly, it would be wrong to think that Canadian governments are paralysed by federal-provincial conflict, or that federal-provincial agreement is impossible. There are notable successes: in fiscal arrangements and equalization; in establishment of the welfare state through federal-provincial cooperation; even in the economic summits of last year which, if they did not lead to the joint medium-term economic policy some hoped for, did produce some consensus on basic directions for policy. Despite the acrimony over oil pricing and revenues, it could be argued that the present trade-offs between producers and consumers and between federal and provincial governments, achieved through intergovernmental negotiation, are as fair to all sides as one could imagine any other process producing. Similarly, in a great many areas federal-provincial cooperation proceeds largely unnoticed. . . .

. . . There is little evidence of fundamental alienation from Ottawa, and considerable evidence that citizens of all provinces, including especially Quebec, are becoming more alike in their basic views about government and policy. Communities are at once more divergent and more alike. Most citizens have little difficulty in maintaining dual loyalties to province and centre. Regional differences are indeed important but they alone do not sustain the tremendous emphasis on regional/provincial divisions which dominates Canadian political debate. The point is that it is *these* divisions, however, which are mobilized and expressed by political leaders, since federalism structures institutions on the basis of territory; and it blurs and fragments interests defined in other ways. It is much too simplistic to ascribe federal-provincial conflict solely to the machinations of power-hungry politicians, but there is a germ of truth there. . . .

In response to these contradictory pressures of political independence and policy interdependence, intergovernmental relations have steadily grown more pervasive. In some ways they have come to overshadow Parliament and legislatures — yet nowhere are they given constitutional status.

More and more provincial governments — most recently Ontario and Saskatchewan — have felt it necessary to establish separate Ministries of Intergovernmental Affairs. Ottawa recently also established a ministerial portfolio in the area. This has provoked some interesting tensions within some governments as the professional federal-provincial bureaucrats, commited to the *process* of intergovernmental relations, to some extent displace line ministries and the finance department officials who have traditionally been the prime movers in the area. Several intergovernmental secretariats form the beginnings of a separate administrative apparatus to serve the process. Interprovincial conferences have taken on a new role; no longer largely social occasions, they are increasingly forums for interprovincial bargaining and for developing joint positions to take to Ottawa. The Western Premiers' Conference and the more ambitious but perhaps less successful Council of Maritime Premiers have moved to develop more coordinated regional positions.

• • •

Despite all the problems, I think we must strengthen the machinery of federal-provincial collaboration. It is inevitable that broad national policies will cut across whatever jurisdictional lines we draw. A return to the consensus on federal dominance now seems quite impossible in the foreseeable future. Nor is the purely confederal system realistic. If neither model can prevail, we must provide a place for continuous dialogue between them.

Many proposals have been put forward for improving the machinery. They range from the very modest — such as a constitutional requirement for annual first ministers' conferences — to the very elaborate, the most important of which are the various proposals for a House of the Provinces, building direct provincial representation into the central government itself. I have argued in favour of such proposals, but they have come under considerable criticism — for creating a house of obstruction, eroding accountability, and so on.

Many commentators balked at blurring the distinctions between the two levels by building provinces into the federal government itself. Those are important objections: I still see many merits to the proposal but I think the really important thing is to provide a forum for continual interaction between Ottawa and the provinces, and to recognize the vital significance of intergovernmental relations by giving the process explicit recognition in the constitution and by building it into our normal political process. It must not remain hived off and separate. We must create a setting in which each government's actions in the federal-provincial arena are subject to debate, assessment and criticism. Governments must be placed under strong incentives to consult with others before undertaking actions which affect them. There must be a setting for public deliberation between governments of the broad economic and social issues which cut across jurisdictions. In short, we must institutionalize the process further.

An alternative to the House of the Provinces proposal is the creation of a permanent intergovernmental forum — we might call it the Council of the Federation — which would not be part of the federal Parliament but rather a body located, so to speak, between it and the provinces. It would be the focus for federal-provincial debate and the umbrella under which the various existing ministerial committees and secretariats would operate.

Responsibility for organizing and managing the Council would be undertaken by a permanent committee of federal and provincial ministers responsible for intergovernmental relations. It would be served by a small secretariat such as the existing Canadian Intergovernmental Conferences Secretariat, responsible for organizing meetings. Together the ministerial committee and secretariat would be responsible for preparing agendas and for providing a follow-up to agreements. The Council would be the setting in which at least annual first ministers' meetings would take place. It would also be required to schedule regular public meetings of ministers in specific policy areas — thus incorporating, for example, regular discussions of economic policy and budgets by finance ministers, ministers of transportation, and ministers responsible for education, social policy and so on. All federal-provincial agreements would be tabled in the Council.

The Council would have to be structured to take account of the dual aspects of federal-provincial meetings — as forums for deliberation, discussion and public education — which requires that they be open, and as arenas for hard bargaining — more akin to cabinet discussion — which requires privacy. Unfortunately a Council forced to be always public would simply drive the real business of federal-provincial relations elsewhere.

The important goal here is strengthening the incentives to consult, inform and mutually educate. I would resist making the Council a formal legislative body, giving it a formal veto over federal policies, or allowing it to make binding decisions. I do not think that is consistent with the need for accountability in a parliamentary system. Each government must remain responsible for its own actions to its own legislature.

However, in some areas, the Council would have formal responsibilities related to the maintenance of the federal system itself. It would rafify Supreme Court appointments. It would be the mechanism which would mandate use of the broad federal discretionary powers now in the constitution: the spending power, the declaratory power and the declaration of emergencies under the peace, order and good government clause. All are so potentially subversive of provincial power that provincial consent is required. The requirement of provincial approval would discipline Ottawa to explore its own arsenal of policy tools and consult fully with the provinces. For these, but not for most other debates, a formal set of voting rules would be necessary.

Such a Council would formalize and legitimate the executive process of intergovernmental relations and make it open and comprehensible. It will remain, however, an executive process and further efforts must be made to make the actions of governments in intergovernmental relations more accountable to legislatures. The growth of ministries of intergovernmental affairs demonstrates that the federal-provincial dimension is a vital aspect of almost all policy. It is essential that, as in other areas, these activities be subject to legislative scrutiny; hence every legislature should establish a permanent standing committee on intergovernmental relations, to focus debate on the government's actions. One other small point: some proposals for a freedom of information act have exempted federal-provincial, along with international, relations, national security and the like from its provisions. That seems to me completely unjustified.

No miracles flow from these very modest proposals. Indeed they recognize, formalize and build on what already exists. But they do provide a framework where the real issues of national and regional development can be discussed more creatively and openly than the present ad hoc and mysterious process permits.

But we must, in the longer run, also seek to build other linkages which strengthen the integrative forces in the country. As I said at the outset, to rely almost entirely on the intergovernmental mechanism to reconcile centre and periphery, French and English, is to place an intolerable burden on a fragile structure. Thus, while strengthening this mechanism, we must at the same time look elsewhere: and in particular to political parties. This means not only making the federal parties more regionally representative, but also strengthening the ties between federal and provincial party systems, increasing mobility between federal and provincial governments, and so on. We need to knit the country together in many ways and define goals and issues in non-regional terms. If we could do that — and recent proposals for reform of the electoral system offer some promise — in the long run, federal-provincial negotiations might one day become what their present structure and membership best equip them to be: agencies for administrative cooperation. . . .

A FISCAL AND ECONOMIC PERSPECTIVE*

Gérard Veilleux

Issues of the Past Two Decades

The first question, then, is what substantive issues have governments been talking about in the economic and fiscal field in the 1960s and 1970s? I propose to give you a list — in rough chronological order — which will touch upon the most important issues and, at the same time, give some indication of the range and diversity of the subject matter. . . .

If we go back to the early 1960s, we find that government concerns focused on such matters as the share of income tax and succession duties, the replacement of tax rental agreements by tax collection agreements, the level of funding and distribution of equalization, the use of shared-cost programs, and Quebec's delayed and unwilling participation in certain national programs such as hospital insurance and the Trans-Canada Highway.

Moving forward to the mid-1960s, the principal concerns were income tax sharing, the level of funding and distribution of equalization, the development of the Canada Pension Plan, the use of shared-cost programs, the new concept of contracting out, post-secondary education, the Canada Assistance Plan, and the harmonization of the fiscal policies of the two levels of governments.

* From an article entitled "Intergovernmental Canada: Government by Conference? A Fiscal and Economic Perspective" in *Canadian Public Administration*, 23, 1, Spring, 1980, published by the Institute of Public Administration of Canada. By permission.

By the late 1960s and early 1970s, the matters of principal concern were the fiscal and economic aspects of constitutional change, the introduction and financing of medicare and, of particular importance, the long-drawn-out debate over federal income tax reform.

By the mid-1970s, attention focused increasingly on three relatively new problems: natural resources, inflation and the block funding of federal conditional transfers to provinces. Discussions relating to natural resources concerned the sharing of sharply increased economic rents from oil and gas, the domestic pricing of these resources, their export, and the equalization of the increased revenues derived by the producing provinces. Discussions relating to inflation focused on the indexing of the personal income tax and on a three-year system of price and wage controls. Discussions on block grants centred on important new arrangements for funding hospital insurance, medicare and post-secondary education.

Other issues in the mid-1970s concerned federal administration of provincial income tax credits and the related need for greater flexibility in the tax collection agreements, the social security review, western alienation, federal expenditure ceilings on contributions to shared-cost programs, termination of the 1972 income tax revenue guarantee, and the tri-level approach to problems of municipal government.

The late 1970s have seen governments grappling with a large number of fiscal and economic issues. These have included expenditure restraint, a return to constitutional discussions, a move to the block funding of existing programs of federal aid to municipal government, a joint industry-by- industry review of the economy (conducted for governments by special task forces), consultations concerning the provincial implications of international trade negotiations, a federal budgetary proposal for a jointly financed temporary reduction of provincial sales taxes, the allocation of revenues from lotteries, a review of the formula for allocating the taxable income of corporations by province, the further escalation of economic rents from natural resources, and certain problems concerning the degree of conditionality which attaches to the new block grants. . . .

This list invites two important conclusions. First, the range of issues dealt with has been remarkably broad and wide-ranging. Secondly, there have been important shifts in emphasis in matters discussed by governments over the course of the past two decades. In the early part of the period, discussions focused mainly on matters of taxation, tax sharing, the provision of major new public services and the use of shared-cost programs as a means to this end. Governments are still concerned with these matters but they have become less dominant. An increasing proportion of intergovernmental relationships is concerned with other matters, particularly economic policy issues relating to the structure and longer-term development of the economy. . . .

Accomplishments of the Past Two Decades

Before referring to the accomplishments of governments I should note, by way of background, that the Canadian economy has undergone considerable change since 1960. Thus, during the period from 1960 to 1979 the population of Canada has expanded by almost six million — from 17.9 million to 23.7 million — or by almost 33 per cent. At the same time, the labour force has grown from a little over 6.4 million to approximately 11.2 million — or by almost 75 per cent. The GNP, expressed in constant (1971) dollars, has increased from a little over $53 billion to more than $130 billion — or by roughly 145 per cent.

The government sector has shared more than proportionately in this expansion. Changes in this sector, covering a span of twenty years from 1958 to 1978, are summarized in Table 1. This table not only indicates the growing importance of the public sector in Canada, but also the pronounced changes in its composition, with a large increase in the provincial-municipal share and a corresponding decrease in the federal government share.

It is against this background that one should look at intergovernmental achievements during the 1960s and 1970s. These have, in my view, been impressive. We have maintained Canada's joint and uniform system of income taxation while, at the same time, implementing various reforms and making numerous changes to give provinces flexibility to meet their varying needs. We have developed a comprehensive system of fiscal equalization

TABLE 1   Government Revenues and Expenditures, 1958, 1978, 1998

Comparative data on the government sector, 1958 and 1978, and projected data on the government sector as of 1998, assuming that the absolute changes in shares which occurred between 1958 and 1978 are repeated between 1978 and 1998

	1958 (1) Total $000,000	(2) Share %	1978 (3) Total $000,000	(4) Share %	(5) Change in shares from 1958 to 1978 %	(6) Projected shares 1998 (Col. (4) & Col. (5)) %
Revenues from own sources						
Federal	5,163	58.2	37,644	45.2	−13.0	32.2
Provincial-municipal	3,705	41.8	45,659	54.8	+13.0	67.8
Total	8,868	100.0	83,303	100.0	—	100.0
Initial expenditures[a]						
Federal	5,930	59.6	49,001	51.8	− 7.8	44.0
Provincial-municipal	4,016	40.0	45,659	48.2	+ 7.8	56.0
Total	9,946	100.0	94,660	100.0	—	100.0
Final Expenditures[b]						
Federal	5,513	55.4	38,144	40.3	−15.1	25.2
Provincial-municipal	4,433	44.5	56,516	59.7	+15.2	74.9
Total	9,946	100.0	94,660	100.0	—	100.0
GNP	34,777		230,407			
Total government expenditures as share of GNP		28.6		41.1	+12.5	53.6

SOURCE: Based upon National Economic Accounts as revised to June, 1979.
[a]*Before* intergovernmental transfers; thus federal transfers to provinces are counted as federal expenditure.
[b]*After* intergovernmental transfers; thus federal transfers to provinces are counted as provincial expenditure.
[*Editor's note:* This table is a consolidation of Tables 1 and 2 in the original.]

which has worked well despite the recent emergence of problems caused by the exceptionally uneven regional distribution of economic rents from natural resources. We have implemented a system of joint financing for hospital insurance, medicare and post-secondary education which has produced high and reasonably uniform standards of these services across Canada, and which now avoids the difficult problems associated with shared-cost programs. We have built up a highly developed system of intergovernmental consultation which enables us to hold frequent discussions on fiscal and economic matters. . . .

In addition to the foregoing accomplishments, we have arrived at a fiscal system in Canada in which total revenues from own sources are divided very evenly between the different levels of government, with the federal government currently having about 45 per cent and the provinces and local governments about 55 per cent. Whether or not this system is now well-balanced is a matter on which informed people would differ. However, few would challenge the view that the state of balance is now much better than it was in 1958 when the federal share of total government sector revenues was 58 per cent compared with only 42 for the provinces. . . .

I might note at this point, however, that some people have begun to wonder whether the decline in the federal share of total public sector revenues and expenditures, as shown in Table 1, has gone too far. Some argue that this share has now reached a point where the federal government is no longer able to exercise an effective policy of fiscal stabilization for the country. Others have concluded that the task is still manageable, but only if it is done jointly by the federal government and the provinces. . . .

With these important accomplishments — and many others could be listed as well — one would expect to find considerable satisfaction with the current state of fiscal and economic federalism, and optimism concerning the future. I think, however, that this would be a misinterpretation of the views of many persons involved with federal-provincial fiscal and economic relations. There is, in fact, considerable concern in Canada today about federal-provincial relations. This is a general concern, and it extends to the fiscal and economic aspects of federalism as much as to other elements. . . .

Future Issues

Let us turn now and look at the future. First of all, what sort of fiscal and economic problems are governments in Canada likely to be looking at in the future? Will they tend to be a repeat of what we have seen in the sixties and seventies, simply with overlays of added complexity? Or will they tend to be relatively new issues bursting upon us as the energy issue did in 1973?

Of course, no one can answer these questions conclusively. However, one may speculate on what the future will bring and I will venture to do so. Earlier, in Table 1, I set out numbers showing changes in the government sector between 1958 and 1978. Columns (2) and (4) of that table showed these changes in terms of shares. [The table also shows] what these shares would become in another twenty years (that is, in 1998), if the changes that took place in the past twenty years were to be repeated in the next twenty. I recognize that this is a simple (if not simplistic) assumption; indeed that is its point: it serves to illustrate how unlikely it is that the trend of the past twenty years can continue unchecked.

The results which Table 1 projects for 1998 are interesting. They show a federal share of total government revenues from own sources of less than one-third, with a federal share of total expenditures after transfers that falls to only about one-quarter. Conversely, the provincial-municipal share of total revenues would be more than two-thirds and their share of total expenditures after transfers would be about three-quarters. These results indicate such a marked imbalance between levels of government that I must disclaim any likelihood of them being achieved. This indeed is one reason why I believe that federal-provincial issues in the next twenty years must differ significantly from those of the past twenty years. Indeed, I believe that shifts of this kind, for example from money issues to non-money issues, have already begun and I believe that this trend will continue.

To begin with, I would suggest that there will be less emphasis on federal-provincial transfer programs, particularly those relating to matters of health, welfare and education — indeed, less emphasis on transfers as a whole. This result is likely for a number of reasons:

1/ federal transfers to the provinces have expanded from $673 million in 1960 to an estimated $10,505 million in 1978 (national accounts basis) and most of the major transfer programs are now relatively mature;

2/ it is evident that little federal money is likely to be available for major expansion of existing transfer programs. Table 1 strongly confirms this conclusion;

3/ with the increased emphasis by provinces on unconditional transfers or block funding, there will be an increasing problem of visibility for the federal government and hence increased reluctance to increase federal funding;

4/ the extensive use of transfer payments as a means of dealing with problems of regional disparities has been questioned in academic and other circles; and

5/ the "law of large numbers" will increasingly inhibit the growth of major transfer programs. Thus, while $3 billion in fiscal equalization payments today may be little larger in relative terms than $500 million was in 1967-68, it is likely to appear much larger.

Notwithstanding these qualifications, because of the practice of reviewing the fiscal arrangements every five years, because of the huge sums involved, and because restraint proposals can be very controversial, this area — despite a decline in its relative significance as noted above — will remain more important than any other. In addition, some individual elements of the fiscal arrangements may increase in importance; equalization could be an example of this because of interregional imbalances arising from the natural resources sector.

Another major subject, that of revenue-sharing of the income tax fields, is also likely to diminish somewhat in importance. This conclusion is also strongly supported by Table 1. Revenue sharing is an area where there are no permanent solutions and where relative or perceived pressures on governments are constantly changing. However, the strong pressures by provinces for increased federal tax transfers, which have characterized most of the postwar era, are likely to decline somewhat in importance for the simple reason that the fiscal position of the provinces relative to the federal government is now greatly improved. This is something which the provinces will have to recognize, although the rhetoric in support of further changes in their favour will undoubtedly continue. The halcyon days of the 1960s may never return.

While intergovernmental transfers and revenue-sharing will decline in relative importance, other areas will tend to become more important. Economic matters relating to the structure and development of the economy will, almost certainly, be among them. These will particularly include issues relating to energy, to the control and development of industry, to the creation of non-tariff barriers on interprovincial trade and to the mobility of capital and labour within Canada. They will also include such matters as international trade, tariffs, banking and the regulation of trade and commerce. The discussion of these economic issues will bring governments increasingly into areas that are under federal jurisdiction, in contrast to the general area of transfer payments, where discussions have tended to focus on matters of provincial jurisdiction, such as health, welfare and education. It will also involve the provinces in areas where they themselves tend to have divergent interests. The latter is a matter of major importance because, as I will suggest, it will increasingly involve the federal government in the role of adjudication and mediation.

The general subject of energy, including its supply and pricing, is likely to be of particular importance for many years to come. Indeed, it may be argued that the single most important challenge in fiscal and economic management of the federation during the 1980s will be to redress the severe inter-regional imbalance brought about by huge increases in economic rents from oil and natural gas.. . . .

Concern with matters relating to industrial development may lead provinces in the direction of making numerous changes in their tax systems, procurement policies, regulatory practices and other matters which can create non-tariff barriers to trade. Changes in the income tax system could jeopardize continuation of the joint arrangements in respect of income taxes which have now been in effect for almost forty years. To the extent that provinces take actions that would weaken the Canadian economic union, they will challenge basic national interests. This area is likely to be one of change and controversy.

Intergovernmental interests in economic matters will likely increase in areas of macroeconomic policy as well, such as fiscal policy, monetary policy and, in general, matters relating to rates of inflation and unemployment and the exchange rate for the Canadian dollar. The provinces, of course, already have important responsibilities in the area of fiscal policy.

Finally, there are the fiscal and economic aspects of national unity, with particular but by no means exclusive reference to the status of Quebec, and the related subject of constitutional reform. In my view, the interaction between economic issues and matters of national unity will tend to be particularly difficult. . . .

Implications for Future Procedures

You will conclude that I foresee important shifts in the types of fiscal and economic issues that governments will be discussing. In general, these shifts will be away from purely monetary issues, such as transfer payments and revenue sharing, and in the direction of intangible economic issues, where the financial implications can seldom be quantified but which relate to the fundamental nature of our economic union. The shifts will also be away from matters of provincial jurisdiction toward matters of federal jurisdiction and/or issues where provinces tend to have divergent interests. In addition, there will be over-riding concerns with issues of national unity which will complicate many economic issues, making solutions more difficult to find.

If shifts of these kinds do occur, how will they affect intergovernmental relations? Will they exacerbate or attenuate the deep-rooted problems to which I have referred? Will intergovernmental agreements and decisions be easier to reach on these new issues than the ones which have been confronted in the past? Will the overall level of tensions between governments increase or decrease?

In general, I am not optimistic about the answers to these questions. I believe that the new issues will be even more troublesome than those we have faced in the past. The new issues seem likely to increase the number and scope of intergovernmental relationships, and the number of joint decisions that could be made. However, the new issues will tend to be intangible in nature and multilateral in scope — and hence difficult for governments to come to grips with. They seem less likely to lend themselves to the finality of legislative solutions or to resolution through the relatively simple, even if second-best, course of unilateral action by a single government. Where problems are money-related, as in the past, they tend to focus on specific programs and usually on federal legislation which, however contentious, is eventually enacted by Parliament and acquiesced in by the provinces. However, where problems relate to the structure and development of the economy, they are more likely to arise from relatively independent actions by any one of eleven governments. In theory, coordination is attainable. In practice, it will be very difficult to achieve.

Alternatives Before Us

. . . I would venture to suggest that there are two basic choices available, that is to say, two alternative directions in which we can go. First, we can continue to move in the direction of increased formal consultation between governments and joint decision-making. Or we can move in the opposite direction toward governmental disengagement, reduced formal consultation and separate decision-making within areas that are as clearly defined as possible. With the first alternative, we would rely more upon government by conference; with the second, less so. For convenience, I shall label these two approaches as the "collaborative approach" and the "classical approach." . . .

There are major advantages of each approach. There are also risks. The collaborative approach may be reaching the limits of what it can accomplish. The classical approach could be dangerous if governments were to opt for it without actually disentangling the responsibilities of the two orders of government. The latter might require changes in the constitutional division of powers. The two alternatives should be studied very carefully in the light of future needs. But irrespective of what changes are made in the methods and machinery governing intergovernmental relationships, the most important determinant of success or failure will be public attitudes and the political will to see problems through to their resolution. Given the difficulties, this will require a high order of statesmanship on the part of all governments. I am confident that it exists.

ESSENTIALS OF FEDERAL FINANCES*

Canadian Tax Foundation

The vast phenomenon of the revenue and expenditure structure of the national government . . . is an operation involving outlays of over $50 billion annually, a staff of employees running to several hundred thousand, and a range of activities that touches the life of nearly every Canadian citizen. Simply maintaining an organization of this size has profound effects on the financial system of the country, but in addition, deliberate use is made of both the revenue and the expenditure apparatus to exert an influence on the economy. . . .

Government by Legislation

One important fundamental is that almost every dollar of revenue raised or spent by governments under our democratic system has been previously authorized by laws passed by the elected representatives. The federal tax system, for example, is contained in four main statutes: the Income Tax Act, the Excise Tax Act, the Excise Act, and the Customs Tariff. These statutes are enacted by Parliament and remain in force until amended. The statutory origins of the expenditure program are somewhat more involved. Various pieces of legislation (for example, the Old Age Security Act) are passed by Parliament from time to time, authorizing the expenditure of funds sufficient to carry out the purposes of the Acts. There are dozens of such predetermined forms of expenditure in the federal accounts; perhaps the best example of all is the interest on the national debt, which is a contractual obligation of the government. Each year, in addition, there are amounts to be spent on nonrecurring programs or for purposes for which no previous statutory provision has been made. In order to maintain the rules of parliamentary control of annual outlays (the principle of the

* From *The National Finances, 1980-81*, Toronto, Canadian Tax Foundation, 1981, Introduction. By permission.

budget), *all* amounts to be spent in the year are gathered together in one detailed presentation (the Estimates) and submitted to Parliament for approval.

The Estimates are referred to 16 Standing Committees of the House of Commons, each specializing in a particular area. The Standing Committees are obliged by parliamentary rules to report back to the House, normally by May 31. In addition, the opposition may, during allotted days, bring forward selected items of estimates before a committee of the whole House for debate, possible amendment, and eventual decision. The House grants approval by passing Appropriation Acts, providing the required funds for the government.

A Governor General's Warrant may be issued under section 21 of the Financial Administration Act when payment is urgently required for the public good. This section is applicable during any period when Parliament is prorogued or adjourned and when no appropriation is available for making payment. An Order in Council signed by the Governor General may permit the appropriation of moneys. Such warrants may be issued only in the fiscal year for which the expenditure is required; they must be published in the *Canada Gazette* within 30 days of the date they are issued; a statement showing all warrants issued, with amounts, must be presented to Parliament by the Minister of Finance within 15 days after commencement of the next ensuing session; and the Auditor General must include in his report every case where special warrant has authorized the payment of money.

For both revenue and expenditure, the granting of approval by Parliament — that is, the enactment of a statute — is the end result of a rather involved procedure of submission for approval and subsequent accountability, the full details of which are not important for present purposes. Certain documents that emerge in the course of this procedure, however, contain much information. . . .

The Estimates

The main source of information on programs of expenditure for any prospective year is a large volume known as the Main Estimates. This document is a complete — or almost complete — statement in detail of the amounts of money required by the government to carry out its various activities during the coming year. It is divided into departments, and under each department details of proposed expenditures are given. These Main Estimates might be called Parliament's handbook to government activities. It is more than a handbook, however, because Parliament must authorize these expenditures by passing individually several hundred "votes" under which the total is classified. It does not always work out that the full amount of money appropriated by Parliament is spent during the year, but the shortfall is seldom very large. More commonly, it is necessary for a department to ask for more money from Parliament. Under-provisions or new expenditures frequently become known before the end of the session at which the Main Estimates have been introduced, and these are covered by the submission of Supplementary Estimates (A), (B), etc. Frequently also during the year, after Parliament has risen, additional expenditures must be made for unforeseen contingencies, and parliamentary approval for these is given by the passage of further Supplementary Estimates in the succeeding session.

Since the fiscal year is the 12-month period commencing on April 1, the President of the Treasury Board will normally submit the Main Estimates to Parliament in the preceding February or March so that they may be considered as time permits during the parliamentary session. . . . An important additional source in recent years has been the minutes of the standing committees discussing the Estimates of the individual departments . . .

Budget Speech

In the parliamentary process, the budget speech follows next after the Estimates. In fact it may follow at a very long interval, the time depending on the exigencies of the business of the House, the state of the economy, and other factors. The traditional purpose of the budget speech is to review the general position of the government's accounts for the old year and to make proposals for the year ahead; to relate the expenditure program for the new year, as presented in the Estimates, to the expected revenues from existing tax sources; and to propose any changes in taxation deemed necessary. The budget speech, therefore, is of greatest interest in connection with revenues, since its main purpose is to formulate the tax changes required to support the expenditure program. . . .

The *Economic Review* is published in April by the Department of Finance regardless of when the budget is brought down. The publication gives a broad review of past, present, and future economic factors that will affect the outlook of business and the nation's finances. This review is of interest to the businessman and citizen at large, and because of its authoritative and comprehensive character, is now very influential in the business community. It is supplemented by elaborate and up-to-date tables of economic data. . . .

The Public Accounts

The Public Accounts, a three-volume report to Parliament, gives the fiscal result in detail for revenues, expenditures, debt, and other financial operations for the year. When Parliament is in session, the accounts are usually tabled in October of the year in which the fiscal year ended. . . .

Departmental Reports

In addition to the general financial compilations and reports issued by the Department of Finance, each operating department and most governmental agencies issue annual reports. These contain more detailed information on departmental activities. . . .

FEDERAL GOVERNMENT BUDGETARY REVENUES AND EXPENDITURES, 1980-81 (ESTIMATES)

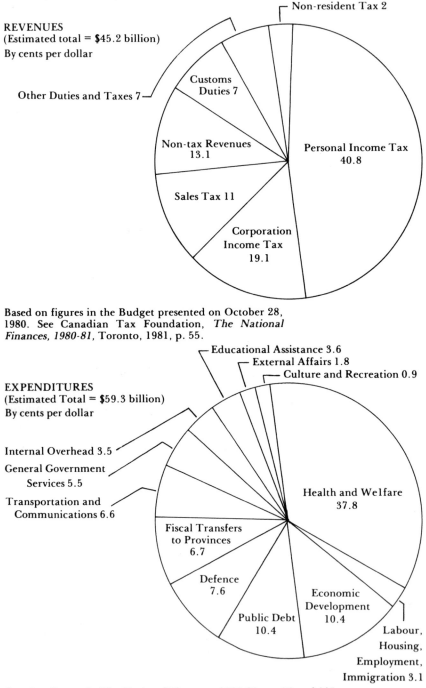

REVENUES
(Estimated total = $45.2 billion)
By cents per dollar

Non-resident Tax 2

Customs
Duties 7

Other Duties and Taxes 7

Non-tax Revenues
13.1

Personal Income Tax
40.8

Sales Tax 11

Corporation
Income Tax
19.1

Based on figures in the Budget presented on October 28, 1980. See Canadian Tax Foundation, *The National Finances, 1980-81*, Toronto, 1981, p. 55.

EXPENDITURES
(Estimated Total = $59.3 billion)
By cents per dollar

Educational Assistance 3.6
External Affairs 1.8
Culture and Recreation 0.9

Internal Overhead 3.5

General Government
Services 5.5

Transportation and
Communications 6.6

Health and Welfare
37.8

Fiscal Transfers
to Provinces
6.7

Defence
7.6

Economic
Development
10.4

Public Debt
10.4

Labour,
Housing,
Employment,
Immigration 3.1

Based on figures in *The National Finances, 1980-81*, pp. 53 and 105.

PROVINCIAL REVENUES AND EXPENDITURES, 1981-82
EXAMPLE: ONTARIO BUDGET, 1981-82

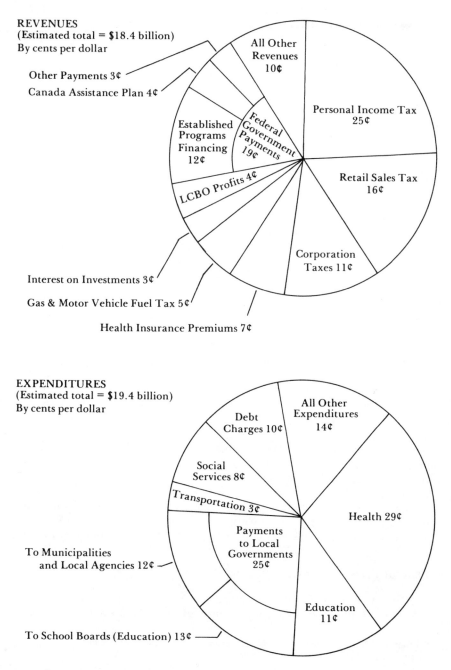

REVENUES
(Estimated total = $18.4 billion)
By cents per dollar

Other Payments 3¢
Canada Assistance Plan 4¢

All Other Revenues 10¢

Established Programs Financing 12¢

Federal Government Payments 19¢

LCBO Profits 4¢

Personal Income Tax 25¢

Retail Sales Tax 16¢

Corporation Taxes 11¢

Interest on Investments 3¢

Gas & Motor Vehicle Fuel Tax 5¢

Health Insurance Premiums 7¢

EXPENDITURES
(Estimated total = $19.4 billion)
By cents per dollar

Debt Charges 10¢

All Other Expenditures 14¢

Social Services 8¢

Transportation 3¢

Payments to Local Governments 25¢

Health 29¢

To Municipalities and Local Agencies 12¢

Education 11¢

To School Boards (Education) 13¢

From the *Ontario Budget, 1981*, Toronto, Ontario Government Bookstore, 1981, p. i and Budget Paper C, p. 30.

Other Sources

Statistics Canada prepares the national accounts and other special analyses of government activities, such as the number of persons employed. The Department of National Revenue compiles and publishes annually detailed analyses of income tax statistics. . . .

FINANCIAL ARRANGEMENTS AND FEDERAL PAYMENTS TO OTHER GOVERNMENTS*

Canadian Tax Foundation

The federal government now uses four basic methods to transfer fiscal resources to the provinces, territories, and municipalities: the reduction of federal tax in order to provide tax room for the provinces, tax abatements, general purpose transfers, and specific purpose transfers.

The provinces and the territories levy their own personal income taxes, expressed as a percentage of the federal tax and collected by the federal government in all provinces except Quebec. Over the nine agreeing provinces, the rates range from 38.5 to 58.0 per cent of federal tax, and they are expected to produce $6.8 billion in 1980-81. We have estimated that a further $5.0 billion would be collected in Quebec, including $.9 billion attributable to the special federal abatement of 16.5 per cent of basic federal tax granted in compensation for opting out (see below). Provincial corporation income taxes, which are designed to take up or in some cases to exceed the federal abatement, are expected to yield $1.2 billion in the eight provinces and the territories that have a collection agreement with Ottawa. Ontario and Quebec collections are estimated at $1.6 billion.

General purpose transfers to the provinces, municipalities and territories are expected to total $4.3 billion in 1980-81. These grants to the provinces are principally equalization payments under the Federal-Provincial Fiscal Arrangements Act, statutory subsidies, and income tax on certain public utilities. Payments to the territories cover the deficiency on ordinary account, capital needs, and amortization of debt. The general payments to municipalities take the form of grants in lieu of taxes on federal property.

The federal government also makes specific purpose transfers or grants-in-aid to the other levels of government for purposes such as hospital insurance, medicare, welfare assistance, and regional development. . . .

Federal-Provincial Fiscal Arrangements

A complete history of federal-provincial fiscal arrangements is available in the 1966 Foundation publication entitled *The Financing of Canadian*

* From *The National Finances, 1980-81*, Toronto, Canadian Tax Foundation, 1981. Chapter 10. By permission.

[*Editor's note:* See also the article by Prime Minister Pierre E. Trudeau, "In Defence of Federalism," *infra*, Chapter 6.]

Federation: The First Hundred Years. This should be supplemented by articles in the *Canadian Tax Journal* for July-August 1972 and 1977. In the following section, only the main features of this complex area of intergovernmental relations are examined. A summary of the arrangements for 1977-82 is also included.

• • •

Total Federal Payments to Other Governments

. . . It is useful to see the whole picture of federal transfers, both general purpose and specific purpose, to other levels of government . . . . Table 10-3 summarizes both general purpose and specific purpose transfers for the years 1970-71 and 1977-78 to 1980-81. The figures for 1979-80 are taken from the Public Accounts and for 1980-81 from the Estimates. The table indicates that federal grants to all other levels of government have risen from $3,825.6 million in 1970-71 to $11,164.2 million in 1978-79. Complete data for specific purpose transfers are not available for the last two years. Payments to Quebec under opting-out arrangements (the difference between the cost of the program and the yield of the tax abatement) and to all provinces in later years with respect to Established Programs Financing do not show the value of the program because the values for the tax points are not shown (as they are in Table 10-1). The payments are considered specific purpose transfers and allocated by function. The recovery of the yield of the special 3-percentage-point abatement to Quebec individual income taxpayers is shown. Before 1976-77, the recovery had been deducted from equalization; it is now deducted from payments compensating for opting out.

In Table 10-3, the figures for other health care in 1977-78 to 1980-81 represent federal payments with respect to the extended health care program, now classified as "health." In previous years, the same services were partially funded under CAP and thus were classified as "welfare." . . .

Table 10.1—Estimated Payments to the Provinces Under the 1977-82 Fiscal Arrangements for the Fiscal Year 1980-81
(Dollar Figures in Millions)

	Nfld.	P.E.I.	N.S.	N.B.	Que.	Ont.	Man.	Sask.	Alta.	B.C.	Total
Equalization (See Table 10-2) ... $	376.4	88.0	449.1	378.7	1,720.8	—	342.6	40.2	—	—	3,395.9
Individual income tax rate 1980 ... %	*58.0*	*51.19*	*52.5*	*52.45*	—	*44.0*	*54.0*	*53.0*	*38.5*	*44.0*	—
Individual income tax collected^a ... $	171.3	31.5	288.2	214.9	—	3,377.8	304.5	361.3	813.9	1,238.3	6,801.6
Corporation income tax rate 1980. ... %	*12-15*	*10*	*10-13*	*9-12*	—	—	*11-15*	*11-14*	*5-11*	*10-15*	—
Corporation income tax collected^a ... $	37.9	5.0	61.5	37.4	—	—	120.7	124.1	352.9	420.1	1,159.6
Share of income tax on certain											
public utilities ... $	4.4	.9	—	—	1.8	25.9	4.4	.2	31.6	2.9	72.0
Statutory subsidies ... $	9.7	.7	2.2	1.8	4.5	5.5	2.2	2.1	3.4	2.1	34.1
Share of taxes on undist. income ... $	.4	..	.7	1.4	13.4	18.5	1.8	1.0	3.6	4.9	45.6
Reciprocal taxation ... $	8.3	2.6	31.7	7.6	31.3	51.3	—	—	—	—	132.8
Adjustments for prior years^b ... $	—	—	—	—	—	—	—	—	—	—	150.0
Less: Youth allowance recovery	—	—	—	—	-158.7	—	—	—	—	—	-158.7
Total payments ... $	608.4	128.7	833.4	641.8	1,613.1	3,479.0	776.2	528.9	1,205.4	1,668.3	11,632.9
Established Programs Financing (EPF)											
Value of federal tax withdrawals (included in above)											
Individual income tax, 13.5 points ... $	45.3	9.4	84.2	62.9	812.0^c	1,345.2	117.1	113.7	361.1	442.0	3,393.1
Corporation income tax, 1 point. ... $	2.7	.5	5.2	3.5	54.4	102.0	8.9	10.4	55.6	33.0	276.0
Cash contribution^d											
Hospital insurance ... $	72.1	15.5	106.0	87.9	549.4	1,000.8	127.9	120.5	210.6	292.9	2,583.6
Medicare ... $	24.8	5.3	36.5	30.3	189.2	344.6	44.0	41.5	72.5	100.8	889.5
Post-secondary education ... $	45.9	9.8	67.5	55.9	349.5	636.7	81.4	76.7	134.0	186.3	1,643.7
Extended health care ... $	15.6	3.3	22.9	19.0	169.2	230.1	27.6	26.0	55.8	70.8	640.4
Prior year adjustments^b ... $	—	—	—	—	—	—	—	—	—	—	-125.1
Total value of EPF ... $	206.4	43.9	322.3	259.5	2,123.7	3,659.5	406.9	388.9	889.5	1,125.8	9,301.2

^aNet after provincial credits and reductions; includes surtaxes. ^bDistribution by province not available. ^cExcludes $464.5 million as value of additional 8.5 personal income tax points due Quebec for opting out of EPF. ^dExcluding associated equalization included in equalization payment above.

SOURCE: Department of Finance.

Table 10.3—Summary of Federal Contributions to the Provinces,
Municipalities, and Territories for the Fiscal Years Ending
March 1971 and 1978 to 1981

	1971	1978	1979	1980	1981[a]
			millions of dollars		
(A) Payment to provinces					
General purpose transfers					
Equalization....................	927.4	2,383.5	2,747.2	3,321.4	3,395.9
Share of federal estate tax	60.4	—	—	—	—
Adjustments for prior years........	—	na	—	—	150.0
Share of income tax on certain					
public utilities	23.9	45.9	81.8	66.3	72.0
Grants in lieu of provincial					
property tax....................	2.9	7.0	2.0	5.3	7.0
Income tax guarantee	—	600.4	121.6	72.1	—
Share of tax on undist. income	—	15.3	16.8	15.9	45.6
Reciprocal taxation...............	—	46.6	100.4	105.3	132.8
Statutory subsidies	31.8	34.1	34.0	34.1	34.1
Sales tax reduction program........	—	—	23.2	64.8	—
Recovery re youth allowances	−27.5	−122.5	−131.3	−157.8	−158.7
Total general purpose transfers......	2,995.8			3,527.3	3,678.7
Specific purpose transfers					
Hospital insurance	801.9	1,754.0	2,252.7	2,456.8	2,583.6
Medicare.......................	400.5	596.4	715.4	814.7	889.5
Other health....................	42.6	488.9	563.8	576.8	640.4
Welfare........................	563.1	1,431.7	1,724.5	1,646.2	1,886.5
Education: Post-secondary	388.3	1,095.5	1,365.4	1,493.7	1,643.7
Other.................	178.3	238.7	212.8	—	—
Transportation and					
communications	44.7	110.4	142.8	—	—
Other.........................	230.3	503.8	510.8	—	—
Total specific purpose transfers......	2,649.6	6,219.4	7,488.2	—	—
Total payments to provinces	3,668.1	9,229.6	10,484.1	—	—
(B) Payments to local governments					
General purpose transfers	53.0	118.3	135.0	129.0	149.0
Specific purpose transfers	51.0	188.2	261.9	—	—
Total payments to local governments .	104.0	306.6	396.9	—	—
(C) Payments to territories					
General purpose transfers	34.6	226.1	231.4	262.9	268.4
Specific purpose transfers	18.9	24.5	51.8	—	—
Total payments to territories	53.5	250.6	283.2	—	—
TOTAL FEDERAL PAYMENTS ...	3,825.6	9,786.7	11,164.2	—	—

[a]Preliminary

SOURCE: Statistics Canada, *Federal Government Finance*, Cat. no. 68-211, various years;
Public Accounts; Department of Finance.

BIBLIOGRAPHY

Federalism and Federal Problems

(See also Bibliography in Chapter 2)

Aitchison, J,H., "Interprovincial Co-operation in Canada," in Aitchison, J.H., (ed.), *The Political Process in Canada*, Toronto, U.T.P., 1963.

Albrecht-Carrie, R., "The Canadian Dilemma," *J.C.S.*, IX, 1, February, 1974.

Armstrong, C., *The Politics of Federalism: Ontario's Relations with the Federal Government 1867-1942*, Toronto, U.T.P., 1981.

Bakvis, H., *Federalism and the Organization of Political Life: Canada in a Comparative Perspective*, I.I.R., Queen's University, 1981.

Bastien, R., *La solution canadienne*, Montréal, Editions de la presse, 1979.

Berkowitz, S.D., and Logan, R.K., (eds.), *Canada's Third Option*, Toronto, Macmillan, 1978.

Bernard, A., *Politics in Canada and Quebec*, adapted by J. Driefelds, Toronto, Methuen, 1981.

Black, E.R., *Divided Loyalties: Canadian Concepts of Federalism*, Montreal, McG.-Q.U.P., 1975.

Black, E.R., and Cairns, A., "A Different Perspective on Canadian Federalism," *C.P.A.*, IX, 1, March, 1966.

Blackman, W.J., "A Western Canadian Perspective on the Economics of Confederation," *C.P.P.*, III, 4, Autumn, 1977.

Boisvert, D., *Evaluating the Federalist Responses*, Discussion Paper 2, Kingston, I.I.R., Queen's University, 1978.

Bothwell, R., Drummond, I., and English, J., *Canada Since 1945: Power, Politics and Provincialism*, Toronto, U.T.P., 1981.

Breton, A., Breton, R., Bruneau, C., Gauthier, Y., Lalonde, M., Pinard, M., Trudeau, P.E., "Manifeste pour une politique fonctionelle," *Cité libre*, XV, 67, mai, 1964. [English translation in *Canadian Forum*, XLIV, 520, May, 1964.]

Breton, A., and Scott, A., *The Economic Constitution of Federal States*, Toronto, U.T.P., 1978.

Breton, A., and Scott, A., *The Design of Federations*, Montreal, I.R.P.P., 1980.

Brown, D., *The Federal Year in Review, 1977-78*, Kingston, I.I.R., Queen's University, 1978.

Brown, D., *Intergovernmental Relations in Canada: the Year in Review, 1979*, Kingston, I.I.R., Queen's University, 1980.

Burns, R.M., "Uncertain Life of Cooperative Federalism," *Q.Q.*, 78, 4, Winter, 1971.

Burns, R.M., (ed.), *One Country or Two?*, Montreal, McG.-Q.U.P., 1971.

Burns, R.M., *Conflict and Its Resolution in the Administration of Mineral Resources*, Kingston, Queen's University, I.I.R., 1975.

Burns, R.M., et al., *Political and Administrative Federalism*, Canberra, Centre for Research on Federal Financial Relations, Australian National University, 1976.

Burton, T.L., *Natural Resources Policy in Canada: Issues and Perspectives*, Toronto, M. & S., 1972.

Byers, R.B., and Reford, R.W., (eds.), *Canada Challenged: The Viability of Confederation*, Toronto, C.I.I.A., 1979.

Cairns, A.C., *From Interstate to Intrastate Federalism in Canada*, Discussion Paper 5, Kingston, I.I.R., Queen's University, 1979.

Cairns, A.C., "The Governments and Societies of Canadian Federalism," *C.J.P.S.*, X, 4, December, 1977.

Cairns, A.C., "The Other Crisis of Canadian Federalism," *C.P.A.*, 22, 2, Summer, 1979.

Canada, Federal-Provincial Relations Office, *Federal-Provincial Programs* and *Activities: A Descriptive Inventory*, Ottawa, 1977.

Caplan, N., "Some Factors Affecting the Resolution of a Federal- Provincial Conflict," *C.J.P.S.*, II, 2, June, 1969.

Carty, R.K., and Ward, W.P., (eds.), *Entering the Eighties: Canada in Crisis*, Toronto, O.U.P., 1980.

Cohen, M., "The Judicial Process and National Policy — A Problem for Canadian Federalism," *McG.L.J.*, 16, 2, 1970.

Creighton, D.G., *The Road to Confederation: The Emergence of Canada, 1863-1867*, Toronto, Macmillan, 1964.

Crépeau, P.A., and Macpherson, C.B., (eds.),*The Future of Canadian Federalism; l'Avenir du fédéralisme canadien*, Toronto, U.T.P., Montréal, Les Presses de l'Université de Montréal, 1965.

Croisat, M., "Planification et fédéralisme," *C.P.A.*, XI, 3, Fall, 1968.

Dehem, R., *Planification économique et fédéralisme*, Montréal, Les Presses de l'Université Laval, 1968.

Dubuc, A., "Une interprétation économique de la constitution," *Socialisme 66, Revue du socialisme international et Québécois*, 7, janvier, 1966. [English translation in *Canadian Forum*, XLV, 542, March, 1966.]

Dunton, D., "Recognized, Equitable Duality," *J.C.S.*, 12, 3, 1977.

Dyck, R., "The Canada Assistance Plan: The Ultimate in Cooperative Federalism," *C.P.A.*, 19, 4, Winter, 1976.

Elton, D., Engelmann, F.C., and McCormick, P., *Alternatives: Towards the Development of an Effective Federal System for Canada*, Calgary, Canada West Foundation, amended report, May, 1978.

Evans, J., (ed.), *Options*, Proceedings of the Conference on the Future of the Canadian Federation held in the University of Toronto, October, 1977, Toronto, U.T.P., 1977.

Fairweather, G., "Canada: A Faltering

Exemplar of Federalism," *J.C.S.*, 12, 3, 1977.

Fortin, P., "La dimension économique de la crise politique canadienne," (Comment by K. McRoberts), *C.P.P.*, IV, 3, Summer, 1978.

French, S.G., dir., *La confédération canadienne: qu'en pensent les philosophes*, Montréal, 1979.

Gallant, E., "The Machinery of Federal-Provincial Relations: I," and Burns, R.M., "The Machinery of Federal-Provincial Relations: II," *C.P.A.*, VIII, 4, December, 1965.

Gélinas, A., "Trois modes d'approche à la détermination de l'opportunité de la décentralisation de l'organisation politique principalement en système fédéral," *C.P.A.*, IX, 1, March, 1966.

Hawkins, G., (ed.), *Concepts of Federalism*, Proceedings of 34th Couchiching Conference, Toronto, C.I.P.A., 1965.

Hicks, U.K., *Federalism Failure and Success: A Comparative Study*, Toronto, Gage, 1978.

Hockin, T.A., *et al.*, *The Canadian Condominium: Domestic Issues and External Policy*, Toronto, M. & S., 1972.

Hodgins, B.W., and Smith, D., "Canada and Québec: Facing the Reality," *J.C.S.*, 12, 3, 1977.

Hodgins, B.W., Wright, D., and Heick, W.H., *Federalism in Canada and Australia: The Early Years*, Waterloo, W.L.U.P., 1978.

Institute of Intergovernmental Relations, *Federalism and Intergovernmental Relations in Australia, Canada, the United States and Other Countries: A Bibliography*, Kingston, Queen's University, 1967; *Supplementary Bibliography*, 1975; *Supplementary Bibliography*, 1979.

Institute of Intergovernmental Relations, Queen's University, Economic Council of Canada, *The Political Economy of Confederation*, Ottawa, S. and S., 1979.

Johnson, A.W., "The Dynamics of Federalism in Canada," *C.J.P.S.*, I, 1, March, 1968.

Kear, A.R., "Co-operative Federalism:

A Study of the Federal-Provincial Continuing Committee on Fiscal and Economic Matters," *C.P.A.*, VI, 1, March, 1963.

Kom, L., *The Federal Year in Review, 1976-77*, Kingston, I.I.R., Queen's University, 1977.

Kwavnick, D., "Quebec and the Two Nations Theory: A Reexamination," *Q.Q.*, 81, 3, Autumn, 1974.

Lalande, G., *In Defence of Federalism: The View from Quebec*, Toronto, M. & S., 1978.

Lamontagne, M., *Le fédéralisme canadien*, Québec, Les presses universitaires Laval, 1954.

Leach, R.H., "Interprovincial Cooperation: Neglected Aspect of Canadian Federalism," *C.P.A.*, II, 2, June, 1959.

Leach, R.H., (ed.), *Contemporary Canada*, Toronto, U.T.P., 1968.

Lederman, W.R., "The Concurrent Operation of Federal and Provincial Laws in Canada, " *McG.L.J.*, IX, 1963.

Lederman, W.R., "Unity and Diversity in Canadian Federalism: Ideals and Methods of Moderation," *C.B.R.*, LIII, 3, September, 1975.

Leeson, H.A., and Vanderelst, W., (eds.), *External Affairs and Canadian Federalism: The History of a Dilemma*, Toronto, H.R.W., 1973.

Leslie, P., *Equal to Equal: Economic Association and the Canadian Common Market*, Discussion Paper 6, Kingston, I.I.R., Queen's University, 1979.

Lortie, P., "The Changing Strains of Federalism," *Policy Options*, I, 3, September-October, 1980.

Lower, A., "The Prime Minister and the Premiers," *Q.Q.*, 87, 4, Winter, 1980.

Lower, A.R.M., Scott, F.R., *et al.*, *Evolving Canadian Federalism*, Durham, Duke University Press, 1958.

McRoberts, K., "English Canada and the Quebec Referendum: The Stakes and the Dangers," *J.C.S.*, 12, 3, 1977.

McWhinney, E., *Comparative Federalism, States' Rights and National Power*, Toronto, U.T.P., 2nd ed., 1965.

Mallory, J.R., "Confederation: The Ambiguous Bargain," *J.C.S.*, 12, 3, 1977.

Martin, J., *The Role and Place of Ontario in the Canadian Confederation*, Toronto, O.E.C., 1974.

Maxwell, J., and Pestieau, C., *Economic Realities of Contemporary Confederation*, Montreal, C.D. Howe Research Institute, 1980.

May, R.J., "Decision-making and Stability in Federal Systems," *C.J.P.S.*, III, 1, March, 1970.

Meekison, J.P., (ed.), *Canadian Federalism: Myth or Reality?*, Toronto, Methuen, 3rd ed., 1977.

Moore, A.M., "Fact and Fantasy in the Unity Debate," *C.P.P.*, V, 2, Spring, 1979.

Nicholson, N.L., *The Boundaries of the Canadian Confederation*, Toronto, Macmillan, 1979.

Ontario, Advisory Committee on Confederation, *First Report*, Toronto, Government of Ontario, 1978; *Second Report, The Federal-Provincial Distribution of Powers*, 1979.

Ontario Advisory Committee on Confederation, *Background Papers and Reports*, Toronto, Q.P., Vol. I, 1967; Vol. II, 1970.

Prévost, J.-P., *La crise du fédéralisme canadien*, Paris, Presses universitaires de France, 1972.

Reuber, G.L., "Economic Problems of Canadian Confederation," *Q.Q.*, 85, 3, Autumn, 1978.

Reynolds, R., and Sidor, N., *Research in Progress on Canadian Federalism and Intergovernmental Relations*, Kingston, I.I.R., Queen's University, 1979.

Russell, P., (ed.), *Nationalism in Canada*, Toronto, McG.-H., 1966.

Ryerson, S.B., *Unequal Union*, Toronto, Progress, 1968.

Savoie, D.J., *The Canada-New Brunswick General Development Agreement*, Montreal, McG.-Q.U.P., 1981.

Schultz, R., *Delegation and Cable Distribution Systems: A Negative*

Assessment, Discussion Paper 11, Kingston, I.I.R., Queen's University, 1981.

Schwartz, M.A., "The Social Make-up of Canada and Strains in Confederation," *C.P.P.*, III, 4, Autumn, 1977.

Scott, A., *Divided Jurisdiction over Natural Resources*, Discussion Paper 10, Kingston, I.I.R., Queen's University, 1980.

Scott, A., (ed.), *Natural Resource Revenues: A Test of Federalism*, Vancouver, U.B.C.P., 1976.

Scott, F.R., *Essays on the Constitution: Aspects of Canadian Law and Politics*, Toronto, U.T.P., 1977.

Silver, A.I., *The French-Canadian Idea of Confederation, 1864-1900*, Toronto, U.T.P., 1981.

Simeon, R., (ed.), *Confrontation and Collaboration: Intergovernmental Relations in Canada Today*, Toronto, I.P.A.C., 1979.

Simeon, R., "Intergovernmental Relations and the Challenges to Canadian Federalism," *C.P.A.*, 23, 1, Spring, 1980.

Simeon, R., (ed.), *Must Canada Fail?*, Montreal, McG.-Q.U.P., 1977.

Simeon, R., *Natural Resource Revenues and Canadian Federalism: A Survey of the Issues*, Discussion Paper 9, Kingston, I.I.R., Queen's University, 1980.

Simeon, R., *Opening Statement to the Special Committee on the Constitution*, Discussion Paper 4, Kingston, I.I.R., Queen's University, 1978.

Simeon, R., *Thinking About Change*, Discussion Paper 1, Kingston, I.I.R., Queen's University, 1978.

Smiley, D.V., *The Rowell-Sirois Report*, Carleton Library No. 5, Toronto, M. & S., 1963.

Smiley, D.V., "Public Administration and Canadian Federalism," *C.P.A.*, VII, 3, September, 1964.

Smiley, D.V., "The Two Themes of Canadian Federalism," *C.J.E.P.S.*, XXXI, 1, February, 1965.

Smiley, D.V., *The Canadian Political Nationality*, Toronto, Methuen, 1967.

Smiley, D.V., "As the Options Nar-
row: Notes on Post-November 15 Canada," *J.C.S.*, 12, 3, 1977.

Smiley, D.V., "Territorialism and Canadian Political Institutions," *C.P.P.*, III, 4, Autumn, 1977.

Smiley, D.V., *The Association Dimension of Sovereignty-Association: A Response to the Quebec White Paper*, Discussion Paper 8, Kingston, I.I.R., Queen's University, 1980.

Smiley, D., *Canada in Question; Federalism in the Eighties*, Toronto, McG.-H.R., 3rd ed., 1980.

Smiley, D., "The Challenge of Canadian Ambivalence," *Q.Q.*, 88, 1, Spring, 1981.

Sproule-Jones, M.H., *Public Choice and Federalism in Australia and Canada*, Canberra, Centre for Research on Federal Financial Relations, Australian National University, 1975.

Stein, M., "Québec and Canada: The Changing Equilibrium between 'Federal Society' and 'Federal Political System'," *J.C.S.*, 12, 3, 1977.

Stevenson, G., *Unfulfilled Union: Canadian Federalism and National Unity*, Toronto, Macmillan, 1979. (Reprinted and reissued by Gage, 1980.)

Swainson, N.A., *Conflict Over the Columbia: The Canadian Background to an Historic Treaty*, Toronto, I.P.A.C., 1979.

Thorson, J.T., *Wanted: A Single Canada*, Toronto, M. & S., 1973.

Thur, L.M., (ed.), *Energy Policy and Federalism*, Toronto, I.P.A.C., 1981.

Trudeau, P.E., *Federalism and the French Canadians*, Toronto, Methuen, 1968.

Underhill, F.H., *The Image of Confederation*, Toronto, C.B.C., 1964.

Veilleux, G., *Les rélations intergouvernementales au Canada, 1867-1967: les mécanismes de coopération*, Montréal, Presses de l'Université du Québec, 1971.

Veilleux, G., "Intergovernmental Canada: Government by Conference? A Fiscal and Economic

Perspective," *C.P.A.*, 23,1, Spring, 1980. (See also comments by Dupré, J.S., *ibid.*)

Walker, M., (ed.), *Canadian Confederation at the Crossroads: The Search for a Federal-Provincial Balance*, Vancouver, The Fraser Institute, 1978, (Toronto, Macmillan, 1979).

Westmacott, M., "The National Transportation Act and Western Canada: A Case Study in Cooperative Federalism," *C.P.A.*, 16, 3, Fall, 1973.

White, W.L., Wagenberg, R.H., Nelson, R.C., and Soderlund, W.C., *Canadian Confederation: A Decision-Making Analysis*, Toronto, Macmillan, 1979.

Wilden, A., *Le Canada imaginaire*, Québec, Presses Coméditex, 1979.

Wiltshire, K., "Working with Intergovernmental Agreements — the Canadian and Australian Experience," *C.P.A.*, 23, 3, Fall, 1980.

Zukowsky, R.J., *Intergovernmental Relations in Canada: The Year in Review, 1980*, Vol. I, *Policy and Politics*, Vol. II, *Struggle over the Constitution: From the Quebec Referendum to the Supreme Court*, Kingston, I.I.R., Queen's University, 1981.

Consociationalism and Pluralism

Lijphart, A., "Consociation and Federation: Conceptual and Empirical Links," *C.J.P.S.*, XII, 3, September, 1979. (With Comment by K.D. McRae, *ibid.*)

Lijphart, A., *Democracy in Plural Societies: A Comparative Exploration*, New Haven, Yale University Press, 1977.

McRae, K.D., (ed.), *Consociational Democracy: Political Accommodation in Segmented Societies*, Toronto, M. & S., 1974.

McRae, K.D., "The Plural Society and the Western Political Tradition," *C.J.P.S.*, XII, 4, December, 1979.

Noel, S.J.R., "Consociational Democracy and Canadian Feder-

alism," *C.J.P.S.*, IV, 1, March, 1971.

Ossenberg, R.J., (ed.), *Canadian Society: Pluralism, Change and Conflict*, Scarborough, P.-H., 1971.

Thorburn, H.G., "Canadian Pluralist Democracy in Crisis," *C.J.P.S.*, XI, 4, December, 1978.

Finances

Bastien R., "La structure fiscale du fédéralisme canadien: 1945-73," *C.P.A.*, 17, 1, Spring, 1974.

Birch, A.H., *Federalism, Finance, and Social Legislation in Canada, Australia, and the United States*, Oxford, Clarendon Press, 1955.

Bird, R.M., *The Growth of Government Spending in Canada*, Toronto, C.T.F., Paper No. 51, 1970.

Bird, R.M., *Financing Canadian Government: A Quantitative Overview*, Toronto, C.T.F., 1979.

Bird, R.M., (ed.), *Fiscal Dimensions of Canadian Federalism*, Toronto, C.T.F., 1980.

Boadway, R.W., and Kitchen, H.M., *Canadian Tax Policy*, Toronto, C.T.F., 1980.

Boadway, R.W., *Intergovernmental Transfers in Canada*, Toronto, C.T.F., 1980.

Breton, A., "A Theory of Government Grants," *C.J.E.P.S.*, XXXI, 2, May, 1965. (See also "Notes," *ibid.*, XXXII, 2, May, 1966; Breton, A., "A Theory of the Demand for Public Goods," *ibid.*, XXXII, 4, November 1966, and "Notes," *ibid.*, XXXIII, 1, February, 1967.)

Burns, R.M., "Federal Provincial Relations: The Problem of Fiscal Adjustment," *C.T.J.*, 20, 3, May-June, 1972.

Burns, R.M., *The Acceptable Mean: The Tax Rental Agreements, 1941-62*, Toronto, C.T.F., 1980.

Canada, Parliamentary Task Force on Federal-Provincial Fiscal Arrangements, [Breau Committee], *Fiscal Federalism in Canada*, Ottawa, S. and S., 1981.

Canada, [Benson, E.J.], *The Taxing*

Powers and the Constitution of Canada, Ottawa, Q.P., 1969.

Canada, [Trudeau, P.E.], *Federal-Provincial Grants and the Spending Power of Parliament*, Ottawa, Q.P., 1969.

Canada, [Trudeau, P.E.], *Income Security and Social Services*, Ottawa, Q.P., 1969.

Canada, Minister of Finance, *Report of the Tax Structure Committee to the Federal-Provincial Conference of Prime Ministers and Premiers*, Ottawa, February 16-17, 1970.

Canada, *Dominion-Provincial Conference on Reconstruction; Submission and Plenary Conference Discussion*, Ottawa, K.P., 1946.

Canada, *Report of the Royal Commission on Dominion-Provincial Relations* [Rowell-Sirois Report]; *Book I, Canada: 1867-1939; Book II, Recommendations; Book III, Documentation*; Ottawa, K.P., 1940, 3 vols. (Reprinted in one volume, 1954.) Also Appendices 1-8.

Canada, *Report of the Royal Commission on Taxation*, [Carter Commission], Ottawa, Q.P., 1966, 6 vols. (See also the Commission's individual research studies, Nos. 1-30, especially No. 23, J.H. Lynn, *Federal-Provincial Relations*, Ottawa, Q.P., 1967.)

Canadian Tax Foundation, *Provincial and Municipal Finances, 1981*, Toronto, C.T.F., 1981.

Clark, D.H., *Fiscal Need and Revenue Equalization Grants*, Canadian Tax Papers No. 49, Toronto, C.T.F., 1969.

Dehem, R., and Wolfe, J.N., "The Principles of Federal Finance and the Canadian Case," *C.J.E.P.S.*, XXI, 1, February, 1955.

Doern, G.B., (ed.), *How Ottawa Spends Your Tax Dollars: Federal Priorities, 1981-82*, Toronto, Lorimer, 1981.

Doern, G.B., (ed.), *Spending Tax Dollars: Federal Expenditures, 1980-81*, Ottawa, School of Public Administration, Carleton University, 1980.

Dupré, J.S., "Tax-Powers vs Spending Responsibilities: An Historical Analysis of Federal-Provincial Finance," in Rotstein, A., (ed.), *The Prospect of Change*, Toronto, McG.-H., 1965.

Dupré, J.S., " 'Contracting out': A Funny Thing Happened on the Way to the Centennial," *Report of the Proceedings of the Eighteenth Annual Tax Conference*, Toronto, C.T.F., 1965.

Dupré, J.S., *Intergovernmental Finance in Ontario: A Provincial-Local Perspective*, Toronto, Q.P., Ontario, 1968.

Dupré, J.S., *Federalism and Policy Development: The Case of Adult Occupational Training in Ontario*, Toronto, U.T.P., 1973.

Foot, D.K., *Provincial Public Finance in Ontario*, Toronto, U.T.P., 1977.

Graham, J.F., Johnson, A.W., Andrews, J.F., *Inter-Government Fiscal Relationships*, Canadian Tax Paper No. 40, Toronto, C.T.F., December, 1964.

Head, J.G., "Evolution of Canadian Tax Reform," *D.L.R.*, I, 1, September, 1973.

Johns , J.A., "Provincial-Municipal Intergovernmental Fiscal Relations," *C.P.A.*, XXI, 2, Summer, 1969.

LaForest, G.V., *The Allocation of Taxing Powers Under the Canadian Constitution*, Toronto, C.T.F., 2nd ed., 1981.

Mackintosh, W.A., *The Economic Background of Dominion-Provincial Relations*, Toronto, M. & S., 1964.

May, R., *Federalism and Fiscal Adjustment*, Ottawa, Q.P., 1968.

Moore, A.M., Perry, J.H., and Beach, D.I., *The Financing of Canadian Federation: The First Hundred Years*, Canadian Tax Paper No. 43, Toronto, C.T.F., 1966.

Moore, M., "Some Proposals for Adapting Federal-Provincial Financial Agreements to Current Conditions," *C.P.A.*, 24, 2, Summer, 1981.

Oates, W.E., (ed.), *The Political Economy of Fiscal Federalism*, New York, Princeton University Press, 1977.

Oates, W.E., *Fiscal Federalism*, Don Mills, Ontario, Harcourt Brace Jovanovich, 1972.

Ontario, *Report of the Committee on Taxation* [Smith Committee], Toronto, Q.P., 1967, 3 vols.

Perry, J.H., *Taxation in Canada*, Toronto, U.T.P., 3rd ed., rev., 1961.

Perry, J.H., *Taxes, Tariffs, and Subsidies: A History of Canadian Fiscal Development*, Toronto, U.T.P., 1955, 2 vols.

Perry, D.B., "Federal-Provincial Fiscal Relations: The Last Six Years and the Next Five," *C.T.J.*, 20, 4, July-August, 1972.

Phidd, R.W., and Doern, G.B., (eds.), *The Politics and Management of Canadian Economic Policy*, Toronto, Macmillan, 1978.

Quebec, *Report of the Royal Commission on Taxation* [Bélanger Report], Quebec, Q.P., 1965.

Robinson, A.J., and Cutt, J., (eds.). *Public Finance in Canada: Selected Readings*, 2nd ed., (Chapter III), Toronto, Methuen, 1973.

Simeon, R., *Federal-Provincial Diplomacy: The Making of Recent Policy in Canada*, Toronto, U.T.P., 1972.

Smiley, D.V., "The Rowell-Sirois Report, Provincial Autonomy, and Post-War Canadian Federalism," *C.J.E.P.S.*, XXVIII, 1, February, 1962.

Smiley, D.V., *Conditional Grants and Canadian Federalism*, Canadian Tax Paper No. 32, Toronto, C.T.F., February, 1962.

Smiley, D.V., "Block Grants to the Provinces: A Realistic Alternative?," *Report of the Proceedings of the Eighteenth Annual Tax Conference*, C.T.F., Toronto, 1965.

Smiley, D.V., *Constitutional Adaptation and Canadian Federalism Since 1945*, Document 4 of the Royal Commission on Bilingualism and Biculturalism, Ottawa, Q.P., 1970.

Smiley, D.V., and Burns, R.M., "Canadian Federalism and the Spending Power: Is Constitutional Restriction Necessary?," *C.T.J.*, XVII, 6, November-December, 1969.

Strick, J.C., "Conditional Grants and Provincial Government Budgeting," *C.P.A.*, 14, 2, Summer, 1971.

4

REGIONALISM

Regionalism has been given renewed emphasis lately because of several factors. One is the greater assertion of power by the provinces which are usually identified with regions; another is the inclination to view regionalism as a rather natural and healthy reaction to the growth of central power in Ottawa; and the third is the tendency of provinces themselves to divide their own large geographic areas and administrative structures into regional units. Thus the traditional concept of regions within Canada (comprising the Atlantic provinces, Quebec, Ontario, the Prairies, and British Columbia) has been supplemented by the notion of regions within provinces.

These developments have both negative and positive aspects, as Professor David Bell points out in his brief but lucid introductory article. One suggestion that always emerges is the proposal to amalgamate the Maritime or Atlantic provinces into a region and the Prairie provinces into another region, each with a single government. This solution is usually more popular in Central Canada than in the east or west. However, the excerpt from the *Newsletter* of the Atlantic Provinces Economic Council supports the case for Maritime union with strong arguments. On the other hand, Professor Norman Ward's article is a devastating critique of the notion of Prairie union.

The problem of regional economic disparities, which has been with us ever since Confederation, has recently received attention from the provincial premiers and the prime minister when they discussed and drafted the new Canadian constitution. The Canadian Charter of Rights and Freedoms contains a clause aimed at reducing disparities in opportunities. (See *supra*, Chapter 2, The Canadian Charter, Part II.) Although the problem has elicited much declamation and considerable study dating back to at least the Rowell-Sirois Commission, there have been no effective solutions. The causes of regional economic disparities and recommendations to overcome them are put forward in the Economic Council of Canada's publication *Living Together: A Study of Regional Disparities*. Highlights from it are contained in the final selection in this chapter.

An article by Douglas Fullerton on the same subject which has been omitted from this edition appeared in the fourth edition of *Politics: Canada*, pp. 101 to 107. The introduction to Chapter 4 in the fourth edition noted also a number of additional items pertaining to regionalism which appeared in earlier editions of this book.

A good deal of literature, including a number of valuable, commissioned, specialized studies, has been stimulated by this renewed interest in regionalism.

Since it is too voluminous to be noted item by item in the bibliography appended to this chapter, students seeking further references should consult both federal and provincial sources. The bibliography in this chapter does refer, however, to many of the more general recent publications on regionalism.

The bibliography also contains references to publications in general on provinces, territories, and municipalities, including regional government. There are cross-references to bibliographies in other chapters on related subjects.

REGIONALISM IN THE CANADIAN COMMUNITY*

David V. J. Bell

The Two Faces of Regionalism

. . . "Regionalism in Canada," with its connotations of tension and conflict, seems antithetical to the notion of "the Canadian community," which connotes harmony and consensus. But regionalism, like drama, has two faces. Negative regionalism, to be sure, displays the frown of conflict and disintegration, manifested when one region is pitted against another, or against the national government. Positive regionalism, however, features the smile of cooperation and integration, the joining together of people living in a given territory to form a new political entity. In this sense, regionalism refers not to the opposite of community, but to the existence of community at a sub-national level.

This essay examines Canadian regionalism in both its positive and negative aspects. . . . Quebec regionalism has not been examined [here]. . . . The focus on negative regionalism is really equivalent to the study of provincialism; while the assessment of positive regionalism amounts to an evaluation of inter-provincialism. The latter concern will direct our attention to the Prairies and the Maritimes, which at present are the only conceivable settings for "positive regionalism." After exploring the relationship between regionalism and federalism, the essay concludes with a brief, tentative speculation about the future of Canadian regionalism.

Negative Regionalism in Canada: Challenges to Community

The history of negative regionalism in Canada predates Confederation itself. In 1784, New Brunswick broke away from Nova Scotia in response to the regional aspirations of the newly arrived loyalist settlers. Similarly, Upper Canada was carved out of the enormous territory of Quebec in 1791. The failure to include Prince Edward Island within Confederation in 1867, and the Manitoba Rebellions led by Louis Riel, both represent regional challenges to national solidarity in Canada. Indeed, at some point in Canadian history, virtually every conceivable region has violently or peacefully asserted its autonomy vis-à-vis the larger entity.

* Published here originally from an essay written in 1971 by the author who is Professor of Political Science and Dean of Graduate Studies, York University. By permission of the author.

Essentially, negative regionalism is simply a form of political cleavage with a territorial basis, best understood in the context of a general theory of political cleavages. . . .

Regional cleavages can interact with a variety of other political cleavages. It is widely believed among social scientists that conflict is positively correlated with the number and importance of reinforcing cleavages in a society. To the extent that this view is correct, it allows us to predict whether regional cleavages are likely to lead to low conflict or to relatively high conflict. The crucial consideration is the number of *other* cleavages that reinforce the regional one. Clearly, the least explosive combination includes a territorial or regional cleavage that is *not* reinforced by class, racial or religious-linguistic division; while the most explosive situation arises where *all* cleavages reinforce the territorial one. A hypothetical example of such a situation would feature a geographically concentrated racial minority, practising a different religion from the rest of society, all of whose members belonged to one social class. Perhaps the closest real world case exists in South Africa.

The situation in Canada is difficult to pinpoint. There is little doubt that economic, linguistic, and ethnic differences do reinforce regional cleavages *to a certain extent*. Economically, there is a fairly recognizable distinction between the "have" provinces (Ontario, British Columbia and to a lesser degree the Prairie Provinces), and the "have not" (all of the Atlantic Provinces and Quebec). Ironically, this line coincides exactly with the eastern boundary of Ontario. Linguistically, of course, the first fact of Canadian politics is the regional concentration of the French minority . . . [although] a significant portion of this minority is found in regions other than Quebec. A classic, if somewhat overstated, assessment of this cleavage was written nearly forty years ago by A.R.M. Lower. . . .

> The French-English cleavage is the greatest factor in Canadian life, not only because it is a racial and linguistic cleavage, but because it coincides with an economic cleavage, a legal cleavage, a cultural cleavage, a religious cleavage, and a philosophical cleavage.

Ethnically, Canadian regions display distinct patterns. The often celebrated "mosaic" truly exists only in the Prairies, while other regions are composed largely of members of the French or British "charter groups." The percentage of non-British/French population in the provinces ranges from a low of less than four per cent in Prince Edward Island to a high of over 53 per cent in Saskatchewan. . . .

Beyond these (and similar) crude estimates, precise measures of the degree of reinforcing cleavages in Canadian society have never been developed. . . .

Even multiple reinforcing cleavages do not produce the conflict characteristic of negative regionalism automatically. Besides the objective existence of cleavage, conflict presupposes subjective awareness of the cleavages and the *interpretation of the cleavage as an "unjust"* one. The suffix of the term implies that, like other "isms," regionalism contains a strong subjective component. It is impossible to discuss regionalism in a political context without considerable attention to the beliefs, values, and attitudes of the inhabitants of the "region." Only when this subjective factor is present does a region take on political (as opposed to economic or geographical) significance. Indeed, perceptions are probably more important than the objective situation in determining the nature and extent of conflict. Do the inhabitants of a given region (a) perceive themselves as possessing a regional identity? (b) believe that their region is the object of "unjust" discrimination? If so, negative regionalism is likely to occur in the form of inter-regional or regional-national conflict.

Taking these questions separately, it is generally agreed that regional identities have been much stronger in Canada than say in the United States. Again precise measures are lacking, but stimulating speculations are not. J.M.S. Careless . . . observes that

> Regional, ethnic and class identities have all tended to fit together more than to develop national identification in Canada. The ultimate conclusion, indeed, might seem to be that the true theme of the country's history in the twentieth century is not national building but region building.

Part of the explanation for the existence and virility of this aspect of regionalism can be traced to the traditional absence of any effective national alternative to regional identity. Even today, the character of Canadian national identity remains confused and uncertain, a reflection of at least three factors: the French-English cleavage; the fact that nearly one-third of Canada's population is composed of members of ethnic groups other than the "charter" British and French minorities; and the ambiguous psychological consequences of the Loyalist tradition in Canada.

Throughout Canadian history, repeated efforts have been made to discover or invent a national identity capable of integrating these diverse elements. . . .

One significant obstacle to "the transfer of loyalty from the region to the nation" is the persistence of feelings of regional injustice. Examples could be culled from virtually every region in the country, but for the purpose of illustration it is perhaps sufficient to draw on the experience of the Maritimes and the Prairies. Probably because compared to Ontario and British Columbia these have been among the disadvantaged provinces economically, one finds almost endemic to politics in these areas a profound sense of regional injustice and exploitation. But "Prairie injustice" has non-economic roots as well. Westerners, for example, still resent the fact that the Eastern provinces created Confederation, while the Western provinces were creatures of it. One noted Westerner went so far as to suggest that, "In some respects, the Prairie Provinces were conceived as a sort of colony of Central Canada.". . .

The image of the West as an exploited colony is still a vivid one. The only available survey data touching on the issue, gathered by David K. Elton in Alberta during 1968, support the hypothesis of widespread alienation in Western Canada. Sixty-one per cent of his respondents agreed that "the Eastern Canadians receive more benefits than do Western Canadians from being part of the Dominion of Canada." . . . Despite these rather high feelings of perceived injustice, at present less than ten per cent of Albertans seem interested in radical movements such as annexation or secession. By the same token, few are genuinely interested in Prairie union as a solution to the problems that lie behind negative regionalism. Again, Elton's survey showed only 23 per cent agreement with the idea that "the three Western provinces should join together and form one large province." Even a relatively high degree of negative regionalism apparently does not guarantee the basis for positive regionalism. As far as the idea of regional integration is concerned, "hating Toronto," to paraphrase humorist Eric Nicol, "is not enough."

Distrust of "Upper Canadians" enjoys an even longer tradition in the Maritimes. George Rawlyk illustrates convincingly his assertion that "Since 1867, two important ingredients in Nova Scotian regionalism have been an often profound dislike of Upper Canada and 'Upper Canadians' and also a basic distrust of Confederation itself." These negative attitudes, Rawlyk continues, almost amount to a "paranoid style," which he defines as a tendency to ascribe to Ottawa and Toronto all blame for Nova Scotia's economic and social decline. . . . Even today, Maritime alienation is remarkably strong. An opinion survey of all three provinces, conducted in connection with the Deutsch Commission investigations, showed that a higher proportion (40 per cent as compared with 33 per cent) of Maritimers felt they had "most in common" with Maine rather than Ontario! A whopping 25 per cent declared that they "would be in favour of political union with the United States"; and fully 63 per cent favoured closer economic ties with their Southern neighbours. By contrast, David Elton's survey of Albertan opinion turned up only five per cent support for Western separatism.

Positive Regionalism in Canada: The Extension of Community

The other face of regionalism, its positive side, involves the attainment of regional integration. In studying integration, it is important to distinguish the integration of people into a community directly as individuals, from the integration of existing communities into a larger whole. The former is largely a social phenomenon, probably understood as well (or as poorly) by humanists as by social scientists. The latter is largely a political phenomenon, ". . . a set of political decisions made by those who have the authority to commit their communities to collective action." Despite the elitist connotations of this approach, the focus on political decision-making as the crux of integration is particularly appropriate to the analysis of positive regionalism. For regional integration in Canada, at least as we have defined it, is equivalent to the amalgamation of two or more semi-sovereign provinces. . . .

Analysts as diverse as civil servants and geographers commonly divide Canada into five "regions." Three of the five regions, Ontario, Quebec, and B.C., coincide with existing provincial boundaries. The other two, the Maritimes and the Prairies, do not. "Regional integration" usually refers to the idea of union among two or more of the provinces in the latter category. At an earlier stage in Canadian history, the phrase might have connoted Upper and Lower Canada. No one seriously proposes this motion nowadays. By contrast, the "idea of Maritime Union" was the theme of an important Conference held at Mount Allison University in 1965; the question "One Prairie Province?" was discussed at an even larger conference held at the University of Lethbridge in 1970. A few weeks after the Maritime Union conference, the governments of Nova Scotia and New Brunswick established a commission to investigate "the advantages and disadvantages of a union . . ." In 1968 (after the characteristic lapse of three years) P.E.I. joined in sponsoring this project. What are the prospects for regional integration in these two areas?

Obstacles to Western unification are as numerous as they are difficult. In a brilliant, thorough analysis, Norman Ward virtually buried the idea of "one prairie province" under an avalanche of hypothetical problems. . . . [See Ward's article, below.]

But do his points apply as well to the idea of Maritime union? The members of the Royal Commission headed by John J. Deutsch to examine the feasibility of just such a union felt that the potential benefits of union far outweighed the expected costs. Their *Report*, finally completed in 1970, strongly recommended that amalgamation take place according to a suggested timetable covering five to ten years.

Several factors might account for the more optimistic conclusions reached by the Commission. In the first place, the idea of Maritime union predates its Prairie equivalent (which Ward dates from 1925) by over a century, going back at least as far as 1808. A much smaller area than the Prairies (less than one-third its size), the Maritimes are considerably more disadvantaged. . . . Perhaps these considerations alone account for the far greater degree of inter-provincial co-operation currently taking place in the Maritime provinces. A thorough inventory turned up 181 organizations (probably about four times the number that exist in the Prairies) whose activities range from academic to agricultural pursuits.

A number of these inter-provincial organizations have been assisted or created by the Federal Government itself! In fact in 1969, the Government set up a Department of Regional Economic Expansion whose explicit purpose is to foster co-operation in economic development at the regional level, especially in the poor regions of the country (including all of the Atlantic provinces and certain areas of the West). . . .

In line with this philosophy, the new Department has taken control of many of the "ad hoc" federal agencies and policies (including the Atlantic Development Board, the Agricultural rehabilitation and Development Agency [ARDA], and the "Cape Breton Development Corporation") set up since World War II to deal with regional disparities in income, unemployment rates, etc., that resulted from Canada's uneven economic development. These policies, a Government study concluded in 1968, had managed only to prevent further widening of inter-regional gaps. Much greater effort would be needed, the report continued, to *reduce* regional inequalities. So far, like its predecessors, the Department has confined its activity to economic measures, shying away from such political issues as regional amalgamation of two or more provinces. Nevertheless, the political relevance of reducing regional economic inequality in Canada need not be laboured. Much of the support for negative regionalism grows out of the search for solutions to regional economic problems.

Indeed, the single most significant consideration that lay behind the Deutsch Commission's recommendations was undoubtedly the nature and scope of the economic and social problems that the Maritimes shared jointly. According to the *Report* (pp. 30-31):

> What is needed is the ability to develop and to carry out plans, policies, and programs on a regional basis. The economies of the Maritime Provinces are individually too small and too inter-dependent for the effective planning and execution of development programs in the face of present-day social and technological trends.

Reviewing the alternative courses of action available to the Maritimes, the Commission found that, despite the possibility for achieving some of the necessary objectives through "informal co-operation," a much higher and more formalized level of co-operation would be necessary. Though to be sure, a great deal might be accomplished through the setting up of *ad hoc* agencies to implement specific programmes, such a practice would result in additional burdens of administrative and overhead costs, while failing to provide the executive authority capable of carrying out these policies. The only way to avoid these disadvantages, they concluded, would be through a full political union rather than a lower level administrative or economic union.

According to the opinion survey conducted in connection with the *Report*, there is already much support for these recommendations. Sixty-four per cent of the respondents surveyed indicated that they would vote in favour of "complete union into a single province." More significantly, perhaps, opinion was approximately evenly divided in all three provinces, a situation precisely the opposite of that which exists in the Prairies. The vast majority of the respondents felt that Maritime union would bring more industry to the Maritimes, provide more jobs, make possible the greater development of natural resources, and also improve governmental efficiency. These expectations may or may not be correct. The important consideration *politically* is that they exist and are widely held.

So persuasive were the Commission's findings, that the three Maritime Provincial premiers moved quickly to follow the timetable set out for them. By the fall of 1971, they were already one year ahead of the suggested schedule in a number of important areas. It seems that the future of regional integration in the Maritimes is quite promising. Whether amalgamation of the three provinces will provide the solutions to the Maritimes' critical problems, of course, remains to be seen. Only when the time comes for action, rather than talk, will the movement toward Atlantic Union meet its crucial test. . . .

What is the relationship between negative regionalism and positive regionalism? A comprehensive answer to this question would fill many volumes. Several fascinating insights emerge, however, from a consideration of the paradoxical effect upon regionalism of federalism.

Regionalism and Federalism

Federalism (i.e., the existence of separate sub-national political units which are theoretically autonomous in at least one important sphere) is in theory an important facilitator of regionalism for the following reasons:

1. Federalism provides an explicit reminder to the citizen of a dual political status and identity. Indeed, citizens of the United States are legally referred to as citizens of the State wherein they reside. Canadian practice tends not to make explicit this dual citizenship notion, referring instead to "citizens" of Canada and "residents" of the provinces, although Quebec is becoming an obvious exception.

2. The existence of the provincial governments provides a career structure for politicians whose chief responsibility is to a sub-national community. Moreover the nature of the general relationship between sub-national and national political units almost automatically invites the provincial politician to appeal to localistic sentiments by attributing all evils and unpleasantness to the "tyrannical domination" of the national government, thereby exacerbating negative regionalism. Such "projection" of blame occurs in virtually any system/sub-system political arrangement regardless of level, considerations of nationality, class, etc. . . .

3. Provincial political authorities, like their national political counterparts (though usually to a lesser degree) are able to regulate social processes such as transportation, communications, and economics to encourage the development of sub-national socio-economic systems, Thus indirectly, federalism contributes to the strengthening of the "structural underpinnings" of provincialism. This influence even extends in Canada and elsewhere to the important spheres of education, where emphasis on provincial rather than national concerns can have lasting effects on the cognitive aspect of community. Through manipulation of the education process, young people may be inculcated with a provincial rather than a national identity.

4. Though in the U.S. few states are large enough to constitute potentially self-sustaining eco-political systems, Canadian provinces often do approximate self-contained systems, or do so in combination with two or three other provinces. Thus in Canada geography reinforces regionalism in a simpler and more direct way than in other countries such as the U.S. ("The South," for example, comprises at least 13 separate states.)

While contributing to the centrifugal forces associated with negative regionalism, federalism in some ways provides an ideal solution for resolving or minimizing potentially disintegrative conflicts inherent in regional differences. If a society is deeply divided at the mass level on religious, social or other grounds, separation of the various sub-cultures into reasonably autonomous regions permits the functioning of a system of "consociational democracy" in which the political elites display towards each other the "sense of community" lacking in the society at large. Precisely this function is served by the federal system in Canada. . . .

Though on several occasions in Canadian history, regional discontent (especially in the West) has given birth to political movements, none of these has seriously challenged the integrity of the nation. The Progressives in the "twenties" were quickly absorbed by the Liberal Party. The CCF/NDP almost from its inception embraced national aspirations which precluded its remaining a party with a purely regional outlook. Social Credit followed with a similar path, though with less success. In the past, without exception, political movements which started out deeply committed to regional or provincial objectives either collapsed before ever challenging the federal government, or themselves became involved in the national political process.

The "nationalization" of political *groups* originally regional in orientation operates on the individual level as well, as Noel observes:

> Time after time, provincial politicians with no more attachment to the federal system than the mass of their constituents become transformed in Ottawa into cabinet ministers intent on making the system work.

This is not to say that Ottawa is untouched by regional influences. Regional considerations play a large role in determining selection of cabinet ministers, for example. But the Canadian political system probably allows less scope nationally for regional factors than, say, the American. Party discipline all but prevents American style regional "bloc-voting" in the lower House; while in the weak Canadian Senate, regional representation is minimal, with approximately one-half of the seats reserved for the central regions of Ontario and Quebec. . . . Ironically, under the present electoral rules, political unification in either the Maritimes or the West would further *reduce* the representation of these regions in Parliament! [See Ward.] Furthermore, while *conceivably* strengthening the Maritimes or Western voice in some Ottawa circles, amalgamation would *definitely* reduce regional representation in such crucial gatherings as Federal-Provincial Conferences.

Another obvious point, too often underemphasized or overlooked entirely, is the fact that political unification is "bad business" for the provincial politicians and civil servants who must ultimately take the decisions to amalgamate. Not only does unification eliminate many lower-level elite positions (e.g., MPP or MLA), but it also cuts the number of high level posts (premier, cabinet minister, deputy minister, etc.) by about two-thirds. A professional politician or bureaucrat is as unlikely as anyone else to embrace fondly the opportunity of reducing his occupational life chances. . . .

In short, federalism in Canada has had a paradoxically ambivalent effect on regionalism. Though a contributing factor to "negative regionalism," especially at the popular level, the federal system fosters nationalism among the political elites through myriad subtle mechanisms and adjustments. Yet federalism tends to discourage regional integration because such a move would eliminate or reduce career opportunities for the political elite.

Conclusion: The Future of Regionalism in Canada

It is possible to discern two trends, operating simultaneously but in opposite directions, to shape the future of regionalism in Canada and elsewhere. One trend sees the extension beyond existing political boundaries of problems (such as economic development and the protection of the environment) the effective solution of which requires greater cooperation among political leaders whose current orientation tends to be narrowly local. The other trend involves a growing concern for preserving local autonomy in the fact of a sprawling, faceless bureaucracy that seems to grow like topsy. Tension between these two trends makes it difficult, if not impossible, to predict the future of regionalism. Projecting the first trend leads one to predict the increasing amalgamation of smaller political units into larger entities. In Canada this would mean a reduction in the number of provinces from ten to, say, five and perhaps even fewer. Projecting the second trend, however, leads one to expect increased momentum of the centrifugal forces that drive smaller units farther and farther away from co-operation. In Canada this could conceivably mean the breakup of the Confederation into ten (or more!) independent nations.

Perhaps the truth lies somewhere in between these two projections: *ad hoc* agencies for regional cooperation will probably continue to develop in response to specific problems that are regional in nature. Where local governments are unable to reach agreement on dealing with these issues, it is quite conceivable that the national government will intercede to encourage (or perhaps to coerce) the "necessary" degree of co-operation. At the same time, however, the progress toward actual political amalgamation will encounter many obstacles, as the molasses-like movement toward political union in Europe clearly shows. The prospects for Maritime Union seem high, but probably not as high as the Deutsch Comissioners would like us to believe. The likelihood of one Prairie Province is almost non-existent. In other words, [former B.C. Premier] W.A.C. Bennett's plan for five Canadian provinces is unlikely to materialize, though the present number may be reduced from ten to seven or eight.

All of this assumes stability of the status quo with regard to Quebec. It is, of course, tempting to back away quietly from the painful task of discussing regionalism in a Quebec-less Canada, imagining such an enterprise "unthinkable," or a likely cause of "future shock." . . . Indeed, procrastination is particularly encouraged by the tendency to treat the Quebec case as *sui generis*, thereby blinding ourselves to an otherwise unmistakable observation about the *general* malaise of Canadian federalism today. As our analysis indicates, negative regionalism is not limited to Quebec but rather is widespread throughout the country. Moreover it lies behind much of the sentiment in favour of regional integration. Not only, however, is the achievement of regional union unlikely to take place (for the reasons outlined above), but consequences of unification if it did occur are also totally unknown and (at present) unknowable. Perhaps Atlantic Union is the solution to the incredible regional disparities in Canada (which, as Merrill, 1968, reports are much worse than those in the United States). But perhaps not! Then what?

If negative regionalism is to lead to anything other than increasing frustration and anger, fresh thinking must be brought to bear on this problem, which, despite the particular sensitivity of its Quebec manifestation, is truly national in scope. Conceivably, the Department of Regional Economic Expansion might become the vehicle for an entirely new policy. It is too soon yet to tell, though early indications suggest that the Department has merely brought together under one administration the old policies which were clearly shown to be unsatisfactory. For example, no attempt has been made, as far as I know, to decentralize regional planning from Ottawa to the affected regions themselves. A major defect of the earlier policies lives on.

We find ourselves behaving exactly the way De Tocqueville described the Americans, "infinitely varying the consequences of known principles and . . . seeking for new consequences rather than . . . seeking for new principles." If ever Canada needed creative political imagination — and the bold leadership capable of implementing new ideas — the time is now. How have other nations acted to overcome negative regionalism? A number of models should be examined, including the interesting Yugoslavian attempt to confront similar problems by loosening their federation and giving greater autonomy to regional governments. This, according to Paul Fox and several other political scientists, is precisely what is happening in Canada on a *de facto* basis as a result of many factors, including changes in the relative significance of the responsibilities accorded the provinces under the B.N.A. Act. Fox points out, for example, that provincial expenditures in Ontario increased "more than 1300 per cent between 1947 and 1967." I am not suggesting, therefore, that Canadian federal-provincial relations are static; but that we have paid too little attention to the normative problem of what political arrangements will best serve Canada's social goals. Whatever approach is followed, the new policies must embrace broad concerns that go beyond the narrow horizons of economic planning.

The future of the Canadian community hinges in large part on how the political elites respond to the challenges posed by regionalism.

ARGUMENTS FOR MARITIME UNION*

APEC

A few days ago the Atlantic Provinces Economic Council presented its Submission to the Maritime Union Study. In it APEC states that it "fully endorses not only the concept of Maritime Union but also wishes to express deep concern that a single Maritime Province be created as the result of a political union of the provinces."

• • •

Three basic arguments for political union of the Maritime Provinces are set forth in the APEC submission. All evolve from fundamental economic reasoning. One is that the reasons for separation of the Maritime Provinces in the nineteenth century now appear to be reasons for union. Another is the increased quality and quantity of services which a single Maritime Province, having one administrative, judicial and economic framework, could provide from the limited provincial government revenues available to the three provinces. Still another basic reason for Maritime Union, the Council contends, is the psychological impact it would likely have on the population of the region.

---

* From the *APEC Newsletter*, 13, 3, April, 1969. By permission. For the full text of the submission, see Atlantic Provinces Economic Council, *Submission to the Maritime Union Study*, Halifax, April, 1969, mimeographed.

The acceptance of Union as an instrument for guiding the future should also motivate the region towards acceptance of still other changes — in a rapidly changing world — an attitude and condition regarded by many as a prerequisite for economic growth and development.

(1) If we look at the reasons for the separation of the Maritime Provinces into three separate entities, the state of the economy and the socio-political feeling at that time, a strong argument evolves for union of the provinces at this time. Although Prince Edward Island has always been a separate province since its creation in 1769, the province of New Brunswick was not established until 1784. What is now New Brunswick was originally part of Nova Scotia under British rule but due to numerous pressures at the end of the American Revolution, Nova Scotia was partitioned off at the isthmus so that the peninsula and the mainland became separate provinces.

Although political and social pressures influenced the British to create the province of New Brunswick, the basic underlying reason which gave rise to the move was the existing state of communications. The political motive was to create small enough units so that the British would not receive the harassment they had recently experienced from the Thirteen States. The social problem was that the primarily Loyalist population in New Brunswick feared being governed from Halifax which was both remote and peopled with what they felt were "Republican sympathizers." There was also the problem of geographical, cultural and occupational diversity both between and within the provinces.

The basic reason for separation, however, was that of communications, both in the plain old-fashioned connotation of the word — that of getting from point A to point B — and in the sense of the spread of information and ideas. Today, with relatively good transportation systems and the rapidity of such forms of transportation as air travel; the predominance of radios, televisions and newspapers; and a highly educated public, the population is not only more mobile but much better informed than at any time in the history of the region. Thus, since there has been such a dramatic change in the economy of the region and in life in general, and since the reasons for separation now seem so archaic, it would seem that Maritime Union is the logical step to be taken in an age where a total systems approach is the order of the day.

(2) The Council feels that much of the rationale for Maritime Union is economic in nature. Although Maritime Union is often endorsed on the understanding that the implementation of administrative, judicial and economic co-ordination will ultimately lead to political union, the Council contends that although some informal institutional arrangements may be made towards the creation of a union, the presence and rigidity of present institutions in the region can only be overcome through complete Maritime political union.

. . . APEC believes that the Maritime Provinces are facing a threat today, more serious than in the history of the region.

The threat, as we see it, is both internal and external. Internally, it is the rapidly rising demand for services in the three provinces and the resultant increases in provincial government expenditures, while increases in revenues needed to pay for these services fail to keep pace. Externally, the threat is that if the three provincial governments do not strive to act, together, through union, to increase the level of efficiency (in the pure economic sense of the word — of producing the optimum output at minimum cost) and the quality of services offered, demands for federal funds to cover increased costs in these provincial responsibilities could lead to the provincial governments finding themselves in the unenviable position of becoming mere "colonies" of Ottawa.

One example which shows quite clearly the opportunity for increased efficiency in the region is the excessive number of departmental employees in the three provinces relative to population as compared to other Canadian provinces.

For instance, in 1967, there were 24,106 persons employed in departments of the three provincial governments to cater to a population of 1,486,000. This represents a ratio of one employee per 61.6 of population. These ratios in the three provinces were: Prince Edward Island, 1:50.0; Nova Scotia, 1:56.1 and New Brunswick, 1:73.6. The ratio for the nation excluding British Columbia, and the Atlantic Provinces on the other hand, was 1:106.1 with ratios ranging from 1:71.4 in Alberta to the 1:117.1 in Quebec and 1:114.9 in Ontario. In fact, for the figures available, the ratios for all of the other provinces are higher than those in the Atlantic Provinces with the exception of Alberta's, which was lower than that of New Brunswick.

This, of course, has important implications in dollars and cents terms. If the ratio in the Maritime Provinces (1:61.6) had been the same as that for the rest of Canada, (1:106.1), only 14,006 would have been employed, instead of the actual 24,106. An increase in productivity in this one aspect of government activity would have meant a gross payroll (if paid the Maritime Provinces' average of $3,743) of approximately $52 million in 1967. This increased efficiency then would have been worth almost $38 million — a relative saving of over 40 percent. It must be pointed out that it would probably be unrealistic to expect the ratio to approach that of the nation as a whole, at the present economic state of the region because of the unique factors which characterize it. This is particularly relevant when our smaller total population and our relatively larger rural populations are considered. These and other factors pose a problem since the economics of scale in the provision of public services cannot be called into play. However, even though the suggested savings figure may be high there is another significant factor. Salary scales for civil servants could be upgraded and greater challenge offered to attract a larger proportion of more highly qualified personnel.

In its Submission APEC analyzes the revenue and expenditure figures of the Maritime Provinces and the rest of the Canadian provinces for the period 1953-67. The figures used are net figures since these are the closest approximation available on which to make comparisons both on a province-to-province and a year-to-year basis.

This analysis reveals that not only has the composition of each side of the provincial financial accounts changed, but also that growth in some segments far outdistanced that in others over the 1953-67 period. Another observation is that although there are some similarities between all the Canadian provinces on one hand, and the Maritime Provinces on the other, in the direction of changes in components, there are some very marked differences in the magnitude of the changes.

Looking first at total net general revenue, it becomes evident that the revenue of all provinces combined has grown at a faster rate than it has for any of the Maritime Provinces. While the rate for All Provinces was 11.6 percent per year, the rates of the three Maritime Provinces were 10.9 percent, 9.3 percent and 8.4 percent for Prince Edward Island, Nova Scotia and New Brunswick, respectively, for the period. Although there is a significant difference between the rates of increase of All Provinces and the Maritime Provinces in total net general revenue, a more significant difference exists in the composition of the aggregate in the region as opposed to the other provinces.

The most striking aspect of the components which combine to make up total net general revenue is the conspicuousness of the amount and growth of revenue received from the other governments by the provincial governments in the region. Firstly, revenue from other governments has increased at more than twice the yearly rate for All Provinces in each of the Maritime Provinces — by 7.9 percent in Prince Edward Island and New Brunswick, and 7.2 percent in Nova Scotia, compared to 3.6 percent in All Provinces. Secondly, the proportion of total net general revenue received from other governments (almost exclusively the federal government) has remained consistently much higher in the Maritime Provinces than for All Provinces, and the gap is widening. Whereas the proportion received by the Maritime Provinces was almost double that of All Provinces in the early 1950s, it is now almost four times as high, at a level approaching 40 percent as opposed to about 10 percent.

The dominance of revenue received from other governments in the Maritime Provinces has, of course, repercussions on the relative size of revenues received by the provincial governments from other sources. For instance, total Tax Revenue for All Provinces increased from 38.7 percent of total net general revenue in 1953 to 68.0 percent in 1967. For the Maritime Provinces it increased from 27.7 percent to 44.3 percent. Both Tax Revenue and Non-Tax Revenue increased at substantially higher annual rates in All Provinces than in any of the three Maritime Provinces.

Looking at provincial expenditures, total net general expenditures of All Provinces increased at an average rate of 12.5 per cent per year compared to the lower rates in the Maritime Provinces — Prince Edward Island, 11.1 percent; Nova Scotia, 10.3 percent; and New Brunswick, 8.9 percent. Putting both net general revenue and net general expenditures together, the most obvious conclusion that can be drawn is that spending seems to be growing faster than revenues, not only in the Maritime Provinces, but, also, in most of the other provinces as well. Over the 1953-67 period, the average yearly rates of increase in spending were greater than in revenue for all the entities considered: 12.5 percent as opposed to 11.6 percent for All Provinces, 11.1 percent versus 10.9 percent for Prince Edward Island (inflated by the heavy increase in revenue at the end of the period), 10.3 percent versus 9.3 percent for Nova Scotia, and 8.9 percent versus 8.4 percent for New Brunswick.

Since the tables used were adjusted for comparability, it is probably safe to say that the differences are of a greater magnitude than reflected in the annual rates of increase, even when it is realized that the rates are compounded for every year from 1953 to 1967.

Comparison of the figures for Gross Provincial, Regional and National Products with the respective net general expenditure figures reveals a general movement across the nation towards spending a larger proportion of output. Not only have provincial government expenditures in the Maritime Provinces exceeded increases in output, but also Maritime Provinces' governments continue to spend a significantly higher proportion of output than do All Provinces.

APEC's Submission emphasizes the importance of the increased efficiency which could come about as the result of political union of the three Maritime Provinces.

Surely, three provinces with combined populations of only 1,486,000 do not require three departments of agriculture, fisheries, forestry, health and welfare, etc. In fact, the population after union, would probably be significantly less than three-quarters of Metropolitan Toronto or Montreal. For instance, in 1966, the total population of the Maritime Provinces was equivalent to about 68 percent of the population of Metropolitan Toronto (2,159,000) and approximately 60 percent of the population of Metropolitan Montreal (2,437,000). With the implementation of political union for the Maritime Provinces, at least some of the economies of scale may come into play.

Not only would political union with the resultant accompanying administrative, judicial and economic unions mean dollars and cents savings for government in the region, but it could also lead to an increase in the quality of services.

(3) The Submission also stresses the value of political union of the Maritime Provinces to the industrial and overall economic development of the region. It points out that the establishment of priorities and the successful implementation of policy can only be achieved by changing the institutions which have been built up to deal with industrial development. Since their establishment, many of them in the last decade, duplication and rivalry have occurred not only between provinces but within provinces as well. . . . It would seem then that it is the institutional framework within which each development planning agency is set — that of individual provinces — that needs to be abolished before complete coordination and cooperation can be achieved. Maritime Union seems to be the most logical answer. . . . By concentrating growth at growth points, the spin-off to the rest of the Maritimes could lead to a faster sustained rate of growth for the entire region.

• • •

ONE PRAIRIE PROVINCE: HISTORICAL AND POLITICAL PERSPECTIVES*

Norman Ward

The union of the three Prairie provinces into one seems so obviously to offer a solution to some of the problems of a chronically vulnerable area that it is hardly surprising that unification is a recurring theme in western Canadian history. . . .

It would be unfair, however, to dismiss all unification schemes as examples of restlessness. The Prairies' common resource base; their shared problems of exporting, at the mercy of world markets, raw materials that do not lend themselves to fancy packaging or any other kind of differentiation that might help them sell; and their consistent victimization (as they see it) at the hands of absentee merchants, bankers and manufacturers who produce the machinery, canned goods and mortgages so indispensable to life on the plains; all these provide good reasons for huddling together in search of a comfort that no outside element is likely to supply. If in union lies strength, One Prairie Province suggests not only larger muscles in grappling with the rest of the world, but a healthy loss of weight as overlapping layers of political and bureaucratic fat are reduced. And with rapid developments in communication and transportation, the larger unit is generally attractive, for if largeness works for hospital and school districts, why not for provinces? A brief visit to the uninhabitable parts of any North American metropolis might of course raise some doubts as to whether largeness of itself brings virtue; but in our drearier cities one of the facts of life rests on the absence of space — and space is one thing the Prairies still have.

They had it in the beginning in such abundance, indeed, that sheer size was one of the chief reasons why three provinces were established in the first place. The Prairies, Prime Minister Sir Wilfrid Laurier said in 1905, were "altogether too large an area to be made into one single province according to the size of the other provinces.". . .

There is a history of suggestions for Prairie union, and it is varied and long; not so long, to be sure, as Maritime union, whose historian has traced it back to 1806, and subtitled his work "A Study in Frustration." The internal pressures towards Prairie union, as with the Maritimes, commonly coincide with perceived pressures from outside the region; and the striking similarities between Prairie and Maritime union, based as they are on a common search for an antidote to central Canadian influence and a remedy for the ailment now called alienation, suggest that the two may be worthy of joint study as a phenomenon associated with a twentieth century form of colonialism that can exist among political units that are theoretically equal in law and constitution but not in economics. . . .

To begin with, one cannot contemplate Prairie union without almost being overwhelmed by the sheer magnitude of the task. With one single ma-

* From Elton, D.K., ed., *One Prairie Province? Conference and Selected Papers*, Lethbridge, *Lethbridge Herald*, 1970. By permission.

jor exception — the absence of a dichotomy separating English-speaking from French-speaking — the unification of the Prairies is by almost any measurable standard an incomparably larger union than was Confederation itself; and it is important to remember that Confederation was possible partly because the Fathers could settle many vexing problems by assigning to the provinces, as separate entities, many subjects of legislation which in a unified Prairie will have to be consolidated. The combined area of the Prairie provinces is now three-quarters that of the modern area of the four provinces created in 1867; but both Ontario and Quebec are now at least twice the size they were in 1867. A far higher proportion of the Prairie area is privately owned than is the case to this day in Ontario and Quebec, holding promise of an almost infinite complexity if property and civil rights are to be unified under one set of laws. The population of the Prairies is roughly comparable to the Canada of 1867; but the population of 1867 demanded from its Dominion and provincial governments combined services costing, in round figures, twenty million dollars. The combined budgets of the three Prairie provinces alone in 1970 are almost exactly a hundred times greater, at two billion. The total number of public servants in both Dominion and provincial jurisdictions in 1867 is difficult to determine with precision, but seven thousand would be a generous estimate; the Prairie provinces today employ seventy thousand. The variety and quality of the services offered today by the Prairies' modern governments is vastly greater than the simple activity of 1867. On the eve of Confederation for example, the combined provinces of Nova Scotia, New Brunswick and Canada were spending annually $2.6 million on transportation, including roads and bridges; Saskatchewan alone in 1969 was spending twenty-five times as much on highways. The original provinces in 1866 spent 9½ per cent of their budgets on education, and less than 5 per cent on public welfare; today they spend roughly one-third on education, and another third on health and welfare. I am not suggesting that the massive nature of these changes means that unification of the Prairie provinces is impossible; I am suggesting that the enterprise would require a colossal amount of political and administrative energy, at a time when the same skills might be better utilized elsewhere. After 1867, the relatively simple adjustment of governmental accounts, and the sorting out of public works and their related debts, nonetheless took several years.

Quantity alone is a misleading indicator of the kinds of adjustments that would be necessary for Prairie unification. Property and civil rights; health, welfare and labor legislation; and local electoral laws, are all under provincial jurisdiction in Canada, and the three Prairie provinces have all read differing meanings into them. Alberta has pioneered among the three with a provincial ombudsman, and Manitoba with an independent commission for drawing constituency boundaries; the Saskatchewan legislature has repeatedly rejected both these developments. Saskatchewan pioneered with hospitalization and medicare, and political rights for civil servants, and all of these have come more slowly to Alberta and Manitoba. Utilities that are under public enterprises in Saskatchewan and Manitoba, are private in Alberta. Saskatchewan has compulsory public automobile insurance, but the other two provinces do not. Legal minimum wages are different in the provinces, and so are provisions for separate schools. All three Prairie provinces experimented with dropping the voting age before the Dominion got around to it, but not simultaneously, and not to the same level.

These examples (and there are dozens more) support two separate propositions: if, as is commonly asserted, one of the great advantages of federalism is that it permits widespread local experimentation in public policy, the reduction of three active laboratories to one would mean a serious loss to both the region and the country; and the differing kinds of experimentation that the three have indulged in denotes that the provinces are politically a lot more different than a superficial look at their common economic problems might suggest. (And even economically, it may be added parenthetically, the provinces are more different than they appear.) The first of these propositions, given the known facts of prairie history, hardly needs demonstration. The second leads one to ponder why Alberta's reaction to the modern period was to turn to Social Credit, Saskatchewan's to the Co-operative Commonwealth Foundation, and Manitoba's to a long run of coalition governments that did not include either Social Credit or the C.C.F. Alberta has had the United Farmers of Alberta and Social Credit. . . . Saskatchewan did have one Conservative administration, but never more than a handful of Social Crediters in the legislature. Manitoba, though given to coalitions in the past, is the only one of the three to have had fairly conventional periods of history with alternating Liberal and Conservative governments, but it has recently turned to the New Democratic Party. The parliamentary tradition itself varies among the Prairie provinces, for both C.C.F. and Liberal governments in Saskatchewan, for example, have had to be tolerant of large robust oppositions of a kind that have at times virtually disappeared from the other two.

The party history of the provinces is such as to make one wonder if a single Prairie legislature would ever know anything but minority governments. . . . The most strongly entrenched party in one province was by far the weakest in the other two. . . . The Liberals, on the other hand, who in 1966-67 were in power in one province and formed the official opposition in one other, would, on an even distribution of that vote over our single-member constituencies, form the government of One Prairie Province. A similar test of the elections of 1959-60 provides a roughly similar result, with the parties in the same order but a little more closely bunched.

Exercises such as these are only exercises; but they do emphasize that, barring coalition or minority governments, a unified Prairie province would mean that three differing administrations would be reduced to one, an inevitable step away from diversity towards uniformity. All the Prairie minority groups, whatever their language, would similarly find themselves reduced from three governments to one more scattered group doing the same with one government, but one now larger and that much more remote. Unless the single province's legislature was to be as large as the current three together, provincial constituencies will have to be larger too; and since one of the great advantages that provincial parties on the Prairies have over their federal counterparts is the relative proximity of the elected provincial member to his constituents, at least some of that would be lost in union. Further, unless a drastic change occurs in the patterns of population growth on the Prairies, within a single province, seats in the assembly would inevitably gravitate from east to west, away from Saskatchewan and

Manitoba, in that order, and towards Alberta. I think to put all this in a single sentence, that unification of the Prairie provinces would for a long time impose severe strains on representative democracy on the plains, with an accompanying loss of attention to local particularities. Federalism, as one wise Canadian scholar has observed, is probably the best known method of applying democracy to huge areas.

Yet even in the existing Prairies the benefits of representative democracy have not penetrated very convincingly into the provinces' northern halves. The large proportions of those populations that are uniformly poor, unorganized, and Indian or Metis, have been known about for years; yet even in Saskatchewan, the alleged socialism of the C.C.F. seemed peculiarly reserved for citizens of European descent, and it is only within the past year that a special service to take utilities into the north was organized under the province's public power corporation. In 1969 the first wholly Indian community to have gas piped to it was added to the corporation's books. If one takes into account the whole range of labor, education, health and welfare policies under provincial control, and the differing impacts of these on the northern and southern halves of the provinces, it is difficult to conclude from the record that the northern halves are likely to be better off under one government. I do not mean to suggest that nothing has been done, or that there are not sincere and able men concerned about the Prairies' northern poor. What I am saying is that the people of the north have enough difficulty now under the governments they have: how much better off will they be if the government is made that much larger and more remote, and preoccupied for years with fitting together the political and administrative jigsaw puzzles that unification will make of the south?

The north's problems are partly economic, of course, which serves to remind us that many political problems are inseparable from economics. Let me cite two that seem to be of almost pressing relevance where One Prairie Province is concerned. . . . It is inconceivable that the Dominion should take over the current debts of the Prairie provinces, totalling (in the last year for which official statistics are readily available) nearly one billion dollars in direct debt, and an additional nine hundred and fifty million of additional obligations, mostly guarantees on bonds and debentures. . . . This total burden is unevenly distributed: in the year cited, the direct per capita debt in Alberta was $27, that in Saskatchewan $587; the per capita indirect debt in Alberta was $349, in Saskatchewan $38. If in that year the provinces had had to meet all their obligations, the per capita burden would have been $805 in Manitoba, $625 in Saskatchewan, and $376 in Alberta. Manifestly, any consolidation of those debts would have involved a considerable transfer of burdens to the taxpayers of what is now Alberta.

Statistics are notoriously unreliable, of course, and taking one recent isolated year from a sequence does not permit one to come to precise conclusions; the point is that large variations, in matters of fundamental importance to politics, do exist among the Prairie provinces, and the story is much the same no matter what yardstick one uses. If one takes public school enrolment for the latest year for which official figures are available, and divides it into the total income of school boards, the boards in Manitoba spent $311 for each pupil, in Saskatchewan $363, and in Alberta $399; Alberta school boards, that is, spent over 20 per cent more on each pupil than Manitoba. The differences do not end there: Manitoba boards in that year received 59 per cent of their total income from local taxation, Saskatchewan 55 per cent, and Alberta 51 per cent. The boards' relative net bonded indebtedness showed a different picture: in Saskatchewan the boards' debts totalled 68 per cent of one year's revenue, in Alberta 108 per cent. Teachers' salaries also reveal major variations, with Alberta paying the largest annual average by a considerable margin.

Here again, these figures are not to be taken as gospel: what is significant about them is the consistent pattern of variation revealed, suggesting the scope of what would be involved in unification. In a united province all services provided by the single government will have to be levelled out, for it is hardly reasonable to expect Manitoba and Saskatchewan to accept membership in it as permanent poor relations. The pattern also indicates that in financial terms the burden will be largely Alberta's unless, as appears improbable, the taxpayers of Alberta are prepared to have all services levelled downwards in each individual instance to whichever of the three provinces has been spending the least.

These generalizations are sound of internal adjustments, and they are also relevant to an important external circumstance: under existing Dominion-provincial financial relations, Manitoba is a regular "have not" province, and Saskatchewan has just reentered that category after having briefly escaped from it. As have-nots, Manitoba and Saskatchewan together receive in federal subsidies, distinct from shared-cost programs, about fifty million dollars a year more than Alberta. Whether or not One Prairie Province would be a have or have-not province rests on a calculation I do not have the information to make; but whether it qualifies or not, Alberta is sufficiently wealthier than Manitoba and Saskatchewan that the creation of One Prairie Province would unquestionably shift a major financial burden from Ottawa to Alberta. If, indeed, a united Prairie province qualifed as a "have" province, that whole fifty million — or whatever it might be — would have to be found within the province; and if it could be found within Manitoba and Saskatchewan, they would not be qualifying for the subsidies now. The alternative, of course, would be to eliminate the governmental services the money pays for.

And if One Prairie Province now is going to cost Alberta taxpayers a great deal, it must be added that a different kind of burden will rest on Manitoba and Saskatchewan. In a general sense, since Canada is internally what is generally called a free trade area, nobody on the Prairie will gain access to any new markets merely by the elimination of two artificial boundaries. But in a particular sense, the inevitable shifting of both political and economic weight westward within a single province has important implications for the central and eastern section: in a word, they may well find in significant aspects of their politics that they have merely exchanged Toronto for Edmonton or Calgary.

This westward gravitation is nowhere more apparent than in the certain fate of Prairie seats in Parliament if one province is formed. It is often said that one good reason for merging the provinces is that it will give muscle to our parliamentary representation by providing one bloc of western seats, and one legitimate comment on that is that it will be muscle in grave danger of immediate atrophy. To begin with, given the Prairies' demonstrated political proclivities, there is no reason whatever to assume that the federal western members will act any more as a bloc than they usually do now. Secondly, even if they do, but are on the Opposition side in the Commons (another familiar pattern) a western bloc of members may not be in a position to do the west much good. Thirdly, acting as a bloc would in any event stimulate the formation of other blocs, and the two central provinces between them have one hundred and sixty-two seats to the Prairies' forty-five. And in One Prairie Province, those forty-five would be a lot less secure than they are now.

That conclusion rests on two separate bases: the Prairie's changing share of Canada's population, and the rules governing the distribution of seats in the House of Commons. . . .

One of the rules governing the distribution of seats says that no province, at any one redistribution, can lose more than fifteen per cent of the number of seats to which it was entitled at the last redistribution. Once a province's representation drops to thirteen, it can drop only one seat at the next redistribution, because two seats would be more than fifteen per cent. Saskatchewan has already been saved once by the 15 per cent rule, and under present projections will be saved one seat in 1971; Manitoba will probably not need the rule in 1971, but it will in 1981. The Prairies, in short, need the protection of the rule, but its protection would become all but meaningless under a united province.

That observation receives added point from another calculation: no province can have fewer seats in the Commons than it has senators, and as a result the three Maritime provinces, which have unusually large quotas of senators in relation to their size, will get six extra seats in 1971. Unlike seats added to the House of Commons under the 15 per cent rule, seats saved by the senatorial floor come out of a fixed basis provincial membership of 261, and therefore the extra Maritime seats come at the expense of the other provinces. It is virtually certain that in 1971 two of the Maritimes' bonus of six will come at the expense of the Prairies. . . . With all these special protections for provinces whose populations are becoming smaller fractions of the Dominion total, it is important to note that by 1971 one M.P. in Prince Edward Island will represent 27,500 people, in New Brunswick 62,300, and in Nova Scotia 76,500; but the comparable Manitoba figure is 81,500, Saskatchewan's is 79,000, and Alberta's is 83,400. All these averages are based on projections which the 1971 census may to some extent upset; but there can be little doubt that for the next census or two the three provinces will have a strong case to make about their parliamentary representation which they will lose automatically once united. [See Chapter 9 of this book for new arrangements.]

The same argument, in a different way, has strength in connection with Dominion-provincial conferences, which are obviously playing an increasingly important part in Canadian politics. If the Maritime provinces unite (and they have shown few signs of hustling into that) One Prairie Province would have one seat out of seven at the conferences: if the Maritimes do not unite, one seat out of nine. Given the small size of the conferences, and the forceful nature of most of our premiers, it is difficult to accept unquestioningly the view that the Prairie would be better off with those odds than they are now with three voices out of eleven. It is impossible to guess how Prairie representation in the federal cabinet might be affected by union, but if prairie seats in the Commons drop sharply, the present boundaries are a better safeguard for three prairie ministers than a united province would offer.

Since so much of this paper has been negative comment on One Prairie Province, I should like to conclude it by suggesting that most of the benefits of union, without its birth pangs and fitful childhood, could be achieved through devices such as the Prairie Economic Council, which has already effected a major agreement over water resources. All three provinces have common law systems; and all three have demonstrated an impressive capacity for co-operation in the past: Prairie highways, for example, do not end abruptly at provincial boundaries, but run straight into other highways. There is no need to multiply examples; but there may be a need to emphasize that increasing co-operative ventures among the provinces may in the long run be cheaper, both in monetary and non-monetary terms, than union.

No doubt there is now some wasteful duplication of political and administrative facilities that might conceivably be eliminated through union; although offhand I cannot recall a single example of a government growing smaller because of major reorganization. Size of itself seems to create new demands for research and the seeking of new ways to keep competent staff employed. The prime costs of modern government, in any event, are largely substantive rather than administrative: if one could reduce to zero the administrative costs of a provincial department of education, for example, the entire cost of maintaining and manning the school system would remain. If one could eliminate entirely the indemnities of legislative members and cabinet ministers, the resultant reduction in provincial budgets would be almost imperceptible. The machinery of government, although it has grown astoundingly in recent decades, has long since ceased to be the main cause of public expenditure: it's the machinery's end products — highways, university and school systems, hospital, health and welfare benefits — that really cost money, and there is no reason to suppose that Prairie union would reduce the demand for any of those.

Still the Prairies' political record is such as to indicate that if the prairie citizens want union, they will get it. After all, as a disgruntled champion of Maritime union, after speaking well of the benefits to be gained from that, said over sixty years ago: "We cannot do it while separated. We are ignored by the Dominion Government; the West gets whatever it asks for . . . "

REGIONAL DISPARITIES IN CANADA*

Economic Council of Canada

"Ever since Confederation," the Economic Council pointed out in its *First Annual Review* of 1964, "the notion of 'balanced regional development' has been an implicit, if not explicit, objective of national policy."

* From Economic Council of Canada, *Living Together: A Study of Regional Disparities*, Ottawa, Supply and Services, 1977. Reproduced by permission of the Minister of Supply and Services.

Over the past decade and a half, the pursuit of this goal has become considerably more precise — and more pressing. . . . A number of policies and programs have been initiated or expanded by governments at all levels in an effort to achieve this objective.

Some discernible progress has been made, even though it has been uneven. Particularly in the Atlantic provinces, income disparities have been reduced. In more recent years, there has been a slight reduction in relative unemployment levels and some slowing or reversal of the outflow of migrants to greener pastures, which had posed a threat to the economic, political, social, and cultural viability of the regions they left behind. A somewhat greater measure of equality of opportunity has also been created in all regions. In relation to the vast amount of time, money, and effort that has been devoted to the task, however, success in achieving a better regional balance has been disappointing. . . .

• • •

Do Regional Disparities Exist?

There is no universally accepted criterion for judging whether life is really better in some parts of Canada than in others, but a wide variety of facts suggest that individual well-being does indeed differ from one region to another. After more than 350 years of settlement, people have certainly not distributed themselves uniformly, either among or within the provinces. On the contrary, with the exception of centres where the local industry is based on natural resources, there is something of an inverse relationship between the density of population, on the one hand, and the harshness of the climate and the relative distance from major markets in the United States, on the other. Presumably, people and businesses have to be compensated in some way if they are to be encouraged to locate in the colder, more isolated regions and pay the higher transportation costs to markets that these regions face. The compensation and job opportunities offered in these regions in the past have obviously not been sufficient to attract many people. But, even in the more populated regions, disparities of income and opportunity exist. The probability of being rich or poor and finding a job differs even among these places.

The material well-being of a society depends not only on absolute wealth and purchasing power, but also on their distribution among individuals and families. Because there are returns to scale in family living, the same income per capita goes farther if a society is primarily comprised of families rather than individuals living alone. There will also be less discontent in society if the wealth is not unduly concentrated in the hands of a few or if the income distribution does not change too quickly. These factors differ from region to region. For example, in 1970 the average Newfoundland family had roughly one more child and about one-third less income than its Ontario counterpart and, apart from housing, it faced a higher cost of living; these factors help explain why Newfoundland is an area of net out-migration and Ontario is not.

• • •

Personal Income Per Capita

There has been a persistent pattern of regional disparity in per capita incomes over the past half century, although there has been a very slow convergence towards the national average, especially since 1954 (Chart 1). Historical events have caused some notable variations in these patterns. . . .

Unemployment

Giving a man a job solves a lot of problems. Unfortunately, the unemployment rates show that the success with which people find and hold jobs differs markedly from region to region (Chart 2). The pattern of regional disparities in unemployment is as persistent as that of differences in income per capita, and it favours the same regions, with only one exception; whereas income per capita is higher in British Columbia than in the Prairies,

CHART 1

INDEX OF PERSONAL INCOME PER CAPITA, CANADA, BY REGION, 1926-75

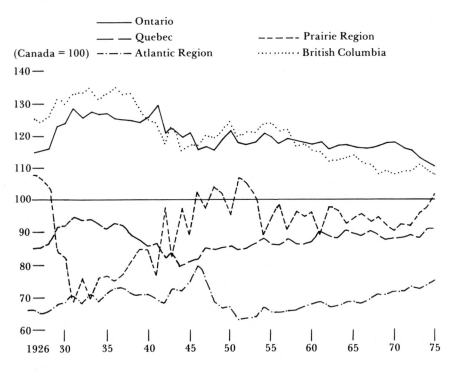

Source: Data from Statistics Canada

the reverse is true for unemployment. From 1953 to 1975, the unemployment rate in British Columbia averaged 6.0 per cent, nearly twice the rate of 3.3 per cent recorded in the Prairies. The unemployment rate in the Atlantic region was the worst, at 8.6 per cent, while the second worst rate was in Quebec, at 7.0 per cent. A point that is less obvious is that, when unemployment across Canada increases, it increases most in the regions where it is already the highest. Past experience shows that an increase of 2 percentage points in the Canadian unemployment rate is typically accompanied by an increase of roughly 3.7 points in the Atlantic region, 2.6 points in Quebec, 1.3 points in Ontario, 1.7 points in the Prairie region, and 1.9 points in British Columbia. . . .

CHART 2

UNEMPLOYMENT RATE, CANADA, BY REGION, 1953-75

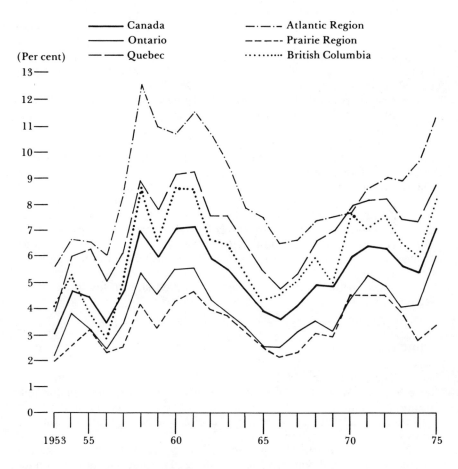

Source: Data from Statistics Canada

Technology, Management, and Other Factors

Besides industrial structure, output per worker, labour quality, and capital stock, a great variety of factors influences the productivity performance of an industry. They include the adoption of new technology, the efforts dedicated to research and development, managerial ability, aggressiveness in seeking markets, worker attitudes, natural resource endowment, the size of a city in which a firm is located, the economic environment of the manufacturing and service industries, returns to scale, local and export market demand, and the cost of transportation.

The contributions of these factors to regional differences in output per worker are estimated residually under management, technology, and other factors. . . . Together they account for about one-third of the regional variations in output per worker of the provincial economies and the goods-producing industries and for a much larger share in the manufacturing sector. Much more significantly, where low income is a really serious problem — in the Atlantic region — these residual factors are very much more important. In Newfoundland, Nova Scotia, and New Brunswick, they never account for less than 60 per cent of the difference from the national average. It would be difficult to rank the residual factors in order of importance, but it is generally thought that technology and managerial ability play a crucial role.

The most important single reason why Canada produces twice as much per capita as it did a generation ago is that it uses far more advanced technology today. More capital per head, a better-educated work force, a greater degree of specialization and scale, resource development, and other factors, all play a role; but none is individually as important as technology.

Canada's five regions are far enough apart and weakly enough linked that differences in their average levels of technology may well exist and persist among them. The Atlantic region, for example, may be ahead of Ontario in a few technological areas but, on average, its level of technology could be lower; this, in turn, could account for a part — perhaps an important part — of the gap in productivity per worker between the two regions. It should not be concluded, however, that regions where technology is less advanced have failed to adopt any technical innovations, but simply that, in general, new methods of production are adopted later in low-productivity regions. . . .

Summary

. . . There were more children per family in 1971 in Quebec than in Ontario and the West, but its reduced birth rate suggests that, in the near future, it will have fewer children per family and a smaller youth dependency ratio. As a result, its income per capita can be expected to converge towards that of the western provinces.

An important matter is Quebec's relatively slow rates of growth in population and employment. Quebec's share of the national population has declined about 2.5 percentage points since 1947 and is now back to what it was in 1921. Population projections indicate a further decline of some 1 to 4 points by the year 2001. Since the francophone population is concentrated in Quebec, these figures have implications for the ability of French- speaking Canadians to make their voices heard in a federation whose population is slowly becoming more anglophone.

Whether one looks at income per capita or purchasing power per family, the Atlantic region has the lowest incomes. Newfoundland and Prince Edward Island are in an unfavourable position relative to Nova Scotia and New Brunswick. This low standard of living is confirmed by social indicators on housing, health, and education. The Atlantic region also has the poorest (least symmetrical) income distributions, apart from that for the dual society in the Northwest Territories. Its wages and salaries per employed worker are the lowest, and its unemployment rates are the highest. In a period of recession, its unemployment rate rises the most, and its unemployed workers stay out of work the longest. Since its workers have a lower incentive than others to enter the labour force, it is not surprising that Atlantic participation rates are so low.

In sum, regional disparities in incomes and job opportunities are indeed substantial and remarkably persistent in spite of the amount of labour migration that has taken place over the years.

Conclusions and Recommendations

Disparities in Canada are surprisingly large — certainly larger than many of us expected and larger than they need to be or ought to be. And it does not seem likely that migration of individuals in search of better opportunities can make any major contribution towards eliminating them in the foreseeable future. As far as the sources of disparities are concerned, a number of seldom discussed causes have turned out to be of great importance. In particular, the roles of human capital, demand, technology gaps, urbanization, and perhaps even government expenditures for non-regional purposes have all been underemphasized relative to the emphasis traditionally placed on the roles of industrial structure, physical capital, resource endowments, and transportation. A recognition of the importance of these rarely discussed causes leads us to believe that the arsenal of effective policy weapons could be broadened with little or no increase in taxes and that there is scope for much more provincial action; we are therefore optimistic about what can be done. Present federal efforts through DREE are small, but they do seem to be having fruitful results, as do the large expenditures on equalization payments. Finally, and this is far from being a conventional caveat, there is an enormous amount of research still to be done. The factors underlying regional disparities have turned out to be extraordinarily complex.

The Size of Disparities

. . . Our investigation in Chapter 4 shows that regional differences in rates of unemployment and rates of employment growth cannot be gainsaid; they are large and clear-cut. Income disparities, however, do vary quite a bit, depending on the method of measurement. It depends on whether one speaks of families or of individuals, of earned income or of total income, and whether one takes into account regional differences in price levels and tax rates, and so on. While the Atlantic provinces remain poor no matter how one looks at income, it is less certain that there are significant income differences among the other provinces. Social indicators also cloud the disparity issue somewhat, for who can say categorically that lower divorce and suicide rates, for example, do not outweigh lower incomes and poorer job opportunities?

All this being said, we are impressed that no amount of juggling with statistics can lead any reasonable person to deny that economic well-being is sharply affected by the region in which one happens to be born or brought up. In short, disparities are real.

Migration as a Cure

At the beginning of our research, we thought that natural economic mechanisms, migration of people, and movements of firms might suffice to resolve Canada's regional disparity problems, particularly the unemployment and income problems in the Atlantic region and Québec, if they were permitted and encouraged to operate freely. That does not seem to be the case. While no published data exist to determine whether firms are relocating in an equilibrating fashion, information is available on the migration of people, and it does not seem to be doing the job.

It could, of course, be argued that out-migration is stopping the disparities from getting wider, especially in the Atlantic region; but that is not the same as narrowing them. The same is true for Quebec; and, for this province especially, it is worth stressing that any increase in out-migration, regardless of whether it cured unemployment and income problems, could be seen as a cure that was worse than the disease. It is less certain whether Atlantic residents would feel this way. . . . But migration as a complete cure for the Atlantic region's unemployment and income problems would probably be a very long and slow process. Even with double the average outflow of the past twenty years, it would be many decades before substantial alleviation of the problems was achieved. Thus, while the individual initiative implicit in the migration process should be encouraged by providing more information on what is possible, it is not realistic to rely solely upon migration as a solution to regional disparities in the Atlantic region or, for that matter, anywhere else.

Rarely Discussed Causes of Disparities

We have shown that regional differences in income are very closely related to differences in productivity. Yet the most commonly cited cause of regional problems — poor industrial structure — can only explain a very small part of the productivity differences. Capital per employee, corrected for industrial structure — another frequently hypothesized cause of productivity differences — does better. But most productivity problems cannot be explained by poor industry structure or by lack of capital. At least three other less commonly considered factors are important.

First, labour quality differs among provinces, and by enough to explain a significant and policy-correctable part of the productivity differences. Most of the variation in labour quality appears to be traceable to differences between provinces in educational attainment — this despite the great effort that has gone into education over the last decade or so. Second, there is some evidence that the achieved level of technology is not geographically uniform within Canada. It has not so far proved feasible to pin down the quantitative importance of these technology gaps in accounting for regional productivity differences; but they do exist, and it would not seem impossible to close them up somewhat. . . . Finally, productivity is also favourably affected by the proportion of a region's population that resides in cities and, up to a limit of perhaps a population of 1½ million or so, by the proportion that resides in the larger cities.

Variations in industry structure, capital availability, educational attainment, technology, and urban structure are not the only sources of regional productivity differences. A more complete listing would also include differing potential for the exploitation of scale economies, varying ability to exploit comparative advantage resulting from regional differences in market accessibility and transportation cost, and variations in the quality and quantity of available mineral and agricultural resources as one moves across the land. There can be little doubt that these factors partially explain why Newfoundland's productivity is lower than Ontario's. But the emphasis in this report has been on those factors which are not only important for productivity but are also fairly readily amendable to influence by government policy. . . .

Broadening the Policy Arsenal

Canada presently has three weapons designed specifically to fight regional disparities. They are, in decreasing order of importance in terms of the proportion of total federal expenditures that these programs represent, equalization payments, the Department of Regional Economic Expansion, and the Manpower Mobility Program. It is possible that, dollar for dollar, small programs can be more effective than large ones. Equalization payments correct for the inability of certain regions to generate enough output and income to pay for an adequate level of government services, by transferring money from the richer provinces to the poorer ones. The Department of Regional Economic Expansion has the more complex task — less certain in its effectiveness — of correcting the inability of certain regions to generate output and income by encouraging firms to settle and expand there and by otherwise generating development opportunities. Manpower mobility programs get people out of a region where they cannot earn, or cannot earn enough, and help them to go where they can.

The attack on disparities can move beyond these programs, and at not much cost, except in terms of ingenuity and will. Our analysis of the determinants of productivity shows that the power of certain regions to generate output and income can be enhanced by paying closer and more direct attention to educational disparities, by seeking out and closing technological gaps, and by nurturing a more economically efficient urban structure. These three methods have one important characteristic in common in that action on all of them is almost certainly best taken by provincial ministers. There is also some scope for action by private businessmen in the provinces. Pulling oneself up by one's own provincial bootstraps is more feasible than has hitherto been thought.

If productivity is one bootstrap that the province can pull upon, aggregate demand is the other. Our analysis has shown that relatively deficient demand is an important cause of regional unemployment disparities and that the cure for it rests, to a significant degree, in the hands of the provincial finance ministers of Quebec, the Atlantic provinces, and British Columbia. We shall be more specific below. The federal government could support those provinces that undertook their own fiscal stabilization policies and could also manage its own national stabilization policy in a more regionally sensitive manner.

Finally, it may be possible from time to time to twist general federal policy in a regionally beneficial manner. The regional side effects of federal expenditures and federal policies, as a whole, need to be continuously monitored. . . .

Recommendations

1. We recommend that the governments of the provinces where incomes and educational attainment are lower than the national average examine ways of improving the educational attainment of new entrants to the labour force and of increasing the ease with which mature members of the labour force can upgrade their education.

2. We recommend that, in the provinces where incomes are lower than the national average, each minister of industrial development or his equivalent, in co-operation whenever possible with private industry associations and trade unions, investigate what is the best applicable technology in each provincial industry, including service industries, with a view to encouraging its adoption where it is not yet in use.

3. We recommend that, in provinces where incomes are lower than the national average, any existing or future urban strategy give full consideration to the productivity advantages in manufacturing that may be gained by working with, rather than against, the tendency for population to drift from rural to urban areas and from smaller to medium-sized urban settlements.

4. We recommend that the growth of satellite cities of intermediate size, in the vicinity of Montreal and Toronto, be encouraged by the provincial governments concerned.

5. We recommend that industry trade associations, trade unions, and other appropriate institutions undertake formal studies to determine why productivity levels in their own industry differ from province to province and that they disseminate the results together with appropriate recommendations.

6. We recommend that all provincial governments, but especially those in low-income provinces, consult with appropriate educational institutions on ways to expand training in formal techniques of management available to existing and potential managers in the province.

7. We recommend that the governments of all provinces, but especially those where unemployment rates are above the national average, calculate each year the amount by which the provincial budget would be in surplus or deficit if the provincial economy were operating at full capacity.

8. We recommend that, in all the provinces where unemployment rates are usually higher than the national average, except Newfoundland, each provincial government continuously assess how much of its unemployment is due to demand deficiency and stimulate demand by increasing the full-employment budget deficit or decreasing the full-employment budget surplus, as the case may be.

9. We recommend that the governments of New Brunswick, Nova Scotia, and Prince Edward Island attempt to agree among themselves, each year, on appropriate joint changes in the full-employment budget surplus or deficit.

10. We recommend that the mix of fiscal policy instruments used by the federal government for cyclical stabilization purposes be chosen in such a way as to increase the proportion of national demand going to high-unemployment regions.

11. We recommend that the cost of relocating any particular federal activity for the purpose of creating jobs rather than achieving better local provision of federal services be compared always with the cost of creating a similar number of jobs through other programs involving direct subsidies.

12. We recommend that the federal government publish, every two or three years, a breakdown, by province and territory, of the location of its cash expenditures and tax receipts.

13. We recommend that the federal government review the terms under which assistance is available for moving workers to temporary jobs and consider undertaking a social experiment to discover whether the benefits of financial assistance to temporary mobility initiatives by the private sector would exceed the costs to the taxpayer.

14. We recommend that a survey, or surveys, be taken to determine the degree of awareness among the unemployed of job opportunities outside their province of residence, as well as their degree of knowledge about federal programs of mobility assistance.

15. We recommend that, as part of a strategy of full employment, the ministers of labour in high-unemployment provinces gradually move to a situation where their minimum wages are not higher than in any province where unemployment is lower than the national average.

16. We recommend that the federal government very gradually move to a situation where the wages of its own employees in each province are more closely related to wages for comparable workers in the private sector.

• • •

UNEMPLOYMENT RATE – 1981

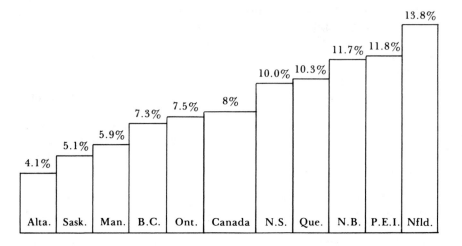

PERSONAL INCOME PER PERSON – 1979

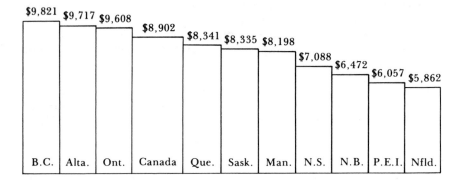

From *The Toronto Star*, February 21, 1981. By permission.

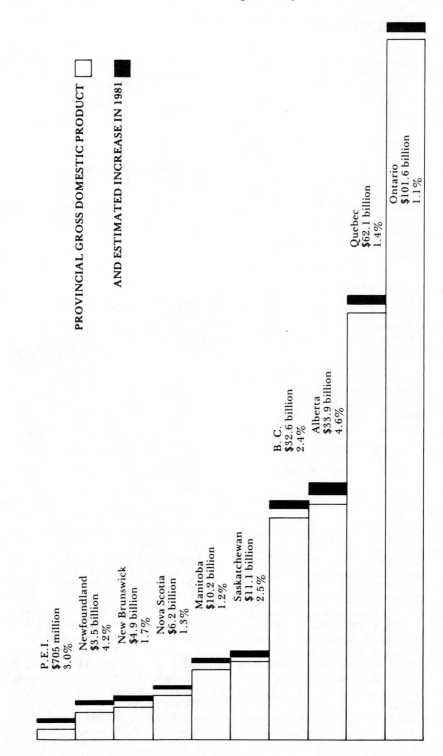

PROVINCIAL GROSS DOMESTIC PRODUCT

AND ESTIMATED INCREASE IN 1981

P.E.I.
$705 million
3.0%

Newfoundland
$3.5 billion
4.2%

New Brunswick
$4.9 billion
1.7%

Nova Scotia
$6.2 billion
1.3%

Manitoba
$10.2 billion
1.2%

Saskatchewan
$11.1 billion
2.5%

B. C.
$32.6 billion
2.4%

Alberta
$33.9 billion
4.6%

Quebec
$62.1 billion
1.4%

Ontario
$101.6 billion
1.1%

BIBLIOGRAPHY

Regionalism

(See also Bibliography in Chapter 10)

Alexander, D., "New Notions of Happiness: Nationalism, Regionalism and Atlantic Canada," *J.C.S.*, 15, 2, Summer, 1980.

Auer, L., *Regional Disparities of Productivity and Growth in Canada*, Ottawa, E.C.C., 1979.

Beck, J.M., *The History of Maritime Union: A Study in Frustration*, Fredericton, Maritime Union Study, 1969.

Bercuson, D.J., (ed.), *Canada and the Burden of Unity*, Toronto, Macmillan, 1977.

Blake, D.E., "The Measurement of Regionalism in Canadian Voting Patterns," *C.J.P.S.*, V, 1, March, 1972.

Breton, A., and Breton, R., *Why Disunity? An Analysis of Linguistic and Regional Cleavages in Canada*, Montreal, I.R.P.P., 1980.

Brewis, T.N., and Paquet, G., "Regional Development in Canada: An Exploratory Essay," *C.P.A.*, XI, 2, Summer, 1968.

Brewis, T.N., *Regional Economic Policies in Canada*, Toronto, Macmillan, 1969.

Brym, R.J., and Sacouman, R.J., (eds.), *Underdevelopment and Social Movements in Atlantic Canada*, Toronto, New Hogtown Press, 1979.

Cameron, D., (ed.), *Regionalism and Supranationalism*, Toronto, I.R.P.P., 1980.

Cameron, D.M., "Regional Integration in the Maritime Provinces," *C.J.P.S.*, IV, 1, March, 1971.

Campbell, A.B., Regan, G.A., and Hatfield, R.B., "The Move toward Maritime Integration and the Role of the Council of Maritime Premiers," *C.P.A.*, 15, 4, Winter, 1972.

Card, B.Y., (ed.), *Perspectives on Regions and Regionalism*, Edmonton, University of Alberta Bookstore, 1969.

Careless, A., *Initiative and Response: The Adaptation of Canadian Federalism to Regional Economic Development*, Montreal, McG.-Q.U.P., 1977.

Chi, N.H., "Regression Model of Regionalism: A Critique," with reply by W.P. Irvine, *C.J.P.S.*, V, 2, June, 1972.

Copithorne, L., *Natural Resources and Regional Disparities*, Ottawa, E.C.C., 1979.

Copithorne, L., "Natural Resources and Regional Disparities: A Skeptical View," *C.P.P.*, V, 2, Spring, 1979.

Daniels, M., "The Birth and Shaping of Regional Policies," *Policy Options*, 2, 2, May-June, 1981.

Dehem, R., *et al.*, "Concepts of Regional Planning," *C.P.A.*, IX, 2, June, 1966.

Economic Council of Canada, *Living Together: A Study of Regional Disparities*, Ottawa, S. and S., 1977.

Fergusson, C.B., "Maritime Union," *Q.Q.*, LXXVII, 2, Summer, 1970.

Forbes, E.R., *The Maritime Rights Movement, 1919-1927: A Study in Canadian Regionalism*, Montreal, McG.-Q.U.P., 1979.

Fox, Paul, "Regionalism and Confederation," in Wade, M., *infra*.

Gartner, G.J., "A Review of Cooperation Among the Western Provinces," *C.P.A.*, 20, 1, Spring, 1977.

Gertler, L.O., *Regional Planning in Canada*, Montreal, Harvest House, 1972.

Gibbins, R., *Regionalism: Territorial Politics in Canada and the United States, A Comparative Analysis*, Toronto, Butterworths, 1981.

Glenday, D., Guindon, H. and Turowetz, A., (eds.), *Modernization and the Canadian State*, Toronto, Macmillan, 1978.

Governments of New Brunswick, Nova Scotia, P.E.I., *Royal Commission*

Report On Maritime Union, [Deutsch Report], Fredericton, 1970.

Hawkins, G., (ed.), *The Idea of Maritime Union*, Report of a Conference sponsored by the C.I.P.A., and Mount Allison University, Sackville, N.B., 1965.

Helliwell, J., "National Fiscal and Monetary Policies: A Regional Interpretation," *BC Studies*, 13, Spring, 1972.

Hockin, T.A., *et al.*, *The Canadian Condominium*, Toronto, M. & S., 1972.

Hodgetts, J.E., "Regional Interests in a Federal Structure," *C.J.E.P.S.*, XXXII, 1, February, 1966.

Howland, R.D., *Some Regional Aspects of Canada's Economic Development*, Ottawa, Q.P., 1957.

Husband, D.D., "National Versus Regional Growth: Some Issues," *C.P.A.*, 14, 4, Winter, 1971.

Irvine, W.P., "Assessing the Regional Effects in Data Analysis," *C.J.P.S.*, IV, 1, March, 1971.

Krueger, R.R., Sargent, F.O., de Vos, A., and Pearson, N., (eds.), *Regional and Resource Planning in Canada*, Toronto, H.R.W., rev. ed., 1970.

Lithwick, N.H., "Is Federalism Good for Regionalism?," *J.C.S.*, 15, 2, Summer, 1980.

Lomas, A.A., "The Council of Maritime Premiers: Report and Evaluation After Five Years," *C.P.A.*, 20, 1, Spring, 1977.

Lotz, J., *Understanding Canada: Regional and Community Development in a New Nation*, Toronto, NC Press, 1977.

Manzer, R., *Canada — A Socio-Political Report*, Toronto, McG.-H.R., 1974.

Marchak, P., "The Two Dimensions of Canadian Regionalism," *J.C.S.*, 15, 2, Summer, 1980.

Matthews, R., "The Significance and Explanation of Regional Divisions in Canada: Towards a Canadian Sociology," *J.C.S.*, 15, 2, Summer, 1980.

Mathias, P., *Forced Growth*, Toronto, J.L.S., 1971.

Merrill, G., "Regionalism and Nationalism" in Warkentin, J., (ed.), *Canada: A Geographical Interpretation*, Toronto, Methuen, 1968.

Migué, J.-L., "Politiques régionales: traitement du malade ou maladie du guérisseur?," *C.P.A.*, 21, 2, Summer, 1978.

Neill, R.F., "National Policy and Regional Development: A Footnote to the Deutsch Report on Maritime Union," *J.C.S.*, IX, 2, May, 1974.

Phillips, P., *Regional Disparities*, Toronto, Lorimer, 1978.

Plumptre, A.F.W., "Regionalism and the Public Service," *C.P.A.*, VIII, 4, December, 1965.

Pratt, L., Stevenson, G., (eds.), *Western Separatism: The Myths, Realities and Dangers*, Edmonton, Hurtig, 1981.

Quesnel-Ouellet, L., "Régionalisation et conscience politique régionale: la communauté urbaine de Québec," *C.J.P.S.*, IV, 2, June, 1971.

Rawlyk, G.A., (ed.), *The Atlantic Provinces and the Problems of Confederation*, St. John's, Breakwater, 1979.

Rawlyk, G.A., Hodgins, B.W., and Bowles, R.P., *Regionalism in Canada: Flexible Federalism or Fractured Nation?*, Toronto, P.-H., 1979.

Roberts, S., "How the West was Lost," *Policy Options*, 2, 2, May-June, 1981.

Schwartz, M., *Politics and Territory: The Sociology of Regional Persistence in Canada*, Montreal, McG.-Q.U.P., 1974.

Simeon, R., "Regionalism and Canadian Political Institutions," *Q.Q.*, 82, 4, Winter, 1975.

Simeon, R., and Elkins, D., "Regional Political Cultures in Canada," *C.J.P.S.*, 7, 3, September, 1974.

Smith, D.E., "The Third Canada [An Alienated West]," *Policy Options*, 2, 2, May-June, 1981.

Wade, M., (ed.), *Regionalism in the Canadian Community, 1867-1967*, Toronto, U.T.P., 1969.

Ward, N., "The Significance of the Senators [in Representing the

West]," *Policy Options*, 2, 2, May-June, 1981.

Whalen, H., "Public Policy and Regional Development: The Experience of the Atlantic Provinces," in Rotstein, A., (ed.), *The Prospect of Change: Proposals for Canada's Future*, Toronto, McG.-H., 1965.

Yeates, M., *Main Street: Windsor to Quebec City*, Toronto, Macmillan, 1975.

Provinces and Territories

(See also Bibliography in Chapter 8)

Armstrong, C., *The Politics of Federalism: Ontario's Relations with the Federal Government, 1867-1942*, Toronto, U.T.P., 1981.

Artibise, A.F.J., *Western Canada Since 1870: A Select Bibliography*, Vancouver, U.B.C.P., 1978.

Atlantic Provinces Economic Council, *The Atlantic Vision — 1990: A Development Strategy for the 1980's*, Halifax, 1979.

Beck, J.M., *The Government of Nova Scotia*, Toronto, U.T.P., 1957.

Bellamy, D.J., Pammett, J.H., and Rowat, D.C., (eds.), *The Provincial Political Systems: Comparative Essays*, Toronto, Methuen, 1976.

Bercuson, D.J., "Regionalism and Unlimited Identity in Western Canada," *J.C.S.*, 15, 2, Summer, 1980.

Bishop, O.B. *et al.*, (eds.), *Bibliography of Ontario History, 1867-1976: Cultural, Economic, Political, Social*, Toronto, U.T.P., 1980, 2 vols.

Brock, G., *The Province of Northern Ontario*, Cobalt, Highway Book Shop, 1978.

Caldarola, C., (ed.), *Society and Politics in Alberta*, Toronto, Methuen, 1979.

Canada, *Report of the Advisory Commission on the Development of Government in the Northwest Territories*, [Carrothers' Report], Ottawa, Q.P., 1966.

Canada, Report of the Special

Representative, *Constitutional Development in the Northwest Territories*, Ottawa, S. and S., 1980.

Careless, J.M.S., (ed.), *The Pre- Confederation Premiers: Ontario Government Leaders, 1841-1867*, Toronto, U.T.P., 1980.

Chandler, M.A., and Chandler, W.M., *Public Policy and Provincial Politics*, Toronto, McG.-H.R., 1979.

Dacks, G., *The Politics of Canada's North*, Toronto, Methuen, 1981.

Donnelly, M.S., *The Government of Manitoba*, Toronto, U.T.P., 1963.

Dosman, E.J., *The National Interest: The Politics of Northern Development, 1968-75*, Toronto, M. & S., 1977.

Eager, E., *Saskatchewan Government: Politics and Pragmatism*, Saskatoon, Western Producer Prairie Books, 1981.

Elkins, D.J., and Simeon, R., *Small Worlds: Parties and Provinces in Canadian Political Life*, Toronto, Methuen, 1980.

Elton, D.K., (ed.), *One Prairie Province? Conference and Selected Papers*, Lethbridge, Lethbridge Herald, 1970.

Fleck, J.D., "Restructuring the Ontario Government," *C.P.A.*, 16, 1, Spring, 1973.

Gibbins, R., "Models of Nationalism: A Case Study of Political Ideologies in the Canadian West," *C.J.P.S.*, X, 2, June, 1977.

Gibbins, R., *Prairie Politics and Society: Regionalism in Decline*, Toronto, Butterworths, 1980.

Hanson, E.J., "The Future of Western Canada: Economic, Social and Political," *C.P.A.*, 18, 1, Spring, 1975.

Hodgins, B.W., *et al.*, *The Canadian North*, Scarborough, P.-H., 1977.

Krueger, R.R., "The Provincial-Municipal Government Revolution in New Brunswick," *C.P.A.*, XIII, 1, Spring, 1970.

Lajoie, A., *Les structures administratives régionales: déconcentration et décentralisation au Québec*, Montréal, Les Presses de l'Université de Montréal, 1968.

Leadbeater, D., (ed.), *The Political Economy of Alberta*, Toronto, Lorimer, 1981.

Lotz, J., *Northern Realities*, Toronto, New Press, 1970.

MacDonald, D.C., (ed.), *Government and Politics of Ontario*, Toronto, Van Nostrand Reinhold, 2nd ed., 1980.

MacKinnon, F., *The Government of Prince Edward Island*, Toronto, U.T.P., 1951.

Mayo, H.B., "Newfoundland's Entry into the Dominion," *C.J.E.P.S.*, XV, 4, November, 1949.

Neary, P., (ed.), *The Political Economy of Newfoundland, 1929-1972*, Toronto, C.C., 1973.

Oliver, P., *Public and Private Persons: The Ontario Political Culture, 1914-34*, Toronto, Clarke, Irwin, 1975.

Pryke, K.G., *Nova Scotia and Confederation, 1864-74*, Toronto, U.T.P., 1979.

Rea, K.J., *The Political Economy of the Canadian North*, Toronto, U.T.P., 1968.

Richards, J., and Pratt, L., *Prairie Capitalism: Power and Influence in the New West*, Toronto, M. & S., 1979.

Richmond, D.R., *The Economic Transformation of Ontario: 1945-73*, Toronto, O.E.C., 1974.

Rohmer, R., *The Green North*, Toronto, Maclean-Hunter, 1970.

Rowat, D.C., (ed.), *Provincial Government and Politics: Comparative Essays*, Ottawa, Carleton University, 2nd ed., 1973.

Rowat, D.C., (ed.), *Provincial Policy-Making: Comparative Essays*, Ottawa, Carleton University, 1981.

Schindeler, F.F., *Responsible Government in Ontario*, Toronto, U.T.P., 1969.

Stevenson, G., and Pratt, L., (ed.), *Western Separatism: Myths, Realities and Dangers*, Edmonton, Hurtig, 1981.

Tindal, C.R., "Regional Development in Ontario," *C.P.A.*, 16, 1, Spring, 1973.

Municipalities

(See also Bibliography in Chapter 8)

Andrew, C., Blais, A., et des Rosiers, R., "Les échevins et la formulation des politiques: note méthodologique," *C.P.A.*, 20, 2, Summer, 1977.

Andrew, C., Blais, A., et des Rosiers, R., "Les élites politiques, les bas-salariés et la politique du logement à Hull," *C.P.A.*, 21, 1, Spring, 1978.

Antoft, K., (ed.), *A Guide to Local Government in Nova Scotia*, Halifax, Institute of Public Affairs, Dalhousie University, 1977.

Aubin, H., *Les vrais propriétaires de Montréal*, Montréal, Editions l'Etincelle, 1977.

Axworthy, J., (ed.), *The Future City*, [Government in Winnipeg], Winnipeg, I.U.S., University of Winnipeg, 1971.

Axworthy, L., and Cassidy, J., *Unicity: The Transition*, Winnipeg, I.U.S., University of Winnipeg, 1974.

Axworthy, L., and Gillies, J.M., (eds.), *The City: Canada's Prospects and Canada's Problems*, Toronto, Butterworths, 1973.

Baine, R.P., and McMurray, A.L., *Toronto, An Urban Study*, Toronto, Clarke, Irwin, 1970.

Baine, R.P., *Calgary: An Urban Study*, Toronto, Clarke, Irwin, 1973.

Beck, J.M., *The Evolution of Municipal Government in Nova Scotia, 1749-1973*, Halifax, Q.P., 1973.

Bernard, A., Léveillé, J., and Lord, G., *Profile: Edmonton* (Political and Administrative Structures of the Metropolitan region), Ottawa, I.C., 1974: *Profile: Montreal*, 1974; *Profile: Ottawa-Hull*, 1975; *Profile: Hamilton-Wentworth*, 1975; *Profile: Quebec*, 1975.

Bettison, D.G., Kenward, J.K., Taylor, L., *Urban Affairs in Alberta*, Edmonton, U.A.P., 1975.

Bolduc, R., "Incidence du rôle accru de l'Etat sur la démocratie locale," *C.P.A.*, 23, 1, Printemps, 1980.

Bourne, L.S., *et al.*, (eds.), *Urban Futures for Central Canada*, Toronto, U.T.P., 1974.

Brownstone, M., *et al.*, *Politics and the Process of Reform of Urban Government: The Winnipeg Experience*, Ottawa, Ministry of State for Urban Affairs, mimeo., 1971.

Burns, R.M., "Government in an Urban Society," *C.P.A.*, 14, 3, Fall, 1971.

Cameron, K., (ed.), *Municipal Government in the Intergovernmental Maze*, Seminar Publication, Toronto, I.P.A.C., 1980.

Canada, *Directory of Canadian Urban Information Sources*, Ottawa, Ministry of State for Urban Affairs, 1977.

Chevalier, M., and Choukroun, J.-M., "Urban Change and the Urban Future," *C.P.A.*, 14, 3, Fall, 1971.

Crawford, K.G., *Canadian Municipal Government*, Toronto, U.T.P., 1961.

Dickerson, M.O., Drabek, S., Woods, J.T., (eds.), *Problems of Change in Urban Government*, Waterloo, W.L.U.P., 1980.

Divay, G., et Colin, J.-P., *La communauté urbaine de Montréal: de la ville centrale à l'île centrale*, Montréal, INRS, Urbanisation, 1977.

Donnelly, M.S., *et al.*, "Aspects of Municipal Administration: A Symposium," *C.P.A.*, XI, 1, Spring, 1968.

d'Entremont, H., and Roberdet, P., "More Reform in New Brunswick: Rural Municipalities," *C.P.A.*, 20, 3, Fall, 1977.

Feldman, L.D., (ed.), *Politics and Government of Urban Canada: Selected Readings*, Toronto, Methuen, 4th ed., 1981.

Feldman, L.D., and Graham, K.A., *Bargaining for Cities: Municipalities and Intergovernmental Relations — An Assessment*, Toronto, Butterworths, 1979.

Gertler, L., and Crowley, R., *Changing Canadian Cities: The Next 25 Years*, Toronto, M. & S., 1977.

Goldrick, M.D., "Present Issues in the Growth of Cities," *C.P.A.*, 14, 3, Fall, 1971.

Goldrick, M.D., "Perspectives on Governing the Regions and the Metropolis in the Future," in *Lessons from Regional Government*, London, Ontario, University of Western Ontario, 1979.

Gordon, D.R., *City Limits: Barriers to Change in Urban Government*, Don Mills, Ontario, Musson, 1973.

Graham, K.A., *et al.*, *Local and Regional Government in the Northwest Territories*, Kingston, Institute of Local Government, Queen's University, 1980.

Groupe de travail sur l'urbanisation, *L'urbanisation au Québec*, Québec, Éditeur officiel, 1976.

Hanigan, L., *et al.*, *Les communautés urbaines de Montréal et de Québec, premier bilan*, Montréal, Presses de l'Université de Montréal, 1975.

Hardwick, W.G., *Vancouver*, Don Mills, Ontario, C.-M., 1974.

Harvey, E.R., *Sydney, Nova Scotia: An Urban Study*, Toronto, Clarke, Irwin, 1971.

Hebel, J.J., "Approaches to Regional and Metropolitan Governments in the United States and Canada," *C.P.A.*, X, 2, June, 1967.

Higgins, D.J.H., "Municipal Politics and Government: Development of the Field in Canadian Political Science," *C.P.A.*, 22, 3, Fall, 1979.

Higgins, D.J.H., *Urban Canada: Its Government and Politics*, Toronto, Macmillan, 1977.

Jackson, *The Canadian City*, Toronto, McG.-H.R., 1973.

Joyce, J.C., (ed.), *Challenging Tomorrow Today: Insights Into Municipal Administration*, Montreal and Toronto, Renouf, 1979.

Kaplan, H., "Politics and Policy-Making in Metropolitan Toronto," *C.J.E.P.S.*, XXXI, 4, November, 1965.

Kaplan, H., *Urban Political Systems: A Functional Analysis of Metropolitan Toronto*, Toronto, C.C., 1967.

Léveillée, J., *Developpement urbain et politiques gouvernementales urbaines dan l'agglomeration Montréalaise, 1945-1975*, Montréal, Département de Science politique, Université du Québec à Montréal, 1978.

Lightbody, J., "Electoral Reform in Local Government: The Case of Winnipeg," *C.J.P.S.*, XI, 2, June, 1978.

Lightbody, J., "The Reform of a Metropolitan Government: The Case of Winnipeg, 1971," *C.P.P.*, IV, 4, Autumn, 1978.

Lithwick, N.H., (ed.), *Urban Canada — Problems and Prospects*, Ottawa, C.M.H.C., 1970.

Lithwick, N.H., "An Economic Interpretation of the Urban Crisis," *J.C.S.*, VII, 3, August, 1972.

Lithwick, N.H., "Urban Policy-Making: Shortcomings in Political Technology," *C.P.A.*, 15, 4, Winter, 1972.

Lithwick, N.H., and Paquet, G., (eds.), *Urban Studies: A Canadian Perspective*, Toronto, Methuen, 1968.

Massam, B.H., "Local Government in the Montreal Area," *C.J.P.S.*, VI, 2, June, 1973.

McAllister, A.B., *An Approach to Manpower Planning and Development in Canadian Municipal Government*, Toronto, Monograph Series, I.P.A.C., 1979.

McRae, K.D., *The Federal Capital: Government Institutions*, Studies of the Royal Commission on Bilingualism and Biculturalism, No. 1, Ottawa, Q.P., 1969.

Médam, A., *Montréal interdite*, Paris, Presses Universitaires de France, 1978.

Meynaud, J., et Léveillée, J., *La régionalisation municipale au Québec*, Montréal, Nouvelle Frontière, 1973.

Miles, S.R., Cohen, S., and Koning, G., *Developing a Canadian Urban Policy: Some Problems and Proposals*, Toronto, Intermet, 1973.

Nader, G.A., *Cities of Canada*, Vol. I, *Theoretical, Historical and Planning Perspectives*; Vol. II, *Profiles of Fifteen Metropolitan Centres*, Toronto, Macmillan, 1976.

Newfoundland, *Report of the Royal Commission on Municipal Government in Newfoundland and Labrador*, [Whalen Report], St. John's, Q.P., 1975.

Nova Scotia, Royal Commission on Education, Public Services and Provincial-Municipal Relations, *Report*, [Graham Report], Halifax, Q.P., 1974, 4 vols.

O'Brien, A., "Local Government Priorities for the Eighties," *C.P.A.*, 19, 1, Spring, 1976.

Ontario Economic Council, *Issues and Alternatives — 1977: Intergovernmental Relations*, Toronto, 1977.

Perks, W.T., and Robertson, I.M., (eds.), *Urban and Regional Planning in a Federal State: The Canadian Experience*, Toronto, McG.-H.R., 1979.

Plunkett, T.J., *The Financial Structure and the Decision-Making Process of Canadian Municipal Government*, Ottawa, C.M.H.C., 1972.

Plunkett, T.J., *Urban Canada and its Government: A Study of Municipal Organization*, Toronto, Macmillan, 1968.

Plunkett, T.J., and Betts, G.M., *The Management of Canadian Urban Government*, Kingston, Institute of Local Government, Queen's University, 1978.

Powell, A., (ed.), *The City: Attacking Modern Myths*, Toronto, M. & S., 1972.

Québec, *Rapport sur l'urbanisation*, Québec, Editeur officiel, 1975.

Quesnel-Ouellet, L., "Changement dans les structures municipales," *C.J.P.S.*, VI, 2, June, 1973.

Richardson, B., *The Future of Canadian Cities*, Toronto, New Press, 1972.

Ridler, N.B., "PPB: Its Relevance to Financially Constrained Municipalities," *C.P.A.*, 19, 2, Summer, 1976.

Robarts, Hon. J.P., *Report of the Royal Commission on Metropolitan Toronto*, Toronto, Ontario Government Bookstore, 1977, 2 vols.

Robinson, I.M., *Canadian Urban Growth Trends*, Vancouver, U.B.C.P., 1981.

Rose, A., *Governing Metropolitan Toronto: A Social and Political Analysis, 1953-1971*, Los Angeles, University of California Press, 1972.

Ross, R.K., *Local Government in Ontario*, Toronto, Canada Law, 2nd ed., 1962.

Rowat, D.C., *The Canadian Municipal System: Essays on the Improvement of Local Government*, Carleton Library No. 48, Toronto, M. & S., 1969.

Rowat, D.C., "The Problems of Governing Federal Capitals," *C.J.P.S.*, I, 3, September, 1968.

Rowat, D.C., *The Government of Federal Capitals*, Toronto, U.T.P., 1973.

Rowat, D.C., *Your Local Government: A Sketch of the Municipal System in Canada*, Toronto, Macmillan, 2nd ed., 1975..

Roy, J., *Montréal, ville d'avenir*, Montréal, Les Editions Quinze, 1978.

Sancton, A., "The Impact of Language Differences in Metropolitan Reform in Montreal," *C.P.A.*, 22, 2, Summer, 1979.

Spelt, J., *Toronto*, Don Mills, Ontario, C.-M., 1973.

Stetler, G.A., and Artibise, A.F.J., *The Canadian City*, Toronto, Carleton Library No. 109, M. & S., 1977.

Tennant, P., and Zirnhelt, D., "The Emergence of Metropolitan Government in Greater Vancouver," *BC Studies*, 15, Autumn, 1972.

Tennant, P., and Zirnhelt, D., "Metropolitan Government in Vancouver: The Strategy of Gentle Imposition," *C.P.A.*, 16, 1, Spring, 1973.

Tindal, C.R., *Structural Changes in Local Government: Government for Urban Regions*, Toronto, Monograph Series, I.P.A.C., 1977.

Tindal, C.R., and Tindal, S.N., *Local Government in Canada*, Toronto, McG.-H.R., 1979.

Trevor, P., (ed.), *Regional Government in Ontario*, Don Mills, Ontario Science Research Associates, 1971.

Weller, G.R., "Local Government in the Canadian Provincial North," *C.P.A.*, 24, 1, Spring, 1981.

Whalen, H.J., *The Development of Local Government in New Brunswick*, Fredericton, 1964.

Wolforth, J.R., *Urban Prospects*, Toronto, M. & S., 1971.

Young, D.A., "Canadian Local Government Development: Some Aspects of the Commissioner and City Manager Forms of Administration," *C.P.A.*, IX, 1, March, 1966.

5

ENGLISH CANADA
AND NATIONALISM

Nationalism has become much more vociferous in both English Canada and Quebec in the past 20 years. Despite the threat of separatism in Quebec, the change is more remarkable in English Canada. Quebec has had a long tradition of French-Canadian nationalism and has produced a continual flow of literature on the subject, but English Canadians have not displayed as much interest in Canadian nationalism until recently.

Some French Canadians are inclined to take the lack of English-Canadian nationalist literature as proof of the non-existence of a significant English-Canadian national spirit. That such an assumption is unwarranted is obvious from the facts of Canadian history which have amply demonstrated that many English-speaking Canadians have devoted themselves to building a nation with its own distinctive characteristics.

For the most part, however, these efforts have been defensive rather than expansionist. In the first half of our national existence they were directed towards emancipating Canada from its colonial position within the British Empire. That goal was attained by the achievement of Dominion status in 1931. More recently, English-Canadian nationalists have found themselves engaged in a second phase of defensive action, this time directed against the absorption of Canada by an omnipresent and almost overwhelming American culture, which is both national and continental. As the political power of the United States has waxed mightily in the post-war period and the thrust of North American economic continentalism has grown more pronounced, English-speaking nationalism has become increasingly strident. Its substance, however, is usually negative rather than positive, long in criticism and short in the development of any theory of Canadian nationalism, unless it is Marxist. The country still awaits the birth of a doctrine of Canadian nationalism, although there are some who believe that such an event should be aborted.

Professor Gad Horowitz's article in this chapter deplores this fear of nationalism and makes the case for a necessary and salutary Canadian nationalism. Professor Charles Taylor's essay develops the argument further in one of the best-reasoned justifications of Canadian nationalism. A major flaw in this philosophy is underlined in a passage from Professor John Porter's well-known book on Canadian society. For further arguments pro and con Canadian nationalism, a reader should consult the bibliography, whose length indicates the mounting interest in the subject. One of the most useful sources on this topic is *Nationalism in Canada*, a book of essays edited by Professor Peter Russell.

A selection from one of the essays in this book concludes this chapter and leads into the next. In his article "The National Outlook of English- speaking Canadians," Professor Kenneth McNaught explains the nature of English-Canadian nationalism, particularly for the benefit of French Candians.

The chapter concludes with a bibliography listing works dealing with Canadian nationalism and Canada-U.S.A. relations.

ON THE FEAR OF NATIONALISM*

Gad Horowitz

Canada is, and has always been, a relatively stable and peaceful society. Our political tradition, in its substantive content and even more in its rhetoric, has emphasized above all, the theme of moderation. The tradition may have served us well in the past, but it must now be transcended if Canada is to survive. Let us not mince words; survival is the issue. The fear of political annexation is not realistic: but the prospect of total economic and cultural integration into American society is real and immediate.

Our political and intellectual elites, true to the Canadian tradition, are moderately concerned about the impending demise of their country, and moderately determined to do something to prevent that demise, on condition that whatever is done, be moderately done. This moderation will be the death of us. One of the sources of contemporary moderation is a genteel fear of nationalism that pervades the English Canadian establishment. The continentalist elements of establishment use this fear of nationalism cynically, in the interest of greater American nationalism of which we are a part. . . .

There are . . . elements of the establishment which are not continentalist, which might be prepared to do something if it were not for their genuine fear of nationalism. Americanization, they would agree, is an evil which we ought to avoid if we can, but nationalism is an even greater evil — it is the malevolent force which has bathed the world in blood.

The moderate view is that Canadian nationalism would be more harmful to Canada and to the world than the Americanization of Canada. This view is false because it is based on a model of nationalism which is not applicable to Canada. The nationalism that has bathed the world in blood is not the nationalism that seeks to prevent the integration of Canada into American society.

There are, to begin with, crucial distinctions to be made among the nationalism of expansionist great powers, the nationalism of small states struggling to preserve some degree of independence and the nationalism of colonized people seeking self-determination. The first of these is never justifiable. The other two nearly always are. Canadian nationalism is clearly

---

* From *Canadian Dimension*, IV, 4, May-June, 1967. By permission.

that of the small state: our relationship with the United States is analogous to the relationship of Finland with the Soviet Union. The Americans and the Soviets need not fear conquest by the Canadians and the Finns. The Canadians and the Finns are no threat to their great neighbours. The shedding of blood is simply not in this picture. Second of all, there is a difference between the nationalism that disrupts established states and the nationalism that preserves or consolidates existing states. Examples of the disruptive type are the nationalisms that destroyed the Austro-Hungarian Empire and the nationalisms that today threaten to destroy and dismember India and Nigeria. These nationalisms, though they are often justifiable reactions to alien domination, are usually accompanied by bitter chauvinistic hatred of neighbouring peoples and often result in the shedding of blood. The mutually antagonistic chauvinism of English and French Canada are potentially analogous to those of Austro-Hungary, India and Nigeria. The intra-Canadian nationalist extremisms which threaten to tear this country apart are correctly feared, not only by our moderates, but by all Canadians with the exception of a fringe of separatists and a fringe of Orangemen. But the Pan-Canadian nationalism which seeks to preserve a Canadian state in some form, and to prevent the digestion of both English- and French-Canadian societies by the United States, is an entirely different matter.

Canada exists. The nationalism that preserves its existence is not disruptive.

Third, there is a difference between racist nationalism and other types of nationalism. This is a distinction which should require no elaboration. Canadian nationalism has nothing to do with race, nothing to do with blood and soil. . . .

Finally, there is a difference between what might be called doctrinal and non-doctrinal nationalism. A doctrinal nationalism perceives the nation as the embodiment of a specific set of values, such as Communism, Liberalism, Catholicism and fascism. This leads it to relate to the outside world in a paranoid manner. The values incarnated in the nation may be viewed as the unique possession of the nation — a treasured possession, which can only be tarnished and mutilated by contact with the outside world. If this is the case, the nation will be isolationist — in a sense, it will turn in on itself and shun the outside influences as a potential corruptor. Another possibility for doctrinal nationalism is the view that the nations have universal unique validity, and that the nation has a special mission to impose these values on the rest of the world by force, by persuasion, or by forceful persuasion. This is the messianic subtype of doctrinal nationalism.

Within its own borders, doctrinal nationalism imposes a rigid ideological conformity. The only legitimate ideology is the national ideology. Adherents of other ideologies are, at best, barely tolerated deviates and at worst, witches to be burned at the stake. I have, of course, been describing the nationalism of the United States. The doctrine of its nationalism is liberalism, individualism, "democratic capitalism." To adhere to a different ideology is to be un-American, a deviate or a witch. . . .

Canadian nationalism cannot be doctrinal. On the contrary, its purpose must be to preserve on the northern half of this continent, a society which does not share the liberal conformitarianism, the isolationism and the messianism of the United States.

What is the doctrine of Canadian nationalism? The moderates cannot answer this question, because there is no such doctrine. There is no unique set of Canadian values which is to be preserved from corruption by outsiders and/or imposed on them by forceful persuasion. Certainly Canadian nationalists are anxious to diminish the economic and cultural influence of the United States in Canada — not in order to preserve some unique set of Canadian national values, but in order to preserve the possibility of building, in this country, a society which is better than the Great Society. It needn't be uniquely Canadian as long as it isn't a copy of the United States. It could be anything. It could be a replica of Sweden, or if you like, of North Korea, Albania or Ireland, or Spain or Yugoslavia, or Cambodia, or all of them. The point is not to preserve all aspects of Canadian society which differentiate it from the American simply because they are uniquely ours, but to preserve those distinctive aspects of Canadian society which make it better than American society and above all, Canada's freedom of action to become something — who knows what it will be — different from Flint, Michigan. If the United States were Utopia, I would not be a Canadian nationalist; but the United States is not Utopia. . . .

Canadian nationalism is not "anti-Americanism" necessarily in a sense of hatred of all things American just because they're American. There is much we can learn from the United States . . . but it should be intended learning for our purposes, not automatic imitation, not unconscious absorption.

The problem of Americanization can be faced without chauvinism, but also without a fake, self-effacing, embarrassed cosmopolitanism. It can be faced; without building Chinese walls, without "restricting the free flow of ideas." It can be faced positively, by taking control of our economy into our own hands and (this is just as important) releasing our production and distribution of ideas from a dam of market forces by assigning a very high priority to the subsidization of Canadian cultural production of all sorts, on a scale very much larger than anything contemplated at the moment. By cultural production, I mean not only the arts, but anything that can be published or broadcast. The use of the state for nation-building purposes is not a new idea in Canada. We need a National policy not of cultural tariffs and taxes, but of cultural bounties and subsidies.

The purpose of Canadian nationalism is not to close Canada to the world, but to open Canada to the world by keeping out the United States. The fears of our moderates are entirely groundless.

NATIONALISM AND INDEPENDENCE, AN ECONOMIC PROBLEM*

Charles Taylor

• • •

Common Purposes

. . . Are there common purposes, big and prepossessing enough to justify our common existence, or should we face the fact that Canada is not worth it, and wind it up? (Meaning, I guess, break up into constituent parts, some of which join the U.S.A.) Both alternatives need much more serious examination than they have received.

As far as the first is concerned, I believe that there are such common purposes, and without claiming to express them definitively, I think they can be described in three main categories. First, Canada's vocation is to develop the five great regions as full-scale societies. . . .

This need not mean flying in the face of objective economic cost factors in order to pay for a country. The way an economy would develop without government intervention is not necessarily any more "natural" or "economic" than the way it develops if planned. Planned development can turn the tide in an underdeveloped region without increasing, and often decreasing, the cost to the nation as a whole. Indeed the principal aim of uniting these diverse regions into one body politic can only be their combined development. If we let this drop, or pursue it half-heartedly, as has been the case for the last century, then there is good reason to ask why Canada should exist. But combined development does constitute a goal which would mean a fuller and more prosperous life for the vast majority of Canadians. . . .

. . . We have somehow to develop a mode of existence where different cultures can grow and be fully themselves without paying the price of isolation, while helping, that is, to enrich each other. We have to develop a society in which diversity is welcomed as richness and not feared as the prelude to division. . . .

Thirdly, once we exist as a country, we cannot avoid our obligation to play a role on the international scene. Without launching into illusions of grandeur bred by our exceptional position immediately after the last war, we can nevertheless see a certain strategic role in the attempt to preserve peace for a middle power, rich, relatively trusted in all parts of the world, although white, and relatively free from deep involvement in the multiple mutual hatreds which crisscross the globe.

This statement of aims is very summary and imperfect. But any discussion of Canadian nationalism cannot be carried on properly unless these, or similar cards, are laid on the table. Since Canadian nationalism can only be prospective, we have to be able to express, even somewhat inarticulately,

* From *Canadian Dimension*, IV, 4, May-June, 1967. By permission.

what our purposes are. But for those who are unconvinced by this three-fold purpose, or who are unmoved by it, let us examine the alternative.

Sometimes people speak of "joining the U.S.A.," as though this was a real option for Canada. But it could never be the object of a common decision by Canadians, as, for instance, we could decide one day to amend the constitution. Parts of what is now Canada could join the U.S.A. only if the country broke up, perhaps partly in disagreement over this. It is hardly likely that nationalism, for instance, in French Canada could ever be overcome to the point where Quebec would consent to be part of a fifty-first state, thus brusquely drawing a line under 350 years' history.

Secondly, it is not all that likely that the Americans would be eager to have us. The days of manifest destiny are past, or perhaps this policy has taken more subtle forms. It can, of course, be interesting to the U.S.A. to control Canadian policy more closely; but is it not much more valuable to them to have as a neighbour a middle power, with all the trappings of independence, which keeps its own intractable internal problems to itself and nevertheless does what it is told?

We should not assume that a viable alternative to refloating Canada is annexation. It may just be break-up, or short of this, a kind of twilight zone of fictitious independence, more and more under remote control from Washington. Indeed, we are already entering a twilight zone of this kind.

When seen in this light, the alternative to a viable Canadian nationalism can hardly be called attractive. Canadians would be reduced to the status of very second class citizens. We would have to follow policies made in Washington without even the opportunity which anyone has living south of the border to influence these policies by our votes. . . .

Paralytic Continentalism

The alternative to Canadian nationalism is not a far-seeing policy of rational welfare on an international basis, but instead a gradual slide into satellite status which will make it more and more difficult to solve even our problems of economic development with the full measure of freedom we require. The alternative is a policy of paralytic continentalism. And the tragedy is that that policy is being followed today, unavowedly, by the Liberal government. . . .

But all this wouldn't work if there weren't a half-conscious connivance on the part of important sections of the electorate. Obviously, many Canadian electors do not want to face the choices. They prefer the hypocritical phraseology, because it hides the stark choice, whose implications are somewhat frightening. There is clearly in Canada a widespread lack of confidence, a sense of inferiority vis-à-vis the U.S.A., a failure of nerve. Again and again, in the course of a political campaign, one finds electors who say: that would be wonderful, but would the Americans let us do it? For these people and many others, the limits of possibility are drawn much more narrowly than they are in fact. They feel beaten in advance. The political activity of the Liberal party both feeds this mood and profits from it. . . .

Nub Is Economic

The nub of the question is in the end economic. One of the underpinnings of paralytic continentalism is the commonplace idea mentioned at the beginning of this paper, that our choice lies between economic nationalism and a high standard of living. Once again, as in the attitude toward nationalism in general, the possibilities open to us are arbitrarily reduced to two, of which one is so plainly unacceptable that it forces us to the other. . . .

Very often the question is posed in terms of the inflow of foreign capital, the lever by which the foreign take-over of the Canadian economy has occurred. The choice then seems to be: either we own our own economy but do without foreign capital, or we grow rich faster at the expense of foreign take-over. But this stark alternative ignores many crucial questions; for instance, what form does the capital inflow take, loan capital or direct investment? The difference is important for future control; what kind of economy is being built by this inflow? This is perhaps the most crucial question of all.

Or else nationalism is seen in traditional terms, as the erection of higher tariff barriers, as a kind of super "National Policy." It is not hard to show the ill effects of a policy of this kind. Indeed, the "satellitization" we now suffer is in part conditioned by the National Policy. But to pretend that the only alternative to paralytic continentalism is a desperate grab at autarchy is absurd.

The real choice lies elsewhere. The political economy of independence concerns principally a nation's foreign trade position, in this day and age at least. This is more important than who owns its industry, although it is evident that this latter factor can itself affect the foreign trade position (and in all likelihood does in our case, to a significant extent). . . . Canada's lack of independence from the U.S.A. springs in large part from the fact that most of our trade is with our neighbours to the South and that we are in deep and chronic deficit with them. This means that the extent to which they can hurt us, while hurting themselves relatively little, is at a maximum. Fortunately, a reduction in their Canadian trade, although far from disastrous for the U.S. as a whole, would hurt certain sectional interests who therefore constitute a standing lobby in Washington against such measures. Canada is very fortunate that the U.S.A. is not a monolithic society and that the vast engine of government can still be immobilized by lobbies. Otherwise, we would have suffered a grisly fate long ago.

The major problem of Canadian independence is therefore the problem of developing a more favourable balance of trade, which in turn is the problem of developing a more competitive economy. How does this dovetail with our other, domestic economic objectives? One of our most pressing problems, as revealed by the reports of the Economic Council of Canada, is the development of our economy to give jobs to our rapidly growing labour force. In the opinion of the Economic Council, this will require greater diversification into secondary industry. If we want to pursue the objective of combined development of the different regions of Canada — and it will become more and more difficult to justify the country's existence if we don't — we must also try to bring about a wider geographical spread of this new secondary industry. But this industry has to be competitive internationally. We cannot increase Canadian employment in secondary industry simply by raising the tariff barrier; or rather we solve the problem in this way only at the cost of a depressed standard of living — if even this solution is possible for a country like Canada in an era of lowering trade barriers.

Thus both the needs of national independence and those of our own basic economic objectives require the development of an economy with a greater component of secondary industry, and which is more competitive internationally — not only vis-à-vis the U.S.A., but in the Atlantic and also the world arena. What, then, is the relation of foreign economic penetration to these objectives?

The relation is basically threefold. First, the growth of foreign, principally U.S., direct investment in Canada means a high, growing and never- ending service of this borrowing in the form of dividends. Of course, Canada has something to show for these payments, namely the plant or whatever built by direct investment. But to build the same plant on loan capital which is paid off over a period of years and then becomes Canadian- owned is much less costly in the long run to the balance of payments. Loan capital is therefore preferable to direct investment from the point of view of the above objectives.

Second, foreign direct investment has largely taken a form which has given a certain shape to the Canadian economy. In its secondary sector it is to a significant degree an economy of subsidiaries and branch plans of large international (mostly American) companies. This has two very important effects. First, our economy is very much influenced by the policy of large international companies toward their branch plants in the fields of exports, research and development, sales and purchases between units of a given international company, and so on. Moreover, certain evidence presented recently by Eric Kierans seems to show that this influence has been very negative in certain aspects and threatens to become more so.

It would appear that for a great many international corporations the role of a foreign subsidiary is principally to increase the market for the parent corporation. The foreign subsidiary therefore plays an important role in buying components from the parent, paying consultant fees, etc., to it, and in so doing, augmenting the profit of the parent company and helping it to amortize its capital. It is not so important that it make profits on its own and remit revenue in the form of dividends. The interest of the subsidiary for the parent is that it allows it to penetrate a foreign market. Where the profit is taken, at the level of the subsidiary or at the centre, is secondary; many, perhaps most, corporations prefer to take it at the centre.

It is clear that this practice is bad for the host country, for the policy puts a premium on the subsidiary's buying from the parent, i.e., on increasing the host country's imports and thus depressing its balance of trade. Some such factor seems to be operating in the trade between Canada and the U.S.A. . . .

How much does this adverse balance reflect a natural superiority of the American parent as a supplier? Very little, it would appear, for the policy of buying from the parent is very price-resistant. And one can easily understand why, for a component bought even at a higher price from the parent factory means a greater profit to the corporation as a whole, which profit is taken at the centre, at the expense of the periphery. Thus a study of the National Industrial Conference Board showed that Canadian industry had much higher material costs than U.S. industry. . . .

This is one way, then, in which the "branch plant economy" does not serve the objectives outlined above. But in another, perhaps more serious way, it leads to a structure of the Canadian economy which is in the long run not going to be internationally competitive. It is not just that units of production which are tied to the purchase of high-cost components from parent companies are not likely to be very export-competitive. What is at stake is the shape of our economy.

The joint result of our tariff policy and foreign investment has been the placing in Canada of a large number of relatively small-scale units of production, as each major company tries to secure its share of the market. This result, of course, sins against the principle of achieving economies by large-scale operations; but this does not deter the large corporation for whom the marginal investment pays off in market penetration. The global result, however, is that Canada has an economy which in some sectors is made up of a large number of small productive units, more than a country of our size would warrant. . . .

In a sense, the Canadian economy must be unique in the world, for it is to some extent a miniature of the American economy. Now the Americans can afford to enter every field of economic endeavour and set up three or more corporations in oligopolistic competition. But this is an absurdity for a country the size of Canada. The only way that a country our size can survive economically is to specialize and achieve pre-eminence in a limited series of lines, as successful small European countries have done. We have only managed to set up this crazy patchwork quilt because of the economics of the international corporation which makes a high-cost additional outlet an interesting proposition.

Many Canadians are satisfied that the accident of geographic location and the tariff has induced American industry to set up this patchwork quilt which we could never have afforded on our own. But this is a very short-sighted attitude. For apart from the disadvantages to our balance of payments resulting from the policy of these corporations, this type of economy does not provide us with the basis for the rapid development toward competitiveness which we are going to need. Branch plant industry tends to be high cost; more, by its marginal nature it tends to be less resistant to the pressures of economic recession. . . .

But the most serious drawback is that there is no basis for dynamism. The new developments of research, the initiative which profits by them, the ability to re-adapt and break out in new fields — very little of that is resident in the branch plant economy; it belongs to the centre. The Canadian patchwork quilt, the miniature of the American economy, is an expensive present; it deprives us of the basis of autonomous re-adaptation toward greater competitiveness. It is a mechanism whereby the capital accumulated through sales in Canada and all the leverage that that implies for research and innovation go to centres of decision outside the country, for whom our problems and objectives must be of very secondary concern. It is also a mechanism whereby those Canadians who can make a contribution in research and innovation are attracted irresistibly in large numbers south of the border. Whereas what Canada needs is to achieve greater competitiveness by concentrated efforts in research and development which will give us pre-eminence in a limited number of fields, the branch plant economy offers us the uncertain status of marginal off-shoots of a larger economy whose major levers of adaptation lie forever beyond our reach. It does not seem the part of wisdom to entrust our entire future to a structure of this kind.

Defensive Action

If we want to achieve our objectives of combined development toward a more diversified and competitive economy and thus ensure Canadians a rising standard of living and maintain our independence, we have to take action in the three domains outlined above in which the growth of foreign ownership and the branch plant economy represents a danger to us.

1. We have to try to reduce the proportion of direct equity investment in Canada's borrowing abroad. This will mean, of course, less investment made by foreign enterprise, and more initiative from inside Canada which, however, will make appeal to outside loan capital, or perhaps even enter into partnership with outside investors. The consequent reduction in the proportion of new investment accounted for by direct foreign investment, mostly of large international companies, will not be a bad thing in itself, as will be seen below, as well as improving the future pattern of our foreign indebtedness.

2. We need a brace of measures to ensure that the affiliates of international corporations which are and remain here behave in a way more consonant with Canadian interests. That these companies are capable of adapting their policies in a significant way if they feel the political pressure to do so is shown by their recent behaviour in a number of fields. . . .

The measures will have to include the proposal put forward by Eric Kierans, and recently echoed by Walter Gordon (*A Choice for Canada,* p. 110), to amend the Companies Act so as to force disclosure of the dealings between affiliates and their foreign parents. When we reflect that an essential element of the pressure that the U.S. government exerts on its international corporations to obey its guidelines is the requirement that they make regular reports on their foreign payments transactions, we can see how totally defenceless we have left ourselves in the past. If public disclosure and censure is not enough, tougher measures will have to be taken. But we must ensure that foreign subsidiaries do their part to maintain our balance of payments, and above all that they supply themselves in Canada when cost is no greater.

3. But these measures will be far from sufficient if the pattern of our economy itself as it develops under the impetus of branch plant investment remains the same. Here we have to supply a missing factor. Our historical situation made it inevitable that we have recourse for our development to foreign capital. But the shape that this foreign investment has taken was determined in part by ourselves: first, by our tariff policy, which made it an

interesting proposition to set up a branch plant here, but second by a lack of indigenous entrepreneurship. The Canadian economy is increasingly being designed by outsiders because it is not being designed by Canadians. If we are going to alter the pattern of our economy toward a more competitive diversified economy, we have to supply that entrepreneurial element. This is also an essential part of the goal described above: if we are to rely more on loan capital, there has to be the Canadian initiative in making the investment for which the foreign loan is required, instead of leaving both initiative and financing to outsiders.

But both because of the inadequacy of Canadian private entrepreneurship and because of social objectives that our development must meet (particularly that of combined regional development), it is clear that this entrepreneurial element will have to be public; it will have to be supplied by government planning. This means something much more ambitious than a Canadian Development Corporation, genre Walter Gordon. This latter proposal would simply allow Canadian private capital to do on a slightly larger scale what they are already doing. What we need on the other hand is the kind of planning which will invest heavily in research and feasibility studies, which will be able to devise new favourable fields of investment for Canada and determine what is required to maintain our competitive advantage, and then will go out and find the investment funds required. A Canada Development Corporation under public control, as a lever in the hands of a planning authority, would play a valuable — indeed indispensable — role in this. But this is a far cry from the Gordon proposal. What we need in short is to design our own economy; and we can only do this through our governments (the provinces must also do their part). This is the crucial measure.

What then of the pre-occupation with foreign ownership per se? — this is in my opinion not a major problem. Its effects, as we have seen, are partially bad, but the way to tackle the problem is along the line of these ill effects. That the above policies would result in a reduction in the proportion of the Canadian economy owned by foreigners is, however, clear. The attempt to reduce foreign direct investment would, if successful, slow down the growth of foreign ownership; the new rules governing the behaviour of foreign subsidiaries might discourage some further investment in this field. And if planned development took place in the context of a phased multilateral reduction of tariff barriers — which should be one of the prime aims of our policy — the interest in branch plant investment would be further reduced. But the major factor tending to reverse the trend towards greater foreign ownership would be a growing element of Canadian entrepreneurship which would flow from government planning. Foreign ownership grows because investment opportunities are met by foreign entrepreneurs, and because many Canadian firms are themselves integrated into foreign units by takeover. The only way to reverse this trend effectively is to increase the component of Canadian entrepreneurship in the economy.

But although the inseparable result of the above policies would be to reverse the proportion of foreign ownership, it would divert us from our main task to make foreign ownership a preoccupation in itself. There may be a case for legislation against foreign take-over in certain sensitive areas, but the attempt to "buy back" foreign-owned industry is fundamentally misguided. For instance, the aim of Walter Gordon to see Canadians given the opening to take minority holdings in foreign corporations runs counter to our main objectives. Gordon renews his plea for this kind of investment in his recent book (*A Choice for Canada*, pp. 98-100). But the argument remains very unconvincing. It is unlikely that minority holdings by (patriotic?) Canadian investors will have very much effect on the behaviour of international corporations; not half so much as government arm-twisting will, in any case. And since it will need a substantial amount of government arm-twisting to induce international corporations to depart from their usual policy of 100% ownership, we may as well save our elbow grease for our principal objective. If we really want to gain control over policy through the stock market, it would be much more sensible to invest a concentrated block in the parent company in the U.S.A.; but that is another type of adventure.

The decisive objection, however, against the policy of buying minority holdings in foreign corporations is that it would mean immobilizing scarce investment resources in the present inadequate structure of the economy. It would mean investing in the branch plant economy, when what we need is to get away from it. . . .

It should be clear that the alternative to paralytic continentalism is not some irrational grasping at autarchy in the form of higher tariff barriers or an expulsion of foreign capital. The nub of the alternative is a policy of public Canadian entrepreneurship, and the policy would involve a drive to lower tariff barriers. The aim would be to escape the exceptional and abnormal reliance of our economy on the branch plant. What then sows confusion abut this alternative, and what makes it possible for Liberal politicians to drag across the stage the ghouls and hobgoblins of autarchic stagnation? What, in short, lies behind the failure of nerve so characteristic of large sections of the electorate today?

Problem Is Political

The problem is political. For the alternative I have been trying to outline to be a reality and a source of hope for large numbers of Canadians, it would have to appear as a live political option. But for this, in turn, this policy must find a constituency within the Canadian electorate which can be organized around it. And this is the source of the trouble. The normal constituency for this alternative has not yet crystallized, indeed, it has been a largely passive component of the Canadian political scene in the past.

Canada, to a greater extent than other comparable countries, has been under political leadership close to the financial and business elite. This group has had a decisive voice in both the traditional parties which have succeeded each other in office. . . .

Now this elite presided in a sense at the birth of the country. It was largely their ambition toward cross-continent development in rivalry to the U.S.A. which powered Confederation and helped shape the economic development of the new state. The crucial political fact underlying the present dominance of paralytic continentalism is that this same social group has over the decades come to accommodate itself to continental integration. The successors to the entrepreneurs of British North America, the builders of transcontinental railroads, are the managers of branch plants and those who service them in one way or another. This draft toward integration lies behind the slowly growing hegemony of continentalism in the old political parties. . . .

The alternative policy is only possible if a new political alliance can be formed to take power at the federal level for the first time without the business elite as its vital centre. Because of the nature of the objectives which are the basis of the alternative — planned development of all regions — this alliance could only be founded on the natural political constituency of reform. In any country, this includes middle and lower income groups, but in Canada reform has shown a potentially wide appeal among the people of less advantaged regions and among those who do not belong to the ethnic and confessional group which has virtually monopolized the key posts in the economy and to a significant degree in government as well.

• • •

This has a direct repercussion on Canadian unity. To achieve this by elite brokerage is no longer enough; it has to become real at the base of the political society as well. Unless the association with English Canada comes to have more significance — and value — for the average Quebecer than it has today, the future of Canada is bleak indeed. And the same could undoubtedly be said for the average English-Canadian in relation to French Canada. . . .

Biculturalism and hence the Canadian future require a widespread sense of the value of the Canadian union among non-elites. It requires, therefore, in the same way as a viable Canadian nationalism, a break with elite politics and the creation of an alliance across the regions of the groups which have been kept under greater or lesser degress of political tutelage in the past. The problems of unity and nationalism are therefore inextricably intertwined, and both are linked to a polarization of Canadian politics along socio-economic lines.

The alternatives before Canada: nationalism or continentalism, are therefore far from being as simple as they may first appear. Nor does this question constitute an isolated one. It enters into the heart of our political life as a nation and touches on a set of choices which may set the mould of our politics for generations. In a short space of time we must choose between the continental drift of the elites, and the building of a new political alliance. This implies obviously, too, a political choice in the direct partisan sense. For the building of this alliance is already being attempted by the New Democratic Party.

NATIONAL UNITY: CANADA'S POLITICAL OBSESSION*

John Porter

Canada has no resounding charter myth proclaiming a utopia against which, periodically, progress can be measured. At the most, national goals and dominant values seem to be expressed in geographical terms such as "from sea to sea," rather than in social terms such as "all men are created equal," or "liberty, fraternity, and equality." In the United States there is a utopian image which slowly over time bends intractable social patterns in the direction of equality, but a Canadian counterpart of this image is difficult to find.

• • •

It would probably be safe to say that Canada has never had a political system with this dynamic policy [emerging from the polarization of the right and the left, such as is found in Talcott Parsons' analysis of the American political dynamic or in British experience or in Marxism]. Its two major political parties do not focus to the right and the left. In the sense that both are closely linked with corporate enterprise, the dominant focus has been to the right. One of the reasons why this condition has prevailed is that Canada lacks clearly articulated major goals and values stemming from some charter instrument which emphasizes progress and equality. If there is a major goal of Canadian society it can best be described as an integrative goal. The maintenance of national unity has over-ridden any other goals there might have been, and has prevented a polarizing, within the political system, of conservative and progressive forces. It has never occurred to any Canadian commentators that national unity might in fact be achieved by such polarization. Rather a dissociative federalism is raised to the level of a quasi-religious political dogma, and polarization to right and left in Canadian politics is regarded as disruptive. Consequently the main focus of Canadian politics has been to the right and the maintenance of the *status quo*. The reason that the Liberal party in Canada was in office so many years until 1957 was not because it was a progressive party, but because it served Canada's major goal of national unity.

The major themes in Canadian political thought emphasize those characteristics, mainly regional and provincial loyalties, which divide the Canadian population. Consequently integration and national unity must be a constantly reiterated goal to counter such divisive sentiments. The dialogue is between unity and discord rather than progressive and conservative forces. The question which arises is whether the discord-unity dialogue has any real meaning in the lives of Canadians, or whether it has become, in the middle of the twentieth century, a political technique of conservatism. Canada must be one of the few major industrial societies in which the right

* Reprinted from *The Vertical Mosaic: An Analysis of Social Class and Power in Canada*, by John Porter, Toronto, University of Toronto Press, 1965, pp. 368-369. By permission. © University of Toronto Press, 1973.

and left polarization has become deflected into disputes over regionalism and national unity.

Canada's major political and intellectual obsession, national unity, has had its effect on the careers of men who take on political roles. It has put a premium on the type of man whom we shall label the administrative politician and has discounted the professional political career in which creative politicians can assume leadership roles. Creative politics at the national level has not been known in Canada since before World War I, when the westward thrust to Canada's empire was still a major national goal. Since the empire of the west was secured, national goals of development have not been known. . . .

THE NATIONAL OUTLOOK OF ENGLISH-SPEAKING CANADIANS*

Kenneth McNaught

Two Founding Races?

Probably because the alternative is so clumsy, the terms "English- Canadian" or "English" are used interchangeably in Quebec to signify those people in the rest of Canada who do not speak French or who are not of French descent. Yet these terms are wildly misleading. They imply the existence in Canada of only two races, and thus that any revision of Confederation must be based upon a dialogue or bargaining process between these two races. Each term also carries the suggestion that the words "Canada" and "Canadian" have come to mean "English Canada" and "'English Canadian." Thus the problem in Quebec eyes concerns the relations between the "two nations"; and it is a striking fact that "nation" and "race" are virtually interchangeable terms in Quebec. . . .

Having established that Canada is composed of two races (or nations, or cultures), the argument goes on to say that only the French nation is really conscious of its own identity and destiny and that without Quebec, Canada would become balkanized. The "English" race or culture is so amorphous that it depends upon the French-Canadian nation to keep it from falling into the arms of the United States or from breaking up into regional fragments. At the same time, it is this enfeebled English-Canadian race which has triumphantly imposed its image on Canada and made necessary the French-Canadian revolution. Strange argument. . . .

The most striking facts about the English-speaking view of Canada are that it rejects racial nationalism and is the product of a deep commitment to slowly evolved historical tradition. . . .

• • •

* From Peter Russell, (ed.), *Nationalism in Canada*, Toronto, McGraw-Hill Company of Canada Ltd., 1966. By permission of the author and publisher.

At the time of Confederation, indeed, all the supporters of the movement, French- and English-speaking alike, talked of the founding of a new nationality. No amount of quibbling about the different meanings attached by "English" and "French" to the word "nation" can obscure the fact that in the 1860s a political nationality was being founded. The debate and conferences leave absolutely no room for doubt on the matter. Nor is there room to doubt that English-speaking Canadians, then and even more now, thought of Canadian nationality as something that included people of French, British and other origins and which would move steadily toward its own sense of identity. That identity was not to be homogeneous in the American sense, but diverse. It would, and has guaranteed to various minorities (especially the French-speaking minority) particular rights with respect to language, religion, land-holding, military service, hunting and fishing.

Yet, while local differences of culture and law were to be guaranteed (especially in Quebec), there was never any question of an "equality of two founding races." The "races" were, in fact, not equal. A central purpose of Confederation was to recognize this fact and to avoid the frictions which the "two nations" idea had created during the unhappy political evolution under the 1841 Act of Union.

In order to maintain minority rights within Quebec and the other provinces, without at the same time permitting Quebec to become a state within a state, the predominance of Ottawa and the rights of the Canadian majority there (however it might be composed) had to be accepted. . . .

Any survey of Canadian political history reveals that the idea of two "founding races" (each with the expectation of its own developing nationality) has been and must be destructive of the idea of Canada. . . .

Pragmatism and "The Compact"

A large part of contemporary Quebec's distrust of "English Canadians" stems from a fixed belief that they are inveterate centralizers. In fact, of course, centralization has never been a fixed goal of English-speaking Canadians. At the time of Confederation Macdonald encountered stiff opposition to an overblown central government from the Maritime Provinces and, in some respects, from the Grit elements within the coalition government of the united province of Canada. Indeed, it was one measure of his pragmatism and of his faith in the idea of a political nationality that he abandoned his preferred goal of legislative union as opposed to a federal pattern of government. Again, the great political-legal battles of the 1880s and '90s between Mowat and Macdonald, the "better terms" campaign in the Maritimes with its peak in the secession resolutions presented by W.S. Fielding in Nova Scotia, and the near-rebellion in Manitoba over the C.P.R. monopoly, all attest to a jealous regard for provincial rights on the part of a majority of English-speaking Canadians.

It is certainly true that English-speaking Canadians have also frequently turned to the central government for the fulfilment of some of their aspirations. But very often this has been for the protection of regional rights or opportunities. In the struggle over Manitoba Schools, for example, the division of Canadian opinion was not simply Quebec against the rest. A very large number of English-speaking Canadians believed that the remedial power of the federal government should be used to sustain minority rights within a province. Furthermore, in many of the instances of apparent English-speaking Canadian support for centralization, a major purpose has been that of using the economic powers of Ottawa to equalize provincial opportunities — not for the purpose of producing a bland national con-formity, but for the purpose of preserving viable provincial or regional dif-ferences of culture. This has been illustrated particularly in the various phases of the Maritimes Rights movement and in the western Progressive movement.

The point is that English-speaking Canadians have always seen the Cana-dian political state as one in which there is a necessarily shifting balance between the central and provincial powers. Their willingness today to undertake a major redressing of that balance is simply one of many historical examples of a continuing process. Nor is the process always dic-tated by reasons of ideology or politics. Frequently it has had a strong material basis. In the 1880s, the 1920s and the 1960s, the almost indepen-dent prosperity of Ontario and British Columbia has been a considerable factor in these provinces' ready acceptance of "co-operative federalism."

Yet despite the cyclical provincial-rightism of English-speaking Cana-dians, there is an equally consistent reassertion of the validity of the nation, and it is this that seems most to irritate the *nationalistes* of Quebec. It does so because they vastly underrate the complexity and change in the idea itself. . . . Much of the reason for this change — an acceptance of multi-racialism, or multi-culturalism — is to be found in the confidence produced by the simple fact of Canadian survival. And since that survival has clearly depended upon a flexible response to regionalism, racial feeling and religious differences, tradition has planted firmly in the minds of English-speaking Canadians the idea that their national loyalty is to national diversi-ty. Unhappily this seems trite only to English-speaking Canadians.

Quebec's Complaints

Quebec, despite these facts of the English-speaking Canadian development, still charges that in the past English-speaking Canadians have broken "the compact" — by refusing to honour the guarantees to the French language in Manitoba, by refusing to extend language privileges to French-Canadian minorities in other provinces, by imposing conscription for overseas service in the interests of British imperialism and by excluding French Canadians from a share of the senior positions in the federal civil service. Less convinc-ingly, but with even greater heat, Quebec charges that the English-speaking power élite has used its combined political-economic domination to exclude Quebeckers from managerial and ownership status in the province's in-dustry. The result of this arrogant domination, argue the Quebeckers, was to render their province a "reservation" or "colony" to be exploited by the English-Canadian and American capital, which adroitly financed such un-savory politicians as Maurice Duplessis and used demagogic pseudo- nationalism as a blind behind which to extend their economic control. The answer to such colonialism was, of course, revolution.

Again we find inconsistency in the Quebec argument. . . . From declaring that the Quiet Revolution is justified because "English Canada" broke the compact, the ideological directors of Quebec pass to the assertion that the original agreement never was good enough. Now it is not enough merely to undo the grievances within the original framework. It is necessary to break the structure altogether and establish two racial states. . . .

In dealing with this nimble logic, English-speaking Canadians are both baffled and resentful. But to say that they have not drawn up any thin red line of verbal battle, that they have generally preferred the familiar paths of compromise and conciliation, is not to say that they have no convictions. I have already noted that the English-speaking Canadians have a very definite concept of Canadian historic amalgam of the original and undoubted purposes of Confederation plus modifications enjoined by the facts of immigration and growth. Reluctance to contend directly with the ever more extreme racial nationalism of Quebec (except by way of concession) is also explained by a compound of causes.

First, strangely, is acceptance of much of the case put forward by Quebec. Most English-speaking Canadians agree that there has been injustice along the way. In the Manitoba schools question, that injustice was a specific and unconstitutional denial to French Canadians of rights and expectations spelled out in 1867 and 1870. In the case of conscription in 1917 there was extremely bad political management of the policy itself, and Quebec opinion was still further inflamed by the contemporaneous and deliberate prohibition by Manitoba and Ontario of teaching in the French language in public schools. . . .

The Present Condition

. . . Most Canadians sympathize entirely with the feeling of exclusion which is the basis of the Quiet Revolution's triumph. Indeed, most English-speaking Canadians who have followed Quebec affairs (and there are many more such people than Quebeckers care to admit) admire the new and forthright willingness to use the government of Quebec to achieve collective purposes: to broaden the base of social welfare and to halt the takeover by American capital. But these are purposes which are agreeable to most Canadians, and they are repelled by the new Quebec insistence that such goals can be achieved only through virtually independent "provincial states." That insistence is bound to render difficult or impossible the achievement of similar goals at the national level since it will rob Ottawa of the essential powers of economic planning — indeed it has already placed grave impediments in the path of such planning.

But guilt feelings and admiration for the new positive approach to the use of government are only half of the explanation of the English-speaking Canadian reluctance to spell out its mounting resistance to racial nationalism and to a new straightjacket constitution. The non-French Canadians know that they have attained a genuine sense of Canadian independence and that the growth of this feeling is not the result of logic-chopping and perpetual rewriting of constitutional formulae. It is the result of deep belief in growth by precedent and the converse suspicion that it is dangerous to commit to words the inner nature of human or social relationships. Since these two facts of feeling and philosophy lie at the heart of the matter, they are worth a further word.

First, independence. Since the enunication in the 1860s of a new nationality, and despite the chronic outcropping of British loyalties, English-speaking Canadians have moved steadily towards independence. From one precedent to another down to the separate declaration of war in 1939 and the notably "un-British" stand taken at the time of the Suez crisis [in 1956] they gradually severed the constitutional and, to a considerable extent, the emotional ties with the "mother country." Not infrequently, as the career of Mackenzie King amply demonstrates, this process was hastened by an almost too sensitive recognition of Quebec's anti-British creed. Even with respect to the Commonwealth, as opposed to specifically British interest, it would take exceptional daring to assert that the English-speaking majority does not place its primary loyalty with the United Nations or with Canada itself before its concern for things British. The plain fact is that non-French Canada has experienced a sense of independence extending much further beyond the constitutional aspect than has Quebec. It is not without reason that some English-speaking Canadians begin to suspect Quebec of frailty in its protestations of independent goals. . . .

Canadians of British descent have always regarded the political process as essentially pragmatic-experimental. They have shied away from detailed and comprehensive definitions of political and social relationships, preferring to see change come by the establishment of precedents which then become the justification of future decisions. That is why they have continued to hold to the English common law, and that is why civil liberties in English-speaking Canada have been more carefully cherished than they have in Quebec. This is why, too, they adjust more easily to multi-racial nationality than does Quebec. A broadening of rights by precedent — such as the instituting of simultaneous translation in Parliament, the proliferation of dominion-provincial consultations, revision of the appointments policy in the federal civil service and crown corporations, or such other possibilities as special Supreme Court panels of judges trained in the Quebec Civil Code to hear cases arising under that Code — it is this method of change that appeals to English-speaking Canadians.

By contrast, French Canadians prefer to systematize and codify the law, the constitution and, indeed, a broad range of social relationships. Because of these philosophic characteristics and a natural proclivity to verbalization, French Canadians mistake the nearly silent and the usually flexible English-speaking attitude as an absence of conviction or determination. No misunderstanding could have more disastrous and predictable consequences. The point has been well taken by some of the very originators of the Quiet Revolution — by those, in particular, who saw that revolution not only as a movement for social justice but also for the liberalization of Quebec. Of these, Pierre-Elliott Trudeau is perhaps the outstanding example. . . .

BIBLIOGRAPHY

(See also Bibliography, Chapter 1)

Canadian Nationalism

Bell, D., and Tepperman, L., *The Roots of Disunity: A Look at Canadian Political Culture*, Toronto, M. & S., 1979.

Berger, C., (ed.), *Imperialism and Nationalism," 1884-1914*, Toronto, C.C., 1969.

Brady, A., "The Meaning of Canadian Nationalism," *International Journal*, XIX, 2, Summer, 1964.

Calvet, A.L., and Crener, M.A., "Foreign Business Control: The Canadian Experience, 1973-1977," *C.P.A.*, 22, 3, Fall, 1979.

Canada, *Foreign Ownership and the Structure of Canadian Industry* [Watkins Report], Ottawa, Q.P., 1968.

Canada, *Report of the Royal Commission on National Development in the Arts, Letters, and Sciences* [Massey Report], Ottawa, Q.P., 1951.

Carty, R.K., and Ward, W.P., (eds.), *Entering the Eighties: Canada in Crisis*, Toronto, Oxford, 1980.

Cook, R., "The Canadian Conservative Tradition: An Historical Perspective," *J.C.S.*, VIII, 4, November, 1973.

Cook, R., *The Maple Leaf Forever: Essays in Nationalism and Politics in Canada*, Toronto, Macmillan, 1971.

Crispo, J.H.G., *Mandate for Canada*, Don Mills, Ontario, General Publishing, 1979.

Cross, M.S., (ed.), *The Frontier Thesis and the Canadas: The Debate on the Impact of the Canadian Environment*, Toronto, C.C., 1970.

Drummond, R., "Nationalism and Ethnic Demands: Some Speculations on a Congenial Note," *C.J.P.S.*, X, 2, June, 1977.

Editorial Committee, "A Citizen's Guide to the Herb Gray Report," *The Canadian Forum*, LI, 611, December, 1971.

Federal-Provincial Committee on the Foreign Ownership of Land, *Report to the First Ministers*, Canadian Intergovernmental Conference.

Feldman, E., and Nevitte, N., *The Future of North America: Canada, the United States and Quebec Nationalism*, Cambridge, Harvard University Press, 1979.

Friedenberg, E.Z., *Deference to Authority: The Case of Canada*, White Plains, N.Y., M.E. Sharpe, 1980.

Gagne, W., *Nationalism, Technology, and the Future of Canada*, Macmillan, Toronto, 1976.

Geddes, G., (ed.), *Divided We Stand*, Toronto, Peter Martin, 1977.

Gibbins, R., "Models of Nationalism: A Case Study of Political Ideologies in the Canadian West," *C.J.P.S.*, X, 2, June, 1977.

Godfrey, D., and Watkins, M., (eds.), *Gordon to Watkins to You*, Toronto, New Press, 1970.

Gordon, W.L., *Troubled Canada*, Toronto, M. & S., 1961.

Gordon, W., *What is Happening to Canada?*, Toronto, M. & S., 1978.

Gordon, W., *Storm Signals: New Economic Policies for Canada*, Toronto, M. & S., 1975.

Gordon, W., *A Choice for Canada*, Toronto, M. & S., 1966.

Grant, G., *Lament for a Nation: The Defeat of Canadian Nationalism*, Toronto, M. & S., 1965.

Gray, Herbert E., *Foreign Direct Investment in Canada*, Ottawa, Government of Canada, 1972.

Hardin, H., *A Nation Unaware: The Canadian Economic Culture*, Vancouver, J.J. Douglas, 1974.

Harvey, T.G., and Harvey, S., *Political Culture in a Canadian Community*, Toronto, C.C., 1973.

Heisey, A., *The Great Canadian Stampede: The Rush to Economic Nationalism*, Toronto, Griffin House, 1973.

Hutcheson, J., *Dominance and Dependency: Liberalism and Na-*

tional Policies in the North Atlantic Triangle, Toronto, M. & S., 1978.

Johnstone, J.C., Young People's Images of Canadian Society, Studies of the Royal Commission on Bilingualism and Biculturalism, No. 2, Ottawa, Q.P., 1969.

Laxer, R.M., Canada Ltd., The Political Economy of Dependence, Toronto, M. & S., 1973.

Laxer, J., and Laxer, R., The Liberal Idea of Canada: Pierre Trudeau and the Question of Canada's Survival, Toronto, Lorimer, 1977.

Levin, M., and Sylvester, C., Foreign Ownership, Toronto, Musson, 1972.

Levitt, K., Silent Surrender, Toronto, Macmillan, 1970.

Lightbody, J., "A Note on the Theory of Nationalism as a Function of Ethnic Demands," C.J.P.S., II, 3, September, 1969.

Litvak, I.A., and Maule, C.J., The Canadian Multinationals, Toronto, Butterworths, 1981.

Lloyd, T., and McLeod, J.T., Agenda 70: Proposals for a Creative Politics, Toronto, U.T.P., 1968.

Marchak, P., In Whose Interests?: An Essay in Multinational Corporations in a Canadian Context, Toronto, M. & S., 1979.

Mathie, W., "Political Community and the Canadian Experience: Reflections on Nationalism, Federalism, and Unity," C.J.P.S., XII, 1, March, 1979.

McKillop, A.B., "Nationalism, Identity and Canadian Intellectual History," Q.Q., 81, 4, Winter, 1974.

Meisel, J., "Political Culture and the Politics of Culture," C.J.P.S., VII, 4, December, 1974.

Migué, J.-L., Nationalistic Policies in Canada: An Economic Approach, Montreal, L'Institut de recherches C.D. Howe, 1979.

Morse, S.J., "Being a Canadian: Aspects of National Identity Among a Sample of University Students in Saskatchewan," Canadian Journal of Behavioural Science, 9, 1977.

Morton, W.L., The Canadian Identity, Toronto, Madison, 1961.

Newman, P.C., Home Country, Toronto, M. & S., 1973.

Niosi, J., The Economy of Canada: A Study of Ownership and Control, Montreal, Black Rose, 1978.

Ostroy, B., The Cultural Connection, Toronto, M. & S., 1978.

Resnick, P., The Land of Cain: Class and Nationalism in English Canada, 1945-1975, Vancouver, New Star Books, 1977.

Roblin, D., "A New National Policy and Canadian Nationalism," C.P.A., 16, 4, Winter, 1973.

Rotstein, A., "Is There an English-Canadian Nationalism?," J.C.S., 13, 1, Summer, 1978.

Rotstein, A., The Precarious Homestead: Essays on Economics, Technology and Nationalism, Toronto, New Press, 1973.

Rotstein, A., and Lax, G., (eds.), Getting It Back: A Program for Canadian Independence, Toronto, Clarke, Irwin, 1974.

Rotstein, A., and Lax, G., (eds.), Independence: The Canadian Challenge, Toronto, M. & S., 1972.

Rugman, A.M., Multinationalism in Canada: Theory, Performance, and Economic Impact, Boston, Martinus Nijhoff, 1980.

Russell, P., (ed.), Nationalism in Canada. Toronto, McG.-H., 1966.

Safarian, A.E., Foreign Ownership of Canadian Industry, Toronto, McG.-H., 1966.

Safarian, A.E., "Foreign Investment in Canada: Some Myths," J.C.S., VI, 3, August, 1971.

Smiley, D.V., The Canadian Political Nationality, Toronto, Methuen, 1967.

Smiley, D.V., "The Federal Dimension of Canadian Economic Nationalism," D.L.R., 1, 3, October, 1974.

Smiley, D.V., "Canada and the Quest for a National Policy," C.J.P.S., VIII, 1, March, 1975.

Stevenson, G., "Foreign Direct Investment and the Provinces: A Study of Elite Attitudes," C.J.P.S., VII, 4, December, 1974.

Symons, T.H.B., To Know Ourselves:

The *Report of the Commission on Canadian Studies*, Ottawa, Association of Universities and Colleges of Canada, Vols. I and II, 1975.

Teeple, G., (ed.), *Capitalism and the National Question in Canada*, Toronto, U.T.P., 1972.

Young, R.A., "National Identification in English Canada: Implications for Quebec Independence," *J.C.S.*, 12, 3, 1977.

Canada and the U.S.A.

Axline, A., Hyndman, J.E., Lyon, P., and Molot, M., (eds.), *Continental Community? Independence and Integration in North America*, Toronto, M. & S., 1974.

Baldwin, D.A., and Smallwood, F., (eds.), *Canadian-American Relations: The Politics and Economics of Interdependence*, Hannover, N.H., Dartmouth College, 1967.

Beigie, C.E., and Hero, A.O., (eds.), *Natural Resources in U.S.-Canadian Relations*, Boulder, Col., Westview Press, 1980, Vol. I.

Cairns, A., "Political Science in Canada and the Americanization Issue," *C.J.P.S.*, VIII, 2, June, 1975.

Canadian-American Committee, *The New Environment for Canadian-American Relations*, Montreal, Private Planning Association of Canada, 1972.

Clark, S.D., "Canada and the American Value System," in *The Developing Canadian Community*, Toronto, U.T.P., 2nd ed., 1968.

Cook, R., and McNaught, K., *Canada and the U.S.A.*, Toronto, Clarke, Irwin, 1963.

Cullen, D., Jobson, J.D., Schneck, R., "Towards the Development of a Canadian-American Scale: A Research Note," *C.J.P.S.*, XI, 2, June, 1978.

Dickey, J.S., (ed.), *The United States and Canada*, Englewood Cliffs, N.J., P.-H., 1964.

Fox, A.B., *et al.*, *Canada and the United States: Transnational and Transgovernmental Relations*, New York, Columbia, 1976.

Lipset, S.M., *Revolution and Counter-Revolution*, New York, Basic Books, 1968, chapter 2, "The United States and Canada."

Lumsden, I., (ed.), *Close the 49th Parallel, etc.: The Americanization of Canada*, Toronto, U.T.P., 1970.

McCaffrey, G., (ed.), *The U.S. and Us*, Proceedings of the 37th Couchiching Conference, Toronto, C.I.P.A., 1969.

Mathews, R.D., "The U.S. and Canadian Intellectual History," *J.C.S.*, VI, 4, November, 1971.

Morchain, J., (ed.), *Sharing a Continent: An Introduction to Canadian-American Relations*, Toronto, McG.-H.R., 1973.

Murray, J.L., (ed.), *Canadian Cultural Nationalism: The Fourth Lester B. Pearson Conference on the Canada-U.S. Relationship*, Toronto, Macmillan, 1978.

Pope, W.H., *The Elephant and the Mouse*, Toronto, M. & S., 1971.

Presthus, R., (ed.), *Cross-National Perspectives: United States and Canada*, Leiden, Brill, 1977.

Preston, R.A., (ed.), *Perspectives on Revolution and Evolution*, Durham, N.C., Duke University Press, 1979.

Preston, R.A., (ed.), *The Influence of the United States on Canadian Development: Eleven Case Studies*, Durham, N.C., Duke University Press, 1972.

Purdy, A., (ed.), *The New Romans: Candid Canadian Opinions of the U.S.*, Edmonton, Hurtig, 1968.

Redekop, J., "A Reinterpretation of Canadian-American Relations," *C.J.P.S.*, IX, 2, June, 1976.

Redekop, J., (ed.), *The Star-Spangled Beaver*, Toronto, Peter Martin, 1971.

Swanson, R.F., *Canadian-American Summit Diplomacy, 1923-1973*, (speeches and documents), Carleton Library No. 81, Toronto, M. & S., 1975.

Taylor, C., *Snow Job: Canada, the United States and Vietnam (1945-1973)*, Toronto, Anansi, 1974.

Tupper, S.R., and Bailey, D., *One Continent, Two Voices: The Future of Canada-United States Relations*, Toronto, Clarke, Irwin, 1967.

Willoughby, W.R., *The Joint Organizations of Canada and the United States*, Toronto, U.T.P., 1979.

Wise, S.F., and Brown, R.C., *Canada Views the United States: Nineteenth Century Political Attitudes*, Toronto, Macmillan, 1967.

6

FRENCH CANADA

While French Canada encompasses more than Quebec, the centre of attention in the past two decades has been that province where the "Quiet Revolution" of the 1960s transformed a whole society rapidly by modernizing its socio-economic and cultural conditions. One repercussion was a revival of the nationalism which is latent in Quebec.

Nationalism was embraced by all of Quebec's political parties but by none more successfully than the separatist movement, which emerged with passion in the mid-sixties. Initially divided into factions and small parties, the movement was welded together by René Lévesque, a former Liberal cabinet minister, who created the Mouvement Souveraineté Association and then converted it into the Parti Québécois in October, 1968. Having secured the adhesion of two small separatist parties which had won modest support in the provincial election in 1966, the P.Q. slowly but steadily advanced to power in the next three elections, winning 23 per cent of the popular vote in 1970, 30 per cent in 1973, and 41 per cent in 1976.

Quebec has now had a separatist government since November 15, 1976, when Premier Lévesque's party won 71 of the 110 seats in the National Assembly. Although the P.Q. was committed to obtaining political sovereignty for Quebec in economic association with Canada, the government has not yet been able to achieve its aim. The constitutional status of the province remains the same despite two major events that offered the possibility of change.

The first was the long-proposed referendum which the P.Q. government finally held on May 20, 1980. Having assiduously pursued a gradualist approach to avoid alarming moderates, and having prepared and pre-tested a cautious question asking Quebecers whether they wished to give the government power merely to negotiate sovereignty-association with Canada, the Péquistes were dismayed to discover that 60 per cent of the electorate replied "No." What was even more disconcerting to the separatists was that a majority of francophones apparently had voted negatively, since only 15 of the 110 ridings had had a majority saying "yes."

Buoyed up by what seemed to be a forthright rejection of the main plank in the P.Q.'s platform and encouraged by the fact that the P.Q. government had lost every one of 11 by-elections since the party had come to power, the Liberals under Claude Ryan pressed for a general election. When it arrived on April 23, 1981, it was the Liberals' turn to be surprised. Premier Lévesque humiliated all of the opposition parties by winning a more resounding victory than that in 1976. The P.Q. captured 80 seats in an assembly which had been increased to 122 members and even more significantly won 49 per cent of the popular vote. The Liberals also actually did better than they had in 1976, increasing their seats from 26 to 42 and their percentage of the vote from 34 to 46, but the psychological disappointment was interpreted as defeat. The two minor parties paid the price of the others' gains; the Union Nationale and the Créditistes suffered drastic reductions in their votes and their representation in the Assembly was wiped out.

The apparent contradiction between the results of the general election and the results of the referendum reflected the ambiguous mood which still seems to prevail in Quebec.

This chapter repeats several items from the fourth edition since they are still very pertinent. The interview with René Lévesque reveals as much about the man as about the party he leads. Similarly, the program of the Parti Québécois, presented here in its 1980 version, indicates that the party is as much concerned with social democratic goals as with political independence. The full text of 46 pages is a slate for comprehensive and intensive socio-economic reform and development of French-Canadian culture.

Prime Minister Trudeau's argument "In Defence of Federalism," given more than 15 years ago, is still one of the best expositions of the advantages of federalism to Quebec and the weaknesses of separatism. The editor's article points out that separatism is not a new phenomenon in Canada. It has been, in his view, a recurrent "death wish" which has plagued the country from its inception.

Three items which appeared in this chapter in the fourth edition have been omitted. "The Battle of the Balance Sheets — Has Quebec Gained or Lost Money?" (fourth edition, pp. 152-154) has been replaced by an abridged article by three economists who examine in a much more sophisticated and thorough manner the same question of whether Quebec would benefit or suffer financially from leaving Confederation. Juris Dreifeld's article, "Nationalism and Socialism in French Canada," has been omitted from this edition because of a lack of space. It will be found in the fourth edition, pp. 162-175. The table entitled "Quebec Provincial Election Results, 1960-1976," which appeared on p. 176 of the fourth edition, has been omitted since the same data can be found now in Chapter 18.

A final item gives the question and the results of the vote on the Quebec referendum on sovereignty-association that was held on May 20, 1980.

The bibliography at the end of this chapter is long but by no means exhaustive since the number of books and articles on the subject of Quebec is very extensive, especially in French, and continues to grow. The two Montreal daily newspapers, *Le Devoir* and *La Presse*, are undoubtedly the best sources of information and commentary on the rapidly changing Quebec scene. *The Globe and Mail* and *The Toronto Star* also give good coverage. A monthly magazine, *Report*, which was devoted to covering developments in Confederation, particularly in Quebec, has unfortunately ceased publication.

RENE LEVESQUE TALKS ABOUT SEPARATISM — AND OTHER THINGS*

(From an interview in 1975 with René Lévesque, the leader of the Parti Québécois, conducted by Greg-Michael Troy, editor, *Medium II*, before the Parti Québécois won power and Mr. Lévesque became Premier.)

* From *Medium II*, student newspaper, Erindale College, University of Toronto, February 27, 1975. By permission.

Two Nations

Question: So, would you call Canada a nation?

Answer: . . . A nation just doesn't mean the state, however, in English it mostly is the state; in other words if you have a government you have a nation. So Canada is a nation by English definition only because it is political. In French, you have a second meaning, which is a more basic definition: people who have a common history, a common language, a sort of common community feeling of being an entity that wants to live together. Another example on an international level might be Scotland. I think Scotland is a nation. I think the Scottish people are beginning to come of the same opinion. They forgot it for awhile. The Basques are a nation both in France and Spain. The Slovaks are a nation. But the English definition of nation often means "there's the government, there's the nation." So I suppose on that basis, in English you would call Canada a nation. In French we couldn't say "la nation canadienne" that easily.

Q: That sounds curiously a lot like what Chaput wrote about in his book: "Why I am a Separatist" . . . two nations within Canada.

A: That goes away back, I mean it's always been a sort of semantic defence for French Canadians, being a minority, being cooped up mostly in Quebec, at least the only place where we can make any decisions worthwhile. It's always been a sort of, I don't know, a bone of contention between the two groups because the moment we say that there are two nations, "les deux nations," you've got a hell of a lot of good old Anglo-Saxon stock that get up and say "No. No, there's only one nation, one country." . . . one everything, but that's a lot of "crap." Eventually, if the Quebec people are a nation, that will be one particular problem they will have to face. If they want to be a nation both culturally and bureaucratically, that's something else again. But that's what we're working for. So in your sense, there will be two nations, definitely, one with a Quebec government and the other with a government wherever you want to put it, Winnipeg or Toronto. Also, an association between two sovereign states, like the Common Market might be possible.

No Canadian Identity

Q: If Canada is two nations, loosely confederated under one flag, and the English nation has this growing trend towards nationalism, how does this affect the separatist movement or the Parti Québécois?

A: Not much! Because Canadian nationalism is more or less a throwback to John A. Macdonald except in modern costume. The Canadian federal state was set up, I think mostly, on the grounds of being scared of the United States. . . . Canadian nationalism is mostly the same thing today only under a different guise. American economic control doesn't seem to create the same kind of reaction in Quebec. We have had our own leftist groups, however, who would like to kick the Americans out, and even a few romantics tied into the image of Che Guevara, but that was a few years back.

Q: It's died down now?

A: Yet, it has and in a way it's kind of sad because at least the kids were actively involved. Right now what you see is a sort of disinvolvement among the people between 18-22, the college age level. Thank God at the high school level — I'm speaking of Quebec — it seems to be picking up again; they're becoming curious about politics and seem to be a little less subcultural. But it's hard to gain people's interests because it's all par for the course now, and it will be until Quebec makes up its mind. It's all very classical, and being very classical is a problem. We in Quebec think of Canada as a very artificial creation conned upon our forefathers whom we now call the "Fathers of Confederation," but who were really nothing but average politicians of the time who made money out of scandals like the Canadian Pacific. Confederation was conned upon people who were not consulted, because we were just colonies afraid of the American design for annexation. Canada never gelled into a real country, not even after a hundred years. . . . A Canadian is just someone who lives here. That's all. There's no national entity.

Q: . . . and the Parti Québécois isn't asking the same question? Isn't searching for a national entity? Isn't frustrated with the same sort of results?

A: We don't have to go out and search to find it. Look, walk around the streets or walk somewhere where you will find French people of your generation and ask 10 of them, the first 10 you meet who are between 18-30, ask them "Are you a Canadian? A French Canadian or a Québécois?" 9 out of 10 of them don't need a philosophical discussion, 9 out of 10 will answer ". . . well what the hell, I'm Québécois." That's the way they see themselves and that's basic.

Conditioned by Propaganda

Q: About as basic as a pair of Levi's pre-faded blue jeans, which are mass-produced to meet the needs of a highly propagandized generation. Every young generation accepts what appears to be different, exciting. The emphasis is not on whether it is right or wrong, but rather on the social appeal. The Parti Québécois is appealing to the new consciousness because you are different. . .

A: You are conditioned by social propaganda and Canadian propaganda. But what I mean is this: every god-damn thing in Canada that has real power — business, big-money, the Federal Government and presently the Quebec provincial government — are all extremely powerful propaganda tools. The C.B.C. is another example along with every other god-damn media who promote Canadian unity. Yet in spite of all that, the new generations in Quebec are growing up and calling themselves Québécois.

Q: Granted, but what I'm basically asking is what makes your propaganda better than the Federal government's? As one gets older it becomes harder to distinguish one political party from the other . . . basically they're all structure with ravenous appetites for controlling people.

Parti Québécois Different

A: Yes, that's a problem that nobody has solved yet, not in Mao's China or the United States. Nobody has devised the perfect political system, not even the future system where people will participate (a lot of people use the word participation), in other words a system that allows people to be decision makers on all levels. I think, however, you have to drive towards that. The Parti Québécois is doing so. We're the only party that I know of in North America that has had the idea and tries to implement it. For instance we're the only damn party I know of that has never taken a cent from any corporation and refuses to. One of our basic regulations states: people are voting, we're not a corporation and we're not a union either. In other words we're a party of and for the people. You can't create a revolution in people's minds. People change slowly, and that change becomes noticeable when people become more conscious of the fact that they hold the power. And that's the best thing we can hope for.

Q: A few years ago Vallières wrote a book titled "Le Temps de Choisir" . . . in it Vallières displayed a rather radically inclined Marxist temperament. . . . Do you support Vallières' political and economic philosophies?

A: Take a guy who starts with a Marxist attitude and is honest about it. (We have a few in the party, a few of quality, but there are others who call themselves Marxists and don't know what they're talking about.) He believes in it. Why the hell should we refuse him? He's working with the party. His Marxist ideas can be very stimulating, but the Party's platform and the Party's attitude doesn't go that far at all; so isn't that normal? . . . But there are people who are more radical and I hope to God we get more of them because we need them at least for now.

Bilingualism

Q: In Chaput's book, *Why I am a separatist*, he stated that the Québécois fear bilingualism and that ". . . bilingualism is a meaningless word, a sin against nature." Would you agree with this?

A: NO! Consider bilingualism at the personal level. In other words a person living in Toronto is kind of cooped up and very narrow-minded. Canada is not that big an entity in the world if he only speaks English. The same would apply here. The more French-Canadian kids become bilingual, or even trilingual, the better, because we're in a global village. The world is shrinking and we know damn well when the Arabs decide something about oil we're affected the next day. We should be open to the whole world. So bilingualism or trilingualism on a personal level is ideal. The Party pushes for better English teaching, but on the other hand, collectively, community-wise in Quebec, the basic official language and the language of promotion should be French. There's no contradiction in that.

French Survival

Q: When I lived in Montreal a couple of years ago I came to notice how critical the Québécois are of themselves.

A: Yes, even in many ways they have complexes. I think every colony has that. You have inferiority complexes on the English-Canadian side facing the American border. What the hell.

Q: How has the French culture survived then? How do you explain the existence, the continued existence of loyalty towards the culture?

A: That's a hell of a good question because we're in a transition period. What kept the French culture going, at least the French language and some rather minor cultural achievements, was mostly the fact that we were a very rural society; basically, a peasant society tied to the church and tied to tradition. One saying we have held for generations in Quebec is "The language is the guardian of religion," in other words, the English were Protestants and the French were Catholics. That was more or less a rule of thumb. Plus we were a peasant rural-based social structure. Over a hundred years ago Montreal was mostly an English city, and even Quebec City which is 95 percent or more French was at least in good proportion English. That kept, basically like a museum piece, the French language and traditions going. Quebec's birth rate was extremely high as it is in peasant or underdeveloped societies, and that's what we were in many ways. Things are different now. Since the Second World War there has been a sort of acceleration of development in Quebec, notably in education (what was called the Quiet Revolution). The old fashioned traditional crutches just broke down. For example, the church is practically non-existent; certainly it is not a framing influence anyway. The same with rural life. The peasant-based society has practically disappeared. Quebec is a part of North America, which has changed more rapidly than any other place. From country people to city people. All the old traditional reasoning, the traditional vision of French cultural survival has broken down. What's going on now is a modernization, let's say a catching up process with ups and downs. We have a very fragile cultural identity now that we're not tied to religion, not tied to a traditional outlook or a country-based outlook of being homogenized by big cities. Out of all this is growing a new identity, a new cultural identity and this is what the PQ is working on. What we had before were people who called themselves French Canadians, but French Canadians were just another minority. Now the French people are becoming conscious that they themselves are really a national majority and that they better get themselves an institutional framework to replace what broke down 20 years ago.

Socialism Growing

Q: You've worked with the Liberal Party; you were a part of the Mouvement Souveraineté Association; you've held some different and varying political views. Now as the leader of a very solid party — the Parti Québécois — don't you fear having to cater to individual socialistic philosophies within the party? Won't this slow down the process of creating an institutional framework?

A: I don't see it that way, that we'll have to cater to socialists. "Creeping Socialism" is all over the place, it all depends on how you adapt to it. We're going to become more and more socialistic if we want to survive. That, in a sense, is world wide. . . .

After Victory

Q: How would you go about creating a central bank for Quebec?

A: Quebec is not completely underdeveloped. A central bank is not exactly like creating the world. You have for instance *"Les Caisses des peuples"* which has well over 3 billion dollars accumulated, a pension fund. It administrates open market operations and does it as well as anyone else. We have competent people and the creation of a central bank is not the end of the world.

Q: All right, what if the Royal Bank with 12 billion dollars, the 8th or 9th largest bank in the world, were to withdraw all its capital from Quebec?

A: All *its* monies they can get out and the sooner the better. But Quebec money, Quebec-owned assets, will they go out with that?

Q: The Royal Bank's Head Office is here in Montreal. Its accumulated assets are from across Canada, not just Quebec. What about loans, investments in Quebec corporations?

A: Loans will have to be honored and things like that, but look, why make it such a problem when it will only be a technical operation once we've made a political decision. The Government is set up in Quebec, a referendum is held, people say yes or no. . . . We want it or we want out, if we want out then Canada has a decision to make. Are they going to use the army, in other words, dishonor themselves? We're making a gamble that Canada can normally accept a political decision that will be very clear. Once that's made there'll be a transition period with problems — taxes become Quebec taxes, the banking system becomes a Quebec banking system, trust companies (if they are allowed to continue) will become Quebec-based trust companies — and that's it. I mean it was done in Jamaica, it was done in Nigeria, it was done in Kenya, so why the hell shouldn't it be done in Quebec? There are at least a hundred different models over the last thirty years of countries doing it, so it's not the end of the world.

Q: You raised an interesting point about the Canadian armed forces and this is really the only firm control Trudeau has over Quebec.

A: There are basically two ways of changing political organizations, one is guns and the other is votes. If ever Canada should have the temptation against a clear decision in Quebec to use guns, then woe to Canada.

P.Q. Not Majority

Q: Vallières said the majority of all the Québécois are separatists. Is that true?

A: No. If Vallières said that he meant deep down, past the frustrations every Québécois has the old dream of independence. I would say even the most rabid Quebec federalist, if you were able to scratch down to his basic beliefs would say "oh well, maybe tomorrow, but we're not ready now, perhaps one day it should happen." I suppose on that basis of dreams 80 percent are separatists. If that's what Vallières talks about he's right. If he's talking about nowadays — everybody knows we're not a majority, but we're growing.

Q: Disregarding fanciful philosophies, Mr. Lévesque, and all the "open-eyed" dreams of the Parti Québécois, what do you think your growth capacity is?

A: Look, I'll give you an example, suppose we win, it'll be a bare majority because it's hard to change institutions and it's hard to change a regime that's over a hundred years old, so we win with a 45-50 percent of the vote, then we form a government and there has to be negotiations and pressure and counter pressure and eventually a referendum on what people want. Eventually Quebec officially becomes a country, then it's not 50 percent but 80 percent of the Québécois who will say, ". . . oh, it's not the end of the world, now it's done, now we believe in it because it answers an old normal dream," but in the meantime it's one hell of a job.

• • •

Peaceful Revolution?

Q: Once you have raised the consciousness of the Quebec people to believe in "great expectations," what happens to the store clerk in Trois Rivières who you've turned into a violent revolutionary? How is he supposed to return to his old role? Or can he?

A: Firstly, a basic revolution doesn't mean you have to kill people, a revolution is simply a change that occurs within a hundred years, in other words a rather quick change is a revolution. It can be guns, it can be votes, but the real revolution is that people change their minds — their outlook towards something new. That's a revolution. You have cultural revolutions, you have political revolutions, and they can be tied together, in the sense that we want to change the basic political institutions, in the sense that we want to take the French culture from being just a "hanger on" in North America to becoming its own home and developing it as we think it should, in the sense that we want a society that would be a hell of a lot fairer than now. We want to have co-management of enterprise, in other words we want to see people who are the labor capital to have as much say as the people who are money capital. That's a long process; even unions don't know how to tackle that because they're used to fighting the boss. And all this means a sort of revolution. So in that sense we are making people revolutionaries.

Q: Again, let's assume you're the leader of the first national Quebec government, what happens if you find you can't fill all the promises you've made and you can't adhere to all the philosophical principles you've set?

A: Well, supposing we win the next election and over a transition period the Parti Québécois is in power and I'm there, all right, and four or five years later they kick us out, well, someone else takes over, what the hell. . . .

Q: Exactly, now instead of guns as weapons you're using words and ideologies as the weapons to free yourself from the colonial identity.

A: Yes, we're talking about wars; politics under a different guise, yes well it's always some sort of a war, but if you can keep it verbal it can kill less people, won't it? But it's always war in a sense, yes you're right.

English and Immigrants

A: Out of 6 million people in Quebec only about 750,000 are English-speaking. Quebec is made up of many ethnic groups and we have finally come to the decision we weren't going to become one of them. Look, a Jewish family moves in, an Italian family moves in, a Greek family moves in and 9 out of 10 of them will join the English group, they assimilate themselves with the English while still maintaining their Jewish, Italian and Greek heritage, but they prefer to linguistically join the English group which immediately ties them to the English majority. In other words they're in Quebec as a sort of ghetto tied to Ottawa, Toronto, New York or simply to the English-speaking American continent. It's more productive, more profitable for them to do that. So when you see us, based on a French majority in Quebec, trying to yank Quebec out of Canada, well, the ethnic groups don't like it because it's pulling them out of a majority situation. So you say there's tension, bad feeling in some fields, well if these few hundreds of thousands of people don't like it, then they can get the hell out. If they want to live with us they'll share equal rights. We're not going to stop promoting our own nationalism just because some guys don't like it, the hell with that. There's bad feeling tied to that but we can't help it. There was more frustration and more god-damn exploitation for the French majority over generations by people who stepped on their heads and told them to speak "white" than you can imagine, but you weren't there. Now we're not even telling the English to speak French, we're even guaranteeing them schools if they want to stay here, but if they stay here they become a minority, an official, definite and final minority. If they don't like it when the day comes; then the hell with them. We're not going to go down the drain just because some Italian or English group doesn't want Quebec to make its own decision.

People are Learning

Q: The televison behind you, Mr. Lévesque, when the waiter saw you come in he switched the channel from an English station.

A: I didn't notice.

Q: Yes, but have you noticed that people, especially the Québécois, are individualists out for themselves, perhaps for economic gain, who knows, but it appears to me that the movement you helped create promotes a communal identity "vive la nation de Québec," but in reality people are only interested in what they personally own.

A: I don't think we can change that, at least not in the foreseeable future. Everybody is going to keep on being number one, I guess, and out for himself. But, what is sinking in Quebec is that even if you are an individualist and you still call yourself a Québécois or part of a French-speaking group it is more profitable for you to be part of a dominant healthy society than to be a minority and considered inferior.
A lot of people are learning that.
A lot of people are learning.

THE PROGRAM OF THE PARTI QUÉBÉCOIS*

[Editor's note: this is a very abridged version of the highly detailed 1980 program of the Parti Québécois which in the original is 46 pages long. Many of the headings, introductory commentaries, and specific detailed clauses, including some entire sections, have been omitted. However, the selections quoted are verbatim.]

General Objectives

A Parti Québécois government therefore pledges to:
1. Obtain political sovereignty for Quebec through democratic means, and propose an economic association to Canada that would be mutually advantageous to both parties.
2. Provide Quebec with a constitution that would achieve a good balance between effective government and true democracy.
3. Decentralize the administration and place more importance on municipalities, at both the local and regional levels.
4. Guarantee the impartiality of the judicial system and make it more accessible to everyone.
5. Pursue a foreign policy of peaceful co-operation.
6. Affirm Quebec's rights over its territory.

Achieving Independence

Quebecers form a people which has the right to choose its collective future. This right to self-determination is contained in the United Nations' Charter that Canada signed as an adherent, along with more than 82 other countries of the world.
Since the people of Quebec live in a democracy, it is for the people to itself decide on its future. . . . For the first time in our history, we will choose the political system under which we wish to live democratically by means of a referendum vote.
Quebecers will be asked to accept or reject a precise project for a new agreement between equals with the rest of Canada: sovereignty-association. They will be asked to give the government of Quebec a mandate to transform the present federal system into an association between two sovereign states.

* From the *Official Program of the Parti Québécois, 1980 edition,* adopted at the 7th National Convention, held in Quebec, June 1-3, 1979, and provided by the P.Q. in January, 1982.

This change necessarily implies negotiations with the rest of Canada, bearing both on the content of a treaty of association defining joint competencies and on the competency transfer-mechanisms. . . .

In the event that English Canada, contrary to its own best interest, refuses any form of equitable association, the Quebec Government pledges it will again consult with Quebecers, to ask them for a different mandate. The Governnent will, at that time, propose to them that Quebec's independence be brought into effect without preferential association with Canada. . . .

Sovereignty-Association

More than 80% of Quebecers, no matter what their origin or their political opinion, want a fundamental change now, a new agreement between the two founding nations, between equals.

The Act of 1867 has never been adapted to meet our needs and aspirations. Presented to Quebec as a solemn pact between two founding peoples, the Canadian Constitution will have in effect confirmed Macdonald's vision of Canada: an essentially anglophone country with a French minority concentrated in Quebec. We were 33% of the Canadian population. Now we are 26%. We will be 20% in 20 years from now. Our influence in the Federal parliament diminishes year by year.

This diminishment reduces the equality between the two nations to more and more of an illusion. Some would like to regain this equality in a "renewed federalism." Now that's a myth that is hard to kill. Repeatedly, since the time of Honoré Mercier, whenever we try to assert ourselves, "renewed federalism" is brought up as a safety valve to reduce the pressure and maintain the status quo. Renewed federalism is impossible because it implies a significant transfer of Ottawa's powers to the profit of our government in Quebec. It comes down to depriving Canadians in other provinces of part of their national government in order to give an incomplete national government to Quebecers. That's both too much for Canadians to put up with, and too little for Quebec. In other words, no federal-type system can satisfy the aspirations of both peoples simultaneously. This is the fundamental reason for all of the interminable political debates that have debased Quebec's political climate for decades.

Quebecers, indeed just like English-Canadians, want two things: to be master of their own house, and to work in co-operation with their neighbours, between equals. English Canadians already have their national government in Ottawa and it only remains for them to adjust their federalism to take regional diversity into account. Justice, equality, and dignity now demand that we also have our own in Quebec. No association that is sound, mature and efficient can be based on inequality between partners or domination of one by the other.

Fortunately, federalism is not the only way to conciliate the sovereignty of peoples and their necessary interdependence. More than 50 countries, organized in a dozen associations between sovereign states, show us the way to the future. In the case of Quebec and Canada, 200 years of shared history have forged mostly economic links between us without deadening the desire for sovereignty.

Two sovereign States, i.e. Quebec and the rest of Canada, could create a Quebec-Canada Association administered by a Joint Council of ministers delegated by each government. This decision-making body would maintain the present economic community on the basis of a treaty of association specifying the competencies to be exercised conjointly. Each State would collect all taxes from its territory and remit to the joint Council any funds necessary for carrying out conjoint plans and projects. Each of the two States would be able to legislate in all of the domains on its territory.

. . . Sovereignty-association would put an end to the interminable constitutional conferences, to the unprofitable tenseness of relations between the two peoples, and to the costly inefficiency of two levels of rival Governments. . . .

A Parti Québécois Government therefore pledges to:

Propose to the rest of Canada that an association of sovereign States be formed which, in the economic domain, will provide for free movement of goods . . . establishment, in common, of the tariff protection judged necessary with regard to third countries . . . reciprocal recognition of each party's right to protect domestic agricultural production . . . [Provide for] free movement of workers between the two States . . . recognition of the dollar as the only lawful money . . . the refitting of central banking institutions as communal institutions . . . freedom of circulation of capital between the two States . . .

Arrange to create conjointly with the government of Canada the institutions required for the proper functioning of the Quebec-Canada association . . . in accordance with the general principle of parity . . . a decisional body formed by ministers delegated by each of the governments; decisions will be made by a vote of unanimity, each State having one vote. . . . Create a Court of Justice of the Association, consisting of judges named in equal number by each government, settling any dispute that might arise between the two States, . . . acting as a tribunal hierarchically superior to the national tribunals . . .

Reassert and defend Quebec's inalienable rights over all its territory including Labrador and the coastal islands in Nouveau-Quebec's zone, the continental shelf, the 200-mile coastal limit, the territory of parks known as Federal, as well as the Quebec portion of the region of the Federal Capital; reclaim possession of the arctic islands and territories which are presently Canadian. . . .

The Electoral System

A Parti Québécois government therefore pledges to:

Maintain the present system of voting but add the element of proportional representation, so that a third of the seats in the National Assembly are reserved for members of Parliament elected by a preferential vote granted to recognized political parties; that is, to parties that had elected at least 10 members of Parliament or had obtained at least 10 per cent of the vote. No member of Parliament having the right to be elected . . . by List for more than two consecutive mandates. . . .

Prohibit the publication or dissemination of the results of public opinion polls seven (7) days prior to an election. . . .

Municipalities

Increase local authority by giving certain powers now exercised by the Quebec government back to the municipalities and increasing the financial resources available to them; and by favouring the creation, on demand, of neighbourhood councils which would be elected by universal suffrage and share responsibilities with the municipal council. . . .

Create regional municipalities . . . [which] would be responsible for establishing free day-care centres and would receive the necessary funds. . . .

Business

Recognize that the economy is directed by various forces — such as public (mixed or otherwise), private, or co-operative enterprise — and foster, as the main form of economic intervention, an extensive increase in the public sector (State and mixed enterprise). . . . Encourage the creation and development of small- and medium-sized Quebec companies (private or co-operative) through various forms of fiscal and technical assistance. . . . Direct public subsidies toward the expansion of the co-operative sector. . . . Authorize the Society for Industrial Reorganization . . . to take over any profit-making company that closes up shop or moves out of Quebec. . . .

Financial Institutions

Make the financial system more democratic by making sure that the shares of financial institutions . . . are acquired primarily by co-operative institutions, public authorities; and Quebec citizens . . . and by favouring the establishment of co-operative investment groups. . . . Supplement Quebec's financial system with public institutions specializing [in granting credit]. . . .

Abolish private "finance" companies dealing in small loans. . . . Through incentives, encourage the creation of mutual companies and life insurance co-operatives. . . . Establish a comprehensive, compulsory public automobile insurance plan.

Through legislation, if necessary, ensure that the majority of Quebecers' savings that are channelled into financial institutions are reinvested in Quebec . . . and make life insurance companies invest in Quebec whatever monies they have collected, minus administrative costs.

Economic Development

Modernize and restructure Quebec's economy. . . . Achieve this reorganization and renewal through a plan of action drawn up by an equal number of representatives from workers and other sectors of the population, business, and public bodies. . . . Adhere to the main objectives of this plan and see that they are respected . . . by regulating the entrance and exit of savings and profits, and by requiring that financial and business organizations reinvest in Quebec a substantial part of these savings. . . . Promote and control the expansion of heavy industry. . . . See to the creation of a motor-vehicle industry. . . .

Social Policy

. . . See that all workers are unionized. . . . Speed up the conversion of the commercial sector of goods and services into a co-operative one in which the co-operatives would be managed by employees and consumers. . . . Recognize the inalienable right of all people to housing. . . . See that all public institutions such as local community service centres, hospital centres . . . and low-income housing units . . . are operated, as much as possible, on a co-operative basis and that a majority of the people serving on the boards of directors are people who use their services. . . .

Make sure that the guaranteed family income could not go below the poverty line . . . [it] would be indexed. . . .

Compensate for the financial burden of raising children by absorbing this cost into Quebec's minimum guaranteed income program. . . . Set up a complete system of day-care services. . . .

Provide objective, positive information on family planning through government birth control centres . . . Inform the population about the various contraceptive methods . . . making them available free of charge . . . Recognize maternity and paternity leave . . . Make sure that a woman can obtain an abortion from her physician and that the cost is covered by health and hospital insurance . . .

Expand the health insurance scheme so that it covers: all aspects of medicine and surgery . . . all curative and preventive measures necessary . . . and the costs incurred in the purchase of artificial limbs. . . . Abolish profit-making establishments. . . . Make health professionals salaried employees. . . . Establish a free, State-financed ambulance service. . . . As soon as possible, pass regulations to make medium-sized and large companies hire a minimum percentage of handicapped people and provide them with transportation. . . . Encourage anti-nicotinism and the respect for non-smokers . . . by introducing an information campaign on the nefarious effects. . . .

Working Conditions

Raise the minimum wage to $3 an hour . . . indexed to the cost of living and the national growth rate. . . . Minimum paid vacation period of four weeks each year. . . . [Assure] that the pregnant employee obtain a maternity leave at full (100%) salary for a period of twenty (20) weeks, costs of leave to be assumed by the State. . . . Permit workers to take their retirement starting at the age of 55 years if they desire to, while also assuring for them the possibility of working to an advanced age and beyond 65 if they desire to. . . .

Cultural Policy — Language

Make French the working language in Quebec in all areas of activity. . . . Make French the only official language of Quebec. This implies that, at the end of . . . five (5) years, French would be the only language of the State, its public bodies, and institutions. . . . Make sure that public and private signs . . . are in French. The practice of translating French proper names into English would be prohibited. . . .

Provide the anglophone minority with English language education at all levels, subject to the following provisions: teaching in such institutions was carried out partly in French and that all pupils or students demonstrated a suitable knowledge of the French language and Quebec culture . . . and access to English-language institutions would be restricted to children attending such institutions at the time the language law went into effect; their brothers and sisters; the descendants of citizens who had done their elementary school studies in English in Quebec or were doing so at the present time; new immigrants, regardless of their mother tongue, will attend French schools. . . .

[Editor's note: At its biennial convention on December 5, 1981, the Parti Québécois altered its program by changing its long-standing position on sovereignty- association. A majority of delegates voted to abandon linking sovereignty to economic association with the rest of Canada. The P.Q. would be free to campaign for sovereignty alone. Moreover, sovereignty could be declared without the party gaining a majority of votes in an election or a referendum. Winning a majority of seats would be sufficient approval.

Premier Lévesque did not take kindly to this radical departure from the policy of *étapisme* which he and his intergovernmental affairs minister Claude Morin had carefully cultivated. Lévesque, who was also president of the P.Q., threatened to resign from politics if the party did not retract the convention's decision. The premier received an overwhelming vote of confidence from his cabinet and caucus and then gave the rank-and-file an opportunity to support him by initiating a mail-in referendum.

Members were asked to answer the following three questions with a single yes or no:

Do you accept as fundamental principles of our action the following:

1. That Quebec's accession to sovereignty come through democratic means, of which the key element must be the agreement of the majority of citizens;

2. That our party program, while eliminating the obligatory connection between sovereignty and association, continue to match sovereignty with a concrete offer of mutually advantageous economic associations with Canada;

3. That the party reaffirm its respect and openness toward all Quebeckers, whatever their cultural or ethnic origin, and especially by recognition of the right of the anglophone minority to its essential establishments, schools and others?

When the results of the referendum were released on February 9, 1982, Mr. Lévesque's position was confirmed by a landslide. About half (143,000) of the party's 300,000 members had taken the trouble to return their ballots and 95 per cent of them supported the premier.

These results were ratified by a reconvened P.Q. convention held on February 13-14. Although Mr. Lévesque had regained control of his party, he had compromised by accepting some modifications in the P.Q.'s original position. The obligatory connection between sovereignty and association was abandoned in favour of a new emphasis on sovereignty accompanied by an "offer" of economic association with Canada. In short, sovereignty and association are no longer linked together inseparably. The party can campaign in the next election on the platform of sovereignty alone. Moreover, though it is accepted that sovereignty is dependent on a majority vote of citizens and not just on a majority of seats, the party is not obliged now to hold a subsequent referendum on the issue. If the P.Q. wins a majority of votes in an election, it can move towards independence without further approval. However, Mr. Lévesque did not rule out the possibility of holding a referendum on a separatist constitution if the party was elected by either a majority or minority of votes.]

IN DEFENCE OF FEDERALISM*

Pierre-Elliott Trudeau

. . . Strictly from the point of view of economic objectives, the question is not to determine whether Quebec will govern itself by means of a sovereign state, or remain integrated with Canadian society, or will be joined to the United States. . . . What is important, in the last analysis, is for it to make sure that its *per capita* income will increase at the fastest possible speed; and, to achieve that, Quebec's economy must become extremely efficient, technologically advanced, fairly specialized, and capable of putting the best products at the best price on all the world's markets.

In fact, our province has too limited a population to support *alone* a modern industrial development, based on mass production and benefitting from the great economies of scale. By necessity, we have to depend on non-Quebec markets, and for that reason we have to be able to meet all competition.

In concrete terms that means that Quebec's economy must in no way be isolated, but rather integrated in a wider complex where we will find at the same time both markets and competitors.

Now it is very important to note that, whatever one says, most of the constitutional uproar at present in vogue in our province leans towards isolation. Thus some people are proposing to give the government of Quebec jurisdiction (more or less exclusive over) banks, immigration, the employment of labour, foreign trade, tariffs and customs, and many other things. This may be a praiseworthy goal — seizing one's economic destinies — but from all the evidence, it also indicates a desire to use legal instruments to protect our capital, our business men, and our higher ranks of management from foreign competition. That's a sure way to make our factors of production inefficient, and to ensure that our products will be rejected by foreign markets. Quebec will then have to require its consumers to "buy at home" to dispose of its products, and finally it will be the workers and farmers who will have to pay the dearest for them (either in prices or in subsidies). This line of reasoning applies just as well to steel as to blueberries; and it's erroneous to think that working people have some long-run advantage in being converted into a captive market.

●   ●   ●

In a general way, the present constitution gives to the provinces, hence to Quebec, wide jurisdiction over matters that will permit them to obtain the objectives [they want]. The provinces have complete jurisdiction over education, and it is above all by that means that labour and management

* Translation by the editor of a portion of speech entitled "Le réalisme constitutionnel," given by the author to the founding Convention of the Quebec section of the Liberal Federation of Canada (QLF), in Quebec City, March 26, 1966. By permission of the author, who at the time of writing was the Member of Parliament for Mount Royal and a Parliamentary Secretary to the former Prime Minister Lester B. Pearson, and who is now the Prime Minister of Canada.

can acquire the scientific and financial knowledge that will enable them to act efficiently in an industrial age. . . .

• • •

Welfare objectives sometimes conflict with economic objectives. . . . It would be too simple if one could merely say: welfare first, economics second. But one must be careful: scarcely any state can transgress with impunity the laws of economics and technology. Any state that would try to do it, for praiseworthy welfare objectives, would impoverish its economy and by the same act make the welfare goals unattainable. In fact, a determinedly progressive welfare policy can be devised and applied only if the economy is fundamentally sound. All social welfare measures, from children's allowances to old age pensions and forthcoming free education and health insurance, will be dead letters if the economic infrastructure is not capable of carrying the load and paying the cost of such programs. . . . In short, it is necessary to oppose the dislocation of the country because it would have the effect of weakening our economy and consequently of making it less able to pursue the welfare objectives and to pay for their cost.

Moreover, the Canadian constitution recognizes the widest provincial responsibility for social welfare matters. It allows each provincial government to apply in its own area the social philosophy that best suits its population. The diversity that results from this can provoke a healthy emulation among the provinces in the taxes and the benefits that will thus fall upon their respective taxpayers. Canadian federalism offers its citizens multiple choice, which adds to their democratic liberties. Within the whole Canadian economy, labour and capital will tend to move towards the mixture of fiscal burdens and social services that suit them best. Obviously, for reasons of language, the French-Canadian taxpayer will be relatively less mobile, but this is all the more reason for the Quebec government to choose with care and as democratically as possible its welfare and fiscal policies. . . .

• • •

. . . I would prefer to safeguard in every possible way the freedom and diversity that are offered by the decentralization of federalism. That is why I think it is urgent to negotiate agreements among provinces for the purpose of establishing at least in the large industrial provinces certain minimal standards of welfare legislation.

In this connection I can only see as incongruous and premature the preoccupation in certain quarters with constitutional reforms that would permit the provinces to conclude by themselves foreign treaties. As long as Quebec, for example, has not concluded with other Canadian provinces agreements on trade union legislation, is it very urgent, is it even economically wise, to bind itself by conventions in respect to standards established in other countries? Moreover, Quebec is always invited to have representatives on Canadian delegations to the International Labour Organization, and our province has never grasped how to field a team that could ensure continued and serious participation.

In an analogous realm, the province just recently has been able to enter into certain agreements with France, without overstepping constitutional legality. I agree obviously with this sort of formal arrangement whereby Quebec can gain the greatest benefits; but I am not otherwise overwhelmed by "the image" that Quebec can project on the international stage. I think, for instance, that Quebec has better things to do than to appear at all the UNESCO meetings, while serious negotiations have not been undertaken with a neighbouring province relative to the education of the French-speaking minority there.

My second remark involves those provinces that are too poor to be able by themselves to reach minimal standards of social welfare. Under the existing constitution the central government can mitigate these inadequacies by means of equalization payments, and this arrangement has to remain. From this point of view, I regret the last year between Quebec and Ottawa about the sharing of federal tax revenues. A theory of taxation that doesn't take into account the needs of the recipients, and which seems to claim that a given group of taxpayers must receive in return at least the equivalent of what it pays for taxes, repudiates the whole redistributive functions of taxation, and declares itself to be irrevocably reactionary.

My third remark concerns the concepts of planning and counter-cyclical policy which both involve a kind of intervention by the state in economic processes, on behalf of welfare goals like full employment and planned development. . . . Under the Canadian constitutional system both sorts of policies assume a certain collaboration between the central government and the provincial governments. The first is no doubt chiefly responsible for the overall economy, but its actions can't be effective if they are not coordinated with those of the second . . . This paper suggests not constitutional changes, but a more systematic recourse to consultation and agreements between the federal and provincial authorities. . . .

[In regard to cultural aims] let us propound first that what creates vitality and value in a language is the quality of the group that speaks it. The question which arises then is whether the French-speaking people in Canada must concentrate their efforts on Quebec, or whether they should take the whole of Canada as the base of their operations.

In my opinion, they must do both, and I believe that for this purpose they couldn't find a better device than federalism.

For cultural values, in order to be disseminated fully, require a nice blend of protection and non-interference by the state. On one hand, the state has to ensure the protection of cultural values which without it would run the risk of being engulfed by a flood of dollars, but on the other hand, cultural values, even more than those based on economics, wither away quickly if they are removed from the test of competition.

That is why, in the matter of cultural aims, Canadian federalism is ideal. While requiring French Canadians, in the federal sector, to submit their way of doing things (and especially their political forms) to the test of competition, the federal system allows us at the same time to provide for ourselves in Quebec the form of government and the educational institutions that best suit our needs.

• • •

That is the reason that I am for federalism. . . . With the exception perhaps of marriage and of radio and television broadcasting, federal jurisdiction applies almost exclusively to those areas where the cultural aspect is reduced to a minimum. . . .

The provinces, on their side, have jurisdiction over all those matters that are purely local and private — over education, natural resources, property and civil rights, municipal institutions, highways, welfare and labour legislation, and the administration of justice. . . .

At one extreme, Quebec has to flee from the temptation of isolation, where one could certainly feel safe from all danger, but would also be barred from progress. At the other extreme, I would be opposed to Quebec taking its stand in a unitary Canadian state, or annihilating itself in a bigger American melting-pot. Nationalism for nationalism, I don't think that a kind of pan-Canadianism or a pan-Americanism is less imbued with chauvinism than the French-Canadian sort! . . .

I can only condemn as irresponsible those who would like to see our people invest undetermined amounts of money, time, and energy in a constitutional adventure that they have not yet been able to state precisely, but which would consist more or less vaguely in scuttling Canadian federalism in order to substitute for it hazy designs of sovereignty from which would emerge something like an independent Quebec, or associated states, or a particular status, or a Canadian common market, or a confederation of 10 states, or something else to be invented in the future — that is after political, economic, and social chaos will have been guaranteed.

Canadian federalism must evolve, of course. But it certainly has been evolving, very substantially, in the last hundred years without the constitution requiring wholesale changes. Periods of great decentralization have alternated with periods of intense centralization in the course of our history, that is, according to the conjunction of social and economic forces, external pressures, and the strength and astuteness of our politicians. Now if there is any immediate basic fact in politics — and at the same time a verifiable proposition in most industrial countries — it is that the state is obliged today to devote a continually increasing portion of its continually increasing budget to those areas which, in the Canadian constitution, fall under the jurisdiction of the provincial governments. In other words, Canadian federalism is evolving at present towards a period of great decentralization.

This reality becomes more obvious if one looks at the total of governmental expenditures apart from transfer payments between governments. . . .

Thus, demographic, social and economic forces are in the process of transferring to provincial governments an enormous addition in power, without having to change a single comma in the constitution. The fact that some of our French-Canadian politicians and intellectuals have chosen this precise moment to demand imperatively that the country provide itself with a new constitution seems to us to be extraordinarily untimely. . . .

SEPARATISM — CANADA'S DEATH WISH*

Paul Fox

The first thing to be noted about Quebec's current separatist movement is that it is not new. It is no exaggeration to say that the history of Canada as a nation is the story of one long-running battle against divisive forces which would split it apart. In Freudian terms, Canada's attempts to fulfil its urge to national life have been accompanied by a contrary destructive death urge.

As a people we have had to fight not only against climate, which has kept us isolated in pockets (especially in winter), but against geography as well. The natural dividing lines in North America run north and south rather than east and west along the Canadian-American border.

With their backs against the Appalachian mountain range, Maritimers have found traditionally that they have had far more in common — in trade, in industries, in outlook — with New Englanders than with "Upper Canadians," as they still call the residents of central Canada. The latter find that they look south for business and pleasure rather than east or west. Montrealers and Torontonians will visit New York, Buffalo, or Florida often before they visit even each other, let alone Halifax, Calgary, or Vancouver. Prairie folk drift across a border created by men rather than by nature when they go to Chicago or the Midwest; and British Columbians, on the far side of the forbidding Rocky Mountains, feel much closer to the American Pacific states, as they are, than to the rest of Canada.

These natural obstacles have bred strong local sentiments in Canada, and it is against these tendencies that the nation has had to struggle ever since its birth on July 1, 1867.

Confederation brought together three scattered, undeveloped and under-populated British colonies, Nova Scotia, New Brunswick and "Canada," as the union of what are now Ontario and Quebec was called. Though two other Atlantic colonies were included in preliminary consultations, they would not join in forming the new dominion. Prince Edward Island pursued its separate way for another six years and Newfoundland did not enter until 1949.

Meanwhile, many of the citizens in two of the three charter Confederation colonies wanted to withdraw. So serious was the opposition to union by the New Brunswick government that it had to be pushed out of office by the British governor, to make way for a more favourable government whose election was secured by financial contributions from Upper Canada. Nova Scotia was no more enthusiastic. Halifax celebrated Canada's first national birthday by draping its main street in black, and in the federal election which ensued the province as a whole elected 18 out of 19 MPs pledged to repeal the act of union.

Out west, in what was to be Manitoba, Louis Riel led a rebellion against encroachment from Ottawa and set up a short-lived republic. Sixteen years

---

* Revised in January, 1982, from an article which appeared originally in the *Family Herald*, March 15, 1962. By permission.

later he made a second attempt in the North-West Rebellion. British Columbia entered as a province in 1871 but haggling over the terms of union and threats to secede continued for years.

Here are examples of genuine separatism, expressed in deeds, not just in words. And the spirit is not dead yet. A ludicrous illustration occurred a few years ago when a tiny municipality in Northern Ontario threatened to withdraw from the province if it did not get the road it wanted. Now the West is talking separation.

Thus separatism as a sentiment in Canada is common. It is the obvious form of protest of local groups which feel their interests are being threatened by the larger national entity. It is the outlet psychologically for the frustrations of a minority which recognizes rationally that it must buckle under to the majority but cannot accept the inevitability of it without a desperate kick, like a child lashing out against an overwhelming parent.

This is not said to deride the cause of separatism, merely to explain it. On a broader scale, many Canadians today express the same emotion in fighting off the encircling embrace of the United States.

French-Canadian separatism is accentuated by differences in language and religion. The Gallic tongue and Roman Catholic faith mark off French Canadians distinctively from English-speaking Protestants. But these are only attributes of their fundamental differences, and despite all the hullabaloo to preserve them, they are not the cause of Quebec's separatism. The fight is nothing less than an endeavour to maintain a way of life which is 350 years old, a separate and distinctive French identity in a sea of North American Anglo-Saxonism.

The depth and intensity of this distinctive culture is what has made separatism in Quebec the prototype of such movements, and the most traditional, enduring, and serious of its kind. The nearest analogy that comes to mind is the successful persistence for centuries of the Jewish people in preserving their Hebraic separateness in a world full of Gentiles.

Separatism in Quebec therefore is not new. It is a theme which has often been voiced in French-Canadian history, especially at critical moments, such as 60 years ago by the Abbé Lionel Groulx and those who dreamed of an independent republic of "Laurentie". . . .

But it would be a mistake for English Canadians to dismiss the current song of protest as one more turn on the same old disc. It is the old refrain, but something new has been added also — a modern, accelerated tempo.

A revolution has occurred in Quebec recently. In the last 20 years, Quebec has commenced going through a transformation which is more significant and shattering than anything that has occurred in French Canada since the conquest.

Industrialization, urbanization, and modernization have arrived in French Canada with a bang. In the short space of a few years Quebec has entered into a transition that has taken half a century to run its course in other parts of Canada. For years these forces were blocked by the traditionalist patterns of thought of church and state. This Old Regime, as it might well be called, was personified by the late Premier Maurice Duplessis. With his death in 1959 and the fall of his Union Nationale party from power in the election of June, 1960, the dam burst. New ideas, new forces came surging to the surface. Most of these poured into courses more constructive than separatism, but the general spill-over of energy revived separatism in some quarters and gave it fresh grounds to feed upon.

Thus the present separatist movement in Quebec is old and new at the same time. . . .

If the separatists succeeded and Quebec split off from Canada, could it maintain itself for long as a progressive, dynamic national state? Is it not a backward step to split into a smaller unit? The trend of evolution is from the single cell to the multi-cellular. The path of economic and political development in the world is towards integration, not disintegration. Witness the growth of corporations, trading blocks, and regional groupings of nations in Europe and elsewhere. This does not mean that individuality is lost sight of. We do not necessarily all become identical because we become more interrelated. There is still room for diversity in unity — the two are not mutually exclusive. In fact, integration may promote individual development. Is the average modern Frenchman, German, and Englishman not a more developed and distinctive human creature living at a higher level in contemporary integrating Europe than his ancestor was in a more divided and primitive medieval Europe?

The challenge for French Canadians is to retain their distinctiveness while still remaining Canadians in an expanding world. It is a challenge that English Canadians also face in their relationship to the United States. The feat for French Canadians is admittedly more difficult and they are deserving of sympathy and assistance in their attempt to be themselves while moving ahead together. Many of the separatists' complaints against English Canadians are justified. But the solution is not to reverse the process of history. Should Ontario depart from Canada because Ontario pays more taxes into the federal treasury than other provinces? Should Anglo-Saxon Protestants in Montreal become separatists and withdraw from Quebec if French Canada becomes a separate state? Many of the Separatists' arguments can be turned against them. Separatists should remember that not all the costs of biculturalism are paid by the minority; English Canadians as well as French Canadians make sacrifices in the interest of national unity. . . .

WOULD QUEBEC BE BETTER OFF IN OR OUT?*

Pierre Fortin, Gilles Paquet, Yves Rabeau

In the months since November 15, 1976, the question of the costs and benefits bestowed upon Quebec as a result of her belonging to the Canadian federation has become the basis for much political debate in Canada. Using necessarily scanty information and more or less explicit assumptions, various analysts have proffered conjectures as to the costs and benefits of alternative political arrangements. More complete and reliable documentation and analyses will be necessary before it is possible to suggest a complete balance sheet on which to base firm conclusions. . . .

* From an article entitled "Quebec in the Canadian Federation: A Provisional Evaluative Framework" in *Canadian Public Administration*, 21, 4, Winter, 1978, published by the Institute of Public Administration of Canada. By permission.

Basic Questions

At the heart of any cost-benefit analysis is the definition of *possible alternatives*. The costs and benefits of Quebec's membership in Confederation must be measured by what Quebec can get from an alternative arrangement (for example, independence or some third option like sovereignty- association). What makes it difficult to calculate a net benefit or cost is the fact that such calculations depend entirely on what the alternative is and what it offers. Since the alternative is not clearly formulated at the present time, the anticipated costs and benefits are highly dependent on individual conjectures as to the alternative organizational arrangement contemplated and the type of performance expected from it.

Another central issue is the *cost of transition* to another organization system. For in the presence of major transitional costs, even if certain net benefits could be expected from organizational rearrangements, such costs could turn the anticipated net gain into a net loss. . . .

In any such discussion, there is the danger of falling into a trap that Jacques Ellul has labelled "the political illusion" — the illusion that there is a political solution to every problem and that institutional rearrangement is a magic wand to solve them all: political sovereignty has never been either a necessary or a sufficient condition for the elimination of economic disparities. . . .

Finally, we have asked two separate questions: would Quebec improve its standard of living if it left Confederation? and, would political independence make it easier for Quebec to solve its economic problems? To these questions we have not given equally satisfactory answers.

In all cases of desire for independence, that first question is always raised in the initial period of debate. The sort of accounts which transpire from these exercises are constructed from unreliable data and a pyramid of shaky assumptions which make these debates rather inconclusive. The most popular of these estimates use public sector accounts and assume that federalism is a zero-sum game. This implies that public accounts suffice and that if one party gains the other must have lost. The possibility that these accounts are incomplete or that all parties might gain or lose is not envisaged. . . .

It is unfortunate that so much time has been spent on this question, for it is in many ways a red herring: if Quebec has anything to gain from separation, it must be greater scope for independent policies better adapted to the needs of her economy. The second question is therefore both more interesting and of greater import. It focuses on the impact of separation on the capacity of the independent economy to get access to a higher potential output, on its capacity to improve its likelihood to make full use of this potential, and on the capacity of the independent economy to modify its income distribution and its economic organization more easily in the preferred way. . . .

An Excursus on Economic Accounts

The inference of a rise or fall in the standard of living of Quebeckers after independence, on the basis of the fact that it is now a "losing" or "gaining" region in the balancing of receipts and expenditures of the federal government, is one of those bizarre pieces of economic reasoning which was sold to Quebeckers in the spring of 1977 by both parties to the debate. The variety of results one may obtain from the calculation of Quebec's net gain or loss in its dealings with the federal government shows how volatile such calculations are and how important it is to excavate the assumptions on which they are based.

First, it must be recognized that a very high proportion of federal spending is effected for the country as a whole by the federal government. This leaves open the question of how the net benefit from these expenditures should be apportioned among the citizens of the different regions. This is the case for external affairs, national defence, some portion of the transcontinental transportation system; immigration, foreign aid, and so on. The benefits from those expenditures are often apportioned among the provinces on a pro rata basis defined by the population distribution among the provinces. This is somewhat arbitrary. A more realistic approach would require that one determine what quantity of these services each province would demand if it were free to do so. Such a demand would, according to some, bear a close relationship to income levels and accordingly it is argued that benefits should be apportioned to each province according to its share in Canada's national income.

A priori, it is not possible to claim that one method is to be preferred to the other, but the calculations made on the basis of these different assumptions result in differences of hundreds of millions of dollars per year in the apportionment of benefits from federal services. For instance, in 1974 the federal government spent in the neighbourhood of $9 billion for national services. On a population pro rata, Quebec would have received $2,457 million (27.3 per cent of the total), whereas on an income-share basis, Quebec would purportedly have received $2,232 million (24.8 per cent of the total). This is a difference of some $225 million in the calculations based on the different sets of assumptions for this one year.

Secondly, even though it might be possible to identify one province unambiguously as the recipient of a particular federal "public good" it does not follow that one may apportion the total benefit to this province if in fact the public good has not been produced there, but is the result of a production process initiated in another province. If the federal government, for instance, were to give to Quebec an aircraft manufactured in Manitoba, according to the standard GDP approach adopted by Statistics Canada Regional Accounts, the total benefit would be allocated to Manitoba. According to the benefits method, which attempts to measure the benefits actually received, the total benefit would be allocated to Quebec. A more realistic apportionment would obviously lie somewhere between these two extremes. For if Quebec had had the choice, it would presumably have had the aircraft manufactured in Quebec, with the consequent number of jobs and income flow increased in Quebec instead of Manitoba, through the usual multiplier effects. A more accurate account of the net benefits would subtract from the value of the aircraft received the income not generated in Quebec as a result of the decision of the federal government to have it manufactured in Manitoba.

Finally, on the tax side, the problem of the regional allocation of the burden of taxation in the case of corporate profits and/or federal indirect taxes introduces yet more indeterminacy in the process of calculation of net costs or benefits. Who exactly pays these taxes which constitute a good portion of the federal revenues? To what extent are these taxes reducing the business profits and to what extent are they shifted forward to the consumers all over the country? In practice, it is not possible to ascertain accurately the portion of these taxes paid by the producers and the portion paid by the consumers. . . .

Those difficulties notwithstanding, analysts have produced a variety of estimates which, as could be expected, range widely from substantial net costs to substantial net benefits for Quebec over the period 1961 to 1975. Two points, however, would appear not to be in dispute. 1/ For nearly all methodologies, Quebec shows a deficit prior to 1965, a deficit which is disappearing progressively and is transformed into a surplus in the 1970s; depending on the methodology used, the reversal comes closer to 1965 or to 1975; all sides agree that Quebec shows a net gain in recent years, especially since the explosion of federal social programs and the beginning of oil subsidies. 2/ From the arguments used, it would appear that the concerns of Quebec have as much to do with the *type* of federal spending in Quebec as with the *amount* of spending; Quebec receives an above-average share of federal social security payments, but receives less than its share in federal investment and development spending.

Quebec in the World Economy

Would the options open to an independent Quebec in the international economy be more advantageous than those available under the present federal system?

The debate on this question suggests that there would seem to be a whole range of possibilities for Quebec to choose from in redefining where it would fit within the system of international interdependence: a free trade area or a customs union with a clutch of countries, a common market or an economic union with clusters of partners, or complete free trade arrangements with the rest of the world. Moreover, it is suggested that within this range of broad options, there is some additional margin of manoeuvrability for differential use of policies and the development of new policy instruments, like a Quebec currency, for instance.

While indeed Quebec's withdrawal from the federation would undoubtedly provide an opportunity for fitting its economy differently into the world economy, the possible options are not equally feasible or attractive and the new capacity for solving Quebec's economic problems that they afford is often limited. For instance, a strategy of *economic autarky* which would wall in the Quebec economy behind trade barriers even higher than those which already exist cannot be regarded as a reasonable option. Such a strategy would result in retaliation against Quebec's exports from the rest of Canada and of the world. This is not insignificant since 30 per cent of Quebec's manufacturing shipments goes to the rest of Canada and another 15 per cent to external markets outside Canada. Such a strategy could only lead to a decline in the production runs, a drop in productivity and a fall in the standard living of Quebeckers. This polar case in the range of options does not appear therefore to be either attractive or capable of helping Quebec solve its economic problems.

More reasonably, Quebec might negotiate new arrangements with other countries involving different obligations and different forms of interdependence with the rest of the world. There is a family of such possible arrangements which differ markedly in their consequences. There is, for instance, a substantial difference between a *free trade area* (which allows free movement of goods and services among partners), a *customs union* (which allows the free movement of goods and services among partners who agree on a joint trade policy with the rest of the world), a *common market* (which allows the free movement of goods, services, labour and capital among partners who agree on a joint external policy with the rest of the world in these respects) and an *economic union* (which allows the free movement of goods, services, labour and capital among partners who agree on a joint external policy with the rest of the world *and* on the coordination of their internal policies: monetary, fiscal and industrial).

Such new arrangements would have to be negotiated in full recognition of the changing nature of the world economic process and of the peripheral role of Quebec within it. . . .

Would an independent Quebec turn out to be more vulnerable than the present Canadian economic union in the face of this world economic process? It would appear likely that Quebec's bargaining power on its own would not be as strong as the one Canada as a whole holds in the negotiation of international arrangements. Why then does Quebec want a new deal and the right to bargain alone for alternative arrangements with the rest of the world? This has less to do with the existence of a federal structure than with some discontent with the way federalism currently works. Canada, including Quebec, may well be able to negotiate better arrangements than Quebec alone, but this does not ensure that Quebec's actual share of the benefits from such agreements would necessarily be greater than what it can achieve alone.

The distinction is important, for much of the basis for Quebec's demands is a conviction that the federation is unresponsive to regional demands. Indeed, various provinces have complained about the same type of malfunctioning and have raised questions about the capacity of the federal structure to yield the desired regional benefits: if an orange tree keeps on bearing apples, one comes to wonder if it is really an orange tree. The central issue is the functioning of the federation, the way in which collective benefits are shared within the federation, rather than the existence of the federal structure *per se*. . . .

On the monetary and financial fronts, the latitudes of an independent Quebec would also be rather limited. Quebec exists in an integrated North American capital market and there are important flows of labour and capital among the provinces. In a small and open economy such as that of an independent Quebec, where capital and labour are mobile, a Quebec currency would not be the universal panacea some would like it to be. Even more than for Canada as it stands now, the scope for an independent monetary policy would be severely limited by the close commercial and financial links with the United States.

Economic Structure and National Policies

. . . Quebec did not fully take part in the first wave of industrialization, based on coal and iron. Consequently, between 1870 and 1935, a significant gap developed between Quebec and Ontario industrial structures. The second industrial revolution based on hydro-electricity and non-ferrous metals will carry Quebec, but the beginnings have left their mark . . . with more heavy industry in Ontario and light industry relatively more important in Quebec.

While technological and geographical factors were important in the experience of Quebec's socio-economy, it must be added that Quebec was brought into industrial capitalism somewhat reluctantly and once in the game did not necessarily play it well . . . the capacity of the Quebec economy to transform has remained much lower than the same measure for Ontario. . . .

This weaker and belated support from the state for industrialization and the slower rate of structural transformation and capacity to transform in Quebec have had, in combination with the geotechnical constraints, a disastrous effect on Quebec's economy: the exodus of population to the United States, especially in the 1870-1930 period, drained the province of a significant portion of its population, and perhaps the most entrepreneurial portion at that. . . .

While these forces may explain much of the experience of the Quebec socio-economy, there may be residual and not insubstantial effects ascribable to the workings of the federation within which Quebec lives. The federal government has formulated over time a variety of national policies designed to promote growth and development in Canada as a whole and an array of sectoral policies designed also for the pursuit of national interest. These policies do not necessarily have the same effect or impact on the different regions and/or groups in Canada. In some cases, such differential incidences are intended and planned, but in many other cases the unintended consequences of general policies were adopted without having been fully understood or analysed.

To a certain extent, the differential impact of national policies on regions is a consequence of the unique characteristics of the regions themselves: geographical coordinates, cultural fabric, specific level of development, differential infrastructure, specific quality of human resources, more or less enlightened complementary provincial policies among others. However, the differential impact of the national policies may also be due to the . . . *national character* of these policies — policies that may make the country as a whole better off but leave one or many regions worse off.

The federal government has not kept any explicit accounting of the effects of its national policies and has therefore not attempted to develop equalization policies taking these effects into account. The current financial equalization system is an attempt to ensure that per capita fiscal capacity is almost the same for all provinces. It is designed to ensure citizens of each province a level of public services which does not depart too much from the national average. But such equalization does not take into account the differential impact on the pattern of development of each region. In short, there is no equalization of the development effects of these policies. . . .

It has been argued by many that the impact of federal decisions on Quebec development has often been detrimental. Cases in point would be the federal transport policy promoting east-west movement of goods, the opening of the St. Lawrence Seaway, the auto pact, and the creation of the Borden line. It is claimed that the cumulative effect of these federal decisions taken in the national interest has strengthened the relative position of the Ontario region in the national economy, and that one can detect no systematic effort to compensate for those negative development effects on Quebec. . . .

It is probably true that in most cases the benefits of these national policies for the Canadian economy as a whole were larger than the losses ascribable to their having acted as impediments to growth and development in Quebec. However, inasmuch as slower regional growth has meant lower provincial fiscal revenues which the equalization payments from the federal government have only partially offset, these negative development effects are not negligible. The matter is made somewhat worse when one aggregates these many national policies, for their cumulative impact would appear to foster Ontario growth more or less systematically while no effective effort is undertaken to promote the orderly industrial adjustment of Quebec industries, such as textiles. It is true that tariffs and quotas have been used to prevent massive layoffs in the face of foreign competition, thereby forcing Canadian consumers to purchase high-cost goods from the low-productivity labour-intensive plants in Quebec, but little has been done to promote a program of industrial adjustment which would help those industries with structural problems in the transition toward their specialization in more productive lines, or toward a redeployment of their manpower over a reasonable period. . . .

[It is not] clear what type of economic development strategy an independent Quebec might substitute for the current policies, and indeed whether Quebec is in a position to solve its structural problems better alone. It would appear quite clear that whatever Quebec does, it will not be able to restructure its economy without taking full cognizance of the constraints imposed by geography, technology, comparative advantage and the central importance of the forces shaping the new international division of labour. However, there seems to be some considerable latitude for improvement of the current development policies in a Quebec perspective.

Whether or not Quebec could obtain a better deal by launching the necessary radical industrial adjustment alone or within the context of a broader economic unit like Canada is an open question. While one might argue that the broader unit would provide the basis for a smoother adjustment path within the constraints mentioned above, the reluctance of the federal government to recognize the necessity of some measurement of the provincial effects of federal decisions and its refusal up to now to recognize the need for a decisive industrial strategy highlight the high costs of transactions within the present federal system and must have an important bearing on this difficult choice.

On balance, it must be recognized that the transition costs would be higher for an independent Quebec, but the rigidities and insensitivities of the federal administration to the realities of the differential regional impact of their national policies might make this gamble look like the preferable alternative.

Quebec's Full Utilization of Its Economic Potential and the Role of Federal Stabilization Policies

If the federal decisions on matters of national development policies have had a somewhat negative influence on Quebec's economic potential. . . . it may be said that the cumulative effect of such national development policies amounts to reducing the economic potentialities of Quebec.

One may also wonder whether stabilization policies which are largely under the jurisdiction of the federal government have encouraged the full utilization of the economic potential of Quebec as it is. The record of the federal authorities in the postwar period is not all that impressive when one examines its marksmanship in the pursuit of the standard objectives of sound macroeconomic policies. Indeed, one might wonder whether Quebec might not have been able to do better for itself it if had acted alone. It most certainly would do much better in a federal system providing better for regional stabilization needs.

For some twenty years, Quebec's average unemployment rate (7.4 per cent) has been higher than the national average (5.6 per cent). Moreover, over the business cycle, Quebec's unemployment rate fluctuates more widely around its average than the unemployment rate in the rest of Canada and this fluctuation lags somewhat behind that of Ontario. These differences between the behaviour of unemployment in Quebec as contrasted with the rest of Canada are sufficient to suggest that a regionalized stabilization policy is worthy of consideration. Such a regionalization would take into account the regional stabilization needs and reduce regional unemployment rates.

The federal government has found it difficult up to now to provide for regional discrimination in its taxes or expenditures, or to implement regionally different interest rates. Indeed, the problem has been regarded by the federal government as politically unpalatable. This has led Ottawa to gear its stabilization policies to the management of national averages. . . .

The alternative would appear to be for Quebec to take over *de facto* the responsibility for stabilization by using her own policy instruments. This is not as feasible as it might at first appear, for the provinces do not have the same borrowing power as the federal government. Moreover, they do not have the sort of fiscal margin of manoeuvrability necessary to undertake the task of economic stabilization. In a sense, the provinces are largely program administrators.

The reason for this is a certain imbalance between the distribution of fiscal fields and the constitutional distribution of spending powers between the federal and provincial levels. On the one hand, the central government draws more than half of its fiscal revenues from the income tax, which is the fastest growing source of public revenue. It follows that autonomous federal revenues increase much faster than those of the provinces. On the other hand, federal spending power is concentrated in sectors for which there is a fairly slow growth in public demand (defence, immigration, external affairs), whereas the provincial spending power falls largely into the areas of booming demand (health, education, social security, urban affairs). Thus, the federal government is blessed with a comfortable margin of latitude between its revenues and expenditures, while the provinces are constantly faced with significant deficits before they can entertain the possibility of any stabilization policy action. Between 1971 and 1976, the central government was able to reduce income taxes by $4 billion and to spend over $5 billion on new initiatives, displaying therefore a margin of manoeuvrability of $9 billion. During the same period, the provinces had to raise their taxes by nearly $0.8 billion and did not undertake any new spending initiatives. In short, they had a negative margin of manoeuvrability.

On the balance of evidence, it would appear that federal decisions in matters of stabilization policy have indeed had detrimental effects on Quebec's full utilization of its economic potential. . . .

It would appear clear that much could be accomplished on this front either by a federally coordinated regionalized stabilization policy or by a judiciously run stabilization policy controlled by Quebec after independence. These gains would have to be compared, however, with the added costs of coordination implied by such a regionalized stabilization policy in the federal state, and with the additional difficulties involved in running an independent stabilization policy in the new small and open independent economy of Quebec. The gains for Quebec would appear to be relatively greater in the former context, in the event that it *could* be implemented.

Distribution of Income and Organization of Production

The composition of external and internal, private and public, and deliberate or accidental forces that have shaped the Quebec economy has generated patterns of distribution of income and wealth and forms of economic organization that may not correspond closely to the wishes of Quebeckers. What additional freedom would an independent Quebec gain in restructuring them?

Over the years, Quebeckers have expressed concern about both sets of issues, but mainly about the distribution of income. This has remained paramount in the consciousness or the subconscious of Quebeckers until the "second XXe siècle." More recently, however, a greater concern for the organization of production has emerged. Indeed, it has been suggested that the distribution of income is a reflection to a great extent of the peculiar organization of production in Quebec. Consequently, it has been argued that simple political arrangements conducive to better opportunities or income for francophones in Quebec might not be more than superficial correctives: what would be necessary is the restructuring of the organization of production on the basis of a recognized right to development along self-determined lines for Quebec.

Whether or not an independent Quebec would be able to modify its distribution of income and wealth and to reorganize its production process in a substantial way within the contraints imposed by the external forces and the discipline imposed by the new Quebec society is not an open question. An independent Quebec would have latitudes to reorganize the production process and to redistribute income: the experience of the last decade or so has demonstrated beyond reasonable doubt that the provincial state, even within the present context and with the limitations imposed on its operations by the federal constraints, has been able to do so. The real question is whether Quebec could do it better *given her circumstances* within the federation or independently. . . .

If Quebec were to become independent, one might expect, however, more substantial efforts to redistribute income in favour of the "nationals" and in particular, in favour of the new middle class. Moreover, one would expect from the experience of the last two decades a more substantial degree of state intervention to redesign the economic organization so as to make better use of Quebec's human and material resources.

The overall transformation is likely to be more difficult and costly if Quebec is to attempt it alone rather than within the context of the federation; but it is by no means impossible, and much could be learned about these possibilities from the experience and aspirations of small open economies like Belgium. Moreover, to the extent that the federal government appears reluctant to relax its grip on the system and to allow such flexibility as would be necessary to effect such adjustments in Quebec's socio-economy, the temptation to go it alone is increased. . . .

Conclusion

The central question facing Quebec in its decision to stay in the federation or to opt out is one which hinges in the final analysis on the opportunity costs of centralized and decentralized government. In that sense, Quebec's interest in exploring the possibilities of independence is part of a sweeping movement christened by Phelps-Brown as the "dispersive revolution": "the demand by the individual for more participation in industrial and political decision-making." This has grown both as a result of the alienation felt by the citizen after the bureaucratic takeover, but also as a result of the greater "variance in the distribution of preferences of citizens for different types of services and their method of finance . . . as the degree of centralization increases." . . .

Be that as it may, our preliminary overview shows that Quebec may argue persuasively that there is an opportunity cost in staying in the federation *as it functions at present.* While it is not easy to tally up our cautious qualitative calculations into a simple net balance, especially in the face of such uncertainties about the exact nature of the alternatives considered and about the costs of transition, it is possible to suggest that, on balance, and in the light of our preliminary analysis:

—the regional economic accounts are not entirely conclusive in answering the question as to whether Quebec would improve its standard of living if it left the federation; there is also a danger that such woolly calculations might become accredited and deflect the discussion into fruitless data-massaging exercises;

—the present federal system has malfunctioned in a variety of ways, and *its rigidities,* much more than the federal system *per se,* are the source of the frustrations and alienation of Quebeckers;

—the margins of latitude open to independent policies by an independent Quebec would be rather narrow at the international level, but might be significant at the level of structural policies and stabilization operations; —there would be room for modifications and improvement in the distribution of income and the organization of production in an independent Quebec; —the rigidities injected by the federal bureaucracy into the functioning of the federation and into the debates between bureaucracies is bound to be of great import for Quebec in the qualitative calculations of the costs and benefits of opting out. It is therefore imperative for those interested in making the federation viable to focus on the functioning of the system and not merely on some new constitution . . . If the workings of the federation are a variable and not a given in the bargaining process, the benefits that Quebec would gain by withdrawing from the federation as it is working now could rapidly melt away.

THE REFERENDUM QUESTION AND RESULTS

The question which appeared on the Quebec referendum ballot on May 20, 1980, was as follows:

The Government of Quebec has made public its proposal to negotiate a new agreement with the rest of Canada, based on the equality of nations;

This agreement would enable Quebec to acquire the exclusive power to make its laws, levy its taxes and establish relations abroad — in other words, sovereignty — and at the same time, to maintain with Canada an economic association including a common currency;

No change in political status resulting from these negotiations will be effected without approval by the people through another referendum;

On these terms, do you agree to give the Government of Quebec the mandate to negotiate the proposed agreement between Quebec and Canada?

The official results were as follows:

Answer	Popular vote	Percentage
Yes	1,485,851	40.4
No	2,187,991	59.6

BIBLIOGRAPHY

(See also the Bibliographies in other chapters, especially in Chapters 3, 8, 10, and 15)

Albert, A., "Conditions économiques et élections: le cas de l'élection provinciale de 1976 au Québec," *C.J.P.S.*, XIII, 2, June, 1980.

Albert, A., "La participation politique: les contributions monétaires aux partis politiques québécois," *C.J.P.S.*, XIV, 2, June, 1981.

Allard, M., *The Last Chance, The Canadian Constitution and French Canadians,* Quebec, Editions Ferland, 1964.

d'Allemagne, A., *Le colonialisme au Québec,* Montréal, Éditions Rénaud et Bray, 1966.

Arès, R., *Nos grandes options politiques et constitutionnelles,* Montréal, Bellarmin, 1972.

Association des économistes québécois, *Économie et indépendance,* Montréal, Éditions Quinze, 1977.

Baker, D.N., "Quebec on French Minds," *Q.Q.,* 85, 2, Summer, 1978.

Barbeau, R., *Le Québec, est-il une colonie?,* Montréal, Éditions de l'homme, 1962.

Bauer, J., "Patrons et patronat au Québec," *C.J.P.S.,* IX, 3, September, 1976.

Beaudry, M., Cloutier, E., et Latouche, D., *Atlas électoral du Québec 1970-1973-1976,* Québec, 1979.

Bélanger, M., "Le rapport Bélanger, dix ans après," *C.P.A.,* 19, 3 Fall, 1976.

Benjamin, J., *Comment on fabrique un premier ministre québécois,* Montréal, Éditions de l'Aurore, 1975.

Benjamin, J., et O'Neill, P., *Les mandarins du pouvoir,* Montréal, Éditions Québec-Amérique, 1978.

Bennett, A., *Quebec Labour Strikes,* Montreal, Black Rose, 1973.

Bergeron, G., *La Canada français après deux siècles de patience,* Paris, Seuil, 1967.

Bergeron, G., *Du Duplessisme à Trudeau et Bourassa, 1956-1971,* Montréal, Éditions Parti pris, 1971.

Bergeron, G., *Incertitudes d'un certain pays: le Québec et le Canada dans le monde, 1958-78* , Québec, Les presses de l'Université Laval, 1979.

Bergeron, G., *L'indépendance, oui mais . . .* , Montréal, Éditions Quinze, 1977.

Bergeron, G., *Ce jour-là . . . le Référendum,* Montréal, Les Éditions Quinze, 1978.

Bergeron, G., et Pelletier, R., *L'état du Québec en devenir,* Montréal, Édition Boréal Express, 1980.

Bergeron, L., *The History of Quebec: A Patriot's Handbook,* Toronto, N.C. Press, 1971.

Bernard, A., *La politique au Canada et au Québec,* Montréal, Les Presses de l'Université du Québec, 2eme ed., 1977. (English version: Methuen, 1981.)

Bernard, A., *Québec: Élections 1976,* Montréal, Éditions Hurtubise HMH, 1976.

Bernard, A., *What Does Quebec Want?,* Toronto, Lorimer, 1978.

Bernard, A., et Laforte, D., *La législation électorale au Québec, 1790-1967,* Montréal, Les Éditions Sainte-Marie, 1969.

Boily, R., *Québec, 1940-1969, Bibliographie,* Montréal, Les Presses de l'Université de Montréal, 1971.

Boisvert, M.A., *Les implications économiques de la souveraineté association,* Montréal, Les Presses de l'Université de Montréal, 1980.

Bourgault, P., *Québec, Quitte ou Double,* Montréal, Ferron, 1970.

Bourque, G., et Destaler, G., *Socialisme et indépendence,* Montréal, Éditions Boréal Express, 1980.

Bourque, G., et Légaré, A., *Le Québec: la question nationale,* Paris, Petite Collection Maspero, 1979.

Brady, A., "Quebec and Canadian Federalism," *C.J.E.P.S,* XXV, 3, August, 1959.

Brichant, A., *Option Canada: The Economic Implications of Separatism for the Province of Quebec,* Montreal, The Canada Committee, 1968.

Brière, M., et Grandmaison, J., *Un nouveau contrat social,* Ottawa, Les Éditions Leméac, 1980.

Brossard, J., *L'accession à la souveraineté et le cas du Québec,* Montréal, les Presses de l'Université de Montréal, 1976.

Burns, R.M., (ed.), *One Country or Two?,* Montreal, McG.-Q.U.P., 1971.

Cabatoff, K., "Radio-Quebec: A Case Study of Institution-Building," *C.J.P.S.*, XI, 1, March, 1978.

Cameron, D., *Nationalism, Self-Determination, and the Quebec Question,* Toronto, Macmillan, 1974.

Canada, *A Preliminary Report of the Royal Commission on Bilingualism and Biculturalism,* Ottawa, Q.P., 1965.

Canadian Broadcasting Corporation, *Quebec: Year Eight,* Glendon College Forum, Toronto, C.B.C., 1968.

Chaput, M., *Why I am a Separatist,* Toronto, Ryerson, 1962.

Chaput-Rolland, S., *My Country: Canada or Quebec,* Toronto, Macmillan, 1966.

Chaput-Rolland, S., *Regards 1970-71: les heures sauvages,* Montréal, le Cercle du livre de France, 1972.

Chodos, R., and Auf der Maur, N., (eds.), *Quebec: A Chronicle 1968-1972,* Toronto, J.L.S., 1972.

Clift, D., *Quebec Nationalism in Crisis,* Montreal, McG.-Q.U.P., 1982.

Clift, D., et Arnopoulos, D.M., *Le fait anglais au Québec,* Montréal, Éditions Libre Expression, 1979.

Cloutier, E., et Latouche, D., (dirs), *Le système politique québécois,* Montréal, Hurtubise HMH, 1979.

Coleman, W.D., "From Bill 22 to Bill 101: The Politics of Language under the Parti Québécois," *C.J.P.S.,* XIV, 3, September, 1981.

Comeau, P.A., "La transformation du parti libéral Québécois," *C.J.E.P.S.,* XXXI, 3, August, 1965.

Constitutional Committee of the Quebec Liberal Party, *A New Canadian Federation,* [The Beige Paper], Montreal, 1980.

Cook, R., *Canada and the French-Canadian Question,* Toronto, Macmillan, 1966.

Cook, R., (ed.), *French-Canadian Nationalism,* Toronto, Macmillan, 1969.

Corbett, E.M., *Quebec Confronts Canada,* Toronto, C.C., 1967.

Cotnam, J., *Contemporary Quebec: An Analytical Bibliography,* Toronto, M. & S., 1973.

Cuneo, C.J., and Curtis, J.E., "Quebec Separatism: An Analysis of Determinants with Social-Class Levels," *C.R.S.A.,* II, 1, February, 1974.

DeBané, P., and Asselin, M., "Quebec's Right to Secede," (A Minority Report of the Special Joint Committee of the Senate and House of Commons on the Constitution), *The Canadian Forum,* LII, 616, May, 1972.

Desrosiers, R., *Le personnel politique québécois,* Montréal, Les Éditions du Boréal Express, 1972.

Dion, G., "Secularization in Quebec," *J.C.S.,* III, 1, February, 1968.

Dion, L., *Le Québec et le Canada: les voies de l'avenir,* Montréal, Les Éditions Québecor, 1980.

Dion, L., *Québec: The Unfinished Revolution,* Montreal, McG.-Q.U.P., 1976.

Directeur général des élections du Québec, *Référendum: Reçueil de la législation,* Québec, Éditeur officiel du Québec, 1980.

Dixon, M., Jonas, S., Vaillancourt, P., (eds.), *Québec and the Parti Québécois,* San Francisco, Synthesis Publications, 1978.

Dofny, J., and Arnaud, N., *Nationalism and the National Question,* Montreal, Black Rose, 1978.

Dolment, M., et Barthe, M., *La femme au Québec,* Montréal, Presses Libres, 1973.

Drache, D., (ed.), *Quebec: Only the Beginning,* Toronto, New Press, 1972.

Dumont, F., *La vigile du Québec, Octobre 1970: L'impasse?,* Montréal, Éditions Hurtubise, 1971. (English edition: Toronto, U.T.P., 1974.)

Dupont, P., *How Lévesque Won: The Story of the PQ's 1976 Election Victory,* Toronto, Lorimer, 1977.

Feldman, E.J., (ed.), *The Quebec Referendum: What Happened and What Next? A Dialogue the Day*

After with Claude Forget and Daniel Latouche, May 21, 1980, Cambridge University, Consortium for Research on North America, 1980.

Forsey, E., *Freedom and Order, Collected Essays,* Carleton Library No. 73, (Part IV), Toronto, M. & S., 1974.

Fournier, P., "The Parti Québécois and the Power of Business," *Our Generation,* XII, 3, Fall, 1977.

Fournier, P., *The Quebec Establishment: The Ruling Class and the State,* Montreal, Black Rose, 1976.

Fréchette, P., "L'économie de la Confédération: un point de vue québécois," *C.P.P.,* III, 4, Autumn, 1977.

Fullerton, D.H., *The Dangerous Delusion: Quebec's Independence Obsession,* Toronto, M. & S., 1978.

Gagnon, G., Sicotte, A., Bourassa, G., *Tant que le monde s'ouvrira pas les yeux ou les créditistes de la vus par eux-mêmes,* Montréal, Éditions Quinze, 1977.

Garigue, P., *Bibliographie du Québec, 1955-1965,* Montréal, les Presses de l'Université de Montréal, 1967.

Garigue, P., *L'option politique du Canada français,* Montréal, Éditions du lévrier, 1963.

Gélinas, A., *Les Parlementaires et l'administration au Québec,* Montréal, Les Presses de l'Université Laval, 1969.

Gélinas, A., *Organismes autonomes et centraux de l'administration Québécoise,* Montréal, les Presses d'UQAM, 1976.

Gellner, J., *Bayonets in the Streets, Urban Guerrillas at Home and Abroad,* Don Mills, Ontario, C.-M., 1974.

Gold, G., and Tremblay, M.-A., *Communities and Culture in French Canada,* Toronto, H.R.W., 1973.

Gow, J.I., "Les Québécois, la guerre et la paix, 1945-60," *C.J.P.S.,* III, 1, March, 1970.

Gow, J.I., "L'administration québécoise de 1867 à 1900: un État en formation," *C.J.P.S.,* XII, 3, September, 1979.

Gros D'Aillon, P., *Daniel Johnson, l'égalité avant l'indépendance,* Montréal, Éditions Alainstanké, 1979.

Guidon, H., "Social Unrest, Social Class, and Quebec's Bureaucratic Revolution," *Q.Q.,* LXXI, 2, Summer, 1964.

Groupe des Recherches Sociales, *Les électeurs Québécois,* Montréal, 1960.

Haggart, R., and Golden, A., *Rumours of War,* with new introduction by R. Stanfield, Toronto, Lorimer, 2nd ed., 1979.

Hamilton, R., and Pinard, M., "The Bases of Parti Québécois Support in Recent Quebec Elections," *C.J.P.S.,* IX, 1, March, 1976.

Hamilton, R., and Pinard, M., "The Independence Issue and the Polarization of the Electorate: The 1973 Quebec Election," *C.J.P.S.,* X, 2, June, 1977.

Hamilton, R., and Pinard, M., "The Parti Québécois Comes to Power: An Analysis of the 1976 Quebec Election," *C.J.P.S.,* XI, 4, December, 1978.

Harvey, F., "La question régionale au Québec," *J.C.S.,* 15, 2, Summer, 1980.

Hudon, R., "The 1976 Quebec Election," *Q.Q.,* 84, 1, Spring, 1977.

Hudon, R., "The 1979 Federal Election and the Quebec Referendum," *Q.Q.,* 86, 4, Winter, 1979.

Institute of Intergovernmental Relations, *The Question: Debate on the Referendum Question, Quebec National Assembly, March 4-20, 1980,* Kingston, Queen's University, 1980.

Institute of Intergovernmental Relations, *The Response to Quebec: The Other Provinces and the Constitutional Debate,* Kingston, Queen's University, 1980.

Irvine, W.P., "Recruitment to Nationalism: New Politics or Normal Politics?," *C.J.P.S.,* V, 4, December, 1972.

Jean, M., (dir.), *Québécoises du 20e siècle,* Montréal, Presses Libres, 1974.

Johnson, Daniel, *Égalité ou indépendance,* Montréal, Les éditions renaissance, 1965.

Jones, R., *Community in Crisis: French-Canadian Nationalism in Perspective,* Carleton Library No. 59, Toronto, M. & S., 1967.

Joy, R., *Languages in Conflict,* Carleton Library No. 61, Toronto, M. & S., 1972.

Jutras, R., *Québec libre,* Montréal, Les éditions actualité, 1965.

Kwavnick, D., "Quebec and the Two Nations Theory: A Re-examination," *Q.Q.,* 81, 3, Autumn, 1974.

Kwavnick, D., "Québécois Nationalism and Canada's National Interest," *J.C.S.,* 12, 3, July, 1977.

Kwavnick, D., "The Roots of French-Canadian Discontent," *C.J.E.P.S.,* XXXI, 4, November, 1965.

Kwavnick, D., (ed.), *The Tremblay Report,* Carleton Library No. 64, Toronto, M. & S., 1973.

Lacoursière, J., and Huguet, H.-A., *Québec, 72-73: Bilan,* Montréal, Éditions fides, 1974.

Lamontagne, L., *Le Canada français d'aujourd'hui,* Toronto, U.T.P., 1970.

Larocque, A., *Défis au Parti Québécois,* Montréal, Éditions du Jour, 1971.

LaTerreur, M., *Les tribulations des Conservateurs au Québec, de Bennett à Diefenbaker,* Québec, les Presses de l'Université Laval, 1973.

Latouche, D., Lord, G., Vaillancourt, J.-G., *Le processus électoral au Québec: les élections provinciales de 1970 et de 1973,* Montréal, Hurtubise HMH, 1976.

Latouche, D., et Poliquin-Bourassa, D., (dirs.), *Le Manuel de la Parole, Manifestes Québécois,* Montréal, Éditions du Boréal Express, Vol. 2, 1900-1959, 1978.

Laurin, C., *Ma traversée du Québec,* Montréal, Les éditions du Jour, 1970.

Lemieux, V., Gilbert, M., Blais, A., *Une élection de réalignement: l'élection générale du 29 avril 1970 au Québec,* Montréal, Éditions du Jour, 1970.

Lemieux, V., *Le quotient politique vrai — le vote provincial et fédéral au Québec,* Québec, Les Presses de l'Université Laval, 1974.

Lemieux, V., *Parenté et politique: L'organisation sociale dans l'Île d'Orléans,* Québec, les Presses de l'Université Laval, 1971.

Lemieux, V., *Quatre élections provinciales au Québec,* Québec, les Presses de l'Université Laval, 1969.

Lemieux, V., et Hudon, R., *Patronage et politique au Québec, 1944-1972,* Montréal, Boréal Express, 1975.

Léonard, J.-F., (dir.), *La chance au coureur: Bilan de l'action du gouvernement du Parti Québécois,* Montréal, Éditions Nouvelle Optique, 1978.

Le référendum; un enjeu collectif, Cahiers de recherche éthique 7, Montréal, Fides, 1979.

Leslie, P., *Equal to Equal: Economic Association and the Canadian Common Market,* Kingston, I.I.R., Queen's University, 1979.

Lévesque, R., *Option Québec,* Montréal, Les éditions de l'homme, 1968. (English edition: Toronto, M. & S., 1968.)

Lévesque, R., *La souveraineté et l'économie,* Montréal, Les éditions du Jour, 1970.

Lévesque, R., *La solution: le programme du Parti Québécois,* Montréal, Les éditions du Jour, 1970.

Lévesque, R., *My Quebec,* Toronto, Methuen, 1979. (French version, *La Passion du Québec,* 1978.)

Linteau, P.-A., Durocher, R., Robert, J.-C., *Histoire du Québec contemporain: de la Confédération à la crise (1867-1929),* Montréal, Éditions du Boréal Express, 1979.

Lithwick, N.H., and Winer, S.L., "Faltering Federalism and French Canadians," *J.C.S.,* 12, 3, 1977.

Lower, A., "The Problem of Quebec," *J.C.S.,* 12, 3, July, 1977.

Macleod, A., *Les commissions parlementaires et les groupes de pression à l'Assemblée nationale du Québec: évaluation d'une tentative de politique consultative parlementaire,* Notes de recherche, Numéros 6-7, Département de Science politique, Université du Québec à Montréal, 1977.

Macleod, A., "Nationalism and Social Class: The Unresolved Dilemma of the Quebec Left," *J.C.S.*, VIII, 4, November, 1973.

Mallea, J., (ed.), *Quebec's Language Policies: Background and Response*, Québec, Les Presses de l'Université Laval, 1977.

Marier, R., "Les objectifs sociaux du Québec," *C.P.A.*, XII, 2, Summer, 1969.

McGraw, D., *Le développement des groupes populaires à Montréal (1963-1973)*, Montréal, Les éditions cooperatives Albert St-Martin, 1978.

McRoberts, K., and Posgate, D., *Quebec: Social Change and Political Crisis*, Toronto, M. & S., rev. ed., 1980.

Mellos, K., "Quantitative Comparison of Party Ideology," *C.J.P.S.*, III, 4, December, 1970.

Meyers, H.B., *The Quebec Revolution*, Montreal, Harvest House, 1964.

Meynaud, J., *Réflexions sur la politique au Québec*, Montréal, Éditions de Sainte-Marie, 1968.

Milner, H., *Politics in the New Quebec*, Toronto, M. & S., 1978.

Milner, S.H., and H., *The Decolonization of Quebec*, Toronto, M. & S., 1973.

Monière, D., *The Development of Ideologies in Quebec*, Toronto, U.T.P., 1981. (French version, 1977.)

Monière, D., *Les enjeux du référendum*, Montréal, Québec-Amérique, 1979.

Monière, D., et Vachet, A., *Les idéologies au Québec*, (Bibliographie), Bibliothèque nationale du Québec, 1976.

Monnet, F.-M., *Le défi québécois*, Montréal, Éditions Quinze, 1977.

Morf, G., *Terror in Quebec: Case Studies of the FLQ*, Toronto, Clarke, Irwin, 1970.

Morin, C., *Le combat Québécois*, Montréal, Éditions Boréal Express, 1973.

Morin, C., *Le pouvoir Québécois . . . en négotiation*, Montréal, Éditions du Boréal Express, 1972.

Morin, C., *Quebec versus Ottawa: The Struggle for Self-government, 1960-72*, Toronto, U.T.P., 1976.

Morris, R.N., and Lanphier, C.M., *Three Scales of Inequality: Perspectives on French-English Relations*, Montreal, Academic Press, 1977.

Murray, V., *Le parti québécois: de la fondation à la prise du pouvoir*, Montréal, Cahiers du Québec/ Hurtubise HMH, 1976.

Murray, V., et Murray, D., *De Bourassa à Lévesque*, Montréal, Éditions Quinze, 1978.

Niosi, J., *La bourgeoisie canadienne: La formation et le développement d'une classe dominante*, Montréal, Éditions Boréal Express, 1980.

Octobre 1970: Dix Ans Après, Montréal, Les Presses de l'Université de Montréal, 1980.

Oliver, M., "Quebec and Canadian Democracy," *C.J.E.P.S.*, XXIII, 4, November, 1957.

Orban, E., *Le conseil législatif de Québec*, Montréal, Bellarmin, 1967.

Orban, E., "La fin du bicaméralisme au Québec," *C.J.P.S.*, II, 3, September, 1969.

Orban, E., *Un modèle de souveraineté-association? Le conseil nordique*, Montréal, Hurtubise HMH, 1978.

Orban, E., (dir.), *La modernisation politique du Québec*, Québec, Éditions du Boréal Express, 1976.

Painchaud, P., (dir.), *Le Canada et le Québec sur la scène internationale*, Montréal, Les Presses de l'Université du Québec, 1977.

Paré, G., *Au-delà du séparatisme*, Montréal, Collection les idées du jour, 1966.

Parti Pris, *Les Québécois*, Paris, Maspero, 1967.

Pelletier, R., *Les militants du R.I.N.*, Ottawa, Éditions de l'Université d'Ottawa, 1974.

Pelletier, R., *Partis politiques au Québec*, Montréal, Hurtubise HMH, 1976.

Pinard, M., *The Rise of a Third Party,* [Social Credit in Quebec], McG.-Q.U.P., enlarged ed., 1975.

Pinard, M., et Hamilton, R., "Le référendum québécois," *Policy Options,* 2, 4, September-October, 1981.

Québec, Assemblée nationale, *Répertoire des parlementaires québécois, 1867-1978,* 1980.

Québec, Conseil exécutif, *La nouvelle entente Québec-Canada: Propositions du gouvernement du Québec pour une entente d'égal à égal: la souveraineté-association,* Québec, Éditeur officiel, 1979. (English version: *Québec-Canada, A New Deal,* 1979.)

Québec, *Loi régissant le financement des partis politiques,* Québec, Éditeur officiel, 1979.

Québec, Ministère des Affaires culturelles, *Bibliographie du Québec, 1821-1967,* Québec, Éditeur officiel, 1980.

Québec, Ministère des Affaires intergouvernementales, *Quebec's Traditional Stands on the Division of Powers, 1900-1976,* Québec, Éditeur officiel, 1978.

Québec, Ministère du Développement Économique, *Challenges for Quebec: A Statement on Economic Policy, Synopsis, Policy Objectives and Measures,* Québec, Éditeur officiel, 1979.

Québec, *Le rapport de la commission royale d'enquête sur l'enseignement,* (le rapport Parent), Québec, l'imprimeur de la reine, 1963-1966, 3 vols.

Québec, *Le rapport de la commission royale d'enquête sur la fiscalité,* (le rapport Bélanger), Québec, l'imprimeur de la reine, 1966.

Quebec, *Report of the Royal Commission of Inquiry on Constitutional Problems* (Tremblay Report), Quebec, 1956, 4 vols.

Quinn, H.F., *The Union Nationale: Quebec Nationalism from Duplessis to Lévesque,* Toronto, U.T.P., 1979.

Rayside, D., "Federalism and the Party System: Provincial and Federal Liberals in the Province of Quebec," *C.J.P.S.,* XI, 3, September, 1978.

Reid, M., *The Shouting Signpainters: A Literary and Political Account of Quebec Revolutionary Nationalism,* Toronto, M. & S., 1972.

Rioux, M., *Quebec in Question,* Toronto, J.L.S., 1971.

Rioux, M., *La question du Québec,* Montréal, Parti Prix, 1978.

Rioux, M., and Martin, Y., *French-Canadian Society,* Vol. 1, Carleton Library No. 18, Toronto, M. & S., 1964.

Rotstein, A., (ed.), *Power Corrupted,* Toronto, New Press, 1971.

Rowat, D.C., (ed.), *The Referendum and Separation Elsewhere: Implications for Quebec,* Ottawa, Department of Political Science, Carleton University, 1978.

Roy, J.-L., "Dynamique du Nationalisme Québécois (1945-1970)," *Canadian Review of Studies in Nationalism,* 1, 1, Fall, 1973.

Roy, J.-L., *La marche des Québécois — le temps des ruptures (1945-1960),* Montréal, Éditions Leméac, 1976.

Roy, M., *L'Acadie perdue,* Montréal, Éditions Québec-Amérique, 1978.

Ryan, C., *A Stable Society,* Montreal, Éditions Heritage, 1978.

Saywell, J., *The Rise of the Parti Québécois, 1967-1976,* Toronto, U.T.P., 1977.

Scott, F., and Oliver, M., (eds.), *Quebec States Her Case,* Toronto, Macmillan, 1964.

Séguin, M., "Genèse et historique de l'idée séparatiste au Canada français," *Laurentie,* 119, 1962.

Shaw, W., and Albert, L., *Partition, The Price of Quebec's Independence,* Foreword by Eugene Forsey, Montreal, Thornhill Publishing, 1980.

Siegfried, A., *The Race Question in Canada,* Carleton Library No. 29, Toronto, M. & S., 1966. (Reprint from 1906.)

Sloan, T., *Quebec, The Not-So-Quiet Revolution,* Toronto, Ryerson, 1965.

Société St. Jean Baptiste de Montréal, *Le fédéralisme, l'acte de l'amérique du nord britannique et les Canadiens français*, Mémoire au comité parlementaire de la constitution du gouvernement du Québec, Montréal, Les éditions de l'agence Duvernay, 1964.

Soldatos, P., (dir.), *Nationalisme et intégration dans le contexte canadien*, Montréal, Centre d'Études et de Documentation européenne, Université de Montréal, 1980.

Spicer, K., *Cher péquiste . . . et néanmoins ami*, Montréal, Les Éditions la Presse, 1979.

Stein, M., *The Dynamics of Right-Wing Protest: Social Credit in Quebec*, Toronto, U.T.P., 1973.

Stratford, P., (ed.), *André Laurendeau: Witness for Quebec, Essays*, Toronto, Macmillan, 1973.

Taylor, M.G., "Quebec Medicare: Policy Formulation in Conflict and Crisis," *C.P.A.*, 15, 2, Summer, 1972.

Tellier, L.-N., *Le Québec, État nordique*, Montréal, Éditions Quinze, 1977.

Thomson, D., (ed.), *Quebec Society and Politics: Views from the Inside*, Toronto, M. & S., 1973.

Treddenick, J.M., "Quebec and Canada: Some Economic Aspects of Independence," *J.C.S.*, VIII, 4, November, 1973.

Tremblay, R., *L'économie québécoise: histoire, développement, politiques*, Montréal, Les Presses de l'Université du Québec, 1976.

Troisième Congrès des Affaires Canadiennes, *Les nouveaux Québécois*, Québec, Les Presses de l'Université Laval, 1964.

Trudeau, P.E., "Some Obstacles to Democracy in Quebec," *C.J.E.P.S.*, XXIV, 3, August, 1958.

Trudeau, P.E., *Federalism and the French Canadians*, Toronto, Macmillan, 1968.

Trudeau, P.E., (ed.), *The Asbestos Strike*, Toronto, J.L.S., 1974. (French version, Montréal, Les Éditions du Jour, 1970.)

L'Urbanisation au Québec, Rapport du Groupe de Travail sur l'Urbanisation, Québec, Éditeur officiel, 1976.

Usher, D., "The English Response to the Prospect of the Separation of Quebec," (with comments by D.L. Emerson and D. Latouche), *C.P.P.*, IV, 1, Winter, 1978.

Vadeboncoeur, P., *To Be or Not to Be, That is the Question!*, Montréal, l'Hexagone, 1980.

Vaillancourt, F., "La Charte de la Langue Française du Québec," *C.P.P.*, IV, 3, Summer, 1978.

Vaillancourt, F., "La situation démographiques et socio-économique des francophones du Québec: une revue," *C.P.P.*, V, 4, Autumn, 1979.

Vallières, P., *Choose!*, Toronto, New Press, 1972.

Vallières, P., *Nègres blancs d'Amérique*, Montréal, Éditions Parti Pris, 1968. (English edition, Toronto, M. & S., 1971.)

Vallières, P., *Un Québec impossible*, Montréal, Québec-Amérique, 1977.

Wade, M., (ed.), *Canadian Dualism: Studies of French-English Relations*, Toronto, U.T.P., 1960.

Wade, M., *The French Canadians*, Vol. I, 1760-1911, Vol. II, 1912-1967, Toronto, Macmillan, 1970.

Wood, J.R., "Secession: A Comparative Analytical Framework," *C.J.P.S.*, XIV, 1, March, 1981.

II PROCESS

7

THE ROLE OF PUBLIC OPINION

Public opinion is shaped by many different forces. One of them allegedly is the publication of public opinion polls. Some observers believe that these influence the way citizens vote. Assuming the worst, several MPs have introduced bills in the House of Commons in the past few years to ban the publication of public opinion polls during election campaigns. However, the House thus far has not seen fit to follow the example of British Columbia and some European countries and prohibit such publication. There also has been concern about the increasing predilection of governments, parties, and candidates to conduct private polls for their own advantage. These problems are superimposed upon the basic questions of the methodology of the polls and their accuracy.

It is surprising that despite the concern with polls almost nothing definitive has been written on the subject in Canada. Professor Hugh Whalen's article, which he prepared originally for an earlier edition of this book and which he has rewritten and enlarged for this edition, stands as the one major Canadian piece of literature on polling. It examines all of these questions, concentrating in particular on the Gallup Poll in Canada. References alluded to by Professor Whalen can be found in the bibliography at the end of this chapter. Richard Gwyn's account of the actual techniques used in interviewing for a Gallup poll that appeared in the fourth edition at pp. 205-206 has been omitted from this edition.

Pressure groups and lobbying also influence public opinion. More has been written about their activities in Canada than about public opinion polls. One of the basic works is Professor Paul Pross's book in the McGraw-Hill Ryerson Series in Canadian Politics entitled *Pressure Group Behaviour in Canadian Politics,* Toronto, McGraw-Hill Ryerson, 1975, which brings together a number of studies of individual interest groups. References to additional works are contained in the bibliography at the conclusion of this chapter. Two articles which appeared in the fourth edition, pp. 206-212, Clive Baxter's "Lobbying — Ottawa's Fast-Growing Business" and W.D.H. Frechette's "The C.M.A. — Spokesman for Industry," have been replaced in this edition by a more recent article by David Blaikie describing the $100 million-a-year lobbying business in Ottawa.

Professor Ken Bryden's essay deals with a subject that is of great concern to a number of Canadians, namely, how to make our political process less bureaucratic and more democratic by increasing the public's input into policy-making and administration. He reviews the literature and experiences we have had and offers some suggestions for further improvement.

Students interested in how the media, politicians, and manipulators manufacture "pseudo-news" should consult Daniel J. Boorstin's splendid book, *The Image: A Guide to Pseudo Events in America,* listed in the bibliography. An amusing and informative account of one manipulator at work is contained in Ron Haggart's article in this chapter.

The media are very significant in influencing public opinion. Concern about the impact of the media, and in particular the dangers arising from the growing concentration of ownership of the press, radio, and television, has led to two major public investigations in the past decade. Senator Keith Davey's Special Senate Committee on Mass Media analyzed the industry thoroughly and published its valuable three-volume report in 1970. So few of its recommendations were acted upon that a royal commission was appointed in 1980 to examine newspapers once again. The Kent Commission report which appeared less than a year later severely criticized daily newspaper publishing in Canada and offered some strong suggestions for improvement. The essence of its findings and recommendations are reproduced in this chapter.

David Surplis's article on concentration and control in Canadian media and Ron Lowman's article on the Ontario Press Council which appeared in the fourth edition from pp. 215-221 have been replaced in this edition by the Kent Commission excerpt and an extract from the recent annual report of the Ontario Press Council that describes its work.

The bibliography contains references to recent Canadian literature on polling, pressure groups and lobbying, participation, and the media. Students should keep an eye peeled for Professsor Arthur Siegel's forthcoming book, *Politics and the Media in Canada,* which will be published in the McGraw-Hill Ryerson Series in Canadian Politics in the near future. References to elites and power have been transferred to the bibliography in Chapter 1.

THE REWARDS AND PERILS OF POLLING*

Hugh Whalen

Polling Comes of Age: Its Basic Dynamics

Polling is now undertaken even among the East-Bloc nations. There, however, its use is rigidly confined to the state agencies and party institutions. In the West, by contrast, the growth of opinion measurement and analysis has occurred in natural fashion across all social sectors, encumbered by neither a state ideology and command economy nor the leaden hand of bureaucratic formalism. For this reason, the number of commercial, governmental and university-related organizations specializing in mass-opinion survey research has risen dramatically since this article was initially prepared some fifteen years ago. Given their high-growth environment, pollers have thus become much more active and — one can but guess

* Written in August, 1980, based in some degree on an original article prepared and published in 1966 in the second edition of *Politics: Canada* and published here with permission of the author, who is Professor of Political Science, Memorial University of Newfoundland. For references, see the bibliography.

— much better remunerated purveyors of increasingly sophisticated "soft" communications services to a widening range of private-sector clients: advertising and public relations firms, other business enterprises, labour and professional groups, issue-specific advocacy groups, university research and specialized public policy institutes, and assorted, all-purpose think tanks.

Political and Administrative Polling

Here polling has increased in a spectacular manner. That competitive, ambivalent yet nervously congenial relationship between pollers and top political leaders, which emerged clearly after 1960, has developed even further and seemingly matured during the last decade.

Government leaders today are systematically made aware of mass-opinion soundings when devising major policy departures, when determining near-term electoral strategy and public relations tactics, and when timing critical action. The influence of these inputs is never uniform, due to situational and stylistic variations. So the relationship between poll indicators and political action is always empirical and contingent.

But in Canada, Mr. Trudeau's decision to defer calling an election toward the end of his fourth year in office in 1978 revealed a strong reliance on precisely those indicators. Likewise, opposition party eagerness to inflict parliamentary defeat of the Clark minority government's budget late in 1979 was influenced in no small part by poll reports indicating a strong shift in electoral advantage to the Liberals.

Indeed, if electoral truth were told, polling activity can now be said to influence anything from the content and emphasis of a leader's television speeches to his choice of social associates and neckties, to party slogans on the bumper sticker of the farm truck. Pre-election activity by "political consultants" in an appropriate manner determines the design of expensive party advertising programs, the location of appropriate target areas for campaign emphasis and de-emphasis, the choice of leadership styles and the behaviour of mass media.

Particularly in the United States, though increasingly in Europe and other countries as well, party leadership contests and primary election activities involve a far greater use of opinion surveys than was formerly apparent, thus adding a new cost dimension in public affairs. During 1968, some 1,400 separate polls were conducted in the United States in connection with presidential and congressional elections. We should hardly be surprised if in 1980 that number finally exceeds 3,000. Polling activity not only influences the decisions of candidates to enter, remain in contention, or to withdraw from primary elections and other forms of leadership competition. As the case of the late U.S. presidential candidate Hubert Humphrey so dramatically attests, it may even become a factor determining their ability to obtain the money contributions needed for effective participation.

In all democratic states, incumbent party leaders and their competitors must in any case now operate in an environment where leadership performance and potential are systematically monitored in relation to mass-opinion flows. Accordingly, all top leaders and their principal advisors must possess a substantial expertise in actual polling techniques and in the interpretation of poll results. There are some instances now on record where principal incumbent leaders, including one recent U.S. president and one Canadian provincial premier, have retired completely from public life mainly on the strength of negative poll results.

There were important "demonstration effects" produced both by American administrative practice and in consequence of certain pathbreaking mass-opinion studies commissioned in Canada, not by bureaucrats, but by the research staffs of legislative committees, royal commissions, task forces and some of the numerous "side-car" advisory bodies. It was these units, for instance, that sponsored the first major publicly funded and technically acceptable survey studies in areas such as housing policy, bilingualism, government information, citizen action groups, and immigration.

There now issues from the Office of the Prime Minister and the Privy Council Office, where a powerful general opinion research facility has been developed, through literally scores of federal and provincial departments, regulatory bodies and crown corporations, an annual flow of contract awards for mass-opinion research that number in the hundreds. Examination of the substantive nature of this polling activity — often either euphemistically or unwittingly styled "reality checks" by those required to justify it — will indicate that in a short span almost every conceivable public agenda item has been examined, from youth culture to affirmative action proposals for women, to the use of freeway noise barriers, to provincial education issues, to energy problems, to federal farm assistance policy — even to the quality of advertising appearing in the electronic media!

What budgetary and political implications can be drawn from these developments? Much polling activity in this as in other areas is effectively screened not only from public but also from formal legislative scrutiny. Given the all-pervasive cloak of Canadian administrative secrecy, together with an understandable taciturnity on the part of commercial polling firms in these confidential matters, next to no precise annual estimate can be made of its probable budgetary cost. For a similar reason, the impact of polling on policy advisors and formal decision-makers remains obscure, except for the increasing visibility of "poll-junkies" in the hurly-burly of bureaucratic politics.

Individual surveys of any significance can range in price from $20,000 to $200,000 or more, depending on their scope and purpose along the many possible motivational, attitudinal, behavioural or factual dimensions of study. When recently put under strong opposition pressure, the Ontario government has conceded that in the period 1977-1980 it has spent some half a million annually on these surveys. It is my own view that, particularly during any pre-election year, the global amount of opinion contracting in Canada for public-sector purposes is likely now to fall in the $8–10 million range.

Individuals who advocate more openness in government, some media commentators and more recently, opposition legislators, have begun to adopt a critical posture on this matter, so far with little evident effect. In their turn, government leaders continue to justify publicly funded polling on the grounds of political and administrative necessity.

One estimate of the ratio of secret to publicly available studies is ten to one. In any case, Prime Minister Trudeau, in April, 1980, allowed that some surveys in highly sensitive areas may elicit the kind of information that it would not be "in the public interest" to distribute widely. One of his opposition critics then responded by suggesting that, not infrequently, prior ministerial knowledge of the answer distributions to certain questions placed on mass-opinion surveys funded by taxpayers necessarily confers upon government members an unwarranted partisan political advantage. The federal government subsequently released the results of a number of surveys.

The Canadian Polling Community

By international standards, the Canadian mass-opinion survey community is of modest size. Its profile, however, is complex in nature, consisting of three separate elements: first, an all-purpose market analysis group serving business needs and government/party requirements; second, a smaller group supplying syndicated and other studies to the mass media; and third, a mixed group consisting of representatives from the university and policy research sectors.

In the first category are eight leading polling companies, of which Canadian Facts Ltd. and Goldfarb Consultants Ltd. are the most important. Beyond this core group some additional twenty firms have been engaged in significant research during the past decade. Some of these have worked solely for political parties, while others have been engaged almost exclusively in private market or audience research. Polling enterprises associated with the names of Harris, Quayle, Teeter, Crowe, Elliott, Caddell and Neopolitan lie in the first category, though some larger commercial companies (e.g., Goldfarb) have also worked extensively with the parties.

Apart from the two main audience-rating firms (A.C. Neilson Co. and the Bureau of Broadcast Measurement), other polling firms active during the 1970s include, among others, Canadian Inter-Mark Ltd., Elliott Research Corporation, Canada Market Research Ltd., Nationwide Market Research Corporation, SORECOM Inc., Canadian Opinion Research, BM1, Media Trends Research Corporation, Contemporary Research Ltd., Multi-Reso Inc., Burke Marketing Research, Cambridge Research Institute, Adcom Research Ltd., and National Polling Trends Ltd. Most of these firms are headquartered in Toronto and Montreal with the larger units having permanent regional city branches. Certain companies serve regional and provincial markets. Among the main polling units there are some inter-corporate connections, not all of which are readily discoverable. A few are subsidiaries of U.S. parent companies. With some exceptions, the political party polling operations have depended heavily on U.S. expertise.

Some opinion research units are multi-purpose ventures combining survey work with advertising and public relations. At present, there are some 300 or more Canadian companies actively engaged in agency advertising and dispensing more than \$3 billion annually to television, radio, newspapers, magazines and other media.

There is in the polling community as well the usual indeterminate number of very small units, including not a few single-person ventures, that drift in and out of the confraternity. In this category we place the growing number of all-purpose planning-engineering-research consulting companies whose service product-mix often includes a limited expertise in mass-opinion surveying.

Finally, certain business associations such as the Canadian Federation of Independent Business and the Conseil du Patronat sometimes undertake survey work.

Second, there are generally more visible media-service organizations, of which the Canadian Institute of Public Opinion, founded in 1941, is the prototype. The CIPO Gallup franchise has since 1973 been held by Nationwide Market Research Corporation. Somewhat similar polling organizations have recently emerged in Quebec, including the Centre de Recherche sur l'Opinion Publique (CROP), l'Institut Québécois d'Opinion Publique (IQOP) and INCI. A group in the School of Journalism at Carleton University has also become active in pre-election and other forms of mass-opinion polling. In the main, these agencies provide syndicated or special- assignment services for Canadian mass media, including three television networks, daily and weekly newspapers and magazines. The actual interviewing for the CIPO is undertaken by Canadian Facts Ltd., a company which is strong in the field of nation-wide sampling operations.

Lastly, there are a small number of mass-opinion analysis units located in the university and policy research communities. The most important of these are the York University Behavioural Institute's Survey Research Centre, Windsor University's International Business Studies Unit and the recently established Institute for Research in Public Policy. The first of these organizations is Canada's foremost opinion research facility and is linked to the major U.S. data-banks and research centres at Ann Arbor, Chicago, New York and elsewhere. The last organization is a mixed private and public think tank with a very broad research mandate, including the analysis of opinion trends.

There are also a number of individual Canadian scholars who have engaged themselves as entrepreneurs in the polling field. Possibly the most visible members of this group at present include Professors Regenstreif, Pinard, Hamilton, Tigert, Cloutier, Fletcher, Drummond, Le Duc and Frizzell, all of whom undertake design and interpretive work mainly for the media but sometimes as well for governments. They generally have not been engaged as "pollsters" with the political parties. The remaining elements in the polling community are associated with academic research and government institutions, two areas beyond the immediate purview of this study.

Two general observations on the polling community are worth making. First, the detailed operational character and the technical performance record of Canadian mass-opinion research has never been subjected to critical examination by any disinterested authority. In contrast, American polling practices were thoroughly examined in the late 1940s by the U.S. Social Science Research Council and have again been the subject of inquiry by the American Statistical Association. The first of these examinations followed a general polling failure in the 1948 presidential election. In Britain, a similar though somewhat less formalized examination has been in progress for some years, due mainly to the problems associated with major polling failures in that country during three general elections in 1970 and 1974. There have been some polling failures in Canada, as we indicate later, but none has caused a sufficient concern to generate any general review of the polling community's performance.

Second, it has long been apparent in the United States and Britain that leaders of polling organizations and their top staffs have been prepared — indeed have been anxious — to engage professionally in serious discussion of survey technique, to report upon opinion research experiments, and to convey suggestions for improved procedures based upon actual research experience. In those countries there has similarly developed an extensive technical literature on mass-opinion analysis by academic writers. In Canada, on the other hand, leaders of polling organizations have contributed virtually nothing in this regard. One will search the non-trade literature in vain for books or articles that deal in a technical fashion with the problems of mass-opinion research in a Canadian setting. The CIPO, for instance, has not once in its nearly forty years of operation ever troubled to supply its subscribers with a comprehensive description of its sampling, estimating and post-sample adjustment procedures.

Much the same can be said in relation to members of the academic community who have specialized in this area. Their contribution has been minimal on the central problems of investigative technique, even though some of them have published widely in fields where opinion poll results are a primary data consideration.

Canadian mass-opinion research, in short, has clearly come of age in the sense that its principal business consultants have steadily extended their private and public markets, thus embedding themselves more securely as intermediaries in the strategic networks of the national and regional communications systems. In this process, however, there has been small evidence of real maturation.

Practice and Malpractice

In the autumn of 1977, two polling studies were made public on Quebec popular attitudes to the emotionally charged issues of separatism, federalism and sovereignty-association. The first study was performed by Goldfarb Consultants Ltd. for Southam Press, using in-home interviews, and the second by the Centre de recherche sur l'opinion publique (CROP) for Readers Digest, using its normal telephone interview method. Both firms are among the most highly regarded polling organizations in Canada. The Goldfarb study surveyed 502 Quebecers as a sub-unit in a national sample of 2,000; the CROP sample numbered 1,356 Quebecers but only 823 were interviewed.

Each poll reported what seemed to be different conclusions and a first-rate controversy ensued. The Goldfarb study found that the proportion of Quebecers favouring separatism had declined from 33 per cent in February 1977 to 25 per cent in July, and that, of this latter proportion, only 10 per cent favoured outright separation from Canada with the remainder preferring independence within some form of economic union. The implication was that the appeal of Mr. Lévesque's strategy was on the decline.

The CROP survey, on the other hand, found that his appeal was indeed growing: 38 per cent indicated a preference for sovereignty-association, 44 per cent were against that option and 18 per cent were undecided or declined to answer. But, on a subsequent question, when asked if, in an actual referendum, Mr. Lévesque should seek merely a *mandate to negotiate sovereignty-association,* 50 per cent answered in the affirmative, compared with 34 per cent who disagreed. Taking into account only those who were decided, answers to this last question yielded the proportions 60 per cent favourable and 40 per cent unfavourable. Adding even more credence to these results was the further finding that barely 14 per cent of the sample was satisfied with the *status quo* of federalism.

This initial poll result, together with others which followed it showing similar trends, have come to be widely regarded as the most influential factors which eventually induced the Lévesque government, some two years later, to formulate its referendum question in terms of a mandate merely to negotiate. There seems little doubt that in the history of polling, this Quebec case will stand as one of the clearest examples illustrating the actual impact of opinion research on governmental action.

The Accuracy of Polling

In a recent letter to *The Globe and Mail* (February 19, 1980), Mr. Mark Lovell of the Professional Marketing Research Society, essentially a group of market analysts serving business clients, made bold to say: "Competently run polls today are very accurate. At the last U.K. general election, eight of nine election eve polls were accurate within 0.5 per cent."

This is a broadly accurate observation with respect to the 1979 British general election. But Mr. Lovell generalized over much in light of the many troublesome poll failure precedents which go unmentioned. In fact, in the 1979 election Mrs. Thatcher's party achieved a seven point lead over the Labour Party. Among the six final polls (published before election day), the projected results were (in relation to the actual + 7 Tory lead): Gallup + 8, RSL + 11.5, Marplan + 8, Mori (1) + 4, Mori (2) + 3, NOP - 1. Among the final polls published on election day, the results were: Mori (1) + 5.5, Gallup + 2.5, Marplan + 6.5, NOP + 7 and Mori (2) + 8.

When dealing with the empirical evidence of polling failure in electoral contests, it has become a common response for pollers since 1948 to insist that after all they are not *really* engaged in forecasting, predicting or "crystal-ball gazing." They claim only to be measuring party preference distributions in a dispassionate technical fashion and reporting, within accepted error limits, their best final pre-election estimates. In recent years, however, it has also been standard practice immediately after elections for the Canadian Gallup Poll to editorialize upon its record of accuracy (within its own error tolerance limit) — except, that is, in 1957 and 1980, when a measure of error has indeed been conceded. Public criticism of polling error, when it is even noticed, tends to be deflected by polling partisans to the alleged general misunderstanding of the nature of mass-opinion survey technique.

Probability Sampling and Polling

All statistical error or variance that is naturally associated with mass-opinion sampling refers to the numerical range of probable error that would likely occur were an infinite number of particular poll results generalized for the entire (usually adult) population, or universe. Estimates of the limits of this variance, therefore, are derived from the theory of probability, or at least that part of it called the "normal law" which presents itself graphically as a bell-type, normal distribution curve. Originally called the "law of error," its presence can be inferred from any number of empirical experiments that involve sampling the results of operations like coin-spinning, die-rolling, various modes of astronomical observation, and so on.

Suppose, for instance, that in a large urn there are ten million beans, exactly half of which are kidney (brown) and half are navy (white). Suppose also that, not knowing this real distribution, we attempt to estimate the proportion of each bean-type in the container by drawing a *randomized* sample of 2,000 beans. With successive samples of this size, there is a 50:50 chance that, on average, each of the two bean sub-samples will contain *approximately* 1,000. If the sampling experiment were repeated a hundred, a thousand or an infinite number of times, it is conceivable — though at the very highest level of improbability — that one or more samples might yield, say, 1 kidney and 1,999 navy beans, or *vice versa*. But when any substantial number of samples are summarized in terms of their result frequency, they will show a "central tendency" to cluster approximately on either side of the predicted result norm of 50 per cent.

Sample variance, therefore, is a measure, expressed as a range, of the deviations to be normally anticipated in sampling experiments. Concretely, if 5,000 such bean sampling experiments were actually conducted by randomized method, it might be shown that in 68.3 per cent of them (14 times in 20) the proportion of kidney beans appearing would fall in the range 51.5–48.5 per cent. With such a number of sample readings, and with 2,000 beans in each sample, then, the error of estimate is 50% ± 1.5. It might also be shown that in 95.4 per cent of the sampling experiments (19 times in 20) the error of estimate is 50% ± 3.0. Finally, it might be shown that in 99.7 per cent of them (19.8 times in 20) the sample variance is 50% ± 4.5.

From this simple example, it can be seen that coherent results of error estimation in sampling theory necessarily require very specific assumptions in three distinct areas. First, the assumed frequency rates (*confidence limits*) of sampling result observation; second, the assumed size of the sample; and, third, an assumed random process of sample selection. Accordingly, in working from hypothesized result norms to the predictions of probable error, it is apparent that the size of sample variance depends on the particular confidence limits which are adopted: the higher the confidence limit used, the wider the range of normal error to be expected, or vice versa.

Most polling organizations now operate at a 95 per cent confidence limit so their sample proportion result distributions are deemed to be accurate 19 times out of 20 within so many points of variance. It can be demonstrated within this framework that, in any large number of sampling exercises, a *decrease* in confidence limits from 95 to 68 per cent will produce a *reduction* in sample variance by about one-half. Conversely, an increase in confidence limits from 95 to 99 per cent will involve an increase in sample error by just under one-third, in order to net those few and infrequent events of very low probability.

To illustrate the central interdependence between statistical confidence limits and sample size, let us take another simple example. Suppose that, in a perfectly executed random national opinion survey, 40 per cent of respondents (eligible voters) indicate a preference for the leader of Party X. What range of sample variance is theoretically associated with projecting this proportional result as a proxy for all eligible voters in the country? The answer here is straightforward, but it requires two formulae. At a 68 per cent confidence limit, the error is calculated in the range: $\pm \sqrt{\dfrac{p(100-p)}{n}}$.

At a 95 per cent confidence limit, the error range is: $\pm 1.96 \sqrt{\dfrac{p(100-p)}{n}}$, where p = 40 and n = the appropriate sample size. The resulting sample variances that appear as between these two confidence limits, and each of eight selected variations in sample size, are set out, by applying our formulae, as in Table 1.

Table 1: Ranges of Statistical Error in Example: 40% for Party X

Sample Size	Confidence Limit 68% ERROR (±) %	Confidence Limit 68% RANGE OF ESTIMATE %	Confidence Limit 95% ERROR (±) %	Confidence Limit 95% RANGE OF ESTIMATE %
100	4.9	44.9 - 35.1	9.6	49.6 - 30.4
200	3.5	43.5 - 36.5	6.9	46.9 - 33.1
400	2.5	42.5 - 37.5	4.9	44.9 - 35.1
600	2.0	42.0 - 38.0	3.9	43.9 - 36.1
750	1.8	41.8 - 38.2	3.5	43.5 - 36.5
1,000	1.6	41.6 - 38.4	3.1	43.1 - 36.9
1,500	1.3	41.3 - 38.7	2.5	42.5 - 37.5
3,000	1.0	41.0 - 39.0	2.0	42.0 - 38.0

It is apparent from Table 1 that, within a 95 per cent confidence limit, the reported 40 per cent sample preference for the leader of Party X, when projected for the entire electorate, is subject to an error tolerance which varies inversely with the number of individuals sampled. A sample of 400, for instance, will have a projected error of 40% ± 5, whereas a sample of 3,000 will have one of only 40 ± 2. But, at whatever confidence limit adopted, it is also clear that the *rate of reduction* in estimated variance, associated with *increasing* numbers in the sample, *diminishes* substantially in the case of samples in the 1,000 - 3,000 and higher ranges.

In accordance with the theory of probability sampling, and in spite of the long-standing general complaint regarding the use of unrepresentative, allegedly under-sized polling samples, it is evident that the statistical variance inherent in randomized selection procedures is determined equally by the adopted confidence limits of pollers and by the size of their samples, *but in no manner by the size of the population under study.* Moreover, the precision of sample estimates increases only as the square root of the number interviewed. It is a rule of thumb that, at a 95 per cent confidence limit, samples in excess of 2,000 individuals must be enlarged roughly *four* times in order to reduce the expected range of error by *one-half.* For this reason, once any sample attains a critical number threshold, in relation to research objectives, each additional person interviewed contributes less and less to the reduction of sample variance. These propositions hold even when the populations under study are as widely divergent as, say, the entire adult populations of Canada, the United Kingdom and the United States — three countries whose comparative population proportions lie approximately in the range 1:2.5:10.

There are two additional dimensions of sample variance that deserve very brief notice. The first relates to the size of sample proportion results. A different degree of variance, for instance, is associated with a poll result indicating, say, a 50 per cent preference for the leader of Party X than one reporting only 20 per cent for the leader of Party Y. As a general rule, there is a tendency for the estimated range of error to rise as the proportions near 50. Therefore, reported poll proportions that are either very low or very high will tend to be more accurate than those in mid-range.

Second, there exists a source of complexity in determining error tolerances when dealing with sub-groups within the population. Most polling organizations do not confine their error-control activity to aggregate proportional result distributions alone. They seek as well reliable data on the degree of sample variance associated with sub-aggregates such as men and women, old and young, urban and rural residents, more and less educated strata, partisans of Party X and Party Y, individuals within higher and lower social status and income groups, residents of different geographic regions, and so on. Sometimes these requirements force an increase in the size of samples. When probability methods of selection are used, individuals in the above groups are likely to be represented in any sample roughly in proportion to their frequency within the total population. As with our earlier example on bean selection, in any human sample drawn at random, males and females will tend to be included in roughly equal proportions. Thus, in a sample of 1,500, when survey results for males and females separately are sought at a level of accuracy equivalent to those expected in relation to the two groups in combination, it is evident that the size of each sub-sample should be almost doubled. All major polling organizations have devised techniques for making these fine adjustments in the error tolerances associated with such sub-group levels of inference.

Estimates of the limits of error in probability or random sampling, in summary, are thus derived from the basic theory of chance occurrence; they specify in a manner the degree to which actual poll results may be expected to differ, 19 times in 20, from those that would have been obtained had the entire adult population in fact been interviewed. An accurate determination of this range of statistical variance, however, presupposes a thoroughly randomized selection of sample respondents that is grounded operationally in the principle of "known probability." Otherwise, the purely theoretic error projections will not serve as reliable predictors of errors associated with the concrete results of actual survey practice. But such a stringent selection requirement can only be realized in the real world when *every* individual in the *entire* population under investigation has an *equal,* and thus a *known,* chance of actually being interviewed.

Notwithstanding much improvement in selection technique during recent decades, it must not be supposed that such an exacting norm is attained in real-world polling practice. Indeed, we do not fault our pollers for failing to achieve what is palpably impossible. We fault them rather for failing to convey adequately to the public the degree to which their estimating and technical operations in fact lie quite outside, and are therefore entirely unrelated to, the abstract, substantially idealized framework of pure statistical inference described above. For it is not the randomly distributed, calculable error tolerances inferred from the body of probability theory, so much as these non-random errors associated with design and procedural defects, that are the source of real trouble.

There exists, for certain, a long, dreary litany of these well-known negative polling characteristics: poorly designed surveys; undersized or unrepresentative samples; ineffective interviewing which contributes to approval-seeking responses; excessively dichotomized, badly formulated or poorly worded questions; interviewer cheating; the excessive inclusion of extraneous questions (piggybacking); respondent fatigue; intentionally misleading replies and outright non-cooperation; inadvertent or intentional misjudgment in post-survey corrections, adjustments and trend-weighting exercises; "cooking the results," whether for fraudulent reasons or for partisan and competitive advantage; computational and data processing failures and a host of others, including the communication of wrong results through accident. We cannot simply deny this massive evidence of dysfunction even when aware of efforts to deal with it. A policing function is impractical; professional monitoring may help; but the vagaries of self-discipline will prevail.

Neither can we assume that judgmental and other secondary errors are self-cancelling. Nor can we believe that there exists, or can ever be ascertained, any coherent relationship between the two distinct sources of error. But a consistent attribution of near-accuracy in, say, pre-election poll performance almost systematically by reference exclusively to the idealized criteria of error estimation, effectively screens off general awareness of the many judgmental and procedural factors which equally serve as partial explanations of variations in observed polling forecast error. In pre-election polling, as we shall later notice, moreover, there are certain special factors such as undecided vote intentions which tend to increase the significance of these latter factors.

In general, if a poller exercises correct judgment or is plain lucky in appraising the many political, non-statistical variables operative during the election campaign, he may well achieve minimum forecast error even with substantial statistical error. If, on the other hand, he deals inexpertly or unluckily with political trends, he may obtain large forecast error even with minimal statistical error. And just how the law of compensating error will tend to effect behaviour within these limits is unclear.

Sample Selection Procedures

Finally, a brief note on actual sampling technique is in order. Successive attempts to secure a greater element of randomization in poll sample selection during recent decades has produced a number of important departures in opinion survey procedure. The quota-stratified sampling technique so widely used in the formative years of polling has been gradually displaced by area-probability sampling methods.

In the former method, pollers sought to extract representative examples through establishing an equivalence among their respondents proportional to the occurrence of their characteristics (age, sex, occupation, education, etc.) in the population as a whole. However, interviewers in the sample areas were often permitted such a wide discretion in the choice of respondents from among the different strata that effective knowledge regarding the probabilities of selection could not be guaranteed. The error tolerances specified in sampling theory were often thus incongruent with actual sampling errors. In early quota polls there often tended to be bias toward women and middle and upper-class strata in opinion samples.

The area-probability method which is now widely used comes much closer to achieving a selection process that is verifiable in relation to some known probability, since in principle every adult can be associated with but one occupied dwelling unit, which in turn can be associated with one, and only one, segment of land.

In an earlier version of this paper, we described the detailed process as follows:

(1) choice of the characteristics of the population to be sampled; (2) in the case of a national sample, division of the country into classes of the appropriate *areal units,* usually of a politico-geographic nature (counties, rural municipalities, villages, towns, cities) from which random selections are made; (3) the units so selected, in turn, are divided into smaller *area-segments* (rural areas delineated by rail lines, roads, rivers and power lines; town and city blocks) from which further random selections are made; (4) the area segments so selected in turn, contain *occupied dwelling units* (each consisting of one household) from which a number are selected by prescribed (randomized) method; (5) the occupied dwelling units so selected, in turn, contain one or more *adults* (or eligible voters) from which a sample of one or more is drawn according to rule.

In early stages, much of the process is undertaken in survey offices, using maps, aerial photographs, tables of random numbers and other equipment. The last two steps, however, are performed by interviewers in accordance with strict rules designed to prevent subjective bias in selection. Interviewers thus have no discretion whatever in regard to the area wherein they work. They begin at some predetermined point in, say, a designated city block and must move in a specified direction using a randomized, prescribed method of selecting a fixed number of respondents. The Gallup and other major polling methods are very rigorous in these matters: interviewers, for instance, are not permitted to begin interviews in corner houses on a block; but, being confined to private households, they do not contact individuals in prisons, hospitals, hotels, religious institutions and military establishments. Using these methods, the American Gallup organization now samples almost the entire U.S. adult population, for ordinary purposes, with a small sample of 1,500 respondents drawn from 350 separate cluster areas.

Canadian Gallup practice, undertaken by the Canadian Institute of Public Opinion (CIPO), a separate entity, uses broadly similar procedures. Miss Clare Hatton, its current director, has referred in a recent interview to her method as "modified-probability" sampling. Traditionally, Canadian practice has involved some mixture of area-probability and random-quota methods, with the latter being confined to rural sectors. For many years, the standard size of the Canadian sample was about 700 in-home respondents, but in late years has been increased to approximately 1,000. For final pre-election surveys, this number is doubled. Interviewers are mature women, not men. Interview costs in 1972 ranged between $4-10, but have since increased.

No detailed specifications of CIPO's procedures are available in the technical literature. As we have indicated earlier, all polling organizations adjust their sample results by weighting and other procedures designed to achieve what they consider to be accurate result projections — "to correct known and measurable bias," for instance, the tendency of Canadian respondents to report preference for the Liberal Party to a degree unwarranted by their accustomed voting behaviour. This process is sometimes called "balancing the sample." Its real implication for CIPO forecasts is obscure.

Opinion surveys may, of course, involve different methods of sample selection than those described above. Mass opinions can be studied by single- or multi-wave mailed questionnaires, using a random selection of names from postal or electoral lists. A recently popular polling method, undoubtedly due to cost-effective reasons and the ease of securing sample dispersion, has been the telephone poll. In Canada, this procedure has been widely adopted by Quebec polling organizations, such as CROP, among others. The major American polling groups have experimented with these devices but few who engage in public polling ventures have actually adopted them. There has also been some combination of telephone and in-home surveys. Telephone polls are relatively quick and cheap to undertake; it has been estimated that the average telephone survey can be completed in a twenty-four hour period at a cost somewhere between 50-60 per cent less than that of a personal interview survey.

Nonetheless, these polls have major defects. Interview exhibits, such as simulated ballots, cannot be used. Determination of respondent age, occupation and ethnicity may often prove to be difficult. The proportion of the population not now having telephones is low (10%) but there are regional differences in this respect as there are in relation to particular subgroups in the population. A number of American studies have shown a substantial bias in telephone surveys toward higher-income strata, toward the non-Southern regions, and toward Republican Party supporters.

No comparable study results are available publicly in Canada, but pollers in Quebec have provided some scanty information, mostly impressionistic, to legislative committees and the press. Mr. Claude Gousse has claimed, for example, that ten minutes is the average maximum time during which effective telephone responses can be obtained, and that there are particular difficulties with multiple-choice questions. He also found that, if men instead of women do the interviewing, the rate of "no" answers may increase by 5 per cent. In all Quebec telephone polls, non-contact and refusal rates have been very high. A CROP poll reporting ten days before the Quebec Referendum, for instance, obtained only 856 respondents out of 1,500 chosen by random telephone selection.

Polling and Election Forecasting

We wish now to examine the *public* record of poll forecasting activity in greater detail, to develop some measures of poll performance, to assess the probable impact of polling on voting behaviour, and also to study the reactions of academic practitioners, media users and political leaders.

Gallup-type polls have "gone wrong" in forecasting election results, particularly in 1936 and 1948 in the United States, and during 1951, 1970, and 1974 in Britain. Gallup forecasts in Canada have failed in 1957 and 1980. At sub-national levels, particularly in the U.S. and in British by-elections, poll forecasts have been more erratic than at the national levels. The Canadian record at provincial levels, for certain pollers, has not been outstanding.

It seems apparent that poll election forecasting will tend to be most accurate, within its accepted error limits, only (1) when general and major sectional opinion dispositions are quiescent in nature; (2) when long-term party identification patterns are not in process of significant adjustment as in the U.S. during 1936; (3) when salient issues do not surface naturally during election campaigns, and are not introduced late in the contests by party leaders as in Britain during 1970; (4) when there are no long periods of single-party dominance, as in Canada during the postwar era, where significant vote margins separate the main contending parties. (It may be indicated that during the postwar period, Canada has had only four out of thirteen elections that were closely contested, as compared with three out of nine in the U.S., and seven out of eleven in Britain. The criterion of "close contest" here used is roughly any election result in which the two principal party contenders are separated by less than 4 percentage points.)

For this reason, the incidence of polling forecast failure in recent years has been more pronounced in Britain than in Canada or the United States. Indeed, the American Gallup-type organizations have probably established a world record in polling accuracy, as a result of their recent success in predicting the outcome of three very close presidential races in 1960, 1968 and 1976. In Britain, on the other hand, it has been clear throughout postwar elections that poll forecasts have been unambiguous only during the few reported landslide victories in 1945, 1959, 1966 and 1979. In Canada, as we have indicated, polling forecasts have traditionally been made, with few exceptions, in a much more favourable dominant-party setting.

Whether the sample selection method for pre-election forecasting involves in-home or telephone interviews, there are two central problems that require the exercise of fine poller judgement and that are, in consequence, the source of great uncertainty. First, a final estimation of the proportion and characteristics of eligible voters who in fact choose not to exercise the franchise may be wide of the mark. In the 1980 federal election, for instance, only 69 per cent of Canada's eligible voters cast their ballots, a rate well below the 75 per cent average voting turnout in all thirteen elections since 1945. There is as well a substantial regional variation in this overall rate of voter participation: in 1980, for instance, preliminary data suggest the following patterns: Ontario (non-Toronto), 71.8%; Toronto, 73.0%; Quebec (non-Montreal), 69.7%; Montreal Island, 65.7%; British Columbia, 71.2%; P.E.I., 80.4%; Saskatchewan, 71.6%; Alberta, 60.8%; Newfoundland, 59.3%.

Some studies have shown that variations in participation rates are also sensitive to variables like social status and political party preference as well as to regional forces influencing mass voter behaviour. Differences in turnout rates among these strata can thus affect the delicate balance in final-poll vote share allocations that are entirely separable from election influences themselves. Some pollers have ignored this problem almost entirely and either put their trust in self-erasing errors or assume that the incidence of non-voting will distribute itself among all strata in a uniform fashion.

In almost any pre-election poll, it can be anticipated that the "Undecided/No-opinion" proportion of respondents will normally range between 10-15 per cent. Most pollers consider this a matter of high importance, particularly in trend studies of party preference where, in the words of Roll and Cantril, the undecideds are often regarded as "a bellwether to changing loyalties, since people tend to go through an undecided phase in the process of shifting from one party to another" (p. 131).

In the matter of reducing the proportion of undecided voters in pre-election samples, a number of procedures have been developed over the years. First, questions must be formulated in specific terms: e.g., the standard CIPO question: "If a federal election were to be held today, which party's candidate do you think you would favor?" Second, if in response a firm answer is not secured, a question is then asked to elicit the respondent's partisan "leanings." Third, a "secret ballot" in lieu of a verbal response is used to record expressed voter preference. Respondents are given a paper with the names of the major parties and leaders upon which they mark their preference and fold the paper before placing it in the "ballot box." American studies have shown that the "leaning" probe tends to reduce the number of undecided responses by one-half. The secret ballot device reduces it even further. (This device, of course, cannot be used in telephone surveys.)

Under volatile electoral conditions or in very close contests, these procedures will still leave a substantial number of undecided voters concerning whom the poller must exercise his experienced judgment. Are "leaning" respondents to be counted with the same weight as those whose intentions have been clearly established? What portion of the undecided group will actually vote? It has often been assumed that most of its members will not vote, but some retrospective poll studies in Britain have reported that as many as two-thirds of them do in fact vote.

The most common practice in the end is to distribute the undecideds, the most uncertain sample group of all, in a manner that assumes that they will indeed vote exactly as the remaining sample group. It is obvious that a substantial risk is attached to the use of such procedure and, should a poller be unlucky, his final projection could be seriously in error. The chance of being unlucky, however, depends upon the prevailing degree of electoral volatility and the closeness of the election. In 1980 during the federal election and the Quebec referendum, some Canadian polling organizations reported final proportions of undecided voters that achieved record levels above 20 and even, in one case, above 40 per cent of all respondents. This pattern is examined more fully below.

There is a principal difficulty encountered when interpreting polling forecasts in a parliamentary system. Polls project only a proportional distribution of the popular vote by party, not a party distribution of elected legislators. The CIPO, for instance, has never attempted to forecast parliamentary seat distributions; thus its polling projections have lacked an essential, concrete predictive result ingredient. Attempts to achieve this end in Britain have proved to be almost completely unreliable.

Canadian Poll Forecast Performance, 1945-1980

With these general considerations in mind, we turn next to the forecast record of the Canadian Gallup organization in thirteen federal elections since 1945. There are three elements of forecast error with which we are here concerned: first, the standard sample variance deviations in *percentage points* accepted by the CIPO and based upon its confidence limit of 95 per cent, as applied to each of the four party-categories of forecast; second, the actual *percentage* error deviations for each of the four party vote-categories. This is the purest measure of poll forecast error — some will say, indeed, some have said already, an unrealistically pure measure. It indicates the sum of all positive and negative percentage polling deviations, *measured from a 100 per cent base of the actual vote proportions* in each of the four vote-categories. (For instance, if it is forecast that a party will receive 10 per cent of the vote and in fact it receives only 5 per cent, the sample point-variance is -5, but the percentage-variance is -50 per cent.) Finally, for each election we measure as well the CIPO forecast error in terms of actual votes and compare it with the winning party plurality and with the electoral participation or voter turnout rate. The Institute's performance in thirteen elections is summarized in Table 2.

In the 52 all-party instances of separate vote forecast during 13 elections, the CIPO has succeeded 17 out of 52 times in achieving a point error below 1.0 per cent. On the whole, this 1:3 ratio is quite favourable for its record. But the CIPO also badly overestimated the electoral strength of the Liberals in 1957, 1965 and 1980. To a lesser extent, and only on one occasion, has it underestimated Liberal vote totals, namely in 1979. The CIPO record of forecasting P.C. voting fortunes is somewhat more variable. In only three elections has it overestimated that party's vote: in 1949, 1958 and 1979; it did, however, substantially underestimate it in three elections: 1957, 1965 and 1980. For the CCF-NDP, the CIPO record is more stable, except that in 1972 and again in 1980 relatively severe percentage overestimates are recorded. Finally, the forecast deviations for "others" tend on the average to be quite low, with one notable overestimate in 1962 and another on the

Table 2 Calculated Errors of C.I.P.O. Pre-Election Final Forecasts, 1945-1980*

YEAR	LIBERAL	PROGRESSIVE CONSERVATIVE	CCF-NDP	OTHERS
1945	−4.6 (−1.9)	+5.8 (−1.6)	+9.0 (+1.4)	−6.8 (−1.1)
1949	−3.0 (−1.5)	+4.4 (+1.3)	+11.9 (+1.6)	−18.9 (−1.4)
1953	+2.5 (+1.2)	0 (0)	−2.7 (−0.3)	−10.1 (−0.9)
1957	+17.4 (+7.1)	−12.6 (−4.9)	−6.5 (−0.7)	−15.8 (−1.5)
1958	−1.8 (−0.6)	+4.5 (+2.4)	−15.8 (−1.5)	−9.1 (−0.3)
1962	+2.2 (+0.8)	−3.5 (−1.3)	−11.1 (−1.5)	+27.3 (+3.0)
1963	−1.7 (−0.7)	−2.4 (−0.8)	+6.9 (+0.9)	+4.8 (+0.6)
1965	+9.4 (+3.8)	−10.5 (−3.4)	−0.6 (−0.1)	−5.3 (−0.5)
1968	+3.3 (+1.5)	−7.6 (−2.4)	+5.9 (+1.0)	−1.6 (−0.1)
1972	+1.3 (+0.5)	−5.7 (−2.0)	+18.6 (+3.3)	−20.5 (−1.8)
1974	−0.5 (−0.2)	−1.1 (−0.4)	+10.4 (+1.6)	−16.7 (−1.0)
1979	−5.2 (−2.1)	+5.8 (+2.1)	+6.1 (+1.1)	−18.0 (−1.1)
1980	+8.4 (+3.7)	−13.8 (−4.5)	+16.2 (+3.2)	−70.6 (−3.3)

* Percentage error is the unbracketed column; percentage point error is bracketed.
SOURCES: Reports of the Chief Electoral Officer (1972-1980); J.M. Beck, *Pendulum of Power: Canada's Federal Elections*, (1945-1968); CIPO final pre-election forecasts (1945-1980). 1980 official results are based on preliminary C.E.O. aggregates.

low side in 1980. All of these "third party" and "others" errors involve relatively small voting populations.

To the extent that a party's support strength is even marginally diminished by an underestimated poll vote forecast (bandwagon effect), CIPO has been rather more favourable to Liberals than Conservatives. There is, unfortunately, no easy way to estimate such an effect. Taken in the main, however, the CIPO has over the years achieved an average point error within its accepted sample variance tolerance of ± 4 points, except in 1957 and 1980. These exceptions are significant. By its own formula, Gallup results are supposed to fall within the accepted limits of error 19 times in 20.

Table 3 provides data on all estimates of CIPO forecast error, together with the total votes cast in elections and the rates of voter turnout.

An examination of these cumulative error deviation patterns facilitates an understanding of CIPO forecast errors in rather more concrete terms than is ordinarily apparent when the discussion is confined, as it usually is, to sample variance point errors. The latter, clearly, are highest in 1957 and 1980. A look at the total *percentage* vote deviation column reveals as well a substantial cumulative error in 1949, 1957, 1958, 1962, 1972, 1979, and 1980, all of them exceeding ± 30 per cent. In the last three cases, however, the relatively high numbers are attributable mainly to errors associated with the CCF-NDP and other categories.

The vagaries of the electoral system explain the somewhat erratic behaviour between the error deviations expressed in votes and the winning party pluralities. In two instances, 1957 and 1979, P.C. governments were elected with a fewer number of votes than the Liberals; in 1958 Mr. Diefenbaker's government achieved an absolute majority (53.6 per cent) of all votes cast, the only occasion during all the elections. During this period Liberal governments have all been elected with pluralities, Mr. St. Laurent's government in 1949 coming closest to achieving majority support with 49.5 per cent of all votes cast.

Table 3: Measures of CIPO Cumulative Forecast Error

	TOTAL VOTE (thousands)	TURN- OUT %	TOTAL PERCENTAGE ERROR ±%	CIPO POINT ERROR ±%	ERROR IN VOTES (thousands)	WINNING PARTY PLURALITY (thousands)
1945	5,246.1	75	26.2	6.0	314.8	710.6
1949	5,849.0	74	38.2	5.8	339.2	1,161.4
1953	5,641.3	68	15.3	2.4	135.4	1,001.7
1957	6.606.0	74	52.3	14.2	938.1	−129.6*
1958	7,287.3	79	31.2	4.8	349.8	1,460.7*
1962	7,690.1	80	44.1	6.6	507.5	3.7
1963	7,894.1	80	15.8	3.0	236.8	702.2
1965	7,713.3	75	25.8	7.8	601.0	599.6
1968	8,125.8	76	18.4	5.0	406.3	1,142.1
1972	9,667.5	77	46.1	7.6	734.7	334.7
1974	9,515.9	71	28.7	3.2	304.5	733.4
1979	11,455.7	76	35.1	6.4	733.2	−482.8*
1980	10,946.5	69	109.0	14.7	1,609.1	1,301.4

* In 1957 and 1979 Progressive Conservative wins were achieved with fewer votes than the Liberals; in 1958, Mr. Diefenbaker received a majority (53.6%) of the total vote.
SOURCE: Table 2 and reports of the Chief Electoral Officer.

The CIPO record in 1962 is of some interest. In that election, Mr. Diefenbaker was returned to office with a minority status in parliament. The cumulative point error in that year was a moderate ± 6.6, but the percentage error reached its fourth-highest level in all thirteen elections. The vote error exceeded half a million and the government's vote plurality stood at just under four thousand, the Liberals achieving 37.2 and the Progressive Conservative 37.3 per cent respectively. This represents high forecast accuracy in a very close contest.

It has sometimes been suggested, most recently in 1980, that polling forecast error is closely related to voter turnout. This generalization does not hold strongly in Canadian federal elections over the postwar years. In five elections there was a clustering about the line of proportionality between the incidence of non-voting and CIPO cumulative point error. But in another five cases there was absolutely no correlation. The most anomalous elections in this last respect are those of 1953, 1957, 1962, 1972, and 1974. The coefficient of correlation for this relationship in all elections is calculated at +0.23, a negligibly positive result which reflects its box-like dispersion pattern on a scatter-diagram.

There are several other polling organizations, in addition to CIPO, that have begun to engage widely in federal election forecasting during the 1970s. They include the Carleton University School of Journalism group under Professor Frizzell, and the polling activity of Professor Regenstreif, most of whom supply polls or analyses to the media. For technical and other reasons, the accuracy of polling forecasts by these groups or individuals cannot be fully examined. But in 1979, and to a much greater extent in 1980, polls themselves became salient issues in the campaigns. Table 4 shows the percentage point errors in the final vote forecasts commissioned by the CBC and CTV networks compared with the CIPO errors during the two most recent federal elections.

Table 4: Selected 1979 and 1980 Election Poll Forecasts:
Percentage Point Errors

	Liberal 1979	Liberal 1980	P.C. 1979	P.C. 1980	N.D.P. 1979	N.D.P. 1980	Other 1979	Other 1980
CIPO	−2	+4	+2	−5	+1	+3	−1	−3
CBC	0	+3	+5	−3	−3	−1	−2	+1
CTV	−1	−1	+5	0	−1	+2	−3	−1
Actual Vote %	40	44	36	33	18	20	6	3

SOURCE: Various issues, *The Globe and Mail.*

These data suggest that in both elections there were serious poll errors. In 1979 the CBC and CTV polls badly overestimated P.C. electoral strength (+5%), while in 1980 the final CIPO estimate erred in the opposite direction (−5%). The most accurate of the three polls in 1980 was that commissioned by the CTV network which forecast the exact vote proportion achieved by the Progressive Conservatives and missed the true Liberal proportion by only −1 point. It is noteworthy that among these three final polls in 1980 there were obvious differences in the proportions of "Undecided/Won't Answer" respondents. While CIPO reported only 11 per cent of its sample in this category, the CBC and CTV polls had the extraordinarily high ratios of 24 and 40 per cent respectively. As we have suggested earlier, this matter is a source of increasing difficulty for pollers in an age of growing alienation, distrust and electoral volatility.

Polling in Quebec has grown rapidly in the last decade. Several public opinion institutes (CROP, IQOP, etc.), together with a number of polling companies and academics have been engaged visibly in the media, government and election surveying activity. Throughout the last decade, and notwithstanding the public salience of their activities, Quebec's pollers have not achieved anything like the forecast accuracy attained by the opinion surveys summarized above. In successive Quebec elections, and in the Quebec Referendum of 1980, Quebec poll forecasts have produced point errors well beyond accepted tolerance limits. Relying mainly on telephone surveys, CROP in 1970 experienced a wide point error in its election forecasts: Liberals (−7), P.Q. (+1), U.N. (−5). But these error margins were reduced in the 1973 Quebec election: Liberals (−4), P.Q. (0), U.N. (+1). During the 1976 election, poll forecast variances continued to be substantial. Two of the principal poll results are summarized in Table 5.

Table 5: Two 1976 Quebec Election Poll Forecasts: Percentages

Poll	Liberal		P.Q.		U.N.		Other	
Le Devoir	27	(−7)	50	(+9)	14	(−4)	9	(+2)
Pinard-Hamilton	27	(−7)	50	(+9)	13	(−5)	10	(+3)
Actual %	34		41		18		7	

% Unbracketed is percentage forecast; bracketed is percentage point error.
SOURCE: Various Quebec newspapers.

The bias in these two polls went heavily against the Liberals (−7), and against the U.N. (−4, −5), and even more strongly toward the *Péquistes* (+9), who directly assumed office under Mr. Lévesque. On all but two of these eight forecasts, allowable sample variances of 3 per cent were exceeded, and in the case of the two P.Q. forecasts, the point errors stood at three times the allowable tolerances.

It is somewhat more difficult to appraise poll performance in relation to the Quebec Referendum. Four of the latest polls to report projected the results indicated in Table 6.

Table 6: May 20, 1980 Quebec Referendum: Late Poll Forecasts in Percentages

Date of Report	Poll	Yes	No	Undecided/ Don't Know/ Won't Say
April 28	CIPO	38	36	26
May 11	IQOP	38	42	21
May 16	Pinard-Hamilton	37	49	14
May 19	CROP	40	37	23
Final Results		40	60	

SOURCE: Various press accounts.

It is clear that all of these polls came close to forecasting the final Yes result, but only the Pinard-Hamilton poll was able to detect the final, almost complete, shift of the undecided or won't-answer respondents to the victorious No camp. After distributing the undecided, the Pinard-Hamilton poll forecast a 43-57 result.

In earlier editions of this article, we have examined the polling record of Professor Regenstreif during the 1960s and early 1970s. It has been far from outstanding. There is no necessity to repeat that evaluation here. One of Canada's earliest "pollsters," best remembered for having forecast the rise of Social Credit in the federal election of 1962, he has in recent times continued "judgmental samplings" in federal and provincial elections, but since 1972 has relied more heavily on publicly interpreting the results of polls conducted by other pollers for the media. Indeed, in a strict sense, he was never a poller at all. But Professor Regenstrief's more recent predictive efforts include two that are worthy of the record. First, in September 1975, two days before the Ontario election, he allowed in *The Toronto Star* that the Liberals would win the election, and that (in terms of seats) the Conservatives and New Democrats would follow, in that order. In the event, the Conservatives won and the Liberals came third in seats, but second in votes. Finally, approximately one month before the Quebec Referendum in 1980, he announced that the Yes forces would likely win the referendum by a narrow margin.

Taken at large, then, the record of public poll performance in Canadian election forecasting is extremely mixed. From the standpoint of its long-term record, the CIPO Gallup affiliate compares favourably with its sister Gallup group in the United States and has a far superior record to the group in Britain. We have examined average poll performance in the three countries (Canada, thirteen elections; U.S. and Britain, eleven elections), which indicates the approximate comparative position. In elections from 1945 to 1980 in Canada, the actual vote percentage point-spread between Liberals and Progressive Conservatives has averaged 10.1. The difference between this actual spread and CIPO forecast point-spread in final election surveys has averaged 3.9, or only 38.6 per cent of the actual spread. In American presidential elections from 1936 to 1976, the equivalent Gallup ratio is 39.8 per cent. But in Britain, for reasons suggested earlier, the Gallup ratio rises dramatically to 62.5 per cent. (The size of these comparative measures, it will be seen, varies inversely with average Gallup forecast performance.) This result mirrors the fact that total vote differences between the two contending parties in Britain have always been relatively small, and that, correspondingly, the Gallup poll failure has been more frequent.

The Consequence of Polling and its Future

Many hate, as well as distrust, the polls. To begin, there is the "brake on progress" thesis. Social critics and activists who constitute the real counter-elite in public affairs often condemn the polls as tending to institutionalize a conservative, anti-innovative mass impulse at the very heart of public affairs. Non-competitive and losing politicians hate the polls. Many do not believe the polls but live or die by them.

Pollers and their partisans, however, have always stressed the essential intermediating function of mass-opinion research as an embodiment of the democratic ideal of popular participation in affairs. Thus Miss Hatton has said: "We at Gallup feel that modern polling on vital issues of the day, both political and social, is the only way of insuring that the people of Canada are able to express their views."

Many commentators and not a few politicians have suggested that so far from having only a disinterested concern with the measurement of opinion and intention, polling activity itself exercises a powerful influence on the opinions and intentions that it claims to measure. During election campaigns, for instance, it is often held that the publication of poll results tends to interfere with what ought to be the autonomous decision function of the electorate. Beyond these arguments there is the problem created for party leaders during the final stages — even in 1980, in Mr. Clark's case, at the opening of the campaign — with unfavourable poll findings.

Three main and one subsidiary "poll effect" hypotheses have been suggested. First, a supposed "bandwagon" effect, in which voters are stimulated to change their intentions in order to be on the winning side. Second, it is sometimes held that polls trigger an "underdog effect" and that (temporarily) weak leaders and candidates are the real beneficiaries. Third, because of alienation and distrust, or because a foregone electoral conclusion is projected, it is sometimes argued that publicity surrounding poll forecasts promotes a "withdrawal effect" that tends to lower participation rates in voting. Finally, consistently weak parties are said to be placed at competitive disadvantage because of a "compartment effect," due to poll results indicating long-term electoral weakness. (This last assertion seems rather insubstantial, since actual election results convey the same message.)

As one might expect, the evidence on these issues provided in the literature of electoral behaviour is inconclusive. Pollers, of course, have done their best to refute each hypothesis. Given the lack of conclusive empirical generalization on the matter, there are good grounds for caution. It seems clear, nonetheless, that the psychology of voting is infinitely complex, certainly that its determinants include many forces other than those alleged above. Next, there is what may be termed the fallacy of saliency. There is a large inattentive public; increasingly people *dislike* to read and write; in our large metropolitan centres an increasing proportion of voters do not well *understand* either English or French.

There is some evidence that as many as three-quarters of all voters in any (non-critical) election already have their minds made up when the first polls are reported and that these dispositions are not significantly altered during the campaign. But last-minute marginal shifts in vote intentions, as in Britain during 1970, have indeed occurred. Through the entire postwar era something rather more than one-fifth of all Canadian voters have supported "third parties" in spite of their persistently low poll ratings. There is, therefore, good reason to believe that poll reports, even supposing they "filter down" through the media in effective fashion, have a minimal impact on the voter's decisional calculus — if any such broad-gauged rational phenomenon really exists.

While there is no strong reason to believe that polls produce the systematic effects alleged, neither can it be established that in any *close* election they have *not* marginally influenced the outcomes. Hence, Mr. Eddie Goodman's retrospective comment on the 1965 election: "The bad poll rating the Conservatives got was wrong — but those polls cost us seven or eight seats. The whole course of Canadian history might have been changed if we had won these seats."

In 1972 prohibition on the publication of poll results during election periods was introduced in France in elections for the National Assembly. Some years ago, a similar ban was introduced in provincial elections in British Columbia. The Barbeau Commission on Election Expenses in 1966 recommended such a measure for Canadian federal elections. More recently, there have been investigations and preliminary discussions on the issue in the Quebec, Ontario, and Nova Scotia legislatures. In recent memory, a number of federal MPs have introduced private member's bills requiring poll proscriptions: e.g., Peters, N.D.P. (1967); Reynolds, P.C. (1976); Coates, P.C. (1970, 1976); Herbert, Lib. (1978); Whiteway, P.C. (1978).

Press and other media reactions to these proposals have been negative, as increasing numbers of columnists and editorialists deal with controversial matters projected in survey findings. General attitudes toward the polling-ban issue are also negative. Two recent Gallup Reports, the first in 1977 and a second in 1980, indicated slightly more than one-third in favour of prohibition with 57 and 53 per cent opposed and 11-13 per cent undecided. An earlier Gallup finding was that a good majority of Canadians felt that government ought to be more responsive to public opinion, in case of any doubt on the point. Citizens in most democracies, broadly speaking, are manifestly tolerant of polling and quite permissive regarding the use and alleged misuse of poll materials by the mass media.

In this paper we make no plea for a prohibition of polls — only a plea for greater information and greater understanding of their nature. A healthy popular scepticism toward polling is also required.

HARD SELL ON THE HILL IS A $100 MILLION BUSINESS*

David Blaikie

OTTAWA —
There's a shadow army, hundreds strong, of slick, persuasive executives who spend an estimated $100 million a year wooing cabinet ministers, senators, legislators and government staff.

They're on the payrolls of private corporations and public interest groups, and their purpose is to use their connections and persuasive powers to move Canada's political policies in directions favorable to their bosses.

They are lobbyists, but they prefer to be called government liaison experts, advisers, or public relations officials — just as they prefer to wield their power quietly and unobtrusively.

Their Headquarters

One of their main headquarters is three blocks south of Parliament Hill, at 130 Albert St., 19 nondescript storeys rising into the national capital skyline.

A sign above the main entrance identifies it as the Varette Building, but in some circles it's referred to as the lobbyists' building.

Through its two revolving doors passes a steady stream of executives — well-dressed, well-paid and little-known.

The building's directory lists a varied collection of national organizations and groups anxious to be close to the federal government: The Canadian Petroleum Association; the Canadian Trucking Association; the Canadian Bar Association; the Canadian Association of Equipment Distributors; the Canadian Frozen Food Association and the Alliance of Canadian Travel Associations.

Similar organizations are next door, in the Royal Trust Building, and in dozens of other office towers around Ottawa.

This is a growth industry in the capital.

Special interest groups multiply unchecked, and almost unnoticed, despite the cutbacks, restraint and belt-tightening within the government itself.

Representing business, consumer, agriculture, health or sports groups, they are here only because government is here, because it is better to ask for something in person than by telephone or mail.

The estimate that they do a $100 million plus business is only a guess, of course — no one knows how big lobbying is and there is no way yet to find out.

But all agree it's big and getting bigger.

* From *The Toronto Star*, January 20, 1979. By permission.

Should Register

Walter Baker, Progressive Conservative House Leader in Parliament, thinks something should be done to keep track of lobbyists.

For the past several sessions, he has introduced a private bill calling for a parliamentary registry for lobbyists. The measure has little hope of passing with the Tories in opposition but would be given "some priority" if the Conservatives win this year's election, Baker told The Star.

The Grenville-Carleton MP is not opposed to lobbying — in fact he thinks it's essential to effective government — but "it's time we knew who the players are," he argues.

Legislation governing the activities of lobbyists is non-existent. Many are as anonymous as those coming and going each day on Albert St.

Baker's bill require[s] all of them, even those on the fringes of the business, to identify themselves publicly. It would apply to any person seeking to influence any parliamentary matter.

"That's a wide net," Baker concedes, "but it would be healthy."

A fine of $5,000 could be levied for each month a lobbyist failed to identify himself and make his activities known to the registry office.

"We've become a society of groups. Collectively these organizations are strong and influential," Baker says.

The increase in groups and organizations establishing headquarters in Ottawa over the last decade has been spectacular. The city telephone book used to list them all in a few columns. Now it takes four pages of fine print, more than 500 names.

And there are so many national associations that they've formed an association of their own: the Canadian Association of Executives.

A major reason is the growth of government itself. Ten years ago the federal budget was $10 billion. Now it is nearly $50 billion. Lobbying has grown at a comparable rate.

"As the issues which governments deal with become more complex and more pervasive, so too must the reaction (by affected groups) become more comprehensive," says Tom Burns of the Canadian Exporters Association.

Burns took over the 500-member organization, a major lobbying force in Ottawa, after years of senior service within the government. He was an assistant deputy minister at trade and commerce when he left a year ago.

Can Contribute

"All special interest groups can contribute to the understanding by government of these complexities — be they in the business field, the consumer field, health, sports or whatever," he argues.

These men (only a handful yet are women) command high salaries, often well in excess of $50,000, and their employers believe they are worth every penny.

David Mundy, like Burns, is a former assistant deputy minister at trade and commerce. Now he heads the powerful Air Industries Association. Henry de Puyjalon, formerly of the Treasury Board, represents the Canadian Construction Association, another powerful lobby. Ernie Steele, also an ex-Treasury Board official, heads the Canadian Association of Broadcasters.

Steele previously headed the Canadian Grocery Manufacturers Association and his slot there was filled by David Morely, another ex-bureaucrat.

A less visible but more significant layer of modern-day lobbyists includes influential lawyers, accountants, consultants and free-lancers.

Some, like Bill Lee, who ran Prime Minister Pierre Trudeau's heady first election campaign in 1968, have formed their own companies and work on retainer for corporate clients.

These companies' services range from simple advice on how to deal with government to "door-opening" chores that get corporate executives into the offices of cabinet ministers or senior bureaucrats.

Lee's company, Executive Consultants Ltd., is one of several now flourishing in Ottawa. (His partner for a time was Bill Neville, who now is principal assistant to Opposition Leader Joe Clark.)

One of the newest and best-known consulting firms is headed by a couple of ex-deputy ministers, Simon Reisman (finance) and Jim Grandy (trade and commerce.)

Caused Flap

Their activities caused a flap in Parliament when it was learned they acted for Lockheed Aircraft Corp. in its successful bid to supply Canada's billion-dollar new long-range patrol aircraft.

The outcry prompted the government to announce guidelines designed to restrict the activities of such senior bureaucrats for a period of two years after they leave the public service.

House Leader Baker says guidelines are not good enough. The Tories would pass legislation enforcing such conflict-of-interest rules, he told The Star.

Men like Reisman and Grandy are highly visible, but this is not the case with accountants and lawyers who do battle with the government on behalf of clients.

Much of their activity goes on unnoticed in places such as the justice department, where all federal legislation is drafted. Small changes won here can save headaches (and dollars) for clients.

The same applies to the regulations that follow passage of legislation. A favored target here is the finance department.

Gowling and Henderson, the city's biggest law firm, and Herridge Tolmie are among the most influential legal firms in Ottawa lobbying circles.

One of the most lobbied government departments is trade and commerce, with its vast jurisdiction over business matters and its potential for conferring grants, subsidies and aid of other sorts via a maze of federal programs.

Peter Thomson, executive assistant to Trade Minister Jack Horner, says he gets up to 100 calls a day asking for favors of one sort or another. Many callers want a meeting with the minister.

"When they can't see him personally, they often settle for me, and I carry their representations to the minister," Thomson says.

Like most holding influential government jobs, Thomson values his contact with lobbyists and special interest groups.

"It's an important information source, greatly appreciated in many cases," he said.

"The demands on a minister's time are impossible to appreciate. We welcome people who come in here, sum up their case quickly and succinctly — and know when to leave."

Herb Gray, MP for Windsor West and a former consumer and corporate affairs minister, agrees that bureaucrats and legislaters need and benefit from the expertise of special interest groups and lobbyists. But he supports Baker in calling for a registry.

Gray also worries about the imbalance between power and merit among the groups.

"Some have more resources than others, particularly the business community. They get their views across with greater ease. That's a fact. There's nothing wrong with this but it does mean that governments should be careful in the weight they attach to these views."

In Gray's mind, the most powerful lobbies in Ottawa are the business community, agriculture, labor and consumer groups. The most powerful individual groups are the Chamber of Commerce, the Canadian Manufacturers' Association, the Canadian Federation of Agriculture, the Consumers Association of Canada and the Canadian Labor Congress, he says.

Labor's Clout

A spokesman for Finance Minister Jean Chretien tends to agree, citing many of the same groups. But he says the CLC's clout is damaged by its unwillingness at times to meet with government, and its ideological association with the New Democratic Party.

York Centre MP Bob Kaplan sees a regular stream of special interest representatives in his capacity as head of the Commons finance, trade and economic affairs committee.

Most seek information on how the committee operates and want to know when and where they can argue their case, says Kaplan.

Like most who deal with lobbyists, he says the question of impropriety or unethical conduct does not arise.

"I've never been offered a bribe or benefit or anything of that sort. It never happens."

Baker said he has never heard, let alone experienced, anything he would consider improper conduct by lobbyists. The possible exception is the practice by some foreign embassies of offering free tours of their countries to MPs and senators.

"This in my view is wrong. It is an attempt to influence an individual with the hope that it will somehow favorably affect policy somewhere down the line," Baker argues.

As for the kind of lobbying practised by Canadian interest groups today, Baker feels we're going to see more of it.

"It's as important for an organization to properly present itself to government as it is for a client in the courtroom to present himself before the judge. He does that, of course, through the auspices of his mouth-piece.''

Bureaucrats Targetted

Modern lobbying goes far beyond efforts to influence votes. Some consider a cause lost, or in serious trouble, if it is not won in the public service before it reaches Parliament.

Studies indicate that, except for cabinet ministers, MPs and senators rank well down the list of favored ''targets.'' Senior bureaucrats with influence over policy, those capable of swaying events by simply writing a memo, are among the most closely watched.

Lobbyists come in a wide variety of forms.

The easiest to identify are men like Tom Burns, of the Canadian Exporters Association, who hold senior executive positions on national associations — the Canadian Association.

And, again like Burns, a former assistant deputy minister, they increasingly come from the senior ranks in the public service.

They are well-connected and move easily through the corridors of power. They frequent the best restaurants, socialize at the best clubs. They move unobtrusively and win battles without causing a ripple.

A telephone call here, a drink there, lunch with an old friend or perhaps a squash game is often all it takes to solve a problem or, equally important, head off trouble.

A lobbyist's day might begin as it does for many in Ottawa, with a cup of coffee and a morning paper. Information, from many sources, is the blood of life.

There is mail to check and, always, the telephone. A lobbyist is apt to spend more time on the telephone than anywhere else.

Some national associations have huge memberships. The Canadian Construction Association, for example, has 15,000 and headquarters demands can be endless. A member may want a government contract checked or ask to have its name added to some government list. A company president may want a meeting with a particular bureaucrat or cabinet minister.

Noon hour often means lunch with a client or some useful contact at a good downtown restaurant. The Chateau Laurier and Four Seasons hotels are favored meeting places.

Back at the office, the afternoon may be taken up with reports, letters or internal meetings. And often there's a dinner meeting before heading home.

High calorie intake is a professional hazard.

Kill Bill

Does lobbying work?

The answer, often, is ''yes.'' Just as the old adage suggests, the squeaky wheel is very good at getting the grease.

The most celebrated, and almost certainly the most successful, lobby of this decade has been that of the Canadian business lobby against reformed marketplace competition laws.

The fight dates back to the end of the 1960s and the high-minded early days of the Trudeau administration, when sweeping consumer-oriented changes in competition laws were proposed by the Economic Council of Canada.

That alone, without legislation actually being drafted, was enough to galvanize the country's biggest companies and business groups into full-scale action.

The effort was immense and sustained — behind the scenes cajoling, public speeches, letter-writing, countless meetings and thousands upon thousands of pages of critical briefs. It had an impact.

The first Competition Act wasn't even introduced in Parliament until 1972, and only then as a draft bill open to debate and alteration. Still, it provoked unbridled corporate outrage.

There were plans to crack down on misleading advertising, to control mergers and monopolies, and give citizens hurt by corporate skulduggery the right to embark on class actions for damages. That and more.

So savagely were the proposals attacked that the government backed down and went back to the drawing board. Ron Basford, the consumer and corporate affairs minister responsible, went on to another portfolio.

Herb Gray, who later assumed the portfolio, tried another tactic in 1973 by breaking the legislation into two bills and trying to get the least contentious through.

Many of the thorniest questions such as mergers and monopolies were left for the second bill.

The first bill finally became law on Jan. 1, 1976, long after Gray had left the portfolio. It had merit but it was a far cry from Basford's original plan.

Gone, largely because of lobbying pressure, was the brave new proposal to allow class action suits. In its place was a weak half-measure allowing individuals to sue separately.

Gone also was the concept of a Competition Tribunal to supervise enforcement of the new, far-reaching changes planned at the outset. Instead, the government settled for an expanded version of the Restrictive Trade Practices Commission.

Still, there were pluses. Consumer groups applauded a series of moves in the legislation to crack down on unscrupulous advertising and selling practices.

When the second bill was eventually presented to Parliament it too, was met with an all-out onslaught from business.

The result: More modifications. Merger and monopoly provisions were softened, and business was given the right to appeal to cabinet the decisions by the competition tribunal. Originally, all the tribunal's rulings were to be final.

And then what happened?

The bill died on the House of Commons order paper with the completion of the last session of Parliament in October. It has not been reintroduced.

Who Are Lobbyists?

Which are the major lobbying groups vying for a favoured position in the halls of Parliament? There are so many associations trying to influence government thinking that they've formed an association of associations — the Canadian Association of Executives. Here's a sample:

The Canadian Chamber of Commerce
Canadian Federation of Agriculture
Canadian Manufacturers Association
Canadian Labour Congress
Consumers Association of Canada
Canadian Bar Association
Canadian Medical Society
Canadian Exporters Association
Air Industries Association of Canada
Canadian Association of Chiefs of Police
Canadian Construction Association
Canadian Association of Broadcasters
Canadian Cable Television Association
Tourism Industry Association of Canada
Canadian Food Processors Association
Pharmaceutical Manufacturers Association of Canada
Mining Association of Canada
Canadian Petroleum Association
Canadian Wildlife Federation
Canadian Telecommunications Carriers Association
Grocery Products Manufacturers Association of Canada
Canadian Teachers Federation
Canadian Automobile Association
Canadian Trucking Association
Canadian Textiles Institute

[Editor's note: See also for Senators as lobbyists, J. McMenemy's article, *infra*, Chaper 14.]

PUBLIC INPUT INTO POLICY-MAKING AND ADMINISTRATION *

Ken Bryden

● ● ●

Models of Public Input

Proposals for enhancing public input are logically subsumed into two main models. These in turn are derived from the two basic models of democratic

* From *Canadian Public Administration*, 25, 1, Spring, 1982, published by the Institute of Public Administration of Canada. By permission.

government: representative democracy and direct democracy. The derived public input models will be designated here as the representation model and the direct participation model.

Representation Model

Considering this model in its pure form, its essential characteristic is that public input occurs preeminently through popularly elected representatives. In the cabinet-parliamentary variant that is of most immediate concern to us, accountability and responsiveness are guaranteed by a chain of responsibility from the cabinet to parliament and ultimately to the people at election time. The fact that public servants are not elected does not vitiate the model because they supposedly do not make policy but only administer the policy made by the elected representatives. Moreover, they are brought into the chain of responsibility by the fact that they are subject to ministerial direction and control. This model, if it ever was an adequate description of reality, has become increasingly inadequate with the growing complexity of society and the rise of mass democracy. The public service is in fact involved intimately and continuously in policy-making. Moreover, every link in the chain of responsibility is tenuous. Ministerial control over the public service is no more than partly effective part of the time. The same can be said of ministerial accountability to parliament, especially under majority government, while general elections held only every few years hardly provide more than limited, sporadic accountability of elected governments and members to the public.

. . . Many have been directing their attention during the past generation to reforms designed to enhance accountability and responsiveness. Such reform proposals can be classified into five main categories.

(A) ENHANCING THE ROLE OF PARLIAMENT
Many well-informed analysts place major emphasis on reforms aimed at making the classical model more effective. . . .

There have been active movements for parliamentary reform in the United Kingdom since the 1930s and in Canada since about 1960. These have resulted in substantial changes in parliamentary procedure, in the structure and function of parliamentary committees, and in the resources made available to private members — all with the purpose of bringing the actual performance of parliament more into line with that envisaged in the classical model. The fact that progress has been substantially less than many had hoped is indicated by what appears to be increased concern in recent years for parliamentary reform. At the same time, the very fact that interest in the subject is lively and even growing suggests that enough progress has been made that concerned and informed critics do not see it as a hopeless cause.

(B) DEMOCRATIZING POLITICAL PARTIES
Parties have traditionally been regarded as having a central role in channeling public input into policy-making and administration. A leading political sociologist of a generation ago described them as "major mediators" be-

tween voters and governments in modern democracies and as "the agency by which public opinion is translated into public policy." The argument has been carried even further by democratic socialist and labour parties organized along the lines of Duverger's model of the "mass party." Supporters of these parties argue that the key to democratic government is a political party in which rank-and-file members have ultimate control over party policy and leadership. This kind of party has not been the norm in Canada. Only the now-defunct Progressive and United Farmer parties, the CCF/NDP and the Parti Québécois could be said to conform to the mass model in their structure and functioning. During the 1960s and early 1970s, however, the Liberal and Progressive Conservative parties moved in the direction of more democratic structures.

In the case of those two parties, reports are mixed as to the effect of such changes but it seems reasonable to presume that accountability sessions and leadership reviews have some effect on party policy, and indirectly on government policy, if the party is in power or on the verge of assuming power. In the case of the "mass" or membership-based parties, the presumption is even stronger. . . .

At the same time, such participation does not actually represent significant public input into the policy process. That has been true even in those cases, rare in Canada, where a membership-based party has held provincial office. As a long-time participant/observer in the CCF/NDP, I can assert that only a small fraction of those voting for the party hold membership in it, that only a small fraction of the members participate in party activities on a consistent basis, and that only a fraction of those participants ever stand for election as delegates to conventions (partly because many cannot afford the time and money involved in attending conventions). Representation at conventions and conferences of other parties is probably at least as narrow as for the NDP. Even the mere holding of membership in political parties is limited overall to less than 5 per cent of the eligible Canadian population.

(C) EXPANDING PRESSURE POLITICS

Many writers see interest groups as playing the most significant role in channeling public input into the policy process. Indeed, this is the dominant theme of contemporary American pluralism which, like many things American, has had substantial spillover effects in Canada. . . . The most sophisticated exposition of this pluralist model has been Dahl's concept of "polyarchal democracy" or simply "polyarchy." In that model the vital between-election interaction of groups with each other and with the authorities serves to keep a wide range of interests to the fore and to prevent any particular group from dominating. "Thus the making of governmental decisions is not a majestic march of great majorities united upon certain matters of basic policy. It is the steady appeasement of relatively small groups." . . .

In his more recent writings, however, Dahl has been less sanguine about polyarchies, stating *inter alia:* "They all fall short of the criteria for a democratic process. They ought to be democratized further." This points to the limitations of interest groups as channels of public input. There is abundant empirical evidence in western democracies that a wide variety of disadvantaged groups are regularly excluded from the political process and that this applies as much to interest group activity as to other activities. Indeed, Verba and Nie concluded that in the United States interest groups are *"more* likely to skew government policy in favour of particular participant groups,'' specifically the well-educated and well-to-do. Reviewing the limited data available for Canada, Mishler found that although more than half of Canadians belonged to at least one voluntary association (one of the highest rates in western democracies), actual participation in those groups is much less. Stanbury revealed in melancholy detail how the government's intention to toughen up Canada's competition law was reduced to a shambles by the vigorous and unremitting opposition of business groups and their allies in the media, with the voice of the consumer interest being drowned out in the din.

It is worth noting, however, that in the competition policy case it was the government of elected ministers, not the public service, that capitulated. Proposals for reform emanated from public servants, and there is no suggestion that their views changed materially during the long, ignominious retreat. Lang's study of legislative reform in the pharmaceutical field, designed to reduce the prices of prescription drugs, also showed public servants holding firm in their belief in the need for reform. Here, however, the outcome was different, at least in the immediate situation. The Canadian Pharmaceutical Manufacturers' Association, an organization of mainly U.S. companies with only limited understanding of how the Canadian policy-making system worked, were unable to apply the kind of pressure produced by the alliance of major business organizations in the competition policy case, while the public servants, working quietly behind the scenes, succeeded in making their case prevail. . . .

Attempts have been made in recent years to bring excluded groups into the process by providing them with public funding. Traditionally such funding consisted of small grants to endeavours considered worthy, largely in the charitable domain. Though this kind of funding has increased, it has been overshadowed by funding designed to help groups to make an input into the policy process. The latter has often fallen short of its objectives, has had unintended consequences, and/or has been ephemeral in its effects. It is often also a reflection of a symbiosis between public administrators and interest groups in which the latter serve the purposes of the former as much as they gain access to the policy process. They nevertheless do gain access and it may well be access denied to them before. The banner example has undoubtedly been the case of native peoples. Millions of dollars have been made available over the last number of years to Indian bands and associations, and also on a smaller scale to the Inuit, with the result that these groups have acquired access previously undreamed of. . . .

(D) MULTIPLYING ACCESS POINTS

Another method that has been used to broaden public input has been to increase the number and range of access points through revivification of old devices and development of new devices — including royal commissions, parliamentary committees, task forces, advisory councils, white papers and green papers.

Royal commissions have been used traditionally by Canadian governments for assistance in devising policies to deal with complex problems (and sometimes to put hot potatoes into cold storage), but in the opinion of one of Canada's most distinguished public servants [Robert Bryce] (now retired), it was not until the Royal Commission on Bilingualism and Biculturalism that deliberate efforts were made to induce public input. Such activity has since become almost a recognized part of commissions' work. A notable example has been provided by Ontario's Royal Commission on Electric Power Planning which treated public input as a key ingredient in its massive inquiry. Parliamentary committees, also a traditional device, have developed even more than commissions into access points, touring the country to hear the views of interested groups and individuals on numerous policy questions. Task forces have been devised to provide less formal and speedier procedures than royal commissions, and the most recent development is the parliamentary task force to supplement the work of parliamentary committees. Advisory councils and committees have been established in a growing number of policy areas, partly to provide interested groups with regular access so that policy-makers and administrators will be better informed about the consequences of their decisions. The white paper, a traditional device copied from the United Kingdom, has been given a new life and meaning in encouraging input, and the green paper, a relatively recent invention, has also been taken over from the United Kingdom to encourage public discussion and comment at a quite early stage in policy formation.

There is no question that the above devices have opened up the policy process enormously to public input. It is doubtful, however, if they have reduced significantly the elitist character of the policy process. In fact, they may even have done the opposite by opening up new channels to those whose resources are such that they are already the predominant outside influences. The case of tax reform in the late 1960s is instructive. Here several of the devices referred to were involved, starting with a massive public inquiry by a royal commission, followed by extensive representations to the Minister of Finance, leading to publication of a white paper which then became the subject of public hearings and reports by committees of both houses of parliament. Yet, the rich and powerful dominated the proceedings at all stages. The taxpayer of small means, who probably did not grasp the implications of the proposals anyway, was not heard from. The upshot was that the royal commission's recommendations for greater equity in the tax system were watered down substantially in the white paper, and the white paper's proposals were watered down even more drastically in the overhaul of the Income Tax Act in 1971.

(E) MAKING BUREAUCRACY "REPRESENTATIVE"

In all the foregoing proposals, the public service is implicitly viewed as passive, reacting to stimuli from without whether channeled through representative assemblies, political parties, interest groups or a combination thereof. Many writers shift the emphasis and argue that restructuring the public service itself rather than the input channels to it is the key to enhanced accountability and responsiveness. . . . The essence of the idea, as Kranz put in, is that "the ratios of each racial-ethnic minority group and women at all levels in a particular government agency equal that group's percentage in the population in the geographic group serviced by that agency.'' In other words, representation in this context takes on the character of a representative sample — what Mosher has designated as "passive" representation to distinguish it from the "active" representation claimed for representative institutions. . . .

Such evidence as is currently available suggests that perceptible if not dramatic progress is being made in Canada's federal public service in the direction of making it more representative in the passive sense. Campbell and Szablowski found in 1976 that personnel above the clerical grades in the central agencies were drawn from a substantially broader social and demographic base than discovered by Porter in 1953 for comparable personnel in the public service generally. Campbell and Szablowski concluded that passive representation in Canada in the later period exceeded that of any other western democracy. Among other things, the occupational status of the fathers of public servants was considerably lower on average than in the earlier period or in other countries. In addition, there was a marked increase in the proportion from western Canada. Francophone Quebec was underrepresented in Finance but this was offset by overrepresentation in the other central agencies, while Finance had a strong contingent of westerners. Only the Atlantic provinces appeared to be significantly underrepresented overall. With that exception, educational achievement was the most important factor in gaining employment in the central agencies. . . .

Direct Participation Model

The key to the difference between the representation and direct participation models is to be found in the distinction made by Verba and Nie between "instrumental" and "consummative" participation. The former refers to participation directed to the achievement of other ends, the latter to participation as an end in itself. . . .

The requirements of instrumental participation are adequately satisfied in the representation model of public input. If an individual's motive is to advance his own interests to the maximum extent possible, he will necessarily take into account the costs and benefits involved in any course of action. . . . Interest group activity will broaden and deepen electoral politics by providing continuous input into the system, but such activity will be confined to small coteries of interest group leaders who will often have to offer special inducements to keep the generality of their members in the fold. . . .

Proponents of consummative participation deny that the foregoing is genuine participation at all. . . . The unique quality of democracy, it is argued, is to be found in the ethical thrust of Rousseau, J.S. Mill and other classical theorists who valued consummative participation above all else because it alone enabled human beings, all of them and not just a privileged few, to develop their potential to the full. . . .

The problem with consummative participation is that the bureaucratic society in which we live requires large-scale, geographically extensive organization, whereas it is feasible for individuals to participate directly and thereby share power only in small, localized units. To the radical left, which reached its zenith in the 1960s, the way to overcome the difficulty was to bring the existing order down by continuous confrontation ("extra-parliamentary opposition") in a revised version of the syndicalist general strike. . . . More prosaic champions of consummative participation, lacking the élan of syndicalist faith, have concentrated their attention on fostering participation in the small unit, hoping thereby to provide building blocks for a more participatory society overall. The concept of worker participation in the management of industry (democratization of the workplace) has enjoyed a revival, with particular interest being taken in the western European and Yugoslav experiments and the Israeli kibbutzim. Worker participation, however, has hardly got beyond the discussion stage in North America. Here the emphasis has been on encouraging other forms of participation.

There was in fact a spectacular upsurge of citizen participation in the 1960s. Starting with the civil rights movement in the United States, it spread over that country and into Canada, manifesting itself in confrontation at the universities and uprisings in the ghettos, as well as in less violent forms, including a host of neighbourhood, environmental, consumer and other action programs. Such participation, however, continued to be of the instrumental kind to a considerable degree: it represented an expansion, one is tempted to say an explosion, of pressure politics. . . .

At the same time, there were also pronounced tendencies toward consummative participation in this upsurge of activity, and such tendencies were supported and even stimulated by governments. The central thrust of this phase of activity was in the direction of devolving power to the neighbourhood level and establishing "neighbourhood governments." The Kennedy War on Poverty and the Johnson Great Society gave a fillip to the movement. . . .

Canada had its own watered-down War on Poverty centred at first on the ill-starred Company of Young Canadians and followed by more modest programs such as Opportunities for Youth, Local Initiatives, New Horizons and Neighbourhood Improvement. The Secretary of State's Department and National Health and Welfare undertook substantial funding of disadvantaged groups (in addition to the large-scale funding of native groups already referred to). Provincial and urban governments stimulated and supported local activities in innumerable ways.

Overall evaluation of these programs is well-nigh impossible because of their variegated nature. In the United States critics claimed that the programs were characterized by bungling, internal bureaucratic conflict and goal displacement. Other investigators claimed, however, and they were the majority, that useful work had been done in stimulating participation in neighbourhood and other small groups. Nonetheless, no one denies that results fell well short of expectations. Though association with the anti-poverty program encouraged involvement of the poor, and blacks in particular took advantage of the opportunity, the participation curve overall was still skewed in favour of the middle and upper classes. . . .

Looking at the broad picture of citizen participation across Canada and North America in the last decade or so, it is clear that, though there has been much activity, there has been little devolution of power. Certainly we are still a long way from Pateman's ideal of equal participation and equality of power. Yet citizens' groups can point to achievements even if many of these have been of a negative, defensive character. Even defensive achievements are indicative of successful instrumental participation, and there is no doubt that that kind of participation has expanded. Progress towards consummative participation, however, has been slow and tentative.

Where Do We Go From Here?

Enhancing public input into the policy process is a complex and ever-changing puzzle to which there is probably no ultimate solution. It is a continuing challenge to which a variety of responses is needed and perhaps different responses at different times. All of the responses discussed above have limitations. None of them, however, could be fairly described as having failed utterly. Parliamentary reform has in fact expanded the opportunity for the elected representative to play a part in the policy process. There are accountability procedures in political parties that did not exist before. There are more opportunities for citizens to make an input than there used to be. At least some previously excluded groups are being heard and are having some effect on policy. The public service is coming to reflect better the composition of the society it serves. All these changes together have opened up the policy process to a degree that can be fully appreciated only if one compares the present situation with the tight bureaucratic control of the 1950s.

Nevertheless, there is a long way to go. To a considerable extent, the effect of opening up more channels has been to provide still greater opportunities for those with superior resources. The rich and the powerful are still most likely to be heard and have influence. All that can be said is that they are probably less likely to have their own way than they were in, say, C.D. Howe's day. And, what is of even greater concern to some people (depending on their underlying philosophy of government), such advances as have been made have been largely in the realm of instrumental participation. It is not to be inferred that such participation is unimportant. On the contrary, protecting and advancing one's own interests is an integral part of democratic citizenship, especially when those interests are threatened as they so often are today. The problem is not that self-interest is illegitimate but that many legitimate interests are submerged. Having said that, however, one is impelled to reassert the fundamental tenet of classical democratic theory, that full democratic citizenship can be achieved only with the full realization of the potential of every individual citizen. And that requires consummative participation.

In fact, this paper will go further and argue that it will only be within a framework of expanding consummative participation that instrumental participation will achieve fruition in the sense that there will be recognition of all relevant interests. Devising strategies to achieve greater participation, whether instrumental or consummative, will be an ongoing process in which we will learn by experience just as (one hopes) we have learned from the experience of the last two decades. . . .

An Information Network

Lack of resources is a major cause of failure of public input into the policy process, and information is an essential resource. Without it the public will not even understand public policy, much less make intelligent input. Freedom of information legislation has become something of a political football in Canada. . . . This is not to deny the importance of freedom of information legislation; rather it is to assert that by itself such legislation is not enough. More is required: what one writer has described as an "information network." More specifically, as the same writer has put it, what we need is not "more information per se" but "more *relevant* information, well organized and easily accessible," as well as "cheap and efficient ways of communicating with one another and with the appropriate political decision-makers."

Modern technology, in which incidentally Canada is a leader, has brought within the realm of immediate possibility a country-wide interactive computer-based network with an easily operated terminal in every home. There is really no limit to the information that can be stored in such a system and retrieved by any citizen at the home terminal. The aim should be to make the information bank as comprehensive as possible. This should apply, and the point needs emphasis, not only to information in the possession of governments but also to that held by major corporations and associations. . . .

There remains, however, what is probably the most difficult question of all. How do we prevent monopoly control of the information network and resultant slanting of the information fed into it? . . . To place the system under government control does not necessarily meet the problem, because the world is full of governments that are at least as manipulative as private monopolists. In our own situation, however, experience with a quasi- independent corporation like the Canadian Broadcasting Corporation gives rise to the hope that a publicly owned agency with built-in safeguards of its independence, and an alert parliamentary opposition and public to ensure that the safeguards are not violated, will prevent the information network from being turned into an instrument of propaganda. . . .

Devolution of Authority

It has almost become part of the conventional wisdom that responsibility for policy on any issue should devolve on the lowest level of government capable of handling it. . . . The fact is that there has been a powerful tendency in the last century for responsibility for policy to move to higher levels of government, not the reverse. Notwithstanding some contemporary mythology, this has not been due in any substantial measure to bureaucratic hunger for power. Rather, it has been due to the pressures of an increasingly complex society where fewer and fewer problems have mainly local dimensions.

In any event, there is precious little real evidence that lower levels of government are more responsive than higher. It is often asserted that provincial governments are closer to the people and therefore more responsive than the federal government. There has, however, been no systematic study of this question and litanies of complaints from opposition politicians and disgruntled individuals and groups suggest that the problems of bureaucracy are similar at both levels. . . .

I am not here attacking the principle of territorial division of power. Unquestionably such division is necessary and desirable, especially in a geographically extensive country like Canada. What I am arguing is that such division does not by itself overcome the problems of bureaucracy. . . .

It is therefore necessary to devise other, complementary ways of devolving authority. Schumacher, the prophet of smallness, was convinced that "large-scale organization is here to stay," and argued that as a consequence: "The fundamental task is to achieve smallness *within* large organization." . . .

In the realm of government in Canada, there have been many attempts to provide substantial administrative discretion to local units, especially in the delivery of services to people. Not having given more than perfunctory study to such experiments, I am not in a position to evaluate them. Intuitively, however, one feels that they make sense even though they are bound to make the maintenance of uniform standards more difficult. . . .

A More Participatory Society

The thesis of this paper is that public input into policy-making and administration by all the people, and not disproportionately by small groups of privileged elites with exceptional resources at their command, will be achieved only to the extent that we are able to move to a more participatory society. The preconditions of such a society include continuing development of all the strategies discussed in the first part of the paper. They also include the informational network and devolution of authority discussed so far in this part. There are two additional, even more important preconditions that will be outlined here.

First, it is necessary to involve more people more regularly in actual policy decisions. That can be achieved in part through the neighbourhood governments and administrative decentralization already discussed. The direct participatory process must be rounded out, however, by being extended to the workplace, which continues to be central to most people's lives. In fact, the workplace is probably the most important locus of participation, since decisions made there have greater immediacy for the individual than those made almost anywhere else. Taking part in those decisions will help to prepare the individual for participation in neighbourhood decision-making. And the combination of participation in those small units, economic and geographic, can give him/her the experience for more effective input to more remote authorities with larger areas of jurisdiction. . . .

The strongest argument in favour of a hierarchical structure in the workplace is that it is essential to efficiency. There is a growing body of evidence, however, that this is not necessarily so. [Abrahamsson has said:]

. . . the gains in efficiency which are achieved by fractionalization of tasks, may be counteracted in the long run by a greater rate of sickness and psychological stress among workers. . . . work engagement as well as productivity figures often rise faster in plants and departments which employ new forms of work organization than in plants that do not use these new forms.

. . . The principle of democracy in the workplace is equally applicable to the public service in its own internal functioning. True, the argument of efficiency is reinforced by the argument of accountability in justifying hierarchical structures in the public service. That, however, is an *à priori* argument with little empirical foundation. . . . We should be prepared to at least consider the other possibility, that participation will foster a sense of responsibility that will strengthen rather than weaken accountability. It could also make for greater responsiveness to the public.

The final precondition of a more participatory society, and one that is fundamental to all the others, is to move in the direction of a more equal society, one in which there is greater equality of economic resources and social status. In our previous discussion, it was noted time after time that procedures designed to broaden input into the policy process were defeated by the fact that those with large resources were able to take undue advantage of them. As long as that situation prevails, public input will continue to be predominantly elitist in character. On the other hand, [as Kalodner has noted],

(With) a redistribution of wealth and political power to achieve greater equality of access to our political, economic and social institutions . . . we may find that many existing political and social institutions will work better than many of our citizens now believe possible.

• • •

THE BRILLIANT CAMPAIGN TO MAKE PUBLIC OPINION*

Ron Haggart

At the end of last year, things were going rather badly for the Spadina Expressway project. The newspapers, reporting as usual the organized opinion of the community, were full of stories all blackly against another super-highway.

Controllers Won't Back Expressway, reported the *Star*. Planner Faces Opponents, said another headline. Chaos Feared if Expressways Slice Up Metro, said the *Globe and Mail*.

Meetings of 12 associations of taxpayers, and then of 85 associations, were reported under headlines like "Shame If It Carries" and "Spadina Results 'Bad As H-Bomb' ".

Suddenly, about the middle of January, the climate of public opinion radically changed. Citizens' associations and ratepayers groups, with all the

* From *Toronto Daily Star*, February 26, 1962. By permission of the publisher.

fervor of an Algerian riot, appeared to be lining the streets, urging the reluctant politicians to hurry up with the Spadina highway.

This new public opinion was recorded in the *Telegram* of Jan. 12: "New life for the Spadina Expressway . . ." the paper reported, "emerged today with growing public support for the $67 million project. The expressway plan will be revived at Metro roads committee on Jan. 22 by ratepayer groups who are demanding that it be built immediately."

These demands from the citizens were heard at a number of meetings called by the roads committee of the Metropolitan council, and on Jan. 29 the extent of the swing in public opinion was recorded by *The Star:* "Champions of the Spadina combined expressway and rapid transit line," it reported, "outnumbered the opposition by better than three to one. . . ."

The single, most important hand behind the magical change in public opinion was a short, sharp bundle of hyperthyroid salesman's energy named Irving Paisley. He runs a prosperous insurance agency near Bathurst and Lawrence and is a councillor in North York.

"There is no doubt about it, that it was going the other way until I took over," Paisley has said of his success in this campaign.

Mr. Paisley's technique was to arrange for masses of approving briefs and statements to descend on the politicians who were making the decision.

Briefs from 25 ratepayer organizations, all enthusiastically in favour of the Spadina Expressway, were submitted to the Metropolitan roads committee.

Of these, Mr. Paisley wrote at least eight. He was the author of the briefs from the Winston Park Ratepayers' Association, the West Glen Ratepayers' Association, the Blackwood-Ranee Ratepayers' Association, the Joyce Park Ratepayers' Association, the Maple Leaf Ratepayers' Association, the Faywood Ratepayers, the Beverley Hills Ratepayers' Association, the Danesbury Ratepayers, and the Hillmount-Viewmount Ratepayers' Association.

An example of Mr. Paisley's genius in the arts of creative public opinion was the brief in support of the Spadina Expressway submitted by the West Glen Ratepayers' Association.

Mr. Paisley describes this association as being "defunct." He went to see Mrs. Dorothy Somers, the secretary of the association, and she agreed that the Spadina Expressway was a good idea.

Mr. Paisley then phoned three members of the executive of the West Glen ratepayers and they, too, agreed with Mr. Paisley's enthusiastic support of the expressway. Mr. Paisley then wrote a brief which said " . . . I am instructed by the executive of the West Glen Ratepayers' Association to place on record its wholehearted support of construction of the Spadina Expressway." Then followed two pages of well-reasoned argument in favour of the highway.

The brief was signed by Mrs. Dorothy Somers, secretary. Curiously, Mrs. Somer's name was spelled incorrectly, appearing with two m's in this official communication from the West Glen ratepayers.

Another example was the brief from the Winston Park ratepayers. John O'Hagan, who lives on Winston Park Blvd. and publishes a paper in Woodbridge, is listed as president.

Mr. Paisley describes this organization as being "defunct."

Mr. Paisley visited Mr. O'Hagan at his home and got his agreement to the project, although Mr. O'Hagan told him he could not speak for the organization. Mr. Paisley went back to his insurance office on Bathurst St. and phoned a few members of the executive of this organization. Mr. Paisley then wrote the brief of the Winston Park ratepayers and took it back to Mr. O'Hagan for his signature.

The brief began: "I am instructed by the members of the Winston Park Ratepayers' Association to urge your committee . . ."

In this case, the members represented totalled approximately four.

In the case of the Hillmount-Viewmount Ratepayers' Association ("We endorse this project which should be put under way as quickly as possible"), Mr. Paisley telephoned the president, Albert Glazer, in hospital where Mr. Glazer was recovering from an operation, and repeated the creative process as before.

The brief from the Beverley Hills ratepayers, which was also written by Mr. Paisley, was signed "Isobel Walker, per." Nothing followed the "per," but that, too, was Mr. Paisley.

Twenty-five copies of each of the 25 briefs had to be submitted to the Metropolitan roads committee. Stencils for at least 10 of these were cut in Mr. Paisley's insurance office. He and his staff worked all one Saturday night until 1 o'clock in the morning turning out the material.

They were so overworked they had to send two of the briefs downtown to have the stencils typed by a friend of Mr. Paisley's. These two stencils (the ones from Winston Park and West Glen) were typed in the offices of Webb and Knapp, the land developers who are building the shopping plaza for Eaton's and Simpson's which will get its entrance from Highway 401 by way of the Spadina Expressway.

Almost all of the briefs from the 25 citizens' associations were mailed to the Metropolitan officials from Mr. Paisley's office, or dispatched downtown by taxicab from Mr. Paisley's office.

Mr. Paisley organized a car pool so that citizens could go down and hear the deliberations of the roads committee, and he wrote and mailed out to his constituents 9,076 copies of a leaflet supporting the Spadina Expressway.

He paid for the postage with a cheque for $136.29 drawn on the account of his insurance agency.

This brilliant campaign had the desired results. *The Telegram* reported on Feb. 5: "The ratepayers appeared to be evenly split, but growing support for the project was indicated as North York councillor Irving Paisley presented letters from 10 more groups in his township, representing 15,000 people."

And the [*Toronto Daily*] *Star* on Feb. 6 was able to report: ". . . a 3½-hour session which saw 36 briefs presented — 28 of them in favour of the big transportation complex."

"I do have a knack for organization," Mr. Paisley says.

FINDINGS AND RECOMMENDATIONS*

Royal Commission on Newspapers

Freedom of the press is not a property right of owners. It is a right of the people. It is part of their right to free expression, inseparable from their right to inform themselves. The Commission believes that the key problem posed by its terms of reference is the limitation of those rights by undue concentration of ownership and control of the Canadian daily newspaper industry. . . .

Concentration engulfs Canadian daily newspaper publishing. Three chains control nine-tenths of French-language daily newspaper circulation. Three other chains control two-thirds of English-language circulation. Additional chains bring the circulation in English under concentrated ownership to three-quarters of the total. In seven provinces — all but Ontario, Québec, and Nova Scotia — two-thirds or more of provincial circulation is controlled by a single chain. Often chain owners of daily newspapers also control community newspapers, broadcasting stations, periodicals, and major interests outside the media. We define a chain as the ownership of two or more daily newspapers in different urban communities by a single firm.

Fateful Decade

Canadian newspapers went through a decade of wrenching change before the traumatic "rationalization" of 1980 — the series of takeovers, mergers, agreements, and closings that brought about the appointment of this Commission. There is no reason to think that the trend of ownership changes, with increasing concentration, has ended. The years ahead will see more, unless the law is changed.

The daily paper is an urban phenomenon. The bigger the city, the more newspaper journalism it generates. Toronto, Montréal, and Vancouver alone account for 44 per cent of all daily newspaper circulation in Canada. In the 1970s, Canada's burgeoning metropolitan centres called up new patterns. Old general-interest newspapers died, new pop tabloids soared. Eight papers that accounted for 15 per cent of Canadian circulation in September, 1970, were gone 10 years later. The increase in morning tabloid circulation during the decade was almost exactly equal to the 1970 circulation of the defunct papers. It also was equal to the net increase in all daily newspaper circulation during the 1970s. The competition of television for public attention intensified, and daily newspapers also had to keep a weather eye on radio, community newspapers, and magazines as claimants for audience and hence for advertisers' dollars. . . .

Within these broad patterns there were significant secondary movements. Weekend circulation, including the introduction of new Sunday editions, grew faster than weekday. Circulation of afternoon papers was slightly

* From *Royal Commission on Newspapers,* Ottawa, Supply and Services, 1981. Reproduced by permission of the Minister of Supply and Services, Canada.

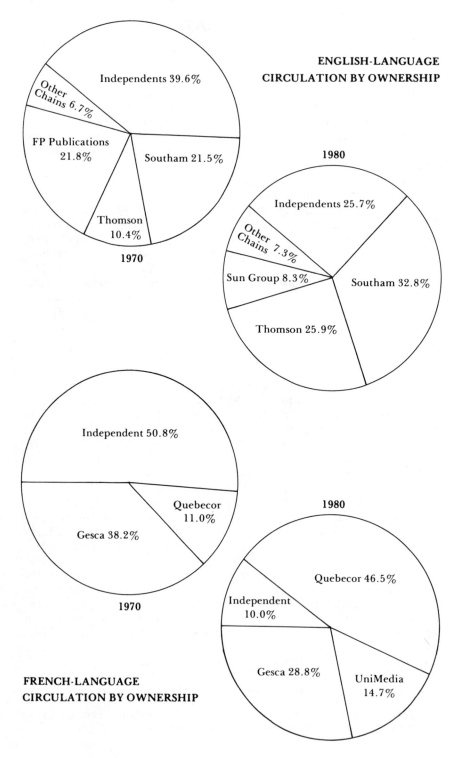

ENGLISH-LANGUAGE
CIRCULATION BY OWNERSHIP

Independents 39.6%

Other Chains 6.7%

FP Publications 21.8%

Southam 21.5%

Thomson 10.4%

1970

1980

Independents 25.7%

Other Chains 7.3%

Sun Group 8.3%

Southam 32.8%

Thomson 25.9%

Independent 50.8%

Quebecor 11.0%

Gesca 38.2%

1980

1970

Quebecor 46.5%

Independent 10.0%

Gesca 28.8%

UniMedia 14.7%

FRENCH-LANGUAGE
CIRCULATION BY OWNERSHIP

lower in 1980 than in 1970, while morning circulation increased by two-thirds during the decade. Afternoon papers were still dominant, at 63 per cent of total circulation, at the time of our survey in September of 1980. But since that time one major paper in Québec, *La Presse,* as well as the smaller *Le Quotidien,* have switched from afternoon to morning. The trend-setting province now has only one French-language afternoon paper, *Le Soleil.* . . .

The people who have been involved in all these changes and exertions in the daily newspaper industry number about 22,000, including employees of news services. About a quarter of that number — 5,500 — are editorial employees, directly responsible for the journalistic content of the papers. Finally, a little over half this group, about 2,900, are original content providers: reporters, photographers, editorialists, feature writers, reviewers, and so on. The remainder are editors, copy-editors, and other support staff. . . . During the decade [1970-80], the aggregate weekly circulation of all daily newspapers in Canada increased from 27,850,500 copies to 32,445,000, a gain of 16.5 per cent. This was a shade above the rate of population growth but represented a nine per cent decline in relation to number of households.

The number of newspaper titles in Canada increased from 114 in 1970 to 117 in 1980, the end of September being the date of our survey in each year; that is, the figure takes account of the closing of the Winnipeg *Tribune* and the Ottawa *Journal* on August 27, 1980, the immediate event that triggered the appointment of this Commission. The count does not include the new Winnipeg *Sun* (no relation to the Toronto *Sun*), which went to publication five days weekly, the minimum for consideration as a daily newspaper, only in the spring of 1981. The count does include both titles of two-in-one newspapers, which we define as two titles put out by one owner from the same plant, containing much of the same editorial material and sharing a good deal or all of the same staff, but aimed at distinct markets — mainly out of town in the morning, in town in the afternoon. An example is The Halifax Herald Limited which publishes the morning *Chronicle-Herald* and the afternoon *Mail-Star.*

Within the total figures for 1970 and 1980, independent titles decreased from 45 to 29, while chain-owned titles increased from 69 to 88, or 75 per cent of the total. Every region experienced changes. . . .

Reviewing the situation across the country in June, 1981, we find three urban communities reduced since 1970 from two newspapers to one, Victoria, English-speaking Ottawa, and English-speaking Montréal. The number of newspapers in both French-speaking Montréal and Québec City has been reduced but there is still competition. New entrants have offset losses, at least in numbers, in Toronto and Winnipeg. There is only one clear case of an increase in numbers in a single market, Edmonton going from one to two. Greater Halifax, it is true, has a second newspaper, but it is too restricted in circulation to be considered competition in the whole market.

Across the country, the number of major cities with two or more resident newspapers dropped from 10 to eight between 1970 and 1981. The total number of newspapers in the 11 cities which had more than one newspaper in either 1970 or 1981 has gone down from 26 to 22. We do not count the separate titles of the two-in-one newspapers here, since we are trying to get an idea of the number of major cities with competition between local dailies, and two- in-one titles can hardly be said to compete with each other. If we include Southam's Vancouver *Sun* and *Province* in this category, we are down to seven urban communities with local competition: Edmonton, Calgary, Winnipeg, Toronto, French-speaking Montréal, Québec City, and St. John's. These account for 49 per cent of daily newspaper circulation in Canada. . . .

Nationwide Concentration

In our cross-country survey, we found many dominant positions: Southam with two-thirds of the circulation in both British Columbia and Alberta. Armadale with more than four-fifths in Saskatchewan, Thomson with almost nine-tenths in Manitoba, two-thirds in P.E.I., and more than four-fifths in Newfoundland, the Irvings with nine-tenths in New Brunswick. Only three provinces — Ontario, Québec, and Nova Scotia — do not have two-thirds or more of their circulation in the hands of a single chain.

Chains accounted for 77 per cent of all copies of daily newspapers published in Canada in September, 1980, an increase from 58 per cent 10 years earlier. The movement in the past decade has been clear-cut. Except for the sale of the Sherbrooke *Record* by the Sterling chain to an independent owner, it has been all the other way: from independent to chain, and from chain to chain in the case of the biggest transaction in the history of Canadian newspapers, the purchase of FP Publications by Thomson in January of 1980. FP had been, by a shade, the highest-circulation chain in 1970, with 21.8 per cent of English-language circulation. . . .

Ownership of Daily Newspapers as at September, 1980

Owner	Number of titles owned	Location	Aggregate weekly circulation (in thousands)
Thomson	40	Various	6,865
Southam	14	Various	8,693
Sterling	11	Mostly B.C.	292
Gesca (Desmarais)	4	Québec	1,711
Bowes	3	Alberta	
		Ontario	93
Irving	5	New Brunswick	793
Toronto Sun	3	Alberta	
		Ontario	2,197
UniMédia (Francoeur)	2	Québec	871
Northumberland (Johnston)	2	Ontario	41
Quebecor (Péladeau)	2	Québec	2,762
Armadale (Sifton)	2	Saskatchewan	715
Torstar	1	Ontario	3,522
Independent	28	Various	3,890
Total	117		32,445

The Thomson Group

Thomson Newspapers Limited and its subsidiary companies reported owning, at December 31, 1980, 128 newspapers: 52 in Canada, 40 dailies and 12 weeklies; 76 in the United States, 71 dailies and five weeklies. Kenneth Thomson confirmed at a public hearing that growth is a continuing objective, and growth has certainly occurred. Since December, 1973, the Thomson holdings have increased from 100 newspapers: 48 in Canada, 34 dailies and 14 weeklies; and 52 in the United States, 46 dailies and six weeklies. . . .

Southam Inc.

Southam Inc., unlike the Thomson group, has no interests outside the broad field of what it refers to as the communication/information industry.

Southam publishes 14 daily newspapers, the weekly business newspaper *Financial Times of Canada,* 39 business publications, 24 annuals and directories, and 13 newsletters and looseleaf services. In addition it operates 10 printing plants and 53 trade shows and exhibitions. It has significant interests in other media operations: a near 50 per cent interest in two dailies, the Brandon *Sun* and the Kitchener-Waterloo *Record,* and a substantial interest in Selkirk Communications Limited which has extensive radio, television and cable interests in Canada and abroad. . . .

Sterling Newspapers

The third largest chain in number of newspapers, but not in circulation, is Sterling Newspapers, created since the time of the Special Senate Committee on Mass Media. Sterling Newspapers became a division of Western Dominion Investments Company Ltd. in 1979. The Sterling chain comprises 11 daily newspapers, nine in interior and northern British Columbia, one in Saskatchewan, and one in Prince Edward Island. The chain also includes seven weekly newspapers, three in the vicinity of Vancouver, one in the lower Fraser Valley, three in the B.C. interior and one in Saskatchewan.

Western Dominion is a private company, one of many controlled by Warspite Securities Limited, the main holding company of the Black Group. According to an information circular issued by Argus Corporation Limited, Conrad M. Black, his brother G. Montegu Black, and members of their families own directly or indirectly 75 per cent of Western Dominion. . . .

Power Corporation of Canada (Desmarais)

The four dailies that form a part of the Power/Desmarais group are owned, through a series of companies, by Gesca Ltée. Gesca is owned by Paul Desmarais; its relationship with Power is established through an "income debenture which effectively provides that all the earnings and any realized changes in the incremental value of the equity of Gesca Ltée accrue to the debenture holder," Power Corporation. . . .

Armadale Company Limited (Sifton)

Michael Sifton has two dailies in Saskatchewan, the Saskatoon *Star-Phoenix* and the Regina *Leader-Post*. These two dailies now form part of a mixed conglomerate enterprise which includes airport operations, real estate and other investments, as well as radio stations in Regina, Winnipeg and Hamilton. There are no public data on the Armadale operations since all are held through private companies. . . .

Torstar Corporation

Torstar is a conglomerate. The day-to-day operations of the Toronto *Star* newspaper are managed separately from those of Torstar. Other enterprises which Torstar controls include Comac Communications Limited, Metrospan Printing & Publishing Ltd., Harlequin Enterprises Limited, and Neilsen-Ferns International Limited.

In addition it has a 50 per cent partnership interest with Southam in Infomart and a one-third interest with Southam and Thomson in Today Magazine Inc. A one-third block of shares in Western Broadcasting Company Ltd. was sold in June, 1981.

In February, 1981, Metrospan added to its 14 community papers those of Inland Publishing Co. Limited, thereby giving it 27 community papers circulating in and around metropolitan Toronto. This purchase also included Inland's extensive commercial printing facilities in Mississauga, Ontario. . . .

The Readers' Opinion

. . . Two out of three Canadians think their local daily is doing a good or an excellent job in fulfilling its responsibilities to the public. Older people are more likely to think this way than the young. . . . The people of British Columbia are most critical of their newspapers' performance, followed closely by those of Atlantic Canada.

Our research indicates that 89 per cent of all adults read at least one newspaper in the course of a week. Canadians spend an average of 53 minutes reading daily newspapers on a typical weekday, and 66 minutes during the weekend; 69 per cent read five or more issues a week. Those most likely to read newspapers are over 35, have the highest household income ($25,000 or more), and are highly educated.

More than half of all Canadians, some 54 per cent, are very loyal to their newspaper. These are adults who look upon newspapers as part of their daily lives. Young adults are less likely than their elders to be consumers of news. They read newspapers less, just as they listen to less news on radio or television. However, they are more inclined than older people to read books or magazines. This generation, influenced by television since childhood, may well be questioning the traditional meaning of "news."

Our study reveals — or confirms, depending on one's point of view — that there is no one superior source of information. Rather, there are preferences for one or the other, according to the type of news or type of information wanted. Television, for instance, is considered best for national and international news; but for local coverage, newspapers come first. . . .

Television edges out daily newspapers as the preferred source of news by a slight margin. But — and this may be a salutary warning — more than half of Canadians believe that television will become even more important in this sector. In general, the future of the newspaper and the radio seems to them unpromising. Francophones show a marked preference for television. These facts add up to important indications that newspapers must define a new role for themselves, one that complements the TV screen. The coming of videotex is going to hasten this development.

NEWSPAPERS   RADIO   TELEVISION

Which of the three information media, newspapers, radio or TV. . .

Keeps you up-to-date

27%	27%	52%

Is most fair and unbiased

29%	32%	53%

Is most influential

23%	14%	67%

Is most essential to Canada

35%	24%	52%

Is most essential to your community

53%	25%	27%

Is most essential to you personally

39%	28%	39%

Presents widest range of opinions

44%	18%	43%

Is most believable

34%	28%	54%

Most Canadians believe that newspapers help make their community a more pleasant place to live. Nonetheless, 78 per cent think that newspapers tend to sensationalize the news. And 72 per cent think newspapers play down facts that could offend their advertisers. Forty per cent think that dailies give too much space to advertising. . . .

Recommendations

In this final chapter we set out our recommendations to the Government of Canada. We propose a Canada Newspaper Act designed to secure for the press of Canada the freedom that is essential to a democratic society from coast to coast. . . .

The Rules of Ownership

The Canada Newspaper Act must contain provisions to prevent any further increase in concentration and to reduce the worst features of the concentration that has hitherto been allowed. . . .

While the local monopoly of a newspaper is a problem in itself, often reflected in profit maximization by impoverishment of editorial content, the worst feature of concentration is not the ownership of several newspapers by one company; it is their ownership by a "conglomerate," a company having, or associated with, extensive other interests. Therefore the Newspaper Act should prohibit the purchase of a newspaper business by a company or person, or any association of persons or companies not at arm's length, if the total net value of the assets employed in non-newspaper business by the company, person, and any associated companies or persons, exceeds the net asset value of the newspaper which is to be purchased. . . .

. . . The provision we propose for the Newspaper Act is that a company or person, or associates of a company or person, owning a daily newspaper may acquire an additional newspaper or newspapers only if:

(1) The total number of daily papers owned thereby does not exceed five.

(2) The circulation of daily newspapers thereby owned does not exceed five per cent of the circulation (measured on a weekly total basis) of all daily newspapers in Canada. At present, this is equivalent to an average daily circulation, for papers published six times a week, of 270,000. A paper could not acquire others beyond that total circulation level for the chain.

(3) The point of publication of any acquired newspaper is not less than 500 kilometers distant from any other paper in the same ownership (500 kilometers is roughly the length of Nova Scotia from southeast to northeast, and the breadth of Manitoba from east to west). . . .

We turn now to the minimum measure of divestment that we consider to be required in order that the degree of concentration should be more tolerable than it is. While the economic reality of daily newspaper monopoly in most communities has to be accepted, there is no economic necessity for the same ownership of other media in the same community. . . .

. . . A reasonable guideline to provide in the legislation would be that the proprietor of a newspaper may not own or control a television or radio station or a cable system if 50 per cent or more of the population within good reception reach of the electronic medium live in the areas where the newspaper is generally available by home delivery or by box or newsstand sales. . . .

. . . We propose that the Newspaper Act provide that the proprietor of a daily paper may not own or control a newspaper published less frequently (a weekly or a twice-weekly) which is, in all or in any significant part of the area in which the daily circulates, either the sole weekly or a dominant weekly facing only minor competition. . . .

Divestments of Dailies

. . . The principle to be embodied in the Canada Newspaper Act is that no company or person or associated companies or group of companies or persons not at arm's length should continue to own or control two or more papers (other than "two-in-one" papers, that is, morning and afternoon papers published from the same plant under the same editorial control) which are the sole or predominant (that is, having 75 per cent or more of the circulation) newspapers in one language published in a province or in a distinct region clearly separated in communications generally, and in newspaper circulation, from other regions. . . .

In New Brunswick, the principle to be expressed in our proposed Newspaper Act requires that the Irving interests divest themselves of either their two-in-one papers in Saint John or their similar Moncton papers. They would also have to decide, under the rules against cross-media ownership, whether to keep the Saint John papers or their television and radio stations.

In Saskatchewan, for reasons given by way of example in Chapter 13, the principle requires that Armadale divest itself of either its Saskatoon or its Regina paper. . . .

We propose that the Press Rights Panel should under the legislation be instructed fully to review the effects of concentration, particularly on a regional basis, at intervals of not more than five years. It would take account of events meantime, and be empowered to order further divestments if it considered them to be required in accordance with the spirit and guidelines of the Act. . . .

The most important divestment we propose is not, however, regional but national; it arises from the special position of the *Globe and Mail,* with its national character recently achieved by printing in Calgary and Ottawa, as well as Toronto; at the time of writing this Report, the intention to add two other printing locations, in Vancouver and in the Maritimes, has been announced. . . .

It is in our judgement an entirely unacceptable concentration of power that this paper should be owned by the Thomson organization which also owns a third of the other daily newspapers in Canada. There are no economic advantages to the union. . . . We therefore propose that the Canada Newspaper Act should stipulate that a company owning or controlling a daily newspaper which is printed in two or more distinct locations in separate provinces of Canada shall not, either directly or through associated companies, own or control any other daily newspaper in Canada. Thomson would thus be required to divest itself, within five years, either of the *Globe and Mail* or of its other papers. . . .

Investment Incentive

. . . We propose that the Newspaper Act provide a special inducement for the purchase of shares in companies which acquire newspapers in consequence of the Act, and provided that the shares are bought within one year after the date of commitment to buy the paper. We have in mind tax haven provisions roughly comparable to those used to encourage film production in Canada.

In order to encourage diversity of ownership, we would limit the benefit to purchases, by any one purchaser, of not more than five per cent of the equity shares of the divested company or shares issued by a company in acquiring a divested newspaper property. Up to this limit, the investment in shares would be eligible for capital cost allowances taken at such rate as suited the investor for tax purposes, though not over a longer period than that for which the shares are retained or a maximum of say, five years.

The Freedom of the Editor

. . . The role and responsibilities of the editor-in-chief must be clearly defined. The fact that contracts for editors are not common in the Canadian newspaper industry is symptomatic of the lack of status commonly accorded to the editorial function. To correct this, the Canada Newspaper Act would require that, if the proprietor of a newspaper has other interests of greater value (that is, it is not an "individual" paper), the editor-in-chief must be appointed under a written contract. The nature of the contract should be detailed in the statute.

The contract should set out a comprehensive statement of principles for the conduct of the newspaper, adhered to by both the proprietor and the editor-in-chief. The Statement of Principles adopted in 1977 by the CDNPA would be a satisfactory model. The contract might provide, further, any more specific description of the paper's objectives which the proprietor thought appropriate. Most important, it must express the editor-in-chief's full responsibility for policy in accordance with the statement of principles and objectives. . . .

The editor-in-chief would be required to make, not later than January 31 each year, a report on the paper during the previous 12 months. The report would review performance against the standards set out in the editor's contract. It would state the amount and structure of the editorial budget; the amount of any tax credit or surtax arising from the newspaper's operations in the last financial year; and the size of the news hole and its relation to advertising space. It would enable the editor to discuss such matters as the numbers and qualifications of editorial staffing; the utilization of news services; the topics of in-depth reporting; the coverage of major trends and developments in international, national, provincial and local news; and so on. This report would be delivered to an advisory committee and be published in the newspaper as soon as made. . . .

The statute would require the creation, by each newspaper other than an "individual" paper, of an advisory committee. The proprietor would appoint two members of the committee. The journalistic staff of the newspaper would elect, by secret ballot, two of their number. The "constituency" would be all persons, except the editor-in-chief or his nearest equivalent, employed full-time in writing and/or editing the paper, provided they have been so employed for at least 12 months before the date of the ballot. . . .

These four people, representing the proprietor and the journalists, would be the "in-house" committee members. There would be three other members resident in, and representative of, the community for which the newspaper is published. They must have no financial interest in, or — apart from ordinary advertising — any business or professional relation with, the newspaper or any other business or businesses in which the newspaper proprietor has an interest.

Within these limitations, the "in-house" members would nominate two representative members for the committee. . . . The two committee members appointed by this process would themselves choose a third representative, who would take the chair. . . .

The Press Rights Panel

. . . We propose that the Newspaper Act should create a Press Rights Panel within the Canadian Human Rights Commission. It would consist of a chairman and two other members. Its association with the Human Rights Commission would make it an independent agency reporting to Parliament through the Minister of Justice. While it would be housed in the Commission and share its services, the Panel would not be subordinate to it. Its membership would be appointed by the Governor-in-Council for fixed terms, of seven years for the chairman, five years for one member and three years for the other; this would minimize the possibility of loss of continuity by simultaneous change of personnel in a small body.

Many of the functions of the Panel have been referred to, but, for convenience, these are restated here along with the more general functions:

(1) It would provide, if requested, guidance to the advisory committees of newspapers. In the remote but never completely impossible chance of an impasse in the proceedings of such a committee, the Press Rights Panel would have power to intervene to appoint one or more members to the committee. In that event it would be required to make a public statement of its actions and the reasons for them.

(2) The Panel would receive, from all newspapers, reports of the proceedings of advisory committees, including a full copy of the editor-in-chief's contract.

(3) It would receive the annual reports of editors-in-chief, and the committees' comments on them.

(4) It would certify to Revenue Canada whether a newspaper proprietor is in full compliance with all of the terms of the Canada Newspaper Act.

(5) It would receive confirmations of intent regarding divestments.

(6) In cases of doubt it would make a final determination whether, under the terms of the Act, divestment is required in situations of cross-media ownership of daily papers with other media; for this purpose it would have authority to make reasonable exceptions, within the spirit of the Act, from the exact application of the arithmetical guidelines.

(7) At intervals of not more than five years it would review the concentration of newspaper ownership, particularly on a regional basis, and have power to order further divestments if it found that they were required, in the spirit and intent of the Act.

(8) It would have authority to extend, for good reason and within the limits specified earlier, the maximum time allowed for divestment.

(9) It could qualify application of the rule against "conglomerate" acquisitions of divested papers, if there were good reason to do so.

(10) It would receive notice of intended closings and, in the event of a proprietor failing to arrange the satisfactory sale as a going concern of a newspaper which it wished to cease publishing, the Panel would determine whether a sale of physical assets was at least as remunerative to the proprietor as any offer available for the business and, if it found otherwise, would prohibit the sale of assets.

(11) It would review and rule on acquisitions of newspapers that involve small chains, with modest flexibility in the application of the statutory guidelines.

(12) It would recommend to government whether a special tax inducement to the purchase of shares in companies acquiring or starting daily papers should be extended to the starting of weeklies and magazines.

(13) In relevant matters, the Panel would, like a Human Rights Tribunal established by the Canadian Human Rights Commission, have the powers of a superior court of record.

(14) The Panel would be empowered to require from all newspapers such information as is strictly necessary to its functions. This would include identification of the ultimate proprietor of each newspaper and complete, up-to-date identification of all business interests with which the ultimate proprietor is in any way associated.

(15) More generally, the Panel would be charged to observe the performance of newspapers in Canada in light of the intent and terms of the Canada Newspaper Act and to publish annually a review of that performance with any comment and advice to newspapers or government that it deems appropriate. In this function, the Panel would in effect act as a kind of ombudsman for the press generally, in something of the same way that the Official Languages Commissioner does in his field. Whether it has much to do in this respect will depend, essentially, on the newspapers themselves.

Tax Credit and Surtax

. . . We propose that the tendency of some newspapers to skimp on their editorial service to their communities should be counteracted by a system of tax credits and surtax. The legislation should provide that every company publishing a daily newspaper or newspapers must report, as part of its tax returns, a statement of the ratio of editorial costs to its total newspaper revenues. For financial years ended on or before March 31 each year, Revenue Canada, in conjunction with the Press Rights Panel, would calculate the percentage of editorial expense to the total of gross revenues from newspaper circulation and advertising for the industry as a whole. This calculation would simply record the average performance of the newspapers.

Our proposed tax measure is that the tax liability of a newspaper-owning company would be reduced by 25 per cent of any amount by which its paper's editorial expenses have exceeded the sum resulting from multiplying the paper's revenues by the ratio of editorial expense to revenues which was the average for all daily newspapers during the previous year. Symmetrically, if a paper's editorial expense falls short of the average industry level, in relation to revenues, the proprietor company would be subject to a surtax equal to 25 per cent of the deficiency. If the company owns more than one newspaper, the calculations would of course be made for each paper and the sum would become the net tax credit or surtax of the company. . . .

News Services

. . . The Commission, therefore, recommends that the Newspaper Act should include an incentive for both types of service, the CP co-operative and a competitive commercial operation. The incentive would be to expand and improve their provision of Canadian material — that is, of Canadian news and of international news written by Canadians stationed or travelling abroad. . . . The device proposed is a matching grant to help cover increased expenditures. . . .

664 COMPLAINTS SINCE '72*

Ontario Press Council

Report on Complaints, 1980

Since its beginning in mid-1972, the Press Council has received 510 specific complaints about the conduct of member newspapers. One in every three (33.53 per cent of the total) either had their complaint adjudicated or received satisfactory redress from the newspaper involved. . . .

Proportionately, people who complained about non-member newspapers had much less luck. The Council can deal with these complaints only if the newspapers agree. In 56 of 149 complaints over the eight years, the non-member newspapers involved chose not to have the complaints heard. However, in 19 complaints the newspapers did provide the redress that satisfied the complainants and in another seven they agreed to adjudications. The adjudications and the satisfactions amounted to 26 per cent of complaints. . . .

These three classes of complaints — against members, against non-members and general — totalled 665 in the eight years. The Council adjudicated 94 and the newspapers satisfied 104, for a percentage of 29.8.

* From Ontario Press Council, *8th Annual Report, 1980,* Ottawa, 1981. By permission.

People interested in the Council frequently asked about the "withdrawn or "abandoned" category. It covers cases where the complainants did not respond in any way to the Council's efforts to deal with their complaints.

The following tabulation shows the number of complaints in 1980 compared with 1979 and with 1972-78:

Totals	1980	1979	1972-78
Complaints	71	76	517
Adjudicated or being adjudicated	12	18	64
Newspaper satisfied complaint	6	17	81
Withdrawn or abandoned	40	27	337
Active at year-end	2	—	—
Disallowed by Council	2	—	7
Non-member newspaper:			
— declined adjudication	9	14	29
— didn't reply	—	—	3
AGAINST MEMBER NEWSPAPERS			
Complaints	48	57	405
Adjudicated or being adjudicated	11	14	62
Satisfied by newspaper	5	17	63
Withdrawn or abandoned	30	26	273
Active at year-end	1	—	—
Disallowed	1	—	7
AGAINST NON-MEMBERS			
Complaints	23	19	107
Adjudicated	1	4	2
Disallowed	1	—	—
Active at year-end	1	—	—
Satisfied by newspaper	1	—	18
Withdrawn or abandoned	10	1	63
Newspaper:			
— declined adjudication	9	14	29
— didn't reply	—	1	3
AGAINST NEWSPAPERS IN GENERAL			
Complaints	—	—	5

Nature of Complaints

Complaints about news stories topped the field once again in 1980 with 32 or 45 per cent of the complaints total of 71. But the proportion showed a drop from 1979 when 37 (48.7 per cent) of the 76 complaints concerned news stories.

Complaints of inaccurate or erroneous reporting, usually the leader in the news story category, dropped to three (4.2 per cent) in 1980 from 11 (14.4 per cent) in 1979.

Complaints involving the issue of public access to newspapers — through advertising, letters to the editor or other ways — numbered eight (11.3 per cent) compared with 10 (13.2 per cent) in 1979.

Advertising content stirred up seven grievances in 1980 (9.8 per cent) against four (5.3 per cent) in 1979.

The miscellaneous category showed an increase to 29 (40.8 per cent) in 1980 from 22 (28.9 per cent) in 1979. This category covers complaints that cartoons, comments, headlines, pictures, practices or conduct were biased, derogatory, inaccurate, irresponsible, misleading, objectionable, racist, sexist or unfair.

The following table shows the number and nature of complaints in 1980, 1979 and 1972-78. The number adjudicated is shown in brackets. The 1980 totals include adjudication of complaints received that year but scheduled for adjudication early in 1981.

	1980	1979	1972-78
ACCESS			
Advertising	1	2	23 (7)
Letters to the Editor	7 (3)	8 (2)	54 (12)
Other access	—	—	23 (2)
	8 (3)	10 (3)	100 (21)
ADVERTISING (content)			
Improper	—	—	3
Misleading	—	2	21 (3)
Objectionable	—	4 (1)	10
Unethical	2	1	4
Unfair policing standards	—	—	1
	2	7 (1)	39 (3)
NEWS STORIES			
Biased, prejudiced, dishonest	4 (1)	2 (2)	25 (1)
Damaging	4	—	—
Derogatory	—	—	6 (2)
Discriminatory	—	3 (1)	7 (1)
Distorted, falsified	2	—	6 (1)
Erroneous or inaccurate	3	11	51 (9)
Incomplete or inadequate	5 (2)	4	20
Incompetent	—	1	39
Irresponsible	—	1 (1)	20 (3)
Misleading	6	4	32 (5)
Objectionable	2 (1)	5 (2)	44 (2)
Sensational	1	1	3
Unfair	5 (2)	5 (1)	40 (6)
	32 (6)	37 (7)	293 (30)
MISCELLANEOUS			
Biased, derogatory, inaccurate, irresponsible, misleading, objectionable, racist, sexist, unethical or unfair:			
— cartoons	1	2 (1)	10 (2)
— comment	6 (2)	13 (1)	24 (3)
— headlines	2	2 (2)	12 (3)
— pictures	9	2 (1)	19 (1)
— practices	—	2 (1)	11 (1)
— conduct	11	1	9 (1)
	29 (2)	22 (6)	85 (11)

continued

	1980	1979	1972-78
SUMMARY			
Access	8 (3)	10 (3)	100 (19)
Advertising content	2	7 (1)	39 (3)
News stories	32 (6)	37 (7)	293 (30)
Miscellaneous	29 (2)	22 (6)	85 (11)
	71 (11)	76 (17)	517 (63)

• • •

[Editor's note: By April 1982, membership in the voluntary Ontario Press Council had grown to 10 of the province's 46 daily newspapers, one bi-monthly, six bi-weeklies and 31 of Ontario's 282 weeklies. The Council, which is composed of 10 representatives of the public and 10 from the member newspapers in addition to a neutral chairman, has an annual budget of approximately $100,000 provided by the member newspapers.

Quebec and Alberta also have press councils. Quebec's was formed in 1973 and Alberta's in 1972. The Alberta Council includes five of the province's seven daily newspapers.]

BIBLIOGRAPHY

Public Opinion and Polling

Albig, W., *Modern Public Opinion,* New York, McG.-H., 1956.

Bellavance, M., and Gilbert, M., *L'Opinion publique et la crise d'octobre,* Montréal, Éditions du Jour, 1971.

Bogart, L., *Silent Politics: Polls and the Awareness of Public Opinion,* New York, Wiley, 1972.

Christenson, R.M., and McWilliams, R.O., (eds.), *Voice of the People,* New York, McG.-H., 1967.

Dion, L., "Democracy as Perceived by Public Opinion Analysis," *C.J.E.P.S.,* XXVIII, 4, November, 1962.

Dion, L., "Régimes d'opinions publiques et systèmes idéologiques," *Écrits du Canada Français,* XII, 1962.

Fenton, J.M., *In Your Opinion,* Boston, Little, Brown, 1960.

Gallup, G., *A Guide to Public Opinion Polls,* Princeton, Princeton University Press, 1948, 2nd ed.

Gallup, G.H., *The Sophisticated Poll Watcher's Guide,* Princeton, 1972.

Gallup, G., and Rae, S.F., *The Pulse of Democracy: The Public Opinion Poll and How It Works,* New York, Simon and Schuster, 1940.

Hennessy, B.C., *Public Opinion,* Belmont, California, Wadsworth, 1965.

Katz, D., *et al.,* (eds.), *Public Opinion and Propaganda,* New York, H.R.W., 1960.

Kish, L., *Survey Sampling,* New York, John Wiley, 1965.

Lane, R.E., and Sears, D.O., *Public Opinion,* Englewood Cliffs, N.J., P.-H., 1964.

LeDuc, L., "The Measurement of Public Opinion," in H.R. Penniman, (ed.), *Canada at the Polls: The General Election of 1974,* Washington, AEIPPR, 1975.

Lippmann, W., *Public Opinion,* New York, Macmillan, 1960.

Lipset, S.M., "Polling and Science," *C.J.E.P.S.,* XV, 2, May, 1949, and *ibid.,* XVI, 3, August, 1950.

Maghami, F.G., "Political Knowledge among Youth: Some Notes on Public Opinion Formation," *C.J.P.S.,* VII, 2, June, 1974.

Mendelsohn, H., and Crespie, I., *Polls, Television and the New Politics,* Scranton, Chandler, 1979.

Pinard, M., "A House Divided," (A review of poll results re sovereignty association, 1962-80), *Report on Confederation*, 3, 6, May, 1980.

Qualter, T.H., "The Manipulation of Popular Impulse, Graham Wallas Revisited," *C.J.E.P.S.*, XXV, 2, May, 1959.

Qualter, T.H., *Propaganda and Psychological Warfare*, New York, Random House, 1962.

Regenstreif, S.P., *The Diefenbaker Interlude: Parties and Voting in Canada, An Interpretation*, Toronto, Longman, 1965.

Rogers, L., *The Pollsters, Public Opinion, Politics, and Democratic Leadership*, New York, Alfred A. Knopf, 1949.

Roll, C.W., and Cantril, A.H., *Polls: Their Use and Misuse in Politics*, New York, Basic Books, 1971.

Roper, E.B., *You and Your Leaders, Their Actions and Your Reactions*, New York, William Morrow, 1958.

Schneck, R., Russell, D., and Scott, K., "The Effects of Ruralism, Bureaucratic Structure, and Economic Role on Right-Wing Extremism," *C.J.P.S.*, VII, 1, March, 1974.

Schwartz, M., *Public Opinion and Canadian Identity*, Scarborough, F. and W., 1967.

Teer, F., and Spence, J.D., *Political Opinion Polls*, London, Hutchinson, 1973.

Webster, N., "Moving Toward Poll Ban," *The Globe and Mail*, May 4, 1978.

Wheeler, M., *Lies, Damn Lies, and Statistics: The Manipulation of Public Opinion in America*, New York, Liveright, 1974.

Pressure Groups and Lobbying

(See also Bibliography in Chapter 1, Social Issues)

Abella, I., (ed.), *On Strike*, Toronto, J.L.S., 1974.

Berry, G.R., "The Oil Lobby and the Energy Crisis," *C.P.A.*, 17, 4, Winter, 1974.

Blishen, B.R., *Doctors & Doctrines: The Ideology of Medical Care in Canada*, Toronto, U.T.P., 1969.

Clark, S.D., *The Canadian Manufacturers' Association: A Study in Collective Bargaining and Political Pressure*, Toronto, U.T.P., 1939.

Dawson, H.H., "An Interest Group: The Canadian Federation of Agriculture," *C.P.A.*, III, 2, June, 1960.

Dawson, H.J., "The Consumers' Association of Canada," *C.P.A.*, VI, 1, March, 1963.

Dawson, H.J., "Relations between Farm Organizations and the Civil Service in Canada and Great Britain," *C.P.A.*, X, 4, December, 1967.

Dion, L., *Société et politique: la vie des groupes. Dynamique de la société libérale*, Québec, Les Presses de l'Université Laval, 1972.

Dion, L., *Les groupes et la pouvoir politique aux Etats-Unis*, Québec, Les Presses de l'Université Laval, 1965.

Dion, L., *Le Bill 60 et la société québécoise*, Montréal, Ed. HMH, 1967.

Dion, L., "A la recherche d'une méthode d'analyse des partis et des groupes d'intérêt," *C.J.P.S.*, II, 1, March, 1969.

Dion, L., "Politique consultative et système politique," *C.J.P.S.*, II, 2, June, 1969.

Englemann, F.A., and Schwartz, M.A., *Political Parties and the Canadian Social Structure*, Toronto, P.-H., 1967.

Friedland, M.L., "Pressure Groups and the Development of the Criminal Law," in Glazebrook, P.R., (ed.), *Reshaping the Criminal Law: Essays in Honour of Glanville Williams*, London, 1978.

Goldstein, J., "Public Interest Groups and Public Policy: The Case of the Consumers' Association of Canada," *C.J.P.S.*, XII, 1, March, 1979.

Granatstein, G., *Marlborough Marathon: One Street Against a Developer*, Toronto, Hakkert and J.L.S., 1971.

Horowitz, G., *Canadian Labour in Politics*, Toronto, U.T.P., 1968.

Kwavnick, D., "Pressure-Group Demands and the Struggle for Organizational Status: The Case of Organized Labour in Canada," *C.J.P.S.*, III, 1, March, 1970.

Kwavnick, D., *Organized Labour and Pressure Politics: The Canadian Labour Congress, 1956-1968*, Montreal, McG.-Q.U.P., 1972.

Kwavnick, D., "Pressure-Group Demand and Organizational Objectives: The CNTU, the Lapalme Affaire, and National Bargaining Units," *C.J.P.S.*, VI, 4, December, 1973.

Lang, R., *The Politics of Drugs: A Comparative Pressure-Group Study of the Canadian Pharmaceutical Manufacturers Association and the Association of the British Pharmaceutical Industry (1930-1970)*, London, Saxon House, 1974.

Litvak, I.A., and Maule, C.J., "Interest-Group Tactics and the Politics of Foreign Investment: The Time-Reader's Digest Case Study," *C.J.P.S.*, VII, 4, December, 1974.

Manzer, R., "Selective Inducements and the Development of Pressure Groups: The Case of Canadian Teachers' Associations," *C.J.P.S.*, II, 1, March, 1969.

Phillips, D., *Interest Groups and Intergovernmental Relations: Language Policy-Making in Canada*, Discussion Paper 3, Kingston, I.I.R., Queen's University, 1978.

Presthus, R., *Elites in the Policy Process*, Toronto, Macmillan, 1974.

Presthus, R., *Elite Accommodation in Canadian Politics*, Toronto, Macmillan, 1973.

Presthus, R., "Interest Groups and the Canadian Parliament: Activities, Interaction, Legitimacy, and Influence," *C.J.P.S.*, IV, 4, December, 1971.

Pross, A.P., "Canadian Pressure Groups in the 1970s: Their Role and Their Relations with the Public Service," *C.P.A.*, 18, 1, Spring, 1975.

Pross, A.P., (ed.), *Pressure Group Behaviour in Canadian Politics*, Toronto, McG.-H.R., 1975.

Rusk, J., et al., "The Lobbyists — A Booming Trade at the Ear of Government," *The Globe and Mail*, October 25, 27, 28, 1981.

Stanbury, W.T., *Business Interests and the Reform of Canadian Competition Policy, 1971-1975*, Toronto, Methuen, 1977.

Tardif, G., *Police et politique au Québec*, Montréal, Les éditions de l'aurore, 1974.

Taylor, M.G., "The Role of the Medical Profession in the Formulation and Execution of Public Policy," *C.J.E.P.S.*, XXVI, 1, February, 1960.

Thompson, F., and Stanbury, W.T., *The Political Economy of Interest Groups in the Legislative Process in Canada*, Toronto, Butterworths, 1979.

Thorburn, H.G., "Pressure Groups in Canadian Politics: Recent Revisions of the Anti-Combines Legislation," *C.J.E.P.S.*, XXX, 2, May, 1964.

Woods, H.D., *Labour Policy in Canada*, Toronto, Macmillan, 1973.

Participation

(See also Bibliographies, Chapters 1, 8, 10)

Budden, and Ernst, J., *The Movable Airport*, Toronto, Hakkert, 1973.

Carter, A., *Direct Action and Liberal Democracy*, Don Mills, Ontario, Musson, 1973.

Connor, D.M., *Citizens Participate — An Action Guide for Public Issues*, Oakville, Ontario, Development Press, n.d.

Draper, J.A., (ed.), *Citizen Participation in Canada*, Toronto, New Press, 1971.

Greason, G.K., and King, R.C., *The Citizen and Local Government*, Toronto, Macmillan, rev. ed., 1967.

Hunnius, G., *Participatory Democracy for Canada*, Montreal, Black Rose, 1971.

Keating, D., *The Power to Make It Happen*, Toronto, Green Tree, 1977.

MacKinnon, F., *Postures and Politics: Some Observations on Participatory Democracy*, Toronto, U.T.P., 1973.

Massey, H.J., *People or Planes*, Toronto, C.C., 1972.

Massey, H., and Godfrey, C., *People and Places*, Toronto, C.C., 1972.

New Brunswick, *Participation and Development: The New Brunswick Task Force Report on Social Development and Social Welfare*, Fredericton, Q.P., 1971.

Pateman, C., *Participation and Democratic Theory*, Toronto, Macmillan, 1970.

Schindeler, F., and Lanphier, C., "Social Science Research and Participatory Democracy in Canada," *C.P.A.*, XII, 4, Winter, 1969.

Sproule-Jones, M., and Hart, K.D., "Political Participation," *C.J.P.S.*, VI, 2, June, 1973.

Vrooman, P.C., "Power Dilemma in Citizen Participation," *Canadian Welfare*, 48, 3, May-June, 1972.

Wilson, H.B., *Democracy and the Work Place*, Montreal, Black Rose, 1974.

The Media

Adam, G.S., (ed.), *Journalism, Communication and the Law*, Toronto, P.-H., 1975.

Audley, P., *Voices of Our Own: A Study of Canada's Communication Industries*, Toronto, Lorimer, 1981.

Babe, R.E., "Public and Private Regulation of Cable Television: A Case Study of Technological Change and Relative Power," *C.P.A.*, 17, 2, Summer, 1974.

Bellan, R., "Newspaper Monopoly-Busting: The Case for Public Funding of Competition by Second Papers," *Policy Options*, 2, 1, March-April, 1981.

Boorstin, D.J., *The Image: A Guide to Pseudo-Events in America*, New York, Harper and Row, 1964.

Braddon, R., *Roy Thomson of Fleet Street*, London, Fontana Books, 1968.

Briggs, E.D., Romanow, W.I., Soderlund, W.G., Wagenberg, R.H., "Television News and the 1979 Canadian Federal Election," a paper presented at the Founding Meeting of the Canadian Communication Association, Montreal, June, 1980.

Bruce, C., *News and the Southams*, Toronto, Macmillan, 1968.

Cabatoff, K., "Radio-Québec: une institution publique a la recherche d'une mission," *C.P.A.*, 19, 4, Winter, 1976.

Canada, *Report of the Royal Commission on Publications*, [O'Leary Report], Ottawa, Q.P., 1961.

Canada, *Royal Commission on Newspapers*, [Kent Commission], Ottawa, S. and S., 1981.

Canada, Senate, *Report of the Special Senate Committee on Mass Media*, [Davey Report], 3 vols., Ottawa, Q.P., 1970.

Canadian Facts Ltd., *Report of a Study of the Daily Newspaper in Canada and its Reading Public*, Toronto, 1962.

Canadian Study of Parliament Group, *Seminar on Press and Parliament: Adversaries or Accomplices?*, Ottawa, Q.P., April, 1980.

Chodos, R., and Murphy, R., (eds.), *Let Us Prey*, Toronto, James Lorimer, 1974.

Cocking, C., *Following the Leaders: A Media Watcher's Diary of Campaign '79*, Toronto, Doubleday, 1980.

Cook, R., *The Politics of John W. Dafoe and the Free Press*, Toronto, U.T.P., 1963.

Donnelly, W., *Dafoe of the Free Press*, Toronto, Macmillan, 1968.

Eggleston, W., "The Press in Canada," *The Royal Commission on National Development in the Arts, Letters, and Sciences,* [Massey Report], Ottawa, K.P., 1951.

Ferguson, G.V., and Underhill, F.H., *Press and Party in Canada: Issues of Freedom,* Toronto, Ryerson, 1955.

Fletcher, F.J., "The Contest for Media Attention: The 1979 and 1980 Federal Election Campaigns," in Reader's Digest Foundation, *Politics and the Media,* Montreal, 1981.

Fletcher, F.J., "The Mass Media in the 1974 Election," in Penniman, H.R., (ed.), *Canada at the Polls: The General Election of 1974,* Washington, AEI, 1975.

Gordon, D.R., *Language, Logic, and the Mass Media,* Toronto, H.R.W., 1966.

Gordon, D.R., *National News in Canadian Newspapers,* Report for the Royal Commission on Bilingualism and Biculturalism, Ottawa, May, 1966.

Gow, J.I., "Les Québécois, la guerre et la paix, 1945-1960," *C.J.P.S.,* III, 1, March, 1970.

Hamlin, D.L.B., (ed.), *The Press and the Public,* Toronto, U.T.P., 1962.

Harkness, R., *J.E. Atkinson of the Star,* Toronto, U.T.P., 1963.

Hunt, R., and Campbell, R., *K.C. Irving: The Art of the Industrialist,* Toronto, M. & S., 1973.

Irving, J.A., (ed.), *Mass Media in Canada,* Toronto, Ryerson, 1962.

Kesterton, W.H., *A History of Journalism in Canada,* Toronto, Carleton Library, M. & S., 1967.

Levy, H.P., *The Press Council: History, Procedure and Cases,* Toronto, Macmillan, 1967.

Lyman, P., *Canadian Culture and the New Technology,* Toronto, Lorimer, 1981.

MacDonald, D., (ed.), *Confederation Dialogue: The Press and the Confederation Debate,* Montreal, Canadian Daily Newspaper Publishers Association, 1978.

McDayter, W., *A Media Mosaic: Canadian Communications Through a Critical Eye,* Toronto, H.R.W., 1971.

McLuhan, M., *Understanding Media,* New York, McG.-H., 1964.

Ontario Press Council, *8th Annual Report, 1980,* Ottawa, 1981. (Previous Reports for 1972-1973 to 1979).

Peers, F.W., *The Politics of Canadian Broadcasting, 1920-1951,* Toronto, U.T.P., 1969.

Peers, F.W., *The Public Eye: Television and the Politics of Canadian Broadcasting, 1952-1968,* Toronto, U.T.P., 1978.

Reader's Digest Foundation and Erindale College, *Politics and the Media,* Reader's Digest Foundation, Montreal, 1981.

Robinson, G.J., and Theall, D.F., *Studies in Canadian Communications,* Montreal, McGill University, 1975.

Royal Society of Canada, *Special Symposium on Communications into the Home,* Ottawa, 1972.

Rutherford, P., *The Making of the Canadian Media,* Toronto, McG.-H.R., 1978.

Salter, L., *Dimensions of the Message: Communication Studies in Canada,* Toronto, Butterworths, 1981.

Shea, A., *Broadcasting: The Canadian Way,* Montreal, Harvest House, 1963.

Singer, D.B., *Communications in Canadian Society,* Toronto, C.C., 2nd ed. rev., 1975.

Soderlund, W.C., Wagenberg, R.H., Briggs, E.D., and Nelson, R.C., "Regional and Linguistic Agenda-Setting in Canada: A Study of Newspaper Coverage of Issues Affecting Political Integration in 1976," *C.J.P.S.,* XIII, 2, June, 1980.

Stewart, W., (ed.), *Canadian Newspapers: The Inside Story,* Edmonton, Hurtig, 1980.

Toogood, A., *Broadcasting in Canada*, Ottawa, Canadian Association of Broadcasters, 1969.

Trueman, P., *Smoke and Mirrors: The Inside Story of Television News in Canada*, Toronto, M. & S., 1980.

Wagenberg, R.H., and Soderlund, W.G., "A Content Analysis of Editorial Coverage of the 1972 Election Campaigns in Canada and the United States," *The Western Political Quarterly*, XXVIII, March, 1975.

Wagenberg, R.H., and Soderlund, W.G., "The Effects of Chain Ownership on Editorial Coverage: The Case of the 1974 Canadian Federal Election," *C.J.P.S.*, IX, 4, December, 1976.

Wagenberg, R.H., and Soderlund, W.G., "The Influence of Chain Ownership on Editorial Comment in Canada," *Journalism Quarterly*, 52, Spring, 1975.

Weir, E.A., *The Struggle for National Broadcasting in Canada*, Toronto, M. & S., 1965.

Zolf, L., *Dance of the Dialectic*, Toronto, J.L.S., 1973.

8

POLITICAL PARTIES

More has been published on the subject of political parties than on almost any other aspect of Canadian politics, as the length of the bibliography in this section indicates. Three books in the McGraw-Hill Ryerson Series in Canadian Politics should be consulted in connection with this chapter. They are William Christian and Colin Campbell, *Political Parties and Ideologies in Canada: Liberals, Conservatives, Socialists, Nationalists,* Toronto, 1974, Conrad Winn and John McMenemy, *Political Parties in Canada,* Toronto, 1976, and Joseph Wearing, *The L-Shaped Party, The Liberal Party of Canada, 1958-1980,* Toronto, 1981.

This chapter begins with an edited version of one of the most popular recent scholarly articles which deals with political parties: Alan Cairns' provocative analysis of "The Electoral System and the Party System in Canada."

The remainder of the chapter is devoted to explanations and critiques of the party system and to descriptions of the ideologies of our three principal federal parties. Professor McLeod's article summarizes the major interpretations of the Canadian party system while the essay by the editor sketches briefly the historical evolution and problems of our main parties. Flora MacDonald's reflective critique of our parties' performance, which appeared in the third edition, pp. 227-230, has been omitted here. Mr. Roussopoulos, who is identified with the New Left, denounces the whole system as outmoded.

In the domain of ideology, Robert L. Stanfield, the recent leader of the federal Conservative party, gives his appreciation of the principles and philosophy of modern Canadian Conservatism, while the late Prime Minister Lester B. Pearson does the same for Liberalism. Another former national party leader, David Lewis of the N.D.P., analyzes contemporary socialism. The N.D.P. Waffle Manifesto and David Lewis' reply to it, which appeared in the third edition, pp. 242-247, have been omitted.

Three charts indicate the constitutional organization of the Liberal, Conservative, and New Democratic parties.

The long bibliography is divided into four sections: federal parties and politics, provincial politics, city politics and political biographies.

THE ELECTORAL SYSTEM AND THE PARTY SYSTEM IN CANADA, 1921-1965*

Alan C. Cairns

This paper investigates two common assumptions about the party system: (i) that the influence of the electoral system on the party system has been unimportant, or non-existent: and (ii) that the party system has been an important nationalizing agency with respect to the sectional cleavages widely held to constitute the most significant and enduring lines of division in the Canadian polity. Schattschneider, Lipset, Duverger, Key and others have cogently asserted the relevance of electoral systems for the understanding of party systems. Students of Canadian parties, however, have all but ignored the electoral system as an explanatory factor of any importance. The analysis to follow will suggest that the electoral system has played a major role in the evolution of Canadian parties, and that the claim that the party system has been an important instrument for integrating Canadians across sectional lines is highly suspect.

• • •

The Basic Defence of the System and its Actual Performance

If the electoral system is analyzed in terms of the basic virtue attributed to it — the creation of artificial legislative majorities to produce cabinet stability — its performance since 1921 has been only mediocre. Table 1 reveals the consistent tendency of the electoral system in every election from 1921 to 1965 to give the government party a greater percentage of seats than of votes. However, its contribution to one-party majorities was much less dramatic. Putting aside the two instances, 1940 and 1958, when a boost

TABLE 1   Percentages of Votes and Seats for Government Party, 1921-1965

	% Votes	% Seats		% Votes	% Seats
1921	40.7	49.4(L)	1949	49.5	73.7(L)
1925†	39.8	40.4(L)	1953	48.9	64.5(L)
1926	46.1	52.2(L)	1957	38.9	42.3(C)
1930	48.7	55.9(C)	1958	53.6	78.5(C)
1935	44.9	70.6(L)	1962	37.3	43.8(C)
1940	51.5	73.9(L)	1963	41.7	48.7(L)
1945	41.1	51.0(L)	1965	40.2	49.4(L)

† In this election the Conservatives received both a higher percentage of votes, 46.5%, and of seats, 47.3%, than the Liberals. The Liberals, however, chose to meet Parliament, and with Progressive support they retained office for several months.

Note: The data for this and the following tables have been compiled from Howard A. Scarrow, *Canada Votes* (New Orleans, 1963), and from the *Report of the Chief Electoral Officer* for recent elections.

* From the *Canadian Journal of Political Science*, I, 1, March, 1968. By permission of the author and publisher.

from the electoral system was unnecessary, it transformed a minority of votes into a majority of seats on only six of twelve occasions. It is possible that changes in the party system and/or in the distribution of party support will render the justification increasingly anachronistic in future years.

If the assessment of the electoral system is extended to include not only its contribution to one-party majorities, but its contribution to the maintenance of effective opposition, arbitrarily defined as at least one-third of House members, it appears in an even less satisfactory light. On four occasions, two of which occurred when the government party had slightly more than one-half of the votes, the opposition was reduced to numerical ineffectiveness. The coupling of these two criteria together creates a reasonable measure for the contribution of the electoral system to a working parliamentary system, which requires both a stable majority and an effective opposition. From this vantage point the electoral system has a failure rate of 71 per cent, on ten of fourteen occasions.

● ● ●

The Effect on Major and Minor Parties

Table 2 indicates an important effect of the electoral system with its proof that discrimination for and against the parties does not become increasingly severe when the parties are ordered from most votes to least votes. Discrimination in favour of a party was more pronounced for the weakest party on seven occasions, and for the strongest party on seven occasions. In the four elections from 1921 to 1930 inclusive, with three party contestants, the second part was most hurt by the electoral system. In the five elections from 1935 to 1953 inclusive, the electoral system again worked against the middle ranking parties and favoured the parties with the weakest and strongest voting support. In the five elections from 1957 to 1965 inclusive, there has been a noticeable tendency to benefit the first two parties, with the exception of the fourth party, Social Credit in 1957, at the expense of the smaller parties.

The explanation for the failure of the electoral system to act with Darwinian logic by consistently distributing its rewards to the large parties and its penalties to the small parties is relatively straightforward. The bias in favour of the strongest party reflects the likelihood that the large number of votes it has at its disposal will produce enough victories in individual constituencies to give it, on a percentage basis, a surplus of seats over votes. The fact that this surplus has occurred with only one exception, 1957, indicates the extreme unlikelihood of the strongest party having a distribution of partisan support capable of transforming the electoral system from an ally into a foe. The explanation for the favourable impact of the electoral system on the Progressives and Social Credit from 1921 to 1957 when they were the weakest parties is simply that they were sectional parties that concentrated their efforts in their areas of strength where the electoral system worked in their favour. Once the electoral system has rewarded the strongest party and a weak party with concentrated sectional strength, there are not many more seats to go around. In this kind of party system, which Canada had from

1921 to Mr. Diefenbaker's breakthrough, serious discrimination against the second party in a three-party system and the second and third party in a four-party system is highly likely.

TABLE 2   Bias of Electoral System in Translating Votes into Seats

Year	Rank order of parties in terms of percentages of vote				
	1	2	3	4	5
1921	Libs. 1.21	Cons. 0.70	Progs. 1.20		
1925	Cons. 1.017	Libs. 1.015	Progs. 1.09		
1926	Libs. 1.13	Cons. 0.82	Progs. 1.55		
1930	Cons. 1.15	Libs. 0.82	Progs. 1.53		
1935	Libs. 1.57	Cons. 0.55	CCF 0.33	Rec. 0.05	Socred 1.68
1940	Libs. 1.43	Cons. 0.53	CCF 0.39	Socred 1.52	
1945	Libs. 1.24	Cons. 1.00	CCF 0.73	Socred 1.29	
1949	Libs. 1.49	Cons. 0.53	CCF 0.37	Socred 1.03	
1953	Libs. 1.32	Cons. 0.62	CCF 0.77	Socred 1.06	
1957	Libs. 0.97	Cons. 1.087	CCF 0.88	Socred 1.091	
1958	Cons. 1.46	Libs. 0.55	CCF 0.32	Socred 0	
1962	Cons. 1.17	Libs. 1.01	NDP 0.53	Socred 0.97	
1963	Libs. 1.17	Cons. 1.09	NDP 0.49	Socred 0.76	
1965	Libs. 1.23	Cons. 1.13	NDP 0.44	Cred. 0.72	Socred 1.51

Independents and very small parties have been excluded from the table.

The measurement of discrimination employed in this table defines the relationship between the percentage of votes and the percentage of seats. The figure is devised by dividing the former into the latter. Thus 1 — (38% seats/38% votes), for example — represents a neutral effect for the electoral system. Any figure above 1 — (40% seats/20% votes) = 2.0, for example — indicates discrimination for the party. A figure below 1 — (20% seats/40% votes) = 0.5, for example — indicates discrimination against the party. For the purposes of the table the ranking of the parties as 1, 2, 3 . . . is based on their percentage of the vote, since to rank them in terms of seats would conceal the very bias it is sought to measure — namely the bias introduced by the intervening variable of the electoral system which constitutes the mechanism by which votes are translated into seats.

Table 3 reveals that the electoral system positively favours minor parties with sectional strongholds and discourages minor parties with diffuse support. The classic example of the latter phenomenon is provided by the Reconstruction party in the 1935 election. For its 8.7 per cent of the vote it was rewarded with one seat, and promptly disappeared from the scene. Yet its electoral support was more than twice that of Social Credit which gained seventeen seats, and only marginally less than that of the CCF which gained seven seats. The case of the Reconstruction party provides dramatic illustration of the futility of party effort for a minor party which lacks a sectional stronghold. The treatment of the CCF/NDP by the electoral system is only slightly less revealing. This party with diffuse support which aspired to national and major party status never received as many seats as would have been "justified" by its voting support, and on six occasions out of ten received less than half the seats to which it was "entitled." The contrasting treatment of Social Credit and the Progressives, sectional minor parties, by the electoral system clearly reveals the bias of the electoral system in favour of concentrated support and against diffused support.

TABLE 3   Minor Parties: Percentages of Seats and Votes

	Progressives		Reconstruction		CCF/NDP		Soc. Credit		Créditiste	
	votes	seats	votes	seats	votes	seats	votes	seats	votes	seats
1921	23.1	27.7								
1925	9.0	9.8								
1926	5.3	8.2								
1930	3.2	4.9								
1935			8.7	0.4	8.9	2.9	4.1	6.9		
1940					8.5	3.3	2.7	4.1		
1945					15.6	11.4	4.1	5.3		
1949					13.4	5.0	3.7	3.8		
1953					11.3	8.7	5.4	5.7		
1957					10.7	9.4	6.6	7.2		
1958					9.5	3.0	2.6	—		
1962					13.5	7.2	11.7	11.3		
1963					13.1	6.4	11.9	9.1		
1965					17.9	7.9	3.7	1.9	4.7	3.4

Distortion in Party Parliamentary Representation

No less important than the general differences in the way the electoral system rewards or punishes each individual party as such, is the manner in which it fashions particular patterns of sectional representation within the ranks of the parliamentary parties out of the varying distributions of electoral support they received. This sectional intra-party discrimination affects all parties. The electoral system consistently minimized the Ontario support of the Progressives which provided the party with 43.5 per cent, 39.7 per cent, and 29.4 per cent of its total votes in the first three elections of the twenties. The party received only 36.9 per cent, 8.3 per cent, and 10 per cent of its total seats from that province. Further, by its varying treatment of the party's electoral support from Manitoba, Saskatchewan, and Alberta it finally helped to reduce the Progressives to an Alberta party.

An analysis of CCF/NDP votes and seats clearly illustrates the manner in which the electoral system has distorted the parliamentary wing of the party. Table 4 reveals the extreme discrimination visited on Ontario supporters of the CCF from 1935 to 1957. With the exception of 1940, CCF Ontario voting support consistently constituted between 30 and 40 per cent of total CCF voting support. Yet, the contribution of Ontario to CCF parliamentary representation was derisory. During the same period there was a marked overrepresentation of Saskatchewan in the CCF caucus. The 1945 election is indicative. The 260,000 votes from Ontario, 31.9 per cent of the total CCF vote, produced no seats at all, while 167,000 supporters from Saskatchewan, 20.5 per cent of the total party vote, were rewarded with eighteen seats, 64.3 per cent of total party seats. In these circumstances it was not surprising that observers were led to mislabel the CCF an agrarian party.

The major parties are not immune from the tendency of the electoral system to make the parliamentary parties grossly inaccurate reflections of the sectional distribution of party support. Table 5 makes it clear that the electoral system has been far from impartial in its treatment of Liberal and

TABLE 4   Percentages of Total CCF/NDP Strength, in Seats and Votes coming from
Selected Provinces

	N.S.	Que.	Ont.	Man.	Sask.	Alta.	B.C.
1935 votes	—	1.9	32.7	13.9	18.8	7.9	24.8
seats	—	—	—	28.6	28.6	—	42.9
1940 votes	4.5	1.9	15.6	15.6	27.0	8.9	26.2
seats	12.5	—	—	12.5	62.5	—	12.5
1945 votes	6.4	4.1	31.9	12.5	20.5	7.0	15.4
seats	3.6	—	—	17.9	64.3	—	14.3
1949 votes	4.3	2.3	39.2	10.6	19.5	4.0	18.6
seats	7.7	—	7.7	23.1	38.5	—	23.1
1953 votes	3.5	3.7	33.4	10.1	24.6	3.7	19.7
seats	4.3	—	4.3	13.0	47.8	—	30.4
1957 votes	2.4	4.5	38.7	11.6	19.8	3.8	18.6
seats	—	—	12.0	20.0	40.0	—	28.0
1958 votes	2.7	6.6	37.9	10.8	16.3	2.8	22.2
seats	—	—	37.5	—	12.5	—	50.0
1962 votes	3.8	8.9	44.0	7.4	9.0	4.1	20.4
seats	5.3	—	31.6	10.5	—	—	52.6
1963 votes	2.6	14.6	42.6	6.4	7.3	3.4	21.5
seats	—	—	35.3	11.8	—	—	52.9
1965 votes	2.8	17.7	43.0	6.6	7.6	3.2	17.3
seats	—	—	42.9	14.3	—	—	42.9

Note: Percentages of votes do not total 100 horizontally because the table does not include
Newfoundland, Prince Edward Island, New Brunswick, or the territories where the
CCF/NDP gained a few votes but no seats.

TABLE 5   Liberals and Conservatives: Percentages of Total Parliamentary Strength and
Total Electoral Support from Quebec and Ontario

	Conservatives				Liberals			
	Ontario		Quebec		Ontario		Quebec	
	seats	votes	seats	votes	seats	votes	seats	votes
1921	74.0	47.1	—	15.5	18.1	26.6	56.0	43.8
1925	58.6	47.4	3.4	18.4	11.1	30.1	59.6	37.8
1926	58.2	44.9	4.4	18.7	20.3	31.7	46.9	33.4
1930	43.1	38.9	17.5	24.0	24.2	33.7	44.0	30.6
1935	62.5	43.1	12.5	24.7	32.4	34.4	31.8	31.5
1940	62.5	48.6	2.5	16.4	31.5	34.4	33.7	31.2
1945	71.6	52.7	3.0	8.3	27.2	34.6	42.4	33.3
1949	61.0	43.6	4.9	22.6	29.0	31.9	35.2	33.2
1953	64.7	44.2	7.8	26.0	29.8	32.6	38.6	34.2
1957	54.5	42.9	8.0	21.7	20.0	31.1	59.0	38.1
1958	32.2	36.2	24.0	25.7	30.6	33.3	51.0	37.8
1962	30.2	36.9	12.1	21.6	44.0	39.2	35.0	28.6
1963	28.4	37.8	8.4	16.0	40.3	39.1	36.4	29.3
1965	25.8	37.4	8.2	17.3	38.9	38.6	42.7	30.0

Conservative voting support from Ontario and Quebec. For fourteen consecutive elections covering nearly half a century, there was a consistent and
usually marked overrepresentation of Quebec in the parliamentary Liberal
party and marked underrepresentation in the parliamentary Conservative

party, with the exception of 1958. For ten consecutive elections from 1921 to 1957, Ontario was consistently and markedly overrepresented in the parliamentary Conservative party, and for eleven consecutive elections from 1921 to 1958, there was consistent, but less marked, underrepresentation of Ontario in the parliamentary Liberal party. Thus the electoral system, by pulling the parliamentary Liberal party toward Quebec and the parliamentary Conservative party toward Ontario, made the sectional cleavages between the parties much more pronounced in Parliament than they were at the level of the electorate.

The way in which the electoral system affected the relationship of Quebec to the parliamentary wings of the two major parties is evident in the truly startling discrepancies between votes and seats for the two parties from that province. From 1921 to 1965 inclusive, the Liberals gained 752 members from Quebec, and the Conservatives only 135. The ratio of 5.6 Liberals to each Conservative in the House of Commons contrasts sharply with the 1.9 to 1 ratio of Liberals to Conservatives at the level of voters.

Given the recurrent problems concerning the status of Quebec in Canadian federalism and the consistent tension in French-English relations, it is self-evident that the effects of the electoral system noted above can be appropriately described as divisive and detrimental to national unity. . . . The electoral system has placed serious barriers in the way of the Conservative party's attempts to gain parliamentary representation from a province where its own interests and those of national unity coincided on the desirability of making a major contender for public office as representative as possible. The frequent thesis that the association of the Conservatives with conscription in 1917 destroyed their prospects in Quebec only becomes meaningful when it is noted that a particular electoral system presided over that destruction.

The following basic effects of the electoral system have been noted. The electoral system has not been impartial in its translation of votes into seats. Its benefits have been disproportionately given to the strongest major party and a weak sectional party. The electoral system has made a major contribution to the identification of particular sections/provinces with particular parties. It has undervalued the partisan diversity within each section/province. By so doing it has rendered the parliamentary composition of each party less representative of the sectional interests in the political system than is the party electorate from which that representation is derived. The electoral system favours minor parties with concentrated sectional support, and discourages those with diffuse national support. The electoral system has consistently exaggerated the significance of cleavages demarcated by sectional/provincial boundaries and has thus tended to transform contests between parties into contests between sections/provinces. . . .

Party System as a Nationalizing Agency

. . . One of the most widespread interpretations of the party system claims that it, or at least the two major parties, functions as a great unifying or nationalizing agency. Canadian politics, it is emphasized, are politics of moderation, or brokerage politics, which minimize differences, restrain fissiparous tendencies, and thus over time help knit together the diverse interests of a polity weak in integration. It is noteworthy that this brokerage theory is almost exclusively applied to the reconciliation of sectional, racial, and religious divisions, the latter two frequently being regarded as simply more specific versions of the first with respect to French-English relations. The theory of brokerage politics thus assumes that the historically significant cleavages in Canada are sectional, reflecting the federal nature of Canadian society, or racial/religious, reflecting a continuation of the struggle which attracted Durham's attention in the mid-nineteenth century. Brokerage politics between classes is mentioned, if at all, as an afterthought.

The interpretation of the party system in terms of its fulfilment of a nationalizing function is virtually universal. Close scrutiny, however, indicates that this is at best questionable, and possibly invalid. It is difficult to determine the precise meaning of the argument that the party system has been a nationalizing agency, stressing what Canadians have in common, bringing together representatives of diverse interests to deliberate on government policies. In an important sense the argument is misleading in that it attributes to the party system what is simply inherent in a representative democracy which inevitably brings together Nova Scotians, Albertans, and Quebeckers to a common assemblage point, and because of the majoritarian necessities of the parliamentary system requires agreement among contending interests to accomplish anything at all. Or, to put it differently, the necessity for inter-group collaboration in any on-going political system makes it possible to claim of any party system compatible with the survival of the polity that it acts as a nationalizing agency. The extent to which any particular party system does so act is inescapably therefore a comparative question or a question of degree. In strict logic an evaluation of alternative types of party systems is required before a particular one can be accorded unreserved plaudits for the success with which it fulfils a nationalizing function.

. . . The basic approach of this paper is that the party system, importantly conditioned by the electoral system, exacerbates the very cleavages it is credited with healing. As a corollary it is suggested that the party system is not simply a reflection of sectionalism, but that sectionalism is also a reflection of the party system.

The electoral system has helped to foster a particular kind of political style by the special significance it accords to sectionalism. This is evident in party campaign strategy, in party politics, in intersectional differences in the nature and vigour of party activity, and in differences in the intra-party socialization experiences of parliamentary personnel of the various parties. As a consequence the electoral system has had an important effect on perceptions of the party system and, by extension, the political system itself. Sectionalism has been rendered highly visible because the electoral system makes it a fruitful basis on which to organize electoral support. Divisions cutting through sections, particularly those based on the class system, have been much less salient because the possibility of payoffs in terms of representation has been minimal.

Parties and Campaign Strategy

An initial perspective on the contribution of the parties to sectionalism is provided by some of the basic aspects of campaign strategy. Inadequate attention has been paid to the extent to which the campaign activities of the parties have exacerbated the hatreds, fears, and insecurities related to divisive sectional and ethnic cleavages.

The basic cleavage throughout Canadian history concerns Quebec, or more precisely that part of French Canada resident in Quebec, and its relationships with the rest of the country. The evidence suggests that elections have fed on racial fears and insecurities, rather than reduced them. The three post-war elections of 1921, 1925, and 1926 produced overwhelming Liberal majorities at the level of seats in Quebec, 65 out of 65 in 1921, 59 out of 65 in 1925, and 60 seats out of 65 in 1926. . . . In view of the ample evidence documented by Graham and Neatby of the extent to which the Liberal campaigns stirred up the animosities and insecurities of French Canada, it is difficult to assert that the party system performed a unifying role in a province where historic tensions were potentially divisive. The fact that the Liberals were able to "convince Quebec" that they were its only defenders and that their party contained members of both ethnic groups after the elections scarcely constitutes refutation when attention is directed to the methods employed to achieve this end, and when it is noted that the election results led to the isolation of Canada's second great party from Quebec.

More recent indications of sectional aspects of campaign strategy with respect to Quebec help to verify the divisive nature of election campaigning. The well-known decision of the Conservative party in 1957, acting on Gordon Churchill's maxim to "reinforce success not failure," to reduce its Quebec efforts and concentrate on the possibilities of success in the remainder of the country provides an important indication of the significance of calculations of sectional pay-offs in dictating campaign strategy. The logic behind this policy was a direct consequence of the electoral system, for it was that system which dictated that increments of voting support from Quebec would produce less pay-off in representation than would equal increments elsewhere where the prospects of Conservative constituency victories were more promising. The electoral results were brilliantly successful from the viewpoint of the party, but less so from the perspective of Quebec, which contributed only 8 per cent of the new government's seats, and received only three cabinet ministers.

In these circumstances, the election of 1958 was crucial in determining the nature and extent of French-Canadian participation in the new government, which obviously would be formed by the Conservatives. Group appeals were exploited by the bribe that Quebec would get many more cabinet seats if that province returned a larger number of Tory MPs. Party propaganda stimulated racial tensions and insecurities. . . .

The significance of Quebec representation in explaining the nature of the Canadian party system has often been noted. Meisel states that the federal politician is faced with the dilemma of ignoring the pleas of Quebec, in which case "he may lose the support of Canada's second largest province without the seats of which a Parliamentary majority is almost impossible. If he heeds the wishes of Quebec, he may be deprived of indispensable support elsewhere." Lipson describes Quebec as the "solid South" of Canada whose support has contributed at different times to the hegemony of both parties, a fact which is basic in explaining the strategy of opposition of the two major parties. An important point is made by Ward in his observation that Liberal dominance in Quebec contributes to the electoral system which "by throwing whole blocks of seats to one party" fosters for that party a "special role as protector of the minority," while other parties are baffled by their inability to make significant breakthroughs in representation. Prophetically, as it turned out, he noted the developing theory that opposition parties should attempt to construct parliamentary majorities without Quebec, thus facing French Canadians with the option of becoming an opposition minority or casting themselves loose from the Liberals.

Ward's analysis makes clear that the special electoral importance of Quebec and the resultant party strategies elicited by that fact are only meaningful in the context of an electoral system which operates on a "winner take all" basis, not only at the level of the constituency but, to a modified extent, at the level of the province as a whole. It is only at the level of seats, not votes, that Quebec became a Liberal stronghold, a Canadian "solid South," and a one-party monopoly. The Canadian "solid South," like its American counterpart, is a contrivance of the electoral system, not an autonomous social fact which exists independent of it. . . .

Quebec constitutes the most striking example of the sectional nature of party strategy, electoral appeals, and electoral outcomes. It is, however, only a specific manifestation of the general principle that when the distribution of partisan support within a province or section is such that significant political pay-offs are likely to accrue to politicians who address themselves to the special needs of the area concerned, politicians will not fail to provide at least a partial response. The tendency of parties "to aim appeals at the nerve centers of particular provinces or regions, hoping thus to capture a bloc geographical vote," and to emphasize sectional appeals, are logical party responses within the Canadian electoral framework.

Electoral System and Party Policy

. . . The inquiry can be extended by noting that the electoral system affects party policies both directly and indirectly. The direct effect flows from the elementary consideration that each party devises policy in the light of a different set of sectional considerations. In theory, if the party is viewed strictly as a maximizing body pursuing representation, party sensitivity should be most highly developed in marginal situations where an appropriate policy initiative, a special organizational effort, or a liberal use of campaign funds might tip the balance of sectional representation to the side of the party. Unfortunately, sufficient evidence is not available to assert that this is a valid description of the import of sectional considerations on party strategies. The indirect effect of the electoral system is that it plays an important role in the determination of who the party policy makers will be.

The indirect effect presupposes the preeminence of the parliamentary party and its leaders in policy making. Acceptance of this presupposition requires a brief preliminary analysis of the nature of party organization, especially for the two major parties. The literature has been unanimous in referring to the organizational weakness of the Liberals and Conservatives. Some of the basic aspects and results of this will be summarily noted.

The extra-parliamentary structures of the two major parties have been extremely weak, lacking in continuity and without any disciplining power over the parliamentary party. The two major parties have been leader-dominated with membership playing a limited role in policy making and party financing. Although there are indications that the extra-parliamentary apparatus of the parties is growing in importance, it can be safely said that for the period under review both major parties have been essentially parliamentary parties. . . . Thus, the contribution of the electoral system to the determination of the parliamentary personnel of the party becomes, by logical extension, a contribution to the formation of party policies. Scarrow has asserted that "it is the makeup of the parliamentary party, including the proportional strength and bargaining position of the various parts, which is the most crucial factor in determining policy at any one time." While this hypothesis may require modification in particular cases, it is likely that historical research will confirm its general validity. For example, the antithetical attitudes of Conservatives and Liberals to conscription in both world wars were related not only to the electoral consequences of different choices, but also reflected the backgrounds and bias of the party personnel available to make such key decisions. . . .

The significance of the electoral system for party policy is due to its consistent failure to reflect with even rough accuracy the distribution of partisan support in the various sections/provinces of the country. By making the Conservatives far more a British and Ontario-based party, the Liberals far more a French and Quebec party, the CCF far more a prairie and BC party, and even Social Credit far more of an Alberta party up until 1953, than the electoral support of these parties "required," they were deprived of intra-party spokesmen proportionate to their electoral support from the sections where they were relatively weak. The relative, or on occasion total, absence of such spokesmen for particular sectional communities seriously affects the image of the parties as national bodies, deprives the party concerned of articulate proponents of particular sectional interests in caucus and in the House, and, it can be deductively suggested, renders the members of the parliamentary party personally less sensitive to the interests of the unrepresented sections than they otherwise would be. As a result the general perspectives and policy orientations of a party are likely to be skewed in favour of those interests which, by virtue of strong parliamentary representation, can vigorously assert their claims.

If a bias of this nature is consistently visited on a specific party over long periods of time, it will importantly condition the general orientation of the party and the political information and values of party MPs. It is in such ways that it can be argued that the effect of the electoral system is cumulative, creating conditions which aggravate the bias which it initially introduced into the party. To take the case of the Conservative party, the thesis is that not only does the electoral system make that party less French by depriving it of French representation as such, but also by the effect which that absence of French colleagues has on the possibility that its non-

French members will shed their parochial perspectives through intra-party contacts with French co-workers in parliament. . . .

While a lengthy catalogue of explanations can be adduced to explain the divergent orientations of Liberals and Conservatives to Quebec and French Canada, the electoral system must be given high priority as an influencing factor. A strong deductive case therefore can be made that the sectional bias in party representation engendered by the electoral system has had an important effect on the policies of specific parties and on policy differences between parties. Additionally, the electoral system has helped to determine the real or perceived sectional consequences of alternative party policy decisions. . . .

In some cases the sectional nature of party support requires politicians to make a cruel choice between sections, a choice recognized as involving the sacrifice of future representation from one section in order to retain it from another. This, it has been argued, was the Conservative dilemma in deciding whether or not Riel was to hang and in determining conscription policy in the First World War. Faced with a choice between Quebec and Ontario, in each case they chose Ontario. It should be noted that these either/or sectional choices occasionally thrown up in the political system are given exaggerated significance by an electoral system capable of transforming a moderate loss of votes in a section into almost total annihilation at the level of representation. If only votes were considered, the harshness of such decisions would be greatly mitigated, for decisions could be made on the basis of much less dramatic marginal assessments of the political consequences of alternative courses of action.

Electoral System and Perceptions of the Polity

A general point, easily overlooked because of its elementary nature, is that the electoral system has influenced perceptions of the political system. The sectional basis of party representatives which the electoral system has stimulated has reduced the visibility of cleavages cutting through sections.

. . . A hasty survey of political literature finds Quebec portrayed as "the solid Quebec of 1921," western Canada described as "once the fortress of protest movements," since transformed "into a Conservative stronghold," eastern Canada depicted in the 1925 election as having "punished King for his preoccupation with the prairies," and the Conservative party described in 1955 as "almost reduced into being an Ontario party," when in the previous election 55.8 per cent of its voting support came from outside that province.

The use of sectional terminology in description easily shades off into highly suspect assumptions about the voting behaviour of the electorate within sections. One of the most frequent election interpretations attributes a monolithic quality to Quebec voters and then argues that they "have instinctively given the bulk of their support" to the government or it is claimed that "the voters of Quebec traditionally seem to want the bulk of their representation . . . on the government side of the House. . . ." Several authors have specifically suggested that in 1958 Quebec, or the French Canadians, swung to Diefenbaker for this reason. . . . A recent analysis of New Brunswick politics argues that the strong tendency for MPs from that province to be on the government side of the House "must be" because "it seeks to gain what concessions it can by supporting the government and relying on its sense of gratitude."

The tendency of the electoral system to create sectional or provincial sweeps for one party at the level of representation is an important reason for these misinterpretations. Since similar explanations have become part of the folklore of Canadian politics it is useful to examine the extremely tenuous basis of logic on which they rest. Quebec will serve as a useful case study. The first point to note is the large percentage of the Quebec electorate which does not vote for the party which subsequently forms the government, a percentage varying from 29.8 per cent in 1921 to 70.4 per cent in 1962, and averaging 48 per cent for the period 1921 to 1965 as a whole. In the second place any government party will tend to win most of the sections most of the time. That is what a government party is. While Quebec has shown an above-average propensity to accord more than fifty per cent of its representation to the government party (on eleven occasions out of fourteen, compared to an average of all sections of just under eight out of fourteen) this is partly because of the size of the contingent from Quebec and its frequent one-sided representation patterns. This means that to a large extent Quebec determines which party will be the government, rather than exhibiting a preference for being on the government or opposition side of the House. This can be tested by switching the representation which Quebec gave to the two main parties in each of the eleven elections in which Quebec backed the winner. The method is simply to transfer the number of seats Quebec accorded the winning party to the second main party, and transfer the latter's Quebec seats to the former. This calculation shows that had Quebec distributed its seats between the two main parties in a manner precisely the opposite to its actual performance, it would have been on the winning side on seven out of eleven occasions anyway. It is thus more accurate to say that parties need Quebec in order to win than to say that Quebec displays a strong desire to be on the winning side.

One final indication of the logical deficiencies of the assumption that Quebec voters are motivated by a band-wagon psychology will suffice. The case of 1958 will serve as an example. In 1957 when there was no prediction of a Conservative victory, Quebec voters gave 31.1 per cent of their voting support to the Conservative party. In 1958 that percentage jumped to 49.6 when predictions of a Conservative victory were nearly universal. On the reasonable assumption that most of the Conservative supporters in 1957 remained with the party in 1958, and on the further assumption, which is questionable, that all of the increment in Conservative support was due to a desire to be on the winning side, the explanation is potentially applicable to only one Quebec voter out of five.

In concluding this critical analysis of a segment of Canadian political folklore it is only necessary to state that the attribution of questionable motivations to Quebec or French Canada could easily have been avoided if attention had been concentrated on voting data rather than on the bias in representation caused by the single-member constituency system. The analysis of Canadian politics has been harmfully affected by a kind of mental shorthand which manifests itself in the acceptance of a political map of the country that identifies provinces or sections in terms of the end results of the political process, partisan representation. This perception is natural since elections occur only once every three or four years while the results are visible for the entire period between elections. Since sectional discrepancies between votes and seats are due to the electoral system, it is evident that the latter has contributed to the formation of a set of seldom-questioned perceptions which exaggerate the partisan significance of geographical boundaries.

Electoral System, Sectionalism, and Instability

Individuals can relate to the party system in several ways, but the two most fundamental are class and sectionalism. The two are antithetical, for one emphasizes the geography of residence, while the other stresses stratification distinctions for which residence is irrelevant. The frequently noted conservative tone which pervades Canadian politics is a consequence of the sectional nature of the party system. The emphasis on sectional divisions engendered by the electoral system has submerged class conflicts, and to the extent that our politics has been ameliorative it has been more concerned with the distribution of burdens and benefits between sections than between classes. The poverty of the Maritimes has occupied an honourable place in the foreground of public discussion. The diffuse poverty of the generally underprivileged has scarcely been noticed.

Such observations lend force to John Porter's thesis that Canadian parties have failed to harness the "conservative-progressive dynamic" related to the Canadian class system, and to his assertion that "to obscure social divisions through brokerage politics is to remove from the political system that element of dialectic which is the source of creative politics." The fact is, however, that given the historical (and existing) state of class polarization in Canada, the electoral system has made sectionalism a more rewarding vehicle for amassing political support than class. The destructive impact of the electoral system on the CCF is highly indicative of this point. It is not that the single member constituency system discourages class-based politics in any absolute sense, as the example of Britain shows, but that it discourages such politics when class identities are weak or submerged behind sectional identities.

This illustrates the general point that the differences in the institutional contexts of politics have important effects in determining which kinds of conflict become salient in the political system. The particular institutional context with which this paper is concerned, the electoral system, has clearly fostered a sectional party system in which party strategists have concentrated on winning sections over to their side. It has encouraged a politics of opportunism based on sectional appeals and conditioned by one party bastions where the opposition is tempted to give up the battle and pursue success in more promising areas.

A politics of sectionalism is a politics of instability for two reasons. In the first place it induces parties to pay attention to the realities of representation which filter through the electoral system, at the expense of the realities of partisan support at the level of the electorate. The self-interest which may induce a party to write off a section because its weak support there is discriminated against by the electoral system, may be exceedingly unfortunate for national unity. Imperfections in the political market render the likelihood of an invisible hand transforming the pursuit of party good into public good somewhat dubious.

Secondly, sectional politics is potentially far more disruptive to the polity than class politics. This is essentially because sectional politics has an inherent tendency to call into question the very nature of the political system and its legitimacy. Classes, unlike sections, cannot secede from the political system, and are consequently more prone to accept its legitimacy. The very nature of their spatial distribution not only inhibits their political organization but induces them to work through existing instrumentalities. With sections this is not the case.

Given the strong tendency to sectionalism found in the very nature of Canadian society, the question can be raised as to the appropriateness of the existing electoral system. Duverger has pointed out that the single-member constituency system "accentuates the geographical localization of opinions: one might even say that it tends to transform a national opinion . . . into a local opinion by allowing it to be represented only in the sections of the country in which it is strongest." Proportional representation works in the opposite manner for "opinions strongly entrenched locally tend to be broadened on to the national plane by the possibility of being represented in districts where they are in a small minority." The political significance of these opposed tendencies "is clear: proportional representation tends to strengthen national unity (or, to be more precise, national uniformity); the simple majority system accentuates local differences. The consequences are fortunate or unfortunate according to the particular situation in each country."

Sectionalism and Discontinuities in Party Representation

It might be argued that the appropriate question is not whether sectional (or other) interests are represented proportionately to their voting support in each party, but simply whether they are represented in the party system as a whole proportionately to their general electoral strength. This assertion, however, is overly simple and unconvincing.

An electoral system that exaggerates the role of specific sections in specific parties accentuates the importance of sectionalism itself. If sectionalism in its "raw" condition is already strong, its exaggeration may cause strains beyond the capacity of the polity to handle. By its stimulus to sectional cleavages the electoral system transforms the party struggle into a struggle between sections, raising the danger that "parties . . . cut off from gaining support among a major stratum . . . lose a major reason for compromise."

This instability is exacerbated by the fact that the electoral system facilitates sudden and drastic alterations in the basis of party parliamentary representation. Recent changes with respect to NDP representation from Saskatchewan, Social Credit representation from Quebec, and the startling change in the influence of the prairie contingent in the Conservative party, with its counterpart of virtually eliminating other parties from that section, constitute important illustrations. The experience of Social Credit since 1962 and more recent experience of the Conservative party reveal that such changes may be more than a party can successfully handle.

Sudden changes in sectional representation are most pronounced in the transition from being an opposition party to becoming the government party. As Underhill notes, it is generally impossible to have more than one party with significant representation from both French and English Canada at the same time. That party is invariably the government party. This has an important consequence which has been insufficiently noted. Not only are opposition parties often numerically weak and devoid of access to the expertise that would prepare them for the possibility of governing, but they are also far less national in composition than the government party. On the two occasions since the First World War when the Conservatives ousted Liberal governments, 1930 and 1957, their opposition experience cut them off from contact with Quebec at the parliamentary level. Even though the party was successful in making significant breakthroughs in that province in 1930 and especially in 1958, it can be suggested that it had serious problems in digesting the sudden input of Quebec MPs, particularly in the latter year.

The transition from opposition to government therefore is a transition from being sectional to being national, not only in the tasks of government, but typically in the very composition of the party itself. The hypothesis that this discontinuity may have serious effects on the capacity of the party to govern is deserving of additional research. It is likely that such research will suggest a certain incongruity between the honorific status symbolically accorded Her Majesty's Loyal Opposition, and an electoral system which is likely to hamper the development in that party of those perspectives functional to successful governing.

The Electoral System as a Determinant of the Party System

Students of Canadian politics have been singularly unwilling to attribute any explanatory power to the electoral system as a determinant of the party system. Lipson has argued that it is not the electoral system which moulds the party system, but rather the reverse. Essentially his thesis is that parties select the type of electoral system more compatible with their own interest, which is self-perpetuation. He admits in passing that once selected the electoral system "produces a reciprocal effect upon the parties which brought it into being."

Lipson's interpretation is surely misleading and fallacious in its implication that because parties preside over the selection, modification, and replacement of particular institutions, the subsequent feed-back of those institutions on the parties should not be regarded as causal. In the modern democratic party state, parties preside over the legal arrangements governing campaign expenses, eligibility of candidates, the rules establishing the determination of party winners and losers, the kinds of penalties, such as loss of deposits, which shall be visited on candidates with a low level of support, the rules establishing who may vote, and so on. Analysis is stifled if it is assumed that because these rules are made by parties the effect of the rules on the parties is in some sense to be regarded as derivative or of secondary interest or importance. Fundamentally, the argument concerns the priority to be accorded the chicken or the egg. As such it can be pursued to an infinite regression, for it can be asserted that the parties which make a particular set of rules are themselves products of the rules which prevailed in the previous period, which in turn. . . . It might also be noted that parties which preside over particular changes in electoral arrangements may be mistaken in their predictions about the effect of the changes. It is clear that the introduction of the alternative ballot in British Columbia in 1952 misfired from the viewpoint of its sponsors, with dramatic effects on the nature of the provincial party system which subsequently developed.

The only reasonable perspective for the analyst to adopt is to accept the interdependence of electoral systems and party systems and then to investigate whatever aspects of that interdependence which seem to provide useful clues for the understanding of the political system.

In a recent article Meisel explicitly agrees with Lipson, asserting that parties are products of societies rather than of differences between parliamentary or presidential systems, or of electoral laws. This argument is weakened by its assumption that society is something apart from the institutional arrangements of which it is composed. It is unclear in this dichotomy just what society is. While it may be possible at the moment when particular institutions are being established to regard them as separate from the society to which they are to be fitted, this is not so with long-established institutions which become part and parcel of the society itself. Livingston's argument that after a while it becomes impossible to make an analytic distinction between the instrumentalities of federalism and the federal nature of the society they were designed to preserve or express is correct and is of general validity. To say therefore that parties are products of societies is not to deny that they are products of institutions. The only defensible view is once again to accept the interdependence of political and other institutions which compose society and then to establish the nature of particular patterns of interdependence by research.

Confirmation of the view that electoral systems do have an effect on party systems is provided by logic. To assert that a particular electoral system does not have an effect on a particular party system is equivalent to saying that all conceivable electoral systems are perfectly compatible with the party system and that all conceivable party systems are compatible with that electoral system. This is surely impossible. Any one electoral system has the effect of inhibiting the development of the different party systems which some, but not necessarily all, different electoral systems would foster. To accept this is to accept that electoral systems and party systems are related.

Approaches to a Theory of the Party System

This paper has suggested that the electoral system has been an important factor in the evolution of the Canadian party system. Its influence is intimately tied up with the politics of sectionalism which it has stimulated. Sectionalism in the party system is unavoidable as long as there are significant differences between the distribution of party voter support in any one section and the distribution in the country as a whole. The electoral system, however, by the distortions it introduces as it transforms votes into seats, produces an exaggerated sectionalism at the level of representation. In view of this, the basic theme of the paper in its simplest form, and somewhat crudely stated, is that statements about sectionalism in the national party system are in many cases, and at a deeper level, statements about the politics of the single-member constituency system.

The suggested impact of the electoral system on the party system is relevant to a general theory of the party system but should not be confused with such a general theory. The construction of the latter would have required analysis of the import for the party system of such factors as the federal system, the relationship of provincial party organizations to the national party, the nature of the class system, the underlying economic and cultural bases for sectionalism, a parliamentary system of the British type, and many others. For this discussion all these have been accepted as given. They have been mentioned, if at all, only indirectly. Their importance for a general theory is taken for granted, as are the interdependencies they have with each other and with the electoral system. It is evident, for example, that the underlying strength of sectional tendencies and the weakness of class identification are interrelated with each other and with the electoral system, as explanations of sectionalism in Canadian politics. For any one of these to change will produce a change in the outcomes which their interactions generate. We are not therefore suggesting that sectional tendencies are exclusive products of the electoral system, but only that that system accords them an exaggerated significance.

Concentration on the electoral system represents an attempt to isolate one aspect of a complex series of interactions which is only imperfectly understood and in the present state of our knowledge cannot be handled simultaneously with precision. In such circumstances the developments of more systematic comprehensive explanations will only result from a dialectic between research finding at levels varying from that of individual voters through middle-range studies, such as Alford's recent analysis of class and voting, to attempts, such as those by Scarrow and Meisel, to handle a complex range of phenomena in one framework.

We can conclude that the capacity of the party system to act as an integrating agency for the sectional communities of Canada is detrimentally affected by the electoral system. The politicians' problem of reconciling sectional particularisms is exacerbated by the system they must work through in their pursuit of power. From one perspective it can be argued that if parties succeed in overcoming sectional divisions they do so in defiance of the electoral system. Conversely, it can be claimed that if parties do not succeed this is because the electoral system has so biased the party system that it is inappropriate to call it a nationalizing agency. It is evident that not only has the electoral system given impetus to sectionalism in terms of party campaigns and policy, but by making all parties more sectional at the level of seats than of votes it complicates the ability of the parties to transcend sectionalism. At various times the electoral system has placed barriers in the way of Conservatives becoming sensitively aware of the special place of Quebec and French Canada in the Canadian polity, aided the Liberals in that task, inhibited the third parties in the country from becoming aware of the special needs and dispositions of sections other than those represented in the parliamentary party, and frequently inhibited the parliamentary personnel of the major parties from becoming attuned to the sentiments of the citizens of the prairies. The electoral system's support for the political idiosyncracies of Alberta for over two decades ill served the integration of that provincial community into the national political system at a time when it was most needed. In fact, the Alberta case merely illustrates the general proposition that the disintegrating effects of the electoral system are likely to be most pronounced where alienation from the larger political system is most profound. A particular orientation, therefore, has been imparted to Canadian politics which is not inherent in the very nature of the patterns of cleavage and consensus in the society, but results from their interplay with the electoral system.

The stimulation offered to sectional cleavages by the single-member constituency system has led several authors to query its appropriateness for national integration in certain circumstances. Lipset and Duverger have suggested that countries possessed of strong underlying tendencies to sectionalism may be better served by proportional representation which breaks up the monolithic nature of sectional representation stimulated by single-member constituency systems. Belgium is frequently cited as a country in which proportional representation has softened the conflict between the Flemish and the Walloons, and the United States as a country in which the single-member constituency system has heightened cleavages and tensions between north and south. Whatever its other merits, the single-member constituency system lacks the singular capacity of proportional representation to encourage all parties to search for votes in all sections of the country. Minorities within sections or provinces are not frozen out as they tend to be under the existing system. As a consequence, sectional differences in party representation are minimized or more accurately, given proportionate rather than exaggerated representation — a factor which encourages the parties to develop a national orientation.

EXPLANATIONS OF OUR PARTY SYSTEM*

John T. McLeod

[The] tedious similarity between [our] two major parties may be one reason for the difficulty of formulating any general theory explaining the Canadian party system. In the nineteenth century it was customary to interpret the two-party system in Macaulay's terms as the reflection of the division of mankind into those who exalt liberty above all else and those whose primary concern is social order. This "literary" theory was invoked by Laurier and given lip-service by Mackenzie King, but it is not taken seriously by contemporary scholars. It is also possible to regard our national parties as mere collections of interest groups in search of power, but the student will search in

* From "Party Structure and Party Reform," in *The Prospect of Change: Proposals for Canada's Future,* edited by A. Rotstein, Toronto, McGraw-Hill of Canada, 1965. By permission of the author and publisher.

vain for any satisfactory interpretative theory suggesting how the vague "interests" are brought together or kept together, now by one party, now by another. In more fashionable terms of behaviourism and "images," Professor Mallory has attempted to explain the success or failure of Canada's major parties by stressing a leader's ability to capture the "national mood." Mallory argues that the important factor is "that at any given time only one party is in tune with a national mood — and that party is likely to stay in power until the mood changes and leaves it politically high and dry." However, Mallory fails to enlighten us as to how or why political moods change. Suggestive as the concept may be, it is not clear how "moods" may be created or identified, nor is it clear whether a leader creates the mood or whether the mood calls forth the leader.

How then do we make sense of the Canadian party system? Perhaps Mallory is most helpful when he gets down to fundamentals and insists that "The most important thing about Canadian politics is that they are parochial rather than national." There persists a certain narrowness of viewpoint in the various sections of the Canadian population. The politics of each region tend to be rather introverted. Canada is composed of five major regions: the Maritimes, Quebec, Ontario, the Prairies, and British Columbia. Each of these regions possesses different political traditions and each contends with rather different social and economic problems. Our heterogeneous population is divided not only into segments of rural and urban, rich and poor, United Empire Loyalists and recent immigrants, but also and most important into a dualistic pattern of English and French. These cleavages make Canada an exceedingly difficult nation to govern. Democratic political parties attempt primarily to organize the population into majorities, but majorities are painfully difficult to attain when the electorate is so fragmented.

Faced with these difficulties, our major parties must inevitably be flexible and broadly inclusive if they are to be national. Above all, they must attempt to harmonize and conciliate the various conflicting interests of the society, and to do so they must emphasize the modest but essential virtues of moderation and compromise. In a nation lacking unity or cohesion, the national political party becomes the shock-absorber of domestic conflicts . . . the principal task of the national political party is to discover some means of bringing the various regions and interests closer together. . . .

Thus it is not surprising that our parties are constantly preoccupied with the search for simple common denominators of slogans and policies on which it may be possible to unite enough of the diverse elements of the population to win elections. . . . Issues for which no common denominator can be found tend to be evaded or solutions postponed.

. . . Intellectually tempting as it might be, further political polarization into radical and conservative camps seems to be a luxury which Canadians have been unable to afford. The chief function of the party in this country has always been to prevent new cleavages and to draw the divergent elements together into a majority by whatever means possible. . . .

All of this is readily understandable and familiar; however, it does not explain why a party may be more successful at one time than at another in working out broadly acceptable policies and controlling the seats of power.

What more can be offered toward an explanation of the Canadian party system?

In the absence of a generally accepted theory of party operation, the most helpful informing hypothesis is that of Macpherson and Smiley, who have set forth the concept of single party dominance. Macpherson's analysis of the rise of Social Credit in Alberta yields the suggestion that Alberta has never had an orthodox system of two evenly matched parties frequently alternating in office. Instead, Alberta reveals a pattern of one massive party completely overwhelming its opposition and remaining in power for a long period of uninterrupted years. This deviation from the two-party norm is what Macpherson has dubbed the "quasiparty system." Smiley takes American experience as his starting point and quotes Samuel Lubell to the effect that in American national politics, the prolonged dominance of one party has been the usual state of affairs. . . . Smiley defines single party dominance as a system in which "one political party retains such overwhelming strength over a period of at least a decade that the major political issues of the community are fought out and the major conflicts of interest resolved within that party."

When the concept of a single party dominance is applied to the Canadian party system its relevance is at once apparent. Our politics since Confederation have normally been dominated by one broad middle-of-the-road party which has so effectively occupied the centre of the stage that the opposition has been squeezed off into the wings. There have been three major periods of such single party dominance in Canada. John A. Macdonald's Tories easily dominated our politics from 1867 until 1896, slipping from office only briefly in the aftermath of the Pacific Scandal. The Liberals under Laurier had things very much their own way from 1896 until 1911. After the interval of the coalition government of 1917, Mackenzie King and his hand-picked successor dominated our political life from 1921 until 1957 with only two short interruptions, and held office for one comfortably undisturbed period of 22 years. Altogether, these three leaders were in power for 56 of the 98 years since Confederation. We have not had frequent alternation between Liberal and Conservative governments, but long periods in which one party was clearly predominant.

Our experience at the provincial level also bears out the importance of the concept of single party dominance. Although the Maritime provinces for the most part seem closer to the classic pattern of the two-party system, most of the other provinces have demonstrated their adherence to the pattern examined by Macpherson and Smiley. Alberta never had a two-party system. The Liberals were in power there from 1905 to 1921 with only negligible Conservative opposition; the United Farmers of Alberta held sway from 1921 to 1935, and Social Credit was so securely entrenched there that in the [1963] provincial election the opposition won only three of the sixty-three seats. [Since 1971 the Conservatives have dominated the scene, winning 74 out of 79 seats in 1979.] In Saskatchewan the Liberals were the dominant party from 1905 to 1944, the Tories managing to win only one election during the whole period; after 1944 the CCF held power in the Wheat Province for twenty years. A series of non-partisan coalition governments in Manitoba during most of the 1922 to 1958 period kept that province in the quasi-party pattern, while [in 1981] in Ontario the Conservative party [had been in power thirty-eight years continuously]. . . .

Inevitably, there is a high premium placed on artful leadership. In the absence of binding principles the leader of the party becomes the focal point of the member's loyalty. Personality rather than philosophy is the key to office. That leader succeeds who can best command the support of, and work out accommodations between, the most numerous interests. . . . A successful leader becomes the major symbol of his party; the party stands for what he stands for, and his pronouncements become party dogma. Whether it is Macdonald or Laurier, King or Diefenbaker, "The Chief" is the mainspring of the machine, and absolute power to formulate policy is concentrated in his hands. The most adroit conciliator will be longest in power.

If a party is to stay long in office its leadership must also reflect the duality of the Canadian nation. The most successful prime ministers have appeared to share their power with a lieutenant who represents the other major language group. An English-speaking leader must have an able French Canadian at his side; a French Catholic first minister must have a prominent English Protestant colleague. Macdonald leaned heavily on Cartier, Laurier on Fielding and Sifton, Mackenzie King on Lapointe and St. Laurent. The fundamental importance of this vestige of the pre-Confederation dual prime-ministership is emphasized by the failure of Borden, Meighen, or Diefenbaker to find such a lieutenant from Quebec. The inability of the Conservative party to win a parliamentary majority in any two successive elections in the twentieth century is often ascribed to this failure.

To become dominant, a national party must achieve a considerable degree of support from Quebec. The voters of Quebec traditionally seem to want the bulk of their representation at Ottawa on the government side of the House. This desire to find representation on Mr. Speaker's right is not peculiar to Quebec but appears to be shared by most of the major interest groups of the country. . . . Their desire for spokesmen in the cabinet helps to promote the "bandwagon" effect which broadens the support of the government party and strengthens single party dominance.

It follows that the cabinet of a dominant party includes a congeries of elements which have little in common except a willingness to support an attractive leader and an eagerness to have a voice in the councils of state. The wide divergencies of opinion inside the governing party make conflict the rule rather than the exception within the cabinet. The major clashes of interest within the nation are likely to be expressed not between competing parties but inside the dominant party. . . . Argument between the parties on the floor of the House and on the hustings is superseded by argument behind the closed doors of cabinet and caucus; major issues are resolved mainly in secret, and the fruitfulness of open democratic debate to educate the voter is stultified. Elections do not often decide issues, and a danger arises of public apathy or contempt toward the ordinary democratic processes.

With the normal role of the opposition so greatly diminished, the minority party tends to be preoccupied with mere posturing and manoeuvering, attempting to splinter off dissident groups from the dominant party and waiting to exploit the inevitable schisms within the government ranks. An opposition leader will not usually try to compete with the governing party by emphasizing a sharply different approach to policy-making, but will concentrate on the omissions and shortcomings of cabinet policy in order to persuade groups supporting the dominant party that they would get a "better deal" if the ins and outs were reversed.

Moreover, when a transfer of power does take place, the new administration will alter the emphasis of government programs, but the basic orientation of policy will change very little. The new cabinet, like the old, will be concerned with placating the major interest groups, and one of the most important of these will still be corporate business. . . .

By definition, however, in a system of single party dominance, the ins and the outs do not exchange places very often, and a further characteristic of the system is that the opposition group will be very weak. The opposition may be weak numerically, as in the national parliament during 1958-62 or in Alberta since 1963, but, more often and more important, after a long period out of office, the opposition may be weak qualitatively. It will lack the practical experience of power which would enable it to probe and criticize the technicalities of government more effectively. A former minority party, when it does finally achieve power, may be so accustomed to negative opposition that it finds difficulty in formulating for itself constructive alternative policies. Like a nagging wife, it may know what it objects to but not what it wants. The traditional weakness of the opposition in Ottawa has been suggested as one of the reasons why most of the provincial governments are frequently controlled by the minority party or by third parties. The most effective opposition to the nationally dominant party then comes from the provincial capitals, and the device of federalism helps to redress the political imbalance.

Following a shift of power, a newly elected government may not be able to profit from the technical advice of the civil service if, over two decades or more, the senior civil servants have become intimately identified with the previously dominant party. This was apparent in Ottawa in 1957-58, and in Regina in 1964; in both cases the civil service had become closely linked with the government party over a long period of years and, through no necessary fault of its own, had become compromised in the eyes of the incoming administration. The complexity of modern government and the enormous technical demands on it make it imperative that a highly competent staff of civil service experts be built up, but when single party dominance has been the rule, a change of government may tend to destroy the top echelon of the old bureaucracy, or at least make it less useful to the new cabinet. With a lack of experienced administrative advisors, the incoming government will have a harder time to find its feet, and new policy innovations are less likely to be attempted or to be successful.

The resulting stagnation of policy and the fact that most governments bog down in the middle of the road are reasons for the rise of third parties. Sameness of policy creates areas of discontent, and third parties appear as vehicles of protest against the inertia of single party dominance. Professor Pinard has argued that third parties arise not only where dissident feelings against the majority party are strongest, but where the traditional minority party has become so weak as to be discounted as an effective means of expressing protest. The prolonged success of one party may so eviscerate the organization of its customary opponents that only a new party will be regarded as an effective alternative to the government.

The role of third parties in Canada has been not only to express sporadic electoral discontent but also to capture provincial governments, to formulate more concrete ideologies, and to seek a balance-of-power position in the national parliament at times of transition when no party has a clear majority. Most important, third parties like the [CCF/NDP], and the Ginger Group before it, have served to popularize radical policy innovations and to push the government party off its conservative stance in the political dead-centre. The influence of third parties on policy has far exceeded their power as measured in numbers of seats won. The origins of such positive departures from the middle of the road as old age pensions, unemployment insurance, hospitalization insurance, and medicare can be attributed largely to the influence of third parties.

Why? There is no general agreement among scholars as to why this pattern of politics has been so prevalent in Canada. Although there is no one explanation which is entirely satisfactory, a number of hypotheses deserve consideration.

Macpherson's analysis of the quasi-party system in Alberta rests on the proposition that the conditions necessary for this pattern to emerge are a "quasi-colonial" economy and a "largely *petit-bourgeois*" class structure of independent agrarian producers. The argument is that Alberta's economy produces staples for distant markets, that the producers are dependent upon and united in their resentment of external capitalist interest, and that the independent small farmer gives the prairie society a virtual homogeneity of class consciousness. "The peculiarity of a society which is at once quasi-colonial and mainly *petit bourgeois* is that the conflict of class interest is not so much within the society as between that society and the forces of outside capital. . . ." Macpherson contends that as Canada's economy becomes increasingly dependent upon that of the United States, our position more closely approximates that of a quasi-colonial nation which is therefore likely to live under a quasi-party system.

Although Macpherson does not explain why the Alberta farmers turned to the political right under Social Credit while their neighbours in Saskatchewan veered to left under the CCF, his book remains one of the most provocative pieces of social analysis published in Canada. We must weigh seriously the argument that the Canadian economy is a precarious one *vis-à-vis* the American industrial giant, and that single party dominance may be an expression of a Canadian will to bind our people more closely together and consolidate our politics in the face of external threats to our regional or national interest. Macpherson may exaggerate the importance of class as a factor in our politics, but at least it should be evident that the great bulk of our population regards itself as middle-class, that the predominant social ethos in Canada is a *bourgeois* ethos, that our major parties are principally middle-class parties financed by business, heavily influenced by the compact social elite, and led by middle-class men highly sensitive to commercial interests. If Canada does not possess class homogeneity, surely our closest approximation to a prevailing class consciousness is a middle-class consciousness. Can we seriously doubt that the relative absence of sharp class conflict in Canada is a primary factor in the existence of single party dominance?

Canada's preoccupation with the centrifugal forces of regional diversity and English-French duality may lead to a more orthodox interpretation which avoids emphasis on class. Political scientists are fond of referring to regional, economic, ethnic, and religious differences in the population as "structural cleavages." Professor Maurice Pinard has argued that "Such cleavages strongly alienate a region from one of the two major parties and tie it to a single party as the sole [principal?] defender of its interest, hence leading to one-party dominance." It may be possible for the bulk of the population to be persuaded at a given time that only one party possesses the requisite leadership to be able to form a strong majority government and act as the broker of interests, effectively smoothing over the structural cleavages. Many writers have also noted that the single-member, simple-plurality electoral system amplifies the number of seats held by the winning party, reduces the seats held by the minority parties, and gives further institutional impetus to the system of single party dominance.

Whatever the reasons for the prevalence of the single party dominance pattern, some of the main implications and results of this phenomenon are apparent. It may be useful to review the most striking corollaries of the system.

First, there will be a deliberate avoidance of ideological issues by the national parties. This tends to render the parties more alike, to narrow the voter's range of choice between them, and to make our politics more gray and dull. Both parties will attempt to gain the dominant position by emphasizing their ability to include and conciliate most of the major contending interests in the nation, and to do so they will exalt pragmatism, compromise, and moderation. They will keep their "principles" as vague and nebulous as possible and avoid divisive philosophizing at all costs. . . . The parties compete not for the political right or left but for the centre. Their supreme role must be as unifying agents, and their chief method of operation must be compromise.

Periods of minority government in the twentieth century can be regarded as periods of transition during which no one party was able to achieve a position of national dominance. . . .

There are sound reasons to indicate that minority governments can provide effective administrations, but the old parties both laud "stable" majority government as infinitely preferable. The persistent re-appearance of minority governments since 1921 might suggest that coalition between a major and a minor party would prove attractive as a means of providing solid majority administrations, but Canada's parties have stoutly resisted coalition except at times of extreme crisis. We have had only two coalition governments in Canada, one at Confederation and one in 1917. Both worked; that is to say, both accomplished things and in neither case did the process of government break down. . . .

At present there appears no immediate prospect of national coalition government. Instead, the foregoing analysis suggests that we are in a period of transition in which neither party is yet able to attain a dominant position. It is a situation of great uncertainty, but one pregnant with possibilities, for transition periods such as this are times when new directions of policy may be sought and fundamental premises re-examined. . . .

POLITICS AND PARTIES IN CANADA*

Paul Fox

Canadian politics and political parties tend to be characterized by the word "moderate." Like Britain and the United States, to which Canadian political parties owe a good deal in formative influences, Canada is a predominantly middle class nation with middle class values. This is reflected in the fact that radical parties of either the right or the left are virtually non-existent and that those parties which do exist seek the golden mean in order to get the maximum number of votes.

This tends to diminish the differences between parties and to make them difficult to pinpoint. In some cases it is more a matter of history and traditional loyalty that distinguishes them rather than logic or the planks in their platforms. This is very apparent in comparing the two parties which have dominated Canadian politics since the country became a dominion in 1867, the Conservatives and the Liberals.

The Conservatives originated in Canada as the colonial equivalent of the British Tory Party. In pioneer days they were ardently loyal to the Crown and stood for the maintenance of the British connection. Under their first great leader, Sir John A. Macdonald, who was prime minister almost continuously from 1867 until his death in 1891, the party broadened its appeal by incorporating some of the opposing Liberals and by devising a "National Policy" which stressed the development of the country from sea to sea, the construction of transcontinental railways, and the fostering of industry and commerce by the adoption of relatively high tariffs.

These elements left their mark on the party for many years, so much so that it was stigmatized by farmers and French Canadians for decades. The farmers complained that it was the party of "big business," sacrificing the agrarian interests of the three wheat-growing prairie provinces to the financial and commercial demands of the large metropolitan centres (Toronto and Montreal) in the more populous and wealthier provinces of Ontario and Quebec. The French Canadians, Roman Catholic in faith and predominant in Quebec, were alienated by the militant Protestantism and pro-British sentiments of some of the leading Conservatives. When one Conservative government in the nineteenth century executed Louis Riel, a Roman Catholic rebel with French-Canadian blood in his veins, and another Conservative government rigorously implemented universal military conscription during World War I (which French Canadians considered to be a "British" war), the Conservative party went into an eclipse in Quebec from which, after four decades, it recovered in the elections of 1957 and 1958, but only spasmodically as it turned out.

In every general election from 1917 to 1957, with one exception, the Conservatives never won more than half a dozen seats in this French-Canadian province which, because of its size, has about one-quarter of the total number of seats in the House of Commons. Conservative weakness in Quebec combined with meagre support in the western agrarian provinces

* Revised in November, 1981.

explains to a large extent why the Tories went out of power nationally in 1921 and remained out, except for five years, until 1957.

The two elections within ten months in 1957 and 1958 brought about a striking change. In the former, the Conservatives under Mr. Diefenbaker secured nine seats out of 75 in Quebec. This provided a bridgehead for future operations. In the succeeding election Mr. Diefenbaker won 50 Conservative seats in Quebec.

At the same time Mr. Diefenbaker, himself a western Canadian who had sat as a western M.P. for 18 years, was able to revive the cause of Conservatism in that part of the country by the sheer force of his own personality. . . .

The result of the election on March 31, 1958 was the most decisive victory in the history of Canadian federal government; the Conservatives were returned with 208 seats out of a total of 265. It was an astonishing revival for a party which had almost disintegrated during the long period of Liberal ascendancy.

Unfortunately for the party, its fortunes varied with its leader's. Mr. Diefenbaker's popularity and command of the situation waned almost as rapidly as they had waxed. The 1962 election returned the Conservatives to the status of a minority government, and the 1963 election found them defeated by the Liberals who have been in power ever since except for 1979-80.

Like its British forebear, the Liberal party in Canada commenced as a reform movement. It was a fusion, after Confederation, of small-scale pioneer farmers of British stock and the more radical and progressive elements in the French-Canadian society known as "Rouges." The colours adopted by the party were red and white in contrast to the Conservatives' blue and white, a distinction that was quite valid. From its birth the Liberal party tended to be more egalitarian, proletarian, and nationalistic. With the advent to leadership of Sir Wilfrid Laurier, a Roman Catholic French Canadian from Quebec, the party became strongly bi-ethnic and succeeded in gaining power in 1896 and holding it till 1911. World War I and the conscription issue split its two wings apart; most French Canadians and Laurier opposed conscription, while many leading Anglo-Saxons abandoned Laurier and entered a wartime coalition government headed by the Conservatives.

From this crisis the party was rescued by the genius of William Lyon Mackenzie King, who, following his election as leader in 1919, set the Liberals on the path towards a broadly based middle-of-the-road social welfare state. By many artful compromises Mackenzie King kept himself and his party in power almost continuously from 1921 until his retirement in 1948, thereby establishing a personal record as the prime minister in Canada who had held office the longest, 21 years and five months.

He was succeeded by Louis St. Laurent, the second French Canadian (both Liberal) to be prime minister. Though Mr. St. Laurent tried to continue Mr. Mackenzie King's victorious tactics of maintaining the centre-of-the-road policy while moving forward, the process of aging had rendered the Liberal government less flexible and less dynamic, and in 1957, after 22 continuous years of power, during which it had won what appeared to be very comfortable electoral pluralities, the party was narrowly defeated by

Mr. Diefenbaker's resuscitated Conservatives who secured 112 seats to the Liberals' 105. Mr. St. Laurent resigned as prime minister and subsequently retired as leader, being replaced by his former secretary of state for external affairs, Mr. Lester B. Pearson. But Mr. Pearson and his Liberals were no match for Prime Minister Diefenbaker's Conservatives, who in the 1958 election reduced the number of Liberal seats to 49.

Under Mr. Diefenbaker the Conservatives appeared to take over the mantle of the Liberals as the party of moderate reform and progress appealing to the diverse geographical, economic, religious, and ethnic groups in the country. However, the Liberals regained their ascendancy in 1963, winning a minority-government victory that they repeated in 1965, largely by appealing to the middle and upper middle class voters in large urban centres.

The new Liberal leader chosen in 1968, Mr. Pierre Elliott Trudeau, was able to enhance this urban, middle-class support, and to win a majority government by combining it with his general personal appeal throughout the country. In 1972 Mr. Trudeau lost his majority and was reduced to leading a minority Liberal government. But in 1974 he regained his majority, winning 141 seats. In 1979 the Liberals lost power to the Conservatives but Mr. Clark's short-lived government lasted only nine months when Mr. Trudeau led the Liberals back to office in 1980 with a majority victory of 147 seats.

Additional proof of the middle-class nature of our politics is that there is no party in Canada on the extreme right wing and the party farthest to the left is virtually extinct. The Communist Party (formerly called the Labour Progressive Party) never had much success in Canada. It elected on only one occasion a federal member of Parliament and his career ended ignominiously in prison when he was convicted of conspiracy to turn over government secrets to the Soviet Union in wartime. This assisted in convincing most Canadian voters, if they needed further evidence, that the party was more interested in serving the Kremlin than the Canadian people, and subsequent events such as the Soviet restrictions on Jews and the repression of the Hungarian revolt created serious dissensions within its own ranks. Party membership has fallen to a few thousand and in the federal election of 1979, only 71 Communist candidates were nominated and together they received only 9,159 votes out of the 11,452,620 ballots cast, or approximately 0.08 per cent. In the same election, the Marxist-Leninist party ran 144 candidates who won 14,231 votes, amounting to 0.12 per cent of the total.

Further proof of the need to seek the middle of the road in Canadian politics is presented by the history of minor parties. Canada has had a number of these but as yet none has been strong enough to form a government at Ottawa. For the most part they have tended to be regional parties representing special interests, in particular western prairie farmers who have been prone to organize their own political movements in protest against the wealthier, more populous "east" (actually central Canada — Ontario and Quebec). Following the discontents of World War I the farmers created their own Progressive party which, at its zenith in 1921, sent 64 members to the House of Commons and acquired the balance of power. The party quickly dissolved, however, because of the centrifugal nature of its ultra-democratic organization and its lack of firm leadership. In 1935 the Social Credit party, which espoused unorthodox monetary doctrines and stirred up strong emotional and religious support, elected 17 members to Parliament from Alberta and Saskatchewan, but after reaching a high point of 19 in 1957 it was wiped out completely by the Conservative landslide in the following year. It gained great support in Quebec in 1962, electing 26 MPs from that province alone (for a total of 30) but subsequently the Quebec wing split away, electing nine *Ralliement des Créditistes* in 1965 to five for Social Credit. In 1968, the English-speaking Social Credit party was eliminated in Parliament, winning no seats at all, while the *Créditistes* continued with 14 seats. In 1972 Social Credit won 15, in 1974 only 11, in 1979 6, and in 1980 none at all. It would seem that both wings of the party are dead.

A party that attempted to fuse the agrarian interests of the west and the labour forces of the east was born during the depression of the 1930s with the cumbersome title of the Co-operative Commonwealth Federation. Dedicated to the principles of democratic socialism, it has tried to become the Canadian equivalent of the British Labour party but it has not had the success of its model. The number of seats it has won has fluctuated widely, from seven in its first trial in 1935 to 28 in 1945 and back to eight in 1958, though throughout the period its share of the popular vote varied between about eight and ten per cent. After reorganizing itself as the New Democratic Party in 1961, its fortunes improved electorally. It won 22 seats in 1968, 31 in 1972, 11 in 1974, 26 in 1979, and 32 in 1980.

The dilemma of the CCF-NDP is that it has been squeezed into an almost impossible position left-of-centre in politics in which it can scarcely find sufficient unique ground on which to make a stand. It fears moving left lest it be accused of being communist, which it abhors, and it cannot move right into the mixed field occupied by Conservatives and Liberals without losing the identity it desires as a working class party. While it is thus stuck on the horns of a dilemma, the Conservatives and Liberals have appropriated many of its social welfare planks. Its chief obstacle is the hard fact of Canadian middle class democracy. Like all radical and sectional parties it can consider broadening its appeal only at the risk of losing its claim to existence. . . .

In the sphere of the provinces, each government, whatever its political stripe, finds that its most fruitful tactic is to set itself up as the defender of provincial rights against the central administration, particularly in the fields of taxation, finance, and resources. This has become so commonplace that some theorists have suggested that the real opposition to the government of the day at Ottawa comes not in the traditional manner from the benches to the left of the Speaker in the House of Commons but from the provincial regimes, whether or not they are of the same political complexion as the federal government. This may or may not be true but it is undeniable that any provincial administration tends to make much more of an issue out of its wrangles with Ottawa than out of its own party ideology.

Dogma is either ignored or soft-pedalled and the provincial governments seek to become all things to all people — or at least to all voters. Like federal governments, the provincial administrations move according to the inexorable fundamental law of Canadian politics towards the centre of the road, or perhaps it would be more precise to say they spread themselves all over the road. Whatever the official label of the party, whatever the planks in its platform before election, it tends to become moderate and eclectic when it obtains power. This has applied to radical parties like the United Farmers, Social Credit, and the CCF, but it also works in reverse sometimes with Conservatives and Liberals. Thus, a Conservative government in Ontario urged the public ownership of a natural gas pipeline and played a leading role in the achievement of national hospital insurance, while the CCF government in Saskatchewan made a determined effort to attain more private capital investment in its natural resources. In Alberta, Social Credit, which drew its strength originally from rural farms, became the darling of business men. In Manitoba, the Roblin Conservative government was probably more progressive than the Liberal-Progressive government it replaced. Thus, the party names do not mean too much in Canada, both provincially and federally, and it is often difficult to establish differences clearly. . . .

THE SYSTEM IS OUTMODED — SAYS THE NEW LEFT*

Dimitrios Roussopoulos

Most people in Canada are fed up with "politics" — by which they mean the machinery of political decision-making. At the moment this feeling has no political expression, although anger, despair and frustration expresses itself in many acts of violence.

Our existing political institutions were developed at a time when a far less bureaucratized and centralized society existed. The party system in Canada, for instance, existed before universal suffrage; the parties represented special group interests in existence before the founding of Canada.

Power today is monopolized in immense bureaucracies which have become political institutions by virtue of the role they play in society. The power of the gigantic corporations is informal, to be sure, but there is little doubt that they have drawn off real power from our formal political institutions. Couple this development with the concentration of power at the top of the parliamentary pyramid, and both the legislature and the electorate are reduced to ritual.

This concentration of power, plus the new manipulative methods of conditioning public attitudes and motivation through the mass media, which celebrate the "values" of a society of compulsive consumption, raise in our minds a questioning of the value of the electoral and parliamentary system of representative democracy.

The issues that divided the political parties in this country are artificial — questions of *management* rather than *basic policy*. The important questions of the day — the growth of liberal totalitarianism, the wasteland between people and government, the lack of quality in our lives and the purposelessness of our society, racialism, the arms race, Viet Nam and so on — are not usually put before the people.

Politicians and opinion-makers exert strenuous efforts to fix our attention on ritual, in this case the casting of the vote. Voting, as a result,

* From the *Toronto Daily Star*, April 6, 1970. By permission.

becomes an isolated, magical act set apart from the rest of life, and ceases to have any political or social meaning except as an instrument by which the status quo is conserved. Electoral pageantry serves the purpose of a circus — the beguilement of the populace. The voter is reduced to voting for dazzling smiles, clean teeth, smooth voices and firm handshakes.

If we could vote for those who really control the country — for example, the directors of the Royal Bank of Canada, the governors of universities, social welfare agencies, industrial corporations and the shadows behind the ministries — then the trappings of liberal democracy would soon become transparent. The real power centres lie far beyond the people's influence at elections. They remain constant *whatever* party is "in power." So the only possible argument for participating in electoral politics, for voting during federal or provincial elections, is that marginal benefits may be gained.

This is obviously a serious conclusion to reach and to recommend — or at least to sanction — for it implies that the political parties, without exception, cannot operate within the province of deep political concern. This is not to say that "it makes no difference" who wins an election; it is rather to say that the "difference" is so slight or lies in such relatively trivial areas that one might very well bypass the area of electoral politics as being irrelevant to any fresh and profound issue of political circumstance.

To the New Left the elaborate procedures and structures of "representative" or parliamentary democracy (which is only one form), born in the 19th century and embroidered on since, stand as ossified caricatures. We live in a society where the majority of people passively consent to things being done in their name, a society of managed politics. The techniques of consultation are polished, but they remain techniques and should not be confused by anyone with participation.

Herbert Marcuse reformulated the libertarian insight that in our type of society any conventional opposition group inevitably assumes the values of the system it opposes and is eventually absorbed by it. In Canada, as elsewhere, this is the fate of socialists and social democrats.

The object of Canada's power elite and its supporting institutions is clear. It is to muffle real conflict; to dissolve it into a false political consensus; to build, not a participatory democracy where people have power to control a community of meaningful life and work, but a bogus conviviality between every social group. Consensus politics, essential to modern capitalism, is manipulative politics, the politics of man-management, and it is deeply undemocratic. Governments are still elected, to be sure, MPs assert the supremacy of the House of Commons, but the real business of government is the management of consensus between the powerful and organized elites.

Consensus politics is not intended for any large-scale structural change. It is the politics of pragmatism, of the successful manoeuvre within existing limits. Every administrative act is a kind of clever exercise in political public relations. Whether the manoeuvres are made by a Conservative, Liberal or New Democrat hardly matters, since they all accept the constraints of the *status quo.*

The product of this system is an increasing rationalization of the existing sources of power. The banks, corporations, the federations of industrialists, the trade union movement are all given a new and more formal role in the political structure. And to the extent that the "public interest" is defined as including these interests it also excludes what, on the other side, are called "sectional" or "local" interests — namely those of the poor, the low-paid and unorganized workers, youth in general and the backward regions. . . .

What we face is not simply a question of programs and ideologies; what we face primarily is a question of institutions. Certain institutions in our society will simply no longer yield fundamental social and political change.

Many people, along with the New Left, are concerned with such issues as: the boredom and conformity of life in the midst of a society of cybernetics; the human need for *creative* work; the continued experience of raw, naked exploitation at the work-place and at home; the power of the state over society, of centralized political entities over community, of the older generation over the younger, of bureaucracy over the individual, of parental authoritarianism over youthful spontaneity, of sexual, racial, cultural and imperialist privilege over the unfettered development of human personality.

At the same time, many of us believe that we have a qualitatively new order of possibilities — the possibility of a decolonialized Canada, of a free, non-repressive, decentralized society based on face-to-face democracy, community, spontaneity, and a new sense of human solidarity. This we believe amidst a technology so advanced that the burden of toil and material necessity could be removed from the shoulders of our people.

In the face of this kind of *revolutionary* change, electoral politics are meaningless, for elections are not won on these grounds; they are won amid tired formulas, old slogans and self-fulfilling prophecies. They are won by proposing changes of degree, not of kind; by working for adjustment, not transformation.

So the New Left in this country, as in other industrial-technological societies, has concluded that there is no alternative but to withdraw our allegiance from the machines of electoralism, from the institutions of "representative" democracy, to forgo the magic rite of voting and to create instead an extra-parliamentary opposition.

The idea is to build a coalition of individuals and groups with a common critique of liberal democracy. The coalition will range from radicals to revolutionaries — from those who believe it still useful to support candidates who while campaigning will also criticize the inadequacies of the system of representation, to those who seek to encourage the development or new constituencies of the self-organized powerless, of producers who control what they produce, of people who control their environment and neighbourhood *directly*. New forms of freedom need to be experimented with — workers' control, participatory democracy (which means control, not consultation), direct democracy — in a period where technology is laying the basis for a decentralized post-scarcity society. . . .

An extra-parliamentary opposition is primarily an act of negation. To paraphrase the philosopher Kolakowski, it is a wish to change existing reality. "But negation is not the opposite of construction — it is only the opposite of affirming existing conditions."

CONSERVATIVE PRINCIPLES AND PHILOSOPHY*

Robert L. Stanfield

Parties are Conciliators

. . . First, I would like to make a few comments on the role of political parties such as ours in Canada. Not only is it unnecessary for political parties to
disagree about everything but some acceptance of common ground among
the major parties is essential to an effective and stable democracy. For example, it is important to stability that all major parties agree on such
matters as parliamentary responsible government and major aspects of our
constitution.

I would like to emphasize too that in the British tradition political parties
are not doctrinaire. . . . In our parliamentary tradition, which is substantially the British tradition, parties have a unifying role to play. . . .
However, a truly national political party has a continuing role to try to pull
things together: achieve a consensus, resolve conflicts, strengthen the fabric
of society and work towards a feeling of harmony in the country. Success in
this role is, I suggest, essential if a party is to maintain a strong position in
this country. This role of a national political party, and success in this role,
are particularly important in countries as vast and diverse as Canada and
the United States.

It is partly because of this that I do not favour the [Senator Ernest] Manning thesis which urges polarization of political view points in this country.
In Canada, a party such as ours has a harmonizing role to play, both
horizontally in terms of resolving conflicts between regions, and vertically
in terms of resolving conflicts between Canadians in different walks of life.
It is not a matter of a national party being all things to all people — this
would never work. But a national party should appeal to all parts of the
country and to Canadians in all walks of life, if it is to serve this essential
role, and if it is to remain strong.

Conservatives Stress Order

Turning now to the consideration of the Conservative Party as such, I
would not wish to exaggerate the concern of British Conservatives through
the years with principles or theory. After all, they were practising politicians
for the most part, pragmatists dealing with problems, and of course, politicians seeking success. There are, however, some threads we can follow
through the years. I am, of course, not suggesting that we in Canada should
follow British principles or practices slavishly. Nor would I argue that our
party in Canada has followed a consistent pattern. I believe it has frequently
wandered far from the conservative tradition that I believe to be valuable,
and conservative principles I accept.

British Conservative thinkers traditionally stressed the importance of
order, not merely "law and order," but social order. This does not mean

* From a working paper presented to the federal Caucus of the Progressive Conservative Party
by the former National Leader, November 14, 1974. By permission.

that they were opposed to freedom for the individual; far from it. They believe that a decent civilized life requires a framework of order.

Conservatives did not take that kind of order for granted. It seemed to them quite rare in the world and therefore quite precious. This is still the case. Conservatives attached importance to the economy and to enterprise and to property, but private enterprise was not the central principle of traditional British conservatism. Indeed the supreme importance of private enterprise and the undesirability of government initiative and interference was Liberal nineteenth century doctrine. It was inherited from Adam Smith and was given its boldest political statement by such Liberals as Cobden and Bright. It was they who preached the doctrine of the unseen hand with practically no reservation.

Restrictions on Private Enterprise and Government

The Conservative concept of order encouraged Conservative governments to impose restrictions on private enterprise where this was considered desirable. We all studied William Wilberforce and his factory legislation when we were in school. These were logical measures for Conservatives to adopt; to protect the weak against the excesses of private enterprise and greed. That is good traditional conservatism, fully consistent with traditional conservative principles. It is also good Conservatism not to push regulation too far — to undermine self-reliance.

Because of the central importance Conservatives attached to the concept of order, they naturally favoured strong and effective government, but on the other hand they saw a limited or restricted role for government for several reasons. Because a highly centralized government is quite susceptible to arbitrary exercise of power and also to attack and revolution, Conservatives instinctively favoured a decentralization of power. National government had to be able to act in the national interest, but there had to be countervailing centres of power and influence. In the past, these might consist of church or the landed gentry or some other institution. Today in Canada, the provinces, trade unions, farm organizations, trade associations and the press would serve as examples. . . .

Man and the World Imperfect

Another reason why Conservatives traditionally saw a limited role for government was because Conservatives were far from being Utopians. They adopted basically a Judeo-Christian view of the world. . . . They certainly saw the world as a very imperfect place, capable of only limited improvement; and man as an imperfect being. They saw evil as an ongoing force that would always be present in changing form. It would therefore not have surprised Edmund Burke that economic growth, and government policies associated with it, have created problems almost as severe as those that economic growth and government policies were supposed to overcome.

A third reason for Conservatives taking a limited view of the role of government was that men such as Edmund Burke regarded man's intelligence as quite limited. Burke was very much impressed by how little man understood what was going on around him. . . .

Burke questioned whether any one generation really had the intelligence to understand fully the reasons for existing institutions or to pass judgement on those institutions which were the product of the ages. Burke pushed this idea much too far, but Conservatives have traditionally recognized how limited human intelligence really is, and consequently have recognized that success in planning the lives of other people or the life of the nation is likely to be limited. Neither government nor its bureaucracy is as wise as it is apt to be believed. Humility is a valuable strain in Conservatism, provided it does not become an excuse for resisting change, accepting injustice or supporting vested interests. . . .

The National View

There is another important strain to traditional Conservatism. Conservatism is national in scope and purpose. This implies a strong feeling for the country, its institutions and its symbols; but also a feeling for all the country and for all the people in the country. The Conservative Party serves the whole country and all the people, not simply part of the country and certain categories of people. . . .

I suggest that it is in the Conservative tradition to expand the concept of order and give it a fully contemporary meaning. The concept of order always included some concept of security for the unfortunate, although the actual program may have been quite inadequate by our present-day standards.

The concept of order certainly includes the preservation of our environment. And the concept of order, linked to Conservative concern for the country as a whole, certainly includes concern about poverty.

Social Goals

For a Conservative in the Conservative tradition which I have described, there is much more to national life than simply increasing the size of the gross national product. A Conservative naturally regards a healthy economy as of great importance, but increasing the size of the gross national product is not in itself a sufficient goal for a civilized nation, according to a Conservative. A healthy economy is obviously important, but a Conservative will be concerned about the effects of economic growth — what this does to our environment, what kind of living conditions it creates, what is its effect on the countryside, what is its effect on our cities; whether all parts of the nation benefit or only some parts of the nation, and whether a greater feeling of justice and fairness and self-fulfilment result from this growth, thereby strengthening the social order and improving the quality of national life.

. . . Any particular economic dogma is not a principle of our party, fond as most Conservatives may be of that particular dogma at any particular time.

At any given time our party is likely to contain those whose natural bent is reform and those whose natural bent is to stand pat or even to try to turn the clock back a bit. I think it is fair to say that Conservative statesmen we respect most were innovators. They did not change Conservative principles, but within those principles they faced and met the challenges of their time.

Traditional Liberalism started with the individual, emphasizing liberty of the individual and calling for a minimum of government interference with the individual. Conservatives, on the other hand, emphasized the nation, society, stability and order.

In this century, Liberals have resorted to the use of government more and more. Today big government and Liberalism are synonymous in Canada. . . .

Some Conservatives want to move to the old individualistic position of nineteenth century Liberalism — enshrining private enterprise as the most fundamental principle of our party, and condemning all government interference. The Conservative tradition has been to interfere only where necessary, but to interfere where necessary to achieve social and national objectives. Conservatives favour incentives, where appropriate, rather than the big stick.

Of course, it has always been and remains important to Conservatives to encourage individual self-reliance; and certainly red tape and regulation have today gone too far, especially in the case of small business. Self-reliance and enterprise should be encouraged, but Conservatism does not place private enterprise in a central position around which everything else revolves.

Conservatism recognized the responsibility of government to restrain or influence individual action where this was in the interests of society. Whether a government should or should not intervene was always a question of judgement, of course, but the Conservative tradition recognized the role of government as the regulator of individual conduct in the interests of society. . . .

Reform and Justice

. . . I would not suggest that Conservatives have tried or would try to build a radically different society from that which they have known. But to reform and adapt existing institutions to meet changing conditions, and to work towards a more just and therefore a truly more stable society — this I suggest is in the best Conservative tradition. . . .

This is a period when true Conservative principles of order and stability should be most appealing. Principles of conservation and preservation are also high in the minds of many Canadians today, and a Conservative can very legitimately — and on sound historical ground — associate with these. Again I emphasize that these kinds of bedrock principles are national in scope and reflect an overriding concern for society at large.

Enterprise and initiative are obviously important; but will emphasis upon individual rights solve the great problems of the day: I mean the maintenance of acceptable stability — which includes price stability, acceptable employment, and an acceptable distribution of income? Would we achieve these goals today by a simple reliance on the free market, if we could achieve a free market?

It would certainly be appropriate for a Conservative to suggest that we must achieve some kind of order if we are to avoid chaos; an order which is stable, but not static; an order therefore which is reasonably acceptable and which among other things provides a framework in which enterprise can flourish. That would be in the Conservative tradition. . . .

LIBERALISM*

Lester B. Pearson

. . . The Liberal Party is the party of reform, of progress, of new ideas. The Conservative Party, by its very name, stresses conservation and caution. . . .

What, then, are the principles that have inspired and guided the Liberal Party in its service to the Canadian people? The fundamental principle of Liberalism, the foundation of its faith, is belief in the dignity and worth of the individual. The state is the creation of man, to protect and serve him: and not the reverse.

Liberalism, therefore, believes in man; and that it is the purpose of government to legislate for the liberation and development of human personality. This includes the negative requirement of removing anything that stands in the way of individual and collective progress.

The negative requirement is important. It involves removal and reform: clearing away and opening up, so that man can move forward and societies expand. The removal of restrictions that block the access to achievement: this is the very essence of Liberalism.

The Liberal Party, however, must also promote the positive purpose of ensuring that all citizens, without any discrimination, will be in a position to take advantage of the opportunities opened up; of the freedoms that have been won . . . Liberalism is the political principle that gives purpose and reality to this kind of progress.

Liberalism stands for the middleway: the way of progress. It stands for moderation, tolerance, and the rejection of extreme courses, whether they express themselves in demands that the state should do everything for the individual, even if it means weakening and destroying him in the process, or in demands that the state should do nothing except hold the ring so that the fittest survive under the law of the jungle.

In other words, Liberalism accepts social security but rejects socialism; it accepts free enterprise but rejects economic anarchy; it accepts humanitarianism but rejects paternalism.

The Liberal Party is opposed to the shackling limitations of rigid political dogma, or authoritarianism of any kind, which is so often the prelude to oppression and exploitation. It fights against the abuse of power either by the state or by persons or groups within the state. . . .

* From Introduction to J.W. Pickersgill, *The Liberal Party*, Toronto, McClelland and Stewart, 1962. By permission of the publisher.

Liberalism, also, while insisting on equality of opportunity, rejects any imposed equality which would discourage and destroy a man's initiative and enterprise. It sees no value in the equality, or conformity, which comes from lopping off the tallest ears of corn. It maintains, therefore, that originality and initiative should be encouraged, and that reward should be the result of effort. . . .

But how can freedom . . . be made meaningful in the face of today's industrial and economic pressures? Government must keep pace with the changing needs of the times and accept greater responsibilities than would have been acceptable to a Liberal a hundred years ago. That is why the Liberal Party favours social and economic planning which will stimulate and encourage private enterprise to operate more effectively for the benefit of all.

Liberalism must always remember that responsibility is the other side of freedom. . . .

In short, freedom and welfare must be kept in a healthy balance or there will be trouble. This essential balance can be achieved by applying to every proposal for further intervention by the state the question, will it truly benefit the individual; will it enlarge or restrict his opportunity for self-expression and development?

The Liberal purpose remains the creation of opportunity for men and women to become self-directing, responsible citizens. This means, as we have seen, the simultaneous pursuit of freedom and welfare. . . .

For the progress Canada has made, and will make, national unity has been essential. The necessity for doing everything possible to maintain and strengthen this unity has been the cornerstone of Liberal policy from the very beginning of its history. Moreover, Liberalism has understood that national unity must be based on two races, cultures, traditions, and languages; on a full and equal partnership of English- and French-speaking Canadians. . . .

Canada is a federal state in which the constitutional and historic rights of the provinces must be preserved. It is important also that the provinces must not be separated by economic inequality which would make national unity difficult, if not impossible. The Liberal Party, therefore, considers it a duty of the federal government to help equalize the distribution of income and wealth and development among the provinces. . . .

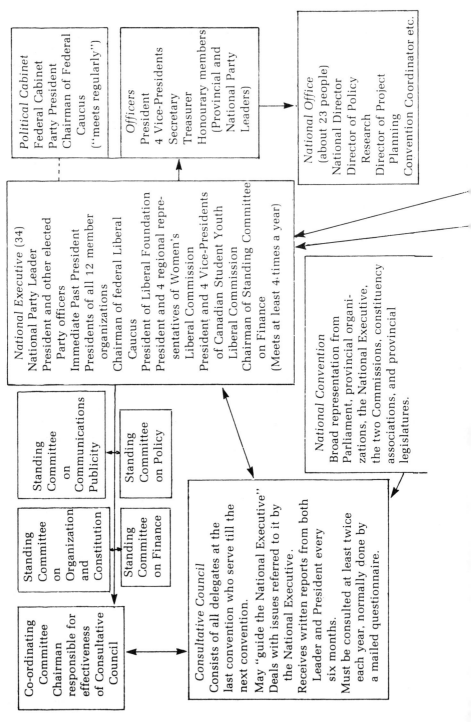

Constitution of the Liberal Party of Canada*

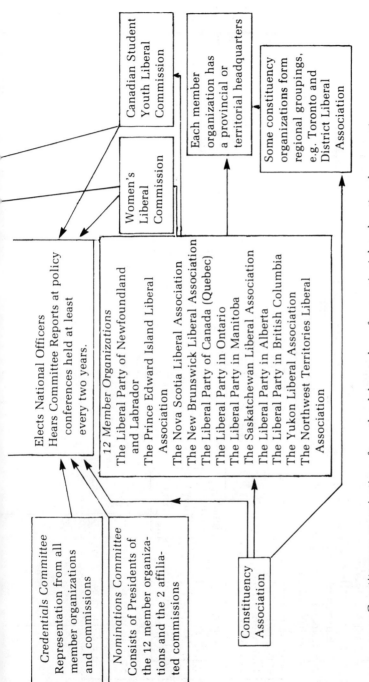

Elects National Officers
Hears Committee Reports at policy conferences held at least every two years.

Credentials Committee
Representation from all member organizations and commissions

Nominations Committee
Consists of Presidents of the 12 member organizations and the 2 affiliated commissions

Constituency Association

Women's Liberal Commission

Canadian Student Youth Liberal Commission

Each member organization has a provincial or territorial headquarters

Some constituency organizations form regional groupings, e.g. Toronto and District Liberal Association

12 Member Organizations
The Liberal Party of Newfoundland and Labrador
The Prince Edward Island Liberal Association
The Nova Scotia Liberal Association
The New Brunswick Liberal Association
The Liberal Party of Canada (Quebec)
The Liberal Party in Ontario
The Liberal Party in Manitoba
The Saskatchewan Liberal Association
The Liberal Party in Alberta
The Liberal Party in British Columbia
The Yukon Liberal Association
The Northwest Territories Liberal Association

Constituency organizations form the delegate base for provincial and national conventions. Both the provincial and the federal constituency associations belong to the provincial organization.

* The chart is based on the party "constitution" as well as occasional organizational changes described in Liberal Party documents. The arrows indicate the direction of the flow of personnel.

From C. Winn, J. McMenemy, *Political Parties in Canada*, Toronto, McGraw-Hill Ryerson, pp. 168-173. By permission.

Constitution of the Progressive Conservative Association of Canada*

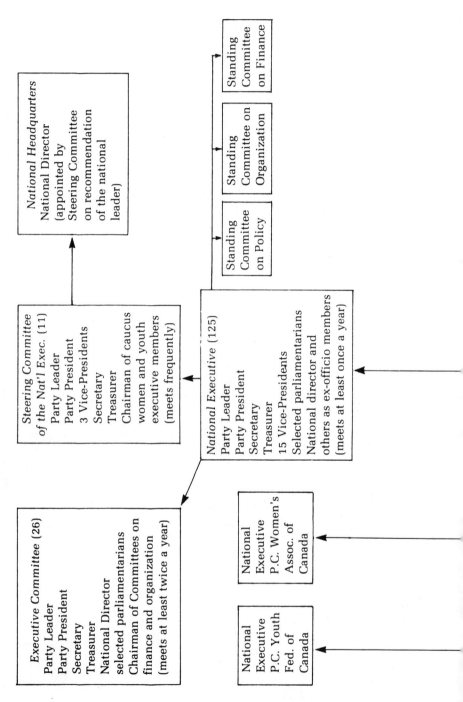

National Headquarters
National Director (appointed by Steering Committee on recommendation of the national leader)

Steering Committee of the Nat'l Exec. (11)
Party Leader
Party President
3 Vice-Presidents
Secretary
Treasurer
Chairman of caucus
women and youth
executive members
(meets frequently)

National Executive (125)
Party Leader
Party President
Secretary
Treasurer
15 Vice-Presidents
Selected parliamentarians
National director and
others as ex-officio members
(meets at least once a year)

Standing Committee on Policy

Standing Committee on Organization

Standing Committee on Finance

Executive Committee (26)
Party Leader
Party President
Secretary
Treasurer
National Director
selected parliamentarians
Chairman of Committees on
finance and organization
(meets at least twice a year)

National Executive P.C. Women's Assoc. of Canada

National Executive P.C. Youth Fed. of Canada

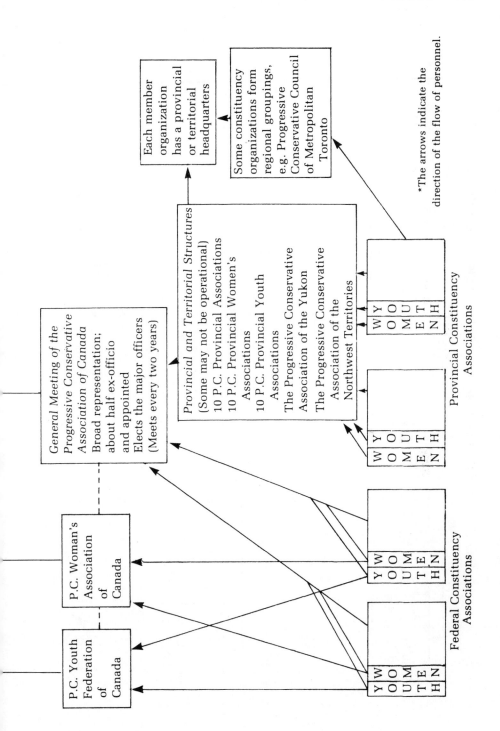

Each member organization has a provincial or territorial headquarters

Some constituency organizations form regional groupings, e.g. Progressive Conservative Council of Metropolitan Toronto

*The arrows indicate the direction of the flow of personnel.

Provincial and Territorial Structures (Some may not be operational)
10 P.C. Provincial Associations
10 P.C. Provincial Women's Associations
10 P.C. Provincial Youth Associations
The Progressive Conservative Association of the Yukon
The Progressive Conservative Association of the Northwest Territories

General Meeting of the Progressive Conservative Association of Canada Broad representation; about half ex-officio and appointed Elects the major officers (Meets every two years)

P.C. Woman's Association of Canada

P.C. Youth Federation of Canada

WOMEN / YOUTH

Provincial Constituency Associations

YOUTH / WOMEN

Federal Constituency Associations

Constitution of the New Democratic Party*

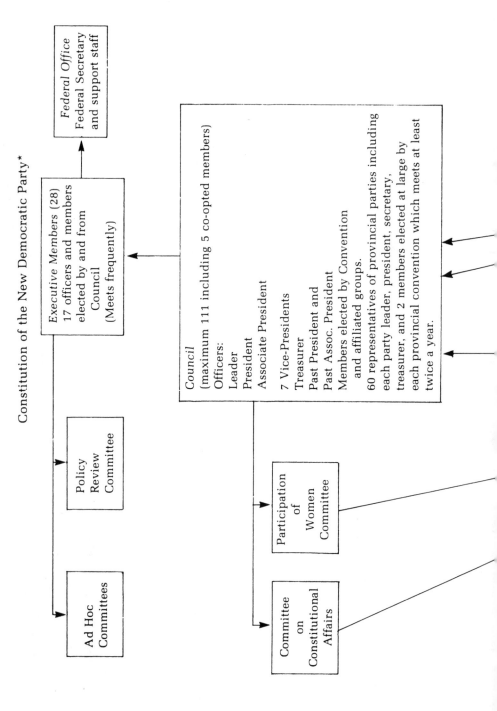

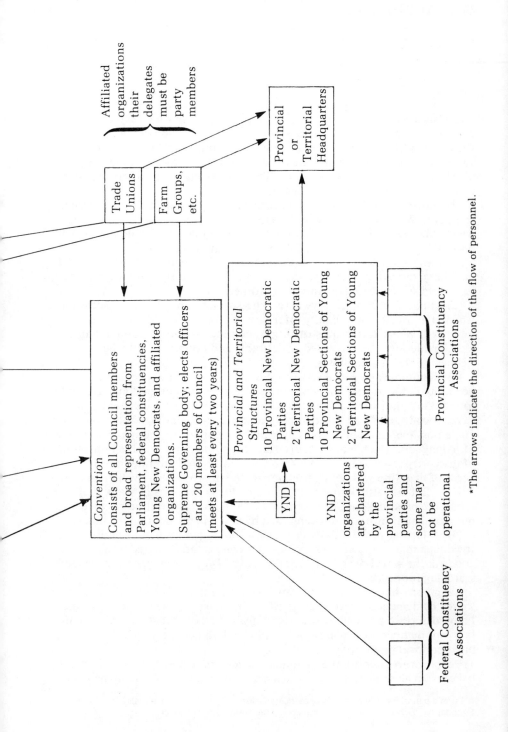

*The arrows indicate the direction of the flow of personnel.

Affiliated organizations their delegates must be party members

Trade Unions

Farm Groups, etc.

Provincial or Territorial Headquarters

Convention
Consists of all Council members and broad representation from Parliament, federal constituencies, Young New Democrats, and affiliated organizations.
Supreme Governing body; elects officers and 20 members of Council (meets at least every two years)

Provincial and Territorial Structures
10 Provincial New Democratic Parties
2 Territorial New Democratic Parties
10 Provincial Sections of Young New Democrats
2 Territorial Sections of Young New Democrats

YND

YND organizations are chartered by the provincial parties and some may not be operational

Provincial Constituency Associations

Federal Constituency Associations

SOCIALISM TODAY*

David Lewis

. . . What are the ends which socialism seeks to achieve? They are, broadly, the following:

(1) A classless or egalitarian society within the borders of a nation. Socialists have proclaimed as their goal a society from which exploitation of man by man and of class by class or of group by group will be eliminated; where every person will have an equal opportunity to share in a rich and varied life and to develop his talents, whatever they may be, to the full, both at work and during leisure hours. This — the classless society based on equality — is the major aim of democratic socialism.

(2) Equality among all nations, regardless of colour, race, or economic standard. We strive for a world based on the brotherhood of man from which the practices of imperialism and the ignominy of colonialism will disappear; a world in which the more advanced economic societies will assist the less developed ones without the price in human exploitation which has characterized overseas expansion in the last centuries. We want a classless world society based on universal brotherhood.

(3) Human freedom everywhere. The socialist dream is of a society in which the worth and dignity of every human being is recognized and respected, where differences of origin, of religion and of opinion will not only be tolerated, but accepted as desirable and necessary to the beauty and richness of the human mosaic.

(4) Economic and social security. Socialists seek not only equality of opportunity but a constant advance in the opportunities offered and available to mankind; not only a fair division of the cake, but a constantly larger cake. Socialists long ago recognized that modern technological advance has made possible, and will increasingly make possible, an economic standard of living from which material suffering, economic want and the oppression of insecurity can disappear. We know, of course, that meeting the economic needs of mankind will not by itself create the life for which the human spirit strives. But we also know that if it can break the prison walls built by economic pressures and insecurities, the human spirit will be released and our moral and cultural values enriched by new and greater opportunities.

(5) A lasting peace based on freedom and equality within nations and freedom and equality among nations. This end is today shared by all men of goodwill the world over, but socialists have always been among the leaders searching for peace. . . .

Let me say immediately that I am well aware that some of these aims are shared by democratic non-socialists. . . . However, some of the aims which I have described are held by socialists only and all of them together form the fabric of democratic socialist philosophy and do not form the fabric of any other political philosophy.

People who support the capitalist society as a desirable social system believe in a class society and not in a classless one, they believe in inequality

---

* From a pamphlet *A Socialist Takes Stock*, published by the Ontario Woodsworth Memorial Foundation, Toronto, 1965. By permission of the author and publisher.

and not in equality; they believe in the right of one nation to make profits at the expense of another, just as they believe in the right of one group within a nation to make profits at the expense of the rest; they believe in the right of the sons and daughters of the rich to have greater opportunities than those of the poor; and even as regards freedom they place the rights of property above those of human beings or, at least, on an equal footing. All these concepts the socialist passionately rejects.

At the other extreme, those who believe in the communist society reject in practice all of the aims of socialism, despite their deceitful words and slogans. In every communist land there has been established a new, but no less evil, class society. The elite of the communist party, the membership of that party, the civil service in government as well as in the party, the secret police, and the army, form a class or classes which are the top of a social pyramid as clearly defined as the pyramid of wealth to which we are accustomed and, if anything, much more oppressive and evil in its consequences. It is unnecessary to remind you that the communist state stifles freedom and enthrones uniformity and conformity as the absolute duty of every citizen. Domination by the chief communist state over other nations and states, rather than equality among nations, has been the communist practice. . . .

• • •

What means has the socialist proposed for building the road to this [socialist] society? Briefly, they are, I think, the following:

(1) We must emphasize, first, the determination of the socialist to pursue at all times only democratic procedures and to base his actions on the consent of the people freely expressed. To use any form of dictatorship to achieve so-called desirable ends is a perversion of our basic ideas of freedom and will in practice also pervert the ends. . . .

(2) A constant and continuing improvement in the existing standards of living and in the social services provided by the state. . . .

(3) The third means which the socialist has proposed, and when he has had the chance, has used, is that of social planning. The socialist rejects the capitalist theory that an unregulated law of supply and demand should control the destinies of society and its members. He believes that it is both necessary and possible for society collectively to plan at least its economic future and to regulate the production and distribution of goods and services so as to achieve an expanding economy of full employment and fair share for all members of society. . . .

(4) The fourth means which the socialist has proposed is that of public ownership, whether it be ownership by the state — federal, provincial or municipal — or ownership by a collectivity of citizens in the form of co-operatives, credit unions or the like. There are three main reasons behind the socialist belief in public ownership.

First and foremost, that the modern concentration of wealth and property places too much power, both economic and political, in the hands of too few people or, what is even worse, in the hands of giant corporations which, by their very nature, are without heart and without soul. . . .

Secondly, nationalization has been proposed by socialists because the job of social planning is made more difficult by the power of private corporations and would be made much easier by public ownership of the key levers in the economy.

Thirdly, the growth and power of private corporations have imposed on society a standard of values which perverts the best ideals of man. . . .

• • •

Among democratic socialists there is, and always has been, agreement about the ends. On the other hand, there is, always has been and probably always will be, disagreement about the means. . . .

Perhaps first among socialist controversies is the question of the extent to which the tool of public ownership can or should be used by socialists in modern society. . . .

Until fairly recently it had been accepted by most socialists as axiomatic that nationalization of industry would automatically bring with it greater social and political freedom and a release from the obstacles to the widest liberty which private economic power produces. . . .

The developments in the Soviet Union, in particular, and in other communist states as well, have completely shattered these assumptions and have shown them to have been and to be entirely false. In the communist societies all wealth, or almost all wealth, has been taken over by the state. But, instead of greater freedom, there is actually no freedom at all. . . .

Similarly, we have learned from the actions of the Soviet Union . . . that there are pressures toward aggression and war other than economic ones and that the lust for power and the zeal of fanaticism are at least as powerful forces endangering peace as economic competition and conflicts. . . .

Socialists can, therefore, no longer regard nationalization as an automatic panacea for all ills, but must regard it merely as one tool that is available in appropriate circumstances for the furtherance of socialist ends.

The experience of the Scandinavian countries, the history of the Roosevelt era in the United States, and developments during the last war have all shown that there are available in the modern economy tools of control and of planning which can be effectively applied without actually replacing private with public ownership in all spheres. . . . The use of fiscal and financial policies to influence the volume and direction of investments, to redistribute income, and to stimulate purchasing power has been demonstrated as a practical tool for economic planning, at least in periods when there is no major depression. . . .

In all modern societies there is growing up a considerable body of social welfare legislation which produces what are known as "transfer payments." These — unemployment insurance benefits, old age pensions, family allowances, farm support payments and the like — provide a constant stream of purchasing power into the hands of large sections of the people. . . .

BIBLIOGRAPHY

Federal Parties and Politics

(See also Bibliography in Chapter 10, Voting Behaviour)

Abella, I.M.,*Nationalism, Communism, and Canadian Labour: The CIO, the Communist Party, and the Canadian Congress of Labour, 1935-1956*, Toronto, U.T.P., 1973.

Avakumovic, I., *The Communist Party in Canada: A History*, Toronto, M. & S., 1975.

Avakumovic, I., *Socialism in Canada: A Study of the CCF and NDP in Federal and Provincial Politics*, Toronto, M. & S., 1978.

Baum, G., *Catholics and Canadian Socialism: Political Thought in the Thirties and Forties*, Toronto, Lorimer, 1980.

Brodie, M.J., and Jenson, J., *Crisis, Challenge and Change: Party and Class in Canada*, Toronto, Methuen, 1980.

Brown, P., Chodos, R., Murphy, R., *Winners, Losers: The 1976 Tory Leadership Convention*, Toronto, Lorimer, 1976.

Buck, T., *Lenin and Canada*, Toronto, Progress Books, 1970.

Canada, *Report of the Committee on Election Expenses*, Ottawa, Q.P., 1966.

Caplan, G., *The Dilemma of Canadian Socialism*, Toronto, M & S., 1973.

Carrigan, O., *Canadian Party Platforms: 1867-1968*, Toronto, C.C., 1968.

Chandler, W.M., "Canadian Socialism and Policy Impact: Contagion from the Left," *C.J.P.S.*, X, 4, December, 1977.

Cherwinski, W.J., "Bibliographical Note: The Left in Canadian History, 1911-1969," *J.C.S.*, IV, 4, November, 1969.

Christian, W., and Campbell, C., *Political Parties and Ideologies in Canada: Liberals, Conservatives, Socialists, Nationalists*, Toronto, McG.-H.R., 1974.

Clarke, H.D., and Price, R.G. *Recruitment and Leadership Selection in Canada*, Toronto, H.R.W., 1973.

Coates, R.C., *The Night of the Knives*, Fredericton, Brunswick Press, 1969.

Conway, J.F., "Pluralism in the United States, Russia, and Canada: Explaining the Roots of Canada's Third Parties," *C.J.P.S.*, XI, 1, March, 1978.

Cook, R., (ed.), *Politics of Discontent*, [Essays on Aberhart, Pattulo, H.H. Stevens, George McCullagh], Canadian Historical Readings, U.T.P., Toronto, 1967.

Cook, R., "The Canadian Conservative Tradition: An Historical Perspective," *J.C.S.*, VIII, 4, November, 1973.

Courtney, J.C., *The Selection of National Party Leaders in Canada*, Toronto, Macmillan, 1973.

Courtney, J.C., "Recognition of Canadian Political Parties in Parliament and in Law," *C.J.P.S.*, XI, 1, March, 1978.

Cross, M.S., *The Decline and Fall of a Good Idea: CCF-NDP Manifestoes 1932 to 1969*, Toronto, New Hogtown Press, 1974.

Cunningham, F., *Understanding Marxism: A Canadian Introduction*, Toronto, Progress, 1978.

Dawson, R.M., *The Conscription Crisis of 1944*, Toronto, U.T.P., 1961.

Denman, N., *How to Organize an Election*, Montreal, Les éditions du jour, 1962.

Dimension Staff, et al., "New Democratic Party: Essays," *Canadian Dimension*, 7, 8, April, 1971.

Dion, L'Abbé G., et O'Neill, L'Abbé L., *Le chrétien et les élections*, Montréal, Les éditions de l'homme, 8me ed., 1960.

Dion, L'Abbé G., et O'Neill, L'Abbé L., *Le chrétien en démocratie*, Montréal, Les éditions de l'homme, 1961.

Dion, L., "A la recherche d'une méthode d'analyse des partis et des groupes d'intérêt," *C.J.P.S.*, II, 1, March, 1969.

Dion, L., "Politique consultative et systeme politique," *C.J.P.S.*, II, 2 June, 1969.

Duverger, M., *Political Parties*, Toronto, Methuen, 1979.

Elkins, D.J., "The Perceived Structure of the Canadian Party System," *C.J.P.S.*, VII, 3, September, 1974.

Engelmann, F.C., and Schwartz, M.A., *Canadian Political Parties: Origin, Character, Impact*, Toronto, P.-H., 1975.

English, J., *The Decline of Politics: The Conservatives and the Party System 1901-20*, Toronto, U.T.P., 1977.

Epstein, L., "A Comparative Study of Canadian Parties," *The American Political Science Review*, LVIII, 1, March, 1964.

Finlay, J.L., *Social Credit: The English Origins*, Montreal, McG.-Q.U.P,, 1972.

Fox, Paul, "Early Socialism in Canada," in Aitchison, J.R., (ed.), *The Political Process in Canada*, Toronto, U.T.P., 1963.

Gibbons, K.M., and Rowat, D.C. (eds.), *Political Corruption in Canada: Cases, Causes and Cures*, Carleton Library No. 95, Toronto, M. & S., 1976.

Granatstein, J.L., *Canada's War, The Politics of the Mackenzie King Government, 1939-1945*, Toronto, O.U.P., 1975.

Granatstein, J.L., *The Politics of Survival: The Conservative Party of Canada, 1939-1945*, Toronto, U.T.P., 1965.

Grant, G., *Lament for a Nation*, Toronto, Carleton Library Series No. 50, M. & S., 1971.

Greenslade, J.G., (ed.), *Canadian Politics: Speeches by F.M. Watkins, Stanley Knowles, J.R. Mallory and H.D. Hicks*, Sackville, Mount Allison University Publication No. 4, 1959.

Gwyn, R., *The Shape of Scandal, A Study of a Government in Crisis*, Toronto, Clarke, Irwin, 1965.

Hamelin, M., (ed.), *The Political Ideas of the Prime Ministers of Canada*, George Vanier Lectures, No. 1, University of Ottawa, 1970.

Harbron, J.D., "The Conservative Party and National Unity," *Q.Q.*, LXIX, 3, Autumn, 1962.

Heasman, D.J., "Political Alignments in Canada: The Fragmentation of Canadian Politics," *Parliamentary Affairs*, XVI, 4, Autumn, 1963, and XVII, 1, Winter, 1963-64.

Heggie, G.F., *Canadian Political Parties, 1867-1968: A Historical Bibliography*, Toronto, Macmillan, 1977.

Heron, C., *Imperialism, Nationalism, and Canada, Essays from the Marxist Institute of Toronto*, Toronto, New Hogtown Press, 1977.

Hogan, G., *The Conservative in Canada*, Toronto, M. & S., 1963.

Horn, M., *The League for Social Reconstruction: Intellectual Origins of the Democratic Left in Canada 1930-1942*, Toronto, U.T.P., 1980.

Horowitz, G., "Tories, Socialists and the Demise of Canada," *Canadian Dimension*, II, 4, May-June, 1965.

Horowitz, G., "Conservatism, Liberalism, and Socialism in Canada: An Interpretation," *C.J.E.P.S.*, XXXII, 2, May, 1966.

Horowitz, G., *Canadian Labour in Politics*, Toronto, U.T.P., 1968.

Horowitz, G., "Toward the Democratic Class Struggle," in Lloyd, Trevor and McLeod, Jack, (eds.), *Agenda 1970*, Toronto, U.T.P., 1968.

Horowitz, G., "Notes on 'Conservatism, Liberalism and Socialism in Canada,'" *C.J.P.S.*, XI, 2, June, 1978.

Hudon, R., "Pour une analyse politique du patronage," *C.J.P.S.*, VII, 3, September, 1974.

Irvine, W.P., "The 1972 Election: The Return of Minority Government," *Q.Q.*, LXXIX, 4, Winter, 1972.

Irvine, W., *The Farmers in Politics*, Toronto, Macmillan, 1978.

Johnson, J., *The Party's Over*, Toronto, Longman, 1971.

Johnston, R., and Percy, M.B., "Reciprocity, Imperial Sentiment, and Party Politics in the 1911 Election," *C.J.P.S.*, XIII, 4, December, 1980.

Kelly, F., (ed.), *The Canadian Voter's*

Guide, Toronto, M. & S., 1979.

Knowles, S., *The New Party,* Toronto, M. & S., 1961.

Kornberg, K., Smith, J., and Bromley, D., "Some Differences in the Political Socialization Patterns of Canadian and American Party Officials: A Preliminary Report," *C.J.P.S.,* II, 1, March, 1969.

Kornberg, A., Smith, J., and Clarke, H., "Attributes of Ascribed Influence in Local Party Organizations in Canada and the United States," *C.J.P.S.,* V, 2, June, 1972.

Kornberg, A., Smith, J., Clarke, H.D., *Citizen Politicians — Canada: Party Officials in a Democratic Society,* Durham, N.C., Carolina Academic Press, 1979.

LaPierre, L., McLeod, J., Taylor, C., Young, W., *Essays on the Left,* Toronto, M. & S., 1971.

Laponce, J.A., "Canadian Party Labels: An Essay in Semantics and Anthropology," *C.J.P.S.,* II, 2, June, 1969.

Laurendeau, A., *La crise de la conscription,* Montréal, Éditions du jour, 1962. (English edition, Toronto, M. & S., 1962).

Lavau, G., "Partis et systèmes politiques: interactions et fonction," *C.J.P.S.,* II, 1, March, 1969.

Leduc, L., "Party Decision-making: Some Empirical Observations on the Leadership Selection Process," *C.J.P.S.,* IV, 1, March, 1971.

Lemieux, V., "Pour une science politique des partis," *C.J.P.S.,* V, 4, December, 1972.

Lemieux, V., "Esquisse d'une théorie organisationnelle des partis," *C.J.P.S.,* X, 4, December, 1977.

Leslie, P.M., "The Role of Political Parties in Promoting the Interests of Ethnic Minorities," *C.J.P.S.,* II, 4, December, 1969.

Levant, V., *Capital and Labour: Partners? Two Classes — Two Views,* Toronto, Steel Rail Publishing, 1977.

Levitt, J., "The Federal N.D.P. and Quebec," *J.C.S.,* 12, 3, August, 1977.

Lewis, David, *Louder Voices: The Corporate Welfare Bums,* Introduc-

tion by Eric Kierans, Toronto, J.L.S., 1972.

MacDonald, J., and J., (eds.), *The Canadian Voter's Guidebook,* Don Mills, Ontario, F. and W., 1972.

McGuigan, M., and Lloyd, T., *Liberalism and Socialism,* Toronto, Exchange for Political Ideas in Canada, 1964, [pamphlet].

McHenry, D.E., *The Third Force in Canada: The Cooperative Commonwealth Federation, 1932-1948,* Berkeley, University of California Press, 1950.

MacKinnon, F., *Postures and Politics,* Toronto, U.T.P., 1973.

MacQuarrie, H., *The Conservative Party,* Toronto, M. & S., 1965.

Masters, D.D., *The Winnipeg General Strike,* Toronto, U.T.P., 1973.

Meisel, J., *Working Papers on Canadian Politics,* Montreal, McG.-Q.U.P., second enlarged edition, 1975.

Meisel, J., "The Stalled Omnibus: Canadian Parties in the 1960s," *Social Research,* XXX, 3, Autumn, 1963.

Meisel, J., *Les transformations des partis politiques canadiens,* Cahiers de la Société canadienne de Science politique, no. 2, 1966.

Meisel, J., "Canadian Parties and Politics," in Leach, R.H., *Contemporary Canada,* Toronto, U.T.P., 1968.

Meynaud, J., *Argent et politique,* Montréal, Collège Jean-de-Brébeuf, 1966.

Morley, J.T., "Comment: The 1974 Federal Election in British Columbia," *BC Studies,* 23, Fall, 1974.

Morley, T., "Canada and the Romantic Left," *Q.Q.,* 86, 1, Spring, 1979.

Morton, D., *With Your Help, An Election Manual,* Ottawa, New Democratic Party, 1966.

Morton, D., *Social Democracy in Canada,* Toronto, Samuel, Stevens, Hakkert, 1977.

Morton, W.L., *The Progressive Party in Canada,* Toronto, U.T.P., 1950.

Muller, S., "Federalism and the Party System in Canada," in Meekison, J.P., (ed.), *Canadian Federalism:*

Myth or Reality, Toronto, Methuen, 2nd ed., 1971.

Murray, D., "The Railliement des Créditistes in Parliament," *J.C.S.,* VIII, 2, May, 1973.

Neatby, H.B., *The Politics of Chaos: Canada in the Thirties,* Toronto, Macmillan, 1972.

Neill, R.F., "Social Credit and National Policy in Canada," *J.C.S.,* III, 1, February, 1968.

Newman, P.C., *The Distemper of Our Times, Canadian Politics in Transition: 1963-1968,* Toronto, M. & S., 1968.

Newman, P.C., and Fillmore, S., *Their Turn to Curtsey — Your Turn to Bow,* (Election Handbook), Toronto, Maclean-Hunter, 1972.

Nicholson, P., *Vision and Indecision: Diefenbaker and Pearson,* Don Mills, Longmans, 1968.

Oliver, M., (ed.), *Social Purpose for Canada,* Toronto, U.T.P., 1961.

O'Toole, R., *The Precipitous Path: Studies in Political Sects,* Toronto, Peter Martin Associates, 1976.

Paltiel, K.Z., *Political Party Financing in Canada,* Toronto, McG.-H., 1970.

Paltiel, K.Z., "Party and Candidate Expenditures in the Canadian General Election of 1972," *C.J.P.S.,* VII, 2, June, 1974.

Peacock, D., *Journey to Power: The Story of a Canadian Election,* [1968], Toronto, Ryerson, 1968.

Penner, N., *The Canadian Left: A Critical Analysis,* Toronto, P.-H., 1977.

Penner, N., *Winnipeg 1919,* Toronto, J.L.S., 1973.

Perlin, G.C., *The Tory Syndrome: Leadership Politics in the Progressive Conservative Party,* Montreal, McG.-Q.U.P., 1980.

Pickersgill, J.W., *The Liberal Party,* Toronto, M. & S., 1962.

Pinard, M., "Third Parties in Canada Revisited," *C.J.P.S.,* VI, 3, September, 1973.

Pinard, M., *The Rise of a Third Party: A Study in Crisis Politics,* McG.-Q.U.P., 1975.

Posner, M., "Canada's Federal Political Parties: Their Ideologies and Histories," *Canada and the World,* 38, 6, February, 1973.

Preece, R., "The Anglo-Saxon Conservative Tradition," *C.J.P.S.,* XIII, 1, March, 1980.

Preece, R., "The Myth of the Red Tory," *Canadian Journal of Political and Social Theory,* I, 1, 1977. (Comments by G. Horowitz, *ibid.,* I,3; W. Christian, II, 2; Reply, II, 2.)

Proulx, J., *Le panier de crabes,* Toronto, M. & S., 1971.

Quinn, H.F., *The Union Nationale: A Study in Quebec Nationalism,* Toronto, U.T.P., 2nd ed., 1979.

Rayside, D.M., "Federalism and the Party System: Provincial and Federal Liberals in the Province of Quebec," *C.J.P.S.,* XI, 3, September, 1978.

Rayside, D.M., "The Impact of the Linguistic Cleavage on the 'Governing' Parties of Belgium and Canada," *C.J.P.S.,* XI, 1, March, 1978.

Regenstreif, P., "Note on the 'Alternation' of French and English Leaders in the Liberal Party of Canada," *C.J.P.S.,* II, 1, March, 1969.

Richardson, B.T., *Canada and Mr. Diefenbaker,* Toronto, M. & S., 1962.

Robin, M., *Radical Politics and Canadian Labour 1880-1930,* Kingston, Queen's University, 1968.

Rodney, W., *Soldiers of the International: A History of the Communist Party of Canada, 1919-1929,* Toronto, U.T.P., 1968.

Rose, W., *Social Credit Handbook,* Toronto, M. & S., 1968.

Roussopoulos, D., (ed.), *The New Left in Canada,* Montreal, Our Generation Press, 1970.

Scarrow, H.A., "Distinguishing Between Political Parties — The Case of Canada", *Midwest Journal of Political Science,* IX, 1, February, 1965.

Schwartz, M.A., *Politics and Territory: The Sociology of Regional Persistence in Canada*, Montreal, McG.-Q.U.P., 1974.

Smiley, D.V., "The Two-Party System and One-Party Dominance in the Liberal Democratic State," *C.J.E.P.S.*, XXIV, 3, August, 1958.

Smiley, D.V., "The National Party Leadership Convention in Canada: A Preliminary Analysis," *C.J.P.S.*, I, 4, December, 1968.

Smith, D.E., *Feminism and Marxism: A Place to Begin, A Way to Go*, Vancouver, New Star, 1977.

Smith, D., *The Regional Decline of a National Party: Liberals on the Prairies*, Toronto, U.T.P., 1981.

Stewart, W., *Divide and Con*, Toronto, New Press, 1973.

Sullivan, M., *Mandate '68, The Year of Pierre Elliott Trudeau*, Toronto, Doubleday, 1968.

Taylor, Charles, *The Pattern of Politics*, Toronto, M. & S., 1970.

Teeple, G., (ed.), *Capitalism and the National Question in Canada*, Toronto, U.T.P., 1972.

Thompson, R.N., *Canadians, It's Time You Knew*, n.p., The Aavangen Press, 1961.

Thompson, R.N., *Commonsense for Canadians: A Selection of Speeches*, Toronto, M. & S., 1964.

Thorburn, H.G., (ed.), *Party Politics in Canada*, Scarborough, Ontario, P.-H., 4th ed., 1979.

Truman, T., "A Scale for Measuring a Tory Streak in Canada and the United States," *C.J.P.S.*, X, 3, September, 1977.

Underhill, F.H., *Canadian Political Parties*, Canadian Historical Association Booklet No. 8, Ottawa, 1957.

Underhill, F.H., "The Revival of Conservatism in North America," *Transaction of the Royal Society of Canada*, LII, Series III, June, 1958.

Underhill, F.H., *In Search of Canadian Liberalism*, Toronto, Macmillan, 1960.

Ward, N., "Money and Politics: The Costs of Democracy in Canada," *C.J.P.S.*, V, 3, September, 1972.

Wearing, J., "Party Leadership and the 1966 Conventions," *J.C.S.*, II, 1, February, 1967.

Wearing, J., "A Convention for Professionals: The PCs in Toronto," *J.C.S.*, II, 4, November, 1967.

Wearing, J., "The Liberal Choice," *J.C.S.*, III, 2, May, 1968.

Wearing, J., "The Trudeau Phenomenon," *C.J.P.S.*, II, 3, September, 1969.

Wearing, J., *The L-Shaped Party: The Liberal Party of Canada, 1958-1980*, Toronto, McG.-H.R., 1980.

Whitaker, R., *The Government Party: Organizing and Financing the Liberal Party of Canada, 1930-58*, Toronto, U.T.P., 1977.

White, G., "One-Party Dominance and Third Parties," *C.J.P.S.*, VI, 3, September, 1973.

Wilbur, J.R.H., *The Bennett New Deal: Fraud or Portent*, Toronto, C.C., 1968.

Williams, J.R., *The Conservative Party in Canada, 1920-1949*, Durham, Duke University Press, 1956.

Wilson, W.A., *The Trudeau Question, Election 1972*, Don Mills, Ontario, Paperjacks, 1972.

Winham, G.R., Cunningham, R.B., "Party Leader Images in the 1968 Federal Elections," *C.J.P.S.*, III, 1, March, 1970.

Winn, C., McMenemy, J., *Political Parties in Canada*, Toronto, McG.-H.R., 1976.

Young, W.D., *The Anatomy of a Party: The National C.C.F. 1932-61*, Toronto, U.T.P., 1969.

Provincial Politics

(See also Bibliography, Chapter 4, Provinces and Territories, and Chapter 10. For Quebec, see Chapter 6.)

Aucoin, P., "The 1970 Nova Scotia Provincial Election," *J.C.S.*, VII, 3, August, 1972.

Badgley, R.F., and Wolfe, S., *Doctors' Strike: Medical Care and Con-*

flict in Saskatchewan, Toronto, Macmillan, 1967.

Barr, J.J., *The Dynasty: The Rise and Fall of Social Credit in Alberta*, Toronto, M. & S., 1974.

Black, E.R., "British Columbia: The Politics of Exploitation," in Shearer, R., (ed.), *Exploiting Our Economic Potential: Public Policy and the British Columbia Economy*, Toronto, H.R.W., 1968.

Blais, A., "Third Parties in Canadian Provincial Politics," *C.J.P.S.*, VI, 3, September, 1973.

Caplan, G.L., *The Dilemma of Canadian Socialism: The CCF in Ontario*, Toronto, M. & S., 1973.

Doern, R., *Wednesdays Are Cabinet Days*, [Schreyer Government in Manitoba], Winnipeg, Queenston House, 1981.

Elkins, D.J., and Simeon, R., *Small Worlds: Parties and Provinces in Canadian Political Life*, Toronto, Methuen, 1980.

Flanagan, T.E., "Electoral Cleavages in Alberta During the Social Credit Reign, 1935-1971," unpublished, University of Calgary, December, 1972.

Frank, J.A., and Kelly, M., "Étude préliminaire sur la violence collective en Ontario et au Québec, 1963-73," *C.J.P.S.*, X, 1, March, 1977.

Gagan, D.P., (ed.), *Prairie Perspectives*, Toronto, H.R.W., 1970.

Gibbins, R., "Models of Nationalism: A Case Study of Political Ideologies in the Canadian West," *C.J.P.S.*, X, 2, June, 1977.

Grayson, J.P., and Grayson, L.M., "The Social Base of Interwar Political Unrest in Urban Alberta," *C.J.P.S.*, VII, 2, June, 1974.

Higginbotham, C.H., *Off the Record: The C.C.F. in Saskatchewan*, Toronto, M. & S., 1968.

Hooke, A., *Thirty Years Plus Five: I Know, I Was There*, Edmonton, Institute of Applied Arts, 1971.

Irving, J.A., *The Social Credit Movement in Alberta*, Toronto, U.T.P., 1959.

Jackman, S.W., *Portraits of the Premiers: An Informal History of*

British Columbia, Sidney, B.C., Gray, 1969.

Kavic, L.J., *The 1200 Days, A Shattered Dream: Dave Barrett and the N.D.P. in B.C., 1972-75*, Coquitlam, B.C., Kaen Publishers, 1979.

Knox, P., and Resnick, P., (eds.), *Essays in B.C. Political Economy*, Vancouver, New Star Books, 1974.

Levesque, T.J., and Norrie, K.H., "Overwhelming Majorities in the Legislature of Alberta," *C.J.P.S.*, XII, 3, September, 1979.

Lipset, S.M., *Agrarian Socialism: The Cooperative Commonwealth Federation in Saskatchewan*, New York, Anchor Books, Doubleday, 1968.

MacDonald, D.C., (ed.), *Government and Politics of Ontario*, Toronto, Van Nostrand Reinhold, 2nd ed., 1980.

MacGregor, J.G., *A History of Alberta*, Edmonton, Hurtig, 1972.

Macpherson, C.B., *Democracy in Alberta: The Theory and Practice of a Quasi-Party System*, Toronto, U.T.P., 1953.

Manthorpe, J., *The Power and the Tories: Ontario's Politics — 1943 to the Present*, Toronto, Macmillan, 1975.

Matthews, R., "Perspectives on Recent Newfoundland Politics," *J.C.S.*, IX, 2, May, 1974.

Matthews, R., "The Smallwood Legacy: The Development of Underdevelopment in Newfoundland, 1949-1972," *J.C.S.*, 13, 4, Winter, 1978.

McCormack, A.R., "The Emergence of the Socialist Movement in British Columbia," [1880-1904], *BC Studies*, 21, Spring, 1974.

McGeer, P.L., *Politics in Paradise*, Toronto, Peter Martin, 1972.

Molot, M.A., and Laux, J.K., "The Politics of Nationalization," [NDP government's takeover of potash in Saskatchewan], *C.J.P.S.*, XII, 2, June, 1979.

Morrison, D.R., *The Politics of the Yukon Territory, 1898-1909*, Toronto, U.T.P., 1968.

Munro, J.M., "Highways in British

Columbia: Economics and Politics,'' *Canadian Journal of Economics*, 8, 1975.

Neary, P., "Party Politics in New-foundland: 1949-1971: A Survey and Analysis," *J.C.S.*, VI, 4, November, 1971.

Neary, P., "Politics in Newfoundland: The End of the Smallwood Era," *J.C.S.*, VII, 1, February, 1972.

Neary, P., (ed.), *The Political Economy of Newfoundland, 1929-1972*, Toronto, C.C., 1973.

Nelles, H.V., *The Politics of Development: Forests, Mines and Hydro-Electric Power in Ontario, 1849-1941*, Toronto, Macmillan, 1974.

Nichols, H.E., *Alberta's Fight for Freedom*, [A History of Social Credit], n.p., 1963, 5 Vols.

Noel, S.J.R., *Politics in New-foundland*, Toronto, U.T.P., 1971.

Ontario Historical Society, *Profile of a Province, Studies in the History of Ontario*, Toronto, Ontario Historical Society, 1967.

Ormsby, M., *British Columbia: A History*, Toronto, Macmillan, 1958.

Paine, R., *Political Rhetoric in the New Newfoundland*, St. John's Breakwater Books, 1981.

Palmer, H., and Palmer, T., "The 1971 Election and the Fall of Social Credit in Alberta," *Prairie Forum*, 1, 1976.

Parti Acadien, *Le Parti Acadien*, B.P. 354, Petit-Rocher, New Brunswick, 1972.

Persky, S., *Son of Socred: Has Bill Bennett's Government Gotten B.C. "Moving Again"?*, Vancouver, New Star, 1979.

Phillips, P.A., *No Power Greater: A Century of Labour in British Columbia*, Vancouver, Federation of Labour Borg Foundation, 1967.

Robin, M., (ed.), *Canadian Provincial Politics: The Party Systems of the Ten Provinces*, Scarborough, P.-H., 2nd ed., 1978.

Robin, M., *Pillars of Profit: The Company Province, 1934-1972*, [British Columbia], Toronto, M. & S., 1973.

Robin, M., *The Rush for Spoils: The Company Province, 1871-1933*, [British Columbia], Toronto, M. & S., 1972.

Robin, M., "The Social Basis of Party Politics in British Columbia," *Q.Q.*, LXXII, 4, Winter, 1966.

Rowat, D.C., (ed.), *Provincial Government and Politics: Comparative Essays*, 2nd ed., Ottawa, Carleton University, 1973.

Schultz, H.J., "The Social Credit Back-benchers' Revolt, 1937," *Canadian Historical Review*, XLI, I, March, 1960.

Schultz, H.J., Ormsby, M.A., Wilbur, J.R.H., and Young, B.J., *Politics of Discontent*, Canadian Historical Readings, No. 4, Toronto, U.T.P., 1967.

Sharp, P.F., *The Agrarian Revolt in Western Canada*, Minneapolis, University of Minnesota Press, 1948.

Simeon, R., and Elkins, D.J., "Regional Political Cultures in Canada," *C.J.P.S.*, VII, 3, September, 1974.

Sinclair, P.R., "The Saskatchewan C.C.F. and the Communist Party in the 1930s," *Saskatchewan History*, XXVI, 1, Winter, 1973.

Smith, D.E., "Interpreting Prairie Politics," *J.C.S.*, VII, 4, November, 1972.

Smith, D.E., *Prairie Liberalism, The Liberal Party in Saskatchewan 1905-1971*, Toronto, U.T.P., 1975.

Spafford, D., "Highway Employment and Provincial Elections," *C.J.P.S.*, XIV, 1, March, 1981.

Stein, M.B., *The Dynamics of Right-Wing Protest: Social Credit in Quebec*, Toronto, U.T.P., 1973.

Swainson, D., (ed.), *Historical Essays on the Prairie Provinces*, Carleton Library No. 53, Toronto, M. & S., 1970.

Swainson, D., (ed.), *Oliver Mowat's Ontario*, Toronto, Macmillan, 1972.

Thomas, L., *The Liberal Party in Alberta: A History of Politics in the Province of Alberta, 1905-1921*, Toronto, U.T.P., 1959.

Thorburn, H.G., *Politics in New Brunswick*, Toronto, U.T.P., 1961.

Tyre, R., *Douglas in Saskatchewan: The Story of a Socialist Experiment*, Vancouver, Mitchell Press, 1962.

Walker, R.R., *Politicians of a Pioneering Province*, Vancouver, Mitchell, 1969.

Ward, N., and Spafford, D., (eds.), *Politics in Saskatchewan*, Toronto, Longman, 1968.

Weller, G.R., "Hinterland Politics: The Case of Northwestern Ontario," *C.J.P.S.*, X, 4, December, 1977.

Whalen, H., "Social Credit Measures in Alberta," *C.J.E.P.S.*, XVIII, 4, November, 1952.

Wilson, B., *Politics of Defeat: The Decline of the Liberal Party in Saskatchewan*, Saskatoon, Western Producer Prairie Books, 1981.

Wilson, J., "The Canadian Political Cultures: Towards a Redefinition of the Nature of the Canadian Political System," *C.J.P.S.*, VII, 3, September, 1974.

Wilson, J., "The Decline of the Liberal Party in Manitoba Politics," *J.C.S.*, X, 1, Spring, 1975.

Wilson, J., and Hoffman, D., "The Liberal Party in Contemporary Ontario Politics," *C.J.P.S.*, III, 2, June, 1970.

Woodward, C.A., *A History of New Brunswick Provincial Election Campaigns and Platforms 1866-1974*, Toronto, Micromedia, 1976.

Young, W.D., *Democracy and Discontent: Progressivism, Socialism and Social Credit in the Canadian West*, The Frontenac Library, Toronto, Ryerson, 1969.

Zakuta, L., *A Protest Movement Becalmed*, [Ontario CCF], Toronto, U.T.P., 1964.

City Politics

(See also Bibliography, Chapter 4, Municipalities, and Chapters 6 and 10.)

Artibise, A.F.J., and Stelter, G.A., *The Usable Urban Past: Planning and Politics in the Modern Canadian City*, Toronto, Macmillan, 1979.

Aubin, H., *City for Sale*, Toronto, Lorimer, 1977.

Barker, G., Penney, J., and Seccombe, W., "The Developers," *Canadian Dimension*, IX, 2-3, January, 1973.

Bettison, D.G., Kenward, J., and Taylor, L., *The Politics of Canadian Urban Development: The Urban Affairs of Alberta*, Edmonton, U.A.P., 1973.

Caulfield, J., *The Tiny Perfect Mayor: David Crombie and Toronto's Reform Aldermen*, Toronto, Lorimer, 1974.

Clarkson, S., "Barrier to Entry of Parties into Toronto's Civic Politics: Towards a Theory of Party Penetration," *C.J.P.S.*, IV, 2, June, 1971.

Clarkson, S., *City Lib: Parties and Reform*, Toronto, Hakkert, 1972.

Colton, T.J., *Big Daddy: Frederick G. Gardiner and the Building of Metropolitan Toronto*, U.T.P., 1980.

Dennis, M., and Fish, S., *Programs in Search of a Policy*, Toronto, Hakkert, 1972.

Easton, R., and Tennant, R., "Vancouver Civic Party Leadership: Backgrounds, Attitudes, and Non-civic Party Affiliations," *BC Studies*, 2, Summer, 1969.

Fraser, G., *Fighting Back: Urban Renewal in Trefann Court*, Toronto, Hakkert, 1972.

Freeman, B., and Hewitt, M., (eds), *Their Town: The Mafia, the Media and the Party Machine*, [Hamilton, Ontario], Toronto, Lorimer, 1979.

Gauvin, M., "The Reformer and the Machine: Montreal Civic Politics from Raymond Prefontaine to Méderic Martin," *J.C.S.*, 13, 2, Summer, 1978.

Granatstein, J., *Marlborough Marathon*, Toronto, Hakkert, 1971.

Granatstein, J.L., *et al.*, "Cityscape '72," *The Canadian Forum*, LII, 616, May, 1972.

Kay, B.J., "Voting Patterns in a Non-partisan Legislature: A Study of Toronto City Council," *C.J.P.S.*, IV, 2, June, 1971.

Leo, C., *The Politics of Urban Development: Canadian Urban Ex-*

pressway Disputes, Toronto, Monograph Series, I.P.A.C., 1977.

Lorimer, J., *A Citizen's Guide to City Politics,* Toronto, J.L.S., 1972.

Lorimer, J., *The Real World of City Politics,* Toronto, J.L.S., 1972.

Lorimer, J., *The Developers,* Toronto, Lorimer, 1978.

Lorimer, J., and MacGregor, C., (eds.), *After the Developers,* Toronto, Lorimer, 1981.

Lorimer, J., and Ross, E., (eds.), *The City Book: The Planning and Politics of Canada's Cities,* Toronto, Lorimer, 1976.

Lorimer, J., and Ross, E., (eds), *The Second City Book: Studies of Urban and Suburban Life,* Toronto, Lorimer, 1977.

Masson, J.K., and Anderson, J.D., (eds.), *Emerging Party Politics in Urban Canada,* Toronto, M. & S., 1972.

Maud, L.R., "The Politics of Local Government Progress," *C.P.A.,* 17, 3, Fall, 1974.

McKenna, B., and Purcell, S., *Drapeau,* [Montreal], Toronto, Clarke, Irwin, 1980.

Nowlan, D., and Nowlan, N., *The Bad Trip — The Untold Story of the Spadina Expressway,* Toronto, House of Anansi, 1970.

Rose, A., *Governing Metropolitan Toronto: A Social and Political Analysis, 1953-1971,* Los Angeles, University of California Press, 1972.

Roussopoulos, D., (ed.), *The City and Radical Social Change,* Montreal, Black Rose, 1979.

Sewell, J., *Inside City Hall,* Toronto, Hakkert, 1971.

Sewell, J., *Up Against City Hall,* Toronto, J.L.S., 1972.

Shackleton, D., *Powertown: Democracy Discarded,* Toronto, M. & S., 1977.

Spurr, P., *Land and Urban Development,* Toronto, Lorimer, 1976.

Stein, D.L., *Toronto For Sale,* Toronto, New Press, 1972.

Vancouver Urban Research Group, *Forever Deceiving You — The Politics of Vancouver Development,* Vancouver, Vancouver Urban

Research Group, 4632 West 11th St., 1972.

Weaver, J.C., *Shaping the Canadian Cities: Essays on Urban Politics and Policy, 1890-1920,* Toronto, Monograph Series, I.P.A.C., 1977.

Political Biographies

Aiken, G., *The Backbencher: Trials and Tribulations of a Member of Parliament,* Toronto, M. & S., 1974.

Archer, J.H., and Munro, J.A., (eds.), *One Canada: Memoirs of the Rt. Hon. John G. Diefenbaker: The Crusading Years, 1895-1956,* Toronto, Macmillan, 1975.

Banks, M.A., *Edward Blake: Irish Nationalist: A Canadian Statesman in Irish Politics, 1892-1907,* Toronto, U.T.P., 1957.

Barrette, A., *Mémoires,* Montréal, Beauchemin, 1966.

Beal, J.R., *The Pearson Phenomena,* Toronto, Longman, 1964.

Beaulieu, P., (ed.), *Ed Schreyer: A Social Democrat in Power, Selected Speeches and Interviews of Premier Schreyer of Manitoba,* Winnipeg, Queenston, 1977.

Beck, J.M., *Joseph Howe, Voice of Nova Scotia,* Carleton Library, Toronto, M. & S., 1964.

Beeching, W., and Clarke, P., *Yours in the Struggle, Reminiscences of Tim Buck,* Toronto, NC Press, 1977.

Benson, N.A., *None of It Came Easy: The Story of J.G. Gardiner,* Toronto, B. and M., 1955.

Black, C., *Duplessis,* Toronto, M. & S., 1977.

Borden, H., (ed.), *Robert Laird Borden: His Memoirs,* Toronto, Macmillan, 1938, 2 vols.

Borden, R.L., *His Memoirs,* Carleton Library, Toronto, M. & S., 1969, 2 vols.

Borden, R.L., (ed. by H. Borden), *Letters to Limbo,* Toronto, U.T.P., 1971.

Bothwell, R., *Pearson, His Life and World,* Toronto, McG.-H.R., 1978.

Bothwell, R., and Kilbourn, W., *C.D. Howe: A Biography,* Toronto, M. & S., 1979.

Bourassa, A., Bergevin, A., and Nish, C., (ed.), *Henri Bourassa, Biography, Bibliographical Index, and Index of Public Correspondence, 1895-1924,* Montreal, les éditions de l'Action Nationale, 1966.

Bourassa, A., (ed.), *Henri Bourassa,* Montréal, les éditions de l'Action Nationale, 1966.

Bourassa, R., *Bourassa/Quebec!,* Montreal, Les Editions de l'Homme, 1970.

Brand, J., *The Life and Death of Anna Mae Aquash,* Toronto, Lorimer, 1978.

Brown, R.C., *Robert Laird Borden: A Biography,* Vol. I, *1854-1914,* Toronto, Macmillan, 1975; Vol. II, *1914-1937,* 1980.

Butler, R., and Carrier, J.-G., *The Trudeau Decade,* Toronto, Doubleday Canada, 1979.

Camp, D., *Gentlemen, Players and Politicians,* Toronto, M. & S., 1970.

Camp, D., *Points of Departure,* Ottawa, D. and G., 1979.

Careless, J.M.S., *Brown of the Globe,* Vol. I, *The Voice of Upper Canada, 1818-1859,* Toronto, Macmillan, 1959; Vol. II, *Statesman of Confederation, 1860-1880,* 1963.

Casgrain, T., *Une femme chez les hommes,* Montréal, Éditions du jour, 1972.

Chalout, R., *Memoires politiques,* Toronto, M. & S., 1969.

Creighton, D., *John A. Macdonald: The Young Politician,* Toronto, Macmillan, 1952; *The Old Chieftain,* 1955.

Dafoe, J.W., *Laurier: A Study in Canadian Politics,* Carleton Library, Toronto, M. & S., 1963.

Dawson, R.M., *William Lyon Mackenzie King: A Political Biography, 1874-1923,* Vol. I, Toronto, U.T.P., 1958.

Dempson, P., *Assignment Ottawa,* Don Mills, General Publishing, 1968.

Desbarats, P., *René: A Canadian in Search of a Country,* Toronto, M. & S., 1976.

Donaldson, G., *Fifteen Men: Canada's Prime Ministers from Macdonald to Trudeau,* Toronto, Doubleday, 1969.

Drury, E.C., *Farmer Premier: The Memoirs of the Hon. E.C. Drury,* Toronto, M. & S., 1966.

English, J., *Borden: His Life and World,* Toronto, McG.-H.R., 1977.

English, J., and Stubbs, J.O., (eds.), *Mackenzie King: Widening the Debate,* Toronto, Macmillan, 1978.

Esberey, J.E., *Knight of the Holy Spirit: A Study of William Lyon Mackenzie King,* Toronto, U.T.P., 1980.

Ferns, H.S., and Ostry, B., *The Age of Mackenzie King: The Rise of the Leader,* London, Heinemann, 1955.

Gibson, G., *Bull of the Woods: The Gorden Gibson Story,* Vancouver, Douglas and McIntyre, 1980.

Gordon, Walter, *A Political Memoir,* Toronto, M. & S., 1977.

Graham, R., *Arthur Meighen,* Vol. I, *The Door of Opportunity,* Toronto, Clarke, Irwin, 1960; Vol. II, *And Fortune Fled,* 1963; Vol. III, *No Surrender,* 1965.

Granatstein, J.L., *Mackenzie King: His Life and World,* Toronto, McG.-H.R., 1977.

Gwyn, R., *Smallwood: The Unlikely Revolutionary,* Toronto, M. & S., rev. ed., 1972.

Gwyn, R., *The Northern Magus: Pierre Trudeau and Canadians, 1968-80,* Toronto, M. & S., 1980.

Haliburton, E.D., *My Years with Stanfield,* Windsor, N.S., Lancelot, 1972.

Heaps, L., *The Rebel in the House: The Life and Times of A.A. Heaps, M.P.,* London, England, Niccolo, 1970.

Humphreys, D.L., *Joe Clark: A Portrait,* Ottawa, D. and G., 1978.

Hustak, A., *Peter Lougheed: A Biography,* Toronto, M. & S., 1979.

Hutchison, B., *The Incredible Canadian,* [W.L.M. King] Toronto, Longman, Green, 1952.

Hutchison, B., *Mr. Prime Minister, 1867-1964,* Toronto, Longman, 1964.

Institut canadien des affaires publiques, *Nos hommes politiques*, Montréal, Éditions du jour, 1964.

Johnson, L.P.V., and MacNutt, O., *Aberhart of Alberta*, Edmonton, Institute of Applied Arts, 1970.

Kendle, J., *John Bracken: A Political Biography*, Toronto, U.T.P., 1979.

La Marsh, Judy, *Memoirs of a Bird in a Gilded Cage*, Toronto, M. & S., 1969.

Lapalme, G.E., *Memoires*, Vol. 1-3, Montreal, Leméac, 1969-73.

Laporte, P., *The True Face of Duplessis*, Montreal, Harvest House, 1960.

La Roque, H., *Camilien Houde, le p'tit gars de Ste. Marie*, Montréal, Les éditions de l'homme, 1961.

Leclerc, A., *Claude Ryan: A Biography*, Toronto, NC Press, 1980.

Lewis, D., *The Good Fight: Political Memoirs, 1909-1958*, Toronto, Macmillan, 1981.

Lovick, L.D., (ed.), *Tommy Douglas Speaks: Till Power is Brought to Pooling*, Lantzville, B.C., Oolichan Books, 1979.

Mardiros, A., *William Irvine: The Life of a Prairie Radical*, Toronto, Lorimer, 1979.

McGregor, F.A., *The Fall and Rise of Mackenzie King: 1911-1919*, Toronto, Macmillan, 1962.

MacInnis, G., *J.S. Woodsworth, A Man to Remember*, Toronto, Macmillan, 1953.

McKenna, B., and Purcell, S., *Drapeau*, Toronto, Clarke Irwin, 1980.

McNaught, K., *A Prophet in Politics: A Biography of J.S. Woodsworth*, Toronto, U.T.P., 1959.

Munro, J.A., and Inglis, A.I., (eds.), *Mike: The Memoirs of the Right Honourable L.B. Pearson*, Vol. II, *1948-1957*, Toronto, U.T.P., 1973; Vol. III, *1957-1968*, 1975.

Nadeau, J.M., *Carnets politiques*, Montréal, Éditions Partis Pris, 1966.

Neatby, H.B., *William Lyon Mackenzie King, 1924-1932: The Lonely Heights*, Vol. II, Toronto, U.T.P., 1963; Vol. III, *1932-39: Prism of Unity*, 1976.

Neatby, H.B., *Laurier and a Liberal*

Quebec: A Study in Political Management, Toronto, M. & S., 1973.

Newman, P.C., *Renegade in Power: The Diefenbaker Years*, Carleton Library No. 70, Toronto, M. & S., 1963.

Nolan, M., *Joe Clark: The Emerging Leader*, Don Mills, Ontario, F. and W., 1978.

Oliver, P., *G. Howard Ferguson: Ontario Tory*, Toronto, U.T.P., 1977.

Pearson, L.B., *Mike: The Memoirs of the Right Honourable Lester B. Pearson*, Vol. I, *1897-1948*, Toronto, 1972; Vol. II, *1948-1957*, 1973; Vol. III, *1957-1968*, 1975.

Phillips, N., *The Mayor of All the People*, [Memoirs], Toronto, M. & S., 1967.

Pickersgill, J.W., *My Years with Louis St. Laurent*, Toronto, U.T.P., 1975.

Pickersgill, J.W., *The Mackenzie King Record*, Toronto, U.T.P., Vol. I, *1939-1944*, 1960; with Forster, D., Vol. II, *1944-1945*, 1968; Vol. III, *1945-1946*, 1970; Vol. IV, *1947-1948*, 1971.

Prang, M., *N.W. Rowell: Ontario Nationalist*, Toronto, U.T.P., 1975.

Provencher, J., *René Lévesque, portrait d'un québécois*, Montréal, Éditions la presse, 1973. (English edition, Toronto, Gage, 1975.)

Radwanski, G., *Trudeau*, Toronto, Macmillan, 1978.

Roberts, L., *C.D.: The Life and Times of Clarence Decatur Howe*, Toronto, Clarke, Irwin, 1957.

Roberts, L., *The Chief: A Political Biography of Maurice Duplessis*, Toronto, Clarke, Irwin, 1963.

Roche, D., *The Human Side of Politics*, Toronto, Clarke, Irwin, 1976.

Rolph, W.K., *Henry Wise Wood of Alberta*, Toronto, U.T.P., 1950.

Ryan, O., *Tim Buck: A Conscience For Canada*, Toronto, Progress Books, 1975.

Salutin, R., *Kent Rowley, A Canadian Hero*, Toronto, Lorimer, 1980.

Savage, C., *Our Nell: A Scrapbook Biography of Nellie L. McClung*, Saskatoon, Western Producer Prairie, 1979.

Schull, J., *Laurier, The First Canadian*, Toronto, Macmillan, 1965.

Schull, J., *Edward Blake: The Man of the Other Way, 1833-81*, Toronto, Macmillan, 1975.

Schull, J., *Edward Blake: Leader and Exile, 1881-1912*, Toronto, Macmillan, 1976.

Schultz, H.F., "Portrait of a Premier: William Aberhart," *Canadian Historical Review*, XXXV, 3, September, 1964.

Sévigny, P., *This Game of Politics*, Toronto, M. & S., 1965.

Shackleton, D., *Tommy Douglas*, Toronto, M. & S., 1975.

Shaw, B., (ed.), *The Gospel According to Saint Pierre*, (Trudeau), Richmond Hill, Pocket Books, Simon and Schuster, 1969.

Sheppard, C.A., *Dossier Wagner*, Montréal, Éditions du Jour, 1972.

Sherman, P., *Bennett*, [W.A.C.], Toronto, M. & S., 1966.

Siggins, M., *Bassett: John Bassett's Forty Years in Politics, Publishing, Business and Sports*, Toronto, Lorimer, 1979.

Smallwood, J.R., *I Chose Canada*, [Memoirs], Toronto, Macmillan, 1973.

Smith, D., *Gentle Patriot — A Political Biography of Walter Gordon*, Edmonton, Hurtig, 1973.

Steeves, D.G., *The Compassionate Rebel: Ernest E. Winch and His Times*, Vancouver, Evergreen Press, 1960.

Stevens, G., *Stanfield*, Toronto, M. & S., 1973.

Stewart, M., and French, D., *Ask No Quarter: A Biography of Agnes MacPhail*, Toronto, Longman, Green, 1959.

Stewart, W., *Shrug — Trudeau in Power*, Toronto, New Press, 1972.

Stinson, L., *Political Warriors: Recollections of a Social Democrat*, Winnipeg, Queenston House, 1975.

Stursberg, P., (ed.), *Diefenbaker: Leadership Gained, 1956-62*, Toronto, U.T.P., 1975.

Stursberg, P., *Diefenbaker: Leadership Lost, 1962-67*, Toronto, U.T.P., 1976.

Stursberg, P., *Lester Pearson and the American Dilemma*, Toronto, Doubleday, 1980.

Stursberg, P., (ed.), *Lester Pearson and the Dream of Unity*, Toronto, Doubleday, 1978.

Thomson, D.C., *Alexander MacKenzie: Clear Grit*, Toronto, Macmillan, 1960.

Thomson, D.C., *Louis St. Laurent: Canadian*, Toronto, Macmillan, 1967.

Thordarson, B., *Lester Pearson, Diplomat and Politician*, Toronto, O.U.P., 1974.

Trudeau, Margaret, *Beyond Reason*, New York and London, Paddington Press, 1979; *Consequences*, M. & S., 1981.

Trudeau, P.E., *Conversation with Canadians*, Toronto, U.T.P., 1972.

Van Dusen, T., *The Chief*, (Diefenbaker), Toronto, McG.-H., 1968.

Waite, P.B., *Macdonald: His Life and World*, Toronto, McG.-H.R., 1975.

Wallace, W.S., *The Macmillan Dictionary of Canadian Biography*, Toronto, Macmillan, 3rd ed., 1963.

Ward, N., (ed.), *A Party Politician: The Memoirs of Chubby Power*, Toronto, Macmillan, 1966.

Watkins, E., *R.B. Bennett*, Toronto, Kingswood House, 1963.

Westell, A., *Paradox: Trudeau as Prime Minister*, Scarborough, P.-H., 1972.

Wilbur, R., *H.H. Stevens, 1878-1973*, Toronto, U.T.P., 1977.

Young, W.D., "M.J. Coldwell, The Making of a Social Democrat," *J.C.S.*, IX, 3, August, 1974.

Zink, L., *Trudeaucracy*, Toronto, Toronto Sun, 1972.

Zolf, L., *Dance of the Dialetic*, Toronto, J.L.S., 1973.

9

THE ELECTORAL PROCESS

Although there has been a good deal of discussion recently about revising the electoral system in Canada, the major aspects of it which were dealt with in the fourth edition of *Politics: Canada* remain the same.

Thus, this chapter repeats most of the items which appeared in the previous edition. Where relevant, however, they have been brought up to date and revised to include the most recent developments.

The first item reproduces the essentials of the Representation Act, 1974, which inaugurated changes that still apply. It is accompanied by a table showing recent alterations in the distribution of seats in the House of Commons and a forecast of what is to come when the 1981 census results are taken into account.

In 1974, Ottawa and Ontario followed Quebec's example of 1963 and enacted laws controlling election expenditures and contributions to parties and candidates. All three statutes are in the contemporary vein, seeking to make elections more democratic by curbing spending and broadening the base of campaign financing. The second article in this chapter explains the federal legislation while the amusing article by Walter Stewart describes who contributes what to which federal party's election pot. Daniel Stoffman's article in the fourth edition identifying donors and expenditures in Ontario has been replaced by Rick Haliechuk's more recent piece on much the same subject.

Gerald Utting's and Val Sears' *realpolitik* accounts of how the professionals package and sell politicians are so graphic and revealing that they have been carried over from the fourth edition.

The article describing the various steps taken in holding a federal election and the two tables accompanying it have been carried over also. The tables have been updated to show party standings in the House of Commons resulting from each of our federal general elections from 1867 to 1980. The tables show, as well, the number of seats won by parties by province in 1980 and 1979 and the discrepancies between percentages of votes and seats won by parties in 1980 and 1979. For similar tables for the 1974 and 1972 elections, see p. 306 in the fourth edition. For the 1968 and 1965 elections, see p. 259 in the third edition.

The final item is a revision of the editor's previous article on the pros and cons of applying proportional representation to Canada, taking note of the recent spate of interest and publications on the subject.

Electoral reform is one of the recurring passions in Canadian politics and it would appear that its time has come again. During the past few years, the Pépin-Robarts Task Force on Canadian Unity, Prime Minister Pierre Trudeau, NDP leader Ed Broadbent, and a number of scholars have displayed interest in revising our electoral system to make representation more reflective of the actual distribution of popular votes and our federal parties more representative of the whole country.

The editor's article, "P.R. for Canada," reviews these proposals and notes the recent literature on the subject. While the literature is listed in the bibliography at the end of this chapter, three particularly useful items should be singled out. Professor William Irvine's monograph, *Does Canada Need a New Electoral System?*, though brief, is the definitive Canadian study of the issue. His article, "Power Requires Representation," in *Policy Options*, 1, 4, December-January, 1980-81, should be read also. For a thorough critique of the various proposals and their underlying assumptions, a student should read Professor John Courtney's article, "Reflections on Reforming the Canadian Electoral System," in *Canadian Public Administration*, 23, 3, Fall, 1980.

Three books in the McGraw-Hill Ryerson Series in Canadian Politics have dealt with the electoral process: T.H. Qualter, *The Election Process in Canada*; W.E. Lyons, *One Man, One Vote*; and K.Z. Paltiel, *Political Party Financing in Canada*. All were published in 1970.

NEW ARRANGEMENTS FOR REPRESENTATION IN THE HOUSE OF COMMONS*

23 Eliz. II, c. 13

An act to provide for representation in the House of Commons, to establish electoral boundaries commissions and to remove the temporary suspension of the Electoral Boundaries Readjustment Act

[Assented to 20th December, 1974]

Her Majesty, by and with the advice and consent of the Senate and House of Commons of Canada, enacts as follows:

SHORT TITLE

1. This Act may be cited as the *Representation Act, 1974*.

Part I: British North America Act

2. Subsection 51(1) of the *British North America Act, 1867*, as enacted by the *British North America Act, 1952*, is repealed and the following substituted therefore:

"**51. (1)** The number of members of the House of Commons and the representation of the provinces therein shall upon the coming into force of this subsection and thereafter on the completion of each decennial census be readjusted by such authority, in such manner, and from such time as the

* From *Canada Gazette, Part III*, Vol. 1, No. 2, Ottawa, 1974. Reproduced by permission of the Minister of Supply and Services Canada.

Parliament of Canada from time to time provides, subject and according to the following Rules:

1. There shall be assigned to Quebec seventy-five members in the readjustment following the completion of the decennial census taken in the year 1971, and thereafter four additional members in each subsequent readjustment.

2. Subject to Rules 5(2) and (3), there shall be assigned to a large province a number of members equal to the number obtained by dividing the population of the large province by the electoral quotient of Quebec.

3. Subject to Rules 5(2) and (3), there shall be assigned to a small province a number of members equal to the number obtained by dividing

(a) the sum of the populations, determined according to the results of the penultimate decennial census, of the provinces (other than Quebec) having populations of less than one and a half million, determined according to the results of that census, by the sum of the numbers of members assigned to those provinces in the readjustment following the completion of that census; and

(b) the population of the small provinces by the quotient obtained under paragraph (a).

4. Subject to Rules 5(1)(a), (2) and (3), there shall be assigned to an intermediate province a number of members equal to the number obtained

(a) by dividing the sum of the populations of the provinces (other than Quebec) having populations of less than one and a half million by the sum of the numbers of members assigned to those provinces under any of Rules 3, 5(1)(b), (2) and (3);

(b) by dividing the population of the intermediate province by the quotient obtained under paragraph (a); and

(c) by adding to the number of members assigned to the intermediate province in the readjustment following the completion of the penultimate decennial census one-half of the difference resulting from the subtraction of that number from the quotient obtained under paragraph (b).

5. (1) On any readjustment,

(a) if no province (other than Quebec) has a population of less than one and a half million, Rule 4 shall not be applied and, subject to Rules 5(2) and (3), there shall be assigned to an intermediate province a number of members equal to the number obtained by dividing

(i) the sum of the populations, determined according to the results of the penultimate decennial census, of the provinces (other than Quebec) having populations of not less than one and a half million and not more than two and a half million, determined according to the results of that census, by the sum of the numbers of members assigned to those provinces in the readjustment following the completion of that census, and

(ii) the population of the intermediate province by the quotient obtained under subparagraph (i);

(b) if a province (other than Quebec) having a population of

(i) less than one and a half million, or

(ii) not less than one and a half million and not more than two and a half million

does not have a population greater than its population determined according to the results of the penultimate decennial census, it shall, subject to

Rules 5(2) and (3), be assigned the number of members assigned to it in the readjustment following the completion of that census.

(2) On any readjustment,

(a) if, under any of Rules 2 to 5(1), the number of members to be assigned to a province (in this paragraph referred to as "the first province") is smaller than the number of members to be assigned to any other province not having a population greater than that of the first province, those Rules shall not be applied to the first province and it shall be assigned a number of members equal to the largest number of members to be assigned to any other province not having a population greater than that of the first province;

(b) if, under any of Rules 2 to 5(1)(a), the number of members to be assigned to a province is smaller than the number of members assigned to it in the readjustment following the completion of the penultimate decennial census, those Rules shall not be applied to it and it shall be assigned the latter number of members;

(c) if both paragraphs (a) and (b) apply to a province, it shall be assigned a number of members equal to the greater of the numbers produced under those paragraphs.

(3) On any readjustment,

(a) if the electoral quotient of a province (in this paragraph referred to as "the first province") obtained by dividing its population by the number of members to be assigned to it under any Rules 2 to 5(2) is greater than the electoral quotient of Quebec, those Rules shall not be applied to the first province and it shall be assigned a number of members equal to the number obtained by dividing its population by the electoral quotient of Quebec;

(b) if, as a result of the application of Rule 6(2)(a), the number of members assigned to a province under paragraph (a) equals the number of members to be assigned to it under any of Rules 2 to 5(2), it shall be assigned that number of members and paragraph (a) shall cease to apply to that province.

6. (1) In these Rules,

"electoral quotient" means, in respect of a province, the quotient obtained by dividing its population, determined according to the results of the then most recent decennial census, by the number of members to be assigned to it under any of Rules 1 to 5(3) in the readjustment following the completion of that census;

"intermediate province" means a province (other than Quebec) having a population greater than its population determined according to the results of the penultimate decennial census but not more than two and a half million and not less than one and a half million;

"large province" means a province (other than Quebec) having a population greater than two and a half million;

"penultimate decennial census" means the decennial census that preceded the then most recent decennial census;

"population" means, except where otherwise specified, the population determined according to the results of the then most recent decennial census;

"small province" means a province (other than Quebec) having a population greater than its population determined according to the results of the penultimate decennial census and less than one and a half million.

(2) For the purposes of these Rules,

(a) if any fraction less than one remains upon completion of the final calculation that produces the number of members to be assigned to a province, that number of members shall equal the number so produced disregarding the fraction;

(b) if more than one readjustment follows the completion of a decennial census, the most recent of those readjustments shall, upon taking effect, be deemed to be the only readjustment following the completion of that census;

(c) a readjustment shall not take effect until the termination of the then existing Parliament.''

3. This part may be cited as the *British North America Act (No. 2), 1974,* and the *British North America Acts, 1867 to 1974* and this Part may be cited together as the *British North America Acts, 1867 to 1974-75.*

● ● ●

Increase in Seats in House of Commons by Province, 1974-1984-85

	1974	1975-80*	1984-85***
Ontario	88	95	105
Quebec	74	75	79
British Columbia	23	28	33
Alberta	19	21	27
Saskatchewan	13	14	14
Manitoba	13	14	15
Nova Scotia	11	11	12
New Brunswick	10	10	10
Newfoundland	7	7	8
Prince Edward Island	4	4	4
Northwest Territories	1	2**	2
Yukon	1	1	1
Total	264	282	310

* As determined by the application of the *Representation Act, 1974,* for which see the immediately preceding item.

** Increased by the *Northwest Territories Representation Act,* which is the short title of *An Act to increase the representation of the Northwest Territories in the House of Commons and to establish a commission to readjust the electoral boundaries of the Northwest Territories,* 23-23 Eliz. II, C. 28, 1975.

*** As determined by the *Representation Act, 1974,* on the basis of the official results of the census of 1981. Because of the length of time assigned to the several stages of readjusting the boundaries of electoral districts, it is predicted that the increase in seats will not be in effect before 1984-85.

FEDERAL ELECTION EXPENSES ACT AIDS PARTIES AND CAMPAIGN FINANCING

After many years of discussion, Parliament has passed legislation which will provide financial assistance to political parties and candidates as well as putting limits on spending. The Election Expenses Act, which came into

force on August 1, 1974 after the federal election of July 8, covers a number of aspects of financing:
— it creates a federal income tax credit system for individuals donating to parties or candidates;
— it requires the registration of political parties that wish to receive benefits under the Act;
— it limits the expenditures of parties and candidates in elections and defines election expenses;
— it requires disclosure of the names of donors of more than $100 to registered parties and candidates;
— it provides stiff penalties for infractions of the Act;
— it reimburses candidates for a portion of their campaign costs.

Tax Credits

The Income Tax Act will now permit a taxpayer to deduct from his federal income tax payable a portion of a political contribution that an individual makes to a registered political party or to a candidate. Contributions may be made annually to a political party or to a party or a candidate during an election. To be eligible for a tax credit, the contribution must be made only to a registered agent of a party or to an official agent of a candidate.

A tax credit is more than merely a deduction from taxable income since the credit is a direct reduction of the federal income tax payable in any given year on an individual's tax form. For instance, if a person must pay $100 in federal income tax in a certain year but has made a donation of $100 to a registered party or candidate, he would receive a tax credit of $75 and therefore have to pay only $25 in federal tax. Thus, by contributing to a party or candidate, the citizen "saves" paying a certain amount to the treasury. The anticipation is that this arrangement will broaden the basis of financing of the democratic process without costing the citizen very much.

The amount of the tax credit varies with the amount of the contribution up to a maximum credit of $500 in any one taxation year. Thus the tax credit will be:
— 75 percent of a contribution up to $100;
— $75 plus 50 percent of a contribution of more than $100 but not more than $550;
— for donations of more than $550, the lesser of $300 plus 33⅓ percent of the amount by which the donation exceeds $550 or $500 for a contribution of $1150.
The following table gives a few examples:

Total Contributions	Tax Credit	Actual Cost to Contributor
$ 10	$ 7.50	$ 2.50
25	18.75	6.25
50	37.50	12.50
100	75.00	25.00
1150	500.00	650.00
	(maximum)	

A taxpayer may contribute, of course, any amount he or she wishes to a party or parties or a candidate or candidates, but the maximum tax credit allowed in any one year for all donations is $500. Receipts for tax credit purposes can be issued only by a registered agent of a party or during an election also by an official agent of a candidate.

Donations may take the form of money or the provision of goods and services. The Canada Elections Act now requires political parties and candidates to list the "commercial value" of goods and services (other than volunteer labour) donated or provided as election expenses. The Act also defines "commercial value."

Registered Political Parties

A "registered political party" is defined in the Canada Elections Act as a political party which was either represented in the House of Commons on the day before the dissolution of Parliament immediately preceding the election, or 30 days before polling day had officially nominated candidates in at least 50 electoral districts in Canada.

The following political parties met these requirements at the election on February 18, 1980 and were qualified as registered political parties:

Communist Party of Canada
Liberal Party of Canada
Libertarian
Marxist-Leninist Party of Canada
New Democratic Party
Parti Rhinocéros
Progressive Conservative Party of Canada
Social Credit Party of Canada
Union Populaire

Limitation of Election Expenses

The Election Expenses Act limits the amounts of money that political parties and candidates can spend in a federal election.

A *party* may not spend more than 30 cents for each elector registered on the preliminary voting lists in every constituency in which that party has an official candidate. Thus, if registered party A had 80 candidates running and each of the electoral districts of these candidates had 35,000 names on the preliminary voters' lists, the total amount that party A could spend would be $840,000 (i.e., 30 cents × 35,000 × 80).

A *candidate* also is limited in his election expenses. He or she may not spend more than the sum of $1 for each of the first 15,000 voters on the preliminary voting list, 50 cents for each of the next 10,000 voters, and 25 cents for each voter exceeding 25,000. Here are a few examples for constituencies with varying numbers of voters:

Constituency	A	B	C	D	E
No. of voters	15,000	25,000	50,000	60,000	75,000
Spending limit	$15,000	$20,000	$26,250	$28,750	$32,500

Definition of Election Expenses

Election expenses are strictly defined in the new Act. They include the "commercial value" of goods and services donated, except for volunteer labour. They also include the cost of media, time and space, personal labour, refreshments, etc. Any goods that are donated and have a commercial value (i.e., the equivalent purchase price) over $100 must be listed as election expenses.

Disclosure

All registered political parties are required to file returns giving their election expenses and their annual receipts and expenses. Candidates must file returns covering the receipts and expenses of their election campaigns. Money that is given to candidates by their political party must be listed by the candidate as a contribution.

All contributions of more than $100 to registered parties and to candidates must be disclosed. The name of the individual or corporate donor must be given. No contributor can donate through a third party.

Each registered party and candidate must appoint an auditor who is required to report the receipts and expenses. All statements of contributions and expenditures by parties and candidates must be filed with the Chief Electoral Officer and become available for public inspection.

Stiff penalties are provided for an offence against the new Act. The maximum penalty for non-compliance is a fine of up to $25,000 and the possibility of a prison term for the official agent. A party can also be fined a maximum of $25,000.

Reimbursement of Candidates

If a candidate receives at least 15 percent of the valid votes cast in his or her electoral district and has provided all the information required by the Act, he or she is entitled to a reimbursement from the Receiver General of Canada of an amount consisting of the following:
— a return of the $200 deposit required from a candidate;
— the cost of postage of a first-class mailing to every voter on the preliminary voters' list;
— 8 cents for each of the first 25,000 voters on the preliminary list;
— 6 cents for each voter thereafter;
— in certain large ridings the actual value of a candidate's travelling expenses to a maximum of $3,000.

[For accounts of the first reports filed under the new Act, which give parties' receipts, expenditures, and names of donors for the year 1975, see three articles by Geoffrey Stevens in *The Globe and Mail*, January 10, February 10, and February 11, 1976. For 1979, see *The Globe and Mail*, July 11, 1980. For 1980, see *ibid.*, July 4, 1981.]

PAYING THE POPLOLLIES*

Walter Stewart

If a man is known by the company he keeps, a politician is known by the company that keeps him. For years Canadians didn't know to whom their elected officials were indebted (they could guess, but they didn't actually know), and now we do, and I, for one, was happier before my cynical suspicions were confirmed. Now that political donations are a matter of public record, it is clear that the two old-line parties are the poplollies of corporations, and the NDP is the poplolly of the unions. (Poplolly is a sound old word; there are newer ones, like mistress.)

This disquieting news comes from an examination of the financial returns submitted by the parties to the chief electoral officer for the year 1980.

At the federal level, donations to the major parties break down this way:
Conservatives — $7,564,120
Liberals — $6,217,795
NDP — $4,920,447

The Marxist-Leninist party fared worst at the trough, with total donations of $756; it was nosed out by the Parti Rhinoceros at $810. The Conservatives fared best (they always do), and the money came mostly from corporations. In fact, corporations accounted for $4,367,936 of all Tory funds, or 58%, and $3,730,983 of all Liberal funds, or 60%, while unions provided $1,702,828 of the NDP's money, or 37%.

The dream of the individual Canadian putting his money where his outrage is has not come to pass, although thc NDP has come closer than the other parties. The NDP received donations from 62,428 individuals, while the Tories persuaded 32,720 voters to dip into their wallets, and the Liberals worked the same magic on 17,670 individuals.

In all, 112,818 Canadians coughed up cash, and got a tax rebate, to support the three main parties — one out of every 209 of us. Or, to put it another way, 23,597,600 of us bitch about politicians, but we can't persuade as many people as reside in Saskatoon to part with any money, even with a tax kickback, to bring about any of the changes we're hollering for. That leaves it up to the corporations and the unions to fund the political process. Take them out of the play, and we could hold our general elections in the Charlottetown skating rink.

The average individual donation was $129 to the Liberals, $93 to the Tories and $45 to the NDP. Public corporations disgorged an average $7,032 per donor, and the average union donation to the NDP was $1,887.

It may be that when the corporations and the unions hand over cash, they are doing so merely as public-spirited citizens, with no thought of tangible return. It may be, too, that every time an angel sneezes, a flower blooms, but I wouldn't count on it.

The largest single donor anywhere to anyone is the Canadian Labor Congress, which dumped $435,934.52 into the NDP coffers, almost a dime out of every dollar that the federal NDP gets. But the public lists are replete

* From *Today Magazine*, November 21, 1981. By permission.

with donations to the Liberals and Conservatives of 30, 40 and 50 thousand dollars from oil companies, construction firms and pipeline corporations.

Then there are the banks. Canada's five largest banks each drop $50,000 into the laps of each of the two old parties — half a million dollars laid out to copper the banks' bet with any government smarting under the lash of having to raise interest rates. The banks don't part with a penny, needless to say, for the NDP.

There are other insights here, too, down among the lists of individual donors. Joe Clark gave $500 to the Conservative Party, while Ed Broadbent gave his party $1,025, and William Kashtan, the Communist Party luminary, donated $1,648 to his.

And Pierre Elliott Trudeau? Not one thin dime. At least no one can say he's trying to curry favor with government.

SHOULD ONTARIO ELECTION SPENDING BE LIMITED?*

Rick Haliechuk

Now that it has been confirmed the Conservatives spent a record amount of money to win the 1981 Ontario election, a full-scale review of election spending laws is needed, politicians say.

It's been six years and three elections since the Election Finances Reform Act, which limits contributions and provides for public subsidies of candidates' expenses, was passed.

Spokesmen for the three major parties say the law is good and has helped broaden the base of political party support. But they say now is a good time to open it to public scrutiny to see what changes may be needed.

"The major problem is you can still be spent into the ground by a very wealthy party," says Liberal Leader Stuart Smith, one of the victims of the Tory machine last spring.

New Democratic Party Leader Mike Cassidy, another victim, also wonders if massive amounts of money impede "the democratic desires of the electorate."

Both leaders have announced their resignations in the wake of the beating their parties took at the polls.

. . . The recently appointed executive director of the Conservative party agrees the time for a review may have arrived.

"I think after an election is the best time," Bob Harris said.

Main Features

Some of the main features of the law:
☐ There are no overall spending limits, but candidates and parties may spend only 25¢ per voter on media advertising;
☐ Contributions are limited to $8,000 in any year in which there's an election and to $4,000 in a non-election year;

* From *The Toronto Star*, September 20, 1981. By permission.

☐ The source of donations of $100 or more must be publicly disclosed;
☐ If a candidate gets 15 per cent of the vote in his riding, he's entitled to public subsidies.

Smith, who quickly points out his party lost the 1981 election on its own merits, believes there should be a limit on overall spending.

"I think in the interests of fairness and democracy in the future, spending limits are necessary, if you're not to have one party just simply totally dominating."

Under federal election spending laws, there are limits imposed on candidates, but no limits on contributions.

Cassidy takes a somewhat different approach, arguing that there should be spending limits on the individual candidate, but not on the central party.

"You don't want a situation where the parties are under such tight wraps that we can't get the message across," said Cassidy, whose party spent $624,600 in this year's campaign compared to $3.3 million for the Conservatives and $1.2 million for the Liberals.

Harris concedes it's fair comment to suggest the money the Tories spent almost guaranteed them victory.

"Same ability"

"But I don't think that money won us the election, any more than the lack of money lost the Liberals the election."

He gave no firm position on the issue of limiting spending, but stressed if the other parties had as much money as the Tories, they'd probably spend as much.

"Everybody has the same ability (under the law) to raise money."

But, as the song says, nobody does it better than the Tories. In 1980, they collected just over $2 million in contributions, as they filled their war-chest for the 1981 campaign and they raised another $2.3 million during the campaign.

That raises the question of whether contributions should be limited to registered voters only, and not to companies and trade unions, as is now the case.

Only voters can contribute to political parties in Quebec, and both the Liberals and Parti Quebecois raised more money in 1980 than the Ontario Tories did.

In part, that is due to a tradition of individual involvement in political party financing in Quebec, Smith says.

"It's terribly important, it's more important in Ontario to have this tradition than it is to have the survival of any of the three parties," the outgoing Liberal leader stressed.

"That is a tradition where ordinary citizens come to understand that they and they alone support the political system as well as the government."

Neither Smith nor Cassidy say decisively that only voters should be able to contribute in Ontario, but both argue that further steps must be taken to broaden the financial base for all the parties. . . .

Smith suggested a system by which a voter could donate money to a party through his income tax return.

Public Subsidies

Still another controversial aspect of Ontario's laws concerns public subsidies, designed to help candidates pay off their campaign expenses. In the 1981 campaign, it's estimated those tax subsidies will amount to more than $2 million.

But the problem, critics say, is that the subsidies are paid out regardless if a candidate made money during his campaign. All a candidate need do is receive at least 15 per cent of the vote in his riding, and he's entitled to a subsidy of 25¢ for each of the first 25,000 voters in his riding, and 14¢ per voter above that.

Thus Industry Minister Larry Grossman, for example, received a $6,000 tax subsidy even though he collected so much money he had to shovel $40,000 into the Tory party's coffers, and still wound up with a $10,000 surplus.

Critics argue this perpetuates the winning candidate's stay in office, by giving him a substantial sum of money to finance his next campaign.

HOW TO PACKAGE A POLITICIAN*

Gerald Utting

Some might call him refreshing in an age of ideology, where even elections to zoological society boards can be couched in the terms of class warfare. Others might call him an exponent of the Politics of Cynicism.

But Hal Evry, Los Angeles political campaign consultant, calls himself a realist. He believes would-be politicians should be aware that people are motivated only by three things: self-preservation, sex and the desire to make money. They neglect this basic fact to their peril, he told a group of politicians and public relations men at a recent seminar in Toronto. The audience paid $100 a head to hear him.

Evry has run campaigns for hundreds of aspirants to office in the United States, from constable in Cucamonga to governor in New Mexico. . . .

Evry told them what every politician and would-be politician doesn't want to hear — that his looks are more important than his opinions in winning the public, that it's usually better to be silent than silver-tongued, to avoid controversy because it's better to win than to be right.

Evry, who claims he can get almost anyone elected to office if his advice is followed, said eight out of 10 people don't like strangers they meet, including candidates, and insists nobody listens to speeches except a tiny minority of politically oriented people.

Different Art

Essentially, Evry's message is that, while being an elected politician may be a skilled art for responsible and serious men and women, getting elected is

* From *The Toronto Star*, July 28, 1975. By permission.

quite a different art; that where an office-holder may need courage and integrity, a candidate needs to be recognized and liked.

Recognition and being liked, in Evry's book, depend not on the inner strengths of a man but on his marketability. A candidate is not too different to a can of shoe polish or a box of breakfast cereal in this light — he's something to be packaged and sold to the public by a professional ad-man who takes the trouble to do as much market research about how people vote as he would about people's preferences in the snap, crackle, pop market.

Since 1958, Evry's organization in Los Angeles has handled the campaigns of 350 candidates, half of them running for Congress. The rest have been candidates for state office, including would-be governors and county executives.

Some of the candidates he has handled: Sam Yorty, rambunctious ex-mayor of Los Angeles, a Republican; George Wallace, Democrat governor of Alabama and sometime hopeful for the U.S. presidency; Winthrop Rockefeller, former governor of Arkansas; Governor David Hall of Oklahoma, a Democrat; Senator Alan Cranston of California, a Democrat; and Senator Ted Stevens of Alaska, Republican.

"About 92 or 93 percent of our candidates have won," Evry told The Star. "The 7 or 8 percent who lost, in my estimation, did so because they didn't follow our advice; they felt they wouldn't stoop to hucksterism, or something like that, and they just wasted their money."

Evry's firm charges a basic fee of $5,000 a month for running a campaign for the U.S. Senate or a state governorship candidate, and $2,500 to $3,000 a month for a House of Representatives or local race. "Whatever else it's going to cost the candidate depends on how many voters he has to reach," said Evry. . . .

IQ Minimum

"I use two criteria: Does he have enough money to win or lose? And is he or she intelligent enough to do the work when elected? A person who has made enough money to be able to afford to run has passed one sort of test in society. And I insist that the candidate must take an IQ test, and prove he's got an IQ of at least 120, before I'll take him on."

Before asking what right someone has to run, he said, shouldn't concerned people be asking rather: Who should be allowed to vote?

"I don't think anyone should be allowed to vote unless they know what it is all about," he said. "But in my country, as in Canada, there are no standards for running and no standards for voting, not even literacy.

"We set standards for barbers and butchers in California, but not for voters and politicians. That doesn't seem right. I have my own standards in accepting clients, which is more than society does."

Every would-be politician, said Evry, claims he wants to serve his country or better his community. "You want to see some of the crazy people who say that to me.". . .

The first thing an aspiring politician must realize, Evry said, is that the incumbent he wants to unseat has everything going for him. "'In the United States, 95 percent of incumbents are re-elected. Why? Recognition is with them, and the public relates recognition or notoriety with superiority. The public believes someone who has already been elected can do the job.

"What you have to do to overcome this is to act as if you were the incumbent. Make people think you are the incumbent rather than the guy himself.

"Get yourself a platform long before the election. Form your own groups with names that sound awfully official. Use words like Parliament, Mayor, Council. . . . Form the Mayor's Purity Committee, say, with yourself as president. Make press statements. If the media don't report your meetings, take advertisements and report them yourself.

"All you need is a group of three or four people. Look at how Nelson Rockefeller formed his very own Commission on National Objectives before he got the vice-presidency. Everyone took it seriously."

Next, said Evry, you've got to find out what the potential voters are worrying about. "I send out researchers who ask, 'What's bugging you?'" The findings, he said, are often very different from the concerns that dominate the headlines and TV newscasts.

The candidate must also realize, Evry said, that most people don't give a hoot about elections. "In municipal elections about 70 percent don't even vote. The man who wins does it with about 15 percent of the potential voters." The important thing, he said, is to find out who votes and make sure they know your name and like your image.

The best way to do this, said Evry, is by putting most of your advertising into TV.

He said most campaign literature is simply thrown in the garbage, so if the candidate wants to pass brochures out they should be as cheap as possible.

Campaigning should be fun, "so if knocking on doors is your idea of fun, by all means do it, but it won't get any votes." . . .

After the candidate has established a platform, said Evry, he should keep his mouth shut during the actual campaign, relying instead on TV plugs, billboards ("high recognition factor"), sniping (the U.S. term for lawn signs) and gimmicks that enhance recognition but don't make enemies.

One of his best-known gimmicks was the one he used in the campaign of the late Ivy Baker Priest, a former U.S. federal treasurer, for the office of state treasurer in California. He got her to try to throw a silver dollar across the Sacramento River on George Washington's birthday, in imitation of Washington's feat in throwing a coin across the Rappahannock River. The silver dollar fell short into the river, and a carefully rehearsed Mrs. Priest told reporters: "That just goes to show a dollar doesn't go as far today as it used to." The picture was carried by newspapers all over California and right across the U.S.

Evry calls this "news that I make up — free advertising (except for my fee) — and it doesn't take much of the candidate's time."

The most effective way to get a vote, said Evry, is a personal letter from a respected friend urging the voter to back the candiate. The least effective is a bumper-sticker ("Your friends hate you for asking them to use stickers").

He said candidates should try to associate themselves with respected symbols — pictures of Congress (or Parliament) on literature and letters, and in the U.S. pictures of George Washington, Thomas Jefferson and other historic figures.

His own firm's letterhead makes use of the ideas — it has a big colour picture of the Capital in Washington spread across it, even though the office address is in Los Angeles.

He said before candidates launch into a series of speeches and controversies, they should remember that Brazilian voters once elected a hippo to office and that Panamanians even voted for a can of shoe polish.

Say Nothing

Don't be drawn into issues promoted by the media, he said. "No newspaper can help you, but they can hurt you. Don't talk to reporters. Better not to say anything than be quoted as saying something you really didn't mean.

"Avoid issues. You're bound to alienate someone. There's no law saying you have to tell a reporter anything and no law saying you have to tell the voter anything."

Campaign literature should consist mainly of direct mail, Evry said. The latest idea is to totally avoid metered mail. "Use as many stamps as possible on a letter — don't use one where you could use 10, it looks more sincere and personal." Machine-written handwriting is good, he said, and a candidate can get supporters to give him lists of names for "Dear Friend" postcards that appear to have been written by a friend but are in fact manufactured by the campaign agency.

One of Evry's successful campaigns involved flooding a small district with 3 million signs saying just, "Three cheers for Milligan," an unknown who said nothing, made no speeches but romped into office over his more tasteful opponents. . . .

Evry thinks Canadian campaign techniques in general are so bad "it embarrasses me."

One Canadian who takes Hal Evry seriously is Ralph Bruce, a chiropractor turned campaign consultant who lives in Val d'Or, Quebec. He said that he was worried about crime in that mining community and decided to run for the city council. "I called Hal in Los Angeles and asked his advice. I followed it, and became the first English-Canadian alderman elected in many years — and with a record majority." . . .

Bruce said the fee he aims at for a provincial riding is $4,000 and thinks a seat can be won for a total expenditure of $20,000 to $25,000. The candidate should start working on getting his image before the public a year in advance of the election, said Bruce, who was trained by Evry's organization in California. . . .

Can Canadians be sold politicians the way they are sold soap?

Same Here

Evry said: "People universally have the same interests. Canadians may think they are different to Californians, but really it's only the climate that's different.

"You can say the political system is different, that parties are different, but parties are people. There's no such thing as a party machine. The voters are people and independent people.

"The swinging vote decides the election and the majority of people aren't going to be influenced by what the media think are the issues, they don't even bother to read the political reporting. In the last presidential election in the United States, more people watched Sandford and Son on TV than the election results. . . ."

SELLING THE LEADER*

Val Sears

Jerry Goodis was having a real fine day.

The man who gave you, adwise, Hush Puppies, Speedy Muffler King and Hiram Walker had a new client: the Prime Minister of Canada.

And here he was, down in Kensington Market with cameraman Dick Leiterman running hundreds of feet of great film through Dick's Arriflex as Pierre Elliott Trudeau went among The Ethnics.

"And you, sir," asked Jerry of a Portuguese gentleman after Trudeau had passed, "what do you think of the Prime Minister?"

"Wonderful man," said the Portuguese gentleman as Dick's camera whirred. "The Liberals allowed me into this country. I have made good here. And that Mr. Trudeau is a strong leader. This country needs a strong leader . . . just like they have in Russia."

Zap. Cut. Hold, it, Dick.

"Cut the Last Bit"

"Now," said Jerry Goodis, the other day, "we might — I'm not saying we will — but we just might cut out that last bit."

This is selling-of-a-prime-minister time. And the boys from the ad agencies are very sensitive about the handling of this new and exciting product — the 1974 federal election campaign.

There's Goodis, from Goodis Goldberg Soren Ltd.; Norm Atkins, from Camp Associates Advertising Ltd. for the Progressive Conservatives; and Manny Dunsky, whose Montreal-based agency turns up everywhere the New Democratic Party forms a government.

They are, naturally, twitchy about discussing details of their work. Atkins obviously has read *The Selling of The President*, a devastating book on the huckstering of President Richard Nixon, and now won't even talk to his shoeshine boy. Dunsky's office shifts inquiries to NDP party publicists in Ottawa. Jerry Grafstein, a Liberal laywer who heads a temporary consortium of ad agencies, is somewhat more forthcoming.

He lets you know this much: "I like a juicy campaign — and this one's going to be juicy."

---

* From *The Toronto Star*, May 31, 1974. By permission.

But the salesmen are there all right. And you'd better believe what you see on the screen — on CBC free-time broadcasts and private network commercials — represent hundreds of hours of hard, sweaty image making.

There's big money as well. In the 1972 campaign, the Conservatives were estimated to have spent $960,000 on national broadcasting alone: the Liberals, $557,000 and the New Democrats, $163,000. . . .

"Film Lies"

But for the ad agencies the Big Apple is still television, particularly the four hours of CBC free time that has been alloted to all four parties on the basis of Commons standings.

Jerry Goodis, whose book *Have I Ever Lied to You?*, and a stable of blue-ribbon clients, has made him the best known among the current political admen, is a dedicated Liberal.

He doesn't wince — as some of the others do — at the use of the word "selling" applied to politicians.

"Why is it immoral to sell a politician?" he wonders. "Everybody sells something. Sure you try to emphasize the candidates' strong points. Why not? When you're chasing a girl you don't tell her you've got bad breath." This is his first campaign.

"Mr. Trudeau is easy to film. In this campaign he's angry and excited. He's a man who's witty, charming, warm, full of humanity, and we're going to try and get that across on television." . . .

All three parties are leaning heavily in this campaign on a simulated news-documentary technique by using man-on-the-street interviews and campaign scenes carefully edited to create the best impression of the candidate.

John Griffin, a veteran news documentary cameraman who has filmed for all three parties and is currently working on the NDP campaign, says this technique makes him uneasy.

"People watching TV really don't distinguish between news and partisan political broadcasts done this way," he says. "Film lies all the time. We don't shoot empty chairs in a meeting hall, for instance. And you can manipulate film to do anything you want with it.

"We may have to film 100 people to get half a dozen who say what the party would like them to say." . . .

At a meeting of party communications chiefs from all provinces at the Hyatt Regency Hotel last week, there was almost solid agreement on one thing: Trudeau was the selling point. . . .

The Conservatives have produced a detailed campaign manual to be distributed to all of their candidates under the title, Winning Ways. It contains everything a candidate may have wanted to know about campaigns but might be afraid to ask.

No Bare Legs

Such as: On television — "Get black or dark knee length socks. A show of bare leg on men is distasteful to viewers. Directors usually advise people who are a little chubby or tending to baldness to go light on sideburns."

On outdoor advertising: "It will make your campaign look big and powerful."

The Liberals prefer a much briefer graphics book and a series of educational sessions in which candidates and their managers are briefed on campaign techniques.

Certainly, after the debacle of the last campaign on the theme, The Land is Strong, the Liberals are exercising a great deal more political control over the admen.

Grafstein, a veteran Liberal backroom boy, now stands between the ad agency consortium and the party itself.

"There'll be no advertising man saying 'we can get this past those big dumb politicians this time,'" he says, "because one of the 'dumb' politicians is going to be right in the room. . . ."

ELECTING A CANADIAN GOVERNMENT*

One of the most important powers exercised by the prime minister is the right to ask that the Governor General dissolve Parliament and give orders that writs of election be issued. . . .

In this manner the machinery for conducting a general election in Canada is put in motion. On instructions from the Governor in Council (in other words, the cabinet) the Chief Electoral Officer, an independent official chosen by the House of Commons, issues the writs of election to the returning officer in each constituency or riding. These officers direct the preparation of voters' lists, appoint deputy returning officers for each polling subdivision in the constituency, receive nominations of candidates and provide for the printing of ballots.

The voters' lists are compiled by enumeration of the electors, which begins 49 days before the election. Enumerators [in twos], representing the two opposing political interests that received the highest numbers of votes in the constituency in the preceding election, make a door-to-door list of urban voters. (Only one enumerator is required in rural ridings.) Preliminary lists of electors are posted in public places, such as telephone poles, so that any voter may protest the inclusion or omission of any name. The official list of eligible urban voters must be compiled at least 42 days before the election date. Final revision of voters' lists must be completed 12 days before the election. . . .

The returning officer in every constituency designates the locations of the polling stations. In a recent election, the number of polling stations within each riding ranged from 27 to 458, and the number of voters who cast their ballots in each station was between 2 and 350. Each deputy returning officer and his poll clerk supervise the conduct of the polling on election day, under the scrutiny of two agents for each candidate. The Canada Elections Act requires a voter to fold the ballot paper as directed so that the initials on the back and the printed serial number on the back of the counterfoil can be seen without unfolding it, and hand it to the deputy returning officer, who

---

* Revised by the editor in January, 1982, and reprinted originally from the Bank of Montreal *Business Review,* May 29, 1962. By permission.

ascertains, without unfolding it, that it is the same ballot paper as that delivered to the elector. If it is the same, the officer is required in full view of the elector and others present to remove and destroy the counterfoil and himself deposit the ballot in the box. After the poll is closed, the ballots are counted by the deputy returning officer in the presence of the poll clerk and party scrutineers, and the ballots, locked in the ballot box, are forwarded to the returning officer. Although the results of the election are usually made public on election night, the official addition of votes for all of the polling divisions in the constituency is made by the returning officer who subsequently issues a declaration of election in favour of the candidate who obtained a plurality; that is, more votes than any other candidate. (In case of a tie, the returning officer, who is not otherwise permitted to vote, may cast the deciding ballot.) This candidate will become the parliamentary representative for the constituency.

In federal elections in Canada the ballot bears in alphabetical order the names of the candidates in the constituency and their party affiliation if the party has met the requirements as a registered party. (A candidate may list also his address or occupation.) To qualify to be on a ballot, a party must register in advance with the Chief Electoral Officer and have members in the previous House of Commons or run at least 50 candidates in the current election.

When a person wishes to become a candidate for election to the House of Commons, he must take certain formal steps in order to have his name appear on the ballot. To assure his candidacy any elector (that is, a person 18 years of age or over who is a Canadian citizen and is not disqualified) must file nomination papers endorsed by 25 other electors and make a deposit of $200 with the returning officer for the constituency within the time prescribed in the Elections Act. It is possible for a candidate to seek election in a constituency in which he does not reside. The deposit of each candidate is refunded if he polls at least half the number of votes of the winning candidate; if less, the deposit is forfeited to the Crown. In a recent election such forfeitures totalled some $75,000.

● ● ●

The campaign which follows the announcement that an election will be held usually lasts for a month to six weeks. The facilities of air transport, television, and radio have done little to reduce the pressure on the contestants; on the contrary, they are subjected to increased demands for their presence. The leading members of the various parties are presented with schedules well nigh impossible to meet as they cross and re-cross the country, giving speeches, meeting thousands of people, making countless appearances on platforms, and before the press, consulting with their campaign managers and advisors, and performing multitudinous other duties. All electioneering must end two days before election day.

In 1980 there were 11,016,899 votes cast for 1,497 candidates running in 282 single-member constituencies across Canada. The turn-out was rather less than recently, attaining only 70 per cent. Only 0.6 of the ballots cast were spoiled.

By electing their M.P. from their riding, the voters were also indirectly choosing their next government. The leader of the party that has the largest number of candidates elected to the House of Commons is traditionally invited by the Governor General to take office as prime minister and form a cabinet which governs the country. Usually, the party that forms the government has a majority of seats in the Commons, but in recent years this has become less common and there have been a number of minority governments. In the past 60 years there have been eight occasions — in 1921, 1925, 1957, 1962, 1963, 1965, 1972, and 1979 — when the party winning the largest number of seats has still had less than half the total number in the House and therefore functioned as a minority government.

General elections must be held at least once in five years, although the prime minister is free to choose a date before that time to call an election. The costs are considerable. The Chief Electoral Officer's requirements for

Canadian General Elections, 1867-1980
Party Standings in House of Commons

Date of Election		Party Standing							
	Cons.	Lib.	Prog.	C.C.F.-N.D.P.	S.C.	S.C.R.	Other	Total Seats
August 7-September 20, 1867	101	80						181
July 20-September 3, 1872	103	97						200
January 22, 1874	73	133						206
September 17, 1878	142	64						206
June 20, 1882	139	71					1	211
February 22, 1887	126	89						215
March 5, 1891	121	94						215
June 23, 1896	88	118					7	213
November 7, 1900	80	133						213
November 3, 1904	75	138					1	214
October 26, 1908	85	135					1	221
September 21, 1911	134	87						221
December 17, 1917	153*	82						235
December 6, 1921	50	116	64				5	235
October 29, 1925	116	99	24				6	245
September 14, 1926	91	128	20				6	245
July 28, 1930	137	91	12				5	245
October 14, 1935	40	173		7	17		8	245
March 26, 1940	40	181		8	10		6	245
June 11, 1945	67	125		28	13		12	245
June 27, 1949	41	193		13	10		5	262
August 10, 1953	51	171		23	15		5	265
June 10, 1957	112	105		25	19		4	265
March 31, 1958	208	49		8				265
June 18, 1962†	116	100		19	30			265
April 8, 1963	95	129		17	24			265
November 8, 1965	97	131		21	5	9	2	265
June 25, 1968	72	155		22		14	1	264
October 30, 1972	107	109		31	15		2	264
July 8, 1974	95	141		16	11		1	264
May 22, 1979	136	114		26	6			282
February 18, 1980	103	147		32				282

*Unionist.
†Figures include results of service vote and deferred election in Stormont held July 16, 1962. C.C.F. became N.D.P. July 31, 1961.

Results of Federal General Elections in 1980 and 1979
Seats Won by Parties by Province in 1980 (1979 results in brackets)[1]

Province	Lib.	P.C.	N.D.P.	S.C.	Totals
Newfoundland	5(4)	2(2)	(1)		7(7)
Prince Edward Island	2	2(4)			4(4)
Nova Scotia	5(2)	6(8)	(1)		11(11)
New Brunswick	7(6)	3(4)			10(10)
Quebec	74(67)	1(2)		(6)	75(75)
Ontario	52(32)	38(57)	5(6)		95(95)
Manitoba	2(2)	5(7)	7(5)		14(14)
Saskatchewan		7(10)	7(4)		14(14)
Alberta		21(21)			21(21)
British Columbia	(1)	16(19)	12(8)		28(28)
Yukon		1(1)			1(1)
Northwest Territories		1(1)	1(1)		2(2)
Totals	147(114)	103(136)	32(26)	(6)	282(282)

Discrepancies Between Percentages of Seats Gained and Percentages of Valid Votes Won by
Parties Nationally in 1980 (1979 results in brackets)

	Lib.	P.C.	N.D.P.	S.C.
Seats[2]	52.1(40.4)	36.5(48.2)	11.3(9.2)	(2.1)
Valid votes[3]	44.3(40.1)	32.4(35.9)	19.8(17.9)	1.7(4.6)

[1]From *Report of the Chief Electoral Officer, Thirty-Second General Election, 1980,* and *Report of the Chief Electoral Officer, Thirty-First General Election, 1979.*
[2]Calculated from data given in the Chief Electoral Officer's *Statutory Report, 1980,* p. 32, and *Statutory Report, 1979,* p. 37.
[3]From sources given in footnote 1. Percentages do not total 100 since votes for other parties have been omitted.

staff and supplies amount to about $35 million and in addition there are the expenditures by party organizations as well as by individual candidates. In 1980 the federal Liberal party spent $9.8 million, the Conservatives $10 million, and the NDP $6 million. In addition candidates probably spent more than $10 million for which they were reimbursed a very large percentage by the federal government under the new Election Expenses Act. After the 1979 election, for example, the federal government returned $8,517,781 to candidates and $2,016,249 to parties.

P. R. FOR CANADA?*

Paul Fox

Most voters would probably be quite shocked if they were told that they were rarely ruled by a majority, that there is every chance that a Canadian government — federal or provincial — will not likely represent a majority of the voters, and that more people will probably vote against a government than for it.

* Revised in January, 1982, based on an article by the author which appeared originally in *The Financial Post,* August 8, 1953. By permission.

Yet that has been the case in many provincial elections and in 17 out of the last 19 federal elections. Only twice since 1921 has the winning party got more than 50 per cent of the national popular vote (the Liberals won 51.5 percent in 1940 and Mr. Diefenbaker about 53.6 percent in 1958).

Minority Wins

How do minority wins occur? The winner may win by a plurality, that is, he gets more votes than any of his several opponents, but he may not get more than 50 percent of the total. For example, in a certain Ontario riding recently the Liberal candidate received a vote of 14,035, the Progressive Conservative 11,155, the NDP 8,302, the Communist 1,413, and another candidate 307. The top man thus had 14,035 votes for him and a grand total of 21,177 against him.

When this sort of thing is repeated in constituency after constituency, a party may win an election by obtaining more seats than any other part or all the other parties combined and still not have had even half the citizens voting for it.

The appearance of important smaller parties, like the NDP and Social Credit, has had a lot to do with this sort of outcome. But the minor parties aren't the real cause of the weakness. The actual defect is in the election machinery. It works in such a way that the party that wins the election ordinarily gets far more seats in the House of Commons than its share of the popular vote entitles it to.

At the same time, the opposition parties usually get far fewer. In every election since 1896 the incoming government has ridden into power with more seats than its portion of the national vote gave it. Sometimes the discrepancies have been really shocking.

In 1979, for instance, when the Conservatives under Joe Clark won the federal election, they polled only 35.9 percent of the popular vote but secured 48.2 percent of the seats.

The next year, the shoe was on the other foot. Pierre Elliott Trudeau and the Liberals recaptured the government with only 44.3 percent of the votes, but that gave them 52.1 percent of the places in the Commons.

The N.D.P. paid the price of the lop-sided victory in both elections. In 1979 the N.D.P. got nearly 18 percent of the vote but only nine percent of the seats, in 1980 approximately 20 percent of the vote and 11 percent of the places.

These figures also show how our election system multiplies a slight shift in voting at the polls into a big landslide in seats for the winner. In 1979, for example, the Conservatives increased their seats from 95 to 136 (about 43 percent) with a shift of only 0.5 percentage points in votes. In 1980, it was the Liberals' turn. They increased their popular vote by only four percentage points but that was sufficient for them to regain power by getting a 28 percent increase in seats. Conversely, the Conservatives dropped only 3.5 percentage points in votes but lost 24 percent of their seats.

Provincial election results are sometimes even more ridiculous. In the Quebec election which brought the separatists to power in 1976, the Parti Québécois, which had been grossly underrepresented in the Assembly, suddenly became overrepresented by jumping from six seats to 71 although its share of the popular vote went up from 30 to only 41 percent. In other words, a 30 percent increase in votes produced a 1,000 percent increase in seats.

Absurd results like these bring our present system of voting into question and raise the issue, what can be done to remedy the defects? The answer is "not much" as long as we retain our existing plurality system (or "first past the post") which permits a candidate to win by not getting a majority but only more votes than the next runner-up.

Should we scrap our present system then and try something different? Few Canadians realize that we came close to doing this in the 1920s.

Alternative Voting

In 1924, and again in 1925, the federal government introduced a bill to abolish our present method of election and to replace it by Alternative Voting. These bills were never passed. But about the same time, Manitoba and Alberta switched over to the new system, followed by British Columbia in 1952, though they all dropped it later.

The big difference between Alternative or Preferential Voting and our present federal method is that the voter gets as many choices as there are candidates and marks his ballot in order of his preference: 1, 2, 3, 4, 5, and so on. When the polls close, the first choices for each candidate are counted, and if no one has a clear majority the contestant with the fewest votes is dropped and the second choices on his ballots are distributed. If there's still no majority, the next lowest man is put out and and his second choices on his ballots are distributed. And so it goes until someone finally gets a majority.

The great advantage to this method, (which is used in Australia for the House of Representatives) is, of course, that it ensures that the winner finally gets a majority and that nobody gets in by a plurality. But that's about all it does. It doesn't solve the problem of the wasted votes for the losing parties and it doesn't give the minorities any representation. It can also encourage a little skullduggery because by means of it two parties can cooperate at an election to knock out a third. (Party A and Party B pass the word along to their supporters to vote their own party first and the other party second, but under no circumstances to cast a ballot for Party C.) This is what happened in B.C. in 1952.

The truth is that no system of voting will guarantee equal weight to all votes and fair representation to minority groups so long as we stick to our present method of electing only one member of parliament from each constituency.

The big weakness of single-member districts is that only one person and one party can be chosen to represent all the voters living in that area.

This is unreal if there are many different points of view in the riding. The only sure way of giving them representation is to enlarge the constituency so that it has a number of seats and to fill these seats in proportion to the way the electorate votes.

Proportional Representation

This, in a nutshell, is the system of voting known as Proportional Representation. It had quite a vogue in Canada about 40 years ago when cities like Winnipeg, Calgary, Edmonton, and Vancouver adopted it. It is still popular in some countries like Denmark, Ireland, and Israel. Australia uses it for senate elections.

There are about as many different systems of proportional representation as there are ideas about government. Somebody once counted 300 varieties, but they all work much the same way. Under the Hare System, which is probably the best known in Canada, electors go to the polls and vote for all candidates in order of preference. There will likely be a large number of candidates, at least as many as there are persons to be elected multiplied by the number of political parties, for each party will want to nominate a full slate. A minimum of five candidates is essential to make P.R. work well.

The quota necessary for election is figured out by dividing the number voting by the number of seats to be filled plus one, the one being added to reduce the quota a bit to allow for such contingencies as spoiled ballots.

The next step is to count the first choices for each candidate. Anyone who has secured the quota is declared elected. If he has more than the quota, his surplus is transferred to the second choices. If none of the hopefuls has a quota, or if too few have it, then the man with the least first choices is eliminated and the second preferences on his ballots are distributed as marked. If this is not enough, the next lowest candidate is put out and his second choices are allocated. This goes on until the required number of candidates reaches the quota.

The supporters of P.R. say it has been tried in Canada in cities like Winnipeg and that it has worked well. They argue that its greatest asset is that it eliminates the startling discrepancy between the popular vote for parties and the number of seats they win in the legislature.

Representation in parliament of political parties becomes identical to the proportion of votes they get at the polls: no more plurality wins, no more narrow-majority wins for one party in a lot of constituencies and a huge "wasted" vote for the other parties; no more over-representation of one party and under-representation of the others with a small knot of voters swinging an election one way or the other and converting a small shift in votes into a landslide in seats.

Instead, there would be an exact mathematical similarity between proportion of popular vote and proportion of seats and completely unbiased treatment for both minor and major parties. There would also be a seat for any minority that could muster a quota, and as many seats for the larger groups as would be proportional to their voting strength.

If P.R. is such a a cure-all, why not adopt it in Canada?

Disadvantages

Oddly enough, the best argument for it is also the best argument against it. The fact is that P.R. produces *too* accurate a resemblance between public opinion and representation in parliament.

If we used it across the country, it would be rare for a party to get a majority in the House of Commons, at least judging by the voting since 1921. This would change completely the basis of our system of cabinet government, which depends on the party in power having enough strength to get its legislative programme through parliament. A party without a majority would be forced to battle every proposal through the Commons, or to enter into a coalition with some other party or parties.

There are other arguments against P.R. A favourite is that it multiplies the number of parties because it gives them a better chance of securing representation in the legislature. This is not as true as most people think. In France and Belgium, for example, there are no more parties now than there were before P.R. was introduced.

But there is a danger in a country like Canada, which has strong regional feelings and interests, that P.R. might foster a large number of regional parties in the federal House. Even under the existing system, the tendency in that direction is strong. Another difficulty is that P.R increases the size of constituences in thinly populated areas to almost unreasonable dimensions. If P.R. were put into effect in Canada and no riding were to have less than five members, it might well be, for example, that the whole of Manitoba outside of Winnipeg and its suburbs would become one or two gigantic electoral districts. Candidates would have a tremendous and expensive task trying to campaign over such a huge area and the voters might never get a glimpse of their MPs.

Actually, none of the disadvantages of P.R. is really significant except the one overwhelming argument that if it were introduced all across Canada it would jeopardize our system of parliamentary government. And that limitation is so serious that is makes it impossible to recommend the wholesale adoption of P.R. in this country.

Is there no solution, then?

The remedy seems to be to mix the two systems together judiciously to get the good effects of each. This could be done quite easily. One way would be to retain our present system for large rural areas while substituting P.R. for it in large, densely populated urban centres. This was first suggested and debated in Parliament 60 years ago. Vancouver, Toronto, and Montreal would be obvious places to start.

If that kind of combination is not acceptable, there is another possibility which has been receiving a good deal of attention lately.

Recent Proposals

Recently, there has been renewed concern about the damaging effects that our present voting system has on the representativeness of our political parties. Because they are squeezed out of getting members elected in certain regions even though they have respectable popular votes there, all of our parties are less than representative of the whole country. The Conservatives, for instance, are almost without members in Quebec, the Liberals have no MPs west of Winnipeg, and the NDP has less representation in Southern Ontario and Montreal than its popular support warrants.

Lacking MPs from entire regions, the parties appear to be less than national — and they are, to the extent that these regions have no voice in the party caucus.

Yet if seats in the Commons had been assigned to parties in proportion to their vote by province in the 1980 election, the Conservatives would have won nine seats in Quebec, the NDP four, and the Liberals 16 or more in the West.

The Pépin-Robarts Task Force on Canadian Unity was so disturbed by this weakness in our present system that it said, "The regional polarization of federal political parties corrodes federal unity." To overcome it and to give the parties better regional representation, the Task Force recommended a mixed electoral system. While the present plurality, single-member system would be continued for the current 282 constituencies, an additional 60 seats would be allocated in proportion to the popular vote for parties, either by province or nationally using the d'Hondt formula.

The accompanying table shows what the results would have been if the Pépin-Robarts' proposal had been applied in the 1980 election.

Composition of the House of Commons following the Federal Election of February 18, 1980, if Pépin-Robarts' Proposal Had Been Applied

Province	Lib.	Cons.	N.D.P.	Créd.	Rhino	Total
Newfoundland	5	2				7
Prince Edward Island	2	2				4
Nova Scotia	5	6	1			12
New Brunswick	7	3				10
Quebec	74	12	3	1	1	91
Ontario	59	46	12			117
Manitoba	4	5	7			16
Saskatchewan	3	7	7			17
Alberta	6	21	1			28
British Columbia	9	16	12			37
North		2	1			3
Totals	174	122	44	1	1	342

Comparing this distribution of seats to the actual outcome which was given in a previous table (Results of Federal General Election in 1980, Seats Won by Parties by Province), it is clear that all three main parties would have benefitted by obtaining greater regional representation.

The essence of the Pépin-Robarts' plan caught on, particularly in light of the misshapen results of the 1980 election. Soon after the election, the leader of the federal NDP, Ed Broadbent, proposed that 50 new members be added to the House of Commons, ten for each of five regions, in proportion to the parties' shares of the votes in each region. The Canada West proposal was very similar. Saskatchewan Premier Allan Blakeney suggested a House with 182 members elected directly in single-member constituencies and another 100 selected by proportional representation. The Quebec Liberal party, following their leader, Claude Ryan, proposed a completely proportional system.

In a book which is the most definitive Canadian study of the problem, Professor William Irvine of Queen's University devised a mixed system which, like Mr. Broadbent's, is somewhat similar to the one used in West Germany since 1949. There would be 188 constituency seats and 166 "provincial seats" based on P.R. If a party did not secure a percentage of constituency seats equal to its proportion of the popular vote in the province, its deficiency would be made up by giving it the required number of provincial members from a ranked list of candidates submitted in advance by the party itself. (This is similar to the List system of P.R. used in Israel and elsewhere.)

In a well-reasoned article noted in the bibliography, Professor John Courtney has commented critically on these various proposals and the assumptions on which they are based. Federal Conservative Leader Joe Clark and Premier Peter Lougheed of Alberta have declined to accept the new systems, no doubt because that very acceptance would make it even more difficult for the Conservatives to dislodge the Liberals from power. The Liberals, with only two exceptions, have won the greatest number of votes in the last 15 federal elections, even in 1979 and 1957 when they lost the government.

Having already expressed suport for P.R. during the 1980 campaign, Prime Minister Trudeau said he was interested in Mr. Broadbent's proposal, and his government promised in the subsequent Throne Speech to set up a parliamentary committee to study alternatives to the present system of voting.

However, this promise was muted in January, 1982 when the government announced postponement of the committee's establishment to a later session of Parliament. There appeared to be opposition to the idea of a new electoral system from within the Liberal caucus as well as from within the NDP party itself. MPs and others expressed dissatisfaction with having two different kinds of members in the House. Liberals were reported to be worried also by the prospect of their block of members from Quebec being diminished, particularly if the Parti Québécois fulfilled its threat to run candidates federally and got them elected by means of the new system.

BIBLIOGRAPHY

(See also the Bibliographies in Chapters 8 and 10)

Adamson, A., "The Referendum in Canadian Experiences," *Policy Options,* 1, 1, March, 1980.

Boily, R., *La réforme électorale au Québec,* Montréal, Éditions du Jour, 1970.

British Columbia, *Royal Commission on Electoral Reform,* Victoria, B.C., 1978, 3 vols.

Cairns, A.C., "The Electoral System and the Party System in Canada," *C.J.P.S.,* I, 1, March, 1968.

(Reprinted in *Politics: Canada,* Chapter 8.)

Cairns, A.C., "The Strong Case for Modest Electoral Reform in Canada," A paper delivered to the Harvard University Seminar on Canadian-United States Relations, 1979.

Canada, *Report of the Committee on Election Expenses,* [Barbeau Committee], Ottawa, Q.P., 1966, 2 vols.

Canada, Task Force on Canadian Unity, [Pépin-Robarts Report], *A Future Together: Observations and Recommendations*, Ottawa, S. and S., 1979.

Courtney, J.C., "Recognition of Canadian Political Parties in Parliament and in Law," *C.J.P.S.*, 11, 1, March, 1978.

Courtney, J.C., "Reflections on Reforming the Canadian Electoral System," *C.P.A.*, 23, 3, Fall, 1980.

Daniels, S.R., *The Case for Electoral Reform*, London, Allen and Unwin, 1938.

Dobell, W.M., "A Limited Corrective to Plurality Voting," *C.P.P.*, VII, 1, Winter, 1981.

Finer, S.E., *Adversary Politics and Electoral Reform*, London, Wigram, 1975.

Gargrave, A., and Hull, R.M., *How to Win an Election: The Complete Practical Guide to Organizing and Winning Any Election Campaign*, Toronto, Macmillan, 1979.

Hermens, F.A., *Democracy or Anarchy? A Study of Proportional Representation*, N.Y., Johnson Reprint Corp., rev. ed ., 1972.

Horwill, G., *Proportional Representation: Its Dangers and Defects*, London, Allen and Unwin, 1925.

Humphreys, J.H., *Proportional Representation*, London, Methuen, 1911.

Irvine, W.P., *Does Canada Need a New Electoral System?*, Kingston, I.I.R., Queen's University, 1979.

Irvine, W.P., "Power Requires Representation," *Policy Options*, 1, 4, December-January, 1980-1981.

Johnson, W., "Time to Reconsider Electoral Reform?," *The Globe and Mail*, May 31, 1979.

Johnston, R., and Ballantyne, J., "Geography and the Electoral System," *C.J.P.S.*, X, 4, December, 1977.

Lakeman, E., and Lambert, J.D., *Voting in Democracies*, London, Faber, 2nd ed., 1959.

Lakeman, E., *How Democracies Vote*, London, Faber, 1970.

Landes, R.G., "Alternative Electoral Systems for Canada," A paper

presented to the Annual Meeting of the C.P.S.A., Montreal, 1980.

Lemieux, V., "New Proportional Representation System Needed," *Star-Phoenix*, Saskatoon, June 18, 1979.

Lemieux, V., *Le quotient politique vrai*, Québec, Les Presses de l'Université Laval, 1973.

Lightbody, J., "Swords and Ploughshare; The Election Prerogative in Canada."*C.J.P.S.*, V, 2, June, 1972.

Long, J.A., "Maldistribution in Western Provincial Legislatures; The Case of Alberta," *C.J.P.S.*,, II, 3, September, 1969.

Lovink, J.A.A., "On Analysing the Impact of the Electoral System on the Party System in Canada," *C.J.P.S.*, III, 4, December, 1970. (Reply by A.C. Cairns, *ibid.*)

Lovink, J.A.A. "Is Canadian Politics Too Competitive?," *C.J.P.S.*, VI, 3, September, 1973.

Lyons, W.E., *One Man — One Vote*, Toronto, McG.-H., 1970.

MacKenzie, W.J., *Free Elections*, London, Allen and Unwin, 1958.

Manitoba, Law Reform Commission, *Working Papers on Electoral Systems*, Winnipeg, 1976, mimeo.

Milnor, A., *Elections and Political Stability*, Boston, Little, Brown, 1969.

Murray, D., "Proportional Representation is un-British, but is it un-Canadian?," *Report on Confederation*, 1, II, October, 1978.

Ontario Commission on the Legislature, *Third Report*, September, 1974. (Re: election financing.)

Paltiel, K., *Political Party Financing in Canada*, Toronto, McG.-H., 1970.

Pasis, H.E., "The Inequality of Distribution in the Canadian Provincial Assemblies," *C.J.P.S.*, V, 3, September, 1972.

Pitkin, H.F., *The Concept of Representation*, Berkeley, University of California Press, 1967.

Pitkin, H.F., (ed.) *Representation*, New York, Atherton, 1969.

Qualter, T.H., "Representation by

Population: A Comparative Study,"
C.J.E.P.S., XXXIII, 2, May 1967.
Qualter, T.H., "Seats and Votes: An
Application of the Cube Law to
the Canadian Electoral System,"
C.J.P.S., I, 3, September, 1968.
Qualter, T.H., *The Election Process in
Canada*, Toronto, McG.-H., 1970.
Québec, Ministère d'État à la réforme
Electorale et Parlementaire, [R.
Burns], *Un Citoyen, un Vote*, [Livre
vert sur la réforme du mode de
scrutin], Québec, Éditeur Officiel,
1979.
Rae, D., *The Political Consequences
of Electoral Laws*, New Haven,
Yale, 1967.
Ross, J.F.S., *Elections and Electors*,
London, Eyre & Spottiswoode, 1955.
Sancton, A., "The Latest Redistribu-
tion of the House of Commons,"
C.J.P.S., VI, 1, March, 1973.
Sancton, A., "The Representation Act,
1974," *C.J.P.S.*, VIII, 3, September,
1975.
Sankoff, D., and Mellos, K., "La
régionalisation électorale et
l'amplification des proportions,"
C.J.P.S., VI, 3, September, 1973.
Schindeler, F., "One Man, One Vote:
One Vote, One Value," *J.C.S.*, III,
1, February, 1968.
Simpson, J., "After Rep by Pop to
Get Rep by Prop?," *The Globe and
Mail*, March 20, 1979.
Smith, J.E., "Proportional Represen-
tation Would be a False Cure," *The
Toronto Star*, April 27, 1980.
Spafford, D., "The Electoral System
of Canada," *American Political

Science Review*, LXIV, 1, March,
1970.
Stevens, G., "Electoral Systems," a
four-part series, *The Globe and
Mail*, August 6, 7, 8, 9, 1974.
Stevens, G., "Financing Election Cam-
paigns," *The Globe and Mail*, October 11, 12, 13, 1973; November 9,
10, 1973; June 27, 28, 1974.
Stewart, W., *Divide and Con, Cana-
dian Politics at Work*, Toronto, New
Press, 1973.
Surich, J., and Williams, R.J., "Some
Characteristics of Candidates in the
1972 Canadian Federal Election," A
paper delivered at the Annual
Meeting of the C.P.S.A., Toronto,
1974.
Twiss, J.E., "The Impact of Electoral
Redistribution and Reallocation of
Seats on the Party System," A paper
presented at the Annual Meeting of
the C.P.S.A., London, Ontario,
May, 1978.
Ward, N., *The Canadian House of
Commons: Representation*, Toronto,
U.T.P., 2nd ed., 1963.
Ward, N., "A Century of Constituen-
cies," *C.P.A.*, X, 1, March, 1967.
Ward, N., "The Representative System
and the Calling of Elections,"
C.J.P.S., VI, 4, December, 1973.
Wearing, J., "How to Predict Cana-
dian Elections," *Canadian Commen-
tator*, February, 1963.
Westell, A., "Election System
Undemocratic," *Star-Phoenix*,
Saskatoon, June 9, 1979.
Westell, A., *The New Society*, Toron-
to, M. & S., 1977.

10

VOTING BEHAVIOUR

The study of voting behaviour in Canada has grown rapidly in the past twenty years, as the length of the bibliography at the end of this chapter indicates.

A number of items might have been reprinted here but the two chosen have been selected because they deal with very important general questions that are asked frequently: namely, what are the factors which lead Canadians to vote as they do, and what is the nature of Canadian political culture?

The chapter selected from the book *Political Choice in Canada*, by Professors Clarke, Jenson, LeDuc, and Pammett, examines several basic questions about Canadian voting behaviour: the extent to which voters change their support for parties from election to election, and the impact on voters of leaders, candidates, and specific issues. Using data from the 1974 national sample of the population relating to the federal general elections of 1972 and 1974, the authors find *inter alia* that political partisanship is flexible rather than enduring, that the popularity of leaders is highly variable — though their influence in attracting votes is more important than that of candidates — and that short-term issues are more significant than long-run issues.

The authors also add some very important general comments. "Divisions between the sexes, age groups, rural and urban areas, or social classes have only very limited electoral significance in federal politics. Even religion and ethnicity, traditionally the deepest cleavages in Canadian politics, are not strongly related to voting behaviour. In a sense, then, many Canadians approach electoral choice relatively free of those societal forces which might tend to 'predetermine' their votes. . . . there is no evidence that region or province of residence *per se* has a major impact on the way individual voters make up their minds." These are strong statements which deserve attention.

Professor John Wilson's provocative article, "The Canadian Political Cultures: Towards a Redefinition of the Nature of the Canadian Political System," tackles the popular contemporary question of the nature of Canadian political culture. Using voting behaviour data as well as other evidence, he argues that we should abandon the traditional notion of Canada as a country having two political cultures, English and French. Instead we probably have a number of different political cultures corresponding to provincial divisions or groups of provincial divisions which are at different stages of political development. His arguments are intriguing, controversial, and important.

The article by Professor Wilson entitled "Politics and Social Class in Canada: The Case of Waterloo South," which appeared in the fourth edition, pp. 338-350, has been omitted from this edition.

POLITICAL CHOICE*

Harold D. Clarke, Jane Jenson, Lawrence LeDuc, Jon H. Pammett

. . . The level of volatility in Canadian electoral behaviour is considerably higher than might be suggested by an examination of aggregate data alone, or by models of the electoral process which stress the significance of long-term forces. In particular, the proportion of variance in voting choice explained by short-term factors for those groups of voters whose partisan attachments we have characterized as "flexible" is impressive, and it should be emphasized that flexible partisans constitute the majority of the Canadian electorate, as measured by the 1974 national sample. When the additional contributions to processes of political change of those persons who do *not* vote in all elections (transient voters) are also considered, the potential for significant variation in electoral outcomes over relatively short periods of time would indeed seem to be high. In this chapter, we shall examine the outcome of the 1974 election in this context, and consider the implications of our argument that there is considerable potential for large fluctuations in Canadian election outcomes over relatively short periods of time. The shift which took place between the 1972 and 1974 elections, separated by less than two years, is, in many respects, a case in point.

The 1974 Election

The Liberal majority victory of 1974, following upon the near defeat of 1972, created the impression of a substantial voter shift in favour of the Liberals, particularly at the expense of the minor parties. In all, 39 seats changed hands between the two elections, the Liberals gaining 32 seats over their 1972 total on an overall improvement of 4% in the popular vote. The NDP was seen by many as the big loser of the election, dropping 15 seats from its 1972 total of 31, but it suffered a net reduction of only about 2% in its total share of the popular vote. The Conservatives, with no appreciable change in their share of the popular vote, nevertheless suffered a net reduction of 12 seats from their 1972 total.

The overall pattern of the election result presents a montage of somewhat conflicting images. On the one hand, the shift in parliamentary seats is a substantial one, and many regional and individual constituency results display considerable volatility. But the total shift in popular vote from 1972, or indeed from other recent elections, is a modest one, producing an

---

* Abridged by the editor from Chapter 12, *Political Choice in Canada,* Toronto, McGraw-Hill Ryerson, 1980, abridged edition. The numbers of the Tables and Figures in the original have been retained in the edited version. By permission.

electoral result that might be considered "typical" by the standards of longer term patterns.

These conflicting impressions reflect certain characteristics of Canadian electoral politics that we have alluded to earlier. The overall pattern is suggestive of considerable aggregate stability, which tends to obscure the rather considerable movement actually taking place in the electorate. Certainly, most observers of the 1974 campaign and election outcome hypothesized that a substantial shift of voters toward the Liberals had in fact taken place. The most common explanations advanced for this shift emphasized concern for majority government, mistrust of the Conservative position on wage and price controls, or a favourable judgement of the leadership of Prime Minister Trudeau. While each of these factors, together with others, contributed to the result, it should not be surprising in light of our previous discussion to find that virtually all such shorthand explanations of the 1974 election result contain elements of oversimplification. In this chapter, we will demonstrate that beneath the simple aggregate differences in party support in 1974 lies a myriad of patterns of movement suggestive of anything but unidirectional shifts in the electorate or of overall electoral stability.

The first indication of the degree of electoral change in 1974 is found in a direct comparison of respondents' 1974 vote with reports of voting behaviour in the 1972 election. About one respondent in five voting in the 1974 election reported a partisan choice *different* from that of 1972. In addition, another 11% of our 1974 sample consisted of those who did not vote in the 1972 election by choice or because they were new voters eligible for the first time in 1974. Over this relatively short period, then, approximately one-third of the total electorate was subject to change. Change emanates from one of three specific sources: *vote switching;* intermittent *non-voting,* or movement into and out of the electorate by some portion of a pool of transient voters; and electoral *replacement* resulting from the death or aging of some voters and the coming of age and entry into the electorate of others. The relative strength of these several forces, as estimated from the 1974 sample, is indicated in Figure 1.

It is possible, of course, to emphasize either stability or change in this discussion. On the one hand, it might be argued that the choice of the *same* party by two-thirds of the electorate in two successive elections constitutes a considerable degree of electoral stability. On the other, the turnover of more than one-third in a period of less than two years might be viewed as a very considerable level of change, particularly in light of the fact that the same parties, leaders and many of the candidates appear in these two particular elections. The Liberals, after all, moved from a position of near defeat to a parliamentary majority with a net gain of only 4% of the total popular vote. One might imagine such a result being accounted for by a very small movement of voters in one particular direction, by a larger movement of voters in several different directions, or by some combination of circumstances between these possibilities.

There are a number of characteristics of the direction of movement of the 1974 sample (Table 1) which merit attention. First, and perhaps most important, is the finding that the net result of the pattern of switching from 1972 to 1974 was actually *away* from the Liberals. Half again as many voters are found to have switched from the Liberals to the Conservatives as switched

FIGURE 1
Stability and Change in the Canadian Electorate, 1972–74[a]

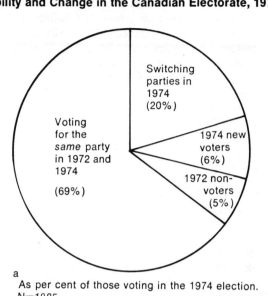

a
As per cent of those voting in the 1974 election.
N=*1885*.

from the Conservatives to the Liberals in 1974. Had the election been fought between these two groups of voters alone, the data suggest that a different result might have been obtained. Nor is the election outcome adequately explained by the movement of supporters of the minor parties toward the Liberals. Although the NDP shows a net loss of support in the sample, nearly as many respondents are found moving from the Liberals *to* the NDP as from the NDP to the Liberals. Similarly, the overall magnitude of the 1972 NDP voters moving to the Conservatives is about equal to that of the NDP to Liberal shift, while a slightly smaller group of 1972 PC voters now voting NDP is found. In several ways, then, the pattern of switching displayed by those voters who supported different parties in 1972 and 1974

TABLE 1 1974 Vote by Behaviour in the 1972 Election (diagonal percentages)

| | | 1972 Behaviour | | | | | |
		Liberal	PC	NDP	Social Credit	Did Not Vote	Not Eligible
	Liberal	39.6	4.2	2.4	0.6	3.3	3.3
1974	PC	6.3	19.9	1.7	0.4	1.5	1.3
Vote	NDP	1.7	0.9	7.6	0.3	0.8	0.8
	Social Credit	0.6	0.1	—	2.1	0.1	0.4

100%
(N = *1791*[a])

[a]Voters in the 1974 election only. Other parties and spoiled ballots excluded.

runs counter to expectations which might be formed on the basis of the aggregate vote patterns, or much of the post-election commentary.

While it is clear that a considerable amount of switching did indeed take place, Table 1 fails to disclose the expected net shift to the Liberals that many observers believed had occurred. Instead, it would appear that the Liberals realized a small net *loss* of their 1972 electoral support. The pattern disclosed by Table 1 suggests, however, that this net loss was more than redressed by the impact of the new voters and transient voters. Although these two groups combined comprise only 11% of the 1974 electorate, the fact that their behaviour more heavily favours a single party than does that of switchers indicates that they may have had more effect on the actual outcome of the 1974 election.

A slightly different way of looking at the success with which each of the parties held its 1972 vote and at the behaviour of the transient and new voters can be obtained from a recalculation of the figures shown in Table 1. For example, both the Liberals and Conservatives enjoyed about equal success in retaining their 1972 supporters (70% and 69% respectively), and both were more successful in this regard than the NDP or Social Credit parties (54% and 49%). Table 1 indicates that the Liberals had lost more 1972 supporters than the Conservatives in absolute terms. However, it is also true that they held an approximately equal *proportion* of their 1972 support. Similarly, the NDP lost fewer voters in absolute terms but, since it had fewer to start with, its proportional loss of 1972 support was significantly greater than that of the two major parties.

A further observation may be made with regard to the nature of the impact of the transients and new voters. Although newly eligible voters are somewhat less likely to vote than members of the permanent electorate, their strong support for the Liberal party in 1974 is clearly evident. The behaviour of the transient voters is particularly important because, although their effect on the result in 1974 is about equal to that of the new voters (Table 1), their *potential* impact on election outcomes is much greater, since transient voters move *out* of the electorate as well as *into* it. We have argued . . . that the proportion of the electorate which votes only in *some* elections may be as much as one-sixth of the total of eligible voters. In any given election, only between one-quarter and one-third of this group may exercise their franchise. In any pair of elections, the transient group may be seen to include persons moving *into* the active electorate as well as persons moving *out* of it, at least temporarily. Of the 1972 supporters of a given party, some did not vote in 1974 (14%, 13%, and 16% for the Liberals, Conservatives, and NDP respectively, and a slightly higher 22% for Social Credit), and thus moved out of the 1974 electorate. At the same time, slightly under half of those persons who did *not* vote in 1972 did so in 1974. While the loss experienced by each of the parties due to 1972 supporters moving out of the electorate is approximately equal in proportional terms, the group moving into the electorate was strongly Liberal, and accounts for the total electoral effect of the transient voters favouring the Liberals, shown in Table 1. The preference shown for the Liberals in 1974 by those who had not been in the active electorate in 1972 tended to offset the loss to the Liberals contributed by those members of the permanent electorate who switched to other parties. In summary, the data do not support the commonly held notion that it was a large-scale migration of 1972 Conservative or NDP voters that best accounts for the 1974 Liberal victory. There was such a shift, nationally and in most of the provinces, but it was more than offset by a switch of 1972 Liberals away from that party. The greater contribution caused by heavy Liberal voting in 1974 of those groups which were not in the active electorate in 1972 underscores the argument that we must consider the implications of more than one source of electoral change in any analysis of 1974 or of other elections.

The evidence indicates that the electoral effects of relatively large changes in the electorate (e.g., switching) can be offset by smaller sources of change when the latter are concentrated in a particular direction. It is not possible to determine from the 1974 study alone whether such is a common occurrence in elections in Canada. Certainly, we can easily imagine alternate sets of circumstances in elections that might produce different patterns. . . .

The 1974 data indeed suggest a number of larger questions. Is it usual for short-term forces, such as issues, leaders, or candidates, to pull groups of voters in different directions and thus produce a kind of cancelling effect in electoral outcomes? What mobilizes transient voters and causes them to enter the electorate at certain times? Are they more likely to move in a single direction, or are they sometimes subject to the same cancelling effects that have been observed here with respect to switchers? And considering the new voters that enter the electorate for the first time in each election, are there long-term forces affecting this group which might account for their strong support of the Liberals in 1974? Such a finding could have significant implications for the nature of the party system in Canada over the next generation. Or are new voters, like certain other groups in the electorate, subject to powerful short-term forces which may produce different electoral outcomes over relatively short periods of time? Most of these questions are ones that cannot be completely answered by a single survey of a particular election. But much of our foregoing analysis of partisanship, images of parties and leaders, the role of issues, etc., is relevant to such questions. We will probe the 1974 patterns further with respect to some of these larger questions, keeping the volatility and/or stability of political choice in Canada in mind.

Long-term and Short-term Forces in Canadian Elections

Most electoral change in Canada which takes place over relatively short periods of time is accounted for by the flexible partisans, transient voters, and new voters entering the electorate at a given point in time. Table 2 (omitted here) indicates that, at least in 1974, there were distinct differences in the directional movement of these several groups. The analysis of the 1974 vote undertaken in Chapter Eleven in *Political Choice in Canada* suggests the argument that the several types of voters identified in the electorate are motivated by different forces, some of which are of a long-term nature and others of which are short-term in character and therefore more volatile in their electoral effects. Specifically, the analysis indicated that issues are more important determinants of the vote for the flexible, high-interest partisans, while other short-term forces (particularly leaders and candidates) are more related to the voting choice of low-interest groups.

Thus far, we have attempted to treat the long-term component of electoral behaviour in Canada only as a kind of control variable, allowing the several long-term elements affecting voting behaviour to be summarized by past voting choice. We have found, however, that this component, so defined, is the primary determinant of voting choice for the durable partisans, and a less important (although nevertheless significant) predictor for the other groups. Let us examine long-term forces more closely. At least some of the sociodemographic attributes described as weak correlates of voting behaviour in Canada in Chapter Four in *Political Choice in Canada* — for example, religion or ethnicity — are nonchanging elements, at least at the individual level. Others, such as region, social class, or socio-economic status, while more mutable, will in fact not change for most individuals or, at minimum, will do so only infrequently. These, too, might be considered as part of a long-term component of electoral behaviour, to the extent that they correlate with a partisanship that is durable for a portion of the electorate.

It has also been demonstrated, in Canada as well as in other countries, that partisanship for some voters is traceable to processes of family socialization, i.e., the "inheritance" of partisan attachment together with other reference group loyalties such as religion or ethnicity. The argument that the long-term component of electoral behaviour in Canada, particularly for durable partisans, is the product of processes of socialization across generations would be rendered more plausible if it can be shown that there is a strong relationship between the partisan attachments of voters and their parents. Such a finding would also provide at least a partial explanation of the persistence of religious, regional, and ethnic cleavages in Canadian electoral politics.

The fact that more than one-third of the electorate in 1974 report having changed their party identifications one or more times suggests that the power of intergenerational transmission of partisanship in Canada may be limited. For the entire 1974 sample, of those able to recall their parents' partisanship, only 37% and 29% had the same party identification as their father and mother respectively. Not surprisingly, such continuity is greater for durable than for flexible partisans. Even among durable partisans, however, only slightly more than half have the same partisanship as their father and somewhat fewer agree with their mother's partisanship. These data indicate that the long-term force of parental political socialization, at least insofar as party identification is concerned, is limited in Canada for *all* groups of voters. There is little evidence to support an interpretation of the persistence of societal cleavages predicated primarily on the hypothesis that inter-generational transfer of partisanship can explain the present partisan predispositions of most voters.

This conclusion is further supported by a multivariate analysis of partisanship. Even for durable partisans, only about one-third of the variance in partisanship can be explained by long-term factors such as region, religion, or family socialization. The pattern of relationships, coupled with the modest proportion of variance explained, demonstrates that assumptions about the nature of partisanship as a long-term force on voting choice need to be made with considerable care. The overall rate of inter- generational partisan disagreement is such that large discontinuities in the partisan composition of the Canadian electorate could occur across a single generation. Taken in conjunction with the earlier reported finding that 36% of the respondents in the 1974 survey report changing their party identifications one or more times, the evidence strongly indicates the limitations of partisanship as a long-term stable force on the vote.

The analysis of several of the more important perennial forces in Canadian electoral behaviour is sufficient to dispel the possibility that the various short-term factors found to be important in 1974 — issues, leaders, candidates — might constitute mere rationalizations of long-standing partisan ties for large numbers of voters. Elections in Canada are more than contests which repeatedly produce particular results reflective of fundamental patterns of long-term cleavages. On the other hand, the finding that long-term forces are relatively weak in Canada, and that short-term factors, such as issues, leaders, or candidates, are important determinants of *individual* choice by itself tells us little about the nature of electoral outcomes. Within the range of possibilities suggested by our analysis of individual behaviour, a number of different types of election outcomes could clearly occur. With respect to issues, it has been argued that a degree of salience must exist, and also that there must be a link to a party made by the voter before any effect on individual choice is likely to occur. Further, an issue will not affect the *outcome* of an election unless it meets both of the above conditions, and in addition exhibits a "skewness" of opinion, i.e., operates in such a way as to favour one party more than the others. If this latter condition is not met, the issue may have a significant effect on *individual* voting choice, but an insignificant effect on the actual *outcome* of the election because approximately equal numbers of votes may be gained and lost by a particular party as a result of it.

It is possible to apply these conditions to the effect of party leaders and candidates in elections, as well as to issues. Unless leaders or candidates are salient to individual voters, it is unlikely that they, any more than issues, will be able to affect behaviour. In addition, the link to parties is automatic in the case of leaders and candidates, since each carries the party label. And finally, leaders or candidates, like issues, can affect electoral outcomes only if attitudes toward them are skewed, because a leader or candidate who gains and loses equal numbers of votes in an election will not significantly alter the fortunes of his party.

Leaders, issues, and candidates are each likely to hold a different type of significance for specific electoral outcomes, just as they have different effects on the individual voter. Their significance may also vary when measured over a period of time greater than a single election. Although leaders are normally a factor in more than one election, their personal popularity may fluctuate widely over relatively short periods of time, and it is evident that their effect is primarily short-term in nature. The same argument can be advanced in the case of local candidates. While individual candidates may enjoy high personal popularity and/or a long tenure in office, their independent effects on electoral behaviour are essentially short-term.

Where the appeal of a leader or candidate is merely an artifact of partisanship, or of longer term factors which correlate with partisanship, their unique effect on individual voting choice will be minimal. However, both leaders and candidates appear to have effects on individual voting choice over and above those which might be explained by long-term factors or by partisanship alone. Where such is the case, the directional impact of such effects is quite evident. Our analysis in Chaper Eleven in *Political Choice in Canada* of the specific effects of leaders and candidates demonstrated that a positive rating of a party's leader or candidate enhanced the share of the vote obtained by that party, even among those persons whose perception of the party itself was negative.

The actual impact of leaders or candidates on electoral *outcomes* is, however, considerably less certain. There is no reason to expect that, either in a particular election or over a more substantial period of time, candidate effects will normally operate so as to favour a particular party. In 1974, the Conservatives appear to have enjoyed a slight advantage in overall candidate effects, but the total electoral impact of such advantage was very small (Table 3). It seems reasonable, then, to argue that candidate effects, even though they are of importance in individual voting choice, will generally not be critical in electoral outcomes, given that all parties will, on occasion, win or lose certain constituencies because of the strength or weakness of the particular local candidate. But the circumstances where such a phenomenon operates so as to decisively favour one party more than the others will be relatively rare in a political system as large and diverse as that of Canada.

By contrast, the possible effects of the party leaders on electoral outcomes are more likely to be significant. First, the appeal of leaders, unlike that of candidates, is more likely to be national in scope, although there are, of course, important differences across regions. In 1974 all indications are that the appeal of party leaders worked to the advantage of the Liberal party. Mr. Trudeau's popularity was greater than that of Mr. Stanfield and the other party leaders in every province, save Nova Scotia, and among nearly all major subgroups of the population. Further, Table 3 indicates that, among those who assigned the most importance to the personal qualities of the party leaders in their voting decision, the effect is overwhelmingly toward the Liberals among all three groups of voters — persons remaining with the same party, those switching from another party, and those entering or re-entering the active electorate in 1974. Unlike the candidate effects which appeared to show a slight trend toward the Conservatives, the movement toward the Liberals among the more leader-oriented segment of the electorate in 1974 is large enough to be of potential significance in the outcome.

This pattern is not surprising, given the relative importance of party leaders in individual voting choice demonstrated in our multivariate analysis in Chapter Eleven, particularly for the flexible low-interest groups together with other measures demonstrating the advantage which Mr. Trudeau enjoyed in personal popularity over his opponents in 1974. It is possible, however, to suggest other patterns that might occur in other elections. Certainly, there may be circumstances in which perhaps two or more party leaders enjoy high personal popularity among certain voters, thus creating a situation in which the effects on individual voting choice are relatively high but the effect on the outcome of an election rather low because approximately equal numbers of voters are being gained and lost by each leader. Also, one might project instances in which *no* party leader is sufficiently attractive to voters, or enjoys enough of an advantage over his opponents, to affect either behaviour or outcomes. . . . Yet, the pattern shown by the 1974 data must also be a fairly common one in which one party leader, enjoying either a permanent or temporary advantage in personal popularity, is able to significantly improve the position of his party among those groups of voters for whom party leaders are the most salient feature of the political system.

TABLE 3 Summary of Electoral Effects of Leaders and Candidates, 1974
(as percent of total 1974 voters[a])

Most important factor in vote	Liberal	PC	NDP	Total
a. Leader/Leadership				
% Switching to	1.3	0.3	0.2	1.8
% Remaining	7.5	1.4	0.5	10.4
New Voters/Transients	1.0	0.3	0.1	1.4
Total	9.8	2.0	0.8	13.6
b. Local Candidate				
% Switching to	0.9	1.5	0.3	2.7
% Remaining	3.2	3.9	0.7	7.8
New Voters/Transients	0.4	0.7	0.1	1.2
Total	4.5	6.1	1.1	11.7

[a]N = *1891*. Social Credit, "other," and spoiled ballots not shown in table.

The several types of electoral situations in which issues as determinants of behaviour may also affect the outcome of an election can be conceptualized similarly. We have already noted in our previous analysis that issues differ considerably in salience and in the degree to which they are linked to parties by the electorate. In order for an issue to affect the outcome of an election, opinion must be skewed in such a way as to consistently favour a particular party.

The issues of the 1974 election provide several examples of combinations of these conditions, all of which are undoubtedly commonplace in a number of other electoral situations. An issue, such as bilingualism, for example, operated so as to favour the Liberals (Table 4), but its low salience in 1974 assures that it can have little effect on the outcome when the voters mentioning this issue are considered as a proportion of the total electorate. At the other extreme is the dominant issue of the 1974 campaign — inflation — which, although mentioned as the most important issue by one-third of the total electorate, displays little in the way of a pattern which might be said to clearly affect the election outcome. Of those mentioning inflation and switching in 1974, the trend was away from the Liberals, while the pattern of those not switching favoured that party slightly. The trend of new voters and transients mentioning inflation as the most important issue also favoured the Liberals. In summary, the Liberals appear to have realized a slight advantage in the *total number of votes* associated with the inflation issue. However, it is evident that the actual electoral effects of the inflation issue in 1974 were very much less than might be suggested by the salience of the issue alone. It is evident that the inflation issue in that election failed to operate as a valence issue, a shortcoming which might at first appear strange, given the potential anti-government thrust of such an issue. In other circumstances, one might well imagine the high salience of general economic issues being more explicitly transformed into votes against the government of the day. However, the interaction between attitudes toward the economy and short-term economic policies is a complex one, and the willingness of voters to affix "blame" for the ills of the economy is governed by more than a set of economic indicators.

The patterns produced by the other two issues singled out in Table 4 are also interesting. Both of these issues have a much lower initial potential to affect the outcome of the election than does inflation, because they were salient only to a relatively small proportion of the electorate. Wage and price controls and majority government are mentioned as "most important" by enough respondents in 1974 to cause us to notice them, but the numbers certainly cannot be considered large. These two issues, while salient in 1974 to approximately equal proportions of the total electorate, exhibit quite different electoral effects. The wage and price controls issue, like the more general inflation issue, displays an absence of any clear directional trend. As a policy initiated by the Conservatives in the campaign, it

TABLE 4 Summary of Potential Electoral Effects of Four Selected Issues in 1974 (as percent of total 1974 voters[a])

Most important issue	Liberal	PC	NDP	Total
a. Inflation				
% Switching to	2.3	3.7	1.3	7.3
% Remaining	10.8	8.0	3.0	21.8
New Voters/Transients	2.0	0.8	0.8	3.6
Total	15.1	12.5	5.1	32.7
b. Wage and Price Controls				
% Switching to	0.4	0.6	0.2	1.2
% Remaining	1.7	2.2	0.9	4.8
New Voters/Transients	0.5	0.3	x	0.8
Total	2.6	3.1	1.1	6.8
c. Majority government				
% Switching to	1.0	0.5	0.1	1.6
% Remaining	3.2	0.7	x	3.9
New Voters/Transients	0.4	—	—	0.4
Total	4.6	1.2	0.1	5.9
d. Bilingualism				
% Switching to	x	x	—	0.1
% Remaining	0.8	0.2	0.1	1.1
New Voters/Transients	x	x	—	0.1
Total	0.9	0.3	0.1	1.3

[a]N = *1891*. Social Credit, "other," and spoiled ballots not shown in table.
x Less than 0.1%.

appears to have attracted some voters to that party and repelled others. Among all three groups — the switchers, the constant supporters of one party, and the voters entering or re-entering the electorate in 1974 — the slight trend toward the Conservatives among those mentioning the wage and price controls issue is largely offset by an approximately equal number of voters moving in the opposite direction. An issue displaying these characteristics, even though it may affect individual voting choice, cannot be said to have affected the outcome of the election.

Majority government, on the other hand, displays a quite different pattern. Although not highly salient to the electorate (it is mentioned as the "most important" issue of the election by only about 6% of those voting in the 1974 contest), the majority government issue operates in favour of the Liberals, thus producing a potential electoral effect which, although small, is statistically significant and indeed larger than that exhibited by issues which are salient to more people. It is, of course, not surprising to find this pattern. As noted in Chapter 8 in *Political Choice in Canada*, majority government has historically been a Liberal issue, given that it has most often been the Liberal party which held the best chance of forming a majority government. In fact, it may be seen in Table 4 that the majority government issue in 1974 is associated primarily with Liberals *remaining* with their party, and does not appear to have generated substantial switching of votes away from the minor parties. It may, however, have *prevented* some votes from being lost by the Liberals to other parties as a result of other short-term forces. While this is clearly a speculative interpretation, it is evident that majority government, like bilingualism, exhibits the type of skewness which is essential for an issue to exert a genuine effect, however small, on the outcome of an election. To the extent that it was more salient in 1974 than was the bilingualism issue, the electoral effects are greater. An equally salient issue, such as wage and price controls, or a much more salient issue, such as inflation, does not display this essential characteristic.

Although we have attempted here to abstract from the electorate distinct issue, leader, and candidate subgroups for purposes of this analysis, it should, of course, be recognized that a number of joint effects may also exist, combining some of the characteristics of the "leader," "issue," and "candidate" groups examined here. Some respondents, for example, mention issues such as inflation in combination with an answer identifying the leader or the candidate as the most important reason for their 1974 vote. A number of these different leader-issue and candidate-issue combinations exist, making generalization about all but the largest ones difficult. However, respondents mentioning such combinations tend to display some of the characteristics shown by those in the candidate, leader, or issue groups alone (Tables 3 and 4). Voters, then, who mention both leaders and an issue as "most important" to them in 1974 show evidence of having been influenced by both in the direction of their vote, as do those mentioning candidates and an issue, or any of the numerous other combinations.

The several short-term forces which we have examined in the 1974 context are illustrative of a number of different types of electoral effects, some of which may vary from one election to another as the salience of issues or leaders increases or decreases, or as the advantage to a particular party changes. We have argued that local candidates, although they may affect individual voting choice, will rarely affect electoral outcomes on a national scale because of the improbability that a single party can gain an advantage in a large enough number of constituencies to truly alter the result. On the other hand, leaders, also important in individual choice, will be most likely to affect the outcome of an election in those situations where *one* leader is highly salient to voters (or where positive and negative perceptions combine), a situation which obtains in the 1974 case with Mr. Trudeau. We can easily imagine, however, electoral contests where two strong leaders might exert offsetting effects, or other situations where no leader is highly salient.

On the other hand, issues cover a broader range of possibilities, and the four examined in our analysis of the 1974 outcome illustrate a number of these. An issue which is not sufficiently salient to the electorate clearly will not exert any effects on individual choice, and therefore will not affect an election outcome. Issues of modest salience, such as majority government or wage and price controls in 1974, may or may not affect the outcome of an election, depending on the ability of a single party to cause such an issue or issues to operate to its advantage. The possibility that elections are won or lost as much by aggregations of small numbers of voters who respond to *different* short-term factors as by larger numbers is a very real one, and issues such as majority government demonstrate such potential. Undoubtedly, there are other issues, both in 1974 and in other elections, which might display such a pattern, and which either singly or in concert are capable of contributing to a particular result. Further, it is evident that the potentially most important issues — those of very high salience, such as inflation — may ultimately prove in a given election to be among the least important in explaining the result. However, the potential for such an issue to operate quite differently in other electoral circumstances should not be dismissed. Finally, a number of joint effects must be considered, since leaders, candidates, and issues do not appeal to mutually exclusive categories of voters. The 1974 results, although illustrative, necessarily leave untested a number of possible combinations.

The Changing Electorate

We have examined the balance of long-term and short-term factors in electoral behaviour in Canada, and particularly the operation of these factors in 1974. On that occasion, about one person in five was found to have voted for a different party than that which was supported in the previous election. For some of these switchers, the change in voting choice may have caused, or been caused by, a change in partisanship, while for others the decision to switch was a function of various short-term forces specific to the election. In both instances, the type of change resulting is that often referred to as *conversion,* i.e., a change in the attitudes of voters who are already part of what we have classified earlier as the "permanent electorate." In the earlier part of this chapter, however, we have argued that a quite different type of change is also important in Canadian elections, i.e., that caused by voters who move into and out of the active electorate (transient voters) and by new voters entering the electorate in a given election. In fact, the evidence presented would suggest that these sources of change taken together were more important in explaining the particular outcome of the 1974 election than was the total movement within the permanent electorate. Such a source of change is of course quite different than conversion, in that it represents a change not in attitudes but in the actual composition of the electorate at a particular point in time. This type of electoral change may be referred to as *replacement*, i.e., the substitution of one group of voters for another in a particular electorate.

Although the emphasis of much of our analysis of electoral behaviour in 1974 has been on those types of change which might be classified as conversion, the importance of replacement should not be minimized, particularly when more than one election is considered. Over the short period between the 1972 and 1974 elections, we estimate that nearly one-quarter of the active electorate changed. Such change emanates from one of three sources — the turnover of non-voters, the entry of new voters, and the death of a small proportion of the total electorate. While we are dependent upon the survey data for reports of non-voting in 1974 or in previous elections, better estimates of the impact of new voters or the death of older voters can be made from census data (Figure 2).

As is seen in Figure 2, our analysis of change between the 1972 and 1974 elections in some respects underestimates the impact of electoral replacement under "normal" electoral circumstances, given the shortness of that time period. If we project a four-year span between elections as "normal," the impact of new voters and of the death rate would each be about double that observed in the 1974 sample. Therefore replacement, as a potential

Figure 2
Electoral Replacement [a]

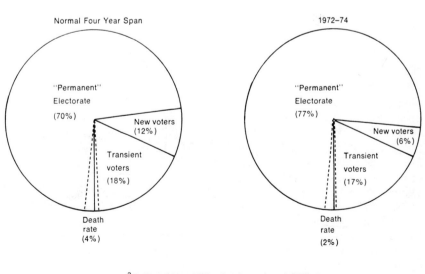

[a] Estimated from 1974 national sample and 1971
census data.
Source: *Census of Canada, 1971.*

source of change, will not normally be any less than that observed in 1974 and may in some other circumstances be much greater. Census data also indicate that although birth rates have been declining in recent years, this demographic trend has not yet been observed in the form of a reduction in the number of new voters entering the electorate. Hence, with each successive election, the absolute number of new voters entering has been larger, and the effect of this group as a percentage of the total eligible electorate has therefore been greater. Of course, participation represents an important qualification of this observation, since younger people are somewhat less likely to vote or to participate in politics than are older voters. Nevertheless, it is not an overstatement of the demographic data to observe that the electorate has been getting progressively younger, and of course the addition of 18-20 year olds to the electorate in 1970 increased this proportion. In 1974, nearly one-third of all eligible voters were under thirty years of age, while about half of the eligible electorate was between the ages of 30 and 59, (Fig. 3).

A slightly different way of looking at these data is in terms of the time when eligible voters first entered the electorate. More than one-quarter of the 1974 voters entered the electorate during the Trudeau/Stanfield era (Figure 3). If the group entering between Diefenbaker's accession to power in 1957 and the beginning of the Trudeau/Stanfield era are added, together they comprise half of all eligible voters. Only about 18% of the 1974 electorate consisted of voters who had been eligible to vote prior to the beginning of World War II. We refer to these "time of entry" groupings as "age cohorts" to signify the common electoral experiences of the several groups.

The significance of a characterization of the Canadian electorate as a changing entity depends on additional evidence which is less obvious. We have already suggested that rates of intergenerational partisan agreement

Figure 3
Distributions of the Eligible Canadian Electorate, 1974

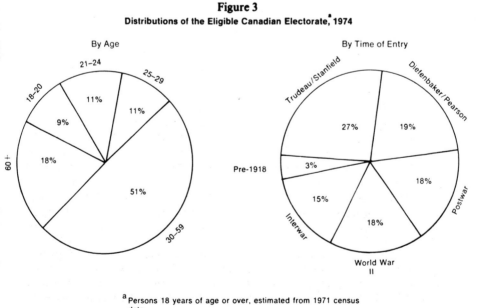

a Persons 18 years of age or over, estimated from 1971 census
data.
Source: *Census of Canada, 1971.*

tend to be relatively low in Canada, thereby decreasing the probability that new voters entering the electorate will merely perpetuate old alignments. We have shown earlier . . . that partisanship tends to be unstable for many voters over relatively short periods of time. Since it is often argued that conditions at the time of entry into the electorate are significant in the formation of political attitudes, each wave of new voters is likely to respond to at least some new forces, their behaviour relatively unconstrained by pre-existing societal cleavages, parental partisanship, or other long-term forces. All of the evidence previously examined — the flexibility of partisanship, the relative weakness of long-term forces, the short-term nature of party images, and the importance of leaders and issues — suggest the high potential for change in the electorate from one election to another. When we consider as well the fact that a substantial number of voters moves into the electorate at a given time, the potential for fluctuations becomes quite impressive. While these changes will not necessarily produce different electoral outcomes, they cannot be ignored in any analysis of the nature of political choice in Canada.

Although the potential for change resulting from conversion and replacement combined is very high, there is little evidence that younger voters currently entering the electorate are harbingers of any fundamental realignment. The major characteristics of political choice that we have documented throughout this book would appear to be well established in nearly all age groups, and we would not, therefore, expect that Canadian politics will somehow be "different" as the result of infusions of new voters. There is a potential for such differences to develop, but there is little evidence in our data to support a contention that the nature of political choice will be altered in the near future as a result of electoral replacement. Rather, the level of volatility, already high in the electorate, is likely to remain so.

An examination of the components of partisanship among the six age cohorts (Table 5) (omitted here) discloses only slight differences between them. There has been no significant increase in the number of voters without partisan attachments, nor is partisan instability higher in the younger cohorts. There is a slightly larger proportion of "weak" partisans in the youngest (Trudeau/Stanfield) cohort, and a statistically significant difference between the six groups, but this observation in itself constitutes scant evidence of meaningful generational differences in the intensity of partisanship. . . . In short, the data do not constitute convincing evidence of any "erosion" of partisanship or of a potential alteration in the nature of the Canadian party system. As noted earlier, the levels of flexibility of partisanship in Canada are already quite high, and the data may be best constructed as evidence that they are likely to remain so.

There are, however, some directional differences in the political orientation of the younger cohorts which are of potential significance for future election outcomes. The percentage of voters who identify themselves with the Conservative party appears to decline steadily with each successive cohort, falling to a low of 18% among the youngest (Trudeau/Stanfield era) cohort (Figure 4) (omitted here). This decline appears to be accompanied by a modest increase in the proportion of voters identifying with the NDP, which rises to a level nearly equal to that of the Conservatives in the youngest cohort. Identification with the Liberal party, on the other hand, remains relatively constant across the cohorts, and shows no sign of weakening or of growing stronger among those voters who first entered the electorate after the accession of Mr. Trudeau.

One cannot, of course, conclude from a single survey that such patterns are "generational" in character rather than perhaps reflecting tendencies of voters to change over the course of their lives. However, some of the trends suggested by this analysis of direction of partisanship among the six age cohorts are corroborated by a comparison of data from the three national election surveys, thereby providing slightly stronger, although still far from conclusive evidence. For example, the percentage of the national sample identifying with the Progressive Conservative party declines from 28% in 1965 to 24% in the 1974 survey. Few differences are observed, however, with respect to the *intensity* of partisanship, or the proportion of respondents without a party identification.

While these directional trends are worth noting, they must of course be carefully qualified. We have already noted that partisanship for many voters is unstable over relatively short periods of time, and that the proportion of flexible partisans in the electorate generally is substantial. Further, we have observed in this chapter that the partisanship of younger voters tends to be weaker, whether due to normal life cycle patterns or to a gradual overall weakening of partisanship within the system. Therefore, we would not want to attempt to make projections regarding possible future election outcomes on the basis of the direction of respondent partisanship alone, given our understanding of its fundamental characteristics.

Summary and Conclusions

The Liberal Party has won most of the Canadian federal elections held in this century. Our analysis suggests that its success has been founded, not only on long-term stable loyalty to that party, but also on its ability to consistently turn many of the short-term factors affecting the bulk of Canadian voting decisions to its advantage. In 1974, on almost all the issues of the campaign, and with respect to leaders as well, more voters found the Liberals to their liking than other parties.

The implication of our analysis, however, is that the pattern of Liberal dominance is more apparent than real. The composition of the electorate changes substantially at each election with infusions of newly eligible voters and mobilization of different groups of transient voters. In addition, there is a substantial amount of vote-switching from one election to the next. Since many of these switchers, transients, and new voters are motivated by the issues, party leaders, and local candidates associated with a particular election, the possibilities for dramatic election reverses, such as the Conservative victories in 1957 and 1958, are always present. These occurrences may be relatively infrequent because patterns of vote-switching often tend to be countervailing, as they were for the 1972-74 period. Given the right combination of electoral forces, however, sudden changes of the electoral fortunes of any party are quite possible.

Possibilities for large-scale electoral change are enhanced by the characteristics of the electorate's psychological attachments to political parties. A majority of Canadians are flexible in their partisanship, either because they support different parties in federal and provincial politics, because they have changed their allegiance in the past, or because they are only weakly attracted to any of the parties. Further, people evaluate the parties in ways which are easily susceptible to change and party images are dominated by references to current policies or leaders, or by the parties' recent performance in government, opposition, or the campaign itself. Reasons given for changing partisanship are consistently related to issues, policies, or leaders. Frequently such reasons involve negative references to the party being left behind, which indicates that the party favoured this time could be abandoned with the same alacrity should a different mixture of short-term factors arise. In sum, flexible partisans are open to changing their parties, and of course their votes, should any particular set of electoral circumstances make such a change appear desirable.

The popularity of political leaders is highly variable, and public attitudes toward any specific politician may warm or cool with startling rapidity. This is because the images of party leaders are dominated by impressions of their style and personality, or, less frequently, by their stands on issues of the day. The instability of leader effects is accentuated by the propensity of parties losing elections to replace their leaders in hopes that a new face will capture the public fancy, erase memories of defeat, or help disassociate the party from an unpopular policy proposal.

The nature of election issues is frequently short-term as well, with their salience largely depending on whether or not they were emphasized in the campaign. In 1974, inflation, an issue emphasized by all parties during the campaign, was the most frequently mentioned issue. In contrast, bilingualism, a relatively long-standing issue in Canadian politics and one on which most voters had opinions, was only infrequently recognized as an election issue. It is obvious, however, that in a future campaign, the reverse may be true. In general, the relevance of an issue in a specific election is a function of its salience to groups of voters and the extent to which parties and the mass media emphasize it.

The importance of short-term factors in Canadian electoral behaviour is enhanced by the inability of social or demographic divisions in the population to manifest themselves at election time. Divisions between the sexes, age groups, rural and urban areas, or social classes have only very limited electoral significance in federal politics. Even religion and ethnicity, traditionally the deepest social cleavages in Canadian politics, are not strongly related to voting behaviour. In a sense, then, many Canadians approach electoral choice relatively free of those societal forces which might tend to "predetermine" their votes.

Neither do Canadians seem constrained by loyalties to regions of the country or levels of the federal system as they enter the polling booths. While there are certainly regional variations in aggregate electoral outcomes, there is no evidence that region or province of residence *per se* has a major impact on the way individual voters make up their minds. The proportion of flexible partisans in all regions, including Quebec, is sufficiently high to suggest that presently observed regional differences in support for various parties may be subject to substantial change in any given election. Indeed, the range of subjective perceptions of region is so complex that it is not likely to fit well with the simplification of issues and images that takes place at election time. And despite the fact that many citizens "feel closer" to one or the other level of government, they seem quite capable of distinguishing between them and making the necessary electoral choices at both levels. Finally, the negative feelings many Canadians manifest towards various elements of the political system may inhibit the development of long-term loyalties, and enhance the effects of short-run factors in the electoral arena.

Any Canadian election is decided by the collective behaviour of durable and flexible partisans, transients, and new voters. Durable partisans — and the electorate contains a substantial number of these — are more likely to cast ballots for "their" party, be motivated in this choice by long-term loyalty to it, and be more immune to forces of change. For such voters, short-term elements in elections, such as issues, leaders, or candidates, tend to reinforce rather than counter the effects of partisan attachment. Flexible partisans, on the other hand, who form a majority of the electorate, are more likely to contemplate alternatives and consider voting differently during an election campaign. In any specific election, the number of these people who actually do change the direction of their votes will be determined by their evaluation of issues, candidates, and leaders. Similarly, many voters who are newly eligible or re-entering the electorate after an abstention will decide their votes relatively unencumbered by long-term partisan ties. Thus, each time the nation goes to the polls, the potential for change, whether great or small, is present. Large numbers of voters from all generations respond to the short-term stimuli they encounter in the period leading up to and during the campaign. For much of the Canadian electorate, the vote decision is a matter of political choice.

THE CANADIAN POLITICAL CULTURES: TOWARDS A REDEFINITION OF THE NATURE OF THE CANADIAN POLITICAL SYSTEM*

John Wilson

Although the character of political competition has changed radically in Canada in the years since Confederation, our perception of the nature of the national political system has hardly changed at all. Lord Durham's famous image of "two nations warring in the bosom of a single state" serves . . . to describe what is generally regarded as the most fundamental distinction in modern Canadian politics. . . . Few areas of Canadian society have escaped the impact of the differences between French and English Canada . . . the distinctions are often held to be so great that it has become customary to think of Canada as having what the modern language of comparative political analysis would call two political cultures.

* Abridged by the editor from the *Canadian Journal of Political Science*, VII, 3, September, 1974. The numbers of the Tables and Figures in the original have been retained in this extract. By permission.

Such a conclusion is, on the face of things, so obvious that it barely seems worthwhile to challenge it. There is some ground, however, for supposing that the easy division of the country into French and English misses more subtle variations which with further examination may be shown to have some significance. No one would deny, for example, that there are important differences in political practice (to say nothing of historical experience) within English Canada, even if they do not always seem to match the grand contrast between the two founding cultures. Yet these differences have persisted over a long period of time, and while they might ordinarily be dismissed as little more than idiosyncratic variations in the "rules of the political game" from one part of English Canada to another, they may nonetheless reflect the existence of more profound differences in attitudes and orientations to the political system which rival in their magnitude the difference which is customarily perceived between French Canada and the result of the country taken as a whole. There is a possibility, in other words, that Canada contains more than two political cultures.

If it is granted, for a moment, that such differences can be shown to exist, it seems probable that they will be associated with individual provinces. That is not to suggest that each province is so different from all the others that there are 10 distinct political cultures in Canada — it may well be that several of them are so much alike in this respect that there is no point in making a distinction — but rather that each province constitutes, in effect, an independent political system and has on that account a political culture of its own.

* * *

TABLE I As far as you are concerned personally which government is most important in affecting how you and your family get on?
(horizontal percentages)*

Residents of	Federal	Provincial	Local	All combinations	None	Don't know	N
Newfoundland	38	38	8	4	—	12	48
Nova Scotia	40	29	16	5	—	10	116
New Brunswick	22	47	13	1	—	17	99
Quebec	28	44	12	4	1	11	754
Ontario	33	35	19	3	1	9	970
Manitoba	31	41	12	8	1	7	139
Saskatchewan	36	40	11	5	—	8	139
Alberta	34	40	15	4	1	6	235
British Columbia	28	47	20	3	—	2	250
Total	31	40	15	4	1	9	2767

* Data from the 1968 national election survey by Prof. John Meisel.

To all of this may be added the evidence which is presented in Table I, that in almost every part of the country people regard their provincial government as more important than the federal government when it comes to dealing with issues which are crucial to their well-being, and the suggestion of at least one recent study that this tendency is likely to increase rather than decrease in the future. In short, there does not seem to be any compelling reason for not accepting the proposition that Canada is in reality a loose collection of 10 distinct political systems. By definition, therefore, we have at least 10 political cultures. But that is no more than a technical observation, based on the argument that every independent political system must have at least one political culture. On the face of things, the differences which are commonly acknowledged to exist within English Canada have nothing to do with differences in attitudes and orientations to the political system — they are almost entirely behavioural in character — and there is therefore still no ground for supposing that we have more than two *distinct* political cultures.

Such a judgement, however, overlooks what appears to be, on reflection, an important characteristic of many of the differences which the now-flourishing literature on regionalism in Canadian politics has identified. Whether it is significant variations in the relationship between social class and voting behaviour, or the persistence over time of different "climates of opinion," or even the frequently noticed differences in philosophy between parties bearing the same name but acting in different provincial systems, there is an unmistakable suggestion that the provinces are by no means all at the same stage of political development. Indeed, the moment the comparison between them is cast into this context a whole range of differences which had hitherto seemed to have no particular significance suddenly appear in a new light. . . .

The possibility that these differences may represent more fundamental kinds of distinctions arises of course, from the fact that the concept of political culture is itself usually presented in developmental terms. That is to say, where there are significant dissimilarities in the dominant political attitudes and orientations of different communities, they are generally associated with considerable differences, in the extent to which each has developed along a scale leading from a less advanced to a more advanced stage of political development. If, therefore, it can be established that only certain kinds of political institutions and behaviour are likely to occur at specific stages of political development, it follows that there is some possibility that the existence of a particular kind of behaviour may be taken as a signal to the existence of a particular political culture. That is not to say that there is a causal relationship between political behaviour and political culture, but rather that *both* are consequences of a more important underlying factor.

I take that factor to be the stage of economic development which the society in question has reached, and in particular the dominant economic and social relationships of the time. No doubt it would be necessary to undertake a much more sophisticated analysis to establish the point, but perhaps it will be sufficient for the immediate purpose to observe that it seems probable that the political institutions and processes which are appropriate for a society dominated by independent producers (whether large or small), who on that account may perceive themselves to be in control of their own destiny, are not likely to be appropriate for a society dominated by a large number of people who are dependent on someone else for their livelihood and who are not the least bit likely to so perceive themselves. It seems probable as well that attitudes and orientations to the political system will vary for similar reasons.

• • •

The history of Canadian party politics is well known. For roughly 50 years, from Confederation to the end of the First World War, the system was dominated without serious challenge by the Liberals and Conservatives. Since that time, beginning with the election of 1921, it has been necessary to describe the structure of Canadian party competition as, at the very least, that of a "two-plus" party system, while in more recent years it has frequently been argued that there are three "major" political parties in Canada. . . . In the modern era there has been a high degree of variations from one province to another in each federal party's rate of success.

The conventional wisdom has been to ascribe these differences to the obvious differences in economic well-being of different parts of Canada, or to speak of the growing regionalism of Canadian party politics. . . . But if Canada is in fact composed of 10 distinct political systems, it is entirely possible that a more accurate description of national party competition would recognize that there are provincially based cases of both two-party and three-party systems at the federal level, and that it is these differences which require explanation. To put the point in a deliberately oversimplified way, it could be said that there is no national party system at all but rather a loose association of 10 distinct provincial systems which, because of wholly understandable variations in their patterns of behaviour, are bound to aggregate at any federal election to the peculiar hybrid which Canada appears to be.

Such a characterization of our circumstances disposes of the odd position which Canada is usually held to occupy in comparison to the other systems in the literature on democratic party politics. By denying the existence of the national party system altogether, attention is focused on the behaviour of its regional components where, as might be expected if it is agreed that there are in fact 10 independent political systems in Canada, the pattern of party competition in both federal and provincial elections more closely resembles norms which have been drawn from the experience of other countries. That is to say, while there are several cases of multiparty systems, most of the Canadian provinces are dominated at both levels by competition between two electorally strong parties.

• • •

. . . While two-party dominance may indeed be the hallmark of a stable political system there are, far from the one to which the literature customarily refers, at least three analytically distinct types of two-party systems. They have, of course, the usual attributes of all two-party systems but they appear to occur at different stages of a system's development and they may be distinguished precisely because they serve societies which are fundamentally different in their leading interests. For the moment we may call them Type 1, Type 2, and Type 3 two-party systems.

A Type 1 system is the kind which is usually found in preindustrial or beginning industrial society. It is dominated by two great parties of the left and the right whose ideological divisions are rooted in the circumstances of that kind of society. That is to say, while both of them may serve the interests of the owning class, one of them is likely to be a party of aristocracy — or of the landed gentry, or if one likes, simply an agricultural party — and the other is likely to be a party of the master manufacturers — a party of trade and commerce or, in a very narrow sense, a capitalist party. Apart from the policy differences which disagreement over the most important sector of the economy is likely to produce between them, the two parties may also be distinguished in terms of the social characteristics of their electoral support. Although very little is known about voting behaviour in this early period of the development of the British and American systems, it seems probable that partisan division was also based on such religious or racial conflicts as may have existed in the two societies as well as on the obvious clash between rural and urban interests. Indeed the latter, which may be characterized as an economic dispute, was likely rather less important simply because the differences of opinion on which it was based were not as intense (being essentially an argument between owners of different kinds of resources) as were the apparently fundamental disagreements of, let us say, Catholic and Protestant. In any case, there is no hint in the preindustrial two-party system that political life turns upon questions of economic equality. Nor should there be, because the circumstances of preindustrial and even beginning industrial society are not such as to raise these issues.

Both the Type 2 and Type 3 two-party systems are more modern. What happens to the preindustrial party system is that as the structure of the society changes, that is to say, as it industrializes, so it becomes clear that the older party system is inadequate. With the development of industrial society a new interest appears which was not previously of any consequence — namely a wage-earning class — and as its cohesiveness grows through the organization of trade unions, cooperative societies and the like, it becomes necessary for the party system to adjust to accommodate its demands.

The Type 2 and Type 3 two-party systems arise out of the process of adjustment. Historically, the process appears to have taken the following form. When the new interest represented by the labouring class grows to the point where its demands constitute a threat to the older regime, there is first of all an attempt to co-opt it into the older structure. Generally speaking, the parties of the landed gentry have been more successful at this than others, since they were able to recognize the common interest which they shared with the new working class in being opposed to the excesses of unrestricted individualistic capitalism. But the combination cannot last for very long because the party of the landed gentry, given the nature of its perception of the most important issues, fairly quickly becomes irrelevant as the rate of industrialization increases, unless it can alter its thinking in a significant way. At this somewhat more advanced stage of the process, the party of the master manufacturers may also be able temporarily to attract the support of certain sections of the working class, since it can claim a superior understanding to that of its opponents of the needs of the new society. In time, however, it must also adjust as its adherents come to terms with problems of that society which interfere in a fundamental way with principles they had earlier espoused. Issues such as state interference to provide for the education of the working class, or legislation to regulate the conditions of work in the factories, strike at the roots of laissez-faire liberalism. In fact, both of the older parties must adjust or face extinction.

Out of this period of adjustment two quite different kinds of two-party systems emerge. Either the new labour interest is successfully co-opted on a long-term basis by the accommodation of one or both of the older parties to its demands, or the least adjustable of the older parties is eliminated from serious contention in the system and replaced by a new party which is more easily able to meet the requirements of representation in a developed industrial society. Since it has been the more common amongst the Western nations we may characterize the latter outcome of the period of adjustment as a Type 2 two-party system, that is to say, one where elimination has occurred. The Type 3 two-party system is thus one where accommodation has occurred.

Both the Type 2 and Type 3 two-party systems are found, of course, in what we may call advanced industrial society. . . .

The conclusion of this much of the analysis seems inescapable. The effect of the argument is to suggest that the four quite distinct kinds of party system which it is claimed can be found in the political history of the most prominent English-speaking nations correspond to three rather different points on a time scale of economic, social, and political development: preindustrial society, industrializing society, and advanced industrial society. If this is so then it must also be the case that not only will there be important and perhaps fundamental differences between the dominant social and political institutions at different points on the scale — due to the very different needs and interests of the societies which each point represents — but the leading political beliefs and values at each point are likely to vary substantially as well. There can hardly be any doubt that this will be true of the first and third points — mid-twentieth-century America bears very little resemblance to the United States of the Civil War — even if it is less obviously certain to be the case with the second. In other words, if it is possible to argue with some degree of certainty, through an examination of the kind of development which has taken place in the party system, that different political communities are at different stages of political development, it is open to us to advance the hypothesis (I put it no higher than that) that they also have different political cultures. We may now turn to a more careful analysis of the Canadian case.

It has already been suggested . . . that treating Canada as a single unit . . . is highly misleading. It is not just that examples of provincially based two-party and three-party systems exist in different parts of the country in federal elections; in nearly every instance, as Table III demonstrates, the *same kind* of system (if not always the same leading participants) also exists at the provincial level. Only Quebec and to some extent Saskatchewan appear to be exceptions to the rule in the years since the end of the Second World War and here, of course, it is the intervention of parties in federal elections which have no comparable history of provincial activity during the period (Social Credit in Quebec and the Conservatives in Saskatchewan) which affects the relationship. Without that intervention it might very well be argued that both are cases of two-party systems, along with the very obvious examples of the four Atlantic provinces. These observations add considerable weight to the suggestion that it would be more accurate to view the Canadian system as simply a loose aggregation of 10 distinct provincial systems.

But the data in Table III are cast in the conventional mould of comparative analysis of party systems. They make no attempt to distinguish, in particular, between the character of the various two-party systems which are found in Canada, and because they are only averages over a relatively brief space of time they may hide important features of each system's development.

The modified histograms which are presented in Figures V and VI [omitted here] are much more useful in this respect. To begin with, they confirm the impression gained from the data in Table III that the same kind of party system exists in each province in both federal and provincial elections. However, while they also appear to settle the question of Saskatchewan (which seems in Figure VI [omitted here] to be a wholly conventional example of a Type 2 two-party system very similar to the British case) they do not provide an immediate explanation of the situation in Quebec and at the same time indicate both Alberta and British Columbia may be special cases. No one familiar with the political history of these two provinces will find that very surprising. Ontario and Manitoba, on the other hand, are very clear cases of three-party systems (although the process of adjustment seems to have gone further in Manitoba) and there seems to be little doubt that the

TABLE III Average Percentage Share of the Popular Vote Won by the Two Leading Parties in Federal and Provincial Elections in the Canadian Provinces held after 1945*

	Federal elections (1949-74)	Provincial elections (1947-74)
Prince Edward Island	97	99
New Brunswick	91	97
Newfoundland	96	96
Nova Scotia	92	93
Quebec	79	90
Saskatchewan	75	84
Ontario	82	78
Alberta	76	78
Manitoba	72	74
British Columbia	66	70

SOURCES: *Report of the Chief Electoral Officer* (or other official agency) for each jurisdiction for the years shown. For the 1974 federal general election results were obtained directly from the Canadian Press immediately following election day and are therefore to some extent incomplete.
* Elections held just at or near the end of the Second World War have been excluded because of the extent to which they appeared to be unrepresentative cases. Their inclusion, however, would not materially affect the data. In the table the provinces are ranked according to the two-party share of the vote in provincial elections.

four Atlantic provinces should be classified as Type 1 two-party systems. The implications of these findings are startling enough to require rather more detailed examination.

The idea that Saskatchewan is an advanced industrial society (because it appears to have a Type 2 two-party system) is perhaps, a little difficult to accept. Yet when its electoral history is compared to that of the other provinces it is clear that only Saskatchewan has *passed through* a period of three-party activity of the kind which the British paradigm suggests is typical of the transformation from preindustrial or beginning industrial society to a more advanced stage of political development. Moreover, it is the only contemporary two-party system in the country where the contest is between an older party and the Canadian equivalent of the British Labour party — the NDP. The contrast between Saskatchewan and the other clear cases of two-party systems (in the Atlantic provinces) is in fact quite striking. Figure VII [omitted here] presents in graphic form the history of Saskatchewan's development alongside that of Nova Scotia, and the very obvious difference between the two should be enough to dismiss any significance which might be attached to the fact that in the 1970s they are both equally competitive systems. But if Saskatchewan has a Type 2 two-party system further investigation should show that its dominant political values are of a kind only appropriate in an advanced industrial society. How could this be the case in a province which, despite other changes, still has a larger proportion of its work force engaged in agriculture than has any other part of Canada?

The stress which has been laid on the idea that it is the development of industrial society as such which brings about the kinds of changes represented by the British paradigm disguises an important aspect of the analysis. What really matters, of course, where the evolution of new political values and different political institutions is concerned, is the *perception* that individuals have of their role in the system. An agricultural society where the independent producers who dominate it are genuinely independent (or can lead themselves to believe that they are) would therefore be expected to exhibit political behaviour of a kind which is typical of a preindustrial society. But where this is not the case, where, that is to say, there are only nominally independent producers who in fact perceive that they are inescapably dependent for their well-being on the will of others who are outside their control, it is entirely likely that an otherwise thoroughly agricultural society will behave very differently. There is a good deal of evidence to suggest that exactly these kinds of circumstances prevailed in Saskatchewan when the CCF first came to power, and that their impact has not been seriously diminished. For in fact the experience of Saskatchewan farmers in the 1930s — and especially that of wheat farmers — was of a degree of economic insecurity and uncertainty wholly beyond their capacity to control as individuals which was so debilitating in its effect upon their life chances that it may be compared to the early experience of the urban working class in Great Britain in the later part of the nineteenth century. But it was precisely that experience which led to the formation of the Labour party and to the demand for government action to mitigate the harsher evils of industrialization. It seems reasonable, therefore, to conclude that the modern party system which has grown in Saskatchewan from the effects of the depression on a wheat economy may be taken as evidence that it has reached a stage of political development analogous to that of modern Britain. This, in turn, suggests that further investigation might be expected to show that there exists in the province a collection of attitudes and orientations to the political system of a kind which is typical of a more advanced political system.

But it would be difficult to make the same claim for the Atlantic provinces. Figure VIII [omitted here] presents graphically the development of the provincial party systems in New Brunswick, Prince Edward Island, and Newfoundland, and while there are minor differences between them and Nova Scotia (such as the existence in the latter of the physically and culturally isolated mining communities of Cape Breton Island, which have from time to time exhibited the electoral behaviour at least of an industrial society) it is clear that none of them has ever experienced a degree of third-party activity even remotely comparable to that of Saskatchewan. Nor is there any reason to believe that they may be examples of a Type 3 two-party system where the established parties have accommodated themselves to the new kinds of demands which arise in an industrial society, for those kinds of pressures, if they have ever been present in Atlantic Canada, appear never to have constituted the threat to the system which they have elsewhere.

It is true, of course, that in both New Brunswick and Nova Scotia, the farmers' movement enjoyed a brief moment of success immediately after the First World War, but in neither case was their intervention as dramatic as it was at about the same time in Ontario and the prairie provinces. Both groups disappeared almost as quickly as they had risen, less through any concessions which were made to them by the older parties than because the reason for their protest had little to do with the nature of the society. In Nova Scotia in particular, where there had been an attempt to produce the much more serious coalition of forces represented by the Farmer-Labour party (a union which in the 1930s was to become the basis for the development of the CCF in Saskatchewan), nothing could be accomplished because neither group perceived itself as sharing with the other a lasting grievance with the structure of the system. As a result, the movement quickly fell apart through internal bickering in much the same way that the Farmer-Labour government collapsed in Ontario in 1923. And unlike Ontario, support for the later development of the CCF and the NDP has never materialized in a serious way in Nova Scotia outside of Cape Breton Island.

In short, because they are all reasonably clear examples of what I have called a preindustrial or beginning industrial party system, the four Atlantic provinces should be expected to exhibit — if the proper data were available — that set of attitudes and beliefs which are typical of underdeveloped political systems. It is possible that a further distinction could be made between Newfoundland on the one hand, where there is already some evidence to suggest that the dominant political attitudes are even less developed than this, and the three Maritime provinces on the other (although it seems likely that Prince Edward Island, given the almost "pure" state of its party system, will be closer to Newfoundland than to its immediate neighbours). But whether we attach names to these phenomena or not, there can hardly be any doubt that Saskatchewan is at the opposite end of a time scale of political development as compared to the Atlantic provinces, which is to say — if the significance I have attached to that scale is properly placed — that the two areas are likely to have radically different political cultures. We come now to the three provinces which were earlier held to present a problem for the analysis: Quebec, Alberta and British Columbia. As it happens, despite the many obvious differences which it has with the rest of Canada, Quebec is the least difficult of these cases. Inspection of her electoral history as recorded in Figure IX [omitted here] shows that so long as the Union Nationale is regarded as nothing more than the continuation of an older conservative tradition in the province (a proposition which would not now attract much dissent) Quebec has had more or less the same kind of two-party development — at least until the election of 1970 — that has dominated in Atlantic Canada. The extraordinary bursts of activity by groups other than the two established parties, which appeared in the provincial histogram in Figure VI [omitted here], are now seen to be entirely due to intermittent success for a number of different nationalist groups of varying ideological character. And while it may be arguable that the circumstances which led to the demise of the Action Libérale Nationale in 1936 and the coming to power of Maurice Duplessis represent exactly the kind of accommodation which occurs in the emergence of a Type 3 two-party system, the record of the Duplessis governments from that time on surely demonstrates that Quebec remained locked in the grip of political values typical of preindustrial or beginning industrial society.

Of course industrial development occurred, but its political consequences never materialized either because the Church made sure through its control of the education system and the organization of Catholic trade unions, cooperatives, farmers' associations, and the like that disruptive tendencies would not get out of hand, or because the state itself suppressed them. Thus, "the potential for conflict was rarely given a chance of becoming activated, because, more than elsewhere, the choices open to the lower classes were dictated by established elites who were monolithic enough to render the appearance of reformist or radical alternatives most unlikely."

It is possible, however, that these circumstances are now changing. The result of the 1973 election suggests that the Parti Québécois is not simply a nationalist movement of the kind which has emerged from time to time in the past — no such group has ever increased its share of the vote in the election immediately following its first appearance — even if it does not yet seem to have the kind of support which would be expected if it were the harbinger of a new left-wing development in the province. Given the pattern of the change which occurred in the paradigm case of Great Britain (and the time which it took) it is a trifle premature to argue that the 1970 election in Quebec represents a period of transition (marked by a high degree of multiparty competition) and that with the 1973 result the province has now established a Type 2 two-party system. It nonetheless seems probable that Quebec has entered the transitional phase, which is to say that it has reached a stage of political development broadly analogous to that of Great Britain in the 1920s. In other words, further investigation might be expected to show that Quebec has a more advanced political culture than any of the Atlantic provinces, even if it falls short of the stage which Saskatchewan is said to have reached.

Alberta and British Columbia, on the other hand, are obviously a different matter. Were it not for the extraordinary size of the black areas in each of these cases in the modified histograms presented in Figures V and VI [omitted here], the movement over time in Alberta would suggest the presence there of a Type 3 two-party system (Social Credit and the Conservatives accounted between them for 87 per cent of the votes cast in the 1971 provincial election) while British Columbia would appear to be either still in the transitional phase or an example of yet another Type 2 two-party system. Although the extent of the support enjoyed by the two older parties varies substantially between federal and provincial elections in Alberta, there appears to be a clear trend in the province towards a regeneration of that support after a long period of three-party activity. By contrast, the Liberals and the Conservatives do not seem to be recovering in British Columbia.

The reason for the size of the black areas in both cases is, of course, the presence of an abnormally high level of support (compared with the rest of Canada) for the Social Credit party. This suggests a need for a slight elaboration of the general theory of the development of party systems which will, perhaps, account for the activity of a party such as that which is represented by Social Credit and will at the same time enable us to make more sense of the Alberta and British Columbia systems.

There are several reasonably well-known facts of political life in the two provinces which, taken together, indicate the direction in which an explanation lies. The first is the extent to which the purpose of the Social Credit party has been to provide a bulwark against the development of socialism in Canada. While this aim was less stridently proclaimed in Alberta (no doubt because the threat was not as great) it always constituted the central theme of Premier Bennett's campaigns in British Columbia. In this connection it is important to recognize that although the idea of coalition against the CCF was considered in several other provinces (notably in Manitoba and Ontario) British Columbia presents the only open case in Canadian history of the Liberals and Conservatives joining forces to the extent that they became, in effect, one party. After the abortive election of 1941 had failed to reduce the socialist menace to the province, the two parties began to work together in the legislature and in 1945 and 1949 actually ran a single coalition candidate in each constituency. These tactics, not surprisingly, substantially reduced the number of CCF MLAs, but had no impact on the level of the CCF vote. In fact, support rose for the party to very nearly 40 per cent in 1945, falling back to 35 per cent in 1949. Two things, however, are important about this period in British Columbia history. The first is that the coalition of the Liberals and the Conservatives effectively forced the BC electorate to abandon, for nearly a decade, such ties to one or the other of the older parties as they may have previously entertained, thus paving the way for the rise of the Social Credit party. The other, and perhaps more important, consequence of these events is that a strong sense of the importance of defeating the CCF must have been left in the minds of British Columbians by the behaviour of the older parties.

These observations suggest that the role of the Social Credit party, at least in British Columbia, was to act as a substitute for the original parties of the system when they proved incapable of doing the job which the conservative element in an industrial society is expected to do. In Alberta, on the other hand, the party came to power as a reaction against the bankruptcy not only of the original parties in the system (which had, in any case, been reduced by 1935 to mere shadows of their former strength) but also of the radical farmer alternative which had governed the province since 1921. In both systems, therefore, the left had been discredited either by its performance (the link between the UFA leadership and the CCF was well understood in 1935) or by the inordinate fear of what it might do which was generated by the behaviour of the older parties.

One other aspect of the more recent electoral history of the two provinces has a bearing here — the kinds of voting shift which occur between the parties between federal and provincial elections. The record of the earlier period in Alberta is uncertain (although the aggregate data are very suggestive: the Social Credit party never fared as well in federal elections as it did provincially and the beneficiary appears always to have been the older parties) but since 1957 the Conservative party has won the lion's share of flagging Social Credit strength at the federal level. In British Columbia as well, both the Liberals and Conservatives appear to gain in federal elections at Social Credit expense while the CCF/NDP vote has often been nearly identical between the two levels. And, of course, in the provincial system it was the Conservatives who were the main victims of the rise of Social Credit, just as it appears to have been a mild resurgence on their part which contributed to the defeat of the Bennett government in 1972.

These facts all suggest that there are other purposes to be served by new third parties than simply the representation of the interests of the working class. The general theory requires that as industrialization proceeds an adjustment in the older party must take place, but it is entirely possible that two quite different kinds of change may be necessary. Ordinarily, one of the two original parties at least is able to adjust to the new circumstances, but it is wholly consistent with the theory to suggest that where neither is able to do so there will be a need for *two* new parties. Since it is usually the rather different demands of the working class to which one or the other of the older parties cannot adjust (because the change that is required is simply not philosophically acceptable to the party's former understanding of things) it is generally the case that the new party which appears is oriented to labour. But it is equally possible that either one or both of the established parties cannot develop the flexibility which has become the hallmark of modern European conservatism, and that the middle class on that account is in danger of going without representation in the new society. In these circumstances we would expect a new party of the right to appear as well as a new party of the left. There would then follow the period of transition in which the nature of the new party system worked itself out and the result would still be either a Type 2 or a Type 3 two-party system,, although the leading actors might not be the ones we would normally expect.

Still, their functions would be the same, and it is the recognition that this is likely to be the case which provides a solution to the problem presented in the first instance by Alberta and British Columbia. It seems to me probable that in both provinces dissatisfaction with the ability of either of the older parties to perform one of the principal functions of conservatism in an industrial society — namely, to counterbalance the strength of the left — is what led to the rise of Social Credit. . . .

The character of the Alberta and British Columbia systems becomes clear immediately. The former is, apparently, a case of a Type 3 two-party system, which is to say that it is at more or less the same stage of political development as Saskatchewan. Further investigation should therefore show that the Alberta and Saskatchewan political cultures are identical, even if the leading issues in the political life of the two provinces are not always going to be the same, and that both of them are rather more advanced in this respect than any other part of Canada. For the reconstitution of British Columbia history in Figure X [omitted here] shows that it is not a Type 2 two-party system at all but is instead still in the transitional stage.

That observation brings us to a brief examination of the clear three-party systems which exist in Canada. Figure XI [omitted here] presents graphically the history of the development of the system in British Columbia, Manitoba, and Ontario. Inspection of the BC graph demonstrates the extent to which the analysis which has just been completed provides an explanation of that province's situation. The relationship between the decline of the Conservative party and the success of Social Credit is very clear. What is perhaps more striking, however, is the broad similarity which exists between the pattern of all three systems. All of them, of course, are *industrializing* provinces. It is one of the great fallacies of eastern high school education that Manitoba is a prairie province like the others, yet there is no end of evidence to suggest otherwise. It is not simply that the province's life is dominated by the great metropolis of Winnipeg in a way that Alberta and Saskatchewan have not been dominated by their leading cities, but also that a good part of the Manitoba economy is taken up with primitive industry — forestry and mining — rather *like* British Columbia and Ontario, and *unlike* Alberta and Saskatchewan.

Three-party systems occur, according to the theory, only during the period of transformation in the political institutions and values of a society which is bound to take place as industrialization advances. We should therefore expect to find, with further investigation, that British Columbia, Manitoba and Ontario all have similar political cultures and that these will bear traces of both the less-developed attitudes and orientations to the political system which the theory argues are associated with a Type 1 two-party system and the more advanced political values and beliefs which appear after the transition to a Type 2 or Type 3 two-party system.

That suggests that when the 10 provinces are considered together there is a possibility that there are at least three distinct political cultures in Canada because it appears to be the case that at least three rather different stages of political development can be identified as existing from one part of the country to another. Table IV summarizes the apparent implications of the analysis on the assumption that this is the case, but it is worth noticing that if the argument I have been making has any validity at all there are no less than two (although not the two which are commonly recognized) and perhaps as many as five distinct sets of attitudes and orientations to the political system now flourishing from coast to coast. If there are only two it seems probable that the kind of investigation which would be required to establish the fact would discover a distinction between five developed and five undeveloped provincial systems, while the groups shown in Table IV could be expanded by putting Newfoundland and Quebec into individual categories of their own on the ground that each is too different from its neighbours to be lumped together with them. But whatever number is finally agreed upon there can hardly be any doubt that our conventional image of a system based simply on conflict between French and English Canada is inadequate.

TABLE IV The Canadian Political Cultures in 1974

Underdeveloped	Transitional	Developed
Newfoundland	Quebec	Alberta
Prince Edward Island	Ontario	Saskatchewan
New Brunswick	Manitoba	
Nova Scotia	British Columbia	

If differences at the level of the political culture of the kind I have suggested cannot, in the nature of the case, be shown to exist without a much more elaborate study, it is at least possible to pursue the idea of different degrees of political development. Given the character of the argument it is comparatively easy to define the nature of a number of other differences which ought to be associated with each stage in the process of change. In terms of the social structure, for example, there should be a less open stratification system in the less developed provinces, and while social classes will of course exist everywhere we would not expect to find them harnessed to the politics of the less developed systems in the way they are in an advanced industrial society such as Great Britain. Instead, we might expect to find that other social cleavages — such as religious affiliation and ethnic origin, which the earlier analysis has suggested are more meaningful political divisions in a preindustrial or beginning industrial society — are the major determinants not only of voting behaviour but of other aspects of electoral politics as well. I propose, however, to examine only two areas where certain kinds of findings could be taken as a demonstration of the existence of at least the different stages of development I have characterized for the Canadian provinces. Both are really variations of the same idea — that social class is a more important political cleavage in an advanced system while religious affiliation is more significant in an underdeveloped system — but the different illustrations of the proposition are, perhaps, intriguing.

The general relationship between the three variables of party support, social class, and religious affiliation which it is claimed exists in each of the four different kinds of party systems I have isolated is set out in the models presented in Figure XII. The society is assumed in each case to be equally split into two social classes (based on economic division) and two religious faiths, although there is a differing class composition as between the adherents of the religions of the kind which is generally found in the real world. In preindustrial or beginning industrial society religious affiliation is the main determinant of support for the different parties, and members of

FIGURE XII: MODELS OF PARTY SUPPORT IN DIFFERENT PARTY SYSTEMS.

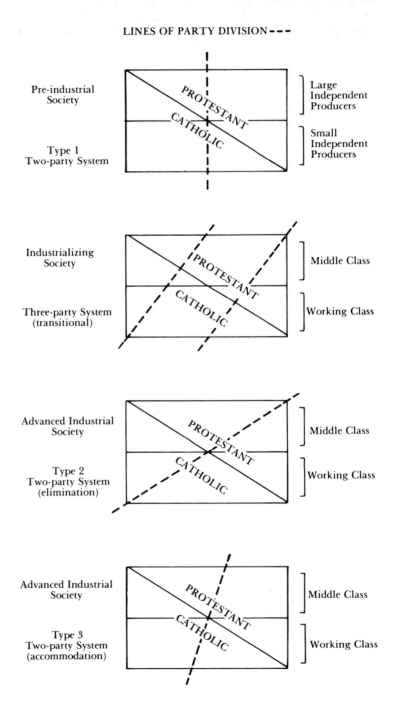

LINES OF PARTY DIVISION - - -

the two social classes appear to be equally distributed between them. In the period of adjustment represented by a three-party system the support bases are less clear. Two of the parties are differentiated along class lines, although not very strongly, and also, apparently, along religious lines. The other party, in the centre both literally and figuratively, seems to have no special support in any group. Finally, the customary pattern of an advanced industrial society where elimination has occurred in the party system (Type 2) shows two strongly class-based parties with religious affiliation being evidently irrelevant, while in a Type 3 system the parties differ in terms of both kinds of support, although neither is very marked, indicating the effect of accommodation.

The most obvious test which can be conducted within this framework is, of course, for the relationship between party support in the electorate and the two socioeconomic variables. The models in Figure XII suggest that a proper inquiry into this question requires a multivariate analysis, even though this will result in certain distributions being based on a very small number of cases — since the size of the sample from which the data are taken was comparatively small in certain provinces — and will force us to combine the Atlantic provinces into one unit. In order to avoid possible error due to the respondent's inability to recall correctly his last provincial vote we will use provincial party identification (as established by a series of questions in the 1968 national survey) as the indicator of partisan support. Those who said they did not belong to a social class as well as those who said they did were pressed to name the class in which they would place themselves, and it is the combination of these answers which is used as the measure of subjective social class in each province. Inspection of the results of this analysis as presented in Table V shows that there does appear to be some relation between the actual behaviour patterns of the provinces and what would be expected in each case on the basis of their supposed stages of political development.

It is quite clear, for example, that in both the Atlantic provinces and Quebec social class has virtually nothing to do with variations in partisanship, while religious affiliation appears to have a considerable impact. A measurement of the effect which each variable has on partisanship towards each of the parties (excluding the NDP and Social Credit in cases where their support is very small) is presented in Table VI, based on Coleman's method for calculating "effect parameters," along with a value which summarizes the effect of each variable for each province. These data indicate that among the provinces west of the Ottawa River the impact of social class and religious affiliations on partisanship is lowest in Alberta, as would be expected if it is an example of a Type 3 two-party system. It may be noticed as well that the effect of religious affiliation is lower than in any other part of the country, which suggests that Alberta is neither a transitional system nor a Type 1 two-party system. Both social class and religious affiliation have an effect in the other four systems, although there is no evidence that Saskatchewan differs from the so-called three-party systems in this respect. Although it is by no means conclusive, the evidence thus leans in the direction of support for the hypothesis that the various provinces are at the different stages of development which the analysis of party systems suggested.

TABLE V The Relationship between Religious Affiliation, Social Class, and Provincial Party Identification in 1968 (in percentages)*

	Protestant		Roman Catholic	
	Middle class	Working class	Middle class	Working class
Atlantic provinces				
Conservative	48	55	35	37
Liberal	47	43	65	63
NDP	3	2	—	—
Social Credit	2	—	—	—
N	62	100	17	41
Quebec				
Union Nationale	18	15	33	36
Liberal	79	77	57	52
NDP	3	8	2	4
Créditiste	—	—	5	7
Nationalist	—	—	3	1
N	33	13	362	231
Ontario				
Conservative	51	39	25	10
Liberal	39	33	66	70
NDP	9	28	9	20
N	330	236	117	125
Manitoba				
Conservative	49	35	18	14
Liberal	34	41	59	67
NDP	12	24	23	19
Social Credit	5	—	—	—
N	41	34	17	21
Saskatchewan				
Conservative	32	23	33	30
Liberal	35	23	47	45
NDP	30	53	20	25
Social Credit	3	—	—	—
N	37	51	15	20
Alberta				
Conservative	41	34	25	35
Liberal	17	12	37	20
NDP	5	7	—	—
Social Credit	37	47	37	40
N	86	68	16	20
British Columbia				
Conservative	14	9	—	12
Liberal	37	26	73	41
NDP	10	25	—	18
Social Credit	39	40	27	29
N	104	69	11	17

* Data taken from the 1968 national survey.

TABLE VI   The Relative Effect of Religious Affiliation and Social Class on Provincial Party Identification*

	Effect of religion				Effect of class				Total effect of	
	Con	Lib	NDP	SC	Con	Lib	NDP	SC	Religion	Class
Atlantic Provinces	.16	.19			.04	.03			.18	.04
Quebec	.18	.23			†	.03			.21	.02
Ontario	.27	.32	.04		.14	.01	.15		.21	.10
Manitoba	.26	.26	.03		.09	.07	.04		.18	.07
Saskatchewan	.04	.17	.19		.06	.07	.14		.13	.09
Alberta	.08	.14		.04	.01	.11		.06	.09	.06
British Columbia	.05	.25	.08	.11	.03	.22	.17	.02	.12	.11

* The measures shown are Coleman's effect parameters for the data presented in Table V. Where no entry occurs, the level of support was too small for useful measurement.
† No effect.

Reliable data dealing with the actual voting behaviour in the provinces — as distinct from party identification — are less easy to find. Tables VII and VIII therefore present the results of two comprehensive surveys conducted in Ontario and Manitoba, showing the relative effect of ethnic origin, as well as religious affiliation and social class, on the vote. Table IX gives Coleman's effect parameters for the three independent variables, and it is clear that in both provinces they have a more or less equal impact on voting behaviour although for Liberal supporters the effect of social class is much less marked than it is with the Conservatives and the NDP. But these findings are exactly what we should expect with systems which are said to be in the transitional stage of development.

A second test of the theory examines the same set of relationships which the models in Figure XII assign to the different systems, but does so in a rather different way. If it is the case that the importance of religion vastly outweighs that of economic position in a preindustrial or beginning industrial society, we should expect that fact to be reflected in the characteristics of those who seek public office in the system, and we should equally expect alternative characteristics to be dominant amongst the same kinds of people in the more advanced systems. That is to say, if one's religion is, on the whole, the independent variable which determines one's party (as should be the case in the Type 1 two-party systems) rather than economic position, then the distribution of religious affiliations amongst each party's candidates should be radically different while their occupational backgrounds should be quite similar. The opposite should be the case in Type 2 two-party systems, and in Type 3 two-party systems there should be no recognizable differences between the parties on either of these variables. The candidates of parties in transitional systems, of course, should exhibit differences on both scores.

The difficulty with this test is the effective absence of reliable data. Entries in the Canadian Parliamentary Guide, while useful, are usually only for a little more than half of all the governing party's candidates, and their selection may very well have been biased by the existence of the characteristics we are looking for. In several provinces, however, the chief electoral

TABLE VII   The Relationship Between Ethnic Identification, Religious Affiliation, Social Class, and Voting Intention in Ontario in 1967 (in percentages)

| | English Canadian* | | | | Not English Canadian* | | | |
| | Protestant | | Roman Catholic | | Protestant | | Roman Catholic | |
	Middle class	Working class	Middle class	Working class	Middle class	Working class	Middle class	Working class
Conservative	56	51	18	16	40	6	27	24
Liberal	32	28	67	44	49	56	64	62
NDP	12	21	15	40	11	38	9	14
N	474	512	73	123	65	53	78	155

* Respondents were asked, "To what ethnic group do you consider that you belong: English Canadian, French Canadian, or another ethnic group?" Nearly two-fifths of the sample said they were "just Canadian" and these cases are not included in the table.

TABLE VIII   The Relationship Between Ethnic Origin, Religious Affiliation, Social Class, and Voting Intention in Manitoba in 1973 (in percentages)

| | British | | | | Non-British | | | |
| | Protestant | | Roman Catholic | | Protestant | | Roman Catholic | |
	Middle class	Working class	Middle class	Working class	Middle class	Working class	Middle class	Working class
Conservative	50	40	53	23	45	34	25	20
Liberal	24	12	20	33	18	15	25	18
NDP	23	48	27	44	33	49	48	60
SC and Others	3	—	—	—	4	2	2	2
N	176	121	16	16	138	111	79	96

TABLE IX The Relative Effect of Ethnic Origin, Religious Affiliation, and Social Class on the Vote in Ontario and Manitoba*

	Conservative	Liberal	NDP	Total effect
Ontario				
Ethnic identification	.11	.15	.04	.10
Religious affiliation	.17	.18	.01	.12
Social class	.11	.05	.17	.11
Manitoba				
Ethnic origin	.10	.03	.12	.08
Religious affiliation	.12	.07	.06	.08
Social class	.14	.02	.17	.11

* The measures shown are Coleman's effect parameters for the data presented in Tables VII and VIII.

officer's *Report* lists the occupations of all candidates and, from time to time, surveys of all candidates in a particular election have been conducted. There is therefore some opportunity to apply a test of this kind of further check on the validity of the theory.

The data in Table X represent a selection from the more reliable sources for the sake of illustration, chosen primarily to give an example of each kind of system. It may be observed, however, that a thorough examination of the available data for all provinces, bearing in mind their limitations, confirms the impression created by Table X that on this count as well the developmental theory gains support. As should be expected, Conservative and Liberal MLAs in New Brunswick divide on religion and not on occupation, candidates for the three parties in Ontario exhibit differences on both variables, and in Saskatchewan occupation rather than religion constitutes the main differences in the backgrounds of members of the two parties — the more so if farmers are thought of as representing, in that province at least, a special kind of working-class movement.

The two tests which have been conducted are, of course, somewhat duplicative in character since they focus on the same set of relationships. But there is no reason why other areas which might be expected to reveal variations in behaviour and practice between the provinces that would reflect the different stages of political development I have hypothesized for them should not be examined. For the possibilities are almost endlessly intriguing. In Ontario, for example, until very recently the opposition was not permitted to question the ministry in an even remotely effective way in the legislature. In British Columbia, until the election of an NDP government there was no Hansard, although in the final years of the Bennett regime summaries of proceedings in the legislature were published. In the realm of party organization, as well, there are fascinating variations from coast to coast. During Mr. Smallwood's rule in Newfoundland nominating conventions were never held to choose provincial or federal Liberal candidates. Instead, the premier held a press conference and announced their names. Or there is the part which electoral and other forms of political corruption have played in Canadian politics. The extent to which patronage remains a crucial element in the political systems of some provinces is also suggestive.

TABLE X   Religious Affiliation and Occupation of Provincial Candidates and Members of the Legislative Assembly — Selected Examples from New Brunswick, Ontario, and Saskatchewan (in percentages)

	New Brunswick				Ontario			Saskatchewan			
	Con	Con	Lib	Lib	Con	Lib	NDP	Lib	Lib	NDP	NDP
Election year	1967	1970	1970	1967	1967	1967	1967	1967	1971	1971	1967
Protestant	81	78	31	31	86	66	56	62	71	64	64
Catholic	19	22	69	69	12	30	18	35	29	24	24
Jewish	—	—	—	—	2	3	6	—	—	—	—
No information*	—	—	—	—	—	1	20	3	14	12	12
N	26	32	26	32	117	117	117	34	1	42	25
Unlisted cases	—	—	—	—	—	—	—	—	—	3	—

	New Brunswick		Ontario			Saskatchewan	
	Con	Lib	Con	Lib	NDP	Lib	NDP
Election year	1970	1970	1967	1967	1967	1964	1964
Professional	29	29	32	48	50	29	19
Commercial	53	59	53	35	11	34	12
Agricultural	9	3	10	10	9	33	49
Manual†	9	9	5	7	30	4	20
N	58	58	117	117	117	58	59

* Despite a full entry in the Canadian Parliamentary Guide no religious affiliation is given. In some cases this may mean that the member has no formal religious affiliation. In the Ontario cases the candidate reported that he had no religion.

† Includes trade union officials.

All of these things in one way or another point to the existence of rather different political values in different parts of Canada, even if we can have no way, given the data now available, of assessing the significance of those differences. If it is accepted, however, that the kinds of distinction which further investigation may discover are likely to be related to the developmental differences which the analysis of party systems suggests, there are a number of immediate consequences for our understanding of the capacity of the national political parties to perform the functions which many people have assigned to them. Whether it is argued that they should seek to eliminate the sectional differences of the past by abandoning the practice of brokerage politics (which it is said merely reinforces the traditional divisions of race, religion and region) in favour of a more "creative politics" based on social class, or simply that the national party system must be able to foster the development of a national political culture, most observers have seen the Canadian party system as playing a critical role in the promotion of greater national unity.

But if the country is indeed divided in the way I have suggested — merely in terms of the extent to which different regions are at different stages of political development — the capacity of class politics to have the unifying effect which is claimed for it disappears. The likelihood of its success as an instrument for promoting greater national unity obviously depends upon all, or nearly all, parts of the country being in a condition which would permit them to respond to this kind of approach. If, however, the different stages of political development I have identified for the various provinces do, in fact, exist it is clear that any attempt by the national parties to appeal to Canadians on class lines will fall on deaf ears over a sufficiently large area of the nation to defeat the purpose. For if only *some* parts of Canada are ready for class politics, each party in order to contemplate national success will have to base its campaign elsewhere in the country on other perceptions of the most important divisions in the electorate. In other words, the practice of brokerage politics will have been preserved by the very behaviour which it is said is most likely to eliminate it.

That is the minimum consequence if the developmental theory of the nature of the Canadian political system is correct. If, however, it is found that the different stages of development which have been identified are sufficiently far apart to be associated with radically different political cultures — if, that is to say, there are in fact different perceptions of what is right and wrong in politics depending upon where one happens to be in Canada — it is difficult to see how any formulation of the task could leave it to the national party system to be an agent for the creation of a national political culture. If the language of politics varies in this fundamental way from region to region, our national leaders will be incapable of speaking to the nation collectively except in times of crisis.

We must therefore either abandon the search for national unity altogether or redefine its meaning in a way which recognizes that our "limited identities" constitute the essence of what it is to be Canadian. If we can accomplish that, and yet remain a nation, we will have taught the world a lesson it sorely needs to learn.

BIBLIOGRAPHY

Voting Behaviour, Political Culture, Socialization, Participation

(See also Bibliographies in Chapters 4, 6, 7, 8)

Alford, R.R., *Party and Society: The Anglo-American Democracies,* Chicago, R.M., 1963.

Anderson, G.M., "Voting Behaviour and the Ethnic-Religious Variable: A Study of a Federal Election in Hamilton, Ontario," *C.J.E.P.S.,* XXXII, 1, February, 1966.

Beck, J.M., "Quebec and the Canadian Elections of 1958," *Parliamentary Affairs,* XII, 1, 1959.

Beck, J.M., "The Election of 1963 and National Unity," *Dalhousie Review,* XLIII, 2, Summer, 1963.

Beck, J.M., "The Electoral Behaviour of Nova Scotia in 1965," *Dalhousie Review,* XLVI, 1, Spring, 1966.

Beck J.M., and Dooley, D.J., "Party Images in Canada," *Q.Q.,* LXVII, 3, Autumn, 1960.

Beck, J.M., *Pendulum of Power: Canada's Federal Elections,* Toronto, P.H., 1968.

Berkowitz, S.D., *Models and Myths in Canadian Society,* Toronto, Butterworths, 1981.

Black, J.H., and McGlen, N.E., "Male-Female Political Involvement Differentials in Canada, 1965-1974," *C.J.P.S.,* XII, 3, September, 1979.

Blais, A., "Politique agricole et résultats électoraux en milieu agricole au Québec," *C.J.P.S.,* XI, 2, June, 1978.

Blais, A., Des Rosiers, R., Renaud, F., "L'effet en amont de la carte électorale: le case de la région de Québec à l'élection fédérale de 1968," *C.J.P.S.,* VII, 4, December, 1974.

Blake, D.E., "Another Look at Social Credit and the British Columbia Electorate," *BC Studies,* 12, Winter, 1971-72.

Blake, D.E., "The Measurement of Regionalism in Canadian Voting Patterns," *C.J.P.S.,* V, 1, March, 1972.

Blake, D.E., "Constituency Contexts and Canadian Elections: An Exploratory Study," *C.J.P.S.,* IX, 2, June, 1978.

Blake, D.E., "1896 and All That: Critical Elections in Canada," *C.J.P.S.,* XII, 2, June, 1979.

Blake, D.E., Johnston, R., Elkins, D.J., "Sources of Change in the B.C. Party System," A paper delivered at the Annual Meeting of the C.P.S.A., Montreal, 1980.

Brodie, M.J., and Jenson, J., *Crisis, Challenge and Change: Party and Class in Canada,* Toronto, Methuen, 1980.

Canada, *Report of the Chief Electoral Officer, Twenty-Ninth General Election, 1972,* Ottawa, I.C., 1973.

Canada, *Report of the Chief Electoral Officer, Thirtieth General Election, 1974,* Ottawa, S. and S., 1975.

Canada, *Report of the Chief Electoral Officer, Thirty-First General Election, 1979,* Ottawa, S. and S., 1979.

Canada, *Report of the Chief Electoral Officer, Thirty-Second General Election, 1980,* Ottawa, S. and S., 1980.

Clarke, H., Jenson, J., LeDuc, L., and Pammett, J., *Political Choice in Canada,* Toronto, McG.-H.R., 1979. (Abridged ed., 1980.)

Cohen, R.I., *Quebec Votes,* Montreal, Saje Publications, 1965.

Copes, P., "The Fisherman's Vote in Newfoundland," *C.J.P.S.,* III, 4, December, 1970.

Courtney, J.C., (ed.), *Voting in Canada,* Toronto, P.-H., 1967.

Courtney, J.C., and Smith, D.E., "Voting in a Provincial General Election and a Federal By-Election: A Constituency Study of Saskatoon City," *C.J.E.P.S.,* XXXII, 3, August, 1966.

Cunningham, R., "The Impact of the Local Candidate in Canadian Federal Elections," *C.J.P.S.*, IV, 2, June, 1971.

Curtis, J., Lambert, R., "Voting, Election Interests, and Age: National Findings for English and French Canadians," *C.J.P.S.*, IX, 2, June, 1976.

Dahlie, J., and Fernando, T., *Ethnicity, Power and Politics in Canada*, Toronto, Methuen, 1981.

Davis, M., "Ballot Behaviour in Halifax Revisited," *C.J.E.P.S.*, XXX, 4, November, 1964.

Davis, M., "A Last Look at Ballot Behaviour in the Dual Constituency of Halifax," *C.J.E.P.S.*, XXXII, 3, August, 1966.

Dean, E.P., "How Canada Has Voted: 1867 to 1945," *Canadian Historical Review*, XXX, 3, September, 1949.

Easton, D., "The Theoretical Relevance of Political Socialization," *C.J.P.S.*, 1, 2, June, 1968.

Elkins, D., "Party Identification: A Conceptual Analysis," *C.J.P.S.*, XI, 2, June, 1978. (Comment by J. Jenson, *ibid.*)

Elkins, D., "The Perceived Structure of the Canadian Party System," *C.J.P.S.*, VII, 3, September, 1974.

Elkins, D., and Blake, D., "Voting Research in Canada," *C.J.P.S.*, VIII, 2, June, 1975.

Elkins, D.J., Blake, D.E., Johnston, R., "Who Trusts Whom to Do What?," A paper delivered at the Annual Meeting of the C.P.S.A., Montreal, 1980.

Elkins, D.J., and Simeon, R., *Small Worlds: Parties and Provinces in Canadian Political Life*, Toronto, Methuen, 1980.

Engelmann, F.G., "Membership Participation in Policy-Making in the C.C.F.," *C.J.E.P.S.*, XXII, 2, May, 1956.

Filley, W.O., "Social Structure and Canadian Political Parties: The Quebec Case," *Western Political Quarterly*, IX, 4, December, 1956.

Fox, P.W., "A Study of One Constituency in the Canadian Federal Elec-

tion of 1957," *C.J.E.P.S.*, XXIV, 2, May, 1958.

Fox, P.W., "Canada's Most Decisive Federal Election," *Parliamentary Affairs*, XI, 3, Summer, 1958.

Gagne, W., and Regenstreif, P., "Some Aspects of New Democratic Party Urban Support in 1965," *C.J.E.P.S.*, XXXIII, 4, November, 1967.

Gilsdorf, R.R., "Cognitive and Motivational Sources of Voter Susceptibility to Influence," *C.J.P.S.*, VI, 4, December, 1973.

Granatstein, J.C., "The Armed Forces Vote in Canadian General Elections, 1940-1968," *J.C.S.*, IV, 1, February, 1969.

Grayson, J.P., "Social Positions and Interest Recognition," *C.J.P.S.*, VI, 1, March, 1973.

Grossman, L.A., "Safe Seats: The Rural-Urban Pattern in Ontario," *C.J.E.P.S.*, XXIX, 3, August, 1963.

Hahn, H., "Voting in Canadian Communities: A Taxonomy of Referendum Issues," *C.J.P.S.*, 1, 4, December, 1968.

Hamilton, R., Pinard, M., "The Bases of Parti Québécois Support in Recent Quebec Elections," *C.J.P.S.*, IX, 1, March, 1976.

Hamilton, R., Pinard, M., "The Independence Issue and Polarization of the Quebec Electorate: The 1973 Quebec Election," *C.J.P.S.*, X, 2, June, 1977.

Hamilton, R., Pinard, M., "The Parti Québécois Comes to Power: An Analysis of the 1976 Quebec Election," *C.J.P.S.*, XI, 4, December, 1978.

Havel, J.E., *Les citoyens de Sudbury et la politique*, Sudbury, Laurentian University Press, 1966.

Hoffman, D., "Intra-Party Democracy: A Case Study," *C.J.E.P.S.*, XXVII, 2, May, 1961.

Irvine, W.P., "Canadian Partisan Identity," *C.J.P.S.*, VII, 3, September, 1974.

Irvine, W.P., "Political Communities in Canada," *Q.Q.*, 86, 2, Summer, 1979.

Jacek, H.J., "Party Loyalty and Electoral Volatility," *C.J.P.S.*, VIII, 1, March, 1975.

Jacek H., et al., "The Congruence of Federal-Provincial Campaign Activity in Party Organizations," *C.J.P.S.*, V, 1, 1972.

Jacek, H.J., McDonough, J., Shimizu, R., Smith, P., "Social Articulation and Aggregation in Political Party Organizations," *C.J.P.S.*, VIII, 2, June, 1975.

Jenson, J., "Party Loyalty in Canada," *C.J.P.S.*, VIII, 4, December, 1975.

Jenson, J., "Party Strategy and Party Identification," *C.J.P.S.*, IX, 1, March, 1976.

Jewett, P., "Voting in the 1960 Federal By-Elections at Peterborough and Niagara Falls: Who Voted New Party and Why?" *C.J.E.P.S.*, XXVIII, 1, February, 1962.

Kamin, L.J. "Ethnic and Party Affiliations of Candidates as Determinants of Voting," *Canadian Journal of Psychology*, XII, 4, December, 1958.

Kay, B.J., "By-Elections as Indicators of Canadian Voting," *C.J.P.S.*, XIV, 1, March, 1981.

Kay, B.J., "An Examination of Class and Left-Right Party Images in Canadian Voting," *C.J.P.S.*, X, 1, March, 1977.

Kim, K.W., "The Limits of Behavioural Explanation in Politics," *C.J.E.P.S.*, XXXI, 3, August, 1965.

Koenig, D.J., et al., "The Year that British Columbia Went NDP: NDP Voter Support Pre- and Post-1972," *BC Studies*, 24, Winter, 1974-75.

Kornberg, A., Smith, J., and Bromley, D., "Some Differences in the Political Socialization Patterns of Canadian and American Party Officials: A Preliminary Report," *C.J.P.S.*, II, 1, March, 1969.

Krause, R.K., and LeDuc, L., "Voting Behaviour and Electoral Strategies in the Progressive Conservative Leadership Convention of 1976," *C.J.P.S.*, XII, 1, March, 1979.

Land, B., *Eglinton, The Election Study of a Federal Constituency*, Toronto, Peter Martin Associates, 1965.

Laponce, J.A., "Measuring Party Preference: The Problem of Ambivalence," *C.J.P.S.*, XI, 1, March, 1978.

Laponce, J.A., *People vs. Politics, A Study of Opinions, Attitudes, and Perceptions in Vancouver-Burrard, 1963-1965*, Toronto, U.T.P., 1969.

Laponce, J.A., "Post-dicting Electoral Cleavages in Canadian Federal Elections, 1949-1968: Material for a Footnote," *C.J.P.S.*, 5, 2, June, 1972.

Leduc, L., "Political Behaviour and the Issue of Majority Government in Two Federal Elections," *C.J.P.S.*, X, 2, June, 1977.

Leduc, L., Clarke, H., Jenson, J., Pammett, J., "A National Sample Design," *C.J.P.S.*, VII, 4, December, 1974.

Lemieux, V., "Les dimensions sociologiques du vote créditiste au Québec," *Recherches Sociographiques*, VI, 2, May-August, 1965.

Lemieux, V., "L'analyse hiérarchique des résultats électoraux," *C.J.P.S.*, 1, March, 1968.

Lemieux, V., "La composition des preferences partisanes," *C.J.P.S.*, II, 4, December, 1969.

Lemieux, V., (ed.), *Quatre élections provinciales au Québec*, Québec, Les Presses de l'Université Laval, 1969.

Lemieux, V., Gilbert, M., and Blais, A., *Une élection réalignment; l'élection générale du 29 avril 1970 du Québec*, Montréal, Éditions du jour, 1970.

Long, J.A., and Slemko, B., "The Recruitment of Local Decision-Makers in Five Canadian Cities: Some Preliminary Findings," *C.J.P.S.*, VII, 3, September, 1974.

Lovink, J.A.A., "Is Canadian Politics too Competitive?," *C.J.P.S.*, VI, 3, September, 1973.

MacDonald, K.J., "Sources of Electoral Support for Provincial Political Parties in Urban British Columbia," *BC Studies*, 15, Autumn, 1972.

McCormick, P., "Voting Behaviour in Alberta: The Quasi-Party System Revisited," *J.C.S.*, 15, 3, Fall, 1980.

McDonald, V., "Participation in the Canadian Context," *Q.Q.*, 84, 3, Autumn, 1977.

Meisel, J., "Religious Affiliation and Electoral Behaviour," *C.J.E.P,S.*, XXII, 4, November, 1956.

Meisel, J., *The 1957 Canadian General Election*, Toronto, U.T.P., 1962.

Meisel, J., "Political Culture and the Politics of Culture," *C.J.P.S.* VII, 4, December, 1974.

Meisel, John, (ed.), *Papers on the 1962 Election*, Toronto, U.T.P., 1964.

Meisel, J., *Working Papers on Canadian Politics*, Montreal, McG.-Q.U.P., 2nd enlarged ed., 1975.

Mishler, W., *Political Participation in Canada: Prospects for Democratic Citizenship*, Toronto, Macmillan, 1979.

Morley, J.T., "Comment: The 1974 Federal Election in British Columbia," *BC Studies*, 23, Fall, 1974.

Morrison, K.L. "The Businessman Voter in Thunder Bay," *C.J.P.S.*, VI, 2, June, 1973.

Morton, D., "The Effectiveness of Political Campaigning: The N.D.P. in the 1967 Ontario Election," *J.C.S.*, IV, 3, August, 1969.

Ogmundson, R.L., "A Note on the Ambiguous Meanings of Survey Research Measures Which Use the Words 'Left' and 'Right'," *C.J.P.S.*, XII, 4, December, 1979.

Ogmundson, R., "On the Measurement of Party Class Positions: The Case of the Canadian Federal Political Parties," *C.R.S.A.*, 12, 1975.

Ornstein, M.D., Stevenson, H.M., Williams, A.P., "Region, Class and Political Culture in Canada," *C.J.P.S.*, XIII, 2, June, 1980.

Palda, K.S., "Does Advertising Influence Votes? An Analysis of the 1966 and 1970 Quebec Elections," *C.J.P.S.*, VI, 4, December, 1973.

Palmer, B.D., *Working Class Culture in Canada*, Toronto, Butterworths, 1981.

Pammett, J.H., "The Development of

Political Orientations in Canadian School Children," *C.J.P.S.*, IV, 1, March, 1971.

Pammett, J.H., Leduc, L., Jenson, J., Clarke, H., "The Perception and Impact of Issues in the 1974 Federal Election," *C.J.P.S.*, X, 1, March, 1977.

Pammett, J.H., and Whittington, M.S., (eds.), *Foundations of Political Culture: Political Socialization in Canada*, Toronto, Macmillan, 1976.

Pammett, J., Clarke, H.D., Jenson, J., LeDuc, L., "Change in the Garden: The 1979 Federal Election," paper presented at the Annual Meeting of the C.P.S.A., Montreal, June 2, 1980.

Penniman, H., (ed.), *Canada at the Polls, 1979 and 1980*, Washington, American Enterprise Institute, 1981.

Penniman, M.R., (ed.), *Canada at the Polls: The General Election of 1974*, Washington, American Enterprise Institute, 1975.

Perlin, G., and Peppin, P., "Variations in Party Support in Federal and Provincial Elections: Some Hypotheses," *C.J.P.S.*, IV, 2, June, 1971.

Philpotts, G., "Vote Trading, Welfare, and Uncertainty," *C.J.E*, 5, 3, August, 1972.

Pike, R., Zureik, E., *Political Socialization*, Vol. 1, Carleton Library No. 84, Toronto, M. & S., 1975; *Socialization, Social Stratification, Ethnicity*, Vol. II, No. 85, 1975.

Pinard, M., "One-Party Dominance and Third Parties," *C.J.E.P.S.*, XXXIII, 3, August, 1967.

Pinard, M., and Hamilton, R., "The Parti Québécois Comes to Power: An Analysis of the 1976 Quebec Election," *C.J.P.S.*, XI, 4, December, 1978.

Regenstreif, P., "The Canadian General Election of 1958," *Western Political Quarterly*, XIII, 2, June, 1960.

Regenstreif, P., "Some Aspects of National Party Support in Canada," *C.J.E.P.S.*, XIX, 1, February, 1963.

Regenstreif, P., *The Diefenbaker Interlude: Parties and Voting in Canada, An Interpretation,* Toronto, Longmans, 1965.

Richert, J.P., "Political Socialization in Quebec," *C.J.P.S.,* VI, 2, June, 1973.

Robin, M., "The Social Basis of Party Politics in British Columbia," *Q.Q.,* LXXII, 4, Winter, 1966.

Rothney, G.O., "Denominational Basis of Representation in the Newfoundland Assembly, 1919-1962," *C.J.E.P.S.,* XXVII, 4, November, 1962.

Ruff, N.J., "Party Detachment and Voting Patterns in a Provincial Two-Member Constituency: Victoria 1972," *BC Studies,* 23, Fall, 1974.

Scarrow, H.A., "Federal-Provincial Voting Patterns in Canada," *C.J.E.P.S.,* XXVI, 2, May, 1960.

Scarrow, H.A., "By-Elections and Public Opinion in Canada," *Public Opinion Quarterly,* XXV, Spring, 1961.

Scarrow, H.A., "Patterns of Voter Turnout in Canada," *M.J.P.S.,* V, 4, 1961.

Scarrow, H.A., "Voting Patterns and the New Party," *Political Science,* XIV, 1, March, 1962.

Scarrow, H.A., *How Canada Votes, A Handbook of Federal and Provincial Election Data,* New Orleans, Hauser Press, 1962.

Schindeler, F., and Hoffman, D., "Theological and Political Conservatism," *C.J.P.S.,* l, 4, December, 1968.

Schwartz, M., "Canadian Voting Behaviour," in R. Rose, (ed.), *Electoral Behaviour: A Comparative Handbook,* New York, Free Press, 1974.

Simeon, R., and Elkins, D., "Regional Political Cultures in Canada," *C.J.P.S.,* VII, 3, September, 1974.

Simmons, J.W., "Voting Behaviour and Socio-Economic Characteristics: The Middlesex East Federal Election, 1965," *C.J.E.P.S.,* XXXIII, 3, August, 1967.

Smith, D.E., "A Comparison of Prairie Political Developments in

Saskatchewan and Alberta," *J.C.S.,* IV, 1, February, 1969.

Smith, J., Kornberg, A., Bromely, D., "Patterns of Early Political Socialization and Adult Party Affiliation," *C.R.S.A.,* 5, 1968.

Sniderman, P.M., Forbes, H.D., and Melzer, I., "Party Loyalty and Electoral Volatility: A Study of the Canadian Party System," *C.J.P.S.,* VII, 2, June, 1974.

Sproule-Jones, M., "Social Credit and the British Columbia Electorate," *BC Studies,* 11, Fall, 1971, and 12, Winter, 1971-72.

Van Loon, R., "Political Participation in Canada: The 1965 Election," *C.J.P.S.,* III, 3, September, 1970.

Warburton, T.R., "Religious and Social Influences in Voting in Greater Victoria," *BC Studies,* 10, Summer, 1971.

Wilson, J., "Politics and Social Class in Canada: The Case of Waterloo South," *C.J.P.S.,* I, 3, September, 1968.

Wilson, J., "The Myth of Candidate Partisanship: The Case of Waterloo South," *J.C.S.,* III, 4, November, 1968.

Wilson, R.J., "Geography, Politics and Culture: Electoral Insularity in British Columbia," *C.J.P.S.,* XIII, 4, December, 1980.

Wilson, R.J., "The Impact of Communications Developments on British Columbia Electoral Patterns, 1903-1975," *C.J.P.S.,* XIII, 3, September, 1980.

Winn, C., and McMenemy, J., "Political Alignment in a Polarized City: Electoral Cleavages in Kitchener, Ontario," *C.J.P.S.,* VI, 2, June, 1973.

Winn, C., and Twiss, J., "The Spatial Analysis of Political Cleavages and the Case of the Ontario Legislature," *C.J.P.S.,* X, 2, June, 1977.

Wiseman, N., and Taylor, K.W., "Ethnic vs Class Voting: The Case of Winnipeg, 1945," *C.J.P.S.,* VII, 2, June, 1974.

Woodward, C.A., *A History of New Brunswick Provincial Election Cam-*

paigns and Platforms, 1966-1974, Toronto, Micromedia, 1976.

Wrong, D.H., "Ontario Provincial Elections, 1934-1955," *C.J.E.P.S.,* XXIII, 3, August, 1957.

Young, W.D., "The Peterborough Election: The Success of a Party Image," *Dalhousie Review,* XL, 4, Winter, 1961.

Zakuta, L., "Membership in a Becalmed Protest Movement," *C.J.E.P.S.,* XXIV, 2, May, 1958.

Zipp, J.F., "Left-Right Dimensions of Canadian Federal Party Identification: A Discriminant Analysis," *C.J.P.S.,* XI, 2, June, 1978.

11

THE EXECUTIVE PROCESS: THE CROWN

Since 1977, when the fourth edition of *Politics: Canada* was published, the argument over whether we should retain the monarchy in Canada appears to have subsided. Whether lack of debate indicates more than lack of interest is an unanswered question. Judged by a Gallup poll on January 3, 1981, Canadians in any case seem to feel increasingly that the monarchy is less important. Seventy-four per cent of the respondents expressed the opinion that the monarchy's importance in Canada was decreasing, compared to the 61 per cent who held that view in 1965.

Canadians were somewhat more enthusiastic about the governor-general. Sixty per cent of the respondents were in favour of retaining the vice-regal position, according to a Gallup poll published on October 31, 1981, while only one in four wanted to abolish it. Lieutenant-governors fared somewhat worse in a Gallup poll released a few days earlier, since only 39 per cent wanted to continue the office while 41 per cent favoured abolishing it. At least there was nothing personal in the opinions, since 70 per cent of the respondents could not name the lieutenant-governor in their province.

Although monarchical persuasion may be waning, republicanism does not seem to be waxing. For that reason, the article by Peter Dempson entitled "We're on the Road to Republicanism," which appeared in the fourth edition, pp. 360-362, has been omitted from this edition. Professor Frank MacKinnon's article defending the monarchy has been retained, however, since it describes clearly and briefly the functions of the governor-general and lieutenant-governors in Canada.

The portion of former Senator Eugene Forsey's classic study of the royal power of dissolution which deals with the governor-general's role in the constitutional crisis in Canada in 1926 has been included for the same reason. The extract from Professor James Mallory's article reproduced here is important also since it describes the most recent case — some would say "probably the last case" — of a lieutenant-governor reserving a bill, which occurred in Saskatchewan in 1961.

Canadians have been remarkably ambivalent about anything smacking of social distinction, whether it be political office or individual honours. There is in North America an egalitarian tendency to deride hierarchy and yet at the same time an eager readiness to accept personal distinction of any kind. The brief article describing the award of honours in Canada indicates the on-again, off-again nature of the practice, culminating in the introduction of an exclusively Canadian honours system in 1967.

Canadians' lack of interest in the Crown is reflected in the relatively few books and articles which have been written on the subject recently. The bibliography at the end of the chapter which lists works on the lieutenant-governors and governor-general is remarkably short.

THE VALUE OF THE MONARCHY*

Frank MacKinnon

A constitutional monarch protects democracy from some peculiarities of political power. It has been retained in our system because it works. Other reasons, such as nostalgic recollections of the past and sentimental ties with Britain, are secondary — to some, irrelevant — and should not obscure basic facts of government. One of these facts is a tendency of man, whether deep-sea diver or astronaut on the one hand or politician on the other, to suffer from the "bends" during rapid rises from one level of pressure and atmosphere to another.

History clearly indicates how common and serious are the "bends" in government. Even small rises from private citizen to mayor may bring on giddiness while major ascents from backbencher to minister or from minister to head of government can cause acute distress of the equilibrium. Constitutions have prescribed various remedies. Complicated procedures select those who are to make the political climb; ascent by stages is sometimes provided — perhaps by planned pauses in the back benches or the opposition; control of those on high is arranged through established contacts with those below; and, most difficult of all, some arrangement must be made to end the stay in political orbit of those who have been there long enough and can not or will not come back by themselves. A sure cure has not yet been devised, however, and the "bends" remain a major occupational hazard of rulers, which some overcome for varying periods and to which others fall quick and tragic victims.

To relieve this difficulty at the heights of political power is the main purpose of the constitutional monarchy. Some human being must be at the summit of government, and much depends on his stability. Unfortunately great talent, public acclaim and hero worship, and even assumptions of "divine right" have not been reliable stabilizers when the head of state wields power. We therefore place two persons at the top: one is at the very summit and he stays there permanently and is accustomed to living at that level; the other is temporary and he is made to understand that his status is sponsored and may be ended at any time.

The monarch holds power in the state on behalf of the people, and he or she is the personal symbol of authority which man finds necessary in every system. Heredity makes his tenure unquestioned and ensures a rigid training

* From *The Dalhousie Review*, Vol. 49, No. 2, Summer, 1969, by permission of the author and publisher.

for the job. Pomp and ceremony attract respect and provide the show which people always expect from heads of state. But the monarch is not allowed to wield the power of head of state by himself; the pomp and ceremony are all that he can manage safely at his level and he must wield the power only on the advice of others.

These others are the sovereign's ministers, especially the prime minister, who is the head of government. A prime minister is almost at the summit but not quite, and that difference is crucial to democracy. He is given no power whatever; he advises the Crown on the exercise of the Crown's power; and that difference is also crucial to democracy. He has no pomp of his own, so that he knows that he is not an indispensable symbol. He is a trustee into whose hands is placed the exercise of power but not power itself.

This separation of pomp and power at the top took centuries to develop and was the result of the mistakes of many sovereigns and ministers. Other arrangements for such separation in other systems did not go so far as the British, who make the monarch so colourful and the prime minister so powerful and responsible an adviser that each, regardless of the per- sonalities concerned, knows his place. . . .

The monarchy therefore serves democracy. It keeps the ministers in sec- ond place as servants of the state — electable, responsible, accountable, criticizable, and defeatable — a position necessary to the operation of par- liamentary government. The people and their parliament can control the head of government because he cannot identify himself with the state or confuse loyalty to himself with allegiance to the state and criticism with treason. He is discouraged from the common tendency of officials, whether elected or not, to regard and make themselves indispensable, to entrench themselves in expanding power structures, to resent accountability and criti- cism, and to scoff at the effects of prolonged tenure of office or advancing years. Moreover, such control avoids the charges of treason, executions, as- sassinations, revolutions, and miscellaneous other expensive upheavals which so often accompany attempts to control and change governments that take themselves too seriously.

The democratic sensibilities of some people are disturbed by the idea of an élite, a symbol, an official who is neither elected nor chosen by someone who is elected. They err if they think the withdrawal of monarchy will remove such elements from government. These elements are characteristic of government itself, whatever its form, and are simply transferred to other institutions when a monarchy disappears. Whatever their system, men will have élites and symbols. Heads of government, elected or not, will take to themselves if they can the prestige and power of monarchs, disguised per- haps, but with the same basic elements; they find them a natural and necessary feature of government authority. The existence of a monarch pro- tects the prime minister from such temptations. . . .

Monarchical phenomena are common in other activities of society. The cult of the celebrity is as dominant in our day as it ever was in history. How often is "I touched him!" heard in a screaming crowd. The elite in athletics have always been admired and well paid. Universities feature academic ceremonial. There are many resemblances between churches and royal courts — the raiment, titles, powers of clergy, even the throne, tiara, and crown. And in the smallest communities the dignities and regalia of fraternal and religious lodges are reminiscent of the potentates and knights of old. These are such natural and acceptable phenomena that it is not difficult to understand government officials taking advantage of them. Man has found, however, that in government it is hard to criticize and advise a tremendous swell in robes or uniform who also has power, a retinue, and a palace. Our system discourages these things as much as possible for working politicians, but, since they are inevitable anyway, they are placed with the Crown, partly to provide a good show, mainly to strengthen the democratic state.

All systems, including democracy, contain the means for their own destruction. It is in time of crisis, when some serious and unexpected dislocation takes place for which there is no normal remedy, that systems break down for good. . . . Parliamentary government presupposes change as required; but such change means orderly alterations of power, not conditions of general panic and destruction. When an electoral system is stalemated, when a parliament breaks down, when a prime minister dies in office and there is no obvious successor, when a leader becomes very ill or insane and everyone knows it but himself and the public — these are among the times when political paralysis is brought on by shock and uncertainty. In such circumstances a constitutional monarch provides a symbol of continuity, order, and authority. He cannot, of course, step in and take over; he can only encourage others and sponsor the search for an orderly solution of the difficulties. He is above suspicion and can command confidence because of his prestige, because he is above politics and ambition for personal aggrandizement, and because he does not exercise power on his own initiative. Even in such modest periods of upheaval as elections, he represents the state as a whole while the parties involved including the government, can oppose each other to even the most vituperative extremes — a process which should never be taken for granted. No political leader can be a symbol of the whole state either in crisis or in elections; nor should he be in a parliamentary democracy. That is the job of a monarch.

There are other purposes of the monarchy: the encouragement of dignity and respect for government, the example of a royal family, the colour of pageantry, the sponsorship of good works and the inevitable social activities of government; the source of honours and awards; a continuing focus of loyalty and emotion; a unifying force among a people; and, in our monarchy, a headship for a family of nations, the Commonwealth. Each of these functions has its own merits and weaknesses. Whether or not we approve of any or all of them, we must remember that none is irrelevant or disposable: each one crops up in some form in every system of government. When a monarchy disappears, other institutions soon take them on. Then trouble begins because of the transfer of such functions to the power structure. Officials and political parties from right to left have found many ways of using them to protect themselves and their powers and prestige from the legitimate operation of democracy. They are in safer hands, and are more effective, with the Crown.

An elected non-political president is often used as an alternative to a monarch. His main problem, aside from the temporary and relatively uninteresting and colourless character of his office, is the ease with which he can be overshadowed by the prime minister and, worse, the ease with which he can compete with the prime minister. Everyone concerned knows exactly where the monarch and his advisers stand in relation to one another and to the people. This arrangement, as already noted, is not so clear in a republic because two elected heads can get in each other's way and trespass on each other's powers.

An elected political president wielding power directly is a completely different institution at the head of a different system of government. He could not function in the parliamentary system as we know it. As every American president has testified, this kind of official also finds burdensome the combination of head of government and head of state.

Which is the "best" system? No one knows; some people tend to think their own is "best" whatever it is; others tend to admire any system other than their own; some are more concerned with the kind of system they have than with how it works. Two things, however, are clear; that systems are not automatically transferable from one place to another — too much depends on the environment; and that any system must allow, not only for logical forms and cherished principles, but also for peculiarities of human nature in government, particularly the hierarchical "bends."

Canadians have retained the Crown as represented by the Sovereign, the Governor-General, and the Lieutenant-Governors. All the reasons for the Crown have applied in both federal and provincial governments, and, on the whole, the relations between the Crown and the Ministers have worked extremely well. The twelve incumbents together cost a little more than two cents per citizen per year. By no stretch of the imagination can the Governors-General or the Lieutenant-Governors be considered to have played any significant role in actual government in our time, or to have obstructed or overshadowed their Premiers. Their job has been to occupy the top levels in their respective jurisdictions and to handle the decorative and emergency functions, while leaving the Prime Ministers and Premiers to handle the powers of government without actually possessing them, and to be electable, responsible, accountable, criticizable, and removable. The Governors-General and the Lieutenant-Governors are something more than constitutional presidents; they have Sovereign's auspices to signify authority, to enhance their prestige, and to clearly mark the line between pomp and power. . . .

Those who worry about the monarchy sometimes doubt the relevance in Canada of the Sovereign herself because she is Queen of several countries. Such a situation is common in Canada; many citizens owe allegiance to outside heads of their businesses, churches, unions, international political parties, and other groups. Nevertheless, a shared head of state is controversial. We need to remember that under our constitution the Sovereign is a part of Parliament and is the formal, ultimate source of political power, and the law sets out the facts of power with clarity for all to see and recognize as authentic. Governments in Canada may have quarrelled over which may do what, but power to govern has itself been unassailable and unquestioned from colonial times to the present. This stability of law is by no means universal around the world in an age when constitutions have been unusually short-lived and unreliable and when human rights have enjoyed only modest protection. Governments and their supporters come and go, but the

Canadian people know that their rights and the powers of their state enjoy a solid, recognized base and the validations of centuries of usage. The sovereign is the legal expression and permanent non-partisan symbol of that fact.

Canadians may some day have their own resident sovereign. Perhaps, when the Queen's reign ends, Prince Charles could become King of the rest of the Commonwealth while Prince Andrew could move to Ottawa to found a purely Canadian dynasty while continuing the stable heritage of constitutional power. Whatever happens, vague or emotional platitudes about monarchical and democratic theory and principle are unrealistic unless considered with the actual practical operation of government and the political performance of men. When the monarchy makes the constitution work as a plan for humans as distinct from a paper declaration, however grand, then it should be recognized as a bulwark of democracy and of the rights Canadians want to enjoy under their parliamentary system.

WAS THE GOVERNOR GENERAL'S REFUSAL CONSTITUTIONAL?*

Eugene A. Forsey

In the Canadian Parliament of 1921-25, the Liberal party, under Mr. Mackenzie King, had 117 members, the Conservatives 50, Progressives, Labour and Independents, 68. For most purposes, however, the Liberal Government enjoyed the support of a majority of the Progressives, so that it was able to carry on for four years without serious difficulty. By September 5, 1925, Mr. King had become convinced of the necessity of seeking at the polls a clear working majority over all other parties. He accordingly advised and secured dissolution. The election was held October 29. It returned 101 Liberals, 116 Conservatives and 28 Progressives, Labour members and Independents. The Prime Minister and eight other Ministers lost their seats.

On November 5, a month and two days before the new Parliament's legal existence could begin, the Prime Minister issued a statement asserting that three courses were open to him: to resign at once, to meet the new House of Commons, or to advise "an immediate dissolution." He had decided to meet the new House, at the earliest practicable moment.

This proved to be January 7, 1926. From then till the House adjourned, March 2, to allow the Prime Minister to find a seat in a by-election and again from March 15, when the sittings resumed, till June 25, the Conservatives made repeated efforts to defeat the Government; but without success. The Government's majorities were: 3, 10, 10, 1, 7, 8, 11, 13, 6, 9, 13, 13, 15, 1, 6, 8. On June 18, a committee appointed to investigate alleged scandals in the Customs Department presented its report. The Conservatives were not satisfied with the report, and one of them, Mr. H.H. Stevens, on June 22, moved an amendment which, among other things, described the conduct of "the Prime Minister and the government" as

* From *The Royal Power of Dissolution of Parliament in the British Commonwealth*, Toronto, Oxford University Press, 1943, pp. 131-140. By permission of the author and publisher.

"wholly indefensible" and the "conduct of the present Minister of Customs in the case of Moses Aziz" as "utterly unjustifiable." On June 23, Mr. Woodsworth (Labour) moved what Keith calls a "non-partisan" sub-amendment which would have struck out the condemnation of the Prime Minister, the Government, and the Minister of Customs, and added a condemnation of various persons on both sides of politics and in the Civil Service and provided for a judicial commission to continue the investigation. The Government accepted this sub-amendment; the Conservatives opposed it. On June 25, it was defeated by a majority of two. Mr. Fansher (Progressive) then moved a second sub-amendment, which would have left in the Stevens amendment the condemnation of the Prime Minister, the Government and the Minister of Customs, and added Mr. Woodsworth's proposed condemnation of other persons, and provision for a judicial commission. The Speaker ruled this out of order. His ruling was challenged, and overruled by a majority of two. A motion to adjourn the debate, supported by the Government, was lost by one; somewhat later, at 5:15 a.m., Saturday, June 26, a second motion to adjourn the debate, also supported by the Government, carried by one. The Fansher sub-amendment had meanwhile been carried without a division, but the Stevens amendment had not been voted on.

During the week-end Mr. King asked for dissolution. The Governor General, Lord Byng, refused. Mr. King thereupon resigned. He announced his resignation to the House, Monday, June 28, saying that he believed that "under British practice" he was "entitled" to a dissolution. He declared that there was "no Prime Minister," "no Government"; declined to take part in a conference on the means of winding up the session; and moved that the House adjourn, which it did, at 2:15 p.m. The Governor General at once sent for Mr. Meighen, and asked him "if he could command a majority in the House to get the work of the session concluded in orderly manner." Mr. Meighen replied that he could, having received informal promises from a number of the Progressives to the effect that they would vote with the Conservatives to get these all-important Bills through, pass Supply, and prorogue. The Governor General then requested Mr. Meighen to form a government, and in the evening he undertook to do so. Next day, during a conference of the Progressives, the Governor General sent for the Progressive leader, Mr. Forke. The Progressives thereupon drew up and gave to Mr. Forke "a confidential memorandum for his guidance". . . . The memorandum was as follows:

> That we assist the new administration in completing the business of the session. That we are in agreement on the necessity of continuing the investigation into the customs and excise department by a judicial commission. . . . That no dissolution should take place until the . . . commission has finished its investigation . . . and that Parliament be summoned to deal with the reports.

Mr. Meighen had accepted office as Prime Minister, but the formation of his Cabinet presented unusual difficulties. Mr. King and his colleagues had not followed the customary practice of holding office till their successors were appointed. They had left the Crown without a ministry, the country without a government, an action which appears to be without precedent in the history of the Empire. Mr. King had refused to engage in a conference on the question of finishing the session's business. The session was almost at an end; but Supply had not been voted; bills to amend the Special War Revenue Act and the Canada Evidence Act, thirteen divorce bills and eight other private bills had passed both Houses and awaited the royal assent. The important Long Term Farm Mortgage Credit Bill was still before the Senate. Under the law as it then stood, if Mr. Meighen formed a government the ordinary way, every one of the 15 or so ministers with portfolio from the Commons, upon accepting office, would automatically have vacated his seat. This would have left the Conservatives and Liberals about equal. The government would have had to seek an adjournment or prorogation of about six weeks to allow time for ministerial by-election. [Later, the Act of 1931, 21-22 George V, c. 52, did away with the necessity for such by-elections.] Mr. King's attitude on the question of a conference suggests that he might have opposed an adjournment. . . . If he had opposed adjournment, it is by no means impossible that, with the Conservative strength reduced by 15 or 16, he could have carried with him enough Progressives to succeed. Mr. Meighen might have got prorogation for six weeks. But either adjournment or prorogation would have involved a long delay, highly inconvenient to the members of Parliament, especially the farmer members at that time of year; prorogation would have killed the Long Term Farm Mortgage Credit Bill, the Montreal Harbour Commission Loan Bill and two private bills; and either adjournment or prorogation would have involved carrying on for six weeks without Supply, which would have been possible but not desirable.

Mr. Meighen therefore announced that, to bring the session to an end promptly, he had "decided to constitute . . . a temporary Ministry . . . of seven members, who would be sworn in without portfolio, and . . . would have responsibility as acting Ministers of the several departments." After prorogation, he would "immediately address himself to the task of constituting a Government in the method established by custom. The present plan is merely to meet an unusual if not unprecedented situation."

The new Government met the House June 29, and proceeded to deal with the business on the Order Paper. The first main item was of course the still unfinished debate on the Stevens amendment. Mr. Rinfret, Liberal, now moved a fresh sub-amendment, which the Speaker declared to be in order. Mr. Geary, Conservative, challenged the Speaker's ruling which was sustained by a majority of one. On a vote on the sub-amendment itself, the new Government received a majority of 12. A further new sub-amendment was then carried by agreement, the Stevens amendment so amended was carried by a majority of 10, and the report of the Committee, as amended, was also carried by 10.

On June 30, the Liberal Opposition moved a vote of want of confidence in the new Government on the ground of its fiscal policy. This was defeated by a majority of seven.

Mr. King followed this up in Committee of Supply by an elaborate cross-examination of the Ministers, designed to show that they were not validly appointed and were therefore not ministers at all. Mr. Lapointe, Liberal ex-Minister of Justice, then raised a question of privilege; that the acting ministers of departments, having really (so he alleged) accepted offices of profit under the Crown, had vacated their seats and had no right to appear in the House. These two propositions, as Mr. Bury, Conservative M.P. for Edmonton East pointed out, are of course mutually exclusive. If the acting ministers of departments were really *Ministers* of departments, there could be no question of the validity of their appointments; if they had not been validly appointed, and were not ministers of departments, then they had not vacated their seats. The two propositions, however, were ingeniously combined in a motion of Mr. Robb, Liberal ex-Minister of Finance:

> That the actions in this House of the Honourable Members who have acted as Ministers of the Crown since the 29th of June, 1926, namely the Honourable Members for West York, Fort William, Vancouver Centre, Argenteuil, Wellington South, and the Honourable senior Member for Halifax, are a violation and an infringment of the privileges of this House for the following reasons:
> — That the said Honourable gentlemen have no rights to sit in this House and should have vacated their seats therein if they legally hold office as administrators of the various departments, assigned to them by Order-in- Council; that if they do not hold such office legally, they have no right to control the business of Government in this House and ask for supply for the Departments of which they state they are acting Ministers.

After debate, this motion was put. Mr. Meighen's seat was of course vacant, which reduced the Conservative strength by one. Mr. Bird, Progressive member for Nelson, broke his pair and voted with the Liberals. As a result, the Government was defeated by one vote. The House then adjourned. Next day, July 2, before it could meet again, Mr. Meighen advised the Governor General to dissolve Parliament. Lord Byng accepted the advice, and Parliament was accordingly dissolved, without prorogation and without royal assent being given to any of the bills which were awaiting it.

These events raised no fewer than eight constitutional questions.

1. Was Lord Byng's refusal of dissolution to Mr. King constitutional in the light of the circumstances as they stood on the morning of June 28?

2. Did the constitutionality of that refusal depend on Mr. Meighen's actually being able to carry on with the existing House of Commons?

3. Did the constitutionality of the refusal depend on the constitutionality of the government of ministers without portfolio?

4. Was the Government constitutional?

5. Was the grant of dissolution to Mr. Meighen constitutional?

6. Was the constitutionality of refusing dissolution to Mr. King on June 28 affected by the grant of dissolution to Mr. Meighen on July 2?

7. Was the manner of dissolution of July 2 constitutional?

8. Did Lord Byng's action relegate Canada to a status inferior to that of Great Britain?

THE LIEUTENANT-GOVERNOR'S DISCRETIONARY POWERS: THE RESERVATION OF BILL 56 IN SASKATCHEWAN*

J.R. Mallory

Before proroguing the legislative session on April 8, 1961, the Lieutenant-Governor of Saskatchewan, Frank L. Bastedo, intimated that he was reserving Bill 56 for the signification of the pleasure of the Governor General. This bill, entitled "An Act to Provide for the Alteration of Certain Mineral Contracts," would have given to the lieutenant-governor in council the power to modify existing mineral contracts, and contained the provision that it would expire on December 31, 1961. After prorogation Mr. Bastedo issued a statement to the press, which said in part, "this is a very important bill affecting hundreds of mineral contracts. It raises implications which throw grave doubts of the legislation being in the public interest. There is grave doubt as to its validity." These doubts were not shared by his constitutional advisers, who informed him that in their view the bill was within the powers of the legislature and advised him to assent to it.

The royal veto — even a suspensive veto, which is what in effect reservation is — is deemed to be dead in most jurisdictions where the British cabinet system operates. No British sovereign since Queen Anne has refused to give assent to a bill, and the exercise of the power to reserve or withhold assent is generally regarded as a relic of colonial thraldom which disappeared when the fetters of Downing Street control were removed. How then can it continue to exist in a Canadian province?

Under the powers conferred upon him by section 90 of the British North America Act, a lieutenant-governor may do one of three things with a bill which has passed through all its stages in the legislature and is presented to him for royal assent so that it is transformed into an Act of the legislature: he may signify that he assents to the bill in the Queen's name; he may withhold his assent; or he may reserve the bill so that it may be considered by the governor general. The first of these three courses is the normal one, and requires no comment. The second is a simple veto; the bill is dead and can be revived only by introducing it again into the legislature, passing it through all its stages, and presenting it again for assent at a subsequent session of the legislature. The third is not a withholding of assent (that is, there is no veto), but the decision as to whether assent will be given or withheld is passed back to the governor general, acting on the advice of his ministers in Ottawa.

Seventy bills have been reserved by lieutenant-governors since Confederation. However, fifty-nine of these were reserved before 1900, most of them in the early days of provincial government. Since 1920 there have been four: three in Alberta in 1937, and the one here considered. The use of these wide discretionary powers of the lieutenant-governor was characteristic of the

* From *The Canadian Journal of Economics and Political Science*, Vol. XXVII, No. 4, November, 1961. By permission of the author and publisher.

period of almost colonial status of the provinces (particularly the western provinces) in relation to the dominion. The revival of the power in Alberta in 1937 caused general surprise. It had become widely believed that the power had become constitutionally obsolete in the same way that the position of the governor general as an imperial officer had disappeared as a result of the achievement of Canadian autonomy. So general was the uncertainty that the federal government referred the whole question of the scope and validity of the powers of disallowance, reservation, and withholding assent to the Supreme Court in the autumn of 1937.

The Supreme Court had no difficulty in finding that these powers continued to subsist, unaffected by changes in constitutional conventions, and the powers were equally valid, whether the legislation was *intra vires* the provincial legislature or not, and that the only limitations on the discretion of the lieutenant-governor were instructions from the governor general.

While the power of the lieutenant-governor is unrestricted in law, it was intended to operate as one of the means by which the federal government could intervene in a province to prevent the enactment of legislation which threatened some wider interest which required protection in the national interest. In other words, the reservation of bills was intended to be a power exercised by the lieutenant-governor acting in his capacity as a Dominion officer. . . .

Sir John A. Macdonald, when minister of justice, caused a minute of council to be adopted in Ottawa in 1882 and communicated to lieutenant-governors in order to make clear to them that they should exercise their power of reservation only when instructed to do so. ''It is only in a case of extreme necessity that a Lieutenant-Governor should without such instructions exercise his discretion as a Dominion Officer in reserving a bill. In fact, with the facility of communication between the Dominion and provincial governments, such a necessity can seldom if ever arise.''

In other words, a lieutenant-governor who reserves a bill on his own authority is acting within the scope of his legal powers, but not within the spirit of the constitution.

Was Mr. Bastedo acting, directly or indirectly, on instruction from Ottawa? The present instructions of lieutenant-governors do not specify any classes of bills which may, or should be reserved. Prime Minister Diefenbaker, when asked in the House of Commons on April 10 whether the bill had been reserved, replied:

> . . . The first information the government received on this matter was on Saturday, when the lieutenant governor telephoned the under secretary of state that he had reserved a bill of the Saskatchewan legislature for the signification of the Governor General's pleasure. . . . We have no other information on the matter. There was no consultation in advance in any way, and any action in this regard would be taken by the lieutenant governor himself.

Two days later, in answer to another question in the House, the Prime Minister made a further statement in which he said:

> . . . The reservation by lieutenant governors have [sic] been generally accepted as dependent on a request from the governor in council. There was no

discussion in this regard, as I have already pointed out. We had no knowledge of the action to be taken by the lieutenant governor. However, the action was taken, and as yet the reasons which the lieutenant governor is required to transmit to the Governor General for the course he followed have not come to hand. As soon as they do the governor in council will take such action as is deemed proper, with full regard to the fact that this government has consistently taken the attitude that if legislation is within the legislative competence of the provinces, except constitutionally in extra-ordinary circumstances there should be no interference with provincial jurisdiction.

Finally, on May 5th, Mr. Diefenbaker tabled in the House the order in council "in which His Excellency the Governor General by and with the advice of Her Majesty the Queen's privy council for Canada declares his assent to Bill No. 56 of the legislature of Saskatchewan passed during the present year and which was reserved by the lieutenant governor of Saskatchewan for the signification of the pleasure of the Governor General in accordance with the terms of the British North America Act." The order in council dealt with the two grounds upon which the Lieutenant-Governor had acted noting that in the opinion of the Minister of Justice the bill was *intra vires* the Saskatchewan legislature, and that "the expression 'conflict with national policy or interest' does not relate solely to a difference of principle or point of view, but must include matters of practical or physical effect, and that in this sense the bill is not in conflict with national policy or interest."

In his statement to the House, the Prime Minister reminded members that the Lieutenant-Governor's action had not been preceded by consultation with the federal government. "I have no hesitation in saying," he said, "that had there been such consultation my colleagues and I would have recommended to the Governor General that the lieutenant governor be instructed not to reserve the bill."

He referred to Macdonald's minute of council in 1882 and noted that "in view of the development of communications since" there should be ample opportunity for consultation before reservation. He then said, "I should point out that while no formal instructions have yet been given to lieutenant governors [never] to reserve a bill unless upon specific instructions, my colleagues and I are now considering whether such formal instructions, should be given." Unfortunately, the *Hansard* reporters omitted that "never," here inserted in brackets, which was in the typewritten text of the Prime Minister's statement. The instructions to lieutenant-governors referred to above seem, however, not to have been issued.

Mr. Bastedo seems to have felt impelled to reserve the bill for two reasons: he thought, contrary to the advice of his own Attorney-General and cabinet, that it was *ultra vires,* and he doubted if the bill was in the public interest. The federal government was unable to subscribe to either of these views. However, even had the Lieutenant-Governor been right, there are other remedies in the constitution which are less reminiscent of the prerogative powers of the Crown as they existed in the days of the Stuart kings. The proper body to decide the question of *vires* is the courts, and there can be little doubt that the interests adversely affected by the bill are able to afford recourse to litigation. Should the bill be regarded as gravely affecting the public interest of the country, then the responsibility for disallowing it — after due deliberation — rested on the federal government. Instead they were dragged into the issue without being given any choice in the matter.

The action of Mr. Bastedo furnishes sufficient reason, if any more is needed, for removing the power of reservation from the constitution. The Lieutenant-Governor acted with complete legality, but his action was wholly alien to the spirit of the constitution. A peculiarity of the British constitutional system is that behaviour which may be legally correct can nevertheless be wholly unconstitutional. This is particularly true in the realm of the prerogative, where wide discretionary powers exist but are in fact strictly confined by a number of conventions of the constitution which Dicey defined as "rules for determining the mode in which the discretionary powers of the Crown (or of the Ministers as servants of the Crown) ought to be exercised."

In Canada, we cannot safely assume that even lieutenant-governors have read Dicey or understand the constitution. In this matter it has now become necessary to bring the law of the constitution closer to political and constitutional realities. . . .

Reservation has one particularly objectionable feature, in that it contains within it a sort of "pocket veto." The federal government is not obliged to do anything at all about a reserved bill. If no action is taken at all, then the bill has been effectively vetoed. Since the bill under consideration would expire in any event on December 31, 1961, inaction would have destroyed its effect completely. Such a course of action would be interference with provincial jurisdiction. As long as the disallowance power remains in existence, reservation is in any event an unnecessary prop to the federal power. The continuance of reservation merely makes it possible for the federal government to be involved by inadvertence in local issues in which it may have no direct interest.

LIEUTENANT-GOVERNORS FEELING FINANCIAL SQUEEZE*

WINNIPEG — Manitoba's Lt.-Gov. F.L. (Bud) Jobin and his wife Donie are often seen in a supermarket loading up a shopping cart with groceries for one of their six monthly receptions at Government House.

Donie Jobin, without full-time housekeeping staff, frequently vacuums through the 23-room official residence.

In Charlottetown, Lt.-Gov. Joseph A. Doiron answers the Government House telephone, just as the Jobins do.

The representatives of the Queen in the provinces say these are just a few of the ways they make ends meet on allowances provided by federal and provincial governments.

"What I am having to do is cut back on functions," said Mr. Jobin. "The average reception for 150 costs between $650 and $700. Knowing that, we've had to turn down requests for receptions."

* From *The Canadian Press*, May 22, 1981. By permission.

In his five-year tenure, the only increases he has received in allowances are $166.16 a month from the federal government and $250 a month from the province. The total doesn't begin to meet price increases of 20 per cent for liquor, 50 per cent for mix, and almost 100 per cent for food.

Mr. Doiron says he has responded to rising costs not by cutting back on the number of receptions, "but what is provided at the receptions."

Occasionally, he has financed functions by dipping into his $35,000 a year salary paid by the federal government.

Mr. Jobin said he is sure he and Doiron are not alone in feeling the pinch.

"I'm not crying," he said. "I went into it. It's just a warning to the next person . . . To do it in the way it has been done for 15 or 20 years, I'm sure a fellow would have to dip into his own pocket."

Excluding the 1,500 people they receive at their annual New Year's levees, the Jobins estimate they entertain about 10,000 people a year. Mr. Doiron said between 6,000 and 7,000 people are received at Government House in Charlottetown.

In addition to his salary, Mr. Jobin receives $27,000 a year from the government and provincial support of $112,900.

Provincial contributions to the offices of lieutenant-governors vary widely, from $7,000 a year in Prince Edward Island to $450,000 in Quebec. As a result, the style of office "has grown in different ways in different provinces," said Saskatchewan's Lt.-Gov. Irwin Mcintosh.

"Saskatchewan has been a low-cost, low-profile operation, but the role is expanding."

Saskatchewan is one of three provinces which don't provide a traditional Government House residence. The lieutenant-governors of Saskatchewan, Alberta and Ontario have suites in hotels or legislative assemblies.

Lt.-Gov. John Aird of Ontario, whose budget from the province last year was $118,204, has office space, a dining room and two salons in the Legislature building at Queen's Park.

"Our lieutenant-governors, in the last few terms have lived in and around Toronto," said Walter Borosa, director of protocol for Ontario government. "His Honor has a home in Toronto.

"We are fortunate to have very adequate facilities in the Legislative building where he can entertain."

THE AWARD OF HONOURS IN CANADA

Paul Fox

From Confederation to the end of the first world war it was customary for some hereditary honours such as knighthoods and companionships in orders of chivalry to be awarded to Canadians. However, during the prime ministership of the Rt. Hon. Robert L. Borden, the House of Commons passed a resolution on May 22, 1919, requesting His Majesty to refrain from granting titular honours to Canadians thereafter. Prime Minister R.B. Bennett's government reversed this policy in 1933 by recommending a number of such awards. Although some honours of this kind were conferred on Canadians in 1934 and 1935, the policy was reversed again when Prime Minister W.L. Mackenzie King took office in the latter year. No titles have been awarded since then.

In 1967 Canada established its own honours system when the Order of Canada was introduced. In 1972 this honours system was amplified by the creation of the Order of Military Merit. To recognize bravery, a Medal of Courage was included in the Order of Canada in 1967. However, no awards of the medal were made and subsequently it was replaced by a series of three decorations.

The Order of Canada, which originally provided for two levels of membership, has had three categories since 1972: Companion (CC), Officer (OC), and Member (CM). The Order of Military Merit has three levels of membership also: Commander (CMM), Officer (OMM), and Member (MMM). The three decorations for bravery are: the Cross of Valour (CV), the Star of Courage (SC), and the Medal of Bravery (MB). A member of an Order or a person receiving a decoration for bravery is entitled to place the appropriate initials after his or her name.

BIBLIOGRAPHY

Lieutenant-Governor

Forsey, E.A., "The Extension of the Life of Legislatures," *C.J.E.P.S.,* XXVI, 4, November, 1960.

Hendry, J. McL., *Memorandum of the Office of Lieutenant-Governor of a Province: Its Constitutional Character and Functions,* Ottawa, Department of Justice, 1955.

La Forest, G.V., *Disallowance and Reservation of Provincial Legislation,* Ottawa, Department of Justice, 1955.

McGregor, D.A., *They Gave Royal Assent: The Lieutenant-Governors of British Columbia,* Vancouver, Mitchell Press, 1967.

Mallory, J.R., "Disallowance and the National Interest: The Alberta Social Credit Legislation of 1937," *C.J.E.P.S.,* XIV, 3, August, 1948.

Mallory, J.R., *Social Credit and the Federal Power in Canada,* Toronto, U.T.P., 1954.

Mallory, J.R., "The Lieutenant-Governor as a Dominion Officer: The Reservation of the Three Alberta Bills in 1937," *C.J.E.P.S.,* XIV, 4, November, 1948.

Saywell, J.T., *The Office of Lieutenant-Governor,* Toronto, U.T.P., 1957.

Governor General

Batt, E., *Monck, Governor-General, 1861-68: A Biography,* Foreword by W.L. Morton, Toronto, M. & S., 1976.

Cobham, Viscount, "The Governor General's Constitutional Role," *Political Science,* XV, 2, September, 1963.

Dufferin, Lady, *My Canadian Journal, 1872-78,* ed. by G.C. Walker, Toronto, Longmans, 1969.

Forsey, E.A., *Freedom and Order: Collected Essays,* Carleton Library No. 73, Toronto, M. & S., 1974.

Franck, T., "The Governor General and the Head of State Functions," *C.B.R.,* XXXII, 10, December, 1954.

Graham, Roger, (ed.), *The King-Byng Affair, 1926: A Question of Responsible Government,* Toronto, C.C., 1967.

Hubbard, R.H., *Rideau Hall,* Ottawa, Q.P., 1967.

Kennedy, W.P.M., "The Office of Governor General of Canada," *C.B.R.*, XXXI, 9, November, 1953.

MacKinnon, Frank, *The Crown in Canada*, Calgary, Glenbow-Alberta Institute, M. & S., West, 1976.

Mallory, J.R., "Canada's Role in the Appointment of the Governor General," *C.J.E.P.S.*, XXVI, 1, February, 1960.

Mallory, J.R., "Seals and Symbols: From Substance to Form in Commonwealth Equality," *C.J.E.P.S.*, XXII, 3, August, 1956.

Mallory, J.R., "The Election and the Constitution," *Q.Q.*, LXIV, 4, Winter, 1957.

McWhinney, E., Mallory, J.R., Forsey, E.A., "Prerogative Powers of the Head of State [The Queen or Governor General]," *C.B.R.*, XXXV, 1, 2, 3, January, February, March, 1957.

Morton, W.L., "Meaning of Monarchy in Confederation," Royal Society of Canada, *Transactions*, Fourth Series, I, 1963.

Saywell, J.T., "The Crown and the Politicians: The Canadian Succession Question, 1891-1896," *Canadian Historical Review*, XXXVII, 4, December, 1956.

Stanley, G.F.G., "A Constitutional Crisis in British Columbia," *C.J.E.P.S.*, XXI, 3, August, 1955.

Willis-O'Connor, H., *Inside Government House*, Toronto, Ryerson Press, 1954.

12

THE EXECUTIVE PROCESS: CABINET, PCO, PRIME MINISTER, PMO

The contents of this chapter are almost entirely different from those in the fourth edition. They reflect what appears to be a change of interest in various elements in the executive arm of government.

When the third and fourth editions of this book were published in the 1970s, there was great interest in the instruments of central executive power — the Prime Minister's Office and the Privy Council Office — which some critics believed Prime Minister Trudeau was building up as part of his alleged "Imperial Presidency." (See Denis Smith's article in the next chapter.)

For whatever reasons, there seems to be much less interest now in both the PMO and the PCO. It may be that the public's concern with any issue is ephemeral, or that observers have accepted centralized power as a *fait accompli,* or conversely that the instruments have not turned out to be as potent and menacing as some critics feared.

The interlude of the Clark government, short-lived as it was (only nine months), probably had something to do with the change, since the new Conservative administration deliberately tried to shift power from the prime ministerial centre to an inner cabinet and seven cabinet committees.

The first article in this chapter sets the scene admirably. Richard Van Loon describes the patterns of cabinet organization in both recent Trudeau governments and in Prime Minister Clark's regime and he reviews the developments in the PMO and PCO. He also discusses the new procedures adopted for designing, controlling, and coordinating policies and managing expenditures, including "the envelope system." In the process he explains the functioning of the Department of Finance, the Treasury Board, the Ministries of State for Economic and Social Development, and the relationship between budgeting and policy priorities. It is an excellent account of current procedures which makes it possible to omit from this chapter several of the articles which appeared in the previous edition dealing with the PMO, PCO, and the Treasury Board.

Although the PMO and PCO may attract less attention than they did, the office of prime minister continues to be in the public eye. Whether or not this indicates that we have moved even further away from popular government — from bureaucracy to personalism — is a good question. In any event, the office of prime minister deserves attention. Marc Lalonde's article provides a good historical description of the position, while Prime Minister Joe Clark's *ex post facto* reflections are not only frank but revealing.

Another pair of articles tells us a good deal about the relationship between a minister and his or her senior advisors. The Honourable Flora MacDonald, speaking from the point of view of a new minister, is highly critical of the web her staff tried to weave around her. On the other hand, the Honourable Mitchell Sharp, who has had long experience as both a minister and a senior bureaucrat, takes quite the opposite view.

The final item is repeated from previous editions. It is a classic account from Sir George Foster's diary of the struggle that goes on among aspiring MPs to get into the cabinet. The fact that it describes an event which happened many years ago does not make it any less relevant for today's reader.

The following items have been omitted from this edition but may be found in the fourth edition at the pages mentioned: Gordon Robertson, "The Changing Role of the Privy Council Office," pp. 373-387; Thomas d'Aquino, "The Prime Minister's Office: Catalyst or Cabal?," pp. 394-408; Paul Fox, "Size and Cost of PMO and PCO," pp. 408-409; Kenneth G. Tilley, "Ministerial Executive Staffs," pp. 409-414; Paul Fox, "The Representative Nature of the Canadian Cabinet," pp. 414-419; and Paul Fox, "Salaries and Allowances of Federal Ministers and Parliamentary Secretaries," p. 421.

For current data on the latter subject, see Robert Fleming's article in the next chapter.

The section in the bibliography in the fourth edition on the political process and policy-making has been transferred to Chapter 15 in this edition.

CABINET ORGANIZATION, THE PMO, PCO, POLICY CONTROL AND EXPENDITURE MANAGEMENT*

R. Van Loon

• • •

Cabinet and Cabinet Committee Structures

Over the past fifteen years the cabinet has evolved from a single decision-making body to a series of committees possessing considerable autonomy within their own spheres of activity. The full cabinet still exists as an entity, although it almost disappeared during the brief span of the Progressive Conservative government in 1979-80. However the bulk of its work is now delegated to a major central committee (Priorities and Planning) and to a series of sectoral committees. In addition the Treasury Board and the closely related Government Operations Committee act as *de facto* boards of management for government while the Legislation and House Planning Committee manages all aspects of the government's legislative program.

* From an article entitled "Stop the Music: The Current Policy and Expenditure Management System in Ottawa," *Canadian Public Administration*, 24, 2, Summer, 1981, published by the Institute of Public Administration of Canada. By permission.

Figures 1, 2 and 3 illustrate the committee structures of cabinet under the Liberals prior to the 1979 election, the Progressive Conservatives in 1979-1980 and the Liberals after they were returned to government in 1980. Under the first Liberal government, the cabinet had nine standing committees, while under the Conservatives there were seven plus the inner cabinet. The second Liberal government maintained the reduced number of committees and replaced the inner cabinet with the Priorities and Planning Committee. Each committee meets regularly, usually once a week. Ministers normally are members of two or three committees, and each committee has a small permanent secretariat which is provided by the PCO and which controls the flow of committee paper work, helps to set committee agendas, writes the committee decisions, acts as the Prime Minister's antenna for that sector of the government's activity and generally facilitates the flow of information from the line departments of government and the other executive support agencies to the cabinet.

In addition to the standing committees, there are also special committees of the cabinet established from time to time to deal with specific policy problems. Some of these sit over extended periods. For example, there is a semi-permanent Labour Relations Committee, which deals with particularly serious national strikes, and there has been, since the advent of the most recent Liberal government, an Ad Hoc Committee on Western Policy.

In the Liberal cabinet between 1975 and 1979, the normal flow of cabinet business was from the sponsoring minister to the PCO secretariat to be placed on the agenda of the appropriate cabinet policy committee. Discussion there produced a "committee recommendation" which then went to Treasury Board, acting as the budgetary watchdog, for consideration of the financial and personnel implications. The Treasury Board recommendation together with the committee recommendation then went to the full cabinet. More often than not recommendations of the policy committees were confirmed, although major discussions could take place and policy committee recommendations could be overturned, particularly when Treasury Board and the policy committee differed.

The structure and operations of cabinet were changed by the Progressive Conservative government in May of 1979. The major structural innovations were the creation of an inner cabinet, the formalization and expansion of the Ministry of State for Economic Development to support the Board of Economic Ministers and the creation of a Ministry for Social Development to support the Social and Native Affairs Committee, while the major innovation in process was the creation of what came to be called the envelope system of financial and policy management. The Ministries of State and the envelope system will be described in more detail below. However, the normal flow of cabinet business under this system was from the sponsoring ministry to a committee of all the deputy ministers in a particular sector. Following discussion there the item might be aborted but more likely was forwarded to the appropriate cabinet committee by the sponsoring minister. Following cabinet committee discussion, a decision, again called a "Committee Recommendation," was prepared and forwarded to inner cabinet. There the CR's were nearly always approved, for a very important feature of the system was the delegation of real decision-making authority to the committees of cabinet. The full cabinet seldom met and at the time of the

FIGURE 1   THE COMMITTEE STRUCTURE OF THE CABINET

(1978 Liberal Version)

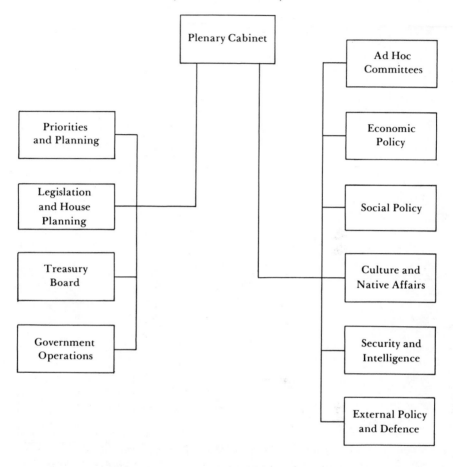

Conservative government's defeat seemed to be on the way to disappearance.

The reincarnated Liberal government of 1980 retained the basic outlines of this structure and process, although the Priorities and Planning Committee was substituted for the inner cabinet and meetings of full cabinet were reinstated.

Both the Conservative inner cabinet and the Liberal Committee on Priorities and Planning have had memberships of about twelve ministers. The Prime Minister acts as chairman and the Minister of Finance, the President of the Treasury Board and the chairmen of the standing committees are members. Other members may be chosen on any basis and although it is too early to divine any precedents, the current practice seems to be to select them so as to provide as much regional representation as possible. These structures have performed several major roles. First, they define the overall priorities of government. Secondly, they allocate budgets to the standing

FIGURE 2   THE COMMITTEE STRUCTURE OF THE CABINET

(1981 Liberal Version)

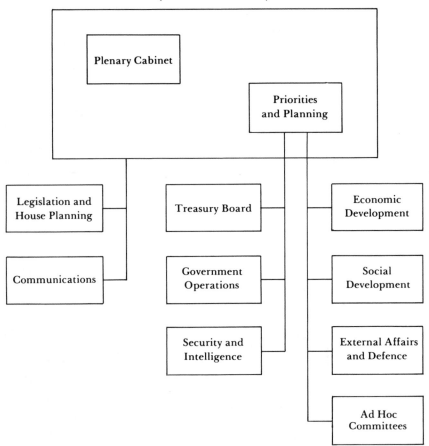

committees by creating the fiscal framework. Thirdly, they review all committee decisions although this frequently amounts simply to ratification.
Fourthly, they deal directly with particularly big or important issues or
those which cut across the lines of responsibility of other committees. Fifth-
ly, they deal with the general issues of federal-provincial relations. Sixthly,
they define the "rules of the game," including the nature of the budgetary
cycle and the very existence of other committees and their supporting
paraphernalia. And finally, they have had some funds and program responsibilities of their own such as equalization payments to the provinces.

In both the Liberal and Conservative versions of this system, the normal
input to a cabinet committee has been a 'memorandum to Cabinet' backed
up by a more detailed 'Discussion Paper.' The memoranda are not made
public but the discussion papers, which contain much of the same information as that in the memoranda, often amplified with considerable technical
detail but without the political considerations and without specific recom-

FIGURE 3   THE COMMITTEE STRUCTURE OF THE CABINET

(1979 Progressive Conservative Version)

```
                    ┌─────────────────────┐
                    │   Plenary Cabinet   │
                    │                     │
                    └─────────────────────┘
```

| Legislation and | | Ad Hoc Committees |
| House Planning | | on Special Issues |

| Security and | | Social and |
| Intelligence | | Native Affairs |

| Economy in | Inner Cabinet | Federal-Provincial |
| Government | | Relations |

| Foreign Affairs | Economic | Treasury |
| and Defence | Development | Board |

mendations, will be public documents under the new Freedom of Information legislation. By far the largest number of these documents are written within the bureaucracy. They may express demands arising within the bureaucracy (for example, when officials ask for change in departmental terms of reference or programs), they may result from clientele demands which have been communicated through bureaucratic channels, or they may represent departmental responses to ministerial requests generated by political communication channels such as caucus, the party organization or the minister's own contacts. However, whatever their basic source, the memoranda are frequently examined closely by ministers, usually starting at the stage of fairly early drafts. Thus the individual minister can have very considerable control over the content of the document, within the real world constraints of his or her time and the limitations on an individual minister's ability to form independent judgments on what are often complex technical issues. The vast majority of memoranda are forwarded by ministers of line departments but memoranda may be forwarded by Ministers of State when the subject is a major policy change cutting across the interests of several departments within the sector, when a major statement of priorities is required, when committee procedures are at issue, or when financial concerns dealing with a whole sector require cabinet committee consideration.

It is important, in considering this taxonomy, to differentiate between partisan considerations and political considerations. The Prime Minister's Office, ministerial staffs, the party structures and the government caucus provide support to ministers because those ministers are of a particular partisan stripe. If the government changes, these people lose their jobs. Indeed, even if the incumbent of a position changes without a change of government, partisan advisors are likely to find themselves jobless. Their support

Figure 4   Executive Support Agencies for Priority Determination
(Classified according to their principal roles)

Partisan Political Advisors	— Prime Minister's Office (PMO) — Individual Ministerial Staff
Process and Procedure Advisors	— Privy Council Office (PCO) — Federal-Provincial Relations Office — Treasury Board
Policy Design and Integration Advisors	— Ministries of State (Social Development, Economic Development) — Department of Finance — Federal-Provincial Relations Office (FPRO)
Financial Advisors	— Department of Finance — Treasury Board Secretariat — Ministries of State for Economic and Social Development — PCO, Priorities and Planning Secretariat
Ad Hoc Advisors	— Royal Commissions, Task Forces, Advisory Committees

is thus for a very particular set of people. By contrast, all other executive support agencies provide support for the government of the day because it is the government and regardless of its political complexion. When it is defeated they provide support for the next government. Being human, they have their preferences as to parties and incumbents but they will generally serve as well as they are able for, in addition to the normal paraphernalia of personal ambition and appreciation of the psychic joys of power, many — perhaps most — are motivated by a professional pride in their work and in the art and responsibility of governing.

Partisan Political Advisors: The PMO

The Prime Minister's Office is always staffed at the senior levels by close partisan advisors and particularly by people whose political, policy and in-tellectual capabilities the Prime Minister respects. The staff grew rapidly in the mid-1970s and currently numbers over one hundred. By contrast R.B. Bennett had a staff of about twelve during the 1930s while King, St. Laurent and Diefenbaker had about thirty staff members and Lester Pearson forty. However, the number of top policy advisors within the PMO has fluctuated widely and about half the staff is there to handle the vastly increased volume of prime ministerial mail.

   The uses a prime minister will make of the PMO will vary from leader to leader and even from time to time. In the early Trudeau years the PMO was avowedly the source of many major policy initiatives. Later, as an election approached followed by a minority government and another election, the PMO became much more concerned with public opinion and the government's response to that opinion. It has tended to remain that way since, with policy innovation proposals coming from other agencies.

There have, however, been important recent exceptions. In August 1978, for example, the PMO and the Prime Minister played the crucial role in producing a major series of restraint proposals. Indeed, it may be that making major policy changes in Canada requires a sudden centralization of authority of the sort which can only occur in the federal government when the Prime Minister, the PMO and a few other major actors in the system take power into their own hands, acting before the web of opposition (which can form rapidly in Ottawa) has had time to materialize.

Process Advisors: The Privy Council Office

The PMO and its non-partisan first cousin, the Privy Council Office, share office space in the immediate vicinity of Parliament Hill, space which symbolizes their role of serving the Prime Minister and, in the case of the PCO, its role of serving the cabinet committees which meet there. Since the late 1960s the role of the PCO has evolved from that of an agency almost entirely concerned with moving paper to cabinet, through an attempt to coordinate all aspects of government policy, to a position as arbiter and problem-solver for much of the machinery and process of government in Ottawa and as briefer of the Prime Minister on the activities of his government. Those latter tasks are now combined with the function of providing major logistical support for the cabinet.

The PCO contains secretariats for each cabinet committee. Normally these consist of some four to eight officers led by an Assistant Secretary to the Cabinet. There are also secretariats or directorates responsible for the machinery of government, for government communications, for legislation and the planning of the parliamentary end of government business, and for senior personnel. The whole structure is headed by Canada's highest ranking public servant, the Clerk of the Privy Council and Secretary to the Cabinet.

To understand the recent evolution of the Privy Council Office and to set our later consideration of other support agencies in context, we will have to understand the general evolution of planning processes and of the interrelationships among central agencies in Ottawa. To achieve that, we will have to go back to the years prior to 1968 when the bureaucratic establishment dominated the formulation and implementation of policy details, and a small group of senior bureaucratic mandarins played a major — some would claim a dominant — role in the process of policy choice.

The influence of the mandarins over the determination of priorities was based on a number of factors, some related to structural features of the system and others to the personal characteristics of the individuals involved. The most important of the structural factors was simply that government was smaller and less complex. There were very few 'old Ottawa hands' and it was possible for them to know each other well. When this was combined with the deputy minister's control over the flow of information within the system and with the fact that deputies normally held office over a considerably longer time than ministers and for longer periods than do current deputies, the potential for very powerful influence existed.

It is probable that the heyday of the mandarins would have passed of its own accord. As government grew more complex and the structures of government became more formal and elaborate, the number of deputies grew too large for easy personal coordination and bureaucratic power became more diffused. Moreover, informal structures of power often vanish simply because they are powerful; their power eventually makes them visible and their visibility makes them a mark for others — such as ministers and MPs — who may hold a more legitimate title to control over the system.

This all coincided with, or perhaps led to, the apparent intention of Prime Minister Trudeau when he took office to temper the influence of the senior public service by providing alternative sources of policy advice. To this end, Prime Minister Trudeau and his advisors appear to have hypothesized that the most effective counter for one bureaucratic institution is another with parallel responsibilities. The political advisory power of the mandarins was to be attenuated through the increase in size and influence of the PMO and their planning functions were to be faced with competition from a revamped PCO using a more systematic approach to the divination and implementation of political priorities.

The growth of the influence of the PCO led to the development of one of three rival planning systems which dominated the Ottawa scene in the mid-1970s. As described by Richard French in *How Ottawa Decides,* the PCO planning system, unlike its counterparts centred in the Department of Finance and the Treasury Board Secretariat, was not clearly based in any single discipline. Rather it drew eclectically from economics, law, political science, sociology, business and public administration and even philosophy. It depended on an attempt to identify broad ministerial priorities and then to use these as a context to frame all the activities of government.

We will return to a consideration of these planning systems again in our conclusions. For now the significant point is that while the PCO did have a very great influence on the policy process in the 1970s and did succeed in investing considerably more decision-making power in the hands of ministers, it eventually ran into limitations which could not easily be overcome within the ambit of its own organizational structure. In part the problems derived from a tendency by the members of departments and other central agencies to view the revamped PCO as an organization of 'upstarts' and 'outsiders.' Although it was composed of regular public service personnel, this was probably inevitable; any new agency will be viewed in that light. Nonetheless, that is a problem which is overcome by time: the larger problems were structural within the organization. While a considerable amount of system-oriented planning capacity was added to PCO, little in the way of other types of technical expertise was put in place. Thus its ability to conduct independent analyses and critiques of policy proposals emanating from departments remained limited.

The causes of these problems may well have lain in good intentions. The other central agencies of the early 1970s, the Treasury Board Secretariat and the Department of Finance, already conducted independent appraisals of most major policy proposals, albeit based upon different sets of premises than those used by PCO. The dictates of efficiency would seem to have argued against too great an expansion of another central agency even if the dictates of establishing an alternative planning system based upon political priorities might have demanded it. But whatever the reasoning, the successive heads of the PCO exhibited a definite reluctance to create another central agency 'monster' in Ottawa.

Another problem plagued the PCO planning efforts of the 1970s: planning was to be based on ministerial priorities, yet the PCO did not succeed in using the statements of priorities which it got from the cabinet. It was, it turned out, at best difficult and at worst impossible to use priority statements as a 'rational' basis for sorting out the diverse proposals emanating from departments and identifying what should be accepted and what rejected. It may be that the ephemeral nature of political priorities doomed such an effort to failure before it started, but the problems were compounded by the lack of an institutional mechanism which would force ministers to trade off one proposal against another in such a way that no matter what anyone *said,* the real priorities of government would emerge and only the more vital of proposals would be accepted. Combined with difficulties of different sorts faced by the planning systems based in Finance and Treasury Board — problems to which we will turn later — the result was a predictable dispersion of government activities and a lack of coherent strategies in fields such as industrial development or social or cultural policy. We will look at more recent attempts to solve these problems in the next section.

Policy Design and Integration Advisors

Among earlier attempts to solve problems created both by a lack of information and by the difficulty of defining priorities was the creation in the early 1970s of Ministries of State for Science and Technology and for Urban Affairs. These were to collect information and, if necessary, conduct research and they were to use the power of superior knowledge and persuasion to provide program integration. However, they had no direct control over departmental budgets, no large budgets of their own and no dedicated cabinet committee through which to report — or to block unacceptable proposals. Unfortunately, contrary to the old adage, it turned out that knowledge is not power — at least not sufficient power to move a large department or a minister set on having his or her way. At the time of this writing only one such ministry — that for Science and Technology — survives and press speculation of its imminent demise is commonplace.

The next stage in this evolution unfolded on the economic development front. By 1978 it was obvious that if Canada was to compete successfully in the world of international trade, some coherent industrial strategy was required. Consequently a Board of Economic Development Ministers was created under the chairmanship of Robert Andras, one of the most powerful cabinet ministers of the late 1970s. The board met regularly over several months but faced persistent problems because, while it discussed policy and while its deliberations were informed by a strong deputy minister and secretariat, there was still no institutional mechanism to force either the integration of policies or the trade-off of one expenditure against another.

The solution to that problem was deceptively simple: give the board (soon to be reconstituted as the Cabinet Committee on Economic Development) responsibility for control of the entire economic development budget. The possibility of the creation of sub-budgets for various policy sectors had been considered in Ottawa on and off since at least the early 1970s. However, such a change implied a significant institutional realignment and, given the rigidities inherent in all large institutions, could not be implemented until the appropriate conjunction of forces appeared. This conjunction was afforded by the arrival of the new Progressive Conservative government in 1979. Newly appointed ministers, without long-established turf to defend, were much more likely to accept a new expenditure management system with its attendant new distribution of powers than was a set of ministers long in place. We have already seen that the return of a Liberal government in March 1980 did not change the trend of this evolution except that the allocation of envelope figures was to be carried out by the reconstituted Cabinet Committee on Priorities and Planning.

The new budgetary envelopes had to be administered and, more important, cabinet committees had to be given support in the making of trade-offs necessary to stay within the limits of the budget envelopes and in ensuring the integration of policy. This job would be most difficult on the economic development and social policy scenes. Thus two new agencies in the form of Ministries of State for Economic and Social Development were created.

The ministries created as an integral part of this new process are relatively small, containing about one hundred staff members. Each engages in long-range planning functions for its sector, helps the cabinet committee to manage the forecast finances for the programs within its envelope (with the management of current year finances being supervised by the Treasury Board) and attempts to ensure policy coordination throughout its sector. Each gains its primary influence by acting as a gatekeeper in the policy and financial management systems: before proposals go to the appropriate cabinet committee they are normally widely discussed with ministry officials and considered by a committee of deputy ministers chaired by the Deputy Minister of State. The cabinet committee is provided with written advice on the basis of these deliberations and in addition the ministry briefs the chairman of the cabinet committee and can use that occasion to forward any objections it may have to a proposal. Coordination and integration within the sector are to be achieved through the overview functions of these agencies and because of the fact that proposals will not normally proceed to cabinet committees before a thorough examination by the ministries. In addition, the ministries themselves may initiate proposals and may retain responsibility for coordinating 'events' such as national sectoral conferences or federal-provincial negotiations in their sector.

Overall policy integration with respect to federal-provincial concerns is the responsibility of the Federal-Provincial Relations Office (FPRO). In the late 1970s there was also a Minister of State for Federal-Provincial Relations but this post has at least temporarily vanished. The place of FPRO in the policy and fiscal management system has been less clearly defined than that of the other central agencies, for the FPRO has not performed a direct gatekeeper role, has no cabinet committee of its own and has therefore relatively little direct influence over departments. It has thus been an agency which departments and other central agencies were sometimes prone to overlook in their day-to-day activities. It has had a significant role in briefing the Prime Minister on the federal-provincial relations aspects of issues and more recently it has performed a major role in the constitutional discussions but the nature of its mandate has set it somewhat apart from other central agencies. In particular the majority of its staff will naturally attempt to improve relations between the federal government and provinces whereas most other departments and agencies, intent upon achieving some set of program goals will, at best, consider federal-provincial relations as a secondary issue and at worst will simply view provinces as an impediment.

Financial Advisors

Figure 4 shows the Department of Finance, the Treasury Board and the Ministries of State for Economic and Social Development both as policy design and integration advisors and as financial advisors. It is in the latter role that Treasury Board and Finance are pre-eminent, but the increasing integration of financial management and policy coordination means that Finance also has important policy integration functions while the Ministries of State have important financial allocation functions.

The Treasury Board is a statutory committee of cabinet. The Board itself is composed of the President of the Treasury Board who is its chairman and is also the minister in charge of the Secretariat, the Minister of Finance (*ex officio*) and five other ministers. The Financial Administration Act, which is the legislation governing the expenditure process, delegates to Treasury Board responsibility as the overseer of the budgetary process. In support of this role Treasury Board Secretariat keeps track of current and projected expenditures within envelopes according to a common set of rules and advises the Priorities and Planning Committee on envelope requirements from year to year, while the office of the Comptroller General advises the Treasury Board with respect to program evaluation and several aspects of administrative policy. The Treasury Board is coming to function more and more as the Board of Management for the government, having responsibility for labour relations, for many aspects of personnel policy, for 'person-year' allocations to departments and for administrative and financial policy. The net result of all this is to make the Treasury Board and its large Secretariat, totalling nearly eight hundred people, highly influential in both financial management and overall management of the public service.

The Department of Finance retains primary responsibility for advising the government on economic policy in general, for many of the transfer payments to the provinces and for the effect of government policies on the economy. It is the primary advisor to the Committee on Planning and Priorities when expenditure allocations are made for the various policy envelopes. Finally, it is responsible for the raising of revenues. This gives it authority over all aspects of the taxation system, including those devices intended to provide financial inducements to people and corporations to behave in certain ways — the so-called tax expenditures. In this area it presumably shares responsibility for the policy aspects of tax expenditures with the cabinet committees directly responsible for policy in these areas, but the rules of this aspect of the system are still unclear.

The Priorities and Planning Secretariat may also be listed as a broadbrush financial advisor, since it plays a major role in advising the Prime Minister when allocations are to be made among envelopes at the time the fiscal framework is established and since it writes the decisions of the Priorities and Planning Committee and hence of the government in this as well as in other respects.

Coordinating the Coordinators

With so many agencies having a role in the coordination and integration of policy, who coordinates the coordinators? In major part this is achieved through the Priorities and Planning Committee of Cabinet where all of the ministerial heads of the integrating agencies sit and where the financial envelopes are established. In this area the role of the Priorities and Planning Secretariat of the PCO is particularly important. It briefs the Prime Minister on all major issues coming before 'his' cabinet committee and since it is there that intractable coordination problems are dealt with, the role of advising the Prime Minister in this respect is obviously crucial to the coordination of the whole system.

Direct formal responsibility for this coordination rests with the Prime Minister but in fact the bulk of the coordination is conducted by the Clerk of the Privy Council; the Priorities and Planning Secretariat reports to him and he controls virtually all bureaucratic access to the Prime Minister and hence to the ultimate source of resolution of coordination problems. In fulfilling this coordination function, the Clerk currently works with an informal committee of senior deputy ministers normally comprising the Secretary to the Cabinet, the Deputy Minister of Finance, the Secretaries of the Treasury Board and of the Ministries of State for Economic and Social Development, the Secretary to the Cabinet for Federal-Provincial Relations and the Under Secretary of External Affairs, with two or three other very senior Privy Council officials normally in attendance.

The role of this senior coordinating committee has evolved from a series of other committees of deputy ministers which went by names such as the Committee of Economic Deputies and DM-10. One of these still exists and has fulfilled several different roles over the last decade. That is the Committee on Senior Officers (COSO). COSO was originally formed to advise the Clerk of the Privy Council and Cabinet Secretary on the evaluation and appointment of deputy ministers and other top officials. It has performed this service continually over the last several years but the current secretary, Michael Pitfield, has also from time to time used COSO to try out new policy ideas and to attempt to achieve better policy integration. More recently COSO has been returned to its original role under the chairmanship of the Associate Secretary to the Cabinet, with the coordinating activities being taken over by the coordinating committee described above.

Handling Policy Proposals

Perhaps one way of understanding the processes which involve this plethora of agencies is to consider the questions which might be asked before a major proposal could become a policy. Initially, an assessment of the amount of demand for the proposal is required. Alternately, since many proposals are generated largely from within the bureaucracy, an assessment of the amount of support for the policy may be what is called for at this stage. This assessment would be carried out partly by the departments and ministers most directly involved and partly by the appropriate Ministry of State.

Some of the most important questions involving a major policy decision concern the financial feasibility and the macro-economic effects of such a step. This financial assessment constitutes another early step in the assessment of a policy proposal. Information from economic forecasts, projections of government revenues and consequent allocations of funds to expenditure envelopes will thus become a vital part of the data required to make any major priority decision, and here the Department of Finance becomes pre-eminent. If Finance is forecasting declining government revenues, then the amount of new money allocated to each sector of government expenditures will be small and, barring the availability of some large expenditure reductions, a cabinet committee will be unable to take on a big new program however desirable it may otherwise be. Similarly, if the Department of Finance opines that a program will create critical economic problems, the cabinet may well be reluctant to move it forward. Since cabinet ministers are not normally economists and since they are too busy to be able to engage in extensive searches for alternative information, they are rather at the mercy of the Department of Finance when dealing with such issues, although countervailing opinions may be advanced by other agencies or by individual departments and a healthy skepticism about economic projections prevails.

Closely connected to the foregoing questions are the problems of how such a program could be fitted in with current government activity in other fields and whether there are sufficient funds available in an expenditure envelope to finance the program. The Ministries of State for Social and Economic Development, working within their respective budgetary envelopes for the next several fiscal years, must determine whether the potential increase in expenditure can be covered or whether the adoption of a new policy will necessitate the deletion of some current programs or an appeal to Priorities and Planning for additional money for the envelope. The Ministry of State must also consider the fit of the proposed program with ongoing programs in its policy area, advise ministers on the fit of the proposal with overall governmental priorities and apprise them of any administrative problems it sees in the proposal. In this last role it will be advised by Treasury Board Secretariat which also retains the right to advise cabinet independently through its minister if it feels its management board concerns have not been adequately dealt with. The ministries may also originate program proposals themselves in order to replace older programs or where a policy cuts across the interests of several departments.

Once the financial and administrative questions have been dealt with, the issue goes to cabinet committee, then to Priorities and Planning and occasionally to the full cabinet. There, in addition to the more technical concerns, ministers will ask the political questions which return full circle to an assessment of the amount of demand for the policy and of its political saleability. Thus, although bureaucratic rationality informs the consideration of the 'middle' questions in the policy process, political rationality has the initial and the final say.

The Budgetary Cycle

We have indicated that the trend of the last several years has been to create a more direct relationship between budgetary process and the determination of policy priorities, hence the budgetary cycle is the final part of the policy process which requires our consideration.

Until the late 1970s, the expenditure budgetary process looked only eighteen months ahead and was used much more as an administrative tool than as an instrument to bring financial considerations into priority determination. The result was a stop-start system of policy-making; if revenues were rising, almost any policy proposed would be accepted by cabinet but when restraint hit, as it did periodically, no new policies would be accepted at all and adjustments could not easily be made. In an attempt to smooth out this situation, more recent attempts have been made to lengthen the budgetary cycle to a multi-year process and to place priority determination within this cycle, while still leaving sufficient flexibility to deal with emergency situations as they arise.

The cycle begins with the preparation by the Department of Finance of four-year projections of economic conditions, the fiscal stance required in the light of these conditions, and consequent projections of government revenues, and with the parallel preparation of expenditure forecasts by Finance and the Treasury Board Secretariat in consultation with the Ministries of State. On the basis of these projections of the overall pie available and of the requirements to finance ongoing commitments, the Priorities and Planning Committee of Cabinet allocates revenues to the various envelopes for the next four years. The making of economic projections is, of course, a risky business at best, while expenditure projections — which themselves depend on economic projections — are equally difficult to make with any accuracy. Nonetheless, if the basic objective is to determine relative priorities and to make them more explicit by assigning dollar values to them, the exercise can still be effective as long as common assumptions are adhered to throughout the system. Moreover the revenue and expenditure forecasts are updated as time passes and the final budgetary assessments for a fiscal year, made near the start of that year, can be quite accurate.

Following the initial envelope allocations, the Ministries of State and the Treasury Board Secretariat compare the funds available to projected expenditures in order to determine how much financial elbow room the sector has for new programs over the next four years or, alternately, how much is required in the way of reduction in current programs in order to provide any such room. Given the rules introduced by the envelope management systems and the commitment to rates of government expenditure growth lower than GNP increases, if the government is to implement any new programs, it must generally create a pool of money to do so (called a policy reserve) by reducing other programs.

The bulk of expenditures — normally over 90 per cent — remains part of the 'A-budget' or 'A-base.' Perhaps the greatest problem facing this or any other attempt to allow governments to change their priorities is the sanctity of that base and the consequent difficulty in creating the policy reserve. However, if we assume that some reserves can be created — as indeed they were in both the Social and Economic policy envelopes during the first year of application of the envelope system by a combination of fairly major program changes, the cutting of some small programs and the reduction of some administrative overhead — then the problem becomes one of sorting out which new proposals will be accepted. At this point the policy process described above comes into play.

The four-year expenditure cycle contains within it a more sharply focused twenty-four-month cycle. Approximately twelve months before the start of a fiscal year the Secretary of the Treasury Board sends a call letter to all departments and agencies asking them to prepare concrete program forecasts accompanied by strategic overviews for the ministries of State for the forthcoming fiscal year. The Minister of State responsible for the envelope supplements the call letter with one of his own specifying the types of assumptions to be used in preparing the strategic overviews. That overview ideally specifies all the forces likely to impinge on departmental expenditures in the twelve to twenty-four-month period for which the program forecast is to be valid. The forecast itself suggests what expenditures departments think will be necessary to cover their ongoing activities during the next fiscal year. A process of bargaining and negotiation ensues among Treasury Board, interested in keeping overall expenditures down, the Ministries of State, interested in keeping expenditures within envelope limits while providing some extra reallocations for the policy reserve, and operating departments, interested in keeping up expenditure levels for their activities and in maintaining maximum amounts of discretionary funds in their own budgets. The bargaining goes through numerous iterations, and to it is added the selection of new policies up to a limit defined by envelope reserves for the approaching fiscal year. The result of all of this is the completion, by the end of December preceding the April 1 start of the next fiscal year, of the Main Estimates. These, in the form of the Blue Book, the size of a metropolitan telephone book, are tabled in the House of Commons early in the new calendar year, are considered in parliamentary committees and passed, usually unchanged, in the form of expenditure votes. These constitute authority for Treasury Board to disburse the funds to departments for expenditure.

In practice this is a very complex process and it is accompanied by procedures for supplementary estimates and for the audit and evaluation of expenditures. It is further complicated by the fact that the whole system is properly described as a rolling cycle. As the Main Estimates are being tabled, the four-year revenue and expenditure projections are being rolled forward one more year, the intermediate years updated, new program forecasts are being prepared, new B-budget reserves created and new policy selections made. Since new policies should be selected in the early stages of the program forecast or program review exercise, the possibility of making adjustments becomes more and more difficult as the time for the tabling of Main Estimates approaches. In order to deal with this rigidity, cabinet committees maintain a reserve fund which can be allocated in emergencies and there is also a Treasury Board operating reserve which can be used to cover cost increases in statutory programs. The whole has been further complicated by inevitable birth pains, not least of which has been the difficulty in making new expenditure decisions early enough to be dealt with as part of estimates.

The image which emerges from this is one of an expenditure management system in a state of considerable flux as governments attempt to grapple with the problem of maintaining enough flexibility to permit the selection of new policies in an era when social and financial pressures appear to preclude any substantial increase in revenues and expenditures. The objectives of Canadian governments — and indeed of governments throughout the Western world — have been quite consistent in this regard since at least the early 1970s, and the historical threads of the attempt to integrate better expenditure management and policy selection processes can be traced back to the 1920s. Whether the 1980 model will succeed where its predecessors have not remains to be seen but since it is unlikely that any system can be wholly satisfactory, an article similar to this in 1990 will probably outline a process different in details but similar in intent and basic outline.

Overview: Summary and Conclusions

The late 1960s saw the sunset of the mandarin system in Ottawa. The mandarin as prime minister, Lester Pearson, had come and gone and the last of C.D. Howe's boys were beginning to fade from the Ottawa scene. The growth of government was creating a system too complex to be managed over lunch at the Rideau Club or from the spacious verandas of the Gatineau Fish and Game Club. If the mandarinate was vanishing, an alternate planning system would be required to take its place. What would fill the vacuum?

In a period characterized by a burgeoning belief in the potential of rational policy analysis and in a world characterized by the division of social science into several disparate ways of viewing the world, it was natural that the vacuum left by the departing mandarins should elicit competition among several alternate systems for the rational planning of government activities. In *How Ottawa Decides,* Richard French defined the three principal policy planning systems which competed in Ottawa in the 1970s.

The oldest was based upon macroeconomics and was centred — one might say it dwelt almost exclusively — in the Department of Finance. Its early apostles were Keynesians, but by the mid 1970s its acolytes were coming increasingly to doubt the efficacy of Keynesian prescription and were moving, hesitantly, towards monetarism. According to French, the combination of their doubts and of a certain aloofness born of the fact that for many years theirs had been the pre-eminent and perhaps the only planning system in town, led the Department of Finance to withdraw to a significant degree from the scrum created by the presence of other planning systems and a proliferating array of planning branches in line departments. Although it has now clearly re-entered the fray, the Finance planning system is the least changed as we move into the 1980s. In spite of continuing doubts about the efficacy for purposes of economic management of the macroeconomics on which it is based, it has tended to maintain its independent status. It is now integrated into the policy and expenditure management process in the ways we have described above but is still clearly identifiable as an independent entity.

The alternate systems were centred in the PCO and in the Planning Branch of Treasury Board. The latter system was based on microeconomics, its watchword was evaluation and its high priest was Douglas Hartle. Its precepts could be stated fairly simply: to make planning more rational it was necessary to evaluate in detail the efficiency and the effectiveness of programs and then to feed the results back to policy-makers who would, when apprised of this rational input, make the 'right' policy choices on the basis of this information. Reams of material has been produced on the difficulties encountered by microeconomic and evaluation-based planning processes. Indeed, a significant quantity of that material has been produced by Hartle himself who quickly grew disenchanted with the potential for introducing the particular definition of rationality he had espoused into political decision-making unless the rules of the game and the incentives and behaviour patterns of politicians and bureaucrats could be drastically altered. Suffice it to say here that the Planning Branch planning system never took hold in Ottawa, nor even managed to dominate its own agency, the Treasury Board. Thus, although some excellent technical work was done by its evaluators and some very interesting findings emerged, the high tide of the Planning Branch system ebbed quickly. The Planning Branch itself disappeared in an austerity move in 1978 and the evaluation function was shifted to the Office of the Comptroller General.

We have already made the acquaintance of the third planning system of the 1970s, based primarily in the Privy Council Office. Its origins, disciplinary underpinnings and leadership were more diffuse than the other two systems and its identity is neither so clear-cut nor so simple to trace. More than anyone else, its leadership is associated with Michael Pitfield; but it was instigated to a considerable degree by Prime Minister Trudeau and it has had several other major proponents. Its intellectual roots, as we noted earlier, were eclectic. Since it grew up in the PCO its source of authority was the cabinet and Prime Minister and its strength derived from its ability to claim the correct interpretation of the words of the ministers and, particularly, the Prime Minister. In a cabinet-centred political system, that is a powerful weapon and in spite of some significant problems it grew to be the dominant planning system of the 1970s in Ottawa.

There is little doubt that it is a variant of the older PCO planning system, informed by information generated within the Finance system, which holds sway in Ottawa in the early 1980s. The central body in this system is the Priorities and Planning Committee of Cabinet which allocates amounts of money to the various expenditure envelopes and which approves decisions made by the envelope subcommittees. It is significant that this is the only standing committee of cabinet which is regularly chaired by the Prime Minister and it is there that many of the major dramas are played out.

We have seen that Priorities and Planning is informed in its deliberations, through a small secretariat headed by the Clerk of the Privy Council, by the economic projections of Finance, the expenditure projections and management precepts of Treasury Board and by the priority statements and working plans of the envelope committees. Coordination of the bureaucracy occurs through the coordinating committee, the sectoral deputy ministers' committees and the Treasury Board management system. The major procedural change from the mid-1970s has been the concentration of control over expenditures within the cabinet policy committees in the envelope system of management, while the major institutional change has been the creation of Ministries of State to support the cabinet policy committees in this policy/budgetary control process.

The policy process now appears to be more decentralized within the cabinet with a major devolution of responsibility to the policy committees. However, it is also probably more centralized towards the cabinet/central agency nexus as a whole, since the pooling of resources in envelope reserves means that individual departments now have less control over expenditure reallocations. Ministers have gained in collective responsibility what they may have lost in individual authority as the titular heads of departments, so that it is possible that the actual portfolio held by a minister will, in time, become a less reliable index of influence than it has been.

Whether the 1980 model of the planning process will work better than its predecessors remains to be seen. Ministers thrive on individual recognition and collective responsibility may sit less happily on the shoulders of the most powerful among them than the visibility and control over resources which has hitherto come from heading an important department. Furthermore, the departments themselves are large and powerful institutions with their own clienteles and with considerable ability to frustrate any planning system should they choose to do so. In the end the politics of the policy and planning process in Ottawa are really a kind of democracy among institutions and coercion is not a particular viable weapon within that system. Indeed, about all that can be predicted with certainty is that no planning and expenditure management process is forever.

THE PRIME MINISTER*

Marc Lalonde

History of the Office

In analyzing the role and function of the prime minister, one must be suspicious of a text book approach. A purely constitutional description of his office would reveal that it has changed little during the past century in

* Adapted by the editor from an article by Marc Lalonde, former Principal Secretary to the Prime Minister, which appeared under the title "The Changing Role of the Prime Minister's Office" in Canadian Public Administration, 14, 4, Winter, 1971, published by the Institute of Public Administration of Canada. By permission.

Canada. A constitutional analysis, however, would be subject to severe limitations. It would inevitably ignore the "pith and substance" of his office which can only be revealed by considering the daily discharge of his responsibilities. In the past decade we have seen a multi-dimensional growth of the demands made on the prime minister in all the roles that he is called upon to fulfil. I do not believe that new constitutional powers have been granted to or assumed by the contemporary prime minister. What has happened instead is that greater demands for his accountability and participation made by ministers, members of parliament, public administrators, the press, pressure groups and the public in general have required the Canadian prime minister fully to assume the powers that he has always had under the constitution.

For some time, many concerned Canadians have been wondering whether the Canadian Parliamentary system is evolving into a presidential system. When asked about this, it is only half jokingly that I usually answer by asking the question, "Why should the Canadian prime minister, who occupies one of the most powerful elected offices in the world, seek to implement a congressional style of government and accept in so doing a reduction of his powers?"

Within the political framework of the British North America Act of 1867 and following British practice, the prime minister is recognized as the chief minister of a committee known as "the cabinet." The cabinet in turn is part of the Privy Council established under section 11 of the British North America Act. Considering the extensive power exercised by the prime minister and the cabinet, it is rather remarkable that the written constitution nowhere mentions the office of prime minister nor specifically the institution of cabinet. Though power is not explicitly vested in the prime minister and cabinet by the law, they exercise it formally through some other body in accordance with the custom of the constitution. The vital aspects of prime ministerial and cabinet power rest, therefore, on constitutional conventions.

Some idea of the basis for the pre-eminent position of the prime minister can be gleaned from an official statement of his functions. . . .

The most recent minute of Council on this subject is P.C. 3374 of October 25, 1935, which reads as follows:

1. A Meeting of a Committee of the Privy Council is at the call of the Prime Minister and, in his absence, of that of the senior Privy Councillor, if the President of the Council be absent;
2. A quorum of the Council being four, no submission, for approval to the Governor General, can be made with a less number than the quorum;
3. A Minister cannot make recommendations to Council affecting the discipline of the Department of another Minister;
4. The following recommendations are the special prerogative of the Prime Minister:
Dissolution and Convocation of Parliament:
Appointment of
   Privy Councillors;
   Cabinet Ministers;
   Lieutenant-Governors; (including leave of absence to same);
   Provincial Administrators;

Speaker of the Senate;
Chief Justices of all Courts;
Senators;
Sub-Committees of Council;
Treasury Board;
Committee of Internal Economy, House of Commons;
Deputy Heads of Departments;
Librarians of Parliament;
Crown Appointments in both Houses of Parliament;
Governor General's Secretary's Staff;
Recommendations in any Department. . . .

While this official statement is useful, it is far from complete. To gain a fuller understanding of the extent of the prime minister's power, it is necessary to examine the fundamental political reality upon which his position rests. He is chosen by a popular convention of a major party; he ordinarily commands substantial and deeply rooted support amongst the electorate; he is the directing force in both cabinet and Parliament; he has a key role in the Commons, answers many questions there, and takes the lead in explaining and defending his government's policies and activities; he must be consulted on important decisions by all cabinet ministers; to a large extent he prescribes the functions of his colleagues and he can, if necessary, advise the Governor General to dismiss a minister; he recommends most important appointments to the cabinet; he has a special responsibility for external affairs; and he has the important prerogative of advising the Governor General when Parliament should be dissolved.

The powers of the prime minister are, therefore, potentially enormous. How they are wielded, however, depends in large measure on his personality and on his interpretation of his leadership role. In the words of Lord Oxford and Asquith, ''The office is what its holder chooses and is able to make of it.''

Prime Minister and Parliament

. . . The traditional duties of the prime minister in the House of Commons have changed very little in the past century. When in the House of Commons, he is inevitably the chief spokesman for the Chamber. He is the dominant figure, and his position and responsibilities are recognized by the House as a whole. . . .

Among those traditional duties is participation in Question Period, undoubtedly one of the institutions most cherished by the Members of the House. . . . Whereas cabinet ministers are frequently called upon to answer questions that touch their respective departments, the prime minister, on the other hand, is expected to answer questions which involve general issues or the interrelationships of the various departments. Attendance by ministers during question period has changed with the introduction in 1968 of the rota system. This innovation frees ministers from attendance in the House for two days of each week, but it also ensures the representation of each government department by its ministers or his parliamentary secretary three days out of five. As for the prime minister, he attends question period on a daily basis and when necessary replies on behalf of his absent ministers.

A vitally important aspect of the prime minister's parliamentary responsibilities concerns his relationship with the government caucus. Every Wednesday morning, unless he is out of Ottawa, he meets with the members of the caucus to hear their questions and opinions and to offer answers and guidance in reply. This weekly meeting with caucus is by no means the only contact between the prime minister and Liberal Members. On the occasion of his daily presence in the House, they have another opportunity to raise various questions with him. . . .

Finally, the prime minister, like all other Members, represents a particular electoral riding and, as such, he has a direct responsibility to his constituents. . . .

Prime Minister and Cabinet

. . . For a time it was popular to refer to the prime minister as *primus inter pares* or as *inter stellas luna minores*. Both interpretations do not do justice to his office. He cannot be first among equals because in a political sense no individual is his equal. It would be wrong, however, to assume that the prime minister stands in a position of unquestionable supremacy over his colleagues in the cabinet. Unlike the President of the United States, the prime minister is not in a position of strength superior to that of the total cabinet. Members of the Canadian cabinet are responsible to the House of Commons; and while they acknowledge the leadership of the prime minister, and will in fact bow to his decisions, they have important political and administrative responsibilities which they must discharge independently of the prime minister. It must also be remembered that ministers who are dissatisfied with their leader retain the weapon of resignation — they can resign of their own free will, and if enough ministers were to resign, a prime minister would face serious difficulties.

One of the most important factors distinguishing the prime minister from his cabinet colleagues is the manner in which he obtains and relinquishes his office. He is requested by the Governor General to form a government, while he himself issues the invitation to all other members. Whenever the prime minister vacates his office, the act normally carries with it the resignation of all those who compose the government; but whenever any other member leaves, the tenure of the remainder is undisturbed.

The powers of the prime minister in cabinet derive from his position as chairman. He controls the agenda and is the principal guiding force in helping the cabinet arrive at decisions. He is both co-ordinator and arbitrator of the executive decision-making process; he is concerned with the total activity of the government and is principally responsible for its policies, style and thrust; he oversees the operation of his colleagues' departments and ensures that harmonious relations exist between his ministers. Supported by the doctrine of cabinet solidarity, his task is to crystallize the collective point of view and to infuse into cabinet decision-making a sense of direction, coherence, efficacy and unity.

The relationship of the prime minister to the various committees of cabinet is most important. He is responsible for appointing members to the standing committees. He also chairs . . . Priorities and Planning. . . . Functioning at the level of Federal-Provincial Conferences, a growing number of which involve him directly, he acts as convenor and chairman, negotiator and arbitrator. The constitutional review process in particular has demanded considerable amounts of the prime minister's time and energy. As chairman of the Priorities and Planning Committee, he concerns himself with the setting of government priorities, planning for the orderly development of integrated policy, and evaluating ongoing programs.

Any discussion of the prime minister's executive duties should include some mention of his control over the power of appointment. . . . The great majority of public servants are now appointed by the Public Service Commission. Nonetheless, with the growth in the number of governmental departments and agencies, a large number of senior appointments are still made by Order-in-Council. Approximately four hundred appointments are made every year by cabinet. While the initiative for recommendations to cabinet for a large number of them lies with individual ministers, the prime minister must ensure that such recommendations carry the assent of his colleagues and have been the subject of adequate investigation. In addition, many appointments [250] are presented to cabinet upon the initiative of the prime minister himself. . . .

Some appointments are a mere formality, others require the prime minister's involvement in numerous hours of consultations and discussions. For instance, a cabinet shuffle is likely to involve individual discussions with most members of the cabinet, or appointments of deputy ministers might require consultations with ministers concerned as well as with senior officials. . . .

Prime Minister and the Party

The prime minister is the leader of his party and is ultimately responsible for its direction. To remain in office he must be master of his party and enjoy its confidence and support. In this respect, the relationship of prime minister and his party has changed little in the last century. What has changed, however, is the role of the party itself as a political instrument and as a vehicle of citizen involvement. Parties are being subjected to a technocratic and professional transformation. More important citizens are seeking greater involvement in influencing party decisions. . . .

The democratization of the Liberal party has affected the position of the prime minister in some additional ways. The constitution of the party now requires the leader formally to "account" to the membership of the party at its biennial National Policy Convention and to submit to a "leadership convention ballot" at the first national meeting of the party following a general election. . . .

A new and important way of ensuring some kind of accountability to the Liberal party and ensuring that it receives the information and support it requires, is the special meetings of cabinet ministers with party officials sometimes referred to as "political cabinet." These meetings take place about every two months and are organized by the P.M.O. In addition to the ministers, the chairman of the parliamentary caucus and the president of the Liberal party attend. The purpose of these meetings is to review the current political situation, to set overall political goals and priorities and to outline political strategy.

An additional method of maintaining liaison between the prime minister and the cabinet, on the one hand, and the extra-parliamentary party, on the other hand, is the various Provincial Advisory Groups sometimes referred to as "troikas." Each Advisory Group is composed of a minister from that province, the chairman of the federal Liberal caucus from that province, and the chairman or representative of the Liberal party organization for that province. They meet from time to time to discuss a variety of subjects ranging from the consideration of government decisions affecting the region to the evaluation of political strategy. . . .

Prime Minister and the Public

. . . Changes in the nature of the body politic have had a profound effect upon relations between the public and the executive, and in particular between the public and the prime minister. The present prime minister came to office at a time when the movement for "direct" or "populist" democracy was gaining momentum across the country. . . .

This new style of politics has required heads of government to make themselves more available to more and more people. Direct communication between the public and the prime minister has required him to devote an increasing amount of time to the media and to travel outside of Ottawa. . . .

But a voice on radio, a TV image or a press report, however faithful, do not sufficiently satisfy the public's desire for communication. Canadian voters also wish face-to-face contact with their political leaders, and more particularly with the prime minister.

One interesting indication of the public's demand on the prime minister's time can be seen from the number of invitations which he receives. In the twelve month period following July 1, 1970, the prime minister received over 3,000 invitations to attend specific functions. In addition he receives, every week, a number of requests from special interest groups desirous of presenting him with their briefs. . . .

It is interesting to note some specific examples of how the prime minister's time is allocated. A recent staff review revealed that his time in Ottawa is divided roughly between 11 or 12 hours per week of cabinet activities, including meetings with individual ministers and cabinet committees; approximately 11 hours of House of Commons activities, including caucus; and approximately 20 hours of miscellaneous activities, including working lunches, meetings with officials, special conferences, meetings with private organizations and citizens. This analysis does not, of course, reveal the full extent of the prime minister's time commitments. To this must be added frequent week-end travel outside of Ottawa on official business as well as numerous hours of study and reading of documents and briefing notes for all activities in which he is involved. . . .

Conclusions

My conclusions . . . stem from my observation of the evolution and possible future development of the office of prime minister.

(i) The prime minister will continue to maintain his pre-eminent position in the government apparatus because of the continuing and pressing need for centralized planning, co-ordination and control. His pre-eminence should not compromise the authority of Parliament. So long as the prime minister remains responsible to the House of Commons, the advent of a *de facto* presidency is impossible.

(ii) The pre-eminent position of the prime minister as a national leader is likely to continue as well. Politics in democratic countries has tended to become more personalized and this phenomenon has unquestionably taken root in Canada.

(iii) The prime minister's contacts with the public, will continue to expand because of the changing nature of public needs, expectations and demands. As a consequence, his symbolic, motivational and pedagogic roles will inevitably increase in importance.

(iv) The prime minister's power and influence is unlikely to emasculate the role of the cabinet or Parliament. The growing demands of the body politic have brought to all these bodies an increase in work, responsibility, power and influence.

(v) If future prime ministers are to meet their expanded responsibilities, they will have to maintain in their service a personal staff of adequate proportions. The alternatives are quite unpalatable — assumption of these functions by the administration or by the extra-parliamentary party.

A PRIME MINISTER'S VIEW OF THE OFFICE*

Joe Clark

. . . It might be useful to discuss some aspects of the Canadian Prime Ministership on the basis of my own experience and observation. I am interested both by the power of that office, which I regard as excessive and which I tried to limit, and the influence of the office — particularly the influence of the office — to encourage a legitimate sense of common cause in a country that is not only diverse but proudly and valuably diverse.

Regarding power in the office of the Prime Minister, I would like to touch for just a moment on an internal question. It has to do with the role of the so-called agencies and principally the power of the Privy Council Office in the Prime Minister's office. I came to that office determined to limit the concentrating ability of the office of the Privy Council which had become, in my judgement, far too tied to the principal interest and the personal priorities of the Prime Minister in a way that undermined the capacity

---

* An abridgement by the editor of a transcript of an address, including a question-and-answer period, given by former Prime Minister Joe Clark to the Eleventh Annual Leadership Conference sponsored by the Centre for the Study of the Presidency in Ottawa, October 19, 1980. By permission.

of the full Cabinet to carry out its responsibility as a representative of regional and other different views, different from the Prime Minister.

The institutional change we established was to give considerably more power to the internal committees of Cabinet and to ensure that the officers of the Privy Council Office, while they would maintain a responsibility for reporting to me and keeping me informed of what was going on as Prime Minister, that those officers would be responsible primarily for serving the various committees of Cabinet to whom responsibility had been devolved, whether in the field of economic development or social and culture policy or external and defence policy or government operations.

I think that was useful as far as it went, but it became clear to me that while it is essential to have the committees of Cabinet with more power at the centre, more power that reaches beyond simply the departments that ministers oversee, it is also important to a system like ours to provide the Prime Minister with the capacity to reach beyond the public service, reach beyond the opinion that comes to him through the normal course of events. . . .

Still speaking of powers, let me turn to a major area of difference between the two systems [in Canada and U.S.A.]. It has to do with the Prime Minister's relationship with Parliament. The theoretical difference is fundamental. The President is constitutionally separate from the Congress, the Prime Minister is inextricably bound to Parliament. From that theory flows an equally fundamental practical difference in the relationship. The President has to earn the support of Congress because he can't control Congress. A Prime Minister, on the other hand, controls Parliament through the very majority that gave him the office. The demand upon a President is to work with Congress through legitimate compromise; the temptation for a Prime Minister is to neglect and even ignore Parliament, except as a rubber stamp of ratification.

Parliament in our system is supposed to be a check and balance against arbitrary action by the Executive; indeed, it is the only effective check and balance, not simply through Parliament's right to concur in legislation or to approve expenditures but also in the daily accountability of the Prime Minister and his Cabinet to the Commons within our system through Question Period. When that accountability is effective, in fact, it is to the supporters of the Parliamentary system one of the most attractive features of our system. But Parliamentary accountability and control, in my judgement, have broken down in Canada to the point where for all practical purposes they do not exist. That has made the office of Prime Minister far more powerful in our country than the office of President in the United States. That prime ministerial power results in part from serious failures in Canada's Parliamentary and electoral practice and in part from the fact that a Canadian Prime Minister is also a party leader and can, when in government, have almost virtually total control of party apparatus and party authority. . . .

The Parliamentary failure, I believe, is evident to any honest student of Canadian affairs. Because the party system is so dominant and because changes of government have been both rare and brief, the consistent purpose of Parliamentary reform has been not to strengthen the Parliament but to strengthen the Executive and to weaken the Parliamentary control that is central to the theory of Parliamentary democracy.

We tried to change that as a government, and indeed I tried to do it very quickly before too many of my ministers became too accustomed to a Parliamentary system that was weighted in favour of the Executive. Our reforms which died with our government increased Parliament's control over government spending, enlarged the capacity of individual private members to introduce initiatives on which Parliament must vote and significantly increased the independent powers of Canadian Parliamentary committees.

Perhaps the most effective evidence to Americans of the present weakness of the committee system in Canadian Parliament, and indeed of the whole Canadian Parliament, is to note that if they had our system in the United States, Sam Ervin would have needed Richard Nixon's approval to launch the Watergate inquiry. Our committees cannot start inquiries into anything without the permission of the people being inquired into. That is a rather significant limitation upon the effectiveness of inquiry. Canada has no means to control and no means to correct the kinds of abuses that Watergate revealed. The only effective control of a majority Prime Minister is at a general election and general elections occur in this country on dates that the majority Prime Minister sets. That speaks to the excessive power of the Canadian Prime Minister which is limited only by the constitutional division of power. . . .

Let me turn to another aspect of the Prime Ministership, an aspect having to do with influence, having to do also with the Prime Minister's relation with the regions of the nation. . . . His regional mandate is tied directly to the electoral strength of his party in various parts of the country and if his party is strong enough in some parts of the country, he can actually run or govern against the interests of other parts of the country. Canada's national politics are divided regionally — neither Mr. Trudeau nor I enjoyed what could honestly be called a national mandate. He is without a single elected representative in three provinces and two territories — more than half the land mass of Canada. I had only two elected Members in Quebec.

That situation imposes a very special and a very personal responsibility on a Prime Minister: to ensure that regions not represented in his caucus have reason to feel that they are understood in his government. One way for the Prime Minister to do that is to bring representatives of the region directly into the government.

Following the 1979 election, I appointed both of our elected Members from Quebec to the Cabinet plus two Senators from that province and a third Senator, Bob de Cotret, who had roots in Quebec and who eventually ran there in the 1980 election. Those Ministers were not put off to the sidelines, they were assigned major portfolios like Justice, Industry, Trade and Commerce and three of them were Members of the so-called "Inner-Cabinet" which was the planning core of our government. In addition to Cabinet appointments recognizing our weakness in Francophone Canada, I also ensured that the Francophone community was well represented among the most senior advisors to the government. Mr. Trudeau has adopted that practice by naming as Ministers of State, Senators from each of the provinces in which he has no elected members.

Beyond ensuring that all regions are personally represented in the government, I think that the Prime Minister must show himself to have a personal commitment to responding to the needs and aspirations of regions in which his party is electorally weak. We tried to do that in Quebec; recently published polls suggest that didn't make us any more popular in Quebec but I believe it did make us more difficult to attack and therefore gave the national government a basis of legitimacy. That challenge of connecting the centre, where government decisions are made, to the parts, where government decisions have impact, is a central responsibility of any national head of government.

. . . Yet there is always a temptation to shut out those regional realities simply because government, like any other institution, concentrates influence where decisions are finally made, and that is usually at the centre. The centre develops a life and a perspective of its own. It was my experience that the best public servants tried to keep some real and direct contact with the country they were governing. That is also true of some influential journalists and commentators, although some others are condescending towards regional personalities and regional perspectives; most politicians, of course, have to go home to some region sometime just to keep themselves electable. Despite all that, there develops an Ottawa mentality that is dangerously insular and that is aggravated by the fact that this is virtually a one-industry city.

. . . The nation is defined on the turf of its administrators. I consider that to be one of the major institutional problems in the country and I raise it here because I believe that it is so significant in Canada now that it can be broken only by the initiative of a Prime Minister. It can be broken only by the insistence of a Prime Minister on reaching out beyond the claustrophobia of the centre. As with so much in government in our short time — we only had the time to get started — that was the reason that my inner Cabinet went to Jasper, the reason my full Cabinet went to Quebec City. I think it makes a substantial difference to meet in different rooms, to walk in different scenery, to have dinner and drinks in places where the people from Ottawa are the visitors.

To illustrate the force of the pressures against even that modest escape from the centre, I was told by my officials that I could not take my full Cabinet to Quebec City because one Minister had to remain always in Ottawa to answer the NORAD telephone just in case it rang. We were able to summon the technological capacity to patch a line through to Quebec City and for one weekend at least no one from the elected government was here in Ottawa. The country survived and the Cabinet learned a lot about the region that we knew least. That Quebec meeting was the exception, and ours, I remind you, was a government that tried to connect the centre to the country.

Those are some observations that I have frankly been looking for an opportunity to make. I would welcome questions and discussions on what we should do with the office of Prime Minister once I am back there again. . . .

Q. My question deals with the problem of isolation. George Reedy says that our President is isolated from reality and therefore makes often uninformed and disastrous decisions. I wonder if this is a problem with the Canadian Prime Minister and with the Canadian Cabinet?

A. . . . Certainly during the time that we were settling in — my party had been out of office for sixteen years and some of my ministers harboured a certain suspicion about the offices they were moving into and the public service, also there was a great deal we didn't know — no question at all, in my judgement, in retrospect we became too isolated, too cut-off from the broader country during that initial settling-in period. . . . I believe that Parliamentary reform and sensitivity to it, the restoration of some real Parliamentary control over the Executive, will go some distance to limit isolation. But I have to say that my experience has been that the simple weight of work that now confronts heads of government, and indeed confronts most ministers, is such that a significant amount of isolation is going to be inevitable so long as ministers and prime ministers and presidents are human because there are limits upon the amount of time and the amount of energy that individuals can expend. If you are as busy as those people tend to be, it is difficult to find the time to reach beyond.

Next time, I will have many more meetings with my Cabinet and its committees outside of this city, not because there is anything wrong with Ottawa except that it's where we usually are. Let me expand for a moment on the Quebec City meeting of the full Cabinet. Not only did we meet there but we made arrangements for each minister to spend the evening in the home of a citizen of Quebec — they weren't all Conservatives because there were thirty ministers and there were probably ten people at each dinner and we don't have three hundred supporters in the city of Quebec — and it gave them the opportunity to sit down in an informal session, as I say, on somebody else's turf, and to learn about a Quebec perspective, or some Quebecers' perspective. I think that is very important. In our system, too, an ability to influence ministers, at least under my government, translated into an ability to influence the Prime Minister. And to a very real degree, the capacity of ministers to break beyond isolation can break a Prime Minister beyond isolation.

Q. Could you comment upon the relationship in your government between the Prime Minister and the other ministers of your Cabinet? What was the balance between the individual leadership of the Prime Minister and the collective decision-making consideration and opposition within the Cabinet?

A. We established formally a system of internal cabinet committees which had very real authority, more authority that I believe they had had before I became Prime Minister. . . . We established a Cabinet committee on economic development under the chairmanship of the Minister of State for Economic Development and very many of the economic development issues were resolved in that committee before they came to the inner Cabinet. Thus it was with the Foreign and Defence Policy Committee, the Social and Native Affairs Committee, with the Government Operations Committee.

We had an inner Cabinet which was the central planning agency on the elected side of our government. Present there were each of the chairmen of the committees of Cabinet. When they had a major problem, something that was out of the ordinary, they would bring it to inner Cabinet; if it was urgent, they would bring it to me directly through a personal meeting.

I think this country is too big for one man to try to govern alone and so we very deliberately established a system of Cabinet committees that would take a large number of the decisions that came before the government of Canada and in practice the rest of the Cabinet accepted the capacity of that section of the Cabinet to discuss all options and come up with decisions that were sound.

Senator de Cotret who was the Chairman of the Economic Development Committee and was without question one of the most effective ministers in my government was also a Francophone. That was done with some deliberateness because I thought it essential that there be at the centre of economic policy as well as elsewhere the ability for a Francophone as well as Anglophone perspectives to prevail.

Q. . . . Do you see any likelihood or desirability of changing the electoral system in some way in favour of a modified proportional representation system?

A. I am glad that you asked that because my answer is no. I don't believe in proportional representation in a large country like this, even a modified system. . . . I think that the present electoral system ensures that the people who are sitting in the House of Commons are people who have a direct connection back to a particular constituency, a particular section of the people of Canada. That is one of the faults with having Senators in your government. I think that having Senators is better than having nobody but I think it is far better to have directly elected people who come from finite constituencies to which they have to go home and where they have to take the flak for whatever their government is doing or not doing.

● ● ●

WHO IS ON TOP? THE MINISTER OR THE MANDARINS?*

Flora MacDonald

As a new Secretary of State for External Affairs, it seemed to me that I ought to establish a foreign policy with the twin objectives that Canada should receive maximum advantage from its foreign relations and that it should play a fully responsible role in the international scene. I was convinced that this required both broad public support for foreign and aid policies and an ability, on my part, to weigh independently the advice I received from public servants.

It is natural that advice from public servants would be based on a continuation of existing policy — policy which, in large part, had had its genesis within the Department. And while it was not necessarily wrong, neither was it necessarily right. A new Minister must be able to assess, for himself or herself, where we have been and where we ought to be going.

* From an address by the Hon. Flora MacDonald to the Annual Meeting of the Canadian Political Science Association in Montreal, June 3, 1980, published in *Policy Options*, 1, 3, September-October, 1980. By permission.

This did not mean a wholesale rejection of everything that had gone on before or was currently in process; but, given my desire to develop a foreign policy attuned to the turbulent 1980s, I was determined that advice as to how we could achieve that goal should come from more than one quarter. It was, and is, natural that senior bureaucrats would have their own methods of gaining approval for the decisions they both needed and especially wanted. A new Minister, just trying to find his or her way through the labyrinth of bureaucracy, is indeed vulnerable to such practices. A new Minister in a new government which had not paced the corridors of power for some sixteen years is not only vulnerable but, indeed, almost without protection.

To reduce this dependency on bureaucratic advice and to provide a mechanism that would ensure political input into the decision-making process, a cabinet committee system was devised by the Prime Minister which aimed to establish a better equilibrium between Ministers and mandarins. While this mechanism was being set up at the cabinet level, I personally moved on two fronts to ensure that I was the recipient of independent advice I considered would be critical to my own survival as an effective Minister.

First, I determined that my personal staff would play a critical role in the evaluation of all sensitive policy issues. Although few in number, their independent and sometimes irreverent analysis of these issues was invaluable.

Secondly, with the co-operation of some interested persons from outside government circles — experts, primarily but not exclusively from the ranks of academe — I had taken the initial steps in developing what I hoped would be a mildly formalized structure to offer ongoing advice.

Without some such protective mechanisms, the Minister is indeed at the mercy of bureaucratic domination, not because of some devious manipulative plot, but simply because that is the way the system had been allowed to develop. To emphasize the point, and the concerns that flow down from it, and because others have documented it so much better than I, I will refer to the memoirs and speeches of several cabinet members who faced a similar situation.

Anthony Wedgewood Benn began a recent lecture, entitled "Manifestos and Mandarins," with the statement:

> . . . It would be a mistake to suppose that the senior ranks of the civil service are active Conservatives (or in Canada, Liberals) posing as impartial administrators. The issue is not their personal political views, nor their preferences for any particular government. The problem arises from the fact that the civil service sees itself as being above the party battle, with a political position of its own to defend.
>
> Civil service policy — and there is no other way to describe it — is an amalgam of views that have been developed over a long period of time. It draws some of its force from a deep commitment to the benefits of continuity, and a fear that adversary politics may lead to sharp reversals by incoming governments of policies devised by their predecessors, which the civil service played a great part in developing.

In a country like Canada with a long history of one-party dominance, this tendency is even more entrenched. Benn goes on to list the techniques employed by the doyens of Whitehall when ministerial views differ from their own:

By briefing Ministers — the document prepared by officials for presentation to incoming ministers after a general election comes in two versions, one for each major party.

It is a very important document that has attracted no public interest, and is presented to a Minister at the busiest moment of his life — when he enters his department and is at once bombarded by decisions to be made, the significance of which he cannot at that moment appreciate.

The brief may thus be rapidly scanned and put aside for a proper reading when the pressure eases, which it rarely does.

Thus Ministers are continually guided to reach their decisions within that framework. Those Ministers who seek to open up options beyond that framework are usually unable to get their proposals seriously considered.

By the control of information — the flow of necessary information to a Minister on a certain subject can be made selective, in other ways restricted, delayed until it is too late, or stopped altogether.

By the mobilisation of Whitehall — it is also easy for the Civil Service to stop a Minister by mobilising a whole range of internal forces against his policy.

The normal method is for officials to telephone their colleagues in other departments to report what a Minister is proposing to do; thus stimulating a flow of letters from other Ministers (drafted for them by their officials) asking to be consulted, calling for inter-departmental committees to be set up, all in the hope that an unwelcome initiative can be nipped in the bud.

Tony Benn's lecture dealt with the interface between cabinet ministers generally and their senior mandarins. Henry Kissinger in his recent book *The White House Years* deals with the particular problems which confront a Secretary of State:

> Cabinet members are soon overwhelmed by the insistent demands of running their departments. On the whole, a period in high office consumes intellectual capital; it does not create it. Most high officials leave office with the perceptions and insights with which they entered; they learn how to make decisions but not what decisions to make. And the less they know at the outset, the more dependent they are on the only source of available knowledge; the permanent officials. Unsure of their own judgement, unaware of alternatives, they have little choice except to follow the advice of the experts.
>
> This is a particular problem for a Secretary of State. He is at the head of an organization staffed by probably the ablest and most professional group of men and women in the public service. They are intelligent, competent, loyal, and hardworking. But the reverse side of their dedication is the conviction that a lifetime of service and study has given them insights that transcend the untrained and shallow-rooted views of political appointees.
>
> When there is strong leadership, their professionalism makes the foreign service an invaluable and indispensable tool of policymaking. In such circumstances the foreign service becomes a disciplined and finely honed instrument, their occasional acts of self-will generate an important, sometimes an exciting dialogue. But when there is not a strong hand at the helm, clannishness tends to overcome discipline. Desk officers become advocates for the countries they deal with and not spokesmen of national policy; assistant secretaries push almost exclusively the concerns of their areas. Officers will fight for parochial interests with tenacity and a bureaucratic skill sharpened by decades of struggling for survival. They will carry out clear-cut instructions with great loyalty, but the typical foreign service officer is not easily persuaded that an instruction with which he disagrees is really clear-cut.

Finally Richard Crossman, in his very revealing diaries, has this to say:

> Now for my impressions of the ministry and of the civil service. The main conviction I had when I got there was that the civil service would be profoundly resistant to outside pressure. Was that true? I think it was. I found throughout an intense dislike of bringing people in, whether they are politicians or experts.
> I should say that in general I have found profound resistance in the civil service to a Minister who brings in outside advisers and experts, and profound resistance to interference by anybody with direct access to the Minister. What they like is sole ministerial responsibility because they are convinced that under this system the amount of outside influence exerted is minimal.

Am I exaggerating when I use these British and American examples of resistance to ministerial attentiveness to outside advice and apply them here in Canada? I do not think so. But I think that this resistance resides almost entirely among those who really have their hands on the levers of power — the senior mandarins. And I sometimes felt they reacted as negatively to the creativity and imaginative proposals of those in the less senior ranks of the foreign service as they did to outside advice. One of my constant frustrations was to find ways in which to penetrate senior management levels so as to tap this well-spring of fresh ideas, creativity and provocative questioning which I know from some experience exists.

I found myself as vulnerable as any new minister in any new government to the techniques Tony Benn attributes to the mandarins in Whitehall. He refers to them as techniques; I often thought of them as entrapment devices. Let me give you some examples:

(a) The unnecessarily numerous crisis corridor decisions I was confronted with — here is the situation; (breathless pause), let us have your instructions.

(b) The unnecessarily long and numerous memos; one of my great triumphs was that, in the wake of an abject plea for mercy, the senior re-write personnel agreed to reduce their verbiage by half.

(c) The late delivery to me of my submissions to cabinet, sometimes just a couple of hours (or less) before the meeting took place, thus denying me the opportunity for a full and realistic appraisal of the presentation I was supposed to be making to my cabinet colleagues. On a number of occasions my aides resorted to obtaining bootleg copies of such documents on their way through the overly complex bureaucratic approval system.

(d) The one-dimensional opinions put forward in memos. I was expected to accept the unanimous recommendations of the Department, though of course there was always the possibility that I might reject it. Seldom, if ever, was I given the luxury of multiple-choice options on matters of major import.

I mentioned earlier that in order to ensure political input into the decision-making process, the cabinet committee system grouped together ministers whose responsibilities were inter-related. Thus, all those ministers whose duties took them into the international field were members of the cabinet committee on foreign and defence policy, the one body where their initiatives could be co-ordinated. I was mandated by the Prime Minister to be chairman of that committee.

As such, I had to be rigorously scrupulous not to allow my departmental interests to prejudice my impartiality as chairman of the committee. The system was designed to provide an independent source of information to ministers, and particularly to cabinet committee chairmen, through the cabinet secretariat of the Privy Council Office. Memos for the chairmen, drafted by secretariat officials, analyzed the issues on the committee's agenda and pointed out the strengths and weaknesses of the various departmental positions. Deputy ministers or other officials participated in such cabinet committee meetings only if the agenda item required their attendance.

There was no comparable committee at the deputy minister level. In my view that would have undermined the decision-making role of ministers.

Not that such a committee of deputy ministers wasn't suggested. It was urged on me in a succession of proposals which I consistently rejected. Such a committee headed by a deputy whose mandate was solely that of chief officer in the department of External Affairs would, I felt, hardly be acceptable to National Defence, Industry, Trade and Commerce, Immigration, etc., as the person to co-ordinate their policies at the bureaucratic level. In addition, such a committee of deputy ministers would usurp or at least conflict with the function of the cabinet secretariat in the P.C.O. One senior mandarin used these words to describe it when he first heard of the proposal: "A mechanism to facilitate conflict."

I thought it was a dead duck; now I hear it has been activated and given the impressive title of Mirror Committee of Deputies. One wonders how many such mirror committees of deputies a cabinet minister can cope with before he or she ends up surrounded by a wall of mirrors each one reflecting the wisdom of the other into infinity. Even Alice in Wonderland might have difficulty in finding her way through what is likely to become a looking glass jungle, presenting the illusion of ministerial control.

Not only did I discover, after the takeover of the current administration, that senior mandarins had been successful in establishing this committee whose very operation must conflict with that of the cabinet secretariat, but I have also been led to believe that during my tenure copies of the private and confidential analysis done for me as a cabinet committee chairman by the P.C.O. cabinet secretariat found their way to my deputy's desk, without my knowledge or indeed without the knowledge of those who drafted the memoranda.

This would have permitted one senior official to be in a position to have access to privileged information not available to other deputy ministers, nor indeed to cabinet ministers other than the committee chairman. One need hardly speculate on the important role control of information plays in the bureaucratic game.

On a more philosophical level, I am concerned that the proliferation of senior management co-ordinating committees — co-ordinating advice not only to senior ministers but now to groups of ministers — will seriously impair the decision-making role of ministers. Such a system effectively filters out the policy options that an entire committee might otherwise consider. Too many bureaucrats, I fear, have the mistaken impression that vigorous debate of policy options by cabinet ministers is an indication that they — the bureaucrats — have somehow failed to properly channel and co-ordinate views before the cabinet meeting takes place.

Regrettably too few Canadian ministers have followed the example of Richard Crossman, Tony Benn, Harold MacMillan, Henry Kissinger or Dean Acheson in providing a first-hand account of the relationship between the minister and the bureaucracy. Regrettably as well, academics in this country have not paid as much attention as they should to the interface between ministers and the senior echelons of their departments.

The effective management of the relationship is what distinguishes parliamentary government from bureaucratic management. As Anthony Wedgewood Benn concluded: "In considering these issues, we do not want to find new scapegoats or pile blame upon ministers or civil servants who have let the system grow into what it is. What matters now is that we should examine what has happened to our system of government with fresh eyes and resolve to reintroduce constitutional democracy to Britain" and, I might add, to Canada.

A REPLY — FROM A FORMER MINISTER AND MANDARIN*

Mitchell Sharp

In a recent article in *Policy Options* Flora MacDonald says "Regrettably too few Canadian Ministers have provided a first-hand account of the relationship between the Minister and the bureaucracy." I am among the few who have done so and I do so again because my account differs substantially from that given by Miss MacDonald.

I have been on both sides of the relationship. For 16 years — between 1942 and 1958 — I was a senior civil servant. Towards the end of that period the media called me a mandarin. For 13 years — between 1963 and 1976 — I was a Minister. In between I was, for 5 years, a businessman.

My previous experience as a civil servant helped me enormously when I became a Minister. I understood the functions of my departmental advisers. I consulted them daily, every morning that I was in town, following the pattern of strong independent Ministers under whom I had served like Ilsley, Abbott and Howe. I asked questions and listened to their answers. Sometimes I agreed; sometimes I didn't. In the end I made my decisions and they carried them out. Once they knew my views they prepared drafts of policy speeches and announcements for my consideration.

Top public servants are powerful persons in the machinery of government at the federal level in Canada. They wield great influence. They do so because they are, in the main, professionals who have been selected for proven administrative ability and who devote their full time to government. In many cases, they have a greater influence upon the course of events than have Ministers, particularly the weaker and less competent Ministers.

This may seem somehow to be anti-democratic but it needn't be and in my experience it isn't. Government is, in fact, a specialized affair which cannot be run successfully by amateurs without professional advice and professional execution. With rare exceptions, in a parliamentary system

* From *Policy Options*, 2, 2, May-June, 1981. By permission.

politicians are amateurs in any field of government administration, at least at the beginning of their political careers.

Few of them will be experts in fiscal and monetary policy, or in nuclear policy, or in foreign affairs, for example, when they offer themselves as candidates in a local constituency. Yet they may find themselves having to make decisions in any or all those complex fields once in office. Prime Ministers are limited in their selection of Ministers to those of their party who have been elected. Sometimes, given the necessity in a federal state for geographical distribution in Cabinet, the choice may be extremely limited.

At a political meeting during the 1968 election campaign, I was asked by a young man in the audience what qualifications I had to be foreign Minister of Canada. I replied that my essential qualification was that I had been elected to Parliament.

Politicians, particularly Ministers, require the best impartial advice that they can get if they are to make wise decisions. Sycophants who echo their boss's views are of little value; indeed they can be positively dangerous as advisers if they are not prepared from time to time to tell their bosses the painful truth that a pet idea is unworkable. That is one of the reasons why I am not in favour of the principle, which is sometimes advanced, that the top positions — the heads of departments — should be filled by those who are in sympathy with the views of the party in power, who should depart with their Ministers when the Government is replaced.

After some 35 years observing the process of government at close range, I am also more convinced than I was at the beginning that there is virtue in continuity in the senior administrative jobs, and in promoting career public servants to them. Competent people are not going to be prepared to enter the public service and make a career of it if they are to be denied access to the top jobs where they can bring their talents fully to bear.

The contrary argument that senior civil servants would resist change in the event that a government with radically different views from its predecessor took office has never been very convincing to me. In the first place, knowing my own country and its political parties, I doubt that any change would be in fact very radical. In the second place, it is precisely under those circumstances, were they to come about, that an experienced senior civil service would be most valuable, one that could guide a new government in the implementation of its innovative policies and enable it to avoid the administrative pitfalls of which it might otherwise not be aware.

I can testify from my own experience and my own observation that changes of government such as occurred in 1957 and 1979 were considered in the civil service as providing a challenge, an opportunity to prove that the service is non-partisan, notwithstanding the long years of Liberal administration. It is useful in this connection to observe that nearly all the deputy Ministers at the time of both changes were drawn from the ranks of public servants who had originally qualified for entry to the public service by the independent Public Service Commission. As nearly as I can determine, something like 80 percent of the present heads of departments are drawn from the ranks of non-political civil servants.

That there were some transitional difficulties in 1957 and 1979 is not surprising. Even when there is no change of government — only change of Minister — there are bound to be some awkward adjustments in relations between the incoming Minister and the incumbent deputy minister, which sometimes necessitate a switch in responsibilities. However, I neither saw nor heard evidence that the transition was difficult because the senior public service was committed to the policies of the previous government and was determined to resist change.

What a new Minister finds — I had the experience four times in my political career — when he or she takes over a department is that the problems are more complicated than they looked to be from the outside and that he or she needs plenty of advice to avoid making mistakes.

There is need, of course, for Ministers to have in their offices men and women to help them perform as Members of Parliament and political leaders. Such temporary appointees, however valuable they may be, are no substitute for permanent non-partisan senior civil servants.

From time to time, too, Governments may wish to be able to call on the services of qualified Canadians from the business or professional world who have special expertise of one kind or another. This they should be able to do and are able to do. I myself inherited a Deputy Minister appointed by the Diefenbaker administration who had not been drawn from the ranks of the permanent public service. I advised Mr. Pearson to retain him, which he did. The test of such appointments should be the competence of the appointee and not his or her personal politics.

Admittedly the system does give rise to serious questions. Do senior civil servants exert too much influence upon the Government? Are Ministers puppets being manipulated by the mandarins, as is sometimes asserted or implied? These are difficult questions to answer satisfactorily because so much depends upon the way individual Ministers react to advice. I don't think anyone who knew him thought that C.D. Howe was manipulated by his civil service advisers, yet he had excellent working relationships with them. The key to that good working relationship was that Mr. Howe gave them his confidence and they responded with loyalty and respect.

When I was a civil servant, I think it is fair to say that individual Ministers and the Cabinet as a whole depended more upon the advice of senior civil servants than they do today and they did so deliberately. When a difficult problem arose, the customary response was to refer it for study and report to a committee of senior public servants. There was also a period during the war and in the immediate post-war years when influential public servants like Clifford Clark, Norman Robertson, Graham Towers and Donald Gordon were active promoters of new ideas and approaches that they persuaded their Ministers and the Cabinet to adopt.

The federal mandarins then, however, were a tightly knit group of personal friends drawn from various walks of life who had been invited to Ottawa to join the public service during both Conservative and Liberal regimes. They were not lifetime civil servants recruited at time of graduation who had risen through the ranks, as is now the pattern.

Today when difficult problems arise, they are more often referred to Ministerial Committees than to committees of civil servants. Innovative ideas still emerge from the civil service, but the process of decision-making at the Cabinet level is so complex nowadays that individual contributions are quickly submerged in a deluge of documentation. The present Ministers,

I suspect, long for a return of the general rule, under which as a civil servant I operated, which was that memoranda for Ministers should not exceed two pages, otherwise they might not be read.

I sympathize with those Ministers who like myself had to wade through pages and pages of memoranda, some of which became available barely in time to be read before decisions had to be taken. However, it was our own fault for letting the system get out of hand.

I sometimes thought that as Ministers we were much too zealous and that, particularly under Mr. Trudeau, we worked far too hard and spent far too much time in Cabinet and Cabinet Committees reading and discussing each other's proposals. Decisions might have taken less time, we might have had a better perspective on events and more time for politics, had we delegated more to our civil service advisers and left more time for reflection.

A first-class non-partisan public service dedicated to the public interest is one of the bulwarks of parliamentary government. It enables the elected amateurs, gifted or otherwise, to make the political decisions and govern the country.

GETTING INTO THE CABINET*

Sir George Foster

[The scramble for a position in the cabinet which occurs when a new government is being formed is well illustrated by excerpts from the diary of Sir George Foster during the cabinet-making period that followed the Conservative victory in the 1911 election. Having served as minister of Finance in five previous Conservative administrations, Foster believed himself entitled to the same post again, and he did not hesitate to let the new prime minister, R.L. Borden, know. The anxieties of the aspirant, the pressures applied to the prime minister, and the inner forces at work are all clearly revealed in a few brief entries.]

Sept. 22. The govt. defeat is a decisive and general one. . . .

Sept. 23. General congratulations pour in from all sides. Left for Ottawa.

Sept. 24. At home in peace and quietness again. Borden came in at noon. Telephoned him, but he was being protected by wife — no communication.

Sept. 25. Now the cabinet-making begins, in the papers and in the clubs. B. keeps to his house and sees those he calls for. No communication.

Sept. 26. Taylor as a middleman suggests Ch. Tariff Comm., with $10,000, as a nice thing, I told him I was not out for office, and would accept none. No other communication.

Sept. 27. Certain parties are in tow. Perley appears to be the manager. Davis-Shaughnessy in evidence. Reporters (Hamilton) at old business. No communication.

Sept. 28. To-night Osler sees me. Financial interests opposed to my being F.M. Would relieve situation if I would remain out. *Globe* criticism feared.

* From W.S. Wallace, *The Memoirs of the Rt. Hon. Sir George Foster*, P.C., G.C.M.G., Toronto, Macmillan, 1933, pp. 155-156, as corrected from the original diary in the Public Archives, Ottawa. By permission of the Estate.

I told him plainly I would not commit suicide. No communication from Borden. Rogers says a portfolio, but not F.M. or Trade and Commerce, seat in Senate.

Sept. 29. The interests seem to be dominant, and Borden doesn't know his mind from day to day. I have advised my friends, and they are at work. No communication.

Sept. 30. To-night at 9 p.m. B. asks me to come up. He skated all around, and finally suggested Sec'y of State. I told him I wouldn't consider it. My old position was what I wanted.

Oct. 1. A quiet day, rest and reading. Hazen is here, and Rogers seems in charge. The Kemp Gooderham-McNab-Graham crowd make up the financial int.

Oct. 2. Fine. More people here. More excitement. Saw Hazen, McLeod, Crockett, Roach, etc. All are strong for me in old position. McGrath had peculiar conference.

Oct. 3. No word from B. Letter from Clouston, and conference with Dobie. Financial interests not adverse. My friends are making things hot.

Oct. 4. More people. More wire-pulling. Deputations galore, and general suspense. B. seems helpless on the surf.

Oct. 5. Called by Chief, and offered Trade and Commerce. Ask why F.M. not given. Ans.: reasons of high politics. My capabilities, honesty and service fully recognized.

Oct. 6. A bothersome day. [Borden] backing and filling. Irresolute and fearful. He is an odd man.

Oct. 7. No word from Borden to-day. Saw Boyce and Smith, who are raging at the outsiders, especially White.

Oct. 8. The day fine. Rested without outside disturbance. . . .

Oct. 9. No announcement yet, and no word from Borden since Friday night. I hear Toronto is bombarding him. Hazen is here — what others I know not.

Oct. 10. This morning the announcement of new govt. The unseemly squabble is ended. Some weak links in the chain. There will be deep dissatisfaction with White. Sworn in at 11 a.m. except Burrell.

[Foster was appointed minister of trade and commerce.]

BIBLIOGRAPHY

(See also Bibliographies in Chapter 8 and Chapter 15)

Banks, M.A., "Privy Council, Cabinet, and Ministry in Britain and Canada: A Story of Confusion," *C.J.E.P.S.*, XXXI, 2, May, 1965. (See also "Comments," *ibid.*, XXXI, 4, November, 1965 and XX-XII, 1, February, 1966.)

Berkeley, H., *The Power of the Prime Minister*, Toronto, Methuen, 1971.
Burke, Sister T.A., "Mackenzie and His Cabinet, 1873-1878," *Canadian Historical Review*, XLI, 2, June, 1960.
Canada, Public Archives, *Guide to Canadian Ministries Since Confederation, July 1, 1867-April 1, 1973*, Ottawa, 1974.

Courtney, J.C., "Prime Ministerial Character: An Examination of Mackenzie King's Political Leadership," *C.J.P.S.*, IX, 1, March, 1976. (Also *ibid.*, J.E. Esberey, "An Alternative View.")

Crane, D., "How Powerful is the Prime Minister?," *The Toronto Star*, August 23, 1980.

D'Aquino, T.P., *Organization of Ministerial Offices — An Organizational Study of Ministerial Offices in Aid of Ministers and Staff*, Ottawa, Prime Minister's Office, 1970.

D'Aquino, T.P., "The Prime Minister's Office: Catalyst or Cabal?," *C.P.A.*, 17, 1, Spring, 1974.

Dawson, R.M., *William Lyon Mackenzie King: A Political Biography*, Vol. 1, *1874-1923*, Toronto, U.T.P., 1958, Chapter 13.

Donaldson, G., *Fifteen Men: Canada's Prime Ministers*, Toronto, Doubleday, 1969.

Fleck, J.D., "Reorganization of the Ontario Government," *C.P.A.*, 15, 2, Summer, 1972.

Fleck, J.D., "Restructuring the Ontario Government," *C.P.A.*, 16, 1, Spring, 1973.

Forsey, E.A., *Freedom and Order: Collected Essays*, Carleton Library No. 73, M. & S., 1974.

Gibson, F.W., (ed.), *Cabinet Formation and Bicultural Relations: Seven Case Studies*, Studies of the Royal Commission on Bilingualism and Biculturalism, No. 6, Ottawa, Q.P., 1970.

Hockin, T., (ed.), *Apex of Power: The Prime Minister and Political Leadership in Canada*, Scarborough, P.-H., 2nd ed., 1977.

Hutchinson, B., *Mr. Prime Minister, 1867-1964*, Toronto, Longmans, 1964.

Irvine, W.P., and Simeon, R.E.B., "The Prime Minister's Mailbag," *C.P.A.*, 19, 2, Summer, 1976.

Jeffrey, B., *A Comparison of the Role of the Minister's Office in France, Britain and Canada*, Ottawa, Library of Parliament Research Branch, October 18, 1978.

Jones, G.W., "The Prime Minister's Powers," *Parliamentary Affairs*, 18, 2, Spring, 1965.

Lalonde, M., "The Changing Role of the Prime Minister's Office," *C.P.A.*, 14, 4, Winter, 1971.

MacQuarrie, H.N., "The Formation of Borden's First Cabinet," *C.J.E.P.S.*, XXIII, 1, February, 1957.

Mallory, J., "The Two Clerks: Parliamentary Discussion of the Role of the Privy Council Office," *C.J.P.S.*, X, 1, March, 1977.

Mallory, J.R., "Mackenzie King and the Origins of the Cabinet Secretariat," *C.P.A.*, 19, 2, Summer, 1976.

Mallory, J.R., "The Minister's Office Staff: An Unreformed Part of the Public Service," *C.P.A.*, 10, 1, Spring, 1967.

Matheson, W.A., *The Prime Minister and the Cabinet*, Toronto, Methuen, 1976.

Morton, W.L., "The Formation of the First Federal Cabinet," *Canadian Historical Review*, XXXVI, 2, June, 1955.

Ondaatje, C., Swanson, D., *The Prime Ministers of Canada, 1867-1968: Macdonald to Trudeau*, Don Mills, General Publishing, 1967.

Pickersgill, J.W., "Bureaucrats and Politicians," *C.P.A.*, 15, 3, 1972.

Pitfield, M., "The Shape of Government in the 1980s," *C.P.A.*, 19, 1, Spring, 1976.

Punnet, R.M., *The Prime Minister in Canadian Government and Politics*, Toronto, Macmillan, 1977.

Robertson, G., "The Canadian Parliament and Cabinet in the Face of Modern Demands," *C.P.A.*, 11, 3, Fall, 1968.

Robertson, G., "The Changing Role of the Privy Council Office," *C.P.A.*, 14, 4, Winter, 1971.

Schultz, R., *et al.*, *The Cabinet as a Regulatory Body: The Case of the Foreign Investment Review Act*, Ottawa, E.C.C., 1980.

Sharp, M., "Decision-making in the

Federal Cabinet," *C.P.A.*, 19, 1, Spring, 1976.

Stewart, I., "Of Custom and Coalitions: The Formation of Canadian Parliamentary Alliances," *C.J.P.S.*, XIII, 3, September, 1980.

Tennant, P., "The NDP Government of British Columbia: Unaided Politicians in an Unaided Cabinet," *C.P.P.*, III, 4, Autumn, 1977.

Ward, N., "The Changing Role of the Privy Council Office and the Prime Minister's Office: A Commentary," *C.P.A.*, 15, 2, Summer, 1972.

Weller, P., "Inner Cabinets and Outer Ministers: Some Lessons from Australia and Britain," *C.P.A.*, 23, 4, Winter, 1980.

13

THE LEGISLATIVE PROCESS: HOUSE OF COMMONS AND PROVINCIAL LEGISLATURES

There has been a change in emphasis in this chapter in this edition. To broaden the scope of the book, more material dealing with provincial legislatures has been selected where it is available and has comparative relevance. Thus the items dealing with the Speaker, the administration of legislatures, and members' indemnities, salaries, allowances and benefits, personal profiles and support services, and House statistics all stem from the provincial legislatures, though the federal House is included in the comparisons.

This broadening of treatment is indicative of the remarkable recent growth in the organization of provincial Assemblies and in the facilities they now provide to their members. It is one aspect of the extent to which provinces have increased their significance within the Canadian system of government in the past few decades. While this development has probably been the most striking characteristic of Canadian government since the second world war, the growth of the sophistication of provincial legislatures as institutions has been particularly rapid in the past five years.

Canadian scholars are now devoting much more attention to the provincial sector, as the bibliography in this and other chapters indicates. But the information about provincial legislatures owes much to the pioneering work of Mr. Robert Fleming, Director of Administration for the Legislative Assembly of Ontario, who has been publishing annually for three years a comparative study of legislatures in Canada. His latest monograph, *Canadian Legislatures: The 1981 Comparative Study,* prepared with the assistance of Mr. J. Thomas Mitchinson, is a mine of valuable information. The excerpts included in this chapter are only a sample of the voluminous data which he and his staff have collected.

Previous editions of *Politics: Canada* have noted that the most pertinent — and probably the most important — facet of the legislative process is the enduring conflict between the executive and legislative branches of government. This adversarial relationship is the essence of the Canadian system of cabinet-parliamentary government and it is reflected in the contents of this chapter.

Professor Denis Smith's provocative article asserting that parliamentary government is being transformed into a presidential system sets the tone. Mark MacGuigan, who is now the Minister for External Affairs, writes of his experiences as a backbench MP, explaining the constraints under which a legislative member works. Geoffrey Stevens, who was then a journalist in the Ottawa Press Gallery, describes the Clark's government proposal, which proved to be abortive, to reform the rules of procedure in the House of Commons. A one-page graphic depicts how a bill becomes law in Parliament.

Donald C. MacDonald, who is a veteran member of the Ontario Legislature, suggests a better method for choosing a Speaker, which by analogy might be applied to the House of Commons and other legislatures. Mr. Fleming's first article describes the improved system of administration which legislatures are adopting, while his second article is an excerpt from his annual monograph which gives so much information about Canadian legislatures.

A number of items which appeared in the comparable chapter in the fourth edition have been omitted from this chapter because they have been overtaken by recent developments. They can be found in the fourth edition at the following pages: Mark MacGuigan, "Backbenchers, the New Committee System, and the Caucus," pp. 431-438; Mitchell Sharp, "An Outline for House of Commons Reform," pp. 440-447; Geoffrey Stevens, "Private Members' Bills — Candidates for Oblivion," pp. 447-449; Paul Fox, "Salaries and Allowances of Members of Parliament, Senators, and Officials," p. 449; and Paul Fox, "Indemnities and Allowances of Members of Provincial Legislatures," p. 450.

The bibliography at the end of this chapter contains references to recent works on the legislative process. Note should be taken too of several new periodicals that provide much information on legislative affairs: *Parliamentary Government,* which is published jointly by the Parliamentary Centre for Foreign Affairs and Foreign Trade in Ottawa and the Institute for Research on Public Policy; the *Canadian Parliamentary Review,* which is the journal of the Canadian Region of the Commonwealth Parliamentary Association; and *Policy Options,* which is published by the Institute for Research on Public Policy.

PRESIDENT AND PARLIAMENT: THE TRANSFORMATION OF PARLIAMENTARY GOVERNMENT IN CANADA*

Denis Smith

• • •

Big government [has] overtaken both Cabinet and Parliament. In Canada as elsewhere in the industrialized world over the last half century, the size, responsibilities, and opportunities for initiative of the permanent administration have expanded enormously. While departments have multiplied and divided, while independent agencies and crown corporations have been born and grown prematurely into monsters, the instruments of Cabin-

* Extract from a paper presented to the Progressive Conservative Party's Priorities for Canada Conference, Niagara Falls, Ontario, October 10, 1969. By permission of the author, who wishes to express gratitude to the Canada Council for a grant to assist research on the condition of Parliamentary government in Canada, of which the paper was a reflection.

et and Parliamentary control of the leviathan have remained negligible. . . .

What may be equally as important as the growing burdens of government is the mythology of Parliamentary government. For the mythology has disguised the reality. We are still bemused by the classic models of Parliamentary government presented with such grace and clarity by Walter Bagehot and John Stuart Mill to an English audience in the mid-nineteenth century. . . . We have, we are told, a system of responsible parliamentary government, in which the public elects individual Members to the House of Commons and the House of Commons, in turn, chooses a Government. Thereafter, while the Cabinet governs, the House holds it responsible for all the actions of the administration, and in the event of parliamentary disapproval, can overthrow the ministry, or force it to seek a fresh mandate from the electorate. The Prime Minister is chairman of the Cabinet; the public service is the loyal and anonymous servant of the Cabinet; the Cabinet is the servant of the House of Commons and only indirectly of the electorate. The theory puts the House of Commons close to the centre of the system, where it is meant to act as "the grand inquest of the nation," influencing, supervising and controlling the actions of the executive.

While the Canadian literature of politics points out that parliamentary control may not be quite up to the theory, the theory is maintained as the ideal. As a result, many of the real forces at work in Canadian politics are underrated or ignored. The tendency is, when describing forces and practices which contradict the model, to see them as aberrations pulling the system away from the Victorian ideal, but rarely as primary forces in their own right which may be basically shaping the system.

. . . But a point may come, in adding up the distortions and aberrations from the norm, when it becomes more comprehensible to abandon the original description and try to put together another one which accommodates the evidence more completely and satisfactorily. I think this point has been reached in understanding how the Canadian system works.

• • •

The best reassessment of the British model — and now a familiar one — is Richard Crossman's introduction to the 1964 edition of Bagehot's *The English Constitution*. Here, Crossman argues that Bagehot's description of the Cabinet in Parliament was falsified soon after publication of *The English Constitution*. The emergence of highly disciplined mass parties took independent power from individual Members of Parliament; the immense new administrative bureaucracy took much ordinary decision-making power away from ministers; and an organized secretariat for the Cabinet, and especially for the Prime Minister, gave the Prime Minister the effective powers of a president. . . .

P.M. Like President

Does the story sound familiar in Canada? It does. The Canadian Prime Minister, indeed, may be further along the road to being a presidential leader than the British, for distinct Canadian reasons.

For one thing, the Canadian House of Commons has never possessed the reserve of aristocratic prestige which once gave the British House of Commons some leverage alongside or against the Prime Minister. For most of its life the Canadian House has been a popular chamber, based on wide popular suffrage; Canadian Prime Ministers have always made their primary appeal for support not *in* the House of Commons, but outside, to the electorate. . . .

The House of Commons is diminished in importance, as compared to the British House in the period from 1832 to 1867, because it is the electorate, not the House of Commons, which chooses and deposes Prime Ministers. The essential influence upon government is the sovereign public, not a sovereign Parliament. Prime Ministers keep their eyes upon the Gallup Polls, and not normally upon readings of the House of Commons' temperature. And the public sees the Government as one man's Government. This public assumption gives the Prime Minister great power over his colleagues.

The fact is a commonplace in Canadian understanding, and yet it is not satisfactorily integrated into the normal liberal model of the parliamentary constitution. We know that general elections are competitions between party leaders for the Prime Minister's office; we concentrate our attention upon the leaders, and the parties encourage us to do so; we see that Prime Ministers, once in office, exercise almost tyrannical power over their ministers and backbenchers; Prime Ministers frequently ignore the House of Commons, or treat it with disdain, unless they perceive that the public is watching (which it only occasionally is); and our Prime Ministers freely admit their own predominance over the House of Commons and the necessity of it. . . .

. . . Given an alert Prime Minister, it is virtually impossible to replace him even by "undercover intrigue and sudden unpredicted *coup d'état.*" He has too many weapons of influence and patronage in his hands, and his adversaries have too few. He is virtually as immovable as an American President during his term of office.

. . . Even without a majority in Parliament, a Canadian Prime Minister is normally secure in office, and scarcely faces the danger of defeat in the House, because one or another of the opposition parties is almost certain to vote with the Government on any division to assure its own survival. . . .

In both the United Kingdom and Canada, the Prime Minister gains his predominance over his colleagues and the House of Commons by winning general elections and exercising the power of dissolution at his own discretion. But in Canada the Prime Minister possesses still more authority granted him from outside Parliament which brings him closer to the American President. He is chosen by a popular convention. The Canadian conventions have increasingly come to duplicate the effects of the American presidential conventions. Under the open embrace of gavel-to-gavel television, the conventions have become as central a part of national political life as the campaigns, and perhaps more central, because of their concentrated drama and intense TV coverage. In the conventions the political process is almost entirely personalized, issues fade away, and the winner is the only one to walk away alive. . . . If anything has accelerated the trend to presidential politics in Canada, it has been the enthusiastic adoption of televised national leadership conventions. . . .

Set against the overwhelming power and public prestige of the Prime Minister are the traditional duties of the legislature. Even if one admits that the power of *overthrowing* governments has been surrendered, the House of Commons is supposed to retain the power and responsibility to provide a public forum of discussion on national issues, to scrutinize spending and legislation, and to safeguard the rights and freedoms of citizens by its vigilant criticism. These are worthy goals; but even *they* fade on closer examination. . . . In its less spectacular, day-to-day performances, the House of Commons normally, if grudgingly, does the work the Government directs it to do, and does so without making much critical impression on Government measures or on the public. This is so because the Government wishes it to be so, and because, until the December, 1968 reforms, the House was the victim of its own diffuse rules, which did not lend themselves to sharp, critical investigation of Government measures.

• • •

President Without Congress

We seem to have created in Canada a presidential system without congressional advantages. Before the accession of Pierre Trudeau, our presidential system, however, was diffuse and ill-organized. But Pierre Trudeau is extraordinarily clear-headed and realistic about the sources of political power in Canada. On the one hand, he has recognized the immense power of initiative and guidance that exists in the federal bureaucracy; and he has seen that this great instrument of power lacked effective centralized political leadership. He has created that coordinated leadership by organizing around him a presidential office, and by bringing order and discipline to the Cabinet's operations. He has made brilliant use of the public opportunities of a party leader, in convention, in the general election, and in his continuing encounters outside Parliament. He has recognized that the public responds first to personalities, not to issues, and so he campaigns for the most generalized mandate. And now, finally, he has successfully altered the procedures of the House of Commons so that it may serve the legislative purposes of an efficient presidential administration.

In doing all these things he has taken advantage of trends and opportunities that already existed. *All* Prime Ministers have been moving — under pressure — in the same direction, but none so determinedly as Prime Minister Trudeau; he has taken the system further, faster, more self-consciously, than it would otherwise have gone. Are we now to be left with this completed edifice of presidential-parliamentary government, in which the House serves the minor purpose of making presidential programs law without much fuss?

Probably not, because the system still contains some fundamental inconsistencies. How clearly the Prime Minister and Members of Parliament see these inconsistencies, I cannot be sure; but they exist, and they will create difficulties. As we have seen, the changes in the rules and practices of the House have *not only* served the *Government's* purposes; they have also, in many ways, benefited individual Members and the opposition parties.

In the course of achieving rules of procedure much more tractable for the Government's purposes, the reforms and the reforming atmosphere have also created a more intractable *membership* of the House, with new and potentially powerful instruments of leverage *against* the Government in their hands. The opposition parties are better equipped by their research funds and their role in legislative committees to criticize the administration from a basis of knowledge. The restrictions of time allocation in the House give these parties an incentive to organize their attacks with more precision and directness than before. Government backbenchers, long silent and frustrated by party discipline, permitted only to express their opinions freely in secret caucus, have been given the taste of greater freedom in the new committees of the House. . . . For the moment, the Government may hold the reins tightly, but the pressures in the House are likely to mount.

• • •

IMPEDIMENTS TO AN ENLARGED ROLE FOR THE BACKBENCHER*

Mark MacGuigan

There can be little doubt that any survey of the Canadian parliament would reveal that the members are massively in favour of parliamentary reform. But the same survey, if it took the trouble to probe the members' attitudes at all, would also show considerable disagreements as to what kind of parliamentary reform they have in mind.

For a start, ministers of the Crown would like to see government business proceed with greater dispatch through the House. Government backbenchers want, in addition, more opportunity to ask questions during the oral question period and to make speeches during the consideration of government orders. Opposition frontbenchers would like to be able to hold up government legislation more effectively and to scrutinize and criticize spending estimates at greater length. Opposition backbenchers also want an opportunity to participate in a more positive way — not simply to frustrate government initiatives but to take some themselves, with a real possibility of affecting legislation. Given the opportunity, the N.D.P. would abolish the Senate. The lone independent member would like to see independent members given the same rights as the spokesmen for the recognized parties. Senators would like a chance to participate more fully in the legislative process.

Nevertheless, I believe there is considerable common ground among members of different parties on parliamentary reform and that the common ground extends at least to a more active and independent role for backbenchers in the committee system. What, then, hinders reform?

* From *Legislative Studies Quarterly*, III, 4, November, 1978, © Comparative Legislative Research Center, University of Iowa. The author, who was a backbench Member of Parliament, is now Secretary of State for External Affairs, Canada. By permission.

The inherent tension between the legislative interest and the executive interest is universally recognized as a principal inhibiting factor. Although this tension is not susceptible of final resolution, it is nevertheless open to accommodation from time to time, and I have argued elsewhere that a new accommodation now would be to the advantage of both the executive and the legislature. The executive cannot concede any additional powers in the Chamber itself. In fact, its greatest need is for tighter control over House business, and this would be the *quid pro quo* the executive would attempt to obtain in a new accommodation. What the executive would yield and backbenchers would therefore gain would be greater freedom of action on parliamentary committees. It would appear from such an analysis that all that is necessary to more fully accommodate all sides is a new bargain. But the reality is much more complex than this analysis, because the inhibition to a creative role for backbenchers is more extensive than the fiat of the executive.

What I want to explore in this paper is the full range of impediments to a creative backbench role in parliament. . . . For such an undertaking, the most basic necessity is an understanding of the character of parliamentary life.

The Situation of the Individual Member

My time in Parliament corresponds almost exactly with the Trudeau years in government (1968-1978). When I was first elected I found myself in a small office on the fifth floor of the Centre Block about the size of a household study. I had one secretary with whom I shared this office, and a single telephone line. As you would imagine, with a single line for both ingoing and outgoing calls for two busy people, there was keen competition for the telephone when I was in the office.

After we were allowed a second secretary in 1969 and I also acquired a parliamentary intern, we were four in this small office (fortunately by then with a second telephone line). There was no privacy either in the office or on the telephone. When, as often happened, I had a visitor whose business necessitated privacy, my staff had to go for coffee, or walk the corridors. (In fairness I should probably note that as recently as six years earlier two MPs and two secretaries had to share similar offices, with a single telephone line for all. As a former minister once remarked to me in exasperation, "I knew that as soon as MPs got full-time secretaries they'd want larger offices.")

As soon as parliamentary committees began meeting in the fall of 1968, I found that parliamentary demands on my time were considerable, and the burden of constituency cases staggering. On the parliamentary side there were the daily question period, which most Members of Parliament wish to attend both for excitement and information, and three half-days of duty service in the House to ensure that the government always maintained a quorum. (This "duty day" requirement has subsequently escalated to include every fourth Friday as well.) I belonged to two standing committees, which met from time to time, frequently during times of estimates and referred legislation. I was soon chairing a special committee study on statutory instruments, which became my major time commitment and lasted for a year.

Then there were caucus meetings — every Wednesday morning from 9:30 to 12:30; and, after caucus committees were formed in 1969, meetings were scheduled with ever-increasing frequency during lunch and dinner breaks. I was also among the majority of members who participated to some extent — a comparatively small extent in my case — in the parliamentary associations (the inter-Parliamentary Union, etc.). Being determined to become bilingual, I participated in twice-weekly French classes on parliament hill, and went every second month or so to the Royal Military College in St. Jean for immersion sessions.

On weekends I commuted the five hundred miles to my constituency in Windsor, to spend the weekend with my family and my constituents. Insofar as possible, constituents' problems were dealt with by telephone, but for the unavoidable personal encounters I had to travel by car to constituents' homes. Although some Members of Parliament had a satisfactory arrangement of rooms in their homes for seeing constituents, I did not. My constituency is a particularly heavy one for civic functions, as the 25-odd ethnic subcommunities expect the presence of their MP at their celebrations. During my early years in parliament I kept a record of the number of events I had to attend. It ran to about two hundred public functions and two hundred visits to constituents' homes a year, both of which I squeezed into weekends and holidays with my family in Windsor. The constituents' problems I brought back with me to Ottawa, but I had to leave my family in Windsor.

Fortunately I had an extraordinarily experienced and able secretary in Ottawa who had come from my constituency and who was able to deal with constituents' problems as well as I could myself — in the beginning, much better. With her help, I managed to cope, but to do so I had to give up almost all social life and all reading except newspapers and magazines. My work day usually finished in my office about 2:00 a.m.

One of the petty limitations on an MP's effectiveness throughout the 28th and 29th Parliaments was his restricted access to the government telephone lines. . . . Only in March of 1976 were MPs given unrestricted access to government telephone lines. About the same time (June, 1976) they were also allowed three telephone lines in their Ottawa offices.

Undoubtedly, however, the biggest change in an MP's working effectiveness has been brought about by his increase in staff. In 1974, constituency offices were established at government expense. (Until then, the member's wife had to bear the burden of constituency calls during the week.) Initially, the constituency secretary was paid at a lower rate than a first-level secretary in Ottawa, but since May 1977, the pay has been the same. Rent and office expenses are also taken care of by the government. Coordinately, there has been an expansion in the MP's Ottawa office. The right to three Ottawa secretaries has been fully recognized since October 1, 1976. This increase from one to four (three Ottawa, one constituency secretary) has meant an enormously increased capacity for work in MP's offices from 1968 to the present.

At the same time, the volume of constituency business has increased. The fact of having a secretary readily available in an office, backed up by a telephone answering service, has probably made people more willing to refer cases to their MP, believing that it is less of an imposition. Certainly, in the days before constituency offices, when constituents had to telephone a member's house, they were often very apologetic for having to disturb him with his family. Probably more important, however, has been the advertising of the availability of the service. Constituents have come to know of the existence of the offices (now available in Ontario also to members of the provincial parliament), and have come to expect the service. The quarterly constituency reports that an MP is allowed now to send to his constituents also draw their attention to his service. My office usually notes a considerable increase in calls immediately after a constituency mailing has been received. . . . The total volume is approximately 3,000 cases a year through the constituency office and a further 2,500 through the House of Commons office.

I might also mention that members who are committee chairmen may receive a large additional volume of mail in that capacity. As chairman of the Standing Committee on Justice and Legal Affairs, I received some 8,000 letters on Bill C-83, the first "gun control bill," in early 1976. . . .

Finally, there are the general political interests of members. Unless a member retains his seat, he will cease to be able to make any contribution to the governmental process. He must see his constituents with their problems, make sure that he is getting an adequate amount of local publicity, keep in constant touch with his key election workers (people whom he ignores between elections are not likely to want to put themselves out for him at election time), and generally appear to be representing the interests of constituents and responsive to the feelings of the party faithful in his constituency. He must also attend regional, provincial, and national political meetings, both to represent his local interests and to make a name for himself personally on the larger scene.

The Government Caucus

From the beginning of the 28th Parliament in 1968 it was clear that some large-scale changes would have to be made in the government caucus. There were a large number of new members who insisted on being listened to, and the prime minister himself appeared from the beginning to be sympathetic to caucus reform.

The decisive change came with a special weekend caucus on June 20-22, 1969. . . . The general principle of consultation, as agreed on at that time, was as follows:

> Before a final decision is made on a bill and before its final drafting, the minister responsible shall discuss the bill in general terms with the Caucus Committee concerned and a subsequent detailed discussion will be held upon the first reading. No bill shall be submitted for second reading until such consultation has taken place or has been renounced by common agreement. A similar procedure shall be followed for major changes relating to government policies for which no legislation is required.

HOW A BILL BECOMES LAW IN PARLIAMENT*

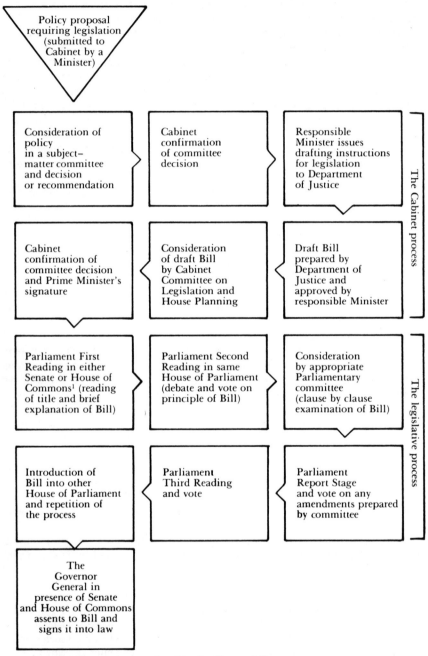

1. All money Bills must be introduced in the House of Commons.

* *From Canada Year Book, 1973, p. 109. Reproduced by permission of the Minister of Supply and Services Canada.*

Although this rule has not always been followed with precision, especially with regard to ministerial statements in the House, it continues to represent the general commitment of the government to the caucus.

The effect of the change has been to greatly increase both the input of the MPs and the number of meetings they have to attend. Initially, it led to the establishment of a system of standing committees of caucus that met simultaneously; however, this system proved impracticable and has been replaced by a system of *ad hoc* committees. All government members are invited to every meeting and meetings are never run simultaneously. The government member who wants to influence policy finds it advisable to attend all of these meetings.

From the beginning of my years in parliament it has been apparent that strong caucus opposition to any government proposal imposes an absolute veto on that proposal. The government has shown time and again that it dare not act in the face of clear caucus opposition. On the other hand, the cabinet is quick to exploit any disagreement among caucus members to enable it to proceed in the desired direction. On the positive side the caucus initially lacked power with respect to the making of policy, but the great reform of 1969 made backbench participation in policy formation more structured and more effective than before. . . . Since then (March 1970) all caucus offices have been filled by election.

The Member as Representative and Legislator

Since I moved into the Confederation Building after the 1972 election I have had a spacious and well-appointed office, with an equally large outer office shared by my three secretaries (and a parliamentary intern, when I have one). It is air-conditioned and carpeted and has padded doors for added quietness. In short, it is both comfortable and efficient, a far cry from the cramped quarters and inadequate services with which I began in 1968. A streamlined telephone system is just being installed, allowing members to make conference calls.

A Member of Parliament is now better able to serve his constituents than ever before. However, the very effectiveness of his service has, along with the greater public awareness of it, increased the volume. The success of constituency offices has therefore led to a greater need for staff in the Ottawa office, since all the more complicated problems from the constituency office have to be forwarded to Ottawa to be dealt with there.

A few members manage to assign one of their Ottawa staff permanently to the role of an assistant, to help in legislative tasks in Ottawa. I have found that impossible. My need for secretarial assistance is such that the entire energies of my four-person staff (in the two offices) are devoted to secretarial and constituency business. I believe my experience is typical of members in this respect. Reform has not yet gone far enough to provide time for policy creativity. I can now finish work at midnight, rather than at 2:00 a.m., but I am still not prepared for my committee hearings at 9:30 a.m., to say nothing of having enough time for general reading.

Here it is crucial to understand the psychology of MPs. In any conflict of roles I believe it is fair to say that they will always give their representational function priority over their legislative one. For one thing, the constituent's problem is there in a very concrete sense. It cannot be dodged, and, while responsibility for the solution may in many circumstances be transferable to someone else (e.g., a minister), responsibility for answering the constituent and for trying to deal with the problem cannot be transferred beyond the MP's office. The MP may even come to assign a greater theoretical, as well as practical, importance to representing his constituents than to solving the problems of the country. He is certainly aware that, if he does not succeed in pleasing his constituents, he will not stay around long to grapple with the problems of the nation.

Perhaps more important, in psychological terms, is that constituency work is easier — not necessarily easier to solve but easier to handle — and MPs are human enough to share the common preference for what is easier! Cases are a world of single instances, presented in readily apprehensible human terms, and most people feel more at home with the concrete. Policymaking involves abstract, conceptualized, and generalized judgements, all of which is hard work. If MPs are to be induced to devote themselves to a task so demanding, they will have at the very least to be assured in their own minds that their constituency work is in good — and a sufficient number of — hands.

Here we come squarely to the principal limitation upon the legislative activity of a Member of Parliament — he is loaded with constituency problems and to a much smaller extent inescapable political duties, which consume the substantial portion of his time and energy and leave him with a very limited amount of both to spend in policymaking. In my view this internal constraint is the principal limitation upon the legislative creativity of the Member of Parliament.

I am just not able to be prepared in advance for a committee meeting, whether it concerns a bill, or estimates, or an investigation. I do not have time to analyze in advance the material that witnesses submit, or that is made available by the government for advance consideration. From ten years' experience in committees I would dare to say that this is also true of all other members except those who are the principal spokesmen for the opposition on a particular committee. The reason they are exceptions is that their party normally makes available to them in their committee function the services of one or two researchers from the party research office, whose duty it is to prepare material and questions in advance. Other members do not have the advantage of such a service and are therefore in fact not prepared for the committee meetings that they attend. Personally, I am constantly forced to draw on my intellectual capital to participate intelligently in committee.

It needs little imagination to see what a transformation would be wrought in a committee meeting if all of the members were prepared. The member or his staff would have studied documentary evidence and interviewed public servants or others in advance. There would be seemingly no end to the questions, and the witnesses would be delighted or embarrassed, as the case might be. The questions would be penetrating, consecutive, and presumably would lead to a new and clearer understanding of the issue by all participants. New areas of concern would be illuminated. The total effect would be that the committee system would be burst open at the seams from the quantity of business, and we might even see attitudes change on one side or the other as a result of a new understanding of the subject matter.

Committees of twenty (and, in two present cases, thirty) could not continue to function at all. No committee larger than ten or twelve would be functional, because all of the members, or at least all of the members who chose to be active, would pursue the subject matter incessantly. The only relieving feature with respect to time would be that something less than 100 per cent of the members ever have an interest in serious policymaking. The others would either not attend at all (as they often do not now) or would remain silent (also not an uncommon feature at the present time), allowing their more concerned colleagues to press on in their search for information.

This would be a different system, and in my view a better one, than we now possess, and it is premised on providing the members with legislative assistance so that they can cope with the legislative dimensions of their positions. I recall that the first time I met an American congressman he had brought his counsel with him to assist in the discussion. I was impressed then, as I have been on other occasions when I have met, say, the foreign policy advisors of various American senators.

There is no scientifically ascertainable number of assistants that would automatically enable a member to be a legislator as well as a representative, but the best estimate I can make as to the desirable number is eight, exactly twice the size of the present staff. That number would provide a constituency staff of two and an Ottawa office of six, including at least two legislative assistants.

Traditional and Partisan Impediments to Reform

I have already touched on the attitudinal impediments to the legislative role of the MP implicit in his preference for his representative role. But there are others.

A reformed committee system might be resisted by older or more traditionalist members who are more accustomed to the House than to standing committees or who regard the manoeuvrability or publicity possible in the House as more advantageous than that in committee.

To a large extent what goes on in the House is show business, a ritual stating of positions by committed antagonists with the only real debate consisting in the wit or forcefulness or verbal ingenuity of the participants. Some members relish it precisely because it is what it is, despite its limited legislative possibilities. Their attitudes are likely to change with time, and especially with the televising of committee proceedings. In any event, I am concerned at the moment with the psychological restraints on members who want to participate in committees.

There are also members who are more concerned with party orthodoxy than with individual participation. For them, whether they are in government or in opposition, the interests of the party are predominant and that of the individual, subordinate. To some extent, as I have suggested, the partisanship that springs up in committees is natural and almost inevitable. But to some extent it is also a result of the fact that there are party stalwarts on both sides who are not prepared to let party lines disappear in the common pursuit of good government.

At present there are comparatively few occasions on which members do not follow party lines in either House or committee, and there are even fewer occasions on which the government majority does not in any event carry the day. It is worth emphasizing that this tendency to vote with one's party is as true of opposition members as it is of government members.

The motivation is probably varied. One explanation is that the desire for promotion keeps most MPs in line, at least most of the time. Promotion for a backbencher consists of becoming a committee chairman, a parliamentary secretary or cabinet minister if on the government side, or a whip, or simply going on a parliamentary trip, though the parties do not in fact closely correlate travelling perquisites with performance. Promotion is undeniably a factor in voting, especially on the government side, and probably also in the official opposition where its members have some realistic hope of someday being in power. But members have not been slow to remark that there is not necessarily an exact correlation between toeing the party line and being promoted. Some notable backbench mavericks have made their way, perhaps because of the publicity they have gained as a result. It is also noteworthy, however, that many effective public critics of their party always vote with it, regardless of what they may have said. Parties can tolerate loose talk more than they can deviation in voting.

There may also be direct pressure by frontbenchers or whips on backbenchers to vote "the right way." At least, this is the suspicion, and it may sometimes be the practice. I have to say, however, that in nine years in parliament I have never seen such pressure operate. I have noticed that government members from time to time have voted against the government, and in the cases in which I have chosen to ask them, I have been told by them that no one ever spoke to them about their vote either before or afterwards. I have not myself had reason to vote against the government, but during the Judges' Affair in early 1976, when I was opposing the position of my party, I left the House with the whip's knowledge rather than vote for the government on an opposition motion, and no one ever questioned my action either before or since. I have heard the present prime minister say many times that "every vote is a free vote" and that in his mind the only sanction is the danger of an election. My personal experience would bear out the truth of this statement.

In my view the most compelling reason for not voting against one's party is the desire to get along with and to be well thought of by one's closest associates. It is, in other words, an in-group feeling that is generated by constant association, a common philosophy, and the desire to keep the party strong. I have remarked how quickly such in-group feeling arises in, say, government members of a committee when opposition members begin to make partisan attacks on the government. The reaction is immediate and almost spontaneous.

It follows that, if there were a general tendency to act more on one's own, this in-group factor would not operate to inhibit going in a different direction from the party. The solution obviously has to be found in developing a general expectation of independent behaviour in committee.

Conclusion

From the viewpoint of the executive, the most urgent reason for parliamentary reform comes from the need for more control over the legislative timetable, but for other Members of Parliament the most pressing necessity is to enlarge the role of backbenchers. This is a common aim of backbenchers in all parties, and should be realizable by means of a compromise that would surrender to the executive more control over the legislative timetable in the House, in return for greater independence for committees.

In fact, a number of changes could predispose the parliamentary system toward a fuller role for individual parliamentarians. The provision of more complete information to members on government activities would enable them to perform their role more effectively. The broadcasting of committee debates via radio and television would provide a greater incentive by making an active member more appreciated by the public. More regular scheduling would enable members to plan their time so that they could better avoid conflicts between their legislative and other functions.

Such changes would help members both in House and in committee, but any great expansion in backbench activity would necessarily have to be in parliamentary committees rather than in the Chamber itself. It is in committees that the detailed and most constructive work of parliament is done, and it is there that the backbencher could make his greatest contribution. This contribution is both legislative, with respect to policy proposals, and critical, with respect to expenditures.

Real improvement in the functioning of the parliamentary committees depends upon the possession and exercise of power by the standing committees: more control over their agenda and budget, the right to specialize, smaller membership and few conflicts in scheduling, an increased status for chairmen, and the loosening of party bonds in both government and opposition. Above all, it depends upon freeing the MP from the bonds that prevent him from achieving his role as legislator. These bonds consist partly of his sense of party loyalty, but principally of his fundamental commitment to serve the interests of his constituents.

The effect of a real reform in committees on the Canadian political system would probably be dramatic. The greater independence that the Member of Parliament came to exercise in committees would be reflected in his general role in the party, and would lead to a greater diffusion of decision-making, especially through the party caucuses. The way to participatory democracy is not through a closer contact between the prime minister or the cabinet and the people, but rather through a more obvious sharing of power in parliament among all members.

The first thing, however, is that a member must be free to participate. He is not fully free to do so if he is restrained by burdensome duties or attitudes. The removal of these structural and psychological impediments is fundamental to enlarging the role of the backbencher.

PROPOSED PARLIAMENTARY REFORMS*

Geoffrey Stevens

Parliamentary procedure is an overwhelmingly boring subject to most Canadians. But it's important. The quality of government we receive depends on more than the will, talent and sensitivity of the administration. It also depends on the ability of Parliament to represent our interests and to examine policies and process legislation in a manner that is expeditious, yet careful.

The proposals set out in the Clark Government's white paper are not revolutionary. But they do strike a reasonable balance between the twin needs of efficiency and careful scrutiny.

One of the most needed reforms is the simple proposal to reduce the size of parliamentary committees to a maximum of 11 members. At present, committee memberships range as high as 31 (Agriculture Committee). With two dozen committees operating, a busy MP may have two or three hearings going on simultaneously. A case can be made for going beyond the white paper — by reducing the number of committees, as well.

Another small, but important reform breaks sharply with parliamentary tradition. The white paper recommends that the Opposition be permitted to question Cabinet ministers about their actions in previous portfolios. . . .

At long last, speeches are to be shortened. Anyone who follows Commons debates is familiar with the pathetic spectacle of an MP trying to stretch 10 minutes' worth of material to fill a 40-minute speech on a subject he knows nothing about to begin with. In the future, 20 minutes, not 40, will be the limit for most speeches. But what's wrong with 10 minutes?

The first hour of the Commons day is all that most Canadians ever see of Parliament, and it is often a ragged spectacle. The white paper would improve it by abolishing the Standing Order 43 procedure which consumes the first 15 minutes — members' requests for unanimous consent (seldom given) to introduce motions on matters which are theoretically of great urgency (but seldom are). The daily Question Period would be lengthened from 45 minutes to one hour. Opposition MPs will like that, although most, if pressed, would admit that 30 minutes is quite enough on many days.

There will be a partial return to the old way of considering departmental spending estimates. Each spring, the Leader of the Opposition will be able to designate two departments whose estimates he wants debated in the Commons (rather than in standing committees). Debate will extend into the summer, if there's a good issue.

It's a way to blockade and embarrass the Government, but it won't improve the quality of the scrutiny of Government spending. The white paper is strangely silent on this point. Nor does it deal adequately with ways to speed up, and improve, the consideration of legislation. One proposal which has been advanced many times, but which is not mentioned in the

---

* From *The Globe and Mail*, Toronto, December 6 and 7, 1979. By permission. The full reference to the White Paper issued by the Clark government under the name of the Hon. Walter Baker, President of the Privy Council and Leader of the Government in the House, is *Position Paper: The Reform of Parliament*, November, 1979.

white paper, is to divide Government legislation into three categories. Minor bills would be given second reading and sent to committee without debate in the Commons. Major bills would be given open-ended debate. Those in the middle would be subject to a time allocation negotiated in advance among the parties. . . .

The white paper is not a perfect document. The reforms it suggests are not as far-reaching as Prime Minister Joe Clark indicated they would be during the election campaign. In Government, the Conservatives are not prepared to endure as much misery as they sought to inflict when they were in opposition.

For example, Commons committees will not have anything approaching open-ended investigatory power. They will be able to *talk* about any subject within their ambit, because the annual reports of departments and agencies will be referred to them automatically, but they will be constrained if they seek to *act*.

If a committee wishes to conduct an investigation, the Government will not be able to reject it out of hand. The inquiry will be deemed to be authorized if at least 50 MPs, 10 or more from each of two political parties, endorse the proposed investigation. But there are a couple of catches. First, no more than five committee investigations will be permitted at any one time (and there are two dozen committees operating at the moment). Second, the research budget for an investigation will have to be approved by the Commons' Commissioners of Internal Economy (a committee of privy councillors controlled by the Government).

To be effective, committees need permanent staff which is expert in the field (say, communications or foreign affairs), as committees in Washington have it. But they won't get it under the white paper proposals. The Government wants, instead, to increase the research staff of the Parliamentary Library. There's nothing wrong with the library researchers. But they are, by the nature of their employ, non-political.

On the positive side, the white paper proposals would compel the Government to respond within 21 days to every committee report. On the negative side, even if the Commons were to vote concurrence in a committee report, it would not be binding on the Government — because this, says the white paper, "would be to invite the destruction of responsible Cabinet government." (Humbug.)

The same reluctance to go all the way is seen in the proposals for private members' bills. At the moment, one hour a day is set aside for private members' business (including bills). The white paper proposes to set aside one full day a week (Wednesday one week, Thursday the next) for 20 weeks per session for private members. This way, a bill would be guaranteed at least 2½ hours of debating time. But there is no guarantee that it would ever come to a vote. It would require a motion supported by at least 60 MPs either to force a vote or to extend the debating time.

Finally, the Government has backed away from its campaign proposal to allow MPs to organize their lives by introducing fixed recesses. "An automatic adjournment at the end of June, or at Christmas or Easter, would deprive the Government of the flexibility it frequently needs," says the white paper. Instead, there will be a device under which adjournment times are fixed in advance, subject always to the Government using its voting strength to shorten or cancel the recess.

BETTER WAY TO CHOOSE HOUSE SPEAKER*

Donald C. MacDonald

Tries for "Continuing" Speaker

The appointment of a "continuing" (as opposed to the misnomer of "permanent") Speaker is the ultimate objective in assuring that the Office of Speaker assist in establishing the independence of the legislative branch. Unfortunately, governments in all jurisdictions in Canada, federal as well as provincial, have been reluctant to move in this direction.

In 1957 Prime Minister Diefenbaker offered the position to Stanley Knowles, veteran CCF/NDP MP for Winnipeg North Centre and acknowledged expert on parliamentary rules. Since the appointment would have been from the opposition ranks, it was assumed to be that of a "continuing" Speaker, though no commitment accompanied the offer. In any case, Knowles did not accept the post because it would have forced him into a non-partisan role, in complete disassociation from the party which he had helped to pioneer.

Lucien Lamoreux was appointed Speaker in the House of Commons following the 1965 election, and was re-appointed in 1968 and 1972. He actually resigned from the Liberal party and ran as an independent in 1968, but since Prime Minister Trudeau was unwilling to officially designate his appointment as that of an "independent," the opposition parties were not disposed to withhold candidates in an election. So that effort to move to an "independent" or "continuing" Speaker also proved abortive.

Some months in advance of the 1981 Ontario provincial election, Premier William Davis raised with Jack Stokes, New Democratic MPP for Lake Nipigon and Speaker for the 31st Parliament, whether he would consider running as an independent. Presumably, this sounding was in consideration of Stokes' re-appointment. But Stokes did not consider the offer acceptable, because the Premier indicated that he could give no assurance that his party would support a second term for Stokes, and there had been no consultation with the Liberal party. As had occurred in the federal field, the first minister did not approach the question of a "continuing" Speaker with sufficient conviction to make its realization possible.

Intermediate Step Possible

But there is an intermediate step along the road to establishing the role of "continuing" Speaker; namely, the manner in which a Speaker is chosen and elected. It is this process which merits review in the wake of experience with the choice of Speaker for the 32nd Parliament in Ontario after the 1981 election.

* Slightly revised version of an article which first appeared in *The Globe and Mail*, Toronto, May 5, 1981. Mr. MacDonald is the MPP for York South and former leader of the Ontario NDP. By permission.

Jack Stokes had been Speaker for three and one-half years in the previous Parliament. He was called by Premier Davis on a Thursday, five days before the opening of the new Legislature, and informed that the new Speaker would be chosen from among the government members. Later that day, George Kerr, a former cabinet minister, was offered the post, but declined for personal reasons. Other candidates were considered but not approached the following day; only late on Saturday was John Turner, MPP for Peterborough, reached, informing him that he was the Premier's choice for the new Speaker. He accepted. The Easter weekend intervened and not until noon on Tuesday, three hours before the opening of the new Legislature, was word of the choice formally telephoned by the Premier to the Leader of the Opposition and the leader of the New Democratic Party. At that point, it was no longer news, because the weekend papers had carried accounts of Turner's being chosen.

That the choice of a new Speaker should be left to such a late date indicates a measure of disrespect for the importance of the high office. The nominee has to scramble to accommodate himself to the duties and practices of the position in a two- or three-day period. This is particularly the case when the nominee has not had the experience of deputy Speaker or any comparable committee chairmanship.

Servant of All the House

Of even greater concern is the implication of such unilateral action on the choice of the Speaker as the chief officer and servant of all members of the House, and not just the governing party. On April 3, 1980, a resolution submitted in my name was debated by the Legislature with regard to the process of choosing and electing officers of the Legislature. With reference to the Speaker, the resolution read: "In order to establish in practice as well as in principle the independence of the Legislature, the nomination of the Speaker should be made by the Premier only after consultation with the leaders of the opposition parties . . . " The resolution was adopted by the House by voice vote, with no opposition being recorded.

The Premier chose to ignore that unanimous view and to assume that a call to the leaders of the opposition parties, literally three hours before the House opened, was tantamount to consultation. If there had been any intention to abide by the spirit of the resolution adopted by the House less than a year ago, that call could have been made on the day John Turner agreed to be the Premier's nominee.

Nobody disputes that a Speaker must be chosen before a Legislature can officially be opened. Without its chief presiding officer, the legislative session cannot legally get underway. Since the process for the choice of Speaker must precede the opening, there is general agreement that it can most appropriately be conducted among party leaders.

During the debate on my resolution mentioned above, Russell Rowe, a former Speaker of the Legislature, stated: "The first part of the resolution I can agree with; namely, the procedure for the election of our Speaker" after consultation with the leaders of the opposition parties. Mr. Rowe added:

In fact, that is basically the way it is done today. The Speaker is now elected by the House in every sense of the word, which implies that any other person's name can be placed in nomination and a true election held. That's the parliamentary way of doing things and I'm sure most of us recall that this is actually what happened in our sister province, British Columbia, just three or four years ago when two people were nominated and a true election was held.

The biennial conference of Speakers from across the world has just been held in Ottawa, with a two-day stay in Toronto, under the auspices of the Ontario Branch of the Commonwealth Parliamentary Association. While there is a similarity about procedures in legislatures which have grown out of the British parliamentary tradition, interesting differences have evolved. After talking to experienced officers of Commonwealth parliaments, it appears there are three processes in operation.

Three Methods of Choice

The first is that followed in Ontario in advance of the opening of the 32nd Provincial Parliament, where the choice is made by the Premier from among the ranks of government party members without genuine consultation with opposition party leaders. This runs the grave risk of the Speaker appearing to be the choice of the governing party rather than the whole Legislature and therefore fails to respect adequately the independence of the Legislature from the executive branch of government.

The second is the procedure followed at Westminster. There the choice of Speaker is made only after extensive consultation and negotiation among all party leaders and whips. The black-balling principle obtains: if any party disagrees about a choice, an effort is made to find a person for whom there is general approval. Significantly, once that decision is made, the formal nomination and seconding in the Commons is made not by the prime minister and the leader of the official opposition, but by backbenchers from each party, as symbolic and substantive reaffirmation that the Speaker is the choice of all members and not just of the prime minister and the government party.

The third procedure is that which is generally followed in Australia. There the government and opposition parties each makes its nomination and the election is fought, with campaigns of varying intensity, and resolved by a vote in the House. Normally the votes follow party lines, though on occasion personalities and differences in perceived capabilities of competing candidates sometimes result in voting across party lines and an opposition nominee being chosen.

There are obvious demerits in this procedure. The choice of Speaker is decided in the arena of partisan politics and there is grave danger that the ultimate choice will not have the whole-hearted support of those who lost in the vote. This will inevitably jeopardize the desirable objective of the Speaker commanding the respect and support of all members of Parliament from the outset of assuming office.

Westminster Model Best

Apparently, Premier Davis finds distasteful the prospect of holding a "true election" among competing candidates. If the emergence of this procedure in Ontario is to be avoided, it can be best done by consultation and negotiation among party leaders along the lines followed at Westminster.

In his response to NDP leader Michael Cassidy's objections to the process, involving no genuine consultation with opposition leaders in the choice of Speaker for the current Legislature, Mr. Davis said: "I hope to spare our very distinguished visitors to the assembly on this first day some internal discussion." If the Premier wants to spare the distinguished visitors who crowd the Legislature on opening day from "internal discussion," but only at the cost of denying the Legislature the right to engage in a genuine election of its chief officer when no consultation has taken place, then there is a solution.

We might consider the procedure followed in Ottawa, where the House of Commons meets in the morning of opening day, with "no strangers in the House," and chooses the Speaker. That would avoid the tedious procedure of the Lieutenant-Governor coming in to open proceedings, having to leave while the Speaker is elected, and only then being able to return and open the Session by reading the Speech from the Throne.

THE ADMINISTRATION OF LEGISLATURES*

Robert J. Fleming

The Emerging Legislatures

The position of administrator in the legislative setting is a comparatively new one. Until recent years, very little attention has been paid to the housekeeping part of legislative operations. The role of a Member of the Legislature was considered to be part-time; pay was extremely modest; and there were few services in terms of staff, offices and equipment, allowances for travel, accommodation or constituency offices. "Sessional Indemnities" were usually paid to Members by the Office of the Clerk and the administrative function in legislatures was a small, relatively unimportant facet of the total operation.

During the late 1960s and early 1970s, this began to change. The work load of legislators everywhere increased substantially, and with it the demand for permanent office space, full-time staff, adequate means of communication and other forms of assistance. This has reached the point where the 1980 annual operating budget of the U.S. Congress exceeds $1 billion; that of the Canadian Parliament is in excess of $100 million; and the

* From *Legislature Administration in Canada and the United States: A 1980 Assessment Including an Overview of the House of Representatives* by Robert J. Fleming, Director of Administration and Secretary of the Board of Internal Economy, Ontario Legislature, Queen's Park, Toronto, September, 1980. By permission.

operating budgets of legislatures in Ontario, Quebec, California and New York are each well over $20 million.

A large percentage of these expenditures represents staff salaries, providing a further illustration of how some legislatures are burgeoning. For instance, in 1979 more than 10,000 staff were employed at the U.S. House of Representatives and in Members' district offices (Congressmen may pay their top staff person up to $52,000). And a survey of Canadian legislatures in 1979 showed that 1,100 staff were employed in various categories in the Quebec National Assembly.

• • •

The Management of the Institution

Management tasks in a modern legislature are extremely varied and usually include: administering Members' salaries, allowances and expenses; offices, furniture and equipment; stationery supplies and postage; telephone services; constituency newsletters; House reporting facilities; restaurant and food services; provision of radio and television coverage of the House; media relations; tours and information; overseeing the hiring of non-partisan staff; library and research services; printing and word-processing systems; preparing legislative estimates; maintenance and housekeeping (which are often looked after by the Ministry of Public Works or Government Services); and security. In addition to these services there are, of course, other services provided by the party caucuses themselves.

The remarkable thing from the perspective of the traditional role of the administrator is that literally every legislature in every U.S. state or Canadian province has taken a different approach to internal administration and organization. Several legislatures view management as a centralized system placing all professional administrative and service units under the Speaker. The majority, however, still divide managerial responsibility among several unconnected offices with the result that authority is diffused and organization is less effective. It is unlikely that this will change in the foreseeable future. . . .

The Speaker, as head of the legislative branch, is chief procedural and administrative Officer of the House and must be in a position to meet the legitimate needs of all Members for staff, office space and equipment, and to provide such services as transportation and accommodation. In order to enable the Speaker to provide these services without restriction and to ensure that legal privileges provided to Members are protected, control over the precincts of parliament is deemed to be a legislative responsibility, separate and distinct from executive influence. Legislative staff are employees of the House rather than the Executive.

In the U.S., the principle of the separation of legislative and executive functions is understood and firmly entrenched. However, in Canada, very little has been done to establish the pre-eminence of the legislature as a distinct body with its own administration. Ontario has gone the farthest of any Canadian province in attempting to remedy this situation. A Commission on the Legislature was established in the early 1970s with a mandate to recommend ways of strengthening the role of Members of the Legislature. Most of the Commission's recommendations have been implemented.

This absence of separation between legislative and executive functions in many legislatures makes it doubly difficult to institute cohesive financial and administrative procedures. The following examples may help to illustrate this dichotomy: the regular employees of the Quebec National Assembly, the Manitoba Legislature and the Nova Scotia Legislature are in fact civil servants (i.e., employees of the Government) rather than employees of the Legislature. In Saskatchewan, the Treasury Board of Cabinet (Executive Branch) is the body responsible for financial management of the Legislature. In British Columbia, the equivalent role to Treasury Board is performed by the Provincial Secretary, a member of the Executive Council. The Legislatures of New Brunswick, Nova Scotia and Prince Edward Island and British Columbia have no finance or administrative offices separate from the Executive. The only Legislatures in Canada where the Speaker has jurisdiction over the entire legislative building are Quebec, New Brunswick and Prince Edward Island. . . .

. . . If economics dictate that the Executive provide legislative services, a workable solution may lie in having all staff performing legislative services reporting to the Speaker regardless of who pays them. The Canadian experience (and that of the U.S., due principally to the multiplicity of policy bodies in most state legislatures) serves to underline that the administrative process is extremely hard to identify or define. Certain procedures have arisen on an *ad hoc* basis over a period of years. These are often ill-defined and illogical, but somehow are workable. . . .

Ontario Commission

. . . The Ontario Commission studying the Legislature recommended a series of sweeping changes: a Board of Internal Economy was created, with power to manage the finances of the Assembly from one central point, and an Administrator was appointed to co-ordinate all financial and administrative functions in the Legislature. In the ensuing five years, in what appeared to be rather laborious deliberation, the Board (consisting of the Speaker as Chairman, three Cabinet Ministers, and a Member from each caucus) succeeded in establishing standards for everything from constituency office funding to equipment and supplies for Members' offices, to salary classification for Legislative Assembly staff. The result of this proliferation of policy-making on the part of the Board is that the operating procedures of the Assembly have been substantially organized into a Manual of Administration containing regulations and operating procedures for financial management and personnel practices of the Assembly. Once policy has been established, the Board does not become involved in the day-to-day administrative machinery used to implement policy.

Ottawa Report

. . . A number of reorganizational studies of major legislative bodies have recommended centralized services: at the Palace of Westminster, the 1974

Report of Sir Edward Compton, followed by the Bottomly Report; in Washington, the 1977 U.S. House of Representatives' Commission on Administrative Review; in Ottawa, the 1979 Report on the Administration of the House of Commons by Mr. James J. MacDonnell, who served as Auditor General from 1973-1980. Of these major studies . . . only the Ottawa Report has been accepted for implementation. . . .

. . . The situation at the House of Commons in Ottawa is somewhat simpler, due principally to the non-partisan role of the Speaker, the strength of the former Auditor General who had determined that the public purse will be well managed, and a Government and opposition parties who realize that the reputation of Parliament is dependent on an efficient and effective administrative branch. As a result, the Auditor General, at the invitation of the Speaker, was able to undertake a remarkably swift review of most aspects of the administration of the House of Commons and actually install an Administrator and a Comptroller, all within an eight-month period. In his report to the Speaker, dated October 31, 1979, James MacDonnell outlined his two key recommendations:

—establish the position of Administrator to co-ordinate and direct the administrative functions of the House of Commons. The Administrator should have equivalent rank to a Deputy Minister and should report directly to the Speaker of the House of Commons;

—establish the position of Comptroller of the House of Commons to develop, co-ordinate and maintain all activities relating to accounting and financial administration and controls of the House of Commons and its Members. The Comptroller should report directly to the Administrator.

The Ontario Legislature too has been a crucible of change over the past five years, and trends and ideas initiated by Ontario are increasingly being used as a benchmark by other provinces instituting administrative reform. . . .

The Role of Administrator

The administrator, as head of a central administration in the legislative environment, is called upon to work in an extraordinarily complex arena surrounded by political, bureaucratic and media pressures. He must implement the dictates of a properly constituted policy committee or board of elected Members, and adhere to procedures and regulations. At the same time, he must do his utmost to serve Members and meet their needs. He must not only be totally impartial, but must be seen to be so. He must be consistent in order to retain credibility, and he must know just how far his authority extends. He is given responsibility for the sound day-to-day management of the public purse, but must be constantly aware that his authority may not be exercised in his own right. He is, after all, only the representative of the Speaker, who has been chosen by the Government with the support of all parties to manage and monitor the affairs of the House from a totally impartial position.

Anticipating the Future

Some legislatures have experienced an enormous growth during the past decade. . . . As more and more states and provinces reach the point where being a legislator is a full-time profession, the need for a professional administrative staff, with the ability to manage the various legislative support services, will increase accordingly. The National Conference of State Legislatures [in the U.S.] has anticipated this growth in administrative support services and has already become a catalyst and information exchange for trends in state legislatures. . . .

In Canada, although there isn't any precise equivalent to NCSL, various groups have been active in collating and distributing information on the day-to-day administration of provincial legislatures. *A Comparative Study of Administrative Structures of Canadian Legislatures,* produced in Ontario, has been well received not only by those working in legislatures, but also by academics, students and other observers of the political scene. . . .

[*Editor's note:* See the following article.]

A COMPARATIVE STUDY OF CANADIAN LEGISLATURES*

Robert J. Fleming and J. Thomas Mitchinson

• • •

Introduction

There is still little hard, factual information available about the day-to-day organization and operation of legislatures in Canada and the United States. . . .

The purpose of the Comparative Study, which is produced annually, is to bring together current information and to conduct an in-depth examination of the internal workings of the various legislative assemblies in Canada, from the standpoint of human resources and administrative organization. Once gathered, this information is correlated in an attempt to determine what patterns of development are emerging. The House of Commons is included in the Study because in many ways it provides a helpful benchmark from which to measure other legislatures.

The Study is divided into five sections: Members' Indemnities, Salaries, Allowances and Benefits; Support Services for Private Members; Administrative Structure; House Statistics; and a Profile of Members elected to every legislature in Canada. A written assessment of the information contained in the various tables and charts precedes each section.

* From *Canadian Legislatures: The 1981 Comparative Study,* edited by Robert J. Fleming and J. Thomas Mitchinson, Office of the Assembly, Queen's Park, Toronto, 1981. Mr. Fleming is Director of Administration for the Legislative Assembly of Ontario and Secretary to the Board of Internal Economy. Mr. Mitchinson is his Executive Assistant. The data reprinted here are only samples of the voluminous information provided in this publication. By permission.

Although no attempt is made in the Study to examine or evaluate procedural reforms which may have taken place in Canadian legislatures in recent years, the Comparative Study indicates that since the mid-1970s all legislatures have been going through substantial change, growth and development with respect to every aspect of their operating and organizational structures. It is anticipated that this will continue at an accelerated pace as more and more legislatures become peopled by full-time legislators and electronic technology in the form of various communication systems begins to take its place in the legislative environment.

The Study examines the backgrounds of the 1,014 men and women currently sitting in the House of Commons and the provincial and territorial legislatures and attempts to ascertain which segments of the population are most strongly represented and whether new trends are developing in terms of the types of people being attracted to federal and provincial politics.

Canadian legislators at the provincial level are now, on the whole, more highly paid and have better facilities at their disposal than their U.S. counterparts. A Québec Member receives $40,600, Ontario $40,000 and five provinces in fact pay their elected representatives in excess of $27,000. Private offices are provided for all Members of legislatures in Canada except the five smallest provinces and territories. In the United States in 1980, only 18 legislatures were able to accommodate Members in private offices. Only seven states paid Assemblymen in excess of $20,000, the highest being Illinois at $28,800. Twenty-three states paid their legislators less than $12,000.

Members' allowances, services and facilities have, in the past few years, been expanded considerably in every province, not only in terms of office accommodation and staffing but also personal insurance and pension provisions, travel and accommodation, telephone, postage, etc.

At the present time eight provinces provide an allowance of some sort to enable Members to engage constituency staff and in some cases to have as many as two constituency offices. This ability to serve constituents did not exist in most provinces prior to 1979.

The financial management of the House of Commons and almost every other legislature in Canada is now centralized under a Board of Internal Economy (the equivalent of Treasury Board for the Government). This development and the trend to include Opposition Members on the Board has come into being only recently.

In the past year professional administrators have been appointed to serve the British Columbia and Saskatchewan Legislatures, with responsibility for overseeing all financial and administrative questions. (Full-time Clerks have also been appointed in British Columbia, Newfoundland, Nova Scotia and New Brunswick.)

These and the many other trends catalogued and charted in the Study indicate that the changes which take place in some legislatures are filtering into other legislatures. It also indicates that "biggest" is not necessarily "best," as some of the smaller legislatures appear to be ahead of some of the larger in terms of services provided to Members and in organizational structure. Across the board, there seems to be no "right" way of doing things, no special uniformity, but rather a variation on some common themes. In short, the Study paints a mosaic where each legislature appears to be reaching its own conclusion but these conclusions bear a remarkable similarity.

Due to the substantial amounts of money involved and the large numbers of professional staff now serving elected Members, it is clear that the Federal Parliament and all provincial and territorial legislatures have recognized the importance of formulating guidelines, and are taking whatever steps are necessary in order to improve internal organization and institute efficient and appropriate financial procedures. Data collected for this Study shows that every legislature, regardless of size, has been able to introduce certain policies and procedures which are both innovative and tailored to individual needs. Although no magic answers exist, sharing of experiences has gone a long way towards simplifying the formulation of appropriate policies and structures for each legislature.

• • •

INDEMNITIES, SALARIES, ALLOWANCES AND BENEFITS

Remuneration for Elected Members

REMUNERATION	H of C	Nfld	P E I	N S	N B	Que
Effective Date	1 Jan 81[1]	1 Apr 81	1 Jan 81	1 Jan 81	1 Apr 81	1 Jan 81
PRIVATE MEMBERS						
Basic Indemnity	43,800	13,680	12,800	15,600	21,980	33,110
% increase at time of last revision	19.48%	8%	5.75%	5.12%	5.76%	6%
Tax-free Allowance	*14,700	6,840	6,300	7,800	8,792	7,500
*tax-free allowance is increased to $18,100 for 23 MPs & $19,500 for 2 MPs						
ADDITIONAL INDEMNITY FOR VARIOUS OFFICE HOLDERS						
Prime Minister	50,000	30,730	34,000	32,000	32,970	43,043
Minister with Portfolio	33,600	18,700	24,000	25,000	21,980	30,580
Minister without Portfolio	33,600	8,657	N/A	7,500–25,000	N/A	30,580
Parliamentary Assistant	7,500	10,000 (1 only)	N/A	N/A	N/A	8,340
Opposition Leader	33,600	18,700	19,700	25,000	21,980	30,580
Third Party Leader	20,200	N/A	N/A	10,000	N/A	12,510
Speaker	33,600	18,700	7,500	15,000	16,485	30,580
Deputy Speaker	17,700	10,000	3,800	7,500	8,242.50	13,900
Deputy Chairman of Committee of Whole	7,500	5,000	N/A	N/A	N/A	N/A
Standing Committee Chairman	N/A	N/A	N/A	1,500	N/A	4,170
Opposition House Leader	16,600	10,000	N/A	1,500	N/A	12,510
Third Party House Leader	7,200	N/A	N/A	N/A	N/A	11,120
Chief Government Whip	9,300	3,090	N/A	2,250 ($75/Mem)	1,500	12,510
Assistant Government Whip	5,400	N/A	N/A	N/A	N/A	6,950
Chief Opposition Whip	9,300	3,090	N/A	1,050 ($75/Mem)	1,500	8,340
Assistant Opposition Whip	5,400	N/A	N/A	N/A	N/A	6,950
Chief Third Party Whip	5,400	N/A	N/A	150 ($75/Mem)	N/A	N/A
Assistant Third Party Whip	N/A	N/A	N/A	N/A	N/A	N/A
Number of Members receiving more than basic indemnity	69(24%)	24(46%)	13(40%)	43(82%)	25(43%)	54(44%)

[1] Legislation passed in July, 1981 provides for automatic annual increases at the beginning of each year amounting to a percentage point less than either the consumer price index or the industrial composite index, whichever is lower. The following amounts are examples of the results of the calculated increases which became effective January 1, 1982: private member's bas-

Ont.	Man.	Sask.	Alta.	B.C.	N.W.T.	Yukon
1 Apr 81	1 Apr 81	1 Jan 81	1 Jan 81	1 Jan 81	1 Apr 81	16 Apr 81
30,000	17,967	16,804	22,050	26,200	14,512	18,750
18.75%	9.1%	9.5%	5%	12.4%	8%	unknown
10,000	8,983	5,896	6,485	13,100	N/A	7,250–9,250
39,200	24,000	32,134	41,265	35,800	39,000	26,300
23,300	20,600	24,175	33,600	30,700	39,000	21,300
11,700	15,600	N/A	23,835	23,200	N/A	N/A
7,200	2,500	5,896	N/A	N/A	N/A	N/A
27,300	20,600	24,175	33,600	24,300	N/A	2,500
13,700	N/A	N/A	N/A	N/A	N/A	1,000
17,200	6,000+$50 per day of work when House is in recess	9,434	20,580	24,300	8,500	6,000
7,200	3,500	5,601	7,665	10,850	5,500	3,000
5,000	2,500	1,500	5,040	N/A	N/A	N/A
3,900	N/A	1,500/sess.	N/A	N/A	4,500	N/A
8,900	2,500	1,500/sess.	N/A	N/A	N/A	2,500
6,700	N/A	N/A	N/A	N/A	N/A	N/A
8,900	2,500	2,500	N/A	N/A	N/A	N/A
6,100/4,400	N/A	1,500	N/A	N/A	N/A	N/A
6,100	2,500	2,500	N/A	N/A	N/A	N/A
4,400	N/A	1,500	N/A	N/A	N/A	N/A
5,000	N/A	750 /sess.	N/A	N/A	N/A	N/A
4,000	N/A	N/A	N/A	N/A	N/A	N/A
72(57%)	27(47%)	36(59%)	32(40%)	23(41%)	9(40%)	9(56%)

ic indemnity, $48,600; tax-free allowance, $16,300; (total for an MP, $64,900); prime minister, $120,400; cabinet minister, leader of the opposition, Speaker of the House, $102,100. The indemnities for the other positions in the list were increased accordingly also.

INDEMNITIES, SALARIES, ALLOWANCES AND BENEFITS

Pension Benefits

c. contribution level
d. eligibility formula

H OF C	c. compulsory contribution of 11% of basic indemnity - optional contribution of up to 11% of all additional indemnities and salaries (excluding tax-free allowance) - contributions of basic indemnity cease when Member has earned full pension d. minimum of 6 years service - no minimum age required
NFLD.	c. 7% of all indemnities and salaries (excluding tax-free allowance) - contributions matched by L.A. d. age plus years of service - 60 (55 for Premier) - minimum of 5 years service and 2 general elections
P.E.I.	c. 6½% of all indemnities and salaries (including tax-free allowance) - L.A. contributes 26% (4 x Member's contribution) d. minimum 50 years of age - 2 general elections or minimum of 8 years elected service
N.S.	c. 8% of all indemnities and salaries (excluding tax-free allowance) - contributions matched by Government d. 10 years elected service or age 55
N.B.	c. 9% of all indemnities (excluding tax-free allowance) - 6% of Ministerial salary - contributions matched by L.A. d. elected service over 10 sessions - no minimum age required
QUE.	c. 8% of basic indemnity (excluding tax-free allowance) - additional indemnities included at option of Member - contributions matched by L.A. d. minimum of 5 years service and 2 general elections - no minimum age required
ONT.	c. 8½% of all indemnities and salaries (excluding tax-free allowance) - contributions matched by L.A. d. age plus years of service - 55 - minimum of 5 years service
MAN.	c. 7% of all indemnities and salaries (including tax-free allowance) d. age plus years of service - 55 - minimum of 8 years service or 2 general elections
SASK.	c. 9% of all indemnities and salaries (including tax-free allowance) - contributions matched by Government - Government increases contribution as age of Member increases (adds 2% if Member between 41-50 - adds 4% if Member 51 and older) d. age 55 - 1 year minimum service required
ALTA.	c. 7% of indemnities (including tax-free allowance) - Ministerial salaries excluded - contributions matched by L.A. d. 5 consecutive years service - no minimum age required
B.C.	c. 4% of all indemnities and salaries (excluding tax-free allowance) - contributions matched by L.A. d. age plus years of service - 60 - Member must be at least 55 years old to be eligible and must have been elected in 2 general elections

| N.W.T. | c. no contribution by Members |
| | d. age 55 - minimum of 6 years service or 2 general elections |

| YUKON | c. N/A |
| | d. N/A |

SUPPORT SERVICES FOR PRIVATE MEMBERS

At Legislature

a. office

| H OF C | — 1 office per Member - space allocated by Speaker (Sergeant-at-Arms) - office supplies and equipment purchased by H of C Administrative Office from either Government department or private supplier |

| NFLD. | — Opposition Leader, Ministers and Premier have separate offices - 1 office to each party for private Members - space allocated by Speaker - office supplies and equipment supplied by Clerk's Office - purchased through Government department |

| P.E.I. | — block of offices supplied to each caucus - space allocated by BOIE - office supplies and equipment purchased by L.A. through Government department |

| N.S. | — each caucus supplied with block of offices - space allocated by Speaker - supplies and equipment purchased by L.A. through Government department |

| N.B. | — each caucus supplied with block of offices - space allocated by BOIE - supplies and equipment purchased by Clerk's Office |

| QUE. | — 1 office per Member - space allocated by Speaker - furniture purchased and supplied by Government department - office supplies and equipment provided by L.A. |

| ONT. | — 1 office per Member (1973) - space allocated by Speaker - office supplies and equipment provided by L.A. from either Government department or private supplier |

| MAN. | — 1 office per Member (1981) - space allocated by Department of Government Services - furniture and equipment provided by Government but maintained and replaced by L.A. - purchases are made through Government Department |

| SASK. | — 1 office per Member (1979) - office equipment and supplies provided by L.A. |

| ALTA. | — 1 office per Member - space allocated by Premier - equipment and supplies provided by Clerk's Office - purchased either from Government department or private supplier |

| B.C. | — 1 office per Member (1978) - space allocated by Speaker - furniture supplied by Government - supplies and equipment provided by Speaker's Office - Speaker purchases through Government department |

N.W.T.	— 1 office for every 2 Members - space allocated by Speaker - equipment and supplies provided by L.A. - purchased through Government department
YUKON	— 1 office per Member (1978) - space allocated by Speaker - equipment and supplies provided by Government (L.A. is part of Government)

SUPPORT SERVICES FOR PRIVATE MEMBERS

At Legislature

b. staff

H OF C	— total allowance of $78,000 for both Ottawa and constituency offices - maximum of $62,304 for Ottawa - any number of employees allowed - staff are employees of Member - no union - Member can order desk top copier and either electronic memory typewriter or word processor and charge to this allowance
NFLD.	— 1 secretary for every 2 Members - salary range is $12,897 to $14,078 for private Members and $15,187 to $16,992 for Ministers and Opposition Leaders - staff are employees of L.A. - no union - BOIE establishes entitlement - salary rates tied to civil service
P.E.I.	— Government caucus has 1 secretary - Opposition caucus has 1 secretary and 1 researcher - salary range for secretary is $15,000 to $17,000 and for researcher is $30,000 - staff are casual employees of L.A. - no union - entitlement established by BOIE - salary rate established by caucus
N.S.	— each caucus given funds for secretarial purposes - number of employees is up to caucus - salary range is $12,910 to $14,582 - salary range tied to civil service - employees are hired for 4 year term by L.A. - no union
N.B.	— each caucus has 3 employees (2 secretaries, 1 research) - salary range for secretary is $13,440 to $20,034 and for research $22,458 to $28,183 - entitlement and salary range established by BOIE - employees of L.A. - no union
QUE.	— 1 secretary per Member - salary range is $15,524 to $17,405 - entitlement established by BOIE - salary range established by civil service - employees are civil servants - no union
ONT.	— 1 secretary/assistant per Member - salary range is $15,451 to $20,968 - entitlement and salary range established by BOIE - employees of caucus - 1 caucus is unionized
MAN.	— 3 secretaries for each caucus - salary range is $13,209 to $15,770 - entitlement and salary range established by BOIE - employees are civil servants - no union
SASK.	— each caucus has pool of full time and sessional employees - salary range is $16,164 to $19,488 - entitlement and salary range established by L.A. - employees of L.A. - no union

ALTA.   — 1 secretary per 4 Members - salary range is $16,188 to $20,988
- entitlement established by BOIE - salary range tied to civil service
- employees are civil servants but are hired only for the life of the parliament - no union

B.C.   — 1 secretary per Member during session - secretarial assistance provided by caucus in off-session - salary range is $1,000 to $1,500 per month
- entitlement and salary range established by Speaker
- employees of L.A. - no union

N.W.T.   — sessional staff supplied by L.A. as required, by secondment through civil service
- pay rates are tied to civil service - inter-session requirements are supplied by Speaker's Office - are casual employees in civil service - some unionized, depending on status in civil service

YUKON   — staff supplied by Clerk's Office on request basis

SUPPORT SERVICES FOR PRIVATE MEMBERS

At Legislature

c. office mail
d. telephone

H OF C   c. no limitations
d. paid by H of C - unlimited access to Government phone network
- unlimited long distance to constituency if not on Government network
- other long distance in Canada must be placed through Government operator - credit cards issued

NFLD.   c. unlimited volume - restricted to legislative business
d. unlimited regular and long distance - paid by L.A.
- unlimited telex
- credit cards issued

P.E.I.   c. only when House in session
d. regular and long distance charged to caucus allowances
- no credit cards

N.S.   c. postage allowance of $1,200 per year per Member included in caucus allowances - costs are charged to caucus
d. allowance of $1,200 per year per Member
- no credit cards

N.B.   c. charged to caucus allowances
d. unlimited regular and long distance within New Brunswick
- credit cards issued

QUE.   c. no limitations - paid by Government
d. regular and long distance paid by Government - no limitations
- credit cards issued - paid for by L.A.

ONT.   c. no limitations - paid by L.A.
d. regular and long distance paid by L.A. - no limitations (Member must verify calls)
- credit cards issued - paid by L.A.

MAN.	c. no limitations - paid by L.A. d. paid by L.A. - long distance limited to calls within Manitoba - no credit cards
SASK.	c. communications allowance equal to 3 x cost of 1st class letter x number of voters in Member's constituency d. unlimited regular and long distance - no credit cards
ALTA.	c. no limitations - paid by L.A. d. unlimited regular and long distance - paid by L.A. - credit cards issued
B.C.	c. no limitations - paid by Government d. unlimited regular and long distance - paid by Government - no credit cards
N.W.T.	c. no limitations - paid by L.A. d. unlimited regular and long distance paid by L.A. - no credit cards
YUKON	c. no limitations - paid by L.A. d. limited to $200 local and $400 long distance per Member per year - no credit cards

SUPPORT SERVICES FOR PRIVATE MEMBERS

In Constituency

a. general
b. categories of allowances

H OF C	a. annual allowance established by BOIE - first established 1973 b. minimum of $15,696 for staff (can use up to $78,000) - up to $8,360 for operation of office - up to $1,000 per parliament to assist Members with purchase of furniture and equipment
NFLD.	a. no program b. N/A
P.E.I.	a. no program - Member may use office space on a weekly basis in any of 5 regional offices run by Department of Community Affairs, free of charge b. N/A
N.S.	a. monthly allowance established by statute - first established 1978-79 b. $75 per month for staff - $60 per month for office - $65 per month for travel within constituency
N.B.	a. no program b. N/A
QUÉ.	a. annual allowance established by statute - first established 1969 b. up to $7,300 for office ($8,600 if Member has 2 offices) - up to $35,000 for staff ($38,500 to $41,100 if Member has 2 offices) - 4% of staff allowance for severance pay - actual operating expenses reimbursed on submission of receipts (no maximum)

ONT.	a. annual allowance established by BOIE - first established 1976 b. up to $8,000 for office - up to $20,318 for staff - 4% of staff allowance for vacation pay - up to $1,000 for postage, stationery and supplies
MAN.	a. annual allowance established by statute b. global allowance of $1,500 - no restrictions on use
SASK.	a. monthly allowance established by statute - first established 1981 b. $694 per month for staff - $589 per month for office
ALTA.	a. annual allowance established by statute - Speaker given authority to increase allowance by up to 10% per year - first established 1979 b. $10,000 for rent, staff, office supplies and miscellaneous items
B.C.	a. annual allowance established by Speaker - first established 1973 b. global allowance of $19,800 - no restrictions on use
N.W.T.	a. monthly allowance established by statute - first established 1975 b. $75 for staff - $15 for postage - $125 for equipment - $1,000 for advertising - $75 for interpreters - $1,500 per year for telephone - Members can use Government offices in constituency rent free
YUKON	a. no program b. N/A

SUPPORT SERVICES FOR PRIVATE MEMBERS

In Constituency

c. staff

H OF C	— MPs must use at least $15,696 of their $78,000 annual staff allowance to hire staff in constituency - no upper limit - staff are employees of Member - pay rate established by Member - no restriction on numbers - on payroll of H of C
NFLD.	— N/A
P.E.I.	— N/A
N.S.	— $75 per month - staff are employees of Member - no restriction on numbers - paid on fee-for-service basis on submission of account
N.B.	— N/A
QUE.	— $35,000 maximum ($38,500 to $41,100 if 2 offices) - staff are employees of Member - pay rate established by Member - no restriction on numbers - on payroll of L.A.
ONT.	— $20,318 maximum - staff are employees of Member - pay rate established by Member - no restriction on numbers - on payroll of L.A.
MAN.	— no specific allowance - included in global allowance

SASK.	— $694 per month - staff are employees of L.A. - pay rate established by statute (½ of top range of Clerk/Steno 3) - 1 employee per Member
ALTA.	— no specific allowance - staff are contract employees of L.A. - paid on fee-for-service basis - 1 employee per Member
B.C.	— no specific allowance - included in global allowance - staff are employees of Member - pay rate established by Member - no restriction on numbers
N.W.T.	— $75 per month - staff are employees of Member - pay rate established by Member - no restriction on numbers
YUKON	— N/A

SUPPORT SERVICES FOR PRIVATE MEMBERS

Caucus Services

c. caucus employees

H OF C	— Government 21 - Opposition 20 - Third Party 9 - employees of caucus - pay rates are established by caucus - benefits same as H of C employees, including pension - no union
NFLD.	— Government 8 - Opposition 13 - employees of L.A. - pay rates are established by BOIE - benefits same as other L.A. staff, including pension - no union
P.E.I.	— Government 1 - Opposition 2 - employees of L.A., hired on contract basis - pay rates are established by BOIE - vacation and sickness benefits only, no pension - no union
N.S.	— Government 3 - Opposition 5 - Third Party 1 (research only) - employees of L.A. - pay rates tied to civil service standards - benefits same as other L.A. staff, including pension - no union
N.B.	— Government 3 - Opposition 9 (research only) - employees of L.A. - pay rates established by BOIE - benefits same as other L.A. staff, including pension - no union
QUE.	— number of employees unknown - employees of caucus - pay rates are established by caucus - benefits established by caucus, including pensions - no union
ONT.	— Government 73 - Opposition 59 - Third Party 50 - employees of caucus - pay rates for secretaries established by BOIE - pay rates for other employees established by caucus - group insurance, hospital, dental and pension provided by L.A. - all other benefits provided by caucus - 1 caucus unionized
MAN.	— total of 9 employees for all caucuses - employees are civil servants - pay rates are established by BOIE - benefits same as other civil servants, including pension - no union

SASK.	— Government 3 - Opposition 5 (research only) - employees of caucus - pay rates are established by caucus - benefits same as civil servants, including pension - no union
ALTA.	— Government 20 - Opposition 6 - Third Party 3 - Independent 2 - employees of L.A. - researchers hired on contract - secretaries hired for length of parliament - pay rates established by caucus - benefits same as other L.A. staff, including pension - no union
B.C.	— Government 10 - Opposition 28 - employees of L.A. - pay rates are established by caucus - optional benefits package equivalent to civil servants, if full time employee - no union
N.W.T.	— N/A
YUKON	— Government 1 - Opposition 1 - Third Party 1 (research only) - employees of caucus - pay rates are established by caucus - benefits established by caucus - no union

ADMINISTRATIVE STRUCTURE

Legislature Budgets

a. 1981-1982
b. 1980-1981
c. % increase

H OF C	a. $112,556,000 b. $100,823,000 c. 10.43%	MAN.	a. $ 3,579,400 b. $ 2,871,900 c. 19.77%
NFLD.	a. $ 3,678,500 b. $ 3,235,300 c. 12.05%	SASK.	a. $ 5,038,690 b. $ 4,360,440 c. 13.46%
P.E.I.	a. $ 943,000 b. $ 868,000 c. 7.96%	ALTA.	a. $ 8,574,471 b. $ 6,815,244 c. 20.52%
N.S.	a. $ 3,628,500 b. $ 3,267,000 c. 9.97%	B.C.	a. $ 7,143,254 b. $ 6,113,160 c. 14.42%
N.B.	a. $ 3,677,900 b. $ 2,856,300 c. 9.52%	N.W.T.	a. $ 2,600,000 b. $ 1,900,000 c. 26.93%
QUE.	a. $ 42,837,700 b. $ 38,132,400 c. 10.98%	YUKON	a. $ 989,000 b. $ 923,000 c. 6.68%
ONT.	a. $ 27,671,600 b. $ 24,254,500 c. 12.35%		

ADMINISTRATIVE STRUCTURE

Employees of the Legislature

a. full time	c. status of employees
b. sessional	d. # earning > $30,000

H OF C	a. 1982	c. employees of H of C - no union
	b. 0	d. unknown

NFLD.	a. 43	c. employees of L.A. (not civil servants) - no union
	b. 4	d. 2

P.E.I.	a. 0	c. casual employees of L.A. - no union
	b. 12	d. 0

N.S.	a. 18	c. civil servants - no union
	b. 36	d. 3

N.B.	a. 30	c. employees of L.A. (not civil servants) - no union
	b. 32	d. 4

QUE. a. 797 (includes 166 in Prov. Auditor's Office and 36 in Ombudsman's Office)
b. 67 (includes 2 in Prov. Auditor's Office and 1 in Ombudsman's Office)
c. civil servants - some employees unionized
d. 162 (includes 69 in Prov. Auditor's Office and 12 in Ombudsman's Office)

ONT.	a. 233	c. employees of L.A. (not civil servants) - no union
	b. 7	d. 18

MAN.	a. 20	c. civil servants - no union
	b. 23	d. 1

SASK.	a. 16	c. employees of L.A. (not civil servants) - some employees unionized
	b. 63	d. 4

ALTA.	a. 88	c. civil servants - no union
	b. 12	d. 6

B.C.	a. 53	c. employees of L.A. (not civil servants) - no union
	b. 100	d. 6

N.W.T.	a. 11	c. civil servants - some employees unionized
	b. 36	d. 2

YUKON	a. 5	c. civil servants - some employees unionized
	b. 6	d. 1

HOUSE STATISTICS

Composition of the House

a. number of elected Members
b. distribution of Members

c. date of last redistribution of seats
d. average number of sitting days per year

H OF C	a. 282 b. Government 147 - Opposition 102 - Third Party 33	c.	1976 146 days
		d.	
NFLD.	a. 52 b. Government 34 - Opposition 18	c. d.	1979 83 days
P.E.I.	a. 32 b. Government 22 - Opposition 10	c. d.	1962-63 40 days
N.S.	a. 52 b. Government 34 - Opposition 15 - Third Party 2 - Independent 1	c. d.	1978 65 days
N.B.	a. 58 b. Government 30 - Opposition 27 - Independent 1	c. d.	1974 70 days
QUE.	a. 122 b. Government 80 - Opposition 42	c. d.	1981 97 days
ONT.	a. 125 b. Government 70 - Opposition 34 - Third Party 21	c. d.	1975 106 days
MAN.	a. 57 b. Government 32 - Opposition 20 - Third Party 3 - Fourth Party 1 - Independent 1	c. d.	1980 90 days
SASK.	a. 61 b. Government 44 - Opposition 15 - Third Party 2	c. d.	1980 96 days
ALTA.	a. 79 b. Government 73 - Opposition 4 - Third Party 1 - Independent 1	c. d.	1979 120 days

B.C.	a. 57	c. 1979
	b. Government 31	d. 150 days
	- Opposition 26	

| N.W.T. | a. 22 | c. 1979 |
| | b. Consensus Government | d. 60 days |

YUKON	a. 16	c. 1978
	b. Government 10	d. 40 days
	- Opposition 2	
	- Third Party 1	
	- Independent 2	
	- Vacant 1	

BIBLIOGRAPHY

Parliamentary Procedure

Beauchesne, A., (ed.), *Rules and Forms of the House of Commons,* with annotations, comments and precedents by A. Fraser, G.A. Birch, and W.F. Dawson, Toronto, Carswell, 5th ed., 1978.

Bourinot, J.G., *Parliamentary Procedure and Practice in the Dominion of Canada,* Toronto, Canada Law Book Co., 3rd ed., 1903.

Canada, Parliament, House of Commons, *Standing Orders of the House of Commons, 1978,* Ottawa, Q.P., 1978.

Dawson, W.F., *Procedure in the Canadian House of Commons,* Toronto, U.T.P., 1962.

Stanford, G., *Bourinot's Rules of Order,* Toronto, M. & S., 3rd rev. ed., 1980.

Stewart, J.B., *The Canadian House of Commons: Procedure and Reform,* Montreal, McG.-Q.U.P., 1977.

Functioning of Legislatures

Adamson, A., "We Were Here Before — The Referendum in Canadian Experience," *Policy Options,* I, 1, March, 1980.

d'Aquino, T., Doern, G.B., and Blair, C., *Parliamentary Government in Canada: A Critical Assessment, and*

Suggestions for Change, Ottawa, Business Council on National Issues, 1979.

Aiken, G., *The Backbencher — Trials and Tribulations of a Member of Parliament,* Toronto, M. & S., 1974.

Aitchison, J.H., "The Speakership of the Canadian House of Commons," in Clarke, R.M., (ed.), *Canadian Issues: Essays in Honour of Henry F. Angus,* Toronto, U.T.P., 1961.

Atkinson, M.M., "Comparing Legislatures: The Policy Role of Backbenchers in Ontario and Nova Scotia," *C.J.P.S.,* XIII, 1, March, 1980.

Atkinson, M.M., "Reform and Inertia in the Nova Scotia Assembly," *J.C.S.,* 14, 2, Summer, 1979.

Atkinson, M.M., and Nossal, K.R., "Executive Power and Committee Autonomy in the Canadian House of Commons: Leadership Selection, 1968-1979," *C.J.P.S.,* XIII, 2, June, 1980.

Balls, H.T., "The Public Accounts Committee," *C.P.A.,* VI, 1, March, 1963.

Bishop, P.V., "Restoring Parliament to Power," *Q.Q.,* LXXVII, 2, Summer, 1970.

Black, E.R., "Opposition Research: Some Theories and Practice," *C.P.A.,* 15, 1, Spring, 1972.

Blair, R.S., "What Happens to Parliament?" in Lloyd, T., and McLeod,

J.T., (eds.), *Agenda: 1970,* Toronto, U.T.P., 1968.

Breaugh, M., "Proposals for a New Committee System in Ontario," *Canadian Parliamentary Review,* 3, 4, Winter, 1980.

Brownstone, M., "The Canadian System of Government in the Face of Modern Demands," *C.P.A.,* XI, 4, Winter, 1968.

Bryden, K., "Executive and Legislature in Ontario: A Case Study in Government Reform," *C.P.A.,* 18, 2, Summer, 1975.

Burke, E., "Speech to the Electors of Bristol," in *Speeches and Letters on American Affairs,* London, Dent, Everyman's library, 1908.

Byers, R.N., "Perceptions of Parliamentary Surveillance of the Executive: The Case of Canadian Defense Policy," *C.J.P.S.,* V, 2, June, 1972.

Byrne, D., "Some Attendance Patterns Exhibited By Members of Parliament During the 28th Parliament," *C.J.P.S.,* V, 1, March, 1972.

Campbell, C., "The Interplay of Institutionalization and the Assignment of Tasks in Parliamentary and Congressional Systems," *International Journal of Comparative Sociology,* 18, 1977.

Campbell, C., and Clarke, H.D., (eds.), "Canadian Legislative Behaviour," *Legislative Studies Quarterly,* III, 4, November, 1978.

Canada, [MacEachen, A.J.], *Members of Parliament and Conflict of Interest,* Ottawa, I.C., 1973.

Canadian Study of Parliament Group, *Seminar on Accountability to Parliament,* April 7, 1978, Ottawa, Q.P., 1978.

Canadian Study of Parliament Group, *Seminar on the Budgetary Process,* Ottawa, Q.P., 1, 1, 1977.

Casstevens, T.W., and Denham, W.A., "Turnover and Tenure in the Canadian House of Commons, 1867-1968," *C.J.P.S.,* III, 4, December, 1970.

Clarke, H.D., Price, R.G., Krause, R., "Constituency Service Among Cana-

dian Provincial Legislators," *C.J.P.S.,* VIII, 4, December, 1975.

Clarke, H.D., "The Ideological Self-Perceptions of Provincial Legislators," *C.J.P.S.,* XI, 3, September, 1978.

Clarke, H.D., Campbell, C., Quo, F.Q., and Goddard, A., (eds.), *Parliament, Policy and Representation,* Toronto, Methuen, 1980.

Clarke, H.D., and Price, R.G., "A Note on the Pre-Nomination Role Socialization of Freshmen Members of Parliament," *C.J.P.S.,* X, 2, June, 1977.

Clarke, H.D., and Price, R.G., "Freshmen MPs' Job Images: The Effects of Incumbency, Ambition and Position," *C.J.P.S.,* XIII, 3, September, 1980.

Clarke, H.D., and Price, R.G., "The Role Socialization of Canadian Legislators: The Case of Provincial MLAs," unpublished paper, Department of Political Science, University of Windsor, 1978.

Clarke, H.D., and Price, R.G., "The Socialization of Freshmen Members of Parliament," in Pammett, J.H., and Whittington, M.S., (eds.), *Foundations of Political Culture,* Toronto, Macmillan, 1976.

Corry, J.A., "Adaptation of Parliamentary Processes to the Modern State," *C.J.E.P.S.,* XX, 1, February, 1954.

Corry, J.A., "Sovereign People or Sovereign Governments," *Policy Options,* 1, 1, March, 1980.

Dawson, W.F., "Parliamentary Privilege in the Canadian House of Commons," *C.J.E.P.S.,* XXV, 4, November, 1959.

Dobell, P., "Parliament and the Control of Public Expenditure," Report to the Royal Commission on Financial Management and Accountability, Ottawa, 1977.

Ducasse, R., "Les deputés et la fonction parlementaire: élements d'une enquête à l'Assemblée nationale du Québec," *J.C.S.,* 14, 2, Summer, 1979.

Fleming, R.J., *A Comparative Study of the Administrative Structures of*

Canadian Legislatures, Toronto, Office of the Assembly, 1980.

Fleming, R.J., and Mitchinson, J.T., Canadian Legislatures: The 1981 Comparative Study, Toronto, Office of the Assembly, 1981.

Forsey, E.A., Freedom and Order: Collected Essays, Carleton Library No. 73, Toronto, M. & S., 1974.

Franks, C.E.S., "The Dilemma of the Standing Committees of the Canadian House of Commons," C.J.P.S., IV, 4, December, 1971.

Fyffe, G., "The Overhaul That's Overdue," Policy Options, 1, 4, December/January, 1980/81.

Gaboury, J.P., and Hurley, J.R., (eds.), The Canadian House of Commons Observed, Ottawa, Les Éditions de l'Université d'Ottawa, 1979.

Hawkins, G., (ed.), Order and Good Government, Proceedings of 33rd Couchiching Conference, Toronto, C.I.P.A., 1965.

Hockin, T.A., "The Advance of Standing Committees in Canada's House of Commons: 1965 to 1970," C.P.A., XIII, 2, Summer, 1970.

Hoffman, D., and Ward, N., Bilingualism and Biculturalism in the Canadian House of Commons, Document 3 of the Royal Commission on Bilingualism and Biculturalism, Ottawa, Q.P., 1970.

Jackson, R.J., and Atkinson, M.M., The Canadian Legislative System, Toronto, Macmillan, 2nd rev. ed., 1980.

Jewett, P., "The Reform of Parliament," J.C.S., 1, 3, November, 1966.

Johnson, J.K., (ed.), The Canadian Directory of Parliament, 1867-1967, Ottawa, Public Archives of Canada, 1968.

Kent, T., "Making Representative Government Work," Policy Options, 1, 1, March, 1980.

Kersell, J.E., Parliamentary Supervision of Delegated Legislation, London, Stevens and Sons, 1960.

Knowles, Stanley, The Role of the Opposition in Parliament, Toronto,

Woodsworth Memorial Foundation, 1957 (pamphlet).

Kornberg, A., "The Social Bases of Leadership in a Canadian House of Commons," The Australian Journal of Politics and History, XI, 3, December, 1965.

Kornberg, A., "Caucus and Cohesion in Canadian Parliamentary Parties," American Political Science Review, LX, 1, March, 1966.

Kornberg, A., Canadian Legislative Behaviour: A Study of the 25th Parliament, New York, H.R.W., 1967.

Kornberg, A., and Mishler, W., Influence in Parliament: Canada, Durham, N.C., Duke University, 1976.

Kornberg, A., and Musolf, L., Legislatures in Developmental Perspectives, Durham, Duke University Press, 1970.

Kornberg, A., Falcone, D.J., and Mishler, W., Legislatures and Societal Change: The Case of Canada, Beverly Hills, Sage, 1973.

Kornberg, A., and Thomas, N., "The Purposive Roles of Canadian and American Legislators: Some Comparisons," Political Science, XVIII, 2, September, 1965.

Kornberg, A., and Thomas, N., "Representative Democracy and Political Elites in Canada and the United States," Parliamentary Affairs, XIX, 1, Winter, 1965-66.

Lamontagne, M., "The Influence of the Politician," C.P.A., XI, 3, Fall, 1968.

Landry, R., "Parliamentary Control of Science Policy in the Quebec National Assembly," Canadian Parliamentary Review, 3, 4, Winter, 1980.

Laundy, P., "Procedural Reform in the Canadian House of Commons," in Lankster, R.S., and Dewor, D., (eds.), The Table: Being the Journal of the Society of Clerks-at-the-Table in Commonwealth Parliaments for 1965, London, Butterworth, XXXIV, 1966.

LeDuc, L., and White, W.L., "The Role of Opposition in a One-Party

Dominant System: The Case of Ontario," *C.J.P.S.*, VII, 1, March, 1974.

Levesque, T.J., and Norrie, K., "Overwhelming Majorities in the Legislature of Alberta," *C.J.P.S.*, XII, 3, September, 1979.

Levy, G., "Delegated Legislation and the Standing Joint Committee on Regulations and Other Statutory Instruments," *C.P.A.*, 22, 3, Fall, 1979.

Lloyd, T., "The Reform of Parliamentary Proceedings," in Rotstein, A., (ed.), *The Prospect of Change*, Toronto, McG.-H., 1965.

Lovink, J.A.A., "Parliamentary Reform and Governmental Effectiveness in Canada," *C.P.A.*, 16, I, Spring, 1973.

Lovink, J.A.A., "Who Wants Parliamentary Reform?," *Q.Q.*, 79, 4, Winter, 1972.

MacDonald, Donald S., "Change in the House of Commons — New Rules," *C.P.A.*, XIII, 1, Spring, 1970.

MacGuigan, M., "Parliamentary Reform: Impediments to an Enlarged Role for the Backbencher," *Legislative Studies Quarterly*, III, 4, November, 1978.

Maine, F.W., "Parliamentary Scrutiny of Science Policy," *Canadian Parliamentary Review*, 3, 4, Winter, 1980.

Mallory, J.R., "The Uses of Legislative Committees," *C.P.A.*, VI, 1, March, 1963.

Mallory, J.R., "Vacation of Seats in the House of Commons: The Problem of Burnaby-Coquitlam," *C.J.E.P.S.*, XXX, 1, February, 1964.

Mallory, J.R., and Smith, B.A., "The Legislative Role of Parliamentary Committees in Canada: The Case of the Joint Committee on the Public Service Bills," *C.P.A.*, 15, 1, Spring, 1972.

March, R., *The Myth of Parliament*, Toronto, P.-H., 1974.

Meisel, J., "New Challenges to Parliament: Arguing over Wine Lists on

the Titanic," *J.C.S.*, 14, 2, Summer, 1979.

Neilson, W.A.W., and MacPherson, J.C., (eds.), *The Legislative Process in Canada: The Need for Reform*, Toronto, Butterworths, 1979.

Normandin, P.G., (ed.), *Canadian Parliamentary Guide, 1981*, (Annual), Ottawa, Box 3453, Stn. C, 1981.

Ontario Commission on the Legislature [Camp Commission], *First Report*, May, 1973; *Second Report*, December, 1973; *Third Report*, September, 1974; *Fourth Report*, September, 1975; *Fifth Report*, October, 1975.

Ontario Legislative Assembly, Standing Procedural Affairs Committee, "Proposals for New Committee System," Toronto, 1980.

Poel, D.H., "The Diffusion of Legislation among the Canadian Provinces: A Statistical Analysis," *C.J.P.S.*, IX, 4, December, 1976.

"Responsible Government Reconsidered," A collection of articles on Parliament, *J.C.S.*, 14, 2, Summer, 1979.

Robertson, R.G., "The Canadian Parliament and Cabinet in the Face of Modern Demands," *C.P.A.*, XI, 3, Fall, 1968.

Robinson, A., *Parliament and Public Spending*, Toronto, Book Society of Canada, 1978.

Rush, M., "The Development of the Committee System in the Canadian House of Commons — Reassessment and Reform," *The Parliamentarian*, 55, 1974.

Schindeler, F.F., *Responsible Government in Ontario*, Toronto, U.T.P., 1969.

Smith, D., *The Speakership of the Canadian House of Commons: Some Proposals*, A paper prepared for the House of Commons' Special Committee on Procedure and Organization, Ottawa, Q.P., 1965.

Smith, D.P., "Parliament Innovates: A New Style of Committee," *Policy Options*, 2, 2, May-June, 1981.

Stanfield, R.L., "The State of the

Legislative Process in Canada,''
Policy Options, 1, 2, June-July,
1980.

Thomas, P.G., ''Parliament and the
Purse Strings,'' unpublished paper,
n.d.

Thomas, P.G., ''The Role of Committees in the Canadian House of Commons, 1960-72,'' unpublished Ph.D.
thesis, University of Toronto, 1975.

Turner, J., *Politics of Purpose,* Toronto, M. & S., 1968, especially
Chapter 2, ''The Member of Parliament.''

Walkland, S.A., (ed.), *The House of
Commons in the Twentieth Century,*
Oxford, O.U.P., 1979.

Ward, N., ''Called to the Bar of the
House of Commons,'' *C.B.R.,*
XXV, 5, May, 1957.

Ward, N., *The Canadian House of
Commons: Representation,* Toronto,
U.T.P., 2nd ed., 1963.

Ward, N., ''The Committee on
Estimates,'' *C.P.A.,* VI, 1, March,
1963.

Ward, N., *The Public Purse: A Study
in Canadian Democracy,* Toronto,
U.T.P., 1962.

White, G., ''The Life and Times of the
Camp Commission,'' *C.J.P.S.,*
XIII, 2, June, 1980.

Williams, R.J., ''The Role of
Legislatures in Policy Formulation,''
in Landry, R., (dir.), *Introduction à
l'Analyse des Politiques,* Québec,
Les Presses de l'Université Laval,
1980.

14

THE LEGISLATIVE PROCESS: THE SENATE

The Senate has been affected by both the wave of change and the mood for reform which have been evident in the Canadian political system in recent years. Although there have been more proposals for reform than actual reforms, there have been three constitutional changes in the Senate in the past seventeen years.

An amendment to the British North America Act in 1965 (14 Eliz. c. 4) required senators appointed thereafter to retire at 75 years of age rather than hold office for life. At the same time, generous pensions were offered to encourage former appointees to retire voluntarily if they were 75 years of age or more. The relevant sections of the statute can be found in the second edition of *Politics: Canada,* pp. 290-293. (It may be noted in passing that this amendment was one of the five enacted by the Canadian Parliament under the authority of the amending power conferred on it by Amendment No. 2 in 1949. See *supra,* Chapter 2 in the present edition.)

In 1975, the B.N.A. Act was amended again to provide for the addition of one senator each for the Yukon and Northwest Territories. The relevant portion of this amendment, which also was passed under the power conferred by Amendment No. 2 in 1949, is reproduced in the first item in this chapter.

In 1982 Canada's new constitution assigned the Senate only a suspensive veto of 180 days over future constitutional amendments. (See the article by the editor in this chapter.)

There has been no shortage of proposals for reform of the Senate. They began almost as soon as the Senate was created at Confederation and they have continued to be offered periodically with recurring bursts of enthusiasm ever since. The Upper Chamber has always been a convenient target for the innocuous discharge of reforming zeal, particularly by prime ministers who have seldom carried through their pious hopes.

The Senate itself has participated in this exercise from time to time, no doubt to ward off a worse fate being imposed upon it from outside. See, for example, the debate in the Senate in 1951 on its own reform, reprinted in part in the first edition of this book, pp. 227-246. See also Senator David Croll's proposals in a debate in the Upper Chamber on March 13, 1973. The latest contribution by the Senate on this subject is the *Report on Certain Aspects of the Canadian Constitution,* presented to the Senate's Standing Committee on Legal and Constitutional Affairs in November, 1980, by one of its subcommittees, reviewing various proposals made by others for reform of the Senate and then offering some suggestions of its own. (For the details, see the article by the editor in this chapter.)

Prime Minister Trudeau has been disposed to consider Senate reform, apparently seriously. The federal government's white paper, *The Constitution and the People of Canada,* published under his name in 1969, offered the provinces a role in the appointment of the Upper Chamber, among other proposed changes. This led to a discussion of the revamping of the Senate as part of the general revision of the constitution and specific proposals were soon presented from a number of quarters, including the provinces and the public. The editor has selected a number of these leading proposals and distilled their essence in the second article in this chapter.

The article by Professor Don Briggs which follows is a critique of the federal government's proposals in 1969. However, the author's comments are so judicious and wide-ranging that his article can be read as a review of the substance of most of the suggestions for reform since then as well. He raises most of the points any reform of the Senate would have to consider.

The dispatch from the Canadian Press is included to show what the Canadian public favours by way of reform. Apparently the public is all for electing the Senate. (So much for some of the intricate federal-provincial schemes for joint appointment.)

The next item gives the indemnities, allowances, and salaries of Senate members and officials on January 1, 1982. The senators do not appear to be underpaid for what they do.

In the final item, Professor John McMenemy tackles another aspect of the Senate. He has brought up to date his article which was published originally in the fourth edition of *Politics: Canada.* It is a hard-hitting critique of the questionable role some senators play as representatives and lobbyists for corporate interests and organizers and bagmen for political parties. Professor McMenemy believes that these roles endanger the independence of Parliament and after reading his article, it is difficult not to agree with him. Any reform of the Senate that eliminated these elements would be an improvement.

The individual items in this chapter in the fourth edition that have not been carried over *in toto* have been incorporated into the editor's article in this edition.

The relatively short bibliography indicates that there is more interest in panaceas for reform than in searching scholarly analysis.

TWO SENATORS ADDED FOR YUKON AND NWT*

23-24 Eliz. II, C.53

An Act to amend the British North America Acts, 1867 to 1975

[Assented to 19th June, 1975]

Her Majesty, by and with the advice and consent of the Senate and House of Commons of Canada, enacts as follows:

1. Notwithstanding anything in the *British North America Act, 1867,* or in any Act amending that Act, or in any Act of the Parliament of Canada,

---

* From *Canada Gazette, Part III,* Vol. 1, No. 9, June 19, 1975, Ottawa, Queen's Printer, 1975. Reproduced by permission of the Minister of Supply and Services Canada.

or in any order in council or terms of conditions of union made or approved under any such Act,
(a) the number of Senators provided for under section 21 of the *British North America Act, 1867,* as amended, is increased from one hundred and two to one hundred and four;
(b) the maximum number of Senators is increased from one hundred and ten to one hundred and twelve; and
(c) the Yukon Territory and the Northwest Territories shall be entitled to be represented in the Senate by one member each.

2. For the purposes of this Act, the term "Province" in section 23 of the *British North America Act, 1867* has the same meaning as is assigned to the term "province" by section 28 of the *Interpretation Act.*

3. This Act may be cited as the *British North America Act, (No. 2) 1975,* and shall be included among the Acts that may be cited as the *British North America Acts, 1867 to 1975.*

SELECTED RECENT PROPOSALS FOR REFORM OF THE SENATE

Paul Fox

The following chronological list contains some of the recent proposals for reform of the Senate with an indication of the essence of their recommendations:

Canada, [Trudeau, P.-E.], *The Constitution and the People of Canada,* Ottawa, Queen's Printer, 1969 — redistribution of membership; reduction in term of office; partial appointment by provinces; suspensive veto; "special responsibility" in dealing with language rights and human rights; absolute veto over appointments to Supreme Court, ambassadorial posts, and chairmanships of cultural agencies.
(For a discussion of these proposals, see *infra,* Briggs' article in this chapter.)

Canada, Special Joint Committee of the Senate and of the House of Commons on the Constitution of Canada, *Final Report,* Ottawa, Information Canada, 1972, Chapter 13 — suspensive veto; continue investigative role; introduction of all bills, including money bills except appropriation bills; increase and redistribute membership; all members to be appointed by federal government but half of new members to be appointed by federal government from a panel of nominees submitted by the provinces and territories; new members to retire at 70.
(For details see *ibid.,* Chapter 13, or *Politics: Canada,* fourth edition, pp. 471-472.)

Canada, *House of Commons Debates,* October 2, 1974, p. 44, Prime Minister P.-E. Trudeau — limited term (e.g., seven years) with possible renewal; suspensive veto; offer to reappoint Conservatives to replace Conservative senators who retire voluntarily.
(See *Politics: Canada,* fourth edition, pp. 472-473.)

Canada, *House of Commons Debates,* October 17, 1974, pp. 490-491, Stanley Knowles — abolish the Senate; no replacement.
(See *Politics: Canada,* fourth edition, pp. 473-474.)
Ontario, Advisory Committee on Confederation, *First Report,* Toronto, Queen's Park, April, 1978 — convert Senate into a House of Provinces whose members would be appointed by the provincial governments and which would have an absolute veto over bills that encroached on provincial jurisdiction and a suspensive veto over bills which had "substantial" provincial interest.
Canada West Foundation, *Alternatives: Towards the Development of an Effective Federal System for Canada,* Calgary, Alberta, amended report, May, 1978 — abolish Senate and replace it with a new House of Provinces composed of 12 provincial and territorial delegations of premiers, cabinet ministers, MLAs, or civil servants; each delegation to have a single weighted vote; distribution of seats by population; suspensive veto over "federal" legislation; joint session of two houses on concurrent legislation.
Canada, House of Commons, *The Constitutional Amendment Bill, Bill C-60,* June, 1978 — replace Senate with a House of Federation composed of an equal number of provincial and federal members (total, 118) reflecting party preferences of federal and provincial electorates after each respective election; suspensive veto; double majority (French and English) required for language bills; veto over appointments to Supreme Court and heads of institutions designated by Parliament (e.g., administrative bodies and Crown corporations).
(Bill received coolly by provincial premiers and subsequently abandoned.)
Canada, Task Force on Canadian Unity, [Pépin-Robarts Report], *A Future Together: Observations and Recommendations,* Ottawa, Supply and Services, January, 1979 — abolish Senate and replace it with a new second chamber called the Council of the Federation, composed of delegations representing provincial governments and led by provincial cabinet minister or premier; 60 members distributed by population up to a maximum per province of one-fifth of total; cannot initiate legislation except constitutional amendments; suspensive veto; absolute veto over appointments to Supreme Court, major regulatory agencies and central institutions (e.g., CBC, Bank of Canada, etc.).
Quebec, Constitutional Committee of the Quebec Liberal Party, *A New Canadian Federation,* [The Beige Paper], January, 1980 — abolish the Senate; no replacement, unicameral Parliament.
Canada, Proposed Resolution for Joint Address re the Constitution of Canada, *Constitution Act,* June, 1980 — suspensive veto on future constitutional amendments.
Canada, Federal-Provincial Constitutional Conference, September, 1980 — federal government ready to consider reform of Senate but over longer period of time than previously and in light of Supreme Court advisory opinion (not decision) that the provinces and senators must agree to reforms; provinces all accept idea of reform but formulas vary.
McWhinney, E., "If We Keep a Senate, It Should Be Elected," *Policy Options,* 1, 3, September-October, 1980 — critique of British Columbia's

proposal based on West German Bundesrat; preference for abolition but alternatively, election.

Ontario, Select Committee on Constitutional Reform, *Report,* Toronto, Queen's Park, October 21, 1980 — increase total membership to 126 composed of Atlantic 30, Ontario 26, Quebec 30, Prairies 26, British Columbia 12, Territories 2; half of members from a province to be chosen by House of Commons following each federal election, half to be chosen by provincial legislature following each provincial election, according to popular vote for parties in the province; ratification of appointments to Supreme Court and major federal boards and agencies; suspensive veto.

Canada, Senate, Standing Committee on Legal and Constitutional Affairs, *Report on Certain Aspects of the Canadian Constitution,* Ottawa, Supply and Services, November, 1980 — retain Senate; prime minister to appoint one-half of members from lists submitted by provinces; fixed term of 10 years renewable for five years by secret ballot of a Senate committee; keep retirement age at 75; increase membership to 126 to include 20 more from West and two more from Newfoundland; suspensive veto of six months.

Kent, Tom, Lecture in Walter L. Gordon Lecture Series Fund, reprinted in *The Toronto Star,* April 7, 1981 — elect Senate by preferential voting for province-wide constituencies; distribution of seats by provinces in rough approximation to population; fixed term of six years; suspensive veto of six months.

Canada, *Constitution Act (Canada Act), 1981-82* — selection, composition, and powers unchanged except that Senate limited to suspensive veto of 180 days re most constitutional amendments.

(See *supra,* Chapter 2, *Constitution Act, 1981-82* Section 47.)

A COMMENTARY ON RECENT REFORM PROPOSALS*

E. Donald Briggs

. . . Like many of his predecessors, Prime Minister Trudeau promised reform of the upper house when he first took office. Since that time . . . some official suggestions for reform have already been put forward. These are contained in the white paper, *The Constitution and the People of Canada,* published in February 1969. [See *ibid.,* pp. 28-34.]

The suggestions are of two sorts. First, on the organizational side, it is proposed that a review of the distribution of Senate membership be undertaken; that the term of office for Senators be reduced to a set number of years (perhaps six, with a possibility of reappointment); and, probably most important, that Senators be "partly appointed" by the provincial governments. Second, on the functional side, it is suggested that the Senate's

* From an article by the author in the *Queen's Quarterly,* LXXVII, 1, Spring, 1970. By permission of the author. The author, who is a member of the Department of Political Science at the University of Windsor, wishes to thank his colleagues, Professor K.G. Pryke and C.L. Brown-John, for helpful suggestions during the preparation of this article.

powers be curtailed in some respects and extended in others. The curtailment would result from providing that "in the general legislative process" the House of Commons would be enabled to over-rule rejection of a bill by the upper house (p. 32). The extension would come from giving the latter "special responsibility" in dealing with legislative measures concerning human rights and the official languages, as well as the right to approve appointments to the Supreme Court, ambassadorial positions, and the chairmanships of cultural agencies. Over these specific matters it is proposed that the Senate should have an absolute veto. . . .

In putting the proposals forward the Government has been motivated by more than the desire to "improve" the Senate. Senate reform and the revitalization of Canadian federalism are apparently seen as closely linked, and the purpose of the suggested changes is stated to be to enable the Senate "to play a more vital role in reflecting the federal character of our country" (p. 28). In these and other suggestions for constitutional change, however, the Government was also concerned with maintaining the customary responsibility of the cabinet to the House of Commons alone — hence the rejection of such ideas as that for a directly elected Senate. The proposed Senate changes are consequently described as providing "the best balance between the principles of responsible and representative government and the need in a federal state for the adequate protection of regional and cultural interests" (p. 32).

There are, however, a number of things about these proposals which are both surprising and puzzling. In the first place, it is not entirely obvious that changes in the method of handling many of the matters over which it is proposed to give the Senate special power are either necessary or desirable in and of themselves. To most Canadians the manner in which ambassadors, for instance, have been appointed has been unobjectionable. It is not easy to see, either, how these proposals are related to, or can be expected to solve, the principal problems of federalism, or what value there may be in them if they do not tend in this direction. Finally, the extent to which they would be effective in reforming or upgrading the Senate may also be questioned, particularly since the new duties proposed for the upper house are plainly of no great significance in terms of the general governmental burden of the central administration.

These considerations are not equally relevant to the organizational proposals, of course, but it may be argued that the latter are unlikely to be effective in improving the position or reputation of the Senate either, unless the functional changes succeed in transforming it into an obviously important body. Each of the proposals has its own weaknesses, however, and they are consequently better discussed individually than collectively.

Organizational Reform

The proposal which by itself seems likely to cause least difficulty is that of a specific term of office for Senators. Sinecures for life or even to age seventy-five have only one thing to recommend them: they ensure that once Senators are appointed they will be relatively immune from pressure by the appointing authority. That this is a principle of paramount importance with respect to judicial and perhaps some other offices is obvious, but its applicability to legislators is considerably more doubtful. It may be argued, in fact, that if the Senate is to become even partly a provincial or regional instrument, then senators should be to some degree responsive to the wishes or policies of their provincial governments. In general, too, a less static membership for the upper house would probably be advantageous. Whether it would prove to be equally desirable to have federally appointed Senators subject to pressure from the federal cabinet is more problematic, but this problem will be taken up more fully below.

In much the same way, the proposal to review the distribution of Senate seats seems, on the face of it, reasonable enough. As the white paper points out, no such review has been undertaken since confederation, though the original regional balance was upset by assigning Newfoundland an extra six seats when it became a province in 1949. There are admitted inequalities — or at least peculiarities — in the present distribution. Not only does the Atlantic region have thirty seats as compared with twenty-four for each of the other regions, but there are inconsistencies as between individual provinces, particularly between those in the east on the one hand and those in the west on the other. It is difficult, for instance, to reconcile New Brunswick's ten senatorial seats with British Columbia's six when the former has fewer than seven hundred thousand people and the latter close to two million.

It may be argued that since representation in the Senate has always been on a regional basis, comparisons of individual provinces in this way are not relevant. Once the possibility of redistribution is raised, however, such inequalities become a legitimate subject for consideration, particularly as the Government in this case has not revealed the basis on which it thinks redistribution should be undertaken. The fact that some Senators are to be appointed by the provinces also promises to make provincial as against regional representation more important than in the past.

Representation in second legislative chambers, of course, especially in federal systems, is not normally on the basis of population; witness the fact that each state in the United States has two Senators when they vary in population from Alaska's two hundred and fifty thousand to New York's seventeen million. Rather, the idea is that interested blocs or geographical areas should be represented to provide a balance with the population-based representation in the lower house. The simplest and perhaps the most logical way of accomplishing this is to give equal representation to each of the federated units, as has been done in the United States. A Canadian Senate composed of ten representatives from each province would therefore be logical, were it not for the fact that this would mean reducing Quebec's share of the total seats from approximately 23.5 per cent to a mere 10 per cent at precisely the time that province is demanding recognition of its special linguistic and cultural position within confederation. Granting, then, that Quebec should be accorded special recognition, other difficulties also appear. The west, for example, and perhaps the Maritimes as well, would be less than happy if their strength were to decline in relation to Quebec's. Ontario might also be a problem, but might feel less strongly about it than the west provided a reasonable balance were maintained between French and English Canada as a whole.

Given such difficulties, however, one is tempted to suggest that it might be better to leave things as they are. In view of the Government's declared intention of making the Senate the guardian of regional and cultural interests, however, this would not be without difficulties either. To date, the Senate has not been of any great importance to any of the provinces, and hence the distribution of its seats has not been of much importance in their eyes either. But, obviously, if it is to be rededicated to their use, this will no longer be the case, and redistribution will almost inevitably be demanded by one or more of them. It was undoubtedly recognition of this fact that led to the Government's somewhat tentative inclusion of such a review in its proposals. Needless to say, the same factors which are likely to make review necessary will also intensify the difficulties of achieving it.

With a minimum of good will on all sides, however, a solution should not be beyond the ingenuity of our collective leadership. Two formulas might be suggested as containing at least some of the elements out of which a solution might be constructed. The first would be to provide for a ninety-seat house in which Quebec would be given one-third, or thirty seats, with the remaining two-thirds being divided equally among the other three regions (twenty seats each). The second, and perhaps from the aesthetic point of view the better, formula would again allow Quebec thirty seats, but out of a total of one hundred and twenty, with each of the other nine provinces having ten. In the first case all three "English" regions would lose strength relative to Quebec, but provided the blocks were equally distributed among the eastern and western provinces (five each), the most glaring inequalities between the provinces of these regions would be eliminated. Under the second formula, Quebec would retain approximately the same proportion of the total seats as she has now (actually a gain of 1.5 per cent), while relative to her the east would make a slight gain and the west a considerable one. Ontario would obviously be the big loser relative to all the other regions, but it may be doubted whether there is any good reason for treating her differently from the other largely English provinces. Either of these formulas, or some variation thereon, would be more logical and would reflect existing political realities more precisely than present arrangements.

Theoretically, therefore, redistribution presents no great problem, and it would certainly seem to be desirable from a number of points of view. Of the organizational proposals, however, both the most substantive and the most uncertain in result is that of making appointments partly provincial. Two obvious and interrelated questions arise from this proposal. First, what does, or should, "partly" mean? Second, why, when the declared object of Senate reform is to create a house which will reflect more precisely "the federal character of our country," are the provinces to be allowed to appoint only some of the Senators but not all of them?

The white paper gives no indication whatever of what the Government may have in mind by "partly," but it does indicate the Government's feeling that while it is necessary to give expression to provincial interests, "the interests of the country as a whole should continue to find expression in the Senate to maintain there an influence for the unity of Canada" (p. 30). Presumably it is that portion of the Senate which will continue to be appointed by the federal cabinet which is expected to be such an influence.

One may sympathize with the objective of giving expression to the interests of the country as a whole, but whether the federal appointment of some Senators is necessary to achieve this, or whether Senators so appointed would actually constitute an influence for unity, is questionable. The Government appears to anticipate that provincially appointed Senators will be so preoccupied with parochial interests that unless some counterbalance is provided, chaos or deadlock or some such catastrophe will result. It should not be forgotten, however, that the Senate is and will continue to be only the second legislative chamber, with no independent existence or mandate of its own. Legislation will continue to be initiated largely by the cabinet and discussed by the Commons from a predominantly national viewpoint, and it will be the duty of the Senate to take the traditional "sober, second look" at what is passed to it from the lower house or directly from the cabinet. As long as cabinet and Commons do their work effectively, therefore, there is little chance that "the interests of the country as a whole" will be neglected or that these interests could be ignored by even the most parochially minded Senate. It is true that provincially oriented Senators may be inclined to be more critical of federal legislative proposals, and critical from a different point of view, than present ones, but this would seem to be precisely the purpose and value of having them in the Senate in the first place: they would bring a new and different perspective to the work of the central government, and it would be hoped that, by so doing, would pave the way for better understanding and more co-operation between the different levels of government.

What the Government means by unity, and what the connection is among it, the presence of federal appointees in the Senate, and the expression of "national" interests, is far from clear in any case. Is it unity within the Senate which is sought? Or concurrence of the Senate with the "national" view of the federal cabinet? One might be excused for suspecting that it is the latter which concerns the Government most, since there seems little reason to assume that the provincial or regional orientation of its members would necessarily mean inability to achieve at least sufficient unity to reach decisions in the upper house. Apart from anything else it is reasonable to suppose that voting would ultimately resolve differences in a provincially oriented Senate as elsewhere in democratic institutions.

The degree to which federal appointees might be able to act as catalysts in reconciling conflicting provincial viewpoints is also doubtful. Federal no less than provincial appointees must be from somewhere, and even if they should in theory be selected at large rather than on a regional or provincial basis, a reasonable distribution over the country would be necessary. When and if federal and provincial views should conflict, minority groups of federal appointees would be likely to find themselves caught between two pressures: to act in accordance with their provinces' interests or views on the one hand, or to conform to central government's view on the other. If they should tend to lean to the latter, they would be less likely to exert influence in the direction of unity than to form simply another faction within the chamber — a "they" group against which opposition might even solidify. If they should tend to "go provincial" on the other hand, any advantage of federal appointment, except that of patronage, would be lost. In neither case would they contribute to Senate unity in any obvious way.

Assuming the validity of this line of reasoning, and assuming that it could not have been overlooked by the drafters of the reform proposals, it follows that the provision for the continued appointment of some Senators by the federal government is likely to have been intended not only to provide patronage but also as a means of preventing or discouraging excessive divergence between the Senate and the cabinet. However, both the need for and the wisdom of attempting to "build in" unity in this fashion must be questioned. Undoubtedly the primary responsibility for governing the country must continue to rest on the federal cabinet and the directly elected representatives in the House of Commons and consequently the forceful expression of their views must be guaranteed. But as it was pointed out above, there is little danger that this would cease to be the case even if the Senate were entirely devoid of "national" spokesmen. Moreover, it must be remembered in this context that except with regard to a very few, not very significant matters, the "new" Senate is not to have a deciding voice in any case: the Commons is to be given power to overrule it in all "general legislative matters." While this is not a power which should be resorted to on any regular basis, it would provide a means whereby the government could, if necessary, ensure that its view of the country's interests would prevail.

Use of this procedure, furthermore, would at least be honest. It would bring differences between federal and provincial authorities into the open and provide an issue upon which voters could ultimately pass judgement. This would be less true if federally appointed Senators either because of their numerical superiority (we are not told that they will not be numerically superior, though we might hope that the Government's intentions are more honourable than that) or for some other reason, were able to circumvent differences within the Senate itself. An "arranged" unity, however, would obviously be no unity at all, and a Senate so constituted as to provide an appearance of unity would, from the point of view of federalism, be no advance over present arrangements. Unfortunately, indications are that the Government is not yet ready to face that fact. But since the Government does not propose giving the Senate sufficiently important functions to cause the provinces to take a very active interest in its deliberations or the performance of its members, all of this becomes somewhat beside the point. The "new" Senate, as it materializes from the present proposals, is simply never likely to be sufficiently concerned with, or important in relation to, the major issues of federalism to make federal-provincial confrontations within it a serious threat to harmony on Parliament Hill. This, of course, makes the Government's concern for unity even more unnecessary.

These factors are of immediate and practical as well as long-term and theoretical importance. Apart from anything else, if the proposed changes in the Senate are to be successful at all, it is essential that the provincial governments should be satisfied that they, or their appointees, will have a real and significant role to play in the new institution. If they are not convinced of this from the outset they are unlikely to take seriously such appointive responsibilities as they are finally accorded, and as a result the quality of Senate membership is likely to give far more legitimate cause for concern than it has to date. The white paper obliquely recognized the importance of this when it expressed the hope that federal and provincial governments "would engage in healthy competition" to ensure that the best men available would be appointed to the upper house (p. 34).

Provincial attitudes are likely to be determined largely by two factors: the proportion of Senate membership to be appointed by them, and the importance of the functions to be performed by the house. The first is self- explanatory in that there is a direct relationship between the number of representatives and the importance of their role. On the other hand, numbers alone mean little if the functions of the house are unimportant. We must consequently turn now to an analysis of the proposals for functional reform. These, unfortunately, are perhaps even more open to criticism than the organizational ones.

Functional Reform

The proposal to accord the Senate "special responsibility" with respect to legislation affecting civil rights and the official languages may seem unobjectionable and natural given the special interest which Quebec in particular has in some of these matters. In terms of the extent of the national government's powers and legislative responsibilities, however, it cannot be said to be particularly significant, nor are civil and language rights matters with which the provinces, with the exception of Quebec, are either especially concerned or especially competent to deal. . . .

Much the same can be said for the confirmation powers which are proposed. On the one hand they seem unlikely to elate the provinces with the opportunities they present for participation in the essentials of the governing process at the national level, and on the other, their inherent value also seems open to question.

The proposal to have ambassadorial appointments, for instance, approved by the Senate will almost certainly come as a surprise to most Canadians. Many, it seems safe to say, will find the reasons behind the proposal puzzling, and the benefits to be derived from such a procedure — for the Senate, the provinces, the country, or the diplomatic corps — perhaps even more so. . . . Moreover . . . there are cabinet prerogatives of far greater potential danger than the right to appoint ambassadors or, for that matter, judges of the Supreme Court, and these proposals would therefore be of comparatively little significance in that connection. . . .

. . . While it is by no means clear that Quebec would consider indirect participation in the appointment of ambassadors (and/or, for that matter, the heads of cultural agencies) a satisfactory substitute for the freedom of action which, as a "nation," she claims as her necessary right, it is clearly something of this kind that the Government hopes to achieve. . . .

The proposal that appointments to the Supreme Court also be subject to confirmation by the Senate has a similar origin and is undoubtedly expected to yield similar advantages. Quebec has also long contested the competence of the Supreme Court to decide constitutional issues between the provinces and the central government. . . . What the Government is now proposing is a compromise, which, as in the case of ambassadors and cultural agencies, concedes the principle but refuses to go the distance. . . .

It may equally be argued that the Government has shown little real interest in Senate reform *per se.* . . . What is more important, however, is that the proposed changes, organizational and functional, collectively constitute only very minor surgery which is at best, calculated to cure some peripheral ills rather than the inherent feebleness of the patient.

By far the most serious and insistent criticism of the present Senate is that it serves no useful function. Unfair as this criticism is in a number of respects, it may be argued that it is the first problem with which reform measures should deal, and that measures which fall short of this goal are not reform in any real sense at all. Since the special tasks visualized for the new Senate are largely ritualistic, and since its power is to be largely confined to these tasks, it seems unlikely that the position or the reputation of the upper house will be substantially improved by the proposed changes.

Both these problems could, at least in principle, be fairly simply solved, and without making the Senate into a rival of Commons in any significant sense. All that would be necessary would be to convert the Senate into what I have elsewhere called a "House of Provinces," [see bibliography for reference] which would be composed of representatives of the provincial governments, and which would be given the power of approving all measures falling within the area of joint federal-provincial responsibility. Such an arrangement would give the Senate the obvious *raison d'être* it has always lacked, and at the same time ensure the continuing interest of more than one province in its operations. . . .

There seems to be here an obvious opportunity to combine the search for appropriate machinery for federal-provincial co-operation with the movement to make the Senate an instrument of federalism. Why should the upper house not become the continuing federal-provincial conference which could thresh out such matters as well as take responsibility for such specific tasks as are contained in the proposals under discussion here? . . .

. . . The key would be to ensure senatorial responsiveness to provincial policies, and this could be accomplished by seconding members of provincial governments to the Senate on whatever basis individual provinces might think desirable. There would thus be no specific term of office for Senators at all (except perhaps for federal appointees, if these should still be regarded as necessary), and perhaps no specific membership as such. This would provide the maximum of flexibility from the provincial point of view, while the importance of the senatorial responsibilities would at the same time ensure that careful consideration would at all times be given to selecting suitable representatives. From the federal point of view such a Senate would be powerful, but with a provision that the Commons could overrule except with regard to matters designated as of legitimate provincial concern, its effective strength would be sufficiently channelled so that the authority of the House of Commons and the cabinet's primary responsibility to it would also be preserved.

Nevertheless, there is no doubt that this would be a radical departure from the traditional concept of the Senate and of second chambers generally, and it is not easy to predict all the consequences which might follow if it were adopted. While it would almost certainly bring the Senate publicity and recognition of the kind it has never before enjoyed, it would not be the type of recognition which Senator Martin and some others have been urging, and it is perhaps not even certain that a "House of Provinces" of this type could to the same extent carry on the kind of work for which these spokesmen consider it to deserve recognition. As they have rightly pointed out, the Senate at present makes a considerable contribution to the governing process by its extensive committee work and by giving detailed and in some cases first-instance study to legislative proposals, thus saving much time for the hard-pressed House of Commons. They believe that these functions could and should be extended still further and it would undoubtedly be useful if they were. Would a House composed largely or entirely of untenured ambassadors of the provinces be able to perform such functions?

The answer is not clear one way or the other, but whether this is the most important consideration may be questioned in any case. The point is that because of a variety of pressures from a variety of sources, means have to be found to institute a new kind of federalism. At the same time, for equally varied reasons, Senate reform seems to have been accepted as desirable and necessary. . . .

. . . Is it to be reformed, or is it, in a phrase recently used by Senator Keith Davey on the CBC, merely to be "tinkered with"? Is it to be made a genuine instrument of federalism and protector of provincial and regional interests, or merely a device for spiking the guns of Quebec? The white paper does not give much ground for encouragement on either score. Certainly if the "reforms" are instituted as proposed the result will be that the Senate will be far worse off than before. Its effective power will have been curtailed and confined to a few largely ritualistic tasks, a fact which will not fail to impress the public as confirmation of its inherent uselessness. The quality of its membership is likely to decline since provincial regimes can hardly be expected to devote much energy or care to the selection of people to perform tasks of little direct importance to them, and since political debts at the provincial level are unlikely to be owed to individuals who are very familiar with or interested in federal affairs. Consequently, not even the traditional functions of the Senate referred to above could be expected to be performed as well as at present. Neither, of course, is all this likely to do anything whatever for the state of Canadian federalism in any general sense.

Real Senate reform cannot be accomplished without giving it something of obvious importance to do. Neither can the real needs of Canadian federalism be accommodated by the Senate without giving it authority over matters of substance. Both mean making the Senate powerful in at least some respects. If that is not a prospect which the Government can accept, it would perhaps be better to leave the Senate as it is, concentrate on extending and publicizing its traditional functions, and look elsewhere for solutions to the problems of federalism. It will certainly be unfortunate, however, if some more serious attempt is not made to solve both problems with one blow by turning the Senate into something approaching a "House of Provinces."

POLL SHOWS CANADIANS FAVOUR ELECTED SENATE*

The Canadian Press

Voters strongly favour an elected Senate, according to a survey conducted for the Calgary-based Canada West Foundation.

The national survey of 1,939 adults between Sept. 14 and Oct. 7 asked which of a number of options should be used if the Senate were reformed.

Nationally, 61 per cent of respondents favoured an elected Senate. Support was consistent with the lowest proportion favouring an elected Senate found in Quebec — 54 per cent.

About 20 per cent of voters wanted a Senate with members appointed by both the federal and provincial governments.

Some 30 per cent wanted the Senate left as it is, 20 per cent wanted it abolished and 31 per cent wanted reform.

The foundation, in a commentary accompanying its summary of the poll results, said the most significant finding is "public support for the institutional *status quo* is very low; less than one Canadian in three supports the Senate as it now stands."

INDEMNITIES, ALLOWANCES, AND SALARIES OF SENATORS*

	Indemnity	Tax-free Allowance	Salary	Total[1]
Senator	$48,600	$7,900		$56,500
Ldr of Govt[2]	48,600	7,900	24,000	80,500
Speaker	48,600	7,900	21,300	77,800
Ldr of Oppn	48,600	7,900	16,600	73,100
Dep Govt Ldr	48,600	7,900	10,400	66,900
Dep Oppn Ldr	48,600	7,900	6,800	63,300
Chief Govt Whip	48,600	7,900	5,400	61,900
Chief Oppn Whip	48,600	7,900	3,600	60,100

* For January 1, 1982. Based on Bill C-83 which amended the *Senate and House of Commons Act,* the *Salaries Act,* and the *Parliamentary Secretaries Act.* The bill was given royal assent on July 10, 1981, but all changes were made retroactive to July 1, 1980. Bill C-83 also provided that in future the indemnity, expense allowance, and salaries will be adjusted yearly by a percentage which will be one percentage point less than either the Consumer Price Index or the Composite Index of Economic Activities, whichever is less.

[1]The total equivalent taxable income would be considerably larger.

[2]When the Leader of the Government in the Senate is a Minister of the Crown, he receives a Minister's salary of $33,600 instead of $24,000.

* From *The Canadian Press,* December 31, 1981. By permission.

BUSINESS INFLUENCE AND PARTY ORGANIZERS IN THE SENATE IMPERIL THE INDEPENDENCE OF PARLIAMENT*

John McMenemy

With one recent exception, scholarly studies of the Canadian Senate have tended to exhibit an unrealistic disregard for the substance and exercise of power. R. MacGregor Dawson described the Senate as a "comparatively unimportant and ineffective body" not far removed from "obscurity and obsolescence." More recently, Richard Van Loon and Michael Whittington reinforced this view that the Senate "is not a very active institution in the policy process."

This attitude towards the Senate ignores the activities of particular senators who have an impact on the informal and formal aspects of the policy process and the electoral fortunes of particular parties. Ironically, their public image of obscurity and obsolescence, reinforced by academic appraisals such as the two mentioned, aids the pursuit of their objectives. Prime ministers make some senatorial appointments precisely to facilitate future party service and many senators may be very useful to private corporations — including such key sectors of the business community as finance, manufacturing, energy, and transportation — which have a direct and continuing interest in federal legislation and administrative regulations and decisions.

Since 1977, when this article was first published, there has been one scholarly assessment of the Senate which has taken major account of the corporate connection. In *The Canadian Senate: A Lobby from Within,* Colin Campbell has published an empirical analysis of senators' standing among the country's elite, the entrenchment of sympathetic reviews of business policy, and senatorial role choices which have led to the creation of this dominant "lobby from within" the parliamentary system.

In 1982, senators' stipends were increased so that they received an indexed parliamentary "indemnity" of $48,600 and a nontaxable expense allowance of $7,900, a free office on Parliament Hill, secretarial service, answering service, franking privileges, free long-distance telephone calls, and limited free air travel. Senators appointed before 1965 who are still sitting hold life-long tenure, while those appointed since then retire at 75 years of age.

This article discusses the active connections of senators with private corporations and the electoral organizations of political parties in the context of the debate on the need for federal independence of Parliament, that is, conflict of interest legislation.

* Revised in March, 1982 from an original article prepared for the fourth edition and published here with the permission of the author who is a member of the Department of Political Science, Wilfrid Laurier University.

The Corporate Connection

A federal Green Paper on conflict of interest which dealt with the conduct of senators and MPs and which included a suggested Independence of Parliament bill was tabled in Parliament in 1973. Two years later, a Senate committee brought down a report which was designed to protect senators from the bothersome business of disclosure or divestiture of private interests. In 1978, the Liberal government introduced independence of Parliament legislation which died on the order paper in the following year. In 1981, no similar legislation was apparently being contemplated by the government. There is, therefore, no federal law requiring parliamentarians to disclose, let alone restrict, directorates, property and financial holdings, and legal or other activities which might be construed as lobbying.

Senators in the cabinet — whose numbers increased in 1980 as a consequence of the increased difficulty of the Liberal party in winning western seats in the House of Commons — are required to follow existing prime ministerial guidelines for ministers. Most senators, however, are bound only by a rule by which they are not allowed to vote on any question in which they have "any pecuniary interest whatsoever, not held in common with the rest of the Canadian subjects of the Crown. . . ." Senators may define "pecuniary interest" in a very narrow way; but, in any case, voting in the Senate or in a committee is not the most effective way to influence a legislative issue.

During the protracted but desultory public discussion since 1973 of parliamentary conflict of interest and the desirability of an Independence of Parliament Act, senators may have become more sensitive to their public appearance. The "business" of sympathetic reviews of federal business policy is currently circumspect compared to the 1960s. In 1964, the Senate's committee on banking, trade and commerce, which is a public focal point for the corporate connection, attracted public attention when dealing with three bills to incorporate banks and three to create mortgage companies. Four directors of established banks were members of the committee, including the (then and still) chairman, Senator Salter Hayden, then a director and shareholder of the Bank of Nova Scotia. The committee readily passed the three bills to incorporate mortgage companies despite reservations on one bill and serious objections to another by the federal superintendent of insurance. The Bank of Nova Scotia was associated with the companies whose incorporation legislation troubled the superintendent.

On the bill to establish the World Mortgage Corporation, for example, Senator T.A. Crerar announced he was a director of the Eastern and Chartered Trust Company which would be closely connected with the new corporation, and he withdrew from the committee. Senator Gordon Isnor acknowledged that he, too, was a director of Eastern and Chartered Trust, but would remain on the committee. Senator Hayden, who was connected with the application through the Bank of Nova Scotia, stood down as chairman because his law firm had drafted the legislation and a law partner had presented it to the committee. However, he remained on the committee to take issue with the federal superintendent of insurance. The acting chairman, Senator Paul-Henry Bouffard, then a director of the Royal Bank of Canada, saw no need to resolve the inconsistency among Crerar's, Isnor's, and Hayden's positions. The senators' critical consideration of the three proposed bank incorporations also drew public attention because of their private interests in established financial institutions.

In 1969, the government conceded in the House of Commons that the current conflict of interest provisions were antiquated and the process that brought forward the Green Paper was begun. In that year, Senator Hayden and his committee were in the spotlight again during their consideration of the Investment Companies Bill. Introduced following the collapse of several financial institutions, the original bill required many companies who were borrowing from the public to make special annual reports, obtain registration certificates and submit to unspecified regulations. Senator Hayden said that none of the 22 companies of which he was a director was affected by the legislation. However, according to an account in *The Globe and Mail*, June 7, 1969, the corporate view was well-represented in his committee:

> Members of Senator Hayden's committee — many of whom are company directors — were openly critical of the broad definition of investment companies. There was also criticism of the broad discretionary powers the bill would give the Government. As a result, a special sub-committee headed by Senator Hayden is working with Government officials to develop mutually acceptable amendments.

Later that year, the two Houses established a joint committee to examine government proposals for tax reforms occasioned by the Royal (Carter) Commission on Taxation. The New Democratic party objected that the senators on the committee had potential conflicts of interest. *The Globe and Mail* of July 25, 1969, agreed:

> Which senators will be on the committee? Why, men who, for the most part, are directors of some of the largest, most important and powerful corporations in the country — banks, financial institutions, distillers, insurance companies, co-operatives, industrial concerns and mining and petroleum companies. . . . What does the Carter Report recommend? Why, stiffer tax provisions for most of these corporations. It suggests that the general or contingency reserves of banks should not be recognized for tax purposes; that financial institutions have been estimating their losses too liberally and should be made to comply with more stringent rules: that depletion allowances give mining and petroleum companies unfair breaks and should be revised. . . . It calls for a tax on capital gains.

At that time, Prime Minister Trudeau was indifferent. "After all," he told the House, Senators "all have interests as taxpayers in what happens in connection with tax reform; it might be difficult to eliminate all people with an interest in taxation."

The government's Independence of Parliament legislation suggested in the Green Paper four years later would have required disclosure of all directorships, regulated the activities of paid lobbyists, and restricted the proportion of a company's stock that a parliamentarian could own. It would also have prohibited parliamentarians from sitting on boards of companies that had more than $1,000 of contracted business annually from the government. An examination of public records by the Canadian Press showed that eight of the 22 members of the Senate's committee on banking held 130 company directorships. These 22 senators accounted for 75 per cent of reported directorships of the then 93 senators. The committee members were executives or directors of businesses in banking, investment and insurance, mining, real estate development, and manufacturing and retailing of pulp and paper products, aircraft parts, feed products, clothing, and soft drinks.

In 1975, parliament debated the government's *Canadian Business Corporations Act* to revise federal private corporation law and amendments to the *Combines Investigation Act*. Senator Hayden, whose committee acted on both matters, was a director of Jannock Corp. Ltd., which grew out of a merger involving Atlantic Sugar Refineries Ltd. In 1963, Atlantic was fined $25,000 for conspiring to fix the price of sugar. At that time, the judge issued an order prohibiting the directors of Atlantic from repeating the offence. In 1975, Atlantic was again in court charged under the *Combines Investigation Act* for activities between 1960 and 1973 — and subsequently acquitted. According to the *Financial Post's Directory of Directors*, Senator Hayden was a director and officer during these years. Another lawyer-director of Jannock Corp. Ltd. was defending Atlantic Sugar. A law partner of the lawyer defending Atlantic Sugar was appointed counsel to Senator Hayden's committee during its examination of changes to the anticombines law.

After consideration by the House of Commons and acting on the advice of Senator Hayden's committee, the Senate made 27 amendments to the government's *Business Corporations Act*. The government asked the House to accept the amendments in one motion on short notice. According to the government spokesman, "the Senate committee . . . acted objectively, fairly and reasonably, arguing clearly and forcefully for each proposed amendment. I felt it impossible not to be responsive to their suggestions. . . . "

Stanley Knowles, NDP House leader and long-time foe of the Senate, had been assured that the amendments were administrative. However, reading them for the first time as the debate proceeded, Knowles realized that almost 25 per cent of the packaged amendments effectively removed directors and officers of corporations from legal liability. He said:

> It strikes me that these are amendments we might expect from the other place. . . . The bill which this House sent to the other place included a provision that in certain instances a conviction could be sought against a corporation or against its officers and directors. Considering the number of officers and directors sitting in the other place, I am not surprised by what has been done.

In recent years, the congenial business review by business-affiliated or oriented senators has continued as a major function of the upper house, though the senators' behaviour seems more circumspect. The banking, trade and commerce committee was closely interested in the last review of the *Bank Act*. In 1979, for example, Senator Sidney Buckwold informed committee colleagues that, as a director of a chartered bank, he would not participate in any vote, but would sit on the committee as the provisions of the legislation were "basically dealt with already" before he was on the committee.

In a review of budget legislation in 1981, committee witnesses included spokesmen for oil companies, the Institute of Chartered Accountants, the Independent Petroleum Association, the Canadian Daily Newspaper Publishers' Association, and the Brewers' Association of Canada. The brewing industry, for example, was concerned about the automatic and quarterly indexing of the excise tax on alcoholic beverages. As their representative was about to be heard, Senator Hartland Molson declared that, because of his private interests, he would not take "an active part" in the meeting.

Also in 1981, the committee completed and sent to the Senate a report on income tax legislation, following representations which included the Canadian Bankers' Association.

According to the *Directory of Directors* (1981) and *Canadian Who's Who* (1980), the following members of the Senate committee on banking, trade and commerce held these positions [for comparative purposes, see the 1975 list in 4th ed., pp. 458-59]:

Jacob (Jack) Austin: chairman, GM Resources Ltd.; director of Giant Explorations Ltd., HCI Holdings Ltd., MSZ Resources Ltd.

Reginald Balfour: director of Colonial Oil & Gas Ltd., Comaplex Resources International Ltd., The Royal Trust Co., Royal Trust Corp. of Canada, Royal Trustco Ltd., Willock Industries Ltd., KCL Enterprises Ltd., Ducks Unlimited (Canada).

A.I. Barrow: president, Halifax Cablevision Ltd.; director, Commodore Co. Ltd., Commodore Commercial Estates Ltd., Chebucto Properties Ltd., Oakland Services Ltd., Palmeters Country Home Ltd.

Louis P. Beaubien: president, Beaubran Corp.; director, Holt Renfrew & Co. Ltd., Inter City Papers Ltd., Marshall Steel Co. Ltd., Quebecor Inc.

Sidney L. Buckwold: vice-president and director, Buckwold's Ltd.; director, Bank of Montreal, Consolidated Pipe Lines Co., Extendicare Ltd., Mutual Life Assurance Co. of Canada, SED Systems Ltd.

Guy Charbonneau: president, Peerless Insurance Agencies Ltd., Charbonneau et Assoc. Ltée, Charbonneau, Ledgerwood, Leipsic, Ryan, Simpson & Assoc. Ltd.; chairman, La Société VS Ltée; director, VS Services Ltd.; member, Montreal advisory board of the Guaranty Trust Co. of Canada.

Jacques Flynn (ex-officio member): director, Savings and Investment American Fund, Savings and Investment Corp. Mutual Fund of Canada Ltd., Savings and Investment Trust.

John M. Godfrey: director, Dover Industries Ltd., Montreal Trust Co., Montreal Trust Co. of Canada.

Salter A. Hayden: chairman, Nelson A. Hyland Foundation; chairman and president, the Orthopaedic & Arthritic Hospital.

Harry W. Hays: director, Canada Permanent Trust Co., Canada Permanent Mortgage Corp., Hiram Walker-Consumers Home Ltd.

E.C. Manning: chairman, Manning Consultants, Ltd.; director, Burns Foods Ltd., Coal Valley Invest. Corp., Fluor (Canada) Ltd., The Manufacturers Life Insurance Co., McIntyre Mines Ltd., Melcor Developments Ltd., OPI Ltd., The Steel Co. of Canada Ltd.

Hartland de Montarville Molson: hon. chairman and director, The Molson Companies Ltd.

Duff Roblin: president, Metropolitan Investigation and Security (Canada) Ltd.

David James Walker: director, Anglo Canada Fire & General Insurance Co., Gibralter Insurance Co.

In 1981, during a committee pre-study of a tax bill, that is, legislation which had been introduced in the House of Commons but not yet in the Senate, Senator John Connolly reminded a witness aggrieved by the legislation that "there are certain problems that arise in connection with the powers of the Senate committee or the Senate itself to vary the take from the proposed tax."

While the Senate has made seemingly technical amendments which have in fact had substantive impact on the regulation of business, it is not always in its legislative competence that the business community receives support from its parliamentary "allies"; otherwise, senators may use their resources to establish a favourable environment for particular business interests elsewhere in the legislative process, notably among ministers and senior administrators.

The matter of lobbying is also important because at least seven members of the committee in 1981 (10 in 1975) were also lawyers. Disagreeing with the assertion that senators were lobbyists, Senators Walker and Connolly have distinguished between lawyers acting on behalf of clients and lobbyists acting on behalf of clients. The press has noted Senator Connolly's representations on behalf of corporations. Speaking of Connolly, Senator Walker, a colleague in law and on the Senate committee, has said:

> Now in the practice of his [law] profession in Ottawa, as may be expected, he has been consulted by corporate and other clients who have problems to be solved within various departments of the federal government. These include tax problems, customs matters, contract settlements and other matters requiring the service of lawyers. . . . I am sure that no official in . . . government . . . would ever feel that, because the honourable gentleman happens to be a senator when he appears before them as a lawyer with a client, he is doing any more than his professional duty requires him to do for a client.

Senator Connolly has observed: "When professional people from outside come [to Ottawa] to interview [government lawyers, accountants, engineers], they do not come to seek favours, they come to try to find solutions for the problems of their clients. . . ."

However, this distinction between the activities of lawyers and lobbyists may be less than clear for nonlawyers who are especially concerned when the lawyer in question is a senator and a member of the committee on banking, trade and commerce.

According to journalist Terrence Belford in *The Globe and Mail,* November 10, 1973, Senator Connolly's clients included Gulf Canada Ltd. and IBM Canada Ltd. Senator Connolly asserted that his relationship with both companies was that of lawyer to client. But Belford quoted Gulf President Jerry McAfee that the senator "occasionally opens doors for us and provides the proper atmosphere" for discussion with government officials: "With his knowledge of the people and scene there . . . he keeps us up to date on who are there, who is who and what is what."

The Active Party Connection

Undeniably, the Senate includes former party activists and leaders. Indeed, Dalton Camp, former president of the national Progressive Conservative party, describes this as "the true value of the senate." According to Camp, "It permits a prime minister to reform his government, to retire ministerial colleagues who are inept or weary, to open seats for newcomers to the cabinet, and to give sanctuary to those who have soldiered in his cause."

Despite indications of reformist intentions in the early years of his ministry, most of Prime Minister Trudeau's appointments reflect the principle of partisan reward and manipulation. Examples of such behaviour occurred in 1979 and 1981. Prior to the election of 1979, Trudeau had "summoned" to the upper house a veteran but disgruntled Conservative MP in the expectation that without him as the Conservative candidate, his seat was ready to be won by the Liberals. In the summer doldrums of 1981, Trudeau similarly honoured a backbench Liberal MP whose parliamentary career was distinguished chiefly by his ability to maintain an already safe Liberal seat through several elections. Along with the appointment to the Senate came announcements of the impending by-election date and the candidacy of Trudeau's principal secretary for the Liberal nomination. However, the Liberals succeeded only in the 1979 case. Although they lost the election of 1979, they gained the seat from the Conservatives and retained it in their victory of 1980. In 1981, the New Democratic party won the by-election in Spadina.

The Senate is less well recognized, however, as a publicly financed and prestigious repository for active party organizers and fund-raisers. In 1975, active Liberal party organizers and fund-raisers in the Senate included M. Lorne Bonnell, Jean-Pierre Côté, John Godfrey, B. Alasdair Graham, Paul C. Lafond, Gildas Molgat, Ray Perrault, Maurice Riel (all these appointed to the Senate by Pierre Trudeau), and Keith Davey, Earl Hastings, Harry Hays, and Richard Stanbury (all these appointed to the Senate by Prime Minister Lester Pearson). Fund-raising aside, recent federal Liberal campaign organizations have included these senators: Keith Davey (co-chairman, responsible for all areas with the exception of Quebec, 1979 and 1980), Jack Austin (chairman, campaign committee for Yukon and Northwest Territories, 1979 and 1980), Derek Lewis (Newfoundland campaign committee chairman, 1979 and 1980), Royce Frith (Ontario campaign committee chairman, 1979), and David Steuart (Saskatchewan campaign committee chairman, 1979). Other campaign chairmen in the provinces included some prominent Liberals from the Commons. The fewer number of senators leading the organization in the 1980 campaign may reflect the party's defeat in 1979 rather than a trend to remove senators from this role in general.

The Conservative party has exploited Senate appointments similarly, although more infrequently since they have been in office for less time. During his nine-month government in 1979-1980, Prime Minister Joe Clark found time to place in the Senate Lowell Murray, who was his 1979 campaign chairman. Clark's action was similar to that of his Conservative predecessor in office, John Diefenbaker, who appointed his key campaign advisor, Allister Grosart, to the Senate in 1962. Also, former Senator Gunnar Thorvaldson, appointed by Diefenbaker, was a fund-raiser for the federal and provincial Conservative parties in Manitoba. According to newspaper columnists Douglas Fisher and Harry Crowe, Senator Thorvaldson's role was to seek "contributions from those who got contracts in Manitoba through the Federal [Conservative] Government and from those out-of-province firms which got contracts from the provincial [Conservative] government."

Conclusion

Scholarly surveys of the Senate usually concentrate on the institution and its inactivity and weak impact on policy and legislation, compared with the House of Commons. When senators are discussed, such assessments usually stress the senators' role as superannuated party supporters. Such analyses usually avoid or minimize the intensive and influential activities of nearly 25 per cent of the senators. These activities relate particularly to the scrutiny of proposed legislation affecting private corporations' organization, practices and activities, and political party organization and fund-raising.

In the latter case, the question arises as to whether the public is well served by its subsidy of high party officialdom appointed by the government party-of-the-day. In the former case, the public may wonder if it is well served by senators, particularly those on the committee on banking, trade and commerce, who have extensive corporate interests and whose intellectual values are those of large-scale business. There has been considerable discussion of conflict of interest legislation for parliamentarians since the publication of the Green Paper in 1973, although no legislation has come forward. Even if senators have become sensitized to the question of personal conflicts of interest, there remains the question of the representativeness of senators and the exploitation of parliament by an internal "business" lobby. The lack of conflict of interest legislation and the Senate's critical views on the Green Paper attest to the relevance of these concerns.

BIBLIOGRAPHY

(See also Bibliography, Chapter 2)

Albinski, H.S., "The Canadian Senate: Politics and the Constitution," *American Political Science Review*, LVII, 2, June, 1963.

Briggs, E.D., "The Senate: Reform or Reconstruction?," *Q.Q.*, LXXV, 1, Spring, 1968.

Campbell, C., *The Canadian Senate: A Lobby from Within*, Toronto, Macmillan, 1978.

Canada, *Rules of the Senate of Canada*, Ottawa, Q.P., 1964.

Canadian Study of Parliament Group, *Seminar on the Senate*, Ottawa, Q.P., 2, 1, 1979.

Dawson, W.F., "Parliamentary Privilege in the Senate of Canada," Address to the 38th Annual Meeting of the C.P.S.A., Sherbrooke, P.Q., June 8, 1966.

Hopkins, E.R., "Financial Legislation in the Senate," *C.T.J.*, VI, 5, September-October, 1958.

Knowles, S., "The Only Sensible Thing To Do With the Senate Is To Abolish It," *Toronto Star*, January 10, 1972.

Kunz, F.A., *The Modern Senate of Canada, 1925-1963, A Re-appraisal*, Toronto, U.T.P., 1965.

Lambert, N., "Reform of the Senate," *Winnipeg Free Press*, Pamphlet No. 30, April, 1950.

MacKay, R.A., "How to Reform the Senate," *Canadian Commentator*, May, 1963.

MacKay, R.A., *The Unreformed Senate of Canada*, Toronto, M. & S., revised edition, 1963.

MacKay, R.A., "To End or Mend the Senate," *Q.Q.*, LXXI, 3, Autumn, 1964.

MacNeill, J.F., "Memorandum for Senator Robertson, re the Senate, Reasons Given by Proponents of Confederation for Constituting a Second Chamber," Ottawa, Senate, February 16, 1950.

Morin, J.Y., "Un nouveau rôle pour un Sénat moribund," *Cité libre*, XV, juin-juillet, 1964.

Orban, E., *Le Conseil legislatif de Québec*, Montréal, Bellarmin, 1967.

Turner, J.N., "The Senate of Canada — Political Conundrum," in Clark, R.M., (ed.), *Canadian Issues: Essays in Honour of Henry F. Angus*, Toronto, U.T.P., 1961.

Watts, R.L., "Second Chambers in Federal Political Systems," *Ontario Advisory Committee on Confederation: Background Papers & Reports*, Vol. 2, Toronto, Q.P., 1970.

15

THE ADMINISTRATIVE PROCESS

This chapter follows the model set by the comparable chapter in the fourth edition. It attempts to present a bird's eye view of the essentials of Canadian public administration. Although much of the material deals with the federal government, many of the principles and procedures which are discussed are practised by Canadian provincial governments, as well.

The introductory item by Professor Thomas Hockin explains the organizational structure of the federal public service. It is accompanied by an up-to-date chart showing in detail the organization of the government of Canada. Within this structure the Treasury Board plays a significant managerial role but its planning and policy-making functions have been tempered recently by competition from other agencies such as the Privy Council Office, the Prime Minister's Office, the Department of Finance, some Ministries, and the Priorities and Planning Committee of cabinet. This shift in power is well described in Richard Van Loon's article in Chapter 12 in this edition, and it should be read in conjunction with this chapter. Its inclusion makes it possible to omit A.W. Johnson's article, "The Treasury Board and the Machinery of Government," which appeared in the fourth edition, pp. 482-497.

Since the Glassco Commission submitted its report on government organization, Ottawa has adopted a number of new managerial techniques, some of which have been emulated in provinces and elsewhere. Professor Douglas Hartle's hard-hitting critique assesses the success of these new procedures and, not surprisingly, finds them wanting.

John Kettle's brief article points out how rapidly public employment is growing in Canada, particularly in the provincial and municipal sectors. His graphics, which forecast that the increase will continue, give some indication of the importance of public employment in this country. He estimates that by 1986 there will be more than two million Canadians — or about 17 per cent of the whole labour force — employed by public authorities.

Since this growing army of civil servants is involved in more and more aspects of citizens' lives as the administrative and welfare state continues to expand, the problem of the conflict of interest of public servants is more acute. In 1973, the federal government issued a set of guidelines for its employees. The order-in-council which proclaimed them is reprinted in this chapter.

As state activity has mounted, Canadians have become increasingly concerned about governmental secrecy and the need for citizens to be able to secure information freely from public sources. The article on this subject in the previous edition from *The Toronto Star* has been replaced by an excerpt from a recent address given by Professor Donald Rowat, who is the leading academic authority on this issue. He compares Canada to Sweden and the United States and makes a plea for improved freedom of information in this country.

The growth of state power has also led to popular support for the creation of an ombudsman to protect citizens' rights. All provinces except Prince Edward Island now have such an office but the federal government lags behind. Professor Rowat, who is also the Canadian authority on the ombudsman, makes it clear in his article that while Ottawa should have such an office, it should be a plural body composed of more than one person. The article from the Canadian Press describing the position in Quebec, which is occupied by a woman, replaces the article in the fourth edition, pp. 514-516, which reviewed the work of the Alberta ombudsman.

The bibliography has been expanded greatly and is now a fairly comprehensive review of recent literature on a number of aspects of Canadian public administration. The sub-divisions are: general, bilingualism and biculturalism, bureaucrats and politicians, collective bargaining, crown corporations and ABCs, financial management and accountability, freedom of information and secrecy and security, management, ombudsman, public policy and decision-making, regulation, and royal commissions.

As the bibliography indicates, there is now a great deal of material published on public administration in Canada. A major source of it is the Institute of Public Administration of Canada which publishes the excellent journal, *Canadian Public Administration,* as well as several series of research studies, monographs, and pamphlets. For government policy-making in particular, students should refer to the quarterly *Canadian Public Policy.* The new magazine, *Policy Options,* carries many articles dealing with issues in public administration and the Institute for Research on Public Policy, which publishes the magazine, also sponsors a number of monographs. Various texts and books of readings are noted in appropriate sub-sections of the bibliography.

THE STRUCTURE OF THE FEDERAL BUREAUCRACY*

Thomas A. Hockin

The public service and those government employees outside public service classifications for all three levels of government in Canada account for over 12 per cent of the country's work force. By the end of 1974, the total number of Federal government employees reached 450,790. Employment at other levels of government pushed the total over 1 million in 1974. The extent to which government is an employer in Canadian society may not be obvious in Ottawa because of the division of government employment into Federal, provincial and local levels and because of its geographical dispersal. (Considerably less than half of Federal employees work in Ottawa.) Also, a large number of employees are engaged in activity which is not visi-

* From *Government in Canada,* Toronto, McGraw-Hill Ryerson, 1976, Chapter 5, "The Federal Public Service." By permission.

bly "governmental," such as the work of the Crown corporations (approximately one-third of all Federal employees are engaged in such corporations).

Levels of government employment are an uncertain measure of the significance of the public service in the over-all life of society. More important is the nature and extent of public service activity itself. In Canada at the Federal level the administrative machine is made up of widely disparate units pursuing many different activities. By 1970 the Federal government was made up of twenty-seven departments, twenty-five boards and commissions, and forty-six Crown corporations.

Let us look first at departments. . . . [See chart "Organization of the Government of Canada."]

All departments except for the Privy Council Office have this much in common: they have been created by statute. This is in contrast to Britain. Yet in Ottawa the cabinet now has liberal discretionary power to alter the duties of departments, thanks to the Transfer of Duties Act of 1918. A department's functions are, of course, defined in large measure by those Acts of Parliament which the minister is expected to administer. The rationale for any group of agencies to be placed into one department or ministry of state varies, from the need to group common functions (such as External Affairs), or common clienteles (Agriculture), or similar processes (Supply and Services), or similar missions (such as the Ministry of State for Science and Technology created in 1971). Other departments are Irish stews, congeries of widely diverse activities (such as the Department of the Secretary of State). Departments also vary widely in size, and in policy influence, from the small but powerful Department of Finance to the enormous yet less powerful Post Office. Some are so enormous and multifaceted, such as Transport, that they have recently had to be fundamentally reorganized to allow the minister and his top public servants time and opportunity to concentrate on at least a minimum of comprehensive policy assessment. A few new departments comprise a large number of staff and executive personnel who have had little experience in the public service (such as in Consumer and Corporate Affairs). Some departments have been at the centre of the Ottawa scene for decades, such as Finance, Justice and External Affairs, and they have enjoyed a good deal more prestige than either their size or their budgets would suggest. Even more striking is the diversity in the geographical dispersal of departments. Some departments, such as Agriculture, Environment, Veterans Affairs, Transport, Manpower, Immigration and Defence, have over three-quarters of their personnel posted outside Ottawa. Some, such as Finance and Justice, have almost all of their personnel in Ottawa. Some departments are deeply involved in fundamental long-range policy-planning, such as the Department of Finance's research branches (in concert with the Bank of Canada's research branch) and some, such as the Department of External Affairs until the late 1960s have indulged in little long-term policy-planning. These wide differences in departmental characteristics are no doubt typical of most bureaucracies in any country. A striking feature of Canadian departmental history is the prescience of the fathers of confederation. In 105 years the number of departments has only grown from fourteen to twenty-seven. Another feature of Federal departments, however, is the tendency to organize departments around what foreign observers would quickly recognize as uniquely Canadian assets: for example, the Department of Indian Affairs and Northern Development, the Department of Fisheries and Forestry, and the Department of Energy, Mines and Resources.

That part of the administrative machine most answerable to Parliament is both *de jure* and *de facto* the government department. Within each department are 'branches' or 'divisions' or 'services' which in turn are usually made up of sub-units ranging in name from corporations, to councils, to agencies. At the top of the departmental pyramid is the minister who is responsible to Parliament (and also to the prime minister and the cabinet) for the work of his department. He is chosen by the prime minister, is a member of the prime minister's political party, and is a Member of Parliament or, very infrequently, a senator. Aside from the 'parliamentary secretary' (another MP who assists the minister in ways defined by the individual minister), the minister is the only official 'political' actor in the department. All 'public servants' in a department are constitutionally subordinate to the minister. In public, departmental solidarity and loyalty to the minister is expected. (Unlike the case in Britain, ministers in Canada do not have 'private secretaries' seconded from the public service to help them with personal political and public relations duties. Instead it is the 'executive assistant' who helps the minister most in these functions. These 'EA's' are usually chosen from outside the public service. A large number of these appointments are filled by young men who are party members and look to a career in politics rather than in the public service). [See Tilley's article, *Politics: Canada* fourth edition, Chapter 12.]

Although not appointed under the provisions of the Civil Service Act, the chief public servant in the department, responsible to the minister for running it, is the deputy minister (or in the case of some departments the 'undersecretary'). In the past, the 'DM' was usually a product of many years' experience in the public service: more often than not his experience was in the department in which he was the deputy. Now it is no longer unusual for a prime minister who wishes to shake up a department, or who wishes to give it a new sense of mission, to choose someone from outside to be its deputy. A number of deputy ministers were changed after Mr. Trudeau took over from Mr. Pearson as prime minister in 1968. Some were appointed from other departments and some from outside the public service. (For example, a western Canadian businessman was named deputy minister of Energy, Mines and Resources by Mr. Trudeau, and a close personal aide of the prime minister was named a departmental deputy minister in early 1973.) The power of the deputy minister is only what the minister chooses to give him except for some managerial authority delegated to him by the Treasury Board and the Public Service Commission. Underneath the DM there are usually assistant deputy ministers (ADM's) or assistant undersecretaries. Departments vary in the number of positions at the ADM level (usually around four). Reporting to ADM's are directors of divisions, or similarly senior line managers. These officers, plus those in ranks immediately below, comprise most of the 'executive' class of the public service. (There were 618 members of this class in 1971.)

The most durable image about the bureaucratic part of the government of Canada is that it is a gigantic administrative pie sliced into hermetically sealed, rigorously hierarchical, departments. This way of looking at the Canadian government is useful as an organizing device for budgetary reporting, for coping with parliamentary accountability, and for certain types of administrative convenience; it is only partially useful as an image of how the government's work integrates or fails to integrate. Although this chapter will concentrate on the role of public servants in *departments* in the formation of public policy it would be remiss not to note that the non-departmental branches of the governmental apparatus, the boards, corporations, and commissions, account for a large part of the bureaucratic machinery. In fact the administrative part of the government of Canada is a collage of departments, boards, commissions, Crown corporations, supra-departmental control and initiating agencies and Federal-provincial committees and interdepartmental committees. More of this collage is represented not by a list of departments but in the list of the bodies and agencies responsible for the 'Ministry'.

The 'Ministry' of the government of Canada is composed of ministers whose answerability goes beyond the mere obligation to answer for departments in Parliament. Most ministers not only represent departments but are answerable in part for the activities of various boards, corporations and commissions. The [chart on Federal Government Organization] gives the names of the various Ministries of the government of Canada and the departments, boards, commissions and corporations which report through the minister to the House of Commons. It must be noted that although ministers are completely responsible for all work done in departments there are other agencies in his Ministry for which he acts only as a 'spokesman' to Parliament. He is not responsible for their activities.

The Federal government contained seventy-one boards and corporations in 1970, a smaller number than in some provincial governments. For example, by the early 1960s Alberta had 123 such bodies and Ontario had 97.

Canada's Federal Crown corporations are important allocators within the Canadian state. They account for considerable resources and expenditures. For example, in the fiscal year 1969-70, Crown corporations obtained from the Federal government a net amount of $2,162 million, comprised of $1,075 million in loans; $656 million in subsidies and other payments to cover operating and capital expenditures; and $449 million for other purposes such as payments of subsidies to private business. A substantial portion of Federal government resources — equal to about one-fifth of the total Federal budget — went to Crown corporations in that year. There were twenty-seven Crown corporations classified as business enterprises, seventeen of these supporting the infrastructure of the economy in transport, communications and finance. Those not classified as enterprises were on the whole engaged in economic or social support services: these included 'thirteen engaged in economic development and support functions of various kinds, six in health and welfare, four in culture and recreation . . . and three in other functions.' Canadian Federal Crown corporations are not involved in judicial functions or day-to-day political considerations and they 'perform at least one of the functions of managing capital assets, lending, making transfer payments and research.'

The growth in the number of these corporations and commissions is noteworthy, but perhaps not exceptional. All countries try to exempt some functions of government from the restraints and patterns of their public service commissions, such as rules on job classification, promotion, staffing and pay. Exemptions are also sought from Treasury departments with their standardized budgetary and financial procedures. All countries also try to take a number of explicit public functions out of 'politics,' so that the minister will not have to be answerable in more detail for the operations of certain public activities than he ordinarily would wish. Canada is no exception. If anything, Canada is becoming unusually prone to those temptations at the Federal and the provincial levels. Still some parliamentary communication is expected from most of these quasi-independent bodies. It has been suggested that the proliferation of such bodies in this century in Canada is in all probability a concession to American influences. Yet apart from a few bodies, such as the Public Service Commission, Canadian agencies bear little resemblance to the 'independent' executive agencies in Washington in that a minister is expected to supply responses from such bodies to Parliament, even if he does not meddle much in their activity. Even the most 'independent' of Canadian agencies is at least expected to provide a minister with information if he asks for it.

Federal boards have considerable independence and power of regulation. The powers of Canadian boards include powers to study, to make policy, to grant licences and to publicize. Some Federal agencies give considerable power to interest groups by giving them representation on the boards; one example is the representation of producers on Federal boards for the marketing of agricultural products. It is also clear that a number of Federal boards wield considerable allocative, structural and regulatory power with little or no cabinet or ministerial influence until the minister decides to change the statutes under which such agencies operate, or unless public or interest-group pressure grows intense enough to force a minister to attempt to persuade such agencies to shift their policy. For example, the powerful Canadian Radio and Television Commission is to be free of political influence, and its mandate includes the power to prescribe classes for broadcast licences, to allocate broadcasting time, to determine time that may be devoted to advertising, and to prescribe the nature of political advertising by political parties. The policy powers of the Canadian Transport Commission are vast. They involve major allocative and regulatory activities. For example, under the National Transportation Act (see Bill 231 in 1967), the grant of power to the Commission under Section 3 of the Act is no more detailed than the direction to investigate for the 'public interest.' The guidelines for granting pipeline licences are little more explicit than 'to serve the public convenience and necessity.' Also 'the Commission shall make investigations, including the holding of public hearing, as in its opionion is necessary or desirable in the public interest', or further 'it may disallow acquisitions if in the opinion of the Commission such acquisition will unduly restrict competition or otherwise be prejudicial to the public interest.' In considering an application for a pipeline certificate the Commission 'shall take into account such matters as appear to be relevant.' However, the Commission is expected to be aware of over-all ministry policy in areas concerned.

Most boards, commissions and Crown corporations, because of their members' fixed tenure of office and statutory power, are officially expected

to operate free of political influence. In practice this expectation is occasionally qualified. First, there is the tendency of the cabinet to appoint to these positions many members who have been party supporters. Second, there is the necessity for many boards or commissions, such as the Canadian Transport Commission, to integrate some of their policy within over-all Ministry and government policy. Third, it is politically advisable for good public relations that corporations such as Air Canada or the Canadian Broadcasting Corporation, or regulators such as the St. Lawrence Seaway Authority, agree to explain to parliamentary committees their policies on various matters. Yet these opportunities for parliamentary probing should not lead one to conclude that such agencies are little different from those agencies clearly integrated into departments. Since there are countless issues with which these independent agencies deal and for which the cabinet and the minister would prefer not to be fully "answerable" in Parliament, ministers are happy, in most instances, to grant them *de facto* power of decision. They simply report their decision to Parliament or let their officers explain the rationale of their decisions in parliamentary committees . . .
[Editor's note: For information on the Treasury Board, see R. Van Loon's article, *supra*, Chapter. 12]

• • •

TECHNIQUES AND PROCESSES OF ADMINISTRATION*

Douglas G. Hartle

I want to say at the outset that, generally speaking, I am not enthusiastic about the new techniques and processes of administration. In my view, those who advocate them are inclined to assume that the problem is much easier than it is. There has been a tendency, which can be traced back to the Hoover Commission in the United States, but which had its counterpart in the Glassco Commission in Canada, which reported in the mid-1960s, to suppose that the public sector was, in some sense, mismanaged relative to the private sector. The basic themes were: 'Let the manager manage' and 'Apply the techniques and processes that have proven successful in the private sector to the public sector.'
    Now in my view the idea that public servants are managers is fallacious. In a well-run system, public servants are not managers; they are policy advisers and/or emissaries (negotiators) and/or administrators. To me the term 'manager' implies a substantial degree of discretion. In a parliamentary system, the bureaucrat should have relatively little decision-making discretion because the minister to whom he reports must take responsibility for the actions of his officials in the House. Any minister who delegates substantial powers to a senior official, who in turn delegates some of these powers to his subordinates, who in turn delegate, *ad infinitum*, is a fool if

* From *Canadian Public Administration*, 19, 1, Spring, 1976, published by the Institute of Public Administration of Canada. By permission. (Professor Hartle was formerly a Deputy Secretary of the Treasury Board.)

he does not specify the ground rules under which they are to proceed. He is, if he does not set forth such rules, inviting political insensitivity at best, and old-fashioned corruption at worst. For the public servant who has a great deal of discretion with little or no accountability is vulnerable both to 'ego trips' on the one hand, where he bestows or withholds favours at his own pleasure, or a candidate for a bribe because the potential beneficiary knows that the power to give or withhold a substantial benefit rests in the hands of a non-elected official. I deplore that substantial body of legislation that confers discretionary powers without any clear methods of holding accountable those who make the decisions.

It is true, of course, that the legislation usually requires that the minister 'decide.' In fact, as we all know, a minister's time is limited, and he is required, by and large, to accept the recommendations of his officials almost automatically.

The Hoover and Glassco Commissions made a fundamental error in my opinion. They were simple-minded in assuming that the techniques and processes that had proven useful in the private sector could be applied, virtually without modification, to the public sector. They forgot, if they ever understood, that there is a fundamental difference between the two sectors. In the private sector, firms that are badly run will ultimately go bankrupt. While no one would claim that the financial statements in the private sector are without their ambiguities, there is a set of accepted accounting conventions that limits the degree of manipulation. For publicly held corporations, if the story told by the profit-and-loss statement is persistently tragic, the shareholders will oust the current corporate managers and replace them with a new set.

In the public sector, there is no equivalent to a profit-and-loss statement. The record of assets and liabilities is virtually meaningless. The shareholders — the voters — have only three alternatives if they find the government's policies are unsatisfactory: they can vote the government out of office (when there is a credible alternative); they can revolt; or they can emigrate. But in reaching their decisions the voters cannot simply examine the equivalent of the profit-and-loss statement of the government of the day. No such statement exists or can exist. The 'generally accepted accounting principles' upon which private sector profit-and-loss statements hinge are disputatious; I cannot see the day when the same degree of consensus, limited as it is (e.g., inflation adjustments), will exist with respect to the assessment of the policy positions of any government.

The basic conflicts between politicians and bureaucrats, the conflicts among special interest groups, and the conflicts between each of these groups and the political-bureaucratic establishment are inescapable. Those who perceive themselves to be losers are unlikely to acquiesce in their losses: those who perceive themselves to be winners are unlikely to be satisfied with their gains. The losers will fight for redress: the winners will fight to retain what they have, and seek more.

Techniques

In the past decade or so there have been at least six techniques introduced that purported to improve government decision: Program Planning and

Budgeting, Operational Performance Measurement Systems, Management by Objectives, Cost/Benefit Analysis, Cost/Effectiveness Studies. I would like to comment on each of them in turn. . . .

Program Planning and Budgeting

While the coroner's report is not yet in, at least in Canada, there seems little doubt the PPB is dead. Some useful things were accomplished, as a comparison of the current *Estimates* with those of a decade ago clearly demonstrates. There is more data presented in a more useful format than there used to be. The new cross-classification of expenditures by agency, by program, by activity, as well as by object of expenditure, is undoubtedly an improvement over the old classification scheme.

Having said this, however, I do not believe that it is an exaggeration to say that the planning and evaluation purposes of PPB have not been realized and are not likely to be. Spending agencies do not take seriously the requests for estimates for their future expenditures. They simply extrapolate the next year's requests at a constant rate. Why should they bother to do otherwise when the numbers are not taken seriously by those responsible for putting together the budget for the coming year? At best, these forecasts are aggregated and presented as one slate to ministers to show that, if restraint is not shown, the system will collapse. This ministers already understand.

Secondly, rarely, if ever, does it make strategic sense for a department to reveal its aspirations during the regular cyclical budgetary review. Better to introduce new initiatives by means of special requests to cabinet outside the regular budgetary cycle where the competition for funds is less and where it can be claimed both that special circumstances warrant emergency action and that funds can be found to finance the new or expanded programs for the balance of the year. To the devil with the financial implications for subsequent years!

Thirdly, the analytical component of PPB, as originally conceived, has been largely ignored. Typically, no analytical work has been undertaken to assess program efficiency and effectiveness. Where it has been carried out it has had minimal effects on budgetary decisions, for reasons I will elaborate upon later.

Why has PPB not realized its earlier promise? I believe that there are several interrelated answers. (1) It was naïve to assume that agreement could be reached as to the objective of each program. Most programs have multiple objectives, and some of them cannot be admitted. Different ministers and officials assign quite different weights to these several objectives at any point in time. Then these weights change. Witness the problems involved in closing a defence base located in a depressed area. (2) What constitutes a program, an activity, a subactivity, or a sub-subactivity is inherently arbitrary. Should our defence spending be considered as one program or as ten programs? What activities should be combined to constitute a program? Why is an activity not a program in its own right, or a subactivity for that matter? (3) When is it in the interest of the minister and officials responsible to take a hard look at what they are doing? Indeed, is it not dangerous even to collect the basic data upon which such an assessment could be based?

(4) Given the ambiguities about objectives, mentioned above, and the lack of consensus about methods, discussed below, how seriously would an analysis designed to support a PPB submission be taken?

Operational Performance Measurement Systems

When an activity (or should I say subactivity?) results in an output that is sufficiently tangible that it can be measured in both quantitative and qualitative terms, and most of the costs associated with the output are clearly assignable to it, it is feasible to calculate the changes over time in unit costs or, what is essentially the same thing, changes in labour productivity. For the past five or six years the Planning Branch of the Treasury Board has been urging departments with repetitive operations to institute such measurement systems. Using Planning Branch officers as advisers, some progress has been made. While it is certainly a rough estimate, I would suppose that the labour productivity of units accounting for perhaps 30 per cent of government employment is now being estimated. The potential is probably something like 70 per cent of federal employment. It must not be forgotten, however, that the wages and salaries paid to this large proportion of federal employees accounts for only a small proportion of federal expenditures. The cost of the Family Allowance would not be materially affected if the application were processed and the cheques issued without labour, materials, space, and equipment. Most of the costs arise because of the dollar amounts stated on the monthly cheques that are distributed to millions of Canadian mothers.

Nevertheless, while not wishing to claim too much for it in terms of potential budgetary-manpower savings, OPMS seems to me a useful advance. Potentially, at least, it can aid the line officer in monitoring the performance of his subordinates; it can also serve as a basis for arguing with the Treasury Board for budgetary increases based on increases in work-load but taking into account some productivity improvements.

There are, however, difficulties. One is the difficulty of measuring the extent to which costs per unit are changing as a result of changes in equipment, space and materials. Theoretically, this problem is soluble, but to the best of my knowledge there is no department that yet measures its total factor productivity. Another problem is that the method cannot deal with overhead costs. Another is that OPMS only copes with changes over time and does not take into account the legitimacy of the base from which the changes are calculated. Fat operations can appear to have remarkable reductions in unit costs with little effort, while lean ones have to struggle for improvements.

The last problem I wish to mention may, however, be overriding. Unless the dollar and manpower budgets arrived at for those activities to which OPMS has been applied in fact reflect the results, the incentive for agencies to maintain, much less extend, OPMS is, to say the least, minimal. There has been a tendency, I am afraid, to have the Planning Branch of the Treasury Board out flogging OPMS to departments while the Program Branch of the Treasury Board has found it expedient to make its recommendations to ministers as though the information were not available. . . .

Management by Objectives

Except in those operations where it is possible to measure changes in unit costs over time, which means essentially the high volume repetitive operations to which OPMS can be applied, I am highly sceptical about the efficacy of MBO. Too often, in my experience, MBO costs more in time and energy than it produces: endless meetings, haggling over jurisdictional territory, drafts and redrafts of statements of objectives to ensure that they are sufficiently vague, no real monitoring of performance against the stated objectives — sometimes because this is impossible and sometimes because it is uncomfortable for the senior officer.

Who is supposed to monitor the monitors? What is his or her motivation for monitoring? If the subordinate can be neither rewarded nor punished on the basis of the results of the monitoring — at least within extremely wide limits of performance — why bother? We all know of cases where the weak, if not totally incompetent, subordinate is given a glowing letter of recommendation as a way of enticing some unsuspecting agency to take him off the hands of the reviewing officer. Good subordinates are often given weak performance appraisals in order to reduce their mobility. . . .

Cost/Benefit Analysis

As I said before, one could quite easily write a book on the subject of cost/benefit analysis. Indeed many have been written. The last time I checked, the Treasury Board Secretariat was on the sixth or seventh draft of its manual. . . .

I have no quarrel with cost/benefit analysis as a technique for ensuring that none of the factors bearing on a project decision is neglected. I do not think this is a trivial advantage. On the other hand, I deplore the facility with which some analysts are able to conjure up estimates of some of the inputted costs and benefits to obtain the ratio they want. It is not surprising, it seems to me, that this technique is looked upon by decision-makers as a tool in the adversarial process, because they would be foolish in the extreme to take the numbers provided by so-called experts as in some sense sacrosanct. As one of my supervisors once put it: 'if anyone around here is going to be arbitrary, it's me.'

I cannot recall any instance where a cost/benefit study played a decisive role in the decision to proceed with or reject any proposed major federal project. Probably this is as it should be, because the technique does not adequately handle the distributional question: who will bear the costs and who will reap the benefits. And distributional questions are necessarily at the forefront of the minds of politicians.

Having said this, however, I would not want to suggest that cost/benefit analysis is valueless. In addition to ensuring that the logic, as distinct from the numbers, is straight, I believe it should be used much more extensively as a decision rule when decision-making powers are delegated. This implies, of course, that superiors take the time to develop the criteria and accept responsibility for the results on which they want project decisions to be reached by their subordinates.

Cost-Effectiveness Studies

I will not belabour this extremely large and important subject for two reasons: first, it is impossible to do justice to it in short compass. Then, a paper of mine on what I thought were the crucial issues was printed in the Journal some years ago. I have not changed my mind about fundamental theoretical issues. I am, however, more sceptical than ever that we will see, in the near future, the emergence of a large set of social-economic statistical indicators that are perceived by the decision-makers, the opinion-makers, and the voters, to fairly reflect the changes, both favourable and unfavourable, that are taking place in this country. Consensus on the 'right' way to measure the changes in the well-being of Canadians is not going to be easily reached. But until it is reached I am not optimistic that cost-effectiveness studies are going to have much impact. As mentioned at the outset, it is difficult to reach agreement on the multiple objectives (effects) of programs. It is difficult to obtain the data to estimate their effects quantitatively. It is also difficult to obtain release of the results unless they are favourable in every respect. I strongly believe, however, that as slow and painful as it is likely to be, we must push on in this direction. Only in this way are we likely to get a more informed electorate and hence a more responsible government.

Processes

There are four processes that I wish to comment upon: the personnel selection-promotion process, the budgetary process, the cabinet committee process, the auditing process. My comments must necessarily be too brief relative to the issues. Here too, each one warrants a book rather than a subsection in a paper. I hope, therefore, that you will forgive my impressionistic approach.

Personnel Selection-Promotion Process

. . . First of all, the whole selection procedure, which was designed to minimize political interference, by and large confers instantaneous tenure on public servants. University tenure is seldom granted until after four or five years and then only after an agonizing appraisal process.

Public servants are inclined to sneer at university faculty members, and sometimes rightly so. But there are more research professorships in Ottawa than there are in all the universities in Canada — men and women with effective instant tenure who have the freedom to pose the question they will research, research it, and then file the answer in their own desks with no accountability.

The annual salaries paid in Ottawa to some professional groups (not to mention overtime pay and perquisites) is nothing short of outrageous. While I hesitate to name names, the economist-statistician group immediately comes to mind. Although I obviously cannot prove it, there seems to be a gross distortion brought about by the fact that those groups with weak bargaining power can opt for arbitration while those who have strong bargaining power (e.g., can inconvenience the public by withholding their services) can opt for the strike route. This is a recipe designed to do in the taxpayer. And do not think that the taxpayer is unaware of what is going on. Tails they lose; heads they lose.

The absence in the past of some kind of career-planning system for individuals is notable, particularly at intermediate and senior levels. How many potentially good men and women retire on the job at painfully early ages? How many progress beyond their level of competence because nobody is keeping track of their level of past performance, or lack of performance?

Budgetary Process

The thing that impresses one is the inconsequential nature of the regular budgetary process and the overwhelming importance of decisions made outside of it, through special memoranda to cabinet.

I have no reason to attribute ulterior motives to the Department of Finance. But the fact is that the growth in revenues has been underestimated year after year. Because the revenue estimates of February form the basis of the *Estimates* of the following February, which do not apply until the fiscal year beginning two to three months later, it is not surprising in a period of rapid growth and/or inflation that the realized revenues exceed those estimated fourteen to twenty-four months earlier. The fact is, however, that departments have recognized that they are foolish to compete for additional funds for new or expanded programs at a time when their requests will be arrayed against so many alternatives. Much better to submit a cabinet memorandum during the fiscal year when the windfall revenue gains are being reluctantly revealed by Finance. Then a quickly prepared memorandum to cabinet showing only that funds are available to finance it for the balance of the current year, with no realistic estimates for the implications for ensuing years, will often do the trick. The real trick is, of course, ultimately played on the taxpayer. For, once having been adopted, it is like practising dentistry on a shark to achieve modifications in the program in the future. To change the metaphor: the marshmallows of the current fiscal year become the bricks of the next fiscal year — through the "A" budget. And the bricks of today become the cornerstones of tomorrow as new and expanded programs are erected on this once quivering foundation.

The problem is, of course, that once launched, new initiatives are more like skyrockets than guided missiles — they follow a course dictated more by the shape of the milk bottle from which they were launched (I here reveal my age since even I know that milk bottles have vanished from the scene) than by the intentions of the persons who lit the fuse.

It is pathetic how little impact PPB, DPMS, MBO, and such techniques have had on these crucial decisions. In the vital decisions these techniques are, at the present time, like a well-intentioned funeral director who, through the magic of cosmetics, puts a good face on a man who has just died a slow and agonizing death from cancer. The illusion is nearly complete. But the family knows the horrors that have been disguised, and the visitors to the funeral home have their suspicions.

The indexing of the personal income tax was an important step forward, for it will reduce the income elasticity of the personal income tax and thereby force the government of the day to face more squarely the political costs of increased expenditures. . . .

Cabinet Committee Process

In the past decade or so we have seen the development of a much greater degree of centralization in parliamentary systems. It is true that some departments have been decentralized, notably DREE and the Post Office at the federal level. But in terms of head office, in the federal government and the government of Ontario — the two with which I am familiar — the Prime Minister's Office and the Cabinet Office have much more senior staff, and certainly claim to have much more influence, than they did in the past. Is this an illusion? If not is it good or bad?

I do not think that the centralization of power in a period of majority government is an illusion. A prime minister or a premier with a clear majority has enormous power. He has power that might well be envied by a benevolent dictator — for who is to say him nay? This power attracts, like a magnet, individuals who wish to influence the exercise of this power, for this confers prestige on them.

Whether it be the effect of television or not, although I am inclined to believe that this is far from unimportant, electorates seem to vote a party leader in or out. Ministers in a majority government are therefore elected because of their leader and can be rejected at pleasure. They tend to become, if they were not already, toothless tigers who gum the policy proposals of the senior bureaucracy in general and the cabinet office in particular. Senior ministers may squirm in their chairs, but too often they do not stand up to be counted.

While it is my impression that majority governments confer great powers on the prime minister, and hence on his bureaucratic subordinates, the reverse is also true. Minority governments are highly dependent upon the performance of particular ministers — whether by virtue of the votes they can deliver as individuals from their own riding or the votes they can deliver by virtue of the policies adopted with respect to their particular portfolio.

Canadians, it seems to me, make a fundamental mistake when they assume that minority governments are indecisive and fraught with conflict. Is there not ample evidence that majority governments are both insensitive and dominated by senior bureaucrats who are playing their games? Are the games of bureaucrats any more attractive than those played by politicians? Frankly, I prefer the latter to the former.

Any prime minister or premier is making a grave error who, by creating a strong Cabinet Office, isolates himself from his own ministers who, if they have been chosen wisely, reflect the views of an important segment of the electorate. Too often the emperor finds he has no clothes only by freezing to death in the harsh Canadian winter. You can imagine which parts freeze first.

In short, I hold the view that too often strong cabinet secretariats, elaborate cabinet briefings prepared by these secretariats, control over cabinet agendas, and so on, isolate prime ministers and premiers from the ultimate reality they must face. This is often done in the name of one of the techniques I have briefly discussed above. To lose an election in the name of PPB, or OPMS, or MBO is no better than to lose it in the name of insensitivity, inactivity, and indecisiveness.

Auditor General

Let me end this paper with a plea. Many of the difficulties referred to above arise not because either politicians or bureaucrats are malevolent — indeed the opposite is the case by my observation — but rather because they respond to the implicit incentive systems within which they operate. They are not bad men but good men who cannot face the terribly painful personal costs of doing good.

One way out of this impasse, short of a revolution, is to have much greater public disclosure of information. The public needs the information that will allow it to identify when a good man is doing good — whether it be politician or bureaucrat. In a state of ignorance, fools and knaves are indistinguishable from wise men and saints.

It is rarely in the interest of a particular minister or official to reveal more than his colleagues: "Better to be silent and thought a fool than to speak up and prove it." Nevertheless, the conspiracy of silence that prevails in our federal and provincial governments seems to me to put their continued existence in jeopardy. There is, in short, a crisis of confidence. It is not in the interest of any individual to speak up; but it is of vital importance that the system as a whole reveal in the future more than it has in the past if its legitimacy is to be maintained.

For this reason, while sceptical of some of the techniques discussed in the earlier part of this paper, I am strongly in favour of the auditor general reporting to Parliament on the extent to which they have been applied, the actions taken on the basis of the results, and the availability of the information to the public.

It is a most imperfect and complicated world. But undue secrecy will not make it less imperfect or less complicated. We do not know how to assess effectiveness of many programs in realizing the aspirations of a multitude of groups. One thing is clear to me, however: I would prefer to trust the partially informed many to the well informed few. This view is reinforced every time I attend a faculty meeting.

BUREAUCRACY GROWS APACE IN PROVINCES AND MUNICIPALITIES*

John Kettle

Cries of "empire-building!" always greet the news that more public servants are at work for Ottawa (and us). Hanging over our heads is the awful

* From *Executive* magazine, October, 1974. By permission.

feeling that the feds are taking over the country, spending all the money, and . . . that more bodies are needed to spend it.

But it ain't so. For years Ottawa has accounted for a declining portion of the labor force as well as a declining portion of total government employment. The empire building (if that's the right word for it) is taking place in the municipal and provincial governments, especially in the provinces. That worried talk in the nation's capital about decentralizing the civil service may not be necessary after all if the trends continue, because the bulk of the country's government employees are already as decentralized as they can be, spread evenly through every province and municipality in the country.

(Incidentally, it is still the same few departments of the federal government that dominate the federal public service today as in the 1960s . . . The Post Office accounts for 19% of the public service, National Defence's civilian workers for another 15%, National Revenue for 8%, Ministry of Transport for 7% — and that's a total of 49% between the four of them. . . .)

We are getting to be a more governed country, if the number of public servants is acceptable evidence. There are now six or seven government employees for every 100 Canadians, and the figure continues to climb. It is climbing, however, almost exactly in step with the labor force. The reason the labor force is a growing part of the population is the changing mix of age groups — more people of working age compared with those below working age. Government's total share remains remarkably steady, at around one in six of all the people with jobs. So really government as a whole is not empire-building either. But if you worry about the epidemic of bureaucrats, the provinces are the governments to watch.

What we are talking of today is a million and a half government employees in Canada, 7% of a population of 22 million and 17% of the people with jobs.

This is a fairly conservative estimate, by the way. I don't know that anyone has added up the numbers before — certainly they aren't assembled by Statistics Canada. Here's what I included (1973 figures):

Federal level:
Departmental employees	290,000	
Crown corporations	145,000	
Armed forces	80,000	
		515,000
Provincial level:		475,000
Municipal level:		
General employees	225,000	
Teachers	255,000	
		480,000
		1,470,000

The various series from 1961 to 1973 required a little fudging. For instance, the government of B.C. only tells Statistics Canada the number of people it employs in institutes of higher learning, leaving them to guess (but not publicly) the number of employees in its departments, Crown corporations, boards, and agencies. I simply assumed the ratio of public servants to population would be the same in that province as in the rest of the country. The figures of municipal employees do not include what I'm sure is a large number of people employed in city transit, city utilities (with the exception of water works employees, who for some reason are counted), and municipal hospitals and school boards. I put in the school teachers on the grounds that they were numerous and easy to isolate. I left the rest because I could see no quick way to uncover national figures or even fake up estimates. One or two of the series had breaks in them when the statisticians decided to collect numbers on a different basis, which required a little juggling.

From these series I found that between 1961 and 1973 federal government employment grew at an average 1.0% a year, provincial government employment at an average 6.9% a year, and municipal government employment at 3.9% a year. Those are big differences, more than enough to skew the old distribution patterns.

I used two different techniques for forecasting. Some of the series are pretty clearly related to the growth of population, the general government or departmental employees most obviously. They grow faster than the population, but then so does the labor force. What I forecast was the ratio of civil servants to citizens; then multiplied by my December 1973 population forecasts. Teachers I related to the number of school-age children, actual and projected. Other series seem to have a life of their own, independent of population growth. The armed forces are winding down, and I simply found an equation that best "explained" or best fit the existing data and extrapolated it. Federal Crown corporation employment has wobbled up and down in the past dozen years, but under the fluctuations there is a faintly growing trend line, and this too I continued.

My extrapolations of employment in 1986:
Federal level:

Departmental employees	450,000	
Crown corporations	145,000	
Armed forces	45,000	
		640,000
Provincial level:		800,000
Municipal level:		
General employees	400,000	
Teachers	300,000	
		700,000
		2,140,000

That's a lot of civil servants, of course, slightly over eight for every 100 Canadians, but still 17% of those forecast to have jobs. What is different about it is the mix between the three levels. In 1986 the provincial governments account for 37% compared with 32% in 1973 and 22% in 1961. Ottawa's share is down to 30% compared with 35% in 1973 and 47% in 1961. Note that the municipal governments' share stays steady throughout the 25 years of records and projections; it is the distribution between the federal

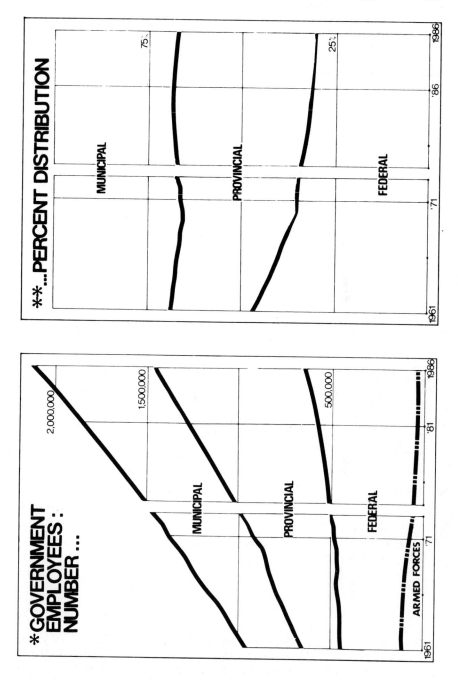

* The chart shows dramatically where the growth in the number of government employees has occurred and is forecast to occur — in the provincial governments. Growth in the federal departments is a little more dramatic than at first appears, since the armed forces have declined and the Crown corporations grow very slowly. Municipal growth comes later. Key figures:

	Federal level	of which armed forces	Provincial level	Municipal level	of which teachers	Total no. of employees
1961	456,953	120,055	213,746	303,362	162,529	974,061
1966	471,180	107,467	319,152	379,407	213,067	1,169,739
1971	491,034	89,563	435,686	462,066	256,924	1,388,786
1976	535,671	72,416	548,767	523,054	269,447	1,607,492
1981	582,932	57,835	672,134	591,841	277,488	1,846,908
1986	640,690	45,488	795,513	699,772	300,948	2,135,975

** The different rates of growth at the various levels of government change the distribution pattern, though of course most people have not noticed it yet. We tend to think of the federal civil service as the main body of government employees, and indeed a few years ago they represented the majority; but no longer. Key figures:

	Federal level	Provincial level	Municipal level
1961	46.9%	21.9%	31.1%
1966	40.3	27.3	32.4
1971	35.4	31.4	33.3
1976	33.3	34.1	32.5
1981	31.6	36.4	32.0
1986	30.0	37.2	32.8

** Here's how the growth in government employees looks on a per-capita basis. The figures are the number of public servants employed at each level for every 100,000 Canadians. At the federal level the ratio actually dropped for a while. Key figures:

	Federal level	Provincial level	Municipal level	Total government
1961	2505	1171	1663	5340
1966	2335	1594	1895	5844
1971	2276	2019	2142	6438
1976	2327	2384	2272	6984
1981	2375	2738	2411	7526
1986	2459	3054	2686	8200

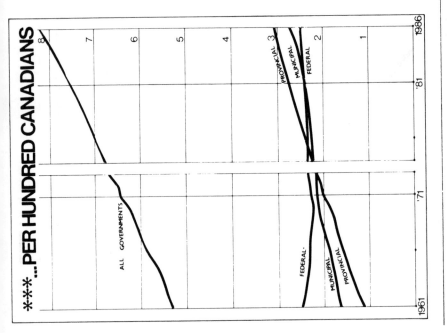

*** PER HUNDRED CANADIANS

* Forecasts based on data from Statistics Canada and other public and private sources. In most cases the extrapolations are "naive" (i.e., judgment-free) mathematical extensions of current trends.

From Executive magazine, October, 1974. By permission.

and provincial levels that moves steadily in favor of the provinces. That's the main news out of this mess of statistics . . . : different government, rather than just more of the same. Presumably we can expect to see some federal politician try to reverse the trend in the next decade or so. We can expect ambitious career civil servants to look increasingly toward the provinces, where the frog pond is growing so much faster. We can also surely anticipate more changes in the federal-provincial tax split. And far off on the time horizon is the promise of another change, the growth of the municipal civil service — largely stimulated in my extrapolations by the return of the teachers as a result of the coincidence of a new generation in the classroom and lower pupil-teacher ratios. My figures do, however, also hint at an eventual speed-up in the growth of regular municipal government employment. I would guess at an increasing demand for tax-paid city services, and, along with that, a little municipal empire-building. But that's one or two decades off.

GUIDELINES TO PREVENT CONFLICT OF INTEREST*

Privy Council

P.C. 1973 — 4065
18 December, 1973

HIS EXCELLENCY THE GOVERNOR GENERAL IN COUNCIL, on the recommendation of the Treasury Board, is pleased hereby to approve the issue of the annexed guidelines to be observed by public servants concerning conflict of interest situations.

Certified to be a true copy
R.G. Robertson
Clerk of the Privy Council

GUIDELINES TO BE OBSERVED BY PUBLIC
SERVANTS CONCERNING CONFLICT OF INTEREST
SITUATIONS

Short Title

1. These guidelines may be cited as the *Public Servants Conflict of Interest Guidelines.*

Guidelines

2. It is by no means sufficient for a person in a position of responsibility in the public service to act within the law. There is an obligation not simply to

* From *House of Commons Debates*, December 18, 1973, p. 8883, Appendix "A." Reproduced by permission of the Minister of Supply and Services Canada.

obey the law but to act in a manner so scrupulous that it will bear the closest public scrutiny. In order that honesty and impartiality may be beyond doubt, public servants should not place themselves in a position where they are under obligation to any person who might benefit from special consideration or favour on their part or seek in any way to gain special treatment from them. Equally, a public servant should not have a pecuniary interest that could conflict in any manner with the discharge of his official duties.

3. No conflict should exist or appear to exist between the private interests of public servants and their official duties. Upon appointment to office, public servants are expected to arrange their private affairs in a manner that will prevent conflicts of interest from arising.

4. Public servants should exercise care in the management of their private affairs so as not to benefit, or appear to benefit, from the use of information acquired during the course of their official duties, which information is not generally available to the public.

5. Public servants should not place themselves in a position where they could derive any direct or indirect benefit or interest from any government contracts over which they can influence decisions.

6. All public servants are expected to disclose to their superiors, in a manner to be notified, all business, commercial or financial interests where such interest might conceivably be construed as being in actual or potential conflict with their official duties.

7. Public servants should hold no outside office or employment that could place on them demands inconsistent with their official duties or call into question their capacity to perform those duties in an objective manner.

8. Public servants should not accord, in the performance of their official duties, preferential treatment to relatives or friends or to organizations in which they or their relatives or friends have an interest, financial or otherwise.

THE RIGHT TO GOVERNMENT INFORMATION — THE CANADIAN CASE*

Donald C. Rowat

In most advanced democracies there is a new trend toward openness in government. Many people have begun to realize that we have inherited from earlier times an undesirable tradition of administrative secrecy. In a true democracy the people have a right to know how they are being governed. In other words, they must have a right of access to government information.

Under a system of discretionary secrecy, while the government may have vast information services, it controls the issuing of information and releases only what it wants to. The public have no clear right to see or make use of the vast store of government records, reports, studies, and statistics that have been paid for with their taxes. Hence, they do not have the full in-

* From *International Review of Administrative Sciences*, 1, 1982. By permission.

formation that they must have if they are to control the government and make wise judgements on public issues. The principle of discretionary secrecy prevents a government from being fully accountable to parliament and the public, and it inhibits the free exchange of information. Thus it prevents the full development of democracy.

By now, several democratic countries have decided that this principle is wrong and ought to be the reverse: all administrative documents should be open to the public except the few that need to be kept secret for good reason, as defined by law. Such countries have adopted a law to establish the principle of governmental openness, called a Freedom of Information Act or Access Act. It provides a right of public access to all administrative documents and information except for specific matters that are narrowly defined in exemptions.

• • •

The country that has had the longest experience with the principle of openness is Sweden. Its constitutional law stating this principle and providing a right of public access to official documents dates back to 1766. Other democratic countries have adopted an access law in much more recent times: Finland (in 1951), Denmark and Norway (in 1970), the United States (1966, revised 1974), and France and the Netherlands (1978). Access laws have also been passed by two Canadian provinces, Nova Scotia (1977) and New Brunswick (1978), and may soon be adopted at the federal level in Canada and Australia.

In Sweden, for over two hundred years the Swedish constitution has provided for open access to official documents and full information to any citizen about administrative activities. This provision was first adopted in 1766, as part of the Freedom of the Press Act, one of the country's four basic constitutional laws. While in most countries all administrative documents are secret unless specific permission is given for their release, in Sweden they are all public except for certain exempted subjects under which they may be withheld. . . .

I will now turn to recent developments in the United States. As you probably know, there has been a stronger tradition of governmental openness in the U.S. than in most other countries. Nevertheless, until very recent years, the release of administrative documents was largely at the discretion of the chief executive, whether federal or state, or the heads of his departments and agencies. At the federal level, it was not until 1946 that provisions were included in a congressional law, the Administrative Procedure Act, which attempted to require the routine disclosure of governmental information. . . . However, the attempt failed, partly because of the vague language of the exemptions. . . .

An important change came with the passage of the Freedom of Information Act in 1966, however. This Act, replacing the provisions of 1946, stated unequivocally that public access to most documents was to be the general rule. More significantly, it listed what types of documents could be kept secret, in nine general categories of exemption, and provided for a means of public appeal against withholding. These provisions finally established the '

Swedish principle of openness: disclosure is the general rule, and documents may not be withheld unless they fall under one of the exemptions specified by law. The categories of exemption, however, are much broader than those of Sweden and hence leave more room for official discretion and judicial interpretation. Difficulties arose in requiring departments and agencies to comply with the Act and in interpreting the meaning of some of the exemptions. For this reason it was amended in 1974. In that year Congress also passed a related Privacy Act, which allows citizens to see personal files being held on them in government agencies, subject to certain exemptions.

The new provisions put into the Freedom of Information Act in 1974 have made it much easier for citizens to enforce their rights. The onus has been put firmly on government agencies to prove why they should not release requested documents, instead of the citizen having to prove why he should have them. . . .

In 1976, the first full year after both the 1974 amendments and the Privacy Act went into effect, the federal departments and agencies received a tremendously increased number of formal requests for access to official documents, the total estimated to be about 150,000. These requests were not only from private citizens, but also from the press, organizations and business firms. Some agencies, like the FBI and the CIA, received thousands of requests from individuals wanting to know whether these agencies kept a file on them and, if so, what was in it. Before the end of the year, such agencies had a huge backlog of unprocessed requests.

● ● ●

In Canada an access law has already gone into effect in two provinces, Nova Scotia and New Brunswick. In Ontario the government has accepted the recommendation of the Commission on Freedom of Information and Individual Privacy that there should be such a law, though it has yet to be enacted. Other provinces are likely to adopt an access law within the next few years.

When Nova Scotia proclaimed its Freedom of Information Act in November, 1977, it became the first jurisdiction in the Commonwealth to adopt such an Act. Its Act followed the general principles of the American Act, except that it provided for an appeal to the legislature instead of the courts. . . . However, it is now generally agreed that the Act's mechanism of appeal is ineffective and a new government has recently introduced a revised Act providing for an appeal to the courts.

New Brunswick's legislature approved a Right to Information Act in June, 1978, but it did not go into effect until January, 1980. Its principles are the same as the American Act except that an appeal can be taken either to the provincial ombudsman or to a judge of the Supreme Court, or first to the ombudsman and then to a judge, who has the power to order the release of documents.

At the federal level in Canada, the new Liberal government, in July, 1980, introduced Bill C-43, the Access to Information Act and the Privacy Act. This bill is now being studied by a committee of parliament. . . . It is a revision of a bill introduced by the previous Conservative government in 1979, except that it includes a Privacy Act, in order to co-ordinate public access to records with private access to personal files. It thus avoids some of the difficulties created in the United States by having two separate Acts.

A good feature of the Canadian bill is that it provides a two-step system of appeal, first to an Information Commissioner, an ombudsman whose decision is only advisory, and then to the Federal Court, which has the power to overturn the minister's decision and order the release of a record. The advantage of having an Information Commissioner is that he would settle most appeals without the need to go to court, thus saving the appellant much time and money. Another good feature of the bill is its provision for an index of government records, so that the public can more easily discover records they may wish to request. A copy of this index is to be kept in every post office in Canada.

Otherwise, however, the Canadian bill is rather weak, because it has fifteen exemptions, compared with nine in the United States. Many of them are broad in scope, so that an official could easily hide a record under one or other of them. And a majority of them exempt a whole class of records, so that an official needs only to prove that a record belongs to one of these classes in order to withhold it. Worse still, five of the exemptions state that documents in that class *must* be withheld, thus going against the spirit of openness and making the bill a kind of Official Secrets Act. For instance, all cabinet and related documents must be kept secret for twenty years unless the Prime Minister gives permission for their release. Also, for most exemptions there is no limit on how long records may be kept secret. The only limit is the government's general rule that most historical records are to be released after thirty years. It appears, then, that the Canadian law will be much weaker than the American Freedom of Information Act.

• • •

WE NEED A FEDERAL OMBUDSMAN COMMISSION*

Donald C. Rowat

Canada's provinces have been world leaders in introducing the concept of the ombudsman as an officer of the legislature to receive and remedy complaints against the administration. He is often pictured as a knight on a white horse charging against big bureaucracy on behalf of the helpless citizen. In 1967, before this office had spread around the democratic world, the governments of Alberta and New Brunswick created ombudsman plans based on the highly successful one that had been introduced in New Zealand in 1962. By now, all provinces except P.E.I. have very successful ombudsman offices in operation.

This new institution has also spread to twenty-four other countries, of which twenty-one have offices at the national level, including such democratic countries as Australia, the United Kingdom, France, Israel and Austria. Yet, Canada's federal government still has no general ombudsman

---

* From *Policy Options*, 3, 2, March-April, 1982. By permission.

office to investigate complaints from the public against its administrative agencies.

Federal Failure

The reasons for this are difficult to divine. The idea of a general ombudsman office for the federal government has been discussed since 1960, and numerous proposals have been made. But the first Trudeau government, instead of creating a general plan, yet recognizing the need for an avenue of public complaints in certain cases, began creating ombudsman-like offices for special purposes. It set up a Commissioner of Official Languages for complaints from the public that they were not dealt with fairly in their own language by federal agencies, a Correctional Investigator for complaints from prisoners, and a Privacy Commissioner for complaints from citizens about access to their personal files held by the government. If the government's current Bill C-43, the Access to Information Act, is ever passed, we will have an ombudsman-like Information Commissioner for complaints against official refusal of access to administrative records. But these offices are all highly specialized and in no sense meet the need for a general ombudsman office to cover all aspects of federal administration.

After delaying action on the idea of a general office for many years, Prime Minister Trudeau in 1976 appointed a committee of senior officials to study the concept of the ombudsman. This committee reported favourably on the idea and recommended a federal plan basically the same as the ones that had already been created in most provinces. In April 1978, the government introduced a bill based on the committee's recommendations but this bill died on the order paper and the government was defeated in May 1979. The new Clark government did not take up the idea, and the second Trudeau government, elected in February 1980, has not revived the bill. As a result, Canada still has no general ombudsman plan at the federal level. Yet the need for such a plan is as great as ever.

Collegial Ombudsman Preferable

One of the basic faults in the federal bill, in my view, is that it provides for the office to be headed by a single ombudsman. I have always maintained that a collegial ombudsman is the most desirable form of organization for populous countries or for the national level in large federations such as Canada. By a collegial ombudsman, I mean several ombudsmen who form a board or commission. The commission decides important cases as a body, but the commissioners specialize in different areas of administration and decide most cases on their own, within guidelines set by the commission.

At the start of the spread of the ombudsman idea in the early 1960s, the notion got fixed in people's minds that the ombudsman institution must be a single person, due to the need for "the personal touch." But the plan began in small countries — Scandinavia and New Zealand — where the workload was small and a single ombudsman could personally make the final decision on all cases. It was therefore argued that the plan was unsuitable for large countries because the ombudsman could not do this — the personal touch would be lost, and the office might turn into a huge bureaucracy like the one that it was supposed to be supervising.

This argument was used despite the fact that the original plan in Sweden already had two ombudsmen, one for civilian and one for military administration, plus the Chancellor of Justice, who was also an ombudsman but appointed by the executive. Finland, too, had an ombudsman plus a Chancellor of Justice. Yet, the idea persisted that the ombudsman must be a single officer. . . .

The Essential is Independence

As early as 1962, I argued that the single ombudsman and the personal touch were not essential characteristics of the office. Instead, the key requirement was independence from the executive and its administration, to assure the complainant of the office's objectivity and fairness.

Britain and France are the only populous countries to have adopted the ombudsman at the national level to date. Having accepted the idea of a single ombudsman without question, they tried to meet the problem of overloading him by requiring that complaints must first be screened through members of the legislature, with the result that the number of complaints handled has been very small in proportion to population. Had they accepted the idea of an ombudsman commission, the prospects of overloading the office with direct complaints would not have been so frightening.

Though in the early years little consideration was given to the collegial idea, several countries have created multiple ombudsman plans in recent years, including, oddly enough, two of the prototype countries, Sweden and New Zealand. In fact, of the twenty-one national plans classified as legislative ombudsmen by the International Ombudsman Institute, eight, or over one-third, have provided for multiple ombudsmen. This trend has gone on largely unnoticed, and the myth that the ombudsman institution must be headed by a single person still persists.

The Austrian Example

In my view the most instructive example of a multiple office is the Ombudsman Commission in Austria. When I visited Austria in 1978, I was pleased to find in operation almost exactly the kind of ombudsman commission that I had advocated in 1962. It is a body of three commissioners, one nominated by each of the three main political parties: the Christian Democrats, the Socialists and the Liberals. Though each commissioner had had a close association with his political party before appointment, they are appointed for a six-year term and, like judges in Commonwealth countries, upon appointment shed any party bias they might have had. In any case, their influence on each other has the effect of keeping them politically neutral.

Each commissioner specializes in an area of the administration and decides minor cases alone. But the commission meets as a body to coordinate its work and to decide important cases. It meets about once a week, and each commissioner is chairman for a year, so that there is no hierarchy among them and no Chief Administrator to dominate the office as in Sweden. Each commissioner gets a summary of all important cases, and any one of them can request that a case come before the full commission for a joint decision.

This form of organization has great advantages for populous countries. It preserves the personal touch by permitting most cases to be decided by single commissioners who have been appointed for this purpose by a legislature, rather than by a nameless bureaucracy at the lower levels of the ombudsman's office. Yet, compared with a system of uncoordinated multiple ombudsmen for special purposes such as has been developing at the federal level in Canada, it preserves the advantages of the single ombudsman's office: consistency of decisions, uniformity of the jurisprudence developed by the ombudsman institution, and efficiency and economy through joint office administration.

For dealing with important or complex cases, this is superior to the single ombudsman, since it adheres to the adage that in such cases, as in the courts, two heads are better than one. And several commissioners standing together can better withstand attempts at executive influence or interference. They are more likely to take on serious cases of maladministration and fight them through to the finish, by giving support to each other. In Austria, for example, if a department refuses to accept a commissioner's informal recommendation, he may then refer the case to the commission, which can respond with the force of a formal recommendation by the whole commission. Also, the commission form meets the problem of omniscience required of a single ombudsman by the appointment of commissioners with different backgrounds and experience. And it helps the office to get away from the aura of the authoritarian hierarchy and one-man rule from the top that is such a characteristic evil of bureaucracy. It is true that with a collegial system some of the image of a knight on a white horse charging against the enemy will be lost, but a stagecoach drawn by a team will get there with far less chance of being wounded.

The Canadian committee of senior officials did discuss the idea of multiple ombudsmen but it recommended a single ombudsman, and this proposal was adopted without question in the federal bill, which died in any case.

My conclusion, then, is that a general ombudsman institution for Canada's federal government ought to be created without further delay, and that it should take the form of an Ombudsman (or Administrative Complaints) Commission.

SHE RIGHTS WRONGS IN QUEBEC — AN OMBUDSWOMAN*

The Canadian Press

The word ombudsman stirs visions in most Canadians of a person who will fight the wrongs — real or imagined — suffered at the hands of government bureaucracy.

Luce Patenaude is the people's champion in Quebec, but there's a snag. Ask most Quebecers who she is and you'll draw a blank stare.

Head of Quebec's 13-year-old ombudsman's office since 1976, 47-year-old Patenaude remains one of the province's best-kept secrets. While ombudsmen in most other provinces — all except Prince Edward Island have them — get a lot of publicity for their attacks on government mismanagement and incompetence, Patenaude works in an atmosphere of anonymity.

Why all the secrecy?

Julien Dube, Patenaude's aide and unofficial deputy, says more publicity would create a bigger workload for the already busy staff of 30, and break the office's $1-million-a-year budget.

Prefers Small Operation

"We'd have to hire more people, and then we'd become a bureaucracy of our own, with the same problems that we are fighting against in other government departments."

That's why Patenaude, a former law professor at the University of Montreal who was appointed in 1976 by then premier Robert Bourassa — a former classmate — has deliberately adopted a low profile, Dube says.

"She doesn't make a lot of noise, but she gets things done efficiently," says Fernand Lalonde, Liberal member of the National Assembly for Montreal's Marguerite-Bourgeoys riding and another former classmate of Patenaude.

Still, Lalonde thinks there should be more publicity from the ombudsman's office because "it seems the office is only known by word of mouth."

Not surprisingly, Patenaude's colleagues know little of her personal life. What is known is that she earns $57,000 a year, is single, dresses simply but stylishly and is said to disdain the official receptions and cocktail parties that abound here.

The ombudsman's office was established by the Union Nationale government in 1968 to investigate public complaints about the way provincial government departments, agencies, and commissions are run.

During the fiscal year 1979-80, 7,718 complaints were received; 4,463 were rejected because they were outside the ombudsman's jurisdiction. Patenaude found 784 complaints valid and was able to obtain corrections in all but six cases.

* From *The Canadian Press*, April 5, 1981. By permission.

Ontario: More Cases

The operation run in Ontario by the almost unknown David Morand has an annual budget of $4.1 million and 122 people on staff. In 1979, the office received 10,572 new complaints and requests for information. Of those, 5,097 required no follow-up.

Twenty-five per cent of the complaints dealt with Workmen's Compensation, another 25 per cent were from Ontario prison inmates and the remainder were of a general nature.

In Quebec, the government's revenue department accounts for the biggest share of complaints.

Other departments that regularly draw complaints are the social affairs ministry about welfare payments, the Workmen's Compensation Board about accident claims and the justice ministry about prison conditions.

Surprisingly, Patenaude investigates more complaints from civil servants than from any other group in Quebec society. The government employees know the office exists — and they use it.

BIBLIOGRAPHY

General

Archibald, K., *Sex and the Public Service*, Ottawa, Q.P., 1970.
Aucoin, P., (ed.), *The Politics and Management of Restraint in Government*, Montreal, I.R.P.P., 1981.
Aucoin, P., and French, R., "The Ministry of State for Science and Technology," *C.P.A.*, 17, 2, Fall, 1974.
Bernard, L., "La fonction publique du Québec dans les années 80," Texte dactylographie d'une conférence fait devant les membres de la section régionale de Québec de l'Institut d'Administration publique du Canada, 23 janvier, 1979.
Bird, R.M., *The Growth of Public Employment in Canada*, Toronto, Butterworths, 1979.
Bolduc, R., "Les questions d'éthique dans les années 1980," *C.P.A.*, 24, 2, Summer, 1981.
Breton, A., and Wintrobe, R., "Bureaucracy and State Intervention: Parkinson's Law?," *C.P.A.*, 22, 2, Summer, 1979.
Cameron, D.M., (ed.), "Power and Responsibility in the Public Ser-

vice," Summary of I.P.A.C. Symposium, *C.P.A.*, 21, 3, Fall, 1978.
Canada, [Treasury Board], *Organization of the Government of Canada*, 1980, Ottawa, S. and S., 13th ed., 1980.
Carson, J.J., "The Changing Scope of the Public Service," *C.P.A.*, XI, 4, Winter, 1968.
Chrétien, Hon. J., "Le profil du gouvernement des années 80," [Decentralization], *C.P.A.*, 19, 1, Spring, 1976.
Cloutier, S., "Le statut de la fonction publique du Canada: son histoire," *C.P.A.*, X, 4, December, 1967.
Cole, Taylor, *The Canadian Bureaucracy and Federalism, 1947-1965*, Denver, University of Denver, 1966.
Des Roches, J.M., "The Evolution of the Organization of Federal Government in Canada," *C.P.A.*, V, 4, December, 1962.
Deutsch, J.J., "The Public Services in a Changing Society," *C.P.A.*, XI, 1, Spring, 1968.
Doerr, A.D., *Machinery of Government in Canada*, Toronto, Methuen, 1981.

Dussault, R., "Le rôle du juriste fonctionnaire dans l'aménagement des relations entre l'administration et les citoyens," *C.P.A.*, 24, 1, Spring, 1981.

Dussault, R., and Bernatchez, R., "La fonction publique canadienne et québécoise," *C.P.A.*, 15, 1, Spring, 1972, and 15, 2, Summer, 1972.

Dussault, R., *Traité de droit administratif: canadien et québécois*, Québec, Les Presses de l'Université Laval, 1974, 2 vols.

Fera, N., "Review of Administrative Decisions under the Federal Court Act (1970)," *C.P.A.*, 14, 4, Winter, 1971.

Foot, D.K., (ed.), *Public Employment and Compensation in Canada: Myths and Realities*, Toronto, Butterworths, 1978.

Forrest, D.G., "Performance Appraisal in Government Services," *C.P.A.*, XII, 3, Fall, 1969.

Fowke, D.V., "Toward a General Theory of Public Administration for Canada," *C.P.A.*, 19, 1, Spring, 1976.

Fox, D., *Public Participation in the Administrative Process*, Ottawa, Law Reform Commission, 1980.

Garant, P., *La Fonction publique canadienne et québécoise*, Québec, Les Presses de l'Université Laval, 1973.

Gélinas, A., (dir.), *L'enterprise publique et l'intérêt public*, Toronto, I.P.A.C., 1977.

Glenday, D.E., *et al.*, (eds.), *Modernization and the Canadian State*, Toronto, Macmillan, 1978.

Granatstein, J.L., *A Man of Influence: Norman A. Robertson and Canadian Statecraft, 1929-68*, Ottawa, 1981.

Grasham, W.E., and Julien, G., *Canadian Public Administration Bibliography*, Toronto, I.P.A.C., 1972. *Supplement I*, 1971-72, 1974; *Supplement II*, 1973-75, 1977; *Supplement III*, 1976-78, 1980.

Heeney, A., *The Things that are Caesar's: The Memoirs of a Canadian Public Servant*, Toronto, U.T.P., 1972.

Hicks, M., "Evaluating Evaluation in Today's Government," [A summary of the Thirteenth National Seminar on evaluating government programs], *C.P.A.*, 24, 3, Fall, 1981. [The papers given at the Seminar are also included in this Number of *C.P.A.*]

Hicks, M., "The Treasury Board of Canada and Its Clients: Five Years of Change and Administrative Reform, 1966-71," *C.P.A.*, 16, 2, Summer, 1973.

Hodgetts, J.E., *Pioneer Public Service: An Administrative History of the United Canadas, 1841-1867*, Toronto, U.T.P., 1955.

Hodgetts, J.E., "Challenge and Response: A Retrospective View of the Public Service of Canada," *C.P.A.*, VII, 4, December, 1964.

Hodgetts, J.E., and Dwivedi, O.P., "The Growth of Government Employment in Canada," *C.P.A.*, VII, 4, December, 1964.

Hodgetts, J.E., McCloskey, W., Whitaker, R., and Wilson, V.S., *The Biography of an Institution: The Civil Service Commission of Canada, 1908-1967*, Montreal, McG.-Q.U.P., 1972.

Hodgetts, J.E., *The Canadian Public Service: A Physiology of Government, 1867-1970*, Toronto, U.T.P., 1973.

Hodgetts, J.E., "The Public Service: Its Past and the Challenge of Its Future," *C.P.A.*, 17, 1, Spring, 1974.

Hodgetts, J.E., and Dwivedi, O.P., *Provincial Governments as Employers*, Montreal, McG.-Q.U.P., 1974.

Hodgson, J.S., *Public Administration*, New York, McG.-H., 1969.

Johnson, A.W., "Education and the Development of Senior Executives," *C.P.A.*, 15, 4, Winter, 1972.

Jolliffe, E.B., "Adjudication in the Canadian Public Service," *McG.L.J.*, 20, 3, 1974.

Judek, S., *Women in the Public Service*, Ottawa, Q.P., 1968.

Keenleyside, T.A., "Career Attitudes of Canadian Foreign Service

Officers," *C.P.A.,* 19, 2, Summer, 1976.

Kernaghan, W.D.K., "An Overview of Public Administration in Canada Today," *C.P.A.,* XI, 3, Fall, 1968.

Kernaghan, W.D.K., (ed.) *Bureaucracy in Canadian Government,* Toronto, Methuen, 2nd ed., 1973.

Kernaghan, K., "Responsible Public Bureaucracy: A Rationale and a Framework for Analysis," *C.P.A.,* 16, 4, Winter, 1973.

Kernaghan, K., "Codes of Ethics and Administrative Responsibility," *C.P.A.,* 17, 4, Winter, 1974.

Kernaghan, W.D.K., (ed.), *Canadian Cases in Public Administration,* Toronto, Methuen, 1977.

Kernaghan, K., "Changing Concepts of Power and Responsibility in the Canadian Public Service," *C.P.A.,* 21, 3, Fall, 1978.

Kernaghan, K., *Ethical Conduct: Guidelines for Government Employees,* Toronto, I.P.A.C., 1977.

Kernaghan, W.D.K., (ed.), *Public Administration in Canada: Selected Readings,* Toronto, Methuen, 3rd ed., 1977.

Kernaghan, K., "Representative Bureaucracy: The Canadian Perspective," *C.P.A.,* 21, 4, Winter, 1978.

Kersell, J.E., "Statutory and Judicial Control of Administrative Behaviour," *C.P.A.,* 19, 2, Summer, 1976.

Kuruvilla, P.K., "Administrative Culture in Canada: Some Perspectives," *C.P.A.,* 16, 2, Summer, 1973.

Laframboise, H.L., "Administrative Reform in the Federal Public Service: Signs of a Saturation Psychosis," *C.P.A.,* 14, 3, Fall, 1971.

Leach, R.H., *Perceptions of Federalism by Canadian and Australian Public Servants: A Comparative Analysis,* Canberra, Centre for Research on Federal Financial Relations, Australian National University, 1977.

Leclair, F., "D'un pouvoir responsable pour l'administrateur public," *C.P.A.,* 21, 3, Fall, 1978.

Love, J.D., "Personnel Reorganization in the Canadian Public Service: Some Observations on the Past," *C.P.A.,* 22, 3, Fall, 1979.

Lyngseth, D.M., "The Use of Organization and Methods in Canadian Government," *C.P.A.,* 22, 3, Fall, 1979.

Ontario, *Committee on Government Productivity,* Report Number Ten, a Summary, Ontario, Q.P., 1973.

Palumbo, D.J., and Harder, M.A., *Implementing Public Policy,* Toronto, D.C. Heath, 1981.

Rich, H., "The Canadian Case for a Representative Bureaucracy," *Political Science,* 27, 1, 1975.

Rowat, D.C., (ed.), *Global Comparisons in Public Administration,* Ottawa, Carleton University, 1981.

Savoie, D.J., "The General Development Agreement Approach and the Bureaucratization of Provincial Governments in the Atlantic Provinces," *C.P.A.,* 24, 1, Spring, 1981.

Self, P., *Administrative Theories and Politics,* Toronto, U.T.P., 1973.

Sigelman, L., and Vanderbok, W.G., "Legislators, Bureaucrats, and Canadian Democracy: The Long and Short of It," *C.J.P.S.,* X, 3, September, 1977.

Stevens, T.J., *The Business of Government,* Toronto, McG.-H.R., 1978.

Tunnoch, G.V., "The Bureau of Government Organization," *C.P.A.,* VIII, 4, December, 1965.

Tupper, A., "The State in Business," *C.P.A.,* 22, 1, Spring, 1979.

White, W.L., and Strick, J.C., "The Treasury Board and Parliament," *C.P.A.,* X, 2, June, 1967.

White, W.L., and Strick, J.C., *Policy, Politics and the Treasury Board in Canadian Government,* Don Mills, Ontario, Science Research Associates, 1970.

Willis, J., "Canadian Administrative Law in Retrospect," *U.O.T.L.J.,* 24, 1974.

Willms, A.M., "The Administration of Research on Administration in the

Government of Canada," *C.P.A.*, X, 4, December, 1967.

Wilson, V.S., *Canadian Public Policy and Administration: Theory and Environment*, Toronto, McG.-H.R., 1981.

Bilingualism and Biculturalism

(See also Bibliography in Chapter 2)

Bakvis, H., "French Canada and the 'Bureaucratic Phenomenon'," *C.P.A.*, 21, 1, Spring, 1978.

Beattie, C., *Minority Men in a Majority Setting: Middle-Level Francophones in the Canadian Public Service*, Toronto, M. & S., 1975.

Blackburn, G.A., "A Bilingual and Bicultural Public Service," *C.P.A.*, XII, 1, Spring, 1969.

Carson, J.J., "Bilingualism in the Public Service," *C.P.A.*, 15, 2, Summer, 1972.

Carson, J.J., "Bilingualism Revisited: or the Confessions of a Middle-aged and Belated Francophile," *C.P.A.*, 21, 4, Winter, 1978.

Cloutier, S., "Senior Public Service Officials in a Bicultural Society," *C.P.A.*, XI, 4, Winter, 1978.

Cote, E.A., "The Public Services in a Bicultural Community," *C.P.A.*, XI, 3, Fall, 1968.

Gosselin, E., Lalande, G., Dozois, G., Boyd, R., "L'administration publique dans un pays bilingue et biculturel: actualités et propos," *C.P.A.*, VI, 4, December, 1963.

Kanungo, R.N., *Biculturalism and Management*, Toronto, Butter-worths, 1980.

Kwavnick, D., "French Canadians and the Civil Service of Canada," *C.P.A.*, XI, 1, Spring, 1968.

Wilson, V.S., and Mullins, W.A., "Representative Bureaucracy: Linguistic/Ethnic Aspects in Canadian Public Policy," *C.P.A.*, 21, 4, Winter, 1978.

Bureaucrats and Politicians

Baccigalupo, A., "Les cabinets ministériels dans l'Administration québécoise," *La Revue administrative*, 20, 1973.

Balls, H.R., "Decision-Making: The Role of the Deputy Minister," *C.P.A.*, 19, 3, Fall, 1976.

Bieler, J.H., Burns, R.M., Johnson, A.W., "The Role of the Deputy Minister," *C.P.A.*, IV, 4, December, 1961.

Blakeney, Hon. A., "Goal-setting: Politicians' Expectations of Public Administrators," *C.P.A.*, 24, 1, Spring, 1981.

Blakeney, A., "The Relationship Between Provincial Ministers and Their Deputy Ministers," *C.P.A.*, 15, 1, Spring, 1972.

Bourgault, J., *Les sous-ministres adjoints du Québec et du Canada en 1973*, Notes de recherche, Université du Québec à Montréal, Département de Science politique, mars, 1978.

Bridges, The Rt. Hon. Lord, "The Relationship Between Ministers and the Permanent Departmental Head," *C.P.A.*, VII, 3, September, 1964.

Brown-John, C.L., "'Party Politics and the Canadian Federal Public Service," *Public Administration* (U.K.), 52, Spring, 1974.

Burns, R.M., "The Role of the Deputy Minister," *C.P.A.*, 4, 4, December, 1961.

Deutsch, J., "Governments and Their Advisors," *C.P.A.*, 16, 1, Spring, 1973.

Forget, C.E., "L'Administration publique: sujet ou objet du pouvoir politique?", *C.P.A.*, 21, 2, Summer, 1978.

Hartle, D.G., "The Public Servant as Advisor: The Choice of Policy Evaluation Criteria," *C.P.P.*, II, 3, Spring, 1976.

Hodgson, J.S., "The Impact of Minority Government on the Senior Civil Servant," *C.P.A.*, 19, 2, Summer, 1976.

Johnson, A.W., "The Role of the

Deputy Minister," *C.P.A.*, 4, 4, December, 1961.

Kenniff, P., *et al.*, *Le contrôle politique des tribunaux adminis-tratifs*, Québec, Les Presses de l'Université Laval, 1978.

Kernaghan, K., "Politics, Policy and Public Servants: Political Neutrality Re-visited," *C.P.A.*, 19, 3, Fall, 1976.

Kernaghan, K., "Power, Parliament and Public Servants in Canada: Ministerial Responsibility Re-examined," *C.P.P.*, V, 3, Summer, 1979.

Lamontagne, M., "The Influence of the Politician," *C.P.A.*, 11, 3, Fall, 1968.

Lemieux, V., *Les cheminements de l'influence: systémes, strategies et structures du politique*, Québéc, Les Presses de l'Université Laval, 1979.

McKeough, W. Darcy, "The Relations of Ministers and Civil Servants," *C.P.A.*, XII, 1, Spring, 1969.

Pickersgill, J.W., "Bureaucrats and Politicians," *C.P.A.*, 15, 3, Fall, 1972.

Plasse, M., "Les chefs de cabinets ministériels au Québec: la transition du gouvernement libéral au gouver-nement péquiste (1976-1977)," *C.J.P.S.*, XIV, 2, June, 1981.

Santos, C.R., "Public Administration as Politics," *C.P.A.*, XII, 2, 1969.

Sharp, M., "Decision-Making in the Federal Cabinet," *C.P.A.*, 19, 1, Spring, 1976.

Tellier, P.M., "Pour une réforme des cabinets de ministres fédéraux," *C.P.A.*, XI, 4, Winter, 1968.

Tennant, P., "The NDP Government of British Columbia: Unaided Politicians in an Unaided Cabinet," *C.P.P.*, III, 4, Autumn, 1977.

Vandervort, L., *Political Control of Independent Administrative Agencies*, Ottawa, S. and S. for Law Reform Commission, 1979.

Collective Bargaining

Armstrong, R., "Some Aspects of Policy Determination in the

Development of the Collective Bargaining Legislation in the Public Service of Canada," *C.P.A.*, XI, 4, Winter, 1968.

Christensen, S., *Unions and the Public Interest: Collective Bargaining in the Government Sector*, Vancouver, Fraser Institute, 1980.

Crispo, J., "Collective bargaining in the public service," *C.P.A.*, 16, 1, Spring, 1973.

Frankel, S.J., *A Model for Negotiation and Arbitration Between the Canadian Government and Its Civil Servants*, Montreal, McG.-Q.U.P., 1962.

Frankel, S.J., *Staff Relations in the Civil Service: The Canadian Ex-perience*, Montreal, McG.-Q.U.P., 1962.

Gunderson, M., (ed.), *Collective Bargaining in the Essential and Public Service Sectors*, Toronto, U.T.P., 1975.

Institute of Public Administration of Canada, *Collective Bargaining in the Public Service*, Toronto, 1973.

Vaison, R.A., "Collective Bargaining in the Federal Public Service: The Achievement of a Milestone in Personnel Relations," *C.P.A.*, XII, 1, Spring, 1969.

Crown Corporations and ABCs

Ashley, C.A., and Smails, R.G.H., *Canadian Crown Corporations*, Toronto, Macmillan, 1965.

Barbe, R.P., "Le contrôle parlementaire des enterprises au Canada," *C.P.A.*, XII, 4, Winter, 1969.

Bridges, The Rt. Hon. Lord, "The Relationship Between Government and Government-Controlled Corporations," *C.P.A.*, VII, 3, September, 1964.

Brown-John, C.L., "Advisory Agencies in Canada: An

Introduction," *C.P.A.*, 22, 1, Spring, 1979.

Corbett, D., *Politics and the Airlines*, Toronto, U.T.P., 1965.

Fournier, P., *Les sociétés d'état et les objectifs économiques du Québec: une évaluation préliminaire*, Québec, Office de Planification et Développement, 1978.

Friedman, W., (ed.), *The Public Corporation: A Comparative Symposium*, Toronto, Carswell, 1954.

Gélinas, A., (ed.), *Public Enterprise and the Public Interest*, Toronto, I.P.A.C., 1978.

Irvine, A.G., "The Delegation of Authority to Crown Corporations," *C.P.A.*, 14, 4, Winter, 1971.

Kristjanson, K., "Crown Corporations: Administrative Responsibility and Public Accountability," *C.P.A.*, XI, 4, Winter, 1968.

Langford, J.W., "The Identification and Classification of Federal Public Corporations: A Preface to Regime Building," *C.P.A.*, 23, 1, Spring, 1980.

Law Reform Commission, *Independent Administrative Agencies*, Ottawa, S. and S., 1980.

Lucas, A.R., and Bell, T., *The National Energy Board: Policy, Procedure and Practice*, Ottawa, Law Reform Commission, 1977.

Peers, F.W., *The Public Eye: Television and the Politics of Canadian Broadcasting, 1952-68*, Toronto, U.T.P., 1978.

Peers, F.W., *The Politics of Canadian Broadcasting, 1920-51*, Toronto, U.T.P., 1965.

Privy Council Office, *Crown Corporations: Direction, Control, Accountability*, Ottawa, S. and S., 1977.

Shea, A.A., *Broadcasting, The Canadian Way*, Montreal, Harvest House, 1963.

Spry, G., "The Decline and Fall of Canadian Broadcasting," *Q.Q.*, LXVIII, 2, Summer, 1961.

Weir, E.A., *The Struggle for National Broadcasting in Canada*, Toronto, M. & S., 1965.

Financial Management and Accountability

Baker, W.A., "Accountability, Responsiveness and Public Sector Productivity," *C.P.A.*, 23, 4, Winter, 1980.

Balls, H.R., "Improving Performance of Public Enterprise through Financial Management and Control," *C.P.A.*, XIII, 1, Spring, 1970.

Balls, H.R., "The Watchdog of Parliament: The Centenary of the Legislative Audit," *C.P.A.*, 21, 4, Winter, 1978.

Canada, *Final Report, Royal Commission on Financial Management and Accountability*, [Lambert Report] Ottawa, S. and S., 1979. (For an extensive review of the Report, see the Seminar Publication of the I.P.A.C., *Financial Management and Accountability*, I.P.A.C., Toronto, 1980. The proceedings of the seminar on the Report are summarized in McLeod, T.H., "The Special National Seminar on Financial Management and Accountability: An Appraisal," *C.P.A.*, 23, 1, 1980.)

Canada, Treasury Board, [D. Johnson], *Guide to the Policy and Expenditure Management System*, Ottawa, S. and S., 1980.

Canadian Study of Parliament Group, *Seminar on Accountability to Parliament*, Ottawa, Q.P., 1, 2, 1978.

Cassidy, R.G., and Neave, E.H., "Accountability and Control in the Federal Government," *Q.Q.*, 87, 1, Spring, 1980.

Denham, R.A., "The Canadian Auditors General — What is their role?," *C.P.A.*, 17, 2, Summer, 1974.

Doern, G.B., and Maslove, A.M., (eds.), *The Public Evaluation of Government Spending*, Toronto, Butterworths, 1979.

Dwivedi, O.P., "Accountability of Public Servants: Recent Developments in Canada," *International*

Journal of Public Administration,
XXVI, 3, July-September, 1980.
Hartle, D.G., *A Theory of the*
Expenditure Budgetary Process,
Toronto, U.T.P., 1976.
Hartle, D.G., *The Expenditure Budget*
Process in the Government of
Canada, Toronto, C.T.F., 1978.
Hartle, D.G., "The Report of the
Royal Commission on Financial
Management and Accountability
(The Lambert Report): A Review,"
C.P.P., V, 3, Summer, 1979.
Hodgetts, J.E., "Government
Responsiveness to the Public
Interest: Has Progress Been
Made?," *C.P.A.,* 24, 2, Summer,
1981.
Johnson, A.W., "The Treasury Board
of Canada and the Machinery of
Government of the 1970s,"
C.J.P.S., IV, 3, September, 1971.
Jordan, J.M., and Sutherland, S.L.,
"Assessing the Results of Public
Expenditure: Program Evaluation in
the Canadian Federal Government,"
C.P.A., 22, 4, Winter, 1979.
Kroeker, H.V., *Accountability and*
Control: The Government Expen-
diture Process, Montreal, C.D.
Howe Research Institute, 1978.
McInnes, S., "Improving Legislative
Surveillance of Provincial Public
Expenditures: The Performance of
the Public Accounts Committees and
Auditors General," *C.P.A.,* 20, 1,
Spring, 1977.
Sinclair, S., *Cordial But Not Cosy: A*
History of the Office of Auditor
General, Toronto, M. & S., 1979.
Steele, G.G.E., "'Needed — A Sense
of Proportion!' — Notes on
History of Expenditure Control,"
C.P.A., 20, 3, Fall, 1977.
Sutherland, S.L., "On the Audit Trail
of the Auditor General: Parliament's
Servant, 1973-80," *C.P.A.,* 23, 4,
Winter, 1980.
Williams, R., and Bates, D.V.,
"Technical Decisions and Public
Accountability," *C.P.A.,* 19, 4,
Winter, 1976.

Freedom of Information, Secrecy, Security

Abel, A.S., "Administrative Secrecy,"
C.P.A., XI, 4, Winter, 1968.
Access to Information: Independent
Administrative Agencies, Ottawa,
Law Reform Commission, 1979.
Canada, Commission of Inquiry
Concerning Certain Activities of the
Royal Canadian Mounted Police
[McDonald Commission], *First*
Report: Security and Information,
Ottawa, S. and S., 1980; *Second*
Report: Freedom and Security under
the Law, Vols. 1 and 2, August,
1981; *Third Report: Certain RCMP*
Activities and the Question of
Governmental Knowledge, August,
1981. (Ancillary studies: Edwards,
J.L., *Ministerial Responsibility for*
National Security, 1980; Franks,
C.E.S., *Parliament and Security*
Matters, 1980; Friedland, M.L.,
National Security: The Legal
Dimensions, 1980.)
Canada, Privy Council Office, *The*
Provision of Government
Information, [The Wall Report],
Ottawa, April, 1974, printed as an
appendix to the Minutes of
Proceedings and Evidence of the
Standing Joint Committee on
Regulations and Other Statutory
Instruments, June 25, 1975.
Canada, Secretary of State, [Roberts,
Hon. J.], *Legislation on Public*
Access to Government Documents,
Ottawa, S. and S., 1977.
French, R., and Béliveau, A., *The*
RCMP and the Management of
National Security, Toronto,
Butterworths, 1979.
Mann, E., and Lee, J.A., *The RCMP*
vs The People, Don Mills, General,
1979.
McCamus, J.D., (ed.), *Freedom of*
Information: Canadian Perspectives,
Toronto, Butterworths, 1981.
Ontario, *Public Government for*
Private People, The Report of the

Commission on Freedom of Information and Individual Privacy, Toronto, Q.P., 1980, 3 Volumes. (See also the Research Publications, Numbers 1 to 17.)

Premont, J., "Publicité des documents officiels," *C.P.A.*, XI, 4, Winter, 1968.

Rankin, T.M., *Freedom of Information in Canada: Will the Doors Stay Shut?*, Ottawa, Canadian Bar Association, 1977.

Relyea, H.C., "The Provision of Government Information: The [U.S.] Federal Freedom of Information Act Experience," *C.P.A.*, 20, 2, Summer, 1977.

Robertson, G., "Official Responsibilities, Privileges, Conscience and Public Information," *Proceedings and Transactions of the Royal Society of Canada*, X, 1972, Toronto, U.T.P., 1973.

Rowat, D.C., (ed.), *Administrative Secrecy in Developed Countries*, New York, Columbia University Press, 1979.

Rowat, D.C., "A Freedom of Information Act: What It Is and Why We Need It," *Quarterly of Canadian Studies*, 4, 3 and 4, 1977.

Rowat, D.C., "The Right to Government Information in Democracies," An Address to the Symposium on Freedom of Information, Tokyo, May 20, 1981.

Rowat, D.C., (ed.), *The Right to Know: Essays on Governmental Publicity and Public Access to Information*, Ottawa, Department of Political Science, Carleton University, 3rd ed., 1981.

Rowat, D.C., "How Much Administrative Secrecy?," *C.J.E.P.S.*, XXXI, 4, November, 1965. (See also "Comments," *ibid.*, XXXII, 1, February, 1966).

Thomas, P.G., "Secrecy and Publicity in Canadian Government," *C.P.A.*, 19, 1, Spring, 1976.

Management

Baccigalupo, A., *Les grands rouages de la machine administrative québécoise*, Montréal, Éditions Agence d'Arc, 1978.

Baker, W.A., "Management by Objectives: A Philosophy and Style of Management for the Public Sector," *C.P.A.*, XII, 3, Fall, 1969.

Baker, W.A., "Administrative Reform in the Federal Public Service: The First Faltering Steps," *C.P.A.*, 16, 3, Fall, 1973.

Bellavance, M., "Le ministère de l'Education du Québec et la gestion de l'enseignement supérieur," *C.P.A.*, 24, 1, Spring, 1981.

Benjamin, J., et O'Neill, P., *Les mandarins du pouvoir*, Montréal, Éditions Québec-Amerique, 1978.

Bolduc, R., "Les cadres supérieurs, quinze ans après [au Québec]," *C.P.A.*, 21, 4, Winter, 1978.

Campbell, C., and Szablowski, G.J., *The Superbureaucrats: Structure and Behaviour in Central Agencies*, Toronto, Macmillan, 1979.

Chartrand, P.J., and Pond, K.L., *A Study of Executive Career Paths in the Public Service of Canada*, Chicago, Public Personnel Association, 1969.

Dobell, W.M., "Interdepartmental Management in External Affairs," *C.P.A.*, 21, 1, Spring, 1978.

Hartle, D.G., "Techniques and Processes of Administration," *C.P.A.*, 19, 1, Spring, 1976.

Henault, G.M., *Culture et management: le cas de l'enterprise québécoise*, Montréal, McG-H., 1974.

Hodgson, J.S., "Management by Objectives: The Experience of a Federal Government Department," *C.P.A.*, XVI, 3, Fall, 1973.

Jacques, J., and Ryan, E.J., "Does Management by Objectives Stifle Organizational Innovation in the Public Sector?," *C.P.A.*, 21, 1, Spring, 1978.

Jain, H.C., and Kanungo, R.N., *Behavioural Issues in Management: The Canadian Context*, Toronto, McG.-H.R., 1977.

Kernaghan, K., (ed.), *Executive Manpower in the Public Service: Make or Buy*, Toronto, I.P.A.C., 1977.

Poncelet, M., *Le management public*, Montréal, Les presses de l'Université du Québec, 1979.

Smart, C.F., and Stanbury, W.T., (eds.)., *Studies on Crisis Management*, Toronto, Butterworths, 1978.

Ombudsman

Anderson, S.V., *Canadian Ombudsman Proposals*, Berkeley, University of California, 1966.

Canada, *Report of the Committee on the Concept of the Ombudsman*, Ottawa, Government of Canada, 1977.

Friedmann, K.A., *Complaining: Comparative Aspects of Complaint Behaviour and Attitudes Towards Complaining in Canada and Britain*, Beverly Hills, Sage, 1974.

Friedmann, K.A., "Controlling Bureaucracy: Attitudes in the Alberta Public Service Towards the Ombudsman," *C.P.A.*, 19, 1, Spring, 1976.

Friedmann, K.A., and Milne, A.G., "The Federal Ombudsman Legislation: A Critique of Bill C-43," *C.P.P.*, VI, 1, Winter, 1980.

Friedmann, K.A., "The Ombudsman in Nova Scotia and Newfoundland," *Dalhousie Law Journal*, 5, 2, 1979.

Friedmann, K.A., "The Public and the Ombudsman: Perceptions and Attitudes in Britain and in Alberta," *C.J.P.S.*, X, 3, September, 1977.

Lavoie, J., *Le protecteur du citoyen du Québec*, Paris, Presses Universitaires, 1977.

Rowat, D.C., "An Ombudsman Scheme for Canada," *C.J.E.P.S.*, XXVIII, 4, November, 1962.

Rowat, D.C., "Recent Developments in Ombudsmanship," *C.P.A.*, X, 1, March, 1967.

Rowat, D.C., *The Ombudsman: Citizen's Defender*, Toronto, U.T.P., 1965.

Rowat, D.C., *The Ombudsman Plan: Essays on the World-wide Spread of an Idea*, Carleton Library No. 67, M. & S., 1973.

Stacey, F., *Ombudsmen Compared*, Toronto, O.U.P., 1978.

Weeks, K.M., *Ombudsmen Around the World: A Comparative Chart*, Berkeley, Institute of Governmental Studies, University of California, 2nd ed., 1978.

Public Policy and Decision-Making

(See also Bibliography in Chapter 1)

Auld, D.A.L., "Social Welfare and Decision-Making in the Public Sector," *C.P.A.*, 16, 4, Winter, 1973.

Baker, W., *Organization Under Stress: The Reorganization of Canada's Department of Public Works, 1970-73*, Ottawa, Centre for Policy and Management Studies, 1980.

Bella, L., "The Provincial Role in the Canadian Welfare State: The Influence of Provincial Social Policy Initiatives on the Design of the Canada Assistance Plan," *C.P.A.*, 22, 3, Fall, 1979.

Bonin, B., (ed.), *Immigration: Policy-Making Process and Results*, Toronto, I.P.A.C., 1977.

Bryden, K., *Old Age Pensions and Policy-Making in Canada*, Montreal, McG.-Q.U.P., 1974.

Canadian Study of Parliament Group, *Seminar on the Budgetary Process*, Ottawa, Q.P., 1, 1, 1977.

Chandler, M., and Chandler, W., *Public Policy and Provincial Politics*, Toronto, McG.-H.R., 1977.

Dobell, R., "How Ottawa Decides Economic Policy," *Policy Options*, 1, 3, September-October, 1980.

Doern, G.B., and Aucoin, P., (eds.), *Public Policy in Canada: Organization, Process and Management,* Toronto, Macmillan, 1979.

Doern, G.B., and Aucoin, P., (eds.), *The Structure of Policy-Making in Canada,* Toronto, Macmillan, 1971.

Doern, G.B., and Wilson, V.S., (eds.), *Issues in Canadian Public Policy,* Toronto, Macmillan, 1974.

Doern, G.B., "Recent Changes in the Philosophy of Policy-making in Canada," *C.J.P.S.,* IV, 2, June, 1971.

Doern, G.B., and Morrison, R.W., (eds.), *Canadian Nuclear Policies,* Montreal, I.R.P.P., 1980.

Doern, G.B., *Government Intervention in the Canadian Nuclear Industry,* Montreal, I.R.P.P., 1980.

Doern, G.B., and Maslove, A.M., (eds.), *The Public Evaluation of Government Spending,* Toronto, I.R.P.P., 1979.

Drury, C.M., "Quantitative Analysis and Public Policy Making," *C.P.P.,* 1, 1, Winter, 1975.

Dupré, J.S., *et al.,* *Federalism and Policy Development: The Case of Adult Occupational Training in Ontario,* Toronto, U.T.P., 1973.

Dwivedi, O.P., (ed.), *Resources and the Environment: Policy Perspectives for Canada,* Toronto, M. & S., 1980.

Falcone, D.J., and Whittington, M.S., "Output Change in Canada: A Preliminary Attempt to Open the 'Black-Box'." Paper presented to the Annual Meeting of the C.P.S.A., 1972.

French, R.D., *How Ottawa Decides: Planning and Industrial Policy-Making, 1968-1980,* Ottawa, Canadian Institute for Economic Policy, Lorimer, 1980.

Fowke, V.C., *Canadian Agricultural Policy: The Historical Pattern,* Toronto, U.T.P., 1978.

Gallagher, J.E., and Lambert, R.S., *Social Process and Institutions: Canadian Studies,* Toronto, H.R.W., 1971.

Gibson, R.B., *The Strathcona Sound Mining Project: A Case Study of Decision-Making,* Ottawa, Science Council of Canada, 1978.

Good, D.A., *The Politics of Anticipation: Making Canadian Federal Tax Policy,* Ottawa, School of Public Administration, Carleton University, Lorimer, 1980.

Gray, J.A., and Gray, P.J., "The Berger Report: Its Impact on Northern Pipelines and Decision-Making in Northern Development," *C.P.P.,* III, 4, Autumn, 1977.

Guest, D., *The Emergence of Social Security in Canada,* Vancouver, U.B.C.P., 1980.

Hartle, D.G., "A Proposed System of Policy and Program Evaluation," *C.P.A.,* 16, 2, Summer, 1973.

Hartle, D.G., *Public Policy, Decision-Making and Regulation,* Toronto, Butterworths, 1979.

Hartley, K., *et al.,* *Energy R and D Decision-Making for Canada,* Montreal, I.R.P.P., 1979.

Hawkins, F., *Canada and Immigration: Public Policy and Public Concern,* Montreal, McG.-Q.U.P., 1972.

Heaver, T.D., and Nelson, J.C., *Railway Pricing under Commercial Freedom: The Canadian Experience,* Vancouver, U.B.C.P., 1977.

Hill, O.M., *Canada's Salesman to the World: The Department of Trade and Commerce,* Montreal, McG.-Q.U.P., 1977.

Hodgetts, J.E., "The Civil Service and Policy Formation," *C.J.E.P.S.,* XXIII, 4, November, 1957.

Johnson, A.W., "Public Policy: Creativity and Bureaucracy," *C.P.A.,* 21, 1, Spring, 1978.

Kirby, M.J.L., Kroeker, H.V., and Teschke, W.R., "The Impact of Public Policy-Making Structures and Processes in Canada," *C.P.A.,* 21, 3, Fall, 1978.

Langford, J.W., (ed.), *Administration of Transport Policy: Emerging Problems and Patterns,* Toronto, I.P.A.C., 1979.

Langford, J.W., *Transport in Transition: The Reorganization of the Federal Transport Portfolio,* Toronto, I.P.A.C., 1977.

Mansbridge, S.H., "Of Social Policy in Alberta: Its Management, Its Modification, Its Evaluation, and Its Making," *C.P.A.*, 21, 3, Fall, 1978.

McAllister, J.A., "The Fiscal Analysis of Policy Outputs," *C.P.A.*, 23, 2, Fall, 1980.

McLaren, R.I., *Civil Servants and Public Policy: A Comparative Study of International Secretariats,* Waterloo, W.L.U.P., 1980.

McMillan, C.J., "After the Gray Report: The Tortuous Evolution of Foreign Investment Policy," *McG.L.J.*, 20, 2, 1974.

Milligan, F., "The Canada Council as a Public Body," *C.P.A.*, 22, 2, Summer, 1979.

Milligan, F., "Program Planning and Control in the Canada Council, 1957-1978," *C.P.A.*, 23, 4, Winter, 1980.

Mitchell, C.M., "The Rule of the Courts in Public Policy Making: A Personal View," *U. of T. Faculty of Law Review*, 3, 1, Spring, 1975.

Morley, J.T., "The Justice Development Commission: Overcoming Bureaucratic Resistance to Innovative Policy-Making," *C.P.A.*, 19, 1, Spring, 1976.

Nossal, K.R., "Allison Through the (Ottawa) Looking Glass: Bureaucratic Politics and Foreign Policy in a Parliamentary System," *C.P.A.*, 22, 4, Winter, 1979.

Ohashi, T.M., *et al.*, *Privatization Theory and Practice: Distributing Shares in Private and Public Enterprises,* Vancouver, Fraser Institute, 1980.

Ontario Economic Council, *The Process of Public Decision-Making,* Toronto, 1977.

Paquin, M., "La répartition du pouvoir de décision dans l'administration publique: l'apport de la théorie de l'organisation," *C.P.A.*, 23, 4, Winter, 1980.

Phidd, R.W., and Doern, G.B., *The Politics and Management of Canadian Economic Policy,* Toronto, Macmillan, 1978.

Pitfield, M., "The Shape of Government in the 1980's: Techniques and Instruments for Policy Formulation at the Federal Level," *C.P.A.*, 19, 1, Spring, 1976.

Prince, M.J., and Chenier, J.A., "The Rise and Fall of Policy Planning and Research Units: An Organizational Perspective," *C.P.A.*, 23, 4, Winter, 1980.

Prost, R., "Connaissance et action: ou les deux faces opposées d'une réforme gouvernementale," *C.J.P.S.*, X, 1, March, 1977.

Rowan, M., "A Conceptual Framework for Government Policy-Making," *C.P.A.*, XIII, 3, Autumn, 1970.

Schultz, R.J., *Federalism, Bureaucracy, and Public Policy: The Politics of Highway Transport,* Montreal, McG.-Q.U.P., 1980.

Simeon, R., "The Federal-Provincial Decision-Making Process," in O.E.C., *Intergovernmental Relations,* Toronto, 1977.

Simeon, R., "Studying Public Policy," *C.J.P.S.*, IX, 4, December, 1976.

Slayton, P., and Trebilcock, M.J., (eds.), *The Professions and Public Policy,* Toronto, U.T.P., 1978.

Stewart, W., *Paper Juggernaut: Big Government Gone Mad,* Toronto, M. & S., 1979.

Studnicki-Gizbert, K.W., (ed.), *Issues in Canadian Transport Policy,* Toronto, Macmillan, 1974.

Taylor, M.G., *Health Insurance and Canadian Public Policy: The Seven Decisions that Created the Canadian Health Insurance System,* Toronto, I.P.A.C., 1978.

Thordarson, B., *Trudeau and Foreign Policy: A Study in Decision-Making,* Toronto, O.U.P., 1972.

Warnock, J.W., *Partner to Behemoth,* [Military Policy], Toronto and Chicago, New Press, 1970.

Wilson, C.F., *A Century of Canadian Grain: Government Policy to 1951,* Saskatoon, Western Producer, 1978.

Wilson, H.T., "Rationality and Decision in Administrative Science," *C.J.P.S.*, VI, 2, June, 1973.

Yelaja, S.A., (ed.), *Canadian Social Policy*, Waterloo, W.L.U.P., 1978.

Regulation

Babe, R.E., *Canadian Television Broadcasting: Structure, Performance and Regulation*, Ottawa, E.C.C., 1979.

Babe, R.E., "Regulation of Private Television Broadcasting by the Canadian Radio-Television Commission: A Critique of Ends and Means," *C.P.A.*, 19, 4, Winter, 1976.

Baldwin, J.R., *The Regulatory Agency and the Public Corporation: The Canadian Air Transportation Industry*, Cambridge, Mass., Ballinger, 1975.

Black, E.R., "Canadian Public Policy and the Mass Media," *C.J.E.*, I, 2, May, 1968.

Beke, J.A., "Government Regulation of Broadcasting in Canada," *Saskatchewan Law Review*, 36, I, Fall, 1971, and 2, Spring, 1972.

Brown-John, C.L., *Canadian Regulatory Agencies: An Introduction*, Toronto, Butterworths, 1981.

Brown-John, C.L., "Defining Regulatory Agencies for Analytical Purposes," *C.P.A.*, 19, 1, Spring, 1976.

Brown-John, C.L., "Membership in Canadian Regulatory Agencies," *C.P.A.*, 20, 3, Fall, 1977.

Boyer, M., *et al.*, "The Impact of Regulation," *C.P.P.*, V, 4, Autumn, 1979.

Campbell, C., and Szablowski, G.J., *The Superbureaucrats: Structure and Behaviour in Central Agencies*, Toronto, Macmillan, 1979.

Doern, G.B., (ed.), *The Regulatory Process in Canada*, Toronto, Macmillan, 1978.

Doern, G.B., *et al.*, "The Structure and Behaviour of Canadian Regulatory Boards and Commissions," *C.P.A.*, 18, 2, Summer, 1975.

Garant, P., *et al.*, "Le contrôle politique des organismes autonomes

à fonctions regulatrices et quasi-judiciaires," *C.P.A.*, 20, 3, Fall, 1970.

Hull, W.H.N., "The Public Control of Broadcasting: The Canadian Australian Experiences," *C.J.E.P.S.*, XXVIII, 1, February, 1962.

Hull, W.H.N., "The Fowler Reports Revisited: A Broadcasting Policy for Canada," Address to the 38th Annual Meeting of the C.P.S.A., Sherbrooke, P.Q., June 9, 1966.

Issues and Alternatives 1978: Government Regulation, Toronto, O.E.C., 1978.

Janisch, H.N., *et al.*, *The Regulatory Process of the Canadian Transport Commission*, Ottawa, Law Reform Commission, 1978.

Reschenthaler, G.B., "Regulatory Failure and Competition," *C.P.A.*, 19, 3, Fall, 1976.

Schultz, R.J., *Federalism and the Regulatory Process*, Toronto, Butterworths, 1979.

Stanbury, W.T., (ed.), *Government Regulation: Scope, Growth, Process*, Ottawa, E.C.C., 1980.

Stanbury, W.T., (ed.), *Studies on Regulation in Canada*, Toronto, Butterworths, 1979.

Trebilcock, M.J. *et al.*, *The Choice of Governing Instruments*, Ottawa, E.C.C., 1982.

Royal Commissions

Bryden, M., and Gurney, M., "Royal Commission Costs," *C.T.J.*, XIV, 2, March-April, 1966.

Canada, *Report of the Royal Commission on Government Organization* [Glassco Report], Ottawa, Q.P., 1962-3, 5 vols.

Canada, *Final Report, Royal Commission on Financial Management and Accountability* [Lambert Report], Ottawa, S. and S., 1979. (See also the section "Financial Management and Accountability" in the Bibliography in this chapter.)

Courtney, J.C., "In Defence of Royal Commissions," *C.P.A.*, XII, 2, Summer, 1969.

Doern, G.B., "The Role of Royal Commissions in the General Policy Process and Federal-Provincial Relations," *C.P.A.*, X, 4, December, 1967.

Gorecki, P.K., and Stanbury, W.T., (eds.), *Perspectives on the Royal Commission on Corporate Concentration*, Toronto, Butterworths, 1979.

Hanson, H.R., "Inside Royal Commissions," *C.P.A.*, XII, 3, Fall, 1969.

Henderson, G.F., *Federal Royal Commissions in Canada, 1867-1966: A Checklist*, Toronto, U.T.P., 1967.

Hodgetts, J.E., "The Role of Royal Commissions in Canadian Government," Proceedings of the Third Annual Conference, I.P.A.C., Toronto, 1951.

Hodgetts, J.E., "Should Canada Be De-Commissioned? A Commoner's View on Royal Commissions," *Q.Q.*, LXX, 4, Winter, 1964.

McLeod, T.H., "Glassco Commission Report," *C.P.A.*, VI, 4, December, 1963.

Mitchell, H., *et al.*, "To Commission or Not to Commission," *C.P.A.*, V, 3, September, 1962.

Ritchie, R.S., Heeney, A.D.P., Mackenzie, M.W., Taylor, M.G., "The Glassco Commission Report," *C.P.A.*, V, 4, December, 1962.

Tunnoch, G.V., "The Glassco Commission: Did It Cost More Than It Was Worth?," *C.P.A.*, VII, 3, September 1964.

Walls, C.E.S., "Royal Commissions — Their Influence on Public Policy," *C.P.A.*, XII, 3, Fall, 1969.

Whalen, H., "Public Participation and the Role of Canadian Royal Commissions and Task Forces, 1957-1969," A paper presented at the Conference of the I.P.A.C., Charlottetown, September 8-11, 1981.

16

THE JUDICIAL PROCESS

The judiciary has attracted more interest in recent years for several reasons. Not only has the Supreme Court of Canada become more significant politically since it was made the final appellate tribunal in 1949, but it has become more prominent publicly because it has been pronouncing the final word on a number of issues which are interesting and relevant to many citizens — in regard to civil rights, for instance, or jurisdiction by the federal or provincial governments. Prime Minister Trudeau has stirred up a wave of interest also by attempting to initiate a number of constitutional and juridical changes. Inevitably, these focussed attention on the courts to a degree that would not otherwise have occurred.

Professor Peter Russell's excellent article in this chapter reviews the Supreme Court's interpretation of the constitution since it became the court of last resort in 1949 with the abolition of appeals to the Judicial Committee of the Privy Council. Professor Russell's original article in *Politics: Canada* dealt with the Supreme Court from 1949 to 1960. In a later edition he extended the review to 1974. In this edition he has added a new portion dealing with recent developments from 1975 to 1980. The three sections, while still retained, have now been combined into one article. Professor Russell's comments on certain civil rights cases can be supplemented by consulting the next chapter which deals with that subject and contains extracts from some of the leading cases.

The second article in this chapter contains the essence of the decisions by the Supreme Court in the celebrated reference case on the new Canadian constitution in 1981. It should be emphasized that because of spatial limitations this extract had to be confined in the main to the bare bones of both the majority and dissenting opinions and it is therefore unfortunate that little or none of the supporting reasoning could be included. For the full text a reader should consult the preliminary publication from which the excerpts are taken or subsequently, when published, the relevant issue of the *Supreme Court Reports*.

Lack of space has led also to the omission of several items which appeared in the fourth edition. They can be found there at the following pages: "The New Federal Court of Canada," p. 547; "Recent Proposals for Reform of the Supreme Court," pp. 547-548; Geoffrey Stevens, "Appointment System Improved," pp. 548-550; "Increased Judicial Salaries, 1975," pp. 550-551; and the Canadian Press, "Lewis St. G. Stubbs, Judicial Rebel," p. 551.

The bibliography in this chapter includes references to judicial review and the judiciary in general. For references to civil rights cases, see the next chapter. For the courts' interpretation of the constitution, see two excellent paperbacks in the Carleton Library Series: Professor Peter Russell's *Leading Constitutional Decisions* and Professor William Lederman's *The Courts and the Canadian Constitution*, both of which are noted in the bibliography.

THE SUPREME COURT'S INTERPRETATION OF THE CONSTITUTION*

Peter H. Russell

I. From 1949 to 1960

In December, 1949, the Supreme Court of Canada became the final court of appeal for Canada. This was accomplished by the simple expedient of an Act of the Dominion Parliament, the constitutional validity of which had been previously established by a 1947 decision of the Privy Council. With the exception of cases in which the litigation had begun prior to December, 1949, no longer could aggrieved litigants carry their case across the Atlantic and plead before the Judicial Committee of the Privy Council that the decision of a Canadian court be reversed. Now a Canadian court, appointed by the Canadian Government, staffed by Canadian jurists, was Canada's highest judicial organ. Canada has passed another — almost the final — milestone on her road to nationhood.

At the time this change was effected it was only logical that interest in it was focussed primarily on the area of constitutional law. In a federal state with a written constitution defining the boundaries of the national and regional legislatures, the court of last resort, through the process of judicial review, can have an enormous influence on the legislative policies pursued by both levels of government. As Professor Kelsen has said, "A court which has the power to annul laws is consequently an organ of legislative power." Indeed, it was as the arbiter of our Constitution — the British North America Act — that the Judicial Committee had become a centre of controversy in Canada. Now, with that tribunal giving way to the Supreme Court of Canada, there was a great deal of speculation as to how this transition would affect the interpretation of the B.N.A. Act.

Looking forward to the new era of judicial autonomy, two rival patterns of hopes and fears were evident. By far the most vociferous viewpoint was expressed by the Privy Council's critics. They had attacked the Judicial Committee for what they regarded as its unjustified and unwise reduction of Dominion power and they now hoped that an indigenous highest court

---

* This article is a combination of three articles written by the author at different times for this book. The first two sections have been published originally as separate articles in previous editions of *Politics: Canada*. The third section dealing with the period from 1975-80 has been prepared for this edition. Professor Russell is a member of the Department of Political Economy, University of Toronto.

would emancipate Canada from the stultifying effects of their Lordships' constitutional conceptions. On the other hand, there were those, mainly in French-speaking Canada, who cherished the Privy Council's constitutional handiwork as a vital bulwark of provincial autonomy against the onslaught of centralizing forces. To these, the abolition of appeals looked ominous. The inclusion of a provision in the Supreme Court Amendment Act of 1949, which guaranteed that three of the nine Supreme Court judges would always come from Quebec, did little to offset their fears. They were more impressed by the fact that the Dominion executive appointed all the judges. Hence, those who subscribed to this school of thought were inclined to heed the warnings of those theoreticians of federalism who insisted that to permit one level of government the exclusive power of appointing the umpire of the federal system constituted a serious deviation from "pure federalism."

It is against this background of speculations that we shall examine the Supreme Court's record of constitutional adjudication from the abolition of appeals in 1949 until the end of 1960. The cases discussed deal only with questions concerning the division of legislative powers. With each of the major issues some attempt has been made to indicate the major contrasts, if any, between the Supreme Court's approach and that of the Privy Council.

The most serious charge in the traditional indictment of the Privy Council's interpretation of the B.N.A. Act was that it had reduced Parliament's power to legislate for "the peace, order and good government of Canada" from the position of a residual clause in the division of powers to the status of an emergency power. For those centralists who pressed for a reinstatement of the Dominion's General power, Lord Simon's judgment in the *Canadian Temperance Federation* case of 1946 had provided a new ray of hope. There, Lord Simon, in maintaining the validity of what was virtually the same statute as was involved in Russell v. The Queen, had gone a long way towards undermining the authority of the emergency doctrine. The true test, he stated, of whether the Dominion's General power could be invoked to uphold legislation was not the existence of an emergency but "the real subject matter of the legislation: if it is such that it goes beyond local provincial concern or interest and must from its inherent nature be the concern of the Dominion as a whole. . . ." The impact of this dictum was partially offset by two later decisions of the Privy Council which returned to the emergency doctrine as the justification for bringing legislation under the General power. Nevertheless, Lord Simon's words were now part of the record, so that, even if the newly emancipated Supreme Court were to assume the yoke of *stare decisis* and consider itself bound by its predecessor's decisions, this opinion could provide the necessary support for extending the scope of the Peace, Order, and Good Government clause beyond emergency situations.

Despite the apparent centrality of "Peace, Order, and Good Government," it has been a key issue in only two of the constitutional cases that have been before the Supreme Court in the past decade. In the first of these cases, *Reference re. Validity of Wartime Leasehold Regulation* (1950), the court was asked to pass on the constitutionality of the Federal Government's rent-control regulations. These orders-in-council had been made under the authority of the National Emergency Transitional Powers Act, which continued those provisions of the War Measures Act that Parliament had deemed necessary for dealing with the economic dislocations arising out of the war. Although the court referred to the Peace, Order, and Good Government clause as the constitutional support for the regulations, in doing so it did not have to go beyond the emergency doctrine. Even this was significant in as much as a number of judges stated that unless there was "clear and immutable" evidence to the contrary, they would not question Parliament's declaration (in the preamble to the Act) that an emergency exists. This policy in the context of an enduring "cold war" situation might well make even the emergency conception of the General power a more fertile source of legislative capacity. It is worth noting that during the 1950s two of the statutes which entailed the widest extension of Dominion power were the Defence Production Act and the Emergency Powers Act.

It was the case of *Johannesson v. West St. Paul* (1952) that provided a more revealing test of the Supreme Court's treatment of "Peace, Order, and Good Government." Here, the constitutional issue revolved around the competing claims of the Dominion Parliament and the Manitoba Legislature to make laws regulating the location of aerodromes. The court was unanimous in sustaining the Dominion's Aeronautics Act and in finding the Manitoba legislation and regulations *ultra vires*. Certainly the most significant aspect of this decision was the test that the court used to determine whether the regulation of civil aviation was a subject-matter of legislation embraced by the "Peace, Order, and Good Government" clause. On this point, four of the five judges who wrote opinions explicitly accepted Lord Simon's test of national importance. Mr. Justice Kellock used these words: "Once the decision is made that a matter is of national importance, so as to fall within the peace, order and good government clause, the provinces cease to have any legitimate jurisdiction with regard thereto and the Dominion jurisdiction is exclusive." Of course the court could dress up this approach in the cautious language of *stare decisis* by referring to Lord Simon's formulation of the national aspect test in the Aeronautics Reference of 1932. But this cannot disguise the fact that in selecting these cases a choice was exercised between contrasting judicial traditions. *Stare decisis* might just as easily have permitted resort to the 1937 Reference cases in which national importance, aside from emergency situations, was rejected as a proper test for invoking the General power.

But it would be a mistake to accept the Johannesson case as a decisive breakthrough. It must be pointed out that the court's validation of the Dominion's Aeronautics Act did not, in itself, constitute an expansion of the central legislature's powers. The Aeronautics Act had been validated previously by the Privy Council in 1932 (although on that occasion Section 132 — the treaty implementing power — rather than the General power had been singled out as the basis of the Act's constitutionality). The effect of the national importance test in the Johannesson case was essentially negative; it prevented a province from encroaching upon a field of legislation already occupied by the Dominion. It may well be that the Supreme Court would be less prepared to adopt Lord Simon's conception of "Peace, Order, and Good Government" if it was required to support the entry of Parliament into an activity already subject to provincial law.

Supreme Court cases since Johannesson v. West St. Paul throw no light on this conjecture. Thus, for the centralist cause, the Johannesson case represents encouragement but hardly victory. The enumerated powers of Section 91, far more than "the residuary power," have served as the vehicle for judicial initiatives. These initiatives, as we shall now see, have generally leaned towards the expansion of the Dominion's powers.

The Judicial Committee's attenuation of the Dominion's Trade and Commerce power had come in for almost as much criticism as its treatment of the General power. There had never been much quarrel with the assumption that some limits would have to be set to Section 91 (2) if a reasonable measure of provincial autonomy were to be preserved. But the restrictive nature of those limits and the inflexible way in which they had been delineated by the judiciary had been the source of much discontent. Although the Trade and Commerce power was occasionally employed by the Privy Council to circumscribe the provinces' powers of trade regulation and as one of a number of supports for Dominion legislation, its emasculation has proceeded so far that as an independent source of constitutional power for significant legislation in the field of economic regulation it had been rendered very nearly useless. Further, for the purpose of drawing a clear line between those forms of trade which could be regulated by the Dominion and those which could be regulated by the provinces, the Privy Council had adopted the categories of inter-provincial and intra-provincial trade. These categories, when applied uncritically to the activities of an interdependent economy, resulted in a division of jurisdiction which precluded efficacious legislation by either the Dominion or the Provinces. The debilitating effects of this approach were felt most severely in connection with marketing legislation. Where produce at the point of which regulation was desirable could not be segregated into that destined for the provincial market and that destined for the extra-provincial market, and where delegation of legislative powers between Parliament and provincial legislatures was precluded, it appeared that judicial construction of the B.N.A. Act had produced a constitutional hiatus.

Since 1949 the Supreme Court has delivered two judgments that cast some light upon its treatment of the Trade and Commerce power. While neither case marks a revolutionary approach, taken together they suggest, to use Professor Laskin's words, "a decided thaw in the hitherto frozen federal commerce power." In the first of these cases, *Reference re. (Ontario) Farm Products Marketing Act* (1957), the court was asked to answer eight questions concerning provisions of and regulations under an Ontario marketing Act. Since it was provincial legislation whose validity was being examined, the Dominion's Trade and Commerce power was referred to only negatively as limiting the application of Ontario's marketing schemes to intra-provincial trade. Even so, the way in which a majority of judges elucidated the distinction between intra-provincial trade (subject to provincial jurisdiction) and inter-provincial or export trade (subject to Dominion jurisdiction) suggested a large area in which Head No. 2 of Section 91 could serve as a constitutional foundation for national economic policies. The court's relatively liberal appraisal of Section 91 (2) did not have any direct bearing upon the outcome of the case: all the judges accepted at face value the wording of the opening question of the Reference Order, to the effect that the "Act applies only in the case of intra-provincial transactions." The significance of this case, then, is to be measured not in terms of its substantive results but in terms of the pragmatic approach to constitutional adjudication which it implies. This approach was most evident in Mr. Justice Rand's opinion from which the following passage is quoted:

> Trade arrangements reaching the dimensions of world agreements are now a commonplace; interprovincial trade, in which the Dominion is a single market, is of similar importance, and equally vital to the economic functioning of the country as a whole. The Dominion power implies responsibility for promoting and maintaining the vigour and growth of trade beyond provincial confines, and the discharge of this function must remain unembarrassed by local trade impediments.

What stands out here by way of contrast with earlier judicial efforts to divide jurisdiction over trading activities is that the point of departure is not fixed categories of Dominion and Provincial economic responsibility but rather judicial notice of the evolving requirements of a national economy.

In the second case, *Murphy v. C.P.R. and A.-G. Canada* (1958), the Trade and Commerce power was invoked as the basis for the constitutionality of the Canadian Wheat Board Act. Here, the court showed that it was prepared to regard the federal commerce power as an independent source of legislative authority broad enough to sustain a Dominion marketing Act, which is of crucial importance to the national economy. However, the facts of this case were such as to qualify the significance of the court's use of Section 91 (2). The impugned provisions of the Act came clearly under the heading "Regulation of international and inter-provincial trade in wheat" and the plaintiff, Murphy, who was challenging the C.P.R.'s refusal to handle his wheat because he had failed to comply with the provisions of the Act, was clearly shipping wheat across provincial boundaries.

The implications of this decision appeared of much greater consequence when the Manitoba Court of Appeal referred to it in the case of *Regina v. Klassen* (1959). Here, in contrast to the Murphy case, the facts posed a more severe challenge to the traditional bifurcation of legislative authority over trade into intra-provincial and extra-provincial compartments. The issue in the Klassen case was whether regulations made under the Canadian Wheat Board Act could be applied to a feed-mill whose business was carried on entirely within a province. Drawing upon the Supreme Court's decision in the Murphy case, the Manitoba court upheld this application of the Dominion statute to *intra-provincial* transactions on the pragmatic grounds that, if the intra-provincial market was severed from the scope of the Act, the whole attempt to create an orderly scheme for marketing the annual wheat crop would be rendered impossible. Considerations of economic policy took precedence over legalistic categories.

From the above cases it seems fair to conclude that if since 1949 there has not been a positive expansion of the scope of the federal commerce power, the Supreme Court has at least demonstrated a more pragmatic and less legalistic approach to the general problem of adjusting national and local interests in marketing matters. Even so, much of the court's work in this area may now be rendered largely academic by its treatment of the delegation question.

During the 1930s and 1940s many of those who viewed the Privy Council's "watertight compartments" treatment of the division of powers as a frustrating obstacle to the effective handling of some of Canada's major social and economic problems looked to the delegation device as the most likely way of hurdling the constitutional barrier. If the Judicial Committee in the course of interpreting the B.N.A. Act had effected a division of authority inappropriate to the needs and resources of the provinces and the Dominion, then, it was argued, at least the legislatures and Parliament should be free to delegate their powers to one another. As for the constitutionality of the delegation device, this question, prior to 1949, had not been canvassed by either the Privy Council or the Supreme Court. The Privy Council's only pronouncement on the subject was made by Lord Watson in 1899, and this was to the effect that delegation by a provincial legislature to Parliament or vice versa was invalid. However, this was simply a remark thrown out in the course of argument and was not central to the case. In his Appendix to the Sirois Commission Report, J.A. Corry, after a thorough examination of the issue, had concluded that it was still an open question.

Thus, when the Supreme Court in 1951 and 1952 was directly faced with the delegation issue, it was breaking rather new and significant ground. The net result of these two cases was paradoxical: first, direct delegation was banned, and then, indirect delegation was approved. In the first case, the *Nova Scotia Inter-delegation* case (1951), the court declared Nova Scotia's Bill 136 *ultra vires*. This Bill constituted an attempt by the Nova Scotia legislature to delegate a part of its law-making authority (in this case in the field of labour law) directly to the Parliament of Canada. In addition, the Bill looked forward to Parliament delegating part of its legislative authority to the Nova Scotia legislature. The judges based their decision on the "watertight compartments" view of federalism. In Mr. Justice Rand's words, this type of delegation was "utterly foreign to the conception of a federal organization."

If the advocates of flexible federalism were at all dismayed by this decision, their anguish was short-lived. The following year, in the case of *P.E.I. Potato Marketing Board v. H.B. Willis Inc.*, the Supreme Court designed an escape from its doctrine of the Nova Scotia Inter-delegation case. Here the issue concerned an attempt by the Dominion in the Agricultural Products Marketing Act (1949) to delegate to provincial marketing boards the power of regulating inter-provincial and export trade in agricultural products. The court ruled that this manner of delegation was constitutionally valid. In order to reach this decision the court distinguished the Nova Scotia case on the grounds that, there, legislative power was being delegated to other legislatures, whereas, in this case, the recipient of the delegated power was the subordinate agency of another legislature. The latter was justified because it involved merely an attempt by Parliament "to employ as its own a Board, or agency, for the purpose of carrying out its own legislation."

Whether or not one agrees with the logic of this distinction, it must be acknowledged that the decision in the Willis case opened a significant chink in the dike which separates Section 91 of the B.N.A. Act from Section 92. Indeed, on at least two occasions since then, the Provinces and the Dominion have resorted to this device of "indirect delegation" to circumvent the effects of other judicial decisions. The most striking example of this occurred after the Privy Council brought down its decision in the case of *A.-G. Ont. v. Winner* (1954). Since the original litigation in the Winner case had begun prior to the abolition of appeals, it was possible to appeal the Supreme Court's decision to the Privy Council. The outcome of this appeal was a victory for the Dominion: the Judicial Committee amended the Supreme Court's judgment and found that the Dominion alone had the power to regulate the operations of inter-provincial bus lines. Within two months representatives of the Federal Government and nine Provinces met to consider the implications of the Winner case. As a result of this meeting the Dominion Parliament passed the Motor Vehicle Transport Act, which was designed to delegate back to provincial licensing boards any of the powers over extra-provincial motor carriers that the Dominion might have won in the Winner case.

Parliament used the same technique again in 1957 to overcome the consequences of another judicial decision. This time, the ruling to be circumvented was part of the decision in Reference re. Ontario Farm Products Marketing Act (see above). In answer to one of the questions in this Reference, the court found that Ontario's incorporation of licensing fees, in its marketing regulations, which were designed to equalize the returns of producers, constituted indirect taxation and was therefore *ultra vires.* Following this, the Dominion Parliament, working on the assumption that a legislative power denied to the Provinces is within the Dominion's orbit, amended its Agricultural Products Marketing Act and delegated the power of imposing equalization levies to provincial marketing agencies. The ironic finale to this episode occurred four years later, when the Supreme Court in the case of *Crawford & Hillside Farm Dairy Ltd., et al. v. A.-G. B.C.* (1960) apparently reversed its position on provincial marketing levies. In this case the court ruled that where a provincial marketing scheme attempts to equalize the returns of producers this is still legislation in relation to trade and not indirect taxation. Consequently, provincial marketing levies such as had been declared *ultra vires* were now valid so long as they applied only to intra-provincial trade. This decision thus rendered superfluous Parliament's earlier amendment to the Agricultural Products Marketing Act.

The Supreme Court's validation of the "indirect delegation" device has undoubtedly opened up another channel of legislative co-operation in the Canadian federal system. This device, when both levels of government are willing to use it, makes it much easier for the national and local legislatures to overcome the difficulties of divided jurisdiction or, as the aftermath to the Winner case suggests, enables them to accommodate political pressures which are not recognized by the courts. In a word, where it is applicable, this device removes the sense of finality from the process of constitutional adjudication.

One of the major laments of the centralist critics of the Privy Council was that tribunal's invalidation of the Dominion's Industrial Disputes Investigation Act (the Lemieux Act) in the Snider case of 1925. The basic purpose of the Lemieux Act was to establish collective bargaining machinery that would be applicable to all mines, transportation and communication agencies, and public service utilities. By finding this statute *ultra vires,* the Privy Council had apparently disqualified the Dominion's efforts to provide a procedure for handling industrial disputes that were national in scope.

In 1955 the Supreme Court in yet another Reference case was confronted with the task of delineating legislative authority in relation to collective bargaining arrangements. In this *Reference re. Validity of Industrial Relations and Disputes Investigation Act,* the court unanimously found the federal statute *intra vires.* The decisive difference between this Act and the Lemieux Act which it had replaced was that it applied only to those activities that were within the legislative authority of Parliament. Consequently, this judgment confirmed the bifurcation of power in the field of labour relations. Whether labour relations in a particular industry are subject to federal or provincial law depends on whether that industry is one that can generally be brought under one of the heads of Section 91 or of Section 92. For instance, in the 1955 Reference, the court was also asked to decide whether employees of a Toronto stevedoring company were subject to the Dominion's Industrial Relations and Disputes Investigations Act. A majority of the court answered this question in the affirmative on the grounds that, since the Company serviced only boats engaged in foreign trade, its activities were subject to Head 10 (Navigation and Shipping) of Section 91.

Mr. V.C. MacDonald has described the Supreme Court's treatment of the labour relations question as "a truly gigantic step from the conclusion of the Privy Council in Snider's case. . . ." This perhaps overstates the case. Certainly the 1955 Reference contrasts with the Snider case to the extent that it denies provincial jurisdiction over collective bargaining in *some* industries. But it must also be noticed that the Supreme Court judgment does not uphold the argument that had prevailed in the lower courts in Canada prior to the appeal of the Snider case to the Privy Council; namely, that the settlement of major industrial disputes was a distinct and independent area of legislative activity and as such was subject to the Dominion's power to legislate for the Peace, Order, and Good Government of Canada. The principal way in which the 1955 decision might lead to an expansion of Federal jurisdiction over labour relations is through the judiciary adopting a generous construction of those industrial activities that are subject to Dominion authority. This has already happened on more than one occasion. In the *Pronto Uranium* case, for example, Judge McLennan of the Ontario Supreme Court ruled that labour relations in uranium mines were subject to the Dominion's legislation because activities related to the production of atomic energy came under the Peace, Order, and Good Government clause.

In the B.N.A. Act there is, of course, nothing comparable to the American Bill of Rights, which explicitly prohibits local and federal legislatures from violating certain basic rights. However, judicial review can affect civil liberties by determining whether the Dominion or the Provinces have the power to restrict fundamental freedom. Prior to 1949 this issue had not been explored in a definitive way by the Privy Council. Consequently, the three constitutional cases in the 1950s which raised civil liberty questions provided rather fertile soil for indigenous judicial seeds.

The three leading cases in this area are also of special interest to the political scientist because they tended to push the Supreme Court into a definite posture in regard to one of the most significant areas of conflicting values in Canadian life. On the surface the three cases would appear admirably suited to play such a role. They all concerned provincial legislation that curtailed some aspect of religious or political freedom; in all three cases it was the Province of Quebec whose legislation was under attack; in all three cases that province's Court of Appeal had upheld the legislation; in all three cases the Supreme Court reversed the decision of the lower court.

Saumur v. Quebec (1953) was the most perplexing of the three. In this case, Saumur, a Jehovah's Witness, challenged a Quebec City by-law forbidding the distribution in the streets of any book, pamphlet, or tract without the permission of the Chief of Police. In a narrow sense Saumur won his case. The Supreme Court on a five to four vote found that the by-law did not prohibit the Jehovah's Witnesses from distributing their literature in the streets. In a broader and more significant sense Saumur and those who view with alarm provincial laws authorizing the police to control the dissemination of opinions lost their case. In the opinions of five of the judges, including the three from Quebec, it was within provincial competence to limit freedom of religious expression. The other four, rejecting the view that the phrase "civil rights" in Section 92(13) refers to liberties such as freedom of religion, ruled against provincial competence in this matter. Saumur's victory, then, did not turn upon constitutional grounds but upon the much narrower opinion of Mr. Justice Kerwin. The latter conceded the constitutional validity of the by-law but reasoned that it did not apply to the Jehovah's Witnesses because it had to give way to the Quebec Freedom of Worship Act. Given the narrow basis of Kerwin's judgment, the Quebec legislature made quick work of the Saumur decision by amending the Freedom of Worship Act so that Jehovah's Witness publications would be clearly classified under the exceptions to the Act.

In contrast to the Saumur case, the case of *Birks & Sons v. Montreal* (1955) was more productive of solid constitutional fruit. The Quebec statute attacked in this case by Henry Birks & Co. required that storekeepers should close their shops on six Catholic Holy days. In a surprising display of unanimity all nine members of the court found the legislation *ultra vires*. Two elements of this decision stand out. In the first place, the court's basic point of departure from the Quebec Court of Queen's Bench lay in classifying the Act as one whose main concern was religious observance and not the regulation of working hours. Second, and this is the important constitutional doctrine, the court ruled that such legislation, which makes the failure to observe a certain religious practice a crime, falls under Parliament's power to enact criminal law (Section [91]).

Certainly the court's most prominent treatment of political freedoms arose in the case of *Switzman v. Elbling and A.-G. Quebec* (1957), which invalidated Quebec's Communist Propaganda Act. This Act, popularly known as the "Padlock Law," prohibited the use of houses for Communist meetings and banned the printing and publication of literature propagandizing the Communist ideology. The Supreme Court's decision here was in line with its earlier decision in the Birks case. With only Mr. Justice Taschereau dissenting, the court determined that the "pith and substance" of the Act was the suppression of Communism and, as such, it was beyond provincial jurisdiction. Once again it was the Dominion's power to legislate in relation to Criminal Law to which the majority referred as the constitutional basis for legislation restricting civil liberty. But, more spectacular and potentially of greater importance to the question of civil liberties in the Canadian Constitution was the doctrine formulated by Mr. Justice Rand and supported by two of his fellow judges, Kellock and Abbott.

Mr. Justice Rand, who has been described by Professor Laskin as the "greatest expositor of democratic public law which Canada has known," throughout these cases attempted to discover within the B.N.A. Act an implicit Bill of Rights that would at least protect fundamental liberties from abridgement by provincial legislatures. In the Winner case of 1951, Rand first brought up the notion of the "Rights of a Canadian Citizen." According to this doctrine, the institution of a common Canadian citizenship was an essential by-product of the nation created by the constitutional Act of 1867. This "citizenship" bears in its wake certain fundamental rights which all Canadians must enjoy and which are constitutionally beyond the range of provincial power. In this case, the particular "Right of a Canadian Citizen," which Rand elucidated as grounds for limiting the scope of New Brunswick's Motor Carrier Act, was the right to the use of highways. In the Saumur case, Rand referred to the phrase "a constitution similar in principle to that of the United Kingdom," which appears in the preamble to the B.N.A. Act, as the constitutional support of fundamental freedoms. This phrase, he reasoned, implies government by parliamentary institutions, a necessary condition of which is freedom of the press and freedom of public discussion. Rand developed this thesis further in the Padlock Law case. Again, he saw in the preamble to the B.N.A. Act a political theory that demands free speech and a free press as essential conditions of a Parliamentary Democracy. Mr. Justice Abbott went one step further than Rand and suggested that this implicit guarantee of free speech meant that "Parliament itself could not abrogate this right of discussion and debate."

Impressive as Rand's ideas may be as exercises in political philosophy, it must be noted that they are still some way from becoming a settled part of our Constitutional Law. In none of the cases in which Rand enunciated his thesis was it either endorsed by a majority or the turning point in the decision. Indeed, the late Chief Justice Mr. Kerwin in the Saumur case explicitly disavowed Rand's use of the preamble to the B.N.A. Act. Nevertheless, while the court as a whole may have declined to be as adventurous as Mr. Justice Rand, it has still partially clarified the constitutional position of civil liberties. After the Birks case and the Padlock Law case, the Dominion's Criminal Law power looms as an effective constitutional restraint on provincial laws that aim at circumscribing political and religious liberties.

Thus far we have examined Supreme Court decisions in those areas of constitutional interpretation which have traditionally attracted the attention of students of Canadian federalism. But these cases by no means give a full picture of the Supreme Court's performance as the umpire of the federal system. In addition to the 12 cases mentioned above, there were 26 other constitutional cases before the Supreme Court in the period under review. While these cases may not have raised what have come to be regarded as the classic issues of judicial review, in many instances they did result in decisions that had a significant impact on the legislative capacities of the Provinces and the Dominion. In the past, political scientists have often been so dazzled by the court's treatment of the General power and Property and Civil Rights that they have been somewhat blind to the importance of some of the other enumerated powers as sources of legislative authority and issues of judicial review.

Two of these rather neglected issues which were prominent in the 1950s were the Dominion's Criminal Law power (Section 91 [27]) and the question of taxation. We have already seen in the Civil Liberties cases how Parliament's Criminal Law power was invoked against provincial attempts to legislate with respect to religious practice and political freedoms. In nine other cases the Criminal Law power was at the centre of the constitutional dispute. In two of these cases the court invoked Section 91(27) to uphold Dominion statutes. The most important of these was *Goodyear Tire & Rubber Co. v. The Queen* (1956) in which the court used Head 27 of Section 91 to sustain provisions of the Combines Investigation Act. This judgment served as a reminder of the extent to which 91(27) can support legislation pursuing economic policy goals. Mr. Justice Rand declared that "it is accepted that head (27) of Section 91 . . . is to be interpreted in its widest sense. . . ." Against this broad interpretation of the Criminal Law power must be balanced the court's tendency to uphold provincial legislation that was being attacked as an infringement of Head 27 of Section 91. This was the basic question in the seven other "criminal law" cases, and in all but one the court found the impugned provincial legislation *intra vires.*

The constitutional prohibition of indirect provincial taxation was the central issue in five cases. It is beyond the scope of this article to examine these cases in any detail, but two cases are significant enough to merit some comment. In *Cairns Construction Ltd. v. Government of Saskatchewan* (1960) the court ruled that Saskatchewan's Education and Hospitalization Tax was *intra vires.* This was a retail sales tax, so that the court's decision provided a further constitutional underpinning for what has become an increasingly important source of provincial revenue. On the other hand, in *Texeda Mines Ltd. v. A.-G. B.C.,* by invalidating British Columbia's Mineral Property Tax, the Court, through Mr. Justice Locke, indicated a severe limitation to the province's powers of taxation. In this instance, although the B.C. tax in form resembled a Saskatchewan tax that had been found valid by the court in 1952, in substance it was ten times higher than the Saskatchewan tax and, consequently, it was distinguished and invalidated.

When the Privy Council was Canada's final court of appeal, the method it employed in constitutional adjudication came in for almost as much discussion as the substance of its decisions. Most of the Privy Council's English-speaking critics were advocates of judicial activism. According to this conception of judicial review, the court's function in a country with a written constitution was to adjust the terms of the constitutional text to the rapidly changing requirements of a dynamic environment. These judicial activists singled out the Privy Council's apparently strict adherence to the principle of *stare decisis* and its literalistic interpretation of the B.N.A. Act as the aspects of its method which precluded the kind of judicial statesmanship they advocated. While the Privy Council's critics looked forward with some optimism to the Supreme Court's emancipation, there were others, not surprisingly associated with the provincial rights view of federalism, who were alarmed at the prospect of any major deviation by the Supreme Court from the Privy Council's traditions. Parliamentary spokesmen of this school of thought went so far as to move, unsuccessfully, an amendment to the Act abolishing appeals which would have made previous Privy Council decisions binding on the Supreme Court.

It is extremely difficult to summarize with any degree of precision the Supreme Court's record with regard to these matters of method. As far as *stare decisis* is concerned, it is clear that the court is under no statutory compulsion to adopt the earlier rulings of the Privy Council as the bases for its own judgments. At the same time it is also clear that *in practice* the Supreme Court since 1949 has never explicitly overruled a Privy Council decision or, indeed, any of its own previous judgments. Thus, the court appears to be somewhere between the position of the United States Supreme Court and its own position prior to the abolition of appeals: unlike its American counterpart it has not officially declared its readiness to discard old judicial precedents when they no longer seem suitable but, in contrast to its own pre-1949 position, it is relatively free to work out its own policy of interpreting and applying Privy Council precedents. This rather ambiguous position becomes, perhaps, more comprehensible if we acknowledge that even when a court formally follows a practice of *stare decisis* this does not necessarily result in as inflexible and predictable a course of decisions as is sometimes suggested. Given rival precedents on the same general question and the art of distinguishing previous cases as different from the one at hand, it is entirely possible for a court, while looking exclusively to past cases for the premises of its reasoning, in fact so to select, ignore and distinguish cases that it is able to evolve its own doctrines of constitutional law.

Stare decisis is naturally linked to that other controversial aspect of judicial review — the unimaginative, literalistic interpretation of the B.N.A. Act as opposed to the statesmanlike adaptation of the constitutional text. Which of these alternative approaches has the Supreme Court tended to follow? Again it is impossible to give a simple answer. It would be misleading to brand the Supreme Court's approach as either distinctively literal or distinctively liberal. If any contrast can be drawn here between the Supreme Court's record and that of its predecessor, it would be in terms of an increasing degree of pragmatism in the court's interpretation of the division of powers, especially in areas affecting economic welfare. In a number of cases, individual judges have based their reasoning not so much on the words of the B.N.A. Act as on the adverse practical consequences they felt would flow from an alternative decision to the one they were giving. For instance, Mr. Justice Locke, in the Johannesson case, based his opinion against provincial regulation of aerodromes partly on his estimation of the "intolerable" state of affairs that would result if the national development of airlines was obstructed by local regulations. Similarly, the court's examination of the concepts of intra-provincial and extra-provincial trade in the Ontario Farm Products Marketing Reference was much more concerned with elaborating a workable scheme for the division of legislative authority than with a close textual scrutiny of the B.N.A. Act. Of course, these are only isolated examples, but still it is in these occasional outbursts of functionalism that we are apt to find some vindication of Edward Blake's opinion that the great merit of a Canadian court of last resort would be in its possession of "the daily learning and experience which Canadians, living under the Canadian Constitution, acquire . . . and which can be given only by residence on the spot."

There is one other aspect of the Supreme Court's method that calls for some comment; that is its practice of having a number of judges write opinions in each case — even in cases where all the judges reach the same result.

This is in marked contrast to the Judicial Committee's custom of publishing only one opinion for every case. No matter how divided their Lordships may have been in private, their public face was always one of unanimity. In contrast to this, the Supreme Court, in the 37 constitutional cases it handled in the period under review, on the average included four opinions in each case.

This rather different practice has been a mixed blessing. The inclusion of the minority's opinion, when the court is split, has the undoubted advantage of displaying the alternative principles of interpretation upon which the case hinged. Also, we know from American experience that the minority opinion of today can become the majority opinion of tomorrow. But, unfortunately, the Canadian Supreme Court has failed to combine this practice of multi-opinion writing with any procedure for co-ordinating the separate opinions. Unlike the United States Supreme Court, the Canadian court does not present a majority opinion which at least indicates the common ingredients of those judgments that determined the outcome of the case. This means that when several judges, constituting the majority in a given case, all write separate opinions, it is extremely difficult to ascertain the common grounds of their disparate arguments and, hence, the basic principles established by the case. For example, in the Saumur case, the five judges who made up the majority all wrote separate opinions and, while they all agreed to allow the appeal, their opinions represented at least three different viewpoints on the central constitutional issue. This disjointed system of opinion writing not only might make it perplexing for the professional lawyer who must somehow determine the net effect of the different opinions, but also, in many cases, it prevents the court from performing what should surely be a necessary adjunct of the process of constitutional adjudication; namely, the clarification of constitutional principles for the public at large.

II. 1960 to 1974

Since 1960 the Supreme Court has played an increasingly prominent role in Canadian public life, although it is still far from assuming as important a position as that occupied by the Supreme Court of the United States. In contrast to its American counterpart, the Canadian Supreme Court's decisions in the area of constitutional law constitute only a minor portion of its work. Still, Canadian expectations about the importance of the Supreme Court's constitutional work have been stimulated rather than tempered by the Court's performance since 1960. These rising expectations have stemmed mostly from the enactment of the Bill of Rights in 1960. But even on the more traditional federal issues, the Court, especially in its more nationalist decisions, has been a focus of political controversy and has continued to have an important influence on the balance of power in Canadian federalism.

Federalism

So far as the classic issues of Canadian constitutional law are concerned — the scope of federal power to legislate for peace, order and good government and the regulation of trade and commerce, as against provincial jurisdiction over property and civil rights or matters of a merely local or private nature — the Supreme Court's decisions have continued to bear a distinct centralist accent. By the mid-1960s there had been more than a 50 per cent turnover in the personnel of the Court since 1952 when the Court in the *Johannesson* case adopted Lord Simon's "inherent national importance" test for invoking the peace, order and good government power. In the *Munroe* case in 1965 and the *Offshore Minerals Reference* of 1967, a very differently constituted Court indicated that the "inherent national importance" test had replaced Haldane's much more restrictive emergency doctrine as the key to the Supreme Court's understanding of peace, order and good government. Regardless of the attraction of these decisions to those of a centralist persuasion, the style if not the substance of these decisions is disappointing. The "national importance" test cries out for judicial opinions like Justice Locke's in the *Johannesson* case, which go beyond purely conceptual and legalistic considerations to the reasons for holding that a particular subject must necessarily be the concern of the national government. But in neither case did the Court accept the challenge of providing a reasoned basis for what were inescapably policy decisions.

In the *Munroe* case, this failure was less objectionable. Here the federal legislation at stake was the National Capital Commission Act, and it was not so unreasonable for Justice Cartwright simply to assert that it is "difficult to suggest a subject matter of legislation which more clearly goes beyond local or provincial interests and is the common concern of Canada as a whole than the development, conservation and improvement of the National Capital Region. . . ."

But the Court's use of the national importance argument to uphold federal rights in the *Offshore Minerals Reference* was far more provocative. It is interesting that the Court's opinion in this highly political case was *per curiam,* that is, unanimous and anonymous — so far as I know the first time in the Court's history that a constitutional decision had been so rendered. Most of the judgment, in fact 23 of its 29 pages, focussed on the question of whether the territory of British Columbia extended past the provincial shore line. After reviewing a body of conflicting statutory and common law authorities, the Court concluded that the provincial territory did not include the sea or the sea-bed adjacent to its coast. The Court might have rested its case there, since not even B.C.'s Premier W.C. Bennett was inclined to press for extra-territorial provincial rights. But the Court went on to offer a positive basis for federal power. With a short nationalist flourish, it asserted towards the end of its judgment that "the mineral resources of our lands underlying the territorial sea are of concern to Canada as a whole and go beyond local or provincial concerns or interests."

The *Offshore Mineral Rights* case was already political enough without this display of dogmatic centralism. Prime Minister Pearson had shown questionable judgment in referring this matter to the Supreme Court at a time when it was the centre of a hot political controversy between Ottawa and a number of provinces. There is no question of the Supreme Court's right to adjudicate a legal controversy between two parties which turns on the question of the ownership of offshore minerals. The rule of law in our constitutional system requires such adjudication. And this adjudication must be authoritative. But there was no case or controversy in the courts on offshore mineral rights. Mr. Pearson chose to take advantage of the reference case procedure and ask the Court for an advisory opinion, presumably with the hope of obtaining a Supreme Court decision favourable to federal interests. This use of the Court was strenuously objected to by both Premier Bennett of British Columbia and Premier Lesage of Quebec. The latter declared that "Quebec is not prepared to allow this question to be decided by the courts, it must be settled by political negotiation." Following the Supreme Court decision in March 1967, Mr. Lesage said that "if French-speaking Canadians' constitutional rights are to be protected, the Supreme Court of Canada, which rules on constitutional questions, must be either changed or altered." Daniel Johnson, who succeeded Lesage as Premier of Quebec, reiterated this position in November 1967.

In the intensely political atmosphere that surrounded this case it is unfortunate that the Supreme Court employed, so glibly, the national dimensions test of peace, order and good government. If the Supreme Court is to retain its effectiveness as the arbiter of our federal constitution, politicians must be careful in exploiting the easy access to the Court which the reference case gives them and the Court itself must take pains to be convincing in justifying decisions which are bound to be highly unpopular in certain quarters. One measure of the ineffectiveness of the Court's decision in the *Offshore Mineral Rights* case is the simple fact that the Court's holding has not been followed.

Turning now to the trade and commerce power, the major breakthrough of the 1950s should be recalled — that is, the Supreme Court's discovery that commerce flows (at least that "commerce" which only the federal parliament can regulate). In the words of Chief Justice Kerwin in the 1957 *Ontario Farm Products Marketing Act* case, "Once an article enters into the flow of interprovincial or external trade, the subject-matter and all its attendant circumstances cease to be a mere matter of local concern." Two cases upholding the federal scheme for marketing the prairie wheat crop followed on the heels of this decision — *Murphy v. C.P.R.* (1958) and, in Manitoba's Court of Appeal, *Regina v. Klassen* (1959). These cases, involving the hard facts of real-life litigation, indicated that with the "flow of commerce" incorporated into our constitutional law, the judiciary might no longer approach the division of powers in the field of economic regulation in terms of the mutually exclusive water-tight compartments of intra-provincial and extra-provincial transactions.

There was no further action on this front until the late 1960s and early 1970s when four cases, three of which concerned Quebec, came before the Supreme Court. The Court's decision in the first of these, *Carnation Co. Ltd. v. Quebec Agricultural Marketing Board* (1968), was favourable to the province. Justice Martland, writing for a unanimous Court, dismissed an attack on Quebec price supports for milk sold to the Carnation Company, most of whose products were exported from the province. Justice Martland acknowledged that the provincial regulations might well have an effect on the company's export trade but that this was not the aim of the legislation. Its prime purpose was to strengthen the bargaining position of milk producers within the province and this was within provincial jurisdiction.

But in the two cases which followed in 1971, the Supreme Court upheld national economic interests which were in conflict with Quebec policies. In both cases, the Court was unanimous. In *Caloil Inc. v. Attorney General of Canada,* the Court upheld the national energy policy which at that time was designed to protect western Canadian producers from competition with cheaper imported oil. The regulations drew a line in Ontario through the Ottawa Valley and banned the sale west of that line of products from Eastern Canadian refineries served by foreign suppliers of crude oil. Justice Pigeon, at the time the newest appointee to the Court, wrote the opinion. He was content simply to classify the federal regulations as being "in pith and substance" concerned with the control of imports and therefore under the federal trade and commerce power. He did not examine the economic aims and consequences of the regulations — in fact, for instance, that the regulations were primarily concerned with the preservation of an appropriate market in central Canada for oil produced in western Canada. Nor did he weigh the need, from a national point of view, of giving this policy priority over provincial interests in local markets and manufacturing. Immediately after the decision, Jacques Parizeau, a well-known separatist economist, at a press conference in Montreal, announced that many of the 1200 workers might be laid off at Caloil's Montreal refinery. This refinery had recently been built largely on the expectation of developing an extensive network of gasoline stations in a market embracing the "golden horseshoe" of south-west Ontario.

The third of the cases, *Attorney General for Manitoba v. Manitoba Egg and Poultry Association,* was a reference case. If all reference cases can be said to be hypothetical, this one must be considered super-hypothetical. Manitoba initiated this reference by asking its own Court of Appeal to assess the constitutional validity of a provincial egg-marketing scheme under which quotas could be applied to any or all of the eggs sold in the province, including those imported from other provinces. Manitoba, in fact, was not an importer of eggs, nor was there any intention of putting this scheme into force in Manitoba. But Quebec was an egg-importer and had imposed quotas on eggs coming on to the Quebec market from Ontario and Manitoba. But no one had challenged the validity of the Quebec scheme in the courts. Hence, Manitoba simply drafted marketing legislation similar to Quebec's and referred it to the courts, hoping, of course, that its own draft scheme (and therefore Quebec's as well) would be held unconstitutional. The Manitoba Court and, on appeal, the Supreme Court of Canada obliged and ruled against the provincial scheme.

The Supreme Court's decision in this case provided the occasion for Justice Bora Laskin's first full-length opinion on a central issue in Canadian constitutional law. Justice Laskin before coming to the bench had for many years been a professor of law at the University of Toronto and in that capacity had established himself as one of the country's leading scholars in the field of constitutional law. He was noted for his trenchant criticism of both the form and substance of the Privy Council's interpretation of the Canadian constitution. He was appointed to the Supreme Court of Canada in 1970 (after five years on the Ontario Court of Appeal) and within three years was to become its Chief Justice.

In many respects his opinion in this case came up to the expectations of those who had applauded his elevation to the Court. The opinion contains a masterful review of the previous cases dealing with trade and commerce. It traces the early reduction of trade and commerce as an all-embracing source of federal power to its virtual attenuation and finally the recent endeavour of the Supreme Court to restore a "necessary balance." The Court's opinion in this case crystallizes this restoration of the federal trade and commerce power as a constitutional basis for national economic policy. The provincial scheme was held to be *ultra vires* because in attempting to impede the flow of commerce across provincial boundaries, it infringed on Parliament's exclusive jurisdiction over trade and commerce. In the words of Justice Laskin, provincial trade wars of the kind which inspired the Manitoba egg marketing scheme "deny one of the objects of Confederation . . . namely, to form an economic unit of the whole of Canada."

Justice Laskin's opinion produced some important dicta on the scope of the federal trade and commerce power, but the case as a whole was seriously flawed by the total absence of any factual evidence to support the Court's view of the legislation's purpose and effect. Justice Laskin himself pointed out at the beginning of his opinion how factual data concerning the importance of imported eggs in the Manitoba egg-market would be relevant to determining the pith and substance of the Manitoba scheme. But even though there were no such data, he was able to satisfy his judicial conscience and reach the conclusion that "the proposed scheme has as a direct object the regulation of the importation of eggs."

Two years later in *Burns Foods Ltd., et al. v. A.G. Manitoba,* the federal trade and commerce power was employed again to cut down a provincial marketing regulation. But on this occasion the Supreme Court's opinion (written by Justice Pigeon) seemed something of a throwback to the earlier, more rigid approach to the division of powers in economic matters. The regulation in question required Manitoba processors to purchase all their hogs from a provincial board. The aim of the regulation was to strengthen the bargaining position of hog producers in the province against the large meat-packing firms. About four per cent of the hogs involved were imported from Saskatchewan. But because the regulation applied directly to this inter-provincial trade, it was ruled null and void by the Court. It is interesting that Mr. Justice Laskin did not take part in this decision.

Besides trade and commerce, and peace, order and good government, there has been the usual trickle of cases on other heads of power. Throughout the 60s and in the 70s, constitutional cases have continued to reach the Supreme Court at the rate of three to four a year. On a purely box-score basis, the outcomes have been considerably more favourable to federal than to provincial interests, as the table below indicates.

Outcome of Supreme Court's Constitutional Decisions, 1950-72

	1950-60	1960-72
Federal law valid	7	13
Federal law invalid	0	0
Provincial law valid	16	18
Provincial law invalid	14	6

Federal authorities have yet to lose a constitutional decision before an independent Supreme Court of Canada, whereas provincial claims have been defeated on numerous occasions. These statistics, coupled with the Court's liberal construction of the key sources of federal power, may be grist for the mill of provincial rights critics of the Supreme Court. Provincial distrust of the Supreme Court was manifest at the Victoria Conference in June 1971. The lengthiest section of the Charter for constitutional reform which emerged from that Conference concerned provincial participation in appointments to the Supreme Court of Canada.

But it would be a mistake to infer from these statistics that in fact the Supreme Court's interpretation of the constitution has consistently embodied a nationalist bias. In a number of the Court's decisions on particular heads of power, a mood of permissiveness and flexibility has been more evident than a pro-federal orientation. On five occasions in the 1960s, the Supreme Court upheld provincial administrative arrangements which were attacked on the ground that they usurped the powers of courts to which the federal government appoints the judges. In five other cases, provincial laws with punitive sections were attacked as infringing exclusive federal jurisdiction over criminal law. All but one of these laws survived judicial review. The device of delegation from the legislature at one level to a board or commission at the other level, a device sanctioned by the Supreme Court in the 1950s, was upheld in two further cases — the *Coughlin* case in 1968 and *The Queen v. Smith* in 1972. In the area of business regulation, Saskatchewan legislation concerning promissory notes *(Duplain v. Cameron,* 1961), an Ontario Act aimed at preventing "unconscionable" interest charges *(A.G. Ont. v. Barfreid Enterprises Ltd.,* 1963), a provincial tax on mining profits *(Nickel Rim Mines Ltd. v. A.G. Ont.,* 1967), and an Alberta Act affecting banks *(Breckenridge Speedway Ltd. v. The Queen,* 1970) were all upheld by the Supreme Court, although each ran up against exclusive federal powers.

An optimistic reading of this relatively charitable treatment of provincial legislation would see it as contributing to "co-operative federalism." It might be more realistic to acknowledge that this judicial restraint has the effect of adding to the areas of law in which the provinces and Ottawa have concurrent jurisdiction. While this trend undoubtedly increased the legislative capacities of federal and provincial legislators, and may in that way contribute to the flexibility of our federal system, it may also make life somewhat more confusing to the Canadian citizen by subjecting him to a welter of legislation on a single subject.

Civil Liberties

[Editor's note: For an extended discussion of Civil Liberties, see also Chapter 17, where in particular the decision in *Lavell and Bedard* is given *verbatim,* abridged.]

The Supreme Court's decisions on civil liberties have attracted far more attention in recent years than have its decisions on the classical issues of federalism. Certainly its decisions in this area have been more divisive of the Court itself. In contrast to the Court's unanimity on most federal issues, it has been closely divided on nearly all cases dealing with civil liberties. Its civil liberties decisions should be divided into two categories: those having to do with the B.N.A. Act and those which concern the Bill of Rights.

Beginning with the 1938 Alberta Press case, the Supreme Court had been evolving two doctrines upon which constitutional protection for certain civil liberties might be derived from the B.N.A. Act. First was Chief Justice

Duff's notion of the rights required for the operation of parliamentary government which, among other things, would include freedom of speech and of the press to debate government policy. A second approach simply relied on exclusive federal jurisdiction over criminal law to preclude provincial legislation attaching penalties to non-conformance with religious customs (*Birks* case, 1955) or outlawing the expression of certain political beliefs (*Switzman* case, 1957). Only the second of these approaches ever gained the support of a majority on the Supreme Court.

Since 1960, there has been little further development of these constitutional "guarantees." The Duff doctrine of implied parliamentary rights has not become established as part of our constitutional law. In the *Oil, Chemical and Atomic Workers International Union* case of 1963, the Court split four to three on the constitutionality of Premier Bennett's legislation preventing trade unions from using union funds collected through a checkoff to support a political party. The majority decided that the law in pith and substance concerned labour relations in the province and therefore was constitutional. But the minority acknowledged that the law could in effect cripple labour-supported political parties and so emphasized its effect on federal elections. Even so, only one of the dissenters, Justice Abbott, saw the issue in terms of fundamental political rights beyond curtailment by both levels of government. The other two dissenting judges, Justices Cartwright and Judson, merely held that provincial legislation relating to federal elections was beyond provincial jurisdiction. Justice Cartwright's minority position was adopted by the majority two years later in *McKay v. The Queen.* The issue here was whether a by-law restricting the posting of signs in a Toronto suburb could validly prohibit the posting of signs by candidates in a federal election. The Court split five to four, the majority holding that this application of a municipal by-law would be an unconstitutional infringement of exclusive federal jurisdiction over Dominion elections. But, again, there was no reliance by the Court on the notion of an implied bill of parliamentary rights in the B.N.A. Act.

In 1969, in *Walter v. A.G. Alberta,* the justices of the contemporary Supreme Court gave further evidence that they were not prepared to find a great deal of constitutional protection for civil liberties in the B.N.A. Act. In this case, Alberta's Communal Property Act, which regulates land purchases by Hutterites and other communitarian sects, was attacked as an unconstitutional provincial restriction of religious freedom. The Hutterites based their argument on the Supreme Court's decision in the 1950s in the *Birks, Switzman,* and *Saumur* cases. But the Supreme Court, in a unanimous decision, held that the Alberta legislation was valid as being primarily in relation to property management.

By 1960 many Canadians were looking beyond the B.N.A. Act to the Canadian Bill of Rights as an instrument through which the judiciary might better protect fundamental rights and freedoms. Granted, the Bill of Rights did not apply to the provinces, and as an ordinary act of Parliament could be set aside at any time by Parliament, still, its enactment in 1960 aroused great expectations.

For many observers, the Supreme Court's treatment of the Bill of Rights adds up to a strange tale of prevarication and confusion. The most consistent element in the Supreme Court's interpretation of the Bill of Rights, until 1973, is that the same judge, Justice Ritchie, has written the majority opinion in the three landmark decisions: *Robertson and Rosetanni* in 1963, *Drybones* in 1969, and the *Lavell and Bedard* case in 1973. Unlike some members of the Court, Justice Ritchie does not admit to changing his mind about the meaning of the Bill of Rights during this period. But it is a challenging exercise in analytical jurisprudence to work out the consistent principles of his decisions.

In *Robertson and Rosetanni,* Justice Ritchie took a conservationist approach to the Bill of Rights. In his view, the Bill's aim was to conserve the basic rights and freedoms Canadians had enjoyed prior to 1960. The Canadian Bill of Rights, he insisted, "is not concerned with 'human rights and fundamental freedoms' in any abstract sense, but rather with such 'right and freedoms' as they existed in Canada immediately before the statute was enacted." In the case at hand, Robertson and Rosetanni were claiming that their conviction under the federal Lord's Day Act for operating a bowling alley on Sunday violated the freedom of religion clause in the Bill of Rights. Justice Ritchie, following his conservationist approach, found that before 1960 the courts of Canada had on a number of occasions declared that Canada enjoyed "freedom of religion" and that when such declarations were made, Canadians also lived under compulsory Lord's Day observance legislation. Therefore, he concluded, freedom of religion as traditionally understood in Canada was not violated by the Lord's Day Act.

Six years later when the *Drybones* case reached the Supreme Court, many observers expected that Justice Ritchie's historical perspective would defeat Drybones' claim for equality under the law as provided for in the Bill of Rights. Drybones, an Indian in the Northwest Territories, had been convicted under a section of the Indian Act which makes it a crime for Indians to have intoxicants or be intoxicated off a reserve. This legislation had been on the statute book for many years prior to 1960. But even so, the mere fact that the law was passed before 1960 did not in Justice Ritchie's view make it immune to the Bill of Rights. Presumably, what was lacking here, in contrast to *Robertson and Rosetanni,* were authoritative statements making it clear that the traditional Canadian conception of equality before the law was compatible with this kind of discrimination against Indians. Justice Ritchie went on to hold that "an individual is denied equality before the law if it is made an offence punishable at law, on account of his race, for him to do something which his fellow Canadians are free to do. . . ." For the first time the Court ruled that federal legislation was rendered inoperative because it violated the Canadian Bill of Rights.

The dissenting opinions in the Supreme Court's *Drybones* decision were as interesting as the majority opinion. Chief Justice Cartwright, who had taken the more radical position in *Robertson and Rosetanni* and written the only dissenting opinion, dissented again. He had given the Bill of Rights question "a most anxious reconsideration" since 1963 and had now concluded that his earlier position had been an "error." To put real teeth in the Bill of Rights would impose a tremendous responsibility on every court in the country, a revolution in our system of government which it could not be assumed Parliament intended to bring about by enacting the Bill of Rights.

Justice Pigeon, the newest Quebec justice on the Court, wrote an even more ardent dissent defending the retention of the British system of parliamentary supremacy.

The *Lavell and Bedard* case, the third land-mark decision, seemed to many to constitute another dramatic turn-about by the Supreme Court. Mrs. Lavell, and another Indian woman, Mrs. Bedard, after leaving an Indian reserve and marrying non-Indians, wished to return and live as members of Indian bands. But under section 12(1) of the Indian Act, an Indian woman who had married a non-Indian was not entitled to be registered as a member of an Indian band, although an Indian man could marry a non-Indian without relinquishing his Indian status. Thus, counsel for the two women hoped to benefit from Justice Ritchie's decision in *Drybones* and claim that the Indian Act by discriminating against women violated the "equality before the law" provision of the Bill of Rights. But Justice Ritchie disappointed them. Writing the majority opinion for a closely divided Court (five to four), he was able to distinguish this case from *Drybones* and dismiss the claim.

For Justice Ritchie, the crucial difference in this case was that the discrimination here applied only within Indian reserves whereas in *Drybones* it pertained to all Indians as members of the Canadian community. Under the B.N.A. Act, there was explicit authorization for federal laws regulating the status of Indians and for over a century the Indian Act had contained this patriarchal provision. Parliament, he argued, could not have intended to change such an established and traditional policy when it passed the Bill of Rights. Later in his judgment he appeared to back away from the definition of "equality before the law" he had given in *Drybones*. There, equality before the law seemed to require a degree of equality *of* the law itself. But now he looked to A.V. Dicey's English definition which emphasizes equality in the way the law is applied rather than of the law itself. "Equality before the law," he wrote, "is to be treated as meaning equality in the administration and enforcement of the law by the law enforcement authorities and the ordinary courts of the land." In his opinion, no such inequality in treatment between Indian men and women resulted from section 12(1) of the Indian Act.

Justice Laskin, soon to become Chief Justice of Canada, wrote a vigorous dissent in the *Lavell* case. The majority's reasoning, he contended, by permitting sex discrimination among Indians "compounds racial inequality even beyond the point that the *Drybones* case found unacceptable." In his view, the Canadian Bill of Rights goes even further than the American Constitution's due process and equal protection guarantees, in that it explicitly prohibits discrimination on the basis of race, national origin, colour, religion or sex. Justice Pigeon's and Justice Abbott's decisions were ironic: Justice Pigeon now concurred with Justice Ritchie for the very reasons he had disagreed with him in *Drybones,* while Justice Abbott disagreed with Justice Ritchie because reluctantly he felt obliged to follow Ritchie's earlier *Drybones* decision. No wonder the public felt confused!

The Supreme Court of Canada certainly cannot be given high marks for clarifying the meaning of the Canadian Bill of Rights. But to be fair, it must be acknowledged that the Bill of Rights imposes on the Canadian Supreme Court a most difficult task — to apply a long list of very abstract ideals to a statute book which is more than a century old. Even in a country where the public and the Court are accustomed to the judiciary's playing a large role in the revision of legislation this would be a remarkable challenge. It is not surprising that in Canada, where traditionally the courts have not been perceived as playing such a role, the Justices of the Supreme Court have been rather wavering and cautious in responding to this challenge.

Their basic caution is further evidenced by the five other Bill of Rights cases the Court decided between *Drybones* in 1969 and *Lavell* in 1973. All concerned various aspects of fair legal procedure. In only one did the Court uphold a claim under the Bill of Rights. This was a case involving the breathalizer amendments to the Criminal Code (*Brownridge v. The Queen,* 1972) where the majority agreed that a person should not be convicted of refusing without reasonable excuse to take a breathalizer test when the refusal is based on the police's denial of the accused's right to counsel. In all of these cases involving the rights of accused persons as against the rights of the police and the prosecution, the Court showed a real reluctance to move boldly in the directions which the Warren Court had taken in the United States, a direction which had done so much to spike the guns of the "law and order" opponents of the U.S. Supreme Court. In Canada, most political criticism of the Supreme Court has come from the other direction, from those who expect the Supreme Court through the application of the Bill of Rights to intervene much more decisively as a reforming influence on legislation and the conduct of government. Even under Chief Justice Laskin's leadership these critics are unlikely to receive much satisfaction in the future.

Organization and Procedure

A few changes in the organization and procedures of the Supreme Court have been made in recent years, all of which reflect the Court's greater self-consciousness of its responsibilities as the nation's final court of appeal. The extremely individualistic pattern of opinion-writing has moderated somewhat. Instead of every justice writing his own opinion, there has been (at least in public law cases) a greater tendency for the majority group of judges to support a single majority opinion. The Court has also been somewhat more inclined to sit as a full court in constitutional cases. In approximately 60 per cent of the constitutional cases it has heard since 1960, all nine judges participated in the decisions, whereas the full court sat for less than 50 per cent of the constitutional cases it heard in the previous decade.

Two other "reforms" should be reported. The Court's bilingual capacities have been enlarged. Since 1970, all of the Court's reported cases have been printed in both French and English in the official reports. Before this, many of the Court's decisions were available in one language only (usually English). For oral presentations, instantaneous interpretation facilities have been installed in the court room. But these are seldom used. The English-speaking judges still seem overly shy about admitting the need for interpretation of French-speaking lawyers' presentations. The other reform is the provision of legal secretaries as research assistants for each of the justices. Law clerks are essentially an American institution. They are usually young law graduates personally selected by each justice. Their introduction to the Supreme Court emphasizes the "research" dimension of the Supreme Court's role. As the second and final court of appeal, its function is not to hear every contested trial decision but to settle those difficult legal questions which often require extensive research and deliberation.

Late in 1974 a much more significant change in the Court's operations was finally implemented. Following many years of agitation by students of the Court and a recent inquiry by a Committee of The Canadian Bar Association, Parliament enacted legislation which would eliminate the automatic right to appeal from the highest provincial courts to the Supreme Court in civil cases involving at least $10,000. In the past this right of appeal accounted for more than half of the cases heard by the Supreme Court. As a result, much of the Court's time was taken up with settling suits which did not raise significant legal issues. This change will free the Supreme Court to devote most of its energies to deciding cases which a panel of three judges has determined raise legal questions of major importance. The establishment of the Federal Court in 1970-71, with an appeal division, also freed the Court from the burden of hearing routine tax appeals. These reforms should enable the Supreme Court of Canada to attain a higher level of performance in a more collegiate manner on an agenda of increasing significance to the nation.

III. Recent Developments 1975-1980

The latter half of the 1970s has witnessed a remarkable increase in constitutional decisions by the Supreme Court of Canada. The Supreme Court Reports for the first five years of the decade contain only nine decisions on the division of powers in the B.N.A. Act. But the Reports for the last five years of the decade record 36 decisions on the division of powers — a fourfold increase. Constitutional litigation has more than increased in volume. Some of the Court's decisions have had a direct bearing on the most important issues in Canadian politics.

It is not easy to account for this significant increase in constitutional cases. Clearly it cannot be attributed to reference cases: only four of the constitutional cases decided by the Supreme Court during the decade were initiated by either level of government referring questions to the courts. Most cases originated with challenges to federal or provincial laws by private individuals, business corporations, labour unions or municipalities. The federal government and a number of provincial governments intervened in nearly all of these cases. The willingness of both levels of government to invest resources in constitutional litigation reflects a more combative era in federal-provincial relations. Judicial decisions rarely settle federal-provincial conflicts, but a favourable court opinion can be an important asset in inter-governmental bargaining. Similarly, governments join litigation in order to defend constitutional assets which an unfavourable court decision might undermine. The rising number of constitutional cases also indicates that both levels of government are increasingly prone to testing the limits of their constitutional powers by unilateral policy initiatives rather than first negotiating more cooperative approaches.

The Division of Powers

How has the Supreme Court responded to this increase in its constitutional case-load? In answering this question we must distinguish between the Court's reputation and the reality of its performance. The decisions which attracted the most political attention tended to favour the federal government and were regarded as significant provincial losses. Cases involving federal losses and provincial gains received much less notice. Generally this is because provincial politicians do not hesitate to complain when the Supreme Court rules against them, whereas federal spokesmen do not denounce the Court when it rules in the provinces' favour. An important consequence of the Court's centralist reputation has been increased provincial government support for constitutional amendments to give the provinces a formal role in the appointment of Supreme Court justices.

The most heralded of the Supreme Court's decisions in the 1970s came in the *Anti-Inflation Act Reference* case of 1976. The Court, by a 7 to 2 majority, found the federal government's programme of wage and price controls constitutional. While the immediate outcome appeared to be a major victory for the federal government, a majority of the judges rejected the most expansive interpretation of the federal parliament's peace, order and good government power. The majority denied that the federal parliament could use the peace, order and good government power to legislate on matters normally under provincial jurisdiction simply because of the inherent national importance of a problem like inflation. Peace, order and good government could be used in the case at hand only because in the majority view there was a temporary emergency sufficient to justify the use of extraordinary powers.

While the rejection of the inherent national importance test may have disappointed ardent centralists, invoking peace, order and good government for the first time as a basis for peacetime legislation dealing with an economic emergency had frightening implications for the provinces. The Court's decision indicated that the onus of proof as to the existence of an emergency lies with those who are challenging the legislation and that in an emergency the federal parliament's powers are virtually unlimited. This decision stimulated provincial interest in giving a reformed federal Upper House representing provincial governments a veto power over the use of federal emergency powers.

Two other areas in which the provinces incurred noticeable losses were natural resources and communications. In the natural resource field the Supreme Court found Saskatchewan legislation unconstitutional in two important decisions. The Court's decision in the *C.I.G.O.L.* (Canadian Industrial Gas and Oil Ltd.) case of 1978 ruled *ultra vires* Saskatchewan's tax and royalty scheme designed to capture for the provincial treasury 100 per cent of the windfall gains resulting from sudden increases in international oil prices. The majority theorized that because provincial oil producers would pass the burden of the tax along to their extra-provincial customers, the levy was an unconstitutional indirect tax and an encroachment on exclusive federal jurisdiction over international and inter-provincial trade and commerce. In a strong dissenting judgment, Justice Dickson pointed out that the majority's theory was 'unreal' in that the Saskatchewan tax in fact had no effect on international prices which were independently determined by international market forces. Although Premier Blakeney bitterly protested this loss, he was able to overcome the entire potential tax loss by introducing an Oil Well Income Tax.

The next year in the *Central Canada Potash* case the Court overturned Saskatchewan's pro-rationing regulations for the province's burgeoning potash industry. These regulations were designed to curtail the supply and control the price of potash entering the international market. Chief Justice Laskin writing for a unanimous court held that, while production controls and conservation measures with respect to natural resources in a province are normally within provincial jurisdiction, provincial legislation primarily aimed at controlling exports from the province infringes upon exclusive federal control over interprovincial and export trade.

These decisions also provoked provincial demands for constitutional reforms. The federal government committed itself to supporting a constitutional amendment which would overcome the *C.I.G.O.L.* decision by giving the provinces the power to levy indirect taxes on non-renewable natural resources. Such an amendment was added to the package of constitutional proposals which Prime Minister Trudeau placed before Parliament in 1980-81. The federal government was not, however, prepared to go so far in reversing the *Central Canada Potash* case. All that it offered was a concurrent provincial power, subject to federal paramountcy, over interprovincial (but not international) trade in non-renewable resources providing there was no discrimination against other provinces.

In the field of communications, the emergence of cable T.V. occasioned two 1978 decisions in which the Court's majority insisted upon the indivisibility of exclusive federal jurisdiction over all aspects of broadcasting. In *Capital Cities Communications*, the Court upheld federal power authorizing the Canadian Radio-Television and Telecommunications Commission (C.R.T.C.) to permit local cable companies to delete advertising from programming picked up from American broadcasts. In the *Dionne* case, the Court ruled that Quebec could not license cable distributors even though they were operating on a strictly local basis within the province. Chief Justice Laskin wrote the majority opinion in both cases. He considered it impractical to separate control of coaxial cable broadcasting or the content of T.V. programming from the exclusive jurisdiction over communications by radio air waves which the Privy Council in the 1932 *Radio* reference assigned to the federal government under Section (10)(a) of the B.N.A. Act. The three Quebec judges dissented in both these cases. In the *Dionne* case Justice Pigeon argued that considerations of practicality were political, not legal, matters and that the provinces should be able to regulate cable T.V. facilities as local works within the province. A third television case in the same year indicated there was a limit to the scope that the Supreme Court was willing to attribute to exclusive federal control over broadcasting. In the *Kelloggs Co.* case, the Court, this time with Chief Justice Laskin and two other judges dissenting, held that regulations passed under Quebec's Consumer Protection Act prohibiting certain kinds of advertising directed at children could validly apply to T.V. broadcasting.

These Supreme Court decisions on broadcasting have also stimulated provincial interest in constitutional change — especially in Quebec, where control over the content of broadcasting is widely regarded as an essential element in provincial control over cultural matters. But no agreement has been reached on the extremely complex issue of defining aspects of broadcasting which could be separated from exclusive federal control and made subject to at least a concurrent provincial jurisdiction.

The most significant provincial gains occurred in two 1978 decisions upholding provincial legislation on matters which closely overlap federal criminal law. The *McNeil* case involved a challenge to Nova Scotia's film censorship regulations which prevented the showing of "Last Tango in Paris." The Court split 5-to-4, the majority upholding the censorship regulations with the exception of one section which it found to be indistinguishable from a section of the federal Criminal Code. In upholding provincial power to censor movies, Justice Ritchie writing for the majority took the position that, "In a country as vast and diverse as Canada, where tastes and standards may vary from one area to another, the determination of what is and what is not acceptable for public exhibition on moral grounds may be viewed as a matter of a 'local and private nature in the Province' within the meaning of Section 92(16) of the B.N.A. Act . . ." In the Dupond case, the Court upheld (6-to-3) a Montreal by-law, which dissenting Chief Justice Laskin referred to as "a mini-Criminal Code." The by-law empowered the city to prohibit assemblies and parades for a period of time when there was reason to believe such gatherings would endanger safety, peace or public order.

These decisions had important civil liberties implications. By continuing a trend towards converting criminal law into a field of concurrent jurisdiction, the Supreme Court moved away from the jurisprudence of the 1950s in which the Court had used exclusive federal power over criminal law as a constitutional limit on provincial laws affecting fundamental freedoms. Further, Justice Beetz's majority opinion in *Dupond* came close to constituting the death knell of the concept of an implied bill of rights in the B.N.A. Act. With reference to the fundamental freedom of speech, Justice Beetz stated that, "None of the freedoms referred to is so enshrined in the Constitution as to be above the reach of competent legislation."

The provinces also scored victories in areas relating to economic powers. In the 1976 case of *Morgan v. P.E.I.*, the Court unanimously upheld provincial power to limit the right of non-residents of the province to buy land in the province. (Although this decision stirred interest in the provision of mobility rights in the Constitution, the actual rights provided for in the new constitutional charter do not extend to land-owning.) The following year, in *Canadian Indemnity Co. v. B.C.*, legislation giving a monopoly control over automobile insurance to British Columbia's Insurance Corporation was found by the Court to be constitutional despite the interprovincial nature of the insurance business. In the same year, for the first time since becoming Canada's highest court of appeal, the Supreme Court found federal legislation unconstitutional in *Macdonald v. Vapor Canada Ltd.* The court unanimously overturned part of the federal Trade Marks Act which in effect established a national code of fair business practices on the grounds that the civil remedies employed by the legislation encroached on exclusive provincial jurisdiction over property and civil rights.

This was not the only federal loss during this period. In two cases decided shortly after the *Vapor Canada* case, the Court found that the federal parliament, in giving the Federal Court of Canada jurisdiction to try suits in which the federal government was a plaintiff, had exceeded its power under Section 101 of the B.N.A. Act to establish courts "for the better Administration of the Laws of Canada." It should be noted that in one of these cases, *McNamara Construction v. The Queen,* the Court reached its decision restricting federal power by explicitly overruling an earlier Supreme Court decision made in 1894.

Perhaps the most significant federal loss occurred in the *Labatts* case reported in 1980. In this case the Court found unconstitutional regulations passed under the Food and Drug Act restricting the use of "light beer" as a generic name to beer with an alcoholic content not exceeding 2.5%. The majority's decision written by Justice Estey imposed a strict limit on the use of the federal trade and commerce power to support a general regulation of trade affecting the whole Dominion where the economic activity involved is not essentially international or interprovincial in character. In these circumstances federal legislation could not be directed at a particular industry like brewing. This decision may seriously curtail the capacity of the federal government to enact consumer protection legislation.

The Canadian Bill of Rights

The increase in cases dealing with the division of powers has not been matched by an increase in cases based on the Canadian Bill of Rights. The Supreme Court's cautious approach to the Bill of Rights has not encouraged lawyers to bring claims based on the Bill before the Court. After the Court's decision in *Lavell and Bedard,* the Supreme Court's reports in the 1970s record only nine decisions on the Bill of Rights. In only one of these, *Cosimo Reale* in 1975, did the Court sustain a claim based on the Bill of Rights. In that case it overturned a conviction on the grounds that a trial judge had not permitted an interpretation of his charge to the jury contrary to section 2(g) of the Bill of Rights.

One of the most significant of the Court's decisions on the Bill of Rights was rendered in 1975 in the *Hogan* case. This case raised the question of whether a court should accept police evidence that has been obtained in a manner which contravenes the Bill of Rights — in this case the right of a person who is arrested or detained to retain and instruct counsel without delay. Hogan had been convicted of impaired driving on the basis of evidence obtained through a breathalyzer test. Before taking the test, he asked for but had been refused access to his lawyer, who was at the police station. The Court's majority refused to give sufficient weight to the Canadian Bill of Rights to modify a principle of criminal evidence which it had developed earlier. This principle was that probative evidence should not be excluded solely on the grounds that it was obtained by the police in an unlawful manner. The Court's decision in the *Hogan* case was a factor in the successful agitation for a clause in the new Charter of Rights giving the courts a discretionary power to exclude police evidence if it was obtained in contravention of entrenched rights and its admission would bring the administration of justice into disrepute.

Two years later the Court dealt a further blow to the Bill of Rights in *Miller and Cockerill v. The Queen.* Here the Court unanimously rejected the argument that Criminal Code provisions retaining the death penalty for the killing of policemen and prison guards (provisions which were subsequently repealed by Parliament) were rendered inoperative by the requirement of Section 2(b) of the Bill of Rights that no law of Canada be construed or applied so as to "impose or authorize the imposition of cruel and unusual punishment." The majority, in an opinion written by Justice Ritchie, seemed to revert to a pre-Drybones position on the general status of the Bill of Rights. Ritchie emphasized that the Bill of Rights was not enacted to create new rights and that therefore the fact that in Canadian history there had never been an absolute right to life meant that it would be wrong to interpret the Bill of Rights as abolishing the death penalty.

Language Rights

The Court's treatment of constitutional language rights was in marked contrast to its restrained approach to the statutory Bill of Rights. In 1979, the Court decided two cases dealing with official bilingualism in Quebec and Manitoba. The *Blaikie* case involved a challenge to a part of Quebec's Charter of the French Language enacted by the P.Q. Government in 1977. The challenged sections were those which made the French language version of laws the only official version and restricted the right of corporate bodies to use English in judicial proceedings. The *Forest* case involved a challenge to Manitoba's Official Language Act enacted in 1890 which went even further in the opposite direction of Quebec's charter in providing for a unilingual English regime in Manitoba. The challenges were based on Section 133 of the B.N.A. Act and Section 23 of the Manitoba Act, 1870, establishing the right to use English and French in the legislature and courts and in the publication of laws in Quebec and Manitoba respectively. The Supreme Court rejected the argument that these constitutional rights were part of the provincial constitution and subject to unilateral amendment by a province under Section 92(1) of the B.N.A. The Supreme Court in both cases found the impugned provisions of the provincial language laws unconstitutional.

The most remarkable feature of the Court's opinions in these cases is the very broad interpretation they gave to entrenched language rights. The Court went well beyond a narrow, literal understanding of the constitutional provisions. It extended the protection of bilingualism in court proceedings to quasi-judicial administrative tribunals and the requirement to print "the Acts" of the legislature in both languages to regulations and other laws passed under delegated legislative powers. The Court stated that this broad approach was justified in dealing with "a constitutional guarantee" and fortified this view by citing some exceptional statements from earlier Privy Council judgments to the effect that the B.N.A. Act should be treated as a "living tree" and given "a broad interpretation attuned to changing circumstances." This language suggests that the Supreme Court might be inclined to be much bolder in interpreting a constitutionally entrenched Charter of Rights than it has been in interpreting the Canadian Bill of Rights.

Amending the Constitution

As the highest judicial arbiter of Canada's constitution, the Supreme Court has faced no more difficult issues than those relating to how the Constitution may be formally changed. Not only are these issues challenging in the sense that there is little by way of established jurisprudence to guide the Court, but also they are issues which touch the most tender political nerves of the nation.

In November 1978 the federal government referred to the Supreme Court a number of questions as to whether the federal Parliament under the limited power conferred on it in 1949 to amend the "Constitution of Canada" could abolish the Senate or replace it with a new kind of federal Upper House more directly representative of the provinces. Such a proposal had been included in the Constitutional Amendment Bill of 1978 which Mr. Trudeau proposed to have enacted by the Parliament of Canada as the first phase of establishing a new Canadian Constitution. The reference to the Court arose when doubts were expressed about the power of Parliament to unilaterally repeal or replace the Senate. The reference questions did not focus on the specific terms of Mr. Trudeau's proposal but canvassed a number of possible upper-house models including some proposed by the provinces.

In answering these questions the Court gave a very restricted interpretation of the federal Parliament's power under Section 91(1) of the B.N.A. Act to amend the Constitution of Canada. The Court held that this power "is limited to matters of interest only to the federal Government." Because the historic purpose of the Senate was to ensure regional and provincial representation in the Senate, the Court concluded that the Senate's fundamental character "cannot be altered by unilateral action by the Parliament of Canada and Section 91(1) does not give that power."

In the Spring of 1981 the Court faced what may be the most momentous judicial decision in Canadian history. The question in this case dealt not with the federal Parliament's powers under Section 91(1) to amend the constitution in Canada, but with its power to proceed unilaterally with a request to the British Parliament to make some fundamental changes in the constitution. These changes included the patriation of Canada's constitution with a comprehensive amendment formula, a charter of rights and freedoms, a commitment to equalization grants and additions to provincial powers over natural resources. The basic question before the Court was whether there was a constitutional requirement of provincial agreement for an amendment which affects federal-provincial relationships or alters the powers of the provinces. This question had been put before three provincial Courts of Appeal by provincial governments that opposed the unilateral federal initiative. The Manitoba and Quebec Courts in 3-to-2 and 4-to-1 decisions denied that there was such a constitutional requirement, whereas the three judges of Newfoundland's Court held that there was. These decisions were appealed to the Supreme Court of Canada. As the result of an agreement amongst the parliamentary parties following months of debate and a prolonged parliamentary deadlock, final passage of the constitutional resolution was postponed until the Supreme Court rendered its decision.

[For the Supreme Court's decisions, see the next item.]

CONSTITUTIONAL DECISIONS, SEPTEMBER 28, 1981*

Supreme Court of Canada

Attorney General of Manitoba et al. v. Attorney General of Canada et al.

A. The Question of Law

THE CHIEF JUSTICE and DICKSON, BEETZ, ESTEY,
McINTYRE, CHOUINARD and LAMER JJ.

I

Three appeals as of right are before this Court, concerning in the main common issues. They arise out of three References made, respectively, to the Manitoba Court of Appeal, to the Newfoundland Court of Appeal and to the Quebec Court of Appeal by the respective Governments of the three Provinces.

Three questions were posed in the Manitoba Reference, as follows:

1. If the amendments to the Constitution of Canada sought in the "Proposed Resolution for a Joint Address to Her Majesty the Queen respecting the Constitution of Canada," or any of them, were enacted, would federal-provincial relationships or the powers, rights or privileges granted or secured by the Constitution of Canada to the provinces, their legislatures or governments be affected and if so, in what respect or respects?

2. Is it a constitutional convention that the House of Commons and Senate of Canada will not request Her Majesty the Queen to lay before the Parliament of the United Kingdom of Great Britain and Northern Ireland a measure to amend the Constitution of Canada affecting federal-provincial relationships or the powers, rights or privileges granted or secured by the Constitution of Canada to the provinces, their legislatures or governments without first obtaining the agreement of the provinces?

3. Is the agreement of the provinces of Canada constitutionally required for amendment to the Constitution of Canada where such amendment affects federal-provincial relationships or alters the powers, rights or privileges granted or secured by the Constitution of Canada to the provinces, their legislatures or governments?

The same three questions were asked in the Newfoundland Reference and, in addition, a fourth question was put in these terms:

4. If Part V of the proposed resolution referred to in question 1 is enacted and proclaimed into force could

   (a) the Terms of Union, including terms 2 and 17 thereof contained in the Schedule to the British North America Act 1949 (12 - 13 George VI, c. 22 (U.K.)), or

---

* Extract from the Supreme Court of Canada, *Constitutional Decisions, September 28, 1981*, Ottawa, Supply and Services, 1981, which is a publication prior to the printing of the official version of the reasons for the Court's judgment in the *Supreme Court Reports*. This extract gives only the decisions, not the reasoning. Reproduced by permission of the Minister of Supply and Services Canada.

(b) section 3 of the British North America Act, 1871 (34-35 Victoria, c. 28 (U.K.))
be amended directly or indirectly pursuant to Part V without the consent of the Government, Legislature or a majority of the people of the Province of Newfoundland voting in a referendum held pursuant to Part V?

In the Quebec Reference there was a different formulation, two questions being asked which read:

Translation

A.   If the Canada Act and the Constitution Act 1981 should come into force and if they should be valid in all respects in Canada would they affect:
(i) the legislative competence of the provincial legislatures in virtue of the Canadian Constitution?
(ii) the status or role of the provincial legislatures or governments within the Canadian Federation?
B.   Does the Canadian Constitution empower, whether by statute, convention or otherwise, the Senate and the House of Commons of Canada to cause the Canadian Constitution to be amended without the consent of the provinces and in spite of the objection of several of them, in such a manner as to affect:
(i) the legislative competence of the provincial legislatures in virtue of the Canadian Constitution?
(ii) the status or role of the provincial legislatures or governments within the Canadian Federation?

The answers given by the Judges of the Manitoba Court of Appeal, each of whom wrote reasons, are as follows:

Freedman C.J.M.:
Question 1 — Not answered, because it is tentative and premature.
Question 2 — No
Question 3 — No

Hall, J.A.:
Question 1 — Not answered because it is not appropriate for judicial response, and, in any event, the question is speculative and premature.
Question 2 — Not answered because it is not appropriate for judicial response.
Question 3 — No, because there is no legal requirement of provincial agreement to amendment of the Constitution as asserted in the question.

Matas, J.A.:
Question 1 — Not answered, because it is speculative and premature.
Question 2 — No
Question 3 — No

O'Sullivan, J.A.:

Question 1 — Yes, as set out in reasons.

Question 2 — The constitutional convention referred to has not been established as a matter simply of precedent; it is, however, a constitutional principle binding in law that the House of Commons and Senate of Canada should not request Her Majesty the Queen to lay before the Parliament of the United Kingdom of Great Britain and Northern Ireland any measure to amend the Constitution of Canada affecting federal-provincial relationships or the powers, rights or privileges granted or secured by the Constitution of Canada to the provinces, their legislatures or governments without first obtaining the agreement of the provinces.

Question 3 — Yes, as set out in reasons.

Huband, J.A.:

Question 1 — Yes

Question 2 — No

Question 3 — Yes

The Newfoundland Court of Appeal, in reasons of the Court concurred in by all three Judges who sat on the Reference, answered all three questions common to the Manitoba Reference in the affirmative. The Court answered the fourth question in this way:

(1) By Sec. 3 of the British North America Act, 1871, *Term 2* of the Terms of Union cannot now be changed without the consent of the Newfoundland legislature.

(2) By Sec. 43 of the "Constitution Act," as it now reads, none of the Terms of Union can be changed without the consent of the Newfoundland Legislative Assembly.

(3) Both of these sections can be changed by the amending formulae prescribed in Sec. 41 and the Terms of Union could then be changed without the consent of the Newfoundland Legislature.

(4) If the amending formula under Sec. 42 is utilized, both of these sections can be changed by a referendum held pursuant to the provisions of Sec. 42. In this event, the Terms of Union could then be changed without the consent of the Newfoundland Legislature, but not without the consent of the majority of the Newfoundland people voting in a referendum.

The Quebec Court of Appeal, in reasons delivered by each of the five Judges who sat on the Reference, answered the two questions submitted to it as follows:

Translation

Question A   i) yes   (unanimously)
             ii) yes   (unanimously)

Question B   i) yes   (Bisson J.A. dissenting would answer no)
             ii) yes   (Bisson J.A. dissenting would answer no)

II

The References in question here were prompted by the opposition of six Provinces, later joined by two others, to a proposed Resolution which was published on October 2, 1980 and intended for submission to the House of Commons and as well to the Senate of Canada. It contained an address to be presented to Her Majesty The Queen in right of the United Kingdom respecting what may generally be referred to as the Constitution of Canada. The address laid before the House of Commons on October 6, 1980, was in these terms:

> To the Queen's Most Excellent Majesty:
> Most Gracious Sovereign:

> We, Your Majesty's loyal subjects, the House of Commons of Canada in Parliament assembled, respectfully approach Your Majesty, requesting that you may graciously be pleased to cause to be laid before the Parliament of the United Kingdom a measure containing the recitals and clauses hereinafter set forth:

> An Act to give effect to a request by the Senate and House of Commons of Canada

> Whereas Canada has requested and consented to the enactment of an Act of the Parliament of the United Kingdom to give effect to the provisions hereinafter set forth and the Senate and the House of Commons of Canada in Parliament assembled have submitted an address to Her Majesty requesting that Her Majesty may graciously be pleased to cause a Bill to be laid before the Parliament of the United Kingdom for that purpose.

> Be it therefore enacted by the Queen's Most Excellent Majesty, by and with the advice and consent of the Lords Spiritual and Temporal, and Commons, in this present Parliament assembled, and by the authority of the same, as follows. . . .

• • •

. . . The law knows nothing of any requirement of provincial consent, either to a resolution of the federal Houses or as a condition of the exercise of United Kingdom legislative power.

In the result, the third question in the Manitoba and Newfoundland cases should, as a matter of law, be answered in the negative and question B should, in its legal aspect, be answered in the affirmative. . . .

• • •

In summary, the answers to Questions 1 and 3 common to the Manitoba and Newfoundland References, should be as follows:

Question 1:   Yes
Question 3:   As a matter of law, no.

The answer to question 4 in the Newfoundland Reference should be as expressed in the reasons of the Newfoundland Court of Appeal, subject to the correction made in the reasons herein.

The answers to the questions in the Quebec Reference should be as follows:

Question A   (i): Yes.
              (ii): Yes.

Question B   (i): As a matter of law, yes.
              (ii): As a matter of law, yes.
There will be, of course, no order as to costs.

• • •

MARTLAND AND RITCHIE JJ. (Dissenting):

Conclusions:

. . . The fact that the status of Canada became recognized as a sovereign state did not alter its federal nature. It is a sovereign state, but its government is federal in character with a clear division of legislative powers. The Resolution at issue in these appeals could only be an effective expression of Canadian sovereignty if it had the support of both levels of government.

The two Houses of the Canadian Parliament claim the power unilaterally to effect an amendment to the B.N.A. Act which they desire, including the curtailment of Provincial legislative powers. This strikes at the basis of the whole federal system. It asserts a right by one part of the Canadian governmental system to curtail, without agreement, the powers of the other part.

There is no statutory basis for the exercise of such a power. On the contrary, the powers of the Senate and the House of Commons, given to them by paragraph 4(a) of the *Senate and House of Commons Act,* excluded the power to do anything inconsistent with the B.N.A. Act. The exercise of such a power has no support in constitutional convention. The constitutional convention is entirely to the contrary. We see no other basis for the recognition of the existence of such a power. This being so, it is the proper function of this Court, in its role of protecting and preserving the Canadian Constitution, to declare that no such power exists. We are, therefore, of the opinion that the Canadian Constitution does not empower the Senate and the House of Commons to cause the Canadian Constitution to be amended in respect of Provincial legislative powers without the consent of the Provinces.

Question B in the Quebec Reference raises the issue as to the power of the Senate and the House of Commons of Canada to cause the Canadian Constitution to be amended "without the consent of the provinces and in spite of the objection of several of them." The Attorney General of Saskatchewan when dealing with Question 3 in the Manitoba and Newfoundland

References submitted that it was not necessary in these proceedings for the Court to pronounce on the necessity for the unanimous consent of all the Provinces to the constitutional amendments proposed in the Resolution. It was sufficient, in order to answer the Question, to note the opposition of eight of the provinces which contained a majority of the population of Canada.

We would answer Question B in the negative. We would answer Question 3 of the Manitoba and Newfoundland References in the affirmative without deciding, at this time, whether the agreement referred to in that Question must be unanimous.

B. The Question of Convention

MARTLAND, RITCHIE, DICKSON, BEETZ, CHOUINARD and LAMER JJ.

The second question in the Manitoba Reference and Newfoundland Reference is the same:

2. Is it a constitutional convention that the House of Commons and Senate of Canada will not request Her Majesty the Queen to lay before the Parliament of the United Kingdom of Great Britain and Northern Ireland a measure to amend the Constitution of Canada affecting federal-provincial relationships or the powers, rights or privileges granted or secured by the Constitution of Canada to the provinces, their legislatures of governments without first obtaining the agreement of the provinces?

As for question B in the Quebec Reference, it reads in part as follows:

Translation

B.   Does the Canadian Constitution empower . . . by . . . convention . . . the Senate and the House of Commons of Canada to cause the Canadian Constitution to be amended without the consent of the provinces and in spite of the objection of several of them, in such a manner as to affect:

(i)   the legislative competence of the provincial legislatures in virtue of the Canadian Constitution?

(ii)   the status or role of the provincial legislatures or governments within the Canadian Federation?

In these questions, the phrases "Constitution of Canada" and "Canadian Constitution" do not refer to matters of interest only to the federal government or federal juristic unit. They are clearly meant in a broader sense and embrace the global system of rules and principles which govern the exercise of constitutional authority in the whole and in the same broad sense in these reasons.

The meaning of the second question in the Manitoba and Newfoundland References calls for further observations. . . .

• • •

It was contended by Counsel for Canada, Ontario and New Brunswick that the proposed amendments would not offend the federal principle and that, if they became law, Canada would remain a federation. The federation principle would even be re-inforced, it was said, since the provinces would as a matter of law be given an important role in the amending formula.

It is true that Canada would remain a federation if the proposed amendments became law. But it would be a different federation made different at the instance of a majority in the Houses of the federal Parliament acting alone. It is this process itself which offends the federal principle.

It was suggested by Counsel for Saskatchewan that the proposed amendments were perhaps severable; that the proposed *Charter of Rights* offended the federal principle in that it would unilaterally alter legislative powers whereas the proposed amending formula did not offend the federal principle.

To this suggestion we cannot accede. Counsel for Canada (as well as Counsel for other parties and all intervenors) took the firm position that the proposed amendment formed an unseverable package. Furthermore, and to repeat, whatever the result, the process offends the federal principle. It was to guard against this process that the constitutional convention came about.

Conclusion

We have reached the conclusion that the agreement of the provinces of Canada, no views being expressed as to its quantification, is constitutionally required for the passing of the "Proposed Resolution for a joint Address to Her Majesty respecting the Constitution of Canada" and that the passing of this Resolution without such agreement would be unconstitutional in the conventional sense.

We would, subject to these reasons, answer question 2 of the Manitoba and Newfoundland References and that part of question B in the Quebec Reference which relates to conventions as follows:

2. Is it a constitutional convention that the House of Commons and Senate of Canada will not request Her Majesty the Queen to lay before the Parliament of the United Kingdom of Great Britain and Northern Ireland a measure to amend the Constitution of Canada affecting federal-provincial relationships or the powers, rights or privileges granted or secured by the Constitution of Canada to the provinces, their legislatures or governments without first obtaining the agreement of the provinces?

YES

B. Does the Canadian Constitution empower . . .by. . . convention
. . . the Senate and the House of Commons of Canada to cause the
Canadian Constitution to be amended without the consent of the
provinces and in spite of the objection of several of them, in such a
manner as to affect:

(i) the legislative competence of the provincial legislatures in virtue of
the Canadian Constitution?

(ii) the status or role of the provincial legislatures or governments
within the Canadian Federation?

NO

THE CHIEF JUSTICE AND ESTEY AND McINTYRE JJ. (Dissenting):

These reasons are addressed solely to Question 2 in the Manitoba and Newfoundland References and the conventional segment of Question B in the
Quebec Reference. Our views upon the other questions raised in the three
References are expressed in another judgment. As will be pointed out later,
no legal question is raised in the questions under consideration in these
reasons and, ordinarily, the Court would not undertake to answer them
for it is not the function of the Court to go beyond legal determinations.
Because of the unusual nature of these References and because the issues
raised in the questions now before us were argued at some length before
the Court and have become the subject of the reasons of the majority, with
which, with the utmost deference, we cannot agree, we feel obliged to answer the questions notwithstanding their extra-legal nature.

• • •

. . . We therefore reject the argument that the preservation of the principles of Canadian federalism requires the recognition of the convention
asserted before us.

While it may not be necessary to do so in dealing with Question 2, we feel
obliged to make a further comment related to the federalism argument. It
was argued that the federal authorities were assuming a power to act
without restraint in disregard of provincial wishes which could go so far as
to convert Canada into a unitary state by means of a majority vote in the
Houses of Parliament. A few words will suffice to lay that argument at rest.
What is before the Court is the task of answering the questions posed in
three references. As has been pointed out, the Court can do no more than
that. The questions all deal with the constitutional validity of precise proposals for constitutional amendment and they form the complete subject-
matter of the Court's inquiry and our comments must be made with
reference to them. It is not for the Court to express views on the wisdom or
lack of wisdom of these proposals. We are concerned solely with their constitutionality. In view of the fact that the unitary argument has been raised,
however, it should be noted, in our view, that the federal constitutional proposals, which preserve a federal state without disturbing the distribution or

balance of power, would create an amending formula which would enshrine provincial rights on the question of amendments on a secure, legal and constitutional footing, and would extinguish, as well, any presently existing power on the part of the federal Parliament to act unilaterally in constitutional matters. In so doing, it may be said that the Parliamentary resolution here under examination does not, save for the enactment of the *Charter of Rights,* which circumscribes the legislative powers of both the federal and provincial Legislatures, truly amend the Canadian Constitution. Its effect is to complete the formation of an incomplete constitution by supplying its present deficiency, *i.e.* an amending formula, which will enable the Constitution to be amended in Canada as befits a sovereign state. We are not here faced with an action which in any way has the effect of transforming this federal union into a unitary state. The *in terrorem* argument raising the spectre of a unitary state has no validity.

For the above reasons we answer the questions posed in the three References as follows:

Manitoba and Newfoundland References:
Question 2: No

Quebec Reference
Question B (i): Yes
        (ii): Yes

BIBLIOGRAPHY

(See also the Bibliography in Chapter 2)

The Courts and Judicial Review

Angus, W.H., "The Individual and the Bureaucracy: Judicial Review — Do We Need It?,"*McG.L.J.*, 20, 2, 1974.

Arvay, J., "Newfoundland's Claim to Offshore Mineral Resources: An Overview of the Legal Issues," *C.P.P.*, V, 1, Winter, 1979.

Barnes, J., "The Law Reform Commission of Canada," *Dalhousie Law Journal*, 2, 1, February, 1975.

Barr, C., "Patterns and Strategies of Court Administration in Canada and the United States," *C.P.A.*, 20, 2, Summer, 1977.

Bossard, J., *La Cour Suprême et la Constitution*, Montréal, Les Presses de L'Université de Montréal, 1968.

Browne, G.P., *The Judicial Committee and the British North America Act,* Toronto, U.T.P., 1967.

Cairns, A.C., "The Judicial Committee and Its Critics," *C.J.P.S.*, IV, 3, September, 1971.

Canada, Law Reform Commission, *Working Papers,* No. 1-14, 1974-74.

Centre for International Business Studies, *The Future of the Offshore: Legal Developments and Canadian Business,* Halifax, Dalhousie University, 1978.

Cheffins, R.I., "The Supreme Court of Canada: The Quiet Court in an Unquiet Country." *Osgoode Hall Law Journal, IV,* 2 September, 1966.

Cheffins, R.I., and Tucker, R.N., *The Constitutional Process in Canada,* Toronto, McG.-H.R., 2nd ed., 1975.

Gertner, E., and Belobaba, (eds.), *The Supreme Court Law Review,* Toronto, Butterworths, Vol. I, 1980; Vol. 2, 1981.

Gibson, D., "— and One Step Backward: The Supreme Court and Constitutional Law in the Sixties," *C.B.R.*, LIII, 3, September, 1975.

Gower, L.C.B., "Reflections on Law Reform," *U. of T. Law Journal*, 23, 1973.

Grant, J.A.C., "Judicial Review in Canada: Procedural Aspects," *C.B.R.*, XLIII, 2, May, 1964.

Griffiths, C.T., Klein, J.F., Verdun-Jones, S.N., *Criminal Justice in Canada*, Toronto, Butterworths, 1980.

Hall, E.M., "Law Reform and the Judiciary's Role," *Osgoode Hall Law Journal*, 10, 2, 1972.

Hogarth, J., *Sentencing as a Human Process*, U.T.P., 1971.

Hogg, P.W., "Judicial Review: How Much Do We Need?," *McG.L.J.*, 20, 2, 1974.

Hunter, I.A., "Judicial Review of Human Rights Legislation: McKay v. Bell," *University of British Columbia Law Review*, 7, 1, 1972.

Joanes, A., "Stare Decisis in the Supreme Court of Canada," *C.B.R.*, XXXVI, 2, May, 1958.

Laskin, B., *Canadian Constitutional Law: Cases, Text and Notes on Distribution of Legislative Power*, Toronto, Carswell, 4th ed., 1973.

Laskin, B., "The Supreme Court of Canada: A Final Court of and for Canadians," *C.B.R.*, XXIX, 10, December, 1951.

Laskin, B., "The Role and Functions of Final Appellate Courts: The Supreme Court of Canada," *C.B.R.*, LIII, 3, September, 1975.

Laskin, B., "The Supreme Court: The First Hundred Years," *C.B.R.*, LIII, 3, September, 1975.

Law Reform Commission, *Judicial Review and the Federal Court*, Ottawa, S. and S., 1980.

Lederman, W.R., *The Courts and the Canadian Constitution*, Toronto, M. & S., 1964.

Lederman, W.R., "Continuing Constitutional Dilemmas: The Supreme Court and the Federal Anti-Inflation Act of 1975," *Q.Q.*, 84, 1, Spring, 1977.

Logan, G.R., "Historical Sketch of the Supreme Court of Canada," *Osgoode Hall Law Journal*, III, 1964.

MacDonald, V.C., "The Privy Council and the Canadian Constitution," *C.B.R.*, XXXIX, 10, December, 1951.

MacDonald, V.C., *Legislative Power and the Supreme Court in the Fifties*, Toronto, Butterworths, 1961.

MacGuigan, M., "Precedent and Policy in the Supreme Court," *C.B.R.*, XLV, 1967.

MacKinnon, F., "The Establishment of the Supreme Court of Canada," *Canadian Historical Review*, XXVII, 1946.

McNaught, K., "Political Trials and the Canadian Political Tradition," *U. of T. Law Journal*, 24, 1974.

McWhinney, E., "A Supreme Court in a Bicultural Society: The Future Role of the Canadian Supreme Court," in Ontario Advisory Committee on Confederation, *Background Papers and Reports*, Toronto, Q.P., Vol. I, 1967.

McWhinney, E., "The New Pluralistic Federalism in Canada," *La Revue Juridique Themis*, II, 1967.

McWhinney, E., *Judicial Review in the English-Speaking World*, Toronto, U.T.P., 4th ed., 1969.

Millar, P.S., and Baar, C., *Judicial Administration in Canada*, Montreal, McG.-Q.U.P., 1981.

Mitchell, C.M., "The Role of the Courts in Public Policy Making: A Personal View," *U. of T. Faculty of Law Review*, 33, 1, Spring, 1975.

Morin, J.-Y., "A Constitutional Court for Canada," *C.B.R.*, XLIII, 1965.

Mullan, D.J., *The Federal Court Act: A Study of the Court's Administrative Law Jurisdiction*, Ottawa, Law Reform Commission, 1978.

Olmsted, R.A., *Decisions relating to the BNA Act, 1867, and the Canadian Constitution, 1867-1954*, Ottawa, Q.P., 1954, 3 vols.

Paus-Jenssen, A., "Resource Taxation and the Supreme Court of Canada: The Cigol Case," *C.P.P.*, V, 1, Winter, 1979.

Peck, S.R., "A Behavioural Approach to the Judicial Process: Scalogram Analysis," *Osgoode Hall Law Journal*, V, 1, April, 1967.

Peck, S.R., "The Supreme Court of Canada, 1958-1966: A Search for Policy through Scalogram Analysis," *C.B.R.*, XLV, December, 1967.

Read, H., "The Judicial Process in Common Law Canada," *C.B.R.*, XXXVII, 1959.

Russell, P.H., "The Jurisdiction of the Supreme Court of Canada: Present Policies and a Programme for Reform," *Osgoode Hall Law Journal*, VI, 1, October, 1968.

Russell, P.H., *Bilingualism and Biculturalism in the Supreme Court of Canada*, Document of the Royal Commission on Bilingualism and Biculturalism, Ottawa, Q.P., 1970.

Russell, P.H., "The Political Role of the Supreme Court in its First Century," *C.B.R.*, LIII, 3, September, 1975.

Russell, P.H., (ed.), *Leading Constitutional Decisions*, Ottawa, Carleton Library Series, revised and enlarged ed., 1982.

Russell, P.H., "The Anti-Inflation Case: The Anatomy of a Constitutional Decision," *C.P.A.*, 20, 4, Winter, 1977.

Russell, P.H., "History and Development of the Court in National Society: The Canadian Supreme Court," *Canada-United States Law Journal*, 3, Summer, 1980.

Scott, F.R., "Centralization and Decentralization in Canadian Federalism," *C.B.R.*, XXIX, 10, December, 1951.

Senate of Canada, *Report to the Honourable Speaker Relating to the Enactment of the British North America Act, 1867*, [O'Connor Report], Ottawa, Q.P., 1939.

Slayton, P., "Quantitative Methods and Supreme Court Cases," *Osgoode Hall Law Journal*, 10, 2, 1972.

Snell, J.G., "The Deputy Head in the Canadian Bureaucracy: A Case Study of the Registrar of the Supreme Court of Canada," *C.P.A.*, 24, 2, Summer, 1981.

Strayer, B.L., *Judicial Review of Legislation in Canada*, Toronto, U.T.P., 1969.

Tarnopolsky, W.S., "The Supreme Court and the Canadian Bill of Rights," *C.B.R.*, LIII, 4, December, 1975.

Weiler, P., *In the Last Resort*, Toronto, Carswell-Methuen, 1974.

Weiler, P., "The Supreme Court and the Law of Canadian Federalism," *U. of T. Law Journal*, 23, 1973.

Judiciary

Angus, W.H., "Judicial Selection in Canada — The Historical Perspective," Address to the Annual Meeting of the Association of Canada Law Teachers, Sherbrooke, P.Q., June 10, 1966.

Jaffary, S.K., *Sentencing of Adults in Canada*, Toronto, U.T.P., 1963.

Lederman, W.R., "The Independence of the Judiciary," *C.B.R.*, XXXIV, 7, August-September, 1956 and 10, December, 1956.

Russell, P.H., "Constitutional Reform of the Canadian Judiciary," *Alberta Law Review*, VII, 1, January, 1969.

Turner, J., *The Federal Court of Canada, A Manual of Practice*, Ottawa, I.C., 1971.

17

PROTECTING CIVIL RIGHTS

For many years Canadians debated whether or not we should have a bill of rights entrenched in the constitution. The pace in favour of such a move picked up when Mr. Trudeau introduced his charter of human rights in 1968. Despite the prime minister's strong personal conviction and advocacy, however, the provinces stoutly resisted his repeated attempts at constitutional conferences to persuade them. They were both unsympathetic to the rigidity of entrenchment and fearful of the potential infringement of their jurisdiction over property and civil rights.

The long-standing debate was finally resolved in November 1981 when the federal government and all of the provinces except Quebec agreed on the substance of the new *Constitution Act, 1981 (Canada Act)* which was approved by the Canadian Parliament in December 1981 and by the United Kingdom Parliament in 1982. Since Part I of the *Constitution Act, 1982* is in fact the *Canadian Charter of Rights and Freedoms*, a bill of rights is now embedded firmly in our new constitution in a prime position.

(For the *Constitution Act, 1981,* including the *Charter,* see *supra,* Chapter 2, where the entire text is reprinted verbatim.)

It remains to be seen whether the *Charter* will fulfill the expectations of those who argued that a bill of rights must be entrenched in the constitution if civil rights are to be protected effectively. Prime Minister Trudeau's adherents certainly believed so, preferring the American and European model of a written, constitutional bill of rights to the existing Canadian practice, inherited from Britain, of resting the protection on judicial interpretation of common law and ordinary statutes. Proponents of entrenchment pointed for support to the Canadian Bill of Rights which was enacted by Prime Minister Diefenbaker's government in 1960 (see the fourth edition of *Politics: Canada,* pp. 557-559) and claimed that it had proved to be ineffectual largely because it was only a mere statute. On the other hand, advocates of the common law tradition argued that constitutional entrenchment gave the judiciary too much power in interpreting the meaning of a bill of rights and that it was preferable, and certainly more democratic and adaptive to changing circumstances, to leave the determination of rights to elected legislatures that could pass laws to establish them and alter them from time to time as conditions and public attitudes warranted. (See D.V. Smiley's excellent exposition of this point of view in his article, "The Case Against the Canadian Charter of Human Rights," in the fourth edition of this book, pp. 567-577.)

It will not be clear which opinion is closer to the truth until the *Charter* has been tested in the courts over a period of years. The outcome will be less categoric than it might have been since the final phase of constitution- making softened considerably the significance of entrenchment. To win provincial assent to the inclusion of any charter in the new constitution, Prime Minister Trudeau was forced to give way on some fundamental points. Thus, in the final draft, the provinces and the federal government were accorded the power to override by legislation some of the most important clauses in the *Charter*, notably section 2 and sections 7 to 15, which list Canadians' fundamental freedoms, legal rights, and equality rights. To permit constitutional rights to be overriden by simple statute makes a mockery of entrenchment, of course. One may well ask why the fathers of the new constitution bothered even to include a charter. The answer from Mr. Trudeau's point of view undoubtedly would be that it is better to have a symbolic charter in the constitution than no charter at all.

However inconclusive as yet the adoption of the *Charter* may be, it does at least mark the end of the theoretical debate about the wisdom of having rights incorporated in a constitution. For that reason this chapter omits a number of items which were included in the fourth edition, pp. 557-577, namely, the Diefenbaker Bill of Rights, Prime Minister Trudeau's proposed charter in 1968, and Professor Smiley's arguments against it.

This chapter does retain, however, two items which appeared in the fourth edition: Rae Corelli's article, "How an Indian Changed Canada's Civil Rights Laws — The Drybones Case," and the Supreme Court's decisions in the Lavell and Bedard cases. Not only are these Supreme Court decisions significant milestones in the litigation of civil rights in Canada but they illustrate some of the issues which undoubtedly will emerge when the courts begin adjudicating the new *Canadian Charter of Rights and Freedoms*. In Drybones the Supreme Court majority suddenly found an imperative in Mr. Diefenbaker's hitherto neglected Bill of Rights which upset a long-standing statute, the Indian Act. In Lavell and Bedard the Court seemed to reverse itself. However, the 5-4 decision was so close and the opposing points of view so convincingly argued that it is a splendid intellectual exercise for a student to read the contradictory judgements and then ask himself or herself, with whom do I agree and why? The finely honed reasoning and conflicting opinions in these cases will no doubt be repeated when the courts commence to interpret the *Charter*.

The final item in this chapter illustrates the work of the Canadian Human Rights Commission which was established in 1978 to assist in protecting civil rights.

Readers should consult also Chapter 16 for a discussion of the Supreme Court's role in civil libertarian cases. Students should see also the comments and proposals about fundamental rights made by the Special Joint Committee of the Senate and the House of Commons in its *Final Report,* Ottawa, Information Canada, 1972, Chapter 9.

References to recent books and articles on civil rights are given in the bibliography at the end of this chapter.

HOW AN INDIAN CHANGED CANADA'S CIVIL RIGHTS LAWS — THE DRYBONES CASE*

Rae Corelli

It was a fateful moment for Canada when, early in the morning of April 10, 1967, Joe Drybones was convicted of having been drunk in a public place (viz., the lobby floor in the Old Stope Hotel in Yellowknife) and fined $10.

* From *The Toronto Star,* January 2, 1970. By permission of the publisher.

Because that was the first act in a 2½ year courtroom drama which was to propel Canada onto the threshold of a revolution in the field of law and civil rights.

The last act was performed six weeks ago by the Supreme Court of Canada which ordered the conviction quashed and the fine refunded on the grounds that the 42-year-old bespectacled and illiterate Indian had been denied equality before the law.

The court's authority for that historic decision?

None other than the much-maligned and ridiculed Canadian Bill of Rights. From the day it was enacted by John Diefenbaker's Progressive Conservative government nearly 10 years ago, the bill had been so thoroughly shunned by the courts that it had virtually no force or effect in Canadian law.

Lawyers had despaired of ever winning a case on the strength of it even though its guarantees of human rights and fundamental freedoms were supposed to take precedence, or so it seemed, over all other federal laws.

The trouble was that no court had ever placed that interpretation on it — until six weeks ago, that is, when the Supreme Court of Canada said that's exactly what the words in the bill meant.

Legal scholars and constitutional law experts across the nation have been excitedly studying the 6-to-3 decision for weeks and now they say it may have an impact on the administration of justice in Canada far beyond their first impressions.

For instance, these experts say, by giving to the Bill of Rights the meaning it did, the Supreme Court of Canada has also given itself — and all other courts in the country — the unprecedented power to over-rule Parliament and throw out unjust federal laws. (The Bill of Rights doesn't apply to provincial law.)

The significance of that is that the day may come when you will be freed by a court — not because you are necessarily innocent but because the law under which you were charged has been found to be discriminatory or manifestly unjust or unduly restrictive.

Says Justice Minister John Turner: "This extremely important decision by the Supreme Court of Canada establishes the paramountcy in law of the Bill of Rights as it relates to federal legislation . . . "

To understand why the decision excites legal experts and where it may conceivably lead, let's examine the bizarre saga of Joe Drybones.

After the RCMP lugged the unconscious Indian away from the Old Stope Hotel (where owner Fred Rasche used to quell mutineers by raining blows on the splintered bar with a five-pound sledge-hammer), they charged him with violating a section of the Indian Act which makes it unlawful for Indians to be drunk off a reservation.

(Since there are no reservations in the Northwest Territories, it's impossible for an Indian to be legally drunk anywhere, including his own home.)

Joe Drybones was convicted, fined the statutory minimum of $10 and let go the following Monday morning (he got boiled on Saturday night). Later that day, lawyer Brian Purdy, a 27-year-old native of Toronto and a graduate of Halifax's Dalhousie University law school, noticed the record of Drybone's conviction in the Yellowknife court office.

It suddenly struck him, Purdy said afterward, that the Indian Act was discriminatory because it contained harsher penalties for drunkenness than those contained in the territorial liquor ordinances under which white men were prosecuted. (For one thing, the white man's law contains no minimum fines.)

Purdy went to see Drybones and explained through an interpreter the law as he saw it. Joe, who didn't have a lawyer at his trial, decided to appeal the conviction.

The appeal was heard June 5 at Yellowknife by Mr. Justice William G. Morrow of the Territorial Court. Purdy based his case largely on section 1 of the Bill of Rights which guarantees "the right of the individual to equality before the law."

Drybones, Purdy said, had enjoyed no such equality. Moreover, he argued, the Bill of Rights is supposed to take precedence over every other law of Canada unless Parliament explicitly decrees otherwise.

Since the Indian Act contained no such decree, Purdy said, the section had to give way to the Bill of Rights and the conviction against Drybones should therefore be set aside.

Morrow agreed. "This portion of the Indian Act is to me a case of discrimination of sufficient seriousness that I must hold that the intoxication sections of the Indian Act (violate) the Canadian Bill of Rights," he said in his judgment.

The crown appealed Morrow's decision to the Territorial Court of Appeal which comprised Chief Justice Sidney Bruce Smith of the Alberta Court of Appeal and two of his colleagues.

Drybones won again. The appeal court said that while it was Canadian government policy to treat Indians differently (often for their own protection) "one would have hoped that that could have been done without subjecting Indians to penalties and punishments different to those imposed on other races."

That judgment finally got the attention of the federal justice department in Ottawa and it launched last-ditch appeal proceedings before the Supreme Court of Canada.

On Oct. 28, 1968, G. Brian Purdy, three years at the bar, found himself in the panelled chambers of the highest court in the nation. Opposing him was a justice department team headed by Assistant Deputy Attorney-General Donald H. Christie.

Chief Justice John R. Cartwright, believing the issue had far-reaching implications for both the courts and the law of the country, had taken the unusual step of assembling all nine judges to hear the argument. Grave and attentive, they gazed down from the 35-foot-wide elevated bench ranged across the end of the chamber.

"It was enough to scare you right out of your socks," said Purdy.

Purdy's entire case was a single sentence 13 typewritten lines long. In it, he repeated his contention that because the Indian Act imposed a more severe penalty than the territorial liquor ordinance, it therefore violated the Bill of Rights and its offending sections should be declared "inoperative."

Then Christie presented the government's case, the court rose and everyone went home to await the decision.

On New Year's Day, 1969, the Old Stope Hotel caught fire and burned to the ground.

All over the Northwest Territories, drunk prosecutions under the Indian Act piled up but were not proceeded with because the Crown was awaiting word on the fate of the law.

Joe Drybones, meanwhile, had long since got his $10 back and had lost interest in the whole affair. Purdy says he doubts whether Joe really comprehended what was going on or, for that matter, if he really knew or cared that there was such a thing as the Supreme Court of Canada.

(In January, 1968, Purdy and a bush pilot spent most of one day scouting the snow desert around Yellowknife by plane, looking for Joe so they could serve him with the notice of the Crown's appeal to the Ottawa court. They finally found him by following his dog-team tracks. "Since he already had his 10 bucks back, I think he thought we were all nuts," said Purdy.)

Then last Nov. 20, more than a year after the case was argued, the Supreme Court delivered its ruling. The 29 foolscap pages shot holes in the Indian Act and transformed the Bill of Rights from a dusty and half-forgotten relic into one of the most important laws in the country.

Mr. Justice Roland A. Ritchie, who wrote the majority opinion dismissing the Crown's appeal, said "an individual is denied equality before the law if it is made an offence punishable at law, on account of his race, for him to do something which his fellow Canadians are free to do without having committed an offence. . . . "

The drunkenness section of the Indian Act, he said, created just that kind of offence and therefore it had to go. . . .

Mr. Justice Emmett M. Hall, agreeing with Ritchie, went so far as to liken the "philosophic concept" of the majority decision to the historic school desegregation order of the United States Supreme Court in 1954. Said Hall:

> The Canadian Bill of Rights is not fulfilled if it merely equates Indians with Indians in terms of equality before the law, but can have validity and meaning only when . . . it is seen to repudiate discrimination in every law of Canada by reason of race, national origin, color, religion or sex . . . in whatever way that discrimination may manifest itself, not only as between Indian and Indian but as between all Canadians. . . .

A judge of the provincial Supreme Court, who asked that his name be withheld, says the Drybones decision is the first time in history that the Supreme Court of Canada has gone beyond its traditional constitutional role of settling arguments over legislative jurisdiction between the provinces and the federal government.

"The court has added a new dimension," he said. "That dimension is that even though the federal government may pass legislation that is completely within its jurisdiction, that legislation shall not stand if its language is such as to create discrimination or the lack of equality before the law.

"The Supreme Court of Canada now employs its own test of a law. It superimposes the Bill of Rights on the statute at issue and if that statute offends, out it goes. It's the biggest decision we've had in years, perhaps ever. Any legislation that affects human rights will be fair game." . . .

THE LAVELL AND BEDARD DECISIONS*

Supreme Court Reports

[*Editor's note:* See also Professor Russell's article, *supra,* Chapter 16 for a discussion of the Supreme Court's recent role in these and other civil libertarian cases.]

Introduction

The Indian Act is a statute of the Parliament of Canada which is chiefly concerned with the internal regulation of the lives of Indians on reserves. Such persons enjoy the use and benefit of Crown lands and have other privileges.

For the purposes of the Indian Act, the definition of "Indian" is laid down in section 2(1) of the Act as follows: "'Indian' means a person who pursuant to this Act is registered as an Indian or is entitled to be registered as an Indian."

Section 12(1) of the Indian Act refines the above definition further: "The following persons are not entitled to be registered, namely . . . (b) a woman who married a person who is not an Indian."

In contrast, the Canadian Bill of Rights, also a statute of the Parliament of Canada, makes the following provision in Section 1 [italics added]:

> It is hereby recognized and declared that in Canada there have existed and shall continue to exist without discrimination by reason of race, national origin, colour, religion *or sex,* the following human rights and fundamental freedoms, namely . . .
> (b) the right of the individual to equality before the law and the protection of the law; . . .

The Lavell and Bedard cases raise the question of whether Section 1(b) of the Canadian Bill of Rights renders inoperative Section 12(1b) of the Indian Act.

Background

Jeannette Lavell, originally a member of the Wikwemikong Band of Indians, married a non-Indian. Accordingly, her name was duly deleted from the Indian Register pursuant to Section 12(1b) of the Indian Act. Mrs. Lavell brought legal action against her exclusion from the Register, first before a judge acting as *persona designata* under the Indian Act, and then before the Federal Court of Appeal. The latter court found in favor of Mrs. Lavell, holding that Section 12(1b) of the Indian Act offended against the Canadian Bill of Rights and was therefore rendered inoperative. The At-

---

* From "Attorney General of Canada v. Lavell," *Canada Supreme Court Reports,* Part 10, 1974, Ottawa, Queen's Printer, 1975, pp. 1349-1392. Reproduced by permission of the Minister of Supply and Services Canada.

torney General of Canada thereupon appealed this decision to the Supreme Court of Canada.

Yvonne Bedard was born and raised on the Six Nations Indian Reserve in the County of Brant until she married a non-Indian in May of 1964. She then resided off Reserve and had two children, but separated from her husband in June of 1970. At this time, she returned to the Reserve to live on a property bequeathed to her by her mother. Thereupon the Council of the Six Nations, whose members were Richard Isaac and eighteen other individuals, served notice that she must dispose of the property, and she duly conveyed her interest in the property to her brother, a registered Indian who then allowed her to continue to occupy the property rent free. Soon, however, the Council of the Six Nations passed a further resolution that Mrs. Bedard must be given notice to quit the Reserve. Mrs. Bedard took action before the Supreme Court of Ontario, which found in favor of Mrs. Bedard, basing its decision on the judgment of the Federal Court of Appeal in the Lavell case. The Council of Six Nations appealed this decision to the Supreme Court of Canada.

The Decision of the Supreme Court of Canada

Having dealt with the two cases together, the Supreme Court found in favor of the respective appellants, namely the Attorney General of Canada and the Council of Six Nations, and against Mrs. Lavell and Mrs. Bedard. Accordingly, this decision reversed the judgments that had been rendered in these two cases by the Federal Court of Appeal and the Supreme Court of Ontario. The final decision was reached by a vote of five justices (CJ. Fauteux and JJ. Judson, Martland, Pigeon and Ritchie) to four (JJ. Abbott, Hall, Laskin and Spence). Reasons for the majority decision were expressed by the written opinion of Mr. Justice Ritchie and supplemented by an additional opinion written by Mr. Justice Pigeon. Reasons for the minority view were given by Mr. Justice Laskin, and supplemented by Mr. Justice Abbott.

The Opinions of the Justices

RITCHIE J.   These appeals, which were heard together, are from two judgments holding that the provisions of s.12(1)(b) of the *Indian Act*, R.S.C. 1970, c. I-6, are rendered inoperative by s.1(b) of the *Canadian Bill of Rights*, 1960 (Can.), c.44, as denying equality before the law to the two respondents. . . .

The contention which formed the basis of the argument submitted by both respondents was that they had been denied equality before the law *by reason of sex*, and I propose to deal with the matter on this basis. . . .

In my opinion the exclusive legislative authority vested in Parliament under [the *B.N.A. Act*] s.91(24) could not have been effectively exercised without enacting laws establishing the qualifications required to entitle persons to status as Indians and to the use and benefit of Crown "lands reserved for Indians." The legislation enacted to this end was, in my view, necessary for the implementation of the authority so vested in Parliament under the constitution.

To suggest that the provisions of the *Bill of Rights* have the effect of making the whole *Indian Act* inoperative as discriminatory is to assert that the Bill has rendered Parliament powerless to exercise the authority entrusted to it under the constitution of enacting legislation which treats Indians living on Reserves differently from other Canadians in relation to their property and civil rights. The proposition that such a wide effect is to be given to the *Bill of Rights* was expressly reserved by the majority of this Court in the case of *The Queen v. Drybones*, [1970] S.C.R. 282 at 298, to which reference will hereafter be made, and I do not think that it can be sustained.

What is at issue here is whether the *Bill of Rights* is to be construed as rendering inoperative one of the conditions imposed by Parliament for the use and occupation of Crown lands reserved for Indians. These conditions were imposed as a necessary part of the structure created by Parliament for the internal administration of the life of Indians on Reserves and their entitlement to the use and benefit of Crown lands situate thereon. They were thus imposed in discharge of Parliament's constitutional function under s.91(24) and in my view can only be changed by plain statutory language expressly enacted for the purpose. It does not appear that Parliament can be taken to have made or intended to make such a change by the use of broad general language directed at the statutory proclamation of the fundamental rights and freedoms enjoyed by all Canadians, and I am therefore of opinion that the *Bill of Rights* had no such effect. . . .

The contention that the *Bill of Rights* is to be construed as overriding all of the special legislation imposed by Parliament under the *Indian Act* is, in my view, fully answered by Pigeon J. in his dissenting opinion in the *Drybones* case where he said, at page 304:

> If one of the effects of the *Canadian Bill of Rights* is to render inoperative all legal provisions whereby Indians as such are not dealt with in the same way as the general public, the conclusion is inescapable, that Parliament, by the enactment of the *Bill,* has not only fundamentally altered the status of the Indians in that indirect fashion but has also made any future use of federal legislative authority over them subject to the requirement of expressly declaring every time "that the law shall operate notwithstanding the *Canadian Bill of Rights.*" I find it very difficult to believe that Parliament so intended when enacting the *Bill.* If a virtual suppression of federal legislation over Indians as such was meant, one would have expected this important change to be made explicitly not surreptitiously so to speak.

• • •

In considering the meaning to be given to section 1(b) of the *Bill of Rights,* regard must of course be had to what was said by Mr. Justice Laskin, speaking in this regard for the whole of the Court in *Curr v. The Queen,* [1972] S.C.R. 889 at pages 896 and 897, where he interpreted sections 1(a) and 1(b) of the *Bill* in the following passage:

> In considering the reach of s.1(a) and s.1(b), and, indeed, of s.1 as a whole, I would observe, first, that the section is given its controlling force over federal

law by its referential incorporation into s.2; and, second, that I do not read it as making the existence of any of the forms of prohibited discrimination a *sine qua non* of its operation. Rather, the prohibited discrimination is an additional lever to which federal legislation must respond. Putting the matter another way, federal legislation which does not offend s.1 in respect of any of the prohibited kinds of discrimination may nonetheless be offensive to s.1 if it is violative of what is specified in any of the clauses (a) to (f) of s.1. It is, *a fortiori,* offensive if there is discrimination by reason of race so as to deny equality before the law. That is what this Court decided in *Regina v. Drybones* and I need say no more on this point.

It is, therefore, not an answer to reliance by the appellant of s.1(a) and s.1(b) of the *Canadian Bill of Rights* that s.223 does not discriminate against any person by reason of race, national origin, colour, religion or sex. The absence of such discrimination still leaves open the question whether s.223 can be construed and applied without abrogating, abridging or infringing the rights of the individual listed in s.1(a) and s.1(b).

My understanding of this passage is that the effect of section 1 of the *Bill of Rights* is to guarantee to all Canadians the rights specified in paragraphs (a) to (f) of that section, irrespective of race, national origin, colour or sex. . . .

It was stressed on behalf of the respondents that the provisions of section 12(1)(b) of the *Indian Act* constituted "discrimination by reason of sex" and that the section could be declared inoperative on this ground alone even if such discrimination did not result in the infringement of any of the rights and freedoms specifically guaranteed by section 1 of the Bill.

I can find no support for such a contention in the *Curr* case in which, in any event, no question of any kind of discrimination was either directly or indirectly involved. My own understanding of the passage which I have quoted from that case was that it recognized the fact that the primary concern evidenced by the first two sections of the *Bill of Rights* is to ensure that the rights and freedoms thereby recognized and declared shall continue to exist for all Canadians, and it follows, in my view, that those sections cannot be invoked unless one of the enumerated rights and freedoms has been denied to an individual Canadian or group of Canadians. Section 2 of the *Bill of Rights* provides for the manner in which the rights and freedoms which are recognized and declared by section 1 are to be enforced and the effect of this section is that every law of Canada shall "be so construed and applied as not to abrogate, abridge or infringe or authorize the abrogation, abridgment or infringement of any of the rights and freedoms herein recognized and declared. . . ." (i.e. by section 1). There is no language anywhere in the *Bill of Rights* stipulating that the laws of Canada are to be construed without discrimination unless that discrimination involves the denial of one of the guaranteed rights and freedoms, but when, as in the case of *Regina v. Drybones,* denial of one of the enumerated rights is occasioned by reason of discrimination, then, as Mr. Justice Laskin has said, the discrimination affords an "additional lever to which federal legislation must respond."

The opening words of section 2 of the *Bill of Rights* are, in my view, determinative of the test to be applied in deciding whether the section here impugned is to be declared inoperative. The words to which I refer are:

2. Every law of Canada shall, unless it is expressly declared by an act of the Parliament of Canada that it shall operate notwithstanding the *Canadian Bill of Rights,* be so construed and applied as not to abrogate, abridge or infringe or authorize the abrogation, abridgment or infringement of the freedoms herein recognized and declared. . . .

In the course of the reasons for judgment rendered on behalf of the majority of this Court in *The Queen v. Drybones supra,* this language was interpreted in the following passage at page 294:

It seems to me that a more realistic meaning must be given to the words in question and they afford, in my view, the clearest indication that s.2 is intended to mean and does mean that if a law of Canada cannot be "sensibly construed and applied" so that it does not abrogate, abridge or infringe one of the rights and freedoms, recognized and declared by the Bill, then such a law is inoperative "unless it is expressly declared by an Act of the Parliament of Canada that it shall operate notwithstanding the *Canadian Bill of Rights."*

Accordingly, in my opinion, the question to be determined in these appeals is confined to deciding whether the Parliament of Canada in defining the prerequisites of Indian status so as not to include women of Indian birth who have chosen to marry non-Indians, enacted a law which cannot be sensibly construed and applied without abrogating, abridging or infringing the rights of such women to equality before the law.

In my view the meaning to be given to the language employed in the *Bill of Rights* is the meaning which it bore in Canada at the time when the Bill was enacted, and it follows that the phrase "equality before the law" is to be construed in light of the law existing in Canada at that time. . . . [Mr. Justice Ritchie proceeds to quote various authorities.]

The relevance of these quotations to the present circumstances is that "equality before the law" as recognized by Dicey as a segment of the rule of law, carries the meaning of equal subjection of all classes to the ordinary law of the land *as administered by the ordinary courts,* and in my opinion the phrase "equality before the law" as employed in section 1(b) of the *Bill of Rights* is to be treated as meaning equality in the administration or application of the law by the law enforcement authorities and the ordinary courts of the land. This construction is, in my view, supported by the provisions of subsections (a) to (g) of section 2 of the Bill which clearly indicate to me that it was equality in the administration and enforcement of the law with which Parliament was concerned when it guaranteed the continued existence of "equality before the law."

Turning to the *Indian Act* itself, it should first be observed that by far the greater part of that Act is concerned with the internal regulation of the lives of Indians on Reserves and that the exceptional provisions dealing with the conduct of Indians off Reserves and their contacts with other Canadian citizens fall into an entirely different category. . . .

Provision for the loss of status by women who marry non-Indians was first introduced in 1869 by section 6 of chapter 6 of the Statutes of Canada of that year. . . . It is thus apparent that the marital status of Indian women who marry non-Indians has been the same for at least one hundred years and that their loss of Band status on marriage to a member of another Band

and acquisition of status in that Band, for which provision is made under s.14 of the *Indian Act,* has been in effect for the same period.

• • •

A careful reading of the Act discloses that section 95 (formerly 94) is the only provision therein made which creates an offence for any behaviour of an Indian *off* a Reserve and it will be plain that there is a wide difference between legislation such as s.12(1)(b) governing the civil rights of designated persons living on Indian Reserves to the use and benefit of Crown lands, and criminal legislation such as s.95 which creates an offence punishable at law for Indians to act in a certain fashion when *off* a Reserve. The former legislation is enacted as a part of the plan devised by Parliament, under s.91(24) for the regulation of the internal domestic life of Indians on Reserves. The latter is criminal legislation exclusively concerned with behaviour of Indians *off* a Reserve.

Section 95 (formerly s.94) reads, in part, as follows:

> 95. An Indian who . . .
>   (b) is intoxicated . . .
> Off a reserve, is guilty of an offence and is liable on summary conviction to a fine of not less than ten dollars and not more than fifty dollars or to imprisonment for a term not exceeding three months or to both fine and imprisonment.

These were the provisions that were at issue in the case of *The Queen v. Drybones, supra,* where this Court held that they could not be construed and applied without exposing Indians as a racial group to a penalty in respect of conduct as to which the Parliament of Canada had imposed no sanctions on other Canadians who were subject to Canadian laws regulating their conduct, which were of general application in the Northwest Territories where the offence was allegedly committed and in which there are no Indian Reserves.

In that case the decision of the majority of this Court was that the provisions of s.94(b), as it then was, could not be enforced without bringing about inequality between one group of citizens and another and that this inequality was occasioned by reason of the race of the accused. It was there said, at page 297:

> . . . I am . . . of opinion that an individual is denied equality before the law if it is made an offence punishable at law, on account of his race, for him to do something which his fellow Canadians are free to do without having committed any offence or having been made subject to any penalty.
> It is only necessary for the purpose of deciding this case for me to say that in my opinion s.94(b) of the *Indian Act* is a law of Canada which creates such an offence and that it can only be construed in such manner that its application would operate so as to abrogate, abridge or infringe one of the rights declared and recognized by the *Bill of Rights.* For the reasons which I have indicated, I am therefore of opinion that s.94(b) is inoperative.
> For the purpose of determining the issue raised by this appeal it is unnecessary to express any opinion respecting the operation of any other section of the *Indian Act.*

And it was later said:

> The present case discloses laws of Canada which abrogate, abridge and infringe the right of an individual Indian to equality before the law and in my opinion if those laws are to be applied in accordance with the express language used by Parliament in s.2 of the *Bill of Rights,* then s.94(b) of the *Indian Act* must be declared to be inoperative.
>
> It appears to me to be desirable to make it plain that these reasons for judgment are limited to a situation in which, under the laws of Canada, it is made an offence punishable at law on account of race, for a person to do something which all Canadians who are not members of the race may do with impunity; in my opinion the same considerations do not by any means apply to all the provisions of the *Indian Act.*

Having regard to the express reservations contained in these passages, I have difficulty in understanding how that case can be construed as having decided that any sections of the *Indian Act,* except s.94(b), are rendered inoperative by the *Bill of Rights.*

The *Drybones* case can, in my opinion, have no application to the present appeals as it was in no way concerned with the internal regulation of the lives of Indians *on* Reserves or their right to the use and benefit of Crown lands thereon, but rather deals exclusively with the effect of the *Bill of Rights* on a section of the *Indian Act* creating a crime with attendant penalties for the conduct by Indians *off* a Reserve in an area where non-Indians, who were also governed by federal law, were not subject to any such restriction.

The fundamental distinction between the present case and that of *Drybones,* however, appears to me to be that the impugned section in the latter case could not be enforced without denying equality of treatment in the administration and enforcement of the law before the ordinary courts of the land to a racial group, whereas no such inequality of treatment between Indian men and women flows as a necessary result of the application of s.12(1)(b) of the *Indian Act.*

To summarize the above, I am of opinion:

1. that the *Bill of Rights* is not effective to render inoperative legislation, such as 12(1)(b) of the *Indian Act,* passed by the Parliament of Canada in discharge of its constitutional function under s.91(24) of the *B.N.A. Act,* to specify how and by whom Crown lands reserved for Indians are to be used;

2. that the *Bill of Rights* does not require federal legislation to be declared inoperative unless it offends against one of the rights specifically guaranteed by section 1, but where legislation is found to be discriminatory, this affords an added reason for rendering it ineffective;

3. that equality before the law under the *Bill of Rights* means equality of treatment in the enforcement and application of the laws of Canada before the law enforcement authorities and the ordinary courts of the land, and no such equality is necessarily entailed in the construction and application of s.12(1)(b). . . .

• • •

LASKIN J.   In my opinion, unless we are to depart from what was said in *Drybones,* both appeals now before us must be dismissed. I have no disposition to reject what was decided in *Drybones;* and on the central issue of prohibited discrimination as catalogued in s.1 of the *Canadian Bill of Rights,* it is, in my opinion, impossible to distinguish *Drybones* from the two cases in appeal. If, as in *Drybones,* discrimination by reason of race makes certain statutory provisions inoperative, the same result must follow as to statutory provisions which exhibit discrimination by reason of sex. . . .

● ● ●

The contentions of the appellants in both cases in appeal, stripped of their detail, amount to a submission that the *Canadian Bill of Rights* does not apply to Indians on a Reserve, nor to Indians in their relations to one another whether or not on a Reserve. This submission does not deny that the effect of s.12(1)(b) of the *Indian Act* is to prescribe substantive discrimination by reason of sex, a differentiation in the treatment of Indian men and Indian women when they marry non-Indians, this differentiation being exhibited in the loss by the women of their status as Indians under the Act. It does, however, involve the assertion that the particular discrimination upon which the two appeals are focussed is not offensive to the relevant provisions of the *Canadian Bill of Rights;* and it also involves the assertion that the *Drybones* case is distinguishable or, if not, that it has been overcome by the re-enactment of the *Indian Act* in the Revised Statutes of Canada, 1970, including the then s.94 (now s.95) which was in issue in that case. I regard this last-mentioned assertion, which is posited on the fact that the *Canadian Bill of Rights* was not so re-enacted, as simply an oblique appeal for the overruling of the *Drybones* case.

The *Drybones* case decided two things. It decided first — and this decision was a necessary basis for the second point in it — that the *Canadian Bill of Rights* was more than a mere interpretation statute whose terms would yield to a contrary intention; it had paramount force when a federal enactment conflicted with its terms, and it was the incompatible federal enactment which had to give way. This was the issue upon which the then Chief Justice of this Court, Chief Justice Cartwright, and Justices Abbott and Pigeon, dissented. Pigeon J. fortified his view on this main point by additional observations, bringing into consideration, *inter alia,* s.91(24) of the *British North America Act.* The second thing decided by *Drybones* was that the accused in that case, an Indian under the *Indian Act,* was denied equality before the law, under s.1(b) of the *Canadian Bill of Rights,* when it was made a punishable offence for him, on account of his race, to do something which his fellow Canadians were free to do without being liable to punishment for an offence. . . .

It would be unsupportable in principle to view the *Drybones* case as turning on the fact that the challenged s.94 of the *Indian Act* created an offence visited by punishment. The gist of the judgment lay in the legal disability imposed upon a person by reason of his race when other persons were under no similar restraint. If for the words ''on account of race'' there are substituted the words ''on account of sex'' the result must surely be the same where a federal enactment imposes disabilities or prescribes disqualifications for members of the female sex which are not imposed upon members of the male sex in the same circumstances.

It is said, however, that although this may be so as between males and females in general, it does not follow where the distinction on the basis of sex is limited as here to members of the Indian race. This, it is said further, does not offend the guarantee of "equality before the law" upon which the *Drybones* case proceeded. I wish to deal with these two points in turn and to review, in connection with the first point, the legal consequences for an Indian woman under the *Indian Act* when she marries a non-Indian.

It appears to me that the contention that a differentiation on the basis of sex is not offensive to the *Canadian Bill of Rights* where that differentiation operates only among Indians under the *Indian Act* is one that compounds racial inequality even beyond the point that the *Drybones* case found unacceptable. In any event, taking the *Indian Act* as it stands, as a law of Canada whose various provisions fall to be assessed under the *Canadian Bill of Rights,* I am unable to appreciate upon what basis the command of the *Canadian Bill of Rights,* that laws of Canada shall operate without discrimination by reason of sex, can be ignored in the operation of the *Indian Act.*

The *Indian Act* defines an Indian as a person who is registered as an Indian pursuant to the Act or is entitled to be so registered. It is registration or registrability upon a Band list or upon a general list that is the key to the scheme and application of the Act. The Registrar, charged with keeping the membership records, is the person to whom protests may be made by a Band Council or by an affected person respecting the inclusion or deletion of a name from the Indian Registrar. By s.9(2) his decision on a protest is final subject to a reference to a judge under s.9(3). The *Lavell* case arose in this way. Section 11 of the Act enumerates the persons entitled to be registered, and it is common ground that both Mrs. Lavell and Mrs. Bedard were so entitled prior to their respective marriages. Section 12 lists the classes of persons not entitled to be registered and the only clause thereof relevant here is subsection 1(b) which I have already quoted. Section 14 has a peripheral relevance to the present case in its provision that a woman member of a Band who marries a person outside that Band ceases to be a member thereof but becomes a member of the Band of which her husband is a member. There is no absolute disqualification of an Indian woman from registrability on the Indian Registrar (that is, as a member on the general list) by marrying outside a Band unless the marriage is to a non-Indian.

Registration or registrability entitles an Indian as a member of a Band (and that was the status of both Mrs. Lavell and Mrs. Bedard prior to their respective marriages) to the use and benefit of the Reserve set aside for the Band. This may take the form of possession or occupation of particular land in the Reserve under an allotment by the Council of the Band with the approval of the responsible Minister, and it may be evidenced by a certificate of possession or a certificate of occupation, the latter representing possession for a limited period only. Indians may make wills disposing of their property, and it may also pass on intestacy, in either case subject to approval or control of the Minister or of a competent court; and in the case of a devise or descent of land in a Reserve the claimant's possession must be approved by the Minister under s.49. Section 50 has only a remote bearing on the *Bedard* case in providing that a person who is not entitled to reside on a Reserve does not by devise or descent acquire a right to possession or occupation of land in that Reserve. It begs the question in that the issue here is whether or not Mrs. Bedard became disentitled to reside on the land in the Reserve which was left to her by her mother upon the latter's death in 1969. The fact that the respondent's brother now holds a certificate of possession of all the land formerly possessed by the mother, that certificate having been issued after the respondent transferred her interest to her brother in February, 1971, does not affect the overriding question of the respondent's right to reside on the land, having her brother's consent to residence thereon.

Indians entitled to be registered and to live on a Reserve are members of a society in which, through Band Councils, they share in the administration of the Reserve subject to overriding governmental authority. There is provision for election of councillors by Band members residing on a Reserve, and I note that there is no statutory discrimination between Indian men and women either as qualified electors or as qualified candidates for election as councillors. Other advantages that come from membership in the social unit relate to farm operations and to eligibility for governmental loans for various enumerated purposes.

Section 12(1)(b) effects a statutory excommunication of Indian women from this society but not of Indian men. Indeed, as was pointed out by counsel for the Native Council of Canada, the effect of ss.11 and 12(1)(b) is to excommunicate the children of a union of an Indian woman with a non-Indian. There is also the invidious distinction, invidious at least in the light of the *Canadian Bill of Rights,* that the *Indian Act* creates between brothers and sisters who are Indians and who respectively marry non-Indians. The statutory banishment directed by s.12(1)(b) is not qualified by the provision in s.109(2) for a governmental order declaring an Indian woman who has married a non-Indian to be enfranchised. Such an order is not automatic and no such order was made in relation to Mrs. Bedard; but when made the woman affected is, by s.110, deemed not to be an Indian within the *Indian Act* or any other statute or law. It is, if anything, an additional legal instrument of separation of an Indian woman from her native society and from her kin, a separation to which no Indian man who marries a non-Indian is exposed.

It was urged, in reliance in part on history, that the discrimination embodied in the *Indian Act* under s.12(1)(b) is based upon a reasonable classification of Indians as a race, that the *Indian Act* reflects this classification and that the paramount purpose of the Act to preserve and protect the members of the race is promoted by the statutory preference for Indian men. Reference was made in this connection to various judgments of the Supreme Court of the United States to illustrate the adoption by that Court of reasonable classifications to square with the due process clause of the Fifth Amendment and with due process and equal protection under the Fourteenth Amendment. Those cases have at best a marginal relevance because the *Canadian Bill of Rights* itself enumerates prohibited classifications which the judiciary is bound to respect; and, moreover, I doubt whether discrimination on account of sex, where as here it has no biological or physiological rationale, could be sustained as a reasonable classification even if the direction against it was not as explicit as it is in the *Canadian Bill of Rights.*

I do not think it is possible to leap over the telling words of s.1, "without discrimination by reason of race, national origin, colour, religion or sex," in order to explain away any such discrimination by invoking the words "equality before the law" in clause (b) and attempting to make them alone the touchstone of reasonable classification. That was not done in the *Drybones* case; and this Court made it clear in *Curr v. The Queen*, [1972] S.C.R. 889 that federal legislation, which might be compatible with the command of "equality before the law" taken alone, may nonetheless be inoperative if it manifests any of the prohibited forms of discrimination. In short, the proscribed discriminations in s.1 have a force either independent of the subsequently enumerated clauses (a) to (f) or, if they are found in any federal legislation, they offend those clauses because each must be read as if the prohibited forms of discrimination were recited therein as a part thereof.

This seems to me an obvious construction of s.1 of the *Canadian Bill of Rights.* When that provision states that the enumerated human rights and fundamental freedoms shall continue to exist "without discrimination by reason of race, national origin, colour, religion or sex" it is expressly adding these words to clauses (a) to (f). Section 1(b) must read therefore as "the right of the individual to equality before the law and the protection of the law without discrimination by reason of race, national origin, colour, religion or sex." It is worth repeating that this is what emerges from the *Drybones* case and what is found in the *Curr* case.

There is no clear historical basis for the position taken by the appellants, certainly not in relation to Indians in Canada as a whole, and this was in effect conceded during the hearing in this Court. In any event, history cannot avail against the clear words of ss.1 and 2 of the *Canadian Bill of Rights.* It is s.2 that gives this enactment its effective voice, because without it s.1 would remain a purely declaratory provision. Section 2 brings the terms of s.1 into its orbit, and its reference to "every law of Canada" is a reference, as set out in s.5(2), to any Act of the Parliament of Canada enacted before or after the effective date of the *Canadian Bill of Rights.* Pre-existing Canadian legislation as well as subsequent Canadian legislation is expressly made subject to the commands of the *Canadian Bill of Rights,* and those commands, where they are as clear as the one which is relevant here, cannot be diluted by appeals to history. Ritchie J. in his reasons in the *Drybones* case touched on this very point when he rejected the contention that the terms of s.1 of the *Canadian Bill of Rights* must be circumscribed by the provisions of Canadian statutes in force at the date of the enactment of the *Canadian Bill of Rights:* see [1970] S.C.R. 282, at pp. 295-296. I subscribed fully to the rejection of that contention. Clarity here is emphasized by looking at the French version of the *Canadian Bill of Rights* which speaks in s.1 of the enumerated human rights and fundamental freedoms "pour tout individu au Canada quels que soient sa race, son origine nationale, sa couleur, sa religion ou son sexe."

In my opinion, the appellants' contentions gain no additional force because the *Indian Act,* including the challenged s.12(1)(b) thereof, is a fruit of the exercise of Parliament's exclusive legislative power in relation to "Indians, and Lands reserved for the Indians" under s.91(24) of the *British North America Act*. Discriminatory treatment on the basis of race or colour or sex does not inhere in that grant of legislative power. The fact that its exercise may be attended by forms of discrimination prohibited by the *Canadian Bill of Rights* is no more a justification for a breach of the *Canadian Bill of Rights* than there would be in the case of the exercise of any other head of federal legislative power involving provisions offensive to the *Canadian Bill of Rights*. The latter does not differentiate among the various heads of legislative power; it embraces all exercises under whatever head or heads they arise. Section 3 which directs the Minister of Justice to scrutinize every Bill to ascertain whether any of its provisions are inconsistent with ss.1 and 2 is simply an affirmation of this fact which is evident enough from ss.1 and 2.

There was an intimation during the argument of these appeals that the *Canadian Bill of Rights* is properly invoked only to resolve a clash under its terms between two federal statutes, and the *Drybones* case was relied on in that connection. It is a spurious contention, if seriously advanced, because the *Canadian Bill of Rights* is itself the indicator to which any Canadian statute or any provision thereof must yield unless Parliament has declared that the statute or the particular provision is to operate notwithstanding the *Canadian Bill of Rights*. A statute may in itself be offensive to the *Canadian Bill of Rights,* or it may be by relation to another statute that it is so offensive. . . .

PIGEON J. (supporting Ritchie J.):   I agree in the result with Ritchie J. I certainly cannot disagree with the view I did express in *The Queen v. Drybones* ([1970] S.C.R. 282, at p. 304) that the enactment of the *Canadian Bill of Rights* was not intended to effect a virtual suppression of federal legislation over Indians. My difficulty is Laskin J.'s strongly reasoned opinion that, unless we are to depart from what was said by the majority in *Drybones*, these appeals should be dismissed because, if discrimination by reason of race makes certain statutory provisions inoperative, the same result must follow as to statutory provisions which exhibit discrimination by reason of sex. In the end, it appears to me that, in the circumstances, I need not reach a firm conclusion on that point. Assuming the situation is such as Laskin J. says, it cannot be improper for me to adhere to what was my dissenting view, when a majority of those who did not agree with it in respect of a particular section of the *Indian Act,* not adopt it for the main body of this important statute.

I would observe that this result does not conflict with any of our decisions subsequent to *Drybones*. In no case was the *Canadian Bill of Rights* given an invalidating effect over prior legislation.

In *Lowry and Lepper v. The Queen* ((1972), 26 D.L.R. (3d) 224) and in *Brownridge v. The Queen* ([1972] S.C.R. 926), the application of criminal legislation, past and subsequent, was held to be subject to provisions respecting a "fair hearing" and "the right to retain and instruct counsel." These decisions are important illustrations of the effectiveness of the Bill without any invalidating effect.

In *Smythe v. The Queen* ([1971] S.C.R. 680) it was held that provisions for stiffer penalties depending on the method of prosecution were not rendered inoperative by the *Canadian Bill of Rights* as infringing equality before the law, although the choice of the method of prosecution always depends on executive discretion.

In *Curr v. The Queen* ([1972] S.C.R. 889) recent *Criminal Code* provisions for compulsory breath analysis were held not to infringe the right to the "protection of the law" any more than the right to the "protection against self-crimination."

Finally, in *Duke v. The Queen* ([1972] S.C.R. 917) these same provisions were said not to deprive the accused of a "fair trial" although proclaimed without some paragraphs contemplating a specimen being offered and given on request to the suspect.

ABBOTT J. (supporting Laskin J.):   I am in agreement with the reasons of Laskin J. and wish to add only a few observations.

I share his view that the decision of this Court in *R. v. Drybones* cannot be distinguished from the two cases under appeal although in these two appeals the consequences of the discrimination by reason of sex under s.12(1)(b) of the *Indian Act* are more serious than the relatively minor penalty for the drinking offence under s.94 of the *Act* which was in issue in *Drybones*.

In that case, this Court rejected the contention that s.1 of the *Canadian Bill of Rights* provided merely a canon of construction for the interpretation of legislation existing when the Bill was passed. With respect I cannot interpret "equality before the law" as used in s.1(b) of the Bill as meaning simply "the equal subjection of all classes to the ordinary law of the land as administered by the ordinary courts" to use the language of Dicey which is quoted in the reasons of Ritchie J.

Unless the words "without discrimination by reason of race, national origin, colour, religion or sex" used in s.1 are to be treated as mere rhetorical window dressing, effect must be given to them in interpreting the section. I agree with Laskin J. that s.1(b) must be read as if those words were recited therein.

In my view the *Canadian Bill of Rights* has substantially affected the doctrine of the supremacy of Parliament. Like any other statute it can of course be repealed or amended, or a particular law declared to be applicable notwithstanding the provisions of the Bill. In form the supremacy of Parliament is maintained but in practice I think that it has been substantially curtailed. In my opinion that result is undesirable, but that is a matter for consideration by Parliament not the courts.

Ritchie J. said in his reasons for judgment in *Drybones* that the implementation of the *Bill of Rights* by the courts can give rise to great difficulties and that statement has been borne out in subsequent litigation. Of one thing I am certain: the Bill will continue to supply ample grist to the judicial mills for some time to come. . . .

[*Editor's note:* For the *Canadian Charter of Rights and Freedoms,* which is part of the new *Constitution Act, see supra,* Chapter 2.]

THE CANADIAN HUMAN RIGHTS COMMISSION FIGHTS DISCRIMINATION*

Liane Heller

OTTAWA — Nine days after Ross Stevenson, a Toronto-based pilot who flies Air Canada jumbo jets to Europe, celebrates his 60th birthday, he'll be grounded . . . unless there's a miracle.

And the designated miracle worker, the Canadian Human Rights Commission, probably won't get there in time.

The Canadian Human Rights Act forbids federal employers such as Air Canada from firing workers — or refusing to hire them in the first place — because of their age.

But there's a catch in federal human rights law that permits the airline to argue, effectively, that its age rules are valid and necessary. Although age discrimination is illegal, the act says it's not against the law to force people to retire "at the normal age" in their profession.

Change in Store

A year from now, that catch — and 13 others like it — may no longer exist. The commission has asked Parliament for sweeping changes to the human rights law that would, if enacted:

□ Do away with mandatory retirement. An employer like Air Canada could still argue that pilot Stevenson should come down to earth at age 61. But there would have to be proof that he's less capable of getting passengers safely to Europe and back at 61 than he was at 60.

□ Extend protection to minority groups that aren't now mentioned in the act, and beef up the current provisions for some of those who already are.

All forms of prejudice against pregnant women and women with children, homosexuals, and mentally or physically handicapped people would be outlawed. So would discrimination based on a person's political belief. And so would sexual harassment.

The federal human rights body, and the act of Parliament that gave it life, are little more than three years old. But the commission, despite its youth, has been able to strike a powerful blow against the forces of discrimination and prejudice.

When the commission first came on the scene, it was using its already potent legislative weapon "like a shotgun," said Ron Atkey, a Toronto lawyer and former minister of employment and immigration in the short-lived Conservative government of 1979-80.

But the agency, said the ex-cabinet minister whose pact with human rights commissioner Gordon Fairweather allowed the commission into the immigration department to investigate complaints, now has developed more accuracy on the firing line.

"They're now using more of a rifle approach," Atkey said.

* From *The Toronto Star*, July 2, 1981. By permission.

Add New Sights

The proposed legislative changes would add new telescopic sights to that rifle.

For example, Stevenson, who turns 60 on Aug. 22, would have a better chance to fly Air Canada planes a few more years.

For almost three years, first alone and more recently with the help of the commission's Toronto office, he's been trying to win that right. . . .

Justice Minister Jean Chretien acknowledges the commission's power to make recommendations independently of government — "it's for them to look at society's problems and find the solutions" — and applauds the commission's move toward "new areas, new standards for dealing with those problems."

But there's "sometimes a disagreement" on the form that solution should take, Chretien said. . . .

Fairweather acknowledges there are improvements to be made, especially in the area of investigating complaints of discrimination.

"I think to a certain extent we were overcome by high-mindedness," he said. "I think we have to pay more attention to the investigation, to have all those areas of discrimination better prepared, so that we can go into a tribunal better prepared."

Earlier this month, for example, the commission's investigators began attending seminars to learn more techniques on collecting crucial evidence needed to make discrimination findings airtight to survive the long haul through the courts.

In about a month one of the commission's most important cases will go to a commission-appointed tribunal, which makes rulings on whether a discrimination claim is valid.

The protagonists, represented by commission lawyer Russell Juriansz, will be 3,000 employees of the Public Service Commission of Canada.

The antagonist will be the federal government.

Millions at Stake

At issue is about $30 million — human rights officials estimate — in compensation for the workers, who say they're paid less than they deserve under equal pay law.

The government has offered a lump-sum settlement of $13 million, but the human rights commission says no.

"That $13 million doesn't cover it," said commission complaints officer Claude Bernier. "We cannot accept a deal. Either there's discrimination or there is not. If there is, and we believe there is, they have to go all the way."

About 2,600 of these people (60 per cent of them women) are food service workers, many of them working in government cafeterias as kitchen help. The others are laundry workers (52 per cent are women) and personnel service workers, such as gatekeepers (60 per cent are women).

These three groups earn as much as 40 per cent less than the mostly male groups who work in building, messenger, custodian and supply jobs. And the commission says such discrepancies are a violation of the equal-pay-for-work-of-equal-value law.

This law says it's illegal to pay one employee less than another if they're both doing work that's of equal value to the employer. And the onus is on the employer to prove that it's not of equal value.

The government agrees, but balks at raising the women's salaries to the highest level of the men's groups. The $13 million should be enough, the Treasury Board argues.

But the commission says no.

Inadequate Staff

Canadians can expect to hear about more cases like McLeod's in coming years, said commissioner Fairweather, and not only in terms of the concept of equal pay for work of equal value.

"I'm told all this equal pay stuff is going to cost money," he said. "Well Parliament was unanimous in passing the bill that put equal pay for work of equal value into the law. They gave me the mandate, and I spend my time weeding, watering and raking the parliamentary garden — shamelessly."

There's already a precedent for the kind of case — group discrimination — Fairweather says will be more important to human rights in the future. In January, 470 federal librarians won $2.4 million in a settlement giving them wage parity with historical researchers.

"Group cases are so essential because they help more people," Fairweather said. "But that doesn't mean we'll be giving up individual cases."

With the possibility of a huge new responsibility — to fight a whole new set of battles for handicapped people and women, if changes to the human rights law go through as planned — it'll be tough going for the commission to add the area of group discrimination to the load.

The human rights commission staff is only about 120 in seven offices across Canada, and its budget last year was only $4.2 million, much of it going to salaries.

In other words, we get a lot for our tax money in this case.

Fairweather doesn't think the operation should expand into a huge bureaucracy, since that's part of what he's fighting.

Charter of Rights

But he could use some help. And that could come in the form of the government-proposed charter of rights and freedoms. . . .

And now there's a rumble around Ottawa that the charter of rights will do away with the necessity of having a federal human rights commission.

But Max Cohen, a lawyer now teaching at University of Ottawa, disagrees.

The charter will indeed be the measuring rod of federal and provincial human rights, but the commissions will still have a purpose, Cohen said.

Particularly the Canadian Human Rights Commission, which has a special role as a federal tribunal with powers to appeal to the Supreme Court of Canada.

Massive Caseload

The court system is expected to take on a massive caseload of constitutional changes — including human rights cases — if the charter is sent to Canada. And eventually, court arguments based on constitutional precedent may become the crucial factor in human rights across Canada.

But there will still be a place for the commission, observers say.

First of all, it provides free advice to Canadians seeking redress for what they think is discrimination.

Secondly, it provides free action on behalf of those who do have a valid complaint under the Canadian Human Rights Act.

Thirdly, it functions as a hypersensitive sounding board for bigotry, prejudice and discrimination across the country.

And lastly, it's been the designated miracle worker so many times in the past three years that people like Air Canada pilot Ross Stevenson will always gravitate toward it — whether they get anything out of it or not.

That's called precedent, as defined by the Canadian Human Rights Commission during the past three years — and for who knows how many years to come.

BIBLIOGRAPHY

(See also Bibliography in Chapter 15, "Freedom of Information.")

Berger, Thomas R., *Fragile Freedoms: Human Rights and Dissent in Canada,* Toronto, Clarke Irwin, 1981.

Borovoy, A., "Civil Liberties in the Imminent Hereafter," *C.B.R.,* LI, 1, March, 1973.

Canada, *Canadian Bill of Rights,* [Diefenbaker Bill, Aug. 10, 1960], *Statutes of Canada,* Ottawa, Q.P., Vol. I, 1960.

Canada, [Trudeau, P.E.], *A Canadian Charter of Human Rights,* Ottawa, Q.P., 1968.

Cosman, R.W., "A Man's House is his Castle — 'Beep': A Civil Law Remedy for the Invasion of Privacy," *U. of T. Faculty of Law Review,* August 29, 1971.

Devall, W.G., "Support for Civil Liberties among English-speaking Canadian University Students," *C.J.P.S.,* III, 3, September, 1970.

Gall, G.L., *Studies in Civil Liberties,* Toronto, Butterworths, 1981.

Haggart, R., and Golden, A.E., *Rumours of War,* Toronto, New Press, 1971.

Hogg, P.W., "The Canadian Bill of Rights — Equality Before the Law, A.-G. Can. v. Lavell," *C.B.R.,* LII, 2, May, 1974.

Hunter, I.A., "Judicial Review of Human Rights Legislation: McKay v. Bell," *U.B.C. Law Review,* 7, 1, 1972.

Kelly, W., and Kelly, N., *Policing in Canada,* Toronto, Macmillan, 1976.

Macdonald, R. St. J., and Humphrey, J.P., (eds.), *The Practice of Freedom: Canadian Essays on*

Human Rights and Fundamental Freedoms, Toronto, Butterworths, 1979.

MacGuigan, M., "The Development of Civil Liberties in Canada," *Q.Q.,* LXXII, 2, Summer, 1965.

Mann, E., and Lee, J.A., *The RCMP vs the People,* Don Mills, Ontario, General, 1979.

Marx, H., "Emergency Power and Civil Liberties in Canada," *McG.L.J.,* 16, 1, 1970.

Russell, P.H., "A Democratic Approach to Civil Liberties," *U. of T. Law Journal,* XIX, 1969.

Sallot, J., *Nobody Said No: The Real Story About How the Mounties Always Get Their Man,* Toronto, Lorimer, 1979.

Schmeiser, D.A., *Civil Liberties in Canada,* London, O.U.P., 1964.

Schmeiser, D.A., "The Case Against Entrenchment of a Canadian Bill of Rights," *Dalhousie Law Journal,* 1, 1, September, 1973.

Scott, F.R., *et al.,* "A Collection of Articles on the Canadian Bill of Rights," *C.B.R.,* XXXVII, 1, March, 1959.

Scott, F.R., *Civil Liberties and Canadian Federalism,* Toronto, U.T.P., 1959.

Sharman, G.C., "The Police and the Implementation of Public Law," *C.P.A.,* 20, 2, Summer, 1977.

Sharp, J.M., "The Public Servant and the Right to Privacy," *C.P.A.,* 14, 1, Spring, 1971.

Smiley, D.V., *The Case Against the Canadian Charter of Human Rights,"* *C.J.P.S.,* II, 3, September, 1969.

Smith, D., *Bleeding Hearts . . . Bleeding Country: Canada and the Quebec Crisis,* Edmonton, Hurtig, 1971.

Tarnopolsky, W.S., "Emergency Powers and Civil Liberties," *C.P.A.,* 15, 2, Summer, 1972.

Tarnopolsky, W.S., *The Canadian Bill of Rights,* Carleton Library No. 83, Toronto, M. & S., 2nd rev. ed., 1975.

Tarnopolsky, W.S., "The Supreme Court and the Canadian Bill of Rights," *C.B.R.,* LIII, 14, December, 1975.

University of British Columbia Law Review, 7, 1, 1972. (See articles pp. 17-137.)

Whyte, J.D., "The Lavell Case and Equality in Canada," *Q.Q.,* 81, 1, Spring, 1974.

18

PROVINCIAL ELECTION RESULTS

A SURVEY OF CANADIAN PROVINCIAL ELECTION RESULTS, 1905-1981*

Loren M. Simerl

The election survey presented here provides a guide to provincial voting statistics, as well as to the nature of the franchise and electoral systems in Canada's provinces over the past seventy-five years. With a few noted exceptions, all voting information in this survey came directly from provincial records and publications. Where accurate party identifications were unavailable from government sources, they were taken from *The Canadian Parliamentary Guide,* newspapers, and the *Canadian Annual Review.*

The choice of 1905 as the starting point for this survey is intended to give the reader a view of provincial elections before the era of third parties began in 1919 in Canada. Moreover, much early provincial election data is unavailable. Only Ontario and Quebec kept voter turnout statistics before 1905. Finally, the provinces of Saskatchewan and Alberta were created in 1905.

Where earlier tabulations of provincial voting data are available, they have been used as a check on the data given here. Inconsistencies have been double-checked.

Efforts have been made to make the percentages of votes for each party reflect its true voting strength. In the provinces of Newfoundland, Nova Scotia, New Brunswick, Ontario, Manitoba, Saskatchewan, Alberta, and British Columbia, where the electoral system tended to distort the relative

* The author, who is Assistant Program Director, Social Planning Council of Metropolitan Toronto, is indebted to Canada's provincial electoral officers and archivists who provided much of the data in this survey, and the Canada Council, which helped make this research possible.

Explanation of the Voter code: The Criteria for Voter Eligibility in
Canadian Provincial Elections

Voter Code	Age	Sex	Citizenship	Reservation Indian Voting	Nature of Other Criteria
a	21	Male	Br. Sub.	no	Wealth
b	21	Male	Br. Sub.	yes	—
c	21	Male	Br. Sub.	no	Anti-Asiatic
d	21	Male	Br. Sub.	no	—
e	21	Male	Br. Sub.	yes	Wealth
f	21	*	Br. Sub.	yes	Wealth
g	21	Both	Br. Sub.	no	—
h	21	Both	Br. Sub.	yes	—
i	21	Both	Br. Sub.	yes	Wealth
j	19	Both	Br. Sub.	no	—
k	21	Both	Br. Sub.	no	Anti-Asiatic
l	21	Both	Canadian	no	—
m	21	Both	Br. Sub.	no	Wealth
n	21	Both	Canadian	no	Wealth
o	18	Both	Br. Sub.	yes	—
p	19	Both	Br. Sub.	yes	—
q	**	Both	Br. Sub.	yes	—
r	18	Both	Canadian	no	—
s	21	Both	Canadian	yes	—
t	18	Both	Canadian	yes	—
u	18	Both	Br. Sub.	no	—

SOURCE: The statutes of the ten provinces.
* Both sexes voted, but not married women.
** The voting age was 21 for men and 25 for women.
Notes: *Sex:* The word "Male" indicates that only men voted.
Citizenship: In 1947 the legal category of "Canadian Citizen" was established. Most provinces, however, continue to allow "British Subjects" to vote, a term which includes members of all Commonwealth countries including Canada.
Reservation Indians: This term excludes specially "enfranchised" Indians and those living off reservations, who could qualify to vote.
Asiatic Law: While in Saskatchewan this law forbade voting by Chinese persons, in British Columbia it applied to Chinese and Japanese persons (1907-1945) and to "Hindu" persons (1909-1945).
Wealth Laws: This is a general category of restrictions which had the effect of denying the vote to the poor and those who received public support, including Indians. Nova Scotia, New Brunswick, and Quebec passed laws to prevent most Indians from voting after they had ended or greatly reduced wealth qualifications. The legal criteria to establish "wealth" usually involved one or more of the following: personal property, real estate, or income, each of which might vary with occupation or locality. Ontario's 1905 "wealth" law applied to only 9 northern ridings.
Language: Although not part of the voter code, British Columbia required its voters to have an "adequate knowledge" of either English or French (1949-1972).

popularity of the various parties, described adjustments in the party percentages removed this distortion. However, the unadjusted, valid votes by party are given for all provincial elections.

Where available, the details of voter turnout are given for each province. They have been adjusted to exclude possible distortions caused by acclamations or missing data. Rejected ballots are included in voter turnout figures for all provinces.

While the election data are set out in comparative format, caution should be exercised in making certain comparisons regarding voter turnout, since voter franchises vary by province and period, as does the thoroughness and method of enumeration.

Abbreviations Used Throughout:

Accl.	Acclamations	Nat.	Nationalist
CCF	Cooperative Commonwealth	NDP	New Democratic Party
	Federation	O.	Others
Comm.	Communist	P./Prog.	Progressive
C./Con.	Conservative	PC	Progressive Conservative
Farm.	Farmer	Proh.	Prohibitionist
El.	Elected	SC	Social Credit
F-L	Farmer-Labour	Soc.	Socialist
I./Ind.	Independent	Temp.	Temperance
Lab.	Labour	UF	United Farmer
L./Lib.	Liberal	3rd	Third Party
L-P	Liberal Progressive	4th	Fourth Party
LPP	Labour Progressive Party		

Prince Edward Island Provincial Elections

Election Date	Seats	Candidates L.	Candidates C.	Candidates O.	Candidates Tot.	Elected L.	Elected C.	Elected O.	Popular Vote L.	%	Popular Vote C.	%	Popular Vote O.	%	Total	ACL	Voter Code
Nov. 18, 1908	30	30	28	—	58	16	14	—	15,488	51.6	14,541	48.4	—	—	30,029	2	e
Jan. 3, 1912	30	24	30	—	54	2	28	—	10,686	39.8	16,189	60.2	—	—	26,875	6	e
Sept. 16, 1915	30	30	30	—	60	13	17	—	17,097	49.9	17,179	50.1	—	—	34,276	—	e
July 24, 1919	30	28	30	2	60	25	4	1	19,241	51.7	17,028	45.7	956	2.6	37,225	—	e
July 24, 1923	30	30	30	7	67	5	25	—	23,087	43.8	27,144	51.5	2,442	4.7	52,673	—	m
June 25, 1927	30	30	30	—	60	24	6	—	34,004	53.1	30,072	46.9	—	—	64,076	—	m
Aug. 6, 1931	30	30	30	—	60	12	18	—	33,833	48.3	36,229	51.7	—	—	70,062	—	m
July 23, 1935	30	30	30	—	60	30	0	—	43,824	58.0	31,780	42.0	—	—	75,604	—	m
May 18, 1939	30	30	30	—	60	27	3	—	40,205	53.0	35,600	47.0	—	—	75,805	—	m
Sept. 15, 1943	30	30	30	12	72	20	10	—	35,396	51.3	31,849	46.1	1,815	2.6	69,060	—	m
Dec. 11, 1947	30	30	30	17	77	24	6	—	40,758	49.8	37,461	45.8	3,598	4.4	81,817	—	m
Aug. 26, 1951	30	30	30	5	66	24	6	—	40,847	51.6	36,971	46.7	1,336	1.7	79,154	—	m
May 25, 1955	30	30	30	—	60	27	3	—	44,918	55.0	36,705	45.0	—	—	81,623	—	n
Sept. 1, 1959	30	30	30	—	60	8	22	—	42,214	49.1	43,845	50.9	—	—	86,059	—	n
Dec. 10, 1962	30	30	30	—	60	11	19	—	43,603	49.4	44,707	50.6	—	—	88,310	—	n
May 30, 1966	32	32	32	—	64	17	15	—	47,056	50.5	46,118	49.5	—	—	93,174	—	s
May 11, 1970	32	32	32	—	64	27	5	—	64,484	58.3	46,075	41.7	—	—	110,559	—	t
April 29, 1974	32	32	32	20	84	26	6	—	61,967	53.9	46,315	40.3	6,786	5.9	115,068	—	t
June 1, 1978	32	32	32	8	72	17	15	—	64,133	50.7	60,878	48.1	1,430	1.1	126,441	—	t
April 23, 1979	32	32	32	6	70	11	21	—	58,180	45.3	68,410	53.3	1,855	1.4	128,445	—	t

Sources: Canadian Parliamentary Guide (1908-1919); Official unpublished results first published by H.A. Scarrow (1923-1955); Results, Provincial Secretary Department (1959-1966); Report of the Chief Electoral Officer (1970-1979). No adequate check upon the party vote is possible for the elections from 1923 to 1955 since the official unpublished results are not available from P.E.I. sources.

Note: The figures given here are based on the combined results for both houses in P.E.I., the Assembly and the Council with half of the total seats in each. Until 1963, voting for candidates of either house was limited by property restrictions, but the restrictions for voting for Councillors were somewhat greater. From 1908 to 1962, an average of 31% of the voters who voted for Assemblymen did not cast a vote for a Councillor.

Note: Before 1970 no records were kept regarding voter turnout.

Acclamations: 1908: 2 Liberals, 1921: 6 Conservatives.

Electoral System: A Single-member, plurality system for each house.

Explanation of Party Totals:
1919: Others: I. (2) 965 (1 El.).
1923: Others: Prog. (5) 1,765; I. (2) 677.
1943: Others: CCF (9) 1,436; I.L. (3) 379.
1947: Others: CCF (16) 3,509; I. (1) 89.
1951: Others: CCF (5) 1,336.
1974: Others: NDP (20) 6,786.
1978: Others: NDP (6) 1,173, I. (2) 257.
1979: Others: NDP (5) 1,655, D.B.P. (1) 200.

| | Voter Turnout | | |
Year	Registered Electorate	Voters who Voted	%
1970	65,201	56,937	87.3
1974	71,429	58,750	82.2
1978	74,857	64,526	86.2
1979	78,517	65,765	83.8

Newfoundland Provincial Elections

Election Date	Seats	Candidates L.	Candidates C.	Candidates NDP	Candidates O.	Candidates Tot.	Elected L.	Elected C.	Elected O.	Elected ACCL	Popular Vote %*	Popular Vote L.	Popular Vote %*	Popular Vote C.
May 27, 1949	28	28	28	—	2	58	22	5	1	—	70.0	109,802	28.0	55,111
Nov. 26, 1951	28	28	23	—	3	54	24	4	—	5	69.0	83,628	29.9	46,782
Oct. 2, 1956	36	35	31	—	11	76	32	4	—	4	66.7	75,883	31.6	36,591
Aug. 20, 1959	36	32	32	18	12	94	31	3	2	1	58.2	75,560	24.8	33,002
Nov. 19, 1962	42	42	35	6	3	86	34	7	1	3	58.7	72,319	36.4	45,055
Sept. 8, 1966	42	42	38	3	7	90	39	3	—	3	59.9	91,613	32.7	50,316
Oct. 28, 1971	42	42	42	19	5	108	18	22	1	—	44.4	102,775	51.3	118,899
March 24, 1972	42	41	41	3	10	95	9	33	—	1	38.0	77,849	59.9	126,508
Sept. 16, 1975	51	51	51	17	32	151	16	30	5	—	37.1	82,270	45.5	101,016
June 18, 1979	52	52	52	51	7	163	19	33	—	—	40.6	95,943	50.4	119,151
April 6, 1982[1]	52	52	52	23	2	129	8	44	—	—	34.9	87,228	61.2	152,943

Source: Chief Electoral Officer, *Report on the Provincial General Election* (1949-1982).

Notes: *The percentages given for party vote are adjusted to exclude the distortions caused by the electoral system. In multi-member ridings, the party per cent is changed by dividing the party vote by the number of members to be elected in each riding.

The vote by party for one riding in which the 1971 election was declared void are not available, although the total vote is known and the results are included in the voter turnout figures.

In two-member ridings the number of "Voters who Voted" is determined by adding the highest candidate vote for each full slate of candidates. Where a party did not run a full slate, the vote is divided by two.

Acclamations: All acclamations were won by Liberals with the exception of one Progressive Conservative in each of the elections of 1956 and 1972.

Electoral System: All ridings used the single-member, plurality system of voting except as described for those elections listed below. In all two-member ridings, voters could mark their ballot twice.

1949-51: Three ridings elected two members each.

1956-72: One riding elected two members.

[1]Preliminary official returns May 12, 1982. (The 1979 voters' list was used in this election.)

Newfoundland

Election Year	NDP	%*	O.	%*	Total	Total Registered Electorate	Registered Electorate in Contested Seats	Voter Turnout Voters who Voted	%	Voter Code
1949	—	—	2,642	2.0	167,555	176,281	176,281	133,189	75.6	q
1951	—	—	1,156	1.2	131,566	176,281	153,318	102,102	66.6	q
1956	—	—	1,964	1.8	114,438	189,240	169,940	111,996	65.9	h
1959	9,352	7.3	12,411	9.7	130,325	189,240	183,434	128,028	69.8	h
1962	4,479	3.8	1,378	1.2	123,231	211,921	200,912	120,394	59.9	h
1966	2,725	1.8	3,548	2.2	148,202	239,616	227,711	145,832	64.0	p
1971	4,075	1.8	5,804	2.6	231,553	265,653	265,653	229,486	86.4	p
1972	410	.2	4,307	1.8	209,074	265,653	255,165	204,033	80.0	p
1975	9,653	4.4	28,879	1.3	221,818	306,247	306,247	222,786	72.7	t
1979	18,507	7.8	2,786	1.2	236,387	322,239	322,239	237,135	73.6	t
1982	9,371	3.7	425	1.7	249,967	322,239	322,239	251,001	77.9	t

Explanation of Party Vote:

1949: Others: I. (2) 2,642 (1 El.).

1951: Others: I. (3) 1,156.

1956: Others: I. (3) 696; CCF (7) 661; I.L. (1) 607.

1959: The votes polled in the NDP column were by pro-labour candidates who ran as the "Newfoundland Democratic Party." Others: United Newfoundland Party (9) 10,639 (2 El.); I. (3) 1,772. (The two elected U.N.P. members had both been previously elected as Progressive Conservatives in 1956.)

1962: Others: I. (2) 740 (1 El.); United Newfoundland Party (1) 638.

1966: Others: I. (7) 3,548.

1971: Others: New Labrador Party (3) 5,645 (1 El.); I. (2) 159.

1972: Others: New Labrador Party (3) 2,548; I.L. (2) 1,259; I. (5) 500.

1975: Others: Lib. Reform Party (28) 26,378 (4 Elec); I.L. (1) 2,185 (El.); 1 (3) 316.

1979: Others: I. (5) 1,303; I.PC. (1) 1,035.

1982: Others: I. (2) 425.

Nova Scotia Provincial Elections

Election Date	Seats	Candidates					Elected					Popular Vote	
		L.	C.	3rd.	O.	Tot.	L.	C.	3rd.	O.	ACCL.	L.	%*
June 20, 1906	38	38	31	—	5	74	32	5	—	2	2	84,359	53.2
June 14, 1911	38	38	37	2	3	80	27	11	—	—	—	99,192	51.1
June 20, 1916	43	43	43	2	1	89	30	13	—	—	—	136,315	50.6
July 27, 1920	43	40	34	12	14	100	29	3	4	7	—	154,627	46.0
June 25, 1925	43	43	41	10	2	96	3	38	—	2	—	161,158	36.9
Oct. 1, 1928	43	43	43	2	—	88	20	23	—	—	—	209,380	48.2
Aug. 22, 1933	30	30	30	3	3	66	22	8	—	—	—	166,170	52.5
June 29, 1937	30	30	30	—	1	61	25	5	—	—	—	165,397	53.6
Oct. 28, 1941	30	30	29	6	—	65	23	4	3	—	—	138,915	53.6
Oct. 23, 1945	30	30	30	20	3	83	28	—	2	(1)	—	153,513	53.0
June 9, 1949	37	37	37	21	1	96	27	7	2	—	—	174,604	50.8
May 26, 1953	37	37	37	16	1	91	22	13	2	—	—	169,118	49.2
Oct. 30, 1956	43	43	43	11	1	98	18	24	1	—	—	159,656	48.0
June 7, 1960	43	43	43	34	1	121	15	27	1	—	—	147,951	42.3
Oct. 8, 1963	43	43	43	20	—	106	4	39	—	—	—	134,873	39.4
May 30, 1967	46	46	46	24	2	118	6	40	—	—	—	142,945	41.8
Oct. 13, 1970	46	46	46	23	2	117	23	21	2	—	—	174,943	46.3
April 2, 1974	46	46	46	46	6	144	31	12	3	—	—	206,648	47.3
Sept. 19, 1978	52	52	52	52	6	162	17	31	4	—	—	175,218	38.5
Oct. 6, 1981	52	52	52	52	6	162	13	37	1	1	—	139,604	33.2

Sources: *Journal of the House of Assembly* (1906-45) and *Election Returns* 1933-1978.

Notes: *The percentages given for party vote are adjusted to exclude the distortions caused by the electoral system. In multi-member ridings, the party per cent is changed by dividing the party vote by the number of members to be elected in each riding.

Notes: *In 1949 the election of one Liberal was declared void and is listed in the Other (O.) Column. No vote figures were given.

Acclamations: 1906: Two Liberals.

Electoral System: In all multi-member ridings voters could place an "X" on the ballot for each of the total number of candidates to be elected.

The number of single and multi-member ridings by the number of members for each riding. (M = Members)

Elections	1M	2M	3M	4M	5M
1906-11	0	16	2	0	0
1916-20	0	14	2	1	1
1925-28	0	16	2	0	1
1933-45	22	4	0	0	0
1949-53	27	5	0	0	0
1956-63	37	3	0	0	0
1967-74	40	3	0	0	0
1978	48	2	0	0	0

Nova Scotia

Election Year	C.	%*	3rd	%*	O.	%*	Total	Voter Turnout			Voter Code
								Registered Electorate	Voters who Voted	%	
1906	66,638	41.6	—	—	7,423	5.2	158,420	—	—	—	f
1911	88,114	45.6	3,410	1.3 Lab.	3,441	2.0	194,157	—	—	—	f
1916	131,844	48.7	1,488	.4 Lab.	727	.3	270,374	—	—	—	f
1920	86,054	26.6	58,727	12.7 Lab.	48,546	14.7	347,954	—	—	—	i
1925	253,697	56.6	12,260	3.1 Lab.	16,847	3.3	443,962	261,570	180,612	69.0	h
1928	218,974	50.3	4,862	1.4 Lab.	—	—	433,216	253,199	179,393	70.9	h
1933	145,107	45.5	2,336	.9 CCF	2,469	1.0	316,082	295,957	254,233	85.9	h
1937	143,670	45.0	—	—	3,396	1.4	312,463	312,817	249,215	79.7	h
1941	106,133	37.5	18,583	8.8 CCF	—	—	263,631	341,788	215,491	63.0	h
1945	97,774	31.7	39,637	15.1 CCF	634	.2	291,558	370,945	238,966	64.4	h
1949	134,312	37.6	32,869	11.3 CCF	749	.3	342,534	369,117	286,694	77.7	h
1953	150,480	41.9	23,700	8.2 CCF	2,065	.7	345,363	370,293	280,661	75.8	h
1956	161,016	48.5	9,932	3.2 CCF	812	.3	331,416	376,894	302,421	80.5	h
1960	168,023	48.0	31,036	9.6 CCF	650	.1	347,660	388,805	318,900	82.0	h
1963	191,128	56.2	14,076	4.4 NDP	—	—	340,077	400,078	311,562	77.9	h
1967	180,498	52.5	17,873	5.6 NDP	498	.1	341,814	405,704	312,647	77.1	h
1970	177,986	46.2	25,259	7.3 NDP	1,464	.2	379,652	453,727	350,852	77.3	p
1974	166,388	38.5	55,902	13.6 NDP	2,220	.5	431,158	507,190	395,089	77.9	p
1978	203,500	46.2	63,979	14.8 NDP	2,008	.5	444,705	542,547	424,418	78.2	p
1981	200,228	47.5	76,289	18.1 NDP	5,002	1.2	421,123	571,296	423,544	74.1	p

Others (votes polled):

1906: I. (5) 7,423 (2 El.).
1911: I. (3) 3,441.
1916: I. (1) 727.
1920: Farmers candidates (14) 48,546. (With one exception Farmer and Labour groups supported each others' candidates.) Elected: Farmer (7).
1925: I. Lab. (1) 8,267, Farm. Con. (1) 8,580. (Both elected with Conservative support.)
1933: United Front (3) 2,469.
1937: Lab. (1) 3,396.
1945: Lab. Prog. (2) 505, I. (1) 129.
1949: I. (1) 749.
1953: I. (1) 2,065.
1956: I. (1) 812.
1960: I. (1) 650.
1967: I. (2) 498.
1970: I. (2) 1,464.
1974: I. (6) 2,220.
1978: I. (6) 2,008.
1981: I. (6) 5,002 (1 El.).

New Brunswick Provincial Elections

Election Date	Seats	Candidates					Elected				A C C L	Popular Vote			
		L.	C.	3rd	O.	Tot.	L.	C.	3rd	O.		L.	%*	C.	%*
March 3, 1908	46	43	43	—	10	96	12	28	—	6	—	87,611	43.5	95,319	46.7
June 20, 1912	48	47	46	—	2	95	2	46	—	—	—	80,532	39.9	123,176	58.6
Feb. 24, 1917	48	48	48	—	—	96	27	21	—	—	—	106,948	52.3	98,469	47.7
Oct. 9, 1920	48	47	27	25	7	106	24	13	9	2	2	147,393	46.5	82,427	27.1
Aug. 10, 1925	48	45	48	3	2	98	11	37	—	—	—	184,700	44.6	217,904	53.2
June 19, 1930	48	48	48	—	1	97	17	31	—	—	—	221,396	47.5	242,922	52.4
June 27, 1935	48	48	48	—	2	98	43	5	—	—	—	340,621	59.0	229,690	40.6
Nov. 20, 1939	48	48	48	1	1	98	29	19	—	—	—	296,838	54.4	243,607	45.3
Aug. 28, 1944	48	48	48	41	—	137	37	11	—	—	—	282,397	47.4	233,371	39.6
June 28, 1948	52	52	52	20	1	125	47	5	—	—	5	332,321	57.2	179,690	32.3
Sept. 22, 1952	52	52	52	12	7	123	16	36	—	—	—	372,140	48.1	369,919	50.1
June 18, 1956	52	52	52	18	2	124	15	37	—	—	—	346,021	45.0	391,775	53.2
June 27, 1960	52	52	52	—	2	106	31	21	—	—	—	418,043	52.4	362,171	46.9
April 22, 1963	52	52	52	3	1	105	32	20	—	—	—	395,543	50.9	367,673	49.1
Oct. 23, 1967	58	58	58	3	—	119	32	26	—	—	—	396,354	50.9	354,070	49.0
Oct. 26, 1970	58	58	58	32	5	153	26	32	—	—	—	354,944	46.2	354,441	51.0
Nov. 18, 1974	58	58	58	35	24	175	25	33	—	—	—	147,272	47.5	145,304	46.9
Oct. 23, 1978	58	58	58	36	29	181	28	30	—	—	—	146,507	44.3	146,808	44.4

Source: *Journal of the Legislative Assembly* 1908-1963, *Report of the Chief Electoral Officer* 1967-1978.

Notes: *The percentages given for party vote are adjusted to exclude the distortions caused by the electoral system. In multi-member ridings, the party per cent is changed by dividing the party vote by the number of members to be elected in each riding. The total provincial vote which is used in the calculation of percentages is given separately in the column labeled "Adjusted Total Vote," which represents the minimum number of voters who cast valid ballots.

The 1967 voter turnout figures exclude rejected ballots. Voters who voted in advance polls in 1967 are estimated by adding together the highest vote polled by one candidate in each party. 1967 estimate is 2,372. In addition 414 ballots are excluded from the 1967 "Voters who Voted" column because there were no accurate comparative figures for registered electorate.

Note: Before 1967 no records were kept regarding voter turnout.

Acclamations: The acclamations in 1920 and 1948 were by Liberals.

Electoral System: In all multi-member ridings voters could place an "X" on the ballot for each of the total number of candidates to be elected. (M = Members).

The number of single and multi-member ridings by the number of members for each riding. (M = Members).

Elections	1M	2M	3M	4M	5M
1908	—	7	4	5	—
1912-20	1	7	3	6	—
1925	3	7	5	4	—
1930-44	1	7	3	6	—
1948-63	—	6	5	5	1
1967-70	4	7	6	3	2
1974-78	58	—	—	—	—

New Brunswick

Election Year	3rd	%*	Party	O.	%*	Total	Adjusted Total Vote*	Voter Turnout Registered Electorate	Voter Turnout Voters who Voted	%	Voter Code
1908	—	—	—	20,723	9.8	203,653	62,374	—	—	—	e
1912	—	—	—	1,907	1.5	205,615	64,175	—	—	—	e
1917	—	—	—	—	—	205,417	64,416	—	—	—	d
1920	64,451	19.6	UF	19,272	6.8	313,543	98,119	—	—	—	g
1925	7,927	1.9	UF	1,330	.4	411,861	141,450	—	—	—	g
1930	—	—	—	183	.1	464,501	147,756	—	—	—	g
1935	—	—	—	1,482	.4	571,793	181,458	—	—	—	g
1939	712	.1	CCF	562	.2	541,719	171,833	—	—	—	g
1944	68,248	13.0	CCF	—	—	584,016	186,187	—	—	—	g
1948	34,415	5.7	CCF	28,634	4.8	575,060	178,196	—	—	—	g
1952	9,490	1.2	CCF	4,858	.6	756,407	221,940	—	—	—	g
1956	11,828	1.7	SC	726	.1	750,350	222,283	—	—	—	g
1960	—	—	—	3,185	.7	783,399	233,865	—	—	—	g
1963	—	—	—	7	.0	763,223	228,880	—	—	—	h
1967	1,247	.1	NDP	—	—	751,671	245,181	313,253	261,135	83.4	h
1970	20,383	2.6	NDP	1,762	.2	731,530	242,559	331,643	269,306	81.2	h
1974	9,092	2.9	NDP	8,322	2.7	309,990	309,990	408,182	312,475	76.6	o
1978	21,403	6.5	NDP	15,774	4.8	330,492	330,492	441,454	333,761	75.6	o

Explanation of Party Vote:

1908: In 1908 and in 1912 the Conservative column refers to both Conservatives and Liberal-Conservatives who supported the Government of Premier Hazen, himself a Liberal-Conservative.

Others: 3 Conservatives ran as pro-Liberal (Government) candidates with Liberal backing, 4,004; 3 Ind. (El.) were pro-Conservative, 9,674; I.L. (3) 6,665 (El.) pro-Conservative; Other (1) 380.

1912: Others: I.L. (2), 1907.

1920: There were no official returns for 12 candidates and their vote was taken from newspaper reports. In 31 of the 48 seats the Liberals faced a unified opposition slate composed of Conservatives, Farmer and Labour candidates, Farmers, or Conservatives and Farmers.

Others: Lab. (4) 16,135 (2 El.); I. (2) 2,682; Soldier (1) 455.

1925: Others: I. (2) 1,330.

1930: Others: I. (1) 183.

1935: Others: I. (2) 1,482.

1939: Others: I.L. (1) 562.

1948: Others: I. (8) 25,500; SC (5) 3,134.

1952: Others: I. (7) 4,858.

1956: Others: I. (2) 1,196.

1960: Others: I. (2) 3,185.

1963: Others: I. (1) 7.

1970: Others: I. (5) 1,762.

1974: Others: Parti Acadien (13) 3,607; I. (7) 3,905; Canada Party (4) 810.

1978: Others: Parti Acadien (23) 11,562; I. (6) 4,212.

Quebec Provincial Elections

Election Date	Seats	Candidates L.	C/UN	3rd.	O.	Tot.	Elected L.	C/UN	3rd.	O.	ACCL	Popular Vote L.	%
June 8, 1908	74	74	64	—	13	151	57	13	—	4	6	131,065	53.5
May 15, 1912	81	83	76	—	11	170	63	15	—	3	1	155,799	53.5
May 22, 1916	81	85	54	—	2	141	75	6	—	—	26	133,473	64.0
June 23, 1919	81	97	21	7	7	132	74	5	2	—	45	87,478	67.5
Feb. 5, 1923	85	88	67	—	24	179	64	19	—	2	8	154,568	53.2
May 16, 1927	85	85	67	—	15	167	73	9	—	3	12	187,799	59.1
Aug. 24, 1931	90	88	90	—	18	196	77	11	—	2	—	260,938	53.3
Nov. 25, 1935	90	90	33	52	28	203	47	17	25	1	3	249,586	46.5
Aug. 17, 1936	90	88	90	—	27	205	14	76	—	—	—	224,344	39.4
Oct. 25, 1939	86	86	84	57'	21	248	69	14	—	3	1	301,631	53.5
Aug. 8, 1944	91	90	90	80	72	332	37	48	4	2	—	523,316	39.3
July 28, 1948	92	92	91	92	36	311	8	82	—	2	—	547,478	36.2
June 16, 1952	92	92	92	23	29	236	23	68	—	1	—	768,539	45.8
June 20, 1956	93	91	93	26	62	272	20	72	—	1	—	827,268	44.8
June 22, 1960	95	95	95	—	63	253	52	42	—	1	—	1,077,135	51.4
Nov. 14, 1962	95	95	95	—	34	224	63	31	—	1	—	1,205,253	56.4
June 5, 1966	108	108	108	73	129	418	50	56	—	2	—	1,099,435	47.3
April 29, 1970	108	108	108	108	141	465	72	17	7	12	—	1,304,341	45.4
Oct. 29, 1973	110	110	110	110	148	478	102	—	6	2	—	1,623,734	54.7
Nov. 15, 1976	110	110	108	110	228	556	26	11	71	2	—	1,134,997	33.8
April 13, 1981	122	122	121	122	161	526	42	—	80	—	—	1,659,924	46.1

Source: Reports of the Chief Returning Officer of Quebec.

Notes: The C/UN column refers to the Conservative Party from 1908 to 1935 when Maurice Duplessis, the then Conservative leader, merged his party with the ALN (National Liberal Action) to form the UN (Union Nationale), which, in effect, displaced the Conservative Party from 1936 to 1973.

Abbreviations: (Quebec): Nat. (Nationalist); BPC (Bloc Populaire Canadien); RIN (Rassemblement pour L'Indépendance Nationale); PQ (Parti Québecois).

Electoral System: Single-member, plurality system.

Acclamations: All acclamations were by Liberals except 3 Conservatives in each of the elections of 1916 and 1919.

Explanation of Party Vote:

1908: Others: I. (9) 7,786 (1 El.); I.L. (2) 3,871 (1 El.); I. Nat. (1) 1,362 (El.); C. Nat. (1) 966 (El.).

1912: Contested the same seat: 3 Liberals in one riding; 2 Liberals in each of two ridings; 2 Labour in one riding. Others: Lab. (4) 3,751 (1 El.); I.L. (3) 3,385 (1 El.); Nat. (2) 2,703 (1 El.); I. (2) 757.

1916: Contested the same seat: 3 Liberals in one riding; 2 Liberals in each of five ridings. Others: Lab. (2) 1,832.

1919: Contested the same seat: 3 Liberals in each of four ridings; 2 Liberals in each of eleven ridings. Others: Democratic Liberals (5) 4,399; Lab. L. (1) 1,457; I.L. (1) 1,716.

1923: Contested the same seat: 2 Liberals in each of five ridings; 2 conservatives in one riding. From 1923 to 1939 candidates declared whether they were Pro-
* Government (G), Opposition (OP), or Other (O). Others: (G): Lab. (2) 4,204; I.L. (6) 2,100. (OP): I. (7) 5,386; Lib. (3) 4,167 (2 El.); Farm. (3) 3,180; Lab. (2) 1,777. (O): Lab. (1) 925.

1927: Others: (G): I.L. (5) 8,232 (2 El.); I. (3) 1,365. (OP): I. (5) 4,686; Lab. (1) 4,432 (El.). (O): Lab. (1) 2,342.
*

1931: Others: (G): I.L. (3) 8,037 (2 El.); I. (2) 2,787; I.C. (1) 711. (OP): I.C. (6) 1,459; Lab. (1) 1,630; I. (1) 106. (O): Lab. (1) 416; I. (1) 323; I. Lab. (1) 65.
*

1935: Others: (G): I.L. (1) 1,541 (El.); L. Lab. (1) 998; I. (3) 615. (OP): ALN; I.L. (1) 1,532. (O): I.L. (4) 3,331; Lab. (2) 2,238; I. (1) 94; I.C. (1) 37.
*

1936: Others: (G): I.L. (11) 9,746; I. (2) 3,765. (OP): I. UN (3) 1,928; C. (2) 1,703; I.C. (1) 167. (O): CCF (1) 1,469; Comm. (3) 1,045; I. (2) 767; People's (1)
* 470; Lab. (1) 79.

Quebec

Election Year	C/UN	%	3rd	%	Party	O.	%	Total	Total Registered Electorate	R.E. in Contested Seats	Voters who Voted	%	Voter Code
1908	99,789	40.8	—	—	—	13,985	5.7	244,839	415,801	391,581	247,091	63.1	e
1912	124,693	42.8	—	—	—	10,596	3.6	291,088	479,521	474,446	294,424	62.1	e
1916	73,147	35.1	—	—	—	1,832	.9	208,452	486,136	336,696	211,229	62.7	a
1919	21,990	17.0	12,596	9.7	Lab.	7,572	5.8	129,636	480,120	238,050	131,084	55.1	a
1923	114,344	39.3	—	—	—	21,737	7.5	290,649	513,224	474,794	294,417	62.0	a
1927	109,105	34.3	—	—	—	21,057	6.6	317,961	567,907	514,857	320,855	62.3	a
1931	213,223	43.5	—	—	—	15,534	3.2	489,695	639,005	639,005	493,885	77.3	a
1935	103,596	19.3	156,078	29.1	ALN	27,101	5.1	536,361	726,551	711,618	551,589	77.5	a
1936	323,812	56.9	—	—	ALN	21,139	3.7	569,295	734,025	734,025	574,255	78.2	a
1939	217,413	38.6	25,523	4.5	ALN	18,730	3.3	563,297	753,310	741,131	570,631	77.0	d
1944	505,651	38.0	191,564	14.4	BPC	109,418	8.2	1,329,949	1,864,692	1,864,518	1,361,109	73.0	g
1948	775,747	51.2	140,036	9.3	UE	50,716	3.3	1,513,977	2,036,576	2,036,576	1,531,753	75.2	1
1952	855,327	50.9	16,039	1.0	CCF	39,358	2.3	1,679,263	2,246,889	2,246,889	1,704,924	75.9	1
1956	956,082	51.8	11,232	.6	SD	51,147	2.8	1,845,729	2,393,350	2,393,350	1,874,508	78.3	1
1960	977,318	46.6	—	—	—	42,144	2.0	2,096,597	2,608,439	2,608,439	2,130,109	81.7	1
1962	900,817	42.2	—	—	—	30,896	1.4	2,136,966	2,721,933	2,721,933	2,166,475	79.6	1
1966	948,928	40.8	129,045	5.6	RIN	147,481	6.3	2,324,889	3,222,302	3,222,302	2,370,510	73.6	r
1970	564,544	19.7	662,404	23.1	PQ	341,681	11.9	2,872,970	3,478,891	3,478,891	2,929,999	84.2	t
1973	146,209	4.9	897,809	30.2	PQ	303,226	10.2	2,970,978	3,758,111	3,758,111	3,025,736	80.5	t
1976	611,678	18.2	1,390,363	41.4	PQ	223,189	6.6	3,360,227	4,023,490	4,023,490	3,430,257	85.3	t
1981	144,104	4.0	1,773,319	49.2	PQ	24,011	.7	3,601,358	4,408,897	4,408,897	3,639,536	82.5	t

Explanation of Party Vote (Con't):

1939: Others: (*G*): C. (1) 2,989 (El.); I. UN (3) 469. (*OP*): Nat. (1) 3,074 (El.); I. L. (2) 539. (*O*): I. (5) 6,281; CCF (1) 2,513; C. (3) 1,679; I. ALN (1) 617; Lab. (2) 281; Comm. (1) 159; I. Lab. (1) 129.

1944: Others: CCF (24) 33, 986 (1 El.); SC (12) 16,542; I. (16) 12,766; I. L. (7) 8,656; I. Workers (2) 8,355; LPP (3) 7,873; I. UN (3) 6,775; Nat. (1) 6,587 (El.); I. CCF (1) 3,015; People's (1) 2,583; Nat. I. (1) 2,124; I. BPC (1) 156.

1948: Others: I. (10) 23,401 (2 El.); CCF (7) 9,016; I. UN (8) 8,649; LPP (1) 4,899; I. L. (7) 2,968; Lab. (1) 1,098; People's (1) 575; I. CCF (1) 110.

1952: Others: I. (6) 14,138 (1 El.); Nat. (1) 9,734; I. UN (7) 5,220; I. L. (7) 4,799; LPP (4) 3,932; I. Lab. (3) 1,027; I. Nat. (1) 508.

1956: The CCF ran under the label "Social Democrat" (SD). Others: I. (7) 33,205 (1 El.); LPP (32) 6,157; I. L. (8) 5,434; I. UN (11) 4,624; Lab. (3) 1,274; L. Lab. (1) 93.

1960: Others: I. (14) 21,563 (1 El.); I. UN (22) 11,155; I. L. (2) 8,205; Comm. (2) 536; Républican L. (1) 188; Soc. (1) 166; Capital Familial (1) 144; UN Lab. (1) 134; I. Lab. (1) 50.

1962: Others: I. (10) 17,835 (1 El.); I. L. (10) 11,209; L'Action Provinciale (11) 1,445; I. UN (2) 336; Comm. (1) 71.

1966: Others: Le Ralliement National (90) 74,670; I. (23) 62,466 (2 El.); C. (5) 6,737; I. L. (2) 2,056; Soc. (4) 905; Comm. (4) 502; Le Partie de la Démocratisation Économique (1) 125.

1970: Others: Ralliement des Créditistes (98) 321,370 (12 El.); NDP (13) 4,374; I. (30) 15,937.

1973: Others: Parti Créditiste (108) 294,706 (2 El.); I. (26) 7,195; Parti Communiste du Québec (Marxiste-Léniniste) (14) 1,325.

1976: Others: Ralliement Créditiste (109) 155,508 (1 El.); Parti Nationale Populaire (36) 31,045 (1 El.); Alliance Démocratique (13) 17,444; I. (15) 10,740; Coalition; nouveau Parti Démocratique du Québec: Regroupement des Militants Syndicaux (21) 3,101; Parti Communiste du Québec (14) 1,770; Parti des Travailleurs du Québec (12) 1,248; No Party Label (8) 2,333.

1981: Others: Parti Communiste (Ouvrier Communiste) (33) 4,958; Parti Libérale de Choix (12) 4,952; I. (26) 4,076; Parti Communiste (Marxiste-Léniniste) (40) 3,298; Parti Libertarian (10) 3,176; Parti Créditiste Sociale Unité (16) 1,284; Parti des Travailleurs du Québec (10) 1,027; Parti Communiste du Québec (10) 768; No party label (4) 472.

Ontario Provincial Elections

Election Date	Seats	Candidates					Elected				ACC L	Popular Vote			
		L	C	3rd	O	Tot.	L	C	3rd	O		L	%*	C	%*
Jan. 25, 1905	98	95	98	—	17	210	28	69	—	1	—	198,595	44.4	237,603	53.5
June 1, 1908	106	90	106	7	29	232	19	86	1	—	6	177,719	41.0	248,194	54.1
Dec. 11, 1911	106	78	106	7	16	207	22	82	1	1	17	142,245	40.1	205,338	54.6
June 29, 1914	111	90	111	4	35	240	24	84	1	2	4	186,284	37.7	270,881	53.8
Oct. 20, 1919	111	67	103	66	52	288	28	25	44	14	4	311,395	24.5	392,389	32.7
June 25, 1923	111	77	103	71	41	292	14	75	17	5	2	202,697	22.1	474,819	48.3
Dec. 1, 1926	112	50	112	20	59	241	14	72	13	13	3	203,966	17.8	638,567	55.7
Oct. 30, 1929	112	84	112	10	30	236	13	90	4	5	8	326,960	32.2	574,730	56.7
June 19, 1934	90	83	90	37	51	261	65	17	1	7	—	735,489	47.1	621,218	39.8
Oct. 6, 1937	90	86	89	39	52	266	63	23	—	4	—	773,608	49.2	619,610	39.4
Aug. 4, 1943	90	89	90	86	17	282	15	38	34	3	—	397,014	30.2	469,672	35.7
June 8, 1945	90	79	90	89	59	317	11	66	8	5	—	475,029	26.9	781,345	44.2
June 7, 1948	90	88	90	81	30	289	13	53	21	3	—	515,795	29.3	725,799	41.3
Nov. 22, 1951	90	88	90	77	16	271	7	79	2	2	—	551,794	31.1	860,898	48.5
June 9, 1955	98	94	98	81	41	314	10	84	2	1	—	577,774	32.8	853,625	48.5
June 11, 1959	98	97	98	80	21	296	21	71	3	1	—	682,590	36.3	868,815	46.2
Sept. 25, 1963	108	107	108	97	25	337	23	77	5	1	—	757,950	35.0	1,052,740	48.6
Oct. 17, 1967	117	115	117	117	17	366	27	69	7	1	—	760,096	31.4	1,022,967	42.3
Oct. 21, 1971	117	117	117	117	33	384	20	78	20	—	—	913,742	27.8	1,465,313	44.5
Sept. 18, 1975	125	125	125	125	60	435	36	51	19	—	—	1,135,103	34.3	1,193,075	35.8
June 9, 1977	125	125	125	125	97	472	34	58	38	—	—	1,053,119	31.5	1,325,359	39.7
March 19, 1981	125	125	125	125	61	436	34	70	33	—	—	1,072,680	33.7	1,412,488	44.4

Source: Chief Electoral Officer, *Ontario Election Returns* (1905-1977).

Notes: *The percentages given for party vote from 1905 to 1923 are adjusted to exclude the distortions caused by the electoral system. In multi-member ridings, the party per cent is changed by dividing the party vote by the number of members to be elected in each riding.

During the period 1905-1923 no figures for registered electorate were kept in ridings won by acclamation and in certain other ridings. For such ridings which were contested, the number of ballots cast has been deleted from the "Voters who Voted" column. The number of contested ridings for which there is no figure for registered electorate is as follows (by year): 1905 (2); 1914 (1); 1919 (9); 1923 (4); 1926 (1). Registered electorate in ridings won by acclamation was 47,809 in 1926 and 102,688 in 1929.

Acclamations: 1908: 6 Con.; 1911: 17 Con.; 1914: 3 Con., 1 Lib.; 1919: 4 Con.; 1923: 1 Con., 1 Lab.; 1926: 3 Con.; 1929: 8 Con.

Electoral System: All ridings used the single-member, plurality system with the following two exceptions.

  1905: There was one two-member riding in which voters could mark their ballots twice.

  1908-1923: There were four two-member ridings in which each voter could cast one ballot for each of the two members to be elected.

Explanation of Party Vote:

1905: Others: I.L. (3) 5,362 (1 El.); Proh. (2) 1,906; Soc. (7) 1,273; I. Temp. (1) 160; I. (1) 100; I.C. (1) 95; Temp. (1) 90.

1908: Others: I.C. (5) 6,107; I. (5) 3,042; Soc. (14) 2,891; Prog. (1) 2,187; I.L. (2) 1,470; L. Temp. (1) 1,017; I. Lab. (1) 544.

1911: Others: I.C. (2) 3,593; I. (5) 3,327; Soc. (7) 3,206; C. Temp. (1) 1,604; Lib. Con. (1) 1,130 (El.).

1914: Others: I. Temp. (5) 6,545; Temp. (4) 6,519; Soc. (10) 3,919; I. (5) 4,807; I.C. (3) 2,896; L. Temp. (1) 2,733 (El.); I.L. (2) 2,236 (1 El.); I. Proh. (1) 1,302; Temp. Con. (1) 1,213; Anti-Temp. Lib. (1) 691; I. Soc. (2) 577.

1919: Others: Labour (20) 107,775 (10 El.); Lab. UFO (5) 25, 324 (1 El.); Lib. UFO (2) 7,448 (1 El.). (The votes of the three preceding groups plus the regular (UFO) United Farmers of Ontario vote totals 395,470 or 36.1% of the adjusted vote.) The remaining votes in "Others" were cast for: I. (14) 38,377; I.C. (3) 14,213; Soldier-Lab. (2) 9,088; Soldier-Ind. (1) 7,472 (El.); I.L. (1) 5,354 (El.); Soldier (1) 2,146; Soc. (3) 637.

Ontario

Election Year	3rd	%*	Party	O.	%*	Total	Registered Electorate in Contested Seats	Voters Who Voted	%	Voter Code
1905	—	—	—	8,986	2.1	445,184	604,666	428,083	70.8	d&a
1908	7,298	1.5	Lab.	17,258	3.4	450,469	622,751	427,131	68.6	d
1911	8,965	1.8	Lab.	12,860	3.5	369,408	583,909	352,455	60.4	d
1914	6,535	1.4	Lab.	33,438	7.1	497,138	697,935	462,649	66.3	d
1919	254,923	23.6	UFO	217,834	19.3	1,176,541	1,378,721	1,028,161	74.6	g
1923	199,393	21.8	UFO	76,183	7.8	953,092	1,655,312	875,032	52.9	g
1926	87,862	7.7	Prog.	216,107	18.8	1,146,502	1,792,757	1,144,617	63.8	g
1929	34,507	3.4	Prog.	78,113	7.7	1,014,310	1,804,932	1,021,229	56.6	g
1934	108,961	7.0	CCF	96,158	6.2	1,561,826	2,130,420	1,577,547	74.0	g
1937	87,490	5.7	CCF	90,425	5.8	1,571,133	2,228,030	1,587,027	71.2	g
1943	415,441	31.6	CCF	31,812	2.4	1,313,939	2,269,895	1,323,712	58.3	g
1945	395,708	22.4	CCF	113,711	6.4	1,765,793	2,469,960	1,781,930	72.1	g
1948	466,274	26.5	CCF	50,169	2.9	1,758,037	2,623,281	1,773,446	67.6	g
1951	339,376	19.1	CCF	24,548	1.4	1,776,616	2,750,709	1,794,922	65.3	g
1955	291,410	16.5	CCF	38,716	2.2	1,761,525	2,905,760	1,784,147	61.4	h
1959	313,834	16.7	CCF	17,334	.9	1,882,573	3,196,801	1,903,845	59.6	h
1963	336,290	15.5	NDP	18,793	.9	2,165,773	3,437,834	2,184,078	63.5	h
1967	626,429	25.9	NDP	10,218	.4	2,419,710	3,685,755	2,439,710	66.2	h
1971	893,879	27.1	NDP	19,783	.6	3,292,717	4,503,142	3,310,776	73.5	o
1975	953,238	28.8	NDP	23,359	.7	3,304,775	4,853,998	3,324,334	68.1	o
1977	935,912	28.0	NDP	27,443	.8	3,341,833	5,123,768	3,361,433	65.6	o
1981	672,824	21.0	NDP	24,492	.7	3,182,484	5,519,204	3,203,281	58.0	o

Explanation of Party Vote (Con't)

1923: Two Conservatives contested the same seat. Two Liberals contested the same seat. Others: Lab. (22) 44,904 (4 El.); Prog. (3) 10,122; I. (14) 16,116 (1 El.); I.L. (2) 5,041.

1926: Two Conservatives contested the same seat in each of two ridings. Others: Proh. (26) 87,814; L. Prog. (9) 45,733 (4 El.); I.C. (7) 22,110 (2 El.); I.L. (7) 20,984 (4 El.); Lab. (3) 14,794 (1 El.); I. Prog. (1) 5,861 (El.); L. Proh. (1) 4,407 (El.); Prog. L. (1) 3,941; I. (1) 3,532; L. Lab. (1) 2,392; L. Lab. Proh. (1) 2,298; Lab. Lib. (1) 2,241.

1929: Two Conservatives contested the same seat. Others: Proh. (8) 25,807; I.C. (7) 21,947 (2 El.); UFO (3) 12,752 (1 El.); Lab. (4) 10,029 (1 El.); L. Prog. (1) 5,449 (El.); Comm. (5) 1,542.

1934: Others: L. Prog. (4) 38,161 (4 El.); I. (15) 17,462 (1 El.); I.L. (5) 12,984; Comm. (14) 9,775; UFO (2) 8,648 (1 El.); Lab. (1) 5,877 (El.); Lab. Soc. (4) 1,526; Farm. Lab. (1) 608; I. Lab. (1) 534; I.C. (2) 344; I. Worker (1) 158; Soc. (1) 81.

1937: Others: I.L. (8) 20,776 (1 El.); L. Prog. (3) 16,920 (2 El.); Farm. Lab. (6) 14,675; I.C. (5) 8,270; UFO (1) 7,296 (El.); I. Lab. (2) 6,377; Lab. (5) 5,455; I. (8) 4,108; LPP (1) 3,343; Social Lab. (11) 2,199; SC (1) 538; Comm. (1) 408.

1943: Two Liberals contested the same seat. Others: LPP (3) 12,037 (2 El.); I.L. (3) 8,252 (1 El.); L. Prog. (1) 4,042; I. (3) 2,593; I. Lab. (2) 2,215; I. CCF (1) 1,513; Soc. Lab. (2) 591; I. Soldier (2) 569.

1945: Others: LPP (29) 43,170 (2 El.); L. Lab. (7) 41,163 (3 El.); I. (14) 11,895; L. Prog. (2) 10,241; Lab. (4) 6,285; Soc. Lab. (2) 710; SC (1) 247.

1948: Others: LPP (2) 17,654 (2 El.); Union of Electors (12) 8,844; I. CCF (1) 8,613; L. Lab. (2) 7,682 (1 El.); I. PC (3) 3,340; I. (1) 1,766; SC (3) 1,104; Soc. Lab. (5) 913; I. Lab. (1) 253.

1951: Others: LPP (6) 11,914 (1 El.); L. Lab. (2) 7,939 (1 El.); I. (4) 1,869; I. Lab. (1) 1,375; I. PC (2) 1,080; Soc. Lab. (1) 371.

1955: One unendorsed PC is counted as a Progressive Conservative. Others: LPP (31) 20,875; I. (5) 9,169; L. Lab. (2) 7,305 (1 El.); I. Lab. (1) 641; I. SC (1) 602; Soc. Lab. (1) 124.

1959: Others: L. Lab. (1) 6,559 (El.); LPP (9) 4,304; I. PC (2) 2,119; SC (5) 1,740; Lab. CCF (1) 1,512; I. (2) 832; White Canada Party (1) 268.

1963: Others: L. Lab. (1) 6,774 (El.); I. PC (1) 5,190; I. (6) 2,656; SC (9) 2,313; Comm. (6) 1,654; I.L. (1) 103; Soc. Lab. (1) 103.

1967: Others: L. Lab. (2) 5,051 (1 El.); I. (5) 2,382; SC (7) 1,906; Comm. (2) 592; Soc. Lab. (1) 287.

1971: Others: I. (23) 16,959; Comm. (5) 1,620; SC (5) 1,204.

1975: Others: I. (15) 10,427; Comm. (33) 9,451; SC (12) 3,481.

1977: Others: Libertarian Party (31) 9,961; Comm. (33) 8,137; I. (33) 9,345.

1981: Others: I. (30) 11,639; Libertarian (12) 7,087; Comm. (18) 5,306; Unparty (1) 460.

Manitoba Provincial Elections

Election Date	Seats	Candidates L.	C.	3rd	4th	O.	Tot.	Elected L.	C.	3rd	4th	O.	ACCL	Popular Vote L.	%*	C.	%*
March 7, 1907	41	40	41	—	—	1	82	13	28	—	—	—	1	29,426	47.9	31,066	50.6
June 11, 1910	41	39	41	—	—	6	86	13	28	—	—	—	1	33,157	44.2	38,117	50.8
July 10, 1914	49	45	49	—	—	9	103	20	28	—	—	1	3	62,798	44.7*	68,352	47.6*
Aug. 9, 1915	47	46	46	—	—	8	100	40	5	—	—	2	1	64,363	56.4*	38,623	35.1*
June 29, 1920	55	50	32	15	24	28	149	21	9	8	9	8	—	50,422	35.1	26,517	18.5
July 18, 1922	55	39	26	19	50	21	155	8	7	6	28	6	2	35,225	23.2	23,539	15.5
June 28, 1927	55	42	41	11	46	18	158	7	15	3	29	1	2	33,852	20.7	44,320	27.2
June 16, 1932	55	11	48	19	52	17	147	—	10	5	38	2	—	5,198	2.0	90,135	35.4
July 27, 1936	55	49	39	20	20	7	135	23	16	7	5	4	1	91,357	36.0	71,927	28.4
April 22, 1941(*)	55C:	41	17	13	3	14	88	28	11	3	3	5	15	58,337	35.6	25,940	15.8
	AC:	1	4	—	9	6	20	—	3	—	2	2	—	701	.4	7,199	4.4
Oct. 15, 1945	55C:	34	18	—	2	11	65	25	13	9	—	3	1	70,475	32.2	34,410	15.9
	AC:	—	—	39	2	19	60	—	—	—	—	3	7	—	—	—	—
Nov. 10, 1949	57C:	45	16	—	—	8	69	31	9	7	—	4	—	77,335	39.2	23,410	11.9
	AC:	—	—	25	—	18	43	—	—	—	—	6	16	—	—	—	—
June 8, 1953	57	50	38	24	44	18	174	32	12	5	2	6	1	105,958	39.6	56,278	21.0
June 16, 1958	57	56	56	43	13	11	179	19	26	11	1	—	—	101,763	35.0	117,822	40.5
May 14, 1959	57	57	57	45	—	6	165	11	36	10	—	—	—	94,452	30.0	147,140	46.7
Dec. 14, 1962	57	57	57	39	12	5	170	13	36	7	1	—	—	108,270	36.4	134,187	45.2
June 23, 1966	57	56	57	53	17	3	186	14	31	11	1	—	—	107,841	33.1	130,102	40.0
June 25, 1969	57	57	57	57	6	7	184	5	22	28	1	1	—	80,288	24.0	119,021	35.6
June 28, 1973	57	50	52	57	3	24	186	5	21	31	—	—	—	88,907	19.0	171,553	36.7
Oct. 11, 1977	57	53	57	57	5	5	177	1	33	23	—	—	—	59,865	12.3	237,496	48.8
Nov. 17, 1981	57	39	57	57	36	6	195	—	23	34	—	—	—	32,373	6.7	211,602	43.8

Source: Summary of Results (1907-1977) found in the 1977 *Statement of Votes.*

Notes: The third party (3rd) column refers to Labour (1920-1932), the Ind. Labour Party (1936), and finally to the CCF/NDP (1941-81). The fourth party (4th) column refers to the Farmer candidates (1920), the United Farmers of Manitoba (UFM) (1922), the Progressives (1927), the Liberal-Progressives (LP) (1932). These farmer-oriented parties (after 1922 led by John Bracken) formally merged with the Liberal Party in the 1936 election and retained their new label of "Liberal-Progressive" until 1961, when the word "Progressive" was dropped. The 4th column refers to (SC) Social Credit (1936-73).

Note: Voter turnout figures exclude rejected ballots from 1907 to 1932.

Note: The percentages given for party vote for 1914 and 1915 are adjusted to exclude the distortions caused by the electoral system. In multi-member ridings, the party percent is changed by dividing the party vote by the number of members to be elected in each riding.

(*) In 1940 Premier Bracken formed a coalition government and during the next three elections candidates declared whether they were for Coalition (C:) or against Coalition (AC:).

Note: Registered electorate in ridings won by acclamation was as follows: 1907 (2,059); 1910 (2,009); 1914 (3,182); 1915 (736); 1920 (6,278); 1922 (3,779); 1927 (6,200); 1936 (2,292); 1941 (75,796); 1945 (32,517); 1949 (73,196); 1953 (5,458).

Electoral System: All ridings in Manitoba used a single-member, plurality system of voting with the following exceptions:

1914-15: 3 two-member districts in which voters could mark two "X's" on their ballot.

1920-45: A 10-member district in Winnipeg used the Hare system of Proportional Representation.

1927-36: All 45 single-member ridings used the alternate system of voting.

1949-53: 1 two-member district and 3 four-member districts used the Hare system.

Acclamations:

1907:	1 Con.	
1910:	1 Con.	
1914:	3 Con.	
1915:	1 Lib.	

1920:	1 Farm., 1 L., 1 Lib.	
1922:	2 UFM	
1927:	2 Prog.	

1936:	1 L-P
1941:	10 L-P, 5 Con., 1 S.C.
1945:	3 L-P, 3 Con., 1 I.
1949:	12 L-P, 4 Con.
1953:	1 L-P

Manitoba

Election Year	3rd	%	Party	4th	%	Party	O.	%	Total	Registered Electorate in Contested Seats	Voters who Voted	%	Voter Code
1907	—	—	—	—	—	—	939	1.5	61,431	76,648	61,431	80.1	d
1910	—	—	—	—	—	—	3,785	5.0	75,059	90,616	75,059	82.8	d
1914	—	—	—	—	—	—	15,654	7.6*	46,804	131,179	112,393	85.7	d
1915	—	—	—	—	—	—	13,901	8.5*	116,887	123,763	93,835	75.8	d
1920	13,811	9.6	Lab.	20,299	14.1	Farm.	32,614	22.7	143,663	203,482	143,663	70.6	g
1922	24,188	15.9	Lab.	49,767	32.8	UFM	19,055	12.6	151,774	218,720	151,774	69.4	g
1927	17,121	10.5	Lab.	52,805	32.4	Prog.	15,114	9.3	163,212	233,453	163,212	69.9	g
1932	41,928	16.5	Lab.	100,721	39.6	L-P	16,580	6.5	254,562	350,476	254,562	72.6	g
1936	30,983	12.2	ILP	23,413	9.2	SC	35,756	14.1	253,436	391,902	258,960	66.1	g
1941	24,350	14.9	CCF	2,723	1.7	SC	22,834	13.9	134,350	329,663	166,388	50.5	g
				9,156	5.6	SC	12,368	7.6	29,424				
1945	73,988	33.8	CCF	2,953	1.3	SC	10,456	4.8	118,703	397,527	220,747	55.5	g
				1,548	.7	SC	24,602	11.2	100,138				
1949	49,933	25.3	CCF				13,359	6.8	114,104	369,644	199,676	54.0	g
							33,099	16.8	83,032				
1953	44,332	16.6	CCF	35,750	13.4	SC	25,318	9.5	267,636	451,905	273,069	60.4	h
1958	58,671	20.2	CCF	5,174	1.8	SC	7,471	2.6	290,901	480,085	292,943	61.0	h
1959	69,594	22.1	CCF				2,902	.9	315,088	484,467	317,581	65.6	h
1962	45,430	15.3	NDP	7,495	2.5	SC	1,776	.6	297,158	491,632	299,920	61.0	h
1966	75,333	23.1	NDP	11,635	3.6	SC	735	.2	325,549	509,469	327,574	64.3	h
1969	128,080	38.3	NDP	4,535	1.4	SC	2,764	.8	334,688	522,203	336,382	64.4	h
1973	197,585	42.3	NDP	1,709	.4	SC	7,290	1.6	467,044	599,712	469,798	78.3	o
1977	188,124	38.6	NDP	1,323	.3	SC	346	.1	487,154	646,670	488,821	75.6	o
1981	228,784	47.4	NDP	8,731	1.8	Prog.	1,402	.3	482,892	670,343	484,790	72.3	o

Explanation of Party Totals and Others:

1907: Others: Lab. (1) 939.

1910: Others: Lab. (1) 1939; Soc. (3) 1,237; I. (1) 306.

1914: Others: I. Lab. (pro-Liberal) (1) 8,205 (El.); Soc. (7) 7,143; I. (1) 306.

1915: Others: I. (5) 10,076 (2 El.); Lab. (3) 3,825.

1920: Two Liberals contested the same seat in two ridings. Two Farmer candidates contested the same seat in two ridings. Others: Pro-Labour: I. Lab. (1) 11,586 (El.); Soc. (2) 4,202 (2 El.); Non pro-Labour: I. (24) 16,604 (5 El.); I. Farmer (1) 404.

1922: Two Labour candidates contested the same riding. I. (19) 15,080 (5 El.); Fusion (1) 3,281 (El.); I. Farmer (1) 694.

1927: Others: I. (14) 11,685 (1 El.); Comm. (1) 2,015; I. Government Supporter (1) 836; I. Prog. (1) 566; Farmer-Lab. (1) 12.

1932: Others: Two Liberal-Progressives contested the same seat in two ridings. Others: I. (12) 8,209 (1 El.); United Workers (Comm.) (2) 4,561; I. Ukrainian (1) 2,685; Soc. (1) 848; I.C. (1) 173.

1936: Others: I. (5) 29,206 (2 El.); Comm. (1) 5,864 (El.); I.L. (1) 686 (El.).

1941: Others: Coalition: I. (14) 22,834 (5 El.); Anti-Coalition: I. (2) 6,615 (1 El.); Workers (Comm.) (1) 4,889 (El.); Sound Money (3) 701.

1945: (Turnout excludes rejected ballots in Winnipeg.) Others: Coalition: I. (7) 6,384 (3 El.); I. L-P (3) 3,248; I.L. (1) 824; Anti-Coalition: LPP (Comm.) (13) 10,566 (1 El.); I. (3) 9,420 (1 El.); I. CCF (2) 4,394; Soc. (1) 222.

1949: Others: Coalition: I. (4) 5,408 (3 El.); Liberal (1) 4,311 (El.); I. L-P (2) 2,625; I.L. (1) 1,015; Anti-Coalition: I. PC (5) 11,388 (3 El.); I. (4) 6,892; LPP (Comm.) (2) 5,243 (1 El.); I.L. (3) 4,094 (1 El.); Con. (1) 3,353 (El.); I. CCF (1) 1,171; I. L-P (1) 860; I. Lab. (1) 99.

1953: Others: I. L-P (6) 11,929 (3 El.); LPP (1) 3,812 (1 El.); I. (11) 9,577 (2 El.).

1958: Others: I. (3) 1,207 (1 El.); LPP (1) 1,207; I. PC (3) 1,223.

1959: Others: I. (3) 1,171; LPP (3) 1,731.

1962: Others: I. (2) 849; Comm. (2) 816; Lib. Lab. (1) 111.

1966: Others: Comm. (2) 638; I. (1) 97.

1969: Others: I. (5) 2,020 (1 El.); Comm. (2) 744.

1973: Others: I. (18) 6,969; Comm. (3) 252; Comm. Marxist-Leninist (3) 69.

1977: Others: Comm. (4) 299; I. (1) 47.

1981: Others: I. (4) 1,141; Comm. (2) 261.

Saskatchewan Provincial Elections

Election Year	Seats	Candidates						Elected						Popular Vote			
		L.	C.	3rd	SC	O.	Tot.	L.	C.	3rd	SC	O.	ACCL	L.	%*	C.	%*
Dec. 4, 1905	25	25	24	—	—	1	50	17	8	—	—	—	1	17,783	52.2	16,180	47.5
Aug. 14, 1908	41	41	40	—	—	3	84	27	14	—	—	—	—	29,798	50.8	28,102	47.9
July 11, 1912	53	53	53	—	—	5	111	45	8	—	—	—	3	50,004	57.1	36,648	41.8
June 26, 1917	59	58	54	7	—	17	129	51	7	—	—	1	17	106,087	56.8	68,899	36.9
June 9, 1921	63	60	4	40	—	48	119	45	2	6	—	10	8	92,775	51.1	7,133	3.5
June 2, 1925	63	62	18	16	—	9	129	50	3	6	—	4	—	127,542	52.7	45,508	14.4
June 6, 1929	63	62	40	53	—	22	140	28	24	5	—	6	—	164,510	46.9	131,701	33.2
June 19, 1934	55	56	52	31	41	8	169	50	—	5	—	—	—	206,188	48.3	114,936	25.9
June 8, 1938	52	53	24	52	1	11	160	38	—	10	2	2	—	200,370	45.8	52,366	9.9
June 15, 1944	52	52	39	52	36	9	153	5	—	47	—	—	—	140,901	36.0	42,511	9.9
June 24, 1948	52	41	9	53	24	11	149	19	—	31	—	2	—	152,394	33.0	37,985	5.5
June 11, 1952	53	53	8	53	53	7	145	11	—	42	—	—	—	211,463	40.7	10,648	1.9
June 29, 1956	53	52	9	55	55	4	171	14	—	36	3	—	—	167,419	32.4	10,955	1.8
June 8, 1960	55	55	55	59	2	5	225	17	—	38	—	—	—	222,066	34.2	94,713	13.5
April 4, 1964	59	58	43	59	6	1	163	32	—	26	—	1	—	269,402	42.5	127,410	16.6
Oct. 11, 1967	59	59	41	59	—	—	165	35	—	24	—	—	—	193,871	45.6	41,583	9.8
June 23, 1971	60	60	16	60	—	2	138	15	—	45	—	—	—	193,864	42.8	9,659	2.1
June 11, 1975	61	61	61	61	—	5	188	15	7	39	—	—	—	142,853	31.7	124,573	27.6
Oct. 18, 1978	61	61	61	61	—	2	185	—	17	44	—	—	—	65,489	13.8	181,045	38.1
April 26, 1982[1]	64	64	64	64	—	57	249	—	56	8	—	—	—	24,044	4.5	289,498	54.4

Sources: Chief Electoral Officer: Returns from the Records of Saskatchewan General Elections, 1905-1948; Election Summaries (1952-1971); Saskatchewan Archives Board, Saskatchewan Executive and Legislative Directory 1905-1970; Election Summaries 1952-1978.

*The percentages given for party vote are adjusted to exclude the distortions caused by the electoral system. In the determination of party percentages, the party vote in multi-member ridings is divided by the number of members to be elected.

Notes: All Voter Turnout data have been calculated from the "Returns from the Records" from 1908-1948. The "Voters who Voted" column excludes votes from polls or ridings where the figures for "Registered Voters" are missing or unreliable. After the Voter Turnout % column a column is included (entitled "Used Seats") which gives the number of seats contested which were used to calculate Voter Turnout.

In multi-member ridings from 1921-29, the number of "Voters who Voted" are determined by adding the highest candidate vote for each full slate of candidates. Where a party did not run a full slate, the vote is divided by the number of members to be elected. After 1930 voters were required to place an "X" on their ballot for as many candidates as there were members to be elected. All turnout figures include rejected ballots.

Acclamations: 1905: 1 Liberal; 1917: 2 Liberals, 1 Ind.; 1921: 16 Liberals, 1 Ind. Prog.; 1925: 8 Liberals.

Electoral System:
All ridings used the single-member, plurality system of voting except as described for those elections listed below. In all multi-member ridings voters placed an "X" by the names of as many candidates as there were members to be elected.

1921-1948: Three ridings elected two members each.
1952-1956: Two ridings elected two members each. One riding elected three members.
1960: One riding elected two members. One riding elected three members.
One riding elected four members.
1964: Three ridings elected two members each. One riding elected five members.

[1]Incomplete official results while recounts were still in progress in four constituencies (Athabaska, Prince Albert, Quill Lakes, and Saskatoon Riversdale). Totals are preliminary, based on official final results in 60 ridings and preliminary Canadian Press results on election night in the four constituencies in which recounts were initiated subsequently.

Saskatchewan

Election Year	3rd	%*	Party	SC	%*	O.	%*	Total	Voter Turnout — Registered Electorate in Contested Seats	Voters who Voted	%	Used Seats	Voter Code
1905	—	—	—	—	—	94	.3	34,057	—	—	—	—	d
1908	—	—	—	—	—	781	1.3	58,681	64,903	45,578	70.2	34	c
1912	—	—	—	—	—	934	1.1	87,586	138,632	80,142	57.8	48	c
1917	—	—	—	—	—	11,664	6.2	186,650	187,718	134,652	71.7	46	k
1921	13,613	8.8	Prog.	—	—	67,262	36.6	180,783	159,256	101,948	65.2	33	k
1925	57,104	25.7	Prog.	—	—	17,605	7.1	247,759	324,909	212,549	65.4	53	k
1929	24,988	7.9	Prog.	—	—	40,061	12.0	361,260	382,509	309,560	80.9	60	k
1934	103,050	24.6	F-L	—	—	5,554	1.2	429,728	443,831	377,363	85.0	54	k
1938	82,568	21.5	CCF	69,720	16.3	35,249	6.5	440,273	448,246	374,589	83.6	49	k
1944	211,365	53.4	CCF	249	.0	2,777	.7	397,803	403,799	322,007	79.7	51	g
1948	236,920	46.4	CCF	40,299	9.1	30,513	6.1	498,111	503,793	419,870	83.3	50	u
1952	290,557	52.4	CCF	21,002	4.3	4,292	.7	537,962	505,679	419,373	82.9	53	u
1956	249,576	43.5	CCF	118,498	21.7	5,250	.6	551,698	510,064	427,918	83.9	53	u
1960	276,897	39.5	CCF	83,761	12.6	1,806	.2	679,243	527,144	443,434	84.1	55	u
1964	268,752	40.2	CCF	2,621	.6	68	.0	668,253	536,392	450,301	83.9	55	o
1967	188,653	44.3	NDP	1,296	.3	—	—	425,403	549,256	427,341	77.8	60	o
1971	248,978	55.0	NDP	—	—	235	.1	452,736	550,850	458,415	83.2	60	o
1975	180,700	40.1	NDP	—	—	2,897	.6	451,023	564,390	453,075	80.3	61	o
1978	228,791	48.1	NDP	—	—	81	.0	475,415	601,142	477,569	79.4	61	o
1982	198,015	37.2	NDP	—	—	20,105	3.8	531,662	630,000	531,662	84.4	64	o

Explanation of Party Vote:

1905: In 1905 and 1908 Conservatives ran as "Provincial Rights" candidates. Others: I. (1) 94.

1908: Others: I.L. (1) 394; I. (2) 387.

1912: The election was declared void in one riding and is not referred to in the tables above. All "Provincial Rights" candidates in 1908 who ran again in 1912 did so as Conservatives. Others: I. (5) 934.

1917: The tables exclude the election of three armed service representatives (votes polled: 12,655). Others: Non-Partisan (6) 5,750; I. (9) 4,440 (1 El.); Lab. (2) 1,474.

1921: Others: I. (35) 46,593 (7 El.); I.C. (3) 6,298 (1 El.); Lab. (3) 6,034 (1 El.) Non-Partisan (4) 5,137; I. Lab. (1) 1,690; Government (1) 1,510; I. Pro-Government (1) (El. by acclamation).

1925: Others: I. (6) 8,703 (2 El.); Lab. L. (1) 4,704 (El.); I.L. (1) 2,653 (El.); I.C. (1) 1,545.

1929: Conservatives, Progressives, and Independents formed a coalition government after the election. Two Progressives contested the same seat. Others: I. (17) 32,778 (6 El.); L. Lab. (1) 4,181; Economic Group (3) 1,942; I.L. (1) 1,160.

1934: Two Liberals contested the same seat. Others: I. (3) 2,949; Lab. (1) 1,420; United Front (3) 1,052; I.L. (1) 133.

1938: Two Liberals contested the same seat. Two Social Credit candidates contested the same seat. Others: I. Lab. (3) 12,047; Unity (4) 11,421 (2 El.); LPP (2) 8,502; I. (1) 2,451; I.C. (1) 828.

1944: The tables exclude the election of 3 armed service representatives (votes polled: 11,610). Others: LPP (3) 2,067; I. (5) 705; I.L. (1) 5.

1948: Others: I. (5) 11,088 (1 El.); Lib. Con. (3) 9,574 (1 El.); I.L. (1) 3,299; LPP (1) 1,301.

1952: Others: I. PC (1) 1,529; I. (3) 1,517; LPP (2) 1,143; I.L. (1) 103.

1956: Others: I. (2) 4,714; Comm. (2) 536.

1960: Others: I. (3) 1,427; Comm. (2) 379.

1964: Others: LPP (1) 68.

1971: Others: I. (1) 189; Comm. (1) 46.

1975: Others: I. Socialist (1) 1,492; I. (2) 1,232; Comm. (2) 173.

1978: Others: I. (2) 81.

1982: Others: WCC (Western Canada Concept) (40) 17,462; I. (7) 1,532; APPS (Aboriginal Peoples Party of Saskatchewan) (10) 1,111. Rejected ballots, 1,480; unopened ballots, 161.

Alberta Provincial Elections

Election Year	Seats	Candidates						Elected					ACCL	Popular Vote			
		L	C	3rd	4th	O	Tot.	L	C	3rd	4th	O	L	L	%	C	%
Nov. 9, 1905	25	27	21	—	—	6	54	22	3	—	—	0	1	14,057	60.7	7,589	32.8
March 22, 1909	41	42	29	—	3	8	82	36	2	—	1	2	9	29,634	59.3	15,848	31.7
April 17, 1913	56	56	56	—	5	15	132	38	18	—	0	0	—	47,544	49.0	43,922	45.3
June 7, 1917	56	49	48	—	1	16	114	34	19	—	1	2	11	54,212	48.1	47,055	41.8
July 18, 1921	61	57	13	43	10	34	157	15	1	38	4	3	2	99,518	34.2	34,548	5.5
June 28, 1926	60	54	56	46	13	14	183	7	4	43	6	0	—	44,722	25.5	40,091	22.9
June 19, 1930	63	36	18	47	11	29	141	11	6	39	4	3	4	46,275	24.6	25,449	13.5
Aug. 22, 1935	63	61	39	45	63	31	239	5	2	0	56	0	—	69,845	23.1	19,358	6.4
March 21, 1940	57	2	0	36	56	71	165	1	0	0	36	20	—	2,755	.9	—	—
Aug. 8, 1944	57	0	0	57	57	70	184	0	0	2	51	4	—	—	—	—	—
Aug. 17, 1948	57	49	0	51	57	16	173	2	0	2	51	2	—	52,655	17.9	—	—
Aug. 5, 1952	61	55	12	41	61	14	183	4	2	2	52	1	1	66,738	22.4	10,971	3.7
June 29, 1955	61	53	26	38	62	23	202	15	3	2	37	4	—	117,741	31.1	34,757	9.2
June 18, 1959	65	51	60	32	64	9	216	1	—	0	61	3	—	57,408	13.9	98,730	23.9
June 17, 1963	63	55	33	56	63	18	225	2	0	0	60	1	—	79,709	19.8	51,278	12.7
May 23, 1967	65	45	47	65	65	14	236	3	6	0	55	1	—	53,845	10.8	129,552	26.0
Aug. 30, 1971	75	20	75	70	75	3	243	0	49	1	25	0	—	6,475	1.0	296,934	46.4
March 26, 1975	75	46	75	75	70	27	293	0	69	1	4	1	—	29,424	5.0	369,764	62.7
March 14, 1979	79	79	79	79	79	19	335	0	74	1	4	0	—	43,792	6.2	408,097	57.4

Sources: Returns (1905-1971), *Statement of Votes* (1930-1948), Edmonton Journal (1975).

Notes: Excluded from the tables above are the results of at-large elections in 1917 and 1944 to elect, respectively, two and three non-partisan armed services representatives.

The party percentages in 1921 only are adjusted to exclude the distortions caused by the electoral system. For that election in multi-member ridings, the party percent is changed by dividing party vote by the number of members to be elected in each riding.

The number of "Voters who Voted" from 1905 to 1926 exclude rejected ballots, and for the elections of 1909 and 1913 the vote in multi-member ridings has been estimated using the procedure of adding the highest vote by one candidate for each party.

Acclamations: 1905: 1 Liberal; 1909: 9 Liberals; 1917: 6 Liberals and 5 Conservatives; 1921: 2 Liberals; 1930: 4 UFA.

Electoral System: All ridings used the single-member, plurality system of voting except as described for those elections listed below.

1909: Two ridings had two members where voters could mark their ballot twice.

1913: One riding had two members where voters could mark their ballot twice.

1921: Two ridings had five members each and one riding had two members where voters could mark their ballot once for each member to be elected.

1926: Two ridings elected five members each using the Hare system of proportional representation (P.R.). The single-member ridings used the alternate system.

1930-35: Two ridings had six members each (Hare P.R.). Others: single-member, alternative.

1940-48: Two ridings had five members each (Hare P.R.). Others: single-member, alternative.

1952-55: One six-member riding and one seven-member riding (Hare P.R.). Others: single-member, alternative.

Explanation of Party Vote:

1905: Contested the same seat: two Liberals in each of two ridings. Others: I. (6) 1,508.

1909: Contested the same seat: two Liberals in each of two ridings. Others: I. (6) 1,695 (1 El.); I.L. (2) 1,311 (1 El.); Lab. (1) 214.

1913: Others: I. (14) 3,639; I.L. (1) 47.

Alberta

Election Year	3rd	%	Party	4th	%	Party	O.	%	Total	Voter Turnout			
										Registered Electorate in Contested Seats	Voters who Voted	%	Voter Code
1905	—	—	—	—	—	—	1,508	6.5	23,154	—	23,154	—	d
1909	—	—	—	1,302	2.6	Soc.	3,220	6.4	50,004	—	43,187	—	d
1913	—	—	—	1,814	1.9	Soc.	3,686	3.8	96,966	—	87,554	—	d
1917	—	—	—	1,328	1.2	Lab.	10,017	8.9	112,612	—	112,612	—	g
1921	83,773	45.4	Farm.	33,987	6.3	Lab.	46,351	8.5	298,177	—	175,980	—	g
1926	70,968	40.5	UFA	14,123	8.1	Lab.	5,233	3.0	175,137	—	175,137	—	g
1930	74,187	39.4	UFA	14,354	7.6	Lab.	27,954	14.9	188,219	293,758	197,141	67.1	g
1935	33,063	11.0	UFA	163,700	54.2	SC	15,786	5.2	301,752	378,249	312,331	82.6	g
1940	34,316	11.1	CCF	132,507	42.9	SC	139,286	45.1	308,864	427,245	320,403	75.0	j
1944	70,307	24.9	CCF	146,367	51.9	SC	65,432	23.2	282,106	421,051	291,908	69.3	j
1948	56,387	19.1	CCF	164,003	55.6	SC	21,748	7.4	294,793	489,311	313,481	64.1	j
1952	41,929	14.1	CCF	167,789	56.2	SC	10,908	3.7	298,335	537,170	318,948	59.4	j
1955	31,180	8.2	CCF	175,553	46.4	SC	18,948	5.0	378,179	589,409	401,018	68.0	j
1959	17,899	4.3	CCF	230,283	55.7	SC	9,195	2.2	413,515	649,678	415,113	63.9	j
1963	38,133	9.5	NDP	221,107	54.8	SC	13,217	3.3	403,444	720,910	404,808	56.2	p
1967	79,593	16.0	NDP	222,271	44.6	SC	13,080	2.6	498,341	779,822	501,108	64.3	p
1971	73,038	11.4	NDP	262,953	41.1	SC	462	.1	639,862	895,442	644,504	72.0	p
1975	76,360	12.9	NDP	107,211	18.2	SC	7,411	1.3	590,170	994,158	590,170	59.4	p
1979	111,984	15.8	NDP	141,284	19.9	SC	5,806	.8	710,963	1,215,490	713,654	58.7	p

Explanation of Party Vote (Con't)

1917: Totals exclude 25,601 votes cast by 13,286 Soldiers and Nurses in an "at-large" district for two special representatives. A special act of the Assembly re-elected by acclamation 11 sitting members who enlisted in the armed services. Others: I. (8) 3,625; Soc. (4) 1,570; I.L. (1) 1,296; Non-Partisan (1) 839 (El.); I. Farmer (1) 439 (El.); Unknown (1) 2,248.

1921: Others: I. (14) 29,691 (3 El.); I.L. (6) 3,666; I. Lab. (5) 5,483; Soc. (2) 2,628; I. Farmer (5) 2,376; I. Prog. (1) 1,744; Non-Partisan (1) 763.

1926: Farmers ran as the (UFA) United Farmers of Alberta. Others: I.L. (5) 2,728; I. (3) 1,254; I. UFA (4) 626; L. Prog. (1) 252; I. Farmer (1) 373.

1930: Others: I. (29) 27,954 (2 El.).

1935: Others: Comm. (9) 5,771; Lab. (10) 5,086; I. (7) 2,740; I.L. (1) 955; United Front (1) 560; I. Lab. (1) 224; I.C. (1) 258; Economic Reconstruction (1) 192.

1940: Others: Ind. Movement (59) 131,172 (19 El.). A grouping of Conservatives, Liberals, and some UFA candidates; Lab. (3) 3,509 (1 El.); I. Prog. (4) 1,726; Comm. (1) 1,067; I.L. (1) 1,136; I. SC (1) 362; I. Farmer (2) 314.

1944: Others: Ind. Movement (36) 47,239 (3 El.); LPP (30) 12,003; Veteran (1) 3,532 (El.); Lab. Union (1) 1,788; Single Tax (1) 480; Farmer-Lab. (1) 390.

1949: Others: I. (7) 9,014 (1 El.); Ind. Citizen's Association (2) 3,969; Lab. (1) 3,579; I. SC (3) 2,958 (1 El.); LPP (2) 1,372; United Lab. (1) 856.

1952: The Conservative column includes: Con. (5) 6,271 (2 El.); and PC (7) 4,700. Others: I. SC (6) 4,203 (1 El.); LPP (2) 1,132; Farmer (1) 655; Lab. (1) 527; Non-Partisan Farmer (1) 463; I. Lab. (1) 2,927; People's (1) 296.

1955: Others: Coalition (2) 4,581 (1 El.); I. (7) 4,225 (1 El.); Lib.-Con. (2) 4,001 (1 El.); LPP (9) 3,420; I. SC (3) 2,721 (1 El.).

1959: Others: I. (2) 3,640; I. SC (2) 2,392 (1 El.); Coalition (1) 2,279; LPP (4) 884.

1963: Others: I. (3) 3,966; I. SC (6) 3,178; Alberta Unity Movement (3) 2,233; Coalition (1) 2,179 (El.); Comm. (4) 527; PC-Lib. (1) 1,134.

1967: Others: I. (7) 6,916 (1 El.); Coalition (2) 3,654; I. PC (2) 1,118; Other (1) 699.

1971: Others: I. (3) 462.

1975: The turnout percent excludes rejected ballots. Others: I. SC (1) 4,428 (El.); I. PC (3) 1,059; Comm. (14) 768; I. (4) 625; I.L. (2) 416; Constitutional Socialist Party (3) 115.

1979: Others: I. (12) 5,449; Comm. (7) 357.

British Columbia Provincial Elections

Election Year	Seats	Candidates						Elected						Popular Vote			
		L.	C.	3rd	4th	O.	Tot.	L.	C.	3rd	4th	O.	ACCL	L.	%*	C.	%*
Feb. 2, 1907	42	40	42	22	—	8	112	12	27	3	—	—	—	23,560	38.0	31,068	47.0
Nov. 25, 1909	42	39	42	20	—	3	104	3	36	3	—	—	—	36,472	33.8	52,462	53.3
March 28, 1912	42	18	46	18	—	6	88	—	40	2	—	—	9	21,261	19.4	51,181	64.6
Sept. 14, 1916	47	46	46	—	—	24	116	37	8	1	—	1	—	90,380	50.9	72,834	41.3
Dec. 1, 1920	47	46	43	14	—	52	155	26	14	2	—	5	—	134,591	36.9	111,380	32.8
June 20, 1924	48	46	48	17	45	12	168	25	16	3	2	2	—	108,322	32.5	102,433	31.6
July 18, 1928	48	46	48	8	—	15	117	12	35	1	—	—	—	146,552	40.9	192,867	52.4
Nov. 2, 1933	47	47	6	46	29	82	210	34	—	7	2	4	—	159,131	42.0	7,114	1.5
June 1, 1937	48	48	43	46	18	31	186	31	8	7	—	2	—	156,074	38.3	119,521	25.7
Oct. 21, 1941	48	48	43	45	—	20	156	21	12	14	—	1	—	149,525	33.6	140,282	28.8
Oct. 25, 1945	48	47*	—	48	16	36	147	37*	—	10	—	1	—	261,147	53.8	(Coalition)*	
June 15, 1949	48	48*	—	48	16	26	138	39*	—	7	—	2	—	428,773	58.9	(Coalition)*	
June 12, 1952	48	48	48	48	47	22	213	6	4	18	19	1	—	180,289	23.3	129,439	15.8
June 9, 1953	48	48	39	47	48	47	229	4	1	14	28	1	—	171,671	23.0	40,780	5.0
Sept. 19, 1956	52	52	22	51	52	22	199	2	1	10	39	—	—	177,922	20.8	25,373	2.8
Sept. 12, 1960	52	50	52	52	52	24	230	4	—	16	32	—	—	208,249	19.5	66,943	6.7
Sept. 30, 1963	52	51	44	52	52	6	205	5	—	14	33	—	—	193,363	17.8	109,090	11.1
Sept. 12, 1966	55	53	3	55	55	15	181	6	—	16	33	—	—	152,155	17.5	1,409	.2
Aug. 27, 1969	55	55	1	55	55	12	178	5	—	12	38	—	—	186,235	18.4	1,087	.1
Aug. 30, 1972	55	50	45	55	55	5	210	5	2	38	10	—	—	185,640	15.5	143,450	13.1
Dec. 11, 1975	55	49	29	55	55	33	221	1	1	18	35	—	—	93,379	6.9	49,796	4.1
May 10, 1979	57	5	37	57	57	22	178	—	—	26	31	—	—	6,662	.4	71,078	5.2

Source: Chief Electoral Officer (1907-1979).

*The percentages given for party vote are adjusted to exclude the distortions caused by the electoral system. When determining party percentages, the party vote in multi-member ridings is divided by the number of members to be elected.

Notes: The number of "Voters who Voted" in 1920 and 1924 exclude rejected ballots and have been estimated in multi-member ridings by adding the top candidate vote for each party which ran a full slate. The vote for candidates which were not part of a full slate were divided by 4 in Victoria and 5 in Vancouver.

The given "Registered Electorate" in 1920 excludes 1,965 persons in one riding won by acclamation.

Acclamations: 1912: 9 Conservatives; 1920: 1 Liberal.

Electoral System: In multi-member ridings voters could place an "X" on the ballot for each of the total number of candidates to be elected, except for the elections of 1952 and 1953 when all ridings used the "alternate" (or preferential) system of voting.

The number of single and multi-member ridings by the number of members for each riding. (M = Members)

Elections	1M	2M	3M	4M	5M	6M
1907-12	31	1	—	1	1	—
1916-20	37	—	—	1	—	—
1924-28	38	—	1	1	—	1
1933	34	3	1	1	—	—
1937	35	3	1	1	—	—
1941-49	36	3	2	—	—	—
1952-53	36	3	2	—	—	—
1956-66	34	6	2	—	—	—
1969-79	41	7	—	—	—	—

Explanation of Party Vote:

1907: The vote for 21 candidates came from newspaper reports. Others: Lab. (6) 1,972; I.L. (1) 197; I. (1) 147.

1909: The vote for 3 candidates came from newspaper reports. Others: Lab. (2) 222; I.C. (1) 154.

*Contested the same seat: 2 Conservatives in each of 2 ridings, 3 Conservatives in one riding.

1912: Others: I. (3) 1,695; I.C. (3) 405.

1916: Others: I. (12) 9,035; Lab. (1) 2,487; I.C. (1) 539 (El.).

1920: The Lab. column includes 10 Federated Lab. 29,532 (1 El.) and 4 Lab. 2,461 (1 El.). Others: I. (18) 35,980 (3 El.); Soc. (7) 12,414 (1 El.); Soldier-Lab. (7) 7,225; Government Aid (2) 5,441; Farmer (4) 3,565; I. Soldier (2) 2,265; I.L. (2) 2,702; Soldier Farm. (3) 1,944; Soldier Farm. (3) 1,740; People's (1) 1,354 (El.); I.C. (1) 697; Farm. Lab. (2) 378; Lab. Soc. (1) 419.

British Columbia

Election Year	3rd	%*	Party	4th	%*	Party	O.	%*	Total	Voter Turnout Registered Electorate in Contested Seats	Voters who Voted	%	Voter Code
1907	6,300	11.1	Soc.	—	—	—	2,316	3.9	63,244	—	—	—	c
1909	11,493	12.1	Soc.	—	—	—	376	.8	100,803	—	—	—	c
1912	9,987	13.9	Soc.	—	—	—	2,100	2.0	84,529	—	—	—	c
1916	4,487	3.5	Soc.	—	—	—	12,061	4.3	179,762	—	—	—	c
1920	31,993	8.7	Lab.	83,517	22.6	PP	76,124	21.6	354,088	199,407	154,818	77.6	k
1924	39,577	8.7	Lab.	—	—	—	11,759	4.6	345,608	225,675	153,289	67.9	k
1928	16,627	4.7	Lab.	—	—	—	5,768	2.1	361,814	245,240	174,934	71.3	k
1933	120,248	31.1	CCF	38,524	11.9	NP	56,206	13.5	381,223	323,540	236,415	73.1	k
1937	119,400	29.5	CCF	4,812	.9	SC	18,122	5.5	417,929	372,781	265,446	71.2	k
1941	151,440	34.4	CCF	—	—	—	12,646	3.2	453,893	417,839	303,901	72.7	k
1945	175,960	39.1	CCF	6,627	1.4	SC	24,013	5.6	467,747	476,222	298,387	62.7	k
1949	245,248	36.9	CCF	11,536	1.9	SC	13,230	2.3	698,823	649,019	477,999	73.6	h
1952	236,562	31.5	CCF	209,049	27.9	SC	13,222	1.6	768,561	793,074	543,456	68.5	h
1953	224,513	32.2	CCF	274,771	37.6	SC	16,104	2.1	727,839	740,006	522,052	70.5	p
1956	231,511	29.4	CCF	374,711	46.0	SC	7,880	1.0	817,397	778,587	509,409	65.4	p
1960	326,094	33.7	CCF	386,886	39.4	SC	8,232	.8	996,404	874,267	628,031	71.8	p
1963	269,004	29.0	NDP	395,079	41.9	SC	1,139	.1	967,675	873,140	608,672	69.7	p
1966	252,753	34.5	NDP	342,751	47.3	SC	2,808	.4	751,876	873,927	596,716	68.3	p
1969	331,813	34.2	NDP	457,777	47.2	SC	1,444	.1	978,356	1,152,598	794,696	68.9	p
1972	448,260	40.1	NDP	352,776	31.2	SC	2,046	.2	1,132,060	1,343,357	929,632	69.2	p
1975	505,396	38.7	NDP	635,482	49.8	SC	6,398	.4	1,290,451	1,559,633	1,088,001	69.8	p
1979	646,188	45.2	NDP	677,607	48.9	SC	3,542	.2	1,405,077	1,673,111	1,155,505	69.1	p

Explanation of Party Vote (Con't)

1924:   Others: Soc. (2) 4,364; I.L. (4) 3,324 (2 El.); I. (4) 3,570; I.C. (1) 276; I. Lab. (1) 225.

1928:   The 3rd party Lab. column includes: Lab. (5) 6,062 (1 El.) and I. Lab. (3) 10,565. Others: I. (13) 4,704; I.C. (2) 1,064.

1933:   The Non-Partisans were led by the former leader of the Conservatives, however only 11 of the 35 Conservatives elected in 1928 ran in 1933 and only 6 of those 11 were clearly Non-Partisan candidates. Others: Unionist (11) 14,394 (1 El.); United Front of Workers and Farmers (20) 4,584; I. (33) 31,435 (2 El.); I. CCF (7) 1,990; Lab. (3) 2,261 (1 El.); Soc. (5) 370; I.L. (2) 1,076; Lab. (1) 96.

1937:   Others: I. (11) 7,341 (1 El.); Lab. (2) 1,787 (1 El.); Comm. (1) 567; Soc. (2) 287; Financial Justice (1) 54; B.C. Constructive (14) 8,086. Soc. Credit (SC) was known as the Social Credit League.

1941:   Others: I. Lab. (2) 3,899; Lab. (4) 2,975 (1 El.); Official Con. (1) 2,161; I. (4) 1,638; Soc. Lab. (4) 950; I. Farm. (1) 388; Emancipation (1) 265; Victory without Debt (1) 209; Religious Political Brotherhood (1) 105; I. Soc. (1) 56.

1945:   The Liberals and Conservatives formed a coalition for the 1945 and 1949 elections. Others: LPP (21) 16,479; People's CCF (2) 2,786; I. (2) 1,532; Lab. (1) 1,289 (El.); I. PC (1) 473; Democratic (1) 423; Soc. Lab. (3) 285; PC (1) 275; I.L. (1) 199; I. Lab. (1) 106; Soc. (1) 105; Prog. L. (1) 61.

1949:   Others: I. (7) 5,163 (1 El.); Union of Electors (12) 2,790; LPP (2) 1,660; Lab. (1) 1,483 (El.); Con. (1) 1,241; People's (2) 607; Soc. Lab. (1) 286.

1952:   Others: LPP (5) 2,514; Christian Democratic (8) 7,176; I. (6) 1,312; Lab. (1) 1,290 (El.); Lab. Rep. (1) 654; Soc. (1) 276.

1953:   Others: LPP (25) 7,496; Christian Democratic (14) 5,036; I. (6) 1,951; Lab. (1) 1,601 (El.); People's (1) 173.

1956:   Others: LPP (14) 3,381; Lab. (1) 1,321 (El.); I. (6) 3,005; People's (1) 173.

1960:   Others: Comm. (19) 5,675; I. (5) 2,557.

1963:   Others: Comm. (4) 849; I. (1) 215; Soc. (1) 75.

1966:   Others: I. (6) 1,711; Comm. (6) 1,097.

1969:   Others: I. (6) 831; Comm. (4) 482; Social Con. (1) 131.

1972:   Others: I. (9) 1,184; Comm. (5) 862.

1975:   Others: I. (16) 4,816; Comm. (13) 1,441; N. Am. Labour Party (4) 141.

1979:   Others: Comm. (9) 1,394; I. (5) 1,098; N. Am. Labour Party (4) 297; Western Independent Party (2) 555; Gay Alliance Towards Equality (1) 126; Independent New Hope Party (1) 72.